Nineteenth-Century Literature Criticism

Topics Volume

Guide to Gale Literary Criticism Series

For criticism on	Consult these Gale series
Authors now living or who died after December 31, 1999	*CONTEMPORARY LITERARY CRITICISM (CLC)*
Authors who died between 1900 and 1999	*TWENTIETH-CENTURY LITERARY CRITICISM (TCLC)*
Authors who died between 1800 and 1899	*NINETEENTH-CENTURY LITERATURE CRITICISM (NCLC)*
Authors who died between 1400 and 1799	*LITERATURE CRITICISM FROM 1400 TO 1800 (LC)* *SHAKESPEAREAN CRITICISM (SC)*
Authors who died before 1400	*CLASSICAL AND MEDIEVAL LITERATURE CRITICISM (CMLC)*
Authors of books for children and young adults	*CHILDREN'S LITERATURE REVIEW (CLR)*
Dramatists	*DRAMA CRITICISM (DC)*
Poets	*POETRY CRITICISM (PC)*
Short story writers	*SHORT STORY CRITICISM (SSC)*
Literary topics and movements	*HARLEM RENAISSANCE: A GALE CRITICAL COMPANION (HR)* *THE BEAT GENERATION: A GALE CRITICAL COMPANION (BG)*
Asian American writers of the last two hundred years	*ASIAN AMERICAN LITERATURE (AAL)*
Black writers of the past two hundred years	*BLACK LITERATURE CRITICISM (BLC)* *BLACK LITERATURE CRITICISM SUPPLEMENT (BLCS)*
Hispanic writers of the late nineteenth and twentieth centuries	*HISPANIC LITERATURE CRITICISM (HLC)* *HISPANIC LITERATURE CRITICISM SUPPLEMENT (HLCS)*
Native North American writers and orators of the eighteenth, nineteenth, and twentieth centuries	*NATIVE NORTH AMERICAN LITERATURE (NNAL)*
Major authors from the Renaissance to the present	*WORLD LITERATURE CRITICISM, 1500 TO THE PRESENT (WLC)* *WORLD LITERATURE CRITICISM SUPPLEMENT (WLCS)*

ISSN 0732-1864

Volume 176

Nineteenth-Century Literature Criticism

Topics Volume

Criticism of Various
Topics in Nineteenth-Century Literature,
including Literary and Critical Movements,
Prominent Themes and Genres, Anniversary
Celebrations, and Surveys of National Literatures

Kathy D. Darrow
Russel Whitaker
Project Editors

THOMSON

★

GALE™

Detroit • New York • San Francisco • New Haven, Conn. • Waterville, Maine • London

Nineteenth-Century Literature Criticism, Vol. 176

Project Editors
Kathy D. Darrow and Russel Whitaker

Editorial
Jeffrey W. Hunter, Jelena O. Krstović, Michelle Lee, Thomas J. Schoenberg, Noah Schusterbauer, Lawrence J. Trudeau

Data Capture
Frances Monroe, Gwen Tucker

Rights and Acquisitions
Edna Hedblad, Emma Hull, Sue Rudolph

Imaging and Multimedia
Randy Bassett, Lezlie Light, Mike Logusz, Dan Newell, Christine O'Bryan

Composition and Electronic Capture
Tracey L. Matthews

Manufacturing
Rhonda Dover

Associate Product Manager
Marc Cormier

LIBRARY OF CONGRESS CATALOG CARD NUMBER 84-643008

ISBN-13: 978-0-7876-9847-8
ISBN-10: 0-7876-9847-4
ISSN 0732-1864

Printed in the United States of America
10 9 8 7 6 5 4 3 2 1

Contents

Preface

Since its inception in 1981, *Nineteenth-Century Literature Criticism* (*NCLC*) has been a valuable resource for students and librarians seeking critical commentary on writers of this transitional period in world history. Designated an "Outstanding Reference Source" by the American Library Association with the publication of is first volume, *NCLC* has since been purchased by over 6,000 school, public, and university libraries. The series has covered more than 500 authors representing 38 nationalities and over 28,000 titles. No other reference source has surveyed the critical reaction to nineteenth-century authors and literature as thoroughly as *NCLC*.

Scope of the Series

NCLC is designed to introduce students and advanced readers to the authors of the nineteenth century and to the most significant interpretations of these authors' works. The great poets, novelists, short story writers, playwrights, and philosophers of this period are frequently studied in high school and college literature courses. By organizing and reprinting commentary written on these authors, *NCLC* helps students develop valuable insight into literary history, promotes a better understanding of the texts, and sparks ideas for papers and assignments. Each entry in *NCLC* presents a comprehensive survey of an author's career or an individual work of literature and provides the user with a multiplicity of interpretations and assessments. Such variety allows students to pursue their own interests; furthermore, it fosters an awareness that literature is dynamic and responsive to many different opinions.

Every fourth volume of *NCLC* is devoted to literary topics that cannot be covered under the author approach used in the rest of the series. Such topics include literary movements, prominent themes in nineteenth-century literature, literary reaction to political and historical events, significant eras in literary history, prominent literary anniversaries, and the literatures of cultures that are often overlooked by English-speaking readers.

NCLC continues the survey of criticism of world literature begun by Thomson Gale's *Contemporary Literary Criticism* (*CLC*) and *Twentieth-Century Literary Criticism* (*TCLC*).

Organization of the Book

An *NCLC* entry consists of the following elements:

- The **Author Heading** cites the name under which the author most commonly wrote, followed by birth and death dates. Also located here are any name variations under which an author wrote, including transliterated forms for authors whose native languages use nonroman alphabets. If the author wrote consistently under a pseudonym, the pseudonym will be listed in the author heading and the author's actual name given in parenthesis on the first line of the biographical and critical information. Uncertain birth or death dates are indicated by question marks. Single-work entries are preceded by a heading that consists of the most common form of the title in English translation (if applicable) and the original date of composition.

- The **Introduction** contains background information that introduces the reader to the author, work, or topic that is the subject of the entry.

- The list of **Principal Works** is ordered chronologically by date of first publication and lists the most important works by the author. The genre and publication date of each work is given. In the case of foreign authors whose works have been translated into English, the list will focus primarily on twentieth-century translations, selecting those works most commonly considered the best by critics. Unless otherwise indicated, dramas are dated by first performance, not first publication. Lists of **Representative Works** by different authors appear with topic entries.

- Reprinted **Criticism** is arranged chronologically in each entry to provide a useful perspective on changes in critical evaluation over time. The critic's name and the date of composition or publication of the critical work are given at the beginning of each piece of criticism. Unsigned criticism is preceded by the title of the source in which it appeared. All titles by the author featured in the text are printed in boldface type. Footnotes are reprinted at the end of each essay or excerpt. In the case of excerpted criticism, only those footnotes that pertain to the excerpted texts are included. Criticism in topic entries is arranged chronologically under a variety of subheadings to facilitate the study of different aspects of the topic.

- A complete **Bibliographical Citation** of the original essay or book precedes each piece of criticism.

- Critical essays are prefaced by brief **Annotations** explicating each piece.

- An annotated bibliography of **Further Reading** appears at the end of each entry and suggests resources for additional study. In some cases, significant essays for which the editors could not obtain reprint rights are included here. Boxed material following the further reading list provides references to other biographical and critical sources on the author in series published by Thomson Gale.

Indexes

Each volume of *NCLC* contains a **Cumulative Author Index** listing all authors who have appeared in a wide variety of reference sources published by Thomson Gale, including *NCLC*. A complete list of these sources is found facing the first page of the Author Index. The index also includes birth and death dates and cross references between pseudonyms and actual names.

A **Cumulative Nationality Index** lists all authors featured in *NCLC* by nationality, followed by the number of the *NCLC* volume in which their entry appears.

A **Cumulative Topic Index** lists the literary themes and topics treated in the series as well as in *Classical and Medieval Literature Criticism, Literature Criticism from 1400 to 1800, Twentieth-Century Literary Criticism,* and the *Contemporary Literary Criticism* Yearbook, which was discontinued in 1998.

An alphabetical **Title Index** accompanies each volume of *NCLC*, with the exception of the Topics volumes. Listings of titles by authors covered in the given volume are followed by the author's name and the corresponding page numbers where the titles are discussed. English translations of foreign titles and variations of titles are cross-referenced to the title under which a work was originally published. Titles of novels, dramas, nonfiction books, and poetry, short story, or essay collections are printed in italics, while individual poems, short stories, and essays are printed in roman type within quotation marks.

In response to numerous suggestions from librarians, Thomson Gale also produces an annual paperbound edition of the *NCLC* cumulative title index. This annual cumulation, which alphabetically lists all titles reviewed in the series, is available to all customers. Additional copies of this index are available upon request. Librarians and patrons will welcome this separate index; it saves shelf space, is easy to use, and is recyclable upon receipt of the next edition.

Citing *Nineteenth-Century Literature Criticism*

When citing criticism reprinted in the Literary Criticism Series, students should provide complete bibliographic information so that the cited essay can be located in the original print or electronic source. Students who quote directly from reprinted criticism may use any accepted bibliographic format, such as University of Chicago Press style or Modern Language Association style.

The examples below follow recommendations for preparing a bibliography set forth in *The Chicago Manual of Style,* 14th ed. (Chicago: The University of Chicago Press, 1993); the first example pertains to material drawn from periodicals, the second to material reprinted from books:

Franklin, J. Jeffrey. "The Victorian Discourse of Gambling: Speculations on *Middlemarch* and *The Duke's Children*." *ELH* 61, no. 4 (winter 1994): 899-921. Reprinted in *Nineteenth-Century Literature Criticism*. Vol. 168, edited by Jessica Bomarito and Russel Whitaker, 39-51. Detroit: Thomson Gale, 2006.

Frank, Joseph. "*The Gambler*: A Study in Ethnopsychology." In *Freedom and Responsibility in Russian Literature: Essays in Honor of Robert Louis Jackson,* edited by Elizabeth Cheresh Allen and Gary Saul Morson, 69-85. Evanston, Ill.: Northwestern University Press, 1995. Reprinted in *Nineteenth-Century Literature Criticism*. Vol. 168, edited by Jessica Bomarito and Russel Whitaker, 75-84. Detroit: Thomson Gale, 2006.

The examples below follow recommendations for preparing a works cited list set forth in the *MLA Handbook for Writers of Research Papers,* 6th ed. (New York: The Modern Language Association of America, 2003); the first example pertains to material drawn from periodicals, the second to material reprinted from books:

Franklin, J. Jeffrey. "The Victorian Discourse of Gambling: Speculations on *Middlemarch* and *The Duke's Children*." *ELH* 61.4 (Winter 1994): 899-921. Reprinted in *Nineteenth-Century Literature Criticism*. Eds. Jessica Bomarito and Russel Whitaker. Vol. 168. Detroit: Thomson Gale, 2006. 39-51.

Frank, Joseph. "*The Gambler*: A Study in Ethnopsychology." *Freedom and Responsibility in Russian Literature: Essays in Honor of Robert Louis Jackson.* Eds. Elizabeth Cheresh Allen and Gary Saul Morson. Evanston, Ill.: Northwestern University Press, 1995. 69-85. Reprinted in *Nineteenth-Century Literature Criticism*. Eds. Jessica Bomarito and Russel Whitaker. Vol. 168. Detroit: Thomson Gale, 2006. 75-84.

Suggestions are Welcome

Readers who wish to suggest new features, topics, or authors to appear in future volumes, or who have other suggestions or comments are cordially invited to call, write, or fax the Associate Product Manager:

Associate Product Manager, Literary Criticism Series
Thomson Gale
27500 Drake Road
Farmington Hills, MI 48331-3535
1-800-347-4253 (GALE)
Fax: 248-699-8054

Acknowledgments

The editors wish to thank the copyright holders of the criticism included in this volume and the permissions managers of many book and magazine publishing companies for assisting us in securing reproduction rights. Following is a list of the copyright holders who have granted us permission to reproduce material in this volume of *NCLC*. Every effort has been made to trace copyright, but if omissions have been made, please let us know.

COPYRIGHTED MATERIAL IN *NCLC*, VOLUME 176, WAS REPRODUCED FROM THE FOLLOWING PERIODICALS:

American Quarterly, v. 48, June, 1996. Copyright © 1996 by The Johns Hopkins University Press. Reproduced by permission.—*American Studies,* v. 20, 2003. Copyright © Mid-America American Studies Association, 2003. Reproduced by permission of the publisher.—*Archiv für Geschichte der Philosophie,* vol. 67, 1985. Copyright © 1985 by Walter de Gruyter & Co., D-10785 Berlin. All rights reserved. Reproduced by permission.—*The Arnoldian,* v. 13, winter, 1985-86. Copyright © 1985. Reproduced by permission.—*Browning Institute Studies,* vol. 11, 1983, for "The Geometry of the Modern City: G. W. M. Reynolds and The Mysteries of London," by Anne Humpherys. Copyright © 1983 by The Browning Institute, Inc. Reproduced by permission of the editors.—*Charles Lamb Bulletin,* January, 2004. Copyright © the Charles Lamb Society and the contributors 2004. All rights reserved. Reproduced by permission.—*Dickens Quarterly,* v. 14, September, 1997; v. 14, December, 1997. Copyright © 1997 by the Dickens Society. All reproduced by permission.—*Dickens Studies Annual,* v. 27, 1998. Copyright © 1998 by AMS Press, Inc. All rights reserved. Reproduced by permission.—*The Eighteenth-Century Novel,* vol. 2, 2002. Copyright © 2002 by AMS Press, Inc. All rights reserved. Reproduced by permission.—*Essays in Arts and Sciences,* v. 16, May, 1987. Copyright © 1987 by the University of New Haven. Reproduced by permission.—*L'Esprit Créateur,* v. 29, summer, 1989. Copyright © 1989 by L'Esprit Créateur. Reproduced by permission.—*The Henry James Review,* v. 24, fall, 2003. Copyright © 2003 by The Johns Hopkins University Press. Reproduced by permission.—*Monatshefte,* v. 86, winter, 1994. Copyright © 1994 by the Board of Regents of the University of Wisconsin System. Reproduced by permission.—*New German Critique,* spring-summer, 1999. Copyright © 1999 by *New German Critique,* Inc. Reproduced by permission.—*Nineteenth-Century Prose,* v. 23, fall, 1996. Reproduced by permission.—*Rivista di Studi Italiani,* v. 9, June-December, 1991. Copyright © 1983 by *Rivista di Studi Italiani.* Reproduced by permission.—*Romance Notes,* v. 36, spring, 1996. Reproduced by permission.—*Shofar: An Interdisciplinary Journal of Jewish Studies,* v. 22, winter, 2004. Copyright © 2004 Purdue University Press. All rights reserved. Reprinted by permission.—*Studies in American Fiction,* v. 30, autumn, 2002. Copyright © 2002 Northeastern University. Reproduced by permission.—*Studies in English Literature, 1500-1900,* v. 12, fall, 1972. Copyright © 1972 The Johns Hopkins University Press. Reproduced by permission.—*Studies in the Novel,* v. 19, fall, 1987. Copyright © 1987 by North Texas State University. Reproduced by permission.—*TriQuarterly,* winter, 1991-92 for "The City as Text: New York and the American Writer" by Morris Dickstein. Copyright © 1992 by *TriQuarterly.* Reproduced by permission of the author.—*Victorian Periodicals Review,* v. 21, fall, 1988. Copyright © University of Toronto Press 1988. Reproduced by permission of University of Toronto Press Incorporated.—*Zapiski Russkoi Akademicheskoi Gruppy v S.Sh.A./Transactions of the Association of Russian-American Scholars in the U.S.A,* vol. 33, 2004. Copyright © 2004 by the Association of Russian-American Scholars in the U.S.A. Reproduced by permission.

COPYRIGHTED MATERIAL IN *NCLC*, VOLUME 176, WAS REPRODUCED FROM THE FOLLOWING BOOKS:

Bailey, Brigitte. From *Roman Holidays: American Writers and Artists in Nineteenth-Century Italy.* Edited by Robert K. Martin and Leland S. Person. University of Iowa Press, 2002. Copyright © 2002 by the University of Iowa Press. All rights reserved. Reproduced by permission of the author.—Baumgarten, Murray. From "London, Dickens, and The Theatre of Homelessness," in *Victorian Urban Settings: Essays on the Nineteenth-Century City and Its Contexts.* Edited by Debra N. Mancoff and D. J. Trela. Garland, 1996. Copyright © 1996 by Debra N. Mancoff and D. J. Trela. All rights reserved. Reproduced by permission of Routledge/Taylor & Francis Books Group, LLC, and the author.—Cherniavsky, Eva. From *That Pale Mother Rising: Sentimental Discourses and the Imitation of Motherhood in 19th-Century America.* Indiana University Press, 1995. Copyright © 1995 by Eva Cherniavsky. All rights reserved. Reproduced by permission.—Dettlaff, Shirley M. From *Melville's Evermoving Dawn: Centennial Essays.* Edited by John Bryant and Robert Milder. Kent State

Thomson Gale Literature Product Advisory Board

The members of the Thomson Gale Literature Product Advisory Board—reference librarians from public and academic library systems—represent a cross-section of our customer base and offer a variety of informed perspectives on both the presentation and content of our literature products. Advisory board members assess and define such quality issues as the relevance, currency, and usefulness of the author coverage, critical content, and literary topics included in our series; evaluate the layout, presentation, and general quality of our printed volumes; provide feedback on the criteria used for selecting authors and topics covered in our series; provide suggestions for potential enhancements to our series; identify any gaps in our coverage of authors or literary topics, recommending authors or topics for inclusion; analyze the appropriateness of our content and presentation for various user audiences, such as high school students, undergraduates, graduate students, librarians, and educators; and offer feedback on any proposed changes/enhancements to our series. We wish to thank the following advisors for their advice throughout the year.

Judaism in Nineteenth-Century Literature

The following entry provides commentary on the treatment of Judaism in nineteenth-century literature. For further information on the portrayal of Jews in nineteenth-century English literature, see *NCLC,* Volume 72.

INTRODUCTION

Although Jewish characters were often stereotypically portrayed in nineteenth-century literature, the shifting ideals of the nineteenth century brought changes in the ways Jews were perceived and in the ways they interacted within society. During the eighteenth century the Enlightenment was pivotal in providing the impetus for a societal reappraisal of the treatment of Jews. Christians began to question the morality of segregating Jewish communities, and as they began to define themselves more as rational individuals, it became less acceptable to deny Jews certain rights.

During the mid-eighteenth century, anyone converting to Judaism or assisting someone in their conversion could face the death penalty. By the late eighteenth century, freedom of religion was allowed in principle. However, in practice, it was forbidden by anti-Semitic legislation. Converts were required to obtain a release from the Christian authorities, yet Christian leaders were not allowed to grant releases. In 1850, the constitution of the North German Confederation instituted freedom of religion. The commercial success of Wilhelm Herzberg's novel, *Jüdische Familienpapiere* (1868), reflected the increased public interest in Judaism that arose from the many debates surrounding the issues of conversion.

As Jews began assimilating into the larger community, the need to retain and defend their religious identity became a more widespread concern. Rabbi Elia Benamozegh wrote *Morale juive et morale chrétienne* (1867) in an effort to illustrate that because Christianity is derived from Judaism, the integrity of Jewish morality cannot be considered inferior to that of Christian morality. According to critic Katharina Gerstenberger, *Ich suchte Dich!* (1898), Nahida Ruth Lazarus's narrative autobiography, is not just a story of the author's conversion to Judaism, but of her personal emancipation as a woman through her declaration of her Jewish identity.

As part of their own Enlightenment, or Haskalah, Jews experienced a new economic and political security along with their rise in social status. Participation in many fields in the arts and sciences became available to Jews, and while they were not universally welcomed, they began engaging in such mainstream pursuits. Immanuel Wolf outlines the importance of the study of Judaism in his "Über den Begriff einer Wissenschaft des Judentums," (1822; "On the Concepts of a Science of Judaism"), and Leopold Zunz asserts in his *Zur Geschichte und Literatur* (1845; *History and Literature*) that the achievements of Jewish scholars in the study of Judaism will lead to better quality of life for all Jews. In order to firmly establish their identity as a people, nineteenth-century Jewish scholars emphasized the importance of establishing and documenting a Jewish historical perspective, which is presented in several popular histories, including Heinrich Graetz's *Die konstruktion der Jüdischen geschichte* (1936; *The Structure of Jewish History*), Abraham Geiger's *Das Judenthum und seine geschichte* (1864; *Judaism and Its History*), and Isak Marcus Jost's *Allegemeine geschichte des Israelitischen volkes* (1832). The study of Judaism expanded and the Jewish connection to Gnosticism became a hotly debated aspect of Jewish history. Graetz, in his *Gnosticismus und Judenthum* (1846), considers Gnosticism a tainting of the Jewish religion, while Moriz Friedländer in *Der vorchristliche jüdische Gnosticismus* (1898) welcomes the discussion of Gnostic ideas and Judaism, asserting that such debate is necessary and beneficial for the expansion of the Jewish religion and to offer an alternative to the Palestinian nationalistic perspective.

Critic Shirley M. Dettlaff examines Herman Melville's use of the dichotomy between Hebraism and Hellenism in his poem *Clarel* (1876). Dettlaff asserts that Melville explores this dichotomy because it mirrors that of the representations of humanity in Victorian interpretations of Greco-Roman versus Judeo-Christian traditions, as well as the concerns of human identity within the Romantic tradition. One German scholar whose commentary on Jews and Judaism has been widely regarded as anti-Semitic, or at best, negative, is Friedrich Nietzsche. Critic Jacob Golomb points out, however, that Nietzsche's views on Judaism and Jews correspond to his general philosophical and psychological tenets, including the Apollonian and Dionysian principles, and the struggle to control, or overcome, oneself. In the lyrics within his *Hebrew Melodies* (1815), Lord Byron utilizes biblical imagery and stories from the Old Testament both to support the cause of Jewish nationalism and offer Romantic commentary on the human condition. George Eliot began research for *Daniel Deronda*

(1876) in 1873, reading Jewish history and viewing firsthand Jewish communities and synagogues in Frankfurt, Germany, and elsewhere in Europe. The novel's eponymous protagonist learns of his Jewish heritage as an adult, and resolves to help realize his brother-in-law Mordecai's vision of a Zionist homeland. The novel concludes with Daniel's departure with his wife for Palestine. Eliot's contemporaries censured *Daniel Deronda* as disjointed and of uneven quality, and this assessment has been shared by modern commentators. While Eliot was disappointed by her audience's failure to accept the work as an organic whole, she was gratified by the praise lavished on her work by Jewish readers. Portions of the novel, including some eloquent affirmations of Zionist ideals and Eliot's warm tributes to Jewish culture, were widely known among Eastern European Jews, who read the novel in translation. Post-nineteenth-century critics have offered numerous analyses of the treatment of Jewish themes in *Daniel Deronda*, which have variously been described as allegorical, mythic, visionary, and symbolic. Critic Bernadette Waterman Ward has opined that Eliot's desire to support the Jewish cause was well intended, but it was ultimately unsuccessful because the Jewish cultural aspects and Zionist message are diluted by the uneven narrative and flat characterization.

Nineteenth-century writers of Jewish and non-Jewish backgrounds fought, through their work, to make countless political, economic, racial, and religious statements about Jewish life, the Jewish identity, and the role of the Jew in mainstream society. While their struggle for equality was not totally realized, the changing views and philosophies of the nineteenth century allowed Jews to achieve a measure of freedom that had previously eluded them.

REPRESENTATIVE WORKS

Matthew Arnold

Culture and Anarchy: An Essay in Political and Social Criticism (essay) 1869

Elia Benamozegh

Morale juive et morale chrétienne: examen comparatif suivi de quelques réflexions sur les principes de l'islamisme (essay) 1867

Lord Byron

Hebrew Melodies (poetry) 1815

George Eliot

Daniel Deronda (novel) 1876

Moriz Friedländer

Der vorchristliche jüdische Gnosticismus (essay) 1898

Abraham Geiger

Das Judenthum und seine geschichte [*Judaism and Its History*] (history) 1864

Heinrich Graetz

Gnosticismus und Judenthum (essay) 1846

*Die konstruktion der Jüdischen geschichte: eine skizze [*The Structure of Jewish History*] (essay) 1936

Wilhelm Herzberg

Jüdische Familienpapiere [as Gustav Meinhardt] (novel) 1868

Theodor Herzl

Der Judenstaat [*The Jewish State*] (history) 1896

Isak Marcus Jost

Allegemeine geschichte des Israelitischen volkes (history) 1832

Nahida Ruth Lazarus

Ich suchte Dich! (autobiography) 1898

Herman Melville

Clarel: A Poem and Pilgrimage in the Holy Land (poetry) 1876

Friedrich Schiller

Über naive und sentimentalische dichtung [*On Naïve and Sentimental Poetry*] (essays) 1795-96; published in the journal *Die Horen*

August Wilhelm von Schlegel

Über dramatische Kunst und Litteratur: Vorlesungen. 2 vols. [*A Course of Lectures on Dramatic Art and Literature*] (lectures) 1809-11

A. Schmiedl

Studien über jüdische, insonders jüdisch-arabische Religions-philosophie (history) 1869

Immanuel Wolf

"Über den Begriff einer Wissenschaft des Judentums" ["On the Concepts of a Science of Judaism"] (essay) 1822; published in the journal *Zeitschrift für die Wissenschaft des Judentums*

Leopold Zunz

Zeitschrift für die Wissenschaft des Judenthums [editor] (journal) 1822-23

Die gottesdienstlichen Vorträge der Juden, historisch en wickelt. Ein beitrag zur alterthumskunde und Biblischen Kritik, zur Literatur-und Religionsgeschichte (history) 1832

Zur Geschichte und Literatur [*History and Literature*] (history) 1845

*This work was written in 1886.

CONTEMPORARY COMMENTARY

The Saturday Review (review date 14 November 1868)

SOURCE: "A Rabbi's View of Jewish and Christian Morality." *The Saturday Review* 26, no. 681 (14 November 1868): 661-62.

[*In the following review of* Morale juive et morale chrétienne: examen comparatif suivi de quelques réflexions sur les principes de l'islamisme *(1867) by Rabbi Elia Benamozegh, the reviewer expounds on Benamozegh's assertion that because Christianity is a branch of Judaism, it could not possess a superior morality with a divine origin.*]

Despite the increased attention given in recent years to Semitic theology, few Christian scholars of repute have addressed themselves to the exploration of the Talmud, the Targums, and the other labyrinths of rabbinical learning. Although the language of these books is easier and more accessible than Sanskrit or Zend, for one student of the Zohar and Midraschims there are a dozen of the Vendidad and the Puranas. Semitic religious quibbles may be a less inviting field of research than Vedic or Zoroastrian philosophy, but many of them are intimately connected with the foundations of the Christian faith. So that, if, as M. Renan asserts, the Buxtorfs and Lightfoots have no worthy representatives now, we ought to be grateful to those learned Jews who from time to time enlighten our darkness on subjects like that which occupies the present volume [*Morale juive et morale chrétienne,* by Elia Benamozegh]. The Italian Rabbi's volume comparing Jewish and Christian morality is interesting, not only for its contents, but also because it has been sanctioned as orthodox by high Jewish theological authority. Some competent observers allege that scepticism on the one hand, and Christianity on the other, are gradually undermining the faith of the peculiar people. Be this as it may, our author does not regard Christianity with the passions of Annas and Caiaphas. To use his own illustration, he deplores that Joseph does not bow down before the white hairs of Jacob, and that Jacob does not embrace and bless Joseph. He calls Christianity a Jewish product of which Jews should be proud. Just as Englishmen may boast of the English origin of American civilization, so Jews may say with pride that the splendid tree of Christianity is a branch from a humble Jewish stock grafted on a Gentile trunk. This branch still bears the mark of the patriarchs, the prophets, and the doctors of the law; if the hands are the hands of Esau, the voice is nevertheless the voice of Jacob.

The Italian Rabbi takes exception to the argument that the superior morality of the Christian code indicates a divine original. That Christianity has owed its triumph to its moral claims he does not deny, but he considers that the natural religious sentiment of man can produce, unaided, ethical systems not inferior in elevation to the doctrines of Christ, quoting in proof hereof the cases of Confucius, Menov, and the sages of antiquity. As compared with Paganism, Christian morals were, no doubt, an advance to a purer, surer, and more independent rule of life. But much of the Messianic moral creed is, in fact—so Mr. Benamozegh argues—a mere repetition of the teaching of the Synagogue. Nor could such fail to be the case. Christianity itself declares that God gave the patriarchs and Moses a moral code. That code must be admitted to have been good, perfect, and absolute, for the Deity could not have promulgated a scheme stamped with the attributes of the mutable and contingent. If this be granted, how, asks this writer, can it be alleged that the same Deity afterwards promulgated a second scheme superior to the first? Men are capable of progress, but progress cannot be predicated of the Absolute, nor can His law be called perfectible. This should be the language of logic, but Christians, according to our author, seem to consider that the divine word is as flexible as mere human doctrine. Moses spoke of man as created in the image of God, whereas Christianity, like Homer, makes God in the image of man. "Il a mis en Dieu," says our author, "la flexibilité de Paul, qui se fait *Juif aux Juifs, Gentil aux Gentils,* les ignobles condescendances des Jésuites aux idolâtres chinois." In the Christian view, he adds, crumbs of truth are scattered to men by degrees, suitable to their readiness to receive them. But this plan seems hard to reconcile with a faith in the permanence of the Messianic system. If by divine command Paul superseded Moses, may not Providence, stooping to man's wants, hereafter efface the doctrines of Paul by a new creed suited to new circumstances and times?

General readers are familiar with the stock objections to the moral code of the Pentateuch. Mr. F. W. Newman in our day, Bolingbroke in the last century, have repeated—the first with something of reverential regret, the second with spiteful glee—the views which St. Augustine combated with so much zeal in the person of Faustus. Whoever is aware that modern Biblical criticism was invented by the Gnostics, not by the Germans, will know that early heresy inferred from the moral imperfections of the Law of Moses that the Jewish legislator was not inspired from heaven. Some of the Gnostics even maintained that only the principle of evil could have ordered the theft of the vases and precious garments of the Egyptians, the unsparing massacre of the nations of Canaan, the murders and executions by command which crowd the sacred annals. The Italian Rabbi, like St. Augustine, argues the points at issue without flying into a spiritual passion; and although his discussion partakes somewhat of the weakness always inherent in defence, his reasons, if not quite new, are stated with an ingenuity which makes them seem so. He says that comparisons of Christian and Jewish morality, to be accurate, should keep in view the distinction between politics and morals. The peculiar people were *Jews* as well as *Hebrews*—members, that is to say, of the Jewish civil commonwealth, and disciples of the monotheistic faith of their father Abraham. The Pentateuch is the political and rituary code of the Jews, ennobled, no doubt, by a spiritual breath from Sinai, but still a system of civil legislation. Politics are not morals; the "Imitation of Christ" does not supersede international law; Thomas à-Kempis is not a refutation of Grotius. The Gospel precepts of humility and patience cannot be applied to nations. What country could turn the cheek to the smiter, and repay injuries with benefits, without becoming the inevitable victim of invasion, conquest, and annihilation? This is the Rabbi's question; he may be unaware that a numerous, perhaps an increasing, school of English politicians recommends this very plan to our Foreign Office. Moses, at any rate, cannot be quoted in support of such diplomatic policy. He saw that the Jews must, as a people, be governed by the rules of political wisdom. He prescribed for them—with what rare foresight the result shows—a system by which they fought their way against ignorance, injustice, and barbarism. In view of the end, the general rules of humanity and morality appeared to suffer some temporary restrictions:—"Sans ces mesures, toute la puissance de Dieu, j'ose le dire, n'aurait pu épargner au peuple d'Israël une prompte, une inévitable destruction." These remarks, if not conclusive, are judicious; they are identical in direction with the line taken by the late Dean Milman where he discusses the war law of the Jews.

The distinction between the political and ethical sides of Old Testament dogmas, the antithesis of Hebrews and Jews, lies at the base of our author's comparison of the morality of the basilica and the synagogue. He tries to show, always with abundance of apt citation, that the morality of the Gospel is, in fact, a copy of that preached by the Law—a copy, as he thinks, deteriorated and obscured. Here, again, we must avoid mistaking a part for the whole. The Old Testament is not the entire Hebrew system, which must necessarily be misunderstood by those who ignore the resources of tradition, of the Talmud, and the Cabbalists. Further, we must not attribute to the Pharisees, for instance, all the sentiments fixed on them by Palestinian prejudice. As a sample of our Rabbi's analysis, we may take the virtue of humility, which, he says, Christianity arrogates to itself as a doctrine of its own special teaching. The sentiment "Blessed are the poor in spirit" was by no means preached for the first time in the Sermon on the Mount. Ancient rabbinical teaching had constantly exalted the humble in spirit and place. Of Hillel the Ancient, who long preceded Christianity, this favourite maxim is recorded—"My lowness shall be my elevation, and my elevation my lowness." In the Talmud we find—"The world to come is to those who bow the knee, the humble, and the bent:" and such sentences abound in the old Rabbinical texts. According to the Mischna, Josua ben Perachia, the preceptor of Christ, taught thus:—"Judge every man favourably;" Hillel said, "Judge not thy neighbour as long as thou hast not been in his situation;" which maxims are equivalent to the Christian, "Judge not, lest ye be judged." In like manner our author confronts the Hebrew and Christian teaching as to pride and anger, dwelling particularly on the command to love our neighbour as ourselves; trying to show, in these as in other cases, that the synagogue had long been familiar with the teaching which is claimed by Christianity as exclusively its own.

As our author always quotes chapter and verse, his arguments have at first sight an impregnable look. They must, however, in the main, stand or fall with the credibility of the Talmudists and the various Rabbinical texts. Now against such credibility the general *primâ facie* evidence is so overwhelming, that arguments in which it is taken as an essential postulate must be classed amongst conjectures rather than amongst proofs. The Talmuds, in their present shape, are hardly earlier than the age of Charlemagne. Of the standard Rabbinical authors some are mere names, concerning which the Jews have been able to do little else than guess. Hillel, for example, is an unknown quantity, who appears, like Zoroaster or Odin, in more incarnations than one, his personality, single, or multiple, being a profound puzzle. As witnesses to matters of fact, the Mischna, Gemara, Zohar, and so forth, must rank below such Sagas as Burnt Njal, and such poems as the *Sháh Náinah*. To find a parallel to the allegorical and cabbalistical nonsense of the Jewish doctors we must turn to Papias, or Philo, or to the modern chemical expositions of the Eddas and the Nibelungen Lied. As a specimen of the flights taken, be it noted that, according to the Talmudists, Moses caused *the entire Pentateuch to be engraved in seventy languages* on the twelve stones beyond Jordan! (Deut. xxvii.). Touching Genesis, some Cabbalists declare that Abraham wrote a work called Séfer Tetsira, or Creation, which work they have even edited and commented, adding complete lists of the angels who were the Masters of the Patriarchs. Very precise details are given about Raziel, the Master of Adam. That intelligent and refined angel brought down from heaven, or elsewhere, a book of wisdom—the Sifra de-Adam harischôn—whose contents are accurately described in the Zohar. No wonder if Luther said that the critics who went for light to the Rabbinical comments on the Bible reminded him of Solomon's captains who traded to India for precious cargoes, but came home laden with apes and peacocks. How far the modern Rabbi mistakes apes for gold may be gathered from the fact that, in a note to an Essay on Islamism which closes his volume, he speaks of the existence of the aforesaid books of Adam and Abraham as being authentically proved by their mention in the Talmud; although, as he says, the Talmud does not expound their contents.

The Saturday Review (review date 5 March 1870)

SOURCE: "Judæo-Arabic Metaphysics." *The Saturday Review* 29, no. 749 (5 March 1870): 325-26.

[*In the following review of* Studien über jüdische, insonders jüdisch-arabische Religions-philosophie *(1869) by A. Schmiedl, the reviewer offers a favorable assessment of Schmiedl's discussion of Judæo-Arabic metaphysical thought.*]

Given that most complex and fragmentary body of literature, ranging from times beyond historic ken down to the fullness of Hellenic culture, which we call collectively the Old Testament; given further those mazes of legal enactments, gorgeous day-dreams, masked history, ill-disguised rationalism, and the rest, which form the Talmud and the Midrash; given also the Kabbalah, and, finally, Plato and Aristotle as developed by Jews and Mohammedans either on the basis of their fundamentally identical creed or independently—what was the attitude of the Synagogue towards all these elements, as far as they treated of the first problems of all religion and all philosophy? What was the process whereby the widely diverging statements and speculations on Creation, the Soul, the Hereafter, the nature of the Deity, contained in those authorities, were sought to be blended and harmonized so as to satisfy both Jewish faith and thought?—a faith fervent and passionate beyond measure, to which all visions and all transcendentalism and allegories were so many historical facts, for all of which death was sweet and holy—and a boldness of thought which, with all reverence, frankly said, as Socrates had said, "That divinely revealed wisdom of which you speak I deny not, inasmuch as I do not know it; I can only understand human reason." The everlasting battle between reason and blind belief in "that which is written" was fought with very grim seriousness in the early period of the middle ages within the bosom of the Jewish Church. And while we survey the history of that controversy as it was taken up and continued in the Christian Church, we blush to find, from the very days of Albertus Magnus, the Doctor Universalis, and Tho-

mas Aquinas, the Doctor Angelicus, down to our own, perfect nests of arguments both on the side of orthodoxy and of rationalism, unconsciously perhaps, but most unmistakably stolen from the mediæval successors of those same Rabbis to whom Jerome owed his Vulgate-lore. To write a history of Jewish metaphysics would indeed be an undertaking worthy to rank with the highest, most difficult, and most interesting and instructive tasks; especially if attempted as a contribution to the history of human rationalism. The religious development from, say, Hillel the "freethinker," who calmly compressed all the Law and the Prophets into the familiar "Be good, my dear," to Maimonides, the "Great Eagle," who more explicitly and scientifically lays down the supreme axiom that every word of the Bible must either be in accordance with rational conclusions or be explained "metaphorically," and who totally denies an "individual" working of Providence; and on to Baruch Spinoza, in whom Goethe—how much of this nineteenth century besides?—lives and moves and has his being—this would indeed be goodly work for a whole life-time.

Our author [A. Schmiedl, in *Studien über jüdische-arabische Religions-philosophie*] has not attempted anything so ambitious. Very far from it. He is satisfied with gathering a few mosaics from the discussions on these metaphysical topics in the Judæo-Arabic schools; and we are duly grateful. In the circumscribed field which he has chosen he has worked conscientiously, and on the whole very successfully. But the curse of wishing to write "popularly" has been upon him, and consequently, being bereft of that very special gift of enthusiasm which is akin to poetry, and which at times is found to lend a strange charm even to the most abstruse subjects, he has so far failed. The mere discarding of learned notes is not always sufficient to make a book either striking or pleasant. Nor has Dr. Schmiedl always been happy in the methodical arrangement of his subjects; whence spring repetitions of a needless and very tedious kind. There is also a looseness of style and language which a little care would have obviated. Having delivered our soul of these slight objections, we shall give a brief glance at the varied contents of the volume itself.

The first disquisition or chapter—the subject of which is taken up again in the second—treats of the Deity as conceived by Jewish philosophy. The existence of God is of course presupposed; or it would no longer be Jewish philosophy. But what about His attributes? Has He any? Scripture, literally taken, seems to affirm this. Yet, taken in a higher sense, as understood by the Alexandrines, the Targum, and the Talmud, it denies it. Philosophy, on its part, found a *contradictio in adjecto* in an absolute Being or Supreme Cause, the sole essence of which is its Oneness and Uniqueness, being considered, either subjectively or objectively, as presenting qualities or *accidences*. This contest between the "Attributists" and "Nonattributists" was indeed one of the fiercest and bitterest, and each camp boasted of brilliant champions. But the latter carried the day, led by no meaner authorities than Ibn Ezra, Jehuda Halevi, and Maimonides. The last of these goes the length of calling the view of his antagonists anti-Jewish. "As well might you say at once that 'He is One but rather Three, besides being Three but rather One.' If you give attributes to a thing, you define this thing; and defining a thing means to bring it under some head, to compare it with something like it. God is sole of His kind. Determine Him, circumscribe Him, and you bring Him down to the modes and categories of created things." The Talmud in its characteristic way relates the story of a precentor who heaped divine epithet upon epithet, and whom a master asked when he had finished—"And have you now quite exhausted God's good qualities?" The Psalms speak of "silence" as the best mode of praising God. Nor is the endeavour which goes through all postexilian literature, of finding a kind of medium between the Inconceivable and the world of matter, foreign to this notion. "Word," or "Holy Ghost," or "Shechinah," are the forms under which Judaism at that early period tried in its speech and thought to approach that which itself, shrouded in the ineffable mystery of the Tetragrammaton, was beyond human thought or approach. Indeed, we should say that the whole Angelology, so strikingly simple before the exile, and so wonderfully complex after it, owes its quick development on Babylonian soil to the same awe-stricken desire which grows with growing culture, removing that inconceivable *Ens* further and further from human touch and ken. At the same time the Talmud protests against anything like the notion of angels interceding on behalf of man. They are nought but messengers, created for the purpose of their message. More clearly still does Maimonides call every natural law, every being, animated or other, so that it fulfils a certain behest, an "Angel." Thus, he says, a prophet is an angel; the elements are angels; the stars are angels; and so are the sea, the winds, and the human intellect. When the Talmud speaks of God as having consulted the angels ("the Circle or Family above") in the fashioning of every part of the human organism, this, he says, shows that everything in creation is done in accordance with the manifold laws of nature, each ruling over its own sphere, and all coming more or less into play in the complicated human frame. Again, when the Talmud reduces the number of angels whom Jacob saw in his dream at Bethel to four, two mounting upwards and two descending downwards, it merely hints at the wondrous weaving and working in the Cosmos by the four fundamental elements—fire and air which strive upwards, and water and earth which tend downwards. And, as if to leave no doubt, the Talmud had further called thinking man superior to the angels. This dictum, however, was fiercely contested in the mediæval

schools. Is man greater because he has a will and may struggle against evil, while the angel can only do what he is bidden? or because man is the centre of creation, even as the earth, according to the astronomy of the period, rests in the middle of the universe? And some schools unhesitatingly doubted and denied the very truth of this opinion enunciated by the Talmud. Is man greater than other creatures? And is he the aim and end of creation, or merely the most perfect organism on earth? Saadia holds the former, Ibn Ezra and Maimonides hold the latter, view. Scripture, argues the first, calls angels "divine beings," and the stars (which the "angels" are supposed to be moving) "sons of God." But remember, Ibn Ezra says, how infinitely larger certain stars are than the whole earth, and do you think that the inconceivably vast host of the heavens can be meant for, and inferior to, the small dust-born human being? Still more sharply does Maimonides ridicule the very notion of "stars or angels" being made for the sake of man, who by the side of these "intelligences" sinks into utter insignificance. The practical consequence of this discussion was that the "honourable mention," not to say "invocation," of angels—which had been stamped out by the Talmud, and which had grown up again by stealth under foreign influences—now received its death-blow. Even the minor masters call it rank idolatry. And the Kabbalists, to whom Angelology is almost the first condition of religious existence, are forced to plead that all those endless varieties of their holy names are but so many anagrams of divine and biblical epithets, and that it is God and not "Patrons" whom they invoke. To stretch the point to the utmost, it was distinctly denied that when Joshua prostrated himself before the angel, he intended to show the angel any reverence. He bowed down before Him who had deemed him worthy of a message—even as a man shows honour even to a dead piece of paper which comes from some one he reveres.

Among the many topics further touched upon in the book before us, such as prophecy, metempsychosis—the notion of which, we may passingly observe, Saadia calls "sheer insanity"—the resurrection, allegorism, &c., we would fain have dwelt somewhat more fully upon the Anthropomorphisms and Anthropopathisms in the Bible, with which Judaism, properly so called, had from the beginning dealt unsparingly. From the Targum, which scrupulously effaces every term which might lead to the thought of a corporeal existence of God, to the Midrash, whose most daring protest against the human similes used even by the prophets Maimonides approvingly quotes; from the broad axiom of the Mishnah, that these things are not to be taken literally—"the Thorah speaking merely in a human way"—to the days when Yedaya Penini could say that at last this Anthromorphistic absurdity had been finally driven even from the obscurest brains—we find one endless series of attempts to get rid of all materialistic interpretation of undoubtedly materialistic terminology. Rough, indeed, is the manner in which Maimonides disposes of the "Voice" on Sinai, or God's "descending thereon"—which the Talmud already declares to be but a figure of speech—and nothing can be more characteristic than the almost contemptuously good-natured manner in which he finally allows the hopelessly unthinking to do as they please about these things. "If some of the short-sighted will not rise to the step to which we endeavour to lift them, let them by all means imagine all such terms (Angels, & c.) to refer to something material—no great harm will come of it." It was indeed only the devotees of Cabbala and Karaism who still protested against these rationalizing Talmudistic views, and their end has been either petrifaction and death, or, worse still, coarse imposture and religious delirium.

We here take leave of our author, grateful for his suggestive and learned "Studies," and hoping soon to meet him again on the same field. But let him not be afraid of bringing with him his whole apparatus next time, however bulky it may be.

JUDAISM IN GERMAN THEORY AND CULTURE

Jacob Golomb (essay date 1985)

SOURCE: Golomb, Jacob. "Nietzsche on Jews and Judaism." *Archiv für Geschichte der Philosophie* 67, no. 2 (1985): 139-61.

[*In the following essay, Golomb presents the main tenets of Nietzsche's psychology, Nietzsche's image of the Jew, and his attitude toward Judaism. The critic asserts that both Nietzsche's admiration and rejection of the Jews stem directly from his psychological doctrine.*]

Several scholars have examined the intriguing issue of Nietzsche's attitude toward Jews and Judaism.[1] Most of these studies dealt with that subject in isolation from the rest of his philosophy. However a balanced understanding of his views on the Jewish question, (or any other topic in his thought) can only be attained from within Nietzsche's general philosophical framework. This applies not only to those who consider Nietzsche a proto-Nazi[2] but also to those of Nietzsche's apologists who, in their fight against the 'Nazi-ization' of Nietzsche, deal with the issue of Judaism in his writings from the narrow perspective of his theory of Races and his social attitudes.[3] These commentators, despite good intentions, disregard the basic point—that Nietzsche's social and cultural attitudes were derived from the basic intuitions of his general philosophy.

This article attempts to show that Nietzsche's attitude toward Judaism is not arbitrary but derived from, and consistent with, the rest of his philosophical-psychological doctrine. His remarks on the Jews and Judaism are applications of this doctrine to the Jewish People taken as a case study. This serves both to corroborate Nietzsche's theory and foster his practical aspirations. From this perspective, Nietzsche's attitude towards Judaism and the Jewish people becomes important yardstick for determining the meaning and integrity of Nietzsche's thought.

Nietzsche's thought, despite its misleading external literary form, is a consistent and unified whole. Nietzsche's own words testify to the fact that there is one uniting theme running through his thought, one "common root" and "fundamental will of knowledge" from which his "philosophical tree" must have arisen and around which his earlier and later views are "entwined and interlaced".[4]

Considering Nietzsche's attitude toward Jews within the wider theoretical framework of his thought enables us to adopt a cooler and more objective tone and to avoid the emotional and apologetic preoccupations of previous expositions. Nietzsche sees the Jews from a philosophical-psychological perspective, not in an impulse or arbitrary way. His review of Jewish "characteristic features" is balanced. He finds a lot of "good" in them, but also a lot of "evil". These terms must be understood in accordance with his philosophical conceptions of "good" and "evil", which lie far beyond the common man's understanding of these concepts. His objective attitude towards the Jewish people is clearly seen in his discussion of the "negative" features of the Jews: he never fails to describe and explain the peculiar socio-economic and historical circumstances which caused the Jews to develop these features.

Nietzsche's statement that in his thought psychology is "the path to the fundamental problems" (*J. G. B.* 23) also applies to his treatment of Jews and Judaism. I try to show that both Nietzsche's rejection and his admiration of the Jews stem primarily from his psychological doctrine. Thus I shall begin with a concise presentation of the main tenets of Nietzschean psychology. After that, I describe the Nietzschean image of the Jew. Finally, I examine Nietzsche's attitude toward Judaism.

1. The Nietzschean Concept of Power

When Nietzsche speaks of the "fundamental problems" (*J. G. B.* 23) he is referring to the "moral intentions" which, for him constitute "the real germ of life . . . in every philosophy" (*ibid.,* 6).

In his attempt to determine the foundations of the germ of life, Nietzsche is in need of a special type of psychology. The main aim of this psychology is to entice the reader to expose in and for himself the roots of his creative powers. In this way Nietzschean psychology becomes a vital means for a positive "temptation" (*Versuchung*) as against the various negative cultural "seductions" (*Verführungen*). Nietzsche seeks to help his reader recognize his power and to use it creatively and morally in authentic patterns of living, which he calls the pathos of positive power. Thus, the concept of power (*Macht*) becomes the central theme of the whole of Nietzschean thought.[5] It becomes what Nietzsche calls the "common root", out of which grows the whole philosophical "tree" (*G. M.* Preface: 2).

Nietzsche explicitly identifies his theory of *Macht* with his "new Psychology", which has "dared to descend into the depth" (*J. G. B.* 23), and become a "morphology" and "*the doctrine of the development of the will* to power" (*ibid.*). This new psychology exposes the basic instinct of the human, all-too-human soul. This instinct is not identical with the hylic pure drive, the animalistic, violent and uncontrollable force which Nietzsche calls *Kraft* and rejects in *The Birth of Tragedy* in his discussion of the "Dionysian barbarian" (*G. T.* 2; 8). However, since Power is also a drive, it integrates the energetic-driving elements of the hylic instincts with the Apollinian components, which moulds the instinctual stream. Thus it is a creative drive embodying the synthesis between the two primary Nietzschean principles—the Apollinian and the Dionysian.

Since man is a creative, instinctive creature, (a sort of *homo faber*), he is also a will to power. Mature Nietzschean thought aims at exposing this psychological substratum in major cultural phenomena: philosophy, religion, science *etc*. However, it is in the moral field *per se,* which is of major interest to Nietzsche, that this principle manifests itself to the fullest and expresses the free, creative overcoming of any natural limitations in ourselves or our surroundings. Therefore, according to Nietzsche, man is nothing but a will-to-power, that is, a will to an authentic and creative morality and culture. The essential element of this key concept of Nietzschean psychology—the will-to-power—is the idea of overcoming one's self (*Selbstüberwindung*). Nietzsche first came to recognize this phenomenon when he discovered the mechanism of Sublimation, anticipating a similar idea in Freud.[6] In the process of *Sublimierung,* Nietzsche discovers a mental mechanism which enables one to attain "self-control" by fighting with "the mighty drive".

Thus, this process exhibits the Hegelian phenomenon of *Aufhebung,* in which some elements are destroyed while others are preserved and raised to a higher level. Hence, the Nietzschean concept of overcoming one's self includes the notions of maturation and development, of an unhindered process of growing up, in which alien elements that do not belong to the person's organic self

and which may prohibit the personality from attaining freedom and creative authenticity, are overcome. To the question why overcome one's self? Nietzsche answers: In order to grow up and attain power. In this sense the will-to-power, which embraces the overcoming of inhibiting elements, is actually identical with the will to selfhood, the will to be a creative and spontaneous person who found his own values and is motivated from within to materialize them. The more quality there is in the will-to-power the more freedom, authenticity and creativity is manifested by the powerful person. The optimal will-to-power is found in the *Übermensch.* The less quality a person's will possesses, the more the person wishes to escape his selfhood and merge with the mob. The mentally sound personality possesses a positive will-to-power and *vice versa.* Such a personality also adopts the "master-morality", in contradistinction to the "slave-morality". The "slave-morality" indicates a negative will-to-power, it is found in those who operate on a qualitatively low level of mental life.

Thus the Nietzschean concept of power is complex. Nietzsche treats the psychology of power in most of his main writings (*Human, All-Too-Human, Dawn, The Gay Science, Beyond Good and Evil, On the Genealogy of Morals*), and consistently distinguishes between the *negative* and the *positive* expressions of power.

Negative power manifests itself in a psychologically weak personality that lacks power and strives incessantly to attain it.

> Es gibt Rezepte zum Gefühle der Macht, einmal für solche, welche sich selber beherrschen können und welche bereits dadurch *in einem Gefühle der Macht zu Hause sind*; sodann *für solche welchen gerade dies fehlt.*
>
> (*M.,* 65)

Such negative power was manifested by the Christians. They constructed their religion out of their craving for power. Since they lacked positive power, they invented "sin", "guilt-feelings", "bad conscience" and the like (*G. M.* II). They used these "inventions" in order to torture their victims and gain advantage over them (*M.* 53). This kind of power—which looks to enhance itself by means of pleasure derived from aggressive, violent or cruel acts—is associated with a tendency to excel at all cost, to win all of life's competitions, to gain prizes, medals, and prestige. People who seek this kind of power lack any feeling of positive power. One who possesses genuine positive power does not feel any need to gain recognition thereby. He does not need to test his power in competitions and trials, but expresses it spontaneously and genuinely. He is in no need whatsoever of pleasures which originate in aggression in order to enhance his feeling of power. The *Gefühl der Macht* is already within him.

PATTERNS OF NEGATIVE POWER

1. Lack or impoverishment of power;
2. Depression; melancholy and suspension of action;
3. Heteronomous dependence upon external circumstances and resources;
4. Violence and cruel exploitation as means for enhancement of power and as resentment;
5. Escape to transcendence and various metaphysical types of comfort and consolation;
6. Castration, Depression and Repression of Instincts;
7. Ascetic patterns of life;
8. Dogmatism and Extremism;
9. Heaviness, passivity and *Akrasia*;
10. Vengefulness and *Ressentiment*;
11. Cowardice and pursuit of security;
12. Nihilism, decadence and fatigue: the preservation of being;
13. Hatred out of fear;
14. Resignation and submissiveness;
15. Pessimism and "thought of death";
16. Fear of natural inclination;
17. The need for system, logic and dialectics;
18. "Internal distress and uncertainty", guilt feelings;
19. Shrewdness, intelligence and spiritualization;

PATTERNS OF POSITIVE POWER

1. Fullness and plentitude of power;
2. Elation; dynamic vitality;
3. Autonomy and creation of values; self-sufficiency;
4. Violence as a spontaneous by-product of the direct manifestation of power;
5. Heroism and greatness;
6. Creative sublimation of Instincts;
7. Aesthetic life;
8. Intellectual tolerance;
9. Lightness and gaiety;
10. Generousity and Nobility;
11. Courage and adventurousness;
12. "Strong instinct", "will to life": enhancement of being;
13. Refined contempt;
14. *Amor fati,* self-acceptance and affirmation;
15. "Thought of life" and sober optimism;
16. Sensualism and acceptance of one's inclinations;
17. "The ability to accept contradiction";
18. Lack of guilt; clear conscience;
19. Spontaneous, direct and impulsive activity.

These two concepts of power are not merely theoretical terms: they also indicate two distinct psychological types, which manifest their respective kinds of power in their everyday patterns of living. In his writings, Nietzsche deals extensively with these two types of power. Below, most of the predicates used to characterize them have been presented in the form of a table. Using the table, it becomes clear that where Nietzsche finds manifestations of positive power in the Jews, he admires and praises them. Where he discovers features that characterize negative patterns of power, he condemns and rejects them. Nietzsche uses the Jews as a case study of his general psychological doctrine; analysis of the Jewish people (as well as the Ancient Greeks and Germans) plays a heuristic and didactic role in his thought.

2. NIETZSCHE'S PERCEPTION OF THE JEW

The above diagram enables us to understand Nietzsche's attitude toward Jews and prevents a distorted understanding due to our own conventional values. Thus, for example, when Nietzsche claims that the Jews are a people endowed with "high intelligence" (*M. A.* 475) and "spirit" (*W. M.* 864; cf. the last item of the above table)—these descriptions will not be considered compliments if we take Nietzsche's psychological views into consideration. According to Nietzsche, the strengthening of the functions of the mind and the over-development of the Apollinian reason cause weakening of the Dionysian power and lead to the destruction of the delicate balance between these two mental principles. The intellect has developed in people with the psychological pattern of the "slave". This is the result of pressure exerted on them by persons with positive power. Out of fear, the "slaves" could not express their drives directly and consequently repress them within themselves. Instead of a spontaneous externalization of their instincts, there appeared in these people a process of *Verinnerlichung* (*G. M.* 2-16). This process helped to generate the intellect and shrewdness with which these "slaves" tried to indirectly overcome their oppressors and regain the powers that had been taken from them. In other words, out of necessity the weak have developed intelligence and powers of reasoning as substitutes for the vital and spontaneous drives which characterize "higher men" who do not need understanding in order to express their power (*G. M.* 1-10). Nietzsche claims that highly developed understanding and reason make one "evil" (*ibid.,* 2-15): "the weak prevail over the strong again and again, for they are the great majority—and they are also more *intelligent*" (*G. D.* 9-14). Thus, because the Jews were "intelligent" and "weak"— they could, despite their being a minority, perform the "miraculous feat of an inversion of values, thanks to which life on earth has acquired a novel and dangerous attraction for a couple of millennia . . . This inversion of values . . . constitutes the significance of the Jewish people: they mark the beginning of the slave rebellion in morals" (*J. G. B.* 195). From this it follows that Nietzsche's attitude towards the Jewish people and their "slave rebellion" is that of a "psychologist of morals" (*ibid.,* 196) and has nothing to do with his historical, nationalistic or theological views and much less with any emotional or capricious bias. It also follows that by referring to Jews as "slaves", Nietzsche does not mean to point out any particular sociological status but only to indicate mental patterns, of negative power.

Patterns of negative power are closely linked to dialectic and a particular form of rational-logical capacity. Nietzsche explains the emergence of the phenomenon of dialectic within the Jewish people by the mechanism "of no other choice": "One chooses dialectic only when one has no other means . . . It can only be *self-defense* for those who no longer have other weapons . . . The Jews were dialecticians for that reason . . . and Socrates too?" (*G. D.* 2-6).

It seems that the reference to Socrates within a passage about the Jews is no mere coincidence, but rather, reflects the fact that his attitude to them was the same. Nietzsche was a sharp critic of Socrates (especially in his first work, *The Birth of Tragedy*). He saw Socrates as the spiritual father of a negative tendency in Western Culture—the omnipresent tendency to put everything into rational form. Both Socrates and the Jews developed the dialectic capacity as a last resort against the destructive human inclinations which Nietzsche named: the "Dionysian barbarian" (*G. T.* 2). Socrates thus brought about an exaggerated Apollinization of culture which encouraged repression of one's Dionysian-vital instincts. But is the development of the Apollinian and rational elements not a necessary condition for the full creative life which Nietzsche favoured? The answer is no, if the consequence of such development is the complete repression of Dionysian instincts that function as the driving factors in creativity and as the raw material for the formation of the sublimative complexes.

According to Nietzschean psychology, the victory of Apollo over Dionysus, of Socratic rationality over the hylic instincts, brings about an impoverishment of life and hinders creativity. The result is the predominance of ascetic tendencies adopted by the "weak", who repress and vitiate their drives and fight the Dionysian vitality of the "mighty". Where there is no Dionysian instinct there is no creation and artistic sublimation. Nietzsche demonstrated this in *The Birth of Tragedy* by contrasting Socrates and Dionysus.

In his later writings Nietzsche continues to elaborate this view by claiming that science rests on the same foundation as the ascetic ideal: "a certain *impoverishment of life* is a presupposition of both of them; the affects grown cool, the tempo of life slowed down, dialectics in place of instinct" (*G. M.* 3-25). If the mind replaces the drives, repression replaces sublimation, the creative vitality weakens and the creating power is diminished. This psychological analysis thus explains how Socrates was responsible for the nihilism and decadence of the West (*G. D.* 2-11).

Like Socrates, the Jews were also responsible for the excessive intellectualization of Europe:

> Jewish scholars . . . have a high regard for logic, that is for *compelling* agreement by force of reasons; they know, with that they are bound to win even where they encounter race and class prejudices and where one does not like to believe them. For nothing is more democratic than logic; it is no respecter of persons and makes no distinction between crooked and straight noses. (Incidentally, Europe owes the Jews no small thanks for making people think more logically and for establishing *cleanlier* intellectual habits—nobody more so than the Germans who are a lamentably *déraisonnable* race who to this day are still in need of having their "heads washed" first.) Wherever Jews have won influence they have taught men to make finer distinctions, more rigorous inferences, and to write in a more luminous and clearly fashion; their task was ever to bring a people "to listen to *raison*".

> (*F. W.* 348)

A careful reading of this passage gives the impression that Nietzsche is expressing an ambivalent attitude towards the Jews, that he does not clearly detest or admire them—just as his attitude towards Socrates is ambivalent.[7] This ambivalence is reflected in the use of the predicates "reasonable" and "spiritual", which are not regarded by Nietzsche as belonging solely to patterns of negative power, but as containing some positive elements as well. Thus, for example, regarding the concept of spirituality, he claims:

> It will be noted that by 'spirit' I mean care, patience, cunning, simulation, great self-control, and everything that is mimicry (the latter includes a great deal of so-called virtue).

> (*G. D.* 9-14)

Self-control and strong discipline are considered positive features of a person since they ensure self-overcoming, that is, the overcoming of chaotic inner drives and their transformation into sublimative-cultural actions. Hence, instead of using the ambiguous term "ambivalence" in describing Nietzsche's attitude towards the Jews (Socrates, Jesus and many others), it is more exact to state that where Nietzsche finds in the Jews patterns of positive power he accepts and admires them, and where he sees patterns of negative power he rejects and condemns them. And since in every folk, nation and individual there is a mixture of positive and negative, a constant vacillation between the positive and negative vectors of power—and there is no one (except the *Übermensch*) who expresses fully and consistently pure patterns of positive power—Nietzsche's attitude toward any man, nation or culture is based on the proportions of the positive and negative features that are actually operative.

Even if someone (or some nation) expresses externally negative patterns, if—on account of the man's history or some feature of his present behavior—it appears to

Nietzsche that he possesses hidden resources of positive power, then Nietzsche strives to assist him to overcome his negative power and to express his positive resources. Nietzsche sees in the Jewish people the residue of its powerful and glorious past, and never tires of emphasizing its most important quality—abundant power and vitality.

* * *

In the same aphorism where Nietzsche mentions the Jews' "higher intelligence" he also refers to their "energy" and their "accumulated capital of spirit and will, gathered from generation to generation through a long schooling in suffering" (*M. A.* 475).

In *The Will to Power*, Nietzsche claims:

> The concept of power, whether of a god or of a man, always includes both the ability to help and the ability to harm. Thus it is with the Arabs; thus with the Hebrews. Thus with all strong races.
>
> (*W. M.* 352)

From this dialectic of power in the Jews, it is clear that corresponding to the immensity of the "damage" that has been inflicted upon the Culture of the West—that is, the intellectualization, moralization and total transformation of values of Western Culture—is an equally immense store of powerful mental resources. The measure of the destruction indicates the power of the destroyer: this is true of the Jews as well as of Socrates and Jesus. Despite the fact that Nietzsche univocally rejects the deeds and influence of both Socrates and Jesus, he admires them for the greatness of their impact. This is true of the Jews as well:

> The people, have won—or 'the slaves' or 'the mob' or 'the herd' or whatever you like to call them—if this has happened through the Jews, very well! in that case no people ever had a more world-historic mission.
>
> (*G. M.* 1-9)

In his references to the Jews' great power we find hints of the psycho-historical explanation that Nietzsche proposes for this power:

> That which partly necessity, partly chance has achieved here and there, the conditions for the production of a stronger type.
>
> (*W. M.* 898)

This passage and others[8] express one of the recurring themes of Nietzschean thought: the dialectics of suffering. Suffering and overcoming suffering enhance power and enable self-overcoming: "What does not destroy me—makes me stronger".

Thus, the diaspora and the constant persecutions of the Jews throughout history became "a school of suffering" and rendered them in a dialectical fashion, immune.

The long and continuous suffering of the Jews brought them positive power, hence Nietzsche's statement that the Jews are "the strongest, toughest and purest race now living in Europe; they know how to prevail under the worst conditions" (*J. G. B.* 251). Furthermore, they have a "plentitude of power *without equal* to which only the nobility had access" (*F. W.* 136). Thus for Nietzsche the Jews are endowed with a long list of positive predicates (see the above table) they acquired due to their history and not due to some alleged biological constitution. Moreover, Nietzsche's references to the Jews as the most "powerful race", in spite of their obvious political and physical weakness, clearly show that there is nothing physical such as brute force in the Nietzschean concept of power, (*Kraft*), and that it always denotes an immune, spiritual power (*Macht*).

Because of the positive power of the Jews, Nietzsche stresses the elevated patterns of being in the Judeo-Hebrew experience, (item *2* in the table), even in the walks of life and forms of thought that manifest negative patterns of power. Thus, Nietzsche emphasizes the Jews' "grand style in morality", "the terribleness and majesty of infinite demands, infinite meanings, the whole romanticism and sublimity of moral questionabilities . . ." (*J. G. B.* 250). He mentions the "sense for the sublime" of the Jews (*F. W.* 135), the "Jewish landscape . . . over which the gloomy and sublime thunder cloud of the wrathful Jehovah was brooding continually" (*ibid.*, 137), where the "sacred prophets" (*M.* 38) wandered.

* * *

The sufferings and distresses of the diaspora not only strengthened the Jews but also worked in the opposite direction: persecution shattered their feelings of power, diminished their self-confidence and suppressed the original *foci* of their positive power. Thus, the Jews had to use various means of strengthening their feelings of power. One of the most conspicuous of these was the tendency to amass fortunes. The Jew became "the genius of money" (*J. G. B.* 251; cf.: *W. M.* 864). This pursuit of money clearly expresses the lack of power. It follows that the desire for wealth stems from negative power (*M.* 204). This *heteronomous* dependence on circumstances and the opportunities they provide for the enhancement of power (item *3* in the table), is counterbalanced, in the Jews, by expressions of autonomy, self-sufficiency and free creation of values (*Z.* 1-15).

Creation of values, even in the most adverse and taxing conditions (*M.* 205) made the Jews a sublime example of "spiritual independence" (*M. A.* 475).

In addition to the pursuit of money, adopted by the Jews for the sake of enhancing their feelings of power, a behavioral patterns expressing resentment and vengefulness developed (item *4* and *10*). Thus, the Jews became "the priestly nation of *ressentiment par excellence*" (*G. M.* 1-16), involved in "the *most spiritual revenge*" (*ibid.,* 1-7). Out of this spirit of revenge and hatred (item *13*), the Jews became the creators of values: ". . . Jewish hatred—the profoundest and sublimest kind of hatred, capable of creating ideals and reversing values . . ." (*G. M.* 1-8).

However with these means of strengthen their feelings of power—pursuit of money and vengeful acts—the Jews did not stoop to physical conquest of Europe, even though they were able to do so (*M.* 205), and Nietzsche admired them for this.

By emphasizing that the Jews were able but unwilling to conquer Europe, Nietzsche underlines their immense power. According to his philosophy of power, political-physical domination is not an expression of the positive predicates but only of *Kraft*. Nietzsche stresses that "if they wanted it—or if they were forced into it . . . [the Jews] *could* even now have preponderance, indeed quite literally mastery over Europe, that is certain; that they are *not* looking and planning for that is equally certain" (*J. G. B.* 251).

This certainty Nietzsche draws from his belief that the Jews are endowed with positive power and do not need political achievements for reassurance. Nietzsche always prefers the spirit which indicates creative power, and the self-mastery needed for the sublimation of drives, to political *Kraft*:

> "Deutschland, Deutschland über alles—I fear that was the end of German philosophy."
>
> (*G. D.* 8-1)

In contrast to the German slogan of *Kraft,* Nietzsche delineates the Jewish attitude: "Geist, Geist über alles". It is here that he finds the more genuine and superior power (*Macht*) of the Jewish people.

Because of the unique circumstances of Jewish existence in the diaspora, this power is not fully operative and is suppressed by negative power. The latter is manifested in various Jewish patterns of conduct the chief aim of which is to preserve life rather than enhance it (item *12*).

Thus, for example, in the economic-financial sphere:

> . . . the instinct of great financiers goes against everything extreme—that is why the Jews are at present the most *conserving* power in our intensely threatened insecure Europe . . . their instinct itself is unswervingly conservative—and 'mediocre'—.
>
> (*W. M.* 864)

Despite the fact that Nietzsche had formerly stressed the dynamic and vital creative powers of the Jews he understands that

a nation in such a life-threatening predicament cannot spontaneously and unreservedly express its positive powers, since it most primarily be concerned with survival.

> (*W. M.* 199)

Nietzsche stresses the Jews' strong instinct for self-preservation: they "tried to prevail after they had lost two of their castes, that of the warrior and that of the peasant" (*ibid.,* 184). His descriptions of "Die Juden, als ein Volk, welches am Leben hing und hängt" (*M.* 74), serve as the background to Nietzsche's speculative explanation of the emergence of Christianity and the awakening of the priestly ethos. These phenomena were powerful expressions of the Jewish instinct for self-preservation:

> . . . the little rebellious movement which is baptized with the name of Jesus of Nazareth represents the Jewish instinct *once more*—in other words, the priestly instinct . . . the 'church' . . . was the lake-dwelling on which alone the Jewish people could continue to exist amid the 'water'—the hard-won *last* chance of survival, the residue of its independent political existence. An attack on this was an attack on the deepest instinct of a people, on the toughest life-will which has ever existed in any people on earth.
>
> (*A.* 27)

In all his writings Nietzsche consistently disparages the so-called "instinct for self-preservation". For him it is by no means the highest value. This is the premise behind his critique of Darwin (see his "Anti-Darwin", in *W. M.* 684; 5) and of the concept of *conatus,* which connotes this instinct. In Spinoza's *Ethics,* this instinct is the essence of being human. Like Socrates, Nietzsche seeks not any life but the "good life", life according to patterns of positive power. What is of utmost concern to Nietzsche is not the mere fact of existence and preservation of life but rather the qualitative enhancement of life: "not self-preservation, but the will to appropriate, dominate, increase, grow stronger" (*W. M.* 689). Hence it is possible to assume that had Nietzsche found in the Jews only the will for self-preservation without any additional positive qualities that made their existence worthwhile—he would not have bothered to mention their strong "life-will". Not preservation of being but its enhancement and intensification is the highest value of Nietzsche's philosophy.

And indeed, Nietzsche finds in the Jews the tendency to preserve themselves not for the sake of life itself, but for the sake of a special kind of life. Thus, the Jews preferred to join the negative power in history—the decadent powers—in order to overcome their decadence and nihilism, which for Nietzsche are always present when the tendency to nullification, self-destruction and death is manifested:

> Psychologically considered, the Jewish people are a people endowed with the toughest vital energy, who placed in impossible circumstances, voluntarily and out

of the most profound prudence of self-preservation, take sides with all the instincts of decadence . . . The Jews are the antithesis of all decadents: they have had to *represent* decadents to the point of illusion. . . .

(A. 24)

Despite the tactical alliance of the Jews with the negative power in history (such as Paul and his Christianity), and despite some manifestations of negative patterns in their life, they continue to express characteristics of the abundant positive power hidden in them. When Nietzsche refers to their negative qualities, he never fails to suggest some historical-cultural explanation why these qualities are such an essential aspect of the life of the Jews:

> Unpleasant, even dangerous, qualities can be found in every nation and every individual: it is cruel to demand that the Jew be an exception. In him, these qualities may even be dangerous and revolting to an unusual degree; and perhaps the young stock-exchange Jew is altogether the most disgusting invention of mankind. In spite of that I should like to know how much one must forgive a people in a total accounting when they have had the most painful history of all peoples, not without the fault of all of us, and when one owes to them the noblest man (Christ), the purest sage (Spinoza), the most powerful book, and the most effective moral law in the world.

(M. A. 475)

The historical-cultural "balance" in the life of the Jews places them on the positive side of patterns of power. Their negative qualities are explained and excused by Nietzsche in one of the following ways:

1. Their physical distress during their political diaspora;

2. The distorting and diversive influence exerted on them by the Christians and especially by the destructive acts of Paul: "the ship of Christianity threw overboard a good deal of its Jewish ballast . . ." (*M.* 68).

In this aphorism, Nietzsche goes on to claim that Paul's Christianity was total and vicious distortion of Judaism, whose adherents were "propelled higher than any other people by the imagination of the ethically sublime" (*ibid., ibid.*).

Thus, Paul, who was "evilly disposed" to the Jewish law and wished to attain "the perfect revenge" (*ibid., ibid.*)—is the main agent of the spiritual impoverishment of Judaism, since he was "the teacher of the *annihilation of the law* . . ." (*ibid., ibid.*). Because of his teachings many of the positively powerful aspects of the Jewish-historical experience were stifled. For example, the strong sensuality of the Jews underwent a process of "repression" (in the Freudian sense) and "castration" because of the introduction of the concepts and ideas of "sin", "guilt", "bad-conscience" (*A.* 25) by Paul and his followers (*F. W.* 139).

It was, therefore, Paul who directed the Jews to the destructive processes of repression instead of keeping them on the road of positive processes of sublimation (of the ancient-Greek types). "With the logician's cynicism of a rabbi" Paul started "that process of decay which had begun with the death of the Redeemer" (*A.* 44)—all this within the Jewish people. Thus as Socrates diverted the ancient Greeks from positive to negative powers, so Paul did to the ancient Hebrews. He succeeded because he "directed himself to the lowest class of Jewish society and intelligence" (*W. M.* 198)—in other words to those of the Jewish people who lacked positive power and therefore were easily tempted by these "books of seduction by means of *morality*" (*A.* 44).

However the Jewish *elite* (and here of course Nietzsche is not interested in the sociological-political meaning of the word but in the sublime psychological patterns of a soul endowed with positive patterns of power) was not tempted by Paul and the New Testament, and despite political exile continued to manifest positive qualities:

1. The Jews have the tremendous and genuine creativity typical of a genius who "above all begets and wants to beget" (*J. G. B.* 248);

2. The Jews approach genius in the sphere of art with Heinrich Heine and Offenbach (*W. M.* 832);

3. The Jews approach genius in the sphere of morality (*F. W.* 136);

4. They excel in the domain of self-criticism which is so vital for the processes of self-overcoming and the attainment of power;

5. They possess a "wealth of passions, virtues, decisions, renunciations, fights, and victories of all kinds" (*M.* 205);

6. The Jews are distinguished above all Europeans in "the way in which they honor their fathers and their children and the rationality of their marriages and marital customs" (*ibid., ibid.*);

7. The Jews have always manifested their "coldest composure and steadfastness in terrible situations" (*ibid., ibid.*);

8. Even in the most adverse circumstances "they . . . have never ceased to believe in their calling to the highest things" (*ibid., ibid.*).

* * *

Nietzsche does not merely suggest, but explicitly bestows upon the Jews a vital role in the Europe of the future. In view of the positive psychological qualities of the Jews, especially their "strong instinct" and abundance of positive power, he sees a very positive prognosis for them. He predicts that the Jews and the Russian will be: "the provisionally surest and most probable factors in the great play and fight of forces" (*J. G. B.* 251). Here he is not hinting at Jewish political-physical domination over Europe, but rather the Jews' spiritual role in the future history of the world, when their plentiful power will flow "into great spiritual men and works . . . into an eternal blessing for Europe" (*M.* 205).

Echoing the Old Testament prophecy about the magnificent future of the nation of Israel and its spectacular salvation, Nietzsche claims that the Jews will once again become the "founders and creators of values". The creation of values is the most significant and prestigious task in Nietzsche's philosophy, which always returns to the "transfiguration of values" and the transfiguration of the nature of our culture and society. The fundamental Nietzschean concept of the "transfiguration of all values" must be understood not as a nihilistic cancellation of all values, but as a gradual transformation from the morality of negative to that of positive power. This does not refer to revolutionary change *ex nihili*—from the complete lack of positive power to its miraculous emergence. In order that a significant change be effected, the changing element must already contain its seed. The process of transfiguration, Nietzsche hints, is already deeply rooted in the cultural history of the West (*F. W.* 117-120), and is even anchored in "a *single* soul" (*J. G. B.* 260), namely, in the mental patterns of the individual who is constantly moving between the opposing fields of negative and positive power. The crucial role that Nietzsche bestows upon the Jews in this world-cultural process of the "transfiguration of all values" (Nietzsche intends his own philosophy to be a catalyst for this process), is best shown via a diachronic, phylogenetic analysis of Judaism, as opposed to the synchronic, ontogenetic exposition developed so far.

3. THE NIETZSCHEAN IMAGE OF JUDAISM

By "ontogenesis" I mean explanation of mental patterns, their development and various manifestations within the life of the individual; "phylogenesis" refers to the patterns of life, conduct and culture of nations—their evolution and genealogy.

The starting point of Nietzsche's philosophical psychology and his discussions of the Jews is always ontogenetic. Then, by projection and generalization, he proceeds to wider, phylogenetic cultural analyses.

In these contexts, the Nietzschean terms "race", "people", "folk" lack the biological and geographical connotations they have in Nazi ideology. Nietzsche refers to the Jews as a cultural-historical entity, as a group of individuals having the same past and present, cohering by virtue of their common fate, experience and future projects (*J. G. B.* 268). Knowledge of the sociological-historical background is thus necessary to understand the individual's mental patterns, since: "One cannot erase from the soul of a human being what his ancestors liked most to do and did most constantly . . ." (*ibid.,* 264).

In order to understand the Jew of the present, in order to direct him toward his future mission, Nietzsche is obliged to reconsider the past of the Jewish people as manifested in history—its genealogy. He distinguishes between the *ancient Hebrews* of the land of Israel and their heroic religion and cult, and the *present day Jews,* scattered in the European diaspora, who are only a weak reflection of their glorious past.

A. THE ANCIENT HEBREWS AND THEIR POSITIVE RELIGION

Before discussing Nietzsche's enthusiasm for the religion and cult of the ancient Hebrews, it is helpful to review his general philosophical attitude toward religious phenomena. This will help us to discredit one of the most popular perceptions of Nietzsche: the view that Nietzsche is a fierce, unshakeable, and unambivalent enemy of religion, that Nietzsche fought religion his entire life. This frequently encountered view is in need of serious qualification and clarification. It is true that Nietzsche unequivocally rejects a specific kind of religion. But he does not reject religious phenomena as such: these phenomena have many positive aspects which he assimilates into his own philosophy. To clarify this issue, along with Nietzsche's distinction between positive and negative power, the complementary, and derivative difference between positive and negative religion must be taken into account.

* * *

Nietzsche claims, in reference to various religious beliefs, that where there is a need to believe, there is a weak will and an individual with impoverished power. Nietzsche's attitude can be summed up by paraphrasing Tertullian's saying—*"credo quia absurdum est"*—into "where I do not want—there I believe". Out of weakness and lack of motivation to overcome and to create, the active and creative willing become a passive faith. This attitude brings Nietzsche to introduce a criterion for the presence of positive versus negative power:

> How much one needs a *faith* in order to flourish . . . that is a measure of the degree of one's strength (or, to put the point more clearly, of one's weakness) . . . The demand that one *wants* by all means that something should be firm . . . this, too, is still the demand for a support, a prop, in short, that *instinct of weakness* which, (to be sure), does not create religious, metaphysical systems, and convictions of all kind but— conserves them.
>
> (*F. W.* 347)

This is, therefore, "negative religion", (Nietzsche points to Buddhism and Christianity as examples) derived from the lack of will and positive, affirmative power. This very psychological need for faith, support, backbone, *etc.* is a clear symptom of negative power and *Akrasia.* Nietzsche, who bases his affirmative morality on the concept of positive power, rejects negative religion, since it establishes this state of feebleness and provides it with a transcendental, "holy" legitimation, thus eliminating the chance that the believer will awaken and try to regain his lost power. When crutches are given to the invalid bereft of power and spirit, Nietzsche thinks, the chance that the invalid will walk unassisted and, by his own resources, overcome his incapacity are very slim indeed. This situation leads him to permanent slavery in a heteronomous prison (*F. W.* 347).

The consequences of the escape to religion extend beyond the religious domain and include most of the cultural and social activities of the human being. He who abrogates his freedom and "self-determination" ends up in a totalitarian system with heteronomous form of government such as the dictatorship of some individual or party. Thus negative religion is the "disease of the will" (*ibid., ibid.*). As such, it must be overcome. This is the main objective of Nietzsche's critique of religion. The healthy individual endowed with positive power does not need this critique, for where there is no sickness there is no need to overcome sickness. Therefore, we can expect to find health and optimum mental power, "a pleasure and power of self-determination . . . of a freedom of the will" (*ibid., ibid.*) where the powerful individual "would take leave of all faith and every wish for certainty". A man who does not need religion is "the *free spirit* par excellence" (*ibid., ibid.*).

Nietzsche is not against negative religion only because it inhibits the development of positive power and blocks the way to auto-creation and freedom. He also rejects it because it actually endangers the vital life itself. Religion, especially in its ascetic forms, does not merely inhibit the will, it also suppresses and represses the instinct for life by its glorification of death and abstinence. And where vital life is repressed there is a great decline in culture and in spontaneous, healthy creativity. Hence religion is not only a symptom of the malady of will and passivity of power, but actively serves the illness and kills the patient. Religion is not merely one nihilistic symptom among many; it leads to absolute nihilism—the nullification of life—and thus is Nietzsche's mortal enemy, for Nietzsche strives to attain the opposite result, the enhancement and vitalization of life. Nietzsche is quite explicit about this nihilistic aspect of negative religion:

> When Christianity came into being, the craving for suicide was immense—and Christianity turned it into a lever of its power. It allowed only two kinds of suicide . . . Only martyrdom and the ascetic's slow destruction of his body were permitted.
>
> (*F. W.* 131)

Nietzsche has another important reason to oppose negative religion, a reason rooted in his doctrine of the morality of positive power:

> "It myself have now slain all gods in the fourth act, for the sake of morality."
>
> (*ibid.,* 153)

Nietzsche eliminates God and wants to freeze (by psychological means) our need for religious faith in order to make room for the morality of genuine power. He realizes that behind the patterns of negative power is hidden the negative religion which justifies them. Hence his war against negative religion is launched "for the sake of the morality of power". This parallels his bitter fight against the morality of negative power—the morality of the "slave" with an ethos of the "bad and guilty conscience".

Negative religion has seduced and continues to seduce people into accepting and justifying their negative, feeble power. To fight this negative seduction (the *Verführung*), Nietzsche is obliged first to halt it, and then to provide positive seduction (the *Versuchung*) which will help them achieve patterns of positive power.

* * *

In this undertaking Nietzsche utilizes several positive aspects of the religious phenomenon, positive in that they help mankind actualize the morality of positive power.

Nietzsche refers to religion in a positive manner in the course of a discussion of the sciences:

> Do you really believe that the sciences would ever have originated and grown if the way had not been prepared by magicians, alchemists, astrologers and witches whose promises and pretensions first had to create a thirst, a hunger, a taste for *hidden* and *forbidden* powers? . . . Even as these preludes and preliminary exercises of sciences were not by any means practiced and experienced as such, the whole of *religion* might yet appear as a prelude and exercise to some distant age. Perhaps religion could have been the strange means to make it possible for a few single individuals to enjoy the whole self-sufficiency of a god and his whole power of self-redemption. Indeed—one might ask—would man ever have learned without the benefit of such a religious training and prehistory to experience a hunger and thirst for *himself,* and to find satisfaction and fullness in himself?
>
> (*F. W.* 300)

Nietzsche claims here and in what follows that religion is not intrinsically absolutely nihilistic. It does not always aim to annihilate life and positive power. Some of its values and ideas have served as a conceptual-emotional reservoir essential to the emergence of human yearning for achievement, for self-perfection, integrity and morality of positive power. Some of God's attributes—for example, those expressing his autonomy, his power and his ability for infinite creation, were the sublime paradigm for Kant's moral theory, and even to-day serve as a model for a being endowed with creative and genuine power (*ibid.,* 337).

Nietzsche indicates that he himself arrived at the concept of positive power from, among other things, this "godlike" model of an ideal being to whom man has attributed the predicates which in his view denote the values most worthy of pursuit. Nietzsche displaces all these attributes from a transcendent God to an *Übermensch.* He could not have done this had there not previously existed in our culture the idea of God, the omnipotent and omniscient being, endowed with perfect positive power.

Nietzsche understands this well and regards the positive components of religions and their all-powerful beings as the "prelude" to his own morality and idea of the *Übermensch.* If negative religion annihilates life and will, and suppresses the development of positive human powers, positive religion (namely the positive components of religion as such) paves the way to the morality and ethos of positive power. This insight into the positive elements of religion is expressed in the following confession:

> But you will have gathered what I am driving at, namely . . . that even we seekers after knowledge today, we godless anti-metaphysicians still take our fire too, from the flame lit by a faith that is thousands of years old, that Christian faith. . . .
>
> (*F. W.* 344)

Nietzsche's transition from the creative-positive power of the Christian God to the creative-instinctual power of the *Übermensch* is only possible due to the pre-existence of Christianity, or more exactly—due to the positive elements of the "Christian faith". However, Nietzsche stresses, one must grasp the Christian faith as springing "only from Jewish roots" and "comprehensible only as a growth on this soil" (*G. D.* 7-4 and cf. *F. W.* 137).

Hence Nietzschean philosophy must be understood as springing from the ancient Hebrews. Nietzsche's morality of positive power and most of his positive ideas grow out of the Christian development of the culture of the ancient Hebrews, exactly as his concepts of the Apollonian and the Dionysian grew out of the ancient Greeks.

* * *

Nietzsche claims that most of the positive components of religion as such, which influenced both his philosophy and the prevalent ethos—were concentrated in the rites and religion of the ancient Jews, namely the Hebrews, in the land of Israel. This is the key to understanding Nietzsche's profound admiration for the ancient Hebrews.

Nietzsche's conscious affinity to expressions of positive power in the religion of the Hebrews manifests itself explicitly in his warm attitude toward the "Jewish Old Testament, the book of divine justice", where "there are human beings, things, and speeches in so grand a style that Greek and Indian literature have nothing to compare with it. With terror and reverence one stands before these tremendous remnants of what once man was . . ." (*J. G. B.* 52).

Coming from a philosopher who is regarded as one of the greatest philohellenes, this is a great compliment to the Jewish Hebrews.

Nietzsche explicitly distinguishes between the Jews in the diaspora and the Hebrews of the Old Testament. This distinction runs parallel to his distinctions between the Old and the New Testaments and positive and negative power:

> The *Old* Testament—that is something else again: all honor to the Old Testament! I find in it great human beings, a heroic landscape, and something of the very rarest quality in the world, the incomparable naïveté of the *strong heart*; what is more, I find a people.
>
> (*G. M.* III-22)

Religion is not only the result of *Akrasia.* Infrequently (as in the case of the Hebrew religion), it functions as a magnified projection of the plenitude of power and positive resources of the people who created it: Show me who your God is and I'll tell you who you are. This theme runs through *Antichrist* and other writings where Nietzsche presents the ancient Jews and their rites in a positive light. Thus, for example, he claims that the Jewish God and his cult were expressions of "consciousness of power, of joy in oneself, of hope for oneself . . . of the self-confidence of the people" (*A.* 25). The Jewish God was the "God of Israel, the god of a people . . . strong, brave, masterful and proud" (*A.* 17), of "people of an inflexible self-will" (*W. M.* 199).

Thus it is not religion as such that interests Nietzsche, but its relation to the key concept of his thought: *Macht.* Hence it is crucial to understand that Nietzsche is not opposed to religion *per se,* but to its misuse and its negative components just as the various types of historical consciousness are not good or bad in themselves, but find their value in the use made of them by various types of personalities, (see Nietzsche's second *Unzeitgemäße Betrachtung* on History):

> The selective and cultivating influence, always destructive as well as creative and form-giving, which can be exerted with the help of religions, is always multiple and different according to the sort of human beings who are placed under its spell and protection.
>
> (*J. G. B.* 61)

Religion can be either "negative" or "positive" (with an exclusive or). It is a function of: (1) The power of the personality that uses it; (2) The use it is put to: a personality with positive power will use the positive elements of religion positively; a negative personality will put religion to negative use. Moreover, Nietzsche emphasizes that positive religion is not the ultimate goal of positive power or of the philosopher who wants to educate us by using positive religion. It is solely a temporary heuristic means. Once religion becomes an end in itself, it becomes *ipso facto* a negative religion par excellence:

> One always pays dearly and terribly when religions do *not* want to be a means of education and cultivation in the philosopher's hand but themselves want to be ultimate ends and not means among other means.
>
> (*J. G. B.* 62)

The independent philosopher, the "free spirit", therefore, "will make use of religions for his project of cultivation and education" (*ibid.,* 61).

This is Nietzsche's attitude toward the religion of the ancient Hebrews. He picks up its many positive aspects for the sake of education and the enhancement of positive power. Nietzsche thinks that such enhancement might work since his object, namely the phenomenon of power, is deeply rooted in the history of mankind and its original religions. This power is very deeply rooted in the religion of the Ancient Hebrews:

> . . . at the time of the kings, . . . Yahweh was the expression of a consciousness of power . . . of a good conscience . . . of the self-affirmation. . . .
>
> (*A.* 25)

Thus, the ancient religion of the Jews becomes a model for a positive religion according to the concept of power developed in his philosophy.

For Nietzsche, Christianity is "the counter-movement" (*ibid., ibid.*) to the morality of positive power of the ancient Hebrews. Similarly, the Judaism of the diaspora is the negative transformation of the positive resources found in the ancient People of Israel.

B. The Present-Day Judaism of Power and its Future Mission

Thus Nietzsche distinguishes between the Hebrew Old Testament and the Christian New Testament and his crucial conclusion is that "the Christians are not the true people of Israel" (*M.* 84). Hence, the "true people of Israel" endowed with positive and genuine power can re-emerge only out of the present day Jews, if they would only return to Hebraicism. In the same way that Nietzsche wanted to return contemporary culture to the

noble and powerful days of the pre-Socratic Greeks, he believed that contemporary Jews ought to return to the glorious and powerful patterns of the past:

> Must the ancient fire not some day flare up much more terribly, after much longer preparation? More: must one not desire it with all one's might? even will it? even promote it?
>
> (*G. M.* 1-17)

But it is not only because of their heroic and powerful past that Nietzsche regards the present day Jews as the most worthy of being the agents of the vital transfiguration of European culture from the negative to the positive ethos of power. The Jews are worthy of this mission because even now, in spite of their politically disastrous predicaments, they are still endowed with abundant resources of positive power. It is due to this very power that they have inflicted so much damage upon Europe. But it can also be very beneficial and "help" Europe (*W. M.* 352). In fact, the Jews have already helped Europe, not so long ago:

> . . . in the darkest times of the Middle Ages, when the Asiatic cloud masses had gathered heavily over Europe, it was Jewish free-thinkers, scholars, and physicians who clung to the banner of enlightenment and spiritual independence in the face of the harshest personal pressures and defended Europe against Asia . . . If Christianity has done everything to orientalize the Occident, Judaism has helped significantly to occidentalize it again and again: in a certain sense this means as much as making Europe's task and history a continuation of the Greek.
>
> (*M. A.* 475)

Nietzsche had been disappointed by Wagner, to whom he had naively assigned the task of reviving the tragic culture of the ancient Greek, a culture endowed with a pathos of positive power. Nietzsche turns to the "new Jews" and sets before them the highest possible mission—to revive and rechannel the positive powers of the ancient Hebrews for the spiritual Renaissance of Europe.

Against the Evangelical negative seduction (*Verführung*) of Christianity, Nietzsche persistently seeks to make the contemporary Jews (instead of Wagner) into the positive counter-enticement (*Versuchung*). In order to effect this Nietzsche first tries to tempt the Jews to return to their positive power and to re-activate it for the sake of Europe. He stresses the "seductive" qualities of the Jews, and their "instinctive ability to create an advantage, a means of seduction out of every superstitious supposition, out of ignorance itself" (*W. M.* 199).

It follows that in the central Nietzschean project of the *Anti-Christ* there is a crucial role for the Jews. They are to become an essential counterbalance against the negative seduction of the Jewish "Christians" and the "Jesuits priests". To achieve this Nietzsche is in great need of those components of positive power rooted in the Jewish people. Thus, Nietzsche hopes to mobilize the Jews to help them in the future transfiguration of values. This is the background for Nietzsche's emotional exclamation:

"What a blessing a Jew is among Germans!"

(*W. M.* 49)

Notes

Few days before his sudden and much regretted death Professor Dr. K.-H. Ilting accepted this article for publication, and I accordingly wish to dedicate it to his memory.

1. C. Brinton, *Nietzsche,* New York 1965, p. 215; M. P. Nicolas, *From Nietzsche Down to Hitler,* New York 1970; A. C. Coutinho, "Nietzsche's Critique of Judaism", in: *Review of Religion* 3 (1939), pp. 161-166; R. M. Lonsbach, *Friedrich Nietzsche und die Juden,* Stockholm 1939; Y. Yovel, "Perspectives Nouvelles sur Nietzsche et le Judaïsme", *Revue des études Juives,* CXXXVIII (1979), pp. 483-485.

2. E. g. A. Bäumler, "Nietzsche und der Nationalsozialismus" (1934), in: *Studien zur deutschen Geistesgeschichte,* Berlin 1937; *Nietzsche der Philosoph und Politiker,* Leipzig 1931.

3. See e. g. R. J. Holdingdale, *Nietzsche: The Man and His Philosophy,* Baton Rouge 1965, pp. 223 f.; W. Kaufmann, *Nietzsche: Philosopher, Psychologist, Antichrist,* Princeton 1968, Ch. 10, pp. 284-306.

4. Nietzsche, *On the Genealogy of Morals,* Preface, 2, trans. W. Kaufmann, New York 1967.

   In order to secure fluent reading—all of Nietzsche's quotations are given in English translations of W. Kaufmann, found in the following books:

   F. Nietzsche, *On the Genealogy of Morals,* hereafter (*G. M.*), New York 1969;

   F. Nietzsche, *Beyond Good and Evil,* hereafter (*J. G. B.*), New York 1966;

   F. Nietzsche, *The Gay Science,* hereafter (*F. W.*), New York 1974;

   F. Nietzsche, *The Birth of Tragedy,* hereafter (*G. T.*), New York 1967;

   F. Nietzsche, *The Will to Power,* hereafter (*W. M.*), New York 1968.

   Quotations from: *Human, all-Too-Human,* (*M. A.*); *The Dawn,* (*M.*); *Twilight of the Idols,* (*G. D.*); and *The Antichrist,* (*A.*) are taken from: *The Portable Nietzsche,* ed. and trans. W. Kaufmann, New York 1954.

5. See my "Nietzsche's Phenomenology of Power", *Nietzsche-Studien,* forthcoming.

6. Cf. my "Freudian Uses and Misuses of Nietzsche", *American Imago,* 37 (1980), pp. 371-385.

7. W. Kaufmann, *Nietzsche,* Ch. 13 "Nietzsche's Admiration for Socrates", pp. 391-411; W. J. Dannhauser, *Nietzsche's View of Socrates,* Ithaca and London 1974.

8. Cf. *M.* 205.

Katharina Gerstenberger (essay date winter 1994)

SOURCE: Gerstenberger, Katharina. "Nahida Ruth Lazarus's *Ich suchte Dich!*: A Female Autobiography from the Turn of the Century." *Monatshefte* 86, no. 4 (winter 1994): 525-42.

[*In the following essay, Gerstenberger claims that Lazarus's autobiography is more than just a detail of her conversion from Christianity to Judaism; it is a narrative on how she asserts herself as a free woman through the declaration of her Jewish identity.*]

Fiction writer, journalist, intellectual, and autobiographer, Nahida Lazarus converted from Christianity to Judaism toward the end of the nineteenth century in a social atmosphere characterized by racial anti-Semitism and secularization. Her 1898 autobiography *Ich suchte Dich!*[1] (re-)constructs the author's experience of religious conversion against the social and discursive background of the contemporary controversies over cultural and racial definitions of "Germanness" and the concurrent deployment of master discourses of racial and sexual difference. The autobiography translates cultural notions of difference and sameness into individual experiences of outsider and insider positions. Conversion to Judaism for Lazarus, who is best known as the wife and biographer of the ethno-psychologist Moritz Lazarus, is a process of claiming and asserting a public voice as a woman. With this essay, I want to put an overlooked female autobiographer back into the literary landscape and suggest a reading of her autobiography as a narrative of multiple conversions and the assertion of Jewish religious identity as an emancipatory female identity.

1. BIO-GEOGRAPHY

Today most of Lazarus's books are virtually unknown and nearly inaccessible, in particular her earlier popular fiction; although her name is listed in numerous literary encyclopedias of the time, the available biographical information tends to be sketchy and incomplete. An unusual degree of geographic mobility as well as relative financial and social independence characterize her life.

Nahida Ruth Lazarus was born as Nahida Anna Maria Concordia Sturmhoefel in Berlin on 3 February 1849, to the writer and feminist Nahida Sturmhoefel[2] and the art historian Max Schasler. Her parents married after she was born and were separated only a few years later. Lazarus spent her childhood and early adulthood in Berlin and in the small village of Flatow in West Prussia, Southern France and Italy, repeatedly crossing national boundaries, moving among cultures and languages. In the mid-1860s she returned to Germany. After short-lived engagements as an actress in Breslau (Wrocław) and Bad Warmbrunn (Cieplice Slaskie Zdrój) in the late 1860s, Lazarus moved to Berlin where she enrolled at an academy for women painters, until in 1873 she married Max Remy (1839-1881), a journalist and art critic for the *Vossische Zeitung*.[3]

Between 1870 and 1890 she wrote and published several popular dramas, novels, and novellas which, according to contemporary sources, enjoyed popular and critical success. Her first theater play, a one-act *Lustspiel,* was produced by the Burgtheater in Vienna as early as 1872,[4] and in the following years her dramas were performed by several Berlin theaters. In the early 1880s she began to write theater and art reviews for various newspapers.[5] After Remy's death, Lazarus remained in Berlin as an independent scholar of Judaism and the Hebrew language. In 1891 she published her first and most important book on Jewish religion and culture entitled *Das jüdische Weib,* which subsequently was translated into English, Hebrew, and Hungarian. Other studies on Judaism followed, including a small pamphlet entitled *Das Gebet in Bibel und Talmud* (1892) and *Culturstudien über das Judentum* (1893).

In the late 1880s she made the acquaintance of the co-founder of ethno-psychology and author of several studies on Judaism, Moritz Lazarus. While he became her teacher of Jewish religion, culture, and philosophy, she became his biographer and chronicler, a role she fulfilled until after his death. In early 1895, at the age of forty-six, she converted to Judaism and shortly thereafter married Lazarus. The couple moved to Meran in 1897, where Moritz Lazarus died in 1903.[6] She published several of her husband's works posthumously, including three autobiographical accounts she had compiled. She died in Meran in January 1928.[7]

Political geography provides an underlying structure for the orchestration of national, racial, and gender relationships in Lazarus's life and work. West Prussia, Northern Italy, Southern France, Sicily, Lower Silesia, Berlin, and Tyrol constitute a set of central and marginal spaces within a European political landscape that in the second half of the nineteenth century was dominated by the idea of the nation-state and the politics of erecting national boundaries to ensure cultural, linguistic, and racial homogeneity. Lazarus spent major parts of her life in geographic locations where nationalisms resulted in repeated re-drawings of the political map. In West Prussia, Lower Silesia, and Tyrol, she experienced geographical peripheries in which German-Protestant culture competed with Polish, Czech, Italian, and Jewish cultures. The political consolidation of nation-states in nineteenth-century Europe reflects the scientific creation of national identities based on the hierarchical constructions of racial difference that placed whites above blacks, Germans above Jews and Slavs. Race, as well as gender, functioned as visible and unalterable markers of sameness and difference, inclusion and exclusion, health and pathology. A cultural product of the late nineteenth century, *Ich suchte Dich!* relies heavily on the stability of these binaries in its desire to establish unambiguous identity categories, while at the same time sharing in the turn-of-the-century fascination with hybrid identities. The necessity to construct Jewishness as a category open to those who are not born into it potentially undercuts the narrative's quest for unambiguous identity positions.

Conversion to Judaism figures as the decisive event around which Lazarus unfolds her autobiographical narrative. Her activities as an actress she omits completely, and her accomplishments as a fiction writer she mentions only in passing; strategies, perhaps, to which she resorts in order to portray herself as a woman who possesses agency yet remains within the social boundaries of acceptable female conduct. The "inconsistencies" that frustrate the critic's desire to invent a coherent version of Nahida/Ruth/Sturmhoefel/Remy/Lazarus revolve around the intersecting axes of the constructions of femininity and the definitions of racial difference that inform Lazarus's work as well as its reception. Her specific uses and definitions of "woman" and "Jew" in the context of turn-of-the-century science, and particularly her category of "the Jewish woman" as an ahistorical ideal, hint at the dilemmas faced by an individual who attempts to intervene in the very discourses of which she is the object. In the German context, the Jew came to be "the marker of what the German was not."[8] For the autobiographer Lazarus, who explicitly justifies her interest in Jewish culture as a philosemitic response to the anti-Semitism she witnessed in Berlin in the early 1880s, the existence of outsider and insider positions possesses very concrete meanings. As a German in non-German contexts, a woman in patriarchal contexts, a convert in both anti-Semitic and Jewish contexts, she has to negotiate three interrelated and hierarchical systems of difference and sameness. In the following reading of *Ich suchte Dich!,* rather than evaluating religious convictions, I will investigate the function of intersecting discourses on Judaism, Jewish women, gender, race, and nation in the formation of a female self as speaking subject of autobiography.

2. LANGUAGE AND AGENCY

The "biographische Erzählung" *Ich suchte Dich!*[9] marks a turning point in the writer's career. Published in 1898, the book features "Ruth," the Hebrew name of all female proselytes, on the cover, confirming the autobiographer's successful search for the God to whom the title appeals. After the publication of her own autobiography Lazarus directed her energies to the dissemination of her husband's scholarly works, the collection of his aphorisms, and, more importantly, the compilation and publication of his autobiographies.[10] Combining the roles of biographer and autobiographer, she assumed an influential position in the positing of her husband as a primary figure within German intellectual life. Central to Moritz Lazarus's autobiographical project are his attempts to assert an identity as a German intellectual and modern Jew, and to write away the "stigma" of his Eastern European Jewish background. Importantly, both autobiographers rely on language in their claims to specific categories of identity. Moritz Lazarus regards his possession of unaccented German, i.e., German without any traces of Yiddish, as his ticket into intellectual German society; similarly, Nahida Lazarus views the systematic acquisition of knowledge about Jewish religion and culture as her entry into the community of those intellectuals who approach Judaism as science. The idea of scientific language as an objective arbiter of knowledge, which endows the voice of everyone who speaks it with equal authority, however, has to contest turn-of-the-century constructions of Jewishness and femininity as biological, visible, and unalterable physical and psychological categories that mark the subject as other. In *Ich suchte Dich!*, essentialist notions of Jewishness as the subject's "true" identity compete with definitions of Jewishness (as well as Germanness) as categories open to those who speak its language. To assert her legitimacy as a Jew, Lazarus's autobiography thus relies on both essentialist identity politics and the Enlightenment belief in education and "objective" language.

Ich suchte Dich! spans the time from the early 1850s to 1895, from the narrator's childhood to her conversion to Judaism in 1895 and her marriage to Moritz Lazarus. In the 220-page narrative, the autobiographical subject appears at first under the author's first name, Nahida; toward the end the autobiographer uses impersonal constructions such as "the young woman" or "the young scholar." The choice of a third-person perspective together with the subtitle "biographische Erzählung" frustrates the reader's expectations to encounter the autobiographical "I" introduced by the title and serves as a reminder of the complexities which govern the relationship between the autobiographical subject and the author. The question of autobiographical identity is further complicated by the use of dialogue as a narrative technique to explore and finally assert the position of the subject. By narrating important sections of her autobi-ography in the tradition of the staged religious *disputatio* between a Jew and a Christian, Lazarus claims and transforms a narrative tradition that excluded women as participants of intellectual exchanges. In these dialogues, the autobiographical subject speaks from the subordinate position of the younger person, the female, and the Jew, whose rational arguments never fail to subvert the authority of her older male Christian interlocutors. The extensive use of dialogues and inner monologues stylistically links *Ich suchte Dich!* to the dramatic conventions Lazarus used in earlier works and gives the narrative the theatrical quality of performed literature. Short sentences, exclamations, and rhetorical questions invite the reader to become involved in the narrative process. The dialogic style of dramatic literature suggests how much persuasive power the author attributes to spoken language as a form of public expression. The text orchestrates a chorus of multiple voices from which the voice of the autobiographical subject emerges as the dominant one. Moreover, the direct speech of the dialogues strategically emphasizes decisive events through the sparing use of the first person singular, the title being one such example.

The choice of a narrative form not commonly used in autobiography raises the question of access to specific discourses. Whereas women were largely excluded from public intellectual exchange in the nineteenth century, they actively participated in the production and consumption of popular literature, including popular theater. While in most cases popular literature endorses conservative constructions of femininity, it also provides women writers, in particular women dramatists, with multiple public voices and personae. *Ich suchte Dich!* contains the conventional, prefabricated language of popular literature and reiterates the gender stereotypes traditionally inherent to the genre. At the same time, the narrative appropriates the dialogue as a high culture form of intellectual exchange between males and turns it into a form of popular female expression. Couching her story of an internal and personal process of religious coming-to-consciousness in the stylized spoken language of public address, Lazarus challenges the gendered split between the private and the public by narrating a private development with a public voice.

3. RACIAL DIFFERENCE AS PRIVILEGE

The opening scene of *Ich suchte Dich!* shows mother and daughter in Italy. Physical difference marks both of them as foreigners in a Mediterranean environment. The mother's tall build and the daughter's blond hair identify the couple as German and attract the attention of passersby. The narrative introduces Germanness as a category of racial difference as seen through the eyes of those who do not share these characteristics and are therefore reduced to the admiration of "superior" racial qualities. The first paragraph suggests an acute awareness of Germanness as a racial category. As privileged outsiders, mother and daughter can afford to ignore the reverence paid to them in a Southern European context. The bond based on family ties and racial sameness, however, is threatened by the mother's chronic respiratory disease. Entitled "Trennung," the introductory chapter delineates the first in a series of interruptions in the relationship between mother and daughter. When the seven-year-old daughter suggests that her mother should remarry to preserve the familial bond, she is immediately silenced by her mother's reprimand. Nahida's father remains notoriously absent throughout the narrative. Lack of a male provider results in the disintegration of the nuclear family unit and forces the mother to transform her musical talents and her language skills, which previously had been the leisure-time activities of an upper-class woman, into a profession that will earn her a living. Organized around the destruction of the mother-daughter dyad, the loss of class status, and the simultaneous assertion of racial privilege, the unspoken absence of the father introduces categories of silence and difference. Silence in a gendered context, caused by the father and enforced by the mother, and difference in a racial context, set the stage for a process of identity assertion through language.

A primary childhood memory that illustrates the close association of difference with social hierarchy and lack of language serves as the background to the impending separation of mother and daughter. More specifically, the scene reveals Nahida's need to refute (imaginary) accusations as a claim to moral superiority. Without any transitional explanation, the text introduces the incident with the emphatic exclamation: "Aber das mit der Jüdin war gewiß kein Unrecht!" (10). Then follows the story of an old Jewish butcher woman who delivered meat to Nahida's family and routinely was teased about her descriptive name, "Veilchen," which did not correspond with the old woman's physical appearance and stigmatized her as an outsider.[11] This lower-class woman is the first Jewish character to appear in the narrative. The diffuse feeling that "Etwas gut zu machen sei" (11) motivates the child to offer the old woman her handshake, convinced that she is doing a good deed. The encounter with a religious as well as social outsider occupies a central position within the narrative. Nahida's pre-verbal philo-Semitic gesture toward "Veilchen" puts her in a position of higher morality vis-à-vis the rest of the family. Moreover, the child's willingness to bridge religious and social differences affords her a position of superiority to the helpless Jewish woman who depends on the little girl's kindness. Jewishness in this context signifies femininity, vulnerability, and the lack of assertive language. Her defense of the Jewish woman provides Nahida with the agency she herself lacks as a victim of her father's infidelity and the breakup of her family.

Difference functions not only a source of isolation, suffering, and silencing but it also instills in her a sense of superior uniqueness.

Surrounded by the massive walls of the house of a Pietist English countess living in Italy, who provides her with the typical nineteenth-century education for upper-class girls, Nahida spends the next years of her life in isolated luxury. The narrative constructs social relationships through a model that pits German against foreign. With her pleasing physical appearance and her artistic talents, "die stets weißgekleidete, blondlockige kleine Deutsche" (24) attracts the attention of the distinguished guests at the countess's house. To be German means to be an isolated yet superior outsider. Nahida's physical appearance becomes the expression of her ability to see through the superficiality and insincerity of the guests at the countess's home. Language, in Nahida's mind, must be the expression of true convictions. She rejects the pedagogical exercise of having to recite the Lord's Prayer in four different languages because of its lack of sincerity (35) and laments her repeated subjection to false accusations and undeserved punishments. The ability to differentiate between truth and pretense and the willingness to suffer for truth's sake form the core of Lazarus's autobiographical self-definition. The child's insistence on genuine and uncorrupted language endows her with the power of speech that must be heard. Possession of true language overcomes the silence of the opening scene.

4. THE RELIGIOUS OTHER AS SEXUAL OTHER

The central chapters of *Ich suchte Dich!* focus on Nahida's experience of Christian religious education, rejecting it as an instrument of silencing and sexually exploiting women. The critique of the representation of women in the New Testament, as well as the position of women within Christian society and its male dominated church organizations, prepares the protagonist's conversion to Judaism. She consequently relies on the writings of the Old Testament in her argumentation. The assumption that Christian society does not provide a secure space for women finds its proof in an incident of sexual harassment. The physically mature and unambiguously feminine fourteen-year-old Nahida (95) finds herself confronted with the sexual demands of an effeminate Protestant minister and teacher, whose ambivalent gender identity makes visible his dangerous and corrupted nature. The narrative reads this incident through a juxtaposition of the spiritual superficiality, vanity, and brutality of the Christian male's hybrid nature with the uncontaminated purity of Nahida's unambiguous racial affiliation, her mature physical femininity, and her unalterable religious beliefs. Nahida's incorruptible femininity and unquestionable Germanness are the visible manifestation of her sexual purity and, by analogy, her essential Jewishness.

Turn-of-the-century discourse frequently creates the religious Other as sexual aggressor and seducer whose transgressions inflict disease upon the victim. At the same time when Lazarus wrote her autobiography, Sigmund Freud recalled in his letters to Wilhelm Fliess the "horrible perverse details" of a primal sexual experience (4 October 1897).[12] In the course of his self-analysis, he notes on 3 and 4 October 1897, he remembered an early childhood incident, which involved "an ugly, elderly, but clever woman" who told him "a great deal about God Almighty and hell." Freud introduces his seductress as an ambiguous sexual and religious Other, linking the woman's ugly but clever nature to her Catholicism. This same female caretaker gave him the opportunity to see her "nudam" and washed him in her own bath water, reddish with menstrual blood. Freud thus derives his theory that all neuroses can be traced back to sexual experiences during very early childhood from his own case. His baptism in the bloody water of the Catholic woman graphically depicts the seduction of the Jewish male by the sexual Other who is also the religious Other. In both Freud's and Lazarus's narrative the ugly nanny and the effeminate priest represent the religious Other as the perverted and dangerous sexual Other that causes disease. Freud seeks to use this reminiscence to resolve his "own hysteria" and goes on to say that should he succeed "I shall be grateful to the memory of the old woman who provided me at such an early age with the means for living and going on living" (3 October 1897). The sexual and religious Other thus causes pathology, but she also provided Freud with the identity of a scientist. In Nahida's case, the "Wunde, die ihr jungfräuliches Gemüt durch jenen Auftritt mit einem Gewissenlosen empfangen" (113) symbolizes her status as a victim, but at the same time justifies her rejection of Christianity. Both Freud and Lazarus read their personal histories through contemporary discourses of sexuality, and both construct a pathologized Other in order to affirm positive and unambiguous identities.

5. FEMININITY ON/AS TRIAL

Education and class privilege afforded Lazarus and her mother a degree of autonomy not available to the majority of women in nineteenth-century Germany and allowed both women to lead unconventional and independent lives without the interference of male relatives or patriarchal husbands. This privileged position perhaps explains why Lazarus does not conceive of her life story in terms of women's demands for political and civil rights. Remaining within the chosen framework of her life story as a narrative of religious conflict and conversion, she interprets her struggle for public expression as the assertion of female religious identity. In the second half of the 1860s Lazarus settled in Berlin. Her extensive travels throughout Europe and the privilege to select a place of residency and a profession freely do not enter into her autobiographical narrative.

The autobiography simply states that Nahida, approximately at the age of seventeen or eighteen, plans "einen Beruf zu ergreifen und sich, auch financiell, selbständig zu machen" (150). Religion is the important category in this chapter entitled "Confessionslos." Upon Nahida's arrival in Berlin, a Jewish doctor and friend tries to persuade her to accept her confirmation into the Protestant church. "Ihre Confessionslosigkeit würde ihr schwere Hindernisse bereiten. Er war ein Jude und hatte viel Erfahrung und Menschenkenntniß" (150). An educated Jew voices a warning against a subject position outside the parameters of clearly defined categories. Nahida opts to remain "confessionslos" (169) after the final attempt to be confirmed fails because of the high-ranking minister's unwillingness to take his female student's religious concerns seriously (157). She dismisses her friends' worries that she might face persecution:

> . . . dann gehe ich fort von Berlin; dann flüchte ich mich zu meiner Mutter und werde sie bitten, mit mir weit weg, in ferne, fremde Länder zu ziehen, meinetwegen zu den Uncivilisirten, wo von Dogmenzwang noch nicht die Rede ist . . . lieber heimatlos als ehrlos durch Lüge und lebenslängliche Heuchelei.
>
> (162)

The position of the outsider and stranger who can lay claim to a genuine identity is both preferable and superior to the low status of those who succumb to lies. "Sie conzentrirte nun alle Gedanken und Kräfte auf Erlangung eines Lebensberufes, der geeignet wäre sie möglichst unabhängig zu machen" (162). A series of religious experiences ranging from bigotry, indoctrination, and sexual assault to the arrogance of the Berlin "Generalsuperintendent" (153) translates into a plan to become independent and self-sufficient. The narrative treats socio-economic independence as a necessary precondition that remains subordinated to the autobiographical subject's quest for Jewish identity. The sexualized and gendered nature of Nahida's religious trials, however, suggests a close relationship between her religious identity and a specifically female project of emancipation.

The years between 1867 and 1872 are conspicuously absent from *Ich suchte Dich!*. The novel-like phrase "Jahre vergingen" (170) effaces Lazarus's engagements as an actress at provincial theaters in Breslau and Bad Warmbrunn and the successful production of her play *Die Rechnung ohne den Wirt* at the Burgtheater in Vienna in 1872. The aura of sexual licentiousness associated with the theater in nineteenth-century Germany might be a reason why she chose not to include her involvement with the theater in her autobiographical narrative.

The chapter "Ein seltsames Erlebniß" (172) about her marriage to Max Remy in 1873, at the age of 24, emphasizes the religious implications which lead to Nahida's decision to marry a man whose appearance "trug den Stempel eines deutlichen, schweren und, wie sich später erwies, unheilbaren Leidens" (172). Reading Remy's name on his business card a few weeks after their first introduction, she knows without any doubt that this man will be her husband. "'Du willst es Gott, also gut,—dann will ich es auch'—" (175). The narrative device of divine interference and legitimation brings to mind the tradition of medieval female mysticism with its erotic fantasies of *unio mystica* as well as the Pietist tradition of individual religiosity outside the sphere of hierarchical church organizations. Both mysticism and Pietism developed highly expressive systems of linguistic representation of the emotional state of the individual soul. Women played a major role in these movements, which read female expression of subjective piety both as a sign of particular closeness to God and, at the same time, as in dangerous proximity to heresy. Nahida's determination to marry an unattractive and ill man is inspired by divine order and does not involve any choice of her own: "Und schließlich—blieb ihr eine Wahl, *da sie so genau wußte, daß er, der Leidende, Unschöne, der Erwählte sei?*" (176). The autobiographical rendition of this relationship calls upon a number of narrative traditions in which the individual undergoes a period of challenging trials and rites of purification to earn an outstanding reward. The "sieben Lehr- und Leidensjahre" (185) evoke the narrative structure of the fairy tale as well as the biblical story of Jacob and his seven-year marriage to Lea, his uncle Laban's unattractive eldest daughter, as the precondition to marry Rahel, her beautiful younger sister. The nature of the trial that precedes the individual's elevation depends on the subject's gender. Envisioning herself in the role of the dutiful wife, Nahida is willing to take an "Abschied von ihrer Kunst" (175) and to dedicate her life to the care and support of her husband. "*Warum—?*" she asks herself. "Warum, da doch Tausende ihres Geschlechts in ähnlicher Lebensstellung ein bequemes, begrenztes Dasein führten, warum war sie, gerade sie ausersehen, durch so seltsame Prüfungen zu gehen?" And she adds: "Vielleicht um noch Anderes, Besseres, Höheres zu leisten? *Vielleicht!*" (186). *Ich suchte Dich!* translates the biblical story of Jacob's service of seven years to win his beloved Rahel into a narrative of a specifically female service. Fulfilling traditional gender expectations as a perhaps necessary precondition for her nontraditional position as a female intellectual, Lazarus's autobiographical protagonist undergoes a transition from artist to housewife and caregiver to scholar and convert.

In a double move which allows her to keep the conventional female role while she simultaneously reverses the traditional gender polarization, Nahida gains agency by providing her invalid husband with unfailing care. A rhetoric of health and disease in the narrative constructs a contrast between the healthy woman and her ill husband, the two of them an "ungleiches Paar—sie, jung, blühend, kraftvoll,—er vorzeitig ergraut, niedergebeugt in seinem Rollstuhl" (183). The figure of Remy takes the place of the mother as an ill partner who depends upon his wife's support rather than providing for her. The shift from the mother to the husband as the victim of disease reverses the division of roles between mother and daughter: Nahida takes on a maternal position not only in relation to her husband but also her own mother. Nahida assumes a traditional gender role as a caretaker and subverts it from within by appropriating a male position of strength. The episode of Lazarus's first marriage, who is thirty-two years old when her husband dies, is inserted between the religious sufferings of her childhood and her adult life as a scholar of Judaism and serves a transitory function in her autobiographical narrative. The autobiography's comment "nun war sie Wittwe geworden, fast ohne zu wissen, daß sie vermählt gewesen" (184) suggests the absence of a sexual relationship between the marriage partners.

Males in this autobiography appear either as sexual aggressors or as asexual. In the context of a conversation with Remy's mother, Nahida relates the story of her unusual first name. Her maternal grandfather, a true Prussian soldier in his professional life but a "weiche, empfindsame Natur" (178) in private, had named his daughter after the virtuous heroine of a novel (179). Establishing a female tradition, even a female literary tradition, her mother had passed on this name, as well as her last name, to her daughter in the absence of an unmentioned father: "Von meinem Vater spreche ich niemals . . . er hat meine Mutter sehr unglücklich gemacht" (180). The grandfather, whose cultural sensitivities keep his unambiguous masculinity under control, remains the only positive male figure. Male sexuality either inflicts disease upon women, as Nahida shows in the cases of her father and the effeminate priest, or disease results in the loss of masculinity, as in the case of her first husband. The stigma of Nahida's illegitimate birth and the presumed unhappiness of her mother, whose character remains peculiarly undeveloped throughout the narrative, translate into a notion of female sexuality as both unrestrained and vulnerable. The Jewish family, which Lazarus portrays in terms of traditional gender roles, becomes the only legitimate and secure space for female sexuality, and, by analogy, a context capable of controlling male sexuality. Drawing on notions of victimization and agency, the autobiography funnels constructions of femininity and female sexuality through definitions of Jewishness.

6. WISSENSCHAFT DES JUDENTUMS

The final chapter of *Ich suchte Dich!* relates the protagonist's public affirmation of a Jewish identity, which now replaces the construction of Nahida as an isolated yet eloquent religious outsider. Alluding to the author's name on the title page, the chapter heading "Die neue

Ruth" (188) indicates the arrival at a new identity—that of the female convert to Judaism. Following the caesura of her husband's death but before the act of conversion, Nahida begins to assert herself as a scholar of Judaism and a public advocate against anti-Semitism. On the basis of her understanding of Jewishness as a religion that safeguards women's socio-sexual position, Nahida's advocacy only includes religious Jews.

Emphasizing the protagonist's altered self-identification, the narrative disclaims earlier contact with Jews such as the observant lower-class Jewish women of her childhood and the Jewish doctor in Berlin—"mit Juden war Nahida bisher . . . gar nicht in Berührung gekommen" (188)—and, importantly, shifts focus to the figure of the middle-class Jewish woman. In the context of *Ich suchte Dich!,* Jewish women of the bourgeoisie exemplify the conflict between Jewish assimilation into German culture and the perceived threat of concurrent secularization with its loss of religious traditions. Jews in theaters and other public places become conspicuous objects of critical observation, "besonders die jüdischen Damen durch ihre Vorliebe für Schmuck und blitzende Brillianten" (188). Lazarus's text here not only evokes "the anti-Semites' image of the middle-class Jew with cultural pretensions"[13] but also links the figure of the Jewish *Emporkömmling* to gender stereotypes, doubling the negative image of the (male) Jew as the negative image of the female Jew. The newly rich female Jew functions as the negative counter image to the figure of the "gute Jüdin" (207), whose activities center on the observant Jewish home. In the construction of the rich Jewish woman "traditional labels ('Jew' and 'Christian') take on the properties of categories of race ('Jew' and 'Aryan')."[14] What links the Jewish women in the theaters to the observant "good" Jewish women is a biological definition that includes the non-religious Jew in a racial definition of "Jew." Outside of the religious context, femininity and Jewishness in this autobiography take on the negative connotations that deny Jews, women, and Jewish women in particular, legitimacy within late nineteenth-century German high culture.

Toward the end of the 1870s, anti-Semitism, "die Schmach des Jahrhunderts" begins "auch in der Familie der jungen Frau ansteckend zu wirken" (189). Reversing the late nineteenth-century trope of the Jew as a disease, the narrative describes anti-Semitism in the language of disease. Anti-Semitism makes Jews visible as an object of sympathetic study and provides Nahida with an opportunity to scrutinize the profundity of her own knowledge. She begins to research the phenomenon of anti-Semitism and to read the current literature on Jewish cultural accomplishments, including Heinrich Graetz's eleven-volume *Geschichte der Juden von den ältesten Zeiten bis auf die Gegenwart* (1853-75) and the Christian biologist Mathias Jacob Schleiden's 1877 book, *Die Bedeutung der Juden für Erhaltung und Wiederbelebung der Wissenschaften im Mittelalter.* Schleiden justifies his hundred-page scientific treatise with his desire "wenigstens den Anfang zu machen, um einen Theil des unsäglichen Unrechts, welches die Christen an den Juden begangen haben, wieder gut zu machen,"[15] a statement of purpose central also to Lazarus's construction of self as a philosemitic child ("das mit der Jüdin war gewiß kein Unrecht") and subsequently as a pro-Jewish scholar. Importantly, both Graez and Schleiden define Judaism as a religious culture distinct from Christian religious practice but united by and within a German cultural context.

The pursuit of knowledge and fear of unscientific "Verwirrung ihres Wissens" (195) leads the young woman to make the acquaintance of the "Präsident des Berliner Zweigvereins der Schillerstiftung [Moritz Lazarus] . . . ahnungslos, daß er ein Jude sei" (197). The narrative introduces Moritz Lazarus with a reference to his prominent position in German high culture, which explicitly renders him invisible as a Jew, and goes so far to ascribe blond hair to the sexagenarian (198), the same physical feature that defines Nahida as German. Not Moritz Lazarus, the Eastern Jew, but Moritz Lazarus, the German intellectual, leads "die bescheidene Frau" (199) to the study of Judaism as science. With his guidance and the help of "gründliche Kenntniß *neuzeitlicher* Thatsachen, der heutigen statistischen Tabellen, der modernen Daten und Zahlen" (193), she appropriates the intellectual tools necessary to defend Jews against anti-Semitism and to assert herself as a scientist and scholar. Significantly, Lazarus approaches the study of Jewish culture through the Biblical language of Hebrew, while Yiddish or German-Yiddish, a language she had used in one of her dramas to stereotype the Eastern European Jewish merchant,[16] is completely absent from the Judaism of the autobiography. The visibly Jewish women in the theater on the one hand, and the invisibly Jewish president of the Schiller society on the other, suggest that access to German high culture and science depends on a unified identity position. The characterization of Jewish women who do not practice their religion as "keine wahren Jüdinnen; sie heißen so, aber sie sind es nicht, sie sind *Zwitterwesen*" (207)[17] betrays a deeply rooted anxiety over boundary transgressions. The image of the body with both male and female sexual organs suggests that an ambiguous sexual gender and racial identity places the individual outside of socially acceptable categories. According to this construction, only "true" Jews, "genuine" Germans, and "real" women can claim legitimate access to high culture and science. The women whose "Jewishness" manifests itself through their jewelry rather than observance become hybrid outsiders. "Eine wahre, gute Jüdin ist nur die, welche das Judentum *kennt, liebt und verehrt*; sie braucht *keine Gelehrte* zu sein, aber mit ihrem ganzen Herzen muß sie an ihrem Judentum hängen!" (208) The less educated Jewish woman thus stands for genuine religiosity in conjunction with authentic femininity. It is the construction of Judaism as a specifically female religious context which enables the autobiographical subject to lay claim to the socially male position of a "Gelehrte" and still place herself within the boundaries of binary gender norms.

Lazarus spent the decade between 1880 and 1890 in Berlin (200), studying Jewish religion, history, and the Hebrew language, enduring, as she formulates it, the specifically female double burden of "Aschenbrödelei" (197) in her own household and the untiring pursuit of "gelehrte Studien" (197). Phrases such as "the young woman" or the "young scholar" instead of the protagonist's first name linguistically mark the transition from child to scholar, suggesting that the author affords her adult autobiographical alter ego a higher degree of respect. The ideal of "Entsagung" (198) links the construction of self as a self-sacrificing woman to the autobiographer's identity as a female scientist who abandons private comforts for the higher cause of her research. In addition, renunciation as a model of male and female conduct in high and popular culture[18] thematically connects Lazarus's autobiographical construction of self and her prolific activities as a writer of popular literature. Biographical and bibliographical entries in contemporary literary encyclopedias note that between 1879 and 1890 Lazarus wrote six dramas,[19] published a collection of novellas[20] and a two-volume novel,[21] all of which belong to the category of popular fiction and appeared under the name of Nahida Remy. In the autobiography, the creation of this voluminous body of work functions merely as a prelude to her activities as a scientific writer. Referring to her 320-page study *Das jüdische Weib* (1896), she writes: "und nun sollte sie auf einem Gebiet, auf dem sie nur Lernende und Empfangende war, *selbständig* etwas schaffen und es wagen, sich damit in die Reihe populär-wissenschaftlicher Schriftsteller zu begeben?" (202, my emphasis). The genre of popular literature provided women writers such as Nahida Remy with the opportunity to participate in the production of literature.[22] With *Das jüdische Weib,* Lazarus asserts in her autobiography, she wrote herself out of the position of the female student, whose learning tellingly equals conception, and inscribed herself, albeit hesitatingly, in the male, i.e., universal category of the author of popular science.

Lazarus constructs the act of religious conversion as a necessary outcome of her systematic scientific study of Judaism. In the introduction to the third edition of *Das jüdische Weib* she states:

> Als ich dieses Buch schrieb, war ich Christin. Heute bin ich Jüdin; ich musste Jüdin werden, nachdem ich durch meine Forschungen *erkannt* und vollends in meinen 'Culturstudien über das Judentum' *bekannt,* was die jüdische Religion bedeutet.[23]

The cognitive process of *Erkennen* precedes but also requires the confessional act of *Bekennen*. The intellectual insight of the adult verifies and retrospectively legitimizes the spiritual knowledge of the adolescent. In the autobiographical reconstruction of the conversion process the academic engagement with Judaism enables the narrator to realize and express the emotional conviction "daß sie im Herzen (wenn auch gänzlich unbewußt) längst *Jüdin* gewesen sei" (213). The declaration, "Ich werde Jüdin," (215) evokes the syntax of the title and gains prominence as one of the few emphatic first-person statements in an autobiographical narrative that treats its protagonist with rhetorical distance.

In 1895, at the age of forty-six, Lazarus converted to Judaism and little later married Moritz Lazarus. The narration of her second marriage recalls the dichotomy of health and illness of her first marriage. On her way from Berlin to Geneva, where the conversion is to take place, the protagonist passes through Freiburg to visit Moritz Lazarus. She finds him to be ill and spends the next six weeks taking care of the seventy-one-year old man. When a doctor suggests a trip to Italy to further his recovery, the need for a travel companion and a nurse prompts student and teacher to get married. Lazarus structures the three central relationships she chose to include in her autobiographical narrative along the division of sickness and health. Her mother as well as both husbands represent ill counterparts to her healthy self. While her mother's illness results in the final breakup of her family, her husbands' poor health in both cases gives the incentive to get married. Unlike her unhealthy mother, the daughter is capable of sustaining marital relationships.

7. AUTOBIOGRAPHY AS VEILED TRANSGRESSION

Lazarus's narrative of conversion, I suggest in conclusion, represents a complex and multifaceted project of identity construction that reaches beyond and outside the adoption of a new religion. Nahida's need to belong to a "Confession" translates into a narrative that in certain ways undercuts the protagonist's desire to create a unified subject position. Probing the meanings of a female gender identity through the binary oppositions of male and female, Christian and Jew, German and Jew, German and non-German, science and literature, high culture and popular culture, *Ich suchte Dich!* both reproduces and challenges conventional notions of femininity.

Despite its virtual absence from the narrative, the mother-daughter relationship demonstrates the contradictions that govern the autobiographer's construction of self in relation to male and female socio-sexual positions. In the daughter's rendition, the mother appears as the victim of an unspeakable and tragic fate. Her death in 1889 in a remote Italian fisher village marks the end of a relationship whose memory proves to be unbearable to the daughter:

> Das Leben und das Ende jedoch der edlen, genialen, aber ach, gegen ihren Willen so ruhelosen Frau waren so unsäglich wehmütiger Art . . . daß die Tochter nie bei der Erinnerung verweilen durfte, wollte sie ihre Fassung bewahren.
>
> Wohltuend ist das Schweigen, wenn man gar zu Viel zu sagen hat!—

(210)

Nahida, the daughter, deliberately oppresses the memory of her mother and, in a reversal of the opening scene, now chooses silence to maintain her own emotional stability. The characterization of her mother as victim gains another dimension in light of the noticeable omission of her mother's activities as a writer, feminist and socialist, pacifist, and nurse during the Italian liberation wars of 1860 and the Prussian-Austrian war of 1866. The daughter reduces the unusual career of Nahida Sturmhoefel, who is said to have published a women's newspaper in 1848,[24] to her suffering, denying her the agency that she possessed as an educated and independent woman who lived in several countries, traveled extensively throughout Europe, and earned her own livelihood as a writer as well as a manual worker. In the final scene of *Ich suchte Dich!* Lazarus portrays herself on the grave of the "edle Schwärmerin . . . , die *auch* ihr Lebelang auf der Suche gewesen" (223, my emphasis). Whereas the mother's life is characterized by a ceaseless but unsuccessful search for a stable and secure identity position, the daughter can bring her autobiographical construction of self to a closure with the emphatic exclamation on her mother's grave: "Ich suchte Dich mein Gott—und habe dich gefunden. Ich suchte dich, mein Judentum, und habe dich gefunden" (223). The characterization of the mother as a beloved but disempowered counterpart and the narrative positioning of her death as the necessary precondition for the daughter's successful completion of the search for an identity suggests that her mother's participation in the women's movement with its demands for women's participation and equal representation in the public sphere could not provide her with a workable model of identity construction. Conversion to Judaism brings Nahida's search for self-identity to a close and makes possible the formation of a narrative "I."

Ich suchte Dich! was published five years prior to Georg Misch's attempt at the first scholarly definition of autobiography. As an "inappropriate" subject of autobiography, to borrow a term from Sidonie Smith,[25] autobiographer Nahida Lazarus claims discursive agency as a woman who both challenges traditional femininity and at the same time seeks to avoid masculine appearances and mannish behavior. The pervasive presence of so-cially and scientifically sanctioned gender norms in this autobiographical narrative exemplifies how a project of individual female emancipation can be firmly embedded in conservatism. Lazarus's text negotiates the desire for a unified subject position and her status as a convert, as someone who occupies a position "in between," not only in terms of religious categories but also in terms of the unstable cultural and social position of the woman who crosses the gendered boundaries from object of study to speaking subject. The process of searching, as the title indicates, takes precedence over the act of finding, and the identity position at which the subject of this autobiography arrives reveals itself to be more complex and subversive than her narrative at first suggests.

Notes

1. Nahida Lazarus, *Ich suchte Dich! Biographische Erzählung von Nahida Ruth Lazarus (Nahida Remy)* (Berlin: Cronbach, 1898).

2. Nahida Sturmhoefel (1822-1889), daughter of a Prussian major, was the founder of a feminist newspaper in Dresden in the late 1840s, and author of several philosophical and lyrical works. See Sophie Pataky, ed., *Lexikon deutscher Frauen der Feder* (Bern: Lang, 1971) 348; Franz Brümmer, *Lexikon der deutschen Dichter und Prosaisten des neunzehnten Jahrhunderts*, 5th ed., 3: 12; and Elisabeth Friedrichs, *Die deutschsprachigen Schriftstellerinnen des 18. und 19. Jahrhunderts. Ein Lexikon* (Stuttgart: Metzler, 1981) 304.

3. Karl A. Leimbach, ed., *Die deutschen Dichter der Neuzeit und Gegenwart. Biographien, Charakteristiken und Auswahl ihrer Dichtungen* (Leipzig, 1899) 429.

4. Österreichischer Bundestheaterverband, *Burgtheater 1776-1976. Aufführungen und Besetzungen von zweihundert Jahren,* 2 (Wien: Ueberreuter, 1979): 305.

5. Adolf Hinrichsen, *Das literarische Deutschland,* 2nd ed., (Berlin, 1891) 1093.

6. Ingrid Belke, ed., *Moritz Lazarus und Heymann Steinthal. Die Begründer der Völkerpsychologie in ihren Briefen,* (Tübingen: Mohr, 1971) xli.

7. Gerhard Lüdtke, ed., *Nekrolog zu Kürschners Literatur-Kalender 1901-1935* (Berlin: de Gruyter, 1936) 407.

8. Sander Gilman, *The Jew's Body,* (New York: Routledge, 1991) 24.

9. The title of the handwritten manuscript reads: "*Ich suchte dich. Eine Erzählung aus dem Leben von Nahida Ruth Lazarus (Nahida Remy),*" Leo Baeck Institute New York, AR 3754.

10. The titles are *Moritz Lazarus's Lebenserinnerungen* (1906), *Erinnerungen eines deutschen Profes-*

sors in der Schweiz (1910), and *Aus meiner Jugend* (1913).

11. On Jewish names see Dietz Bering, *Der Name als Stigma* (Stuttgart: Klett-Cotta, 1988).

12. All references to Jeffrey Moussaieff Masson, *The Complete Letters of Sigmund Freud to Wilhelm Fliess 1887-1904* (Cambridge: The Belknap Press of Harvard UP, 1985).

13. Sander Gilman, *Jewish Self-Hatred. Anti-Semitism and the Hidden Language of the Jew* (Baltimore: Johns Hopkins UP, 1986) 223.

14. Gilman, *Jew's Body* 202.

15. Mathias Jacob Schleiden, *Die Bedeutung der Juden für Erhaltung und Wiederbelebung der Wissenschaften im Mittelalter* (Leipzig, 1877) 1.

16. Nahida Remy, *Nationale Gegensätze* (Berlin, 1884).

17. The addition "sie sind *Zwitterwesen*" appears in the handwritten manuscript only, p. 57.

18. Peter Nusser, *Trivialliteratur* (Stuttgart: Metzler, 1991) 60.

19. *Constanze* premiered at Residenz-Theater in Berlin on 26 April 1879; *Die Grafen Eckhardstein* (1880); *Schicksalswege* (1879) premiered at the Belle-Alliance Theater in Berlin on 9 May 1879 and at the Ostendtheater; her other dramas include *Domeniko, Nationale Gegensätze* (1884), and *Liebeszauber* (1887).

20. Nahida Remy, *Sizilianische Novellen,* (Berlin, 1886).

21. Nahida Remy, *Geheime Gewalten* (Dresden, 1890).

22. Nusser 63.

23. Nahida Remy, *Das jüdische Weib. Mit einer Vorrede von Prof. Dr. M. Lazarus* (Leipzig, 1891) n.p.

24. Pataky 348.

25. Sidonie Smith, "Construing Truths in Lying Mouths," *Studies in the Literary Imagination* 23.2 (1990): 159.

Shirley M. Dettlaff (essay date 1997)

SOURCE: Dettlaff, Shirley M. "'Counter Natures in Mankind': Hebraism and Hellenism in *Clarel*." In *Melville's Evermoving Dawn: Centennial Essays,* edited by John Bryant and Robert Milder, pp. 192-221. Kent, Ohio: The Kent State University Press, 1997.

[In the following essay, Dettlaff examines Melville's development of the philosophical delineations of the differences between Hebraism and Hellenism in his Clarel.*]*

A little more than halfway through Herman Melville's *Clarel* (1876), when the pilgrims visit the monastery of Mar Saba in the Judean desert, the bewildered title character attends a masque in which the Wandering Jew, portrayed by one of the monks, pours forth all the agony in his soul; no sooner has the doleful monk-actor left the stage than a cheerful Greek traveler is heard extolling the joys of life in a pagan song. The sudden juxtaposition of these opposites causes Clarel to question

> if in frames of thought
> And feeling, there be right and wrong;
> Whether the lesson Joel taught
> Confute what from the marble's caught
> In sylvan sculpture—Bacchant, Faun,
> Or shapes more lax by Titian drawn.
> Such counter natures in mankind—
> Mole, bird, not more unlike we find:
> Instincts adverse, nor less how true
> Each to itself. What clew, what clew?
>
> (NN *Clarel* 3.20.32-42)

What clue, indeed? Answering this question becomes a crucial problem for the main character in *Clarel.*[1] Although the surface story of *Clarel* features conflicting religious views that bewilder the title character during his pilgrimage to the Holy Land, what Melville has Clarel and the reader gradually realize is that these debates stem from the two opposing views of human personality generally expressed in the Greco-Roman and Judeo-Christian traditions. The issue involves, in Melville's words, the "old debate" whether man is "ape or angel" (4.35.12). But there is more to it than this rather general contrast: Melville's perception and expression of this dichotomy was influenced by a theory of human personality that eighteenth-century German literary critics had developed and that eventually made its way into English literary culture. It is the human typology that Friedrich Schiller and Friedrich Schlegel had worked out independently during the late eighteenth century and that A. W. Schlegel had popularized in the early nineteenth century. It is the theory of human character that, with a slight twist, Matthew Arnold, during the time that Melville was writing *Clarel,* proposed as Hellenism and Hebraism.

Classicism and Romanticism in German Literary Theory

This basic dichotomy developed in Germany out of independent and slightly different attempts to distinguish between the ancients and the moderns, distinctions that were to some extent inspired by medieval romances, Shakespearean plays, English graveyard poetry, and *Sturm und Drang* literature, much of which Melville knew and admired. These attempts began as interpretations of cultural history but broadened to include a theory of human types. In *Naive and Sentimental Poetry* (1795-96) Schiller presented the more fully developed theory, influenced by Kantian philosophy, when he described ancient poets as "naive" and modern ones as "sentimental" but changed the terms to "realist" and "idealist" when broadening the concepts to distinguish between basic human types. Developing his own similar distinction independently in a series of articles (1797-1800), Friedrich Schlegel used the terms that finally prevailed, "classic" and "romantic," although it was his brother, August Wilhelm, who codified and popularized Friedrich's ideas, along with many of his own, in the well-known and influential *Lectures on Dramatic Art and Literature* (1809-11).

Despite the differences in meaning, the antitheses of these early theorists had a certain basic similarity. Following Winckelmann's familiar but now debunked theories about Greek art, they suggested that the ancient Greeks epitomized one type of human or artist, who was then labeled as naive, realistic, or classical. A. W. Schlegel, whose version of the antithesis in *Lectures on Dramatic Art and Literature* became better known outside of Germany than Schiller's, popularized the familiar stereotype of the Greeks as representatives of classical culture who were fully realized products of nature, healthy human beings raised to feel external harmony with a beautiful, hospitable environment. With objective minds relying primarily upon the operation of the senses and the intellect, they enjoyed internal "harmony of all their faculties" and felt little self-consciousness or internal conflict. They accepted their lot in life as a part of nature and spontaneously expressed this vision in art that was sensuous, beautiful, and full of joy. A major deficiency of their outlook, Schlegel charged, however, was that it never became much more than "a refined and ennobled sensuality," the highest development of "finite nature" (24).

The other kind of human personality, the one that moved beyond man's finite nature to aspire to the infinite and appeared in the most famous literary characters of the period, was the modern, which Schiller called "sentimental" or "idealist" and the Schlegels "romantic." The product of a hostile northern climate, a highly spiritualized Christianity, and a modern civilization alienated from nature, this also-familiar stereotype was seen as a very subjective, divided being. He was torn between his senses, which seek gratification in this world, and his spiritual faculties, which long for something so far transcending the senses that it can never be attained. This *Streben nach dem Unendlichen,* a key concept of *Sturm und Drang* romanticism, propels the typical romantic quest for some unreachable goal. This heightened sense of the ideal also creates an inner discord in the modern's faculties unknown among realists or the ancients, one that is exacerbated by modern introversion and can lead to moral paralysis. Both the northern climate and Christianity have turned the attention of the modern or romantic inward, causing him to be highly reflective

and, according to Schlegel, to develop an "earnestness of mind" (25), all of which qualities, for example, made Hamlet the darling of the romantics. The unbridgeable gap that the idealist perceives between what his imagination intuits and what he experiences in actuality creates a pervasive melancholy, the *Weltschmerz* of Werther, in which, as Schlegel put it, "life has become shadow and darkness" (26). This idealism is not totally negative, however, Schiller noted, since it assumes a superior concept of humanity and a more lofty ethical system. Unlike the realist who, following the rule of practical use, seeks pleasure, happiness, and well-being, the idealist, following the rule of abstract value, longs mainly for a noble heroism and freedom from physical necessity (182-83). Schiller also warned that both types can lead to exaggerated behavior: the realist can sink into coarse, mindless activity, while the idealist can become a rigid, joyless fanatic locked into and enervated by his own mental system (183-84).

Central to the thinking of these theorists is the belief that these types of personality conflict with each other and, yet, both must be combined to provide a complete definition of man. In *Naive and Sentimental Poetry* Schiller asserted that the antithesis between the naive and the sentimental is a psychological antagonism that is as old as mankind, that is "based on inner mental dispositions," and that, being nearly insurmountable, makes true communication between the two types almost impossible (176). Despite the tendency for most humans to belong to one type or another, he felt that both opposites had to be synthesized to produce the fully human person. He held out the hope that the antagonism could be overcome "in a few rare individuals who . . . always existed and always will" (176). And he suggested that in society there should be a class of humans in which both tendencies were developed "so that each would preserve the other from its own extreme" (175). It must be remembered that the aesthetics of these writers were closely related to these theories about personality types, which originated in attempts to distinguish between types of poets. Since these writers believed that the truly great poet is one who can synthesize the senses and the spirit, he must be such a person himself.

It is this theory of characterization that is often dramatized in the *Bildungs-* or *Kunstlerroman* of romantic literature. As M. H. Abrams has observed, in many of the great works of this period that dramatize this dichotomy, like *Wilhelmmeisters Lehrjahr* or *Faust,* the poet's search for identity and fulfillment involves a dialectic between the actual and ideal worlds and eventually culminates in a synthesis of the two. In the typical *Bildungsweg,* the protagonist falls from his innocent, instinctive life of the senses. Some trauma, often an unhappy love affair or death of a loved one, shocks him out of this naive unity with nature, and he enters the romantic state, one characterized by alienation, obsessive thought, interior conflict, melancholy, and unfulfilled yearning. He sets off to search for truth and for a return to this earlier paradise, but he discovers that he cannot go back and instead must struggle forward dialectically through reflection and freedom to achieve a new wholeness or reintegration. In his new, mature state he appreciates both the life of the senses and that of the spirit. It is thus that he is able to create the true art that also unites the diametrically opposed worlds of the senses and of the spirit (Abrams 217-37).

Able to operate in both worlds, the man who achieves this synthesis is not the captive of either. He is free and independent, the most noble human whose development of self transcends the antithesis of the senses and the spirit. Yet even he can never achieve perfection. A crucial point the theorists make is that in the search for the infinite there can be no attainable goal, only progress toward it. As Schiller observed in his poem "The Pilgrim," a work that Melville probably read,

> While I live is never given
> > Bridge or wave the goal to near—
> Earth will never meet the Heaven,
> > Never can the THERE be HERE!
>
> (*Poems and Ballads* 35)

But the quest is not fruitless. Also important for the romanticist, as Abrams notes, citing Faust as an example, is that the fully developed human's "triumph consists simply in the experience of sustaining a desire which never relaxes into the stasis of a finite satisfaction" (245). The great artist, then, constantly striving for the infinite, creates works that are deliberately open-ended, that suggest more to the imagination than can the tidy resolutions that appeal merely to the intellect. The ambitious but inconclusive quest is not evidence of a pessimistic naturalism; it is, instead, evidence of a tragic view of life in which the human has a lofty mental potential in his imagination and a dignity in his ability to choose that surpass the limitations of his physical being or finite mind.

Schiller and the Schlegels, who were at the center of two very powerful German literary circles, influenced other romantic authors and theorists, as well as Coleridge, Byron, Shelley, Madame de Stael, and Carlyle. These were other sources from which Melville could have encountered this dichotomy directly or indirectly before the 1860s. Although there is no external evidence that Melville studied Schiller's theory in *Naive and Sentimental Poetry,* he did, early in his career, read a great deal of Schiller. Nor do we know if Melville actually read A. W. Schlegel's *Lectures on Dramatic Art and Literature,* which was probably Schlegel's most influential work, but apparently he knew enough in 1849 to report in his journal that he had discussed "Schlegel" with George Adler. There is no doubt, however, that

Melville was fascinated by those literary characters who embodied to one degree or another the spirit of what Schiller called the sentimental and Schlegel the romantic: Hamlet, Werther, Faust, Childe Harold, Teufelsdrock. And Melville's early, rather general use of this antithesis can be seen already in *Moby-Dick* and *Pierre,* for instance, in the well-known passage from "The Lee Shore" in *Moby-Dick*: "But as in landlessness alone resides the highest truth, shoreless, indefinite as God—so, better is it to perish in that howling infinite, than be ingloriously dashed upon the lee, even if that were safety! For worm-like, then oh! who would craven crawl to land!" (107).

Melville apparently became more deeply interested in the distinction when in 1862 he read and heavily annotated Madame de Stael's *Germany,* which provides a summary of the Schlegels' dichotomy in chapter 11, "Of Classic and Romantic Poetry." In fact, Melville checked in de Stael a key point that the Germans made, that modern writers stress the personality of the individual more than the ancients did: "In ancient times, men attended to events alone, but among the moderns character is of greater importance; and that uneasy reflection, which, like the vulture of Prometheus, often totally devours us, would have been folly amid circumstances and relations so clear and decided, as they existed in the civil and social state of the ancients" (Cowen 52). His reading of Schiller's poetry at the same time also had an impact on his imagination.

But the culminating influence was probably Matthew Arnold's. Melville's intensive reading of Arnold in the 1860s and early 1870s, the gestation period for *Clarel,* exposed him to Arnold's version of that earlier German dichotomy. Arnold's antithesis was heavily indebted to Schiller and to the Schlegels, as well as to Heinrich Heine, from whom he took the terms "Hebraism" and "Hellenism."[2] Arnold used the dichotomy but not the terms in *Essays and Criticism,* which Melville read and carefully annotated. Melville surely recognized the distinction and its relationship to the earlier theory. Also, Arnold was popularizing the distinction and the terms in a series of essays that were eventually collected in the famous *Culture and Anarchy.* Melville's use of the dichotomy may have been influenced by one of the essays that was originally entitled "Anarchy and Authority":

> Both Hellenism and Hebraism arise out of the wants of human nature, and address themselves to satisfying those wants. But their methods are so different, they lay stress on such different points, and call into being by their respective disciplines such different activities, that the face which human nature presents when it passes from the hands of one of them to those of the other is no longer the same. To get rid of one's ignorance, to see things as they are, and by seeing them as they are to see them in their beauty, is the simple and

attractive ideal which Hellenism holds out before human nature; and from the simplicity and charm of this ideal, Hellenism, and human life in the hands of Hellenism, is invested with a kind of aerial ease, clearness, and radiancy; they are full of what we call sweetness and light. Difficulties are kept out of view, and the beauty and rationality of the ideal have all our thoughts. . . . But there is a saying which I have heard attributed to Mr. Carlyle about Socrates,—a very happy saying, whether it is really Mr. Carlyle's or not,—which excellently marks the essential point in which Hebraism differs from Hellenism. "Socrates," this saying runs, "is terribly at ease in Zion." Hebraism—and here is the source of its wonderful strength—has always been severely preoccupied with a severe sense of the impossibility of being at ease in Zion; of the difficulties which oppose themselves to man's pursuit or attainment of that perfection of which Socrates talks so hopefully, and, as from this point of view one might almost say, so glibly.

(802-03)[3]

However, it would be more accurate to suggest that, rather than being influenced by Arnold, Melville was inspired by Arnold's updating of the then old German dichotomy to present his own modification of it in *Clarel*. What Arnold was trying to achieve in his prose criticism of modern English culture, Melville decided to do for American and European culture, only better—that is, in poetry and according to his own version of the old antithesis.

"Hebrew" and "Hellene" in *Clarel*

The setting of *Clarel,* the Holy Land, where ancient Jewish history has been overlaid by centuries of Greek influence, offered Melville the perfect opportunity to use this dichotomy. Palestine abounds in historical evidence of "Isaiah's dark burden, malison" (4.26.116) as well as "gay Hellene lightheartedness" (3.4.110). Melville uses Arnold's very terms early in *Clarel* when he contrasts a barren tomb with a frieze sculptured on it, suggesting that both the decoration and the sepulcher represent "contraries in old belief— / Hellenic cheer, Hebraic grief" (1.28.33-34). Influenced by a theory of art that stresses the conflict and union of opposites, Melville uses the dichotomy not only to align the characters in opposing groups but to provide a pattern for their interplay. It suggests literary models and rationales for his characters. It supplies thematic as well as scenic contrasts. But, most important, it provides a kind of dialectical pattern for the story of the title character.

First, the Hebraic/Hellenic dichotomy determines character alignment in the story. Melville deliberately highlights the distinction between these "counter natures" and also gives both a mythical dimension when at Mar Saba he juxtaposes the Wandering Jew's complaint and the Greek Merchant's lyric. This pointed contrast suggests that one of Melville's narrative strategies is to confront the pilgrims touring Judea with the desert and all that it represents in order to give them a kind of reality test, during which they reveal their personality type. Regardless of their ethnic origin, characters can be considered "Hellenic" if, to follow Arnold's criterion, they manage to make themselves at ease in Judea, or "Hebraic" if they do not.[4] In responding to the desert, the characters also reveal their moral status, for the issue is not just the identification of personality types but the question of whether one type of life is superior to the other.

According to the paean to a Saturnian Golden Age sung by the Merchant from Lesbos, Melville's Hellenism is roughly the same as the German notion of classicism, a joyful naturalism which extols the worldly, focusing on the bright side of life rather than on the dark. It is represented in the mythic Golden Age, the prelapsarian childhood of the race, an Eden of agrarian peace and harmony, of glorious sensuousness, of culture and "gracious talk" with the gods. Those characters in *Clarel* who can be considered Hellenic, to one degree or another, try to create this world about them. They fail Melville's reality test of the Judean desert by attempting to ignore, trivialize, or escape what it represents: evil or nonbeing, the physical, moral, and intellectual negatives that constitute the dark underside of human existence. Like Schiller, Melville reveals attitudes toward them that vary from bemused tolerance to outright contempt. If they are very young, like Glaucon or the Cypriote, their innocent, mindless enjoyment of life stems from the charming, natural ebullience of youth that as yet has had little or no experience of physical or moral evil. But the older Hellenes, who Melville thinks should know better, have deliberately and thus reprehensively prolonged their moral childhood. Whenever some evil looms into view, they blindly flee it and create only an environment of creature comforts or intellectual certainty. Sensualists such as the Greek Banker, the Merchant of Lesbos, and the Lyonese Jew have created for themselves false Edens in which financial success, convivial gatherings, or hedonistic delights provide a sense of security and block out painful realities. More intellectual Hellenes like Margoth or Derwent create an Arcadia of the mind, Margoth putting his faith in the scientific method, and the Anglican clergyman glossing over the troublesome nineteenth-century doubts about Christianity with an optimistic casuistry.

Even those characters who are ethnically Jewish may reveal a Hellenic temperament, as is the case with the Lyonese, Margoth, Agar, and Ruth. The two women, for instance, neither understand nor sympathize with Nathan's Zionist vision and shrink from the Judaic wasteland. They try, futilely, with potted plants and flowers, with the semblance of family life, to recreate the American homeland, a snug domestic retreat from unwelcome reality. Whether they obscure disturbing realities with food, drink, sex, fellowship, domesticity, success, or religious sophistry, these Hellenes do not have the type of human nature or strength of character to open their eyes to what the desert represents. Melville even extends his character test to the reader of the poem, warning that he may wish to turn back from the desert along with the Syrian Banker (2.13.112-19) or skip a disturbing description (2.35.38-41). Melville understands and appreciates this life but considers it to be limited, agreeing with Schiller in the poem "Guides of Life: The Beautiful and the Sublime," that one may enjoy the beauty of the physical world and yet not grant it the respect that one reserves for a higher experience, the sublime.

It is in his depiction of the Hebraic character that Melville is most indebted to the Hebraic/Hellenic dichotomy. This is the temperament that Melville does respect highly, the embodiment of the sentimental or romantic character whose *Streben nach dem Unendlichen* Melville was describing when he grouped Leopardi, Obermann, and St. Teresa as "all of earnest mind, / Unworldly yearners" (3.1.13-16). He is represented to a great extent by the Wandering Jew, a figure of mythic resonance whose vision is dark, otherworldly, and sublime. Early in *Clarel* (1.13.112-16) Melville recounts his version of the legend of Cartaphilus. In the masque at Mar Saba he dramatizes and renders more generally symbolic the Wandering Jew's anguish: his fall from grace, his guilt and alienation, his search for rest and peace.[5] The key point in Melville's depiction of Cartaphilus and the Hebrew in general is that both have been cast out of Eden and yet strive for the infinite with a "longing which cannot be uttered."[6] Since Melville's Hebrew character has high expectations of life, he is especially sensitive to evils that he encounters. When this type of character is thwarted by some catastrophe of fate and is traumatically shocked, he does not seek relief in the Hellenic joys of life. Goaded, like the German romantic, to search for a better world that his imagination suggests should exist somewhere, he embarks upon the quest to discover some explanation or justification for this evil as well as some respite from the alienation and pain he suffers. One type of Hebrew striver in *Clarel,* the religious zealot—like Nathan, Nehemiah, the Syrian monk, and Brother Salvaterra—having abandoned worldly joys and undertaken the journey, achieves some degree of peace through espousing one of the great religions. However, the more truly Hebraic personality finds institutionalized religion another Hellenic delusion and avoids that, too; he cannot be "at ease in Zion." He is like Moses Mendelssohn, who, according to Rolfe, "though his honest heart was scourged / By doubt Judaic, never laid / His burden at Christ's door" (2.22.86-88). This Hebraic doubter, a Byronic exaggeration of the type—represented also in Celio, Mortmain, Agath, and Ungar—is torn by disbelief and wracked by despair or anger. Like the Byronic hero, he

wanders about the world, unable to find meaning or rest, gradually wearing himself out physically but never relaxing his *Streben nach dem Unendlichen* or lightening his *Weltschmerz.*

One specific way in which Melville develops this difference between Hebraism and Hellenism is through the Pilgrim/Tourist dichotomy presented in the first two cantos of the poem. Melville twice warns Clarel, as well as the reader, that a tour of the Holy Land requires a proper attitude, that of the Hebraic pilgrim, who realizes that the journey is a spiritual one like those taken by the great saints rather than the sightseeing trip taken by a Hellenic tourist. A fellow American traveler returning from Jerusalem points out that his countrymen especially need to put aside their provincial attitudes and adopt "the Semitic reverent mood, / Unworldly" (1.1.93-94), to interpret Palestine correctly, opening their minds to a more profound reality, which they are unaccustomed to and indeed repelled by. For, as the American traveler warns Clarel in what is a key line for understanding Clarel's actions in the poem, "To avoid the deep saves not from the storm" (1.1.99).

A poem entitled "Judaea," which Clarel discovers in his room in Jerusalem, expands on this point, contrasting what the worldly traveler, the tourist, expects from the Holy Land with what the "palmer," the true pilgrim, seeks. The shallow sightseer concentrates on "Sychem grapes," Tabor's garlands, "Sharon's rose," and "Solomon's Song," fabled tourist attractions that appeal to the superficial fancy, whatever diverts and cheers the soul. The true pilgrim, with his more profound imagination, "clings / About the precincts of Christ's tomb" (1.2.119-20) and brings with him out of Judea only a dusty palm. The pilgrim focuses on what for Melville was the most important symbol of the Christian story for modern man: the Crucifixion.

> Imagination, earnest ever,
> Recalls the Friday far away,
> Re-lives the crucifixion day—
> The passion and its sequel proves,
> Sharing the three pale Marys' frame;
> Through the eclipse with these she moves
> Back to the house from which they came
> To Golgotha. O empty room,
> O leaden heaviness of doom—
> O cowering hearts, which sore beset
> Deem vain the promise now, and yet
> Invoke him who returns no call;
> And fears for more that may befall.
> O terror linked with love which cried:
> "Art gone? is't o'er? and crucified?"

> (1.3.181-96)

Of the great Christian mysteries, the Crucifixion and its immediate aftermath of doubt for Christ's followers are central for the sincere modern Christian who realizes that Christ has died again in the contemporary world, this time because of rationalism and science. When the imagination grasps this point, worldly existence loses its meaning, human death becomes terrifying, and the human has no recourse in dealing with evil. The modern Hebraic character is frustrated because his intense spiritual longings have lost their object and he cannot find another. This search is the real quest, the true pilgrimage that Melville is suggesting in *Clarel* as opposed to the conventional tour of the Holy Land.

The Hebrew doubters are on such a pilgrimage: not only have they, like Christ's followers immediately after his crucifixion, begun to doubt Christ, but like Christ they have taken up their cross and are struggling on the *Via Crucis* toward their own inevitable crucifixion. The Wandering Jew is a dark version of or mythic alternative to Christ, whose suffering and alienation may never reach the ultimate reward of reunion with God. As much as Melville admires these Hebraic doubters, he agrees with the German literary theorists and Arnold that they represent only one side of human nature and that characters who synthesize both the Hebraic and the Hellenic are the preferred, if rare, ideal. Obsessed with the dark side of life, the Hebraic doubters lose sight of its bright side and do not transcend and judge it from a tragic perspective, affirming its validity while still aware of its transience and triviality. Just as he had in his earlier works, Melville believed, like Schiller, that such a synthesis must be achieved, that psychological growth is dialectical. But his idea of the synthesis is not like that of some German romantics, a reintegration with nature or any other exterior forces. Unlike Matthew Arnold's synthesis, where balance is maintained by a movement away from the extremes toward the middle, Melville's more heroic idea requires an experience and balancing of the opposite extremes. Most humans cannot achieve this synthesis, perhaps because they lack a sufficiently strong, imaginative personality that can recognize the simultaneous validity of opposites and, what is even more difficult to do without losing their balance, develop an ethical system based upon such a dualistic vision.

In the divine Rama appears such a balance of the Hebraic and the Hellenic, of the classic with the romantic. According to the narrator, mortals with the divine heritage of Rama can experience crippling encounters with evil and still transcend it:

> Though the black frost nip, though the white frost
> chill,
> Nor white frost nor the black may kill
> The patient root, the vernal sense
> Surviving hard experience
> As grass the winter.

> (1.32.20-24)

Being both divine and human, spiritual and sensuous,

> Theirs be the thoughts that dive and skim,
> Theirs the spiced tears that overbrim,
> And theirs the dimple and lightsome whim.

> (1.32.35-37)

Potential guides or models for Clarel who have achieved some kind of Rama-like synthesis include Derwent, Vine, and Rolfe. However, Derwent's rather mindless, superficial attempt to achieve a middle way, which parallels Arnold's Hellenic latitudinarianism, while tempting to Clarel, proves ultimately unsatisfactory. And Vine's synthesis, which errs in the opposite direction, also fails Clarel. Vine represents the second-rate artist of the mere fancy, whose literary taste escapes to the romance of the past and the beauty of nature. An introvert of great personal beauty and sensuousness, he has learned that hedonism and aesthetic experiences do not quench his longing for the infinite. His similarities to Hawthorne have been much commented upon, but he also fits the more general romantic convention of the graveyard solitary and man of sensibility. Some tragic experience has made him a "funeral man," who is first introduced, significantly, reclining before and meditating upon a tomb, brooding about fate and death. Suffering and haunted by the tragic vision, he balances it, somewhat, with an appreciation of beauty, countering the void, not too effectively it turns out, with the sensuous and the symbolic. He has taken the dialectical journey, having been a "Sybarite" and now having become, for some reason that we are not told, a "Carthusian," yet

> Not beauty might he all forget,
> The beauty of the world, and charm:
> He prized it though it scarce might warm.

> (1.29.40-42)

The revelation of the moral weakness behind his reserve suggests the deficiencies of his synthesis as well.

Most closely resembling the Rama figure, however, is Rolfe, to a certain extent Melville's idealized self-portrait, but more significantly his depiction of the great artist. He possesses not the mere fancy, but a powerful imagination that can actively unite the past and the present as well as intuit the sublime in nature. And he possesses the great intellect that Melville considered crucial for the pursuit of truth. Rolfe has achieved a truer synthesis of the Hebraic and the Hellenic than has Derwent or Vine. Like the Hellenes, he has a very genial personality and is an active participant in the world, an erudite raconteur and persuasive debater whose search for the truth has made him knowledgeable about man's outer life, about the social, political, intellectual, and religious aspects of man's history. But all his knowledge of the world has not satisfied an Hebraic *Streben nach dem Unendlichen,* perhaps some explanation for all the evil that his study and personal experience of mankind have revealed to him. Despite his intellectual doubt, he continues his quest for truth, a *Kunstlerweg,* with that "earnestness of mind" that Schlegel stressed, apparently aware that although the goal may be unattainable, one must never relax "into the stasis of finite satisfaction." Not only does his personality represent a synthesis, but as an artist he tries to unite disparate experiences. Like the poet in Melville's poem "In a Garret," who desires to "grapple from Art's deep / One dripping trophy!" Rolfe has returned to the Holy Land

> where evermore
> Some lurking thing he hoped to gain—
> Slip quite behind the parrot-lore
> Conventional, and—what attain?

> (1.31.35-38)

Probing beyond official, sanitized versions of reality, he is the one who often tells stories about other characters' disastrous encounters with fate. Despite his awareness of evil, he is broadly tolerant of people and rejoices in convivial social situations, wholeheartedly joining in the drinking, the song, and even the whimsical talk. When another pilgrim overemphasizes the dark side of reality, Rolfe will contribute a story or comment that rights the balance (2.19.1-16). Rolfe's extremes in behavior reveal that "earnestness and levity" can be united in a "mind / Poised at self-center and mature" (4.3.124-25). Rolfe represents Melville's version of the German ideal, the free and independent, fully developed human and artist who synthesizes the Hebraic and Hellenic, the romantic and the classic, with a definite leaning toward the former. These are the reasons he is the mature model for Clarel, the tyro romantic or modern man of sensibility.

Beyond aligning most of the characters, the Hebraic/Hellenic dichotomy provides an adversarial pattern for the philosophical controversies about modern problems the pilgrims engage in as they travel in the desert. Representative Hebrews and Hellenes debate the issues from their respective viewpoints, the cast of minor characters changing but not the basically antithetical philosophical orientations. The latitudinarian Anglican Derwent can be trusted to argue for the Hellenic side, with the assistance of Margoth, the Merchant from Lesbos, and the Lyonese, all of whom represent well-defined and more extreme positions on the Hellenic spectrum. Speaking for various aspects of the Hebraic vision are Mortmain, Ungar, Rolfe, of course, and others.

The confrontation and alternation of the Hebraic and the Hellenic also function to control the mood of the poem. When a desolate scene or obsessed character threatens to take over, Melville introduces its opposite to remind Clarel and the reader that another choice is possible. Just before Clarel, Vine, and Nehemiah visit the Garden of Olives, the narrator answers his own question, "And wherefore by the convents be / Gardens? Ascetics roses entwine?" (1.3.1-2) by explaining that, like Christ suffering in the Garden, they "defend us from despair." Throughout the poem gardens, oases, and pastoral land punctuate the arid desert, as the pilgrims stop at the Jordan, Mar Saba, and Bethlehem while journeying in the Judean waste. Joyous or convivial episodes at these rest stops are juxtaposed with somber discussions and the deaths of Nehemiah and Mortmain.

CLAREL'S JOURNEY

The Hebraic/Hellenic dichotomy is perhaps most helpful in suggesting the form and significance of the central, if slight and somewhat confusing, story of Clarel's journey toward maturity. Melville casts Clarel as a tyro romantic and sets him on a *Bildungsweg,* during which the divinity student is tested to see which one of the "counter natures in mankind" is his own.[7] The question for Clarel at the beginning of the poem is whether or not he will become a true Hebraic pilgrim, opening his imagination to all the uncertainties that a sincere search for religious truth in the nineteenth century entails, or a Hellenic tourist, preferring merely a superficial, conventional tour of the Holy Land in which he merely exercises his fancy. The tests involve a dialectical process in which Clarel encounters Hellenic or Hebraic alternatives, not just in the intellectual discussions he hears but in his own personal life. Clarel's ultimate test, in the metaphor of the American traveler, is whether he will choose to brave the deep or try to avoid it.

During much of the poem Clarel tries to avoid it, although as a future clergyman on a trip to the Holy Land he would seem a person of Hebraic temperament. When he is first presented to the reader, Clarel is clearly portrayed as a young romantic, the contemplative solitary, in the traditions of Hamlet, Werther, the graveyard poet, and the Byronic hero. He reveals the characteristics that Schiller succinctly set forth in *Naive and Sentimental Poetry* and that Carlyle mocked in *Sartor Resartus.* In fact, the presentation of Clarel reveals all but one of the qualities of the sentimental character that Schiller saw concentrated in *Werther*: "sensitivity to nature, feeling for religion, a spirit of philosophical contemplation," "the gloomy, formless, melancholic Ossianic world," and a "tender effeminacy" (138). The one Wertherian characteristic not present in Clarel at the beginning—a "fanatically unhappy love"—does appear with full melodrama at the end of the poem. Like a graveyard poet, Clarel is first pictured in a tomblike cubicle of a Jerusalem hostel, reflecting very earnestly and rather self-consciously in the posture of the thinker brooding alone, as the last rays of the sun fade away. With features that are "pale, and all but feminine," he discontentedly questions the source of the melancholy that unexpectedly weighs down his spirit his first evening in the Holy City. Disturbed and depressed by the forbidding desert and barren city, he reflects upon their effect on the religious doubts that already plague him. "Earnest by nature" (1.1.107), Clarel is presented as an "Unworldly yearner" who opens his mind beyond book learning and society's official versions of reality to vague hints of another version of reality suggested by "nature's influx of control," even though he is made uneasy by the "clandestine" inklings, "underformings in the mind / Banked corals which ascend from far" (1.1.75-76).

Throughout his stay in Jerusalem, Clarel continues to exhibit characteristics of the tyro romantic. Like Hamlet, he is alienated, lonely, and melancholy; he is uncertain, irresolute, and passive; he is also sensitive and squeamish. Since the ruined city, with its deserted biblical landmarks, religious and cultural diversity, and commercial chicanery, has been stripped of any supernatural aura that he had associated with it, he wanders from one holy place to another, desperately hoping that one shrine or holy person will miraculously stem his increasing doubt. But he is disappointed by one false hope after another, including Nehemiah, the deluded Christian zealot who, ironically, becomes for a time his "guide." Also like the romantic hero, he is inexperienced, introverted, and full of fantasies, constantly reflecting and castigating himself. At the Church of the Holy Sepulcher Clarel's long-sustained reflection about the pilgrimages of various religions culminates in typical romantic inner conflict and self-loathing. Projecting his feeling of guilt upon the situation, he fancies that the sounds of the various religious services are curses aimed at him for his sacrilegious questioning of Christianity, and he actually flees the scene in self-condemnation.

However, Clarel's Hebraicism is superficial, more fanciful than truly imaginative. His increasing doubt opens up the "deep," and he begins to develop the imagination to see it; but he lacks the courage and resolution, the maturity and independence, the strong sense of self, to embark upon it. Because of his youth and inexperience, Clarel is naturally drawn to the more attractive and commonly accepted Hellenic attitude. Clarel unwittingly reveals his weakness when he answers Nehemiah's insistent question about the traditional Christian pilgrimage, "A pilgrim art thou? pilgrim thou?" (1.9.20), by acknowledging, "I am a traveler—no more" (1.9.28).

In key parts of the poem Melville puts Clarel in situations where he is drawn to these opposite poles, represented in Part I by Celio and Ruth. An understanding of Melville's dialectic reveals his attitude toward Clarel's behavior, showing that while Melville tempts the youth with a Hellenic alternative, here Ruth, he really expects Clarel to respond to the Hebraic or heroic alternative,

as represented by Celio. Just how far Clarel has to go to become the true Hebraic doubter is suggested by Celio, whom Clarel meets while touring aimlessly with Nehemiah. He is a mature Hebraic doubter cast in the mold of a Byronic or Shelleyan rebel. When Celio wordlessly recognizes in Clarel "A brother that he well might own / In tie of spirit" (1.11.43-44) and hovers about, Clarel becomes "embarrassed" and does not acknowledge the tie that he too feels. They differ in that Celio has already worked out a way of dealing with his doubts, while Clarel scarcely knows what to do about them. Clarel realizes this fact when he reads the journal of the dead youth, whom he has searched out at last—when it is too late:

> A second self therein he found,
> But stronger—with the heart to brave
> All questions on that primal ground
> Laid bare by faith's receding wave.

> (1.19.26-28)

Unlike Clarel, Celio has had the intellectual and moral strength to move beyond the Christian framework and judge it. His Ecce Homo speech on the Via Crucis accuses Christ of misleading and betraying mankind with promises of immortality unknown to previous generations; it is a speech that, although much less vitriolic, recalls Ahasuerus's polemic against God in Shelley's *Queen Mab*. Celio's subsequent leaving the city walls and being accidentally locked out overnight in Jehoshaphat represents his confrontation with the heart of darkness and links him with the Wandering Jew, with whom he compares himself. Melville suggests that the Hebraic doubter can heroically descend into the dark night of the soul and courageously accept the alienation and anguish that such a journey creates. However, Clarel wanders about Jerusalem in Part I, still significantly more attached to Nehemiah than to Celio, and thus unable to take the first steps on this journey.

Instead, Clarel falls in love. Melville clearly suggests that this course of action, while natural, is an escape to Hellenism.[8] When the supernatural fails Clarel, he puts his faith into the natural—in human love, which gives emotional support but not complete spiritual satisfaction. With their pots of greenery and their family life, Ruth and her mother create for Clarel the only oasis that he knows in the city. Despite their ethnic background, both women close their eyes to the tragic vision. And they help Clarel close his eyes to it also, appealing to the Hellenic strain in his nature. There Clarel immerses himself in a youthful vision of Paradise, one whose power and beauty have fueled myth since the beginning of man, but which Melville sees as basically opposed to the tragic vision symbolized by the crucifix:

> Clarel and Ruth—might it but be
> That range they could green uplands free

By gala orchards, when they fling
Their bridal favors, buds of Spring;
And, dreaming in her morning swoon,
The lady of the night, the moon,
Looks pearly as the blossoming;
And youth and nature's fond accord
Wins Eden back, that tales abstruse
Of Christ, the crucified, Pain's Lord,
Seem foreign—forged—incongruous.

(1.28.1-11)

It is to be expected that for someone of Clarel's age nature's lure is very strong and visions of the future should be idyllic. In this contrast between love's Eden and pain's Crucifixion, Melville makes one of the fullest statements of the Love or Bride/Death motif in the poem, a more specific version of the basic Hellenic/Hebraic dichotomy.

In the latter half of Part I, Clarel vacillates between the Hebraic/Hellenic dichotomy, as he moves back and forth between Ruth's home, on the one hand, and scenes of suffering or thoughts of Celio on the other. Clarel is ambivalent about following Celio's path, and his attraction to Ruth provides an excellent excuse for blocking out of his mind the serious problem of his faith. However, Clarel's need to decide between the two alternatives is succinctly pictured when the narrator describes Clarel's reaction to the arrival of a new group of pilgrims:

Dubieties of recent date—
Scenes, words, events—he thinks of all.
As, when the autumn sweeps the down,
And gray skies tell of summer gone,
The swallow hovers by the strait—
Impending on the passage long;
Upon a brink and poise he hung.
The bird in end must needs migrate
Over the sea: shall Clarel too
Launch o'er *his* gulf, e'en Doubt, and woo
Remote conclusions?

(1.41.67-77)

In this call to the Hebraic quest, Clarel is compared to a bird reluctant to leave the shore and migrate over the sea because of the uncertainty, the hardship, and the possible disaster of the tragic journey. Drawn in opposite directions, Clarel remains indecisive.

Significantly, it is "Fate's herald" (1.42.40) that precipitates a decision, but a waffling one. When Clarel becomes indecisive because he is usually drawn to Hellenic temptations, disastrous events force him in the opposite direction—in this case, the murder of Nathan. Then, using the fact that Ruth and Agar are secluded in mourning as his rationale, Clarel finally does decide to join Rolfe, Vine, and some other travelers on a three-day journey to the Dead Sea and back. But here is no conscious, deliberate choice between the two ways of

life represented by Celio and Ruth. Clarel still hopes to have it both ways. His journey into the desert begins as the pseudo-quest of a mere traveler, since he still does not understand the nature of the true pilgrimage.

The Heart of Darkness

Despite the fact that Clarel's story shifts into the background in Parts II and III, "The Wilderness" and "Mar Saba," his experience in the desert marks a significant advance in his education as he symbolically descends into Jehoshaphat just as Celio did. The trip into the Judean desert is, of course, the archetypal night journey that provides the main story line of the poem. It is a journey into the "heart of darkness," for the remote, uninhabitable wasteland, with its river of death, the Kedron, flowing through it into the Dead Sea, represents totally unmitigated evil, the core of which is nonbeing. "Wishful from everyone to learn" (2.5.10), Clarel observes carefully the responses of the travelers as they progress deeper into the desert. Their reactions, whether they are intellectual or moral, teach Clarel about human nature and prepare him vicariously for his own personal confrontation with death. Clarel begins to realize that there are "counter natures in mankind." Some of the "pilgrims" show themselves to be merely Hellenic tourists and flee. The Greek Banker, who refuses to say the word "death," turns back from the desert, along with his future son-in-law. And others become troubled or quiet. The effect on a Hebraic doubter like Mortmain is to increase his fascination with evil to a frenzy.

The characters that Clarel admires the most, the ones who have achieved some kind of synthesis between the Hebraic and Hellenic—Rolfe and Vine—neither shrink from the experience nor are overcome by it. Clarel is greatly impressed by both Vine and Rolfe in Jerusalem, seeing them both as extraordinary older men who can help him deal with his doubts. In the desert he studies them closely and observes that they take the bleak wasteland in stride, evidence, he thinks, of their already having confronted the specters of pain, death, and doubt in their personal lives and having worked out ways of dealing with them. The youth watches them carefully to understand and emulate their response, but he is still too inexperienced in life to be able to react as they do. While Clarel does have the courage to continue on with the journey, his experience of evil is still abstract and impersonal. Just as the other characters are tested, so is Clarel. Intellectually, he tries to figure out the "clew" to which of the counter natures is right, but as he interacts with the other characters, fate in the form of the desert situation steps in and continues to force him into a dialectic between the Hebraic and the Hellenic. His doubts about religion have been a blow, but one that has not struck at the center of his being; he assumes that there will be other Hellenic comforts in his life. However, Melville withdraws them, one by one, as he assesses Clarel's character.

One of the first Hellenic comforts that is undermined in the desert is friendship. Early in the journey, the lonely, confused Clarel imagines that the introverted, uncommunicative Vine will eventually share his solution to the problem of doubt, that their similar concern with the dark side of life will bind them together in a close friendship. But when, at the Jordan, Clarel's desire for companionship and security becomes a homoerotic overture that Vine repulses, Clarel begins to see that his ordeal must be a solitary one (2.27.121-23) Later in the high desert, Clarel's accidental observation of the fear at the center of Vine's being, a weakness camouflaged by his reserve, suggests that the older man has not been completely successful in dealing with the problems of death or doubt. Clarel reluctantly begins to face the essential isolation of the human condition.

Another of these Hellenic comforts that the desert experience undermines is intellectual certainty. Ready to "woo / Remote conclusions," Clarel at first trusts that there are intellectual avenues to faith, that others more learned than he may have answered the religious questions that are disturbing him. His need seems about to be fulfilled when in the desert the pilgrims bring up and debate major modern questions such as the role of rationalism and science in religion, the evolution and validity of Judaism, Catholicism, and Protestantism, as well as many other topics. These debates constitute much of Parts II and III of the poem and prove informative to Clarel, but they do not provide a certain path to truth. When, at the end of one such discussion in the canto "Concerning Hebrews," Clarel naively asks, "whose the eye that sees aright, / if any?" (2.22.129-30), even Rolfe turns aside "as overtasked." Clarel realizes that all this intellectualizing about faith has come to nothing. He notes that in contrast to the European pilgrims, Djalea, the desert dweller, has achieved a calm there and will not "fall / In waste of words, that waste of all" (3.5.181-82).

Because of his experience in the desert, Clarel's original romantic inner conflict and distrust of self deepens, especially as he contrasts his reactions to those of Rolfe. In his role of the sensitive young gentleman, he tends to shrink repeatedly from Rolfe's wide-ranging and non-partisan intellectual inquiry, becoming increasingly aware of his own weakness and cowardice. Rolfe's ability to look objectively at everything, his ability to "Forego the state / Of local minds inveterate, / Tied to one poor and casual form" (1.1.96-98), frightens Clarel. Early in the journey Clarel chastises himself for being weak and resolves: "This pressure it need be endured: / Weakness to strength must get inured . . ." (2.21.127-28). He realizes that Rolfe's frankness is

> At variance with that parlor-strain
> Which counts each thought that borders pain
> A social treason.
>
> (2.21.130-32)

Yet much later in the poem Clarel still has enough of that genteel, Hellenic "parlor-strain" in him to shrink from Rolfe's "earnest comment's random force" (2.21.123) and to flinch when Rolfe broaches topics that pain or embarrass; for at Mar Saba Clarel feels "quick distaste" because Rolfe uses the sexual allusion "hermaphrodite" when discussing Derwent (3.16.174-76), and he actually turns his head when Rolfe refers to an old battle tactic of setting forth a "King a corpse in armor led / On a live horse" (3.16.208-09). This squeamishness, which reveals Clarel to be still conventional, narrow, and superficial, suggests that even at Mar Saba Clarel has not yet traveled very far in his own pilgrimage. Despite the waning of his faith, his growing distrust in rational discourse, and his disappointment in friendship, he has not yet received the kind of grave psychic wound that will make him so tragically aware of the dark side of reality that he realizes the triviality of mere social improprieties.

At the end of the Mar Saba section, however, Clarel does move closer to such a wound, when he sinks to a new emotional low, in his experience with the mad monk Cyril. It is still a second-hand encounter with death that only prefigures what is to come. But his reaction to it does begin to precipitate his choice of the two "counter natures in mankind." When Clarel is further disappointed in his last faint hope—the possibility that Derwent might offer some acceptable way to faith—and happens upon a grisly vault full of skulls, he is forced by the shrouded monk Cyril, to participate in a demented initiation ritual by uttering the password "death." The shock of fear that this experience arouses in Clarel galvanizes his imagination and marks a significant step forward in his becoming a true pilgrim. For the first time in the poem, he broods about the enigma of death without the Christian promise of an afterlife:

> Die—to die!
> To be, then not to be! to end,
> And yet time never, never suspend
> His going.
>
> (3.24.92-95)

In these lines, which echo Hamlet's famous soliloquy, Clarel applies his loss of faith to the central human mystery[9] as it relates to him personally, and the effect is profoundly disturbing.

CLAREL'S CHOICE: AN ANATOMY OF PSYCHOLOGICAL CONFLICT

This encounter brings about the major internal conflict that puts Clarel back in the center of the story during the last part of the poem, a crucial conflict that Melville develops in complex detail. The conflict has several stages in which Clarel continues to vacillate between the opposite poles, drawn by both but satisfied with neither, developing new arguments for both sides. At first, with Ruth and the Celibate representing the opposite responses to death, the power of the Hellenic attraction seems to wane. The thought of Ruth, previously such a comfort to him, no longer provides much guidance or solace. When Clarel broods about death after seeing the vault of skulls, the image of Ruth he envisions as solace is like a star seen only fitfully during a storm (3.30.6-10). A much more powerful antidote to his encounter with death is the celestial vision he experiences soon afterwards as he observes the celibate monk feeding doves under the Mar Saba palm. As superior to Plato's world of the mind as Plato is to "the Mammon kind" (3.30.51), the spiritual purity of the ascetic monk charms "away half Clarel's care" (3.30.59) and suggests to him that this kind of life is, after all, the best. Significantly, it is the Celibate who offers Clarel the old "hermit-rhyme" recording instances of women causing trouble for men throughout the Old Testament and thus causes Clarel to explore new arguments against this Hellenic alternative. He wonders if his idealized view of marital love can transcend the limitations of the flesh, as he imagined it would, and he questions, with new awareness, if such a love is really "locked, with Self impure" (3.31.48).

But Clarel can no more figure out whether the Celibate's path or marriage to Ruth is right than he could figure out previous riddles. At one point, trying to break out of his futile oscillation, he raises the larger question of whether there are any general or eternal truths at all (3.31.60-63), and later he expresses a thorough skepticism that shocks him.

> What may man know?
> (Here pondered Clarel;) let him rule—
> Pull down, build up, creed, system, school,
> And reason's endless battle wage,
> Make and remake his verbiage—
> But solve the world! Scarce that he'll do:
> Too wild it is, too wonderful.
> Since *this* world, then, can baffle so—
> Our natural harbor—it were strange
> If *that* alleged, which is afar,
> Should not confound us when we range
> In revery where its problems are.—
> Such thoughts! and can they e'en be mine
> In fount?
>
>   (4.3.107-20)

This is the result of Clarel's launching "o'er *his* gulf, e'en Doubt," the logical conclusion that Clarel's experience in the desert has led him to. And his doubt about eternal truth, about worldly truth, and even about his own motives renders him, again like Hamlet, unable to act. When he considers leaving the pilgrimage to rejoin Ruth in Jerusalem, he does nothing:

>   Nay,
> Doubt had unhinged so, that her sway,

> In minor things even, could retard
> The will and purpose.
>
>   (4.16.108-12)

The Hamlet-like moral paralysis that sets in exacerbates his obsessive tendency toward internal debates and self-criticism.

At Bethlehem the conflict intensifies and reaches its climax, this time featuring the Lyonese and Brother Salvaterra. Clarel is attracted to the Franciscan monk from Tuscany for much the same reason that he admired the Celibate at Mar Saba—for his heroic asceticism. But when Ungar suggests that man is totally depraved, Clarel develops a new argument. If Ungar is right, Clarel infers, should not one then "sin out life's petty lease" if nothing is "left us but the senses' sway?" (4.22.64-65). Although he is immediately repelled by this proposition, he begins to toy with a pagan hedonism that along with an abdication of reason seems the legacy of doubt. The question at issue is whether a person with a Hebraic nature can yield himself to "the senses' sway." This question is immediately answered in Clarel's encounter with the Lyonese Jew, who has embraced such a hedonism and, in effect, denied his racial heritage. The Prodigal's arguments against the mysticism of Judaism and his profligate way of life dramatize for Clarel an affirmative answer to the question. Therefore, when Clarel dreams of a desert presided over by the "pale pure monk" and of a pagan city ruled by the prodigal, the power of the Hellenic attraction is revealed as "he felt the strain / Of clasping arms which would detain / His heart from such ascetic range" (4.26.308-10).

However, Clarel's movement toward the Hellenic creates a strong reaction in the opposite direction. At David's well, before he discovers that the Lyonese is an apostate Jew, he expresses that Hebraic yearning for the infinite that he has felt throughout the poem, comparing himself to the biblical David: "But who will bring to me / That living water which who drinks / He thirsteth not again!" (4.28.69-71). And when he naturalistically concludes that this longing of his may just disappear because it has never been fulfilled, he takes himself sternly to task in a crucial passage that suggests a deepened awareness of the "counter natures in mankind" and the demands of his higher nature:

> "But whither now, my heart? wouldst fly
> Each thing that keepeth not the pace
> Of common uninquiring life?
> What! fall back on clay commonplace?
> Yearnest for peace so? sick of strife?
> Yet how content thee with routine
> Worldly? how mix with tempers keen
> And narrow like the knife? how live
> At all, if once a fugitive
> From thy own nobler part, though pain
> Be portion inwrought with the grain?"
>
>   (4.28.74-84)

Here Clarel definitely places himself with the Hebraic characters in the poem, chiding himself for the moral weakness that tempts him to shun the heroic way of life and betray his true self.

After this insight, Clarel's final choice seems puzzling, since he understands clearly at this point what the choices are and what kind of person he is. It is the Hellenic temptation that Clarel chooses after he learns that the Lyonese is by birth a Jew. He denies his Hebraic nature and, giving rein to an emotion that ends all debate, he decides to marry Ruth and take her away from the desert town. He concludes that "One thing was clear, one thing in sooth: / Stays not the prime of June or youth" (4.29.61-62). Although he has some misgivings about rejecting the heroic alternative, Clarel affirms a traditionally romantic naturalism as the only certainty in life, one that is validated by a corresponding impulse from the heart:

> At large here life proclaims the law:
> Unto embraces myriads draw
> Through sacred impulse. Take thy wife;
> Venture, and prove the soul of life,
> And let fate drive.
>
> (4.29.102-06)

The important question here is, "Has Clarel passed the test of choosing the right alternative, has he followed the "clew" to determine his true nature?

Melville suggests that Clarel has not, that he has fallen to temptation in reaching out to "pluck the nodding fruit to him, / Fruit of the tree of life" (4.29.56-57). Melville reveals his disapproval by forcing Clarel to experience the unmitigated terror of the void by removing the tempting alternative, by causing the sudden deaths of Ruth and Agar. Upon seeing the dead bodies of the two women in the Valley of Jehoshaphat, Clarel does finally encounter the heart of darkness and receives the serious psychic wound for which his experience in the desert has been preparing him. No longer abstractly and intellectually weighing arguments, he suffers for the first time what seems to him intolerable agony, melodramatically crying out, "art thou God?" Like a Byronic madman he storms:

> "O blind, blind, barren universe!
> Now am I like a bough torn down,
> And I must wither, cloud or sun!"
>
> (4.30.93-95)

When he feels the anguish that Celio, Mortmain, Ungar, and Agath as well as Rolfe and Vine have experienced, Clarel can truly understand and feel the significance of the crucifixion. Longing for some meaning, some sense of immortality or of a deity, Clarel does not leave Jerusalem when the rest of the travelers do and instead haunts the town during the rest of Lent, experiencing

the liturgy, especially that of Good Friday, with new emotional impact. Finally, he has become the true pilgrim, having realized that his original quest for religious faith was a rather superficial one. After describing both animals and humans burdened by fate wending their way along the way of the Cross, the narrator asks,

> But, lagging after, who is he
> Called early every hope to test,
> And now, at close of rarer quest,
> Finds so much more the heavier tree?
>
> (4.34.45-48)

Clarel's *Bildungsweg* suggests Melville's belief that basically Hebraic personalities cannot escape their destiny of doubt and pain, nor can "Unworldly yearners" ever be satisfied with what is basically a Hellenic mode of life, whether it is the simple appeal to the heart and the senses that Ruth embodies or the more sophisticated religious *via media* that Derwent represents. Clarel's attempt to evade his destiny shows that he did not learn the lesson that Agath's story and Rolfe's story about the mariner were trying to teach. Although some people may try to avoid the evils that fate has in store for them, fate will triumph eventually and force them to assume the cross. This is the lesson that the biblical Jonah as well as Shakespeare's Hamlet had to learn. In choosing to return to Ruth and all that she represents, Clarel willfully challenged fate to "drive" (4.29.106). But now he takes his place with all the others on the *Via Crucis* as "in varied forms of fate they wend" (4.34.41).

While Clarel's story is thus the making of another heroic striver, a Hebraic doubter, Melville, following the path of the early Goethe and Schiller as well as Byron, leaves Clarel at the end of the poem still on his journey. He has not found truth, freedom, or wholeness. He does not achieve a synthesis of the Hebraic and the Hellenic, as did Rolfe. He does not accept his fate. He simply suffers. But the fact that he is last seen walking the *Via Crucis* suggests that he has learned some lessons. Apparently he realizes that the Hellenic path is not his; he has become a tragic figure whom fate, in the form of Ruth's death, forces to continue his quest. There is some question whether the painful loss of faith, friendship, intellectual certainty, and romantic love will actually foster the call to heroism, the *Streben nach dem Unendlichen* of which Clarel has shown only fitful evidence.

In the controversial epilogue of the poem, Melville walks the same tightrope between belief and disbelief in his comments about Clarel's final mental state. He allows the reader to speculate about whether Clarel will find faith or not. Such an open ending is another of Melville's character tests for the reader, who, in giving a Hellenic or Hebraic interpretation, reveals his own personality type and thus his philosophical orientation.

Perhaps Melville suspected that future readers might argue learnedly about the "correct" interpretation of the enigmatic ending of the poem. But he understood quite well that Hellenic readers would project their own optimism upon his remarks about immortality and that Hebraic ones would stress the darker side. One's temperament determines his solution to "The running battle of the star and the clod." Melville points out in the Epilogue:

> Science the feud can only aggravate—
> No umpire she betwixt the chimes and knell:
> The running battle of the star and clod
> Shall run forever—if there be no God.

> (4.35.14-17)

But Melville surely admired the rare few who could resist falling into either category and who could sustain a desire for faith even while seriously considering reasons for disbelief. About the only way of determining whether man is "ape or angel," star or clod, is the purely subjective evidence of man's yearning for the infinite.

It is a measure of Melville's intelligence as well as of his erudition that he perceived so clearly the importance and implications of the early-nineteenth-century German dichotomy between the romantic and the classic, as well as Arnold's distinction between the Hebraic and the Hellenic. Among theorists and artists, this human typology continued to inspire new interpretive twists through the late nineteenth and early twentieth centuries, with Nietzsche taking it in one direction and renaming it Apollonian and Dionysian. Carl Jung, in his psychology of human types, took it in yet another direction, calling it introversion and extroversion. And Thomas Mann used it to dramatize the development of the artist in *Tonio Kroger*. Clearly, Melville's thoughtful application of this theory of personality to *Clarel* places him in the mainstream of late-nineteenth-century and early-twentieth-century European thought.

Notes

1. A few critics have briefly mentioned that in *Clarel* Melville is more interested in human character and psychology than in ideas. Howard describes the poem as one in which Melville's "mind dwelt more upon people than upon philosophy" (307), and Bezanson notes that Clarel "goes increasingly from asking whose beliefs are right to asking who is the right kind of man" (lxix).

2. See Super, who notes that Arnold took the contrast from Heine's *Der Doktor Faust* "Erlauterungen" (439n).

3. See Dettlaff 214-16, where I argue that Melville had read enough of Arnold to understand and use these terms and that Melville may have read "Anarchy and Authority" when it appeared in 1868 (216n).

4. Early critics divided the characters into the ascetic and the worldly, a division that is very similar to the Hebraic and the Hellenic. Sedgwick distinguished "the lighthearted few" from the majority of serious "seekers after spiritual refreshment" (205), and Arvin categorized the youths as those who represent "pleasure-loving worldliness" or "ascetic spirituality" (277). Beginning an interpretation that has since predominated, Howard emphasized another, narrower dichotomy—that of faith *vs.* doubt—asserting that all the characters represent varying degrees in the range between these opposites. Apparently refining Howard, Bezanson suggested three clusters of characters: the centrists, the dark monomaniacs, and the optimistic believers. Brodwin, Knapp, and Kenny have followed basically that same dichotomy.

5. Rosenthal points out the importance of this motif for the poem. However, in not placing the Wandering Jew in the Hebraic part of the basic dichotomy in the poem, Rosenthal applies the motif indiscriminately, I believe, to almost all of the characters and thus weakens the significance of the symbol as an aid to understanding the poem.

6. Arnold uses this quotation from Romans 8:26 to describe Heinrich Heine's Hebraism in *Essays in Criticism* 166.

7. Although most critics have dealt with Clarel's search for faith, few have analyzed the inner drama of Clarel's education. Chase was the first to emphasize the poem as an educational one and to discuss the other main characters as symbolizing "modes of life or thought bearing upon the education of Clarel" (244), but he did not focus on the continuity of Clarel's interior reactions to these characters and the events of the poem. Bezanson saw Clarel as a "lost hero in search of a guide" (liv). Bowen, Miller, and Browne have continued the pattern of briefly discussing Clarel's state at the beginning and the end of the poem and have not analyzed the developing psychological drama. In the 1970s, however, critics began to look more carefully at Clarel's education. Brodwin argued that Clarel's real education involves not just the search for religious faith but a deeper, existential realization of an authentic self after experiencing pain, death, and freedom. Knapp and Ra'ad both looked beneath the surface; but Knapp's interpretation is too optimistic and Ra'ad's argument that Clarel's education develops dialectically only as a reaction to the deaths of characters in the story seems narrow, even though valid.

8. Baym concludes that the erotic "motif" is not just one thread in the complexly woven tapestry of Clarel but the framework for the entire design. Seeing the action of the story as Melville's so-

phisticated rendering of the conventional nineteenth-century conflict between intellect and nature, Baym asserts that Clarel's flight from feminine love into skeptical intellectualizing is ultimately sterile and that salvation lies only in a return to Ruth, a return that Clarel's neurotic fear of sex makes difficult. But the way that women in general are seen in the poem is the traditional biblical or Hebraic one, which while sometimes appearing to admire, still really sees woman as a trap, a snare that will lure man to his doom by personifying those very qualities in himself that he would like to yield to but must transcend if he is to achieve salvation. Thus woman is associated with youth, beauty, charm, pleasure—those very joys that the Hellenes celebrated. Baym, in following and overemphasizing a suggestion of Bezanson's, has pushed her naturalistic and psychological interpretation too far, with the result that it contradicts the major thrust of the poem's theme: the need for the person with the deep-diving imagination to deny the commonplace and become a heroic quester.

9. See Brodwin, who points out that death is the central problem underlying the question of faith and doubt in the poem and asserts that "Faith for Melville is in fact an end condition, a stance one finds oneself in only after confronting and resolving the question of death" (30).

Works Cited

Abrams, M. H. *Natural Supernaturalism: Tradition and Revolution in Romantic Literature.* New York: Norton, 1971.

Arnold, Matthew. "Anarchy and Authority." *Every Saturday* 5 (June 27, 1868): 802-03.

———. "Heinrich Heine." *Essays in Criticism.* Boston: Ticknor and Fields, 1866. 140-73.

Arvin, Newton. *Herman Melville: A Critical Biography.* New York: William Sloane Associates, 1950.

Baym, Nina. "Erotic Motif in Melville's Clarel." *Texas Studies in Literature and Language* 16 (Summer 1974): 315-28.

Bezanson, Walter, ed. Introduction. *Clarel: A Poem and Pilgrimage in the Holy Land.* By Herman Melville. New York: Hendricks House, 1960. ix-cxvii.

Bowen, Merlin. *The Long Encounter: Self and Experience in the Writings of Herman Melville.* Chicago: U of Chicago P, 1960.

Brodwin, Stanley. "Herman Melville's *Clarel*: An Existential Gospel." *PMLA* 86 (May 1971): 375-87.

Browne, Ray. *Melville's Drive to Humanism.* Lafayette, IN: Purdue UP, 1972.

Chase, Richard. *Herman Melville: A Critical Study.* New York: Macmillan, 1949.

Cowen, Wilson Walker. "Melville's Marginalia." Vol. 11. Ph.D. diss. Harvard University, 1965.

Dettlaff, Shirley. "Ionian Form and Esau's Waste: Melville's View of Art in *Clarel*." *American Literature* 54 (May 1982): 212-28.

Howard, Leon. *Herman Melville: A Biography.* Los Angeles: U of California P, 1950.

Kenny, Vincent. *Herman Melville's "Clarel": A Spiritual Biography.* Hamden, CT: Archon, 1973.

Knapp, Joseph G. *Tortured Synthesis: The Meaning of Melville's* Clarel. New York: Philosophical Library, 1971.

Miller, James E. *A Reader's Guide to Herman Melville.* New York: Noonday Press, 1962.

Ra'ad, Basem L. "The Death Plot in Melville's Clarel." *Emerson Society Quarterly* 27 (1981): 14-27.

Rosenthal, Bernard. "Herman Melville's Wandering Jews." In *Puritan Influences in American Literature.* Ed. Emory Elliot. Urbana: U of Illinois P, 1979. 167-91.

Schiller, Friedrich. *Naive and Sentimental Poetry* and *On the Sublime.* Trans. Julius A. Elias. New York: Frederick Ungar, 1966.

———. *Poems and Ballads.* Trans. Edward Bulwer Lytton. London: George Routledge, 1887.

Schlegel, Augustus William. *Lectures on Dramatic Art and Literature.* Trans. John Black. London: Henry G. Bohn, 1861.

Sedgwick, William. *Herman Melville: The Tragedy of Mind.* New York: Russell and Russell, 1944.

Super, R. H., ed. *Lectures and Essays in Criticism.* Vol. 3: *By Matthew Arnold.* Ann Arbor: U of Michigan P, 1962.

Abbreviations

NN *Clarel*   *Clarel: A Poem and Pilgrimage in the Holy Land.* By Herman Melville. Ed. Walter E. Bezanson, Harrison Hayford, Alma A. MacDougall, Hershel Parker, and G. Thomas Tanselle. Evanston and Chicago: Northwestern UP and the Newberry Library, 1991.

Katharina Gerstenberger (essay date 1997)

SOURCE: Gerstenberger, Katharina. "January 31, 1850: Conversion to Judaism is Protected under the Constitution of the North German Confederation." In *Yale Com-*

panion to Jewish Writing and Thought in German Culture, 1096-1996, edited by Sander L. Gilman and Jack Zipes, pp. 186-92. New Haven, Conn.: Yale University Press, 1997.

[In the following essay, Gerstenberger highlights the changes in the reception of and in the discourse about Judaism and conversions to Judaism that took place in Germany during the mid-nineteenth century.]

The *Jüdisches Lexikon* (1930), under the entry "Proselyt" (proselyte), notes that "statistics concerning numbers and motivations of conversions during modern times are not yet available." Whereas Jewish conversion to the Christian denominations was not only common but actually expected in nineteenth-century Germany, Christian conversion to Judaism by comparison remained a limited phenomenon, one regarded with suspicion by the Christian majority as well as by some Jewish commentators. Conversion to Judaism in nineteenth-century Germany, as opposed to conversion in antiquity, was embedded in the context of centuries of Jewish history in a Christian society. Until well into the eighteenth century, throughout Christian Europe both converts and Jews involved in the conversion process faced the death penalty. During the first half of the nineteenth century, conversion to Judaism, which in principle was guaranteed by the Prussian Legal Code of 1794 with its decree of freedom of religion (*Religionsfreiheit*), was in practice frequently prohibited by anti-Jewish legislation. Frederick William III, for example, in his cabinet orders of 1814 and 1834, revoked the right to convert to Judaism. Under penalty of law, the king ordered the Jewish communities not to admit any convert who had not obtained an official release from the Christian community—and forbade Christian leaders to grant secession from Christianity. The constitution of the North German Federation finally instituted freedom of religion in 1850, which was extended to all of Germany in 1871. Austria granted freedom of religion in 1868, and Hungary followed as late as 1895. Jewish scholars such as the Berlin schoolteacher Nathan Samter, who often addressed the subject of conversion to Judaism, situate this particular relationship between Jews and Christians in the larger framework of Jewish legal and social history in Germany.

It was not until the early twentieth century that German-Jewish communities began to include conversions to Judaism in their population statistics; for Germany, the data collected by the regional Protestant churches pertaining to conversions from Protestantism constitute the most comprehensive nineteenth-century source. According to church records, 126 conversions took place in Berlin between 1872 and 1894; in the city of Dresden, nine Protestants converted to Judaism between 1886 and 1903. In Austria, with its significantly higher rate of conversion, the Jewish communities did compile statistics on conversions to Judaism: in Vienna between 1868 (the year in which freedom of religion was granted in Austria) and 1903 more than 2,300 people converted, with women outnumbering men almost two to one. Given that the foremost motivation for conversion was (and is) marriage between Christian-born women and Jewish men, the ban of interfaith marriages in Austria, which was in effect throughout the nineteenth century, explains the comparatively high numbers as well as the overwhelming predominance of female converts. For the year 1903, the *Zeitschrift für Statistik und Demographie der Juden* (*Journal for statistics and demographics of the Jews*) reports twenty conversions to Judaism in all of Germany, excluding Berlin. Although there are no separate figures for baptized Jews who returned to the "religion of the fathers" (*Religion der Väter*), their conversions are treated as specific cases involving the reavowal of an affiliation that has never been fully severed, rather than the adoption of a new religion. Commentators on conversion statistics generally welcomed (re)conversions to Judaism (*Übertritte*) as gains and regretted conversions from Judaism (*Austritte*) as losses to Judaism.

Reaching well beyond its relative numerical insignificance, conversion to Judaism triggered a vital public debate in the second half of the nineteenth century. This issue also has some importance in autobiographical literature as well as in fiction and popular history. In the larger contexts of general secularization and Jewish assimilation, German anti-Semitism, and Zionism, Christian conversion to Judaism marks a critical intersection between Jewish-German and Christian-German identity positions. The Jewish debates surrounding the desirability of converts and the conditions of conversion speak to the larger question of definitions of Jewishness and Judaism in the modern world.

The popular and critical success of Wilhelm Herzberg's epistolary novel *Jüdische Familienpapiere* (*Jewish family papers*; 1868, Eng. trans., 1875) illustrates public interest in an increasing diversity of Jewish identities in nineteenth-century Germany, which the novel depicts as the result of a growing liberalization in Jewish-Christian relationships. Herzberg's protagonist, a young man born to Jewish parents who died in England on their way to America, was raised in the Christian faith by an Englishman. The novel shows him during an extended visit in the house of his uncle, a neo-Orthodox rabbi. As a demonstration of his gratitude, young Samuel, in an early letter to his adoptive father, renews his vow to devote his "earthly life to the poor lost sheep of Israel" (7). Contrary to the protagonist's missionary intentions, religious disputes between uncle and nephew ensue, during which the young man experiences a religious crisis, confesses to his adoptive father his rejection of Christian dogmas, and affirms his Jewish identity. Questions of Jewish identity occupy a central position in this novel, whose protagonist characterizes his conversion as one of conviction rather than as simply a return to the religion of his parents. The rabbi defines a "good Jew" as one who "strictly adheres to the ceremonial laws" (12), but he extends this delineation by suggesting the existence of a Jewish "Nature" that cannot be erased by a Christian "Education" (147). Herzberg affirms the reality of a Jewish essence through an insertion: immediately preceding the letter that relates Samuel's return to Judaism, he relates a lengthy story about a Moroccan Jewess who reveals her Jewish essence by choosing death over forced conversion to Islam. Although on the surface it defines Jewishness as the religious observance within the social community into which the individual is born, the novel simultaneously acknowledges the precariousness of Jewish identity toward the beginning of the second half of the nineteenth century and, through its minor characters, allows for Jewish identity positions outside a purely religious framework. In a contradiction of the rabbi's assertion that Jewish "Nature" guarantees Jewishness, in his own family he suffers the loss (and return) of his oldest son, who, despite the father's dedicated efforts to provide him with a profound Jewish education, married a Christian woman; in a desperate attempt not to lose his younger son to a Christian actress, he begs his son's prospective bride to abandon her profession and convert to Judaism. To maintain the traditional Jewish family unit, the rabbi reluctantly resorts to opening his house to a convert. The actress respectfully declines his invitation, explaining that of the rabbi's two requests, to give up her profession is the one that she cannot fulfill. Even though the erotic relationships between the rabbi's sons and Christian women ultimately fail, Herzberg's novel, which the critics praised as a strong statement in favor of traditional Judaism, in fact probes the boundaries of traditional Jewish society. Conversion to Judaism in this novel is a response to an increase in Jewish-Christian relationships and a counterargument against Jewish conversion to Christianity.

The distinction between "good" and "bad" Jews, as made by Herzberg's rabbi, expresses his regret that in the nineteenth century birth to Jewish parents can no longer be assumed to be positively synonymous with religious observance. Until about 1870, observance of ceremonial law, including circumcision, figures centrally in the Jewish reception and appreciation of converts. Between the years 1843 and 1875, the *Allgemeine Zeitung des Judentums* (*AZJ*) reports more than twenty individual and multiple cases of conversions to Judaism. Although these brief notices contradict each other in their assessment of the commonness or rarity of Christian conversion, without exception the convert's motivation is of central interest to the authors. Strict observance of Jewish law, which in some cases is said to precede the actual act of conversion by decades, represents the most persuasive indication of the convert's

sincerity to become a "good" Jew. Observance of Jewish rituals and dietary laws testifies to the Jewishness of those born into Judaism as well as converts. In the journalistic conversion narrative, the traditionally required recitation of Jewish ceremonial laws, which serves to deter the potential convert, is conventionally followed by the convert's solemn refusal to refrain from conversion. The mention of circumcision and the convert's conduct during the "conversion operation" ("Bekehrungs-Operation") (*AZJ* 30 [1866]: 198) emerge as standard narrative elements designed to illustrate the male convert's integrity; self-circumcision or the new Jew's willingness to bear the financial burden of the medical care necessary for his recovery elicit even higher admiration. The eagerness of a convert to submit to circumcision as a sign of sincerity, as it emanates from the pages of *Allgemeine Zeitung des Judentums* or *Der Israelit,* aims to confirm Judaism's inherent attractiveness perhaps more to the Jewish readership than to prospective converts.

By comparison, reports on female conversions, which commonly attribute the motivation to change religion to the convert's desire to marry a Jew, tend to discredit these conversions as secondary in merit to male religious convictions. In practice, the valuation of conviction over marriage as two distinct motivations translates into the tendency to place male converts above females. In a letter dating back to 1865, Ludwig Philippson, rabbi in Magdeburg and founding editor of the *Allgemeine Zeitung des Judentums,* who insisted that his willingness to accept converts did not contradict his principal objection to seeking proselytes (*Proselyten-Macherei*), treated conviction and marriage as mutually compatible when he explained that he converted a number of people to Judaism upon having "convinced himself that a complete and honest conviction had taken root . . . even if the first motive was marriage" (*AZJ* 79 [1915]: 403). Until well into the second half of the nineteenth century, the convert's ability to demonstrate through observance the integrity of his or her religious belief was believed to reflect converts' self-understanding of Jewish identity as a traditional religious identity.

Around 1870, liberal Jews begin to reexamine the question of converts with the general goal of facilitating conversion. The two issues at the center of this controversy, male circumcision and the presence of men during the ritual bath of women converts, are expressions of a larger development among the Jewish communities away from the primacy of ceremonial law and toward the proclamation of the universal humanist monotheism, which was expected to secure a space for Judaism and Jewish identity within a modern world. Hoping that a "fresh air stream" from America might enliven Judaism in Germany, the great scholar and liberal rabbi Abraham Geiger reported extensively in his *Jüdische*

Zeitschrift für Wissenschaft und Leben (*Jewish journal for science and life*) on the 1869 rabbinical conference in Philadelphia and its deliberations concerning circumcision of proselytes. Reversing the prevalent contention that circumcision serves to deter undesirable converts, Bohemian-born rabbi Isaac Mayer Wise argued that mandatory circumcision, because the procedure was not explicitly required of born Jews, on the contrary might keep away serious converts and attract those with ulterior motivations. It was not until 1892, however, that the Central Conference of American Rabbis passed a resolution to the effect that circumcision did not constitute a requirement for converts; in Germany, circumcision remained an obligation for converts throughout the nineteenth century. Nevertheless, the challenge to make circumcision imperative for male converts, which Ludwig Philippson had considered "indispensable" less than ten years earlier (*AZJ* 26 [1862]: 86), aimed at lowering the boundaries between Jews and Christians and illustrated the self-understanding of Reform Judaism as an integral part of German and European culture. By uncoupling conviction from ritual observance, the Reformers adjusted the conversion process to the dwindling reality of this once decisive difference between Judaism and Christianity and integrated the convert into their understanding of a Jewish identity grounded in spirituality, philosophy, and scholarship.

Concerning the question of female proselytes, the Second Israelite Synod, the 1871 convention of liberal rabbis in Augsburg, again at the initiative of Abraham Geiger, pronounced that two trustworthy Jewish women could serve as witnesses of the ritual bath. Although the brief discussion revealed that, in actual practice, standard rules of moral conduct prevented male presence, the main argument in favor of the motion, the perceived necessity to raise the status of women within Judaism, shows the close connections between the issue of conversion and a reform of Judaism as envisioned by liberal Jews. The Association of Liberal Rabbis of Germany officially adopted the Augsburg decision in 1899.

From the mid-1880s into the first decade of the twentieth century, the history of conversion to Judaism was a topic of interest to a number of Jewish writers. In particular the stories of "famous" converts and their individual cases appeared in both the weekend supplements of Jewish family journals and Jewish "house calendars" (*Haus-Kalender*), and in scholarly journals. Expressions and products of a late-nineteenth-century German-Jewish identity, these narratives no longer questioned the desirability of converts or pondered the requirements for conversion. Rather, the figure of the outstanding proselyte exemplified the attractiveness of Judaism in light of the obstacles and risks that the act of conversion entailed within the convert's particular historical context. The evidence of Christian conversion became a sensitive measuring device for the legal and social position of Jews in European Christian society. The interest in conversion as a specific aspect of Jewish-Christian history was also a response to the contemporary context of anti-Semitism. Because of its plea for tolerance and emancipation, the Enlightenment serves today as the historical referent and positive counterpart to anti-Semitic prejudice, and the French Revolution is celebrated as a liberating turning point in Jewish history.

Among the canonical cases of famous converts, which include Count Potocki, the Polish nobleman who allegedly was burned at the stake in Vilna in 1749, and Anna Constanze von Cosel, mistress and prisoner of the Saxon King August the Strong, the story of Joseph Steblicki drew perhaps the most extensive attention. An educated man and a public figure in his native Nikolai (Silesia), Steblicki converted from Catholicism to Judaism in 1785. His case marks a decisive change in the official treatment of converts because valid law, which called for the death penalty, was overruled by a legal council in Berlin in accordance with the proclamation of freedom of religion under Frederick II. Eduard Biberfeld, who published the transcripts of the Steblicki case in the *Magazin für die Wissenschaft des Judenthums* (*Magazine for the science of Judaism*) in 1893, drew a connection between the Enlightenment period and his own time when he wrote in his introduction: "And what would be more befitting to the understanding of the general cultural development of a period than its treatment of the Jews? . . . Especially in our time, which is so contaminated by the spirit of hate" (183). A year prior to Biberfeld's historical documentation, Marcus Brann in his *Jüdischer Volks- und Hauskalender* (*Jewish people's and house calendar*) had evoked the Steblicki case to contrast the anti-Semitism of contemporary "German Christianity" with the unprejudiced attitude of the Enlightenment. Similarly, Louis Neustadt in his 1894 monograph on Steblicki distinguishes between the Enlightenment spirit of Frederick II and late-nineteenth-century anti-Semitism. Narrative accounts of historical cases such as Steblicki's pursue an additional strategy: the convert's courage to follow his or her religious convictions is meant to throw a critical light on the status of Jewish-Christian relationships. At the turn of the century, most writers introduced their interest in Christian conversion to Judaism with at least implicit references to the spread of anti-Semitism.

Among the "outstanding converts" enumerated in encyclopedia entries and monographs on the subject of conversion, Nahida Ruth Lazarus's name figures prominently as one of the most important and honored converts in late-nineteenth-century Germany. Her conversion took place in early 1895 in Freiburg under the supervision of Rabbi Adolf Lewin. Because the majority of converts to Judaism were women, whose conversions were generally assumed to be motivated by marriage to a Jew, Lazarus's example is both representative and unique. The cases of, for instance, Paula Beer-Hofmann, who converted in 1898 and became the wife of the Austrian writer Richard Beer-Hofmann; Paula Buber (née Winkler), a born Catholic who converted prior to marrying Martin Buber in 1901; and Nahida Lazarus, who after her conversion married her teacher of many years, Moritz Lazarus, the cofounder of ethnopsychology, are similar to the degree that all three women married prominent men. The prevailing assumption that marriage provided the sole incentive for their conversions, however, obscures any sovereign motivations. Nahida Lazarus—in contrast to Paula Beer-Hofmann, whose writings concerning her conversion remain unpublished, and Paula Winkler Buber, who wrote only a short journal article about her conversion—related the story of her conversion before public audiences and published a 220-page autobiographical narrative. Its title, *Ich suchte Dich!* (*I sought you!*; 1898), describes the autobiographer's search, which reaches its completion in the act of conversion and her affirmation of a single God. Lazarus's autobiography is as much the story of her conversion out of the Christian religion as it is the narration of her conversion to Judaism. Her gradual rejection of Christianity, which takes up the major part of the autobiography, draws on two lines of argumentation: the dogmatic insistence on supernatural phenomena in Christian belief (the conventional contention that is central also to Herzberg's novel, whose influence Lazarus acknowledges in her autobiography), and the base position of women in the New Testament. In engaging her older male Christian educators in religious disputations, young Nahida not only confronts Christian dogma but also asserts herself as a woman with a Jewish voice of her own. In her narrative, Lazarus strictly separates her resolve to convert from her subsequent marriage to Moritz Lazarus, who appears in the autobiography as her teacher long before he becomes her husband. Lazarus appropriates the model of conversion that the contributors to the *Allgemeine Zeitung des Judentums* had reserved for male converts: her autobiography privileges religious conviction as an independent motivation. The conversion was already scheduled to take place in Geneva when her decision to marry Moritz Lazarus was brought about by a visit to him on her way to Switzerland.

Lazarus's understanding of her Jewishness as a female convert draws on several different traditions. The autobiographical statement that, prior to her conversion, in her "heart (even if entirely unconsciously) she had long been a Jewish woman" (213) uncouples Herzberg's idea of a Jewish essence from Jewish birth and defines Jewishness as a spiritual constitution based solely in faith. The comparative discussions of Judaism and Christianity in the tradition of the dispute over the true religion, however, do not lead to immediate conversion. Not having undergone Christian confirmation, Lazarus remained without religious affiliation for several years. In

her autobiography, she explains her initial interest in Judaism not as a result of her disenchantment with Christianity, but as a response to the ascent of the anti-Semitism she observed in Berlin in the 1880s. Her desire to defend the Jews against their German attackers led her to the scholarly study of the Jewish religion, history, and people in the tradition of Leopold Zunz (*Wissenschaft des Judentums*), with conversion as the natural outcome of her occupation with Jewish culture, in particular the role of women. Lazarus's path to Judaism combines the traditional quest for religious fulfillment with modern scholarship, both of which are principally open to the sincere male student regardless of the religious community into which he was born. Her academic pursuits against anti-Semitism thus double as a struggle for the recognition of women as intellectuals.

Decrying the decline in religiosity among Jews, enthusiastic critics recommended the convert Nahida Lazarus as an ideal to all born Jews, in particular to Jewish women. In contrast to the perception of converts as foreign elements and a threat to a distinct Jewish identity, Lazarus's reviewers used her example to strengthen a modern yet religious Jewish identity. A former Christian and a woman, the figure of Nahida Lazarus confirmed to her Jewish contemporaries the value and validity of a spiritual Jewishness. At the end of the twentieth century, Lazarus's hope that scholarly proof of Jewish cultural accomplishments could enlighten racial anti-Semites seems perhaps naive. Her positive reception as a scholar and autobiographer by many Jewish historians well into the twentieth century, however, suggests how much her voice was appreciated.

Paula Winkler, a Germanist by training and among the first women to enroll at the University of Munich at the turn of the century, found her way to Judaism through Zionism. In the Zionist weekly *Die Welt*, Winkler, who subsequently published novels and stories under the pseudonym Georg Munk, described her relationship to Jews and the Jewish people and assessed her position as a convert within the Zionist movement in an article entitled "Confessions of a Philozionist" ("Bekenntnisse einer Philozionistin"; 1901). Merging Jewish history with her own family history, Winkler traced her exceptionally positive attitude toward Jews back to her childhood and, importantly, to the stories of her mother, to whom Jewish culture provided intellectual and emotional stimulation as a young woman. The attractiveness of Jewish culture to Christian women is based on the perception that Jewish women enjoy a higher social status than Christian women, a notion that is also central to Lazarus's conversion narrative. Winkler insists that her community knew no anti-Semitic discrimination against Jews but that she failed to understand the special position of Jews (*Sonderstellung*) within Christian society. Both Winkler and Lazarus associated Jewish identity with Christian persecution; subsequently, both writers traced their motivation to convert to Judaism to memories of witnessing such acts of aggression. For Winkler, Zionism provided the means not only to end Jewish suffering but also to preserve Jewishness: "in differentiating lies all your beauty" ("im Unterscheiden liegt all Deine Schönheit," 6), she writes, addressing the Jewish people. Emphatically downplaying her own "value, sense, or meaning" (6) to the Zionist movement, Winkler stresses the strength with which Zionism endows her own life. Winkler met her future husband, Martin Buber, at the Third Zionist Congress in Basel in 1899, where she listened to his speech. In her article, she recapitulates this encounter as a turning point in her life—without mentioning Buber's name or the fact that she was married to him by the time she wrote this text. One of only two short texts she published under her own name, Paula Winkler's conversion narrative occupies a special position within her work.

Jewish writing on conversion, whether literary or carried out in the pages of journals, whether autobiographical or scholarly, responded to shifts in the relationship between the dominant Christian majority and the Jewish minority. Jewish emancipation, Reform Judaism, Zionism, and the continuous struggle for new definitions of Jewish identity in an increasingly anti-Semitic Germany shaped nineteenth-century discourses on Christian conversion to Judaism.

Bibliography

Eduard Biberfeld, "Joseph Abraham Steblicki: Ein Ger Zedek des 18. Jahrhunderts," *Magazin für die Wissenschaft des Judenthums* 20 (1893): 181-98; David Max Eichhorn, ed., *Conversion to Judaism: A History and Analysis* (New York: Ktav, 1965); Ismar Elbogen, Georg Herlitz, Bruns Kirschner, eds., *Jüdisches Lexikon* (Berlin: Jüdischer Verlag, 1927-30); Wilhelm Herzberg, *Jüdische Familienpapiere: Briefe eines Missionärs* (Hamburg: Meissner, 1868); Bernhard Koenigsberger, "Proselyten im Judenthum," *Jeschurun: Organ für die geistigen und sozialen Interessen des Judenthums* 1 (1901): 571ff.; Nahida Ruth Lazarus, *Ich suchte Dich! Biographische Erzählung von Nahida Ruth Lazarus* (Berlin: Siegfried Cronbach, 1898); Louis Lewin, "Jüdische Proselyten in Grosspolen," *Jahrbuch der Jüdisch-Literarischen Gesellschaft,* vol. 7 (1910): 375-78, vol. 9 (1912): 498-503, vol. 11 (1916): 268-71; Louis Neustadt, *Joseph Steblicki: Ein Proselyt unter Friedrich dem Großen* (Breslau: Schatzky, 1894); Jacob Raisin, *Gentile Reactions to Jewish Ideals, with Special Reference to Proselytes,* ed. Herman Hailperin (New York: Philosophical Library, 1953); Nathan Samter, *Judenthum und Proselytismus: Ein Vortrag* (Breslau: Wilhelm Jacobson, 1897); Samter, "Sollen die Juden Mission treiben?" *Allgemeine Zeitung des Judentums* 59, no. 40 (1895): 471-74; no. 41 (1895): 457-89; Samter, "Der Übertritt zum Judenthum: Eine rechtsgeschichtliche Studie," *Allgemeine Zeitung des Judentums* 58, no. 43 (1894): 509-11; and Paula Winkler, "Bekenntnisse einer Philozionistin," *Die Welt* 36 (1901): 4-6.

Michael Brenner (essay date spring-summer 1999)

SOURCE: Brenner, Michael. "Gnosis and History: Polemics of German-Jewish Identity from Graetz to Scholem." *New German Critique,* no. 77 (spring-summer 1999): 45-60.

[*In the following essay, Brenner examines three approaches to the study of the relationship between Gnosticism and Judaism.*]

During the first century after the establishment of *Wissenschaft des Judentums* as an academic discipline, contemporary ideology and politics often colored the work of Jewish historians. As Immanuel Wolf, one of the founders of the *Verein für Cultur und Wissenschaft der Juden,* declared in his outline of *Wissenschaft des Judentums* in 1819, "scientific knowledge of Judaism must decide on the merits or demerits of the Jews, their fitness or unfitness to be given the same status and respect as other citizens."[1] More directly, the scholarly studies of Leopold Zunz served as instruments of emancipation for German Jews. Like Wolf, Zunz believed that "the equality of the Jews in customs and life will follow from the equality of *Wissenschaft des Judentums.*"[2] In his *Gottesdienstliche Vorträge der Juden, historisch entwickelt* (1832), he documented the long tradition of Jewish sermon literature. Thus, he rebutted the claims of the Prussian government, which dismissed German-language synagogue sermons as illegitimate innovations of Jewish liturgy. Zunz's later scholarship also intervened in contemporary politics. In reaction to a decree that forbade Jews from adopting Christian names, Zunz wrote *Die Namen der Juden* to demonstrate that many ostensibly "non-Jewish" names were, in fact, of ancient origin.

Gnosticism, a seemingly remote and obscure religious phenomenon of late antiquity, became another disputed topic in Jewish scholarship, where present interests and conceptions often overshadowed the research into the past. This may be related in part to the new insights into Gnosticism from that time as well as its supposedly subversive elements. More importantly, the controversies over Jewish Gnosticism were born out of the very vagueness of Gnosticism as a religious phenomenon. Because of its ambiguity it lent itself to a variety of interpretations and applications. Whoever looked for a historical battlefield to fight contemporary wars was well served by scholarly discussion concerning the relationship between Judaism and Gnosticism.

In this essay I will show three different approaches taken by scholars in their pioneering studies on Gnosticism and Judaism. For Heinrich Graetz, the early contacts between Gnosticism and Judaism were the infiltration of heretical ideas into the Jewish religion, a process he saw manifest in his own time in the early Reform movement. Just as Rabbi Akiba fought successfully against the intrusion of heresy into the Judaism of his time, so Graetz and other conservative Jews sought to counter the threat from Abraham Geiger and other leaders of Liberal Judaism in Germany.

Fifty years later Moriz Friedländer, a prolific writer and secretary of the Austrian section of the *Alliance Is-raélite Universelle,* published a very different evaluation of Judaism and Gnosticism. He praised the encounter between Gnostic and Jewish ideas as the beginning of a universalization of the Jewish religion, which challenged the narrow-minded nationalistic outlook of the Pharisees in Palestine. The Hellenistic Jewish community of Alexandria, where he located the earliest beginnings of Gnostic ideas, was Friedländer's role model for modern Liberal Judaism.

A generation later, Gershom Scholem took up the subject and went one step further than both Graetz and Friedländer. Where Graetz had viewed Gnosticism as a dangerous element foreign to Judaism, Friedländer had stressed the Jewish origins of Gnosticism, but he had restricted them to antinomian groups within the Jewish Diaspora community of Alexandria. Scholem, however, argued for a Gnostic influence on Judaism from its very heart, in Palestine. His argument was not part of a political or religious debate in the same sense as with Graetz or Friedländer. Rather, it was part of Scholem's scholarly agenda to point to the heterogeneous character of Judaism, from which movements such as Sabbatianism could not be excluded. The integration of Gnosticism into ancient Judaism was a foundational stone in the complex building of Judaism he (re)constructed in his many publications.

Heinrich Graetz: Reform Judaism as Modern Gnosticism

The argument for a Gnostic character of Jewish heretics was first presented by the most important Jewish historian of the nineteenth century, Heinrich Graetz, in his doctoral dissertation on Gnosticism and Judaism (1846). Graetz wrote his dissertation in Breslau, at a time when the aftershocks of the "Tiktin-Geiger debate" of 1838 still divided the local Jewish community. In several anonymous articles, Graetz had backed the position of the Orthodox rabbi of the community, Gedaliah Tiktin, and had polemicized against the Reform "newcomer" Abraham Geiger. As is clear from Graetz's diary notes, he intended to draw historical parallels between Jewish heretics of talmudic times and the contemporary German Reform movement in his dissertation.[3] In its preface he left no doubt that this work, which was dedicated to the founder of modern Neo-Orthodoxy, Samson

Raphael Hirsch, and in whose house he lived as a student, was intended as a polemic against "modern Pantheism." Graetz argued that just as Gnosticism had tried to subjugate rabbinic Judaism in the Tannaitic era, so did nineteenth-century "Pantheism." "The gnostic and antignostic movements within Judaism constitute an exact mirror image of the present time,"[4] he wrote. Recalling his opposition to the Reform movement, it is not difficult to figure out whom Graetz had in mind when speaking about contemporaries who wanted to "adjust Judaism to modern Pantheism." For Graetz, the Jewish Reform movement was a modern version of Jewish Gnosticism, whose leader, Abraham Geiger, was a nineteenth-century heretic. Graetz envisioned himself as a modern Rabbi Akiba who came to rescue the traditional values of Judaism.

In spite of some methodological flaws, his polemical style and his strong biases against "latter-day Gnostics," Graetz's work is still useful for academic purposes. Once the reader becomes aware of the meaning between the lines, it—like many others of his writings—remains a pioneering attempt of scholarship.

Graetz discussed in particular two concrete examples of Gnostic traits in the Talmud which shall be mentioned only briefly here. First, he pointed to the similarities between Gnostic terminology for the creation of the world and the expressions used in the discussions on Ma'asse Bereshith in the Talmud. Second, he mentioned the Gnostic doctrine of aeons and its Jewish counterpart in the form of Midot.

For Graetz, Gnosticism was definitely a non-Jewish phenomenon, rooted in syncretistic Hellenism. Relying on Ferdinand Christian Baur as his authoritative scholarly source, Graetz stated that Gnostic teachings had developed earlier than similar Jewish phenomena.[5] Although Gnosticism had a non-Jewish character, not all Jewish Gnostics were necessarily antinomians. A central piece in Graetz's work was the well-known talmudic story of the four who entered Paradise:

> Four entered Paradise, and these are they: Ben Azzai, Ben Zoma, the Outsider [Aher], and R. Aqiba. Said to them Rabbi Aqiba, "When you get to stones of pure marble [that look like water], don't say, 'Water, water,' for it is said, 'He who speaks falsehood shall not be established before my eyes.'" (Ps. 101:7). Ben Azzai peeked and died. In his regard the scripture says, "Precious in the sight of the Lord is the death of his saints" (Ps 116:5). Ben Zoma peeked and was smitten, and of him the Scripture says, "You have found honey? Eat so much as is enough for you, lest you be filled up with it and vomit it out" (Prov. 25:16). The outsider cut down the shoots. R. Aqiba got out in one piece.[6]

According to Graetz, only the most radical of the four, Elisha ben Abuya (Aher), developed a distinct antinomian position within Judaism. The influence of Gnosticism on Ben Azzai resulted in his asceticism, most notably his celibacy. Ben Zoma's interest for Gnostic theories did not result in practical implications for his way of life. Finally, Rabbi Akiba rose as a strong opponent of this "Gnostification" of Judaism, who was able to vanquish these heretical tendencies.

Thus for Graetz, there existed a group of Jewish Gnostics who did not entirely leave the ground of Halakhic Judaism. Although Graetz never used the term "heretics" in describing the group represented by Ben Zoma or Ben Azzai, he left no doubt that the Jews "contaminated" by Gnostic ideas were lost for Judaism. Their identification with the non-Jewish culture had removed them from the heart of Judaism and turned them into *minim*—Gnostic heretics.[7] Graetz would categorize Geiger in this group.

The paradise [*pardes*] story is an allegory for the fate of such thinkers and, of course, a hint to what might happen to modern Ben Azzais. Graetz always had contemporary parallels in mind when writing about Jewish Gnostics. Just as he distinguished between Ben Azzai/ Ben Zoma and Elisha ben Abuya, he also juxtaposed two different kinds of modern Jewish heretics: those who tried to "adjust Judaism to modern Pantheism" (meaning the Reform movement as led by Geiger) and those who "tried to subjugate it [under modern Pantheism] by apostasy."[8]

The role of Rabbi Akiba in Graetz's interpretation still has to be explained. Graetz equated the term *pardes* with Gnosis, and since Rabbi Akiba was included among those who entered the *pardes,* it means he must have had access to Gnostic teachings. Graetz does not deny this fact. His argument was that Rabbi Akiba had to be exposed to Gnostic teaching in order to oppose it successfully. (When Graetz wrote his dissertation he still believed that Rabbi Akiba was the author of the *Sefer Yetsirah* and that this treatise was an anti-Gnostic polemic using Gnostic language.[9])

We may draw the historical parallel a bit further. Just as Rabbi Akiba had to get acquainted with Gnostic ideas, Graetz had to use the culture and the language of his environment in order to counter its "pantheistic" influence on Judaism. And like Rabbi Akiba, who led Jewish heretics back into mainstream Judaism, Graetz's own writings were intended to create a more conservative Jewish consciousness among nineteenth-century German Jews on the road toward religious reforms and assimilation.

In conclusion, one has to read Graetz's version of Jewish Gnosticism carefully. He perceived variations within Jewish Gnosticism and was very well aware that it was not a monolithic phenomenon. Nevertheless, for Graetz, Gnosticism was essentially alien to Judaism and the

two were therefore incompatible. Any attempt at a synthesis was doomed to fail. Tragic illustrations of this failure were the different fates of Aher, Ben Azzai and Ben Zoma. David Biale aptly summarized Graetz's view as follows: "Gnosticism was a foreign philosophy—it attempted to infiltrate Judaism but was decisively defeated."[10]

THE DEBATE OVER THE ORIGINS OF
GNOSTICISM: MORIZ FRIEDLÄNDER AND THE
HELLENISTIC JEWISH ROLE MODEL

Graetz was not much troubled with the question of Gnostic origins. It was clear to him that they came to Judaism as a foreign element. Therefore the question of origins was irrelevant in the relationship between Judaism and Gnosticism. However, for future generations of Jewish and non-Jewish scholars this was to become one of the most debated issues in their research on Judaism and Gnosticism. Although the founder of modern research on Gnosticism, Ferdinand Christian Baur, claimed an "Oriental" origin for Gnosticism, he also suggested that Gnostic religion could have developed only where the Jewish religion had come into contact with pagan religion and philosophy.[11] This latter thesis was elaborated further by Moriz Friedländer in his not very scholarly monograph *Der vorchristliche jüdische Gnosticismus,* published in 1898. In Friedländer's view, Gnosticism first emerged within the Jewish Diaspora community of Alexandria, out of the encounter between Judaism and Hellenistic culture. It was the task of Hellenized Jews, whom Friedländer admired as a model for modern Jewry, to transform Judaism into a universal religion. The best medium to achieve this aim was the Gnostic doctrine, which was characterized by cosmogonic and theosophical speculations.

The main source of Friedländer's thesis for a pre-Christian Jewish Gnosticism was Philo's description of antinomian parties within Diaspora Judaism (Migr. 86-93). Friedländer equated these antinomian circles with Gnostic sects like the Ophites, the Cainites, the Sethians and the Melchezedekians. He tried to prove that the common basis for these different sects was the distortion of Jewish doctrines, while originally no essential Christian elements could be found in them. Thus the Cainites venerated Cain as the divine power, the Sethians held Seth to be the Messiah and, for the Melchizedekians, Melchizedek was a "Son of God," higher than the Messiah. (Jesus, incidentally, entered the doctrines of the Gnostic sects only much later.) While Friedländer regarded Gnosticism as an Alexandrian Jewish product, he also claimed that it soon entered Palestine. The Mishnah passage, which restricted esoteric learning to a small group of people (Hagiga Jer.77a), was for him proof that cosmogonic and theosophical speculations had taken a heretical turn among Palestinian Jews at an early date.[12]

Friedländer had a clear agenda, evident in other works as well. He claimed that the Judaism of the Greek Diaspora followed "the original traditions, which had been transplanted from the times of the prophets and were widespread in the time of the Maccabees, while the traditions of the Pharisees [in Palestine] were the more recent ones, which had been artificially implanted into the law by a now dominant nationalism."[13] While Orthodox Judaism still followed this wrong and recent path of the nationalistic Pharisees, Friedländer called upon his Jewish contemporaries to return to the older and "genuine" Judaism he saw embodied in the world of Hellenistic culture that was under the influence of Gnostic ideas.

Friedländer's study was rejected by most scholars when it appeared, and it was ignored when the discussion on the sources of Gnosticism was revived at the beginning of the twentieth century.[14] Most participants in this discussion found the origins of Gnosticism neither in Judaism nor in Christianity, but in "Eastern" cultures. This theory was part of a larger trend which, based on archaeological findings, argued for the revision of traditional views as to the origin of ancient culture. The main source of civilization was now seen in the "East"—meaning Iran and Babylon. The most popular expression of this new approach was doubtless Friedrich Delitzsch's book *Babel und Bibel* (1902) which characterized Israelite traditions as mere copies of more ancient "Eastern" myths.[15] The new emphasis on the Eastern origin of Gnosticism, as expressed mainly in the works of Richard Reitzenstein[16] and Wilhelm Bousset,[17] must be seen against this general background of the development of the German *Religionswissenschaftsschule* at the turn of the century.

In a later search for a more integrative definition of Gnosticism, another German Jew, Hans Jonas, saw philosophical and mythological elements combined in his description of a "Gnostic religion" which had exercised a strong influence upon "the spirit of late antiquity," a time he called the "Age of Gnosticism."[18] For Jonas, the essence of this religion was the alienation from the cosmos, a concept which never left Western culture and was most recently expressed by the philosophy of existentialism. Jonas, it should be noted, was then under the influence of both Heidegger and Spengler, and identified himself as an existentialist.

Research on Gnosticism in the second half of the twentieth century is based on the discoveries made near the Egyptian village of Nag Hammadi in 1945. Previously, the main material for scholarship on Gnosticism had been Christian anti-Gnostic polemics. Now vast amounts of Gnostic literature, written in Coptic, could be read. One of the results of this discovery was another revision of the theories on Gnostic origins. The extent to which Biblical motifs pervaded the Nag Hammadi documents led scholars to suspect stronger Jewish origins of Gnosticism than had been previously believed. Adopting this position, they deviated from Jonas who, like the *Religionswissenschaftsschule* before him, rejected the notion of Jewish origins of Gnosticism. Indeed, in his epochal work *Gnosis und spätantiker Geist,* Jonas had not even mentioned the possibility of Jewish origins in Gnosticism. For Jonas, Judaism and Gnosticism were incompatible and opposed.[19]

GERSHOM SCHOLEM: GNOSTICISM AND THE CONCEPT OF A HETEROGENEOUS JUDAISM

As a result of its drive to prove to the Christian world that pure monotheism was an essential idea of Judaism, the nineteenth-century *Wissenschaft des Judentums* could not accept the idea of Gnosticism as part of a "normative" Judaism. Therefore, it was left to a critic of traditional *Wissenschaft des Judentums,* Gershom Scholem, to identify "Jewish Gnostics" with esoteric circles within normative Judaism. For Scholem, Gnosticism and Messianism were the two chief forces behind the development of Jewish mysticism, which his oeuvre reestablished as a central tenet of Judaism itself. But what did Scholem mean by Gnosticism? As several critics have noted, Scholem's discussion of "Jewish Gnosticism" demonstrates the importance of a proper definition of Gnosticism. Edwin Yanauchi has rightly stated that "this one man's Gnosticism may be simply another man's Mysticism, Esotericism, or Eucratism."[20] Scholem would probably have agreed. At a conference at Dartmouth in 1965 Scholem was reported to have said that it did not matter whether one used the term "Jewish Gnosticism" or "Jewish Esotericism" or "Merkabah Mysticism."[21] Certainly his broad definition of the term "Gnosticism" left much room for speculation. For him, it was "a convenient term for the religious movement that proclaimed a mystical esotericism for the elect based on illumination and an acquisition of a higher knowledge of things heavenly and divine."[22]

It is no wonder that leading scholars in the field of Gnosticism have criticized Scholem's lack of clarity in his definition of Gnosticism. Although there is no general agreement on a definition of Gnosticism,[23] most scholars do not question that the dualism between two Godheads—the "good" hidden God and the "evil" Creator—is a central element of Gnostic teaching. Thus Jean Danielou has stated that "it is this radical dualism, therefore, which is the properly Gnostic element."[24] Hans Jonas confirmed this point of view: "A Gnosticism without a fallen god, without benighted creator and sinister creation, without akin soul, cosmic captivity and acosmic salvation, without the self-redeeming of the Deity—in short: a Gnosis without divine tragedy will not meet specifications."[25] And for Kurt Rudolf, Gnosticism was a "dualistic religion" consisting of several schools and taking up a negative attitude towards the world.[26]

However, in his definition of Gnosticism Scholem did not even mention the issue of dualism. The reason for this becomes clear when one understands his principal thesis regarding Jewish Gnosticism. According to Scholem, the Jewish Gnostics—and this means first and foremost the Merkabah mystics—modified the dualistic principle and harmonized it with the basic ideas of Judaism. This approach was rejected, by Hans Jonas amongst others, who criticized "the semantic disserve which Scholem did to clarity when he called his Palestinian Hekhaloth mysticism a 'Gnosis.'"[27]

Scholem's definition of Gnosticism reflects the dilemma of a perceived incompatibility between monotheistic Judaism and a dualistic Gnosticism. If one accepts a strict dualism as the basic premise of Gnosticism and at the same time monotheism as the basic definition of normative Judaism, one cannot argue for Gnostic streams within normative Judaism. To solve this dilemma, one must either define the Jewish Gnostics as heretics or modify the dualistic element in the definition of Gnosticism. Before Scholem, the former was usually preferable: Graetz, who argued that Gnosticism exercised a negative influence upon Judaism, and Friedländer, who, contrary to Graetz, saw Gnosticism as a positive force for Judaism, both agreed that Gnosticism and Judaism were not originally the same. Scholem, however, chose to elaborate upon the latter possibility.

According to Scholem, the earliest form of Jewish Gnosticism was Merkabah mysticism. Scholem rejected Friedländer's equation of heretical Jewish Gnostics with *Minim* and adopted Schuerer's broader definition of this term. For Scholem the Jewish Gnostics were not the heretics against whom normative Jews had to fight, they were themselves part of normative Judaism. Thus he placed them "near the center of rabbinic Judaism, not on its fringes" and spoke about a "truly rabbinic Gnosis." Scholem did not find any heretical traces in Merkabah Mysticism, the speculations around the Holy Throne connected with the Book of Ezekiel, which he identified with Jewish Gnosticism. On the contrary, "all these texts go to great length to stress their strict conformity, even in the most minute detail, to Halakhic Judaism and its prescriptions."[28]

Scholem had already argued that the Merkabah texts were older than previously assumed.[29] In *Jewish Gnosticism,* Scholem elaborated this thesis and stated: "The truth of the matter is that in many respects I was not radical enough."[30] Here he brought evidence that the roots of what he called Jewish Gnosticism went back at least to Mishnaic times. He cited the story of the Four who entered Paradise, which we know already from Graetz's analysis, and demonstrated that it can only be understood in connection with Hekhaloth literature. For Scholem, Rabbi Akiba's warning not to say "water! water!" when they come to the place of "pure marble plates" resembled the description of the gate of the sixth palace in the descent of the Merkabah mystics. Further evidence for the antiquity of Merkabah mysticism can be found in the "Song of the Kine" (Aboda Zara 24b) and its resemblance to celestial hymns used in the Hekhaloth literature. The story of Paul's ascent to Paradise in 2 Corinth. 12:2-4 constitutes, according to Scholem, a link between older Jewish texts and the Gnosis of Tannaitic Merkabah mysticism.

Antiquity can also be proven for the second major type of Jewish Gnosticism—Shiur Komah speculation. Scholem derived this argument from Origen's inclusion of the Song of Songs in the mystical teachings, the study of which was allowed only after reaching full maturity. Scholem rejected the usual Christological interpretation by claiming this was only established after Origen's writings. Instead, the answer must be found in connection to Jewish Shiur Komah speculation. Since the "Song of the Songs" contains a detailed description of the limbs of the lover, who was identified with God, it served as the basic Scriptural text on which the doctrine of Shiur Komah leaned; therefore it was considered as a mystical teaching.[31]

Scholem's conclusions relevant to our discussion can be summarized in two main points: First, he placed Jewish Gnosticism within normative Judaism and rejected the previous equation of Jewish Gnostics with Jewish heretics. Second, he attempted to prove the antiquity of Jewish Gnosticism, which according to him reached back at least until the second century C. E. Scholem did not try to prove, however, that Gnosticism per se was a Jewish phenomenon. He made clear that Jewish Gnosticism predated Christian Gnosticism, but his remark "that, initially, Jewish esoteric tradition absorbed Hellenistic elements" was taken as proof of Scholem's identification of the origins of Gnosticism within the Hellenistic culture.[32]

This issue, however, deserves more reflection. It is true, that in his writings Scholem would not go beyond the thesis of a pre-Christian Jewish Gnosticism and claim that Gnosticism had its roots within Judaism. The reason for this was the lack of evidence and not a belief that Gnosticism ultimately had non-Jewish roots. Some remarks Scholem made privately point to the assumption that he actually believed in the Jewish origins of Gnosticism. Birger Pearson concludes his essay on Friedländer with a footnote referring to a recent letter which Scholem had sent him in which "Professor Scholem stated his belief that the Gnostic revolt did indeed arise from within Judaism."[33] Another statement Scholem made in a discussion with Harold Bloom may be very vague, but reveals much more about Scholem's actual thoughts than the scholarly treatment of the matter in his writings. Bloom recalled: "When, in my puzzlement, I attempted to remind him that Gnosticism itself seemed as much a misreading of Plato as of the Hebrew Bible, so that in some strange sense Gnosticism and Neoplatonism both derived from Plato, Scholem replied triumphantly: 'Exactly so. And where did Plato get everything from? Egypt, who had it from us!'"[34]

Even in his *Jewish Gnosticism* the reader can detect Scholem's sympathy toward an "inner-Jewish" understanding of Gnostic origins. This becomes clear in his polemics against "scholars who have been looking far and wide to establish the source from which it all has come [and] have been remarkably reluctant, or rather, unwilling to allow the theory that Gnostic tendencies may have developed in the very midst of Judaism itself, whether in its classical forms or on its heterodox and sectarian fringes."[35] Scholem explicitly pointed to the Samaritan origins of mythical Gnosticism and argued that if there was a Gnostic tradition in Jewish heretical circles, the same might have been true for orthodox Judaism at an early time as well.[36] After these few remarks, however, he abruptly stopped the discussion of this particular question by writing: "Important and promising as all these alleys of inquiry are, it is with that other aspect of the problem, mentioned above, that I propose to deal here."[37]

All these remarks lead to the conclusion that Scholem did not oppose the thesis of the Jewish origins of Gnosticism. His reluctance to answer the questions related to the origins of Gnosticism must be explained solely by his conviction that he did not have any evidence to prove either Jewish or non-Jewish origins of Gnosticism. He stated that the theories of Jewish origins of Gnosticism[38] are of a "highly hypothetical, if sometimes plausible character." Thus, Harold Bloom states correctly:

> Scholem desired Kabbalah to be wholly Gnostic and yet wholly Jewish, which resulted in his shrewdly desperate insistence that Gnosticism was essentially Jewish in its origins.[39]

In a similar vein, Robert Alter commented on a passage from Idel: "I suspect that if Idel were able to produce convincing proof of Gnosticism as an indigenous Jewish doctrine (as perhaps he may yet do), Scholem would have been delighted by the idea."[40]

CONCLUSION

Apart from their scholarly value, the writings on Gnosticism and its relationship to Judaism discussed here must also be read as historical documents of three German-Jewish intellectuals. Heinrich Graetz's dissertation was a weapon on the battlefield against the growing influence of the Reform movement in Germany. By drawing a dark picture of the Gnostic threat to ancient Judaism he warned against what seemed to him an ob-

vious parallel in his own time. Like Graetz, Moriz Friedländer identified Jewish Gnosticism in the Hellenistic world with the contemporary Jewish Reform movement. Yet he came to the opposite conclusion. An opponent of Orthodox Judaism, Friedländer hailed the successful symbiosis of Gnostic and classical Jewish ideas as the prototype of a liberal and open-minded modern Jewish religion. Perhaps because of their blatantly apologetic character, neither Graetz's nor Friedländer's work on Gnosticism succeeded in exercising any significant influence on the future research in the field.

This, of course, was not the case for Gershom Scholem, who argued from a quite different position. He had left the German-Jewish world of Graetz's and Friedländer's heirs after completing his dissertation at the University of Munich in the early 1920s and was no longer an integral member of German-Jewish scholarship. We should keep in mind, however, that he continued to write many of his works in German both before and after the war, and that his German-Jewish intellectual background formed his scholarly oeuvre in a dialectical way. As a rebellious son of *Wissenschaft des Judentums* he would again and again point to its apologetic character and demand a fundamental revision of its principles. Only Zionism and a Jewish society, he argued, made it possible to leave the narrow path of a "legitimate" view on Judaism and create a scholarship that would not be oriented towards the concrete needs of Jews in a non-Jewish environment.

Scholem's work is characterized by a repeated effort to refute any concept of a clearly defined essence of Judaism. He planted those phenomena, which previous scholars had regarded as marginal to the Jewish experience, into its very heart. Just as Zionism radically transformed the Jewish society of his time, modern Jewish scholarship as Scholem understood it had to radically alter the understanding of the Jewish past. While the early representatives of *Wissenschaft des Judentums* singled out a hypothetical "essence of Judaism," Scholem and other scholars of his generation—confronted with a very different present situation of Jewish society—were eager to prove that Judaism was always heterogeneous. In Scholem's agenda, which David Biale described as a Jewish counterhistory, Jewish Gnosticism played an important part. This may also explain why he insisted on the central role of Gnosticism within Jewish mysticism despite his obvious problems with defining the term in general and in respect to Judaism.[41] In more general terms, Biale has shown that Scholem's research was influenced by a contemporary agenda and was in many ways comparable to the tasks of the predecessors from which he had distanced himself so often:

> Scholem's pluralistic conception of Jewish history and Jewish nationalism was opposed to the [earlier] search

of identity. What his oeuvre showed was not the 'essence' of Judaism, but an anarchical undermining of all essences. Seen in historical context all of his studies of the 'back side' of Jewish history were an 'anarchical blast of wind,' which tried to shake the self-complacency and self-righteousness affecting all nations. But like other national historians he also partook in the 'invention of traditions': His form to embed the Kabbalah within larger structures of Jewish history was the conscious attempt to connect the national rebirth with the forces he regarded as vital in Jewish history.[42]

Notes

I would like to thank Susannah Heschel, Michael A. Meyer, Nils Roemer, and Elliot Wolfson for the valuable comments I received on earlier drafts of this paper.

1. Immanuel Wolf, "On the Concept of a Science of Judaism," *Leo Baeck Institute Yearbook* 2 (1957): 204.

2. Leopold Zunz, *Zur Geschichte und Literatur* (Berlin: Veit, 1845) 21.

3. Only shortly before the completion of his dissertation, Graetz published the first articles signed with his name, in which he criticized Geiger's "Lehrbuch zur Sprache der Mischna" (his series of articles in *Orient* begins in 52 [1844]). A remark on the genesis of his dissertation in his diary (29 June 1845) underlines the real purpose of this work: "One rainy night I was strolling around Oldenbourgstrasse [where Graetz lived with S. R. Hirsch], and not far from the pastor's house the thought occurred to me to describe Acher's apostasy and to lay out its relations with a *parallel.*" Heinrich Graetz, *Tagebuch und Briefe,* ed. Reuven Michael (Tübingen: Mohr, 1977) 149. The original Latin title of his dissertation was: *De auctoritate et vi, quam gnosis in Judaismum habuerit.*

4. "From this perspective the epoch presents an undeniable analogy with our own time; for gnostic dualism one need only substitute modern pantheism along with its direct or indirect emanations, to which Judaism should accordingly be subsumed, as either sophisticated accommodation or as apostasy; *thus in the gnostic and anti-gnostic movements that are internal to judaism one has . . . a true mirror of the present.*" Graetz, *Gnosticismus und Judenthum* (Krotoschin: B. L. Monasch, 1846) vi-vii. (my emphasis).

5. Graetz 35-36.

6. Hagigah 14b, trans. Jacob Neusner.

7. Since Graetz had identified the term *minim* with Gnostics, the discussion about this issue has not yet come to an end. Schuerer has criticized Friedländer for making this equation. Recent critics of this identification include Ithamar Gruenwald, "The Problem of the Anti-Gnostic Polemic in Rabbinic Literature," *From Apocalypticism to Gnosticism. Studies in Apocalypticism, Merkavah Mysticism and Gnosticism* (Frankfurt: P. Lang, 1988) 237ff. and Alan F. Segal, *Two Powers in Heaven* (Leiden: E. J. Brill, 1977) cf. 67 on Elisha ben Abuya.

8. Graetz vi.

9. Graetz 110. Graetz revised his ideas about the authorship and background of the *Sefer Yetsirah* in *Geschichte der Juden,* 4th ed., vol. 5 (Leipzig: Oskar Leiner, 1886) 297. There he claimed that it was written in Gaonic times.

10. David Biale, *Gershom Scholem: Kabbalah and Counter-History,* 2nd. ed. (Cambridge: Harvard UP, 1982) 53. Graetz's view was basically accepted by Manuel Joel who tried to show the influence of Gnosticism on both Palestinian and Diaspora Judaism. See esp. Joel's detailed treatment in his *Blicke in die Religionsgeschichte zu Anfang des zweiten christlichen Jahrhunderts,* vol. 1 (Breslau: Schottlander, 1880) 103-70.

11. Ferdinand Christian Baur speaks about the *Herkunft aus dem Morgenland* in his *Die christliche Gnosis oder die christliche Religions-Philosophie in ihrer geschichtlichen Entwicklung* (Tübingen: C. F. Osiander, 1835). In this work Baur divided Christian, Jewish and Eastern sources of Gnosticism. See esp. 36-68.

12. Moriz Friedländer, *Der vorchristliche jüdische Gnosticismus* (Göttingen: Vandenhoeck & Ruprecht, 1898) 46.

13. Friedländer, *Die religiösen Bewegungen innerhalb des Judentums im Zeitalter Jesu* (Berlin: Reimer, 1905) vi.

14. See esp. Emil Schuerer's review in *Theologische Literaturzeitung* 24 (1899): 167-70, in which he opposed Friedländer's narrow definition of *minim* as Gnostics. With regard to the Jewish origins of Gnosticism in general, Schuerer mainly criticized Friedländer's lack of proofs for this thesis. But note that Schuerer did not reject the thesis of the pre-Christian origins of Jewish mysticism: "To be sure, it is beyond dispute that the beginnings of a Jewish 'Gnosis' (mysticism, kabbalah) extend into the pre-Christian period. However, the contours of these beginnings are too difficult for us to perceive clearly. We cannot, therefore, sketch them with any certainty," (168).

15. See Klaus Johanning, *Der Bibel-Babel-Streit: Eine forschungsgeschichtliche Studie* (Frankfurt/Main: P. Lang, 1988).

16. Richard Reitzenstein, *Poimandres: Studien zur griechisch-ägyptischen und frühchristlichen Literatur* (Leipzig: B. G. Teubner, 1904).

17. Wilhelm Bousset, *Hauptprobleme der Gnosis* (Göttingen: Vandenhoeck und Ruprecht, 1907).

18. Hans Jonas, *Gnosis und spätantiker Geist,* vol. 1 (Göttingen: Vandenhoeck und Ruprecht, 1934).

19. Since the 1950s, however, scholars have been reviving Friedländer's basic assumption from half a century before, and are pointing—in more sophisticated ways—to the Jewish origins of Gnosticism. One of the first modern representatives of the "Friedländer approach" was the Dutch scholar Gilles Quispel. Quispel's first systematic treatment of this topic was his article, "Der gnostische Anthropos und die jüdische Tradition" *Eranos Jahrbuch* 12 (1954): 195-234. Although Quispel argues for the Jewish origins of Gnosticism, he differs on many essential points from Friedländer. For him, Gnosticism is not a product of Diaspora Judaism, but of heterodox streams in Palestinian Judaism. However, Palestinian Judaism was highly Hellenized, too, and thus Gnosticism was—similar to Friedländer's thesis—the product of the combination of Jewish religion and Greek vulgar philosophy [*Vulgärphilosophie*]. More specifically, he found in Gnosticism a combination of Greek views on the universal soul and Jewish ideas concerning *ruah* and *hokhmah*. The diverging positions in Gnosis scholarship clashed at the hundredth general assembly of the *Society of Biblical Literature* in 1964, where both Jonas and Quispel expressed their views. Those papers were published in *The Bible in Modern Scholarship*, ed. J. P. Hyatt (Nashville: Abingdon, 1965) 252-93. While Jonas argued that monotheistic Judaism and dualistic Gnosticism were incompatible, Quispel emphasized the Gnostic motifs in the esoteric traditions of the Palestinian Pharisees. In recent decades the thesis of a Jewish origin of Gnosticism has been adopted by so many scholars that they are no longer concerned with the question whether Judaism was the basis for Gnosticism, but rather if it was Diaspora (Friedländer) or Palestinian (Quispel) Judaism. Thus, in 1973, Birger A. Pearson published an article "Friedländer Revisited," (*Studia Philonica* 2 [1973]: 23-39) in which he tried to strengthen Friedländer's arguments with new evidence from the Nag Hammadi documents. See also Pearson's study, "Jewish Haggadic Traditions in the Testimony of Truth from Nag Hammadi," *Ex Orbe Religionum: Festschrift G. Widengren* I (Leiden: Brill, 1972) 457-70. Even Simone Petrement, who rejects the thesis of a pre-Christian Jewish Gnosticism, had to admit: "Until 1950, this orientalizing and Iranizing theory had been accepted by a good number of scholars. But following that point its success declined. One now elaborated a new hypothesis: Gnosticism had been the offspring of Judaism, to be sure, but of a dissident Judaism. It is this hypothesis that has dominated in nearly all research to this very day." *Le Dieu separé. Les origines du gnosticisme* (Paris: Cerf, 1984) 11-12. A brief summary of those arguments can be found in John G. Gager, *The Origins of Anti-Semitism: Attitudes Toward Judaism in Pagan and Christian Antiquity,* (New York: Oxford UP, 1983) 167-70.

20. Edwin M. Yamauchi, *Pre-Christian Gnosticism. A Survey of the Proposed Evidences* (Grand Rapids: Eerdmans, 1973) 14.

21. Yamauchi 150.

22. Gershom Scholem, *Jewish Gnosticism, Merkabah Mysticism and Talmudic Tradition* (New York: Jewish Theological Seminary, 1960) 1.

23. Compare for example the different definitions proposed at the Congress on the origins of Gnosticism at Messina in 1966. While a scholar like T. P. van Baaren provided a list of not less than 16 points to define the term, other participants offered much broader definitions. T. P. van Baaren, "Towards a Definition of Gnosticism," *Le Origini dello Gnosticismo,* ed. U. Bianchi (Leiden: Brill, 1967) 174-80.

24. Jean Danielou, *The Theology of Jewish Christianity* trans. and ed. John A. Barker (London: Darton, Longman & Todd, 1964) 73.

25. Hyatt 293. See also Shaul Magid, "Gershom Scholem's Ambivalence Toward Mystical Experience and His Critique of Martin Buber in Light of Hans Jonas and Martin Heidegger," *Journal of Jewish Thought and Philosophy* 4 (1995): 245-69.

26. Kurt Rudolf, *Gnosis. The Nature and History of Gnosticism* (San Francisco: Harper and Row, 1987) 2. Modern scholarship tends to distinguish between the term "Gnosis" which stands for the broader meaning of a secret knowledge and "Gnosticism" which characterizes a specific heretical movement in early antiquity. Ithamar Gruenwald accused Scholem of confusing these two terms. See his "Jewish Merkavah Mysticism and Gnosticism," *From Apocalypticism to Gnosticism: Studies in Apocalypticism, Merkavah Mysticism and Gnosticism* 192. But if he did so, he did it consciously, as the following statement by Scholem reveals: "The discussion as to what exactly is to be understood by 'gnosis' has gained in prominence in scholarly literature and at conferences during the last decades. There is a tendency to exclude phenomena that until 1930 were desig-

nated gnostic by everyone. To me it does not seem to matter greatly whether phenomena previously called gnostic are now designated as 'esoteric,' and I for one cannot see the use or value of the newly introduced distinctions (for example, gnosis-Gnosticism and the like)." Scholem, *Origins of the Kabbalah* (Princeton: JPS and Princeton UP, 1987) 21, n.24.

27. A similar criticism can be found in David Flusser's review of Scholem's book: "What the patristic writers included within the term Gnosis was something revolutionary—the rebellion against the God of Israel; and the reviewer can see no point in extending this clear concept into one that is blurred. . . . It would consequently seem more profitable to abandon the terms Gnosis and Gnosticism as a title for esoteric doctrines preserved in talmudic literature as in the Heykhaloth." David Flusser, *Journal of Jewish Studies* XI (1960): 65.

28. Scholem, *Jewish Gnosticism* 10-12. Scholem revealed his ambivalent stand toward Friedländer by remarking that in his writings "quite a grain of truth has been overshadowed by many inconsequential and misleading statements," (9). Compare also his remark where he protects Friedländer against scholars who "have been poking fun" at him (3).

29. Scholem, *Major Trends in Jewish Mysticism,* third ed. (New York: Schocken, 1961) 40-79.

30. Scholem, *Jewish Gnosticism* 8.

31. Scholem, *Jewish Gnosticism* 37-39. Modern scholarship opened anew the question of the character and the antiquity of Hekhaloth literature and reassesses Scholem's earlier understanding of Merkabah mysticism. For new approaches see esp. the work of Peter Schaefer.

32. Scholem, *Jewish Gnosticism* 34; Moshe Idel, *Kabbalah: New Perspectives* (New Haven: Yale UP, 1988) 31. For a similar statement by Scholem see his *Major Trends* 35. Cf. also Idel's reply to the review article by Y. Tishby, *Zion* LIV (1989): 224.

33. Pearson 39, n. 51.

34. Harold Bloom, "Scholem: Unhistorical or Jewish Gnosticism" *Gershom Scholem* (New York: Chelsea House, 1987) 216.

35. Scholem, *Jewish Gnosticism* 2.

36. Scholem, *Jewish Gnosticism* 4.

37. Scholem, *Jewish Gnosticism* 5.

38. Scholem, *Jewish Gnosticism* 3.

39. Bloom 215.

40. Robert Alter: "Jewish Mysticism in Dispute," *Commentary* (Sept. 1989): 56. Two of the "new perspectives" in Moshe Idel's challenge to Scholem's outlook on Kabbalah are related to the topics of the previous discussion and can be summarized as follows: a. In view of the new evidence in Gnosis scholarship Jewish sources have to be regarded as highly influential on the origins of Gnosticism; b. these sources were at the same time transmitted in Jewish circles and served ultimately as the *Urquelle* for medieval Kabbalah.

41. Moshe Idel has pointed this out in detail in a recent article. Idel, "Subversive Katalysatoren: Gnosis und Messianismus in Gershom Scholems Verständnis der jüdischen Mystik," *Gershom Scholem: Zwischen den Disziplinen* eds. Peter Schäfer und Gary Smith (Frankfurt/Main: Suhrkamp, 1995) 80-121.

42. Biale, "Scholem und der moderne Nationalismus," *Gershom Scholem* 271.

Nils H. Roemer (essay date 2005)

SOURCE: Roemer, Nils H. "Recovering Jewish History in the Age of Emancipation and Reform." In *Jewish Scholarship and Culture in Nineteenth-Century Germany: Between History and Faith,* pp. 35-46. Madison: The University of Wisconsin Press, 2005.

[*In the following essay, Roemer discusses the various cultural and intellectual factors that affected the study of Judaism and Jewish history in nineteenth-century Germany.*]

Aside from Jost's *Geschichte der Israeliten,* Jewish historians had produced few valuable essays that reflected the formulation of an ambitious program. With the exception of Jost and Zunz, only a small number of former Verein members continued along the path of Wissenschaft. Its association with religious reform and the battle over emancipation further contributed to its importance and energy. Yet the very quality that allowed Jewish historiography to blossom made it increasingly divisive and hindered efforts to find an institutional home for it outside of the German universities. Moreover, its conflicting nature obstructed attempts to garner a wide-ranging readership. Far from presenting the dominant discourse during this period, the study of the Jewish past still had to vindicate its primary role within the intellectual culture of German Jewry. Yet with Wissenschaft's ascendancy, it confronted criticism for its lack of impact upon the wider Jewish society. Despite this nascent condemnation and the emerging ideological differences, Jewish historians continued to regard Wissenschaft as a tool in the hands of the intellectual elite and not an educational force. In this respect, it functioned as *"historische Aufklärung"* (enlightenment through history) with the purpose of elucidating Judaism's true essence and countering its biased representation in the German public. It was only during the late 1830s and 1840s that the first efforts to popularize Jewish history were made in the form of textbook histories. Simultaneously, Heinrich Heine and Ludwig and Phöbus Philippson had been dismayed by the lack of impact the scholarly representation of Jewish history had had on Jewish education and proposed poetic treatments instead.

For most of the historians, historical scholarship continued to be seen as the supreme instrument in the fight for emancipation and internal reform. As Zunz stated in 1832, "the neglect of Jewish science is intricately bound up with the Jews' civic degradation." The linkage of emancipation and reform also formed the cornerstones of his first comprehensive analysis of Jewish liturgy. The study was sandwiched between a call for emancipation in the first chapter, which was censored out of the first edition, and an appeal for internal reform in the last chapter.[1] In line with this self-understanding, Zunz and Jost engaged in elaborate public defenses of the Jews in the face of Luigi Chiarini's slandering of the Talmud.[2] When the Prussian government attempted to ban Jews from acquiring non-Jewish names, the Berlin community commissioned Zunz to write a treatise that would counter this prohibition in exchange for 100 thaler.[3] Zunz's *Die Namen der Juden (The names of the Jews)* amply illustrated that Jews in the past had had names like Jason, Abu-Hassan, Fischlin, and Esperanza.[4] Similarly, in 1840, the community leaders of Berlin asked Zunz to write about the notorious blood-libel accusation in Damascus, which quickly became an issue that was debated in the European press.[5]

Strung together, emancipation and internal reform nevertheless produced the opposing dynamics of discontinuity and development. In respect to the debate over emancipation, Jewish participants pointed to advances and discontinuities between premodern and contemporary Jewry.[6] Jost made this point clear when in defense of emancipation he wrote, "all of us who were still in our childhood thirty years ago are witnesses to unbelievable transformations. . . . We have wandered, or better, flown through a thousand-year history!"[7] If Jost understood the last few decades as the equivalent of a thousand years, he simply underscored the advancements and discontinuity in light of the accelerated process of social, cultural, and religious transformation. From the 1840s on, however, Jewish historians more strongly grounded current Judaism in the past. Whereas Jost's scholarship presented a program to overcome elements of the Jewish past that were mainly associated with the dark ages of Ashkenazic Jewry and to return Jewish society to its biblical state, other Jewish histori-

ans increasingly reintegrated the premodern period into their conceptions of Judaism's development. Instead of discontinuity, they emphasized change and progress and highlighted the particularistic aspects of Judaism.

Zunz's study presented an elaborate attempt to come to terms with the question of development and continuity and to legitimize the modern sermon in the vernacular. In his magnum opus, Zunz portrayed postbiblical Judaism as a thriving culture and stressed that during those times when there was no Jewish state, cultural creativity nevertheless flourished.[8] Positing an organic development, Zunz bridged the disjuncture between the Israelite religion and rabbinic Judaism. For him, halakhah and haggadah represented the continuation of biblical law and the freedom of prophecy.[9]

In contrast, Jost's 1832 *Allgemeine Geschichte des israelitischen Volkes (General history of the Jewish people)* failed to provide a basic developmental scheme and to differentiate between the various historical epochs. By mostly neglecting Jewish cultural and religious history, Jost did not accord historical agency to the Jews.[10] In a review of Jost's history that appeared in Gabriel Riesser's *Der Jude,* the critic expressed the hope that a history of the Jews would be written that combined political with religious history.[11] A few years later, Abraham Geiger upbraided Jost's history when he declared that the external history of the Jews does not offer a reasonable principle of development. In the external history of the Diaspora, Geiger maintained, "the smell of mustiness of the field of corpses approaches one."[12]

Jost had daringly begun with two attempts at writing a comprehensive history of the Jews. However, more research was needed to bring the development of Judaism into clearer perspective. New studies appeared that charted the Second Temple period, the history of Spanish Jewry, as well as the neglected field of Jewish law. Levi Herzfeld brought the Second Temple period into focus as one of profound religious transformation in which monotheism only slowly took hold.[13] Michael Sachs, a rabbi and preacher in Berlin, published *Die religiöse Poesie der Juden in Spanien (The religious poetry of the Jews in Spain)* in 1845, which brought together a collection of medieval religious poetry in translation and represented to a large extent the German Jewish enchantment with the Golden Age of Spanish Jewry.[14] Concurrently, Zacharias Frankel delved into the realm of Jewish law, and Abraham Geiger described the language of the Mishna.[15]

With this blossoming scholarship, the Jewish public sphere developed. When, in the aftermath of the Napoleonic defeat, many societies excluded Jews from membership, German Jews founded their own societies. In particular, Jewish reading societies emerged within smaller communities during the 1830s, a time when the overwhelming majority of Jews in Germanic lands still lived in small and middle-sized towns.[16] While up until the 1830s most of these reading societies devoted themselves to general education, they slowly took up education in the field of Jewish history. The first such clubs appeared in communities like Baiersdorf in 1837 and Jebenhausen in 1838.[17] In 1842 Abraham Geiger founded in Breslau the Learning and Reading Association *(Jüdischen Lehr- und Leseverein,* later *Israelitischer Lehr- und Leseverein)*. The society, which in 1846 had 110 members, provided them with the opportunity to familiarize themselves with publications on Judaism. To this end, a library was established, and public talks were organized. Geiger gave numerous lectures here during the 1840s that covered almost all periods of Jewish history.[18]

The exact number of these reading clubs and societies is unclear, but their existence increasingly expanded the readership of Jewish periodicals. In 1836 Ludwig Philippson started the *Allgemeine Zeitung des Judenthums.* From its inception, it reviewed scholarly publications and even introduced a special rubric for Jewish history in 1838.[19] Jost edited the *Israelitische Annalen* (1839-41), which was dedicated to Jewish history, culture, and literature of all times and countries. In addition to these periodicals, Julius Fürst published the *Orient* (1840-51), which included a separate literary insert dedicated to scholarship.[20] Abraham Geiger edited the first major scholarly journal, the *Wissenschaftliche Zeitschrift für jüdische Theologie* (1835-47), after he completed his studies at the university in Bonn. Jost claimed in one of his letters to Philipp Ehrenberg that one copy of the *Israelitische Annalen* reached about 50 readers because Jewish reading societies had ordered them. Jost went on to say that the *Orient* had only 115 subscribers in 1841. The total circulation of the *Allgemeine* and the *Orient* was about 700 copies by 1850.[21] Yet despite these advances, with the exception of the *Allgemeine,* none of these journals lasted beyond a few years.

This situation also dominated the reception of the works by Wissenschaft scholars. Zunz bemoaned the lack of an audience for scholarly works in a letter to Meyer Isler in December 1830 when he wrote, "it is a real misfortune to write for Jews! The rich Jews do not pay attention, the Jewish scholars cannot read it, and the fools review it."[22] Zunz's *Gottesdienstliche Vorträge* immediately found 300 subscribers in 1832 from Cracow, Brody, Lemberg, Tarnopol, Odessa, Vienna, Triest, Padua, Copenhagen, Stuttgart, Pest, and Leyden.[23] In view of the wide geographic distribution, the readership was fairly limited. Moreover, only 200 additional copies were sold during the next eight years. It was only at the beginning of the 1850s that the first edition of 750 copies was finally out of print. Twenty years after their initial publication, the 950 sets of Jost's history were still not sold out, and his *Allgemeine Geschichte des is-*

raelitischen Volkes "lay like lead," as he remarked in 1841.[24] A similar fate met the publication of more than one thousand copies of Zunz's *Die Namen der Juden.*[25] Only Ludwig Philippson during this period was more successful in reaching a wider audience, including Christians, when he delivered several public lectures between 1846-47.[26]

Efforts during the 1840s to create a publishing society for the promotion of works on Jewish history and literature similiarly failed. While Gabriel Riesser, Albert Cohn, and other rabbis and teachers lent their support to this cause, only two hundred members signed up.[27] In 1841, Leopold Zunz revitalized the Verein of the 1820s to "support all Jewry" through the nursing of science and art.[28] While over nine hundred copies of the society's statutes were distributed, the response from Jewish communities and individuals remained limited. The society offered the substantial sum of two hundred thaler to the author of the best monograph that answered the question "What was, is, and should the rabbi be?" When after two years no manuscripts were received, the society amended the question to a study of the rabbinate since 1782. Yet no historian responded, and the prize was never awarded. Among the few scholarly projects supported by the society was the publication of Judah Halevi's *Kusari* by David Cassel. Next to these activities the society had a small library for its members, which was hardly ever used.[29] Zunz's lectures during the 1840s about Jewish history and literature equally attracted only a small number of attendees[30] Consequently, the society folded in 1847.[31]

It was this situation that Ludwig Philippson and others addressed with the creation of historical novels. For many Reform-oriented pedagogues, rabbis, and writers, the scholarly treatment of Judaism was, as one observer put it, not successful in overcoming the lack of "Jewish *Bildung,*" since they were for the most part simply not accessible nor particularly effective as teaching tools. Instead, pedagogues demanded the creation of religious folk and youth literature.[32] Historical novels, like Berthold Auerbach's *Spinoza: Ein Denkerleben (Spinoza: the life of a thinker),* Phöbus Philippson's *Die Marranen (The Marranos),* followed by Heinrich Heine's *Der Rabbi von Bacharach (The rabbi of Bacharach),* depicting mostly the history of Spanish Jewry, filled this gap.

While Philippson and others attempted to educate German Jews about their history in the form of historical novels, Jewish history became a subject of instruction in several Jewish and general schools. When, at the end of the 1830s, Moses Elkan and Ephraim Willstätter published the first textbooks, they relied heavily on Jost's *Allgemeine Geschichte.* Yet they nevertheless wanted to educate and further the formation of the heart and the spirit, while pupils had to memorize the material.[33] In contrast to Jost, Willstätter struck a very different tone when he emphasized the importance of historical memory for the Jews to maintain their identity and to remain faithful believers before their God. Illustrating his work with historical examples, he pleaded in his introduction for unity among the Jews based on the common remembrance of Israel's past. To familiarize pupils with Israel's past would further German Jews' integration and maintain their distinctiveness.[34]

In line with Willstätter's understanding of the moral and religious function of historical memory, the reviews clearly indicate that Jewish history was not to be taught as a secular subject. In the eyes of pedagogues, Jewish history instructed students in God's providence, the religious-moral vocation, and the veracity of Judaism. With respect to these educational goals, numerous reviews attacked these early textbooks. The criticisms echoed the early reproach Jost had faced. In these textbooks, Jewish history "appears as a sad and desolate field of human humiliation."[35] Elkan was reprimanded for having slavishly followed Jost and therefore lacked the "warmth with which the Jewish youth could excite themselves for their religion and co-religionists." In particular, the adaptation of Jost's portrayal of Jesus from the perspective of enlightened rationalism was seen as "peculiar objectivity in a textbook for 'Israelite schools.'"[36]

Offered at an affordable price, Elkan's textbook, despite its criticism, had several editions.[37] The readership of this work must, however, have remained fairly limited since only a few Jewish schools offered postbiblical history as a formal field of instruction.[38] Nevertheless, these textbooks and their reception point to a distinct historical tradition that only slowly regained its voice during the 1840s and began to impact more forcefully on the evolution of Jewish historiography in the second half of the nineteenth century. The authors of the textbook histories subscribed to a morally instructive concept of history that was closer in spirit to the moderate German Enlightenment and the first generation maskilim than the critical works that disseminated from the nascent Wissenschaft school.

In contrast to the attribution of the moral and religious significance of the Jewish past, Jewish historians remained critical of any popularizing tendencies of Wissenschaft. They understood the inception of Jewish historiography as the dialectical summation of the previous decades of enlightenment and reform and the telos of their ambitions. In Zunz's study of synagogal sermons, a new epoch in Jewish history began in the 1750s. Taking his cue from Gans's speech, he posited the recent history as a development that progressed from the Enlightenment to the age of education and reform. Zunz understood the fourth period as the outcome of the liberating Wissenschaft.[39] This movement was to raise the

comprehension of Judaism to a new level and was not an educational program. Jost, for example, in his 1832 *Allgemeine Geschichte,* addressed not the general Jewish reading public but, as the subtitle indicates, "politicians, lawyers, theologians and scientifically educated readers."[40] Along these lines, Geiger opposed the popular treatment of Jewish history in the pages of the *Allgemeine Zeitung des Judenthums* as long as the inner connection of the entirety of Jewish history was not fully understood.[41]

Notwithstanding its self-avowed reluctance to educate a broader public, Wissenschaft during the 1840s became a contentious affair and increasingly mirrored the polarization of the Jewish communities in light of the revitalized debates over reform that led to three rabbinical conferences of the 1840s.[42] In the course of the conferences' deliberations, the traditional messianic hope was reshaped in the form of the mission theory that became a cornerstone of Jewish historiography. As Ludwig Philippson declared at the conference, "Every people has its mission in history. The Jews too have their mission: they are the people of religion."[43]

Despite the wish to utilize the conferences to build a unified program for religious reforms, they became the rallying point for divergent voices. Zacharias Frankel walked out of the rabbinical conference over the issue of Hebrew in the services and went on to found the short-lived journal *Zeitschrift für die religiösen Interessen des Judenthums,* which was filled with criticism of the Reform movement. For Frankel, the readiness with which Reform Judaism handed over some of the tenets of Judaism in the expectation of emancipation defiled the memory of those Jews who in the past had gladly sacrificed their lives for them.[44] Frankel was not alone in his discontent with Reform Judaism and its scholarship. Michael Sachs equally attacked it because of its alleged thoroughly negative approach toward Judaism. Like Heinrich Heine, Sachs also deplored the reduction of Judaism to a single idea. In a letter to his friend Moritz Veit in Berlin, Sachs wrote: "They study history as an isolated [object], authors and book titles they investigate with the same fear like the mixture of meat with milk products. They call this meticulous. Sheer foolishness! If there is a Judaism—I only ask that it is not watered down into *Shema Yisrael* and called essence—step into the path that you see and form it further with its own power!"[45]

The divergence intensified when the radical laity in Frankfurt questioned the necessity of circumcision, and members of the Rothschild banking family in Frankfurt commissioned Zunz to write a defense of this institution.[46] In an article Zunz published in 1844, he defended the tradition and challenged the Reformers' readiness to discard elements of the Jewish religion.[47] To jettison the belief in the messiah or the Talmud was, in the eyes of

Zunz, a repudiation of the Jewish past. Zunz, therefore, turned down an invitation to participate in the rabbinical conference in Breslau.[48] In 1845, in his *Zur Geschichte und Literatur* (*On history and literature*), a work that elucidated the history of legal, liturgical, exegetical, and ethical literature of Ashkenazic Jewry, Zunz attacked Reform-oriented scholarship as tendentious and selective. Against these scholars, Zunz argued Jewish history should be studied as an end in itself and not in anticipation of political and social advantages to be gained.[49]

In light of these religious controversies, Jewish scholarship developed more sharply along the lines of denominational differences. Heated debates occurred in Breslau in which the right for free scholarly inquiry was upheld by Abraham Geiger's followers against their traditionalist opponents led by Salomon Tiktin.[50] Concurrent with these controversies, Jewish theologians and philosophers promoted dogmatic theological and philosophical expositions of Judaism and challenged the importance of historical research in an attempt to regain a clearly delineated notion of the essence of Judaism. Philosophical expositions of Judaism by Salomon Formstecher, Samuel Hirsch, and Salomon Ludwig Steinheim appeared for which stages in the divine education, not the contingencies of history, were the only things that mattered.[51] Jost captured the sense of disintegration quite pointedly when he wrote, "Among twenty scholars, and there are barely more who can claim this title, everyone has nineteen pursuers, if not even mockers."[52] Jost may have slightly overstated his point, yet he nevertheless vividly expressed the sense of disunity among Jewish scholars.

As Wissenschaft became more fractured and contested, several Jewish historians became wary of a radical reformulation of Judaism. Reform-minded scholars like the Hungarian Moses Brück pulverized the status of previously sacred texts and rituals and posited the return to the Mosaic level of Jewish law.[53] In contrast, the Reform scholar Abraham Geiger aimed to reassert the importance of historical continuity and wondered how historical studies could "set the course for us to follow."[54] He therefore became increasingly interested in showing how contemporary Judaism was the product of a long development that was still ongoing. Geiger hoped that the historical understanding would not only relativize previously normative texts but construct an image of continuity.[55]

Similar to Geiger, Heinrich Graetz, the new champion of the emerging positive-historical school, reaffirmed the centrality of the historical approach against theological and philosophical expositions of Judaism's core. Graetz, who had established himself as a scholar in his own right with his dissertation from the University of Jena on Jewish gnosticism, published a lengthy pamphlet in Frankel's periodical titled "Die Construction der jüdischen Geschichte" ("The construction of Jewish history"), in which he outlined a program for a history of the Jews. In these reflections on Jewish history, Graetz turned against Samuel Hirsch and Salomon Steinheim when he unequivocally exclaimed "the totality of Judaism is only discernible in its history."[56] With unparalleled sophistication, Graetz combined external and internal aspects of Jewish history, whereby different elements of a multifaceted essence shaped the various epochs in Jewish history. For Graetz, the contingent historical progression represented even in its remote aspects a continuously developing unity.

Unlike the members of the Verein, Graetz utilized the concept of the idea of Judaism in a new fashion. History became the "reflex of the idea," the realm in which the core of Judaism and its manifestations were validated.[57] In their quest for a new historical understanding, Geiger and Graetz regarded the fact that *Judentum* denoted a religion and a people as a major advantage. The historical individuality of the Jewish people testified to the veracity of Judaism's universal teachings. These historians justified Jewish particularism in terms of its universal mission to humanity. Accordingly, Graetz quite confidently concluded his essay by writing that from a historical perspective, Judaism had in contrast to Christianity a "winning game" (*ein gewonnenes Spiel*).[58]

Turning against Christian scholarship, Graetz, like Zunz, asserted that Judaism continued to have an active history beyond the times in which it formed a state.[59] Therefore, Graetz insisted that it was not the destruction of the Second Temple but rather the end of the First Temple period that represented the beginning of a new historical epoch in Jewish history.[60] While Graetz had restructured the flow of Jewish history in order to avoid a Christian reading, he was clearly aware of the far-reaching implications of his approach. It became obvious that the recognition of Jewish history would not only do justice to it but disturb the construction of world history that still had Christianity as its backbone.[61]

This resurgence of expressing Judaism's irreducible role and its particular historical vocation was not restricted to the followers of the emerging positive-historical school. Heine, Geiger and Philippson insisted on the existence of a rich and vibrant post-biblical Jewish culture and directly assaulted Christian scholarship for its biased treatment of Second Temple Judaism in particular and its overall disregard of Jewish scholarship. Their ambition was not exhausted by a reevaluation of Jewish history. In the shadow of the Jewish past, a continuous historical vocation of Judaism in the present and future emerged.

In his dissertation *Was hat Mohammed aus dem Judentume aufgenommen?* (*What did Mohammed adopt from*

Judaism?) in 1833, Geiger argued that Islam did not develop from sectarian Christian movements in Arabia. Rather, Islam came from rabbinic Judaism, which helped to emphasize Judaism's postbiblical historical impact.[62] Similarly, Heine reclaimed Judaism's irreducible role when he revised the commonly assumed direction in the process of the integration of German Jews into European societies: "But it is not Germany alone that possesses the features of Palestine. The rest of Europe too raises itself to the level of the Jews. I say raises itself—for even in the beginning, the Jews bore within them the modern principles which only now are visibly unfolding among the nations of Europe."[63] Judaism thus encapsulated already all the elements of modernity, while Europe still had to follow suit. Ludwig Philippson powerfully expressed a similar notion in 1847. For Philippson, Judaism not only represented a rich past but also provided the blueprint for the ideal modern state and the solution to the social question. Jewish history was also seen as a central element of world history beyond the biblical period.[64]

Despite these advances in the scholarly elucidation of the Jewish past, German universities did not endorse the idea of chairs for Jewish studies. In 1836 Abraham Geiger tried to rally support behind a Jewish faculty at a German university.[65] Calling on both the Christian and Jewish public, Geiger proposed that the resources could be gathered from a soon-to-be-founded society in commemoration of Maimonides' 700th birthday. Geiger posited that Jewish theology could maintain its rank as a scholarly discipline solely in independent institutions dedicated to the free pursuit of knowledge.[66] In 1842 Julius Fürst's initiative followed, which envisioned the establishment of a chair for Jewish studies at the University of Leipzig where he taught Oriental studies.[67] In 1848 Zunz's attempt to secure a faculty chair for Jewish studies at the University of Berlin failed when the commission turned down his request. In a possibly intentional misreading of Zunz's proposal, the commission rejecteed the plan by claiming the university was not the place to educate rabbis and strengthen Jewish parochialism. Since Jews ceased having a state, their history would be taught across the established disciplines such as theology, classical studies, and cultural studies.[68]

In contrast to these initiatives, Ludwig Philippson launched in 1837 a public campaign for the establishment of a Jewish theological seminary. He envisioned an institution devoted to scholarly studies in combination with a seminary for the education of rabbis and teachers. Not affiliated with a German university, this faculty was to be financed by an endowment of 100,000 thaler.[69] According to Philippson's report, the appeal evoked an immediate response among Christians as well as in Jewish circles. He was pleased to see that the influential Paris daily, *Journal des Débats,* the Protestant newspapers *Universal-Kirchen Zeitung* of Frankfurt am Main and the *Hamburger Correspondent* carried favorable articles. Moreover, Abraham Geiger joined the fray with a second publication, *Ueber die Errichtung einer jüdisch-theologischen Facultät (On the establishment of a Jewish theological faculty)*, and enlisted noted Reform rabbis like Samuel Holdheim, Salomon Herxheimer, Meyer Isler, and Immanuel Wolf in this campaign.[70] Despite the initial success, during which more than 1,700 donors made their pledges, only 13,000 thaler were raised. Most of the Jewish communities remained indifferent to this project or may have rescinded their participation because they were fearful of governmental disapproval.[71] With the exception of Heinrich Heine's uncle, Salomon Heine, who contributed one thousand thaler, other Jewish bankers like the Frankfurt Rothschilds gave nothing. Because it lacked the financial backing of wealthy Jewish families and the larger communities like Berlin, Hamburg, and Frankfurt, the project was doomed.

Efforts to institutionalize Jewish historiography were thus frustrated by the increasing fragmentation of Jewish scholarship and communities, as well as the disregard displayed by German academia. With most of the newly founded periodicals having folded, Jewish historians operated in a highly charged, divisive and, ultimately, fairly limited Jewish public sphere. These historians had not acquired the position of the unchallenged arbiters in debates over religious and cultural renewal. For Jewish historians to gain a lasting foothold in the emerging German Jewish culture, they would have to find an institutional home and establish Jewish historical studies also as an educational force. Despite these shortcomings, Jewish historians like Geiger and Graetz had not only defended the centrality of the historical approach against competing disciplines but also underscored Judaism's particularism. They had overcome Dohm's legacy that portrayed Jewish history in the Diaspora as an aberration and instead emphasized development and change over break and discontinuity.

Whereas Jewish scholarship remained embroiled in public disputes, Jewish historians during the next decades appealed to a broader reading public. Established within rabbinical seminaries, historians moreover softened the radical historicizing of Judaism. Lacking a substantial academic readership and wary of the internal disintegration of the communities, Wissenschaft's scholars turned to history as an educational tool to reshape modern Jewish identities and to create a new unity among the conflicting denominations. As we shall see, while the divisions between the historians reached a high point and were intensified by bitter debates with Christian scholars, the creation of Jewish book clubs facilitated during the next decades a lasting and fairly diversified reception of Jewish scholarship.

Notes

1. Leopold Zunz, *Die gottesdienstlichen Vorträge der Juden, historisch entwickelt: Ein Beitrag zur Altertumskunde und biblischen Kritik, zur Literatur- und Religionswissenschaft* (Berlin: Asher, 1832), vii and 479-81.

2. Luigi Chiarini, *Théorie du judaisme appliquée à la reforme des Israélites de tous les pays de l'Europe et servant en même temps d'ouvrage préparatoire à la version du Talmud de Babylone* (Paris: Barbezat, 1830); Leopold Zunz, "Beleuchtung der théorie du Judaïsme Chiarini's (1830)," *Gesammelte Schriften,* 3 vols. (Berlin: Gerschel, 1875-76), 1: 271-98; and Isaac M. Jost, *Was hat Herr Chiarini in Angelegenheiten der europäischen Juden geleistet? Eine freimüthige und unparteiische Beleuchtung des Werkes théorie du Judaïsme* (Berlin: A. W. Hayn, 1830).

3. See Leopold Zunz's letter to Philipp Ehrenberg, November 21, 1836, in *Leopold Zunz,* ed. Glatzer, 189.

4. The *AZJ* favorably reviewed and extensively paraphrased this work. See *AZJ* 2 (1838): 93-95 and 97-98; and *Sulamith* 8:1[1838]: 174-75.

5. Leopold Zunz, "Damaskus, ein Wort zur Abwehr," *Gesammelte Schriften,* 3 vols. (Berlin: Gerschel, 1875-76), 2: 160-71. On the impact of the Damascus affair in general, see Jonathan Frankel, *The Damascus Affair: "Ritual Murder," Politics, and the Jews in 1840* (Cambridge: Cambridge University Press, 1997).

6. Reinhard Rürup, "Jewish Emancipation and Bourgeois Society," *LBIYB* 14 (1969): 67-91.

7. Isaak M. Jost, *Offenes Sendschreiben an Herrn Geh. Ober-Regierungs-Rath K. Streckfuss zur Verständigung über einige Punkte in den Verhältnissen der Juden* (Berlin: Lückritz, 1833), 65.

8. Zunz, *Die gottesdienstlichen Vorträge der Juden,* 2 and 5. This was also singled out as Zunz's accomplishment in the review in *AZJ* 5 (1841): 106-7.

9. See the chapter "Organismus der Haggada," *Die gottesdienstlichen Vorträge der Juden,* ed. Zunz, 304-29. See also Schorsch, *From Text to Context,* 247; and Niehoff, "Zunz's Concept of Haggadah as an Expression of Jewish Spirituality," 3-24.

10. Isaak M. Jost, *Allgemeine Geschichte des israelitischen Volkes, sowohl seines zweimaligen Staatslebens als auch der zerstreuten Gemeinden und Sekten, bis in die neueste Zeit in gedrängter Uebersicht, zunächst für Staatsmänner, Rechtsgelehrte, Geistliche und wissenschaftlich gebildete Leser, aus den Quellen bearbeitet,* 2 vols. (Berlin: Amelang, 1832).

11. See the review in *Der Jude* 1 (1832): 94-96.

12. See Abraham Geiger's review of Jost's *Allgemeine Geschichte des israelitischen Volkes* in *WZjT* 1 (1835): 169-82 and *WZjT* 2 (1836): 504-18 and 565, here 180, as well as Jost's rejoinder. Isaak M. Jost, "Beitrag zur jüdischen Geschichte und Bibliographie," *WZjT* 1 (1835): 358-66. See also Heinemann Jolowicz, "Eine neue Ansicht über die Entwicklungsgeschichte des Judentums," *Der Israelit des 19. Jahrhunderts* 2 (1841): 177-78, 181-83, 185-87, and 189-90. The neglect of cultural history was also criticized in respect to Isaak M. Jost's *Neuere Geschichte der Israeliten von 1815 bis 1845,* 3 vols. (Breslau: Jacobsohn, 1846-47). See the review in *Literaturblatt des Orients* 9 (1846): 129-34.

13. The first volume that appeared in 1847 covered only the period from the destruction of the First Temple up to Esra. Levi Herzfeld, *Geschichte des Volkes Israel von der Zerstörung des ersten Tempels bis zur Einsetzung des Makkabäers Schimon zum Hohen Priester und Fürsten,* 3 vols. (Braunschweig-Nordhausen: Westermann, 1847-57). See also Schorsch, *From Text to Context,* 320-21.

14. The term "Golden Age" stems from Franz Delitzsch, *Zur Geschichte der jüdischen Poesie vom Abschluss der heiligen Schriften des Alten Bundes bis auf die neueste Zeit* (Leipzig: Tauchnitz, 1836), 44, in which he describes the period from 940 to 1040 as the Golden Age of Jewish poetic creation.

15. Zacharias Frankel, *Die Eidesleistung der Juden in theologischer und historischer Beziehung* (Dresden: Arnold, 1840); Zacharias Frankel, *Der gerichtliche Beweis nach mosaisch-talmudischen Rechte. Ein Beitrag zur Kenntniss des mosaisch-talmudischen Criminal-und Civilrechts. Nebst Untersuchungen über die Preussischen Gesetzgebung hinsichtlich der Zeugnisse der Juden* (Berlin: Veit, 1846); and Abraham Geiger, *Lehr- und Lesebuch zur Sprache der Mischna* (Breslau: Leuckart, 1845).

16. Avraham Barkai, "The German Jews at the Start of the Industrialization: Structural Change and Mobility, 1835-1860," *Revolution and Evolution: 1848 in German-Jewish History,* ed. Werner E. Mosse, Arnold Paucker, and Reinhard Rürup (Tübingen: J. C. B. Mohr, 1981), 123-49; and Steven Lowenstein, "The Rural Community and the Urbanization of German Jewry," *Central European History* 8 (1980): 218-36.

17. "Baiersdorf," *AZJ* 1 (1837): 453-54; and Aron Tänzer, *Die Geschichte der Juden in Jebenhausen*

und Göppingen: Mit erweiternden Beiträgen über Schicksal und Ende der Göppinger Judengemeinde 1927-1945, ed. Karl-Heinz Rueß (Weissenhorn: Konrad, 1988), 237.

18. "Breslau," *AZJ* 10 (1846): 52 and 333; "Breslau," 5 (1844): 355-56; and "Breslau," *AZJ* 25 (1861): 223-24. Heinrich Graetz wrote several short articles on the Association. His attitude toward it changed during the course of a year from admiration to sharp criticism. This change of heart was probably partly due to Abraham Geiger's central role in the society. See [Heinrich Graetz], "Breslau," *Orient* 4 (1843): 212, 222-23, and 229-30; and "Breslau," *Orient* 5 (1844): 179-81 and 355-56. See also L. Geiger, *Abraham Geiger,* 129.

19. Ludwig Philippson, "Prospectus," *AZJ* 1 (1837); and "Geschichte: Zur Geschichte der Juden," *AZJ* 2 (1838), 153-55.

20. Isaac M. Jost, "Vorwort," *Israelitische Annalen* 1 (1839): 1-2; and "Ein Wort zur Verständigung über die Tendenz der Annalen vom Herausgeber," *Israelitische Annalen* 1 (1839): 3-6. See Julius Fürst, "Vorwort," *Der Orient* 1 (1840): vi-vii.

21. See the letter to Philipp Ehrenberg from November 1, 1841, in the Isaac Jost Collection, LBI-AR 4294; and Joachim Kirchner, *Das deutsche Zeitschriftenwesen, seine Geschichte und seine Probleme,* 2 vols. (Wiesbaden: Harrassowitz, 1962), 2: 147.

22. Cited after Ludwig Geiger's unpublished manuscript, "Briefe von Leopold Zunz an S. M. Ehrenberg, Philipp Ehrenberg und M. Isler (1916)" in the Leopold Zunz Collection, JNUL 4° 792 V2, 54.

23. See the letter to S. M. Ehrenberg, March 27, 1832, in *Leopold Zunz,* ed. Glatzer, 160.

24. See Jost's letter to Philipp Ehrenberg from November 1, 1841, in the Isaak Jost Collection, LBI-AR 4294; Glatzer, *Leopold Zunz,* 160 and 437; and Schorsch, *From Text to Context,* 236. My reading differs from Schorsch's in respect to Jost. See also Leopold Zunz, *Das Buch Zunz künftigen ehrlichen Leuten gewidmet* in the Leopold Zunz Collection, JNUL 4° 792/C-13, 73d.

25. Ludwig Geiger, "Zunz im Verkehr mit Behörden und Hochgestellten," *MGWJ* 60 (1916): 245-62 and 321-47, here 254-56.

26. See the partial reprint in Ludwig Philippson, "Vorlesungen über Geschichte, Inhalt, Stellung und Beruf des Judenthums," *AZJ* 11 (1847): 1-4, 17-20, 33-37, 49-54, 68-72, 81-86, 97-100, 113-16, and 126-29, which finally appeared as *Die Entwicklung der religiöesen Idee im Judenthume,* *Christenthum und Islam* (Leipzig: Baumgärtner, 1847). See also Kayserling, *Ludwig Philippson: Ein Biographie* (Leipzig: H. Mendelssohn, 1898), 132-34 and 141-45, on the public reception of the lectures and the book that was translated into French and English.

27. "Aufforderung zur Gründung eines israelitischen Literaturvereins," *AZJ* 7 (1843): 334-35; "Der israelitische Kulturverein," *AZJ* 7 (1843): 362-63 and 438; "Der Literaturverein," *AZJ* 7 (1843): 707; and "Aus Württemberg," *AZJ* 8 (1844): 433-34. See also Moritz Kayserling, *Ludwig Philippson: Eine Biographie,* 252.

28. "Der Cultur-Verein zu Berlin," *Israelitische Annalen* 3 (1841): 177-79, here 178, and the documents pertaining to the *Kulturverein* in the Leopold Zunz Collection, JNUL 4° 792/C1.

29. "Der Cultur-Verein zu Berlin," *Israelitische Annalen* 23 (1841): 177-79; "Berlin," *Der Orient* 3 (1842): 139-41; "Berlin," *AZJ* 7 (1843): 579-80; "Berlin," *Der Orient* 4 (1843): 305-6; and "Berlin," *Der Orient* 5 (1844): 252-54 and 259-61.

30. See the letter by Zunz to Bernhard Beer from December 13, 1841, in Glatzer, *Leopold Zunz,* 218. See also Leopold Zunz, *Das Buch Zunz künftigen ehrlichen Leuten gewidmet* in the Leopold Zunz Collection, JNUL 4° 792/C-13, 96.

31. As early as 1844 Zunz wrote to Steinschneider that the association was in crisis. See Alexander Marx, "Zunz's Letters to Steinschneider," *PAAJR* 5 (1933-34): 95-153, here 124. See also "Berlin," *AZJ* 8 (1848): 247; "Berlin," *AZJ* 11 (1847): 299; and "Der Verein zur Unterstützung der jüdischen Lehrer in Preußen," *AZJ* 20 (1856): 31-33.

32. Cohn, "Die Nothwendigkeit religiöeser Volks- und Jugendschriften," *WZjT* 4 (1839): 26-35, here 29-30.

33. Ephraim Willstätter, *Allgemeine Geschichte des Israelitischen Volkes. Von der Entstehung desselben bis auf unsere Zeit. Ein kurzer Abriß nach den vorliegenden Quellen und größern Werken der Geschichte für die ersten Klassen israelitischer Elementarschulen und zum Selbtstudium bearbeitet* (Karlsruhe: Marx, 1836), v, vii, and ix; and Moses Elkan, *Leitfaden beim Unterricht in der Geschichte der Israeliten, nebst einem kurzen Abriß der Geographie Palaestinas für israelitische Schulen* (Minden: F. Essmann, 1839). See also Hermann Baerwald, "Welchen Nutzen gewährt uns das Studium der Geschichte?" (1846) in the Hermann Baerwald Collection, Leo Baeck Institute, New York, AR 744; and *Literaturblatt des Orients* 3 (March 5, 1842): 156-57, here 157.

34. Willstätter, *Allgemeine Geschichte des Israelitischen Volkes,* v-xvii.

35. *Literarisches und homilitisches Beiblatt der AZJ* 3 (1839) 10: 39-40 and 11: 41; *ZrIJ* 2 (1845): 428-29; and *Literaturblatt des Orients* 3 (March 5, 1842): 156-57.

36. *ZrIJ* 2 (1845): 428-29. Jost's *Israelitische Annalen* and the *Orient* reviewed Elkan's textbook more favorably. See *Israelitische Annalen* 1 (1839): 16; and *Literaturblatt des Orients* 3 (1842): 156-57.

37. The book was republished in 1845, 1850, 1855, 1861, and 1870. In 1846 Julius Heinrich Dessauer published a new textbook history. However, he was attacked for plagiarism and the book was reprinted only once in 1870. See Julius Heinrich Dessauer, *Geschichte der Israeliten mit besonderer Berücksichtigung der Kulturgeschichte derselben. Von Alexander dem Großen bis auf gegenwärtige Zeit. Nach den besten vorhandenen Quellen bearbeitet* (Erlangen: Palm, 1846). For the harsh reviews, see *ZrIJ* 3 (1846): 35-40, 72-80, and 156-60 and the rejoinder by Dessauer in *ZrIJ* 3 (1846): 479-84.

38. Wolf Landau, "Wie soll der Religionsunterricht der israelitischen Jugend in unserer Zeit beschaffen sein," *ZrIJ* 1 (1844): 27-36, 73-76, and 129-41, which does not even refer to postbiblical history or any of the already existing textbooks. See the survey of Jewish schools in Franconia "Über das israel. Schulwesen im mittelfränkischen Kreise Baierns," *Israelitische Annalen* 2 (1840): 101-3, which refers only to biblical history. Four years later, several schools in Unterfranken, such as Aschaffenburg, Kissingen, and Niederwerren, introduced postbiblical Jewish history, which, however, was still grouped as "Jewish—especially biblical history." See "Unterfranken," *Der Orient* 5 (1844): 139-40. In contrast, the draft for the *Lehrplan* in Nassau that followed the model of Wiesbaden already included post-biblical history. For instruction in this field, Elkan's textbook is mentioned as is Zunz's timetable of biblical history. In addition to the weekly instruction in Jewish history, the studies on the Sabbath were also meant to include lectures about Jewish history using Jost's *Allgemeine Geschichte des israelitischen Volkes.* See "Nassau," *Der Orient* 3 (1842): 355-57, here 356, and "Goch," *AZJ* 15 (1851): 46-47, where Elkan's textbook is also used.

39. Zunz, *Die gottesdienstlichen Vorträge der Juden,* 450 and 479.

40. Jost, *Allgemeine Geschichte des israelitischen Volkes.*

41. Abraham Geiger, "Jüdische Zeitschriften," *WZjT* 4 (1839): 286-92, and 459-71; and 5 (1844): 372-90 and 447-77, here 466-67. See also Geiger's response to Cohn's suggestion in *WZjT* 4 (1839): 35-36.

42. Steven M. Lowenstein, "The 1840s and the Creation of the German-Jewish Religious Reform Movement," *Revolution and Evolution,* ed. Mosse, Paucker, and Rürup, 255-97.

43. *Protokolle der ersten Rabbiner-Versammlung, abgehalten zu Braunschweig* (Brunswick: Vieweg, 1844), 61; and *Protokolle und Aktenstücke der zweiten Rabbiner-Versammlung, abgehalten zu Frankfurt am Main* (Frankfurt a. M.: E. Ullmann, 1845), 74.

44. Zacharias Frankel, "Ueber Reformen im Judenthume," *ZrIJ* 1 (1844): 3-27, and "Nachbemerkungen des Herausgebers," *ZrIJ* 1 (1844): 60-73.

45. See the letter by Michael Sachs to Moritz Veit from March 17, 1840, in *Michael Sachs und Moritz Veit: Briefwechsel,* ed. Ludwig Geiger (Frankfurt a. M.: Kauffmann, 1897), 35. See also Michael Sachs's criticism of Abraham Geiger's scholarship in the introduction to Sachs's *Die religiöse Poesie der Juden in Spanien* (Berlin: Veit und Camp, 1845), 160-64 and 195.

46. Leopold Zunz, "Gutachten über die Beschneidung (1844)," *Gesammelte Schriften,* 3 vols. (Berlin: Gerschel, 1875-76), 2:191-203; and Ludwig Geiger's appendix to the unpublished manuscript, "Briefe von Leopold Zunz an S. M. Ehrenberg, Philipp Ehrenberg and M. Isler" (1916) in the Leopold Zunz Collection, JNUL 4° 792 V2, 115-16.

47. Zunz, "Gutachten über die Beschneidung (1844)," *Gesammelte Schriften,* 2:191-203. For the critical responses, see "Zunz, Gutachten über die Beschneidung," *Der Israelit des 19. Jahrhunderts* 5 (1844): 221-25 and 253-55. Zunz's statements were praised on the other hand in the Conservative press. See Cassel, "Gutachten über die Beschneidung von Dr. Zunz," *ZrIJ* 1 (1844): 240-44.

48. Zunz, "Gutachten über die Beschneidung (1844)," 196. See Zunz's otherwise unknown letter from 1846 to Abraham Geiger in Ludwig Geiger's unpublished manuscript, "Briefe von Leopold Zunz" (1916) in the Leopold Zunz Collection, JNUL 4° 792 V2, 119, as well as Abraham Geiger's letter to Zunz Geiger, *Abraham Geiger's nachgelassene Schriften,* 5 vols. (Berlin: L. Gerschel, 1875-78), 5: 180-85.

49. Leopold Zunz, *Zur Geschichte und Literatur* (Berlin: Veit, 1845), 3, 17, 158, and 28. See also Schorsch, *From Text to Context,* 277; and the critical review by Abraham Geiger, "Zur Geschichte und Literatur von Dr. Zunz, Literaturblatt," *Der Israelit des 19. Jahrhunderts* 7 (1846): 2-4, 65-68, 69-72, 78-80, and 81-82.

50. Meyer, *Response to Modernity,* 113.

51. S. Formstecher, *Die Religion des Geistes: Eine wissenschaftliche Darstellung des Judentums nach seinem Charakter, Entwicklungsgängen und Berufen in der Menschheit* (Frankfurt a. M.: Joh. Chr. Hermann'sche Buchhandlung, 1841), esp. 197, 204-10, and 312-15; Samuel Hirsch, *Die Religionsphilosophie der Juden oder das Prinzip der jüdischen Religionsanschauung und sein Verhältnis zum Heidenthum, Christenthum und zur absoluten Philosophie* (Leipzig: Hunger, 1842), xv-xxxii, and 457-528; and L. Steinheim, *Die Offenbarung nach dem Lehrbegriffe der Synagoge*, 4. vols. (Frankfurt a. M., 1835-1865), esp. 1:17-31. See also Meyer, *Response to Modernity*, 67-74; and Aharon Shear-Yashuv, *The Theology of Salmon Ludwig Steinheim* (Leiden: E. J. Brill, 1986).

52. See Jost's letter to S. M. Ehrenberg from 1852 in Nahum N. Glatzer, "Aus unveröffentlichten Briefen von I. M. Jost," *In zwei Welten: Siegfried Moses zum fünfundsiebzigsten Geburtstag*, ed. Hans Tramer (Tel Aviv: Verlag Bitaon, 1962), 400-13, here 405.

53. Moses Brück, *Rabbinische Ceremonialgebräuche in ihrer Entstehung und geschichtlichen Entwicklung* (Breslau: A. Schulz, 1837). See Abraham Geiger's review in *WZjT* 3 (1837): 413-26; Meyer, *Response to Modernity*, 160; and Andreas Gotzmann, *Jüdisches Recht im kulturellen Prozeß: Die Wahrnehmung der Halacha im Deutschland des 19. Jahrhunderts* (Tübingen: J. C. B. Mohr, 1997), 177-83.

54. Ludwig Geiger, "Abraham Geigers Briefe an J. Derenbourg (1833-1842)," *AZJ* 60 (1896): 164-66, here 165; and Michael Meyer, "Abrahams Geiger's Historical Judaism," *New Perspective on Abraham Geiger: An HUC-JIR Symposium*, ed. Jacob J. Petuchowski (Cincinnati: Ktav Pub. House, 1975), 3-16.

55. Abraham Geiger, "Die zwei verschiedenen Betrachtungsweisen: Der Schriftsteller und der Rabbiner," *WZjT* 4 (1839): 321-33; "Jüdische Zeitschriften," *WZjT* 4 (1839): 286-92, 459-71; and 5 (1844): 372-39, here 374-75; and "Einleitung in das Studium der jüdischen Theologie," *Abraham Geiger's nachgelassene Schriften*, 5 vols., ed. Ludwig Geiger (Berlin: L. Gerschel, 1875-1878), 2: 1-31, here 5.

56. Heinrich Graetz, "Die Construktion der jüdischen Geschichte," *ZrIJ* 3 (1846): 81-97, 121-32, 361-81, and 413-21. In the following, the edition by Feuchtwanger is cited. Heinrich Graetz, *Die Konstruktion der jüdischen Geschichte*, ed. Ludwig Feuchtwanger (Berlin: Schocken Verlag, 1936), 8.

57. Ibid., 10; and Geiger, "Einleitung in das Studium der jüdischen Theologie," 4-6.

58. Graetz, *Die Konstruktion der jüdischen Geschichte*, 93.

59. Ibid., 49; and Zunz, *Zur Geschichte und Literatur*, 17-21.

60. Schorsch, *From Text to Context*, 284.

61. Graetz, *Die Konstruktion der jüdischen Geschichte*, 49.

62. Abraham Geiger, *Was hat Mohammed aus dem Judentume aufgenommen? Königl. Preussische Rheinuniversität gekrönte Preisschrift* (Bonn: F. Baaden, 1833); and Heschel, *Abraham Geiger and the Jewish Jesus*, 50-75.

63. Heinrich Heine, "Shakespeares Mädchen und Frauen," *Heinrich Heine: Sämtliche Schriften*, ed. Klaus Briegleb, 7 vols. (München: Deutscher Taschenbuch Verlag, 1997), 4: 171-293, here 258. The English translation is quoted here from *The Poetry and Prose of Heinrich Heine*, ed. Frederic Ewen (New York: Citadel Press, 1948), 678.

64. Ludwig Philippson *Die Entwicklung der religiösen Idee im Judenthume, Christenthum und Islam*. The book was republished in 1874. See also Ludwig Philippson, "Geschichte und Vernunft: Ein Gespräch," *AZJ* 14 (1850): 481-83, 511-14, 602-3, and 630-31, here 631.

65. Abraham Geiger, "Die Gründung einer jüdisch-theologischen Fakultät, ein dringendes Bedürfniss unserer Zeit," *WZjT* 2 (1836): 1-21.

66. Salo Wittmeyer Baron, "Jewish Studies at Universities: An Early Project," *HUCA* 46 (1975): 357-76, here 358-59.

67. Monika Richarz, *Der Eintritt der Juden in die akademischen Berufe: Jüdische Studenten und Akademiker in Deutschland, 1678-1848* (Tübingen: J. C. B. Mohr, 1974), 234-37.

68. Ludwig Geiger, "Zunz im Verkehr mit Behörden und Hochgestellten," 338. See also Alfred Jospe, "The Study of Judaism in German Universities before 1933," *LBIYB* 27 (1982): 295-313; and Baron, "Jewish Studies at Universities: An Early Project," 373.

69. Ludwig Philippson, "Aufforderung an alle Israeliten Deutschlands zu Subskriptionen, um eine jüdische Facultät und ein jüdisches Seminar für Deutschland zu begründen," *AZJ* 1 (1837): 349-51.

70. Abraham Geiger, *Ueber die Errichtung einer jüdisch-theologischen Facultät* (Wiesbaden: L. Riedel, 1838); and "Die Errichtung einer jüdisch-theologischen Facultät," *WZjT* 4 (1839): 309-12. See also his letter from January 18, 1838, to M.

Creizenach in *Abraham Geiger's nachgelassene Schriften*, ed. Geiger, 5: 104; Meyer Isler, "Bemerkungen über die Errichtung einer jüdisch-theologischen Facultät," *AZJ* 2 (1839): 153-55, 157-60, and 162-64. Samuel Holdheim delivered a sermon in support of the plan on Shabbat Hanukkah (December 23, 1837). A lengthy excerpt of the sermon appeared in "Die jüdisch-theologische Facultät und das jüdische Seminar für Deutschland," *AZJ* 2 (1838): 58-59.

71. "Liste der Subskribenten zur Begründung einer jüdischen Facultät und eines jüdischen Seminars," *AZJ* 1 (1837): 465-66; 2 (1838): 7-8, 10-11, 19-20, 22-23, 39, 50-51, 71-72, 89-91, 119, 129, 139-40, 167-68, 176, 205-8, 215-16, 222-24, 266-67, 279, 282, 302, 313, 339, 351-53, 372-73, 400-401, 437-38, and 495-96. See Salo W. Baron, "Jewish Studies at Universities: An Early Project," 365.

Abbreviations

AZJ	*Allgemeine Zeitung des Judenthums*
HUCA	*Hebrew Union College Annual*
LBI-AR	Leo Baeck Institute—Catalog Number
LBIYB	*Leo Baeck Institute Yearbook*
JNUL	Jewish National and University Library
MGWJ	*Monatsschrift für Geschichte und Wissenschaft des Judentums*
PAAJR	Proceedings of the American Academy of Jewish Research
WZjT	*Wissenschaftliche Zeitschrift für jüdische Theologie*
ZrIJ	*Zeitschrift für die religiösen Interessen des Judentums*

TREATMENT OF ZIONISM

Thomas L. Ashton (essay date fall 1972)

SOURCE: Ashton, Thomas L. "Byronic Lyrics for David's Harp: The *Hebrew Melodies*." *Studies in English Literature, 1500-1900* 12, no. 4 (fall 1972): 665-81.

[*In the following essay, Ashton discusses Byron's blending of myth, Jewish nationalism, and the "monumental" to create metaphors of man and of man's condition in his* Hebrew Melodies.]

"How the devil should I write about *Jerusalem,* never having yet been there?" quipped Byron in 1816.[1] He found no irony in his having written about Jerusalem only the year before in the *Hebrew Melodies*. Childe Harold had not journeyed to the Temple: The *Hebrew Melodies* are not a collection of hymns or psalms brimming with the faith of the Old Testament. They are merely thirty poems Byron wrote at various times during 1814 and 1815 and then gave to Isaac Nathan (or intended to do so), who in turn set them to music. But it is just this fact that binds the poems together, for they share in the essential unity of Byron's lyric corpus. The Biblical poems are *Byronic*. In their own peculiar way, they almost seem to be a later edition of Byron's *Hours of Idleness,* his best known collection of lyrics.

The First Number of *A Selection of Hebrew Melodies,* bringing together the music of Nathan and the poetry of Byron, was published 6 April 1815. (Shortly thereafter, in May, John Murray published a volume containing only Byron's poems, but misleadingly titled *Hebrew Melodies,* thus accounting for the confusing title by which Byron's *lyrics* have come to be known.) National melodies, made palatable by contemporary composers and poets, were in vogue, and Nathan hoped to profit from the popular taste for the ancient, the sublime, and the nationalistic. By 20 October 1814, Byron had started on the poems. First he gave Nathan some secular love lyrics that he had written in the spring and summer of 1814. Then, warming to the composer, he provided some vaguely Jewish poems. Finally, after marriage to his reforming angel, he sent poems dealing directly with Old Testament subjects. Nathan rejected none of this mixed but valuable gift. He knew better than the pious who hoped to find sacred poetry by Lord Byron in the *Hebrew Melodies*. Only a year earlier, Byron had elaborated on his themes in a letter to Annabella: "I do not believe that there be 50 lines of mine in all touching upon religion."[2] The *Hebrew Melodies* added little to that figure.

"Of Religion I know nothing, at least in its *favour*," wrote Byron to Edward Long in 1807.[3] Four years later he turned to shocking his conservative friend Francis Hodgson, whose attempt to purge the second canto of *Childe Harold's Pilgrimage* was unsuccessful. William Gifford, Murray's editor, was more able. To Gifford, Byron wrote in 1813: "To your advice on Religious topics, I shall equally attend. Perhaps the best way will be by avoiding them altogether."[4] But the *Hebrew Melodies* are not at all free from one kind of peculiarly Byronic religious sentiment. In the same letter, Byron told Gifford that he had attended "a Calvinistic Scotch school where I was cudgelled to Church for the first ten years of my life." What he learned there he did not forget. Annabella believed that his "early Calvinistic impressions, and later Oriental observations, had tended to infix in his mind" what she called a "dark predestinarianism."[5] The Old Testament strain of Byron's *Hebrew Melodies* is bound up with his Calvinistic fatalism. Byron could never accept the full import of his Calvinism.

But he does not spare us the plangent sorrow of the Old Testament wailing complaints. No wonder Annabella called the *Hebrew Melodies* "his gloomy compositions."[6]

If Byron rejected the faiths of Calvinists and Jews as a theme, he did not reject the Bible per se. "Of the Scriptures themselves I have ever been a reader & admirer as compositions, particularly the Arab-Job—and parts of Isaiah—and the song of Deborah," he wrote to Annabella in 1814.[7] The selection is significant: "Arab" Job for the infidel Calvinist, Deborah for its archaic expression and militancy, and Isaiah for its nationalism. These were just the strains to be interwoven in the *Hebrew Melodies,* where the sacred would be sacrificed to the political and the political to the romantic. But where Byron was outright in his rejection of piety, he did not entirely eschew the conventions of the national melodies genre.

Tom Moore helped to create the national melodies style, and Byron learned that style and its meaning from him. The suppressed preface to the Second Number of the *Irish Melodies* explains the politics of those lyrics:

> The annals of Ireland, through a long lapse of six hundred years, exhibit not one of those themes of national pride, from which poetry borrows her noblest inspiration; and *that* history which ought to be the richest garden of the Muse, yields nothing to her but weeds and cypress! . . . The language of sorrow however, is, in general, best suited to our music, and with themes of this nature the poet may be amply supplied. There is not a page of our annals which cannot afford him a subject; and while the National Muse of other countries adorns her temple with trophies of the past, in Ireland, her altar, like the shrine of Pity at Athens, is to be known only by the tears that are shed upon it![8]

The fall from idealized Past occurred so long ago that Irish history affords little material for instilling national pride in the men of the "debased" Present. That is the first task of the national melodist. The lack of triumphal themes and a musical tradition congenial to lamentation turn the Irish melodist into a weeping elegist. This is the meaning of Moore's "Oh! blame not the bard." What else can he do but weep? Irish melodies meant tears as well as pride, and Byron learned of this fusion from them. In the *Hebrew Melodies* he put it to his own use.

Byron joined the national melodies style he learned from Moore and the Jews he read about in the Bible to write the Jacobin airs of old Zion. Irish, Greeks, and Jews were all equally downtrodden: "The Greeks . . . have as small a chance of redemption from the Turks, as the Jews have from mankind in general," wrote Byron.[9] He was not alone in his comparisons; Moore's "The Parallel" is an Irish Melody which compares the Irish and the Jews and finds both their fates miserable. Nor was using the Bible for the purpose of political al-

legory unheard of in Byron's day or any other. Byron's concern for Jewish nationalism was sincere, and in Ravenna in 1820, he was willing to see contemporary events in the light of that cause. To Murray, he wrote when the Austrian armies seemed to be about to cross the Italian border:

> Our "puir hill folk" offered to strike, and raise the first banner, but Bologna paused; and now 'tis autumn and the season half over. "O Jerusalem! Jerusalem!" The Huns are on the Po; but if they once pass it on their way to Naples, all Italy will be behind them. The Dogs—the Wolves—may they perish like the Host of Sennacherib![10]

Byron the national melodist looked at the politics of the Bible in just this way. But the man of causes was not a man of the proletariat. Commoners had his sympathy as the "enslaved," but not as the "mob." Byron's split posture is evident in another of his remarks:

> I love the cause of liberty, which is that of the Greek nation, although I despise the present race of Greeks, even while I pity them. . . . I am nearly reconciled to St. Paul, for he says, there is no difference between the Jews and the Greeks, and I am exactly of the same opinion, for the character of both is equally vile.[11]

Byron's differentiation of the "cause" and the "Greeks" suggests that his lyrics would ultimately be truest to his uniquely romantic consciousness. The Jews would feature in metaphor serving the higher cause of Promethean liberty. While Byron's espousal was sincere, its expression was consistently Byronic. The *Hebrew Melodies* would be more than an occasion for taking political potshots at the Prince Regent by calling him Herod or Belshazzar.

Byron put together nationalism and Jews to write poems about Jewish nationalism, but in those poems, he joined Jewish nationalism and a Calvinistically inclined understanding of the Old Testament to create metaphors of man and of man's condition. In the plight of the exiled Jews, Byron found man's plight, and the tears he shed for fallen nationhood were shed for fallen man as well. "For Byron the homeless Jews wandering in strange lands, whom not even death can reunite, are symbolic of man—just as the modern Greek, enslaved and cowed, is also man," writes Robert Gleckner.[12] Leslie Marchand concurs in part: "Two themes that were congenial to Byron's spirit dominate the lyrics derived from Old Testament sources: one is the deep pathos of the loss of Eden, the wail of a wandering and homeless people, and the other the battle cry of Jewish nationalism. The lost Eden was easily identified in Byron's feelings with the general romantic lament for lost innocence and beauty."[13] Battle cry and wail, the fused sounds of Moore's preface, are merely different sides of the same romantic coin. When Byron gives in to melancholy, life is all darkness and limits. But he remains romantic: condemned to a fallen world, he is not without anger and defiance. Byron was a rebel with a keen awareness of man's limitations. Those limitations made him both rebellious and melancholy. But Byron does not challenge human action by calling it absurd. In the *Hebrew Melodies,* he builds a myth in which Promethean love, negating self-consciousness, mediates real and ideal. His Prometheanism, regardless of its success or failure, turns its back on the fallen state without an exit.

II

The *Hebrew Melodies* are dominated by melancholy and defiance. These feelings define the poles of Byron's response to life *at the time of their writing*. As we have seen, these responses are perfectly suited to the national melodies style, with its emphasis on elegy and heroism, and to the "certain wildness and pathos" that had "become the chief characteristic of the Sacred Songs of the Jews,"[14] and they are thoroughly compatible with romantic consciousness fed on nostalgia and Prometheanism. Recognizing this, we can perceive the Byronic symmetry of the universe of the *Hebrew Melodies.* To Eden soar the generous Promethean heroes; from it fall the selfish tyrants; the fallen lament it, and the beautiful dwell in it. This symmetry is apparent in Byron's version of the Books of Samuel: "Saul," "My Soul is Dark," "The harp the monarch minstrel swept," and the "Song of Saul Before His Last Battle." These poems on Saul and David show us the universe of the *Hebrew Melodies* in microcosm and reveal the essential unity of Byron's vision.

In *Don Juan,* we are told that Samuel rose from the grave "to freeze once more / The blood of monarchs with his prophecies." In the *Hebrew Melodies,* he does just that; all the monarchs of those lyrics (except David) "fall." That word becomes a commonplace describing their fate. While the peculiarities of individual lots need to be accounted for, it is important to recognize Byron's archetype. Nor can we ignore the emphasis on fall by vision or spiritual agency: Saul sees Samuel, Belshazzar sees the handwriting on the wall, the host of Sennacherib is destroyed by the "angel of death," Herod is haunted by the ghost of Mariamne, and Eliphaz the Temanite is chilled by the "Spirit" who passed before him. Men do not overthrow Byron's tyrants; they are destroyed by the specter of their own radical selfishness. In a world of death, selfish pride (expressed as political tyranny) is a sin, because it is an enemy of the love upon which Byron's heavenly "high world" rests. Looking back at the past is as dangerous as looking into the future. In the *Hebrew Melodies,* fall by vision is extended to all men by being equated with fall by memory. Both hope and memory delude man. The "future cheats" him as its hope declines into the fallen present:

> Nor can we be what we recall,
> Nor dare we think on what we are.

Just "what we are" is what Samuel arises to tell Saul. Byron's description of the prophet makes his point: "glassy," "shroud," "withered," "dry," "bony," "shrunken," "sinewless," and "ghastly bare." "Death" stands in Samuel's "fixed eye," because Samuel is death personified. "Saul saw, and fell." Stretched on the ground, he listens to the prophecy: suicide for Saul, and death for Jonathan.

> Crownless, breathless, headless fall,
> Son and sire, the house of Saul!

This is not very different from Daniel's explanation ("Vision of Belshazzar") of the handwriting on the wall:

> Belshazzar's grave is made,
> His kingdom passed away.

Tyrants provide for their own decay ("made"), and the only "kingdom" they inherit is the "grave." Their selfishness is ironic, for ultimately it destroys what it most desires. Thus Herod casts himself down, by his tyrannical destruction of an ideal Mariamne. Because he is the object of his own selfish pity, there is no reference to tears in his "lament." His craving after the ideal is in vain precisely because it is vain. So his tortures are "unconsumed" and "still consuming." Selfhood generates an ironic, frustrating, tyrannous cycle of possession and destruction, unless it is redefined in Promethean terms. This is also the point of "All is Vanity, Saith the Preacher." There the repetition of possessives ("mine" and "my") reveals the vanity at the core of Ecclesiastes's lament. So a "serpent" holds his selfish heart in a symbolic vise-like grip. His many-splendored world galls while it glitters; ironically, Ecclesiastes can recall "no day" of "pleasure unembittered." In "They say that Hope is happiness," we learn why. Memory was hope; now hope is memory because there is nothing to hope for. So in "Sun of the Sleepless," memory is a distant star whose "tremulous" gleam and "cold" light are ironically "distinct but distant," revealing only "what we are."

Selfishness is ironically self-defeating, and in a mutable universe it is doubly so. Sennacherib, "the Assyrian" who "came down," proves this by destroying himself. His fall is as determined as that of a "wolf" leaping into a fold and a "wave" rolling "on deep Galilee." Concentrating the troops into a single rider, Byron dramatizes the fall of the host. This wolf is found lying dead on the ground with "rust on his mail." The wave expires "as the spray of the rock-beating surf," that echoes in the "foam" of the dead steed's last gasp. Sennacherib's destruction stems from the impermanence of human action:[15]

> Like the leaves of the forest when Summer is green,
> That host with their banners at sunset were seen:

Like the leaves of the forest when Autumn hath blown,
That host on the morrow lay withered and strown.

The initial repetition fosters the cycle that is the eventual victor. The falling leaves and the sunset are natural prophecies of the fall of the selfish. All too soon the "banners" are "alone," the "host" has "withered," and the "shining spears" have become rusty "lances unlifted."

Eliphaz the Temanite (one of the "sleepless") meets with Byron's final vision of "what we are." In that vision the twin ironies of selfishness are revealed at once. As in "Saul," initial emphasis is placed on the appearance of the Spirit. Eliphaz beholds "the face of Immortality unveiled." Ironically, that face is "formless." Ultimately *nothing* is unveiled in Byron's dark lyric. The "insecure" Seraph's speech tells us that men are "creatures of clay" who dwell in vain "in the dust!" Because the "clay" (a familiar metaphor) is unenkindled, only the "moth" soars in "From Job." "Surviving" man, it is a symbol of both human insignificance and the futility of selfish aspiration. Wisdom's light is "wasted," because men and moths waste it, and because it resembles the light of the "Sun of the Sleepless."

The dimly-lit, fallen world revealed to Eliphaz may be redeemed. The subsequent history of Saul, made mythic by Byron, makes this clear. "My Soul is Dark" dramatizes I Samuel 16:14-23, the account of David's easing of Saul's melancholy. Though this Biblical episode preceded the raising up of Samuel, it is convenient to think of it as following that event, and to understand Saul's melancholy as stemming from Samuel's prophecy of doom. The heroism proven in the "Song of Saul Before His Last Battle" will then be seen to stem from the inspiration of "the harp the monarch minstrel swept." The evil spirit plaguing Saul is the romantic agony. Because Saul has found out "what we are," Byron tells us that his "heart" has been "doomed to know the worst." To purge this "heavy heart" Music's "sound" shall "charm" forth hope. But only "if in this heart a hope be dear." Only then will David's "melting" strains give rise to the tears that metaphorically quench the melancholic flames which "burn" Saul's "brain." The emphasis falls heavily on the *heart,* for it is ultimately the heart that must restore the fallen universe which the brain forges. When the heart is *wrought to sympathy,* self-consciousness is vitiated. The success of the catharsis depends on Promethean selflessness attested to by genuine weeping.[16] Music is not so much cause as effect: Harmony is a symbol of the mediation suggested by "melting." "My Soul is Dark" is a Hebrew Melody about the cathartic role of Hebrew melodies.

The weeping harpers of Byron's sighing versions of Psalm 137 resemble Saul more than David. But "By the Rivers of Babylon" shows us again that tears are just what is needed. The unconstrained waters of Babylon "which rolled on in freedom below" make an ironic comment on the fall of the captive harpers. Reflection leads to weeping. But though the river's freedom saddens, the expression of that sadness in wailing complaint is immediately followed by defiance drawing its inspiration from the recognition of that natural freedom. The harp of Judah, no aeolian harp, is suspended on the willow. "Its sound should be free" defiantly exclaims the harpist. (The evolution of courage out of tears is emphasized by the change from plural to singular in the middle of the lyric.) Those "tones" shall *never* be "blended with the voice of the spoiler." His selfishness would prohibit harmony and thus redemptive music. The harpers of "In the Valley of Waters," refusing to entertain their captors, threaten: "Our blood they shall spill." Willing martyrdom emerges from genuine tears, and selfhood has been mediated in a catharsis proven by the heart's generosity. Like Manfred, the harpers know that "it is not so difficult to die." In a natural world in which the leaves on "the willow's sad tree" are "dead" and the "wind . . . hath died on the hill" (originally "the wind in the cave of the hill") their gratuitous heroism is not without meaning.

"In the Valley of Waters" and "My Soul is Dark" are analyzed in "The harp the monarch minstrel swept." This seems appropriate because David is the best of Byron's psalmists, and because in his lyric he seems to be reciting the very song played to Saul. The harps of the captive minstrels and David's harp are at once similar and dissimilar. "Its chords are riven," just as the harps of Judah are "all stringlessly hung." But at the close of "The harp the monarch minstrel swept," David's harp has risen and changed its tune. Unselfish heroic aspirations lead to the harp's aspiration or ascent: "Its sound *aspired* to Heaven and there abode!"[17] The riven harp becomes mightier than David's "throne," and its *harmony* commands tyrants of "iron mould," who are "softened" with "virtues not their own," particularly unselfish ones. Harmony is again the symbol of mediation. (In the natural world, "vallies ring," "cedars bow," and "mountains nod," responding to the melodies of the Hebrew Orpheus and approving his heroism.) In the lyric's final stanza, the radical catharsis is elaborated. "Devotion" and "love," the minions of the harp now "heard on earth no more," descend to become the redeemers of Byron's universe. From the heaven within the heart, they "bid the bursting spirit soar," commanding it in "sounds that" only "seem as from above," to free itself from its self and turn real into ideal. This is the music that Saul found irresistible.

Because "The harp the monarch minstrel swept" is at the center of the myth projected in the *Hebrew Melodies,* it symbolizes Byron's own struggle to pass from negation to affirmation. Cancelled fragments and incomplete stanzas show that he was divided between consolation and continued weeping. Before writing the affirmative third stanza of the lyric, Byron cancelled an incomplete stanza beginning darkly: "His glory bids us mourn the more." The present third stanza originally began: "But he is dust—and we are sunk." Cancelling this line, Byron allowed David to rest on his triumphs in heaven. But then he set down a grim incomplete fourth stanza:

> It there abode—and there it rings
> But ne'er on earth its sound shall be—
> The Prophet's race hath passed away—
> And all the hallowed Minstrelsy
> From earth that sound & soul are fled
> And shall we never hear again.[18]

There is no consolation to be found here. "But ne'er on earth" emphasizes our enslavement. What we "never hear" cannot bid us soar. *Happily,* this unfinished stanza was cancelled too. Nathan, however, wished to have another "to help out the melody." Byron replied: "Why I have sent you to Heaven—it would be difficult to go further." In the stanza he finally wrote, Byron made a heaven of earth, and then exclaimed: "Here, Nathan, I have brought you down again."[19]

In his martial monologue, the "Song of Saul Before His Last Battle," Saul "soars" (another commonplace) from Belshazzar's camp to David's realm. Byron told Nathan that though "Saul, who was once gloriously surrounded by strength, power, and the approbation of his God, . . . had *sunk* from this," he could not "but uphold him originally a brave and estimable man."[20] The Promethean tone of Saul's monologue shows us that he regained Byron's original opinion. Napoleon, Byron's "little Pagod," failed; Saul did not, and so Byron remarked to Nathan: "Napoleon would have ranked higher in future history, had he even like your venerable ancestor Saul, on mount Gilboa, or like a second Cato, fallen on his sword, and finished his mortal career at Waterloo."[21] Saul tells the troops to pay no "heed" to his "corse"; ironically, they are to "bury" their arms in the foe. If the men falter, Saul's armor bearer is to slay him. "Mine be the doom which they dared not to meet" threatens the hero in familiar accents. There will be no "heir" to Saul's "royalty." But that is Byron's point: Saul has regained his "royalty." His corpse is "a king's," and his death is "kingly":

> Bright is the diadem, boundless the sway,
> Or kingly the death, which awaits us to-day!

In death, Byron crowns Saul to signify his redemption through heroism. Byron again affirms that redemption and indicates its source in praising the hero of "Thy days are done, thy fame begun":

> The generous blood that flowed from thee
> Disdained to sink beneath:[22]

"Generous" is brought to our attention, because to be generous in a selfish world is heroic. The blood of the hero disdains to sink because it is as selfless as the heart of Byron's "Prometheus":

> Triumphant where it dares defy,
> And making Death a Victory.

Precisely because her death is a "victory," Jephtha's daughter prompts us in her very last line: "And forget not I smiled as I died." Calling to mind Charlotte Corday, the Maid of Saragoza, and Saul, she commands, "Strike the bosom that's bared for thee now."[23] Because the sacrificial element is emphasized, the defiant captive is no less a hero than Jephtha's daughter. So in "Were my bosom as false as thou deem'st it to be," "scattered and scorned," a dying exile heroically affirms his faith. By proving his bosom faith and belief in the "creed" that his tyrant terms a "curse," not by "abjuring" it, the exile unselfishly turns curse into blessing:

> If the Exile on earth is an Outcast on high,
> Live on in thy faith, but in mine I will die.

It is precisely because exiles, outcasts, and slaves must "triumph" in the world "on high" that they *live on* in their "faith," even though doing so implies death at the tyrant's hands. A bosom's faith is its generosity. The selflessness it attests to is ample reason for "making Death a Victory."

The world "on high" to which heroes "soar" is built of love that redeems by vitiating self-consciousness. Its testament and structure are made explicit in "If that High World." Recognizing this from Byron's remark that "to him one of the most convincing reasons for believing in Eternity was that we never *could love enough* in this state of being—that we could not mingle 'soul in soul,'" Annabella wrote, "this is beautifully expressed in the Hebrew Melody."[24] Death liberates only if the eternity of "When coldness wraps this suffering clay" is transformed into heaven by "surviving Love" and "cherished heart." If so

> How sweet this very hour to die!
> To soar from earth and find all fears
> Lost in thy light—Eternity!

"It must be so," Byron announces boldly! Death severs being and soul and being from being. Because of our loved ones, we "cling" ironically to "Being's" paradoxical "severing link" while "striving to o'erleap the gulph" that separates high world ("Eternity") and fallen present ("this state of being").[25] But by doing just that, we affirm the love that makes a heaven of eternity. In that heaven, hearts share the "immortal waters," while the soul, "soul in soul," grows "deathless." Byron was more than half serious when he replied to a woman who had asked what would make him happy in his high world: "The pleasure, Madame, of seeing you there."[26]

Byron's quip is quite to the point. Having affirmed his "high world," he made it the abode of the women who embody his vision of ideal beauty—particularly in the lyrics he composed before deciding on the *Hebrew Melodies,* and before his marriage, but subsequently given to Isaac Nathan along with the Old Testament lyrics. Their subject is secular love, their place is the "high world," and their protagonists are women: Francisca, Mrs. Wilmot Horton (the "she" of "She Walks in Beauty"), Lady Frances Webster (the "thee" of "I Saw Thee Weep"), and Augusta (the "name" of "I speak not, I trace not, I breathe not thy name"). These Eves, like "devotion and her daughter love" in "The harp the monarch minstrel swept," show us that real and ideal may be mediated. Like David's harmonies, their ideal beauty is a symbol of an Eden restored by the unselfish heart.

When the heroine of "I Saw Thee Weep" is melancholy, metaphor transforms her eye into "a violet dropping dew." When she smiles, her smile more than matches "the sapphire's blaze." The continuity of color suggests that ideal beauty mediates conflicting emotional states. More blue than the sapphire, the heroine is happy. This is made explicit when the sapphire's blaze is softened to the "deep and mellow dye" of sunset, that the "shade of coming eve" can scarce "banish." Even when the sun has set, the heart continues to draw strength from the smiles of ideal beauty:

> Their sunshine leaves a glow behind
> That lightens o'er the heart,

This restoring "sunshine" is very different from the light of the "sun of the sleepless." (Byron has exorcised a demon which threatened, in a cancelled line, to "overshadow all below."[27]) In "She Walks in Beauty," grace "softly lighten's o'er" Mrs. Wilmot Horton's idealized face. Her beauty is dark "like the night," because beauty is in the beholder's eye, and because Byron is the beholder. But because the night is "cloudless" and "starry," she is "all that's best of dark and bright," a symbol of mediation, like the *sunset light* of "I Saw Thee Weep." "Mellowed" and "tender," such light is denied to "gaudy" day. The perfection of ideal beauty rests on a delicate balance suggestive of the unique quality of the mediation achieved. "One shade the more, one ray the less," writes Byron, would destroy the "grace" of the earthborn angel. The starlight becomes a halo accenting "every raven tress," providing another example of the harmony "of dark and bright" in Eden. There the starlight shines from within Byron's serene Eve. Its sources are

> A mind at peace with all below,
> A heart whose love is innocent!

Again, in the end, we are returned to the "heart." "Below" tells us where we are, even if we don't believe it, and we do believe, for the "heart" has set the "mind" at ease. The contour of Byron's myth has brought us round from self-consciousness to a love "innocent" and thus selfless.

III

Byron's vision unites the *Hebrew Melodies,* and the artistic execution of that vision, it needs to be added, is very much part and parcel of the unity achieved.[28] Generally Biblical tales and Jewish history are made to serve as the basis of *dramatic* lyrics. Goethe remarked that Byron should have lived "to execute his vocation . . . to dramatise the Old Testament."[29] It was in these dramatic lyrics employing Biblical personae, not in his subsequent dramas, that Byron began to do just that. His peculiar *mobilité* informs the quick-change artistry of the poems, giving rise to his unique mastery of the dramatic lyric. The *Hebrew Melodies* occupy a significant place in the evolution of romantic lyricism, defined by Karl Kroeber as the "gradual transformation of simple narrative structure as the basis of lyric organization into a discontinuous, non-narrative structure."[30] We may overlook this, as Wasserman speaking about romantic lyrics reminds us, because their "superficial appearance" discourages "an intensive metaphysical reading," and because we too often think that Byron is merely impersonating for the sake of it, as Leigh Hunt thought, "he does not so much go out of himself to describe others, as furnish others out of himself."[31] But when we recognize Byron's genius and consider the *Hebrew Melodies* as dramatic lyrics articulating a consistent mythos, the importance of their execution is manifest. They are examples of the "worthy nineteenth-century poem" in which Patricia Ball finds the "coalescence" of "storyteller with his material . . . taking place within and becoming part of the poem itself."[32]

The fusion at the center of Byron's dramatic lyrics gives rise to the monumentality of the *Hebrew Melodies,* that is their ability to enlarge their emotional scope through resonance. Byron makes the lyric form bear the full weight of drama in a single moment. As Francis Jeffrey recognized, the *Hebrew Melodies* express "a depth and force of feeling which though indicated only by short sobs and glances, is here as marked and peculiar as in [Byron's] greater pieces."[33] Roden Noel responded to the same quality of monumentality and amplified Jeffrey's remarks: "Where Byron is effective in drama, it is by lyrically pouring the quintessence of his characters into the mould of one supreme situation, capable of realizing them with the utmost intensity."[34] This is just what Byron has done in the dramatic lyrics of the *Hebrew Melodies.* "Depth," "force," and "intensity" are measures of the monumentality of those poems generated by the resonance or "intensifying reverberation" that enlarges them.[35] Robert Langbaum has observed in his study of Browning's poetic that the speakers of dramatic monologues *burst* into utter-ance in the same sense that the verb is used in connec-tion with song. Just as in opera the singer only wants occasion to burst into an aria the expressiveness of which can hardly be justified by the dramatic situation; so in the dramatic monologue the dramatic situation is less the adequate motive then the occasion for a total outpouring of soul, the expression of the speaker's whole life until that moment.[36]

It is just this quintessential compression fundamental to the dramatic lyric which generates the bursting reso-nance of the *Hebrew Melodies,* giving rise to their monumentality. Nor has Byron neglected to provide the music of his character's intense song. He has taken pains to weave a musical fabric of alliteration, asso-nance, and carefully rhymed stanzas. On this fabric, he stamps his stark designs. The contrast of plangent sound and simple structure contributes to the intensity of his monumental lyrics. Byron refines the lyric to a simple statement uniquely his, and he writes that statement large. In doing so he exchanges the self-conscious for the tragic. In his longer narrative poems, Byron turned autobiography into mythology.[37] By making his Biblical lyrics monumental, he did much the same. Byron's *He-brew Melodies* have a music of their own.

Notes

1. To John Murray, 9 Dec. 1816, *The Works of Lord Byron, Letters and Journals,* ed. R. E. Prothero (London, 1898-1904), IV, 22. Hereafter cited as *L& J.*

2. 15 March 1814, quoted in Ethel C. Mayne, *Life and Letters of Anne Isabella Lady Noel Byron* (London, 1929), p. 92.

3. 16 April 1807, *L& J, II,* 19n.

4. 18 June 1813, *L& J,* II, 221.

5. Quoted in Malcolm Elwin, *Lord Byron's Wife* (London, 1962), p. 270.

6. Elwin, p. 264.

7. 15 February 1814, quoted in Mayne, *Lady Byron,* p. 87. His frequently quoted remark about having read the Bible "through and through" before he was "eight years old" is found in *L& J,* V, 391.

8. *Notes from the Letters of Thomas Moore to His Music Publisher, James Power,* ed. Thomas Crof-ton Croker (New York, 1853), pp. 2-3.

9. *The Works of Lord Byron, Poetry,* ed. Ernest H. Coleridge (London, 1898-1904), II, 192. Hereafter cited as *Poetry.* Byron likened the plight of the Irish to that of the Jews when speaking on Catho-lic Emancipation in Parliament 21 April 1812 (*L& J,* II, 438).

10. 7 Sept. 1820, *L& J,* V, 72. Evidence of proto-Zionism in the *Hebrew Melodies* is discussed by

Joseph Slater in "Byron's *Hebrew Melodies," Stud-ies in Philology,* XLIX (1952), 75-94.

11. James Kennedy, *Conversations on Religion with Lord Byron,* (London, 1830), pp. 246-248.

12. *Byron and the Ruins of Paradise* (Baltimore, 1967), p. 207.

13. *Byron's Poetry* (Boston, 1965), p. 134.

14. *A Selection of Hebrew Melodies* (1815), I, pref-ace.

15. G. Wilson Knight writes: "The Assyrian host chal-lenges the stars and sea, man as against the cos-mos, its co-equal and rival" (*Byron and Shakes-peare* [London, 1966], p. 14).

16. M. G. Cooke writes that the poem dramatizes "the self-conscious mind striving to yield away the self" (*The Blind Man Traces the Circle* [Princeton, 1969], p. 31).

17. My italics. Cooke (p. 27) writes: "David's music embodies immortality in music." But then he adds: "That immortality, lost in fact, is preserved some-how in memory, which thereby serves as a de-fense against the experience of mortality." By-ron's memory is indefensible.

18. From Byron's holograph MS., Ashley 4728, by permission of the British Museum.

19. Isaac Nathan, *Fugitive Pieces and Reminiscences of Lord Byron* (London, 1829), p. 33.

20. Nathan, pp. 42-43, my italics.

21. Nathan, p. 40.

22. Cf. "Though Freedom's blood thy plain bedew; / There 'twas shed, but is not sunk," from "We do not curse thee, Waterloo!"

23. She echoes Zuleika of the *Bride of Abydos* (ll. 655-657), who cries: "Thou ledst me here per-chance to kill . . . my breast is offered—take thy fill!"

24. Quoted in Elwin, p. 284.

25. This conflict is reflected in the contrary attitudes of Anah and Aholibamah as they depart for heaven with their angelic lovers at the close of *Heaven and Earth.* Byron described their journey to Med-win: "The affectionate tenderness of Adah [*sic*] for those from whom she is parted, and forever, and her fears contrasting with the loftier spirit of Aholibamah triumphing in the hopes of a new and greater destiny, will make the dialogue" (Medwin's *Conversations of Lord Byron,* ed. Ernest J. Lovell, Jr. [Princeton, 1966], p. 157).

26. Nathan, p. 22.

27. From Byron's holograph MS., by permission of the Miriam Lutcher Stark Library, the University of Texas, Austin.

28. We can see now just how well the secular lyrics which have nothing to do with the Bible fit in with the *Hebrew Melodies.* The tonal disparity of defiance and lamentation in the Biblical poems need not confuse their thematic unity, and the tonal similarity of the secular poems and their Biblical counterparts helps to suggest the essential thematic unity of those poems. Because of this, "tones" seems preferable to "two voices," to "public-private" and "private-public" voices, and to "various speakers" (Marchand, p. 117; Gleckner, pp. xvi-xvii; W. H. Marshall, *The Structure of Byron's Major Poems* [Philadelphia, 1962], p. 176). In "Oh! snatched away in beauty's bloom," sorrow weeps by the banks of a river, just as the tearful harpers of Judah weep by the rivers of Babylon. The beloved of Byron's "Bright be the place of thy soul" soars to his high world in much the same fashion as the hero of "Thy Days are Done." Finally, the Byron of "I Speak Not—I Trace Not—I Breathe Not" defends his unselfish clandestine love for Augusta as heroically as the exile of "Were my bosom as false as thou deem'st it to be." The flux of tones ranging from tearful to scornful is consistently Byronic. Marchand (*Byron's Poetry,* p. 134) excludes "She Walks in Beauty" from the *Hebrew Melodies* on the grounds that it "is really out of tone with the Hebrew melodies proper." But he sees that "the love songs have much of the haunting sadness and the sense of desolation which informs the poems voicing a wild lament for the lost Jewish homeland." Gleckner says Marchand acted "erroneously, I think" (p. 210*n*) in excluding "She Walks in Beauty." He prefers to keep "apart" (p. 210) Byron's "I Saw Thee Weep." None of these lyrics need to be excluded; each has its place.

29. Quoted in Henry Crabb Robinson, *On Books and Their Writers,* ed. Edith J. Morley (London, 1938), I, 372.

30. *Romantic Narrative Art* (Madison, 1960, rptd. 1966), p. 51.

31. Earl R. Wasserman, *The Subtler Language* (Baltimore, 1959), p. 252; *Examiner,* 2 June 1822, p. 341.

32. *The Central Self* (London, 1968), p. 184.

33. Jeffrey to Moore, 11 June 1815, *L& J,* III, 294-295*n*.

34. *Essays on Poetry and Poets* (London, 1886), p. 57.

35. Cooke, p. 157.

36. *The Poetry of Experience* (New York, 1957, rptd. 1963), p. 183.

37. Harold Bloom, *The Visionary Company* (New York, 1961, rptd. 1963), p. 252 *passim*.

Carol A. Martin (essay date fall 1988)

SOURCE: Martin, Carol A. "Contemporary Critics and Judaism in *Daniel Deronda.*" *Victorian Periodicals Review* 21, no. 3 (fall 1988): 90-107.

[*In the following essay, Martin surveys nineteenth-century critical commentary on the subjects of Judaism, anti-Semitism, and Zionism present in George Eliot's* Daniel Deronda.]

Theodor Herzl, the "father" of modern Israel, recounts in his diary for 25 November 1895, a meeting with Colonel Albert Edward Williamson Goldsmid, who, after dinner on the first night of Herzl's visit to Goldsmid's home, told the visitor a "wonderful story":[1]

'I am Daniel Deronda,' he said. 'I was born a Christian. My father and mother were baptized Jews. When, a young man out in India, I learned of this, I decided to return to my ancestral people. While a lieutenant I went over to Judaism. My family were indignant. The woman I loved was also a Christian of Jewish stock. I eloped with her to Scotland where, to begin with, we had a civil marriage. Then she had to become a Jewess, and we were married in a synagogue. I am an orthodox Jew. It has not prejudiced my position in England. My children Rachel and Carmel received a strict religious upbringing and learned Hebrew at an early age.' That . . . sounded like a novel, [Herzl adds].

(*Diaries* 82-83)

Only six months earlier (7 June 1895) Herzl had noted in his diary that he "must read *Daniel Deronda*" (34) and only two days before, he recorded a conversation with Hermann Adler, Ashkenazic Chief Rabbi of the British Empire, in which he had "expounded my subject," and Adler had replied, "That is the idea of *Daniel Deronda*" (80). Thus, whether he had had a chance to read the work, he was certainly familiar, by the occasion of his meeting with Goldsmid, with the general outlines of this last novel of George Eliot, and especially with the Zionist journey of the hero at the conclusion. Though the *Encyclopadia Judaica* (vol. 7) observes that Goldsmid "is said to have been the model for George Eliot's character Daniel Deronda," [perhaps basing this comment on the quotation above from Herzl's *Diaries*], there is no solid evidence for this, and Eliot scholars have more often accepted Emmanuel Deutsch as a model, sometimes for Deronda, sometimes for Mordecai, if there was indeed one individual model. Nonetheless, this anecdote and the other references

Herzl makes demonstrate the importance some of the chief members of the Anglo-Jewish community attached to the novel and its portrait of Daniel Deronda, a young man brought up as the "nephew" of an English baronet, finding out, like Goldsmid, in adulthood that he is of Jewish parentage and undertaking a journey to the East to establish a homeland for his people. Though the un-awareness of his Jewish parentage makes Goldsmid's life particularly parallel with that of Deronda, travel to the East with a pre- or proto-Zionist motive was, of course, an interest of many members of the Anglo-Jewish community in the 19th century, starting with Sir Moses Montefiore, who in 1838 "had concluded a tentative agreement with Mohammed Ali [of Egypt, who was in rebellion against the Turkish Sultan] for rights to purchase land and settle Jewish colonists in Palestine" (Halpern 255) and who "made seven journeys to the Holy Land, . . . the last, when he was over 90 years old, in 1875" (Bentwich 7), the year before *Daniel Deronda* was published.

The novel was published in parts over eight months, from January to September 1876, and, being a new work by the author frequently referred to as "England's greatest living novelist," it attracted many critical notices. Some of which came out after the conclusion of the last number, but many more appeared as the parts of the novel were published, giving readers interested in watching the development of reactions to fiction in progress a chance to gauge the opinions of critical seers who could have access to only part of the work at a time. Although a few of the regular serial notices, those in the *Athenaeum,* the *Examiner,* and the *Spectator,* have been indexed in Fulmer's bibliography and in Geibel's dissertation, dozens more appeared in London, Edinburgh, and provincial papers in England and Scotland, often appearing regularly with the publication of each new part. Of the few indexed reviews that have been at least partially reprinted, only two reviews of the novel in progress are given in Carroll (short notices from *Academy* and *The Nation,* both for February 1876). Holmstrom and Lerner excerpt five notices published before the novel's completion: *Examiner,* 29 January; *Spectator,* 8 April, 10 June, and 29 July; and *Academy,* 5 February.

These reviews and those published after the novel's conclusion and reprinted in one of these two collections give only a hint of the negative reaction to the "Jewish portion" of the novel to which Eliot refers in her journal and letters and of which some of the critics themselves take note. Thus in her journal for 1 December 1876, Eliot comments: "Since we came home at the beginning of September I have been made aware of much repugnance or else indifference towards the Jewish part of Deronda, and of some hostile as well as adverse reviewing" (*Letters* VI: 314). In July 1876, the critic for the *New Quarterly Magazine* noted what one finds in many of the papers that will be discussed below: "There has been a sensible abatement of the enthusiasm which greeted the appearance of the first chapters of *Daniel Deronda,* among the critics" (514), and an enthusiastic *Westminster Review* noted in the third of its three brief installment reviews that *Daniel Deronda* has experienced a great deal of hostile criticism" (October 1876; 575). Though neither specifies the Jewish portion in particular, discussion of the serial reviews below will reinforce Eliot's own awareness that it was the Jewish portion that presented the problem. The historian Joseph Jacobs, a prominent member of the Anglo-Jewish community, shared this awareness, even to feeling compelled to write an article called "Mordecai: A Protest against the Critics."

CORRESPONDENCE WITH BLACKWOOD

Even before the novel appeared in parts, the "Jewish portion" was a matter of concern to George Eliot and George Henry Lewes. On 1 December 1875, Lewes wrote to William Blackwood, Eliot's publisher: "Your admiration is very cheering to her [Eliot, who needed careful encouragement as she wrote], and I must add that your taking so heartily to the Jewish scenes is particularly gratifying to me, for I have sometimes shared her doubts on whether people would sufficiently sympathize with that element in the story. Though I have reflected that (as) she formerly contrived to make one love Methodists, there was no reason why she should not conquer the prejudice against the Jews." He goes on to anticipate, however, a "fervour of admiration" from "all the Jews of Europe" (VI: 196). On 29 December, again writing to Blackwood, he looks for a large public for the novel: "The Jews alone would constitute an energetic propagandist party, for never have they been idealized and realized so marvelously before" (VI: 205).

Lewes' letter, of course, may have been designed to guide Blackwood's response in his letters to the sensitive author. If so, Blackwood missed the point, or at least didn't take it up sufficiently. Reacting to what she saw as the publisher's lukewarm response to Mordecai, Eliot wrote him on 25 February 1876: "I thought it likely that your impressions about Mordecai would be doubtful. Perhaps when the work is finished you will see its bearings better. The effect that one strives after is an outline as strong as that of Balfour of Burley for a much more complex character and a higher strain of ideas. But such an effect is just the most difficult thing in art—to give new elements—i.e. elements not already used up—in forms as vivid as those of long familiar types" (VI: 223).

Two days later Lewes sent Blackwood a not-too-veiled hint about the effect of his judgment: "I was very sorry to find from your last that you did not take cordially to Mordecai—sorry because I think it on the whole one of the greatest of her creations . . . but mostly sorry because I knew it would damp her. It has cast a gloom over her already desponding mind; she feeling that the public will in general share your imperfect sympathy. All along this has been her vision of the effect which this presentation of the Jewish ideal would have; and I have vainly combated it. But whether it is liked or disliked do it she must and will" (VI: 224). Taking his cue, Blackwood immediately dispatched a letter (29 February) noting "If Mrs. Lewes heard the excited speculations over Mordecai among the privileged few here who have read Book V [not due out until the end of May] she would be more than satisfied with the impression her wonderful Jew is making" (VI: 225). He followed this on 2 March with another letter to Lewes even more fulsome, praising, from Book VI, "the marvelous Mordecai and oh that Cohen family. The whole tribe of Israel should fall down and worship her" (VI: 227)

PUBLIC REACTION

The reaction of the Jewish public justified Lewes' and Eliot's hopes. The first of many notices in the *Jewish Chronicle* was a brief one, on 21 July: "we have received parts 1 to 5 of this the latest novel of the leading living novelist. Beyond stating that the work is of the deepest interest to Jewish readers, and bids fair to equal if not to surpass in merit the previous productions of the author, we think it but just both to writer and reviewer to defer its critical consideration until its completion" (251). At that completion, two notices followed immediately (8 and 22 September), with two further discussions three months later (15 and 22 December). In addition to these items, noted by Geibel, is an article he does not index, on the page following the 15 December essay, in which is recorded a lecture by Dr. Hermann Adler to the Jewish Workingman's Club and Institute, Aldgate, on the previous Saturday, a session presided over by Haim Guedalla, whom the 20th century scholar Ruth Levitt says derived his idea of the exchange of Turkish debt for Israel from George Eliot (27). This is the same Adler whose letter to Eliot which she opened on her return from the Continent to the negative reviews, "gratified me more than anything else of the sort I ever received," as she says in a letter to John Blackwood, 2 September 1876 (VI: 275).

The *Jewish Chronicle*'s response included, in addition to these longer pieces, frequent little notes about such matters as forthcoming translations of *Deronda*—miscellaneous items that testify to the interest the novel was expected to have for the newspaper's readers. Nineteenth-century Jewish support for the novel also included a passionate defense by Rabbi David Kaufmann, which was translated into English in 1878. Twentieth-century studies include those by Baker, Levitt (whose book contains a foreword by Abba Eban describing Eliot as "Among those first visionaries" of an "Israel resurgent," "one woman [who] stands out peerless and apart"), and Shalvi, who edited a collection of essays from a 1976 symposium at the Hebrew University of Jerusalem to celebrate the centenary of the publication of *Daniel Deronda*.

In contrast to this century of testimony, a perceptible change occurs in many serial reviews in the ordinary English and Scottish press, when the so-called Jewish portion begins late in the fifth book, titled "Mordecai." By the time this part appeared, many newspapers had reviewed each of the earlier four books, and though there were some who quarreled with Eliot's decision to publish in installments, a number who objected to her "scientific" diction, and a minority who did not think the novel up to her usual standards (the "usual" usually being the style and subject of *Adam Bede*), the response had been generally enthusiastic. The interest of readers in the character of Gwendolen Harleth had by Book 5 become well established, and it was with annoyance that some reviewers were compelled to turn from her misfortunes to the story of Mordecai. *The Glasgow News* for 15 June lamented thus:

> The new part of 'Daniel Deronda' . . . is called 'Mordecai,' who, however, only makes his appearance towards the close of the number, and does not succeed in making himself particularly intelligible or agreeable. He talks in a very high-flown way about Jews and things Jewish, and apparently is desirous to impart something or other—what [,] it is impossible to say—to the unfortunate hero of the book, who appears to be as fascinated by the gaze of Mordecai as were the wedding guests by the glittering eye of the Ancient Mariner. However, there is happily very little of Mordecai, who is little more at present than a George-Eliotish version of Mr. Disraeli's Sidonia.
>
> (2)

The *Tablet* is more explicit in its objection to Book 4, praising the depictions of the Grandcourts but regretting the book's conclusion: "The catastrophe is strongly and shortly told; but the sudden break and total change of interest in this volume is either an error in art or an unworthy device; we are obliged to leave Gwendolen with Lydia Glasher's diamonds at her feet, receiving her bridegroom with scream upon scream, and to interest ourselves through three long chapters in Deronda's search among the Jews" (27 May; 683).

The objections to the Jewish portion include various broad charges, not all of which were consistent with each other: it is highly objectionable that a young man brought up as an English Christian gentleman should turn around and adopt the Judaism of his parents; Deronda is too idealistic, a "prig" (especially when he does not take the Christian heroine for his wife, but chooses the young Jewess instead); Mordecai is too idealistic, and therefore unbelievable; the Zionist mission is absurd, unbelievable; Judaism is not a religion and the Jews not a people from whom one expects idealistic values or behavior; readers just are not interested in Jews and the whole Jewish plot is therefore tedious and boring. This listing is fairly representative of the tone and ideas of many, though not all reviewers; to these general objections are added a few specific derogatory stereotypes. This last point is simply and quickly illustrated through two examples.

The *Glasgow News* for 1 July finds an anti-Semitic stereotype by Hans Meyrick one of the two "bright flashes" in part 6: "The dialogue is rather dreary, save in the present book, where Hans thinks of Mirah's recovered brother as of 'a fellow all smiles and jewelry—a Crystal Palace Assyrian with a hat on.'" One might argue that because Hans is a comic character, Eliot has set us up to laugh at this stereotype—that the reviewer should settle on this anti-Semitic stereotyping as a "bright spot" is only what the text has directed. But from Eliot's point of view—as established by other incidents in the novel—this comment has the opposite role: it is part of her demonstration of the limits of English vision which she deplored in a letter to Harriet Beecher Stowe, 29 October 1876 (see *Letters*, VI: 301-302), and illustrated not only in Hans but in Lady Mallinger's hope that Mirah will convert to Christianity (267), Amy's wish that Mirah's Jewish religion "would gradually melt from her, and she would pass into Christianity like the rest of the world" (410), and Mrs. Meyrick's "cheerful" acceptance of a "consummation" in which "if Jews and Jewesses went on changing their religion, and making no difference between themselves and Christians, there would come a time when there would be no Jews to be seen" (425). In fact, though Hans and the rest of the Meyrick family are generally portrayed with sympathy, it should be clear from this accumulation of detail that Eliot wishes to demonstrate that anti-Semitism is not restricted to characters so wicked that the reader could never identify with them; quite the contrary, it is the ordinary "well-meaning" and genial English person—like Hans, Amy, Mrs. Meyrick, and Lady Mallinger—who lacks the wider vision that goes beyond prejudice and stereotyping.

Eliot on Anti-Semitism

In her letter to Stowe, Eliot asks (VI, 302), "Can anything be more disgusting than to hear people called 'educated' making small jokes about eating ham, and showing themselves empty of any real knowledge as to the relation of their own social and religious life to the history of the people they think themselves witty in insulting?" A *Sunday Times* review incorporated one of these "small jokes" about another stereotype, that of the Jew as old clothes-dealer: the conversation between Deronda and his mother is "almost wearisome"; "Of

course, Deronda is a Jew. The matter of that has been as little open to doubt as the nationality of Aaron Solomon, the second-hand clothes-dealer, of Petticoat Lane, who, when asked by a magistrate his religion, answered, 'I am a Quaker, don't you shink zo?'" (20 August; 7). Perhaps thinking of this very "joke" (though the stereotype was common enough; see Zatlin), Jacobs, in "Mordecai: A Protest Against the Critics," referring to the problem critics had in seeing Deronda's "easy transition" from Christianity to Judaism, notes that this "initial difficulty" didn't exist for one "who has from his childhood seen the world habited in those Hebrew Old Clothes of which Mr. Carlyle and others have spoken so slightingly" (101).

This conversion of Deronda to Judaism was a sore point with several reviewers, as one might expect in a time of zealous attempts to convert Jews to Christianity, by tract (Lady Mallinger's observation that there is a "Society for the Conversion of the Jews" is Eliot's sardonic comment on this practice) if no longer by threat. Some reviewers felt that it was absurd to propose that an intelligent, cultivated, "English" character like Deronda would accept his Jewish heritage and the role Mordecai envisions for him. The *Liverpool Daily Post* apparently will excuse Disraeli for such fantasies but not George Eliot:

> Perfect, however, [Deronda] is not, for the author makes him play a bad second-fiddle to Tancred as a would-be explorer of an Asian mystery, which is an absurd position for so wise a man. Nobody minded Tancredism in Mr. Disraeli, because it is his function to make mystic epigrams out of absolute nothingness. But from George Eliot we expect no such nonsense. We shall be told that the Hebraic aspirations of Mordecai and the talk of his companions are proved to be almost literally real by an article of Mr. Lewes in the *Fortnightly* for 1865. But it is a very different thing to hear Pan-judaic rhapsodies from the mouths of such men as these, and to make a person of *Deronda's culture, knowledge of the world, and sound Whig education and political and religious polish, a believer in them.*
>
> (8 September; 4; my emphasis)[2]

The Standard concludes that Deronda. behaving in such a fashion, must be a prig. "Is it possible to respect a poor creature who is overjoyed to give up the convictions and faith of a lifetime and to find himself a Jew because he has fallen in love with the pretty face of a Jewess whom he has picked out of a river?" (25 September; 2). The explanation that Deronda accepted his Jewish heritage only because he fell in love with a Jewess is shared by other reviews, including that of the *Morning Post,* which finds it "strange that he should never have even suspected that he was of Jewish origin, and, also, since he had been brought up a Christian, that he should marry Mirah Lapidoth according to the rites of her religion" (17 October; 3), and the *Liverpool Weekly Albion,* which observes: "It is not, then, the ravings of Mordecai that have converted the hero's feelings, but the fact that he is in love with the Jewish girl Mirah. The reader may have guessed as much . . ." (29 July; 7). The *Spectator,* though generally positive about the novel and especially impressed with its "religious" tone, qualifies its praise because the religion in which this tone is conveyed is not Christianity:

> so far as this book conveys the author's religious creed, it is a purified Judaism,—in other words, a devout Theism, purged of Jewish narrowness, while retaining the intense patriotism which pervades Judaism; and that the hero . . . evidently sees nothing in the teaching of Christ which raises Christianity above the purified Judaism of Mordecai's vision.
>
> (9 September; 1131)

Perhaps the most biased representations that Christianity is inherently better than Judaism come in the Roman Catholic *Tablet.* One review is quoted above (page 7), and other notices observed the "tediousness" of Mordecai's history (1 July; 10) and the reviewer's being "bored extremely by the club of Jews" (29 July: 138). In the final notice, the anti-Semitism is overt: claiming to judge the work only from a "purely literary point," the reviewer asserts that Eliot "commits a literary error when she makes Deronda abandon on learning the fact of his Jewish birth all that a modern English education weaves of Christianity and the results of Christianity into an English gentleman's life." Citing Deronda's "tenderness," the reviewer adds:

> then consider the improbability of such callousness that no pain of his at renouncing what must have touched him as a religion of love and sympathy, even though he had never held it as a living faith, is even alluded to. The author does not give a word or hint as to any suffering or regret or difficulty in the change. *Deronda's acceptance of Judaism as a religion is revolting* [my emphasis]; that is not what we are proving; we are calling attention to a grave artistic fault . . . we do not conceive to what rule of duty she has sacrificed her readers' feelings, their sympathy, and the reality and unity of her loveliest character.
>
> (4 November; 587)

This "loveliest character" has been a controversial figure from the earliest critics to the present—viewed at times as one on whom Eliot lavished too much descriptive power and allowed too little room for action. Some of these criticisms have little or nothing to do with Deronda's Jewish heritage or Zionist mission. However, occasional early reviewers clearly found him quite satisfactory as long as it appeared that he would be a love interest in Gwendolen's life, if and when—and many clearly expected it was only a case of "when"—Grandcourt departed the scene. The London *Figaro* reviewer makes the most disingenuous comments and reversals of opinion in expressing his dismay at the outcome. Piqued at having hopes for a union of Gwendolen and

Deronda disappointed, the writer would therefore make Deronda a Christian. In the penultimate review, the reviewer acknowledges the attraction between Mirah and Deronda, but, there still being "sufficient uncertainty," he hopes "All may come right in the end. . . . Gwendolen . . . is, by far, the more suitable wife for Deronda. We shall be angry with him if he does not see that himself" (12 August; 11). The reviewer's disappointment with the last installment leads to the conclusion that Deronda's character is diminished by this wrong choice:

> We suppose that George Eliot, *who would not have spoilt her book if she had made her hero a Christian* [my emphasis], would say that the ties of race had something to do with Deronda's choice. But a man of a very deep and loving nature would, in choosing a wife, surely consider first whether she was dearest in the world to him; the question of race would weigh little. In the opening chapters of "Daniel Deronda," the hero seemed to possess all the virtues; in the closing ones most of them seem to have departed from him. We take leave of him gladly, wondering at our folly in ever enthroning him as a model of well-nigh unapproachable excellence.
>
> (27 September; 12)

Apart from this "flaw," however, it is "noble work. . . . The author's usual care in details is manifested, and that portion of the story in which the woes and triumphs of the descendants of Abraham are expatiated upon is now pathetic, now magnificent . . ." (27 September; 12-13). This writer seems to have missed the vital connections between Deronda's Jewish heritage and the whole thrust of the plot, and would instead reduce the Jewish elements to a kind of Dickens-like caricature—something to amuse and touch us perhaps, but only incidental to what is really a love story.

CONTEMPORARY JEWISH RESPONSE

The hostility, or at the least lack of sympathy, with Deronda's acceptance of Judaism is alluded to by Jewish writers like James Picciotto, author of *Sketches of Anglo-Jewish Life* (1875), and Joseph Jacobs. Jacobs observes "the jar most readers must have felt in the omission of any explanation of the easy transition of Deronda from the Christianity in which he was bred to the Judaism in which he had been born," and finds the answer to this apparent ease in an understanding of Mordecai, of which he sees little in the critics against whom he directs his "protest." The Englishman with great yearnings (like the Englishwoman, Dorothea Brooke, of Eliot's preceding novel) finds little in contemporary life that allows for these yearnings:

> Like Mordecai, Deronda protests against the "blasphemy of the time," that men should stand by as spectators of life instead of living. But before he meets with Mordecai what noble work in life has this young

and cultured Englishman with his thousands a year? This age of unfaith gives no outlet for his deep, spiritual yearnings (nor for those of thousands like him). The old beliefs are gone. . . . Yet there comes to this ardent soul an angel of the Lord (albeit in the shape of a poor Jew watch-mender) with a burning message, giving a mission in life as grand as the most far-reaching idea he could have formed. Is it strange that his thirsty soul should have swallowed up the soul of Mordecai, in the Cabalistic way which the latter often refers to? . . . But is it not strange that the literary leaders of England should have failed to see aught but unsatisfactory vagueness in all the parts of *Daniel Deronda* which treat of the relations of the hero with Mordecai Cohen?

(110)

Jacobs goes on to locate the critics' difficulty in their failure of imagination: "Is it possible that they have failed to see the grandeur and beauty of these incidents because of the lack of that force of imagination necessary to pierce to the pathos of a contemporary tragedy . . . ?" (110) This is a formulation of the problem that Eliot herself might have made.

Picciotto also finds the failure to accept the conversion in the critics' inability to recognize the sympathetic nature of Deronda himself, which "inclines him to take up passionately the cause of wronged individuals as of oppressed races" (596). Given this carefully-established feature of his character, "How far a young man of good social position is likely to break with his former ties to embrace ancient religious forms which must, to say the least, expose him to the ridicule of his late companions, and cause him considerable embarrassment, must be determined by the amount of sacrifice each person is disposed to make on behalf of his convictions" (596). He then notes that there is nothing "inherently improbable" in such a return to an ancestral creed and cites a recent "well-known case" of just such an action, which, though he does not provide the name, must be that of Colonel Albert Goldsmid (596-97).

The Morning Post's reviewer would not accept this test of actual truth. Having expected interest to hinge on the Gwendolen-Deronda relationship, he is disappointed when the novel ends otherwise: "as a matter of fact, the actual *denouement* is made to turn upon the hero's national cravings after a future for the Semitic race to an extent which debars from sympathy *any mind not so wrapped up as his own* in the visionary schemes to which he proposes to devote his life. This may be perfectly true to nature, but in a work of fiction of so high an order we want not so much absolute as possible truth" (17 October; 3; my emphasis). Here again the critic lays the blame on a failure of artistry: reality as it is well known to the English reader becomes the test of possible truth. *The Fortnightly Review* took a similar stand: the problem with the Jewish part is not in whether

such a thing "may as a matter of fact be going on around us, but of what our imagination can effectively realise" (1 November; 605). Eliot addressed the limitations of this idea of reality and of the English imagination in the letter to Stowe cited above. Educated English people

hardly know that Christ was a Jew. And I find men educated at Rugby supposing that Christ spoke Greek. To my feeling, this deadness to the history which has prepared half our world for us, this inability to find interest in any form of life that is not clad in the same coat-tails and flounces as our own lies very close to the worst kind of irreligion. The best that can be said of it is, that it is a sign of the intellectual narrowness—in plain English, the stupidity, which is still the average mark of our culture.

(29 October 1876; VI: 302)

The *Daily News* for 31 August tries to make the issue one of artistry, but the tone and diction indicate the subtext. There are flaws in the novel "as a work of art," the principal flaw being that "the main current of large interests which sweeps through the book, is one which will only carry with it the interest of people whose imaginative sympathies are very quick and eager, or whose knowledge of certain matters is exceptional. *The world in general cares no more for the Jewish part of the story* about Mordecai, with his visions, and Daniel with his theories of Jewish unity, and so on, *than Daniel's mother cared*. The *thing is a weariness* [my emphasis], though of course it ought not to be, and though all of us are to blame for our indifference." The tone of the review's final words indicates the writer's bias: earlier he had noted that readers can't sympathize with Mirah and wish instead that Gwendolen were destined to marry Deronda "though he may not seem a great prize. . . . We are not told whether this lady ever learned to console herself, like Calypso, but it would be pleasant to feel sure that she did, and lives to forget the champion of Panjudaism" (3). Picciotto sees the question of art another way: "Some critics cannot forgive the author" for Deronda's choice of Mirah over Gwendolen; their dissatisfaction may "arise . . . from the fact that Daniel Deronda has become Deronda the Jew. [Gwendolen's "misfortunes" enlist] the full sympathy of the reader. But a man in England is not yet permitted to marry two wives at the same time, and had Daniel Deronda selected Gwendolen, the author would have assuredly committed an artistic error" (599-600). Picciotto concurs in the hope that Gwendolen may be consoled, but the tone and the conclusion about the novel's artistry are significantly different.

THE ZIONIST MISSION CRITICIZED

The most serious misreadings of the text and the most flawed reactions in the view of Eliot and Lewes and of the Jewish readers and critics were centered on the prophetic, consumptive Jewish workman, Mordecai, and on the Zionist mission which Mordecai had envisioned and which Deronda undertakes at the end. From *Scenes of Clerical Life* to *Daniel Deronda,* the purpose of fiction for Eliot is to create imaginatively the lives of others so that readers will have that "fiber of sympathy" that connects them with the lives around them, as the narrator says in the famous chapter 17 of *Adam Bede.* There, of course, Eliot's narrator stresses the need for sympathy with the "common, coarse people, who have no picturesque sentimental wretchedness" but only a very ordinary existence. Some enthusiasts for that doctrine in *Adam Bede* seemed, however, to have forgotten it when they encountered the Jewish portion of *Daniel Deronda,* though it is clear from her letters and journals, as well as from the whole of her fiction, that Eliot in her novels simply applied that doctrine to different groups in different times and places. Writing to Elizabeth Stuart Phelps, 16 December 1876, Eliot makes the connection between *Adam Bede* and *Daniel Deronda* explicit: "there has been no change in the point of view from which I regard our life since I wrote my first fiction—the 'Scenes of Clerical Life.' Any apparent change of spirit must be due to something of which I am unconscious. The principles which are at the root of my effort to paint Dinah Morris are equally at the root of my effort to paint Mordecai" (VI: 318). In a letter to Haim Guedalla, 2 October 1876, she reiterates those principles: "It is my function as an artist to act (if possible) for good on the emotions and conceptions of my fellow-men" (VI: 289). And to John Blackwood, 3 November 1876, she wrote, apropos of the negative reviews, that she had received

> very delightful letters from unknown readers and reported judgments from considerable authorities. A statesman who shall be nameless has said that I first opened to him a vision of Italian life, then of Spanish, and now I have kindled in him a quite new understanding of the Jewish people. This is what I wanted to do—to widen the English vision a little in that direction and let in a little conscience and refinement.
>
> (VI: 304)

Though Lewes hoped that Eliot might create a sympathy for the Jews as she had for Methodists, many of the popular press found Mordecai incomprehensible and repugnant. Thus, his speeches were called "the ravings of Mordecai" (*Liverpool Weekly Albion,* 29 July; 7); "obscure and tiresome . . . Mordecai's harangues" (*Edinburgh Courant,* 4 September; 6). Mordecai is "a very mad Israelite, who half convinces [Deronda] that he himself is one of the chosen people" (The *Standard,* 12 June; 3). "Mordecai, who is meant to be a seer that is half prophet and half poet, is simply a harmless lunatic . . . and [Eliot's] inspired Hebrew is talking like a fool" (*Standard,* 25 September; 2). In an earlier notice, the *Standard* reviewer had expressed his contempt for the discussions of the philosophers' club: in the conversations at The Hand and Banner, "Mordecai is the prin-

cipal orator, and we are bound to say that he is quite as intelligible as the other persons who take part in the discussions" (10 July; 2). Similarly, the *Glasgow News* saw some "bright flashes" in sections of part 6, but "elsewhere we are treated to Mordecai's maunderings about the future of the Jews" (1 July; 2). *The Guardian* (London) had at first a somewhat mixed reaction, finding Mordecai "a sort of modern representative of the ancient prophets who *fancies* [my emphasis] he has found in Deronda a fitting disciple to receive and embody the great ideas with which his soul is full . . ." (21 June; 825). But this paper's final review is quite unsympathetic: Deronda is unrealistic, and

> the Jewish part of the story is simply odd and inexplicable. It has nothing to do with the main plot, *which would move on quite smoothly if it was all cut out,* and its only merit lies in the very vivid picture of the Cohen household which it brings before us. There is a certain grandeur of confused glory, like a sunset of Turner's, about Mordecai's aspirations, but they never assume a shape distinct enough to give us the faintest idea of the practical work to which Deronda's life is henceforward to be dedicated, and, in spite of all his predilections and anticipations, we cannot but fear that he will make a very indifferent Jew. But that mysterious and picturesque race, 'aged, blind, unvenerable,' has evidently a special charm for the author.
>
> (4 October; 1312; my emphasis)

Among 20th century critics, F. R. Leavis is, of course, the most famous advocate of the split between the two parts: "the two stand apart, on a large scale, in fairly neatly separable masses" (79), of which the "good half" should have been admired (if George Eliot had been rightly appreciated) "not the less for the astonishing badness of the bad half" (80), i.e., the Jewish story. Eliot's contemporary Jewish critics do not all dispute Leavis on the separation. Jacobs, for instance, says that "the least observant must have noticed that *Daniel Deronda* is made up of two almost unconnected parts, either of which can be read without the other" (101). Only Kaufmann gives a full defense of the view held by Eliot, who "meant everything in the book to be related to everything else there" (*Letters* VI: 290): "the two narratives which run side by side in 'Daniel Deronda' are to be regarded as pendants mutually illustrating and explaining one another. But it need scarcely be said that the authoress has not fallen into the error of expressly indicating this relation, by crudely holding the two pictures up opposite each other" (Kaufmann 49).

MORDECAI AS JEWISH VISIONARY

Notably a minority view in the general critical response of the 1870s, the Jewish critics share an appreciation for Mordecai as a new version of the visionary in Jewish history and philosophy. The *Jewish Chronicle* sees him less as a realistic character than as "an abstraction of all the higher aspirations and sublimer thoughts of the Hebrew sages and poets. He is a noble type of what the modern Jew should be, rather than what he is" (8 September; 357). The context here suggests that it is not so much the impossibility of a modern Jew in the character of Mordecai, but a prominence of those who do not have his self-sacrificing spirit: the writer for the *Chronicle* (one of the strong advocates of Zionism in the late 19th century; see Bentwich and Shaftesley 215, 227 and *passim*) takes this occasion to chide his audience. Picciotto challenges the critics: Mordecai "is a prophet, a seer, but far from being the absolutely impossible character he has been considered by some critics. Anciently the most eloquent and learned rabbis among the Jews practised trades or handicrafts. Who shall say that among the immigrants from distant climes or among the Jews of Great Britain there is no workman whose whole heart is wrapped up in visions of the future greatness of his race?" He then adds, as an actual parallel, the example, from Lewes' 1866 *Fortnightly* article, of a workman's club for philosophical discussion (601).

The most thorough discussion of Mordecai in relation to possibility comes from Jacobs, who finds evidence of prejudice in the unwillingness of the English critics to accept him: "If Mordecai had been an English workman laying down his life for the foundation of some English International with Deronda for its Messiah Lassalle, he would have received more attention from the critics." Acknowledging that the "past generation of Englishmen has been . . . generous to Jews," Jacobs suggests readers were not "consciously repelled by the idea of a poor Jew being worthy of admiration. But," he adds, "fifteen centuries of hatred are not to be wiped out by any legislative enactment. . . . There remains a deep unconscious undercurrent of prejudice against the Jews which conscientious Englishmen have often to fight against . . ." (107). Mordecai is "a lineal successor of those great leaders of spiritual Judaism who have fought in the van in that moral warfare which Judaism has waged and won against the whole world. . . . A 'nation of shopkeepers' has produced a Milton, a Shelley, a Newman; a 'nation of pawnbrokers,' if you will, has given birth to a Jehuda Halevi, a Spinoza, a Mordecai" (104).

Finding, however, that "English critics . . . have unanimously pronounced [Mordecai] an impossibility," he too has recourse to facts, including the workman's club reported by Lewes and the example of the late Emmanuel Deutsch: "Would that Mr. Deutsch had lived to convince the world in his own burning words that Mordecai is no inert scarecrow of abstractions, but a warm living reality!" (104-105) Kaufmann too defends him in terms of depth of character: "He is one of the most difficult as well as one of the most successful essays in psychological analysis ever attempted by an author; and in his wonderful portrait . . . we see glowing enthusi-

asm united to cabalistic profundity, and the most morbid tension of intellectual powers united to clear and well-defined hopes" (67).

Though Jacobs says that the critics were unanimous in their failure to understand Mordecai, in fact, a few in the Gentile press did not share what Lewes called the "decidedly unsympathetic" attitude of the "Christian public" (*Letters* VI: 294). *The Nonconformist,* for example, notes the subtle development of plot connecting Deronda and Mordecai; of

> most absorbing interest . . . is the strange, half-mystical relation in which Deronda finds himself to the old Jew, Mordecai, at the book shop. We should not wonder if it were to prove for Daniel somewhat as it did for Saul of old. When he went out to find traces of the friends of Mirah, he is probably on the way to find a new kingdom for himself, as well as traces of his own paternity. Anyway, that odd, old, and as it might seem, half-insane Jew . . . who talks now like a weakling and now like a prophet [is not in the book] for nothing. . . . The mixture of Jewish shrewdness with enthusiasm and high ideal forms something original in fiction, though there *have* been such Jews.
>
> (31 May; 555)

Likewise, *The Globe and Traveller* (London), admitting the problem some readers might have in accepting the possibility of such an ideal, compares Mordecai to another Eliot character, Savonarola. Books 5 and 6

> contain one complete and indivisible study of character in the person of the Hebrew poet Mordecai. . . . In him George Eliot has no doubt risked forfeiting a considerable amount of popular interest for the sake of creating the most ambitious bit of portraiture that she has attempted since her historical picture of Savonarola. . . . Many people will find it hard to believe in the possible reality of so dramatic a figure as the consumptive shopman, lodging in a pawnbroker's family, associating with the narrowest and most unsympathetic people, and yet inwardly living in a visionary region where it is hard to decide whether he has in truth the soul of a prophet or the brain of a madman.
>
> (18 July; 6)

Mordecai, the review concludes, is the "most remarkable" character in a novel full of unusual people.

Mordecai and Zionism

Often, objections to the character of Mordecai were inextricable from objections to the Zionist conclusion. Thus, the *Edinburgh Courant* admits it has not considered the

> Jewish element [the story's] strong point. There is much that is simply obscure and tiresome in Mordecai's harangues, and the elaborate studies to which he and Deronda devote themselves, together with the mysterious chest of papers . . . prepare one for valuable dis-

coveries, which are never divulged, and *for a plan rather more definite than that which Deronda announces as the purpose of his mission to the East—viz., to restore a political existence to his people."*

(4 September; 6; my emphasis)

In contrast, Kaufmann (quoted above) referred to Mordecai's "clear and well defined hopes," and Jacobs observes that the "Two ideas [which] dominate Mordecai's arguments . . . resumption of the soil of Palestine by the Jews (which has often been proposed by Gentile writers as a solution of the much vexed Eastern Question), and as a consequence of the third and final promulgation of the Jewish religion to the world, are sufficiently definite ideas, however large and grand they may be" (108). The *Courant* reviewer seems to half-recognize this, for he proceeds thus immediately after the end of the quote above:

> No doubt it was necessary to account in some way for the mystery of Deronda's parentage, and there are passages descriptive of Jewish life and manner which one would not willingly omit. But so far as there is a serious 'purpose' in this part of the story, we must confess to thinking it a failure. There is *nothing new or original* in the representation of Jewish prospects and hopes, and you *might substitute any other oppressed nationality, or simply strike out the Jewish part of it altogether,* without seriously impairing the real interest of the book."

(4 September; 6; my emphasis)

This review puts the novel in a damned-if-it-does, damned-if-it-doesn't situation. On the one hand, the "discoveries" are not "divulged" nor the "plan" made "definite" enough for comprehension. And yet, there is "nothing new or original in the representation of Jewish prospects and hopes." The final sentence is the key: the Jewish part should have been omitted.

In a similar vein, the *Manchester Examiner and Times* cannot accept the idea of personal sacrifice involved in Daniel and Mirah's journey to the East. Discussing the expectations of the readers regarding a possible after-history of the novel's characters, the reviewer reverts to the astonishment of critics who opposed Deronda's conversion on grounds that an Englishman would never give up the joys and benefits of his special position:

> But one task at least we believe even George Eliot would be disposed to consider almost beyond her; we mean a narrative of the result of the efforts of Daniel and Mirah not merely to ameliorate the condition of the Hebrews in the East, but to make a nation of them. Is the satire altogether so unconscious which sets before us so romantic a scheme of philanthropy and the unselfish determination of two young Jews, both sensible of the charms of English civilisation and in a position to enjoy them, at the moment when we are wondering at a marvelous climax in the career of the most conspicuous member of the Jewish family known to modern England?

(31 August; 7)

It is not clear why Disraeli's elevation to the peerage as Lord Beaconsfield (announced 12 August 1876) should make it probable that Eliot was being satirical in having her Jewish characters set out to establish a homeland in the East. Quite the contrary, one might imagine, given Disraeli's own novels.

The issue of satire or seriousness also is raised by the *Manchester Guardian.* Though an early review found "most original" the juxtaposition of "one of the most poetic aspects—actual or possible—of Jewish thought and sentiment"—the character of Mordecai—with "aspects of Jewish life of a totally opposite character"— the family of the Cohens (30 May; 6), the final review declares Deronda not a "true dramatic representation," but rather limited to "description" and "analysis." Perhaps this is why he is judged finally as a passive victim: he

> has his life determined by events rather than by his own character, falls a helpless victim to the fascinations of the Hebrew mentor for whose ideas he consents to become the conduit pipe, and finally takes up for his quest of the Sangraal the promising task of gathering together the outcasts of Israel. It is difficult to say what amount of seriousness George Eliot intends us to attach to the scheme of a grand Jewish colonisation of Palestine and a political re-constitution of the race. That a belief in the genius and destinies of his people, in the persistency of its qualties and the importance of its influence, may be a noble and fruitful inspiration to one of the chosen nation we do not doubt, and such belief might well shape itself in impossible dreams in the brain of a recluse idealist such as Mordecai. But Daniel Deronda acting as a second Moses and leading back his people to the promised land hardly presents himself to our eyes as a serious figure."

(4 September; 6)

The reviewer's attitude is evident in the sarcastic tone of "promising task"; the loaded diction of "helpless victim," "outcasts of Israel," "impossible dreams," and "recluse idealist"; and the disclaimer "we do not doubt." In a madman such "impossible dreams" are credible, but not in a character whom the author has portrayed as perfect, a fact this review goes into considerable detail to establish, before the conclusion quoted above. The reference to the "quest of the Sangraal" is another assumption of the futility of idealism in a modern age, like the reference to Deronda as the "champion of Pan-judaism" quoted above, or the question in *Vanity Fair*: "What is the object of the melodramatic Jewish element in the story? What are we to suppose is the result of the vague and Quixotic design of Deronda?" (14 October; 240).

To conclude that Eliot was satirical, or just not serious in the Zionist plot, is to ignore the gradual development of Deronda's character in the novel:

> . . . while [in the scene with Deronda's mother] we have a distinct manifestation of certain blind determinations and sympathies due to race, we have also with

it a broad human sympathy and susceptibility with which the Jewish idea in itself is not usually associated. And, therefore, it is with the truest creative insight that George Eliot has contrived gradually to draw Deronda into a distinct and conscious sense of inner affinity with Jewish thought and tendency, through a poor idealist like Mordecai, who at once attracts and interests him, and gives play for sympathy, from the striking contrast between his ideas and grand purposes and his most sordid surroundings, and from the manner in which he is debarred from all sympathy in the only approach to intelligent society that is open to him.

(*Nonconformist* 16 August; 823, my emphasis)

Thence too comes the purpose of the debates at the club, which "not a few" may find "somewhat tedious. But they are given as much on account of the thought and sympathies more deeply stimulated by them in Deronda—thoughts and sympathies which are certainly meant to have their own effect on the whole issues of the story" (16 August; 823).

JEWISH TOPIC ONLY FOR JEWS

If some reviewers found the Jewish topic a "weariness" but tried to avoid an appearance of bias by adding "of course it ought not to be" (*Daily News* 31 August; 2, quoted above), other reviewers were quite open about the attitude that Jewish topics are only of interest to Jews:

> *Jews may possibly care* for those parts of the work which have reference to the Cohens in Whitechapel, to Mordecai, and to Deronda's indefatigable efforts to identify his origin with the Hebrew race. *Candid critics will fail to discover* in them anything of special excellence or novelty. The aspirations of Judaism, the consciousness of the great mission which *is said to haunt,* even in these latter days, the remnant of the Jewish race, have been exhaustively described in *Tancred*; and Daniel Deronda himself is nothing more than a hero after Mr. Disraeli's own heart, somewhat more solemn and scientific, as suits the attendant circumstances of George Eliot's novel.

(*The World* 6 September; 20, my emphasis)

Jews *may* possibly care, but anyone else who pretends to care is not telling the truth.

The London *Observer* critic is also sceptical about idealism being a characteristic of modern Jews; he doesn't care for the novel overall but discusses what he calls the "best and most valuable characters." After that

> Mordecai, of course, remains, and with him remain the Jewish family where Deronda discovered him, and all the Jewish lore, Jewish sentiment, and Jewish aspiration which the writer associates with them. But in spite [of Eliot's] erudition and imagination . . . we fear that most persons will find it the most tiresome and the most incredible. We are most of us tolerably familiar with the Jewish race, Jewish traditions, and the lives,

thoughts, and aspirations of ordinary Jews. And we think that most people who are familiar with them will say that though they have great practical talents and many domestic virtues, the attempt to attribute to them as a race exceptional ideality is a sore trial to our faith.

(3 September; 7)

As critics from Joseph Jacobs to Alan Mintz (at the Jerusalem Symposium [Shalvi 137-56] and elsewhere) have pointed out, the failure of idealism in the novel lies in the English society of Gwendolen and Grandcourt, and it is precisely in terms of the contrast between the lack of self-transcendent purpose in the former and the idealistic, but also practical force of the Jewish portion that the novel's critique of contemporary society gains its strength.

Different from the stance of the *London Observer,* that Jewish matters are very familiar, and for *that* reason the story is not credible, is the critic who places the blame on the unfamiliarity of the readers with Jewish topics. The *Daily News* (London) regrets the absence of Eliot's usual "large popular force set in the past" such as the Wesleyanism of *Adam Bede* or the Reformation-era presence of Savonarola in *Romola. Deronda* "is a novel of to-day, and no great historical force exists in it, except perhaps that unfamiliar one, the passion of Jewish nationality. Very great pains have been taken with the Hebrew side of the story, but unfortunately the matter is hard of understanding to the general reader" (June 6; 2). Given these attitudes, one can hardly wonder at Lewes's comments to Edward Downden, whose sensitive review appeared in February 1877 in *The Contemporary Review*: Eliot "has been pained to find many dear friends and some of her most *devoted* readers, utterly dead to all the Jewish part. The phrase uttered to one lady which was reported to me, 'I never *did* like the Jews and I never shall,' expresses pretty plainly the general state of feeling" (*Letters* VI: 336).

POSITIVE ATTITUDES: THE JEWISH PART

Despite these reviews, which explain Jacobs remarks about the negative reception of the novel, there were numerous, occasionally positive comments and even some positive sequences of reviews. Sometimes they touched on the same points that other reviewers handled negatively. For instance, *The Globe and Traveller* for 12 September admits that the novel has caused disappointment, because "It deals with people and with things" not expected in Eliot. But this reviewer celebrates Eliot's taking up a contemporary topic because present life "sadly wants a great painter," and touches on the reading audience's possible lack of sympathy, but not here to justify his own distaste. The review expresses sentiments like Eliot's own. Some contemporary novels have

> injured our readiness of sympathy with what lies outside our common experience—the present, past, and future of the Hebrew race, like the Florentine history in

"Romola," does not readily combine at first sight with our chronic interest in our neighbors and especially in ourselves. It requires more care and thought than can, perhaps, be fairly expected from ordinary readers, who ask, before all else, for easy reading, to harmonise these intensely foreign elements with the central story of Gwendolen Harleth's soul.

                                                        (6)

In a curious coincidence, two of the most generally sympathetic sets of reviews were published in papers at or near the place of what Joseph Jacobs calls "the most striking incident in the mediaeval history of the English Jews" (*The Jews of Angevin England* 385), the siege of Clifford's Tower at York, in which at least 150 Jews perished in 1190. The *York Herald* and the *Yorkshire Gazette* were both enthusiastic. After positive comments on the emerging Jewish story in the 11 May and 7 June numbers, the *Herald* critic betrays a receptiveness not found in the work of many of his peers: Book 6 "sustains [the story's] interest in a remarkable degree. We are held to the page with a fascination few can resist. The character of Mordecai comes out into fine relief and more is made of his poetic ideas than at one time seemed possible. Indeed, he grows upon us until we come to regard him as in many respects finer than Daniel Deronda himself, and drawn with a firmer freer hand. Deronda's state of mind respecting the Jew and the kind of confidence demanded of him is very cleverly portrayed." The discussion at the Hand and Banner is "singularly like reality" and "Mordecai's idea of a restoration of Judaism 'out of a new Jewish polity, grand, simply, just like the old' comes out more distinctly" (5 July; 3).

The next review, in contrast to those deploring Deronda's acceptance of his Jewish heritage, states matter-of-factly: "Deronda is a Jew, and yet he has been brought up as a Christian. He accepts his fate, and with a strange pleasure, born of many subtle experiences and prefigurings." (8 August; 3). Like the reviewer in the *Nonconformist,* this writer sees the development that makes plausible, even inevitable, Deronda's acceptance of his heritage. With this awareness, the final review notes that though "everyone had marked out Gwendolen as the wife of Deronda," it is fitting that the work end as it does (4 September; 6).

The Edinburgh *Daily Review,* whose strong Christian bias causes it to fault the "humanistic" parts of Eliot's work, found Mordecai a "splendid drawing. . . . Mr. Disraeli is a Jew, but how tawdry and unreal his most laboured writing on his own race appears beside this effort of the genius of a woman who was at least born a Christian. She has taken a Hebrew prophet, dressed him in the garb of an old beggar man who, while he mends his watches and keeps an old book shop, lives in a heaven of thought and emotion, to be described only as

that of Ezekiel and Spinoza combined. From the high level of the Greek Baldassarre of 'Romola,' she has unconsciously used the Old Testament to rise to the far higher type of this Semitic dreamer . . ." (30 May; 3). The next review has "no sympathy" with the "mere novel reader [who] will complain that the former half of the book [6] relating to the Jews is spoiled by the somewhat philosophical discussions of the club of poor men," because this section contains "some of the finest passages, certainly some of the most pregnant sayings which George Eliot has ever penned" (27 June; 5). Later reviews do not offer much comment on the Jewish part, so it is hard to see the writer's direction, but overall he is less concerned with the Jewish part *per se* than with the expression of elevated sentiments, especially of a religious character.

I have concentrated on the reactions to Mordecai and Deronda because these formed the bulk of the reviewers' comments on the Jewish aspects of the novel. Reactions to the Cohen family were less divided; most critics found them a vivid and credible picture. One might take exception to the epithets sometimes used for Ezra Cohen—as in the repeated comment of the *Manchester Examiner and Times*: Eliot "enables us to understand the estimate formed by the vulgar, commonplace Cohen" (29 May; 4) and "we should have been sorry to miss . . . the conversation between Deronda and the vulgar, commonplace Cohen" (28 June; 7). The word "vulgar" appears in an otherwise sympathetic review in the *Yorkshire Gazette* (10 June; 8) as well, and the Anglo-Jewish historian James Picciotto refers to the "shrewdness, vulgarity, and kindness of heart" of Ezra Cohen (600). Most reviewers who commented on little Jacob Cohen found him appealing; the *Manchester Guardian,* for instance, noted that "Among the Hebrews in whom the course of the story already abounds its readers will be glad to welcome the reappearance of little Jacob" (30 May; 6). However, the *Tablet,* though finding the study of Mordecai to contain "some of the most strongly original scenes in the book," adds: "The visionary Mordecai printing his Hebrew poetry on the mind of the horrible infant pawnbroker who stands on his head to distract himself during the printing process forms a startling scene" (1 July; 10; my emphasis). The reviews quoted from above are taken for the most part from the daily and weekly papers which responded to George Eliot's last novel as it appeared in installments over eight months in 1876. A full listing of all reviews for each paper cited is given in the Appendix. The reviews heretofore reprinted, or even those indexed merely, provide only a small portion of the evidence that led Eliot to deplore the "arrogance and contemptuous dictatorialness" in the English attitude toward Jews and other "oriental peoples" (letter to Stowe; VI: 301). Lewes and many members of the Anglo- Jewish, as well as the international Jewish community, were likewise dismayed at the critical response and raised the issue of anti-Semitism. The measure of popular resistance to Judaism and to the growing Zionist movement can better be taken from the responses of these ordinary newspapers read by ordinary people than from the quarterlies that appealed to more specialized readerships. Ironically, it was these ordinary readers, who had responded with such enthusiasm to *Adam Bede* and other of her early novels, whose imagination Eliot had hoped, through *Daniel Deronda,* "to rouse . . . to a vision of human claims in those races of their fellowmen who most differ from them in customs and beliefs" (*Letters* VI: 301). If, despite the critical response, the private letters she received and the public commendation of Jewish leaders like Adler, Picciotto, and Jacobs in England and Kaufmann abroad gave her encouragement in the last four years of her life that her effort had been worthwhile, how much more gratified would she have been had she been able to be present, nearly twenty years later, at that historic meeting when Albert Goldsmid declared himself "Daniel Deronda" to Theodor Herzl, or a hundred years later when the centenary symposium met in Jerusalem, proving by the fact of its being that the vision of Mordecai and Daniel was neither inexplicable nor impossible nor impractical.

Notes

1. A much abbreviated version of this essay was delivered as a paper at the first annual colloquium of the Western Association for Interdisciplinary Nineteenth-Century Studies at Scripps College, Claremont, California, 21-22 March 1986. For assistance on the research phase of this work, I would like to acknowledge and thank the staff of the British Newspaper Library in Colindale; for advice and assistance during its preparation, I would like to thank my colleague Norman Weinstein.

2. The *Liverpool Daily Post* mistakenly lists the *Fortnightly* article for 1865 instead of 1866.

Works Cited

Baker, William. *George Eliot and Judaism.* Salzbur: Institut fur Englische Sprache und Literatur, 1975.

Bentwich, Norman. *Early English Zionists, 1890-1920.* Tel Aviv: Lion the printer, n.d.

———. and John M. Shaftesley. "Forerunners of Zionism in the Victorian Era." *Remember the Days, Essays on Anglo-Jewish History.* Ed. John M. Shaftesley. London: Jewish Historical Society, 1966.

Carroll, David, ed. *George Eliot, the Critical Heritage.* New York: Barnes and Noble, 1971.

Eliot, George. *Adam Bede.* Ed. John Paterson. Boston: Houghton Mifflin, 1968.

———. *Daniel Deronda.* Ed. Barbara Hardy. Baltimore: Penguin, 1967.

Fulmer, Constance Marie. *George Eliot: A Reference Guide.* Boston: G. K. Hall, 1977.

Geibel, James Wayne. *An Annotated Bibliography of British Criticism of George Eliot, 1858-1900.* Diss. Ohio State University, 1969. Ann Arbor: UMI, 1970. 70-6780.

Haight, Gordon S., ed. *The George Eliot Letters.* 9 vols. New Haven: Yale U P, 1954-1978.

Halpern, Ben. *The Idea of the Jewish State.* 2nd ed. Cambridge, MA: Harvard U P, 1969.

Herzl, Theodor. *The Diaries of Theodor Herzl.* Trans. and ed. Marvin Lowenthal. 1956. New York: Grosset & Dunlap, 1962.

Holmstrom, John, and Laurence Lerner, eds. *George Eliot and Her Readers, a Selection of Contemporary Reviews.* New York: Barnes & Noble, 1966.

Jacobs, Joseph. *The Jews of Angevin England.* London: David Nutt, 1893; Westmead, England: Gregg International, 1969.

———. "Mordecai: A Protest Against the Critics." *Macmillan's Magazine* 36 (June 1877): 101-111.

Kaufmann, David. *George Eliot and Judaism, An Attempt to Appreciate 'Daniel Deronda.'* Trans. J. W. Ferrier. 2nd ed. New York: Haskell House, 1970.

Leavis, F. R. *The Great Tradition.* New York: New York U P, 1973.

Levitt, Ruth. *George Eliot: The Jewish Connection.* Jerusalem: Massada Ltd., 1975.

Picciotto, James. "Deronda the Jew." *The Gentleman's Magazine* 239 (November 1876): 593-603.

Shalvi, Alice, ed. *Daniel Deronda, A Centenary Symposium.* Jerusalem: Jerusalem Academic Press, 1976.

Zatlin, Linda Gertner. *The Nineteenth-Century Anglo-Jewish Novel.* Boston: Twayne, 1981.

APPENDIX

Newspapers and journals containing 1876 reviews quoted in the text; most of these were part of a sequence of reviews of *Daniel Deronda*; all reviews in the sequence, even if not quoted, are included.

The Daily News (London): 29 January; 6 June; 31 August

Daily Review (Edinburgh): 29 January; 28 February; 28 March; 27 April; 30 May; 27 June; 28 July; 5 September

The Edinburgh Courant: 29 January; 28 February; 30 March; 29 April; 7 June; 6 July; 7 August; 4 September

Figaro (London): 9 February; 22 March; 19 April; 24 May; 28 June; 29 July; 12 August; 27 September

Fortnightly Review: 1 November

The Glasgow News: 29 January; 28 February; 30 March; 6 June; 15 June; 1 July; 28 July

The Globe and Traveller (London): 31 January; 29 February; 10 April; 15 May; 18 July; 12 September

The Guardian (London): 2 February; 15 March; 21 June; 4 October

Jewish Chronicle: 21 July; 8 and 22 September; 15 and 22 December

Illustrated London News: 24 June; 5 August; 9 September

Liverpool Daily Post: 8 September

The Liverpool Weekly Albion (shares material with *Liverpool Daily Albion*; dates are for *Weekly*, which has the more complete reviews): 29 January; 4 March; 6 May; 29 July; 2 September

Manchester Examiner and Times: 29 January, 26 February; 29 March; 27 April; 29 May; 28 June; 27 July; 31 August

Manchester Guardian: 29 January; 28 February; 28 April; 30 May; 4 September

Morning Post (London): 17 October

New Quarterly Magazine (quarterly): notices in April; July; October

The Nonconformist: 2 February; 29 March; 12 April; 31 May; 16 August; 13 September

The Observer (London): 30 January; 12 March; 16 April; 3 September

Spectator: 29 January; 12 February; 8 April; 10 June; 29 July; 9 September

Standard (London): 7 February; 6 March; 3 April; 12 June; 26 June (very brief mention); 10 July; 14 August; 25 September

Sunday Times (London): 20 February; 19 March; 23 April; 14 May; 18 June; 23 July; 20 August

Tablet: 19 February; 11 March; 15 April; 27 May; 1 July; 29 July; 26 August; 4 November

Vanity Fair: 14 October

Westminster Review (quarterly): brief notices in April; July; October

The World (London): 2 February; 6 September

York Herald: 1 February; 1 March; 5 April; 11 May; 7 June; 5 July; 8 August; 4 September

Yorkshire Gazette: 5 February; 18 March; 22 April; 13 May; 10 June; 15 July; 5 August; 23 September

Bernadette Waterman Ward (essay date winter 2004)

SOURCE: Ward, Bernadette Waterman. "Zion's Mimetic Angel: George Eliot's *Daniel Deronda*." *Shofar: An Interdisciplinary Journal of Jewish Studies* 22, no. 2 (winter 2004): 105-15.

[*In the following essay, Ward asserts that while Eliot attempts to support Zionism and portray Jews and Judaism in a positive light in* Daniel Deronda, *she fails to create a compelling or authentic title character. Ward argues that Daniel is simply a racial Jew with no cultural connection to Judaism, nor any understanding of the Zionist movement.*]

George Eliot meant to take a stand against "narrowness and bigotry" with *Daniel Deronda*. Its favorable attitude towards Jews and Zionism gave the book notoriety and influence all over Europe; its hero Daniel discovers he is a Jew halfway through the novel, and his conversion to Jewish nationalism was meant to help foster the establishment of a "Belgium of the East," where many cultures could meet peacefully[1] and mix harmoniously in accord with to Eliot's utopian post-Christian relativism. Eliot gained applause from educated Jews all over Europe for her positive portraits of Jewish life, but the book is among George Eliot's least successful novels artistically, routinely faulted for "stiffness, didacticism and idealization"[2] which leave the eponymous hero "dwindling into a self-righteous prig."[3] Eliot seeks to make Daniel a superior being with almost magical transformative power in the moral sphere. She normally reserves this role for a type of female protagonist I have come to call the Mimetic Angel, building upon the literary insights of René Girard. It is because Eliot equates Jewish ancestry with the social position of women, and gives him no other principle on which to build his moral discernment, that Daniel fails as a fully rounded character.

The novel has two strands of plot. The first strand concerns vain, selfish Gwendolyn Harleth, pointedly described as being like "a very common sort of men."[4] Drawn into the wiles of an evil, tyrannical man by her competitiveness against other girls, she is forced to marry him by a financial disaster, despite knowing of the illegitimate children he is thereby disinheriting. After this moral fall, she reappears occasionally to have crises of conscience in the presence of her slight acquaintance Daniel, before whom she feels a sense of moral inferiority. Gwendolyn makes a sort of Platonic ascent from rebellion against Daniel's moral superiority, which her beauty cannot defeat, through submission to Daniel personally as a sort of lay pastor, into something approaching religious reverence for his virtue.

Eliot's plan to inspire sympathy with Jews depends on the less critically successful sections of the novel focusing on Daniel, raised as an English gentleman without knowledge of his origins, and made sensitive to others' pain by his own fear that he may be a bastard. Eliot gives a feminine cast to Daniel's early moral development: "He had not lived with other boys, and his mind showed the same blending of child's ignorance with surprising knowledge which is oftener seen in bright girls" (p. 141). Gwendolyn's fascination with Daniel rarely intrudes into his life. As he aimlessly considers his career after college, Daniel happens along a riverbank in time to save beautiful, Jewish Mirah from suicide. He joins her search for her long-lost brother, Mordecai, a mystic whose visions of a coming spiritual heir draw him to Daniel when Daniel finds him.

Daniel soon discovers that he is a legitimate son of a Jewish marriage, but his widowed mother rejected both Judaism and him, arranging his English upbringing. He embraces his Jewish identity and rejects the English social world; his crisis comes just when Gwendolyn's husband drowns in an accident for which she feels irrationally responsible. She clearly expects Daniel to take his place in English society as her spouse and life's guide. Instead he sends her off with some remarkably vague moral advice, which she treasures, and marries Mirah. Mordecai dies as a satisfied spiritual progenitor, on the eve of Daniel's journey to Palestine in the interests of Zionism.

The awed, passionate, intimate, sometimes even playful relation between a Jewish believer and God is not important to Eliot's portrait of Mordecai, who indeed spends all his time studying religious writings, but speaks of the Eternal Goodness in the tones of Matthew Arnold. Mordecai is, at best, a rather stiff character; at worst, he is a walking Romantic social theory attached to a cabalism which Eliot carefully documented in her notebooks and attributed to him, as she attributed superstitions to other (usually more fully realized) characters—Adam Bede's premonitions about his father's death, or Dinah Morris's Methodist visions. Joy with a flavor of straightforwardly practiced Judaism—the genuine lightheartedness with which one performs good deeds in accordance with the Law—is left to some minor characters, Mordecai's hosts, the Cohens. Ritual prayer is delegated mostly to Mirah, whose wispy, self-negating saccharinity seems to mark her as a refugee from a Dickens novel. Eliot makes Mordecai primarily a philosopher with Romantic notions about language and a dream of the resurgence of the Jewish people.

Yet Mordecai has visions and enunciates oracles which establish Daniel's identity as a sort of messiah. Eliot corroborates these with her accounts of Daniel's power to save those in moral distress, though the reason for that power never becomes clear; the ethical advice that he gives is not only banal but exceptionally non-specific even for platitudes. Daniel changes Gwendolyn's heart with this:

> Look on other lives besides your own. See what their troubles are, and how they are borne. Try to care about something in this vast world besides the gratification of small selfish desires. Try to care for what is best in thought and action—something that is good apart from the accidents of your own lot.
>
> (p. 383)

This rather dull stuff magically transforms, as does Dinah's passionately Methodist moral guidance in *Adam Bede,* or Maggie Tulliver's resignation garnered from her social oppression and *The Imitation of Christ* in *The Mill on the Floss,* or Dorothea's religiously philanthropic passion in *Middlemarch.* As she listens to this vague exhortation, Gwendolyn becomes Daniel's Eternal Disciple,[5] seeking to imitate him by referring every action and idea to his imagined judgment about its propriety for her.

Gwendolyn's role requires mimetic dependency—an indignity which Eliot is willing to visit upon Gwendolyn but from which the author seeks to protect her hero. René Girard argues convincingly, in many theoretical works, that human desire is inherently aimless, once "basic needs are fulfilled," and that we therefore look to one another imitatively to discover what is desirable. Those who seem to know what they want are the admired "models" or "idols" for this mimesis; and what the imitator ultimately desires is the self-assured *being* of the model. Of course, the direction of desire by observation of what others want is as much a force in geopolitics as in the nursery; Girard first discussed it in nineteenth-century novels in which men appear to be competing for a woman but are in fact competing for one another's admiration. Girard astutely observed that the successful rival can indeed command admiration rather than enmity, if his status as victor is unassailable. The unsuccessful rival often becomes an "eternal disciple" by adopting the values of the model—including, perhaps, the model's contempt for the disciple.[6]

A mild form of this transference of desire is used to sell products with the names of famous sports figures or media idols; but there are grimmer forms of Eternal Discipleship. For reasons ranging from sheer muscle mass to complex social arrangements, a woman is particularly vulnerable to such mimetic frustration in attaining power and glory as to make her bind up her identity in the worth of a male idol. This condition, the "internalized oppression" noted by feminists from the time of Mary Wollstonecraft and John Stuart Mill to the present, can cause an Eternal Disciple to engage in self-hatred for failing to fulfill the idol's wishes, redirecting onto the self even blame that might legitimately attach itself to the idol's behavior. Successful caste systems of all sorts depend on self-subjugation by mimetic inferiors eager to fulfill their submissive roles, and on superiors confident in the propriety of their domination. Rebellion against such a system can, in fact, create social disorders, and new subjugations yet more venomous than those left behind; caste systems do at least create stable social arrangements.

Girard points out that Judaism (and through Judaism, Christianity) unmasks the falsity of the assumption that human admiration is of infinite worth. Not only does divine law take precedence over the granting of supreme power in one's life to other human beings—the persecuted, the weak and the poor may well have claim to spiritual superiority, and certainly "the fat and the strong," in Ezekiel's phrase,[7] have no claim to special veneration. Friedrich Nietzsche despised this "Jewish" point of view, which seemed to reward victims with imaginary powers because they could not take real power and subjugate their betters by sheer strength.[8] But Girard, attacking Nietzsche head-on, lauds the Hebrew prophets for recognizing the futility of the cycle of subjugation and revenge. The clear-eyed denunciation of this evil, rather than the acceptance of the role of disciple to the powerful of the earth, involves a courageous willingness to accept persecution rather than become a rival to the powerful. Only monotheism offers an escape from the cycles of rivalry practiced by various gods and men.

Nevertheless, Nietzsche's analysis goes far in explaining the nineteenth-century British cultural phenomenon of the "Angel in the House," named by the Roman Catholic poet Coventry Patmore but appearing in George Eliot's novels as well. Virginia Woolf seethes about the "Angel in the House":

> She was intensely sympathetic. She was immensely charming. She was utterly unselfish. She excelled in the difficult arts of family life. She sacrificed herself daily. If there was a chicken, she took the leg; if there was a draught she sat in it—in short she was so constituted that she never had a mind or wish of her own, but preferred always to sympathise with the minds and wishes of others.

This Angel in the House had instructions for how a young woman should deal with a man: "Be sympathetic; be tender; flatter; deceive; use all the arts and wiles of our sex. Never let anybody guess that you have a mind of your own."[9] The Angel in the House uses her sexuality to civilize the male brutes around her, and her real power is in the manipulation of others' guilt and desire to dominate. She is a nineteenth-century revision of the insouciantly anti-Christian tradition of Courtly

Love, emerging as the Victorian Pre-Raphaelite poets read Dante. Coventry Patmore, who wrote *The Angel in the House,* reinterpreted divine grace as mediated by Beatrice in Dante's *Divine Comedy*; he made grace itself the symbol for the psychological and moral elevation to which a woman could bring a man. This inversion of the sexual symbolism of his own Christianity, as well as the works of the Hebrew prophets, was the strange outgrowth of a fundamentally Christian idea of a superior being who suffers wrongs without revenge in order that others might be saved. When Eliot wrote, without irony, of "woman's peculiar constitution for special moral influence," she was invoking the notion that someone who refrains from vengeance is especially virtuous and can transform others with her virtue. Nietzsche sneered that Judaism confused the categories of those who restrain their capacity for vengeance and those who are helpless to achieve revenge; like Patmore, Eliot seems to have actually confused those categories. She attributes special power to those who in fact are powerless to avenge wrongs. Eliot's high-mindedness serves her worse than Patmore's sentimentality on this point. Patmore knows why a powerless woman can seem to transform men: utter dependency on his opinion flatters a man in his desire to be idolized. Woman in Patmore sees

> what he admires
> within her glass, and sight of this
> Makes all the sum of her desires
> To be devotion unto his.[10]

Patmore's Angel can manipulate male desire if she will only "on her sweet self set her own price."[11] However, her overmastering desire for male approval limits her price-fixing. Patmore says: "The woman is the man's 'glory', and she naturally delights in the phrases which are assurances that she is fulfilling her function. . . . A woman without this kind of 'vanity' is a monster."[12] Therefore "To rivet and exalt his love / Her mode of candor is deceit."[13] Patmore's Angel thinks not of Truth but of the impression she creates in the eye of her idol, eats up lying flattery, accepts blame for her man's faults rather than requiring him to repent of them, and deceives. The Angel is an Eternal Disciple, unable to compete in *being* with the unreachably superior male; she therefore patterns her behavior in conformity with his perceived desire. If she is unable to fulfill his wishes, she cannot blame him, but must instead channel all the resentments of the marriage onto herself, in order not to disrupt the social ordering of the relationship. Thus she can become like her master—or change him, if he can be brought to attend to her, and see her false humility as heroic suffering for his sake, and become humbly grateful for it. The abnegation of self practiced by an Angel in the House can mimic virtuous selflessness, but operates out of a dependence on the recognition of the idol so desperate that it disregards truth and personal responsibility. Victorians would perceive its fundamental cowardice as unmanly.

Eliot's Mimetic Angels seek to abnegate the self by perfect sympathy. Eliot advocates neither sexual manipulativeness nor deceit, yet, as in Patmore's system, the power of the woman always comes from an intense sensitivity to what more powerful people really want and a desire to provide it. For women, awareness of others' desires comes from subjugation: a master need not know what the slaves want, but the slave had better know what the master wants. Eliot treats this enslaved helplessness as a school of virtue. A feminist critic says, "She could even state that the fact that 'woman seems to me to have the worse share in existence' should be the basis for 'a sublimer resignation in woman and a more regenerating tenderness in man.'"[14]

Eliot seeks to give Daniel a feminine depth of sympathy. This is why she emphasizes a feminine side to him, as she had emphasized a masculine side in his foil Gwendolyn. However, the concrete conditions that produce a condition of dependency are not really his; a rich young man of exceptional manly beauty, he is given an upbringing of extraordinary privilege in the household of an English baronet. His sensitivity is supposed to come from suspecting that he may be illegitimate and that his affectionate guardian may actually be his father. Such a suspicion, especially with assurance of a handsome independent income for life, does not approach the level of insecurity of even a privileged Victorian woman, who literally had no right to any of her possessions without her husband's approval. Eliot's early identification of Daniel with a clever girl is partial evidence of an inability to transfer to men the moral superiority which she attributed to women; her female characters, even if somewhat idealized, can bear this burden of intense sympathy because realism demands that she accurately depict women's dependency.

Although she thinks dependency upon others is the ground of sympathy, Eliot does not want an unmanly male hero, and makes Daniel rebuff the needy Gwendolyn to preserve the independence of what one critic calls "unscrupulous" manhood.[15] Daniel rejects indignantly a singing career which would involve him in constantly soliciting public approval; Gwendolyn, in a deliberate parallel, seeks such a career. This accords well with Victorian views of natural sex roles—but, if not from a dependent supersensitivity to others' desires, whence springs Daniel's ability to efface himself for others?

Daniel's real qualification for the development of this sympathy is evidently his membership by blood in what Eliot calls the "Suffering Race." Eliot makes his Jewishness the equivalent of femininity, perhaps in an un-

conscious identification of the historical oppression of Jews with that of women. Daniel himself is feminized, as we have seen, and Daniel's mother is the source of both his public name and his secret Jewishness. Eliot distances Daniel from actual Jewish culture at the time when his preternatural virtues emerge into action. He is in college and just out of it when he performs his first heroic actions of sympathy. She specifies that he was educated at Cambridge in the 1850s, where, her notes for the book observe, attendance was required at a half-hour's Anglican chapel service every morning. Young men attending had to sign the Articles of Faith of the Church of England in order to matriculate, and again in order to graduate.

Daniel is unable to make up his mind what to do after graduation partly because he embraces a morality too abstract to urge him to any concrete attachments. Untouched by the legal or social disabilities of Jews in Europe, Daniel somehow (and not believably, according to a plethora of critics) has developed the personality that Eliot associates with frustrated spiritual ambitions such as those of her heroines Dorothea, Dinah, and Maggie, or the historical Saint Theresa: a peculiar, preternatural sensitivity which saves Daniel from chilly indifference to all particular good. Eliot does not account for this peculiarity, except to give him a sort of a call of ancestral blood.

Not long before, the French atheist and anti-Semite, Ernest Renan, had published a life of Jesus in which he made Jesus blond and, if a Jew at all, at least one with a great deal of Gentile admixture, raised in "Galilee of the Gentiles" and so preserved from the narrow-mindedness that Renan took pains to connect to the Jews.[16] Except that she gave her hero brown hair, Eliot's Daniel oddly resembles Renan's Jesus, the spokesman of the enlightened rejection of religious establishments (like the one that had refused Renan a professorship just before he authored his *Vie de Jésus*).

Despite his nationalistic destiny in the book, Daniel's dialogue bespeaks abstract philosophical humanism implausibly linked to nationalism; one critic characterizes the interaction between the mystical prophet and his spiritual heir as "Mill vs. Mordecai."[17] Eliot's Daniel develops through the novel into the spokesman of a moralistic Hebraism, in Matthew Arnold's famous construct, warming and particularizing a clear but uninvolved philosophical Hellenism. Mere cosmopolitan Hellenism exposes people to the risk of *anomie,* the indifference to others which is for Eliot the great enemy of human flourishing; the absence of Arnold's "Hebraism" is the source of Daniel's depression and directionlessness after college. Local or ancestral associations can open one's heart to sympathy and thus morality.

This is a Romantic notion; in Eliot it certainly springs from Wordsworth. Racial identity draws Daniel to generous devotion and saves him from motiveless aimlessness.

In the novel, Eliot emphasizes the goodness of having a native place and community to which one can feel a loyalty that raises one above the self.[18] Most of her Jews are generous, though, as she does with women, Eliot does show us some Jews who are boorish and out of touch with larger sympathies. Eliot certainly means the novel to excite sympathy for Jews and encourage Zionism, for she thinks Jews need local roots for their culture, which has been treated as alien to Europe. Eliot introduces Gwendolyn's house by saying,

> A human life, I think, should be well rooted in some spot of a native land, where it may get the love of tender kinship for the face of the earth . . . inwrought with affection, and kindly acquaintance with all neighbors . . . as a sweet habit of the blood. At five years old, mortals are not prepared to be citizens of the world, to be stimulated by abstract nouns, to soar above preference into impartiality.

> (p. 16)

Gwendolyn, rootless, is morally stunted, as is Daniel's mother, who rejected her roots. Eliot recognizes mere family loyalty as narrow and destructive, but she considers one's native place and culture both intimate enough to claim personal attachment and large enough to induce selflessness.

Eliot saw European Jews as connecting the Semitic "east" to the European west, oblivious to the offense which Jewish presence and, much more, Jewish success would give to the surrounding Muslim nations.[19] The novel espoused a political Zionism perhaps more interesting to the British government than to European Jews, but soon was eagerly read and translated around Europe.[20] Though she sees nationalism as a stepstone to universal sympathy, Eliot is anti-assimilationist. Ironically, the idea that national identity and self-determination are moral imperatives strongly influenced real, and ferociously bigoted, politics in the locale to which she sends her newly-fledged fictional Zionist. She contributed almost as much to the intellectual ferment that formed the nation-states in the Middle East as did another Londoner, her fellow secularist, Karl Marx; though the infusion of ideas was not, as Eliot hoped, a force for international harmony.

Eliot creates some truly evil villains beyond our pity, like Gwendolyn's husband, who understands his victims' emotions and manipulates them. But the truly pitiable fate is to lack the sympathy that makes love possible, like Daniel's resentful and ambitious mother. When this character rejects her upbringing for a career outside the bounds of Jewish wifehood, Eliot makes her miserable. Daniel abandons his English upbringing equally, yet Eliot evidently approves his natalist nationalism. Behind Eliot's preference for blood ties over upbringing is a movement from the social morality of Wordsworth towards the German Romantic ideal of blood-and-soil folk culture.[21]

Daniel's imperviousness to his cultural surroundings is rather remarkable. Young Englishmen educated in the fifties and early sixties of the nineteenth century at either Oxford or Cambridge, as Daniel was, would have found moral earnestness immovably linked with Christianity. Compulsory chapel provided a context for generous and self-sacrificing impulses. John Henry Newman's Oxford novel *Loss and Gain* shows late-forties English university life in which discussions of Christian belief engage undergraduates as discussions of downloading music CDs engage them now.[22] The actual letters of students at this time confirm his impression.[23] If a Victorian wanted to create a youth of firm courage and extraordinary, but not effeminately dependent, sympathy, the link between the two would have been what mimetic theory recognizes as anti-sacrificial principle found in both Christianity and Judaism. But when Gwendolyn demands moral advice, Daniel never adverts to the religion in which he has supposedly been educated. Moreover, he embraces a Jewish identity, and engages in the study of religious writings, while specifically resisting Jewish religious belief, although he has just been in contact with either real prophecy and foresight or a series of coincidences bordering on the miraculous.

His nationalism has similar lapses. *Daniel Deronda* does not, as a novel, seriously embrace the larger international struggle in which the character Daniel would be engaged were he to enter upon political Zionism. Eliot does not recognize that national self-determination by its nature divides different peoples, and involves them in larger international rivalries. Daniel, indeed, never refers his mild and sweet moral insights to his political life. He adheres, even at the end, to a value system that is in fact personal and domestic—what one critic calls "the female-centered private goodness of the heart."[24] And so Daniel becomes neither very political nor very religious. Neither does he imitate Mordecai, though he does marry Mordecai's submissive sister.

Were Daniel a woman, he would fit into Eliot's analysis of the social virtues imposed on women by the necessities of dependence. Eliot was optimistic about the possibility of moral progress by means of these, but her novels, more truthful than her theories, offer little hope of it. Social virtues developed by mere dependency contribute in the end to social scapegoating. The nationalistic impulse might engage a man's passions and make the character believable, but such a passion would be too "bigoted," as Eliot characterizes Jews who keep to the traditions of their ancestors without question. History has demonstrated that to fix one's hopes for the development of sympathy upon nationalism, particularly racial self-determination, is no escape from mimetic violence. Eliot's project of using literature to promote sympathy with the victims of scapegoating has rather more hope in it, but Daniel, meant to engage our sympathy, is only nominally a Jew. Daniel is connected by no cultural ties, and no religious ties, to his genetic heritage: he is a Jew in the image of the earnest, ethical, deracinated upper-class English unbeliever.[25] Eliot wanted to free the Jews from scapegoating, but this is eliminating scapegoating by eliminating the "preferential signs of victimization"[26]; she merely scapegoats Jewishness itself rather than Jews.

The novel's title character falls flat because Daniel must preach on his own nonexistent authority. The characteristics Eliot gives him to make him virile and courageous are disconnected from the characteristics she must give him in order to make him a Mimetic Angel. Not by nationalism—which he scarcely seems to internalize—but by submitting his autonomy to a straightforwardly monotheistic religion could his intense sympathy with others be maintained without a terrible dependency on human, ultimately mimetic, opinion. This Eliot could not give to her hero; she felt she had to drive religion out and replace it by social Duty.[27] Her concept of a future was evolutionary and progressive, looking forward to "a generation, that in the onward tendency of human things have risen above the mental level of the generation before them."[28] But progressive evolution favors the superior minds and bodies, and the socially united; a duty to the future is (as readers of Nietzsche demonstrated) easily made a duty to engage in mimetic scapegoating. Abstract humanism, as envisioned in the early days of Eliot's Daniel, might disapprove of victimization but cannot draw one's commitments to action in any particular direction—a failure which is Eliot's equivalent to Hell. Neither the deceptions of the Angel in the House nor the call of blood and soil could in the end satisfy Eliot's desire for truth and benevolence; but she thrust aside the idea of an actual religion, with a real God to whom one can legitimately submit, as insufficiently reverent to individual autonomy. In rejecting the idea that a strong and noble man can in fact give himself over selflessly to God, she ironically produced in her final hero a character with no self, an empty man.

Notes

1. Quoted in William Myers, "George Eliot: Politics and Personality," *Literature and Politics in the Nineteenth Century* (London: Methuen, 1971), p. 123.

2. Deborah Heller, "Jews and Women in George Eliot's *Daniel Deronda*," in *Jewish Presences in English Literature,* ed. Derek Cohen and Deborah Heller (Montreal: McGill-Queen's University Press, 1990), p. 78.

3. James Harrison, "The Root of the Matter in *Daniel Deronda,*" *Philological Quarterly* (1989): 516.

4. George Eliot, *Daniel Deronda,* Oxford World's Classics edition, ed, intr. Graham Handley (Oxford and New York: Oxford University Press, 1988), p. 33.

5. This expression develops from Girard's *Deceit, Desire and the Novel: Self and Other in Literary Structure* (Baltimore: Johns Hopkins University Press, 1965); "eternal" here being a play on "the Eternal Husband," as Girard has put it. René Girard, personal communication at the Stanford Colloquium on Religion and Violence, November 1998.

6. The process Girard describes was, he notes, described by Freud, but all desire was in that theory swallowed up in sexuality; Girard allows desire a greater indifference to its object.

7. Speaking in the name of God, Ezekiel uses an image of people as sheep, saying, "I will seek that which was lost, and will bring back that which was driven away, and will bind up that which was broken, and will strengthen that which was sick; and the fat and the strong I will destroy, I will feed them in justice" (Ezekiel 34:15, *The Holy Scriptures, According to the Masoretic Text: A New Translation with the Aid of Previous Versions and with Constant Consultation of Jewish Authorities.* [Philadelphia: The Jewish Publication Society of America, 5677-1917]).

8. This is, of course, the argument of Nietzsche's *The Genealogy of Morals,* first essay, sections 11-15.

9. Virginia Woolf, "Professions for Women," in *The Death of the Moth and Other Essays* (New York: Harcourt, Brace and Co., 1942), p. 237.

10. Coventry Patmore, *The Angel in the House in Poems,* 9th collective ed., vol. 1 (London: George Bell and Sons, 1906), p. 90.

11. Patmore, *The Angel in the House,* 1.iii.3

12. Coventry Patmore, *The Rod, the Root and the Flower,* second ed., revised (London: George Bell and Sons, 1907), p. 40.

13. *Poems,* p. 124.

14. Heller, "Jews and Women," p. 93.

15. Patricia Vigderman, "The Traffic in Men: Female Kinship in Three Novels of George Eliot," *Style* 32:1 (Spring 1988): 32.

16. Ernest Renan, "Vie de Jésus," in *Œuvres complètes de Ernest Renan,* ed. Henriette Psichiari, (Paris: Calmann-Levy, 1947).

17. Amanda Anderson, "George Eliot and the Jewish Question," *Yale Journal of Criticism* 10:1 (Spring 1998): 41.

18. Anderson, "George Eliot and the Jewish Question," p. 41 *et passim.*

19. The *Q'ran* says, in *Surah* 9, 29-30, "29. Fight those who believe not in God nor the last day, nor hold that forbidden which hath been forbidden by God and His Apostle, nor acknowledge the religion of truth (even if they are) of the people of the Book, until they pay the Jizya with willing submission and feel themselves subdued. 30 The Jews call Uzair a son of God and the Christians call Christ the Son of God. That is a saying from their mouth: (in this) they but imitate what the Unbelievers of old used to say. God's curse be on them: how they are deluded away from the truth!" Ali Yusuf's footnote defines the *jizya* as "a poll-tax levied from those who did not accept Islam, but were willing to live under the protection of Islam, and were thus tacitly willing to submit to its ideals being enforced in the Muslim State, saving only their personal liberty of conscience as regarded themselves" (*The Holy Q'ran, Translation and Commentary,* A. Yusuf Ali [Brentwood, Maryland: Amana Corp., 1983]). *Surah* 6 is also instructive in relation to this question, and Yusuf Ali's footnotes very illuminating. The amount of the *Jizya* is not specified; neither are the strictures by which the People of the Book were to be made to feel themselves subdued; but clearly success and prosperity above that of their Muslim neighbors would violate the proper order of things as set forth in this passage.

20. Susan Myers, "Safely to their Own Borders", *ELH* 60:3 (Fall 1993): 324-54.

21. Monica Cohen, "From Home to Homeland: The Bohemian in *Daniel Deronda*," *Studies in the Novel* 30:3 (Fall 1998): *passim.*

22. See his novel *Loss and Gain* (Oxford: Oxford University Press: World's Classics Edition, 1986).

23. See the correspondence of Gerard Manley Hopkins's circle of college friends from the 1860s in *Further Letters of Gerard Manley Hopkins, Including His Correspondence with Coventry Patmore,* 2d. ed., revised and enlarged, ed. Claude Colleer Abbott (Oxford: Oxford University Press, 1956).

24. Cohen, "From Home to Homeland," pp. 342-3.

25. Anderson, "George Eliot and the Jewish Question."

26. René Girard, *The Girard Reader* (New York: Crossroad, 1996), p. 271.

27. This is part of the modern project of scapegoating religion which René Girard discusses in "Nietzsche versus the Crucified," *The Girard Reader,* pp. 244-61.

28. George Eliot, *The Mill on the Floss,* ed. Sally Shuttleworth (London and New York: Routledge, 1991), p. 249.

FURTHER READING

Criticism

Cowen, Anne, and Roger Cowen. *Victorian Jews through British Eyes.* Oxford, England and New York: Oxford University Press, 1986, 196 p.

   Discusses the perceptions prevalent among Victorians regarding Jews and traces the historical basis for such perceptions.

Elukin, Jonathan M. "A New Essenism: Heinrich Graetz and Mysticism." *Journal of the History of Ideas* 59, no. 1 (January 1998): 135-48.

   Examines Heinrich Graetz's ideas that mysticism was the link between the Essenes and Christianity.

Endelman, Todd M. "Native Jews in the Victorian Age." In *Radical Assimilation in English Jewish History, 1656-1945,* pp. 73-113. Bloomington and Indianapolis: Indiana University Press, 1990.

   Explores the historical and economic developments in the nineteenth century that affected English Jews and the perceptions about Jews, and analyzes the impact of such developments and perceptions on nineteenth-century literature.

Kornblatt, Judith Deutsch. "Vladimir Solov'ev on Spiritual Nationhood, Russia and the Jews." *The Russian Review* 56, no. 2 (April 1997): 157-77.

   Outlines how Solov'ev moved from an interest in the religious or spiritual aspect of Judaism to an understanding of the Jewish national character.

Modder, Montagu Frank. *The Jew in the Literature of England to the End of the 19th Century.* 1939. Reprint. New York and Philadelphia: Meridian Books, Inc. and The Jewish Publication Society of America, 1960, 435 p.

   Researches the portrayal of Jewish characters in English literature and traces economic conditions which significantly affected the social status of the

Jews in England during the eighteenth and nineteenth centuries.

Naman, Anne Aresty. *The Jew in the Victorian Novel: Some Relationships between Prejudice and Art.* New York: AMS Press, Inc., 1980, 238 p.

Compares prejudice against Jews as represented in the writings of Charles Dickens, Anthony Trollope, and George Eliot.

Salmon, Rachel. "Reading Hopkins: A Dialogue between Two Traditions." *The Hopkins Quarterly* 25, nos. 3-4 (summer-fall 1998): 68-75.

Discusses Gerard Manley Hopkins's concept of the hermeneutic dichotomy between Judaism and Christianity.

Spector, Sheila A., ed. *British Romanticism and The Jews: History, Culture, Literature.* New York: Palgrave Macmillan, 2002, 294 p.

Collection of essays assessing the impact of Jewish history and society on the development of British Romanticism.

————, ed. *The Jews and British Romanticism: Politics, Religion, Culture.* New York: Palgrave Macmillan, 2005, 334 p.

A collection of essays that trace how the Enlightenment shaped the relationship of the Jewish community to the larger British society, focusing on politics, religion, and culture.

Thomas, Gordon K. "The Forging of an Enthusiasm: Byron and the *Hebrew Melodies.*" *Neophilologus* 75, no. 4 (October 1991): 626-36.

Looks at the events in Byron's life that led him to compose various poems, including the *Hebrew Melodies.*

Wohlfarth, Marc E. "*Daniel Deronda* and the Politics of Nationalism." *Nineteenth-Century Literature* 53, no. 2 (September 1998): 188-210.

Examines the Jewish theme and plot in *Daniel Deronda* in relation to British nationalism.

Additional coverage of the portrayal of Jews in nineteenth-century English literature is contained in the following source published by Thomson Gale: *Nineteenth-Century Literature Criticism,* **Vol. 72.**

Major Cities in Nineteenth-Century Literature

The following entry contains critical commentary on representations of London, New York City, Paris, Rome, and St. Petersburg in nineteenth-century literature.

INTRODUCTION

Many nineteenth-century writers view the Victorian city as an obstacle to artistic inspiration; the crowds, unsanitary conditions, crime, and pollution, they argue, obscure the natural beauty of the world. Other writers express the opposite sentiment, maintaining that these same aspects of city life provide unique insights into the human condition. These differing impressions of the city are evident in Victorian poetic treatments of London and Paris. Matthew Arnold equates life in London with decay and corruption, and contrasts it with the restorative power and virtue of the natural world, while Charles Baudelaire draws inspiration from the physical devastation of Paris in the mid-1800s and uses the imagery of ruin and confusion to symbolize his own emotional devastation and that of his countrymen. Critics Michael Gassenmeier and Jens Martin Gurr (see Further Reading) trace the development of two opposing views in poetry featuring the city of London, maintaining that the contemporaneous production of poetry that derides and celebrates city life reflects the political and ideological debates that took place in England during the seventeenth and eighteenth centuries. In addition to works featuring London as alternately good and evil, various authors, including Charles Dickens and G. W. M. Reynolds, portray the city as a labyrinth, symbolizing the complexity of modern life.

During and since the nineteenth century, writers have captured New York City residents' historically frenetic pace of life, setting their works in a wide range of locales within the city, such as Central Park, the Bowery, the Tenderloin district, and the New York harbor. Authors such as Edgar Allan Poe, Walt Whitman, Herman Melville, Stephen Crane, and Henry James present New York City as alternately impersonal, cold, power-hungry, corrupt, progressive, hopeful, alive, unforgiving, and ultimately, symbolic of the elusive nature of humanity. Dickens assumes the role of a *flâneur*—a casual urban spectator, intimately knowledgeable of the world he surveys—to relate his impressions of New York City in his *Sketches by Boz* (1836). Whitman, meanwhile, employs the imagery of a constant parade of spectacle abounding in places such as Broadway and the Brooklyn Ferry to communicate his ideas regarding a collective human consciousness.

The French Revolution brought enormous changes to the city of Paris. Victorian novelists participated in, and in many cases guided, the development of a new Parisian reality separate from its monarchic past. Numerous literary guidebooks to Paris were compiled during the post-revolution era, providing sketches of life in modern Paris and attempting to define the new structure as well as comment upon it. "Haussmannization," the redesigning of Paris using London as a model that was undertaken by Napoleon III and Georges Haussmann from 1850 to 1880, sparked a widespread debate over the characterization of Parisians and Paris life. French authors served as reporters, capturing the tangible and intangible aspects of Paris life in great detail, and providing a running commentary on the city's urbanization as well as a frame of reference for the city's residents. Dickens and other contributors to his journal *Household Words* (1850-59) depict a view of Paris during the 1850s that critic Michael Hollington likens to the Paris represented by Baudelaire: a peculiarly beautiful, artificial world that reflects universal human characteristics.

Rome figures prominently in the works of Nathaniel Hawthorne, who in *The Marble Faun* (1860) and *Passages from the French and Italian Notebooks of Nathaniel Hawthorne* (1872) illustrates a mysterious and often dark world to which America owes part of its heritage. Hawthorne and Margaret Fuller, according to critic Brigitte Bailey, examine various American issues through the lens of Roman settings and society. Henry James's novel *Daisy Miller* (1879) is set in Rome; the novel's American characters stand in contrast to their surroundings, and the city is presented through their eyes. Rome also figures prominently in many of James's other works, including *Roderick Hudson* (1878) and *The Portrait of a Lady* (1881). Melville, as evidenced by journal entries made during his travels in Rome, was profoundly inspired by the city's art and culture, and drew upon these impressions to create characters and settings for his fictional works.

Russian authors such as Alexander Pushkin, Nikolai Gogol, and Fyodor Dostoevsky demonstrate the prominence of St. Petersburg during the nineteenth century as both a physical setting and a symbol of a uniquely contradictory Russian world-view. The rapidly changing political and social realities of nineteenth-century Russia greatly affected the literary representation of St. Petersburg, which symbolizes the anxieties inherent in such changes as well as a state of mind in which it becomes possible to live with ambiguity. English author Lewis Carroll, in his 1867 journal entries detailing his travels in Russia, provides an outsider's view of St. Petersburg and reveals his fascination with the city and its people.

REPRESENTATIVE WORKS

Matthew Arnold

Alaric at Rome (poetry) 1840

The Strayed Reveller, and Other Poems (poetry) 1849

Empedocles on Etna, and Other Poems (poetry) 1852

Poems (poetry) 1853

Poems: Second Series (poetry) 1855

Culture and Anarchy: An Essay in Political and Social Criticism (essay) 1869

Honoré de Balzac

Le père Goriot: Histoire parisienne [*Daddy Goriot; or, Unrequited Affection*; also translated as *Old Goriot*] (novel) 1835

*Les parents pauvres. 12 vols. (novels) 1847-48

Comédie humaine. 40 vols. (novels, novellas, and short stories) 1895-98

Anaïs de Bassanville

Le Trésor de la maison. Guide des femmes économes. (domestic manual) 1867

Charles Baudelaire

Salon de 1845 (poetry) 1845

Les fleurs du mal [*The Flowers of Evil*] (poetry) 1857; enlarged editions published in 1861 and 1868

Petits poèmes en prose, Les Paradis artificiels [*Poems in Prose from Charles Baudelaire*] (prose poetry) 1869; also published as *Le Spleen de Paris, petits poèmes en prose,* 1917; also translated as *Paris Spleen,* 1947; and *The Parisian Prowler,* 1989

Art in Paris, 1845-1862. Salons and Other Exhibitions Reviewed by Charles Baudelaire (criticism) 1965

William Blake

Songs of Innocence (poetry) 1789; revised and enlarged as *Songs of Innocence and of Experience: Shewing the Two Contrary States of the Human Soul,* 1794

Robert Buchanan

London Poems (poetry) 1866

Lord Byron

Don Juan, Cantos I-XVI. 6 vols. (poetry) 1819-1824

Lewis Carroll

The Russian Journal, and Other Selections from the Works of Lewis Carroll [edited by John Francis McDermott] (journal and essays) 1935

Arthur Hugh Clough

The Close of the Eighteenth Century, A Prize Poem (poetry) 1835

The Bothie of Toper-na-fuosich, A Long-Vacation Pastoral (poetry) 1848; revised as *The Bothie of Toberna-Vuolich for Poems, with a Memoir,* 1862

Ambarvalia [with Thomas Burbidge] (poetry) 1849

†*Poems* (poetry) 1862

‡*Letters and Remains* (poetry, essays, and letters) 1865

#*Mystery of the Fall* (poetry) 1869

Samuel Taylor Coleridge

Poems on Various Subjects [with Charles Lamb and Robert Southey] (poetry) 1796

Fears in Solitude, Written in 1798, During the Alarm of an Invasion. To Which are Added, France, an Ode; and Frost at Midnight (poetry) 1798

Lyrical Ballads, with a Few Other Poems [with William Wordsworth] (poetry) 1798

Christabel: Kubla Khan, a Vision; The Pains of Sleep (poetry) 1816

Stephen Crane

Maggie: A Girl of the Streets (A Story of New York) [as Johnston Smith] (novel) 1893; revised as *Maggie: A Girl of the Streets,* 1896

The New York City Sketches of Stephen Crane [edited by R. W. Stallman and E. R. Hagemann] (sketches) 1966

Charles Dickens

Sketches by Boz, Illustrative of Every-Day Life and Every-Day People [as Boz] (sketches and short stories) 1836

Oliver Twist (novel) 1838

American Notes for General Circulation (travel essay) 1842

The Life and Adventures of Martin Chuzzlewit (novel) 1844

Household Words. 19 vols. [owner and editor] (journal) 1850-59

Bleak House (novel) 1853

Hard Times for These Times (novel) 1854

Little Dorrit (novel) 1857

Great Expectations (novel) 1861

The Uncommercial Traveller (sketches and short stories) 1861

Our Mutual Friend (novel) 1865

Fyodor Dostoevsky

Prestuplenie I nakazanie [*Crime and Punishment*] (novel) 1866

Pierce Egan

Life in London (novel) 1821

Paul Féval

Les Mystères de Londres. 11 vols. [as Sir Francis Trolopp] (novel) 1844

Margaret Fuller

"These Sad But Glorious Days": Dispatches from Europe, 1846-1850 [edited by Larry J. Reynolds and Susan Belasco Smith] (journalism) 1991

Nikolai Gogol

Mertvye dushi [Dead Souls] (novel) 1842
Sochineniia. 4 vols. (short stories, plays, and novel) 1842

Nathaniel Hawthorne

The Blithedale Romance (novel) 1852
The Marble Faun; or, The Romance of Monte Beni (novel) 1860; published in England as *Transformation; or, The Romance of Monte Beni,* 1860
Passages from the French and Italian Notebooks of Nathaniel Hawthorne (journal) 1872

Victor Hugo

Notre-Dame de Paris [The Hunchback of Notre-Dame] (novel) 1831
Les misérables [Les Miserables] (novel) 1862

Joris-Karl Huysmans

A rebours [Against the Grain] (novel) 1884; also translated as *Against Nature,* 1959
Là-bas [Down There] (novel) 1891

Henry James

‖*A Passionate Pilgrim, and Other Tales* (short stories) 1875
Roderick Hudson (novel) 1876
The American (novel) 1877
Daisy Miller (novel) 1879
The Portrait of a Lady (novel) 1881
Washington Square (novel) 1881

William James

Talks to Teachers on Psychology; and to Students on Some of Life's Ideals (lectures) 1899

Charles Lamb

"The Londoner" (essay) 1802; first published in the journal *Morning Post*

Antoine Joseph Napoléon Lespès

Paris dans un Fauteuil: types, histoires et physionomies (essays) 1855
Spectacles vus de ma fenétre, par L. L. (essays) 1866

Henry Mayhew

London Labour and the London Poor, Nos. 1-63. 4 vols. (journalism) 1851-62

Herman Melville

Mardi: And a Voyage Thither. 2 vols. (novel) 1849
Redburn: His First Voyage (novel) 1849

White Jacket; or, The World in a Man-of-War (novel) 1850
Moby-Dick; or, The Whale (novel) 1851
Pierre; or, The Ambiguities (novel) 1852
Israel Potter: His Fifty Years of Exile (novel) 1855
The Piazza Tales (short stories) 1856
The Confidence Man: His Masquerade (novel) 1857
Battle-Pieces and Aspects of the War (poetry) 1866
Clarel: A Poem and Pilgrimage in the Holy Land (poetry) 1876
John Marr and Other Sailors with Some Sea Pieces (poetry) 1888
Timoleon (poetry) 1891
Billy Budd and Other Prose Pieces (novel and short stories) 1924
Journal of a Visit to London and the Continent by Herman Melville 1849-1850 [edited by Eleanor Melville Metcalf] (journal) 1948

Louis-Sébastien Mercier

Tableau de Paris. 2 vols. [published anonymously; *Paris in Miniature*] (novel) 1781; enlarged edition, 12 vols., 1782-88

Edgar Allan Poe

Tales by Edgar A. Poe (short stories) 1845

Alexander Pushkin

Yevgeny Onegin [Eugene Onéguine] (novel) 1823-31
Pir vo vryemya chumy [A Feast in the City of the Plague] (drama) 1832; also published as *A Feast during the Plague*
Mednyi vsadnik [The Bronze Horseman] (unfinished poetry) 1837
Pikovaya dama [The Queen of Spades] (novella) 1850

G. W. M. Reynolds

The Mysteries of London. 4 vols. (novel) 1845-48
The Mysteries of the Court of London. 8 vols. (novel) 1849-56

Percy Bysshe Shelley

The Poetical Works of Percy Bysshe Shelley. 4 vols. [edited by Mary Wollstonecraft Shelley] (poetry) 1839

Ferdinand Silas

"Les propriétaires vengés" (essay) 1855; published in the journal *Le Bourgeois de Paris*

Emile Souvestre

Philosophe sous les toits; journal d'un homme heureux [Attic Philosopher in Paris] (philosopher) 1853

Eugène Sue

Les mystères de Paris. 10 vols. [*The Mysteries of Paris*] (novel) 1842-43

Edith Wharton

The House of Mirth (novel) 1905
The Custom of the Country (novel) 1913
The Age of Innocence (novel) 1920
A Backward Glance (autobiography) 1934

Walt Whitman

Leaves of Grass (poetry) 1855; revised and enlarged
    editions, 1856, 1860-61, 1867, 1871, 1881-82, and
    1891-92

William Wordsworth

§*Lyrical Ballads* [with Samuel Taylor Coleridge]
    (poetry) 1798
**The Prelude, or Growth of a Poet's Mind, An Auto-
    biographical Poem* (poetry) 1850

*This collection includes the novels *La cousine Bette: Où la passion va-
t-elle se nicher?* (also published as *La causine Bette: Le Père prodigue*),
translated as *Cousin Bette,* 1888; and *Le cousin Pons* (also published as
Le cousin Pons: Les Deux Musiciens), translated as *Cousin Pons,* 1880.

†Among the poems included in this collection are *Amours de Voyage* and
Mari Magno, and some of the songs of *Dipsychus.*

‡Includes a complete version of *Dipsychus.*

#Also known as *Adam and Eve.*

‖This collection includes the short story "The Last of the Valerii," which
was first published in the journal *Atlantic Monthly* in 1874.

§Enlarged editions of *Lyrical Ballads* were published in 1801 and 1802.
A final edition was published in 1805.

**This work was written between 1799 and 1805.

LONDON AND PARIS IN POETRY

William Sharpe (essay date winter 1985-86)

SOURCE: Sharpe, William. "Confronting the Unpoetical City: Arnold, Clough, and Baudelaire." *The Arnoldian* 13, no. 1 (winter 1985-86): 10-22.

[*In the following essay, Sharpe compares and contrasts
the various commentaries on and renderings of life in
London and Paris in poetry by Matthew Arnold, Arthur
Hugh Clough, and Charles Baudelaire.*]

"These are damned times," wrote Matthew Arnold to
his friend Arthur Hugh Clough in 1849, "everything is
against one . . . our physical enervation, the absence of
great *natures,* the unavoidable contact with millions of
small ones, newspapers, cities . . ." (*Letters,* 111). For
many Victorian poets, the sense of living in "damned
times" was perhaps the greatest obstacle to poetic expression, and the infernal urban landscape seemed proof
of their fallen condition. Emblematic of what Arnold
elsewhere called "the unpoetrylessness" of the era, the

Victorian city loomed as the most central and yet least
artistic fact of modern life. When Charles Kingsley's
Alton Locke tried to write about the London slums in
which he grew up, he could only sigh, "All this is
so—so unpoetical" (251). Leigh Hunt, too, observed
that "London . . . is not a poetical place to look at."
"But," he was forced to admit, "surely it is poetical in
the very amount and comprehensiveness of its enormous experience of pain and pleasure. . . . It is one of
the great giant representatives of mankind, with a huge,
beating heart" (213). How was the poet to write about a
subject whose importance was undeniable, but which
was obviously not "poetical" as he understood the term?[1]

The work of Matthew Arnold and Arthur Hugh Clough
provides some of the clearest examples of the metropolitan malaise of Victorian poetry. An analysis of Arnold's writing shows several reasons for his resistance
to urban subject matter: an aesthetic abhorrence of modern life, a Wordsworthian idealization of nature, and the
influence of Biblical archetypes of the fallen city. Arnold's praise of the countryside only thinly veils his
anxiety in the city and dislike of his fellow men. Although his close friend Clough argued for a poetry responsive to the conditions of urban life, Clough's own
city poetry builds upon a characteristically Victorian association of the city with the deeply-felt failure of religion and morality. Clough views the city as a direct assault upon religious faith, sexual probity, and personal
identity.

In their urban prejudices and fears, Clough and Arnold
contrast sharply with their contemporary, Charles
Baudelaire, who confidently asserted in the *Salon of
1846,* "Parisian life is rich in subjects both poetic and
marvellous" (952).[2] The example of Baudelaire provides a useful reference point from which to explore the
inhibitions that prevented Victorian poets from writing
freely about the city. Defying the most entrenched values of his time, Baudelaire prefers the city to the country, the artificial to the natural, urban shock to pastoral
security, sexuality to purity, the infernal to the heavenly.
Far from rejecting the city that threatens to corrupt his
art and morality, he embraces it and uses it to his artistic advantage.

But if Paris encouraged creativity, London seemed to
stifle it: in *The Prelude* of 1805, Wordsworth spoke of
the city as a scene "that lays / If any spectacle on earth
can do / The whole creative powers of man asleep!"
(679-81).[3] At mid-century this Wordsworthian attitude
so pervaded Victorian poetry that even poets determined
to write about London found themselves writing about
the country instead.[4] In Arnold's "The Buried Life"
(1852), for example, oppressive urban surroundings
prompt the poet's "unspeakable desire / After the knowledge of our buried life" (47-48)—which turns out to be
figured in natural terms: "The hills where [man's] life
rose / And the sea where it goes." (97-98)[5]

Arnold's city poems are characterized, not just by an escapist longing for nature, but by an air of social concern for those who must share his "brazen prison." If crowded city streets are not conducive to poetry, at least they make one aware of why refreshment in nature is so necessary to both the artist and the working man. In "Stanzas in Memory of the Author of 'Obermann'" (1852) Arnold even takes Wordsworth to task for irresponsibly neglecting urban themes: "Wordsworth's eyes avert their ken / From half of human fate" (53-54). Accusing him later of having "retired (in Middle-Age phrase) into a monastery," Arnold concludes that Wordsworth "voluntarily cut himself off from the modern spirit" ("Heinrich Heine," 121).

Yet Arnold's poetic treatment of the city is often guilty of the very monastic tendencies of which (only half correctly) he accuses Wordsworth. In "Stanzas from the Grande Chartreuse" (1855), Arnold's own "monkish" retirement even threatens to become literal—seeking to evade the world's call "to life, to cities, and to war" (180), the poet petitions the isolated Carthusian monastery high in the Alps:

> Oh, hide me in your gloom profound,
> Ye solemn seats of holy pain!
> Take me, cowled forms, and fence me round,
> Till I possess my soul again.
>
> (91-94)

The soul-stealing power of Arnold's cities takes on an apocalyptic resonance in the early lyric "A Dream" (written 1849). Here, a voyage down "the darting river of Life" begins in green, sunlit Alpine scenery, but must traverse "burning plains, / Bristled with cities" (36-37) before finally reaching the sea. As in "The Buried Life," Arnold implies that man's maturity must unfortunately be spent amid the burning cities of the plain. Long associated with Sodom and Gomorrah, Babel and Babylon, these cities are versions of the failed human community that writers since Biblical times have measured against the promise of the City of God. In many ways, nineteenth century city poetry from Wordsworth's London to Tennyson's Camelot in *Idylls of the King* is the history of a continuing quest to turn Babylon into the New Jerusalem.

Arnold's longing for the celestial city is evident in *Culture and Anarchy* (1869), where he contrasts his country's religious and social ideals to the reality of modern-day London:

> We all call ourselves, in the sublime and aspiring language of religion . . . *children of God.* Children of God;—it is an immense pretension!—and how are we to justify it? By the works we do, and the words which we speak. And the work which we collective children of God do, our grand centre of life, our *city* which we have built for us to dwell in, is London! London,

with its unutterable external hideousness, and with its internal canker of *publice agestas, privatim opulentia* . . . unequalled in the world!

> (59)

Although Arnold's outrage at "external hideousness" and his perception of private luxury amid public penury are grounded in contemporary observation, his Biblical language points to the timeless nature of this frustrated ideal of the city as a "grand centre of life."

There are only echoes of the heavenly city in Arnold's verse, but the deficiencies of the earthly one consistently stimulate the yearning for a God-infused nature. "Lines Written in Kensington Gardens" (1852) is perhaps the strongest example of the pastoral impulse underlying so much Victorian poetry about the city. In *The Prelude* Wordsworth had spoken of "city smoke, by distance ruralized" (1850, I, 89), and here Arnold tries to achieve that distance both psychologically and physically. Shielded from the city by the park's foliage, the poet luxuriates in his shelter, contrasting its "true" natural life to the maddening noise in London:

> In the huge world, which roars hard by,
> Be others happy if they can!
> But in my helpless cradle I
> Was breathed on by the rural Pan.
>
> (21-24)[6]

In suggesting that by birth he is consecrated to nature, Arnold identifies this setting with infancy where, although helpless, he was more secure than as an adult in the city. An apparently picturesque detail from lines 9-10 confirms this fantasy: "Sometimes a child will cross the glade / To take his nurse his broken toy." Nurse, cradle, child, toy: the poet's alienation from the city is also his separation from childhood. Conscious that there is no longer anyone to fix that broken toy, he associates the responsibilities of adult life with the city, and fears that the peace he seeks "now keeps only in the grave" (28). The park, nursing him amid its screening boughs, provides a momentary deliverance that seems inconceivable in the street just a few feet away.

Seeking as Wordsworth did "among least things / An under-sense of greatest" to support him in the city (*The Prelude*, 1805, VII, 710-11), he prays:

> Calm soul of all things! make it mine
> To feel, amid the city's jar,
> That there abides a peace of thine,
> Man did not make, and cannot mar.
>
> (37-40)

This recasting of William Cowper's famous anti-urban phrase, "God made the country, and man made the town," once again evokes the Victorian quest for the City of God, here in the guise of a Wordsworthian "natural supernaturalism." In the final lines, the strain of city life forces the poet to clamor for repose with increasing desperation: "Calm, calm me more! nor let me die / Before I have begun to live" (43-44). Although Arnold attempts to equate the city with death and nature with life, his reiterated emphasis on "calm" indicates how much the city—and this soul-nurturing refuge from it—has sapped the vigor of the poet's wish to live. He seeks not life, but oblivion.

Beneath Arnold's horror of the city lies a barely concealed aversion to his fellow men, whom he hears "rave" around him. For the poet who dreads "the unavoidable contact with millions of small [natures]," hell is indeed other people, when they are encountered in the teeming city streets. Arnold's insistently pastoral "Lines" recall Tennyson's more direct confession in *Maud,* "And I loathe the squares and streets, / And the faces that one meets . . ." (II, 232-33). The Victorian rush toward nature is equally a flight from men, and the setting of Arnold's poem reinforces this theme. Much of the landscaping of the English city park represents an effort to import the prospects of romantic nature into the city. Unlike the more formal, cultivated and open Parisian parks, such as the Tuileries or Luxembourg Gardens, where the design of the promenades allows the stroller to see and be seen, the meandering walks of Kensington Gardens invite solitude and the contemplation of nature. "Lines Written in Kensington Gardens" may well be the most representative Victorian poem of the city, because everything about it, from the rustic setting to the poet's misanthropic longing for rural peace, is so completely devoted to escaping London.

In striking contrast, the prose poems of *Le Spleen de Paris* show Baudelaire deliberately prowling the well-populated public gardens and streets of his city, noting the physical and emotional mutants of urban life, for whom he feels a perverse affection. Instead of seeking solitude in nature, Baudelaire delights in the activity he called "bathing in the crowd" (243). "The solitary and pensive stroller," he writes in "Les Foules" (1861), "draws a singular intoxication from this universal communion" (244). For him the secret of urban identity lies not in fending others off, but in building a self composed of all their most intimate experiences: "And I go to bed, proud to have lived and suffered in others than myself" (288). In Arnold's poetry, nature is a primal garden to be sought, the city a fallen Bedlam to be escaped, but for Baudelaire geography is less important than the imagination which can transform it. Population and isolation, he insists, are equally at his service: "Multitude, solitude: terms equal and interchangeable for the active and fertile poet. He who does not know how to people his solitude, does not know how to be alone in a busy crowd either" (243-44). The poet who can be himself in the crowd has no need for the anxious pastoralism of "Kensington Gardens."

Charles Kingsley wrote in 1848 that the landscapes of London picture-galleries should be the urban man's passport "beyond the grim city-world of stone and iron" (qtd. in Houghton 80), a substitute excursion for those not fortunate enough to live in the country. Arnold's poem "Consolation" (1852) attempts a similar mental journey beyond the constricting city where "Mist clogs the sunshine" and "Smoky dwarf houses / Hem me round" (1-3). Claiming that even amidst his dejection "countless / Prospects unroll themselves" (7-8), the poet envisions scenes in Tibet, Rome, the Sahara. But there is no creative power in his alienation from the city: he projects himself out of his smoggy surroundings only to picture other lives that might be better or worse than his own, rather than looking inward to participate imaginatively in them. In the end he finds his "consolation" in mere passivity, waiting as impartial time "Brings round to all men / Some undimmed hours" (74-75).

For Baudelaire, however, even the most uncongenial surroundings can stimulate the poet's fertile consciousness. In "Le Cygne" (1859), the very buildings and neighborhoods torn apart by Haussmann's renovation of Paris become elements in an "allegory" of emotional displacement. Like the swan of the title, lost in the city and discovered bathing in a pond of dust, the poet no longer feels he has a natural environment. But like the swan also his habits are fixed—he will continue to be a poet even in this apparently unpoetic place, doing his "bathing" in the crowd and among all the urban "bric-a-brac confus" that now surrounds him. The poet no longer has the choice of viewing his devastated city in the terms of poetic or moral decorum he grew up with; this place of exile has itself become estranged from the considerations of conventional aesthetics. As Baudelaire planned to announce in a later edition of *Les Fleurs du Mal,* the task of the modern poet has become that of transforming the city's muck into the gold of art (180).

Surprisingly, the most important Victorian demand for a new poetry of the city closely parallels Baudelaire's strategy. Can't we, asked Arthur Hugh Clough in 1853, concentrate on the mundane and still see "some central, celestial fact?" (144-45). In his article "Recent English Poetry," Clough seeks, as Wordsworth and Arnold had in their famous prefaces, to define the purview and responsibilities of the modern poet. But the program he proposes—the faithful description of urban life rather than the recollection of rural emotion or noble classical actions—is daringly innovative for the Victorian era. Desiring a poetry where urban objects will be "irradiated with a gleam of divine purity" (146), Clough wants to shift the substance of contemporary poetry from pastoral landscapes to the stark city streets. Poets should "exclude nothing" and "deal with what is here" (145), rather than what might be. Clough's essay stems in part from his disagreement with Arnold about the role of modern poetry. Only the year before Arnold had written to him complaining about the *"blankness* and *barrenness,* and *unpoetrylessness"* of modern life (*Letters* 126). In response, Clough is determined to advance the city's claim to become "the true and lawful haunt" of poetry. As he later wrote, "The dirt and refuse of thy street / My philosophic foot shall greet" ("O Land of Empire, Art, and Love," 1869). Although one may picture London as the "inhuman town," he says, the poetic struggle with it can be a purifying process for both poet and city.

In practice, however, Clough's city failed to provide him with the poetic material he had so eloquently predicted was there. One of his earlier poems, "To the Great Metropolis" (1841), describes a London which has lost its majesty and become "a huge Bazaar, / A railway terminus, a gay Hotel, / Anything but a mighty Nation's heart." The "great heart" Wordsworth sensed in his view of the city from Westminster Bridge has disappeared, along with the feeling of the city's centrality to national life that Arnold notes in *Culture and Anarchy.* Instead of throbbing with life, Clough's London drains the vitality and imagination of those who live there:

> These vulgar ways that round me be,
> These faces shabby, sordid, mean,
> Shall they be daily, hourly seen
> And not affect the eyes that see?

> ("These Vulgar Ways," 1850)

Whereas Wordsworth was most disturbed by the noise and confusion of the city, Clough, like Arnold, fears the personal meanness of its inhabitants, who he feels are an infectious threat to his social and moral integrity.

Clough also associates the city with religious doubts. In "Easter Day, Naples, 1849," for example, the feverish atmosphere of the "sinful" city reinforces or perhaps even prompts the poet's crisis of faith:

> Through the great sinful streets of Naples as I past
> With fiercer heat than flamed above my head
> My heart was hot within me; till at last
> My brain was lightened, when my tongue had said
>
> · · · · ·
>
> Christ is not risen!

But Clough's habit of viewing the city in Biblical terms endures regardless of his personal convictions. In a later poem Clough, like Arnold, depicts the city as a modern Sodom, and prays that

>   upon two million odd
> Transgressors in sad plenty,
> Mercy will of a gracious God
> Be shown—because of twenty.

> ("Blessed Are They Who Have Not Seen," 1862)

Without exception, Clough's poetry shows the city devoid of that "central, celestial fact" that, as a critic, he had thought redeemed it. The Victorian poet constantly measures the present city against an unattainable heavenly one, and inevitably finds himself living in an infernal Babylon rather than the New Jerusalem. Baudelaire, on the other hand, collapses these distinctions: his search for "the New" in "Heaven or Hell, no matter where) (127), shows how these terms designate complementary aspects of the earthly city he loves. For Baudelaire, a truly modern poetry must comprehend with equal assurance "tous les hôpitaux et . . . tous les palais" (79).

Nowhere is the conflict between these two visions of the city more apparent than in the poets' differing responses to the city's sexual aspect. 'Bathing in the crowd" provokes a sensual, uninhibited response in Baudelaire's *flâneur;* for Clough, merely walking the streets threatens sexual violence and even endangers his identity. In "The Contradictions of an Expanding Soul" Clough sees all of urban life as a kind of unavoidable venereal infection, and he wonders how "to escape / Contamination in the jostling street / And foul contagion from diseased base souls."

From the harlot of the midnight streets in Blake's "London" to the tawdry Thames daughters in *The Waste Land,* English poetry, following Revelation, pictures the city as the Whore of Babylon who must be renounced and destroyed before the virginal New Jerusalem can appear. Clough's contribution to the archetype is to place the poet in both the position of the man about to undergo "contamination" and the woman who will cause it, herself a victim of the city's sexual despoliation. Plunging into the crowd, unable to "keep unbroke the precious party wall," he feels like a woman about to be raped: "Alas we seem as women in the world / Amongst rude men unlovered." The sexual violence of urban experience simultaneously strips away both virginity and identity.[7]

Clough's major work, *Dipsychus* (1850), tries to confront this problem.[8] The poem is an extended dialogue between Dipsychus, a young Englishman (whose name means "double-souled"), and a Mephistophelian Spirit. The dramatic tension centers on whether Dipsychus should—or will—give in to the worldly temptations of Venice. An exterior voice aggravating his inner doubts, the Spirit urges him towards life's pleasures, prostitutes chief among them. As the Victorian Everyman, Dipsychus is tempted and tormented by the relentless attack from all sides:

> What is this persecuting voice that haunts me?
> What? whence? of whom? How am I to detect?
> Myself or not myself? My own bad thoughts
> Or some external agency at work,
> To lead me who knows whither?

> (II, 17-21)

Since for Dipsychus merely being in the city is a physical humiliation, the sexual aspect of his agony cannot be minimized. Each time he walks down the street, he is forced "To enter the base crowd and bare [his] flanks / To all ill voices of a blustering world" (VII, 94-95).

In contrast, Baudelaire writes in "Les Foules" that "he who easily marries the crowd knows the feverish *jouissances* of which the egoist will be eternally deprived" (244). The word "jouissance" can mean, as the context of marriage suggests, "sexual bliss," and the poetically fertile course that Baudelaire recommends is precisely what Dipsychus, the "egoist" so concerned with his own search for an ultimate morality, can never dare to know. Overturning as if by intention the terms Dipsychus counts on to keep himself pure, Baudelaire concludes by praising "that holy prostitution of the soul which gives itself fully, poetry and charity, to the unforeseen which reveals itself, the unknown person who passes by" (244). The poet must expose himself to the transitory yet ennobling pleasures of urban experience, but Dipsychus is incapable of such sweet surrender. Despite their attractions, the prostitutes in Clough's poem cannot be "holy"; only the devilish Spirit, with his nagging refrain of "submit, submit," seems to appreciate them:

> 'Tis here, I see, the custom too
> For damsels eager to be lovered
> To go about with arms uncovered;
> And doubtless there's a special charm
> In looking at a well-shaped arm.

(II, 49-53)

Epitomizing the shame of the city, the whores of modern Babylon sway but cannot topple Dipsychus' resolution, since he detects—or imagines he does—"the once fair flushing cheek / Flaccid under its paint" (III, 107-8). The poem ends with the protagonist still physically "pure" but forced to accept the urban values he has fought for so long: "Be it thus—since that it must, it seems. / Welcome O world, henceforth; and farewell dreams!" (XIV, 20-21). Baudelaire depicts the city as the beginning of dreams; Clough regards it as the end of them, and so makes his own search for a modern poetry of the city an impossibility.

In the "Epilogue" (1860) to *Spleen de Paris,* Baudelaire also figures the city as a prostitute, but never considers taking Clough's morally upright stance towards the city's seductions. The poet who would master the city must first court the old whore she is, drunk on her infernal charm that makes him young again. There is no Biblical choice between harlots and brides; he must take her in her entirety, "marrying" the heaven and hell he finds in her streets. Like *Dipsychus,* "Epilogue" has its pimping devil, but here Satan understands the poet's perversely noble compulsion "contempler la ville en

son ampleur / Hôpital, lupanar, purgatoire, enfer, bagne." More than a hospital or a brothel, a purgatory or a hell, the city is finally the "bath" that contains them all, in which the poet must immerse himself if he is to make the city his own.

Even when they lauded the city's potential, the Victorian poets were unable to take Baudelaire's rejuvenating plunge.[9] Nonetheless, *Dipsychus* is remarkable for its refusal to consider escape to the country as a means of addressing urban malaise, and for its dogged resistance to the city's sexual allure, which Clough must have recognized as also being a prime source of its poetic power. Because he is so far from that "easy marriage" of poet and crowd celebrated by Baudelaire, Clough's anguished self-examination provides a unique record of how the Victorian poet tried—and failed—to find a genuine place for the city in his art.

Paraphrasing Blake's "London," one might say that in every poetic voice, in every poetic ban, the Victorians' "mind forg'd manacles" made it impossible for them to engage fully with the city in their art. Arnold wrote to Clough in 1849, "Reflect . . . how deeply *unpoetical* the age and all one's surroundings are. Not unprofound, not ungrand, not unmoving:—but *unpoetical*" (*Letters* 99). But the Victorian aesthetic had to give way: since Arnold's time, the "unpoetical" poetry of modern life—of Symons and Wilde, Eliot and Auden has increasingly sprung from the "unreal city" first opened for exploration by Baudelaire.

Notes

1. In "The Frightened Poets," the first extended discussion of the Victorian poet's troubled relation to the city, G. Robert Stange concludes that "a strange mixture of Romantic gestures, aristocratic pastoralism, and middle-class prudery blinded the poets to the misery and grandeur of their city" (493). For further discussion of the poet's aversion to the city, see Hulin *passim* and Thesing xvii-xviii, 42; for the "enmity" between Victorian poetry and the novel over the value of modern life as a subject of literature, see Conrad 176-216.

2. Quotations from Baudelaire are from *Oeuvres Complètes,* 1961, and translations of the prose are my own. Common features in the social and economic make-up of London and Paris during the nineteenth century seem to justify comparison of the poetry written about the two cities. See Lees 413-28.

3. The English poets were not alone in sensing this problem: Friedrich Engels noted in 1844 that "the inhabitants of modern London have had to sacrifice so much that is best in human nature in order to create those wonders of civilisation with which

their city teems. The vast majority of Londoners have had to let so many of their creative faculties lie dormant, stunted, and unused . . ." (30).

4. Robert Buchanan's *London Poems* (1866) is typical in this respect. Although he proclaims himself ready to make "the busy life of London musical," he finds it impossible to repress a Wordsworthian belief in the underlying value of nature:

> the presence of the mountains
> Was upon me; and the murmur of the sea
> Deepened my mood; while everywhere I saw,
> Flowing beneath the blackness of the streets,
> The current of sublimer, sweeter life. . . .
>
>   ("Bexhill, 1866")

5. For a full survey of Arnold's urban poems, see Thesing 64-77.

6. See Jenkyns 174-79 for a discussion of the cult of Pan who, as god of the countryside, expressed the Victorian nostalgia for nature.

7. Cf. George Meredith's *The Egoist* (1879), where the sexual menace of the city is confirmed by Sir Willoughby Patterne's obsessive desire for a woman who has not been "smirched" by contact with the world; it is hinted that his ego has been threatened by his "metropolitan conquests," who have not admired him sufficiently (Ch. 3). "In London," Sir Willoughby says, "you lose your identity . . . you are nobody . . . a week of London literally drives me home to discover the individual where I left him" (Ch. 11).

8. For extended discussions of *Dipsychus* as a whole, see Chorley 245-66 and Houghton 156-207. Thesing also devotes several pages to the poem, 48-56.

9. One of the rare exceptions can be found in Elizabeth Barrett Browning's *Aurora Leigh* (1857). After a brilliant description of fog overwhelming the city, "as if a sponge / Had wiped out London," the writer-heroine reflects: "Your city poets see such things / Not despicable." For her, to "view the city perish in the mist" is to be rewarded, Baudelairean fashion, "By a sudden sense of vision and of tune" (III, 169ff.). Unfortunately, the passage is unique in her work.

Works Cited

Arnold, Matthew. *Culture and Anarchy.* Ed. J. Dover Wilson. Cambridge: Cambridge UP, 1932.

———. *The Letters of Matthew Arnold to Arthur Hugh Clough.* Ed. H. F. Lowry. London: Oxford UP, 1932.

———. *The Complete Poems.* 2nd ed. Ed. Miriam Allott (New York: Longman, 1979).

———. "Heinrich Heine." *Matthew Arnold: Lectures and Essays in Criticism.* Ed. R. H. Super. Ann Arbor: University of Michigan Press, 1962

Baudelaire. *Oeuvres Complètes.* Ed. Claude Pichois and Y.-G. Le Dantec. Paris: Pléiade, 1961.

Browning, Elizabeth Barrett. *Aurora Leigh and Other Poems.* Ed. Cora Kaplan. London: The Women's Press, 1962.

Buchanan, Robert. *London Poems.* London, 1866.

Chorley, Katharine. *Arthur Hugh Clough: The Uncommitted Mind.* Oxford: Clarendon Press, 1962.

Clough, Arthur Hugh. *The Poems of Arthur Hugh Clough.* 2nd. Ed. F. L. Mulhauser. London: Oxford UP, 1974.

———. "Recent American Poetry." *North American Review.* 77 (1853): 1-20. Rpt. in *Selected Prose Works of Arthur Hugh Clough.* Ed. Buckner B. Trawick. University, Ala.: U. of Alabama Press, 1964 143-171.

Conrad, Peter. *The Victorian Treasure House.* London: Collins, 1973.

Dyos, H. J. and Michael Wolff, eds. *The Victorian City: Images and Realities.* 2 vols. London: Routledge and Kegan Paul. 1973.

Engels, Friedrich. *The Condition of the Working Class in England.* Trans. and ed. W. O. Henderson and W. H. Chaloner. Stanford: Stanford UP, 1968.

Houghton, Walter E. *The Poetry of Clough: An Essay in Revaluation.* New Haven: Yale UP, 1963.

———. *The Victorian Frame of Mind.* New Haven: Yale UP, 1957.

Hulin, Jean-Paul. "Rus in urbe: A Key to Victorian Anti-Urbanism?" *Victorian Writers and the City.* Ed. J.-P. Hulin and Pierre Coustillas. Lille: Pub. de l'Univ.de Lille III, 1979. 11-40.

Hunt, Leigh. "London" (1851). *Table Talk.* New Ed. London: Smith, Elder & Co., 1882. 213-214.

Jenkyns, Richard. *The Victorians and Ancient Greece.* Cambridge, Mass.: Harvard UP, 1980.

Kingsley, Charles. *Alton Locke, Tailor and Poet.* Vol. I. New York: J. F. Taylor, 1898.

Lees, Lynn. "Metropolitan Types: London and Paris Compared." Dyos and Wolff 2:413-28.

Meredith, George. *The Egoist.* Ed. Robert M. Adams. New York: Norton, 1979.

Stange, G. Robert. "The Frightened Poets." Dyos and Wolff. 2:475-94.

Tennyson, Alfred. *The Poems of Tennyson,* ed. Christopher Ricks. New York: Norton, 1969.

Thesing, William. *The London Muse: Victorian Poetic Response to the City.* Athens: U. of Georgia Press, 1982.

Wordsworth, William. *The Prelude: A Parallel Text.* Ed. J. C. Maxwell. Harmonsworth: Penguin, 1971.

LONDON

Anne Humpherys (essay date 1983)

SOURCE: Humpherys, Anne. "The Geometry of the Modern City: G. W. M. Reynolds and The Mysteries of London." *Browning Institute Studies* 11 (1983): 69-80.

[*In the following essay, Humpherys discusses G. W. M. Reynolds's novel* The Mysteries of London, *examining in particular the unifying interplay between seemingly contrasting narrative and thematic elements within the text.*]

In Book VII of *The Prelude* Wordsworth chronicles the months he lived in London and concludes with two images for the modern city. Following his feeling that "The face of every one / That passes by me is a mystery," he sees a blind beggar with his life's history on a card around his neck; this is followed by the spectacle of Bartholomew's Fair. The poet's response to these experiences of urban mystery and multitudinousness is well-known:

> O Blank confusion! true epitome
> Of what the mighty City is herself
> To thousands upon thousands of her sons
> Living amid the same perpetual whirl
> Of trivial objects, melted and reduced
> To one identity, by differences
> That have no law, no meaning, and no end—
>
> (Book VII, ll. 722-28)

Although this picture of modern city life as a whirlwind of countless images without meaning has become a commonplace, Wordsworth's reaction actually posits an urban vision that is provocatively contradictory. While the city confuses with its multiplicity of differences, it also terrifies by its capacity to destroy individuality, to "melt and reduce" all objects "to one identity." Thus, under the surface of Wordsworth's description is a deeper and perhaps more threatening chaos, one that impinges on perception itself. Not only do we experience city life as a lack of coherence and order, but also as profoundly reductive of human potential to type.

It might be that the need to resolve this frightening contradiction contributed to the efforts in the fiction, journalism, and illustration of the nineteenth century to gain control over the modern urban chaos by imposing an order of language and grammar, of image and structure on the seemingly infinite and expanding variety of urban possibilities. But although the nineteenth-century struggled valiantly to perceive and order urban life, the extent of its final failure is seen in the gradual substitution in the twentieth century of a literature of imaginary cities for the nineteenth-century "real" city.

Among the earlier nineteenth-century efforts to achieve control of London life were those of a prolific and once enormously popular journalist and fiction writer, G. W. M. Reynolds, whose mammoth novel *The Mysteries of London,* published in parts from 1844 to 1848, became a model for many imitations in Europe and America. Though at first glance this work seems, with its intricate plot and cast of hundreds of characters, to reflect the multiplicity and reduction to type which Wordsworth found so disheartening, a closer look reveals that several levels of order are imposed on the city through a series of metaphorical diagrams or patterns which structure the meaning of the story. In the relationship of these patterns we will find, rather surprisingly given the resolutely nineteenth-century form of *The Mysteries of London,* an adumbration of a modernist response to the city.

George William MacArthur Reynolds was born in 1814 the son of a post-captain in the Royal Navy. He received an upper-middle-class education at Ashford Grammar School and at the Royal Military College, Sandhurst. In 1830, he left Sandhurst and went to Paris, where he associated with revolutionary groups and began a lifelong involvement with French life and literature. Shortly after he gained full control of his £12,000 estate, he lost it in publishing ventures. In 1836 he was declared bankrupt and returned to England.[1]

There he entered the new world of London journalism, writing for both a middle-class reading public and the evolving lower-class one. He soon plied his astonishingly prolific pen for those on the borderline between the two. Between 1847 and 1859, he wrote some thirty-five or forty million words and became, according to the *Bookseller,* the "most popular writer in England."[2] His formula for success included the use of Gothic conventions, a little soft-core pornography, a clear and forceful style, and brilliant narrative structure. (A common precept given to young Victorian writers, according to E. F. Bleiler, was "characterize like Dickens, plot like Reynolds.")[3] He wrote fifty-eight novels, eleven works of translation, a number of political tracts, and edited eight journals, four of which he himself founded. His most important works are the two journals, *Reynolds Miscellany* (1846-69) and *Reynolds Weekly Newspaper,* which he edited from its founding in 1850 to his death in 1879 (the *Weekly Newspaper* itself continued well into the second half of the twentieth century), and the two serial novels, *The Mysteries of London* (first and second series, 1844-48) and *The Mysteries of the Court of London* (first through fourth series, 1848-55).

In addition to his important contributions to popular literature and the development of the working-class press, Reynolds himself played a role in the late Chartist movement. He knew the leaders and spoke at rallies. Through his radical *Weekly Newspaper,* which in 1855 appears to have had a circulation over a quarter of a million, he was an "important force in the formation of working class opinion," as Louis James and John Saville have claimed.[4] But after 1860 Reynolds wrote little. Despite another bankruptcy in 1848, he eventually made a fortune, and until his death in 1879, he appears to have led a life of ease and respectability.

The Mysteries of London, like much of his work, came out of Reynolds's French experience. The French writer Eugène Sue, whom Reynolds knew, had written an immensely popular novel, *Les Mystères de Paris* (1842-43), which was itself inspired by Pierce Egan's *Life in London* (1821-22) and which in turn inspired a host of imitations in many different languages. One of the offshoots was *Les Mystères de Londre* (1842-43) by another Frenchman, Paul Feval, and Reynolds picked up elements for his work from both Sue and Feval.[5]

The Mysteries of London was published in weekly parts at a penny a piece and became so successful that after the first few months Reynolds began to reissue the novel again from the beginning. In book form the first series is in two volumes of over 400 pages each. Between its first issue in parts and its publication in volume form, it sold over a million copies. Its basic story is about the two brothers, Eugene and Richard Markham, the women they love and who love them, and the depredations of a terrifying criminal, Anthony Tidkins, the Resurrection Man. In the course of this overriding story, the reader is introduced to an absolutely dizzying array of London dwellers of all types, classes, and occupations, and an equally astonishing range of information about everything from the way dice are loaded and liquor adulterated to the way wealth is distributed in the British Isles.

Reynolds's intention thus was to be inclusive, to try to encompass the totality of London as a physical entity and as a habitation for hundreds of thousands of city-dwellers. But he made clear efforts to order and control his material. His first step was to take several familiar plot devices from the Gothic romance and from his French sources that would give a kind of popular mythic resonance to his tale. For example, from Feval, Reynolds picked up the idea of two brothers whose lives run in neatly parallel but totally opposite directions. Using familiar devices and exercising his genius for keeping many stories moving at the same time, Reynolds was able to make all the characters' lives and fortunes

intercept and separate in ways that suggest an urban chain of connection which includes all variety of visible, invisible, and coincidental exchange.

But beyond the function of plot, which in the nineteenth-century novel was frequently a central ordering device, Reynolds has a number of "imaginative diagrams" of London that both impose coherence, differentiate individuals, and suggest meaning. The first such "diagram" is one Reynolds himself asserts throughout the work, namely that the city is constructed on a series of oppositions. When Reynolds used it in *The Mysteries of London,* this image of the "contrasts of London" was conventional, even clichéd, having already been invoked by Pierce Egan, by Dickens, and by dozens of other writers and political cartoonists.[6]

The meaning inherent in the contrasts diagram is introduced by Reynolds in the opening paragraphs of *The Mysteries of London*: "Among these cities [of Western Europe] there is one in which contrasts of a strange nature exist. The most unbounded wealth is the neighbour of the most hideous poverty; the most gorgeous pomp is placed in strong relief by the most deplorable squalor; the most seducing luxury is only separated by a narrow wall from the most appalling misery."[7] Many aspects of *The Mysteries of London* reinforce this image of opposition: most obviously the basic narrative of two brothers whose parallel lives are opposed. The duality is also reflected in the arrangement of society. Like Disraeli, Reynolds sees the modern world in terms of two opposed forces—the haves and the have-nots, the rich and the poor, or, to Reynolds, the aristocracy and the oppressed. (The middle classes as a power hardly exist in *The Mysteries of London*; the bankers and other bourgeois types function mainly as extensions of aristocratic misrule.[8])

Reynolds also structures many of the parts on the principle of contrasts, following scenes of upper-class corruption with those contrasting in setting and sentiment. So the night in the harem of the Marquis of Holmesford (like Lord Steyne in *Vanity Fair* modelled on the notorious and recently deceased Marquis of Hertford) is followed by a heroic scene as Richard leaves to fight for freedom in Italy. A warm and friendly home at Clapton is contrasted to a scene in Bethlem Hospital; the first sight of a criminal's secret hideout is followed by a description of the secret lower chamber of the post office where mail is opened and tampered with.

Although the image of London as one of contrasts is usually as simple as it is insistent, one use of it in *The Mysteries of London* is more subtle. A secret center of power in the criminal world is the Resurrection Man's hideout, first a house in Smithfield and then one in Globe Town east of Bethnal Green. In describing these houses, the author contrasts the seemingly innocent exterior and the evil interior, the harmless appearance against the deadly reality. But beyond this is a contrast between a safe aboveground and a horribly dangerous underground. Both these houses have, buried deep beneath them, a hidden cell used as a private prison where all manner of violence, torture, and unspecified sexual activity are practiced. The Resurrection Man also keeps his money in a cupboard in the underground room. This Dostoievskian image of the threat of the unknown in modern city life, with its implied reference to the hiding place of repressed fears, is as expansive in its connotations as any Victorian image of the nightmare of the city.

Furthermore, the underground cell is part of a recurrent theme in *The Mysteries of London* in which the characters are morally tested by being "buried alive." Though both the good and the evil are subjected to this torture, the final outcome for each is another manifestation of the contrasts of London. The good escape, the evil do not. Some of the uses of this device include a bank clerk, involved in a fraud, who is literally buried alive. But since his motive for his crime was friendship, he is saved and vouchsafed a vision of "the supernal secret of eternity" (I, 340). The hero is threatened by underground burial more than once, but he is never actually incarcerated, except in prison. Three women are buried in the underground cell: one barely manages to escape being murdered there, and another, under the threat of murder "and worse," is forced to surrender her fortune to her brutal aristocratic husband. The descriptions of Bedlam and Newgate invoke images of being buried alive. Finally, the criminals in the work are all buried alive either metaphorically or literally. A murdered, hiding in the underground cell, goes temporarily mad. Crankey Jem rises from the death of permanent transportation to avenge himself on the Resurrection Man. And the Resurrection Man himself (so called for his trade in body-snatching) not only is involved in "bringing to life" the dead and buried, but he himself "rises from the dead" more than once, while in the end he is shut up alive in his own underground prison, blinded, and starved to death. The way in which the literal and metaphoric uses of this device reinforce each other is a good example of the skill with which Reynolds integrated Gothic motifs and social analysis.

The contrasts of London trope was the most obvious way that Victorian writers of all sorts tried to make sense of urban life. Yet ultimately it is not very satisfactory because it both oversimplifies, and, paradoxically, does not clarify. It makes a point about urban life but it does not explain it: it is primarily descriptive. Therefore the best writers of the period who use the "contrasts" theme—writers like Dickens, Mayhew, and Reynolds—project at an abstract level a more complex organization of the city. As one looks at their works closely, the contrasting lines regroup themselves into another image,

another kind of "imaginative diagram," one that pictures the city as a maze or labyrinth.

The usefulness of imaging London as a maze is obvious; it reflects the actual geography of that city, and it also gives figurative meaning to the blind alleys, wrong turns, and unexpected corners that an individual can encounter in his effort to move from place to place in a meaningful way. Also the image of the city as maze, implying that there is a path to the center (in the case of the labyrinth a center guarded by a monster), projects a meaning to city life which we may discover by correctly solving the puzzle of the maze. So in many urban texts, a clever and brave hero or heroine threads the maze of the city to a center where the monstrous source of power is revealed. Dickens uses this imaginative diagram in a number of his works: all roads in *Oliver Twist* lead to Fagin's den; in *Bleak House* Chancery rots at the heart of modern life as does the prison in *Little Dorrit*. One reason Dickens's evocation of the modern city is so powerful in these works is because the geography of the novel and the themes of the novel have the same center: Chancery is both a physical center and a thematic one. Even the many statistical and investigative accounts of the city—by Mayhew, Chadwick, McCulloch, and the parliamentary committees—projected a central controlling force. Their motivation for collecting the "facts" was the conviction that when all these statistical particulars were put together the central "laws" that controlled social and economic behavior would be revealed.

Reynolds too thought he had found the center of the maze of the modern city. In writing both *The Mysteries of London* and *The Mysteries of the Court of London*, he wanted to demonstrate, he said, how the aristocracy had been corrupted by power.[9] Or as Louis James puts it: "the inhumanity of the capitalist system expresses itself in the criminal classes that carry out the predatory desires of the rich."[10] Most of the criminal action in the book, for example, is the acting out of upper-class desires. Even the Resurrection Man's career is seen as the result of "overbearing conduct and atrocious tyranny of the more wealthy part of the community" (I, 191). The banking scandal in the novel is caused by various aristocratic cheats and frauds. The hero's early imprisonment, from which stems most of his troubles, is due to cheating aristocratic friends. And many of the comments about life in nineteenth-century London which Reynolds inserts as narrator make clear his belief that the monster keeping the treasure of a utopian life from the rest of society is the aristocracy. "In a word," the Home Secretary instructs one of his underlings, "you must always shield the upper classes as much as possible; and in order to veil their little peccadillos, bring out the misdeeds of the lower orders in the boldest relief" (II, 288).

And yet, though the image of London as a maze of aristocratic abuse makes sense in terms of Reynolds's plot, it does not adequately encompass the experience of reading *The Mysteries of London*. Despite the integration provided by his assured plotting, despite the descriptive unity of contrast, despite Reynolds's insistence that all the twisting roads of life in the city end up in the same foul dead end of aristocratic abuse, we ultimately experience the city of *The Mysteries of London* as fragmented and empty. For one thing, in *The Mysteries* there is no geographical center to London, a realistic detail, of course, and one way in which the real London, with its multiplicity of centers of power, is reflected in the novel.

The centripetal effect the lack of a geographical center has on the reader is reinforced by other elements in the novel. For example, the many worlds of London, each with its separate mystery, do not seem connected to each other in meaningful ways. The powers of integration instead seem to be chance and coincidence. Although these forces are normal in popular fiction, their pervasiveness in this work undermines the thematic coherence Reynolds insists on. One example: at the end of volume one the hero Richard accidentally bumps into his arch enemy, the Resurrection Man, on the street; the Resurrection Man, in an effort to escape, randomly knocks on a door of what turns out to be the gypsy hideout, where he is given entrance. But unknown to him or them, the gypsies have, also by chance, hidden in the same room in which they put him the very woman who has stolen the Resurrection Man's money. And also unknown to everybody, a mysterious traveller who has sought shelter in the gypsy house for that night is the Resurrection Man's enemy, Crankey Jem. The ruling class's oppression plays no role in the working out of these relationships; escape and revenge are randomly achieved.

One can of course argue that by making all lives subject mainly to chance the author projects a unifying vision of the absence of God and Providence in modern man's affairs. To me the plot devices of coincidence are both too many and too gratuitous to carry the weight of this theme, but in any case a city whose human relationships are ruled by chance is not a city where aristocratic abuse has absolute power.

In addition, two other factors work against the sense that modern urban life has coherent meaning. The diagram of the city as maze suggests, implicitly at least, that the killing of the monster at the heart will usher in a new and better order. Certainly the republicanism of Reynolds and his calls for revolution (albeit a peaceful one)[11] suggest that the elimination of the aristocracy will result in some version of the Heavenly City. But the actual city as pictured by him in the pages of *The Mysteries of London* belies this outcome. Despite his radical politics, Reynolds, in this work at least, seems to have a very dark view of the human potential for good. The nice folk in his novel all hail from other regions than the modern city: the hero is a chivalric stereotype; his closest friends are from outside England; even his working-class benefactor is never seen directly acting in the world. In the host of men and women of all classes who make up the rest of London, Reynolds does not suggest that there is much significant difference in character between the oppressors and the oppressed. Every class has its share of cheats, frauds, hypocrites, and murderers. A seduced and abandoned school girl becomes a tyrannical sadist when she has those she thinks are responsible for her plight in her control. She is in turn murdered by the Resurrection Man, who is working, as usual, for the upper classes. A woman who comes up from below to make a good marriage turns murderess. Interestingly enough, mere sexual license in women does not seem to bother Reynolds, and so there are a number of sympathetically drawn sensual women who are ultimately rewarded for their virtuous actions towards others. But no realistically drawn lower-class character shows much decency, or honesty, generosity or altruism; there are no examples of Dickens's deserving poor, nor any of the complexly generous lower-class figures in Mayhew's surveys. We see no one that we believe would make a better world for us if the aristocracy were gone. The hero himself is no match for the social realities, as Reynolds clearly suggests by having his triumph take place in an imaginary Italian state. He is relatively ineffectual in London. This lack of positive human values undercuts the simplicity of blaming everything on the abuse of power by the ruling class and creates a vision of city life in which every man's hand is against his neighbor, a nightmare version of Wordsworth's evocation of city life. Reynolds recognized this problem but could not face it directly, posing it as an unanswered question: "Is there implanted in the heart of man a natural tendency towards even the blackest crimes—a tendency which only requires the influence of particular circumstances to develop it to its dark and terrible extreme?" he asks rhetorically (II, 263).

A recurrent narrative pattern further limits Reynold's insistence that the mysterious center of city life is the corruption of the aristocracy. The many different stories told throughout the work overtly expose the aristocratic abuse in urban institutions—royalty, religion, fashion, finance, civil and governmental service, social services, criminal organizations, and so on. But a repeated narrative structure in some of these stories complicates this overt assertion. Frequently the institution is represented by a separate building or house: we see the royal family in Buckingham palace, the aristocrat in his town house, the financier in the inner office of the most respected bank in London, the Home Secretary in the Black Chamber of the Post Office, the criminal in his underground cell. A repeated narrative pattern begins outside one of these mysterious buildings. The narrator has us move inward to the center; we frequently must go through various barriers—fences, windows, stairs, doors, corridors. When finally, after some difficulty and danger, we reach the inner sanctum, we find not some evil power figure, but—nothing. The center of the bank is a safe that when opened is empty; the center of the Marquis of Holmesford's fabulous townhouse is his harem, where, titillated by erotic dances, spiced by champagne, caressed by youth, the besotted old aristocrat is impotent. The most bizarre example of this pattern concerns the Queen. In this episode, extending over the two volumes, a London pot boy Henry Holford steals into Buckingham Palace, ostensibly to find out where they keep the plate. He climbs over a fence, slides through a window, creeps through doors, glides down halls, and eventually finds the center of the government itself—Victoria. Hiding under the very couch where Victoria and Albert are courting, he learns that the monarchy is also impotent: Victoria is ignorant, helpless in the hands of her ministers, heir to insanity and scrofula. (Reynolds, however, remains moderately deferential to the person of the Queen herself.)

As we penetrate the mysteries of London with their geographical separateness and coincidental connections, then, we find power fragmented and at the heart of each fragment, not an active emblem of evil, but the void. And while such a vision is coherent, it is not reassuring; it increases the fears of the unspecific and does not eliminate the threat of multiplicity.

Such a dark view of Reynolds's enormously successful novel, however, immediately raises the question, how could such a negative work be so popular with the huge numbers of unsophisticated readers who eagerly bought every number? The resolution to this contradiction lies in the genius of what John Cawelti has called "social melodrama." In his analysis of this convention in *Adventure, Mystery, and Romance,* Cawelti shows that the success of social melodrama results precisely from its unresolved contradiction between a realistic analysis of the corruption of society and a conventional plot that affirms the opposite, namely "the basic melodramatic principle that things are as they should be."[12] We can see this duality at work in Reynolds's novel. For surrounding all the stories, images, and direct statements that suggest otherwise is a formulaic story in which totally conventional rewards and punishments are handed out. The novel begins with the brothers Richard and Eugene parting by a tree on the family estate, promising to meet again in twelve years at the same place to see who has made the best success. The book ends with their final meeting. Richard has gone from a convict prison to be Prince of an Italian State. Eugene has succeeded as city man, as a lover, as a power seeker and power broker, but at the close he is destitute, solitary, and mortally wounded by his various accomplices. Thus the story of Richard and Eugene asserts that Providence does indeed rule, and it supports the conventional values of society: monogamy, virginity, selfless sacrifice are rewarded with success and beauty.

This ultimate contrast in *The Mysteries of London* brings us back once again to Wordsworth.[13] The contradictions in *The Mysteries of London* between form and content also further express that urban lawlessness which confounded the speaker in *The Prelude.* They are the final manifestation of the contrasts of London, here a contrast in the work as a whole between an "overtext" and "undertext." Yet, paradoxically, this apparent lawlessness actually affirms the integrative power of art. For the conventional melodramatic frame of this novel turns out to be the true ordering principle that controls the chaos of the modern city, even as Wordsworth's philosophic mind uses poetic figure and blank verse to control the randomness of Bartholomew's Fair. Of *The Mysteries of London* we cannot say whether the work is dominated by the negations of realism or the affirmations of melodrama; in the final analysis these two forces seem tightly balanced, as, incidentally, do many of the contrasting elements in Reynolds's career as a whole. For us as readers, however, the equilibrium contains and hence makes meaning of the mysterious contradictions of modern urban life: in *The Mysteries of London* we experience not only the "disassociation of sensibility" we are heir to, but also the healing unitary force in the literary conventions through which we express our fragmentation and despair.

Notes

1. Two biographical sketches of Reynolds have been published: E. F. Bleiler, "Introduction" to the Dover reprint of Reynolds's novel *Wagner, the Wehr-Wolf* (New York: Dover, 1975), pp. vii-xviii, and Louis James and John Saville, "G. W. M. Reynolds" in the *Dictionary of Labour Biography* (London: Macmillan, 1976), III, 146-51. Bleiler's volume also includes a thorough bibliography of Reynolds's works on pp. 153-60.

2. *Bookseller* (July 1868), p. 447; (July 1879), p. 660.

3. Bleiler, p. xvii.

4. James and Saville, p. 149.

5. See Louis James, "The View from Brick Lane: Contrasting Perspectives in Working-class and Middle-class Fiction of the Early Victorian Period," *The Yearbook of English Studies* (1980) for a short discussion of the sources and influence of *The Mysteries of London,* pp. 96-97.

6. Louis James, *English Popular Literature 1819-1851* (New York: Columbia University Press, 1976), p. 80.

7. G. W. M. Reynolds, *The Mysteries of London,* 1st Ser., 2 vols. (London: John Dicks, 185?), I, 1-2. Further references will be made parenthetically in the text.

8. Richard C. Maxwell in "G. W. M. Reynolds, Dickens, and the Mysteries of London," *Nineteenth Century Fiction,* 32 (1977), argues that Greenwood (Eugene) is a new kind of middle-class villain (pp. 192-93). Eugene is an interestingly ambiguous figure; if the independent villainy of the middle class exists anywhere in the novel, it is with him. Still he is ultimately as much a victim of upper-class treachery as is his brother.

9. Bleiler, p. xv.

10. James, "View from Brick Lane," p. 100.

11. In volume II, Reynolds expresses the call to peaceful revolution most forcefully:

> "Yes! Most solemnly do I proclaim to you, O suffering millions of these islands, that ye shall not always languish beneath the yoke of your oppressors! Individually ye shall each see the day when your tyrant shall crouch at your feet; and as a mass ye shall triumph over that proud oligarchy which now grinds you to the dust!
>
> "That day—that day cannot be far distant; and then shall ye rise—not to wreak a savage vengeance on those who have so long coerced you, but to prove to them that ye know how to exercise a mercy which they never manifested towards you;—ye shall rise, not to convulse the State with a disastrous civil war, nor to hurry the nation on to the deplorable catastrophe of social anarchy, confusion, and bloodshed,—but ye shall rise to vindicate usurped rights, and to recover delegated and misused power, that ye may triumphantly assert the aristocracy of mind, and the aristocracy of virtue!"

(II, 238)

12. John C. Cawelti, *Adventure, Mystery, and Romance: Formulaic Stories as Art and Popular Culture* (Chicago and London: University of Chicago Press, 1976), p. 261.

13. I am grateful to my colleague Gerhard Joseph for pointing out this final "contrast" to me.

Howard Horsford (essay date May 1987)

SOURCE: Horsford, Howard. "Melville and the London Street Scene." *Essays in Arts and Sciences* 16 (May 1987): 23-35.

[*In the following essay, Horsford examines Herman Melville's journal of his travels in London in 1849 and 1850.*]

None of Melville's "journals," as any reader of them knows, has the dense descriptive or reflective quality of the notebooks of his famous contemporaries, Hawthorne or Emerson or Thoreau. True, there are a number of recognizable elements that find their way into later writings, but even in this, there is certainly nothing like, say, the notebooks of Henry James. Especially is this poverty characteristic of the 1849 record, which is somewhat but not much more than a surface naming of places or things seen, of persons, of meetings with publishers and the occasions of festive dinners.[1] Even the most notable of contemporary events are ignored or only distantly or indirectly alluded to—the sordid death of Poe, for instance, reported as Melville waited to sail from New York; the summer's cholera which had ravaged both London and New York while he drove himself to push *Redburn* through the press and write *White-Jacket*; the frenzy over California; or a last example, the aftermath of the 1848 uprisings in Europe which had preoccupied him in the late additions to *Mardi*. One can tease imagination by thinking of Melville, repeatedly wandering through Soho, brushing past Karl Marx who had just taken refuge there after fleeing Paris in August.

Of course, the lively quality of this journal as compared to the depressed and finally exhausted tone of the 1856-1857 Mediterranean and Levantine journals is significantly different. With only occasional lapses, this earlier daily diary is marked by exuberance and nearly inexhaustible energy—the exuberance of a published young author going to see the sights of London, and perhaps beyond; going with letters of introduction from well-known people and with entree to important publishers; and going perhaps with an inadmissible sense of recess from a punishing summer in a cramped joint household of mother and sisters and brother and young wives and two squalling infants.

But after acknowledging that, what we should very much like is a denser context for those much too bare notations. What were the plays like, and the farces he so thoroughly enjoyed? What can we usefully find out about the people he met, or not least, the implications of the meetings he might have had but did not? What exactly was going on in the vexed business of copyright? Noting Melville's persistent and seemingly indefatigable wandering around—not only to the conventional guidebook sights but repeatedly to and through obscure and out-of-the-way districts—what was he in fact seeing? what kind of life encountering? It is this latter dimension of Victorian London I should like to consider here.

In some instances, he did record a few details of his experiences: the public hanging of the Mannings, or the scene in the Guild Hall the day following the Lord Mayor's banquet are examples, but for a far larger part we have only mere street names or similarly naked allusions. Yet it turns out that these areas which he seems to have sought out were commonly the most desperate, the vilest and most degraded of the greatest commercial metropolis of the western world. By following his bare references with a contemporary city map at hand, and by finding other, sterner and fuller accounts of these aspects of the mid-century city we can begin to get a sense of what he saw, looked for, encountered nearly every day of his stay.[2]

In some indefinite degree, this persistent wandering was probably prompted by his vague notion of doing something with the narrative of Israel Potter (to which he refers late in his entries, December 18th); Walter Bezanson, in his "Historical Note" to the recently issued Northwestern-Newberry Library edition of *Israel Potter* (1982), has surveyed the actual use Melville did make of his journal record. And certainly other experiences also find their way into, notably, the sketches "Rich Man's Crumbs," "Temple II" and "The Paradise of Bachelors," as well as passing allusions and metaphors in novels like *Moby-Dick*. But it is unnecessary to rehearse that aspect again. What can be done, I hope usefully, is to bring together a denser context for a body of allusions which are at best only abbreviated and dispersed throughout the journal. This can, at least partly, supply what Melville himself does not regarding his most interesting experiences.

Take his rather gruesome interest in the public hanging of the Mannings: early on the morning of November 13th, just a week after arriving, he and his friend George Adler made their way across the river to the Surrey County Gaol, paid half a crown apiece for a roof-top vantage to watch the "brutish" mob and the execution. (The trial of George and Marie Manning for the murder of her admirer had been the newspaper sensation of the autumn.) Melville called it "a most wonderful, horrible, & unspeakable scene" (Metcalf, p. 30), and one could, of course, be reasonably content with this unusually (for Melville) lengthy comment. Surely, however, there is greatly added interest in the London *Times'* account and Dickens' first outraged letter printed there the next day, far more detailed and informative. Dickens and Forster had gone at midnight to observe the gathering of the drunken rabble.

> I believe that a sight so inconceivably awful as the wickedness and levity of the immense crowd collected at that execution this morning could be imagined by no man, and could be presented in no heathen land under the sun. . . . [the] screeching, and laughing, and yelling in strong chorus of parodies on Negro melodies with substitutions of "Mrs. Manning" for "Susannah", and the like . . . When the day dawned, thieves, low prostitutes, ruffians and vagabonds of every kind, flocked on to the ground, with every variety of offensive and foul behaviour. Fightings, faintings, whistlings, imitations of Punch, brutal jokes, tumultuous

demonstrations of indecent delight . . . [were everywhere]. When the two miserable creatures . . . were turned quivering into the air, there was no more emotion, no more pity, no more thought that two immortal souls had gone to judgment, no more restraint in any of the previous obscenities, than if the name of Christ had never been heard . . .

The adjoining news account specified that the prisoners, she already veiled and blindfolded, shook hands as they were being hooded, and again just before the drop; that the hanging at 9 a.m. was on the roof in view of 30,000 spectators, at the outskirts of which "were grouped in smaller numbers, a very different class . . . who had paid their two or three guineas to gratify a morbid curiosity, and who . . . from their luxurious homes, came to fill the windows, the gardens, and the housetops of a few miserable little houses . . . ."[3]

However one explains Melville's special effort to reach this grisly, out-of-the-way exhibition as a writer's desire to store up experience, this was certainly a macabre curiosity. More reasonably explicable is his tireless, restless wandering about the unsavory recesses of the city, beginning almost as soon as he arrived. I pass by the *Times* account of the Lord Mayor's procession that first Friday—in Melville's skeptical American eye a "most bloated pomp"—and of the banquet about which he read the next day (Metcalf, pp. 25, 26) after viewing the remains, an experience well-known as the basis of the later sketch, "Rich Man's Crumbs." Instead, let me go on to the further wanderings of that Saturday which has, probably, a different kind of literary connection. Saturday was the day recommended to "upper class" visitors for sightseeing by guidebooks like that compiled by Melville's future dinner acquaintance, Peter Cunningham—this because Mondays were the "workingman's holiday."[4] In the course of the day, Melville had visited the usual highlights of the City from Temple Bar to the Tower, and then somewhat curiously, he walked on along the river through the Docks and the seamy maritime district toward infamous Limehouse (Metcalf, pp. 25-27). The sailor associations, no matter how rough, of course interested him, but a little oddly he walked through the dank Thames Tunnel (one of the very few sights he revisited on his spiritless return to London eight years later) to the dreary (and dangerous) lower-class district of Rotherhithe on the other side. What may have attracted him, however, is suggested by his throwing a coin to a "Poor Jack" before recrossing by boat, using a term in quotation marks with which he might ordinarily be supposed unfamiliar.

"Poor Jack" and "mudlark" were, of course, the usual local terms applied to idle men and boys hanging around the docks to pick up a penny or two for petty services. But *Poor Jack* was also the title of Captain Marryat's 1840 novel about an enterprising Rotherhithe lad, part of the small library installed on Melville's third whaler, the *Charles and Henry*.[5] Naturally this suggests that such a curious excursion to a tourist's nowhere may have been prompted by recollected sentiment, but a further dimension I defer for a moment.

Another otherwise inexplicable venture may also have been partly prompted by literary association. After a too convivial Saturday evening (November 24th) with the family of Joshua Bates, the transplanted banker from New England, Melville rose late into a continuing pea-soup fog and once again walked through and beyond the City into another part of the East End—Whitechapel Road—where, as he notes, "Bayard Taylor stopped" (Metcalf, p. 49). Taylor, whom he had met earlier in New York, and whose astonishing popularity as a travel writer Melville ruefully came to envy, had published *Views Afoot* three years before; it was the account of his footloose, nearly penniless wandering about Europe partly in company with his cousin, the Dr. Franklin Taylor who was Melville's shipboard companion on this trip. But granting this modest personal connection, this was an extraordinarily odd place for walking on a densely foggy Sunday with a heavy head.

Apart from these merely mildly interesting literary associations, what is common to both these otherwise unaccountable excursions into squalor is their part in a remarkably persistent pattern of walks through the misery of mid-century London. Redburn had seen Liverpool's counterpart, but the degradation in London was far more extensive, and by 1849, hideous beyond imagining. Naturally these were the regions most devastated by the summer's cholera, the more crowded, as we might not remember, by the flood of refugees from the Irish famine, and by the ruthless displacements from tenement to tenement due to the construction of new commercial thoroughfares and the railroads' thrust into central London. Melville's new acquaintance, J. C. B. Davis, second in succession to Melville's brother, Gansevoort, as Secretary to the American Legation, expressed a dismay they both felt as Americans; Melville troubles to record an evening's conversation: ". . . I was struck with his expressions concerning the poverty & misery of so large a portion of the London population. He revealed a heart" (Metcalf, p. 51). And conceivably this was a topic, too, when Davis and Melville returned to the city with the benevolent George Peabody after the dinner with Bates and his family. Peabody also was a transplanted New England banker, partner of Junius Morgan; he gave a large part of his fortune to provide public housing for the London poor.

Taylor had merely discreetly named the area of his "humble lodging," but a later, updated and franker encyclopedic guidebook issued by Murray, warned the traveler against the area of Whitechapel with the distressingly recurrent phrase, "one of the very worst localities in London; a region of narrow and filthy streets, yards and alleys, many of them wholly occupied by thieves' dens, the receptacles of stolen property, gin-spinning dog-holes, low brothels, and putrescent lodging-houses,—a district unwholesome to approach and unsafe for a decent person to traverse even in the day time."[6]

Similarly, whatever the initial impetus that earlier took Melville past the Docks along the river, and whatever interest this maritime district would have held in any case for the ex-sailor, it was both notoriously squalid and dangerous. Hawthorne, accompanied by his son Julian, found the region "dingy," "shabby," "dreary," "coarse" and "uninteresting,"[7] but Murray's guidebook expressed the proper Victorian horror at streets that still exhibited the degraded concomitants of sailor life, "flaring drinking, dancing, and music rooms, and haunts of a far worse order. Here, among other 'dens,' are the Chinese opium-smokers' sties" (*London, Past and Present,* III, 150). But this was not a late century development: Ratcliffe Highway (now St. George's Street) along which Melville walked was particularly singled out for lengthy attention in the section on prostitution in Volume IV of Mayhew's *London Labour.*

We may legitimately suppose, as remarked earlier, that the searching out of London's lower life had as a more or less vague purpose the development of a background sense for the contemplated *Israel Potter,* though in the event, the actual novel uses virtually nothing from this personal observation.[8] But beyond this there is an unstated dimension to his persistent wandering about London streets, day and night, that, for all its melodramatic and even lurid potentialities, is nowhere accounted for in his pedestrian daily entries. Certainly guidebooks did not recommend these areas to the visitor! Concentration here on the degraded, however, ubiquitous as it was, of course does not mean to suggest for Melville either a calloused curiosity or in other respects prurient titillation. But it may add a further depth to our understanding of the range of his intellectual concerns and indeed his humane sympathies.

Nevertheless, a somewhat contrary case in point: on the December morning of the day he expected to conclude the sale of *White-Jacket* to Richard Bentley, he looked for old books in Holywell Street; it was a now-demolished short lane angling off the Strand, not far from his lodging in Craven Street (overlooking the river, just southeast of Trafalgar Square and Charing Cross). In a much later, polite description the lane was mentioned for its quaint old architecture, but in fact it was a well-known center for the most salacious Victorian pornography—a shop of the notorious William Dugdale was there—and as well, a haunt of the commonest street drabs. Hawthorne, too, found out this street of second-hand books, but he did record his dismay at the heterogeneous proximity of "sermons and other works of divinity, old editions of the classics, and all such serious matters; while, at stalls and windows close beside them (and, possibly, at the same stalls) there were books with title pages displayed, indicating them to be of the most abominable kind." And that classic of the Victorian underground, *My Secret Life,* described the corner nearby as a place where the streetwalkers shamelessly relieved themselves.[9]

It is likely, of course, that Melville did not write of this because of the women of his family who would be reading his pages, yet again and again he found out the blight of London, so repeatedly as to suggest at least a horrified fascination. A quite early example (November 15th, a week and half after arriving) might have been accidental, yet it would have indicated to him how wide-spread were the plague-spots, not only in the crowded center city or the East End. On this Thursday, everything was officially closed in thanksgiving for the cholera's cessation, so he and his friend, George Adler, went on a long traverse around the north side of the city which ultimately took them through King's Cross. Now this was the area whose chaotic demolition by the London and Northwestern rail line to Euston Station Melville would have had to see from the horse-drawn omnibus as he rode through, though *we* have to depend on Dickens' graphic description in Chapter Six of *Dombey and Son* (1848-1849):

> Houses were knocked down; streets broken through and stopped; deep pits and trenches dug in the ground; enormous heaps of earth and clay thrown up; buildings that were undermined and shaking, propped by great beams of wood. Here, a chaos of carts, overthrown and jumbled together, lay topsy-turvy at the bottom of a steep unnatural hill; there, confused treasures of iron soaked and rusted in something that had accidentally become a pond. Everywhere were bridges that led nowhere; thoroughfares that were wholly impassable . . . carcasses of ragged tenements, and fragments of unfinished walls and arches, and piles of scaffolding, and wildernesses of bricks, and giant forms of cranes, and tripods straddling above nothing.

An 1854 pamphlet calls the area, characteristically, "one of the worst" with its appalling stenches, piggeries, stables, garbage heaps, cesspools, no water and an utter absence of sanitation.[10] Surely, not only Melville's nose but his eye must have been offended, yet he writes nothing of the scene.

Not every such experience, to be sure, was appalling. The very first Saturday night in the city, he persuaded Adler to wander with him through one of the most notorious of these districts, one that as it happens was nearest Craven Street, and through which he later repeatedly found his way (oddly enough, later recommending it to his Uncle Peter Gansevoort—Metcalf, p. 175). This blighted area just beyond the monumental new Trafalgar Square reached nearly as far east as Lincoln's Inn Fields, nearly as far north as the British Museum, and west toward Regent Street; it encompassed the hideous rookery of St. Giles just now devastated by the construction (1849) of New Oxford Street, as well as Leicester Square and Soho, populated by refugees from the Continental uprisings, and centered in the evil area around Seven Dials. We can know this was the district, however, only by Melville's passing reference to "Holborn" (Metcalf, p. 27), even as he wrote cheerfully enough of the evening's "entertainment" as "vagabonding thro' the courts & lanes, looking in all the windows. Stopped in at a Penny Theater . . ." Adler, he says, was afraid, but he himself found it "Very comical."

These theaters, called "Penny Gaffs" by their youthful patrons, flourished by the hundreds throughout the poor districts of London, jerry-built and dangerously flimsy in old warehouses, stables or stores. What amused Melville was singing and dancing of the bawdiest sort, sometimes six or more performances a night, each to two hundred or so ticket buyers; often they included a play or two—for example, *Hamlet* cobbled up in twenty minutes, or outrageous melodramas or farces. To horrified Victorian sensibilities, the young audiences of both sexes were unspeakably rowdy, addicted to the most degraded language and representation. The remarkable journalist, Henry Mayhew, described a visit with a friend to such a place about the time of Melville's visit.

> The audience is usually composed of children so young, that these dens become the school-rooms where the guiding morals of a life are picked up; and so precocious are the little things, that the girl of nine will, from constant attendance at such places, have learnt to understand the filthiest sayings . . . The show that will provide the most unrestrained debauchery will have the most crowded benches; and to gain this point, things are acted and spoken that it is criminal even to allude to.

As Mayhew and his friend approached, they heard and saw what Melville and Adler would have:

> . . . for a great distance off, the jingling sound of music was heard, and the gas-light streamed out into the thick night air . . . The front of a large shop had been entirely removed, and the entrance was decorated with paintings of the "comic singers," in their most "humorous" attitudes. On a table against the wall was perched the band, playing . . . "dancing tunes" with great effect . . .

> The visitors, with a few exceptions, were all boys and girls, whose ages seemed to vary from eight to twenty years. Some of the girls—though their figures showed them to be mere children—were dressed in showy cotton-velvet polkas, and wore dowdy feathers in their crushed bonnets. . . . Some of them, when tired of waiting, chose their partners, and commenced dancing grotesquely, to the admiration of the lookers-on, who expressed their approbation in obscene terms . . .

To discover the kind of entertainment, a lad near me . . . was asked "if there was any flash dancing." With a knowing wink the boy answered, "Lots! Show their legs and all, prime!"[11]

Mayhew devoted six closely printed columns to his indictment of a society that could offer no better entertainment and schooling to its poor. But it is Dickens again who provides us with a fuller sense of the unspeakable degradation of this "heart" of the city that so occupied Melville's wanderings. For *Bleak House* (1852-1853), Dickens located the pestilential graveyard of Captain Nemo and Lady Dedlock's death near the eastern edge, while somewhere in the area, perhaps near Seven Dials, he imagined the horror of Tom-all-alone's with its pitiful denizen, Jo the crossing sweeper. Seven Dials, at the intersection of seven streets, had from the beginning a repellent fascination for Dickens. His friend and biographer, John Forster, recounts of the child:

To be taken out for a walk into the real town . . . perfectly entranced him with pleasure. But, most of all, he had a profound attraction of repulsion to St. Giles's. If he could only induce whomsoever took him out to take him through Seven-dials, he was supremely happy. "Good heaven!" he would exclaim, "what wild visions of prodigies of wickedness, want, and beggary, arose in my mind out of that place!"[12]

And Seven Dials became the occasion for one of the earliest sketches by Boz; though treated with a hand ironic enough for popular essay purposes, the sense of the horrible squalor and the intolerable degradation of humanity is sufficiently evident, as it had to be for Melville. Adopting the viewpoint of a bemused and confused visitor, Dickens wrote (I abridge ruthlessly):

But what involutions can compare with those of Seven Dials? Where is there such another maze of streets, courts, lanes, and alleys? . . .

The stranger who finds himself in "The Dials" for the first time . . . at the entrance of seven obscure passages, uncertain which to take, will see enough around him to keep his curiosity and attention awake . . . From the irregular square into which he has plunged, the streets and courts dart in all directions, until they are lost in the unwholesome vapour . . . lounging at every corner, as if they came there to take a few gasps of such fresh air as has found its way so far . . . are groups of people, whose appearance and dwellings would fill any mind but a regular Londoner's with astonishment.

On one side, a little crowd has collected round a couple of ladies, who having imbibed the contents of various "three-outs" of gin and bitters in the course of the morning, have at length differed on some point of domestic arrangement, and are on the eve of settling the quarrel satisfactorily, by an appeal to blows . . .

In addition to the numerous groups who are idling about the gin-shops and squabbling in the centre of the road, every post in the open space has its occupant, who leans against it for hours . . .

As Melville must have,

The . . . unexperienced wayfarer . . . traverses streets of dirty, straggling houses, with now and then an unexpected court composed of buildings as ill-proportioned and deformed as the half-naked children that wallow in the kennels . . . shops for the purchase of rags, bones, old iron, and kitchen-stuff, vie in cleanliness with the bird-fanciers and rabbit-dealers, which one might fancy so many arks, but for the irresistible conviction that no bird in its proper senses, who was permitted to leave . . . would ever come back again . . . dirty men, filthy women, squalid children, . . . reeking pipes, bad fruit, . . . attenuated cats, depressed dogs, and anatomical fowls, are [components of the "still life"] . . .

From here the description goes on to detail the squalor of the interiors, the crowding, the constant fighting, and the drunken brutality of the inhabitants.[13]

Descriptions like this, or those in *Bleak House* (for example, Chapters 16 or 21), might be supposed overcharged for literary effect, but the quasi-official language of Lord Shaftesbury in 1847 is plain enough about what Melville regularly walked through:

. . . tight avenues of glittering fish & rotten vegetables, with doorways or alleys gaping on either side—which, if they be not choked with squalid garments or sickly children, lead the eye through an almost interminable vista of filth and distress. . . . The pavement, where there is any, rugged and broken, is bespattered with dirt of every hue, ancient enough to rank with the fossils, but offensive as the most recent deposits. The houses, small, low, and mournful, present no one part, in windows, door-posts, or brickwork, that seems fitted to stand for another week—rags and hurdles stuff up the panes, and defend the passages blackened with use and by the damps arising from the undrained and ill-ventilated recesses.

(cited in Sheppard, *London,* pp. 4-5)

Whatever Melville's reasons for not describing such misery, neither did he write anything of the notorious proliferation of prostitution in even the most fashionable streets—unless an oblique reference to a "singular interview" one evening in the Haymarket be such (Metcalf, p. 40). An obviously possible reason is that mentioned before, deference to a prim, "Victorian" prudishness in his wife, mother and sisters, certain to read the journal when he returned home. But if so, this implies an interesting contrast to the genteel Sophia Hawthorne, who certainly read *her* husband's recording of such encounters as he would know she would.

However that may be, with some knowledge of the customary haunts of these women, even little girls—and perhaps males, too, of whom there seem to have been some[14]—we can nevertheless surmise what must have been Melville's almost constant experiences in his afternoon and evening wanderings.

Surely as a one-time sailor he had at least speaking knowledge, and quite possibly more, of dockside doxies, in Liverpool early, or Callao, Valparaiso, Rio, or even New York and Boston, to say nothing of his experiences in Polynesia. And surely it is possible to suppose that a vigorous, exuberant young fellow of 30, one who had seen as much of the world as he, had more than a primly averted eye for what certainly accosted him at every turn, at every hour, day or night. But that supposition has only the authority of our own supposing.

He could not have failed to understand, for example, what he saw in the Burlington Arcade. On the December afternoon of the day he had bought Rousseau's *Confessions* in Holywell Street, and while waiting for Bentley's decision, in one of the elegantly expensive shops of the Arcade he bought a cigar case for his brother Allan, and walked about to pass the time (Metcalf, p. 70). But because this was a very fashionable shopping center, the Arcade was also a promenade for the better class of ladies of pleasure. According to the indispensable Mayhew's supplement, "The Burlington Arcade is a well-known resort of women on the long winter afternoons, when all the men in London walk there before dinner" (IV, 251).

The region near Regent Street, too, through which Melville sometimes passed, was notorious. The once important medical reformer, Dr. William Acton, described "the street connecting Leicester Square with . . . Regent Street . . . [as] a thoroughfare *infested* with loitering prostitutes" and urged the police to clear it. Perhaps because of the Arcade's wealthier patronage, he thought police interference there more questionable on the grounds of "individual freedom," but the Haymarket had acquired such "an evil notoriety" that its frequenting should no longer be tolerated.[15]

That slightly later Volume IV added to Mayhew's *London Labour* spoke of the women soliciting along Regent Street and in the Haymarket at places like the notorious Kate Hamilton's as a higher class, estimating the number at eight thousand, "higher," presumably, than the poor drabs Melville had seen thronging the East End. But in a nice reversal of the familiar self-righteous English view of French morals, the famous historian, Hippolyte Taine, cast a French eye on English vice as he saw it along the Strand and in the Haymarket.

> Every hundred steps one jostles twenty harlots; some of them ask for a glass of gin; others say, "Sir, it is to pay my lodging." . . . The deplorable procession in the shade of the monumental streets is sickening; it seems to me a march of the dead.
>
> (cited in Sheppard, *London,* p. 367)

Peter Cunningham, Murray's exhaustive guidebook compiler, innocently advised tourists expected for the Crystal Palace Exhibition that the Haymarket was a place one must see on an opera or theater night, crowded with a crush of carriages and throngs of people, orderly and disorderly, moving in and out of the brilliantly lighted restaurants, taverns and shops. But editions of *Cruchley's Picture of London* (a copy of which Melville had borrowed from George Duyckinck to bring with him) strenuously cautioned strangers against the sharpers, swindlers, confidence men, pickpockets and prostitutes infesting the neighborhood at all hours.

The many causes of such a proliferation can hardly be enumerated here, but they would certainly include the harshness of the Poor Laws, the dislocations attributable to industrial change, and not least the Irish famine. If Melville never once speaks of this, Hawthorne was not so reticent and once expressed a rather unexpected sympathy with these victims. Nearly as peripatetic as Melville, after walking about the area of Charing Cross and the Strand one evening in 1855, he recorded:

> At every street corner, too, under archways, and at other places of vantage, or loitering along, with some indescribable peculiarity that distinguished her, and perhaps turning to re-tread her footsteps, was a woman; or sometimes two walked arm in arm—hunting in couples—and separated when they saw a gentleman approaching. One feels a curious and reprehensible sympathy for these poor nymphs; it seems such a pity that they should not each and all of them find what they seek!—that any of them should tramp the pavement the whole night through, or should go hungry and forlorn to their beds.
>
> (*English Notebooks,* p. 232)

I remarked earlier that I did not particularly want to consider the material as sources for Melville's later work; this sympathy of Hawthorne's for the plight of women in the comfortable world of Victorian men tempts me, however, to speculate in an unprovable way about the third of Melville's two-part sketches. The other two, "Poor Man's Pudding and Rich Man's Crumbs" or "The Two Temples," make clear thematic contrasts, with the transatlantic geography largely incidental to the purpose. But while it is true enough the convivial feasting of bachelors in London also stands in a simple way against the dreary labor of the New England mill girls, the now recognizable physiological metaphor underlying "The Tartarus of Maids" is not so obviously the opposing counterpart of bibulous masculine bonhomie. Yet I am led to wonder if underlying not only the sardonic irony of "Rich Man's Crumbs" but also both halves of this pairing—however indirect and submerged—may be Melville's acute sense of the painful disparity he repeatedly saw in London, the disparity between the complacent world of prosperous Victorian literary men, publishers, lawyers, bankers and business men, on the one hand, and the appalling misery of the streets, especially in this instance of the women whose only commodity had to be the physiology of their bodies.

Notes

1. First transcribed and edited by his granddaughter, Eleanor Melville Metcalf, as *Journal of a Visit to London and the Continent, 1849-1850,* Cambridge: Harvard University Press, 1948. Except for a few lapses of no consequence, her transcription is reliable, and for convenience I shall cite her edition by page number. Actual quotations, however, follow my reading of the holograph manuscript, a transcription of which I have made for the CEAA-sponsored Collected Edition.

2. The first resource of anyone concerned with the lower life of London is the remarkable compilation of the journalist. Henry Mayhew: the first of the four volumes of his *London Labour and the London Poor* were issued in 1851, hardly more than a year after Melville's visit, with further material and other contributors in the added fourth volume, 1862. I cite the modern reprint, London: F. Cass, 1967. Readily accessible and highly informative modern accounts are Francis H. W. Sheppard's *London, 1808-1870: The Infernal Wen,* Berkeley: University of California Press, 1971, and Richard D. Altick's *Victorian People and Ideas,* New York: W. W. Norton, 1973. *The Victorian City,* ed. H. J. Dyos and Michael Wolff, London and Boston: Routledge and Kegan Paul, 1973, though voluminous is more sociologically abstract and less descriptive; its footnote references and many illustrations, however, are valuable.

3. A recent book with an improbable title has now been wholly devoted to the sensational murder, the police chase, the trial and the executions, including the press accounts of the mutual recriminations and assertions of the other's guilt by husband and wife: *The Woman Who Murdered Black Satin,* by Albert Borowitz, Columbus: Ohio State University Press, 1981.

4. *Modern London,* London: John Murray, 1851, p. xxvi (derived from his *A Handbook for London, Past and Present,* 1849, and aimed at the expected influx of Crystal Palace visitors).

5. Wilson L. Heflin, "New Light on Herman Melville's Cruise in the *Charles and Henry,*" *Historic Nantucket,* XXII, No. 2, October, 1974, pp. 6-27, especially p. 15. Good-hearted boy that Jack is, he often befriends old sailor pensioners at Greenwich Hospital (which Melville himself sought out several days later, November 21). Among them is a Negro from "south of Baltimore" who had fought with Nelson at the Nile—an irresistible parallel to *Billy Budd*'s Baltimore black, a "Trafalgar man" in Chapter 8. Incidentally, there is also in one episode a mate named Stubb.

6. Henry B. Wheatley's modernization of Cunningham's original (see n. 4) as *London Past and Present . . .* , in 3 volumes, London: John Murray, 1891; III, 500.

7. *The English Notebooks,* ed. Randall Stewart, New York: Modern Language Association, 1941, pp. 233-234.

8. The few pages of the penultimate Chapter 25, "Forty-five Years," merely summarize rather barely Melville's version of Potter's dismal life in London after the Revolution; apart from avoiding the historical anachronisms that could have been involved, Melville dispenses with all but a few concrete details: a few bare names like Smithfield, a few domiciles like a "doorless house in St. Giles'," and some meager allusions to his hand-to-mouth attempts to support a wife and child. Far more space is devoted in the preceding Chapter 24 to the single event of Potter's entering London, "the City of Dis," by way of London Bridge—the way Melville himself first entered—developing Melville's journal passage about the immense jostle of the crowds on the bridges and the smoky pall of the City (Metcalf, p. 25).

9. *English Notebooks,* p. 248; *My Secret Life* is cited in Steven Marcus, *The Other Victorians,* New York: Basic Books, 1966; Bantam Books, 1967, p. 99.

10. Quoted by Sir Walter Besant, *London in the Nineteenth Century,* London: A. and C. Black, 1909, pp. 272-273.

11. *London Labour,* I, 40-41; an earlier description can be found in James Grant's edition of *Penny Theatres, from Sketches in London, 1838,* reprinted by the Society for Theatre Research, London, 1952. Mrs. Metcalf also included extracts (p. 106-107) from still other clippings in the Harvard Theater Collection.

12. *The Life of Charles Dickens* (ed. J. W. T. Ley, London: Cecil Palmer, 1928), p. 11.

13. From Chapter V of the "Scenes" section, *Sketches by Boz,* 1836 (vol. 26 of *The Works,* New York: Charles Scribner's Sons, 1900, pp. 81-86).

14. Kellow Chesney (*The Victorian Underworld,* New York: Schocken Books, 1970, 1972) suggests reasons leading him to believe the prevalence of male prostitution was less evident at mid-century than at other times; see pp. 16, 96, and especially 327-329.

15. *Prostitution,* London: 1857; 2d ed. 1870, pp. 232-233.

Murray Baumgarten (essay date 1996)

SOURCE: Baumgarten, Murray. "London, Dickens, and The Theatre of Homelessness." In *Victorian Urban Settings: Essays on the Nineteenth-Century City and Its Contexts,* edited by Debra N. Mancoff and D. J. Trela, pp. 74-88. New York and London: Garland Publishing, Inc., 1996.

[*In the following essay, Baumgarten examines Charles Dickens's renderings of nineteenth-century London street performance, homelessness, and "the transformative theatrical experience that defines this urban world."*]

Urban life in the Dickens universe is a theatrical code. Historians note his accuracy: Nineteenth-century industrial capitalism helped to define the modern city in theatrical terms (Gay passim, Schwarzbach ch. 10). Not only was this a function of the reconstruction of the cities and massive new investment in plazas, parks, and squares, it was also the result of capital accumulation and the increasing democratization of everyday life. Crowds now gathered, not only on ritualized occasions and events—executions, coronations, royal weddings, progresses, parades, and the like—they also congregated in the course of daily business, including commuting to work. The new spaces created by the urban reconstruction of London served as impromptu theatres for street performers who could now take their activities from local side-streets and neighborhood building courts to the potentially larger audiences congregating in these public arenas. Such urban theatrical phenomena punctuate Dickens's novels: Pip and Wemmick in *Great Expectations,* to take only one example, meet on the street amid the crowds going to and from work. Their encounters bear witness to these new experiential conditions, which shape their lives. As Wemmick changes into Jaggers's law-clerk on the way into the City and back into the benevolent son of the Aged P. on his return journey to Little Britain, Pip, standing-in for the Dickensian reader, discovers the transformative theatrical experience that defines this urban world.

Creating the infrastructure that made the modern city possible, the monumental building projects also provided a window into the easier pace of the past in the informal street performances they made possible by the new dramatic staging of the city. At the same time, they made everyone a performer. Lewis Mumford underlines the function of the modern city as encouraging and inciting "the greatest potential number of meetings, encounters, challenges between all persons, classes and groups, providing, as it were, a stage upon which the drama of social life may be enacted, and with the actors taking their turns as spectators and the spectators as actors" (184).

In spite of the new power-relations which maximized competition and which Noddy Boffin defines in *Our Mutual Friend* as "scrunch or be scrunched" (bk. III, ch. 5), nineteenth-century London was also the place of "playful self-making" for all, especially for the working and lower classes. "Through their convivial laughter, their sympathy, their nonhegemonic speech, and their imaginative exuberance" they asserted that "life is not warfare against sin, nor is it only competitive struggle." Without "wealth or status" they yet became "imaginatively adept at exploiting language, gesture, and common reality to transform, with a sense of ceremony, existences which would otherwise be overwhelmed by necessity and utility" (Morris 34-35). From the Artful Dodger in *Oliver Twist* to Rogue Riderhood in *Our Mutual Friend,* Dickens's novels offer a portrait gallery of such figures of transformation.

While the impact of capitalism on Dickens's world has been noted by many scholars, the social economy of theatrical self-presentation which I explore in this essay, following the important work of Robert Garis, has not received similar attention. My discussion traces this motif through several of his novels, focusing on how the city functions to reinforce the theatricalization of appearance and everyday life; I also elaborate its connection to aspects of the picturesque. Furthermore, the ways in which theatrical experience is deployed in the marketplace for economic gain has not been central to current discussions of Dickens's art which also tend to elide the urban experience. In his writings as in his world, the opportunities of London are available to all, including the homeless. The city as marketplace, labyrinth, and stage is the central scene of his work—a measure of his encompassing democratic art.

While Dickens's representations of lower-class life echo those of Mayhew, they also provide a dynamic sense of character and possibility. Where Mayhew's are static and reinforce conventional stereotypes of the poor that, reinforced by an anthropology developing spurious racial distinctions which would make class division a seeming fact of nature (as Thomas Prasch points out in his essay in [*Victorian Urban Settings: Essays on the Nineteenth-Century City And Its Contexts*], "Photography and the Image of the London Poor") Dickens's characters dramatize their situations as part of a strategy of overcoming such barriers. While Silas Wegg is poor and a rogue, the way in which he accepts Boffin's offer to read to him—"No, sir. I never did 'aggle and I never will 'aggle. Consequently, I meet you at once, free and fair, with—Done, for double the money!" (bk. I, ch. 5)—is but one of many instances in *Our Mutual Friend* in which theatrical self-presentation functions to bridge class and social divisions as well as further economic gain.

Nineteenth-century urban reconstruction not only defined the theatre of everyday life, it also helped to create the homeless as a distinct and visible group: a class of people with access to this city stage but without personal location. Like other characters in Dickens's urban comedy, Silas Wegg has no home of his own yet he takes center stage throughout much of *Our Mutual Friend* by setting up his stand on a street corner. At almost the polar opposite of the social scale, Nicholas Nickleby discovers that he too can rely only on his self-presentation and role-playing as levers by which to attain a domicile of his own, in a manner of which Wegg is the undisputed master.

Nicholas Nickleby and *Our Mutual Friend,* among the Dickens novels most concerned with the theater, both focus on clothes-making. In *Our Mutual Friend* Jenny Wren models her dolls' clothing on that of society, while much of *Nicholas Nickleby* takes place in the Mantalini's dressmaking establishment. In both novels, appearances count for so much that clothing is put at its metaphoric center. In both, what a character wears is part of the modern industry of image-making and self-production. Not only his sister Kate but Nicholas as well will discover the power of the projected image, and the temptation to trade upon it for subsistence and possible wealth. Like dressmaking, the production of the self in this world is not a "natural" phenomenon but a technical—and technological—event that articulates the central values of this culture. Here, personality, like Miss LaCreevy's miniatures in *Nicholas Nickleby,* is composed. It is an image framed by the portrait painter's equivalent of a "Claude Glass" which functions to define a picturesque image.[1] Whatever the moral differences among characters, all are arrayed along the same ladder of self-making. Life for Boffin, Bella, Rokesmith, as for Nicholas, Kate, and Crummles, embodies the dressmaking idea, as Carlyle emphasizes in *Sartor Resartus*: we are in a world of cutting out shapes, stitching seams, and sewing on ruffles and borders, and thereby assembling a striking appearance out of the abstract, impersonal materials furnished by the industrial revolution, which began in England with the mass-production of cloth.

Just as appearance is an abstraction in this world, so personal relationships are here mediated by the abstractions of print and money. Thus it is entirely appropriate that Nicholas first learns of the job of tutor to Squeers through the abstract medium of a newspaper advertisement, which his uncle Ralph shows him. This is the beginning of Nicholas's education in the ways of the world. It is part of his introduction to the power available to those who can manipulate print and numbers; it is the beginning of his lessons that social appearance in this world is constructed appearance.

It is his appearance that leads Nicholas to employment throughout the novel. What he must learn in this bildungsroman is how to live up to his projected social role of gentleman. To be a knight and hero in this world is to fulfill the expectations of (aristocratic) appearance—and it is only through Nicholas's apprenticeship to the theatre of Crummles, a troupe that lives out the comic dramas they put on the provincial stage, that he discovers what it means to act his part. After that apprenticeship, he is ready for the fateful encounter with the Brothers Cheeryble, which frees him from the financial grasp of his uncle.

Though we never quite learn what their business consists of, Dickens makes quite clear that the Cheerybles do not engage in the kind of financial sleight-of-hand that characterizes Ralph's activities. Their offices do not depend on the illusion-creating staging of which Ralph is so fond, in which he makes certain that the seedy Newman Noggs plays the role of gatekeeper to intimidate his clients. Nor are the Cheerybles, who are committed to an older style of business, engaged in setting up phony stock ventures which depend on false advertising, as is Ralph Nickleby at the beginning of the novel; and his orchestration of the effort to drive local muffin makers out of business and replace them with a monopoly is the target of Dickens's satire in a scene that not only has the bite of Brechtian satire but functions by synecdoche to condemn all the instances of this morally shabby process.

The two firms are spatially counterposed in the novel; together they suggest the possibilities of urban life. The city thus becomes emblematic of the space between the old and new activities, between an older investment in a stable identity and a modern embrace of opportunity and dynamic self-making. And their intermediary is the market that, while invisible, projects possibilities which in terms of their past histories, impresses the newcomers to the city not just as opportunities but as seemingly malevolent situations.

Like their more privileged contemporaries these new city-dwellers had to learn how to negotiate the city by learning to read its new alphabet and syntax. Among the novelists who took as their task that of deciphering city life, Dickens is primary, teaching his contemporaries what "city-knowing" and "city-thinking" is. The problem he faced is that, as Mary Ann Caws has phrased it, "there is no easy reading of the city or its texts, no simple shuffling about of ironies as covers of the situation." While Dickens informs us "about city misery, physical and mental, about loneliness and loss and powerlessness" in an act of the literary imagination that "we must not lose," it is also not in his work, nor can it be in ours, "an excuse for yet more city-despair, for yet less use of the imagination, political, textual, and personal" (Caws 2; 6).

By contrast with Mayhew and other social observers, even in his darker novels Dickens does not speak for the class divisions so evident in the city or accept them as natural or a social given. Rather, his plots enforce the possibility that the urban world is the site of moral self-making precisely because it brings people together across class and social lines. His is not Mayhew's static image-building but an art of dynamic and evolving situations and figures. The serial format of Dickens's novels enforces this transformational context, as does the city—the central site of his fictional project and personal life—with its ephemeral, transitory, changing experiences of repetition with variation. In his work, the content of the form crosses over like one of Carlyle's metaphors to insinuate change as the form of the content. Whether characters are cannibalistic or altruistic, it defines them whatever their place as part of the same universe of discourse. They speak to and for each other, as evidenced in the impact the Cheeryble Brothers make, even in adversarial confrontation, on Ralph Nickleby. Here Dickens's fictions articulate, as do Carlyle's essays and Marx's critiques, the radical modern notion of species-being. Though their examples are often negative ones like the Irish widow in *Past and Present* who, spurned by Edinburgh charities, dies in the city and infects it with typhus, they reveal the ways in which it is not possible to escape from our common humanity (Marcus 97-99). And while Marx emphasizes the lure of the market and Carlyle the snaring of personality in the labyrinth, Dickens foregrounds the theatrical power of the stage in connecting classes and individuals.

The repeal of English sumptuary laws in the 1820s and 1830s codified the greater freedom to rise and to fall of everyday life. Linkages that had seemed part of the order of things were broken. When characters change their clothes in Dickens—Bella leaving the Boffins, her benefactors, and returning to her family home in the simple dress with which she left; Bradley putting on his schoolmaster's teaching style along with his vest; Twemlow inserting himself into his silk stockings for dinner at the Veneerings—they define their person in terms of the theatrical effect they seek to create and in terms of which they expect to be read. Values which had previously gone without saying now had to be discussed, clarified, and articulated, as John Stuart Mill emphasizes in "The Spirit of the Age," making a distinction between manifest and latent social functions. "For, the obvious and universal facts, which every one sees and no one is astonished at, it seldom occurs to any one to place upon record; and posterity, if it learn the rule, learns it, generally from the notice bestowed by contemporaries on some accidental exception" (226-27). Change has made what seemed familiar strange. Now clothes were no longer directly connected to social class but, as Carlyle reminds us in *Sartor Resartus,* have become costumes to be donned as part of identity-games and role-playing rather than natural concomitants of place and position. As markers of conventions, which remained strong, clothes were now part of the manipulable furniture of self-presentation. Rather than being

tied to place, competence, and craftsmanship as measures of value, clothing was one way of indicating the realm of desired identity. Perhaps that is why the sketch of Monmouth Street Dickens provides in *Sketches by Boz* is so vivid, the clothes turning into the lives of the people who wore them in a dreamer's dance of the imagination.

> We love to walk among these . . . and to indulge in the speculations to which they give rise; now fitting a deceased coat, then a dead pair of trousers, and endeavouring, from the shape and fashion of the garment itself, to bring its former owner before our mind's eye. We have gone on speculating in this way, until whole rows of coats have started from their pegs, and buttoned up of their own accord, round the waists of imaginary wearers; lines of trousers have jumped down to meet them; waistcoats have almost burst with anxiety to put themselves on; and half an acre of shoes have suddenly found feet to fit them, and gone stumping down the street with a noise which has fairly awakened us from our pleasant reverie, and driven us slowly away, with a bewildered stare, an object of astonishment to the good people of Monmouth Street, and of no slight suspicion to the policemen at the opposite street corner.
>
> ("Old Clothes" 75)

Against that sense of possibility and renewed, reconstructed identity in and of the city, we have Carlyle's recurring image of the Jewish peddler, the Old Clothes man whom Mayhew also describes and Dickens evokes, as part of the nightmare possibility of this new world defined not by ascribed status but by the ready money earned through commerce and industry.

In Dickens's world the opportunities for self-presentation are manifold. They take place in the Victorian parlor, in which Mr Podsnap dismisses everything "not English" and Mr Bounderby reiterates his rise from birth-in-a-ditch to industrial and financial eminence in *Hard Times,* as well as Edith Dombey's and Bella Wilfer's self-definition before the bedroom mirror. It is not accidental then, or merely a taste for sociological completeness that brings the poor and the homeless to the center of Dickens's stage; rather, it is in their relations to the hegemonic middle-class that Dickens explores the range of possibilities offered by the urban theatre of modern life.

His exploration focuses on the public world as well as the private realm; he takes us into Chancery and the Inn, and the places in between. In his world, the homeless, whether Silas Wegg or Nicholas Nickleby, perform their self-making in the new public arena articulated by and in nineteenth-century European culture, in and along the modern street. Given its public status and accessibility, the throngs passing through it, and its availability for many purposes, the street superseded all other venues. *Little Dorrit* concludes with Arthur Clennam and Little Dorrit, freed of the imprisonments of the past, leaving the Marshalsea prison, and going out of the church where they have been married into "the roaring streets."

> They paused for a moment on the steps of the portico, looking at the fresh perspective of the street in the autumn morning sun's bright rays, and then went down.
>
> Went down into a modest life of usefulness and happiness. Went down to give a mother's care, in the fulness of time, to Fanny's neglected children no less than to their own, and to leave that lady going into Society for ever and a day. Went down to give a tender nurse and friend to Tip for some few years, who was never vexed by the great exactions he made of her, in return for the riches he might have given her if he had ever had them, and who lovingly closed his eyes upon the Marshalsea and all its blighted fruits. They went quietly down into the roaring streets, inseparable and blessed; and as they passed along in sunshine and shade, the noisy and the eager, and the arrogant and the froward, and the vain, fretted, and chafed, and made their usual uproar.
>
> (826)

Now the homeless and dispossessed individual is part not of the picturesque pastoral or rural Wordsworthian landscape but the stage of urban life. He is not the leech-gatherer emerging from the rocky earth who serves as a moral teacher in "Resolution & Independence" but a figure whose moral value develops in the course of social interactions in an epic tale rather than a lyric meditation. He is not the figure who, as Wordsworth described his experience, emerges from a crowded, indistinct landscape and awakens the poet's mind from his "dreamy indifference" to focus his attention on "a poetical object" (Wordsworth to Lady Beaumont, 21 May 1807, in Wordsworth 145-51). Dickens's characters are part of the panorama of the street—of crowds and action and constant movement—a characteristic feature of Dickens's art. The picturesque individual has been turned into the unusual, eccentric performer on the stage of urban life. Now he is part not of the personal witnessing of the artist who has sought out the picturesque for inspiration but the objective condition of urban spectacle (Nord passim).

Capital city and commercial center, London in Dickens's fiction is the theatrical realm in which everyone, including the homeless, make their entrance. They encounter economic possibility, despair as well as political empowerment, and moral destiny in its streets. One can also trace the connection of the interest in the picturesque with the Victorian habit of "slumming"; the notion that these people are the ruins of urban humanity encouraged the development of social welfare and the rise of the social worker as a profession.

Dickens generalized the pursuit of the rural ruin (modeled on the Gilpinian and Wordsworthian reading of, for example, "Tintern Abbey"), and extended it to London, treated now as if the city were a ruin, its docks and shipyards, its monuments and housing warrens demanding a complex personal decoding. When Kate and her mother follow Newman Noggs to the rooms provided by Uncle Ralph on the ironically named Golden Square, when Kate walks to Madame Mantalini's or Nicholas negotiates the streets leading to the Cheerybles' place of business, they must deploy city habits only to be gained in their exercise. Nothing in their earlier experience prepares them for the confrontations with power and money that await them, and only their newly acquired street smarts will help them in the struggle to overcome them.

To follow the transformation of the picturesque into the Dickensian picaresque also charts the Wordsworthian presence in Dickens's art. *Nicholas Nickleby*, published in 1838 when Wordsworth was poet laureate, is not only a city novel but a travelogue whose main characters journey almost the entire length of England from London northward. It is also a portrait of London as an inhospitable place which echoes Wordsworth's view of the city in Book VII of *The Prelude*. When the Cheerybles talk of their entry into the city, it is "the wilderness of London" they refer to. This is the city of Hungerford Stairs with its Warrens' Blacking factory; it is a place of misery and despair where Oliver Twist will need great luck and much help to survive, and Nicholas Nickleby will be "reduced to the necessity" almost of begging (1:340, 339). And yet, it is only in London that Nicholas and Kate will be able to succeed. Like Oliver they have left the more settled and organized countryside with its orderly villages, for the chaos, anarchy, and opportunity of the city. Yet it is more than economic hope which brings these representative figures to London. The city beckons as a political and moral phenomenon: in a time of great change, it is the site of the story of success, for it is the theatre of possibility. And it is this theatrical trope which defines Dickens's chosen city.

H. M. Daleski has noted that in *Oliver Twist*, "the idea of homelessness is concretized in the image of the street . . . the central image of the novel." Daleski further notes that in looking "back on his work and seeking, in an 1841 Preface, to dissociate it from the genre of the Newgate novel," Dickens claimed that in *Oliver Twist* there were "no canterings upon moonlit heaths, no merry-makings in the snuggest of all possible caverns;" instead, what he had offered were "the cold, wet, shelterless midnight streets of London; the foul and frowsy dens, where vice is closely packed and lacks the room to turn." Those streets would seem "to have taken precedence in his imagination over the foul dens as the habitat of his criminals. But of course it is not only the criminals (and prostitutes) who walk the streets; they are also the wet and shelterless recourse of the law-abiding poor. Oliver is one of these, and when he makes his way to London, he reflects that it is 'the very place for a homeless boy, who must die in the streets, unless someone [helps] him.'" Dickens thus uses "the image of the street to insist on the connection between poverty and crime. Receiving the efflux of the poor, the streets engender criminals." It is precisely when Oliver "finds himself in the streets, homeless and starving," that he is approached by the Dodger, who takes him to the "'spectable old genelman' who will give him 'lodgings for nothink'" (Daleski "Introduction").

In addition to Oliver's victimization, Dickens also represented another aspect of the world of the London streets in his depiction of Wegg. Early in *Our Mutual Friend* this itinerant ballad-salesman sets up his peddler's stand on a corner. Within a matter of hours, Wegg has appropriated his environs, turning them into an ecological niche favorable to his existence by the exercise of his prodigious imagination (Fulweiler 60-61). "He had established his right to the corner by imperceptible prescription. He had never varied his ground an inch, but had in the beginning diffidently taken the corner upon which the side of the house gave." Echoing the habits of his betters, Wegg hangs out his own shingle. "On the front of his sale-board hung a little placard, like a kettle-holder, bearing the inscription in his own small text:

> Errands gone
> On with fi
> Delity By
> Ladies and Gentlemen
> I remain
> Your humble Serv[t]
> Silas Wegg.

Wegg carries his role further: "He had not only settled it with himself in the course of time, that he was errand-goer by appointment to the house at the corner (though he received such commissions not half-a-dozen times in a year, and then only as some servant's deputy), but also that he was one of the house's retainers and owed vassalage to it and was bound to leal and loyal interest in it." Like a consummate actor, his role-playing defines the roles of his counterparts, ignorance not standing in the way of his theatrical trajectory. Though he knows nothing of the house's inhabitants, "he gave them names of his own invention: as 'Miss Elizabeth,' 'Master George,' 'Aunt Jane,' 'Uncle Parker'—having no authority whatever for any such designations—but particularly the last—to which as a natural consequence, he stuck with great obstinacy." Of particular interest is his sense of the house as habitat:

> Over the house itself, he exercised the same imaginary power as over its inhabitants and their affairs. He had never been in it . . . but this was no impediment to his arranging it according to a plan of his own. It was a great dingy house with a quantity of dim side window and blank back premises, and it cost his mind a world of trouble so to lay it out as to account for everything in its external appearance. But, this once done, was quite satisfactory, and he rested persuaded that he knew his way about the house blindfold: from the barred garrets in the high roof, to the two iron extinguishers before the main door—which seemed to request all lively visitors to have the kindness to put themselves out, before entering.

(*Our Mutual Friend*, ch. 5)

It is no accident that when opportunity knocks for Wegg in the person of Boffin, the homeless actor is ready for the role offered him. Reading "The Decline and fall of the Rooshian Empire" to Boffin, Wegg discovers his place in the social order, and once ensconced in the Bower, he quickly defines a place and home for himself, in fact so thoroughly that it is only subterfuge— the performance of Sloppy in the theatrical play devised by Rokesmith and Boffin—that makes it possible to remove this engaging scoundrel from the premises. After all, he has had the impudence to charge extra for poetry. "For when a person comes to grind off poetry night after night, it is but right he should be paid for its weakening effect on his mind" (bk. I, ch. 5).

As his fortunes improve Wegg's canny negotiating style is revealed as part of his public self. His private person, however, is consumed by desperate mood swings, paranoia, and consuming anger: the more prosperity the less he can comprehend it. In him Dickens represents a central aspect of the psychology of homelessness. The same process ignites the outbursts of Betty Higden who responds to the offer to take her sick grandson to the hospital with terror. "'Stand away from me every one of ye!' she cried out wildly. 'I see what ye mean now. Let me go my way, all of ye. I'd sooner kill the Pretty, and kill myself!'" What is at stake here is not a misplaced attack on the Poor Laws and the Workhouses, which, by the time of the writing of *Our Mutual Friend* (1864-65) had been changed, but the response of the working and serving classes to the paternalism of their betters. "'Stay, stay!' said Rokesmith, soothing her. 'You don't understand.'" Betty Higden's response elaborates her and our current city experience. "'I understand too well. I know too much about it, sir. I've run from it too many a year. No! Never for me, nor for the child, while there's water enough in England to cover us!'" Dickens's narrator elaborates her comment, generalizing it in the voice of a fate-defining Greek chorus: "The terror, the shame, the passion of horror and repugnance, firing the worn face and perfectly maddening it, would have been a quite terrible sight, if embodied in one old fellow-creature alone. Yet it 'crops up'—as our slang goes—my lords and gentlemen and honourable boards, in other fellow-creatures, rather frequently!" (bk. II, ch. 9)

In "Night Walks," originally published in 1860 in *All the Year Round* and then reprinted in *The Uncommercial Traveller*, Dickens gives a personal account of what it is like to leave home and be in the streets. He begins "by declaring that an inability to sleep made him walk about the streets all night for a number of nights, and that this afforded him the opportunity of finishing his 'education in a fair amateur experience of houselessness.'" Quickly, he becomes "one of the houseless," and takes us along on his wanderings, "'the restlessness of a great city' forming 'one of the first entertainments offered to the contemplation of us houseless people.'" Then follow numerous references to "those houseless nights," and "the sights that are revealed to his 'houseless eyes,' and the sounds that fall on 'houseless ears.'" But then, as Daleski notes, "Dickens suddenly flashes into the thing itself, becoming Houselessness, like the shade of the Analytical Chemist: 'Houselessness even observed,' we are told, 'that intoxicated people appeared to be magnetically attracted towards each other'; and 'walking the streets under the pattering rain, Houselessness would walk and walk and walk, seeing nothing but the interminable tangle of streets'" (Daleski "Introduction"). Dickens thus brings his reader to a realization of the fundamental impact of homelessness on the human being.

His novels elaborate the theatrical repertory of the modern urban world: from Gothic effect to Romantic surprise, from bourgeois tenacity to paranoid lashing out, from philosophic resignation to schizophrenia, from boredom to the fresh vision of innocence. It is the site of the wonderful and the dreadful possibilities of modern city life, which we, the reader, stalk as part of the progress not only of Oliver and Nicholas but Eugene Wrayburn and Bradley Headstone in *Our Mutual Friend*:

> Having made sure of his watching me. I tempt him on, all over London. One night I go east, another night north, in a few nights I go all round the compass. Sometimes, I walk; sometimes, I proceed in cabs . . . I study and get up abstruse No Thoroughfares in the course of the day. With Venetian mystery I seek those No Thoroughfares at night, glide in them by means of dark courts, tempt the schoolmaster to follow, turn suddenly, and catch him before he can retreat. Then we face one another, and I pass him as unaware of his existence, and he undergoes grinding torments. Similarly, I walk at a great pace down a short street, rapidly turn the corner, and, getting out of his view, as rapidly turn back. . . . Night after night his disappointment is acute, but hope springs eternal . . . and he follows me again to-morrow. Thus I enjoy the pleasures of the chase.
>
> (bk. III, ch. 10)

The first great practitioner of the detective novel, Dickens creates a linguistic universe that in the energy, deftness, and surprise of its syntax thereby simulates the theatrical experience of life in the modern city. As we read his writing we participate in the modern theatrical project of urban life: modern identity has become staged identity.

Note

1. "Claude Glass"—"Claude Lorraine Glass, also Claude Glass: a somewhat convex dark or colored hand mirror used to concentrate the features of a landscape in subdued tones. Sometimes applied to colored glasses through which a landscape etc., is viewed. Named from Claude of Lorraine 1600-1682, the French landscape painter." *Oxford English Dictionary,* Second edition. Oxford: Clarendon Press, 1989, 3: 285.

Works Cited

Caws, Mary Ann. *City Images: Perspectives from Literature, Philosophy, and Film,* New York: Gordon and Breach, 1991.

Daleski, H. M. *Homes and Homelessness in the Victorian Imagination.* Ed. M. Baumgarten and H. M. Daleski, New York: AMS Press, in press.

Dickens, Charles. *The Life and Adventures of Nicholas Nickleby,* London: Oxford, 1987.

Dickens, Charles. *Little Dorrit,* Oxford: Oxford Illustrated Dickens, 1987.

Dickens, Charles. *Our Mutual Friend,* Oxford: Oxford Illustrated Dickens, 1987.

Dickens, Charles. *Sketches by Boz,* Oxford: Oxford Illustrated Dickens, 1987.

Fulweiler, Howard W. "'A Dismal Swamp': Darwin, Design, and Evolution in *Our Mutual Friend,*" *Nineteenth Century Literature* 49:1 (June 1994): 50-76.

Garis, Robert. *The Dickens Theatre,* Oxford: Clarendon, 1965.

Gay, Peter. *The Education of the Senses,* volume one of *The Bourgeois Experience: Victoria to Freud,* New York: Oxford University Press, 1984, 1986.

Marcus, Steven. *Engels, Manchester, and the Working Classes,* New York: Random House, 1974.

Mill, John Stuart. "The Spirit of the Age," in *Newspaper Writings, Collected Edition of the Works of John Stuart Mill.* 33 vols. Toronto: University of Toronto Press, 1986, 22: 227-316.

Morris, Pam. *Dickens's Class Consciousness. A Marginal View,* London: Macmillan, 1991.

Mumford, Lewis. *The Urban Prospect,* New York: Harcourt, Brace, 1968.

Nord, Deborah. "The City as Theatre: From Georgian to Early Victorian London," *Victorian Studies* 31:2 (Winter 1988): 159-188.

Schwarzbach, F. S. *Dickens and the City,* London: University of London, 1979.

Wordsworth, William. *The Letters of William and Dorothy Wordsworth,* ed. Ernest de Selincourt. Oxford: Clarendon, 1967.

Judith Fish (essay date January 2004)

SOURCE: Fish, Judith. "'A Merry Season to Us All, & Auspicious New Year to Our London': Charles Lamb and the Representation of a City." *The Charles Lamb Bulletin,* no. 125 (January 2004): 2-9.

[*In the following essay, Fish assesses Charles Lamb's satirical commentary on the Picturesque within the context of Lamb's writings about London.*]

The titular quote ['A merry Season to us all, & auspicious New Year to our London'[1]] from Charles Lamb refers to the *London Magazine,* but it could just as easily refer to the city in which he was born and with which he enjoyed a life-long love affair. One of Lamb's most well-known pieces on London is 'The Londoner', first published in the *Morning Post* in February 1802, in which he claims that:

> The man must have a rare *recipe* for melancholy, who can be dull in Fleet-street. I am naturally inclined to *hypochondria,* but in London it vanishes, like all other ills. Often when I have felt a weariness or distaste at home, have I rushed out into her crowded Strand, and fed my humour, till tears have wetted my cheek for inutterable sympathies with the multitudinous moving picture, which she never fails to present at all hours, like the shifting scenes of a skilful pantomime.[2]

A few days after this essay appeared, Lamb received a letter from Thomas Manning, then in Paris:

> I should tell you concerning the external appearance of Paris, that I think it much more grand & imposing than that of London. The houses are grand and massy, seemingly built for eternity; & the Palaces are *very very* far superior to any thing in London. The old Louvre and the pavillions [sic] of Madame Pompadour are of most beautiful architecture.[3]

Lamb makes no overt comment upon Manning's sentiments, but instead replies to him with a long letter in which he rather indignantly reproduces large extracts from his essay.[4] His Johnsonian view of London might appear to offer praise for praise's sake, but with Lamb, of course, things are rarely that straightforward. His writing about London serves a two-fold purpose: firstly, Lamb uses it in order to satirise the contemporaneous cult of the Picturesque and the trend for Picturesque tourism which was popular in fashionable circles at the time; and secondly, his presentations of London can also serve as the tool with which he makes himself the playful—or not so playful—antithesis of his friends Wordsworth and Coleridge.

The notion of the Picturesque gained favour at the end of the eighteenth century, when a number of books were published that dealt with the subject. Picturesque aesthetics were of particular importance to wealthy landowners who wanted to have their country estates landscaped in the way advocated by the writings of Uvedale Price (himself the owner of a large estate) and Richard Payne Knight. The most celebrated landscape gardener of the time was Lancelot 'Capability' Brown, who advocated an extremely stylised approach to estate management; too stylised, according to Price, who complained that Brown's contrived planting schemes resulted in trees 'drilled for parade like compact bodies of soldiers' (Copley & Garside p. 21). Another contemporary, Joseph Holden Pott, concluded that Brown's 'sole aim' was 'to form scenes for the poet and the painter'.[5]

This craze soon spread beyond the grounds of stately homes and into the countryside at large, as tourists of the Picturesque travelled around Britain (and in some cases, further afield into Europe) in search of the perfect view. There was an increasing demand for a new genre of literature: the guidebook, which Stephen Copley describes as 'one strand in the burgeoning array of contemporary forms of regional loco-descriptive literature'.[6] One author of such literature was the Reverend William Gilpin, who wrote hugely influential books which prescribed tours of the Wye Valley and the Lake District, amongst other places. Ann Bermingham points out the inherent irony of the situation. The Picturesque according to Price and Knight had been once imbued with exclusivity, but now what they had 'defined as the delicate and sophisticated taste of a select few became the popular pastime of the bourgeois'.[7] Hordes of tourists followed the routes described by Gilpin armed with an array of paraphernalia. As well as maps and guidebooks, they—or rather their servants—would be carrying sketch books, pencils, watercolour sets, barometers, pedometers, and Claude Glasses (named after the seventeenth century landscape painter Claude Lorrain), which were special tinted lenses through which the landscape should be viewed. According to Malcolm Andrews, the Picturesque tourist 'pursued his prey with a Claude Glass rather than a gun. He could fix and compose elusive landscape features in a matter of seconds'. Andrews describes the 'manipulative potential' of the Claude Glass as tourists used it to alter the season or time of day:

> The darkened glass, tinted blue and grey, could suffuse a varied afternoon scene with moonlight. The yellow, or 'sunrise' glass, when used at noon, conveniently afforded a glowing dawn view, 'without the obscuration of the morning mist'. . . . Since the tourist was essentially a visitor, with little time to spare, he could reasonably try to condense twenty-four hours of changing light effects into a couple of hours' play with his Glasses. It was a kind of artistic licence.[8]

It was also necessary given the nature of Gilpin's tours, which are whistle-stop to say the least.

The use of such tools of contrivance as the Claude Glass is symptomatic of the mindset encouraged in the tourist by Gilpin. In his *Observations on the River Wye,* he informs his disciples that,

> Nature is always great in design; but unequal in composition. She is an admirable colourist; and can harmonize her tints with infinite variety, and inimitable beauty: but is seldom so correct in composition, as to produce an harmonious whole. Either the foreground, or the background, is disproportioned: or some awkward line runs across the piece: or a tree is ill-placed: or a bank is formal: or something, or other is not exactly what it should be.[9]

As we can see, Gilpin wants to stylise the landscape to an absurd degree. This is demonstrated when he reaches one of the highlights of his tour: the ruins of Tintern Abbey. Although he acknowledges its beauty, he is frustrated that it has been ruined in what he sees overall as an aesthetically displeasing way:

> Though the parts are beautiful, the whole is ill-shaped. No ruins of the tower are left, which might give form, and contrast to the walls, and buttresses, and other inferior parts. Instead of this, a number of gabel-ends hurt the eye with their regularity; and disgust it by the vulgarity of their shape.

However, Gilpin has a remedy for this, which he tentatively suggests:

> A mallet judiciously used (but who durst use it?) might be of service in fracturing some of them; particularly those of the cross isles, which are not only disagreeable in themselves, but confound the perspective.[10]

Visitors to the abbey complained that their enjoyment was hindered by its surroundings. 'The outside did not entirely answer my expectations,' says one, 'and this I attribute to the miserable approach through a dirty lane bounded by ruinous huts'. Another tourist remarks that, 'At some trifling expense, the surrounding cottages and orchards might be removed; and then the abbey could stand nobly back'd by woods, and open to the water: at present it is shamefully block'd up'.[11]

Both Coleridge and Wordsworth pass telling comments upon the nature of Gilpin's tourists. In a Notebook entry made during the summer of 1800, Coleridge refers to 'Ladies reading Gilpin's & c while passing by the very places instead of looking at the places'. Around the same time, Wordsworth composed a short poem entitled, 'On seeing some Tourists of the Lakes pass by reading; a practise very common':

> What waste in the labour of Chariot and Steed!
> For this came ye hither? is this your delight?

> There are twenty-four letters, and those ye can read;
> But Nature's ten thousand are Blank in your sight:
> Then throw by your Books, and the study begin;
> Or sleep, and be blameless, and wake at your Inn![12]

Lamb's criticism is, characteristically, less explicit. He resented any form of contemporary literature which attempted to be prescriptive or authoritative and often sought to undermine these discourses with the use of parody, irony, and satire. There are two short pieces on London which seem particularly to treat Picturesque literature in this way. The first is entitled 'A Town Residence', published in *The Examiner* in 1813. Lamb begins by asking: 'Where would a man of taste chuse his town residence, setting convenience out of the question?' He answers himself in terms which would not be wholly out of place in a guidebook:

> Palace-yard,—for its contiguity to the Abbey, the Courts of Justice, the Sittings of Parliament, Whitehall, the Parks, & c.,—I hold of all the places in these two great cities of London and Westminster to be the most classical and eligible. Next in classicality, I should name the four Inns of Court: they breathe a learned and collegiate air . . . Next to the Inns of Court, Covent-Garden, for its *rus in urbe,* its wholesome scents of early fruits and vegetables, its tasteful church and arcades,—above all, the neighbouring theatres cannot but be approved of.

Lamb then stalls:

> I do not know a fourth station comparable to or worthy to be named after these. To an antiquarian, every spot in London, or even Southwark, teems with historical associations, local interest. He could not chuse amiss. But to me, who have no such qualifying knowledge, the Surrey side of the water is peculiarly distasteful. It is impossible to connect any thing interesting with it. I never knew a man of taste to live, what they term, *over the bridge.*[13]

Before passing his sweeping indictment of the whole of south London on the grounds of taste, Lamb states explicitly that he is not qualified to do so; that his statement stems from ignorance. By identifying this opinion as arbitrary and ill informed, it could be that he is commenting upon the claims and statements of the authoritative travel writers who dismiss entire towns with a sentence or two.

There is a similar piece entitled 'London Fogs' (date unknown):

> In a well-mix'd Metropolitan Fog there is something substantial and satisfying—you can feel what you breathe, and see it too. It is like breathing water, as we may fancy the fishes do. And then the taste of it, when dashed with a fine season of sea-coal-smoke, is far from insipid. It is also meat and drink at the same time: something between egg-flip and *omelette soufflée,* but much more digestible than either. Not that I would recommend it medicinally—especially to persons that have

queasy stomachs, delicate nerves, and afflicted with bile; but for persons of a good robust habit of body, and not dainty withal (which such, by the by, never are), there is nothing better in its way. And it wraps you all round like a Cloak, too—a patent water-proof one, which no rain ever penetrated. No; I maintain that a real London fog is a thing not to be sneezed at—if you can help it.

Mem.—As many spurious imitations of the above are abroad, such as Scotch Mists, and the like, which are no less deleterious than disagreeable, please to ask for the 'true London particular,' as manufactured by Thames, Coal Gas, Smoke, Steam & Co.—None others are genuine.[14]

On the whole, the text is a rather eccentric one in which Lamb demonstrates his love of London by embracing wholeheartedly even the negative aspects of living in a city. But the final memorandum is the give-away. He uses advertising jargon to portray a natural phenomenon—fog—as a manufactured product, and in doing so, parodies those advocates of the Picturesque who, as we have seen, wish to manufacture the natural landscape and impose contrivance upon it. In particular, Gilpin describes in his *Observations on Cumberland and Westmoreland* the effects of fog, and how although it can be a nuisance in blotting out the landscape, on one occasion this was not unwelcome: 'Tho it is probable some views were obscured, which might have pleased us; it is equally probable, that many of those disgusting features, with which we might have been presented, were softened, and rendered more agreeable to the eye'. However, Gilpin laments that ultimately 'the misty hue was, in general, laid on with too full a pencil'.[15] This is also reminiscent of a passage in *The Prelude*, as Wordsworth describes straining his eyes at the top of Kirkstone Pass, 'as the mist / Gave intermitting prospect of the wood / And plain beneath' (XI: 362-64). For Wordsworth this was an example of sublime nature in his native Lake District, something which the city-dweller Lamb had little time for. He would rather present London fog as being sublime, and in doing so makes himself the antithesis of Wordsworth, who talks of the 'straggling breezes of suburban air' (*The Prelude*, VII: 208).

In *Observations on Cumberland and Westmoreland*, Gilpin also describes at some length the types of people who are suited, in the Picturesque sense, to dramatic landscapes:

The characters, which are most *suited to these scenes* of grandeur, are such as impress us with some idea of greatness, wildness, or ferocity; all which touch on the sublime. Figures in long, folding draperies; gypsies; banditti; and soldiers,—not in modern regimentals; but as Virgil paints them . . . are all marked with one or other of these characters: and mixing with the magnificence, wildness, or horror of the place, they properly coalesce; and reflecting the same images, add a deeper tinge to the character of the scene.

Gilpin quotes from Philip Thickness's account of his travels in Spain on the merits of gypsies; but they have to be the right sort of gypsies, 'the genuine breed', as he says: 'They are extremely swarthy, with hair as black as jet; and form very picturesque groups under the shade of the rocks and trees of the Pyraenean mountains'.[16]

Lamb's response is the Elia essay, 'A Complaint of the Decay of Beggars in the Metropolis'. Although it is primarily a piece of pre-Dickensian social satire, the ironic sideswipe at Gilpin and Thickness is unmistakable when Lamb presents London beggars as an unmissable tourist attraction:

The Mendicants of this great city were so many of her sights, her lions. I can no more spare them than I could the Cries of London. No corner of a street is complete without them. They are as indispensable as the Ballad Singer; and in their picturesque attire as ornamental as the Signs of old London. They were the standing morals, emblems, mementos, dial-mottos, the spital sermons, the books for children, the salutary checks and pauses to the high and rushing tide of greasy citizenry.

Furthermore, where Thickness had stressed the importance of the genuine gypsy, Lamb implores his reader not to reject a beggar on the grounds of dubious authenticity:

Shut not thy purse-strings always against painted distress. Act a charity sometimes. When a poor creature (outwardly and visibly such) comes before thee, do not stay to inquire whether the 'seven small children', in whose name he implores thy assistance, have a veritable existence. Rake not into the bowels of unwelcome truth, to save a halfpenny. It is good to believe him. If he be not all that he pretendeth, give, and under a personate father of a family, think (if thou pleasest) that thou hast relieved an indigent bachelor. When they come with their counterfeit looks, and mumping tones, think them players. You pay your money to see a comedian feign these things, which, concerning these poor people, thou canst not certainly tell whether they are feigned or not.[17]

The differences with Wordsworth are again also clear. In *The Prelude*, Wordsworth describes London as a 'Babel din' (VII: 157) of 'Lies to the ear, and lies to every sense' (VII: 575). It is a 'Parliament of Monsters' (VII: 692) in which nothing is real and nothing can be trusted, including the beggars, whom Wordsworth singles out for their inauthenticity. While Lamb accepts and enjoys this as a part of city life, Wordsworth is disgusted by it. Lamb was often irritated by Wordsworth's dogma, and in this instance he seeks to undermine his high-minded attitude by celebrating the probable falseness of the beggars instead of being offended by it.

However, whilst the respective treatments of the city by the two authors could not be more different, there is at the same time a curious instance of intertextuality. Returning to 'The Londoner', Lamb's description of 'the multitudinous moving picture' which London 'never fails to present at all hours, like the shifting scenes of a skilful pantomime' bears a striking resemblance to a passage in Book Seven of *The Prelude*:

> Add to these exhibitions mute and still
> Others of wider scope, where living men,
> Music, and shifting pantomimic scenes,
> Together joined their multifarious aid
> To heighten the allurement.

(VII: 281-285)

The phrases used by both are surely too analogous for coincidence, but given that *The Prelude* was composed over several years, it is difficult to determine who has influenced whom.

Contention surrounds the relationship between Lamb, Wordsworth, and London. In 1801 Lamb thanks Wordsworth for an invitation to Cumberland, but declines:

> Separate from the pleasure of your company, I don't mu[ch] care if I never see a mountain in my life.—I have passed all my days in London, until I have formed as many and intense local attachments, as any of you *Mountaineers* can have done with dead nature. The Lighted shops of the Strand and Fleet Street, the innumerable trades, tradesmen and customers, coaches, waggons, play houses, all the bustle and wickedness round about Covent garden, the very women of the Town, the Watchmen, drunken scenes, rattles;—life awake, if you awake, at all hours of the night, the impossibility of being dull in Fleet Street, the crowds, the very dirt & mud, the Sun shining upon houses and pavements, the print shops, the *old Book* stalls, parsons cheap'ning books, coffee houses, steams of soups from kitchens, the pantomimes, London itself, a pantomime and a masquerade, all these things work themselves into my mind and feed me without a power of satiating me. The wonder of these sights impells me into nightwalks about her crowded streets, and I often shed tears in the motley Strand from fullness of joy at so much *Life*———. All these emotions must be strange to you. So are your rural emotions to me.—But consider, what must I have been doing all my life, not to have lent great portions of my heart with usury to such scenes?———[18]

Many of the phrases used in this letter were to inform the text of 'The Londoner'. Lamb is trying to demonstrate to Wordsworth that one man's meat is another man's poison. 'I do not envy you', he continues. 'I should pity you, did I not know, that the Mind will make friends of anything. Your sun & moon and skys and hills & lakes affect me no more, or scarcely come to me in more venerable characters, than as a gilded room with tapestry and tapers, where I might live with handsome visible objects'. However, I do not think that personal preference over town or country is the primary focus here. Elsewhere in the letter Lamb comments frankly upon *Lyrical Ballads* and is critical of Wordsworth's poetic dogma:

> I will just add that it appears to me a fault in the Beggar, that the instructions conveyed in it are too direct and like a lecture . . . An intelligent reader finds a sort of insult in being told, I will teach you how to think upon this subject. This fault, if I am right, is in a ten thousandth worse degree to be found in *Sterne* and many many novelists and modern poets, who continually put a sign post up to shew *where you are to feel*. They set out with assuming their readers to be stupid.[19]

Then Lamb adds what Edmund Blunden deems an 'ironical' postscript: 'Thank you for Liking my Play!!' Although it may appear meek and ingratiating this is, according to Blunden, a further, more subtle 'complaint against Wordsworth's egotism'.[20] I would argue the same for Lamb's promotion of his own surroundings over Wordsworth's. Geographical territory is, in this instance, a metaphor for literary territory. It was obviously still irking him when he wrote to Robert Lloyd a week later, declaring, 'Let them talk of Lakes and mountains and romantic dales all that fantastic stuff' before going on to paraphrase much of the letter to Wordsworth. '*A mob of men is better than a flock of sheep*', he concludes.[21] Thirteen years later Lamb prods Wordsworth with a gentle reminder. He has been reading *The Excursion*, and comments that:

> There is a deal of noble matter about mountain scenery, yet not so much as to overpower & discountenance a poor *Londoner* or South-country man entirely, though Mary seems to have felt it occasionally a little too powerfully, for it was her remark during reading it that by your system it was doubtful whether a Liver in Towns had a Soul to be Saved. She almost trembled for that invisible part of us in her.[22]

A sardonically pompous note attached to Wordsworth's poem, 'By their floating Mill', composed in 1806, suggests that the irritation was a mutual one:

> Suggested on the Thames by the sight of one of those floating mills that used to be seen there. This I noticed on the Surrey-side between Somerset-House and Blackfriars' Bridge. Charles Lamb was with me at the time; and I thought it remarkable that I should have to point out to him, an idolatrous Londoner, a sight so interesting as the happy group dancing on the platform'.[23]

Nonetheless, if we were to take Lamb at his word, the very fact of its location on the Surrey side of the Thames would have been enough to quell his curiosity.

With Coleridge, the situation is inverted. In his 1797 poem, 'This Lime-Tree Bower My Prison', Coleridge addressed the piece to Lamb in terms which did not find favour with the addressee:

> Now, my friends emerge
> Beneath the wide wide Heaven—and view again
> The many-steepled tract magnificent
> Of hilly fields and meadows, and the sea,
> With some fair bark, perhaps, whose sails light up

The slip of smooth clear blue betwixt two Isles
Of purple shadow! Yes! they wander on
In gladness all; but thou, methinks, most glad,
My gentle-hearted Charles! for thou hast pined
And hungered after Nature, many a year,
In the great City pent, winning thy way
With sad yet patient soul, through evil and pain
And strange calamity![24]

Lamb's explicit complaint is about the 'gentle-hearted' tag. 'For God's sake (I never was more serious), don't make me ridiculous any more by terming me gentle-hearted in print, or do it in better verses', he says in his first letter on the subject.[25] A week later he elaborates:

> In the next edition of the Anthology, (which Phoebus avert, and those nine other wandering maids also!) please to blot out *gentle hearted,* and substitute drunken dog, ragged-head, seld-shaved, odd-ey'd, stuttering, or any other epithet which truly and properly belongs to the Gentleman in question.[26]

The response appears a little overblown, and one wonders whether the comment, 'do it in better verses' holds the key. Is Lamb in reality more irritated by the way in which Coleridge has patronised and seemingly misunderstood him in relation to his city-dwelling lifestyle?

Lamb had no desire to find an Arcadian perfection in his surroundings, unlike his friends, and unlike the advocates of the Picturesque. As he explains in 'The Londoner', those aspects of the city which might render it imperfect as others perceive it are the very same characteristics which, for him, make it so pleasing:

> The very deformities of London, which give distaste to others, from habit do not displease me. The endless succession of shops, where Fancy (miscalled Folly) is supplied with perpetual new gauds and toys, excite in me no puritanical aversion. I gladly behold every appetite supplied with its proper food. The obliging customer, and the obliged tradesman—things which live by bowing, and things which exist but for homage, do not affect me with disgust; from habit I perceive nothing but urbanity, where other men, more refined, discover meanness. I love the very smoke of London, because it has been the medium most familiar to my vision. I see grand principles of honour at work in the dirty ring which encompasses two combatants with fists, and principles of no less eternal justice in the tumultuous detectors of a pickpocket. The salutary astonishment with which an execution is surveyed, convinces me more forcibly than an hundred volumes of abstract polity, that the universal instinct of man, in all ages, has leaned to order and good government.[27]

London (together with all of its faults) is, for Lamb, a landscape not of horror and revulsion, but one just as worthy of attention as the Wye valley, or the Lake District. It is one matter of personal preference which he uses in order to show that other personal preferences, such as literary ones, should be allowed to stand, and that one individual should not have the right to dictate the tastes of others.

Notes

1. The Charles Lamb Society Collection at Guildhall Library, London, CLS Ms 20. Quoted with permission from the Charles Lamb Society.

2. *The Works of Charles and Mary Lamb,* ed. E. V. Lucas, 7 vols. (London: Methuen & Co., 1903-05), I: *Miscellaneous Prose,* 401-02. Hereafter referred to as *Miscellaneous Prose.* All references to 'The Londoner' are to the text of 1802.

3. G. A. Anderson, ed., *The Letters of Thomas Manning to Charles Lamb* (London: Martin Secker, 1925) 63.

4. *The Letters of Charles and Mary Anne Lamb,* ed. Edwin W. Marrs, Jr., 3 vols. (Ithaca and London: Cornell University Press, 1975-), II: 54-59. Hereafter referred to as *Letters.*

5. Quoted in James A. W. Heffernan, *The Re-Creation of Landscape: A Study of Wordsworth, Coleridge, Constable, and Turner* (Hanover and London: University Press of New England, 1984) 8.

6. Stephen Copley and Peter Garside, eds., *The Politics of the Picturesque: Literature, Landscape and Aesthetics Since 1770* (Cambridge: Cambridge University Press, 1994) 42.

7. Ann Bermingham, *Landscape and Ideology: The English Rustic Tradition, 1740-1860* (London: Thames and Hudson Ltd., 1986) 83.

8. Malcolm Andrews, *The Search for the Picturesque: Landscape Aesthetics and Tourism in Britain, 1760-1800* (Aldershot: Scolar Press, 1989) 67-70. Hereafter referred to as *The Search for the Picturesque.*

9. William Gilpin, *Observations on the River Wye, 1782* (Oxford and New York: Woodstock Books, 1991) 18. Hereafter referred to as *Observations on the River Wye.*

10. *Observations on the River Wye* 32-33.

11. Quoted in *The Search for the Picturesque* 98.

12. William Wordsworth, Poems, in Two Volumes, *and Other Poems, 1800-1807,* ed. Jared Curtis (Ithaca: Cornell University Press, 1983) 535. Hereafter referred to as Poems, in Two Volumes, *and Other Poems.*

13. *Miscellaneous Prose* 155.

14. *Miscellaneous Prose* 351.

15. William Gilpin, *Observations on Cumberland and Westmoreland, 1786,* 2 vols. (Poole and New York: Woodstock Books, 1996), I: 219-20. Hereafter re-

ferred to as *Observations on Cumberland and Westmoreland.*

16. *Observations on Cumberland and Westmoreland,* II: 45-47.

17. *The Essays of Elia,* 133, 137.

18. *Letters,* I: 267.

19. *Letters,* I: 265-9.

20. Edmund Blunden, *Charles Lamb and His Contemporaries: Being the Clark Lectures Delivered at Trinity College Cambridge 1932* (Cambridge: Cambridge University Press, 1933) 63, 129.

21. *Letters,* I: 270-71.

22. *Letters,* III: 96.

23. Poems, in Two Volumes, *and Other Poems* 421.

24. *CC Poetical Works* 1: 179, ll. 20-32.

25. *Letters,* I: 217.

26. *Letters,* I: 224.

27. *Miscellaneous Prose* 402.

NEW YORK CITY

Morris Dickstein (essay date winter 1991-92)

SOURCE: Dickstein, Morris. "The City as Text: New York and the American Writer." *TriQuarterly,* no. 83 (winter 1991-92): 183-205.

[*In the following essay, Dickstein regards the treatment of New York City by authors such as Edgar Allan Poe, Walt Whitman, Herman Melville, and Henry James as "the narrator's effort to* read *a man—the emblem of the urban crowd—who, in the end, cannot be read."*]

If the City is a text, how shall we read it?

—Joyce Carol Oates[1]

Cities are constructions of steel and stone, aggregations of humanity on a grand scale. Architects plan and study cities; historians trace their economic and political influence; urbanists analyze their patterns of development and social interaction. But there is also a symbolism of cities that exerts a powerful hold on our imagination. Ancient Greek and biblical cities, so small by modern standards, crystallized into large, resonant myths: Athens and Sparta, Nineveh and Babylon, Rome and Jerusalem, later even London and Paris.

American cities are too new to carry this weight of symbolic meaning. We have no modern urban texts powerful enough to invest them with the mythic reverberations of such older cities. Instead we have media images that provide the world with instantly recognizable stereotypes. Today most Americans associate New York with images of crime and urban blight, streets of sunless concrete, subways out of Dante's hell. But until recently the prevailing image was the famous skyline: we see it behind the credits of dozens of films.

There were others: the bright lights of Broadway, now threatened by development in the Times Square area; or the Statue of Liberty, which played its symbolic role in 1989 in Tiananmen Square. Fritz Lang claimed that he took the inspiration for the 1926 film *Metropolis* from his first sight of the skyline from the New York harbor. This is a European view: New York as the capital of the future, the image of modernity. As late as the 1960's, New York still had more skyscrapers than all the world's cities combined. By 1940, according to urban historian Kenneth T. Jackson, it "had become the world's largest and richest city."[2]

After the war, movies like *On the Town* could make a powerful impact simply by filming on location. According to dance critic Arlene Croce, who grew up in Providence: "New York had a tremendous glamor in the postwar years; I certainly felt it in *On the Town,* and every time the 20th Century Fox orchestra played 'Street Scene' behind a New York stock shot, which it did constantly in that period, I would be paralyzed with desire."[3] Feeding this fascination were hundreds of song lyrics that reflected New York's genius at self-promotion during this era. From Rodgers and Hart's "Manhattan" to Dubin and Warren's "42nd Street" and "Lullaby of Broadway" to "New York, New York, / It's a Wonderful Town"—now the material for instant nostalgia—New York was synonymous with bubbly wit, urbanity and glamor.

But this bastion of industrial capitalism and urban sophistication was not the city most New Yorkers lived in. What they knew best, what their children eventually wrote about, was Jane Jacobs's New York, a city of separate neighborhoods and ethnic groups, a city of urban villages linked by a gigantic web of trolley-lines, subways, tunnels and bridges, but also a city with a vibrant street-life, that somehow defied the American love affair with the automobile.

Not many American writers were attracted to New York as an icon of modernity. In *Manhattan Transfer* and *U.S.A.,* John Dos Passos tried to imitate the staccato rhythm and headlong energy of the industrial city, which he found so alien to individuality. His work, like Döblin's Joycean novel *Berlin, Alexanderplatz,* epitomizes what the sociologist Georg Simmel describes as "the in-

tensification of nervous stimulation" in city life: "the rapid crowding of changing images, the sharp discontinuity in the grasp of a single glance, and the unexpectedness of onrushing impressions."[4] Dos Passos's montage in *U.S.A.*—a noisy overlay of newsreel headlines, the fragmentary perceptions of the camera eye, and miniature biographies of real people along with the interwoven threads of fictional narrative—is a transposition of urban life into a abstract, collective pattern in which the individual is submerged. As he says at the outset, he wants to write an epic of Everyman, a Whitmanesque Poem of These States, "the slice of a continent . . . the speech of the people." But more than modern life itself, it is his own technique that impoverishes his characters and pinches their inner lives.

The modern look and feel of New York has proved more of a challenge and an inspiration to visual artists, including precisionists like Charles Sheeler and Louis Lozowick, cubists like Max Weber, and futurists like Joseph Stella, who arrived from Italy in 1906. Weber, in a brilliant series of paintings in 1915, including *New York at Night; Rush Hour, New York; New York Department Store* and *Grand Central Terminal,* depicted the city as a hub of modernity and technology. Stella, a few years later in *The Voice of the City of New York Interpreted,* created an explosive but abstract geometry of five vivid New York scenes, in which New York's bridges and buildings, despite their Gothic touches, became almost ready-made cubist images. "New York is what all towns will be tomorrow—geometric," wrote a French visitor, Paul Morand, in 1929. "It is the simplification of line, of ideas, of feelings, the reign of directness."[5]

Finally there were the abstract painters of the New York School after World War II, who were also inspired by the hard-edged geometry of city life. (Mondrian's *Broadway Boogie-Woogie* is perhaps the most famous example.) Working parallel to them were the European-born architects attached to the International Style, who turned from the more decorative and lush skyscrapers of the thirties, such as the Chrysler Building, to the severe formal geometry of the Seagram Building, the Lever House, and many lesser versions of the modernist glass box, which began to give a dismally rectangular quality to the Manhattan skyline.

Only a handful of writers like Hart Crane in parts of *The Bridge* ("To Brooklyn Bridge," "The Tunnel") and William Carlos Williams in his prose experiments of the 1920's tried to celebrate the city by imitating this modernist iconology. They tried to get the buildings, the bridges, the rush of humanity into their very technique. They were reacting against the grim, apocalyptic portrayal of urban life in other modern writers like Eliot, yet Eliot's influence overshadowed theirs. His London in *The Waste Land,* with its Dantesque image

of the crowd flowing across London Bridge, "so many / I had not thought death had undone so many," summarizes the anti-urban fascination and revulsion of so many post-Romantic authors. Eliot's spectral "Unreal City" is virtually an anthology of such writers, for it includes imagery not only of Dante's hell but of Dickens's dustheap in *Our Mutual Friend,* Poe's prophetic 1840 sketch "The Man of the Crowd," and Baudelaire's *"fourmillante cité, cité pleine de rêves,"* which Eliot himself cites in his notes.

Poe's version of New York is called London in "The Man of the Crowd"; in a few pages it introduces an astonishing number of motifs that would later become crucial for the literature of the city. It even introduces the theme of this essay, The City as Text, since it describes the narrator's effort to *read* a man—the emblem of the urban crowd—who, in the end, cannot be read. *Er lasst sich nicht lesen* is the first and last line of the story. The narrator's driving curiosity, his avidity to read the faces of the crowd, propels the story forward, for this is also a fable about interpretation, an open-ended detective story.

This nameless narrator resembles Poe's other curious, brooding protagonists: his detectives, and the fevered, obsessional types who haunt his horror stories. But this man's object is the city itself, more specifically, "the dense and continuous tides of population" rushing past the door of his hotel, which he first observes darkly through the "smoky panes" of his window. Almost a century before the vogue of "mass society," before Le Bon and Ortega and King Vidor's great silent film *The Crowd,* Poe was one of the first to see the crowd as a single complex entity, a creature that seemed to have a life and will of its own. But he also saw it as a mystery, full of anonymous beings and unaccountable energies, something that cried out to be deciphered yet could never truly be known. At first the narrator is detached, shielded, peering out from a distance at the kaleidoscopically changing mass, trying to read the individual faces that reel by him "in that brief interval of a glance."

Then, at the exact midpoint of the story, his attention is absorbed by the idiosyncratic look on a single face, and he leaves his secure vantage point to plunge into the crowd itself. He turns from cinematic observer, before whose "keenest appetency" the street simply unreels itself, into the *flâneur,* the walker in the city, or in this case the stalker in the city. His inscrutable prey, whose behavior is a jumble of puzzling hints and signs, stands for the mystery of the crowd itself. Pursuing him all through the night and the next day, "resolute not to abandon a scrutiny in which I now felt an interest all-absorbing," he finally grows "wearied unto death." He finds the mystery at last impenetrable.

Writers like Dickens and Dostoevsky—and Poe's disciple, Baudelaire—would soon do wonders with the turbulent anonymity of urban crowd, but the American writer who best developed the viewpoint of the *flâneur* was Whitman.[6] It has been argued that Whitman's city is really a version of urban pastoral. Yet Whitman, far more than Poe, made the eddying flow of the crowd not simply the subject of his work but one of its formal principles. Responding to the "aboriginal name" of "Mannahatta" in an 1860 elegy, Whitman described New York as a city of islands nesting in bays and rivers, a city of flowing tides but also of flowing currents of humanity—"tides swift and simple, well loved by me," as well as "immigrants arriving, fifteen or twenty thousand a week. . . . Trottoirs throng'd, vehicles, Broadway, the women, the shops and shows." These busy tides and currents are transmuted into the structure of his best poems.

Whitman loves to make lists. His rolling Homeric catalogs are themselves word-crowds. Think of the exotic place-names that trip so liquidly off his tongue in great inventory poems like "Salut au Monde!" where Whitman becomes the *flâneur* in orbit, reeling off an immense geography, encircling the globe as he had circled the city. Whitman ingests the country and the city, the rivers and the mountains. But the ebb and flow of what Whitman names in these poems, those words that taste so good to him, infuse the whole rhythm and substance of greater poems such as "Song of Myself" and "Crossing Brooklyn Ferry."

If Whitman is not fully a city poet, it's because he takes in city activity as he takes up everything else, as part of an endless current through which he reaches out to the world and assimilates it to himself: "To me the converging objects of the universe perpetually flow," he says in "Song of Myself." Yet unlike many poets who preceded him, who felt swamped and nullified by city life, Whitman takes pleasure in this current, revels in its diversity. For Wordsworth in the seventh book of *The Prelude,* London was summed up in the freakish carnival of St. Bartholomew's Fair, melting individual identity into a monstrous amalgam. But Whitman, for all his stress on selfhood, on personality, relishes the undifferentiated quality of the urban mass. Wordsworth in London feels depressed, spiritually starved, under threat of dissolution. For Whitman this chaos is a plenitude, a blurring of the hard boundaries of the self, the separations of space and time.

Whitman assimilates the city to the rhythm of physical activity, not just the movement of the body but the systole and diastole of its inner pulsations. He personalizes the crowd without individualizing any member of it, not even himself. The "Calamus" poems, at once both sexual and political, express his dream of "a new city of friends," a community which is both plebeian and sensual. Does he takes his pen in hand, he asks, to record

> . . . the vaunted glory and growth of the great city spread around me?—no; But merely of two simple men I saw to-day on the pier in the midst of the crowd, parting the parting of dear friends. . . .

> ("What Think You I Take My Pen in Hand?")

Elsewhere he writes,

> A great city is that which has the greatest men and women,
> If it be a few ragged huts it is still the greatest city in the whole world.

> ("Song of the Broad-Axe")

One of Whitman's most flagrantly sensual tributes to New York as a city of "comrades and lovers" is another "Calamus" poem, which begins daringly, arrogantly:

> City of orgies, walks and joys,
> City of whom that I have lived and sung in your midst will one day make
> you illustrious. . . .

The gaucheness and crude boasting of this last line is a piece of essential Whitman, as well as a piece of New York. He goes on to enumerate what in the city might repay him for making it so famous:

> Not the interminable rows of your houses, nor the ships at the wharves,
> Nor the processions in the streets, nor the bright windows with goods in them,
> Nor to converse with learn'd persons, or bear my share in the soiree or feast;
> Not those, but as I pass O Manhattan, your frequent and swift flash of eyes offering me love,
> Offering response to my own—these repay me,
> Lovers, continual lovers, only repay me.

As usual in Whitman, we have no way of knowing how literally to take these lines. His New York, it would seem, is both a place to pick up men and a metaphorical community of flashing eyes and intersecting glances. ("How the floridness of the materials of cities shrivels before a man's or woman's look!") The urban crowd becomes for him what Nature was for some Romantic poets: a scene of ecstatic fusion.

> I hear the sound I love, the sound of the human voice,
> I hear all sounds running together, combined, fused or following,
> Sounds of the city and sounds out of the city, sounds of the day and night. . . .

> ("Song of Myself")

Emphasizing the body yet himself strangely disembodied, Whitman becomes the tutelary spirit hovering over all human activity—over the little one sleeping in its cradle, the youngsters climbing the bushy hill, the suicide sprawled on the bloody floor of the bedroom. In Whitman's crowded catalog almost every line is a separate story, a concrete naming. These precise jottings are like little poems strung together, through which he plunges breathlessly, as Poe's narrator plunges into the maelstrom on the street. But where Poe's feverish narrator remains detached—observing, weighing, speculating—Whitman's theme, his essential myth, is one of connection, of something far more deeply interfused: "And these tend inward to me, and I tend outward to them . . . And of these one and all I weave the song of myself."

After the audacities of "Song of Myself," Whitman's most daring leap (as well as his greatest city poem) was "Crossing Brooklyn Ferry." There his myth of connection sheds its vagueness and, with an uncanny gift for prophecy, he projects himself fifty and a hundred years into the future. For Whitman, whose life was split between Brooklyn and Manhattan, the ferry became what the Brooklyn Bridge would later be for writers like Hart Crane: a symbol of passage, a poetic crossing that signals their own leaps of imagination. For Whitman it is more—the link between the city and the bay, as well as a bridge between the past, the present and the future. (Many years later Whitman in prose recalled his passion for ferries, comparing the "oceanic currents, eddies, underneath" with "the great tides of humanity also, with ever-shifting movements.")

Whitman's genius in the poem is to imagine not an abstract future but people in the flesh, traversing the same tide a hundred years later, and to insist that they imagine *his* personal reality, even to the point of imagining him imagine them.

> Just as you feel when you look on the river and sky,
> so I felt,
> Just as any of you is one of a living crowd, I was one
> of a crowd. . . .
>
> I too lived, Brooklyn of ample hills was mine,
> I too walk'd the streets of Manhattan island, and
> bathed in the waters around it,
> I too felt the curious abrupt questionings stir within
> me, . . .
> I too receiv'd identity by my body. . . .
>
> What thought you have of me now, I had as much of
> you—I laid in my stores in advance,
> I consider'd long and seriously of you before you
> were born.

Whitman turns our perception of the past and future into an insistent moral demand: that we acknowledge that the people who have once lived and will yet live are as real as we are. But the self-delighting narcissist in Whitman wants more than to be recognized: he wants to be petted, known, loved, he wants to create the future, to dominate it, to merge with it sexually across time and death. The poem itself becomes the medium that "fuses me into you now, and pours my meaning

into you." The city, like the poem, now assures his immortality, and he concludes by laying a benediction upon it, for it is now coeval with his own body, blood of his blood, flesh of his flesh, eddying forward like his own throbbing brain.

If Whitman is the poet of urban euphoria, who saw his work as "a call in the midst of a crowd, / My own voice, orotund, sweeping and final," then Melville, his exact contemporary, created the most powerful contrary vision. Melville did not often write about cities, but in a few texts he gave us indelible images of urban isolation, anonymity and entrapment worthy of Kafka. Alfred Kazin has written about Melville's "angry attachment to his birthplace," where his mother, Maria Gansevoort, came from an illustrious family. There he spent not only some of his early days but his years of neglect and anonymity as a deputy customs inspector, a job too dimly reminiscent of his years at sea. *Moby-Dick* begins in Manhattan only so that Ishmael can describe the crowd at the water's edge, to explain the irresistible fascination of the sea. In *Moby-Dick,* cities represent the safe confinements of domesticity and civilization, but the urban scenes in Melville's other novels are frequently nightmarish. Pierre Glendinning's arrival in New York (in *Pierre*) is a Biblical scene of almost hellish phantasmagoria; Pierre lands in the midst of a chaotic urban crowd—the underclass, as we would call it today—a Babel of sexes, races and languages that fills him "with inexpressible horror and fury."

> In indescribable disorder, frantic and diseased-looking men and women of all colors, and in all imaginable flaunting, immodest, grotesque, and shattered dresses, were leaping, yelling, and cursing around him.

Their language he describes as "words and phrases unrepeatable in God's sunlight, and whose very existence was utterly unknown, and undreamed of by tens of thousands of the decent people of the city." This is not the ordinary urban crowd, certainly not Whitman's benign current of humanity. This is the edge of the city, the boundary line between civilization and chaos. With its thieves'-quarters and brothels and strange foreign tongues, it is the city of vice and crime, an urban archaeology of a buried, invisible stratum of city life.

In *Redburn,* a few years earlier, Melville had sent his hero down to explore another invisible city. Descending from his ship in Liverpool, armed only with a fifty-year-old guidebook his father had once used, Redburn finds barely the faintest resemblance between the city on paper and the "modern" Liverpool. Here change is the law of life and everything old has been torn down and forgotten. (Melville's point is clear: our fathers' experiences, and their guidebooks, now prove less than useless.) Later he comes upon a woman and her daughters starving to death in the street, but he can find no one, not even the police, who will take the least interest in them, except, finally, to dispose of their cadavers. They too belong to the forgotten, the invisible city.

Stopping off in Constantinople on his voyage to the Near East in 1856, Melville himself experienced the narrow streets of the city as a "maze," a "labyrinth." On a long walk, as described in his journal, "found myself back where I started. Just like getting lost in a wood. No plan to streets. Pocket compass. Perfect labyrinth. Narrow. Close, shut. . . . If you could but get up into a tree, soon out of the maze. But no, no names to the streets. . . . No numbers. No anything." The open sea allayed the claustrophobia he felt in the city.

Some of Melville's most arresting short fiction deals with isolation or abandonment, the loneliness at the heart of great cities. In "The Two Temples" he describes a morosely comic incident in which he is first kept from entering Grace Church, then, after sneaking in, accidentally locked in the church, then expelled by the angry beadle. In another scarcely known sketch, "Jimmy Rose," he portrays a great figure of the town, once a wealthy, generous and convivial host, who loses all his money yet continues living—barely, pathetically—on the grudging charity of his former friends. His very house, which the narrator of the story eventually inherits, is now buried in a grim commercial district. Once the center of fashion, it is now in the backwater of "progress," a symbol of the forlorn graciousness of an earlier era. But Melville's most piercing image of isolation in New York can be found in his greatest tale, "Bartleby, the Scrivener: A Story of Wall-Street." Here Melville develops brilliantly what is only rudimentary in "Jimmy Rose," the contrast between the plight of the outcast and the conventional but wholly ineffectual sympathy of the elderly narrator.

Bartleby, with his "pallid haughtiness" and iron resistance, may be the formal subject of the story, but the lawyer who employs him and finally abandons him is unquestionably the central character. Like Poe's Man of the Crowd, Bartleby and his unaccountable "preferences" are ultimately impenetrable; his refusal to examine his own work, to continue copying, or even to vacate his employer's office is certainly outrageous—for those of us who think as this lawyer does. His rebellion, always couched in the same polite formula, "I would prefer not to," is surely the mildest, purest form of negation imaginable, yet no conventional view of the world, no rational ethic of business or society could accommodate it.

Melville's narrative impersonation of the cozy Wall Street lawyer, who is indignant at the loss of a public sinecure and so proud of the patronage of Mr. John Jacob Astor, is a tour-de-force of ironic ventriloquy. Known to all as "an eminently *safe* man," he has always, as he tells us proudly, "been filled with a profound conviction that the easiest way of life is the best." His snug, comfortable existence is disrupted by his troublesome copyist. But despite his liberal tolerance and his strong undercurrent of fascination with Bartleby, he never truly confronts his mysterious shadow and double, whose anonymity and immobility are the hideous underside of his ease and sociability. He can understand Bartleby only through sentimental platitudes about human loneliness which, in a different way, *are* actually the themes of the story. He can conclude by lamenting, with great pathos, "Ah, Bartleby! Ah, humanity!," but his own humanity is too limited to comprehend Bartleby's passive resistance. Try as he may, he can neither help him nor, Pilate-like, wash his hands of him. "In vain I persisted that Bartleby was nothing to me—no more than to anyone else." In him Whitman's notions of urban fellowship and mutual sympathy are tested and found sorely wanting.

Melville's New York, so unlike Whitman's, is a hierarchy of Dickensian clerks, demanding clients, and prudential employers concerned about appearances. Instead of receiving automatic deference, along with a day's work for a day's pay, this Wall Street lawyer is asked to peer into a metaphysical abyss, an exercise for which he is poorly equipped. A lax and tolerant clubman, addressing us in a style of genuine cultivation, he represents not only the business but perhaps also the literary world of the early nineteenth century, with its close links between law, letters, commerce and the easy social world of the gentleman. But his paternalism and sociability cannot encompass the key images of his own working life. Once his office might have commanded an unobstructed view, but now, as Wall Street has prospered, it faces an air shaft and a grimy brick wall. here Bartleby sits, behind a screen, copying, within reach of his master's voice but sequestered from his eyes, cut off from any sense of nature and the outside world, himself facing literally nothing.

If the watchword of Whitman's New York is fusion—the city nesting on bays, the manly contact of hands and eyes—the great theme of Melville's New York is blockage, closure: the dead wall behind the screen which Bartleby, as in a trance, stares at in silent revery. Bartleby's response to blockage is immobility: not to work, not to eat, not to move, above all, not ever to explain himself. At being asked, with a remarkable touch of black humor, if he would like to travel to Europe to "entertain some young gentleman" with his "conversation," Bartleby mildly replies, "I like to be stationary. But I am not particular."

Whitman could write optimistically in *Specimen Days* that "an appreciative and perceptive study of the current humanity of New York gives the directest proof yet of successful democracy." But the relation between

Bartleby and his employer shows the irreducible social, economic and human obstacles to this urban utopia. "I know you," Bartleby finally says to the lawyer, without looking at him, "and I want nothing to say to you." Starving himself to death, he curls up in a fetal position in the courtyard of the Tombs, then already one of New York's horrendous prisons.

Though Melville himself was forgotten after the 1850's, his deeply ambivalent vision of New York lived on in the work of other writers. His treatment of the underclass, of social conflict and urban disintegration, became a staple of the naturalism of the 1890's, while his satiric portrayal of the narrow but comfortable world of the respectable middle class, as represented by the lawyer, became material for the social novels of Henry James and Edith Wharton. Amid the crude commercial values and cataclysmic social changes of the Gilded Age, these two writers, themselves products of New York gentility, painted a picture of the social hierarchy of Old New York that was acidulously critical yet touchingly elegiac.

The naturalists concentrated on the immediate topical world of the slum and the strike, on living conditions and working conditions. Theirs was the modern city just coming into being, with legions of immigrant workers arriving each week, squeezed into crowded, miserable living quarters and unhealthy workplaces. Theirs was the downtown world of the tenement, the sweatshop, the Tammany ward, the union hall, the dance hall, and the gin shop—the now no-longer-so-invisible world that Poe and Melville had begun to excavate. (Melville had even written a prescient sketch, "The Tartarus of Maids," about the dreadful lives of factory girls in a huge New England mill.)

James and Wharton, on the other hand, wrote about the uptown world of the great houses and magnificent dinner parties. They too dealt with the vertiginous rate of change in the city, which so dramatically altered the world they had known. Between 1860 and 1900, New York was transformed from an important commercial port and manufacturing center into a dominant force in the national economy—America's only world city. ("There's only one city that belongs to the whole country," says a character in Howells's 1890 novel *A Hazard of New Fortunes,* a testament to New York's new ascendency.) It was also physically transformed—at the lower end by the tremendous influx of immigrants, at the upper end by the surge of new industry and wealth, which tore down old structures and inexorably pushed the development of the city northward.

In 1898 New York swallowed its own suburbs, incorporating the four outer boroughs, including Brooklyn, which was itself America's fourth largest city. When James returned to New York after a twenty-one-year

absence in 1904, he was struck by the "note of vehemence in the local life," which reflected "the appeal of a particular type of dauntless power."[7] The crude, brash energy of the Gilded Age was everywhere: in the crush of humanity on the electric trolley-lines, in the skyscrapers that dwarfed passersby and blocked his view of the churches of his boyhood, even in the conversation which, like the architecture, he felt, lacked "quiet interspace" (*The American Scene,* p. 95).

James saw New York as the triumph of the onrushing future over the gracious past, of "the economic idea" over any "aesthetic view."[8] He described the skyscraper as "a huge, continuous, fifty-floored conspiracy against the very idea of the ancient graces" (p. 95). His own birthplace on Washington Place, right off Washington Square, had been torn down, with no "tablet" to mark his entrance into the world. "Where, in fact, is the point of inserting a mural tablet, at any legible height, in a building certain to be destroyed to make room for a sky-scraper?" (Just a few years later, James's birthplace would be the site of the notorious Triangle Shirtwaist fire, in which so many immigrant working girls perished. Today the site of this chilling juxtaposition, marked by the plaque James missed, belongs to New York University.)

The disappearance of his birthplace inspired James to write one of his last great stories, "The Jolly Corner," to imagine what his life might have been like if the house had survived, if he had not left home, and had instead become one of the movers and shakers of the new economic order. This is a kind of ghost story, and James imagines his hero's alter ego as a developer, an entrepreneur, an emblem of the buccaneering new city, and of America itself. This alter ego comes to him as a haunting apparition, a Mr. Hyde whose unhappiness and deformity hint at the horrors of his own unlived life. This is "The Beast in the Jungle" as social history.

In *The American Scene* James writes with the same mixture of recoil and fascination about what New York had become in his long absence. On one hand he feels a "sense of dispossession," "a horrible, hateful sense of personal antiquity" (pp. 86, 80). On the other hand he is drawn to the teeming Lower East Side ghetto, even to the Yiddish theater and the crowded cafés, where, in the "torture-rooms of the living idiom," he imagines he hears the "Accent of the Future," a language for which there is no "existing literary measure" (p. 139).

Twenty-five years earlier, James had already marked a changing New York in *Washington Square,* a novella commemorating the world of his own grandmother. Washington Square itself is merely the backdrop of the story but in the early pages, as we learn how "the tide of fashion began to set steadily northward," James fills in the social history of the neighborhood with a tender personal accent, which still echoes in his account of lower Fifth Avenue in *The American Scene*. Though set far in the past, around 1850, the story can be read as the early history of an old maid, the oft-told tale of a woman once disappointed in love, never to love again. But the actual subject of the story, as is so often the case in James, is money. Courted by a smooth and attractive fortune-hunter, Catherine Sloper is "defended" by her cold-hearted, inflexible father, whose cruel sarcasm perfectly matches the cynical opportunism of her would-be lover.

James conveys the social and professional standing of Dr. Morris Sloper with a light irony that points up his limitations and satirizes a society that accords him so much distinction. Like the lawyer in "Bartleby," he has done his duty, won his place in the world, but lacks the milk of charity, the gift of warmth or human understanding. His urban sharpness is his undoing: he doesn't *see* people, he sees through them. The plain Catherine, on the other hand, is very much the simple heart, a creature starved for affection and toyed with unconscionably by father and lover alike. She withdraws, turns her back on the world, seals herself into a corner of the past which is Washington Square. The city has changed but *she* has not. Her frozen fate, itself a kind of closure and entrapment, approaches the grim death-in-life of Bartleby's. Her adamant refusal to marry or to forgive—she is as resolute towards her father and her meddlesome aunt as towards her former lover—is like Bartleby's refusal to copy, or even to move. It bespeaks an iron passivity which is a bleak, oblique form of protest.

By the late 1880's James essentially had put New York and America behind him. He left it to Edith Wharton to develop fully the tragic implications of the Washington Square theme. Old New York and changing New York are not simply the settings of Wharton's novels; they are essentially the protagonists. After James, Edith Wharton was America's most piercingly intelligent social novelist. But her world was tightly enclosed: this was her limitation as well as the basis of her unusual tragic power. Like the ethnic writers who came after her, Wharton wrote about the small world she grew up in and knew best. Most New York writers have been able to grasp the city only through its cacophonous subcultures, but as she grew older and read more anthropology, Wharton came to see even New York's upper classes as a distinct tribe with its own peculiar mores and rituals.

Just such a ritual is the brilliant dinner party at the end of her 1920 novel *The Age of Innocence*, which, "in the old New York code, was the tribal rally around a kinswoman about to be eliminated from the tribe" (Signet edition, 1962, p. 265). As the hero, Newland Archer, fully understands, what's really happening at this dinner

remains unspoken, fenced in by old habits of duplicity, by an iron reserve. Newland's cousin, Ellen Olenska, with whom he had fallen in love, is being sent back to Europe—in style. His "affair" with her, never consummated because of their ingrained New York inhibitions, has been taken for granted, and the whole tribe has now "rallied about his wife on the tacit assumption that nobody knew anything, or had ever imagined anything."

> It was the old New York way of taking life "without effusion of blood": the way of people who dreaded scandal more than disease, who placed decency above courage, and who considered that nothing was more ill-bred than "scenes," except the behaviour of those who gave rise to them.
>
> (p. 266)

Despite the silent accusations that underlie this ritual, Newland and his so-called "lover" get off easily in this "conspiracy of rehabilitation and obliteration," except of course that they will never be together; the deepest part of their lives will remain unlived. Instead, they submit to the Old New York code of family, propriety and respectability—values deeply etched in their own being.

Edith Wharton was the product of these values herself, but in her books, as in her life, she weighed them against other values: passion, spontaneity, art, adventure. The New York she describes in *The Age of Innocence* is narrow-minded, provincial and self-satisfied. When Newland's mother and sister travel abroad, they never dream of actually becoming acquainted with a foreigner. When a penniless French intellectual, who lives on good conversation, inquires about a job in New York, Newland is stymied, for he is unable "to fit M. Rivière into any conceivable picture of New York as he knew it" (p. 165). And Newland's wife May finds the whole idea simply unimaginable: "A job in New York? What sort of job? People don't have French tutors."

The satiric side of this portrait of New York in *The Age of Innocence* is the work of the later, expatriate Edith Wharton, the woman who had to battle her own class and breeding to become a writer, to discover passion, to leave her marriage, the woman who, like so many younger writers of the 1920's, fled the limitations of America for the art, culture and freedom of Europe. For many of these writers, who came from small towns in the Midwest, New York itself was such a refuge: an offshore island, a lonely outpost of European sophistication in a philistine America. But not for Edith Wharton, who had come of age at an earlier time, surrounded by ritual sanctions and constraints.

Yet *The Age of Innocence*, like *Washington Square*, also has its elegiac side. Now that the old New York no longer existed, now that a terrible world war had revealed an uglier, more violent world than anyone had dreamed possible, the staid moral values of that simpler society looked more attractive to Wharton. Even in those earlier days the larger world had looked sordid enough, and Old New York was beginning to feel beleaguered. Newland worried that "the country was in possession of the bosses and the emigrant, and decent people had to fall back on sport or culture" (p. 106).

The ambivalence, the autumnal quality of Wharton's novel, is expressed in her title, for it alludes to a more benign and innocent time, but also to an "invincible innocence" like May's, armored against experience, untainted by imagination, blind to the vast changes in the world around her. Like Harriet Ray in *The Custom of the Country,* she is "sealed up tight in the vacuum of inherited opinion, where not a breath of fresh sensation could get at her" (*CC,* Scribner's edition, p. 83).

These last words give us an intimation of how much more harsh Wharton's vision of New York could be in prewar novels like *The House of Mirth* and *The Custom of the Country.* In these books, set in a twentieth-century New York, the new money is already in the saddle. The old-fashioned values of Washington Square are giving way to the brutal economics of Wall Street and the equally brutal social ethics of Fifth Avenue. Here the rituals of exclusion and displacement no longer take place "without effusion of blood," if they ever did. Instead Wharton almost takes pleasure in pursuing her characters to their inexorable destruction. Lily Bart in *The House of Mirth* and Ralph Marvell in *The Custom of the Country* are perfect products of their social world yet also doomed to collide with it. Neither can play the money game, which is also the marriage game. Lily is trained to be a decorative object, an adornment in some loveless marriage. Ralph is schooled to be cultivated and useless, a gentleman of the old school, like his venerable grandfather. Blinded by their own sensitivities, these characters are no match for the coarse, the calculating and the ambitious—the aggressive new rich whose wealth is grounded in industry, mining, oil, railroads, banking, stock speculation—in short, for all the explosive energies that were transforming the city and the nation.

Faced with these predatory creatures, who have history and economics on their side, the sensitive, indolent, all-too-trusting Ralph Marvell in the end "seemed to be stumbling around in his inherited prejudices like a modern man in mediaeval armour." When his wife proves to have deceived him from the start, when "the whole archaic structure of his rites and sanctions tumbled down about him" (p. 469), he takes his own life. Meanwhile, his unfaithful, unscrupulous wife, the former Undine Spragg, surmounts one obstacle after another, one husband after another, to end up remarried to her first husband, now a successful Wall Street tycoon. As Lily

Bart is the poor but beautiful insider who, tangled up in her own half-understood scruples, becomes the outcast, Undine is the outsider who will stop at nothing to satisfy her longing for financial security and social standing—the very archetype of the survivor.

Wharton is unique in being able to endow this drama of social closure, of exclusion and inclusion, with some of the Melvillean power of tragedy. *The House of Mirth* begins as a social comedy about the marriage market; its wicked irony irresistibly reminds us of *Pride and Prejudice.* But by the time of Lily Bart's death, we're more likely to think of ritual sacrifice than of Shakespearean comedy. If the outcast Lily Bart is a Bartleby figure, then Lawrence Selden, the ironic, worldly lawyer who truly loves her, may remind us of Melville's Pilate-like narrator. Selden too is a well-meaning but ineffectual man who, despite his considerable independence of mind, cannot step out of the circle of his own reticences and prejudices. He can't save Lily because he can't reach out to her, can't help misinterpreting her behavior. A lifetime of proprieties and indirections, an elaborate semiotics of social intercourse, prevents both of them from ever speaking their minds. When he finally overcomes his scruples and comes to get her, she has already killed herself, without quite intending to do so. Even her death had eluded her control.

Edith Wharton brilliantly examines the ground rules of the social game and poignantly portrays its victims, but she too, despite her biting criticism, never really looks outside it. The cruelties of exclusion and hierarchy in New York are her subject, but her novels are as closed in upon themselves as the world she dissects. When Undine Spragg falls out of favor with society, she discovers that she has become invisible. She can go to the opera, yet no one there actually *sees* her. Lily Bart, in her precipitous decline, finds every social avenue simply closed to her. But as far as Wharton shows, there simply *was* no world outside those avenues, no New York apart from what she represents under the names of Washington Square, Wall Street and Fifth Avenue. The new middle-class flats and residential hotels along West End Avenue are worse than death; from the viewpoint of society, they scarcely exist. Lily Bart does seek out a woman who is poor, and takes some comfort from her survival, but she represents nothing significant in the world of the novel. She also spurns the help of a Jewish financier and speculator, whose manners are bad and whose grammar is unspeakable, but who manages to buy his way up from Wall Street to Fifth Avenue.

The naturalistic writers of the turn of the century and the New York ethnic writers who followed them specialized in everything Edith Wharton left out or condemned: the titanic forces of the new economic machine, the despised immigrants who were its first victims but who eventually were able to use it to gain a foothold in New York. In Edith Wharton's New York there are only a handful of streets, all of them instantly readable. Her characters are defined by where they live, when they go out, whom they see; a chance indiscretion tells all. Everyone knows everyone else; their families have intermarried for generations; their very names, like Newland and Archer, are grafts from their family trees. Even Wharton's style of cadenced narrative, cutting irony, and acute social observation suggests the knowing but irreverent insider, whose values continue to reflect the world she criticizes.

How different is the cool journalistic manner of Stephen Crane's *Maggie: A Girl of the Streets* (subtitled "A Story of New York," as Melville had called his tale "A Story of Wall-Street"). Looking for some archetypal city tale, the young Crane gives us a fable of the prodigal daughter: a story of drunken parents, coarse men, and a girl's Hogarthian descent from slum life to prostitution to abandonment and self-immolation—in short, the material of Victorian melodrama. What *is* new about the story, what echoes down through every tenement novel in the twentieth century, through every film from Griffith's *Musketeers of Pig Alley* through *Dead End* to *The Naked City* and *Mean Streets,* is the taste and feel of the overcrowded streets, down to the thousand cooking odors streaming out of the tenement. Like Jacob Riis in *How the Other Half Lives,* Abraham Cahan in *Yekl,* Dreiser in *Sister Carrie,* Jack London in *The People of the Abyss,* and Upton Sinclair in *The Jungle,* Crane discovers a new city foreseen by Whitman and Melville yet excluded from the social fiction of James and Wharton. By reporting so sharply on what most novels left out, Crane became the missing link between Whitman's passionate *flâneur,* dreaming of a "city of friends," and Alfred Kazin's *A Walker in the City,* in which every sight and sound of the old immigrant neighborhood of Brownsville glows and echoes with an astonishing emotional intensity.

I have no room here to explore the riches of the modern ethnic New York novel, which began with works by Cahan, Anzia Yezierska, Michael Gold and Henry Roth and culminated in 1950's novels like Ralph Ellison's *Invisible Man* and Saul Bellow's *Seize the Day,* two more stories about men who feel free, only to find themselves blocked at every turn. These migrants and children of immigrants, authors who knew the invisible New York as they knew their own families, had grown up on the French and Russian novel, on the novel of "society," on modernism, never imagining that their own experiences could be material for an American literature. They were under cultural pressure to assimilate, to blend into the melting pot of a bland American identity.

The world they knew was completely out of keeping with the optimism and gentility of so much American writing. But they had the example not only of Crane but of Dreiser, whose *Sister Carrie* was one of the rare works that took up Whitman's expansive sense of the exhilarating possibilities of the American city as a terrain of ambition and conquest. (As one critic remarks, Carrie is a Maggie who doesn't *have* to be punished.) Yet the book's depiction of the terrible decline of Hurstwood also conveys the other, Melvillean sense of the anonymity of city life as a scene of entrapment, closure and disintegration. Its portrayal of the trolley strike and the lower depths to which Hurstwood sinks—especially in the chapter called "The Curious Shifts of the Poor"—foreshadows the grim social novels of the Depression years.

We began with the symbolism of cities, the real cities that had also become cities of imagination. If the city was originally a symbol of civilization, for twentieth-century writers it became the symbol of civilization in decay. And no city has come to represent crime, poverty, racial conflict and social disintegration more than New York. The underside of the prosperity of cities was always its concentrations of inhuman misery, the vast disparities of fortune and social welfare so close together. Michael Gold's 1930 novel *Jews Without Money* was set three decades earlier, at exactly the moment Henry James was touring the Lower East Side and Edith Wharton was writing *The House of Mirth.* Written in a tone of high excitement, almost manic recollection, it was a Whitmanian prose poem that inverted Whitman's optimism. It was a catalog of squalor and desperation. If the immigrant city *seems* a more open and fluid place than Edith Wharton's tight little world, it was also a city of gruesome enclosure in which people could live their whole lives within a few feverishly crowded blocks.

From Whitman, Gold borrowed the nervous, bustling energy of the plebeian city, the emotional intensity, the wild variety of sights, sounds, smells. The jagged rhythm of New York, which Whitman had caught in the movement of his verse, becomes the style of the city in Yezierska, Gold and Henry Roth, whose bleak, claustral visions of the ghetto are far closer to Melville and Crane than to Whitman. And Roth's *Call It Sleep* brilliantly captures an immigrant child's pervasive *fear* of the city, so full of dark, sexual cellars and dangerous streets, as well as the Babel of strange languages that so disgusted Melville's Pierre.

Like *Call It Sleep,* Ellison's *Invisible Man* is a modern *Bildungsroman,* since the city, as far back as Hawthorne's great story "My Kinsman, Major Molyneux," has always been seen as the site not only of a culture's but also of an individual's coming of age. The prototypical New York writer whom Ellison most resembles is not Whitman or Melville but Horatio Alger, whose moral fables about innocent country boys trying their fortune in the great city became guidebooks for real country boys making their way in large numbers into the urban maze. But Ellison's young hero's invisibility is more drastic than anything encountered by Edith Wharton's social outcasts. Everywhere in the city he finds rampant duplicity: everyone strikes poses, everyone tries to manipulate him. Instead of a success story it becomes a *Candide*-like fable of innocence and experience, exposure and disenchantment. This young man goes not from rags to respectability (as in Alger) but from naivete to cynicism, telling his story from yet another cellar, a Dostoevskyan hole in the ground.

With postwar writers like Ellison and Bellow we move from naturalistic documentation of the darker side of city life to metaphysical rumination, in which New York comes to stand for the collapse of modern society. In Bellow's early New York novels like *The Victim* and *Seize the Day,* the city is a scene not of freedom and possibility, not even of tenements and ghettoes, but of an obscure unease, of blockage and failure that seem to lie at the heart of the human enterprise. It's revealing that Saul Bellow (like Dreiser in *Sister Carrie*) locates the expansive possibilities of city life in Chicago, the rough-and-ready place where Bellow grew up, while ascribing the malaise and disintegration of modern life to New York, the city to which he later came as an aspiring writer. It's a long way from the buoyant adventures of Augie March to the sense of entrapment in *Seize the Day* and the saturnine outlook of Mr. Sammler. By the time of *Mr. Sammler's Planet,* which depicts New York in the "swinging sixties," individual failure and unhappiness have given way to large-scale social apocalypse—epitomized for Bellow by black criminals, disrespectful students and sexually voracious women.

The primitivist fantasies of some modern writers, Bellow says, have become the daily fare of the New York streets: "The dreams of nineteenth-century poets polluted the psychic atmosphere of the great boroughs and suburbs of New York" (p. 33). "From the black side, strong currents were sweeping over everyone. Child, black, redskin—the unspoiled Seminole against the horrible Whiteman. Millions of civilized people wanted oceanic, boundless, primitive, neckfree nobility, experienced a strange release of galloping impulses, and acquired the peculiar aim of sexual niggerhood for everyone" (p. 162). These rancid views have rarely been cited by critics, though they are placed in the mouth of a venerable figure who can hardly be separated from Bellow himself.

In this grim, arguably racist fantasy, New York had become a wholly terrifying city, a locus of appetite and anarchy for the grasping middle class as well as the ferocious underclass. Yet at the very same time, the rest of the world was drawn to the city as a scene of boundless energy and modernity, a safe haven from every kind of persecution, not as the Waterloo of Western

civilization. Once they arrived, their very presence would make Mr. Sammler rueful and anxious.

On this apocalyptic note, our brief trajectory through New York writing must conclude. There are many competing postwar versions of New York that I cannot deal with here: Frank O'Hara's chatty portrait of the city as a movie set and gossip mill inhabited by a few good friends, Pynchon's comic myth of the New York underworld in *V.,* or Donald Barthelme's postmodern New York of "The Balloon" and "City Life." Later we have Richard Price's rough but vital blue-collar New York, the frivolous punk New York of Tama Janowitz and *Between C and D,* the Yuppie New York of Jay McInerney's *Bright Lights, Big City,* the New York *noir* of Paul Auster's metaphysical detective stories, which take us back to the artist-fables of Poe and James, a late echo of Edith Wharton's New York in the engrossing social novels of Louis Auchincloss, and finally Tom Wolfe's insider-reports on a city fractured by race and greed—trendy journalism disguised as fiction.

But they can hardly match the ever-greater power of the movies to create and recreate the city—from *On the Town* and *The Naked City* of the late forties to the recent films of Martin Scorsese, Woody Allen, Sidney Lumet, Susan Seidelman and Spike Lee. Since location shooting became the norm at the end of the sixties, New York has belonged more to the filmmakers than to the writers. Richard Price (in *Sea of Love* and *New York Stories*) has become an adept screenwriter, and many New York novels today are simply embryonic movies. Oddly, Bellow's Juvenalian screed, which he himself has since discounted, was one of the few books that had the vehemence and violence to compete with those visual images. Unlike the work of the filmmakers and younger writers, Bellow's book alludes to the long literary tradition we've described here, but is not nourished by it. Bellow's Sammler is a distant descendant of the *flâneur,* but the *flâneur* as an old man, out of touch, a wisdom-figure who is cranky, brilliant, haughty and dismissive. As Steven Marcus notes, his is a city that can no longer be read, though he reads it, insistently, through the lens of the most perverse modern authors.[9] Many other ethnic groups would follow Bellow's restless, haunted Jews in taking refuge in New York, but Mr. Sammler could only see them as a threat. In him the walker in the city has become a virtual blind man, whose urban text has turned into dark biblical prophecy and fierce social allegory.

Notes

1. Joyce Carol Oates, "Imaginary Cities: America," *Literature and the Urban Experience,* ed. Michael C. Jaye and Ann Chalmers Watts (New Brunswick, NJ: Rutgers University Press, 1981), p. 11.

2. Kenneth T. Jackson, "The Capital of Capitalism: the New York Metropolitan Region, 1890-1940,"

Metropolis 1890-1940, ed. Anthony Sutcliffe (Chicago: University of Chicago Press, 1984), p. 323.

3. Arlene Croce, *The Fred Astaire & Ginger Rogers Book* (New York: Galahad Books, 1972), p. 171.

4. Georg Simmel, "The Metropolis and Mental Life," *Classic Essays on the Culture of Cities,* ed. Richard Sennett (New York: Appleton-Century-Crofts, 1969), p. 48.

5. Paul Morand, *New York,* trans. Hamish Miles (New York: Henry Holt, 1930), pp. 313-14.

6. Walter Benjamin's essays on Baudelaire and nineteenth-century Paris are a classic analysis of the *flâneur* and the urban crowd. See also Marshall Berman's discussions of Baudelaire's prose poems and Dostoevsky's St. Petersburg in *All That Is Solid Melts into Air* (New York: Simon & Schuster, 1982).

7. Henry James, *The American Scene,* ed. Leon Edel (1907; Bloomington: Indiana University Press, 1968), p. 74.

8. In "New York" (1921) Marianne Moore would cite James and play upon his ambivalence. She chooses an offbeat urban subject, the wholesale fur trade, that stands for both commerce and beauty, the savagery of the hunt and the finery of fashion. Although she knows that "estimated in raw meat and berries, we could feed the universe," in the end, she says, quoting James, "it is not the atmosphere of ingenuity . . . it is not the plunder, / but 'accessibility to experience.'" For a commentary, see Charles Molesworth, *Marianne Moore: A Literary Life* (New York: Atheneum, 1990), pp. 240-44.

9. "Almost all the signifying messages have now become contradictory and cancel each other out. . . . The tendency of the whole is to collapse away from meaning (forget about systematic meaning) into incognizability and chaos." Steven Marcus, "Reading the Illegible: Some Modern Representations of Urban Experience," *Visions of the Modern City,* ed. William Sharpe and Leonard Wallock (Baltimore: Johns Hopkins University Press, 1987), pp. 246-47.

Bibliography

Bender, Thomas. *New York Intellect.* New York: Knopf, 1987.

Berman, Marshall. *All That Is Solid Melts into Air: The Experience of Modernity.* New York: Simon & Schuster, 1982.

Choay, Françoise, ed. *L'urbanisme, utopies et réalités.* Paris: Éditions du Seuil, 1965.

Conrad, Peter. *The Art of the City: Views and Versions of New York.* New York: Oxford University Press, 1984.

Gelfant, Blanche Housman. *The American City Novel.* 2nd edition. Norman: University of Oklahoma Press, 1970.

Jaye, Michael C. and Ann Chalmers Watts, eds. *Literature & the Urban Experience.* New Brunswick, NJ: Rutgers University Press, 1981.

Kazin, Alfred. *A Writer's America.* New York: Knopf, 1988.

———, and David Finn. *Our New York.* New York: Harper & Row, 1989.

Lankevich, George J., and Howard B. Furer. *A Brief History of New York City.* Port Washington, NY: Associated Faculty Press, 1984.

Morand, Paul. *New York.* Trans. Hamish Miles. Illustrations by Joaquin Vaquero. New York: Henry Holt, 1930.

Mumford, Lewis. *The Brown Decades.* 2nd edition. New York: Dover, 1955.

———. *The City in History.* New York: Harcourt Brace Jovanovich, 1968.

———. *The Culture of Cities.* New York: Harcourt Brace Jovanovich, 1970.

Pickering, James H., ed. *The City in American Literature.* New York: Harper & Row, 1977.

Pike, Burton. *The Image of the City in Modern Literature.* Princeton, NJ: Princeton University Press, 1981.

Sennett, Richard, ed. *Classic Essay on the Culture of Cities.* New York: Appleton-Century-Crofts, 1969.

Sharpe, William, and Leonard Wallock, eds. *Visions of the Modern City.* Baltimore: Johns Hopkins University Press, 1987.

Sutcliffe, Anthony, ed. *Metropolis 1890-1940.* Chicago: University of Chicago Press, 1984.

Trachtenberg, Alan. *Brooklyn Bridge: Fact and Symbol.* 2nd edition. Chicago: University of Chicago Press, 1979.

Wallock, Leonard, ed. *New York: Culture Capital of the World, 1940-1965.* New York: Rizzoli, 1988.

Weimer, David R. *The City as Metaphor.* New York: Random House, 1966.

Christopher P. Wilson (essay date June 1996)

SOURCE: Wilson, Christopher P. "Stephen Crane and the Police." *American Quarterly* 48, no. 2 (June 1996): 273-315.

[*In the following essay, Wilson examines the effects of Stephen Crane's encounter with police power and corruption, as well as the larger political, social, and cul-*

tural conflicts in 1890s-era New York City, on Crane's literary sketches set in the city's Tenderloin district, and the author's other works. In addition, Wilson explores the limitations of Michel Foucault's Panopticon model of studying culture.]

> Everyone who thinks is likely to know that the right of arrest is one of the most dangerous powers which organized society can give to the individual. . . . Theoretically the first result of government is to put control into the hands of honest men and nullify as far as may be the ambitions of criminals. When government places power in the hands of a criminal it of course violates this principle and becomes absurd.

> —Stephen Crane, unpublished fragment, 1896

In the last decades of the nineteenth century, the district in New York City most saturated by brothels, theaters, and (so often overlooked) many small industries, was the infamous Tenderloin. Situated between wealthy Gramercy Park and Murray Hill on the East and the working-class Hell's Kitchen on the West, the Tenderloin was a border area juxtaposing splendor and want, extravagance and degradation, wealth and crime—and now, vice crime and police reform. As Timothy Gilfoyle recently reminds us, "The Tenderloin" was itself a police nickname, a name reputedly coined by a Tammany cop, Captain Alexander "Clubber" Williams. In police lore, this place name signified a juicy or "choice" cut of police duty, full of exposure to temptation and, concomitantly, opportunities to fatten one's pay. And in the fall of 1896, journalist, novelist, and new literary celebrity Stephen Crane, still riding high from *The Red Badge of Courage* (1895) and the recent reissuing of *Maggie: A Girl of the Streets* (1896), traveled to the Tenderloin to conduct what he called a "study of the life of a New York policeman"—a work that he apparently never even began to write.[1] In its place, we have only the so-called Dora Clark affair, an episode that has come both to represent Crane's strained relations with New York's finest and to explain why his work in Gotham would soon be cut short.

As many scholars know, on September 15 and 16 of that autumn, the following events, as narrated in R. W. Stallman's biography (1968), took place:

> From the Turkish Smoking Parlors [Crane] walked with [two young women] to the Broadway Garden, where another "chorus girl" introduced herself as Dora Clark and joined the group. Unknown to Crane, Dora Clark—also known as Ruby Young—was a streetwalker who had several times been arraigned for soliciting. Crane did not care who they were; it was enough that he had found their types. After he had interviewed them at the Broadway Garden, a resort of ill-repute, he escorted one of the women across the street to catch an uptown cable car, leaving the other and Dora Clark on the corner of Broadway and 31st Street. While they stood there conversing, two men walked swiftly by, as though

in a hurry to get home, and neither they nor the two women took notice of each other. However, the women were just then spotted by [Police detective Charles Becker], not in uniform, from the vestibule of the Grand Hotel. It was 2 A.M. Walking back to [the two women] from the cable-car, Crane suddenly realized that they were being arrested [for soliciting the two men who had walked by] . . . and so Dora Clark spent the night in a prison cell, while Crane debated whether he dared afford to damage his reputation by defending a girl of the streets.

> (220)

As Crane chronicled in his own account of the affair, "Adventures of a Novelist," both local cops and fellow journalists warned him that Clark was a habitual offender. Theodore Roosevelt, recently appointed president of the city's Police Board and a professed admirer of Crane's writing, was noticeably silent in response to a protesting telegram from the author. Nevertheless, Crane went ahead and testified on Clark's behalf on two occasions. Announcing that he must do his "duty as a man" as if "our wives and sisters" were "at the mercy of any ruffian who disgraces the uniform," he appeared first at Clark's criminal trial, which ended in dismissal. Then he testified at a Police Board hearing against Detective Becker that exonerated the policeman and effectively smeared Crane himself as an habitué of bawdy houses and opium dens. Subsequently, his attention already turning to the growing instability in Cuba that would lead to the Spanish-American War, Crane was hounded out of New York by the unforgiving police.[2]

At first glance, this relatively local, short-lived scandal might seem to have little significance for the larger contours of the 1890s, or even for the dawning reform movement that would become Progressivism. Indeed, although this affair was traditionally cited as evidence of Crane's own Progressive credentials—a "soldier" going into "battle" with the "entrenched" Tammany Hall police—that image has virtually evaporated.[3] In the 1970s and 1980s, particularly as textual and poststructuralist interpretation came to the fore, critics stressed instead how Crane's art actually undermined moral certainty, subverting or parodying the moral vocabulary of his middle-class readers and reform itself.[4] Of late, while the image of Crane as parodist persists, his work has also been subject to the general critical rewriting of realism as a social and cultural construction, a trend that has drastically revised our understanding of the relationship between literature and power at the turn of the century. In many quarters, this era's literary realism has now been implicated in the broader middle-class anxiety about urban disorder; realism's aesthetic entails a "spectatorship" aimed at the poor that both exoticizes and hopes to reform them.[5] In perhaps the most challenging variant of this broader case—representative of the general impact of Michel Foucault on cultural study—Crane himself has been cast as having unwittingly supplemented the "policing" powers he seemed to resist. It is this final, Foucauldian variant that will occupy my attention here.

This most recent turnabout, of course, has reflected larger critical trends. Albeit with significant differences, thinkers like Foucault, Jacques Donzelot, and D. A. Miller have articulated the ways literary, journalistic, and social discourses, again by entailing a spectatorial view of lower-class criminality, worked in tandem with the broader machinery of regulation, surveillance, and "biopolitics" that, these writers argue, came of age in the nineteenth century. The dominating blueprint for this system has been, of course, Foucault's Panopticon: the disciplinary complex and mechanism of power that "establishes over individuals a visibility through which one differentiates and judges them," leaving "no zone of shade."[6] In much of recent literary criticism, media analysis, and cultural studies, the term *policing* itself has come to serve as a shorthand metaphor for the surveillance work putatively undertaken by various modes of realistic representation. In a recent influential study of crime reporting, for example, the news media are described as "as much an agency of *policing* as the law-enforcement agencies whose activities and classifications are reported upon." Similarly, in Maren Stange's recent work on documentary photography, Jacob Riis's slide lantern lectures and exhibitions are "woven throughout" with "the idea of photography as surveillance, the controlling gaze as a middle-class right and tool." And thus, in the work of Mark Seltzer and others, Crane's writings on the urban poor have come to exemplify a complex, Foucauldian "realist imperative" of making everything visible, a process which "entails a policing of the real."[7] In a reversal characteristic of the new historicism, of which the studies by Stange and Seltzer are brilliant examples, the agency of the author evaporates while his or her texts become secret agents of power.

What is surprising, however, is how the rhetorical charge of policing, in cultural studies generally and in Crane's case in particular, has developed so independently of the scholarship undertaken by historians, sociologists, and criminologists on police culture, community politics, and power in specific cultural settings.[8] By way of contrast, this article will argue that the Dora Clark episode can best be understood in the context of the particular social, political, and cultural struggles over police power in New York in the mid-1890s, indeed in light of a broad re-"ordination" of liberal authority that Crane's street fictions both consent to and resist.[9] My title is intended to invoke the importance of both the particulars of this history as well as the current theoretical debates over the policing work of representation. On the first front, while it seems inevitable that interpretations of Crane's writing should have changed over the years, ironically certain givens of the Dora

Clark affair have remained virtually intact. In our most recent accounts, of course, Crane seems at best aloof from New York politics, at worst a spotlight-seeking author who, in the words of Christopher Benfey's biography (1992), was "cruising for crisis." Yet these very same accounts, for example, nevertheless continue to take at face value the New York Police Department's (NYPD) claim that Clark had been previously arraigned for solicitation. (Stallman's version set the mold: it convicts Clark by shuffling its scare quotes, saying she is a streetwalker in "chorus girl" clothing.) The New York press, paradoxically, is still often portrayed as offering a slanted yet somehow reliable record of these events.[10] Finally, the police themselves are assigned an even more shadowy role, with the unsupportive Roosevelt either duped, hostile to Crane's impractical chivalry, or distracted by the upcoming national elections. In some quarters, the shorthand label of the *Dora Clark affair* has kept alive even the Victorian, chivalric, anti-Tammany narrative that Stallman and others described. At the very least, we need to explore more fully the fact that, as Joseph Katz has pointed out, Crane directed his protest not at Tammany at all, but at the police department as Roosevelt himself had shaped it.[11] Indeed, we might provisionally rename this the Charles Becker affair, if only to shift the focus from Dora Clark's character—and the general tone of dismissiveness around what even Katz calls this "tawdry little drama"—to the central, quite significant issue of police power under the reformed NYPD.[12]

Furthermore, I hope to show how Crane's relationship to this reconfiguration of police power, far from disappearing from his work, made its way into the sixteen Tenderloin sketches he published in 1896. Hardly detached from their political milieu, these compositions allude directly to the tumultuous time: to the year-long investigations of the Lexow Commission on police corruption in 1894, which exposed extensive corruption, kickbacks, and political partisanship on behalf of Tammany Hall; to the controversy over Roosevelt's strict enforcement of the so-called Raines Law, raising excise taxes on liquor and restricting Sunday commerce of saloons, bawdy houses, and public entertainments; and most of all, to the changing politics of policing prostitution during Roosevelt's self-styled "year of reform." In sum, the NYPD did surface in Crane's shorter work, often as an unstable locus of civil authority undergoing reformation. Crane's Tenderloin experience is significant, in turn, because it illuminates facets of Roosevelt's police reform we might not otherwise see: the interdependence of street surveillance and internal police discipline to his campaign; the seminal role of detectives to vice crusading and that internal management; and the instability of the social terrain that Roosevelt's reforms tried, by a complex style of administrative management characteristic of Progressivism, to reordinate.[13] To sum up Crane's perspective, I will end with a discussion of one of his generally overlooked tales, "An Eloquence of Grief," which represents the mechanics of a police court as a mixture of moral piety, medieval agony, and administrative blindness. Not coincidentally, the police court was the very place a representative from William Randolph Hearst first urged Crane to begin his Tenderloin expeditions and where Dora Clark was herself tried.[14]

Ultimately, by illuminating the dimensions of class, gender, and urban politics in Crane's work, I mean to explore both the applicability and the limits of the now-popular Panopticon model for cultural study. Specifically, I mean to challenge the brittleness of certain abstractions—the media, the gaze, the police—not only in describing such volatile and partisan issues as the enforcement of vice laws, but in characterizing the cultural work of Crane's literary journalism. Despite what one might believe, Foucault himself actually warned against casting news writing within his scheme of surveillance, saying that the private ownership of journalism exposed the utopian cast to the original blueprint of the Panopticon.[15] Indeed, it is perhaps not Foucault's portrait of the Panopticon that best bears comparison to the news coverage of the Charles Becker Affair, but of earlier, pre-Enlightenment juridical "saturnalia," those public spectacles that were sometimes resisted by its summoned audience of citizens. Far from providing a neutral or transparent lens into a stable historical "context," New York newspapers of the 1890s embroiled Crane, Dora Clark, and Charles Becker in a virtual maelstrom of social and political allegories, much as in the famous Helen Jewett murder of the 1830s.[16] Crane's own realism is deeply embedded in this turmoil.

A few final methodological observations concerning this last point. It might well seem, so far, that I am proposing what is commonly deemed a recontextualization, and to a degree I am. My first section takes up this task. In the second part, however, I also mean to show that the Dora Clark affair that Stallman and others described, albeit a logical byproduct of midcentury historical writing, drastically overstated the stability of the historical record itself. From the start, with court transcripts unavailable, Crane's midcentury biographers relied primarily on scrapbooks of news clippings originally compiled by a subscription service, kept by the author and Cora (Stewart) Crane, and subsequently deposited at Columbia University. A familiar collaboration of traditional archival practice and biographical scholarship soon ensued: critics took it as their task to *reconcile* conflicting news accounts into "objective" historical narratives that focused on the risk the "affair" posed to Crane's reputation.[17] However, in my second (and thus in a double sense "mediating") section on the press coverage of the Becker affair, I mean both to recover and remap this saturnalia that has disappeared from academic view. Along the way, I hope to demonstrate

how local partisanship, conventions of crime news, and journalistic dependence on police power shaped the representational field in which Crane worked. Only by selecting a few of these representations could critics have produced the author-centered "history" in the first place.

A corollary to this methodological point informs my third section on Crane's texts themselves. Traditional cultural-historical practice might be to see the news coverage of the Becker affair as background, and in turn to see Crane's journalism merely as subordinate to his better-known canonical work. Recent Foucauldian criticism has tended to conflate Crane's canonical work with "policing" and skip over the news context entirely. Yet far from providing a detached, Panoptical vantage point on the journalistic carnival described above, Crane's own Tenderloin sketches are instead suffused with it. My effort, then, will be to stay with Crane's sketches, to read them collectively, and to demonstrate how they re-present the news field as well as Roosevelt's police reforms. My approach may seem, to some readers, rather diffuse. Yet this is because I do not mean to displace the clippings of Crane's scrapbooks or reconcile them into an "objective," seamless history. Rather, my strategy is partly to recreate those scrapbooks, as an array of representations both surrounding Crane news writing and reemerging within it. These news clippings provide, as it were, the very tissues of Crane's eloquence, or lack of it, in representing Dora Clark's grief.

* * *

Histories of American police departments, particularly of New York's force, are pockmarked with infamous episodes of greed, corruption, and political abuse, extending from the 1890s to the present day. Understandably, then, in a few accounts, Theodore Roosevelt's brief tenure on the NYPD Police Board (1895-1897) seems an oasis of reform vigilance and professionalization. Roosevelt rose to this role on the heels of the Lexow investigations, when civil service reformers joined with Republican "regulars" to elect a fusion candidate, William L. Strong, mayor of New York, temporarily ousting Tammany Hall. Strong then named two Democrats, one mainline Republican, and Roosevelt to the police commission. Once appointed, Roosevelt took the lead, lobbying vigorously for a series of internal reforms presaging the Progressive era's public rhetoric of efficiency, nonpartisanship, and moral crusading. He claimed to base department appointments and promotions on merit rather than party patronage; he installed new entrance exams, putatively setting a higher educational standard; he put policemen in charge of eliminating election fraud. While streamlining the management of internal department matters, he also promised prompt disciplinary action against police brutality and, most importantly, equal enforcement of the Raines Law. This law required any "police officer or constable having notice or knowledge of any violation" of Sabbath alcohol restrictions to report it to his District Attorney, whose duty it was then to prosecute.[18]

Not only did law enforcement under Roosevelt seem more vigorous; to some it was nobly egalitarian. Roosevelt even went on record that Irish Americans still made the best police officers.[19] Many of the reforms I have listed above seem unobjectionable at first glance, nonpartisan in the best sense. Nevertheless, what can easily be overlooked about many of these reforms is that they had highly partisan effects which directly altered the mechanics of street justice in places like the Tenderloin. Moreover, Roosevelt's reforms relied on highly problematic use of surveillance and disguise, techniques with ramifications for police officers and urban citizens as well. Finally, these reforms were largely driven by presumptions about habitual criminality that required paramilitary, "administrative" policing. All of these themes would be central to the Becker affair.

Roosevelt's paramilitary ethos, as historians have recognized, meant sweeping changes for his department. For example, at the daily level, he successfully argued for adoption of the double-breasted British army box coat and U.S. army leggings; the institution of frequent (and surprise) inspections of patrolmen; merit certificates and medals; and regular pistol practice to supplement the police club, a symbol much criticized under Tammany. Roosevelt even implemented a bicycle squad for swifter apprehension of street criminals, a reform that looked forward to future police reliance on the patrol car. Roosevelt's successful campaign with Jacob Riis to abolish the police lodging house also indicated his goal of moving police duties away from the broad community-service functions that patrolmen performed in earlier days, functions both reformers thought of as sentimental and ill advised.

To his public, Roosevelt stressed military discipline as a means of closing loopholes of corruption, instituting better morale, and assuring equal enforcement.[20] Paramilitarism, however, actually complicated the Progressive aura of reform. For one thing, it gave Roosevelt's well-known ethnocentrism more than a minor role in restructuring the department. Irish Americans remained a strong presence on the force. Yet Roosevelt's claim that ninety-four of one hundred policemen appointed during his year of reform were "native born" also implied a subtle distinction resulting from the new entrance exams, which Roosevelt explicitly compared to naturalization tests. Not surprisingly, then, newspapermen like Abraham Gruber, editor of the German-American New York *Staats-Zeitung,* objected to exams that included, for instance, questions on American history.[21] Meanwhile, the value Roosevelt placed on prior military experience, collaborating with this implied

generational cutoff of naturalization, obviously penalized more recent immigrants. Indeed, when Roosevelt praised what he continued to refer to as the Irish "race," he said it was for the "soldierly virtues" it had demonstrated in the Civil War. Irish American appointments proved a useful symbol of nonpartisanship. Yet as recent studies of colonial police forces suggest, Roosevelt may have preferred Irish patrolmen on the force because he thought they might better police their own. So much for egalitarianism.[22]

Collaterally, under the cover of nonpartisan vice enforcement, the reformed NYPD directly challenged the fabric of Democratic political culture. Roosevelt himself fully understood the central role of saloons (and Tammany's police itself) to this seedbed. In his speeches and essays on police management, he agreed with Jacob Riis's assessment that the saloon was a "boy's club" for the worst type of political education. "The saloon is the natural club and meeting place for the ward heelers and leaders, and the bar-room politician is one of the most common and best recognized factors, in local political government." By contrast, Roosevelt himself appointed officers from temperance societies.[23] As far as internal discipline went, a streamlined command structure provided the internal policing Roosevelt needed to overcome entrenched Democratic opposition within the force. To further this end, Roosevelt argued for centralized, hierarchical command led by a single commissioner. As Lincoln Steffens, one of Roosevelt's protégés at the time, put it in an unpublished essay, the ideal requisite for success was one honest man from whom all power flowed. Using the metaphor of military discipline, Steffens wrote that the best course to solidify that command "would be to deprive the police of all discretion in the enforcement of the laws." Although Democratic opposition thwarted the particular goal of a single commissioner, internal surveillance on the force became routine, and not only in Roosevelt's much-publicized midnight inspections. New uniforms, for example, did not simply instill discipline and higher morale; they allowed citizens and police superiors to identify a patrolman on the job and thus monitor his performance. Likewise, standardized police pistols and ammunition could be registered and thus monitored. As Hearst's *New York Journal* (hereafter, *Journal*) noted all too blandly, standardized equipment also facilitated swifter exchanges during riot control.[24]

In turn, detective bureaus, perhaps Roosevelt's main point of pride, became central to this paramilitary command structure. Although Roosevelt exploited the visibility of the box-coat to oversee patrolmen, when it came to the arrest of vice offenders, he preferred to rely upon plainclothes detectives. Roosevelt announced that "there are certain kinds of crime which can be reached only by the use of detective methods—gamblers, keepers of disorderly houses, and law-breaking liquor deal-ers can hardly ever be touched otherwise. It would be almost useless to try to enforce the law against any of them if we were confined to employing uniformed po-lice." Once again, however, Steffens uncovered a less-obvious function that detectives served. Decades before becoming enamored of Bolshevism, and before distanc-ing himself from Roosevelt in the sardonic hindsight of his *Autobiography,* Steffens argued that the key to po-lice reform was to promote one's own appointments as spies. "In other words treat the detectives as a confiden-tial guard, and use them, half for the detection of crimi-nals off the force, half for the capture of criminals on the force." Arguing that trusted roundsmen and captains could be allowed to corral vice into specific districts, Steffens then added: "[t]he detective force of a police department is the key to the system. . . . The man who controls it, controls the situation." As the *New York Times* (hereafter, *Times*) revealed, the detective bureau of the NYPD was in fact called the "Secret Service" branch.[25] For his part, Roosevelt compared detectives to military spies and defended their use even in labor ac-tions. He buttressed his case by referring to the sup-pression of the Molly Maguires.[26]

Charles Becker—a naturalized, Republican-leaning, second-generation German from Sullivan County, New York who had been on the force less than three years—was himself a police detective. Although appointed un-der Tammany, his rate of promotion under Roosevelt was significant. And of course, when he arrested Dora Clark he was in plainclothes.[27] Taken as a whole, his ac-tions in arresting Clark were quite characteristic of the paramilitary order Roosevelt attempted to install. Whereas a beat officer in the Gilded Age, for example, would have normally treated a well-known local drunk more leniently than an inebriated stranger, Roosevelt re-versed these priorities.[28] Instead, Becker was trained in the proactive ethos described by so much sociological work on twentieth-century police culture. As these stud-ies have shown, modern patrol officers are trained to be suspicious, to weed out anything on the street that seems threatening to citizens or to themselves. Becker's ac-tions were not those of a criminal cop or Tammany hack, but quite characteristic of what Jerome Skolnick calls the twentieth-century officer's characteristically "administrative" and "crafts" approach to law enforce-ment.[29] In this emerging framework within police cul-ture, as long as an officer can identify, to his superiors, suspicious behavior that led to the collar, even a "bad arrest"—that is, one not leading to conviction—is nev-ertheless deemed legitimate by his peers (220-21). As Skolnick writes:

> In contrast to the criminal law presumption that a man is innocent until proven guilty, the policeman tends to maintain an administrative presumption of regularity, in effect, a presumption of guilt. When he makes an arrest and decides to book a subject, the officer feels that the

suspect has committed the crime as charged. He be-lieves that as a specialist in crime, he has the *ability to distinguish between guilt and innocence.*

(197; emphasis added)

These days, this rationale negotiates the potential ille-gitimacy of entrapment, not an issue in Clark's arrest. Yet everything about Roosevelt's system emphasized preemptive action against habitual criminals. It was sig-nificant, for example, that the NYPD now adopted the Bertillon system of criminal anthropometry, which added a formula of bodily measurements to repeated of-fenders' files.[30] As Roosevelt himself noted proudly, "We did not possess a particle of that maudlin sympa-thy for the criminal, disorderly, and lawless classes which is such a particularly unhealthy sign of social de-velopment."[31]

Meanwhile, these class attitudes intersected with the gendered character of vice reform. Becker's obvious disdain for Clark, reported in several interviews, was hardly atypical of police-prostitute relations then or now. Although many modern officers realize that it is often more efficient to affect sympathy for the prosti-tute's sense of herself as a working girl, degrading ban-ter has a longer in-house history (Skolnick, 105-6). Crane's "Adventures" provides only one glimpse (660) of how the entire Tenderloin station house relegated Clark to her preassigned role as common prostitute. Clark's prior arraignments, if they existed at all, already positioned her, in police culture, for a pre-scripted role whether she suited the part or not. It also seems likely that Becker treated Clark as a noncomplying player of a new "game" that would not accord her the status of en-tertainer or working girl. And she fought back.[32]

In the aftermath of the arrest, meanwhile, Roosevelt may well have been distracted. But it seems more likely that, in leaving Crane unprotected, Roosevelt saw him-self as closing ranks behind a foot soldier—that is, Becker. This time, contrary to Steffens's more naive outline of the flow of power, preemptive action at the point of conflict actually enhanced discretionary power on the street by men in Roosevelt's secret service. "Equal enforcement" simply provided the cover story.[33] Becker himself could hardly have been confused on this score. We often forget, for instance, that he let the sec-ond "chorus girl" accompanying Dora Clark go (and the "Johns"). In fact, another policeman named Rosen-berg, himself an antagonist of Clark, had been em-broiled in an absurd case of aggressive misidentification just three weeks earlier.[34] As James Richardson reports, arrests for prostitution rose precipitously in the year leading up to Clark's trial: there were 403 convictions from May 1895 to May 1896, compared with only 172 during the previous year.[35]

Roosevelt's crusade, explicitly coordinated with private reform groups, also meant changes in the dynamics of police regulation of prostitution. Indeed, the situation often seemed arcane.³⁶ For instance, the incumbent New York comptroller now complained, with no small irony, that since protection money from brothels had dried up, he needed appropriations to reimburse police officers for the new expenses incurred in securing evidence against prostitutes. (Crane, as we shall see, joked about detectives as profligate spenders.) In fact, Richardson shows how this controversy would lead to the resignation of commissioner Frederick Grant, the man presiding at the Becker hearing. Limited funds might also have meant that Becker had to resort more often to the threat of arrest to enforce his rule on the street.³⁷

Meanwhile, the Raines Law set into motion a blurring of boundaries previously separating various forms of commercial sex, theater, and hotel management. As several historians have shown, "equal enforcement" drove saloons into calling themselves hotels to evade the letter of the law. We might thus reverse the debunking effect of Stallman's scare quotes and take them literally as a reflection of how disorderly urban space had become: Becker's testimony, for instance, positions him in a "hotel" lobby before he goes out to Clark on the street; she and Crane's other companion are "chorus girls," and have come from "entertainment halls." We do not know how Becker was dressed (except, again, that he was in plainclothes); one report nevertheless tells us that Clark had, earlier, mistaken a policeman for a man seeking an assignation. In other words, Becker was intent on reducing the visibility of prostitution and preserving Roosevelt's sense of cultural ordination. However, the ground of urban space was slipping beneath them.³⁸

Indeed, this contest over the meaning of urban space not only casts a different light on Clark's claims, but also on the implicit testimony of the marginal street women, boardinghouse residents, and workingmen whose appearance at these trials has, until now, seemed so comic, "tawdry," or incidental. News reports, for example, mention a janitor, one James O'Connor, and a second woman, Big Chicago May, both probably police collaborators, who testified that Crane frequented the company of thieves and prostitutes. Reports also mention a woman named Effie Ward who, in several accounts, assaulted O'Connor after he testified. Finally, mentioned in the news but minimized in every historian's account are the iron works foreman, the driver, and the cabmen who also testified that they saw Becker brutalize Clark on Sixth Avenue several weeks after her first arrest. In biographical criticism on Crane, these characters all seem bit players. What we have overlooked is that when the police slandered Crane, they reciprocally slandered the residents of the boardinghouse he inhabited and the neighborhood that surrounded it.³⁹

Roosevelt's new political "machine" was thus definitively shaped by ethnicity, exercised within prevailing norms of patriarchal authority, and orchestrated in a class context. Indeed, the above-mentioned chorus from the margins, trivialized even in the nominally Democratic press, opens up yet another class dimension to vice patrols. From one vantage point, Becker's plain-clothes dress might seem a form of disguise, or what we commonly call undercover surveillance. Yet as Skolnick (210) points out, in the so-called victimless crimes Roosevelt stressed, the cop actually stands in as a surrogate complainant for a third party not present to the crime (and in some cases nonexistent). Even the reform-minded newspapers thus pointed to the ambiguity of having a man dressed like a pleasure-seeking "civilian" making vice arrests. The disguise, such as it was, actually made momentarily visible the groups whose tacit political will probably made such arrests possible.⁴⁰

Casting such ironies aside, the Tenderloin campaign was nonetheless waged with utter confidence. Some in the press chimed in. Just two months before the Becker affair, in an article entitled "Tenderloin as It Was," the *Times* carried the department's banner in announcing that "The Sinful district has become meek." The article draws on the report of Captain Chapman to Chief Conlin, the officers who, the *New York World* (hereafter, *World*) would charge, would orchestrate the testimony against Crane's character. The article is virtually a précis of Roosevelt's ethos. Underlining that Captain Chapman had "a fine war record, and that he had shown that he has not forgotten his training as a fighter by his aggressive policy in the suppression of crime,"⁴¹ the *Times* presented the glory days of vice as if they were already a thing of the past. "Since Capt. Chapman has been in command," the *Times* pronounced, "he has pursued a vigorous and aggressive policy against the vicious characters who have always infested the precinct." Now, the *Times* added, "[i]t is . . . possible to walk on Sixth Avenue at all hours of the evening without being accosted by disorderly characters." Sixth Avenue, as Katz has discovered, was the site of Stephen Crane's first protest of a solicitation arrest—one month after this victory proclamation and a month before the Charles Becker affair. Crane in fact once began a sketch about Sixth Avenue, but he did not complete it.⁴²

As the final endorsement of Roosevelt's crusade, the *Times* ran a page-one story arguing that newspapers should desist from illustrations of police detectives, since such sketches jeopardized their undercover work.⁴³ Thus the political absurdity was not only that Dora Clark had been arrested on "sight." Additionally, some voices within the press, the social institution supposedly harboring the cult of "exposure," argued that the policeman arresting her should be allowed to remain invisible. Indeed, in many news reports there is virtually no record of the man identified, originally, as a codefendant in Clark's complaint: another Detective named Conway. Perhaps he was unmentioned so as not to blow his cover.[44]

* * *

For late-nineteenth-century police trials and the NYPD's internal disciplinary hearings, such as the two involving Crane, Clark, and Becker, news reports are virtually the only extant record. Thus far, I have been following customary historical practice, treating news reports as a factual archive. The truth is that news accounts variously disagree, in ways that are factually irreconcilable, over what Dora Clark said in court and what her background was; whether the presiding magistrate in her trial, one Judge Cornell, knew Crane and why; whether Clark pressed her complaint against Becker over Crane's reservations or the reverse; whether Police Commissioner Grant protected Crane's reputation or left it exposed; and more. Moreover, because federal elections approached in this critical autumn, news writers, editorialists, and cartoonists rarely overlooked an opportunity polemically to link street crime to even the most remote items of national debate. In one Republican cartoon, a silver mine operator was cast as a street mugger; in one Democratic news report, an arrested tramp claimed his name was Willie Bryan.[45]

The 1890s, of course, are notorious for volatility in the journalism trade; partisan transcriptions of court proceedings are to be expected. Yet the problem goes beyond factual discrepancies or simple partisan distortions. With the rise of the *Journal* and Joseph Pulitzer's *World*, the purchase of the *Times* by Adolph Ochs in 1896, or the reversal of Charles A. Dana's *New York Sun* (hereafter, *Sun*) of nearly thirty years of partisanship in endorsing William McKinley, the familiar classifications of journalism history—party labels, chronological distinctions, or differentiations by audience—start to come unglued. News conventions around crime reporting were in a considerable state of flux. As I have shown elsewhere, those most committed to the "new" journalism of Hearst and Pulitzer and by partisan ties antagonistic to Roosevelt were ironically the papers most dependent on the police for their staple of crime news. Conversely, the sheets that habitually defended Roosevelt were those most likely to regard crime reporting as a sordid affair.[46] Simultaneously, Roosevelt himself added to the scrambling of local press allegiances by his controversial foreign policy positions and by the aggressiveness of his vigilance about vice. Even without the recurrent political turmoil over the NYPD, the figure of the individual cop on the beat did not, himself, easily conform to prevailing political sympathies. Then as now, the police officer was a fluid representational icon, appearing sporadically in the news as a working-class hero, as a symbol of community order, or as a stock villain in tales of urban corruption.

Nonetheless, it is possible to describe provisionally a local triad of mainstream newspaper styles in these years. Each corner of such a triangle contained several New York papers and represented one location where partisanship, class accents, and conventions of crime reporting formed a common social rhetoric. Necessarily, this triad of newspaper styles was also a fluid configuration, marked by fragile alliances and often crisscrossed by unacknowledged mutual imitation.[47] At one corner stood the largely Republican, "anti-Tammany" cohort of New York newspapers: the *Press*, *Tribune*, and *Times*, the last being locally Democratic and nationally Republican. This cohort habitually adopted a somewhat antiseptic tone toward crime news. They used court reports as non-local or comic column filler, or as occasional news oddities of amusing arrests or unusual court orations. Elites often considered this material "beneath the fold," far less important than political news. Primarily, these papers interpreted their role as providing public notice. The editorial page of the *Times* even ran notices for unfilled positions in the NYPD, assuring applicants that the process under Roosevelt was now "perfectly fair and open."[48] At a second corner stood the more traditionally Democratic sheets—some affiliated with Tammany, like the *Sun*, and others, like the *Brooklyn Daily Eagle*, more mugwumpish—which had always been more at home with crime reporting. At the third corner stood what journalism historians, reflecting the elite denigration of the day, still often call the new "yellow" papers, Hearst's *Journal* and Pulitzer's *World*. These two sheets, in fact, competed vigorously with each other and marked, as we shall see, some distance from their reputed working-class orientation.

Within the first cohort, the Becker affair seems a minor episode indeed. The three anti-Tammany dailies each devoted at most four to six column inches to the Clark and Becker trials. Only the *Press*, which had habitually backed Roosevelt and thereby earned the NYPD's own advertising account, moderately dramatized the affair. Having already experimented with melodramatic reports of brutal crimes and police heroics, often accompanied by set-scene Victorian woodcuts, the paper ran the Becker hearing under the headline "Red Badge Man on a Police Rack." But beneath this medieval banner headline, putatively inside information both minimized the affair and confirmed the case of authorities: that Clark was "well known" by the Tenderloin police and that Crane's present address was a known opium haunt.[49] The undercutting by the *Times* was more subtle. In reporting on the charge against Clark, mistakenly minimized as "loitering" by this paper, the *Times* simply converted all courtroom testimony into the indirect third person, ending with the judge's assurance to Clark that he would guard against any further police harassment. Of Becker's hearing, the *Times* reported only that Crane was "subjected to a very severe cross-examination," and added that Grant upheld Crane in his refusals to answer damaging, but again unspecified, questions. On the whole, in the *Times, Tribune,* and *Press* reports, the dominant impression is of an orderly proceeding, a watchful judicial system responding honorably to rather minor charges. Yet something more complex than mere partisanship, or "surveillance" by the "media," was in play. Rather, within this anti-Tammany reform cohort, upper-class reticence, collaborating with self-styled non-partisanship and identification with governance, worked to mute Crane's charges and reinforce the apparent civility of police and judicial proceedings.[50]

Indeed, these class idioms of civility crossed party lines. They were quite visible within the second cohort, for example on the pages of Dana's *Sun.* In older days, the *Sun* had taken notorious glee in the flops and foibles of day-to-day police management; even in 1896, *Sun* columns were still littered with comedies of drunken patrolmen, mistaken arrests, and absurd court orations. From its example Pulitzer's *World* would learn a great deal.[51] Like the locally Democratic *Times,* the *Sun* did occasionally take a moderate tone toward vice crusading. It cautioned, for example, that enforcement of the Raines Law needed to be more "practical" in its legal approach to probable cause. But now the *Sun*'s attitude toward Dora Clark and her sisters on the street epitomized its recent drift from working-class to elite audiences. The *Sun*'s legal quibbles did little to disguise, in 1896, its new-found enthusiasm for rigorous law enforcement; indeed, even its traditional satire of ineptitude could now be claimed as having endorsed such vigilance. The *Sun*'s long-standing defense of "experience" as the main criterion for public duty—often held up against the rubes, novices, and gentleman amateurs of civil service reform—also made Dana's organ, now, a tacit ally of cops regardless of their political leanings.[52] Therefore, the paper congratulated Roosevelt's NYPD in October not only for increased arrests, but for increased prosecutions of street women, a trend it called "salutary and pleasing." Similarly, its Brooklyn neighbor, the Democratic *Eagle,* praised Roosevelt's judgment about the need to lock up "habitual criminals" and gang associates to preempt subsequent disorder—a policy, again, crucial to the Clark case.[53]

The *Sun* and the *Brooklyn Eagle* thus saw Dora Clark's arrest as a routine affair. Where they differed from the anti-Tammany cohort was in their modest protest of the vilification of "knight-errant" Crane. The *Sun*'s September 17 report gave voice to Clark's complaint of harassment, yet cast her voice in a bourgeois, chiseled diction, which again only enhanced the court's aura of civility while confirming her status:

> "All I have to say is that the charge is false," was the girl's answer. "The charge is founded, not upon fact, but upon the desire of this policeman to assist a couple of brother officers in gratifying a spite they have against me." . . .

> "But you do not deny that you frequent the Tenderloin, do you?" asked the Magistrate.

> "There would be no use in making such a denial," was the answer.

Into this polite melodrama, the "'red badge of courage' flaming on his breast," Crane is cast as the champion of Clark's cause, asserting that "[i]t would be well if others would follow my example." Crane is a righteous gentleman, indeed a man Judge Cornell himself knows and believes. Yet this time, the Judge does not promise to safeguard Clark, but instead warns Dora Clark "against placing [her]self in a position that will justify [her] arrest again."[54] In short, the *Sun* managed to one-up its anti-Tammany opponents by salvaging Crane's chivalry while still casting Dora as a woman of questionable character. The *Sun* did so, as well, without questioning the police in making the initial arrest. Less than four days after the Clark trial, when Charles Becker shot and killed an escaping burglar (as it turns out, a young boy), the *Sun* reported that he had "the reputation of being an efficient policeman." No partisan bickering here.[55]

This cross-partisan support of police authority, however, left the field open for the so-called yellow journals, which punctured all pretense of civility. For example, whereas the *Sun* and *Brooklyn Eagle* had supported an appeals court decision to overturn the extortion conviction of William McLaughlin, an inspector of police implicated in the Lexow scandals, the *World* crowed that "M'Laughlin is Lucky" and couched the court's finding in a rogues' gallery report of police officials still unpunished. In much of its coverage of police affairs, the *World* inherited the *Sun*'s traditional satire to create a believe-it-or-not, proto-Keystone cops pageant. Sunday *World* editions, under the heading of "One Day's Life in Greater New York," included short articles about bears locked in police cells; wildly improbable court reunions; and, perhaps most humorously, the saga of Policeman John Hughes, who said that he never drank to excess until he joined the force.[56] All of this could be done, of course, while these newspapers supported Dora Clark. Thus, although in its editorials the *World* decried Clark's arrest, in its news coverage it used Crane's status as a writer to create a "racy" story of bohemian adventurism. Leading with "With Himself as Hero" and "Crane Had a Gay Night," the *World* cast Crane as "A Novelist in search of Types, [who] Found his Heroine and Saved her [and] Picked up a plot in the streets." Not surprisingly, it is in the *World* that we see that "effie ward pulled the janitor's hair and planted her fist in his face" at the end of the Becker hearing. And if the *Sun* had quoted Clark as saying, ever so civilly, that "I am almost sure to be arrested the very next time I appear in the precinct, no matter if I am simply walking along," the *World* depicted Clark as a more colloquial heroine: "I will be arrested again on sight the moment I show my face in the precinct." Moreover, the *World* reported that Judge Cornell sympathized with Crane not because of shared reform intentions (as the *Sun* claimed), nor because of Crane's literary reputation (as the *Eagle* had). Rather, it was because the author had been sitting up on the bench for a week, studying "types among the prisoners."[57]

One reason for the *World*'s levity, of course, was that Crane worked for its chief circulation competitor, Hearst's *Journal,* which likewise came to Clark's defense. Yet yellow sensationalism did not necessarily generate a common ground regarding police authority. On the contrary, the *Journal* ran by far the most romantic representations of crime busting of any of the papers considered here: contests between reform and Tammany detectives; breathtaking accounts of arrests; and, of course, thrilling exposés of corruption.[58] The *Journal,* then, cast Crane within this heroic idiom and made him a contestant for justice amid a gallery of passionate combatants that included Clark herself. The *Journal*'s elaborate woodcuts, often used to present "authentic" simulacra of news artifacts (checks from Mark Hanna, a diplomat's cane, the actual hand of Laura Jean Libbey), accentuated this gallery effect by recreating the narrative for its audience. Illustrations showed Crane and Clark's evening gambol, their arrest, and their courtroom appearance; in fact, the middle panel inaccurately presented Becker in uniform. Moreover, the *Journal*'s set-scenes unwittingly served to anticipate the dimension of the drama so threatening to its author: they made Crane look like Clark's suitor (or "John"). Crane's role as heroic realist nevertheless rose to save the day.[59]

The *Journal* cast Crane as hero by turning the *World*'s lampooning on its head. As within the *Sun* cohort, within the *Journal* Crane is a valiant knight. Yet it is his skill as a literary realist, not only his gentility, that is put at the service of justice. In the opening of the *Journal*'s first report, Crane is portrayed as an intense writer who, even in the hubbub of the courtroom, concentrates on "the tide of human Misery" passing before him. Clark is led in weeping, under the cruel gaze of officers and onlookers; she is shamed by the charge. Meanwhile, *Journal* sketches seemed to repudiate the popular iconography of the predatory chorus girl, casting Clark in prim, nearly matronly garb and Crane as the man of letters in a studio portrait. In the news text, the courtroom crowd develops a deep sympathy for Clark's plight. The report asserts that her fears of harassment are well-founded and invites admiration of her defiance. She speaks eloquently of her own plight:

> The Magistrate was annoyed, for he had often listened to baseless charges against policemen.
>
> "It's the truth," she cried, "but what is a girl's word against a policeman's? And so he's right, Judge, when he says I've been arrested."

"Haven't you anything definite to say?" asked the Magistrate, sharply.

"I have the truth to say," she replied, defiantly. "I was in Broadway Garden last night with a woman and two men. I know it was late and I suppose I ought to have been in my own room alone—but I wonder if men can understand how deadly lonesome that is? I was out where there were people and lights and music. . ."[60]

If in this report the unsympathetic "reform Police Magistrate" does not recognize Crane, Dora Clark is a quite recognizable literary type: the sentimental working girl of dime novel and story papers whose fall, such as it is, stems from impoverishment, loneliness, and urban temptations. Reciprocally, Crane's role is the male chivalric protector.[61] Indeed, to signify this ready-made role, the *Journal* reported the assurance of Clark's lawyer that two charity organizations had taken an interest in her case. In short, in the *Journal* Clark became one of the unfortunate, where class relationships were subsumed under the sign of the patriarchal protection of womanhood.[62] Thus, even if the *World* and *Journal* came to Clark's defense, they did so only by first positioning her, as the *Journal* illustrations show, in a respectful zone above the Tenderloin itself. When Crane states in court that Clark was, by virtue of her gender, in his "protection," the *Journal* observes: the other "women [in the courtroom] were puzzled. Being of the Tenderloin, it was utterly impossible for them to understand the motive Mr. Crane expressed."[63]

Our traditional scholarship errs in several ways, of course, by having elevated this last narrative as an objective, author-centered, even sentimental history. However, neither can the image of a monolithic, Panoptical media "gaze" with "no zone of shade" capture the competing array of press allegories around this affair. Indeed, one might say that it is precisely by allotting various spotlights and "shading"—that is, by intricate local decisions about what was beneath view or simply out of it—that the New York press competed over and complied with the process of Progressive social reordination. In retrospect, it was the virtual silencing of the affair by both the anti-Tammany cohort and older "Democratic" papers that seemed most collaborative with the police; these papers and their readers might be said to represent Skolnick's absent third party, citizens who would just as soon avoid direct involvement but want the police work done nevertheless. Yet even the yellow papers drew Clark out of the Tenderloin in order to save her. And although we may never know whether a real Dora Clark's voice was silenced by the press's own, we should recognize her resistance despite the odds. We might also notice that the reports of her recurrent grief and shame seem, rather dramatically, to contradict the presumption by the police, the press, and even Crane biographers of her "habitual" status as a prostitute. Indeed, it was this particular contradiction that seemed to leave its mark on Stephen Crane's eye.

* * *

Over time, the chivalric frame Hearst's *Journal* placed around the Dora Clark affair ceded to academic criticism the heroic image of Crane's realism at service of liberal exposé. Even when this image waned in the 1970s and 1980s, descriptions of Crane's writing retained this association with urban exposure. For example, even as he argued that Crane wrote from "a perspective disengaged from that of the typical middle-class viewer," Alan Trachtenberg nevertheless adroitly placed Crane's work as subtly modifying the tradition of "unveilings" of urban mysteries exemplified by Eugene Sue, George Foster, and Jacob Riis himself. Even the most recent Panoptical readings reiterate this power of exposure in order to reverse realism's cultural work; to paraphrase Dominick La Capra, the "new" historicism often seems the "old" upside down.[64] Yet if Crane exposes anything in his sketches of 1896, it is that his Tenderloin was already a reformed, policed space. His musings on systematic police reform, therefore, go out as ironic asides or meditations on the work of an individual patrolman. Taken collectively, his writings offer a kind of postscript on the vice campaign's mop-up stages, sketches where he could turn the victory chants of the *Times* and police captains into loss and lament.[65] Where the Becker affair had shaped his vision, it was in a growing dispiritedness and even ambivalence about police power.

To be sure, Crane's sketches retained the basic parameters of the journalistic genre long devoted to unveiling the city's shrouded mysteries. Taken collectively, Crane's Tenderloin pieces offer a panorama that seems to survey the district from street level to rooftop, entering into zones of urban friction and examining their social mechanics. The moral geography of Crane's sketches typically reduced the city to its microcosmic spaces, to encounters on street corners, in cable cars, bars, and restaurants. Often essentially tour-guide estimates of these haunts, his articles speak in the language of social generalization, the estimation of "how hot" or "how not" a given locale was. Crane's sketches also convey that conventional ambiguity about their speaker, who seems not only knowledgeable about vice but experienced in it. The *Journal* seemed fully ready to capitalize on these traditional generic expectations. When it ran Crane's "The Tenderloin as It Really Is" in the wake of the Clark trial, accompanying drawings depicted three descending social layers, with a woman's visage in the center of each panel. At the top, a maiden gazes longingly out at metropolitan high life; in the middle panel, knowingly, at the working-class world of rough amusement; and at the bottom, drunkenly, through jail bars, at depravity. To an extent, these descending circles evoked the risky pleasures of a border district and portrayed one reason why the author of *Maggie* had been drawn into this affair. Like *Maggie*'s own conclu-

sion, these alternative possibilities signified the relative instability of ordination that the police sweeps tried to fix—that is, at what level the affair could be classified by type (famous author/showgirl or struggling writer/working girl or bohemian opium smoker/prostitute).[66]

Nevertheless, the conventional framing of the *Journal* is misleading. In fact, Crane now seems almost dispirited by how little there is to unveil. For example, in his first article after the Clark trial, "In the Tenderloin: A Duel," Crane begins by characterizing the district as so overwritten about that every common man claims to be an expert. Citizens base their claim, Crane notes ironically, on the "truth which the world's clergy and police forces have collected" (384), a clear reference to campaigns like those of Rev. Charles Parkhurst and Captain Chapman. However, Crane himself characterizes the region as a "corpse" (388) over which requiems are said and where windy anecdotes are told of the "open days" when vice and drink had flourished. Though he partly retracts his epitaph, Crane admits that the "croakers have clinched" one "mighty fact": that the days of "freedom and fraternity" have given way to a more hollow, garish display.[67]

Other Tenderloin pieces similarly deflate expectations of thrilling picturesqueness by citing the lamentable effects police reforms have had on familiar urban scenes. On "New York's Bicycle Speedway," for instance, Crane writes that a "new game" has arisen between "the Bicycle Cop and the Scorcher" replacing the old one of "Fat Policeman on Foot Trying to Stop a Spurt. . . . [T]hey changed all that," Crane writes. "The un-police-like bicycle police are wonderfully clever, and the vivid excitement of other days is gone. Even the scorcher seems to feel depressed. . ." (372). In "Opium's Varied Dreams," the Tenderloin is a once-splendid space in which vice has "retired to private flats" upon the "appearance of reform" and the police (365). Up in "The Roof Gardens and Gardeners of New York," Crane discovers one restaurant, famous for receiving "injunctions," that has shifted to "entertainment" in the aftermath of the Raines Law (380-81). Here Crane refers obliquely to the politics of the new "game" of vice enforcement: prodigal spending by "Central Office detectives" and reporters (378), while the "civil service commission" (379) absurdly monitors the waiters. In a swipe at the paramilitarism of police, Crane muses that "[s]ome day there may be a wholesale massacre of roof-garden waiters" (379), for such establishments are now "what might be called a county of unoccupied land" (381). No so Minetta Lane, which several newspapers puffed as one of "Gotham's Most Notorious Thoroughfares" when Crane explored it. Yet Crane himself reports that it has been reformed over the last two years (401); now saloons are "restaurants" (403), and the police are ever present "under the reign of Police Captain Chapman." "Any citizen can walk through there at any time in perfect safety," Crane writes in mockery of *Times*-like approval, "unless, perhaps, he should happen to get too frivolous" (405). What Crane set between the lines of his columns was a war not in the streets, but one declared on them—and virtually over.[68]

It is important to recognize, however, that even as Crane's writings lament the subduing of pleasure, his depictions of the police themselves cannot easily be categorized as conveying simple distrust of police power. On the contrary, Roosevelt's paramilitarization of the NYPD apparently created a spectacle for Crane's own enrapture. Crane was fascinated with the fortitude, presence, and courage that the cop often embodied in presiding over small dramas of everyday social ordina-tion. Crane's patrolmen appear not, that is, as Victorian villains or buffoons, nor in the mid-twentieth century garb of the crime buster. Rather, they are everyday workmen who arrive at an outbreak of disorder, stanch the flow, and cart the disorderly off stage in a grim and archetypal ritual. In "The Fire," for example, it is the movement of the tower-like (344) policeman's fingers that calls the fire department to battle with the flames of nature. In "When A Man Falls, A Crowd Gathers," a patrolman deters a crowd with a "sweep" of "two huge buckskin gloves" (348). Like his counterpart the fire-man, the patrolman is also cast by Crane (as by Roosevelt) as intrinsically a veteran figure, "evidently in an eternal state of injured surprise at [the civilian crowd's] persistent desire to get a view of things" (344). As Crane puts it in his late novel *Active Service,* the police are part of "the machinery of a finished society that prevents its parts from clashing."[69]

Here again one discovers the limits of fixing Crane's position with a simple partisan label. Even though he resisted the explicit brutality of police and Becker's personal ruffianism, Crane also spoke on behalf of good police "management" and seemed drawn to the cop's military consciousness, which separated him from the gaping public.[70] Both of these latter ideas placed Crane uneasily in the camp of a cross-partisan reform alliance that figured crime enforcement (and, more broadly, achieving political consensus) as largely an administra-tive matter of efficiency and expertise. The ambivalence of Crane's position is perhaps best represented in "When A Man Falls," when a cop arrives to disperse the gathering crowd:

> [H]e came swiftly, his helmet towering above the mul-titude of black derbys [sic] and shading that confident, self-reliant police face. He charged the crowd as if he were a squadron of Irish lancers. The people fairly withered before this onslaught. . . . He was evidently a man whose life was half-pestered out of him by the inhabitants of the city who were sufficiently unreason-able and stupid as to insist on being in the streets. His

> was the rage of a placid cow, who wishes to lead a life of tranquility, but who is eternally besieged by flies that hover in clouds.
>
> (347)

If, again, Crane reads the patrolmen as an intermediary figure, he is also an object of real ambivalence. Seen one way, he is a paramilitary being confident of his su-perior, practical, crafts approach to law enforcement. He keeps those pleasure-seeking spectators at bay "be-fore his threats, his admonitions, his sarcastic ques-tions" as well as the sweep of those gloves. Part of his tool kit, therefore, is a battery of explicit force and bru-tality, but part is also the machinery of language: sar-casm, warnings, and the rhetorical coups that both iden-tify the game at hand and monitor against rule breaking. Like Roosevelt, Crane deploys a number of racist no-tions about Irish character that, the passage implies, suit this man for an advance-guard role: animalistic placid-ity and obedience as well as soldierly fortitude. But here the alliance with reform ended, for in Crane's sketch the cop is also a figure of rage and unreasonabil-ity. Pestered by encounters that are both episodic and dispiritedly routine, he is a man deprived of life and thus angry to see it relished by those taking pleasure in the streets.

Crane's ambivalence, as well as a less-than-heroic self-evaluation, also made its way into perhaps the richest panel in his Tenderloin panorama, "An Eloquence of Grief." As archival research has shown, Crane wrote this tale in September 1896. The tale returns, in a sense, to the scene of the crime: that is, to the police court, where the authority of patrolmen like the one above was often sanctioned. Here Crane sums up not only the machinery of justice in the 1890s but the mixture of pi-ousness, routine, and cynicism that oiled its administra-tion. The sketch depicts a brief hearing involving a ser-vant girl charged with petty theft, and it opens ominously, shot through with the dispirited aura of his other excursions:

> The windows were high and saintly, of the shape that is found in churches. From time to time a policeman at the door spoke sharply to some incoming person. "Take your hat off!" He displayed in his voice the horror of a priest when the sanctity of a chapel is defied or forgot-ten. The court-room was crowded with people who sloped back comfortably in their chairs, regarding with undeviating glances the procession and its attendant and guardian policeman that moved slowly inside the spear-topped railing.
>
> (382)

Crane's imagery, a devious mixture of the Christian and the barbaric, positions the uniformed cop as both priest and usher, who enforces civility to a comfortable audi-ence assembled as if for theater. As the case opens, however, the arresting officer for the case actually at hand is in plain clothes, a sign Crane twists, now, to a demonstration of how "uniform" proceedings are turned from the street into oh-so-civilized proceedings. Rather quickly, Crane turns the setting into a bleak Last Judgment, a mural of bodies brought before an unnamed magistrate, some well-dressed plaintiffs made to depart "one way" while Crane's protagonist, called only "the girl," is turned another, "towards a door with an austere arch leading to a stone-paved passage" (383). The metaphor of Final Judgment is especially macabre in its irony, given that what we are witnessing is only a preliminary hearing. To Crane's eyes, however, this was precisely the dark absurdity that a street arrest like Dora Clark's had represented.

Layered within this imagery is an equally dark rendering of administered justice as a force superseding all democratic resistance by the creation of spectacle. The passive crowd is there for the show but not able to locate the seat of power:

> All persons connected with a case went close to the magistrate's desk before a word was spoken in the matter, and then their voices were toned to the ordinary talking strength. The crowd in the court-room could not hear a sentence; they could merely see shifting figures, men that gestured quietly, women that sometimes raised an eager eloquent arm. They could not always see the judge, although they were able to estimate his location by the tall stands surmounted by white globes that were at either hand of him.
>
> (382)

It is true that in this proceeding, as in the modern forms of power that Foucault describes, authority is recessed from view, so as to thwart incitement to counterviolence. In this sense it operates much like Roosevelt's police department, doing the work of the even-more-invisible "respectable" citizens who supported it. Yet as the blending of medieval and modern iconography in the passage above also suggests, the time frames to which Crane's imagery allude make the proceeding's Foucauldian shape apt in yet another way. In a second sense—in addition to the press's "saturnalia"—it is as if we are witness to the spectacles of punishment that Foucault places in history before the arrival of the Panopticon: that "theatre of hell" where "the cries of the condemned man . . . already signify his irremediable destiny. . . . Hence the insatiable curiosity that drove the spectators to the scaffold . . . there one could decipher crime and innocence, the past and the future, the here below and the eternal" (46).

Nevertheless, it is debateable how decipherable this proceeding really is. In a technical sense, Crane's point of view within the courtroom might seem, as critics have often described the "surveillance" power of realism, as invisible to the action and immune to it. But this stance is only temporary. As if the *World* was right

about Crane's true position, his narrative view shifts from the audience to the judge's bench itself. From this closer vantage point, the distanced, ironic voice gives way to something different from detachment, indeed to melodrama that might have been pasted in from the *Journal's* portrait of Dora Clark:

> In a corner of this space, devoted to those who had business before the judge, an officer in plain clothes stood with a girl that wept constantly. None seemed to notice the girl, and there was no reason why she should be noticed, if the curious in the body of the court-room were not interested in the devastation which tears bring upon some complexions. Her tears seemed to burn like acid, and they left fierce pink marks on her face.
>
> (382)

Here, Crane juxtaposes a close-up of the acidity of suffering against the cold stone backdrop of the court. One cannot overstate how suffused Crane's prose is, in this moment, with the array of news representations surrounding the Becker affair. Like his own scrapbooks, the two main vehicles of Crane's "Eloquence" display an ambivalent counterpoint between a *Times*-like indirect quotation of testimony, the "civil" authority through which the judge decides against the defendant, and a more heated prose of yellow melodrama that is drawn to her agony. Like the Dora Clark in Hearst's *Journal,* this girl "believes that she was lost" (383). And then, at his climax, Crane's counterpoint positions the eloquent cry of this girl against the consciousness of an unnamed, witnessing "man":

> People pity those who need none, and the guilty sob alone; but innocent or guilty, this girl's scream described such a profound depth of woe—it was so graphic of grief, that it slit with a dagger's sweep the curtain of common-place, and disclosed the gloom-shrouded spectre that sat in the young girl's heart so plainly, in so universal a tone of the mind, that a man heard expressed some far-off midnight terror of his own thought.
>
> (383)[71]

The momentary linkage between the girl in agony and her now-terrorized male interpreter is striking. It is possible to read this as a chivalric plea or as an "exposure" of the scene: the curtain of the commonplace rendered. Yet the passage above is pointedly not an appeal based on the unnamed girl's putative innocence. Rather it depicts the violence beneath the proceedings and one's own immobility in the face of it. The girl resists both her preliminary and final convictions; the interpreter, however, seems frozen. Crane's title thus potentially doubles as bitterly self-condemning: there is no eloquent male knight present at all.

Meanwhile, the system rolls on. And as if transposing the male observer's dispirited terror to the reader, our eyes have been dissuaded from realistic objectivity, confidence in secure social ordination, and faith in administered justice. In Crane's denouement, another case comes on. This time, it is a hearing for a routine drunk (or is he, we now ask?) who protests that he is not a habitual offender. Nevertheless, this plea only causes, in the last lines, "[a] court officer [to lift] his hand to hide a smile" (384). Here again, with the "cry" of the girl silenced and Crane's male witness immobilized, the system produces only forgetfulness and further violence. Whatever eloquence remains survives in the smile of the officer, a preemptive vanity to which he is clearly not entitled.

* * *

Given the systematic character of Roosevelt's campaign, it does seem likely, as our received account has it, that Crane soon felt under siege following the Becker hearing and was forced to leave New York. In this respect, that Crane's sketch of Sixth Avenue remained unfinished is telling; even in "An Eloquence of Grief" the author is, as it were, "arrested" in the presence of power. Reforming the Tenderloin was not only contingent on reforming the men who policed it, but as the *Times* recognized, the men who reported on it. Yet on all three fronts the campaign proved incomplete. Even my provisional shorthand label of the Charles Becker affair ultimately proves inadequate. Despite the temptation to scapegoat Becker or personalize his action, the fact is that whatever enhanced power he experienced was itself a byproduct of work discipline from above; soon, Tammany would be in charge again. Roosevelt's vice campaign also had its own limits. If, as the *World* liked to muse, Crane had stayed longer to pick up his plot, he might have seen that the Raines Law, in Gilfoyle's estimate, "produced results entirely contrary to its supporters' intentions"—including a subsequent increase in prostitution.[72]

Meanwhile, as fatalistic as Crane's requiem in "An Eloquence of Grief" can seem, his representation itself points to the limitations of the Panoptical paradigm in deciphering police power. Crane's representation turns, much like the Panopticon can, many of the particulars of ethnicity, gender, and class into a gothic abstraction, Foucault's "machinery that no one owns"; it silences a voice like Dora Clark's and her own agency in pressing her case; and perhaps just as importantly, it overlooks the vocal resistance like that of the audience in the raucous Becker hearing.[73] Furthermore, if Crane's traditionally chivalric image obscures his fascination with authority, the Panoptic revision underestimates how permeated he was with middle-class ambivalence about the power that turn-of-the-century policing represented. Indeed, Crane's uneasy mixture of awe for police veterans, his concern for effective crowd management, and his anxiety over the danger inherent in the police's submerged envy and antipathy for urban frivolity—all of

this makes Crane's posture quite suggestive of how many in the urban middle classes might have viewed police power in these years and after. These conflicted attitudes entangled Crane in a loop of bad faith that made him both exemplify, in the public eye, genteel class paternalism and yet become its opponent when it was more systematically implemented.

From these attitudes, the Spanish-American War could provide little escape. Police actions, in time, would not only be cross-referenced rhetorically from domestic to international fronts, but in a real sense superimposed as a guide to action, as intervention could be legitimated with or without a civil (read: "national") complainant. When Roosevelt declared, in the cloak of nonpartisanship at home, that "[o]ur duty is to preserve order, to protect life and property, to arrest criminals, and to secure honest elections," he might have been providing a blueprint not just for the NYPD, but for future Latin-American policy. (We might also remember that the Spanish-American War was precipitated in part by the illegal search and seizure of an American woman by Spanish forces, an action Hearst's *Journal* virtually invented.)[74] Even the plot of *Active Service*, which depicts a chivalric rescue mission of a newspaperman undermined by a confident showgirl and uncooperative military men, belies one character's assessment that a foreign landscape could be "'a long way from the Bowery'" (151). Perhaps it was only as far as the Tenderloin, a "land" Crane felt had already been occupied.

Notes

Newspaper microfilms for this article were provided by the Lilly Library, Indiana University; the New York State Library, Albany, New York; the library at the State University of New York, Stonybrook; the library at Michigan State University; and the Boston Public Library. I would like to thank the Stephen Crane and Lincoln Steffens Collections, Rare Book and Manuscript Library, Columbia University, which have allowed me to quote from their holdings and use their extensive microfilms. A Boston College Research Incentive Grant funded part of the research. I would like to thank Richard Fox, Paul Lewis, Robin Lydenberg, and especially Judy Smith and Dayton Haskin for their comments on earlier drafts. An early version of this article was delivered to an encouraging audience at Boston University's American Studies Program.

1. This ambition, which dates from the precise week of the Dora Clark episode, was reported in the *Baltimore News,* 14 Sept. 1896, scrapbook clipping in Stephen Crane Collection, Rare Book and Manuscript Library, Columbia University. See also Ellen Moers, "Theodore Roosevelt, Literary Feller," *Columbia University Forum* (summer 1963), 15. Fragment in epigraph from The *New*

York City Sketches of Stephen Crane, ed. R. W. Stallman and E. R. Hagemann (New York, 1966), 259. My account of the Tenderloin's geography is indebted to Gilfoyle's *City of Eros: New York City, Prostitution, and the Commercialization of Sex, 1790-1920* (New York, 1992).

2. Stephen Crane, "Adventures of a Novelist," reprinted in Stallman and Hagemann, *New York City Sketches,* 226-31; "wives and sisters" from the 17 Sept. 1896 article in the *New York Journal,* reprinted here in *New York City Sketches,* 223. Scholarly accounts of this episode were provided by R. W. Stallman, *Stephen Crane: A Biography* (New York, 1968), 218-36; and Olov W. Fryckstedt, "Stephen Crane in the Tenderloin," *Studia Neophilologica* 34 (1962): 135-63. See also Andy Logan, *Against the Evidence: The Becker-Rosenthal Affair* (New York, 1970), 107 and following; Christopher Benfey, *The Double Life of Stephen Crane* (New York, 1992), 171-81; and James Richardson, *The New York Police, Colonial Times to 1901* (New York, 1970), 261-62. Roosevelt actually had dinner with Jacob Riis and Crane in July; see Elting E. Morison, ed., *The Letters of Theodore Roosevelt* (Cambridge, Mass., 1951), 550. In August, Crane had sent "George's Mother" to Roosevelt for comment; Roosevelt had already written him in July, wanting to talk about Maggie. See Stanley Wertheim and Paul Sorrentino, eds., *The Correspondence of Stephen Crane* (New York, 1988), letters from Roosevelt of 20 July and 18 Aug. 1896, 1:241, 1:249.

3. "Soldier" and "battle" quotes from Stallman, *Stephen Crane: A Biography,* 231, 224. Scholars often point out that Becker went on to become, in 1914, the first New York City policeman given the electric chair, for his implication in the murder of a local gambler. Logan's book covers this scandalous episode, alluded to in the Meyer Wolfsheim sections of F. Scott Fitzgerald's *The Great Gatsby* (1925). On the original casting of American realism as a liberal "war" on injustice, see esp. Amy Kaplan, *The Social Construction of American Realism* (Chicago, 1988), 15 and following pages.

4. The best reading of Crane's newspaperwork is Alan Trachtenberg's "Experiments in Another Country: Stephen Crane's City Sketches," reprinted in *American Realism: New Essays,* ed. Eric Sundquist (Baltimore, Md., 1982), 138-54. See also Laura Hapke, *Girls Who Went Wrong* (Bowling Green, Ohio, 1989), 45-67; and Michael Davitt Bell, *The Problem of American Realism* (Chicago, 1993), 146 and following pages. For valuable poststructuralist readings, see Michael D. Warner, "Value, Agency, and Stephen Crane's 'The Monster,'" *Nineteenth Century Fiction* 40 (June

1985): 76-93, and Michael Fried, *Realism, Writing, Disfiguration: On Thomas Eakins and Stephen Crane* (Chicago, 1987).

5. The best revision of realism's middle-class milieu is Kaplan, *Social Construction of American Realism*; on spectatorship and urban disorder, see esp. 44 and following pages. See also, from a Jamesonian perspective, the role of spectatorship described in June Howard, *Form and History in American Naturalism* (Chapel Hill, N.C., 1985), esp. 104-41; Crane's *Maggie* described on 105-6.

6. Panopticism described in Michel Foucault, *Discipline and Punish: The Birth of the Prison,* trans. Alan Sheridan (New York, 1979), esp. 195-228; "visibility" quote on "the examination," from 184, "no zone of shade" as quoted in Frank Lentricchia, *Ariel and the Police: Michel Foucault, William James, Wallace Stevens* (Madison, Wisc., 1988), 69-70. See also "The Eye of Power," an interview reprinted in *Power/Knowledge: Selected Interviews and Writings, 1972-1977,* ed. and trans. Colin Gordon (New York, 1980); Jacques Donzelot, *The Policing of Families,* trans. Robert Hurley (New York, 1979); and D. A. Miller, *The Novel and the Police* (Berkeley, Calif., 1988). See also Lentricchia's discussion of Foucault, 48-49, 57-69.

7. Quote on news media (emphasis added) from Richard V. Ericson, Patricia M. Baranek, and Janet B. L. Chan, *Representing Order: Crime, Law, and Justice in the News Media* (Toronto, 1991), 74. Maren Stange, *Symbols of Ideal Life: Social Documentary Photography in America, 1890-1950* (Cambridge, England, 1989), esp. 18-26; quote on 23. For a comparable account of the role of slum photography in "clearing the streets," see John Tagg, *The Burden of Representation* (Amherst, Mass., 1988), esp. 150 and following pages. Mark Seltzer, *Bodies and Machines* (New York, 1992), 91 and following pages. Quotes here from 95-96; Foucault discussed explicitly on 42-43. Foucault's model is also central to Katrina Irving's excellent "Gendered Space, Racialized Space: Nativism, the Immigrant Woman, and Stephen Crane's Maggie," *College Literature* 20 (Oct. 1993): 30-43.

8. I have discussed the potential discontinuities between revisionist cultural history and the new historicism in "Containing Multitudes: Realism, Historicism, American Studies," *American Quarterly* 41 (Sept. 1989): 466-95.

9. Here and elsewhere my use of "ordination" derives from Robert C. Allen, *Horrible Prettiness: Burlesque and American Culture* (Chapel Hill, N.C., 1991), 54.

10. This is nowhere more evident than in Stanley Wertheim and Paul Sorrentino, *The Crane Log: A*

Documentary Life of Stephen Crane, 1871-1900 (New York, 1994), which selects various newspapers' reports and simply reprints them verbatim. See 204-14.

11. Katz's article first documented Crane's developing quarrel with Roosevelt, a distinction most studies still overlook. See Joseph Katz, "Stephen Crane: Metropolitan Correspondent," *Kentucky Review* 4 (spring 1983): 39-51. "[N]aive or duped" from Stallman, *Stephen Crane: A Biography,* 225, subsequent characterizations from Fryckstedt, "Stephen Crane in the Tenderloin," 157; Benfey, *Double Life,* 176. On Roosevelt's actual whereabouts, see Morison, ed., *Letters of Theodore Roosevelt,* 559. More recently, James B. Colvert's biography, Stephen Crane (New York, 1984), repeats Stallman's account almost verbatim; ironically, even Seltzer, *Bodies and Machines,* cites Stallman's version of the quarrel with "Tammany" (203 n. 10). Meanwhile, Katz's distinction has been overlooked because he, too, frames the Dora Clark episode as stemming from Crane's desire to "exert his own identity" (41) and challenge the isolated "brutes" on the NYPD. The articles Katz recovered from the *Port Jervis Evening Gazette* are "Poor Police Arrangements at the Bryan Meeting," 20 Aug. 1896; "What an Observant Correspondent Sees Worth Noting," 27 Aug. 1896, which mentions the arrest of an "unoffending and innocent woman on 6th Avenue the other night"; and "An Interesting Letter from Our Correspondent," 8 Sept. 1896. Roosevelt's reply to Crane's protest is well-known: see the letter from Roosevelt, 18 Aug. 1896, in Crane's *Correspondence,* 1:249.

12. "Tawdry" from Katz, "Stephen Crane: Metropolitan Correspondent," 43. In fact, there are a few indications that Clark had never been convicted, and that her earlier arraignments also resulted from friction with the police. "Red Badge Man on a Police Rack," *New York Press,* 17 Oct. 1896, 3, reported that Clark testified she had been arrested three times before on the same charge and had been found not guilty.

13. In my account of the administrative ethos in modern liberalism, I am relying particularly on several recent studies: James T. Kloppenberg, *Uncertain Victory: Social Democracy and Progressivism in European and American Thought, 1870-1920* (New York, 1986), 267-77; Robert B. Westbrook, "Politics as Consumption: Managing the Modern American Election," in *The Culture of Consumption,* ed. Richard Wightman Fox and T. J. Jackson Lears (New York, 1983), esp. 148-53; Eugene Leach, "Mastering the Crowd: Collective Behavior and Mass Society in American Social Thought,

1917-1939," *American Studies* 27 (1986): 99-114; and Michael McGerr, *The Decline of Popular Politics* (New York, 1986). See also my own chapter on novelist Robert Grant in *White Collar Fictions: Class and Social Representation in American Literature* (Athens, Ga., 1992), 97-124.

14. On Hearst's solicitation, see the letters from H. R. Huxton in Crane's *Correspondence,* 1:255 and following pages; for Crane's later view of Hearst, see 2:679.

15. Foucault's observation about the private media comes in "The Eye of Power":

> Foucault: . . . almost all of the eighteenth century reformers . . . overlooked the real conditions of possibility of opinion, the "media" of opinion, a materiality caught up in the mechanisms of the economy and power in its forms of the press, publishing, and later the cinema and television. Perrot: When you say they overlooked the media, you mean that they failed to see the necessity of working through the media? Foucault: And failed to see that these media would necessarily be under the command of economico-political interests. . . . Basically it was journalism, that capital invention of the nineteenth century, which made evident all the utopian character of this politics of the gaze.
>
> (161-62)

In *Bodies and Machines,* Seltzer similarly qualifies the fantasy of surveillance by pointing to its "unbalanced" erotics. Fried's influence is central to this qualification.

16. For similar accounts from the penny press, see esp. Dan Schiller, *Objectivity and the News* (Philadephia, 1988), 57-61, 63-65; Alexander Saxton, "Problems of Class and Race in the Origins of the Mass Circulation Press," *American Quarterly* 36 (summer 1984): 211-34; Patricia Cline Cohen, "Unregulated Youth: Masculinity and Murder in the 1830s City," *Radical History Review* 52 (1992): 33-52; and Amy Gilman Srebnick, "The Death of Mary Rogers, the 'Public Prints,' and the Violence of Representation," *Legal Studies Forum* 2 (1993): 147-69.

17. In the collection of obituaries and later reviews housed in Stephen Crane Papers, Rare Book and Manuscript Library, Columbia University, however, I found virtually no mention of this episode. Crane nevertheless worried about it: in a letter to his brother not unlike a last will and testament, Crane insisted that he had acted "like a man of honor and a gentleman in the case" and that his

"Adventures" reported events exactly as they had happened. Letter to William Howe Crane, 29 Nov. 1896, in Crane's *Correspondence,* 1:266.

18. Raines Law quoted in "Misdirected Zeal," *New York Times,* 26 Dec. 1896, 4. Roosevelt's views in "The Laws Must Be Enforced," in *Campaigns and Controversies,* vol. 14 of *The Works of Theodore Roosevelt* (New York, 1926), 181-82—a statement originally given in June 1895; "The Enforcement of Law," 14:183-91, also originally published in 1895.

19. See "The Ethnology of the Police," in *Campaigns and Controversies,* 229, and "Administering the New York Police Force," in *American Ideals/The Strenuous Life/Realizable Ideals,* vol. 13 of *The Works of Theodore Roosevelt,* 129. This talk was originally published in 1897. Roosevelt's opinions on racial inheritance were reiterated in Morison, ed., *Letters of Theodore Roosevelt,* 555; see also *Letters of Theodore Roosevelt,* 495, where he claimed two-thirds of his appointments might have been Roman Catholic.

20. Roosevelt discusses these reforms in "Administering," 127 and following pages. For relevant news articles, see "Police Board in Action," *New York Times,* 7 Mar. 1896, 1; "Bicycle Police to Patrol Whole City," *New York Journal,* 10 Sept. 1896, 3. Statistics from Richardson, 254.

21. For admission to the force, Roosevelt's board installed entrance exams covering five subjects: spelling; penmanship; letter writing; simple arithmetic; and the history, government, and geography of the United States. On the exams and Roosevelt's defense, see Morison, ed., *Letters of Theodore Roosevelt,* 578-79.

22. Roosevelt, "Ethnology," in *Campaigns and Controversies,* 226-35; compare Richardson, *New York Police,* 259-60. Observation on colonial police forces from Maureen Cain's review essay, "Some Go Backward, Some Go Forward: Police Work in Comparative Perspective," *Contemporary Sociology* 22 (May 1993): 320.

23. On the centrality of saloons to working-class culture, see Elliot J. Gorn, *The Manly Art: Bare-Knuckle Prize Fighting in America* (Ithaca, N.Y., 1986), 98-99, 133-34; and Daniel Horowitz, "Underworlds and Underdogs: Big Tim Sullivan and Metropolitan Politics in New York, 1889-1913," *Journal of American History* 78 (Sept. 1991): 536-58. Compare also Roosevelt, "The Law Must Be Enforced," in *Campaigns and Controversies,* 183-91, Riis quoted on 190, and "Administering," 129.

24. Paramilitarism is one theme of Jay Stuart Berman, *Police Administration and Progressive Reform* (New York, 1987), 60-62, and Robert Fogelson, *Big-City Police* (Cambridge, Mass., 1977), 54 and following pages. For Roosevelt's own use of the metaphor, see "Ethnology," in *Campaigns and Controversies,* 232; "Americanism in Municipal Politics," in *Campaigns and Controversies,* 198; and his pep talk to district officers, "The Commissioner's Advice . . . ," *Campaigns and Controversies,* 209. On Roosevelt's views during his tenure, see Edmund Morris, *The Rise of Theodore Roosevelt* (New York, 1979), 481-542.

25. Lincoln Steffens, "A Way to Police Reform," typescript on microfilm, Butler Library, Columbia University. It is unclear whether this is a later version of an unpublished essay Roosevelt had earlier endorsed (see Morison, ed., *Letters of Theodore Roosevelt,* 473), but it seems likely. On Roosevelt's own views on police discretion, see "The Law Must Be Enforced," 181-82. Steffens explicitly points to the outrage following Roosevelt's enforcement of the Raines excise law, saying that policemen who had befriended Roosevelt were later discriminated against within the department. "Secret Service" identified in "Portraits Do Them Harm," *New York Times,* 4 Jan. 1896, 9.

26. The New York state legislature proposed a bill to bar such use in strikes, much to Roosevelt's outrage. For Roosevelt's reasoning on plainclothes "spies," see Morison, ed., *Letters of Theodore Roosevelt,* 618, and 575-76. Writing in the early 1900s, Steffens refers back, in obvious disgust, to the outcry about using "spies" that had accompanied Roosevelt's reforms.

27. Becker's background is discussed in Logan, *Against the Evidence,* 105-6 and passim.

28. Alexander Von Hoffman, "An Officer of the Neighborhood: A Boston Patrolman on the Beat in 1895," *Journal of Social History* 26 (winter 1992): 310-30.

29. Jerome Skolnick, *Justice Without Trial: Law Enforcement in Democratic Society* (New York, 1966); all further citations to this volume in text. A different view on the role of "civility" in police relationships with citizens is provided by Albert J. Reiss, *The Police and the Public* (New Haven, 1971).

30. This difference in priorities should not overlook the fact that, as Eric Monkkonen has shown, most street arrests in the nineteenth century were made at the behest of police, not from civilian complaints. Eric H. Monkkonen, *Police in Urban America, 1860-1920* (Cambridge, England, 1981), 103. "Police Board in Action," *New York Times,* 7

Mar. 1896, 1, reports on adoption of Bertillon System; see also Henry F. T. Rhodes, *Alphonse Bertillon: Father of Scientific Detection* (New York, 1956), 73-99.

31. Roosevelt, "Administering," 127.

32. "Hysteria" from "Adventures," *New York City Sketches,* 230. As one of the few clues to how Becker might have testified, we have "Not a Grudge, He Says," *New York Journal,* 19 Sept. 1896, 5. The article notes that Becker "talks like a man who might have had an education in the public schools." In this report, Becker says he will make no statement, but he adds, "I am ready to make one if Mr. Crane makes a complaint against me. I think I can produce evidence that will surprise him." Following this veiled threat, he says that Crane is mistaken, and that he (Becker) did not take Clark away from a "party of persons with whom she was conversing. . . . To do such a thing would be simply suicidal for a man in my position. I am in this business not for glory, but to earn my living honestly. I wish to retain my position, and, if possible, to get ahead."

33. The more the administrative ethos is allowed to flourish, Skolnick argues, "the more [patrolmen] demand a *lack of constraint upon initiative*" (235; emphasis added).

34. "Respectable Woman Arrested," *New York Sun,* 24 Aug. 1896, 1, also gives a clear sense of Becker's assignment. Discussing Rosenberg, the *New York Sun* reports he is "assigned by Capt. Chapman to arrest women who are in the streets for immoral purposes." Rosenberg is noted by the *New York Sun* as repeatedly having charged women "against whom the evidence was very slight." In this instance Rosenberg, while in plainclothes, arrested a woman merely walking ahead of her husband after he had stepped into a cigar store; Rosenberg, however, swore in court that she solicited him. Somewhat typically, the *New York Times* soft-peddled the episode: see "Policeman Rosenberg's Mistake," *New York Times,* 24 Aug. 1896, 8. In one report, Dora Clark said that the initial spark to her quarrel with Rosenberg was her misidentification of him as a nonwhite man seeking assignation, a story she told to titters in criminal court. See the *New York Sun*'s 17 Sept. report in *New York City Sketches,* 217. The *New York Sun* also revealed that there were, quite simply, a litany of police disciplinary hearings taking place just as Becker was brought up before Commissioner Grant: "Parker Asks Questions," *New York Sun,* 1 Oct. 1896, 8.

35. Arrest statistics from Richardson, *New York Police,* 254.

36. "Officers Moved Around," *New York Press,* 9 June 1896, 3, speculates that Conlin shook up and reassigned patrolmen upon receiving information from the Parkhurst Society. In his resignation letter of 17 Apr. 1897, Roosevelt underscored that he had made the police not only the enemy of the criminal but the "ally of every movement for good" (Morison, ed., *Letters of Theodore Roosevelt,* 594-95).

37. These surrounding controversies are discussed in Berman, *Police Administration,* 103 and following pages; and Richardson, *New York Police,* 254 and following pages. See also "Trouble in Transfers," *New York Times,* 5 Mar. 1896, 10. Funds were made up by the City Vigilance League, according to Berman (105).

38. On the blurring of boundaries, see also Gilfoyle, *City of Eros,* 243-48.

39. These witnesses are mentioned in "Dora Clark Makes Startling Charges," *New York Journal,* 8 Oct. 1896, in *New York City Sketches,* 233.

40. The newspapers reported several cases where plainclothes officers had exceeded their authority or not identified themselves: see "Blackmail Charged Against the Police," *New York Journal,* 22 Sept. 1896, 7; "Policemen Reprimanded," *New York Sun,* 25 Aug. 1896, 3, which discusses policemen Conway and Schroeder of the West Forty-seventh Street station and a "third cop, whose name is withheld," who got into a brawl with a crowd; "The 'Other' Woman Was His Prisoner," *New York Journal,* 8 Sept. 1896, 4, tells of the failure of Conway to bring the correct prisoner to court. Conway, it is noted in the article, "has been acting as a 'plain clothes man,' his duty being to arrest women at night." The *New York Sun* also compared Rev. Charles Parkhurst to an entrapping detective, wining and dining his victims to get them to commit crimes; see Candace Stone, *Dana and the Sun* (New York, 1938), 164 and following pages.

41. This success followed a reorganization of district and precinct lines by Chapman; see "Broadway Squad Change," *New York Times,* 12 July 1896, 16. The *New York World* identified Chapman's orchestration of the testimony of James O'Connor in "Crane Had a Gay Night," 252. In the *New York Press* report of the trial on 17 Oct. 1896, 3, Dora Clark singled out Capt. Chapman as her persecutor.

42. It is reprinted as "Sixth Avenue" in *New York City Sketches,* 117.

43. "Portraits Do Them Harm," 1.

44. Becker's partner is referred to in "S. Crane and Dora Clark," *New York Sun,* 17 Sept. 1896, in *New York City Sketches,* 218.

45. Tramp quoted in "71 Tramps Nabbed," *New York Sun,* 24 Aug. 1896, 5; cartoon is "The Modern Highwayman," *New York Press,* 21 Aug. 1896, 1.

46. On the relationship of police precincts to sensationalism, see Christopher Wilson, *The Labor of Words: Literary Professionalism in the Progressive Era*(Athens, Ga., 1985), 17-39; on this relationship and crime generally in this period, see David Ray Papke, *Framing the Criminal: Crime, Cultural Work and the Loss of Critical Perspective* (Hamden, Conn., 1987), 59-74.

47. Necessarily, this means neglecting key newspapers, notably the immigrant press, for example the German-American *Staats-Zeitung.* Roosevelt himself identified the *New York World* and *New York Journal* as his main nemeses; see "Administering," 125-26. In Morison, ed., *Letters of Theodore Roosevelt,* 470, 488, 502, 508, and passim, he says the *New York Press* stood by him steadily, the *New York Tribune* and *New York Times* more tepidly. Roosevelt claimed the *New York Sun* was compromised by its involvement with the Tammany machine (Morison, ed., *Letters of Theodore Roosevelt,* 508). In substituting "police" news for the conventional "crime" news, I am following the usage suggested in much recent sociological criticism; see, for instance, Steve Chibnall, "The Crime Reporter: A Study in the Production of Commercial Knowledge," *Sociology* 9 (Jan. 1975): 49-66.

48. The editorial page of the *New York Times* was written by Charles Miller, perhaps Roosevelt's closest ally on an earlier New York committee advocating civil service reform. See F. Fraser Bond, *Mr. Miller of "The Times"* (New York, 1931), 106-7, 108. For typical coverage, see "Wanted—Policemen," *New York Times* 17 Sept. 1896, 4; "Work of the Detective Bureau," *New York Times,* 23 July 1896, 12; "Honesty or False Pretense," *New York Times,* 21 Jan. 1896, 4; "Commissioner Parker," *New York Times,* 21 Aug. 1896, 4; "Mr. Roosevelt's Justice," *New York Times,* 24 July 1896, 7. Crane coverage in "Stephen Crane as Champion," *New York Times,* 17 Sept. 1896, 8; "Crane Presses His Charge," *New York Times,* 17 Oct. 1896, 9.

49. For the *New York Press*'s anti-Tammany stands on police reform, see "The Police Bill Decision," *New York Press,* 28 Oct. 1896, 6; "Passion Sways Police Rulers," *New York Press,* 21 Aug. 1896, 9; "Roosevelt Sets Police Guessing," *New York Press,* 22 July 1896, 3; "Police Bribery Openly Charged," *New York Press,* 4 June 1896, 1; "Parker, Pachyderm," *New York Press,* 4 July 1896, 6; and "Mr Parker's Little Handsaw," *New York Press,* 10 June 1896, 6. For some of the *New York Press*'s experimentation in newer areas, see "Stirring Deeds of Police and Firemen," 21 June 1896, 16; "Night Stick Against Knife Saves a Woman from a Brutal Husband," 25 Aug. 1896, 10; "Policeman Kills a Negro Burglar," 31 Aug. 1896, 1; "The Lady Burglar as She Really Is," 7 June 1896, 25; and part of an occasional comic series on the Irish cop, "Casey's Reminiscences of the Ambulance 'Doc,'" 21 June 1896, 16. On Victorian woodcuts and the crime story, compare Stange, *Symbols of Ideal Life,* 11-20. Principal *New York Press* coverage of the Becker episode occurred in "Policeman May Be Tried," 18 Sept. 1896, 4; and "Red Badge Man on a Police Rack," 17 Oct. 1896, 3. This second report says Crane testified that the police had "threatened to blacken his character" to prevent him from testifying. The *Tribune* reports, if anything, trivialized the controversy even further. See "Saved From a Fine By Stephen Crane," *Daily Tribune,* 17 Sept. 1896, 12; "Dora Clark Accuses Two Policemen," *Daily Tribune,* 4 Oct. 1896, 2; "An All-Night Police Trial," *Daily Tribune,* 17 Oct. 1896, 5; "The Letter Reached the Wrong Crane," *Daily Tribune,* 30 Sept. 1896, 11.

50. It is not surprising that Roosevelt thought the *New York Press* was the most loyal to his cause. Due in part to its local Democratic ties, the *New York Times* had, in fact, been a bit tepid on the Raines Law, and the *New York Press* was not. Compare "Misdirected Zeal," *New York Times,* 26 Dec. 1896, 4, with "Money Piles in From Liquor Men," *New York Press,* 2 July 1896, 6.

51. See, for instance, "Policeman Was Drunk," *New York Sun,* 23 Aug. 1896, 4; "Little Rebecca Found," *New York Sun,* 24 Aug. 1896, 1; "Policeman Arrests Detective," *New York Sun,* 10 Sept. 1986, 8; "Chief Conlin's Burglar," *New York Sun,* 13 Sept. 1896, 1; "A Police Court Oration," *New York Sun,* 14 Sept. 1896, 4.

52. See, for example, "Police Law Once More," *New York Sun,* 29 Sept. 1896, 6. On the *New York Sun*'s antipathy to the Lexow report and its support of Tammany, see Stone, *Dana and the Sun,* 135-39, 140-42, 164 and following pages; on its changing audience in the 1890s, see Janet E. Steele, *The Sun Shines for All* (Syracuse, N.Y., 1993), 79-80, 96-98, 119-20; compare Saxton, "Problems of Class and Race," 234.

53. "Roosevelt is Right," *Brooklyn Daily Eagle,* 3 Sept. 1896, 6; "Modern Municipal Reform," *Brooklyn Daily Eagle,* 4 Sept. 1896, 5; "The Ha-

bitual Criminals Act," *Brooklyn Daily Eagle,* 19 Oct. 1896, 6.

54. "S. Crane and Dora Clark," *New York Sun,* 17 Sept. 1896, 5, reprinted in *New York City Sketches,* 217-19; "Novelist Crane Racked," *New York Sun,* 17 Oct. 1896, 8; ["Stephen Crane said in a New York police court,"] *Brooklyn Daily Eagle,* 17 Sept. 1896, 6; "Mr. Crane's Humiliation," *Brooklyn Daily Eagle,* 16 Oct. 1986, 2; "Mr. Crane and the Police," *Brooklyn Daily Eagle,* 17 Oct. 1896, 6, reprinted in *New York City Sketches,* 252-54.

55. "The Police Report," *New York Sun,* 16 Sept. 1896, 6. See also "71 Dock Tramps Nabbed," *New York Sun,* 24 Aug. 1896, 5, describing a police sweep; and "Policeman Kills a Thief," *New York Sun,* 21 Sept. 1896, 5; compare "Boy Burglar Shot to Death," *New York Journal,* 21 Sept. 1896, 1.

56. I discuss the style of *New York World* Sunday editions more fully in Christopher Wilson, White Collar Fictions, 40-47. For typical fare, see "M'Laughlin is Lucky," *New York World,* 21 Oct. 1896, 2; "Police Force Spoiled Him," *New York World,* 16 Sept. 1896, 7; "a few of the things that joining the force taught truly good policeman Hughes," *New York World,* 17 Sept. 1896, 4; "Policemen as Cinderellas," "Reunited in Court," and "Bears Locked in Cells," *New York World,* 18 Sept. 1896, 5. Compare "A New Trial for McLaughlin," *Brooklyn Daily Eagle,* 20 Oct. 1896, 6.

57. "With Himself as Hero," *New York World,* 17 Sept. 1896, n.p., and "Crane Had a Gay Night," *New York World,* 16 Oct. 1896, n.p., both clippings in Stephen Crane Papers, Rare Book and Manuscript Library, Columbia University.

58. For representative fare, see "Conlin Wins The Thief-Taking Match," *New York Journal,* 10 Oct. 1896, 9; "Torn from His Bride," *New York Journal,* 24 Oct. 1896, 3; "Boy Burglar Shot to Death," *New York Journal,* 21 Sept. 1896, 1; "Died Struggling with a Policeman," *New York Journal,* 21 Sept. 1896, 9; "Brave Policeman's Narrow Escape," *New York Journal,* 26 Sept. 1896, 9; "Blackmail Charged Vs. Police," *New York Journal,* 22 Sept. 1986, 7.

59. Main coverage in "Crane Risked All," *New York Journal,* 17 Oct. 1896, 1, reprinted in *New York City Sketches,* 242-48; "Novelist Crane Was True Blue," *New York Journal,* 16 Oct. 1896, 1, also in *New York City Sketches,* 235-38; "A Crime or a Blunder," the *New York Journal*'s call for Becker's trial, *New York Journal,* 18 Sept. 1896, 8; "Dora Clark Doesn't Appear," *New York Journal,* 18 Sept. 1896, 8; "Not a Grudge, He Says," *New York Journal,* 19 Sept. 1896, 5; Crane, "Adventures," in *New York City Sketches,* 229-30.

60. "Stephen Crane As/Brave as His Hero," in *New York City Sketches,* 223.

61. Compare my discussion of chivalric "protectionism" in regard to O. Henry: Wilson, *White Collar Fictions,* 47 and following pages. On contemporary images of the chorus girl, see Allen, *Horrible Prettiness,* 201 and following pages.

62. "Adventures," in *New York City Sketches,* 229-30. More typically, according to Kathy Peiss, "while carefully marking the boundary between the fallen and the respectable, a working woman might appropriate part of the prostitute's style as her own." *Cheap Amusements: Working Women and Leisure in Turn-of-the-Century New York* (Philadelphia, 1986), 66; see also 57-59 on street culture.

63. "Crane Risked All," in *New York City Sketches,* 245.

64. Trachtenberg, "Experiments in Another Country," 148. In part, Trachtenberg actually recoups the realistic claim by casting Crane's news sketches as experiments in rendering the sheer data of experience phenomenonologically. LaCapra's argument is that historians who debunk logocentrism implicitly reclaim interpretive certainty for themselves; see *History and Criticism* (Ithaca, N.Y., 1985), 137-38 and following pages.

65. A similar strategy is at work in the last page of Crane's best war piece, "War Memories," in *Tales of War,* vol. 6 of *The Works of Stephen Crane,* ed. Fredson Bowers (Charlottesville, Va., 1973). Here Crane mocks how "natural-born major-generals" will go on "clucking" about combat where common soldiers remain silent (263).

66. Although many readings, past and present, affirm with certainty that Maggie Johnson "actually becomes a streetwalker" (compare Irving, "Gendered Space," 39), this critical move would seem to reproduce the objectification that it protests. Trachtenberg, "Experiments in Another Country," at least, recognizes that the name Maggie was "virtually generic" (145); "streetwalker" also encodes the ambiguity about space Crane addresses. The finale of *Maggie* not only teases us with several potential misrecognitions—we witness street encounters that may be assignations, solicitations, or pleas for charity—but also makes us wonder whether the "girl of the painted cohorts of the city" is even the Maggie we have been following in the plot. I have written about similar stories of misrecognition, modelled on Crane's example, in Christopher Wilson, "Broadway Nights: John Reed and the City," *Prospects* 13 (1988): 273-94.

67. All subsequent in-text citations from *Stephen Crane: Tales, Sketches, and Reports,* vol. 8 of the Bowers collection. Nearly the exact sentiments are expressed about the Tenderloin in "In the Broadway Cable Cars" and "A Lovely Jag in a Crowded Car" both in *Stephen Crane: Tales, Sketches, and Reports,* ed. Bowers, 8:361-64. This latter is also an intriguing piece in that the presence of a drunk transforms the space of the cable car into a saloon.

68. On the publicity about Minetta Lane, see *Stephen Crane: Tales, Sketches, and Reports,* ed. Bowers, 8:n. 882.

69. Stephen Crane, *Active Service* (New York, 1901), 199.

70. That summer, as Katz shows, when Crane had challenged the reformed NYPD for their "blundering" and "mismanagement" of crowds at a rally for Bryan, he singled out a pattern of "brutality" and "unnecessary harshness" that would not, he wrote, "have been possible under the [Tammany] Byrnes regime." See "Poor Police Arrangements at the Bryan Meeting," reprinted in Katz, "Stephen Crane: Metropolitan Correspondent," 44. On the *New York Sun*'s own standard of "knowing the ropes," see Stone, *Dana and the Sun,* 168.

71. "Eloquence" also seems to realign the elliptical centers of Crane's "An Experiment in Misery"—wherein the testimony of the man denominated the "assassin" is "so profound it is unintelligible" (286), and cries of the flophouse are described as "carving" a scar in the "imaginations" of Crane's "youth" (289). Compare Howard's remarks on the "immobility" of the spectator in naturalism, (126 and passim).

72. Gilfoyle, City of Eros, 243; see also Richardson, New York Police, 253 on the increased incidence of prostitution following the bill's enactment. Intriguingly, "Assaulted a Policeman," *New York Sun* 17 Oct. 1896, 4, also discusses the arrest of a *New York World* reporter named Richard Bell who claimed he was arrested simply because he was about to expose the revival of vice in the Tenderloin.

73. "[M]achinery that no one owns" from "Eye of Power," 156.

74. I refer here to the (misnamed) Clemencia Arango affair, notorious because *New York Journal* sketches provided by Frederic Remington recreated a scene that never occurred. See Arthur Lubow, *The Reporter Who Would Be King: A Biography of Richard Harding Davis* (New York, 1982), 143 and following pages. Roosevelt, "The Law Must Be Enforced," 184. I have already

pointed out the relevance of this emphasis, and the police-beat metaphor generally, for foreign policy. See Christopher Wilson, "Plotting the Border: John Reed, Pancho Villa, and *Insurgent Mexico,*" in *Cultures of U.S. Imperialism,* eds. Amy Kaplan and Donald Pease (Durham, N.C., 1993), 340-61.

William Sharpe (essay date fall 1996)

SOURCE: Sharpe, William. "A Pig upon the Town: Charles Dickens in New York." *Nineteenth-Century Prose* 23, no. 2 (fall 1996): 12-24.

[*In the following essay, Sharpe details Charles Dickens's use of the* flâneur *as a narrator to portray New York City in his* American Notes.]

For a century and a half, partisans of *American Notes* (1842) have been on the defensive, trying to make a case for a book that at its publication was blasted in America and judged disappointing in Britain. While these efforts have had little effect on the book's equivocal reputation, recuperative readers continue to argue that this grumpy, opinionated hodgepodge of genres savaging American life and landscape is really worthy of Dickens after all. Oddly, little attention has been given to the part of the book where Dickens displays himself to be most—and least—at home, his chapter on the city of New York. I believe we can render *American Notes* much more legible if we consider how Dickens structures his representation of urban America by employing a European literary tradition that claimed to be able to read and explain any large city. The tradition of the strolling urban spectator, or *flâneur,* dates from the early seventeenth century, and in English develops through the work of Thomas Dekker, Addison and Steele, Leigh Hunt, and Charles Lamb, among others, before Dickens himself takes up *flâneur*-ship in *Sketches By Boz* (1836). In the nineteenth century, the street-wise sketch produced by the *flâneur* is a standard literary mode for exploring territory unknown to the reader.

The urban tableau is not often recognized as belonging to travel literature *per se,* because it focuses on everyday domestic sights rather than exotic foreign ones. Nonetheless, its function is to make the seemingly inchoate metropolis appear a model of order and organization to armchair adventurers of the middle-class. Reporter, moralist, social critic, and man-about-town, the ostensibly objective *flâneur* is a crucial mediator in the bourgeois public's effort to handle the flux of new signs, sights, and social formations that define the modern city. Gifted observer though he may be, the *flâneur*'s ultimate function is to interpret and, to a degree, obscure social relations—so that readers come away reassured that their city is a wondrous storehouse of incident and character, that indigent urban "types" such as beggars and street vendors are "amusing," and that poverty and misfortune are directly attributable to corrigible moral failings. The New York chapter of *American Notes* shows that Dickens had begun to reconsider the notion of the gentleman *flâneur*, by setting him to work in a time and place where urban growth and democratic ideology were making the refined, disengaged stroller an increasingly implausible and unattractive figure. Moreover, the lowest and most bestial urban figure Dickens describes serves as an ironic portrait of the *flâneur* in America. The "pig upon the town," I will argue, is an urban idler of great distinction who not only helps us understand Dickens' response to the city, but also represents Dickens' reading of the United States as a whole.

I

Dickens was hardly the first *flâneur* to write up his impressions of New York; home-grown journalists had been publishing "man about town" sketches and serials in the pages of the influential *Knickerbocker* magazine throughout the 1830s. But he arrived in New York at a time when Americans were just beginning to see their leading city as the equal of Paris and London; in the press, it was even replacing European cities as the center of fashionable intelligence. In the 1820s and 1830s Americans such as Washington Irving and Nathaniel Parker Willis had made a success of reporting on their strolls through London, but Dickens was the first famous foreign writer to hold the mirror up to Gotham's vanity. This situation created anxieties and expectations on the part of his American audience: Elsewhere in *Notes* Dickens recounts meeting people in a tizzy about what "Boz" will say about them when he writes up the trip.

Sketches by Boz had been hailed as a collection of true and amusing portraits of London life, skilled likenesses produced by an objective observer who had an eye for humorous and quaint incidents. In *Boz* Dickens had adopted the standard persona of the urban spectator: Worldly, bemused, even callous to the feelings of his subjects, claiming for himself the authority and ability to read their lives and determine their characters with a single glance. Like a scientific observer he cataloged urban types and designated certain activities as representative moments in the life of a class, a neighborhood, an occupation. But the very stasis of the urban sketch proved too limiting for Dickens' narrative urge. Against the grain of a genre dedicated to ironically delineating stable patterns of urban life, Dickens introduced a sense of time, change, and mortality, and occasionally allowed himself to comment on the poignancy of the human dramas he could only hint at in the verbal snapshot he took.

His strolls around New York, though much impeded by crowds of curiosity seekers, took Dickens back to his roots as a writer, but he returned to the genre a changed man. At the end of his "Gin-Shop" chapter in *Boz,* he had stressed the decorum of his format: "We have sketched this subject very slightly, not only because our limits compel us to do so, but because, if it were pursued farther, it would be painful and repulsive." In New York, however, Dickens abandoned aesthetic detachment, gave vent to a personal sense of outrage, criticized rather than lauded public institutions, and expressed shock that such a social order be allowed to exist. Although his penchant for comparison occasionally imparts the sense that New York is a second-hand London, Dickens is vivid enough in short stretches to seem to have got the gist of New York's misery a decade before Melville, and a half-century before Jacob Riis. In his best moments, what Dickens adds to the urban sketch is an appreciation for the humanity of his subjects; he provides compassion without condemnation. But his sympathy for the poor and the imprisoned, and his indignation at the conditions which they are forced to endure, ring discordantly in a tradition where enthusiasm of any sort is usually reserved for wonder at the vastness and variety of the city itself. When Dickens visits the city watch house, for example, he exclaims,

> What! . . . Do men and women, against whom no crime is proved, lie here all night in perfect darkness . . . breathing this filthy and offensive stench! Why, such indecent and disgusting dungeons as these cells, would bring disgrace upon the most despotic empire in the world! Look at them, man—you, who see them every night, and keep the keys. Do you see what they are? Do you know how drains are made below the streets, and wherein these human sewers differ, except in being always stagnant?
>
> Well, he don't know.

(139)

The moral crusading that Dickens was able to bring off in his novels sounded shrill and uncontrolled in a format associated with worldly, disinterested sophistication. In short, Dickens appeared to have lost his cool, something neither the genre nor the public could accept.

II

His celebrity made it awkward for Dickens to use the editorial, anonymous "we" so characteristic of urban sketches from *Boz* to *The New Yorker*'s "Talk of the Town." But unwilling to forego narrative complicity with his audience, Dickens begins his tour by inviting the reader to join him: "Shall we sit down in an upper floor of the Carlton House Hotel [on Broadway] and, when we are tired of looking down upon the life below, sally forth arm-in-arm, and mingle with the stream?"

(128). This is the sort of opening, the *flâneur* poised above the crowd and ready to plunge into it at a moment's notice, that Edgar Allan Poe, another experienced practitioner of urban spectatorship, employed in his story "The Man of the Crowd," published two years earlier in 1840.

Like Poe's narrator, Dickens skillfully reads the crowds, setting up a taxonomy of urban types and traits:

> Some southern republican that, who puts his blacks in uniform, and swells with Sultan pomp and power. Yonder . . . is a Yorkshire groom, who has not been very long in these parts, and looks sorrowfully round for a companion pair of top-boots, which he may traverse the city half a year without meeting. . . . The young gentlemen are fond, you see, of turning down their shirt-collars and cultivating their whiskers. . . . Byrons of the desk and counter, pass on, and let us see what kind of men those are behind ye: those two labourers in holiday clothes. . . . Irishmen both! You might know them, if they were masked, by their long-tailed blue coats and bright buttons.
>
> (128-129)

But whereas Poe's narrator never learns the identity of the "man of the crowd" he pursues, Dickens pounces on the Irishmen and wrings from them a sentimental story about their working at first to bring the family over from Ireland and now to send their poor uprooted mother back to the aulde sod to die. Poe, a part-time New Yorker who never left the United States, gave himself the liberty to set his fictional *flâneur*-ish nightmare in a London he had only read about. Dickens, on the other hand, relies on frequent reference to anything familiarly British in order to convey his own sense of "real" New York. His first comparison strikes the keynote of dirtiness that becomes a leitmotif in his descriptions of country and city throughout *American Notes.* "There are many by-streets, almost as neutral in clean colors, and positive in dirty ones, as by-streets in London; and there is one quarter, commonly called the Five Points, which, in respect of filth and wretchedness, may be safely backed against Seven Dials, or any other part of famed St. Giles's" (127-128).

Thus in Dickens' New York the *flâneur* plunges into the stream of life only to bog down in a physical and moral morass. Much as he would later do in *Bleak House,* Dickens makes the connection between all levels of society through the medium of mud. In fact, mud is soon revealed as the native element of the most memorable and representative character in Dickens' New York. Before his evening tramp through saloons and slums via "lanes and alleys, paved with mud knee-deep" (138), Dickens returns his readers to Broadway and the hotel where the tour started, warning:

> We are going to cross here. Take care of the pigs. Two portly sows are trotting up behind this carriage, and a select party of half-a-dozen gentlemen-hogs have just now turned the corner.
>
> (133)

Contemporary sources confirm that Dickens was not exaggerating when he described the presence of pigs all over the city. Photographs show pigs and goats wandering the streets until about 1900. What is exceptional is the special attention Dickens bestows on these porcine *flâneurs,* animal counterparts to the urban idlers observing them, and much better adapted to the muddy milieu:

> Here is a solitary swine, lounging homeward by himself. He has only one ear; having parted with the other to vagrant-dogs in the course of his city rambles. But he gets on very well without it; and leads a roving, gentlemanly, vagabond kind of life, somewhat answering to that of our club-men at home. He leaves his lodgings every morning at a certain hour, throws himself upon the town, gets through his day in some manner quite satisfactory to himself, and regularly appears at the door of his own house again at night. . . . He is a free-and-easy, careless, indifferent kind of pig, having a very large acquaintance among other pigs of the same character, whom he rather knows by sight than conversation, as he seldom troubles himself to stop and exchange civilities, but goes grunting down the kennel, turning up the news and small-talk of the city, in the shape of cabbage-stalks and offal. . . . He is in every respect a republican pig, going wherever he pleases, and mingling with the best society on an equal, if not superior footing, for every one makes way when he appears. . . .
>
> (133-134)

Although Dickens begins with the parallels between his chosen pig and "club-men at home," by the end of the passage the aristocratic polish of the European *flâneur* has given way to an American-style "republican" form of urban rambler. Ever the astute spectator, Dickens quickly deciphers the life-story of the pig from his comportment on Broadway—his casual day, his lack of civility, his interest in cabbage stalks and offal. Assertive of his own equality, this pig is an American in his manners and politics. In his study of the pig, Dickens is not exactly sketching an urban "type" as he did in *Boz,* or animating the inanimate, as he does so often in his novels, but something rarer in his work, investing nature with human attributes in order to make a point about the degraded social and physical environment in which the pig circulates. For if Broadway pigs seem to set themselves up as human, the inhabitants of the Five Points have been reduced to beasts. Touring the filthiest and most degraded slums, Dickens remarks that "many of those pigs live here. Do they ever wonder why their masters walk upright in lieu of going on all-fours? and why they talk instead of grunting?" (136). The poor not only live with pigs but live like them. At the overnight jail Dickens demands, "Are people really left all night, untried, in those black sties?" (139).

Though his documentation of hoggish street-life has broad application to the general ambience of New York's thoroughfares in the 1840s, in his portrait of the republican pig Dickens probably had in mind the American press in particular. When he speaks of his pig-protagonist "turning up the news and small-talk of the city in the shape of cabbage stalks and offal" (134) he alludes to the cheap newspapers who seemed to him nothing but swill-guzzlers with an appetite for the low and filthy. Dickens, as we know, came to detest the popular press during his tour of the United States. Having endured the newspapers' ire because of his appeal for an international copyright law that would have cut into their profits, Dickens collected material for his friend John Forster's subsequent articles denouncing the American press, and thoroughly satirized its moral bankruptcy in *Martin Chuzzlewit*. Here in *American Notes,* Dickens turns directly from pigs to urban amusement, marveling that there are no street acts or other innocent entertainments. Instead, he finds packed barrooms and hundred-proof tabloids:

> What are the fifty newspapers, which those precocious urchins are bawling down the street, and which are kept filed within [the saloon], what are they but amusements? Not vapid, waterish amusements, but good strong stuff; dealing in round abuse and blackguard names; pulling off the roofs of private houses, as the Halting Devil did in Spain; pimping and pandering for all degrees of vicious taste. . . .
>
> (135-136)

The "Halting Devil" is Asmodeus, a stock character found in almost all *flâneur* literature, who publicizes hidden vice by mischievously taking off the tops of apparently respectable houses in order to show the *flâneur* and his readers what scandalous behavior goes on inside. It was in the guise of protecting public morality that the American press made frequent allusion to Asmodeus in the 1840s, emulating his appetite for scandal and, in Dickens' words, "imputing to every man in public life the coarsest and the vilest motives" (136). Thus many readers in America, not merely Dickens, soon came to regard Asmodeus as the patron demon of the muckrakers and sensationalists who were at that time laying the foundation of American mass-market journalism. A few years later, in chapter 47 of *Dombey and Son* (1846-1848), Dickens wished aloud for a benevolent version of Asmodeus who would offer a genuine moral lesson: "Oh for a good spirit who would take the house-tops off, with a more potent and benignant hand than the lame demon in the tale and show a Christian people what dark shapes issue from amidst their homes." Dickens' revulsion at the Halting Devil's work in New York signals not only his disgust with the

American press, but also his increasing dissatisfaction with the detachment and moral duplicity of the urban sketch genre. He finishes the passage by characterizing the swinery of the press as "gorging with coined lies the most voracious maw," and he names a string of its offenses that prompt adjectives like coarse, foul, and vile (136). As Dickens excoriates the press, he seems to be fleshing out his remarks on the pigs a moment earlier: "They are the city scavengers, these pigs. Ugly brutes they are . . ." (134). Wallowing in the muck of the popular press, Dickens implies, Americans cannot help but be fouled by the sty of their own mass culture.

Yet on the other hand, a pig is just what many Americans saw Dickens as being—a visitor who, being shown the best his hosts had to offer, resolutely headed out the back door and plunged into the mire by the barn. He appeared to be interested only in the refuse of the nation. In each major city he devoted almost all his free time to investigating conditions in the prisons, madhouses, asylums, and charity houses, and when he had tired of degradation, mud, and disease, he turned to attack slavery, newspapers, public taste, spitting and hat-wearing indoors, the abuse of copyright, and the rudeness of strangers on steamboats. While he may have been concerned, like many reformers, with better treatment for the imprisoned, the insane, and the poor, Dickens' obsession with these topics gave the impression that his own muckraking tendencies were little better than those he castigated. Because Dickens gave so little attention to the urban wonders that usually filled the *flâneur*'s sketchbook—devoting, for example a short paragraph to all of New York's theatres, gardens, and parks, and no room whatsoever to the idle pleasures of window-shopping or sidewalk superintending that he celebrates in *Boz*—his account seemed imbalanced and prejudiced.

Yet if Dickens' criticism struck his audience as a boorish affront to the national honor, Dickens himself was probably not blind to the parallels between the American *flâneur*-like pig and the pig-like *flâneur* from London who sketched him. Both enjoy the freedom of the streets, and are determined to dine off whatever tidbits of a literary or vegetable nature they are able to sniff out as they roam the town. Dickens appears to know his subject so intimately that points in common emerge, especially when he constructs a psychobiography for his swinish counterparts: "They are never attended upon, or fed, or driven, or caught, but are thrown upon their own resources in early life, and become preternaturally knowing in consequence" (134). Telling what might be his own story, Dickens the urban spectator presents as certain knowledge what he can only have intuited from his own childhood experience as a cast-off piglet.

He also reports on the callousness of the pig-*flâneur*, whose behavior echoes that of the *flâneur* in *Boz,* indifferent to human misfortune and mortality:

He is a great philosopher, and seldom moved. . . . Sometimes, indeed, you may see his small eye twinkling on a slaughtered friend, whose carcass garnishes a butcher's door-post, but he grunts out "Such is life: all flesh is pork!" buries his nose in the mire again, and waddles down the gutter: comforting himself with the reflection that there is one snout the less to anticipate stray cabbage-stalks, at any rate.

(134)

Thus satirizing his own meditations upon the human urban condition in *Sketches by Boz,* Dickens suggests that the static, conventional moralizing of the *flâneur* tradition needs to give way to a more dynamic, partisan, humane, and morally complex view of both self and city. Bringing himself more fully into the field of vision, the compromised observer must acknowledge his own fascination with life in the gutter, and picture his wanderings therein with self-deprecating humor.

III

What is the significance of the promenading pig for the larger landscape of *American Notes*? I believe he functions as a comic contribution to another literary topos, the *rus in urbe* or "country in the city" theme. As the muck-laden urban emblem of the entire untamed mud-ridden nation, the republican pig, of whom Dickens finds frequent reminders throughout the countryside, becomes a caricature of all America. Claiming that the "foremost attributes" of his street-smart pigs are "perfect self-possession and self-reliance" (134-135), Dickens makes these urban pigs who root about in their native soil seem positively Emersonian. And in this capacity they prepare the reader to meet their frontier cousins, who are equally well adapted to their surroundings: "a coarse, ugly breed, as unwholesome-looking as though they were the spontaneous growth of the country" (221).

Far more at home in town and country than any European visitor, American citizen-pigs seem to sprout naturally and inevitably from their ideal landscape. For mud and mire are the chief components of Dickens' entire journey outside the city, just as they were within: In Virginia, his stagecoach sinks nearly to the windows in a bog (178); in Kentucky "the road was perfectly alive with pigs of all ages" (212); in Missouri the coach sinks over the wheels amid pigs and frogs, while away from the road "everywhere was stagnant, slimy, rotten, filthy water" (222). The much-anticipated Mississippi turns out to be "an enormous ditch . . . running liquid mud" (216); Cairo reveals itself as a "detestable morass" (230); and in Ohio his coach founders in the mire one more time (236).

Everywhere Dickens discovers unhealthy, "unwholesome" conditions—St Louis is fever-inducing, ditto for Washington, D.C. and all of the South. Even when fever is absent Dickens cannot refrain from introducing it: "The country around New York is surpassingly and exquisitely picturesque. The climate . . . is somewhat of the warmest. What it would be, without the sea-breezes which come from its beautiful Bay in the evening time, I will not throw myself or my readers into a fever by inquiring" (143). Well before *Bleak House,* Dickens shows himself to be fever-obsessed. Indeed, *American Notes* and particularly the New York chapter often read as a rehearsal for that novel: Mud, rain, and disease abound, mentions of Noah, floods, and rising waters are frequent, urban squalor gets sustained attention, and there is even an old lady in the Hartford insane asylum who proudly declares that she is "an antediluvian" (122). In the sodden American landscape, Dickens encounters a rawness of nature and a rudeness of culture for which the desolation wrought by the Great Flood seems the only literary equivalent, pestilence the only possible consequence, and pigs the only life-form suited to this post-diluvian morass.

New York City is often mistakenly singled out as the least American of all American places, when in fact it is the reverse. With a city-lover's intuition, Dickens grasped that this city *was* the country, confined and under pressure, possessing the least of pastoral nature, but displaying the most of human nature, presenting in an only slightly smaller script what the whole of the nation wrote large. He saw that everything that drew him with the "attraction of repulsion," as he once explained his urban affinities, could be found here—crime, vice, social injustice and institutional abuse, comic characters and miserable wretches, muddy streets and parading pigs to rule them. Cities were the only places Dickens was really equipped to travel in the United States, and New York the only one where he concludes his chapter with an apparently heart-felt good-bye (144). In Dickens' novels the countryside is rarely seen except in relation to cities, against which it takes its value as a refuge, a nurturer and restorer of virtues needed to meet the challenges of urban life. So it might have been in the United States, but Dickens could not find anything in the American wilderness to counterbalance the worst excesses of Broadway, the Tombs, and the Five Points. The pig upon the town who represents both Dickens and his American tour illustrates, finally, what cosmopolitanism can come to when nature and culture have too much in common.

Notes

[There are no corresponding endnote numbers in the text.]

1. On the book's initial reception see "A Note on the Reception of *American Notes*" in Charles Dickens, *American Notes for General Circulation,* ed. John S. Whitley and Arnold Goldman (New York:

Penguin, 1972), pp. 329-331; Jerome Meckier, "The Battle of the Travel Books," *Innocent Abroad: Charles Dickens's American Engagements* (UP of Kentucky, 1990), pp. 75-132; Philip Collins, ed., *Dickens: The Critical Heritage* (London: Routledge, 1971), pp. 118-139; and Edgar Johnson, *Charles Dickens: His Tragedy and Triumph* (Boston: Little, Brown, 1952), I: 441-443. For the present-day reputation of *American Notes,* see Whitley and Goldman, who laud Dickens' effort to connect American ideology, manners, and landscape as "a striking imaginative triumph" (30) but who also call the book a "curious compromise" (28) between travelogue and personal recollection; see also Meckier, who finds that Dickens has surpassed earlier travel writing on the United States by Mrs. Trollope and Harriet Martineau, but nonetheless concludes that *American Notes* "is not among his better efforts" (33).

2. The book's first apologist was its author, who, anticipating a rocky response upon publication, wrote an introduction explaining his aims, his concerns about overly sensitive readers, and his decision not to discuss, for modesty's sake, his own reception in America. John Forster convinced Dickens to omit the introduction for fear that it would look cowardly, but later published it in his biography. See John Forster, *The Life of Charles Dickens* (London, 1904), 1: 304-307. Given this context, critics have tended to read the American chapters of *Martin Chuzzlewit* (1843-1844) as a tacit admission on Dickens' part that he had not "got it right" the first time round in *American Notes,* to the extent that even the most sympathetic readers of the travel book discuss it in tandem with the novel.

3. One reason might be that Dickens had very little to say about New York in *Martin Chuzzlewit* and thus there is less interplay between the texts of travel book and novel. Also, the New York chapter of *American Notes* belongs to an urban genre that differs considerably from Dickens' landscape descriptions of the South and West. For a view of Dickens' New York that complements my own, see Alessandra Lorini, "New York City as Text: Nineteenth Century Representations of the Poor and Their Living Space," *Rivista di Studi Anglo-Americani* 6, No. 8 (1990), pp. 35-45.

4. On the nineteenth-century urban observer before Dickens, see Deborah Epstein Nord, "City as Theatre: From Georgian to Early Victorian London," *Victorian Studies* 31, No. 2 (Winter 1988), 159-188.

5. As Dana Brand writes, the success of the *flâneur* "represents a historically significant accommodation of the bourgeoisie to the urban, cosmopolitan world they were creating." See *The Spectator and the City in Nineteenth-Century American Literature* (Cambridge UP, 1991), p. 186. Brand's book, to which I am indebted for the history of the *flâneur* presented here, convincingly demonstrates that the *flâneur* has an Anglo-American history and cultural significance that exceeds the already distinctive role allotted him in early nineteenth-century France by Charles Baudelaire and later Walter Benjamin.

6. For an overall account of Dickens' 1842 journey, Edgar Johnson's is probably still the best; see Johnson I, 357-426; on Dickens' time in New York see Johnson I: 384-394.

7. Brand, p. 71.

8. "I suppose that Boz will be writing a book by-and-by, and putting all our names in it! . . . at which imaginary consequence . . . he groaned, and became silent." *American Notes for General Circulation,* ed. Goldman and Whitley, p. 242. See also p. 119. Subsequent references noted parenthetically.

9. Brand, pp. 56-57.

10. Charles Dickens, *Sketches By Boz, Illustrative of Every-day Life and Every-day People* (1834-1836; rpt. London: Chapman and Hall, 1850), p. 173.

11. For contemporary descriptions of the hog-, dog-, and goat-ridden "suburbia" north of 25th Street that offered street animals of the 1840s a "home" within an easy commute of downtown, see Eric Homberger, *Scenes from the Life of a City: Corruption and Conscience in Old New York* (Yale UP, 1994), pp. 212-219. Nineteenth-century observers also compared the condition and behavior of the poor to that of pigs: See Homberger, pp. 30-39.

12. See *Garbage! The History and Politics of Trash in New York City,* exhibition and illustrated catalogue, New York Public Library (12 November 1994-25 February 1995). See also Frederick Law Olmsted's complaints about the encroachment of shanties and pigsties upon "better" neighborhoods: letter to Henry H. Elliot, 27 August 1860, *The Papers of Frederick Law Olmsted,* ed. Charles Capen McLaughlin (Johns Hopkins UP, 1980-), vol 3. *Creating Central Park,* ed. Charles E. Beveridge and David Schuyler (1983), 260-261.

13. The association in Dickens' mind between New York and gentlemen pigs of dubious comportment resurfaces in chapter 33 of *Martin Chuzzlewit.* Entering the log cabin of a family he had last seen in the city, Mark Tapley remarks, "'These gentlemen ain't my friends. Are they on the visiting list of

the house?' The inquiry referred to certain gaunt pigs, who had walked in after him, and were much interested in the heels of the family."

14. See Meckier, "The Newspaper Conspiracy of 1842," pp. 39-74. Meckier traces how the newspapers prejudiced public opinion against Dickens and copyright law, and calculates how much profit they gained (and Dickens lost) in the absence of such a law.

15. Also called the limping devil, Asmodeus first made his appearance in *Le Diable Boiteux* by Alain René Le Sage in 1707 (see Brand, p. 26).

16. Contributing to the popularity of Asmodeus-style characters in the late 1840s, novels such as George Thompson's *New York Life* (1849) and Harrison G. Buchanan's *Asmodeus; or, The Legends of New York* (1848) reveled in bringing to light the corruption, hypocrisy, and debauchery they attributed to the upper-class leaders of the city. See David S. Reynolds, *Beneath the American Renaissance: The Subversive Imagination in the Age of Emerson and Melville* (New York: Knopf, 1988), p. 459.

17. New Yorkers did not forget Dickens' pigs, nor were they blind to their significance. Writing on the editorial page of Hearst's *The American* in 1921, Damon Runyon attacked the manners and morals of his own era: "Since Mr. Dickens' time, the pigs of Broadway have changed in form only, having taken on the semblance of humans. You can see them today in streetcars and subway trains, pushing and grunting their way to seats while women stand clinging to straps. You can see them wandering along Broadway, old hogs familiar with every sty in the city, and young porkers just learning the ways of swine, their little eyes eagerly regarding every passing skirt. Of an evening they gather in cabarets, wallowing in illicit liquor and shouting their conversational garbage made up of oaths and filthy stories and scandal. A pig is a pig even when it wears evening clothes." Cited in William R. Taylor, *In Pursuit of Gotham: Culture and Commerce in New York* (Oxford UP, 1992), p. 181.

18. Dickens carefully avoided mentioning the copyright issue in *American Notes,* but the newspapers' outrage at his speeches during the tour made what the papers regarded as his ill-mannered and greedy position on this issue perhaps the best known of all his criticisms of the U.S.

19. Meckier points out that Dickens was hailed upon his arrival as a genuine American in spirit (the *New York Herald* proclaimed that "His mind is American—his soul is republican—his heart is democratic") and thus his "betrayal" was felt all the more keenly: "Negative remarks in *American Notes* cut deeper [than those of Mrs Trollope or Harriet Martineau] because Dickens made them" (p. 16).

20. See, for example, "Thoughts about People": "It is strange with how little notice, good, bad, or indifferent, a man may live and die in London. He awakens no sympathy in the breast of any single person . . ." (*Sketches,* p. 200).

21. In *Martin Chuzzlewit* Dickens reiterates the connection between pigs and people, and between Americans' swinery and the behavior that they regard as exemplary of their democracy. Of Americans' bad manners, Martin comments "A man deliberately makes a hog of himself, and *that's* an Institution" (chapter 34). *American Notes* may be a little fairer, for it does not exempt other North Americans from porcine comparisons: Dickens comes upon "the vilest and filthiest ribaldry that ever human hogs delighted in" scribbled in the visitors' comment book on the Canadian side of Niagara Falls (245).

22. According to Robert Lawson-Peebles, "the American terrain" is a major source of "Dickens's revulsion against America." See "Dickens Goes West," in *Views of American Landscapes,* ed. Mark Gidley and Robert Lawson-Peebles (Cambridge UP, 1989), p. 113. On Dickens' horror at the raw landscape of the American interior, see Meckier, who compares the American portions of *Martin Chuzzlewit* to Conrad's *Heart of Darkness* (pp. 23, 27-28), and see also Rodney Stenning Edgecombe, "Topographic Disaffection in Dickens' *American Notes* and *Martin Chuzzlewit*," *JEGP* [*Journal of English and Germanic Philology*] 93, No. 1 (January 1994), 34-54. Building on Lawson-Peebles' work, Edgecombe argues that Dickens practices "the scenic tapinosis of colonial discourse" wherein the author projects his own social and psychic discomfiture with the foreign country onto its landscape, glamorizing in the process the home country whose shortcomings initially drove him to travel (p. 54).

Alan Trachtenberg (essay date 1996)

SOURCE: Trachtenberg, Alan. "Whitman's Lesson of the City." In *Breaking Bounds: Whitman and American Cultural Studies,* edited by Betsy Erkkila and Jay Grossman, pp. 163-73. New York and Oxford: Oxford University Press, 1996.

[*In the following essay, Trachtenberg asserts that Walt Whitman uses Broadway imagery to impart a "lesson of the city, his vision of ecstatic community," which, Tra-chtenberg argues, "lies in the turn in consciousness which the unspeakable life of the street brings home."*]

"The chief street of a great city," wrote Whitman in 1856, "is a curious epitome of the life of the city; and when that street, like Broadway, is a thoroughfare, a mart, and a promenade all together, its representative character is yet more striking" ("Broadway"). In his poems Whitman's city shares these representative features of Broadway, the conjunction of thoroughfare, promenade, and marketplace: a place of passage, movement of people, goods, and useful knowledge, and a place of display and spectacle, of things in the guise of goods in shop windows and of persons in the guise of exchangeable social identities. "An endless procession," as he writes in the 1856 article, his city is at once material place and mode of perception.

What we seek is that nexus, the rapport between procession as Broadway life and procession as a way of taking life in, processing and representing it. How does the city's materiality, its hidden or obscurely visible political economy and its economy of social relations, figure itself in the tapestry of perception Whitman invents as he sets out to model the city as poetry? Passage from street to poem, itself an endless and intricate procession, is the issue at hand.

Broadway persists in Whitman's memory as the archetypal place of urban instruction, its "representative character" implying but also withholding a pedagogy. In a late poem (1888) he addresses the great city's "chief street" as "portal" and "arena," salutes it as "Thou visor'd, vast, unspeakable show and lesson!" (*LG* 521). What is the visor'd lesson, and why unspeakable? Epitomized by its greatest thoroughfare, Whitman's city brings people together in countless varied and fluid transactions, unutterable in their variety and veiled in their changeableness. People pass blindly and mingle unknowingly with others who are their immanent "you." The street instructs the poet to interrupt the flow without dispersing it, to seize "whoever you are" as the necessary occasion for "my poem," for my coming to be myself.

> Whoever you are, now I place my hand upon you,
>   that you be my poem,
> I whisper with my lips close to your ear,
> I have loved many women and men, but I love none
>   better than you.
>
> O I have been dilatory and dumb,
> I should have made my way straight to you long ago,
> I should have blabb'd nothing but you, I should have
>   chanted nothing but you.
>
> ("To You," *LG* 233)

The audacity of "That you be my poem" confirms the extremity of need: only You gives voice to I, only the fusion of I and You which is the poem brings me to

myself, and you to yourself. Whitman's city is the imaginative space where such things happen—not a place he represents but a process he enacts. The lesson of Broadway, its instruction in the mutuality and interdependence of I and You, constitutes Whitman's poesis: not a speakable lesson but a continuing process, the originating event of his discourse.

A process undertaken and undergone, moreover, as William James understood, not for the sake of sensation alone, the quivering touch or ecstatic vision, but for the sake of a state in which self and other fuse into a new sensation of being, quivered into new identities. Whitman cruises the city in search of significant others—as James will put it, "the significance of alien lives"—and finds his "You" in every encounter. "You have waited, you always wait, you dumb, beautiful ministers. . . . Great or small, you furnish your parts toward the soul" ("Crossing Brooklyn Ferry," *LG* 165). The poet interpolates the other, whether person or thing, as "soul," the You which realizes the I. Soul names the ground on which enactments of new identity occur. James called this way of being in the city "rapture," and in a popular lecture in the late 1890s, "On a Certain Blindness in Human Beings," he recruits Whitman's rapt attention to the city as exemplum of a vision he too wishes to promulgate.

According to James, Whitman "felt the human crowd as rapturously as Wordsworth felt the mountains." James portrays Whitman as "rapt with satisfied attention . . . to the mere spectacle of the world's presence" (James 122-24) and presents this open-eyed receptivity to "mere spectacle" as an antidote to that "blindness," as he puts it, "with which we all are afflicted in regard to the feelings of creatures and people different from ourselves." We cannot see beyond the horizon of the "limited functions and duties" of our practical lives, our "single, specialized vocation," and in that private darkness we nourish our own "vital secrets," blind to "the significance of alien lives" and thus to the fullest significance of our own (James 113). Calling this a certain blindness in human beings, James seems to assert its universality as an existential, transhistorical human condition. Without diminishing the general character of the condition—and James speaks of a person's unknowing relation with her or his dog to underscore that dimension—he also localizes a present version of this blindness with pointed allusions to a common predicament shared by his audience. And he alerts us to seek similar evidence of a historical social condition and predicament in Whitman's rapture and raptness.

James gave his lecture on "a certain blindess" principally at women's colleges in the late 1890s, but his address embraces a larger range of middle-class citizenry, the "we of the highly educated classes (so called)," that is, specialized professionals or students looking forward to academic or professional or corporate careers. Perhaps he chose this theme to perform before young women aspiring to professionalism because he deemed women, for whom professional and academic careers were still novel and scarce, more sympathetic than college men to the insight that the highly educated have drifted "far, far away from Nature."

> We are trained to seek the choice, the rare, the exquisite exclusively, and to overlook the common. We are stuffed with abstract conceptions, and glib with verbalities and verbosities; and in the culture of these higher functions the peculiar sources of joy connected with our simpler functions often dry up, and we grow stone-blind and insensible to life's more elementary and general goods and joys.

> (James 126)

Whitman doubtless helped James write such lines, emboldened him to prescribe that we "descend to a more profound and primitive level," that we learn from "the savages and children of nature, to whom we deem ourselves so much superior" (James 126-27).

This agitation toward a more vigorous, natural, emotional, and risk-filled life signals a distinct motif of the middle-class nineties, a yearning for revitalization, a protest against a metropolitan malaise of conformity and repression among white-collar workers, the new managerial-professional class of incorporated urban America that James addressed. "Deadness" toward the world of others is "the price we inevitably have to pay for being practical creatures," which is to say, incorporated creatures. James tells his young women listeners that it is all right, it is healthy, it is tonic, to go sensuous, savage, and irrational. "The holidays of life are its most vitally significant portions, because they are, or at least should be, covered with just this kind of magically irresponsible spell" (James 129).

Holiday of course grates, seeming to trivialize alien lives by offering touristic excursions to their significance. Diction like "magically irresponsible spell" must have embarrassed James himself, for when he published the lecture in a volume in 1899, he noted in the preface that "it is more than the mere piece of sentimentalism which it may seem to some readers." Those who have read his philosophic essays, he wrote, will recognize the essay's seriousness as an expression of "the pluralistic or individualistic philosophy." By pluralistic universe he means that "truth" being "too great for any one actual mind," we need to learn to see through many lenses, multiple perspectives. "The facts and worths of life need many cognizers to take them in. There is no point of view absolutely public and universal. Private and uncommunicable perceptions always remain over, and the worst of it is that those who look for them from the outside never know *where*" (James vi).

This authorial gloss on the underlying philosophical argument of the essay also glosses the role of Walt Whitman as James's rapturous city poet. Without saying so, James portrays a Whitman who intuits pragmatism, the view that truth is plural and partial, subjective, fragmented, scattered. James alerts us to the presence of "many cognizers" in Whitman's domain, to the significance of scale of perspective, shifts of point of view, positions of the moving eye. As an instance of Whitman's rapt attention toward the crowd and its otherness, James inserts in his lecture a passage from an 1868 letter to Pete Doyle which James found in what he called "the delicious volume" published as *Calamus* in 1897. It is Whitman of the omnivorous and voracious eye describing a ride atop a Broadway omnibus.

> You know it is a never ending amusement and study and recreation for me to ride a couple of hours on a pleasant afternoon on a Broadway stage in this way. You see everything as you pass, a sort of living, endless panorama—shops and splendid buildings and great windows . . . crowds of women richly dressed continually passing . . . a perfect stream of people . . . and then in the streets the thick crowd of carriages, stages, carts, hotel and private coaches . . . and so many tall, ornamental, noble buildings many of them of white marble, and the gayety and motion on every side: you will not wonder how much attraction all this is on a fine day, to a great loafer like me, who enjoys so much seeing the busy world move by him, and exhibiting itself for his amusement, while he takes it easy and just looks on and observes.

> (James 123-24)

It's not so much what or how Whitman sees here that so captivates James, not the city's great promenade and marketplace taken in as a panoramic spectacle, but the flow of the passage, the speaker's taking it easy, his guiltless loafing while life passes by, "this mysterious sensorial life, with its irrationality," as James says later in the lecture.

As urban loafer, flaneur of Broadway coaches and Brooklyn ferries, the Whitman James stages for us plays a crucial demonic role in the argument. Of all the literary authorities James raises in support of his argument (Wordsworth, Emerson, Stevenson, Tolstoy), Whitman looks most the part of disreputable tramp, "a worthless, unproductive being." By his very otherness he demonstrates James's point that you don't have to go to such extremes of errant behavior, that vacations from the office might suffice to see the world in a new, nonhabitual light. The letter to Doyle and the Brooklyn ferry poem show the antithetical conception of productivity and worth which James argues alone makes ordinary everyday conceptions tolerable. Feeling "the human crowd as rapturously as Wordsworth felt the mountains, felt it as an overpoweringly significant presence," Whitman says in effect that "simply to absorb one's mind" in the crowd "should be business sufficient and worthy to fill the days of a serious man" (James 122). For James's Whitman the mere seeing of things means serious business, yielding profits of a different order from those recognized by the practical, productive, specialized world: "To be rapt with satisfied attention, like Whitman, to the mere spectacle of the world's presence, is one way, and the most fundamental way, of confessing one's sense of its unfathomable significance and importance" (James 124-25).

This term, rapt, calls for closer attention. Whitman himself understood the arrogant impropriety of his stance, the insult to the ideology of private ownership in what he found sufficed, his satisfaction in saying "I see, dance, laugh, sing." In the passage which follows in section 3 of "Song of Myself," Whitman acknowledges the voice of the bourgeois superego by asking, in regard to the hugging bedfellow who withdraws at the peep of day leaving behind swelling baskets covered with white towels:

> Shall I postpone my acceptation and realization and
>   scream at my eyes,
> That they turn from gazing after and down the road,
> And forthwith cipher and show me to a cent,
> Exactly the value of one and exactly the value of two,
>   and which is ahead?

> (*LG* 31-32)

The eyes gaze after, naturally rapt; the antithetical condition is to cipher and count, to apply the calculus of ownership to an incalculable act of love.

Rapt attention, then, stands opposite conventional forms of possession, ownership, property. Mulling over the mystery of private property in the years just before 1855, Whitman noted that "the money value of real and personal estate in New York city is somewhere between five hundred millions and a thousand millions of dollars." What does this mean, he asked?

> It is all nothing of account.—The whole of it is not of
> so much account as a pitcher of water, or a basket of
> fresh eggs,—The only way we attach it to our feelings
> is by identifying it with the human spirit,—through
> love, through pride, through our craving for beauty and
> happiness.

> (*NUP* 119)

He might have said through our rapture. In another notebook entry in the same years he wrote: "What is it to own any thing? It is to incorporate it into yourself, as the primal god swallowed the five immortal offspring of Rhea, and accumulated to his life and knowledge and strength all that would have grown in them" (*NUP* 113). In "There Was a Child Went Forth," one of the originally untitled 1855 poems, going forth means swallowing the world: "And the first object he look'd upon, that object he became" (*LG* 364). To be rapt in attention to-

ward someone or something, in Whitman's presumed gloss on James's figure, is to become that person or thing, to incorporate it as nourishment, knowledge, strength.

Yet, to be rapt also says to be seized, carried off, taken from one place to another, transposed, perhaps by force or by emotion, a state of transport, ravishment: James's terms project an excess beyond the figure of exultant poet for whom the city stands in for Wordsworth's "nature," source of ultimate refreshment, verification, and meaning. Rapt and rapturous, with hidden kinship to rape, convey an inchoate sense on James's part of a violence immanent in Whitman's version of the city, in his crowds, in his apparent surrender as passive panoramist to their inducements and promises. Indeed, if we think of "City of Ships" and especially the haunting "Give Me the Splendid Silent Sun," Whitman's Civil War city is filled with the clamor and agitations of war, but signs of siege appear even earlier, a discordant note at the deeper frequencies of his urban vision.

Consider the first appearance of a distinctively urban place in "Song of Myself," the initially untitled opening poem of the 1855 edition. It occurs in what would later become section 8 and presents not an entirely heartening picture: a kaleidoscopic display of colliding images, visual and aural, fragmented narrative shards composing a tableau of untold stories, "living and buried speech" echoing from "impassive stones." An hallucinatory air hovers over this Broadway passage, which seems more typical of Baudelaire or Eliot than the Whitman of William James:

> The blab of the pave, tires of carts, sluff of boot-soles,
>   talk of the promenaders,
> The heavy omnibus, the driver with his interrogating
>   thumb, the clank of the shod horses on the granite
>   floor,
> The snow-sleighs, clinking, shouted jokes, pelts of
>   snow-balls,
> The hurrahs for popular favorites, the fury of rous'd
>   mobs,
> The flap of the curtain'd litter, a sick man inside borne
>   to the hospital,
> The meeting of enemies, the sudden oath, the blows
>   and fall,
> The excited crowd, the policeman with his star quickly
>   working his passage to the centre of the crowd,
> The impassive stones that receive and return so many
>   echoes,
> What groans of over-fed or half-starv'd who fall sun-
>   struck or in fits,
> What exclamations of women taken suddenly who
>   hurry home and give birth to babes,
> What living and buried speech is always vibrating
>   here, what howls restrain'd by decorum,
> Arrests of criminals, slights, adulterous offers made,
>   acceptances, rejections with convex lips,
> I mind them or the show or resonance of them—I
>   come and I depart.

> (*LG* 36)

The scene verges on an implosion into private rage and pain, into passionate disorder. In its fragmented inventorial form the passage resembles a newspaper page, a reenactment of such a page with juxtaposed accounts of riots, street fights, sudden illness, criminals apprehended. What does the poet make of this spectacle in which rich and poor, over-fed and half-starved, fall together in sunstroke or fit? How does the poet relate to the policeman with his star, the figure of coercive authority who pushes his way to the center of the crowd, indeed at the exact center of the passage itself? What does "come and depart" in the closing line (in 1855, "I come again and again") reveal about the poet's place in the scene, the speaker's way of being in such a city place?

The concluding line retrospectively discloses the presence of the poet in a curiously paradoxical posture of minding (in both senses of watching and caring about) and not-minding the scene, gripped yet independent of it: an oddly tentative closure swinging between coming and going, staying and leaving, turning toward and turning away. What can we make of this alternating motion in Whitman's relation to the crowd? James might say that the poet's rapture demands the freedom from practical commitments, from family and job, which coming and going imply. To enjoy the pleasure of merely watching life go by, to stay open to what James calls the "vital secrets" of other people's lives, you had better not make a profession of it.

This pragmatic explanation has merit, for it reminds us that Whitman's posture is that of a person with a definite calling, a vocation of his own to avoid vocations which entrap one within fixed identities. But we seek a formal explanation as well, an account of the form or typical forms of Whitman's representation of his poet in the city: a formal account, moreover, through which we might better understand Whitman's response to the pressures and opportunities of the historical moment.

Perhaps the coming and going or ebb and flow pattern provides an enabling condition for Whitman to confront the crowd in the first place, to confront it "face to face" as a condition of his own being, as the "dumb, beautiful ministers" which minister to harmony with the world at the close of "Crossing Brooklyn Ferry." Section 42 of "Song of Myself" restates the earlier dynamic relation of poet to crowd in somewhat more opaque but paradoxically illuminating terms:

> A call in the midst of the crowd,
> My own voice, orotund sweeping and final.
>
> (*LG* 76)

A voice heard from without yet recognized as originating from within—"my own voice" as "a call" heard from within "the crowd." Whitman's speaker makes the ecstatic claim of the mystic, that he stands at once inside and outside himself, within the crowd which comprises the city, part of it yet detached enough to hear his own voice. The poet minds his own voice calling at once to the crowd and to himself, calling himself through or by means of the crowd: an act of self-interpolation, himself as the "performer" in the following lines:

> Come my children,
> Come my boys and girls, my women, household and
>   intimates,
> Now the performer launches his nerve, he has pass'd
>   his prelude on the reeds within.

And a few lines later, in an ecstatic fit:

> My head slues round on my neck,
> Music rolls, but not from the organ,
> Folks are around me, but they are no household of
>   mine.
>
> (*LG* 76)

The poet comes to himself through the intermediary of the crowd; the call emerges from and expresses the oneness of being close and being distant. Coming and going define a mode of acceptance, Whitman's way of placing himself in the crowd yet holding (or withholding) himself free and aloof from it, far enough away to witness it, to discern its patterns, to re-create it as an element of his own being, what he calls "soul," as in the final lines of "Crossing Brooklyn Ferry": "You furnish your parts toward eternity, / Great or small, you furnish your parts toward the soul" (*LG* 165).

"Crossing Brooklyn Ferry" recapitulates the ebb and flow pattern in the representation of crowd and the self's relation to the crowd. The capacious, vehicular structure of that poem invites the epithet processional, a form of movement, in this case stately, majestic, with great formal feeling, though in the case of the kaleidoscopic panorama in section 8, agitated, uncertain, edgy. In "There Was a Child Went Forth," "Broadway Pageant," "City of Ships," and "Give Me the Splendid Silent Sun," whatever the emotional tonality of the procession its effect is to produce an idea of a totality, an assembly of parts constituting an immanent even if not yet present whole. Processional form signals a hope of unity at the site of difference and conflict: it is Whitman's crowd control, we might say, his way of subduing and containing recalcitrant particulars within his dream of an American oneness—his answer (in the sense of equivalence) to the cop's star or club at the center of the crowd.

We can better approach the problem of dissonance in Whitman's city, then, by looking at his compositions. When Whitman writes to Doyle, "You see everything as you pass, a sort of living, endless panorama," he is being serious about the worth and value not just of seeing but of this particular mode of urban perception, a moving mode of dynamic panorama, the mode of procession. It constructs itself as a recounted movement through city space, a passage which attempts to comprehend a whole in its parts, to create an impression of a totality out of disparate, disjunctive parts.

A mode of this sort had arisen in the popular press of the new industrial metropolises of Europe and the United States in the 1830s and 1840s, and Whitman took as if naturally to the emerging conventions of moving panorama as early as his 1840s newspaper accounts of life in the burgeoning city (*Walt Whitman of the* New York Aurora). As a visual and kinetic form the panorama-procession occupied theatrical space within the city; as a written form in the penny press and periodicals it developed out of the "ramble" familiar to London readers in the late eighteenth century, drew upon the "city mysteries" genre of Sue and Lippard and Poe, and in Whitman's city poems takes a new turn as a nuanced method of structuring and comprehending urban experience. "Crossing Brooklyn Ferry" is Whitman's most exquisitely realized work in the processional mode, but we find it in much of his journalism and incidental prose and in other poems of passage through city space.

James doesn't comment on the formal composition of Whitman's rapturous utterances, except to remark dimly and perhaps archly that "his verses are but ejaculations—things mostly without subject or verb, a succession of interjections on an immense scale." But had he examined the structure within which these interjections performed their work, he might have found in Whitman's processional order evidence of something he evokes earlier in the lecture. Speaking of that moment of swiftly changing consciousness, as when "the common practical man becomes a lover," and "the hard externality give[s] way," illuminating us by "a gleam of insight into the ejective world," James wrote that "the whole scheme of our customary values gets confounded, . . . our self is riven and its narrow interests fly to pieces, then a new centre and a new perspective must be found" (James 118).

New center and new perspective offer a clue to the radically urban mental configuration embodied in Whitman's processional form. It allows the speaker of his poems access to ever changing perspectives from a flexible point of view because it understands the constancy and thus inevitable incompleteness of its need, a permanent, agitating need, for the other, for You. A common pattern in the poems is the idle saunter unexpectedly ruptured, and then a zoom-like shift from wide-field panoramic perspective to close-up scrutiny:

> By the city dead-house by the gate,
> As idly sauntering wending my way from the clangor,

> I curious pause, for lo, an outcast form, a poor dead
>   prostitute brought,
> Her corpse they deposit unclaim'd, it lies on the damp
>   brick pavement,
> The divine woman, her body, I see the body, I look on
>   it alone,
> That house once full of passion and beauty, all else I
>   notice not.

> (*LG* 367)

The shift in perspective away from the clangor of the main thoroughfares to the "outcast form" produces the poem's most dramatic perspectival shift, from within the clangor which knows the prostitute as outcast, to the poet's own outcast act of looking alone on the dead body, the wondrous but ruined house of the corpse, a look in which the surrounding city of substance and power—"the rows of dwellings . . . Or white-domed capitol with majestic figure surmounted, or all the old high-spired cathedrals"—loses its priority and its reality: "That little house alone more than them all—poor, desperate house!"

A similar pattern of a turn in space and a constriction of perspective, a narrowing and sharpening of focus, occurs in "Sparkles from the Wheel":

> Where the city's ceaseless crowd moves on the live-
>   long day,
> Withdrawn I join a group of children watching, I pause
>   aside with them.

> (*LG* 389)

And as in the dead-house poem, this turn is followed by an obsessive close-up and an attendant shift in the long view of the enclosing city space: in this case, the city vastness rising up as if newly perceived from the perspective of the small group of children, poet, and knife grinder, "an unminded point set in a vast surrounding." Moreover, the sparkles from the wheel suggest a new perception, of city substance collapsing into mere sensation: "Myself effusing and fluid, a phantom curiously floating, now here absorb'd and arrested." The effusion and the arrest suggest a pattern of distintegration of substance into sensation, of matter into light, which elsewhere—"There Was a Child Went Forth," for example—accompanies doubts about the reality of appearance:

> The doubts of day-time and the doubts of night-time,
>   the curious whether and how,
> Whether that which appears so is so, or is it all flashes
>   and specks?
> Men and women crowding fast in the streets, if they
>   are not flashes and specks what are they?
> The streets themselves and the façades of houses, and
>   goods in the windows,
> Vehicles, teams, the heavy-plank'd wharves, the huge
>   crossing at the ferries,
> The village on the highland seen from afar at sunset,
>   the river between,

Shadows, aureola and mist, the light falling on roofs
   and gables of white or brown two miles off,
The schooner near by sleepily dropping down the tide,
   the little boat slack-tow'd astern,
The hurrying tumbling waves, quick-broken crests,
   slapping,
The strata of color'd clouds, the long bar of maroon-
   tint away solitary by itself, the spread of purity it
   lies motionless in,
The horizon's edge, the flying sea-crow, the fragrance
   of salt marsh and shore mud,
These became part of that child who went forth every
   day, and who now goes, and will always go forth
   every day.

                             (*LG* 365-66)

An astonishing and immeasurably beautiful enactment of dematerialization, the very condition, in Whitman's processional mode, for fusion of I and You, for integration into a new identity and achievement of the soul.

The very energy of Whitman's processional lines in such a passage, and throughout the majestic "Crossing Brooklyn Ferry," invokes in us a sense of the fragility of the triumph of such lines. They are won against forces of distintegration which Whitman may have understood less gothically than Poe and Melville but with an equal sense of their menace to the integrity of selfhood. But Whitman, like James, also sensed a promise within the decentering forces of the market and of modernity in general, the promise of new registers of selfhood achieved in relation to the "significance of alien lives." He invented his urban processional as a way of moving through the city, through its encountered others, directly to the soul, Whitman's great trope for communal love, labor, and spirit, the only means of attaching the city's incalculable collective wealth, "the money value of [its] real and personal estate," to human experience. Is this not the office of those "dumb, beautiful ministers" in "Crossing Brooklyn Ferry," those persons and things encountered in the crossing no longer alien, who always wait until "[w]e receive you with free sense at last, and are insatiate hence-forward" (*LG* 165)?

This receiving of the world with free sense is exactly the function of Whitman's processionals. Procession dissolves the world into sensation in order to accomplish this reintegration. It is a lesson in a mode of being, a way of remaining within the float even while disentangling oneself from it. No wonder James saw within it, saw even further than he may have realized, a remedy for a certain blindness. Seeing processionally is Whitman's most radically urban way of seeking the soul, a way of freeing people from the hold of money and ownership to seek possession of themselves, in Karl Mannheim's terminology, through the ecstasy (exstasis) which comes with recognition of oneself in others. Whitman's lesson of the city, his vision of ecstatic community, lies in the turn in consciousness which the unspeakable life of the street brings home.

Abbreviations

LG   Walt Whitman, *Leaves of Grass*. Ed. Sculley Bradley and Harold W. Blodgett. New York: Norton, 1973.

LG 1855 Walt Whitman, *Leaves of Grass: The First (1855) Edition*. Ed. Malcolm Cowley. New York: Penguin, 1959.

LG 1860 Walt Whitman, *Leaves of Grass, 1860 Facsimile Text*. Ed. Roy Harvey Pearce. Ithaca: Cornell UP, 1961.

NUP   Walt Whitman, *Notebooks and Unpublished Prose Manuscripts*. Ed. Edward F. Grier. 6 vols. New York: New York UP, 1984.

Bibliography

James, William. *Talks to Teachers on Psychology, and to Students on Some of Life's Ideals*. 1899. Rpt., New York: Dover, 1962.

Whitman, Walt. "Broadway." *Life Illustrated* (Aug. 9, 1856). Rpt. in *New York Dissected*. Ed. Emory Holloway and Ralph Adimari. New York: Rufus Rockwell Wilson, 1936.

———. "The Child's Champion." *The New World* (Nov. 20, 1841): 321-22.

———. *Complete Poetry and Collected Prose*. Ed. Justin Kaplan. New York: Library of America, 1982.

———. *Correspondence*. Ed. Edwin Haviland Miller. 6 vols. New York: New York UP, 1961-77.

———. *Der Wundarzt. Briefe, Aufzeichnungen und Gedichte aus dem amerikanischen Sezessionskrieg*. Ed. René Schickele. Zürich: Rascher, 1919.

———. *Faint Clews & Indirections: Manuscripts of Walt Whitman and His Family*. Ed. Clarence Gohdes and Rollo G. Silver. Durham: Duke UP, 1949.

———. *Franklin Evans, or The Inebriate*. 1842. *The Early Poems and The Fiction*. Ed. Thomas Brasher. New York: New York UP, 1963. 124-239.

———. *Grashalme. Gedichte*. Trans. Karl Knortz and T. W. Rolleston. Zurich: Schabelitz, 1889.

———. *I Sit and Look Out: Editorials from the* Brooklyn Daily Times. Ed. Emory Holloway and Vernolian Schwarz. New York: Columbia UP, 1932.

———. *Leaves of Grass*. Ed. Sculley Bradley and Harold W. Blodgett. New York: Norton, 1965.

———. *Leaves of Grass: A Textual Variorum of the Printed Poems*. Ed. Sculley Bradley, 3 vols. New York: New York UP, 1980.

———. *Leaves of Grass: Facsimile Edition of the 1860 Text*. Ed. Roy Harvey Pearce. Ithaca: Cornell UP, 1961.

———. *Leaves of Grass: The First (1855) Edition.* Ed. Malcolm Cowley. New York: Penguin, 1986.

———. *Memoranda During the War [and] Death of Abraham Lincoln.* Facsimile ed. Ed. Roy P. Basler. Bloomington: Indiana UP, 1962.

———. *Notebooks and Unpublished Prose Manuscripts.* Ed. Edward F. Grier. New York: New York UP, 1984.

———. *Poemas* (1912). Trans. and Intro. Armando Vasseur. Montevideo: García and Co., 1939.

———. *Prose Works 1892.* Ed. Floyd Stovall. 2 vols. New York: New York UP, 1964.

———. *Uncollected Poetry and Prose.* Ed. Emory Holloway. 2 vols. Garden City: Doubleday, Page & Co., 1921. Rpt. Gloucester, MA: Peter Smith, 1972.

———. *Walt Whitman of the* New York Aurora. Ed. Joseph Jay Rubin and Charles H. Brown. State College, PA: Bald Eagle P, 1950.

———. *Whitman's Manuscripts: Leaves of Grass (1860). A Parallel Text.* Ed. Fredson Bowers. Chicago: U of Chicago P, 1955.

PARIS

Priscilla Parkhurst Ferguson (essay date summer 1989)

SOURCE: Ferguson, Priscilla Parkhurst. "Revolutionary Paris and Literary France." *L'Esprit Créateur* 29, no. 2 (summer 1989): 39-49.

[*In the following essay, Ferguson examines the symbolic and practical significance of literary expressions and assessments of the urbanization of Paris following the French Revolution.*]

On the 21st of January 1793, Louis XVI was driven from the Prison du Temple to what had been inaugurated as the Place de la Révolution.[1] The journey lasted almost two hours. The closed carriage and its full military escort passed through streets lined with citizens armed with spikes and guns. Drums attached to the horses covered any expression of sympathy for the condemned king. At the scaffold the king declared his innocence and absolved his executioners, but his attempts to say more were muffled by more drums. The deed accomplished, the severed head was paraded before the impatient by-standers whose shouts of "Vive la liberté" and "Vive la république" ended this performance of what Foucault aptly called the "Spectacle of the Scaffold."

The conspicuous political dimensions of this event have long overshadowed its specifically urban consequences. In beheading the king, the Revolution not only abolished a central symbol of country, it obliterated a vital emblem of the city. At least since the sixteenth century, monarch and inhabitants alike had boasted of Paris as the "capital of the kingdom": whose capital could it be henceforth? Decapitation deprived the city of a *chef,* of its symbolic head. Paris became an organism without a head, truncated, incomplete, a monstrosity. So strong was the association of the city and the monarchy that the execution made much of Paris a symbolic non-sense. The fleurs-de-lys that figured on the seal of the city clearly had to be removed. But what would replace them? Whose city was it? It had been the monarch's city. Who now would, or indeed could, comprehend it? In a very real sense, the city had to be re-written before it could once again be read.

Most obviously, one political regime took over from another and went about the business of creating institutions in its own image. Accordingly, revolutionaries destroyed a number of the more egregious emblems of the past (for which the term "vandalism" was coined). But renewal entails more than demolition. The Revolution had somehow to accommodate the past, and given the imprint of the monarchy upon Paris, symbolic regeneration posed problems of major proportions. The execution of Louis XVI is itself a larger symbol of urban crisis. It bespeaks an immediate need for symbolic re-representation. It requires a drastic rewriting or resymbolization of the urban text. In the nineteenth century, the writer, particularly the novelist, took up that challenge, claiming a new authority over the city as text. To a very considerable extent the integrity of the nineteenth-century novel lies in the reconceptualization it proposed of post-revolutionary Paris.

Struggles over the designation of city space gave a distinctly urban resonance to the larger political conflicts played out in post-revolutionary France.[2] The successful contestation of authority opened the city to definitions from every quarter. The execution of one king, the defeat and subsequent flight of his successors in 1814, 1815, 1830, 1848 and 1870 bespoke the fragility of political authority. With no center, the urban symbol system was in disarray. Into this symbolic void, writers stepped with varying degrees of assurance, to assert the authority of the written word and to interpret the modern city and the society that it both represented and expressed.

The profusion of writing about Paris betrayed a pervasive bewilderment over the state of urban society. If, as Victor Hugo insisted in the 1820s, a post-revolutionary society compelled a post-revolutionary aesthetic, it followed, in turn, that an urbanizing Paris dictated an urban aesthetic. Exactly how that aesthetic might be revolutionary was a subject of great debate. Histories, guidebooks, essays, novels, and poetry about Paris glutted the market, which then asked for more. In 1856, by way of justifying yet another anthology of Paris explorations, Théophile Gautier summed up the situation:

> Avec ce titre magique de Paris, un drame, une revue, un livre est toujours sûr du succès. Paris a sur lui-même une curiosité inextinguible que rien n'a pu satisfaire encore, ni les gros ouvrages sérieux, ni les publications légères, ni l'histoire, ni la chronique, ni l'étude, ni la mémoire, ni le tableau, ni le roman.[3]

Guidebooks proper, with maps and discussions of streets and sights, generally confined themselves to tracking topography and institutions. More indicative of the literary commotion of the period are the "literary guidebooks" that offered directions to the Paris emerging after the July Revolution of 1830. The literary guidebook made a signal contribution to the French literary scene during the middle third of the century, from the fifteen-volume *Paris, ou le livre des cent-et-un* (1832-34) to the work that both capped and depleted the genre, *Paris Guide,* published for the Exposition Universelle of 1867. For Parisians equally interested in and anxious about the world changing before their very eyes, these works offered both information and assurance.

These multi-volume collections largely of vignettes on people, places, events, and institutions capitalized on the expanding reading public that made the serial novel so successful a formula. Publishers raced to get out the next compilation, and writers from all corners of the literary world joined in, from Chateaubriand and Charles Nodier among the older generation, to Lamartine, Balzac, Gérard de Nerval, Alexandre Dumas, Victor Hugo, and a host of others. Even foreigners, Goethe and Fenimore Cooper most prominent among them, were pressed into service. By the 1840s these literary guidebooks carried lavish illustrations by Gavarni, Henry Monnier, and Daumier, to mention only the best-known. The pieces themselves ran the gamut from the short sketches known as *physiologies* (Balzac's "Histoire et physiologie des Boulevards de Paris" in *Le Diable à Paris*), semi-caricatures (Balzac on "L'Epicier") to institutions (the morgue, the insane asylum at Charenton, on public libraries), to events (the cholera epidemic, Cuvier's funeral). These collections were, in short, a rag bag, that offered something for almost everyone.

The model for this urban journalism was Louis-Sébastien Mercier's *Le Tableau de Paris* (1782-88). The decisive innovation of *Le Tableau* was to render the city in terms of its inhabitants rather than its masters.[4] Mercier would not talk, he informed his readers at the outset, about the already fixed, about the monuments and buildings that mark urban space. He would himself fix the transient, the ever mobile public and private behavior. The reader should not expect either topography or history. Mercier was interested in comportment and its "nuances fugitives" (1: iv). In a credo that looks ahead to nineteenth-century realism, Mercier claimed to describe what he saw. His was a picture, a *tableau*; it was definitely not a meditation: "[J]e n'ai tenu dans cet ouvrage que le pinceau du *peintre,* & . . . je n'ai presque rien donné à la réflexion du *philosophe*" (1: ix).

Later observers were well aware that Mercier's talent for fixing changing customs introduced a new level of complexity into the definition of the city, a complexity that seemed to suit their own times. Fifty years after the publication of *Le Tableau de Paris* the publisher Ladvocat placed *Paris, ou Le Livre des cent-et-un* under Mercier's aegis: "il faut faire pour le Paris d'aujourd'hui ce que Mercier a fait pour le Paris de son temps" (1: vi). But in that half century politics had intervened. Mercier's brush would no longer do. "Il faudra pour le peindre une autre plume que celle de Mercier." It was not simply a question of unearthing a contemporary Mercier. No single pen could write the post-revolutionary city: "Quel écrivain pourrait suffire à ce Paris multiplié et tricolore?" (1: vi). According to republican lore the national flag joined the white associated with the monarchy with the red and the blue of the city of Paris: who could deal with this diversity? Who could render what Ladvocat, citing the *Journal des Débats,* called the "drame à cent actes divers" of tricolor Paris? (1: ix). Who, Janin wanted to know in his introductory article, could guide readers through the long gallery of modern customs, "telles que deux révolutions nous les ont faites?" (1: 1). Ladvocat's solution—the solution of the genre—countered diversity of subject with diversity of execution, which is why the literary guidebook can stand as the paradigmatic genre of urban exploration. "Eh bien! donc, renoncez à l'unité pour une peinture multiple, appelez à votre secours toutes les imaginations contemporaines avec leurs coloris si divers" (1: vii).

Mercier clearly gloried in the exuberant diversity he found all around him, sure of his ability to contain that diversity. But overwhelmed by diversity, by sheer numbers, by strange sectors of society and their even stranger inhabitants, his nineteenth-century epigones could not sustain his sense of certainty. Insofar as the fragmentation of the city precluded encompassing the whole, these works could but enumerate their findings. No single point of view could prevail. The classical unities, and even more modern ones, no longer obtained. The social and political revolution called for the collaborative interpretation:

> Ne pouvant pas avoir de comédie à un homme tout seul, nous nous mettons plus de cent pour en faire une;

qu'importe qu'on soit cent ou qu'on soit deux? c'est
même chose pour l'unité; si l'unité y perd, l'intérêt y
gagnera . . .

(1: 14-15)

To judge by the number of works that appeared in this
format, multiple authorship made good commercial
sense. It also made good sociological and aesthetic
sense. Ten years after *Paris des cent-et-un* Jules Janin
reiterated his convictions in the Introduction to undoubtedly the most ambitious of these works, *Les
Français peints par eux-mêmes* (five of the nine volumes concerned Paris) which appeared between 1840
and 1842 and was billed as an *Encyclopédie Morale du
Dix-Neuvième Siècle.* Not only the rapidity of change
but also the fragmentation of Parisian society forced a
new approach to the city. Politics determined the urban
text. "[P]lus la société française s'est trouvée divisée, et
plus l'étude des mœurs est devenue difficile. Ce grand
royaume a été tranché en autant de petites républiques
. . ." (1: ix).

A single writer could grasp the unitary nature of the
king's domain; many chroniclers were needed to comprehend the warring, squabbling republics of a post-
revolutionary age. "Qu'un seul homme se chargeât de
cette histoire, c'était bon autrefois, peut-être quand il
n'y avait en France que la cour et la ville" (1: ix).

The very vogue of these works testifies to the failure of
the definitions they proposed, the failure, in sum, of an
"aesthetic of iteration." In these texts the diverse parts
of the city fail to cohere. The chorus of voices provides
no synthesis, no sense of place, no center. The aesthetic
of iteration founders on the descriptive because there is
no author/ity to turn *description* into *narrative.*[5] Coherence resides in the table of contents, where the order is
logical in the primary, etymological senses of theory
(*logia*) and discourse (*logos*). There is no guide to the
city. These tables of contents take the reader on the textual equivalent of the promenades taken by the *flâneur*
of whom Baudelaire and Benjamin made the figure of
the artist. At the same time these works resemble the
order of the collection, whose heterogeneity Benjamin
took as emblematic of nineteenth-century Paris.

The order of these works becomes *socio-logical,* the
order-disorder of society complacently, uncritically reproduced in an urban text designed to reassure. The
multiple authorship vaunted by Janin and so strongly
supported by publishers and readers reproduced, as indeed it was meant to, the diversity and the disorienta-
tion of urban life. The city was laid out before the reader
like the merchandise displayed in the arcades that Benjamin took as another emblem of modernity and of
Paris. The display of the guidebook was designed to
diffuse attention onto as many points as possible, to entice the potential consumer or reader. The *flâneur,* Benjamin observed, gives himself over to the phantasmagoria of the market.[6]

Rewriting the city demands a special kind of imagination, one that sees beyond the parts to the whole, one
that welcomes system. The great novels of the nineteenth century do just this, and their richness depends,
in good part, on their assumption—quite the contrary of
Janin's—that the city existed intact and that, however
much attention must be paid to the parts, Paris was
more than their sum. The novel replaced the aesthetic
of iteration of the literary guidebooks with an "aesthetic
of integration." The politics of integration and the definition of city space once imposed by the monarch no
longer obtained. In the absence of an urban aesthetic
the writer arrogated the authority of definition. The
kings of the nineteenth century had lost creative power.
Balzac explicitly connected the transformations in the
city, in particular its losses, to the absence of royal authority. He saw no king who fulfilled the *idea* of king-
ship, which he defined in terms of a *gaze* capable of
giving life or taking it away or as a *word* endowed with
the gift of creation. Balzac, of course, was presenting
himself as replacement, the one who could recreate old
Paris.[7]

By the nineteenth century the conjunction of literature
and the city was already a commonplace. Into an urban
space flooded with discourse of every sort the novel
brought a reimagined city, not fragments of a city but a
city made whole. The novel simultaneously expanded
the narrative to contain the city and constricted the city
to fit its narrative. The simplification involved in these
rhetorical strategies of containment is a necessary property of symbolic management. For without such styliza-
tion the city muddles the reader trying to read the urban
text much as it disorients the inhabitant endeavoring to
negotiate the city.

The metaphorization of Paris did not begin in the nineteenth century, but it is then that metaphors and images
acquired a particular intensity.[8] The characteristic and
appropriate trope for the city is metonymy. For metonymic figures, in particular synecdoche, construe the
familiar sights of Paris that, topographically and symbolically, tie its many parts: the Seine, the sewers, the
catacombs, the cemetery, and latterly, the métro. All of
these figures reduce the city to a part, but a part that in
turn contains the city. The reciprocity of synecdoche is
vital to the way these metonymic figures define the city
in its entirety.

One of the most frequent strategies of writers and tourists alike, is to view the city from afar, most strikingly
from a height. Early maps tend to place the observer
somewhere on the horizon, at a point of view that no
one at that time could possibly have. We have all
climbed the towers of Notre-Dame or the Tour Eiffel or,
hélas, the Tour Montparnasse. An adventurous soul in
the nineteenth century might even take a balloon ride.

Or read novels. The view from afar was a staple of city novels, a sub-genre of a more general romantic taste for panorama. The most famous is assuredly Victor Hugo's "chronique de pierre" of mediaeval Paris in "Paris à vol d'oiseau" in *Notre-Dame de Paris* (1831) (Livre 3, ch. 2), which he countered 30 years later in *Les Misérables* (1862) by "les funestes harmonies" of the 1832 Paris insurrection in "Paris à vol de hibou" (4e partie, livre 13, ch. 2). The image analogous to the aerial panorama is the labyrinth in Hugo's celebrated presentation of the sewers in *Les Misérables,* the one and the other *not* the "real" city but a projection of that city.[9] The most striking of Balzac's Parisian panoramas, the most pregnant with meaning, are those from Père-Lachaise: Jules Desmarets at the burial of his wife in *Ferragus* and Eugène de Rastignac's defiant challenge in *Le Père Goriot.*[10] The cemetery is a *site de passage* and a *rite du récit,* a rite of passage and a place of passage, a modern variant of the mediaeval dance of death intended to impress the living with the vanity of life. The cemetery was a city unto itself, "un Paris microscopique," another synecdoche for "le véritable Paris." In Bakhtin's terms, the *topos* of the cemetery constitutes a chronotope, a trope that makes time "artistically visible" and invests Space with "the movements of time, plot and history."[11] This chronotope reinvests the landscape with authorial definition, and the bird's-eye view of the writer substitutes for the superior vantage point that was once the king's.

This "melodramatic imagination" is very much an "urban imagination."[12] A "synecdochal imagination," the ability simultaneously to conceive the part and the whole, is vital to the urban novel because it alone allows the city to be defined as such. Synecdoche bespeaks an "aesthetic of integration." Physiologies and literary guidebooks disperse energy by dividing Paris into parts. Those caricatured are safely Other, they live safely Elsewhere. The urban imagination, on the other hand, insists upon connections between those parts, and, thereby, the capacity to encompass extremes. Père-Lachaise is part of the city, so are the sewers; the infamous rue Soly, where Ferragus lives, is contiguous with the rue Menars, where Madame Jules has her elegant home; the Montagne-Saint-Geneviève of the scruffy Pension Vauquer is inscribed within the Faubourg Saint Germain of Mme de Beauséant's hôtel and vice-versa. Balzac does not allow the reader either to forget or dismiss these connections. Each is a necessary function of the other. Each depends upon the other. The myth of Paris is in turn a function of the insistence upon these almost organic connections. Integration overcomes iteration to create the unity that cannot be reproduced because it does not exist. This creation is the vocation of the writer, and the city thus created a "utopic."[13] It is precisely this utopic that allows us to identify with the city, to know it, or to feel that we do. The utopic is a text for dealing with the city.[14]

This utopic, properly speaking, is revolutionary. The assimilation of the Revolution into literary France is the task, and the glory, of the writer, and the condition of literature. The writer's creation of symbolic unity replaces the monarchy but does so only in full acceptance of the consequences of that which destroyed the monarch. The novel makes its distinctive contribution by restoring the human scale of the city through exemplary (not "typical") figures that give the city expression and definition. Rastignac, Quasimodo, Gavroche, Frédéric, Gervaise, Nana . . . are not only protagonists in novels but actors in a profoundly literary because profoundly revolutionary Paris.

The fusion of the writer and Paris, Paris and modernity, modernity and revolution, is nowhere more arresting than in the work and the persona of Victor Hugo. Nowhere is Hugo more insistent on the connections than in his outsize Introduction to *Paris Guide* of 1867. Given his tenacious and highly publicized opposition to the Second Empire, Hugo was a somewhat audacious choice for a work timed to appear for the Exposition Universelle sponsored by the government. But any work whose title page boasted authorship *par les principaux Écrivains et artistes de la France* had to include Hugo, so great his reputation in France and abroad and so strong his associations with Paris.

By its format *Paris Guide* belongs squarely within the tradition of the literary guidebook. The editors conceived the two large and closely printed volumes as an "entreprise encyclopédique" and had the "conviction absolue de publier l'ouvrage *le plus complet* qui ait été entrepris jusqu'à présent sur Paris" (vi, emphases in text). Yet at the very outset Hugo subverts the aesthetic of iteration with his grandiloquent introduction of over 40 pages. Hugo pays far less attention to the real Paris, its topography or even history, than to the meaning of the city within the progressive development of western civilization. Paris is more than the head of a people (xx), it is the brain of the universe, and, hence, vital to its life: "L'univers sans la ville; ce serait comme une décapitation. On ne se figure pas la civilisation acéphale" (xxv). Thus Hugo returns to the very source of unmeaning. Decapitation exemplifies the loss of meaning for monarchical Paris. Hugo's refusal of decapitation accomplishes the impossible. It puts Paris back together again, makes the city whole, and restores its meaning. That meaning has changed. The language through which Hugo accomplishes this miracle has become the language of revolution. The creator of meaning is no longer the monarch but the writer.

Clearly, Hugo takes *Paris Guide* in the higher sense: the book is a guide to Paris, Paris is the guide to humanity. The Paris seal reproduced on the frontispiece shows a galley whose great billowing sail that literalizes Hugo's impassioned affirmation that "Paris est le point vélique de la civilisation" (xix). Like the winds that converge on one point of the sail, the currents of modern civilization meet in Paris. The history of Paris is a "microcosme de l'histoire générale" (vi). "Paris est la ville pivot sur laquelle, à un jour donné, l'histoire a tourné" (xviii).

This paradigmatic modernity Paris owes to the Revolution: "1789. Depuis un siècle bientôt, ce nombre est la préoccupation du genre humain. Tout le phénomène moderne y est contenu" (xviii). Rome is more majestic, Venice more beautiful, London richer. But Paris has the Revolution: "Palerme a l'Etna, Paris a la pensée. Constantinople est plus près du soleil, Paris est plus près de la civilisation. Athènes a bâti le Parthénon, mais Paris a démoli la Bastille" (xviii).

The Revolution gave Hugo the synecdoche that he needed to encompass modern Paris. The Revolution both explains and justifies the post-revolutionary city, including even the decadent Paris of the Empire (xxxii). Thus the progressive vision of *Paris Guide* counters the pessimism of *Notre-Dame de Paris,* with its bitter lamentation on the lost unity of mediaeval civilization. As the mediaeval world cohered around the Church, so modern society finds its *raison d'être* in the Revolution: "ce puissant dix-neuvième siècle, fils de la Révolution et père de la liberté" (xxxiv). As Notre Dame de Paris signified mediaeval Paris, so the Panthéon, "plein de grands hommes et de héros utiles," represents modern, that is, revolutionary Paris. Saint Peter's may be the larger dome, the Panthéon is the more elevated thought (xxviii).

Paris-Revolution-Art. Literature supplies the crown that Paris bears on its coat of arms: "Ce qui complète et couronne Paris, c'est qu'il est littéraire" (xviii). Hugo in effect crowns himself as the modern writer, claiming legitimacy as a descendant of "cette trinité de la raison": "Rabelais le Père, Molière le Fils, Voltaire l'Esprit . . . c'est Paris" (xxvii). Because poetry and reason make common cause—"La grande poésie est le spectre solaire de la raison humaine" (xxix)—Paris is the guide to humanity, and the poet is the guide to Paris.

* * *

Even as Hugo was writing his revolutionary utopic, Haussmann was drastically rewriting the urban text of Paris, creating a very different city from the one that Hugo knew or imagined. Haussmann produced a Paris to be seen and admired, a bourgeois Paris of parks and broad avenues to compete with the royal Paris of the Ancien Régime. By way of contrast, Hugo's concern was not with the seen but with the seer. His domain was not the material city but the spiritual one. His view of the city took as its vantage point not the towers of Notre-Dame but rather the dome of the Panthéon, the

tomb that radiates above the city like a star ("Le Panthéon . . . a au-dessus de la ville le rayonnement d'un tombeau étoile," xxviii).

In due time, Hugo himself would lie in the Panthéon, among the great men and useful heroes of France. For the moment, in 1867, for *Paris Guide,* he wrote from afar, the distance of his exile allowing him to imagine Paris without the encumbrance of visible realities of the bourgeois city. Hugo staked these claims on the very last page of his introduction to *Paris Guide* with the name of his home on the Isle of Guernsey. Hauteville House does not simply tell the reader where Hugo lives; it is a sign that tells the reader where he stands in relationship to Paris—Hauteville House, high above the city, high within the city. Even in exile Hugo claimed Paris as his own.

It is supremely fitting that Hugo should have been so intimately associated with the Republic and that he, in effect, became its hero. It is also right and proper that the Third Republic should have inscribed this metonym for Paris on the cityscape itself. In 1881, to celebrate the beginning of his 80th year, the street where he lived became the Avenue Victor Hugo. And it was Hugo's burial in 1885 that definitively transformed the Panthéon into a republican sanctuary, what Hugo himself had called the "tomb star." The city itself confirms what Hugo believed as firmly as Carlyle, namely, that the writer is the hero of post-revolutionary society, for it is through the writer that Revolutionary Paris becomes literary France.

Notes

1. Thanks are due the National Endowment for the Humanities for the fellowship and the University of Illinois at Chicago for the leave that supported this work on revolutionary Paris. The argument in the present article is elaborated in "Reading Revolutionary Paris," in Philippe Desan et al., eds., *Literature and Social Practice* (Chicago: University of Chicago Press, 1989).

2. See my "Reading Streets," *The French Review,* 61, No. 3 (February 1988): 386-97.

3. *Paris et les Parisiens au XIXe siècle—Mœurs, arts et monuments* (Paris: Morizot [1856]), p. i. Other works cited below include *Paris, ou le livre des cent-et-un,* 15 vols. (Paris: Ladvocat, 1831-34); *Les Français par eux-mêmes,* 9 vols. (Paris: L. Curmer, 1842); *Paris Guide par les principaux écrivains et artistes de la France,* 2 vols. (Paris: Librairie Internationale, 1867).

4. The *Tableau de Paris* appeared in one volume in 1781, a revised edition in four volumes in 1782, volumes 5-8 in 1783, volumes 9-12 in 1788. Citations are to the 12-volume edition of 1788 (Amsterdam).

5. Philippe Hamon, *Introduction à l'analyse du descriptif* (Paris: Hachette, 1981), p. 183.

6. "Paris, Capitale du XIXème Siècle" (originally written in French in 1939), *Das Passagen-Werk—Aufzeichnungen und Materialien,* 2 vols., ed. Rolf Tiedemann in Walter Benjamin, *Gesammelte Schriften,* 5 vols. Frankfurt/M: Suhrkamp Verlag, 1982), 5: 60. The passage cited above appears in the French version only. For the connection between *physiologie* and *flânerie,* see Richard Sieburth, "Une idéologie du lisible: le phénomène des physiologies," *Romantisme,* No. 47 (1985), 39-60.

7. "Ce qui disparaît de Paris," *Le Diable à Paris,* 1844, in *Œuvres diverses,* 3 vols. (Paris: Conard, 1940), 3: 606-07.

8. Cf. Pierre Citron, *La Poésie de Paris de Rousseau à Baudelaire,* 2 vols. (Paris: Editions de Minuit, 1961), 2: 249-63, 407-44.

9. See Citron, 1: 387-409; Judith Wechsler, *A Human Comedy—Physiognomy and Caricature in 19th Century Paris* (Chicago: University of Chicago Press, 1982), p. 20, points out that three popular literary guidebooks also featured bird's-eye views for their frontispiece (*Le Diable à Paris,* Hetzel, 1845-46, Edmond Texier's *Tableau de Paris,* 1852-53 and *Paris dans sa splendeur,* 1861). Other examples include, Zola: the end of *La Débâcle* with its vision of Paris in flames; the climb of the wedding party up the Colonne de la Place Vendôme in *L'Assommoir;* Jeanne's night at the open window, and Hélène and M. Rambaud at Jeanne's tombstone in the Passy cemetery in *Une page d'amour;* the final vision in *Les Trois Villes—Paris, Œuvres complètes.* The device is by no means limited to French literature. See, for Dickens, "The View from Todgers" in *Martin Chuzzlewit,* 1844; and the historical vision that concludes *A Tale of Two Cities* (1859).

10. Père Lachaise opened in 1804 and by the 1820s was a favorite promenade. Walter Benjamin points to "Das panoramatische Prinzip bei Balzac." *Das Passagen-Werk,* 5: 663. Examples are found in *Les Proscrits* (1831); *La Femme de trente ans* (1831), the beginning of Part IV; *L'Envers de l'histoire contemporaine* (1842-44). See Jeannine Guichardet, *Balzac «Archéologue de Paris»* (Paris: SEDES, 1986), pp. 321-27.

11. M. M. Bakhtin, "Forms of Time and of the Chronotope in the Novel," in *The Dialogic Imagination,* trans. C. Emerson and M. Holquist (Austin: University of Texas Press, 1981), p. 84.

12. See Peter Brooks, *The Melodramatic Imagination—Balzac, Henry James, Melodrama and the Mode of Excess* (New Haven: Yale University Press, 1976).

13. See Louis Marin, *Utopiques: Jeux d'espace* (1793), trans. R. A. Vollrath, *Utopics: Spatial Play* (Atlantic Highlands, N.J.: Humanities Press, 1984).

14. See Michel de Certeau, *L'Invention du quotidien* (1974), trans. S. Rendall, *The Practice of Everyday Life* (Berkeley: The University of California Press, 1984), esp. ch. 3.

Sharon Marcus (essay date 1999)

SOURCE: Marcus, Sharon. "Enclosing Paris, 1852-1880." In *Apartment Stories: City and Home in Nineteenth-Century Paris and London,* pp. 135-65. Berkeley and Los Angeles: University of California Press, 1999.

[*In the following excerpt, Marcus delineates the literary representation of and debate over the redesigning of Paris by Napoleon III and Georges Haussmann.*]

In May 1855 an article by Ferdinand Silas in a short-lived newspaper, *Le Bourgeois de Paris,* playfully exhorted its readers to rebel against landlords and to "break with your effeminate, citified habits . . . return to the savage, patriarchal nature of your ancestors the Gaul. . . . [A]s long as you revel in the hybrid existence that the nineteenth century has set up for you, you will be nothing but dressed-up automatons—serving at best as tenants for your landlords."[1] With this statement, the article dismissed urban modernity as a historical and social degradation that reduced the bourgeois male tenant to a feminized machine. Rejecting any positive view of progress, Silas contrasted contemporary Parisian men unfavorably with their stronger, more masculine forebears.

Silas's article was one of many similar protests against the changes in the Parisian housing market triggered by the developments known as Haussmannization—the construction, by Napoleon III and his prefect of the Seine, Georges Haussmann, of an imperial capital city of monuments and public buildings, broad boulevards, and new infrastructure (sewers, gas and water networks). Haussmann and Napoleon III aimed to improve hygiene, facilitate traffic circulation, and prevent workers from building the barricades used so effectively in older, narrow streets during the 1848 revolution.[2] In so doing, they explicitly took London as a model, in ways that the English themselves rarely registered; . . . most British writers starkly contrasted the two capitals.[3] Yet from 1850 to 1880, French urban planners adapted Paris to London's characteristic urban configurations of squares and parks; generated plans for model workers' housing, which included a translation of Henry Roberts's writings on the subject, commissioned by Napoleon III in 1850; and initiated state-sponsored public health investigations and street improvements similar to ones undertaken in England.[4] Indeed, French officials, who benefited from the powers of a dictatorial, centralized government, were able to institute many of the changes they associated with England on a far grander scale than anything undertaken in London, where a byzantine system of municipal administration made coordinated, wholesale transformations of the urban landscape almost impossible.[5]

French writers also began to take the English house as the prototype of a newly private domesticity, frequently referring, as we will see throughout this [essay], to the need to create a sense of *comfort* and *home,* citing those words in English and often glossing them as having no exact equivalent in French. In a lecture on housing at the 1878 International Exhibition, for example, Charles Lucas praised the suburban villas of London: "The Londoner . . . has all the advantages, all the charms of property, along with a dwelling that provides all the hygiene of the country, and he realizes the dream so dear to the English, and which should be so dear to everyone, of the 'at home,' the home of one's own [*la maison à soi*], in which to raise a family."[6] The internal political shifts effected by the French reactions to the revolutions of 1848 and 1871 made urban observers, domestic advisors, public health reformers, and architects newly amenable to viewing Paris through an English lens that brought into focus a proprietary, masculine domesticity. Under the notoriously conservative regimes of the Second Empire and the early Third Republic, urban and architectural discourses began to oppose what the preceding era had celebrated—the apartment building's capacity to create continuity between the street and the home.

Opposition to the apartment house did nothing, however, to eradicate its role as the predominant Parisian building type. Indeed, by defining every Parisian as either owning or occupying an apartment, the heated and voluminous literature about conflicts between landlords and tenants defined every Parisian in terms of the apartment house. So universally current did the conflict between landlord and tenant become that by 1865 the newly revised edition of François Sergent's *Manuel complet du propriétaire et du locataire* (first issued in 1826) stated in its introduction: "Everyone is either a landlord or a tenant. These two interests are opposed and their contact is constant."[7] That new antagonism stemmed from the dramatic economic shifts in apartment living triggered by Haussmannization: increases in land values and rents (between 1851 and 1857, rents doubled in the city's central arrondissements) promoted an expensive, competitive housing market that pushed poor people to the outskirts of the city, encouraged real-estate speculation, and promoted the construction of larger, more expensive apartment buildings.[8]

The debates about landlords and tenants did not simply register a series of empirical changes, however; their rhetoric also suggested that the cultural understanding of the apartment house had shifted significantly. Thus, even though historical evidence suggests that the sociological profile of landlords did not radically alter between the 1820s and the 1850s (in both periods most landlords did not live in the buildings they owned), the debates of the Second Empire attacked contemporary landlords for no longer being properly paternal; and even though the *portière* continued to be a real presence in apartment houses during the Second Empire, she became far less visible in representations of those buildings.[9] Whereas in a July Monarchy novel like *Le Cousin Pons,* the *portière* had eclipsed both the proprietor and his tenants, in the 1850s writers began to focus on landlords whose failure to be "good family men [*pères de famille*] . . . [and] wise administrators, husbanding the future" induced a corresponding breakdown of familial masculinity in tenants presumed to be exclusively male.[10]

The debates about Haussmannization's effects attributed to both tenant and landlord a shared deviation from newly asserted masculine norms. In a discussion of Haussmannization's ill effects on tenants, Alexandre Weill wrote that "no one lives anymore according to the precepts of the ordinary wisdom and good sense of the family man [*père de famille*]," while Victor Bellet, in a text defending landlords, argued that "today not a single Parisian landlord can deem himself certain of conserving and transmitting to his children the house that he has purchased or received from his forefathers [*pères*]."[11] Writing from different political poles about opposed groups, both Weill and Bellet invoked a breakdown in the attributes of the *père,* particularly in the paternal ability to preserve the qualities of "wisdom and good sense" along with quantities of property.

The emphasis on paternal masculinity as the measure of the apartment house's effect on Parisian life erased women from the debate about Haussmannization's consequences, yet polemicists drew on a metaphorical femininity to explain what ailed the modern apartment building. When Weill opposed the "honesty" of older buildings to new ones whose luxurious facades belied an interior parsimony, he described that architectural artifice as particularly female: "All these petticoated houses are covered with makeup. . . . But as a result the interior is as it were dishonest. . . . Nowhere is there an honest row of large square rooms, with vast courtyards, as the architects of our forefathers used to make them."[12] Weill attacked the facade for the way its attractive exterior masked the truth of its deficient interior; by personifying the facade as female—dressed in women's undergarments and daubed with cosmetics—he folded his architectural critique into a misogynist commonplace about the deceptiveness of women's appearances.

Weill's use of clichés about femininity diverted attention from, by naturalizing, a surprising aspect of his complaint: its deployment of a new criterion for evaluating the apartment house. In the first half of the nineteenth century, as we have seen, Parisian architects and observers understood the apartment house to be a relatively transparent structure. That transparency meant that the apartment house's facade worked less as a boundary between an external, public surface and its internal, private depths, and more as the frame for a series of views into and out of the building. Weill's 1860 lament about dissembling facades implied that the exterior and interior of the apartment house should form a coherent unit but also made clear that the interior should prevail over the facade in any contest between the two: if the facade was more lavish than the interior, both would be corrupted, but for the interior to be more luxurious than the facade would pose no problem.

A new emphasis on the interior became widespread during the period from the 1850s to 1880—years that spanned the Second Empire and the first decade of the Third Republic, forming a unit because the Third Republic's conservative reaction to the Paris Commune uprising of 1871 created significant continuities between the two regimes with respect to urban planning. The new configuration of the interior as a hermetic, concealed, and strictly demarcated place, and the valorization of the involuted domesticity that accompanied that innovation, involved changes in both architectural practices and cultural values. Taken together, those changes produced what I call the interiorization of Paris, the creation of enclosed, private spaces through both physical and discursive means. This [essay] traces the course of interiorization in architectural practice and in urban literature, public hygiene reports, domestic manuals, and architectural criticism, focusing on how those discourses advocated the convergence of interiorization and masculinity. Because the proponents of urban enclosure assumed women's domestic sequestration, they did not have to insist on it; rather, they expended the bulk of their energy on urging *men* to return and adhere to a domestic space. As Eugène Pelletan put it in *La Nouvelle Babylone* (1862), in order to "save the fatherland," it was necessary to "regenerate *men at home*"—a home increasingly conceived of along the English model examined in [chapter three of *Apartment Stories*], a home more and more prescribed as antithetical to the apartment house.[13]

HAUSSMANNIZATION AND THE NEW URBAN LANDSCAPE

My claim that Paris became interiorized after 1850 challenges the received interpretations of Second Empire Paris as a city of spectacle, *flânerie,* and circulation, a Paris making the transition, as the historian Jeanne Gaillard puts it, from an "introverted" to an "extroverted city," a Paris about which the Goncourt brothers famously wrote, "the interior is going to die. Life threatens to become public."[14] My purpose is not to dismiss those understandings of the city, but to complicate them by showing that during the Second Empire, the very notion of a public realm based on mobility, exchange, and visual display developed alongside articulations of urban space as a private realm of intromission and seclusion. The commercial spaces promoted by Haussmann contributed to the formation of a mass, consumer public, but they also produced a reaction against that very notion of the public, a reaction implicit in the Goncourt brothers' comments, which touted interiorization as a nostalgic alternative to an alienating modernity.

Private life did not emerge only as the nostalgic and belated antidote to an expanded public realm; rather, Haussmannization itself directly promoted the containment of urban spaces. Haussmann literally interiorized many of the city's common areas by enclosing activities and sites that had formerly been open and coextensive with the street. Street sellers, artisans, and mechanics were moved from the street into restricted, specialized locations. The open central markets of Les Halles, where women had been highly visible workers, were rebuilt as covered structures. Women had formerly done laundry at various points on the banks of the Seine; after first being restricted to delimited areas of the river, they were then encouraged by Napoleon III's building program to do their laundry indoors, in purpose-built *lavoirs.* The carnival festivals that had periodically overtaken Parisian streets were moved into dance halls.[15]

Haussmannization has historically been associated with a series of *percements* (literally, piercings) that opened up the cramped medieval city to a streamlined, rational network of wide boulevards, but it also consistently filled in open spaces. As the architectural historian David Van Zanten explains,

> A series of existing open spaces that had been markets . . . or street crossings . . . had their centers filled with curbed islands of grass, trees, and flower beds, protected with a grill . . . with traffic channeled around them. . . . [T]here was a tradition of transforming city spaces into interiors on special occasions. . . . [T]he delimitation, enclosing, planting, and manicuring of these spaces made . . . this permanent. . . . [P]ublic

space [was] . . . subdivided, differentiated, and furnished. The voids in the plan of Paris, as they broadened under Haussmann, filled with something new.[16]

Pedestrian sidewalks newly lined with trees, kiosks, newspaper stands, and urinals became physically and visually isolated and protected from the road and its vehicular traffic. By contrast with the adjoining, newly widened roadways, the embellished sidewalks appeared to be relatively interiorized spaces out of doors.

The spatial relationships between buildings and streets also changed in the areas reconfigured by Haussmann, whose emphasis on long, straight boulevards with perspective views of monuments at either one or both ends meant that the majority of new streets were built to direct the pedestrian's view straight toward a statue, column, or civic building. By focusing the pedestrian's gaze on what lay at the end of the street, perspectival organization placed the apartments that lined streets in a peripheral space that dissolved on the edge of vision. That peripherality visually distinguished lines of contiguous apartment buildings from the free-standing monuments that anchored the perspectival vanishing point. At the same time, apartments began to occupy a different plane from the street—a weak vertical plane as opposed to the strong horizontal axis that directed the flow of the street and the pedestrian's gaze. In illustrations of Paris, perspectival views down streets began to replace frontal views of apartment houses, with the perspectival view shifting attention from the mass of the building to the space of the street (often represented as empty) and to the impression of motion along it.[17]

The newly wide boulevards did not form a continuous unit with the apartment buildings that flanked them; rather, boulevards and apartment buildings seemed to occupy distinct spaces, which in turn facilitated perceptions of streets as exterior spaces, apartment buildings as interior ones.[18] Other changes in apartment-house construction and design separated apartment buildings from the spaces external to them, despite the fact that under Haussmann, individual apartment buildings became more tied to urban infrastructure by virtue of improved links to sewage, gas, and water networks. Apartment buildings constructed under Haussmann no longer reserved the ground floor for shops, and Haussmann's zoning practices isolated residential neighborhoods from businesses, thus promoting a view of domestic space as separate from commercial exchange.[19] Second Empire architects also discouraged decorating practices that made domestic interiors resemble streets. In an article whose title—"Des voies publiques et des maisons d'habitation à Paris"—signaled a conceptual separation between roads and houses, Charles Gourlier noted that within houses, wood parquet floors were replacing "pavement" [*dallages*]. Formerly, slabs of concrete, stone, or marble had been used to cover floors inside

apartments and to pave streets, but now they began to be confined strictly to the street. The street thus became a mineral realm whose hard, unyielding durability was perceptibly distinct from the more delicate, vegetal ground of the home.[20]

In and of themselves, however, none of these physical changes in the city's streets and apartment buildings necessarily determined how Parisians would interpret their experience of them. Physically enclosed spaces can promote a sense of privacy, even outdoors, but that sense can be altered by the perceptions of those who occupy them. The equation of interior spaces with the political, social, and subjective characteristics of privacy does not inhere in the spaces themselves but constitutes a possible interpretation of them. It thus remains to be seen, through readings of key prescriptive and descriptive discourses on the structure of Parisian space, whether the users of the relatively enclosed built environment that Paris became after 1851 experienced it as subjectively interior and socially private.

CONTRACTING THE URBAN SUBJECT AND
SEPARATING STREET FROM HOME: THE
DISCOURSE OF URBAN OBSERVATION

The literature of urban observation in the Second Empire and Third Republic aimed explicitly to combine objective descriptions of Paris with subjective reactions to it. Some works exhibited continuities with the *tableaux* and *physiologies* of the July Monarchy, but much urban literature after 1850 differed from that of the July Monarchy in two ways that illuminate the experience of Parisian interiorization.[21] First, many books about Paris deployed a poetics of contraction—to single authors from multiple ones, to the space of an enclosed, individualized consciousness, to smaller and smaller units of time—that they mapped onto their representations of the city. Second, those works began, on a widespread basis, to demarcate the city's streets from its houses by means of a vocabulary of public and private that broke significantly with the urban literature of previous decades.[22]

In contrast to the *tableaux* of the 1830s and 1840s, which had emphasized heterogeneous authorship and an ambitiously global view of the city, works of urban observation written during the Second Empire effected a radical individualization of the urban observer, whose claim to describing the city was now based on an individual consciousness that could interiorize the city subjectively, then reproduce it through the prisms of memory, affect, and imagination. The titles of various works suggested that interiorization often took the form of contraction: contraction to a literal interior, to a single domestic space—*Paris chez soi* (1854), *Paris dans un fauteuil* (1855), *Paris intime* (1859); contraction to a single subjectivity or an individualized point of view—

"Paris à vue de nez" (1867), *Mémoires du boulevard* (1866), *Mes Souvenirs: les boulevards de 1840-1870* (1884); and contraction to a single span of time, either a day or an hour—*Les Heures parisiennes* (1866) and *Entre minuit et une heure: étude parisienne* (1868). The titles of those works often belied their content, creating a contradiction between the interiority implied by a text's descriptive label and the exteriority that its content ascribed to the city. Most of the sketches in Léo Lespès's *Spectacles vus de ma fenêtre* (1866), for example, required the narrator to venture beyond the purview of his window and into the street.[23] Just as during the 1830s and 1840s, the words *Paris* and *ville* provided book titles with marketable cachet, during the Second Empire words that connoted individuals and interiors became equally profitable when applied to books about the city.[24]

The interiorization of the city in urban literature transformed the cataloging euphoria of the July Monarchy observer, who had shuttled from streets to theaters to apartments, into the elegiac melancholy of an enclosed and isolated narrator, whose contact with the urban crowd never claimed to transcend his own omnipresent subjectivity. Such narrators remain familiar to us through the urban lyricism of Baudelaire's *Les Fleurs du mal* and *Petits poèmes en prose* and through the spatial fantasies of Decadent works of the 1880s, such as Huysman's *A rebours* and *Là-bas*, but they were not unique to canonical texts.[25] Emile Souvestre, for example, in *Un Philosophe sous les toits: journal d'un homme heureux* (1850), moved his urban narrator into a garret room, from which the city appears as a distant, impressionistic blur of the allegorical and the banal: "our philosopher gazes upon society from the heights of his garret, as though upon a sea whose riches he does not desire and whose shipwrecks he does not fear." Unlike Balzac's Rastignac, who vows from the heights of Père Lachaise to conquer Paris, or the narrator of Victor Hugo's *Notre-Dame de Paris,* with his bird's-eye view of the city, Souvestre's narrator is both above the city yet still contained within it. The space that he occupies, a garret room, does not differ significantly from the space he observes, since when he looks out, he sees only reflections of his own inner dilemmas. His vantage point emphasizes the urban landscape's disarray rather than its organized legibility. Souvestre's narrator describes "the perspective that opens up in front of my window":

> Overlapping roofs whose peaks entwine, cross, and are superimposed on one another; on top of them jut the pylons of tall chimneys. Yesterday I thought they had an Alpine look to them . . . today all I see are tiles and pipes. . . . [T]he smoke that rises up in light drifts, instead of making me dream of the barred windows of Vesuvius, reminds me of cooking and dishwater; and the telegraph that I make out in the distance over the old tower of Montmartre puts me in mind of the vile gallows whose arms stand up over the city.[26]

The narrator turns this description of Paris into a display of his own subjective powers of perception, and hence into a display of his own interior imagination, by describing the city in terms of images of poetic reverie and contemplation—the ocean, steam and smoke, mountains—and by reminding the reader that his subjectivity has created these images out of the unpromising materials of urban and everyday life—dirty dishes, telegraph poles, and roof tiles. Even the most banal elements of the city are not presented as simple causes (cooking) of an effect (smoke), but instead as products of the writer's subjective associations, as memories and metaphors: "the smoke . . . *reminds me* of cooking and dishwater." He then uses the figure of the voyage to show how his imagination enables him to travel further and see more, within a confined space, than tourists who move freely through the streets: "How many times have my days of rest drifted away in the contemplation of this marvelous spectacle, in the discovery of somber and charming episodes, in seeking, that is, in this unknown world, the travel impressions that opulent tourists seek further below!"[27] By incorporating his views of buildings as he sees them in the present into memories of them in the past, the narrator achieves an even greater mental interiorization of the city that lies outside his room.[28]

Urban literature also contracted the city's sexual topography, considerably reducing the field of erotic encounters. The July Monarchy network that had relayed numerous apartment buildings and streets shrank in Second Empire narratives to the space of a single building. Louis Jacquier's *L'Amour à Paris* (1862), which sorted types of couples, romances, and marital arrangements according to neighborhood, recounts an anecdote about telegraphic communication between lovers who hold up different letters of the alphabet at the windows of facing buildings but subtly associated that practice with an earlier era by noting that such correspondence could now take place only in "certain streets . . . those that are not excessively wide," that is, the streets built before Haussmannization.[29] In Emile Villars's *Le Roman de la parisienne* (1866), whose title attempted to confer an illusory unity on an eclectic collection of poems and stories, two neighbors whose balconies adjoin can successfully seduce one another in "Un Roman par la terrasse," but in a lyrical evocation of "Ma Voisine: impression parisienne," a man fails to make contact with a woman he spies in a building across the street, as though the field of Parisian sexual vision had narrowed to the perimeter of an individual apartment building.[30]

The strong desire and easy ability to see from one building into another that had so marked the July Monarchy literature began to retract into itself to the point of obfuscation. In an 1855 apartment-house romance in which a man falls in love with a woman in the building opposite, Léo Lespès devoted the most space to elaborating *obstacles* to the hero's vision and to detailing the instruments and techniques that painstakingly allow him to incrementally increase his visual access to the woman's apartment. Despite his efforts, however, the story presents the failure of his attempt to penetrate visually an interiorized and feminized space; the hero meets his neighbor only through the intervention of his mother, who brings the woman to him after he falls ill. The street no longer serves as a heterosexual copula that bridges facing interiors, as it did in the *tableaux*; in this text, only a maternal, domestic agent from one interior can link it to the other.[31]

Where a writer like Lespès presented visual penetration of the apartment house as desirable but difficult, other urban observers began to denigrate the value of seeing into apartments altogether. In a *Tableau de Paris* singly authored by Edmond Texier, editor of the leading bourgeois weekly *L'Illustration,* several passages foregrounded the urban observer's inability to penetrate Parisian private life and made female modesty a figure of privacy. Near the beginning of a chapter on "Private Life," his narrator praises buildings whose "modesty" impedes his view of their interiors:

> the observer strolls through the streets in vain, no hospitable breach exposes the houses' varied ramparts to his gaze or gives passage to his curiosity; in vain he scales a height and contemplates this immense and teeming hive of rooftops . . . hoping that a helpful genie will come to unhat all these impenetrable sanctuaries of private life; nothing of the sort! Paris modestly conserves her domiciles; it doesn't let its intimate acts be seen, and at most, it lets itself be guessed at.[32]

Texier insists here on the impossibility of both frontal and aerial views of what lies inside apartment buildings. The very act of describing an interior opens it up to view and signifies the entrance of an exterior agent who makes it accessible to an equally exterior reader/viewer; Texier's highlighted visual impasse, his inability to see inside, *produces* what lies within the apartment building as an interior.

The new opacity of the interior, perceived as a private space impervious to an intrusive gaze, corresponded to a newly emphatic equation of the exterior with the public, defined in terms of theatrical display and spectatorship. In *Ce qu'on voit dans les rues de Paris* (1858), Victor Fournel portrayed the familiar urban figure of the *badaud,* similar to the *flâneur* but defined less by walking than by an almost automatic, involuntary, vacant gawking. The *badaud*'s inner being, according to Fournel, becomes completely identified with the external objects at which he stares; the *badaud* "is no longer a man; he is the public, he is the crowd."[33] Fournel's emblematic public man of the street, characterized as an indiscriminate viewer who absorbs and projects himself into all he sees, does not once enter a house or even observe a house facade from the street. His failure to do so suggests the extent to which writers had begun to equate the public realm with a thoroughfare through which one moved forward, and to distinguish the street from the houses situated directly on it.

As the apartment building's interior came to be seen as less available to external vision, and as the street came to be the sole space in which public life was possible, a new sense arose of a division between the inside and the outside, newly defined as opposed and *competing* public and private spheres. Using pronouns like *on* and *nous* to designate a collective unit that rhetorically included men and women of all classes, writers sketched either an unbalanced economy in which resources that they considered proper to the interior were being disastrously transferred to the exterior, or an ecology in which one system, personified as an aggressor (the exterior) subsumed another (the interior). In an economic narrative that traced the imbalance between interior and exterior resources, Dr. Robinet expressed the fixed proportion of interior to exterior existence with an emphatic formula: "the more one provides air and light outdoors, the less there is on the inside!"[34] The implausibility of this statement is highlighted by Robinet's mathematical locution, derived from the public hygienists discussed [in chapter four of *Apartment Stories*], and suggests the extent to which the opposition of interior and exterior was a matter of metaphor, not physical reality. Théophile Gautier, in a contribution to *Paris et les parisiens au XIXe siècle,* argued for ecological destruction by pointing out that the modern valorization of limitlessness and speed had made the street more important than the home, and that as a result, houses were being destroyed to make space for roads: "[Modern] civilization, which needs room for its frenetic activity and perpetual motion, carves out large avenues for itself in the black maze . . . of the old city; civilization knocks down houses."[35] By moving the relatively literal spatial distinction between "avenues" and "houses" into a more metaphorical antagonism between "civilization" and "houses," Gautier translated spatial difference into a temporal one and transferred houses to a more distant, archaic, fragile era—the time of the "forefathers" often invoked, as we have seen, by critics of Haussmannization.

In the course of designating interior and exterior as spatially separate and opposed, writers also came to construe them as attached to distinct social spheres. Nestor Roqueplan's 1853 *La Vie parisienne* achieved this simply by using the word "and" to link the "interior" to the "familial," and by contrasting "domestic duties" to "exterior ambitions."[36] The "interior" no longer marked a space whose physical difference from the exterior was neutral, obvious, and thus trivial; it became identified with *le foyer,* the family home and hearth.[37] The language of a slightly later work, Alfred Delvau's *Histoire anecdotique des cafés et cabarets de Paris* (1862), highlighted the difficulties of aligning the spatial category "exterior" and the sociopolitical category "public." Delvau invoked "Paris, where one gladly exteriorizes one's self. We find it tiresome to live and die at home. . . . We require public display, big events, the street, the cabaret, to witness us for better or for worse . . . we like to pose, to put on a show, to have an audience, a *gallery,* witnesses to our life."[38] Cafés and cabarets were primarily interior spaces, as were galleries (which referred to sections in the theater, salons, and semienclosed porticoes), yet Delvau labeled them public by virtue of their theatricality and their opposition to the domestic space of "at home" [*chez soi*]. Social exteriorization ("public display, big events") logically and syntactically precedes and grounds the physical exteriority of spaces ("the street, the cabaret").[39]

Writers began to vehemently articulate the qualities and resources they believed should be exclusive to the home, often using a negative logic that condemned the presence in the street of what was absent in the home. In *Les Dessous de Paris* (1860), an anthology of articles originally published in the newspaper *Le Figaro*, Delvau argued that the street had become more homelike than the home:

> As soon as it awakes, Paris leaves its abode and steps out, and doesn't return home until as late as possible in the evening—when it bothers to return home. . . . Paris deserts its houses. Its houses are dirty on the inside, while its streets are swept every morning. . . . All the luxury is outside—all its pleasures walk the streets.[40]

Delvau couched his argument for populated, clean, luxurious houses as a reproach against the streets that had those amenities when houses lacked them. In *Paris nouveau et Paris futur* (1865), Victor Fournel hyperbolically argued that the street offered better shelter than modern apartments: "One doesn't live in them, one perches . . . always in a rush to leave and seek out a little air, a little peace and rest in the street—yes, really, a little rest. . . . Where is a home of one's own [*le chez-soi*] possible in Paris?"[41] Fournel himself provides an answer to his rhetorical question—a home is possible in the street—but the opposition between street and home had become so strong that even his attribution of domestic comforts to the street could only serve as an accusation against both the advantages of Parisian boulevards and the deficiencies of the urban residence.

DOMESTIC MANUALS: KEEPING MEN IN THE HOME

A tendency to conceive of the city as divided into distinctly separate interior and exterior spaces also emerged in the sizable corpus of Second Empire and Third Re-

public prescriptive domestic literature, which warned readers of the need to isolate dwellings from outside influences, both moral and material, and which counseled women not only how to create that privacy but how then to keep their families, and particularly their husbands, within the confines of that delimited residential space.

The domestic manuals of the second half of the nineteenth century, which emphasized the need to maintain a hermetically sealed home, represented a drastic shift from earlier prescriptive literature, which had understood domestic interiors as analogous to the sphere of political administration. The 1821 edition of the *Encyclopédie des dames: manuel de la maîtresse de maison, ou lettres sur l'économie domestique,* for example, defined both the woman and her home in relation to abstract qualities such as comfort and order; a woman's domestic work consisted in realizing those idealized concepts.[42] Pariset's 1821 version of female domesticity argued that the foremost beneficiary of domestic order was the woman herself, and that women became tied to their homes because they designed them to cater to their own comfort and pleasure.[43]

The 1852 reedition of Pariset's work, however, no longer commanded women to stay at home in order to enjoy themselves; it told women to stay at home to clean. At a time when the city was being reconfigured as a more sanitary structure from which excrement and corpses would be efficiently removed, the 1852 domestic manual reformulated the home as a tenuously isolated space from which the housewife had to constantly expel dirt. Hygiene replaced comfort in new appendices on specialized techniques for cleaning silver, parquets, iron, wood, and ivory. The authors advised women to cover stair landings with carpets to keep dirt from the street from spreading into the house, recommended shutters to keep out the sun, and gave advice on how to fend off the atmospheric humidity that could corrode objects and bodies alike.[44] Women were now charged with protecting the interior from the exterior, a task to be carried out in the service of the family unit: "the care one must take to preserve the family's health . . . is one of the most important and dearest duties of a housewife."[45]

The domestic manuals of the Second Empire and the Third Republic constituted a popular and profitable genre directed primarily at a Parisian audience; they offered a guide to cultivating a privacy whose precariousness urban observers highlighted, and they shared with works of urban observation a tendency to posit a competition between an isolated conjugal home and commercialized urban leisure. Louise d'Alq, the founding editor of several magazines and the author of numerous treatises on daily life, wrote in *La Vie intime* (1881): "private life, life in the interior of the family, that is what can really be called life." The comtesse de Bassanville's *Trésor de la maison: guide des femmes économes* (1867), written for families with moderate incomes, argued that the city was a dangerous place because its inimical effects on domestic "regularity" and "order" led women to depart from fixed schedules and fall ill. To shelter the home from the city, de Bassanville urged her readers to create a decor that would mark the difference between urban locales and the domestic interior, as in the following advice about wallpaper: "don't ever use red, unless you want your living-room to resemble a restaurant or a café."[46]

Writers of domestic manuals linked the security of the home's spatial enclosure to a social organization based on the difference between men and women. In a manual called *La Science de la vie,* d'Alq advised that women were made to be mothers, not politicians, and should base their identity and that of their homes on their contrast to the men whom their husbands could encounter outside the home: "Man does not need to come back home [*rentrer à son foyer*] to find a second self; that he could find at his club or at a café."[47] D'Alq's use of the verb *rentrer* constituted the home as an interior and origin for the husband, the place that he entered and to which he "returned." She thus defined the home in terms of two conflated differences: the spatial difference between a central point of return and its peripheral but dangerously attractive satellites; and the gendered difference between the wife and the husband, whose very dissimilarity formed the basis for a complementary marital unit. The spatial difference became gendered by making the home both feminine, in the wife's charge, and conjugal, a place in which husband and wife mingled; de Bassanville articulated the imbrication of space and gender in an appositional chapter title, "De l'intérieur, de la famille."[48] Gender difference in turn became spatialized not only because the wife's difference pulled the husband inside, but also because the wife was defined by her anchored presence in the home, the husband by his ability to stay in that home or leave it, according to where his desires could best be fulfilled.

The verb *rentrer* recurred in many domestic manuals, anchoring an ideology that historians have imprecisely termed one of "separate spheres," a nomenclature that implies a symmetry between men and women that did not exist. Domestic manuals envisioned a system in which men could move between the home and its outside, but women could not; men needed to be persuaded to return to the home, while women had to solicit their desire to do so. Manuals from the early 1860s on taught women "to want, thanks to your efforts, your husbands to be happy to return home, after the preoccupations and exhaustion of days laboriously employed."[49] De Bassanville wrote that "an even more valuable result of establishing clear order in one's home is that it keeps one's husband in the house" and that "with know-how

and worldliness, not only will your house be good, but furthermore it will be pleasant, and your husband and children will desert it as little as they can."[50] Guillaume Belèze wrote that the married woman must "cultivate . . . [and] encourage in her husband a taste for family life" and Adolphe Puissant stated that "a woman's greatest point of pride is the cheerfulness of her interior, of the place that most closely reunites the different members of a single family. Our best companions are those who know best how to keep us in our homes."[51]

The conceptual distinction between domestic interior and urban exterior ultimately collapsed for men, since manuals advised women to lure men into the home by making it resemble, in function if not in form, the very spaces against which they initially defined that home. The home resembled a club by becoming a site of homosocial contact for men, a place where men would "take charge of everything that requires contact with other men," and became like a brothel by becoming a place where women catered to men's desires. As far as women were concerned, however, the home remained a consistently interiorized and even carceral space whose oppressive qualities d'Alq barely bothered to dissimulate: "the domestic hearth, the *at home* [in English in the original] . . . occupies such an important place in life . . . that it always deserves . . . to be taken into serious consideration, especially by a woman, for whom it is her prison, or rather her nest, to use a slightly less harsh term."[52]

Notes

1. Ferdinand Silas, "Les propriétaires vengés," *Le Bourgeois de Paris,* May 12, 1855, 4.

2. On Haussmannization, see Jean Castex et al., *Formes urbaines: de l'îlot à la barre* (Paris: Dunod, 1977), 16-19; Jeanne Gaillard, *Paris: la ville, 1852-1870* (Paris: Champion, 1977); David Harvey, "Paris, 1850-1870," in *Consciousness and the Urban Experience* (Baltimore: Johns Hopkins University Press, 1985), 63-220; David Pinkney, *Napoleon III and the Rebuilding of Paris* (Princeton: Princeton University Press, 1958); David Van Zanten, *Building Paris: Architectural Institutions and the Transformation of the French Capital, 1830-1870* (Cambridge: Cambridge University Press, 1994), 214. Literary critics and art historians also often correlate Haussmann's modernization of Paris with the rise of a representational modernism that emphasized vision itself, particularly fleeting or incomplete views, and generated a culture of the crowd, of spectatorship, and of conspicuous consumption. See, for example, Christopher Prendergast, *Paris and the Nineteenth Century* (Oxford: Blackwell, 1992), 6, 8, 69; T. J. Clark, *The Painting of Modern Life: Paris in the Art of Manet and His Followers*

(Princeton: Princeton University Press, 1984); and Priscilla Parkhurst Ferguson, *Paris as Revolution: Writing the Nineteenth-Century City* (Berkeley: University of California Press, 1994). Feminist accounts of modernism by Janet Wolff and Griselda Pollock demonstrate that the designated agents of modernity and modernism, the *flâneur* and the artist, have been defined as necessarily masculine, and that female artists during the Second Empire inscribed urban strictures on female mobility and spectatorship in their paintings; see *Vision and Difference: Femininity, Feminism, and Histories of Art* (London: Routledge, 1988), 66. Pollock bases her argument in part on Janet Wolff's "Invisible *Flâneuse*" (first published in 1985).

3. Napoleon III had, of course, spent many of his years of exile in London and even had a house in the northern London suburb of St. John's Wood. See Alan Montgomery Eyre, *St. John's Wood: Its History, Its Houses, Its Haunts and Its Celebrities* (London: Chapman and Hall, 1913), vi.

4. Leonardo Benevolo mentions Napoleon III's commission of the Henry Roberts translation in *The Origins of Modern Town Planning,* trans. Judith Landry (Cambridge, Mass: MIT Press, 1967), 119.

5. For good summaries of the street improvements in London, which included the installation of gas streetlights; the paving of streets; improved sewage systems; the razing of docks to embank the Thames; the innovation of an underground subway; the renovation and construction of many new monuments; and the spread of many new building types, including hotels, train stations, and office blocks, see Thomas Burke, *The Streets of London through the Centuries,* 4th ed. (London: Batsford, 1949); Percy J. Edwards, *History of London Street Improvements, 1855-1897* (London: London County Council, 1898); Philippa Glanville, *London in Maps* (London: The Connoisseur, 1992), 41-45; Christopher Hibbert, *London: The Biography of a City* (New York: William Morrow, 1969); and Geoffrey Tyack, *Sir James Pennethorne and the Making of Victorian London* (Cambridge: Cambridge University Press, 1992). Edwards, writing for the London County Council, whose creation in the 1880s finally endowed London with a centralized planning committee, emphasized that the mid-Victorian Metropolitan Board of Works had been able to carry out only local, piecemeal changes because it lacked the central powers of finance or expropriation that Haussmann exercised; James Winter (*London's Teeming Streets* [London: Routledge, 1993], 17, 45) also emphasizes the difference between the modernization of London and Paris.

6. Charles Lucas, *Exposition universelle internationale de 1878, à Paris: compte rendu—conférence sur l'habitation à toutes les époques* (Paris: Imprimerie nationale, 1879), 32. In an article on "The Parks" (in *Gavarni in London: Sketches of Life and Character,* ed. Albert Smith [London: Bogue, 1849], 113), Albert Smith remarked on the difficulty of translating English notions of home into French: "It is fortunate that our English words *home* and *comfort* have no synonyms in their language. If they had, the Parisians would be painfully worried to understand the meaning of them." After 1850, however, Parisian urban discourse claimed to understand the meaning of those concepts very well and, as we will see, suggested various means of making Parisian housing conform more closely to the British concept of home.

7. François Sergent, *Nouveau manuel complet du propriétaire et du locataire,* rev. Charles Vasserot (Paris: Roret, 1865), v.

8. For statistics on rent increases, see Adeline Daumard, *Maisons de Paris et propriétaires parisiens au XIXe siècle, 1809-1880* (Paris: Cujas, 1965). For discussions of Haussmannization's effects on Parisians from a range of political perspectives, see Victor Calland and Albert Lenoir, *Institution des palais de famille: solution de ce grand problème—le confortable et la vie à bon marché pour tous,* 2d ed. (Paris, 1855), which advocated combining property ownership with collective living in a utopian domestic program; for similar critiques of Haussmannization, see Taxile Delord, Edmond Texier, and Arnould Frémy, *Mort aux locataires assez canailles pour ne pas payer leurs termes* (1854; Paris: Editions Seesam, 1990); M. Delamarre, "Question des loyers," series in *La Patrie,* 1861; Alexandre Weill, *Paris inhabitable: ce que tout le monde pense des loyers de Paris et personne ne dit,* 3d ed. (Paris: Dentu, 1860). For a conservative view supporting tenants, see M. de Bussy [pseudonym of Charles Marchal], *Question actuelle: propriétaires et locataires—de la cherté des loyers dans Paris-Lyon-Bordeaux-Lille-Rouen-Marseille, etc. et des moyens sûrs et immédiats d'y remédier* (Paris: Eugène Pick, 1857), 10, 11; for a liberal one, see Louis Bellet, "Les Loyers dans Paris," *La Patrie,* April 3, 1861.

9. On landlords in Paris, see Daumard, *Maisons de Paris,* who notes that during the Second Empire, property ownership did become more concentrated in the hands of the wealthier members of the middle class whose main occupation consisted of investing in real estate, in contrast to the earlier part of the nineteenth century, when many people even in the lower middle-class were likely to own one or two buildings (235, 242). Throughout the

century, however, few landlords lived in a building that they owned (253-254).

10. Victor Bellet, *Les Propriétaires et les loyers à Paris* (Paris: Dentu, 1857), 29, 40.

11. Ibid., 38; and Weill, *Paris inhabitable,* 9.

12. Alexandre Weill, *Qu'est-ce que le propriétaire d'une maison à Paris: suite de Paris inhabitable* (Paris: Dentu, 1860), 2.

13. Eugène Pelletan, *La Nouvelle Babylone* (1862), quoted in Judith F. Stone, "The Republican Brotherhood: Gender and Ideology," in *Gender and the Politics of Social Reform in France, 1870-1914,* ed. Elinor Accampo, Rachel Fuchs, and Mary Lynn Stewart (Baltimore: Johns Hopkins University Press, 1995), 42.

14. J. Gaillard, *Paris: la ville,* 525-531; the Goncourts quoted in T. J. Clark, *Painting of Modern Life,* 34, and 274 n. 17; their comments, emended for publication in 1891, were originally made in 1861.

Gaillard's evidence (in what is otherwise a prodigiously researched work) for the introverted nature of Paris during the Restoration and July Monarchy is scanty and bases its interpretations of physical structures on presentist assumptions that have little to do with the social meanings assigned to those structures in the mid-nineteenth century; compare, for example, her discussion of the *passages* (526), to Nicholas Green, *The Spectacle of Nature: Landscape and Bourgeois Culture in Nineteenth-Century France* (Manchester: Manchester University Press, 1990).

For a departure from a simple view of Second Empire Paris as "extroverted," see Clark, *Painting of Modern Life.* Clark shows that Haussmann's Paris was associated as much with an ability to confound legible imagery as with the provision of ordered spectacle (47-50); ultimately, Clark understands Parisian imagery as a homogenizing substitute for real urban relations, Parisian spectacle as antithetical to "collective life" and "complex negotiation in the public realm," and as contemporary with "[t]he essential separation of public life from private, and the thorough invasion of both by capital" (64). In the art of Manet and other avant-garde painters who concentrated on Parisian subjects, Clark finds not only a dialectic between representations of the effacement of class relations and of their "resilience," but also a way of painting that undermined spectacle by presenting vision as fundamentally lacking (64, 72-76). For Clark, the separation of public life from private life and the intensification of public life through its commodification caused a more positive earlier version of the public to disappear.

In *Art Nouveau in Fin-de-Siècle France: Politics, Psychology, and Style* (Berkeley: University of California Press, 1989), Debora L. Silverman offers an interpretation of the Goncourt brothers' house in which she contends that the "impetus to create . . . [a] home as aristocratic fortress was the new invasive metropolis. . . . To struggle against this menace of invasive public life, the Goncourts enclosed themselves in a world of private interiors" (20). Though like Silverman I identify a Second Empire turn to the interior as "fortress," I disagree with her claims that such interiorization was idiosyncratic, that it depended on eighteenth-century aristocratic models, that it necessarily entailed feminization (34, 36), and that it represented a retreat from the city; rather, interiorization was given both a more recent and a much more ancient historical date; it required that the home be defined as masculine; and it acted on urban space in its entirety, making the notion of a retreat from the urban more complex than Silverman suggests.

For a sense of how the arguments I make in this [essay] could be extended to the realm of visual culture, see Michael Fried's recent comments that interiority, not extroversion, defined the modernity of nineteenth-century French painting (*Manet's Modernism, or, The Face of Painting in the 1860s* [Chicago: University of Chicago Press, 1996]). In his reading of the painters he identifies as "The Generation of 1863" and of Edmond Duranty's 1876 critical essay on *La Nouvelle Peinture,* Fried displaces the usual association of modernity in painting with representations of exterior spaces coded as public. Fried notes that "for Duranty and other art critics of the 1860s and 1870s the effect of modernity was closely linked with representations of types [linked to the revival of the *physiologies* in the 1860s], and that in turn was facilitated, if indeed it was not made possible, by the evocation of the particular closed milieux—the absorptive worlds or cloisters—in which those types had their habitual . . . place" (259). After citing Duranty's description of modern drawing as depending on "the observation of the intimacy of man with his apartment" (260), Fried notes that Duranty's essay elaborates "a theory of the cloister into a theory of the *apartment,* or rather of the relation between the modern urban individual and the particular social spaces—interiors and streets—in which he or she was not just to be found but to be found imprinted, habituated, distracted, absorbed" (260); Duranty offers a vision of "a network of spaces which, for all their seeming openness and accessibility, were fundamentally *closed*" (261).

15. Michelle Perrot, "La ménagère dans l'espace parisien au XIXe siècle," *Annales de la recherche urbaine* 9 (1980): 7, 12, 16, 20; Siegfried Kracauer, *Orpheus in Paris: Offenbach and the Paris of His Time,* trans. Gwenda David and Eric Mosbacher (New York: Knopf, 1938), 25; Clark, *Painting of Modern Life,* 50-52, discusses the removal of work from the streets; see also Haine, *Paris Café,* 156; and J. Gaillard, *Paris: la ville,* 329-330.

16. Van Zanten, *Building Paris,* 217.

17. On the perspectival arrangement of streets under Haussmann, see Anthony Sutcliffe, *Paris: An Architectural History* (New Haven: Yale University Press, 1993), 86. Stylistic differences between apartment buildings and monuments became more marked during the Second Empire; see Sutcliffe (*Paris,* 88) and François Loyer (*Paris: Nineteenth-Century Architecture and Urbanism,* trans. Charles Lynn Clark [New York: Abbeville Press, 1988], 237-238), who argues that even though apartment buildings became larger under Haussmann (about one story taller) and hence more monumental in scale, the structural differences between apartments and monuments increased: apartment buildings were attached in rows of uniform height (strictly enforced according to Haussmann's new building regulations), while monuments were free-standing, volumetric rather than planar, and architecturally unique.

18. As contemporary architectural critics have pointed out, when streets get wider and their function as bearers of traffic overrides all other uses, they both reduce the importance of the buildings that flank them and become spatially and phenomenologically independent of them. See William C. Ellis, "The Spatial Structure of Streets," in *On Streets,* ed. Stanford Anderson (Cambridge, Mass.: MIT Press, 1978), 115-118; and Joseph Rykwert, "The Street: The Use of Its History," in *On Streets,* ed. Stanford Anderson (Cambridge, Mass.: MIT Press, 1978), 14-16.

19. See Castex et al., *Formes urbaines,* 154, who write that as family life began to inscribe itself in distinct sites, in specialized neighborhoods within Paris and specialized rooms within the apartment, "housing itself [began to] function . . . in opposition to the exterior"; see also J. Gaillard, *Paris: la ville,* 531.

20. Charles Gourlier, "Des voies publiques et des maisons d'habitation à Paris," *Encyclopédie d'architecture: journal mensuel,* supplement to 2, no. 9 (1852): 73-96. Gourlier represented a solidly mainstream voice in both architecture and urbanism: trained at the Ecole des Beaux-Arts, he worked as an inspector general and belonged to the Société centrale des Architectes.

21. For examples of continuities between July Monarchy and Second Empire urban literature, see texts such as Maxime du Camp's six-volume *Paris: ses organes, ses fonctions et sa vie dans la seconde moitié du XIXe siècle* (1869-75), which anatomized Parisian history, geography, style, and social mores; several important collectively authored anthologies, such as *Paris chez soi* (1854), *Paris et les parisiens au XIXe siècle* (1856), and *Paris-guide* (1867); and the *physiologies* that enjoyed a brief period of renewal from 1866-69.

22. This transformation occurred gradually over the course of the 1850s. The points of view and techniques of July Monarchy writings on the city persisted in some cases into the 1850s. In 1854, for example, a *tableau* called *Paris chez soi* ("Par l'élite de la littérature contemporaine" [Paris: Boizard, 1854], 3) appeared; its title suggested the nascent interiorization of the city but its introductory chapter, entitled "A travers les rues," suggested the continued ease with which writers could speak interchangeably of homes and streets. Significantly, this volume also maintained the generic tradition of emblazoning the "example of the *Diable boiteux* . . . the immortal Asmodeus" across its opening pages.

23. Léo Lespès [pseud. Timothée Trimm], *Spectacles vus de ma fenêtre* (Paris: Faure, 1866).

24. Attesting to the sale value of words connoting domesticity, two collections of stories by Emile Souvestre that had little or nothing to do with home life carried the titles *Les Anges du foyer* (Paris: Michel Lévy, 1858) and *Les Anges du logis* (Pont-à-Mousson: Haugenthal, 1859).

25. On the transition from July Monarchy to Second Empire views of the city in Balzac and Baudelaire, see Ferguson, who writes (*Paris as Revolution,* 94), "Balzac's controlling narrator gives way to Baudelaire's anguished poet, for whom exploration of the city is a pretext for exploration of the self."

26. Emile Souvestre, *Un Philosophe sous les toits: journal d'un homme heureux* (Paris: Michel Lévy, 1850), 1, 6.

27. Ibid., 31.

28. Ibid., 29-34. The narrator's assimilation of every episode and character that he observes into a reflection, a *miroir* of his own personal dilemma (whether to choose an ambitious new job or remain content with his old one) also contributes to his interiorization of the city's heterogeneity into

the homogeneity of his own consciousness. Baudelaire took up the observation of others through a window as a version of self-observation and self-creation in the prose poem "Les Fenêtres" (in *Le Spleen de Paris: petits poèmes en prose* [1869; Paris: Livres de Poche, 1972], 139-140). "Intérieur," a poem by Emile Villars (in *Le Roman de la parisienne [Mélange]* [Paris: Librairie centrale, 1866], 61, 64), similarly incorporated spaces that earlier writers had conceived of as exterior into a single, encapsulating unit. Villars takes up the familiar theme of a man observing a woman in a building that faces his own. The device of repeating every stanza's first line in its last enforces each stanza's unity by enclosing the varied intervening lines between identical phrases. The first stanza immediately asserts the virtual nonexistence of any visual barrier between the two apartments, which become united by the ubiquity of the observing "I": "Je la vois sans qu'elle s'en doute, / Le soir, derrière la redoute / D'un store presque aérien, / Haut rempart qui ne défend rien. / Je la vois sans qu'elle s'en doute." Though the poem thus begins like a July Monarchy seduction story, it departs from those conventions by concluding with the narrator's sensory incorporation of his neighbor's apartment rather than with any actual movement into it: the narrator does not finally see into his neighbor's apartment, nor enter it; instead, he hears what takes place in it. The poem's final stanza begins and ends with the line, "Plus rien. J'entends le lit craquer [Nothing more. I hear her bed creak]," suggesting that though the woman still occupies a physically separate interior, the poet has incorporated it into his own perceptual apparatus without having physically entered it.

29. Louis Jacquier, *L'Amour à Paris* (Paris: Chez tous les libraires, 1862), 147-148, 155-156. Narrower streets would have been associated with Paris before Haussmann.

30. Villars, "Intérieur."

31. Léo Lespès, "La Guerre des fenêtres: journal du siège d'une jolie femme," in *Paris dans un fauteuil: types, histoires et physionomies* (Paris: Lasalle, 1855), 21-35.

32. Edmond Texier, *Le Tableau de Paris* (Paris: Paulin et Le Chevalier, 1852-53), 56, 276.

33. Victor Fournel (*Ce qu'on voit dans les rues de Paris* [Paris: Delahays, 1858], 263, 261) writes that the *badaud* is a "mobile daguerrotype . . . who retains the slightest traces and in whom the city reproduces its movement and the public spirit reproduces its multiple physiognomy."

34. Jean François Eugène Robinet, *"Finissons Paris!" Observations sur l'édilité moderne* (Paris: Ritti, 1879), 12.

35. Théophile Gautier, "Mosaïque de ruines," in *Paris et les parisiens au XIXe siècle* (Paris: Morizot, 1856), 40. The journalist Fournel, author of several works on Paris, combined the economic and the ecological narratives when he wrote in 1865 that "what the administration, in enlarging the streets, has given the city in terms of air, landlords have taken away in even larger measure by shrinking apartments. . . . [T]he vastness and multiplicity of the new roads has whittled away at space everywhere" (Victor Fournel, *Paris nouveau et Paris futur* [Paris: Lecoffre, 1865], 61).

36. The complete quote is "Never, in any era, has there been less interior and familial virtue than today. Everything that one used to give to intimate affections, to domestic duties, now is transferred to insane and completely exterior ambitions" (Nestor Roqueplan, *Regain: la vie parisienne* [Paris: Librairie nouvelle, 1853], 44).

37. Gustave Claudin, *Paris* (Paris: Dentu, 1862), 80.

38. Alfred Delvau, *Histoire anecdotique des cafés et cabarets de Paris* (Paris: Dentu, 1862), v.

39. Although cafés began to put tables out on the street during this period, the majority of seats were still located inside the building and writers continued to refer to even the largest café as a *maison*. See, for example, Gustave Claudin, *Entre minuit et une heure: étude parisienne* (Paris: Dentu, 1868), 29.

40. Alfred Delvau, *Les Dessous de Paris* (Paris: Poulet-Malassis, 1860), 3-5, 8, 133-135.

41. Fournel, *Paris nouveau*, 61, 71.

42. Pariset's advice (Mme Pariset, *Encyclopédie des dames: manuel de la maîtresse de maison, ou lettres sur l'économie domestique* [Paris: Audot, 1821], 4, 8) on economizing, on choosing and furnishing an apartment, on supervising servants, and on cooking and dressing, emphasized qualities also considered essential to governing or running a business: spatial and temporal regulation, "order" and "regularity." Pariset's use of an administrative metaphor to describe the housewife's financial duties also rendered women's work equivalent to bourgeois men's: "Consider yourself," a friend tells a prospective bride, "a true minister of the interior, and never neglect the direction of your administration." The tendency to equate the home with a political office appeared in other domestic manuals written during the 1820s. Marie-Armande Gacon-Dufour's *Manuel complète*

de la maîtresse de maison . . . ou guide pratique pour la gestion d'une maison à ville et à la campagne (Paris: Roret, 1826) indicated by its very title that the work of the home differed little from work in an administrative or commercial concern—all required skilled *gestion,* a noun meaning management or administration with legal, political, and financial connotations. The 1828 reedition of that work emphasized the financial rewards of the housewife's expertise; its subtitle was *Guide pratique pour la gestion d'une maison et de la parfaite ménagère, ou guide pratique pour la gestion d'une maison à la ville et à la campagne, contenant les moyens d'y maintenir le bon ordre et d'y établir l'abondance,* 2d ed., rev. and expanded by Mme Celnart (Paris: Roret, 1828). Gacon-Dufour's 1826 text opened with an aphorism: "Every mistress of a house probably has her *régime d'administration*" (1). The use of a term as redolent of bureaucratic politics as *régime d'administration* suggested that the housewife performed work equivalent to her husband's; the use of the generalizing adjective *toute* suffused the statement with an imperative, universalizing force that identified all housewives as a class of worker.

43. Pariset wrote of "the imperious sentiment which a woman must feel for her home [*son chez-elle*]" but argued that women experienced a "need to stay in or return to" their homes only because they had made them into private paradises for themselves, not for their families: "she must feel [*se trouver*] better there than anywhere else; she must stay there as much as possible." The use of the imperative word "must [*doit*]" lends authority to this prescription for self-indulgence, while the reflexive form "*se trouver*" emphasizes the self-pleasuring, self-sufficient character of this location (ibid., 23).

44. Mme Pariset, *Nouveau manuel complet de la maîtresse de maison, suivi d'un appendice par Mesdames Gacon-Dufour, Celnart* (Paris: Roret, 1852), 288.

45. Ibid., 315. For a discussion of how domestic manuals targeted women for the inculcation of new standards of cleanliness, see Geneviève Heller, *"Propre en ordre": habitation et vie domestique 1850-1930—l'exemple vaudois* (Lausanne: Editions d'en bas, 1979). On changes in bourgeois attitudes toward dirt, see Alain Corbin, *The Foul and the Fragrant: Odor and the French Social Imagination* (Cambridge, Mass.: Harvard University Press, 1986).

46. La comtesse de Bassanville, *Le Trésor de la maison: guide des femmes économes* (Paris: Brumet, 1867), 35.

47. Louise d'Alq, *La Vie intime,* 2d ed. (Paris: Bureaux des *Causeries familières,* 1881), ix; *La Science de la vie: conseils et réflexions à l'usage de tous* (Paris: Bureaux des *Causeries familières,* n.d.), 206-207.

48. La comtesse de Bassanville, *L'Art de bien tenir une maison* (Paris: Librairie H. Aniéré, 1878).

49. Julie Fertiault, *Le Ménagier français* (Paris: Bureaux du Conseiller des Dames et des Demoiselles, 1863), 7.

50. De Bassanville, *Trésor de la maison,* 6; and *Art de bien tenir,* 2.

51. M. G. Belèze, *Le Livre des ménages: nouveau manuel d'économie domestique* (Paris: Hachette, 1860), 365; Adolphe Puissant, *De l'économie domestique et de l'éducation dans les classes ouvrières* (Paris: Baillière, 1872), 7.

52. D'Alq, *Le Maître et la maîtresse de la maison* (Paris: Bureaux des *Causeries familières,* n.d.), 14.

Michael Hollington (essay date September 1997)

SOURCE: Hollington, Michael. "Dickens, *Household Words,* and the Paris Boulevards (Part One)." *Dickens Quarterly* 14, no. 3 (September 1997): 154-64.

[*In the following first part of a two-part essay, Hollington outlines the writings of Charles Dickens and contributors to his periodical,* Household Words, *on the reconfiguration of Paris.*]

1. GUSTAVE

"October 4, 185-. No. 9. A male child; newly born; weakly and very small; ticket round the neck with the name of Gustave; coarse linen; red stain on the left shoulder; no other mark." This is how Dudley Costello, at the end of his impressive *Household Words* article "Blank Babies in Paris" (17 December 1853), translates the registry entry for a new arrival at the Foundling Hospital in Paris in the Rue d'Enfer. The language may be terse and severely factual, but Costello, responding to Dickens's editorial policy of "dwelling on the romantic side of familiar things," is able to wring metaphor and symbol from his subject. As a kind of Victorian Raymond Williams, he starts by interrogating the etymology of that street name: it comes from Via Inferior, but, Costello remarks: "a poetical imagination soon made the corruption" that ensures that infant orphans in Paris are brought up in the street of hell. The building on that street may be strikingly plain and anonymous ("it lay before us, grey, blank, and dreary, with nothing to relieve the monotony of its general aspect . . .") but the writer is able to imagine its very absence of significant features as pregnant with significance, for it is a place "where no witness might see the trembling mother deposit her new-born child."

Dickens himself, in one of the numerous writings in which orphans play a central role, would later describe a similar psychological moment in his story *No Thoroughfare* (written in collaboration with Wilkie Collins), where a mother passes through the streets of London on her way to Coram Street to deposit her illegitimate child: "As above her there is the purity of the moonlit sky, and below her there are the defilements of the pavement, so may she, haply, be divided in her mind between two vistas of reflection or experience. As her footprints crossing and recrossing one another have made a labyrinth in the mire, so may her track in life have involved itself in an intricate and unravellable tangle" (*CS*, 539-40). Here, in what is unambiguously an imaginative piece of writing, the allegorical tendencies latent in Costello's article come to the fore. In two sentences, the city is imagined as a systematically organized totality of zones of contrasting significance. The first sentence proposes a vertical axis in which high signifies transcendental beauty and purity and low symbolizes physical and moral ugliness and dirt. The second considers the city from a horizontal perspective, and treats the labyrinthine patterns of her hesitant journey through mazy streets to the Foundling Hospital as an emblem of the complex uncertainty of human destiny.

This paper aims to investigate Dickens's critical responses to Paris in the 1850s—that is to say, to the city under Haussmann and Louis Napoleon, in the throes of a painful transition towards *modernity*—as well as those of the writers who worked for him on *Household Words*. But as it does this, it will also examine the important role played by allegory in the articulation of these reactions. We shall be concerned to try to develop some outlines of a Dickensian poetics of the city that has much in common (we may note this at moments only, as we do not have space here to develop the comparison in detail), particularly in its emphasis upon allegory and transcendence, with that of his contemporary Charles Baudelaire. Its emphasis is inevitably upon visual features of the city. It goes without saying that vertical categories like high and low or horizontal ones like straight and crooked are imagined from the standpoint of an observer who looks up and down and round and about at the sights before him, and all the writings we shall examine construct this observer through the imaginary figure of the *flâneur*. In these papers, the figure of the *flâneur* represents a kind of city dilettante of the eye, casually strolling in search of visual experience from which he will remain essentially detached. Paris is essentially imagined as a spectacle which first fixes the observer's gaze, and then lures him on (for the *flâneur* is quintessentially male, and the city regularly female) to pursue and pin down its significance.

But before examining in detail the most obvious theater of this spectacle—the Parisian boulevards and arcades—it would be worth dwelling on Gustave and his surroundings a little longer, for there is a clear link here (via their equivalents in London) with those archetypes. It is striking how the new arrivals are laid out in the foundling hospital as if in a display case:

> . . . directly in front of a blazing fire, on an inclined plane, covered with a mattrass about the size of the stage of Mr Simpson's Marionette Theatre, lay seven or eight little objects all in a row, who might have passed for the Marionnettes themselves only they were much smaller, were anything but gaily attired, and were a great deal too tightly swathed to stir a single peg, whereas the amusing puppets of the Lowther Arcade—but all the world is familiar with the flexibility and grace of their movements.

The ticket round Gustave's neck, though intended to confer identity and to facilitate eventual reclaim, thus also appears to label him as an item for sale in a shopping mall. There are links with Dickens's own article "Dullborough Town," reprinted in *The Uncommercial Traveller*, where "four (five) deceased young people lay, side by side, on a clean cloth on a chest of drawers; reminding me by a homely association, which I suspect their complexion to have assisted, of pig's feet as they are usually displayed at a neat tripe-shop" (*UTRP*, 118-19), with another interesting piece by Costello, "Dead Reckoning at the Morgue" (*HW* 1 October 1853) where, in a "*Salle d'Exposition*," corpses are exhibited, "the clothes . . . hung up over the corpse in such a manner that they can be readily recognised" and "the body itself . . . placed on a dark slab, slightly inclining towards the spectator," and finally with Dickens's "Railway Dreaming," where, again in discussing the morgue, he remarks that "perhaps all the world knows that the bodies lie on incline planes within a great glass window, as though Holbein should represent Death, in his grim Dance, keeping a shop, and displaying his goods like a Regent Street or Boulevard linen-draper" (*HW* 10 May 1856). In mid-century Paris, one might conclude that in their 'progress' from cradle to grave human individuals constantly present themselves, or are presented, as commodities for recognition and/or purchase. In the time of the previous foundling hospital, Costello tells us, a nurse whose charge had died through negligence had only to pop round to the equivalent institution to buy a new one, at the then going rate of twenty sous.

2. FLANERIE

"We are coming to Paris expressly to be looking about us," Dickens wrote to his friend François Régnier of the Comédie Française, announcing a trip in the company of Wilkie Collins in the Carnival season of 1855 (*Letters* 7: 522). The unreliable Robert du Pontavice de Heussey cites a comparable letter to Forster which he mistakenly dates to October 1855, but his translation of its contents brings out clearly the kind of activity envisaged: "Nous avons décidé, W. Collins et moi, que pendant au moins une bonne semaine, nous serions de simples touristes anglais, badauds et flâneurs, et non pas les inimitables écrivains que chacun sait" ("We have decided, Collins and I, that for at least a good week, we would be mere English tourists, idlers and curious, and not the inimitable writers whom everybody knows," Pontavice de Heussey 294; Surveyer 55). Dickens and his companion would be stepping into the incognito of the touristic *flâneurs* strolling around Paris, stopping to inquire here and there about objects and persons that catch their gaze and arouse their curiosity.

But despite the desire to remain anonymous, the object of this ostensibly objectless activity, then or thereafter, *was* in fact writing, as Dickens announced the following year: "I think I have a good idea for a series of Paris papers into which I can infuse a good deal of myself, if Collins comes here (as I think he will) for some time" (*Letters* 8: 24). The project never materialized, partly, perhaps, because Collins was not well enough at the time to withstand the rigours of *flânerie* Dickensian-style, which involved as a mere starter a three hour walk each afternoon. "We breakfast at ten, read and write till two, and then I go out walking all over Paris, while the invalid sits by the fire or is deposited in a cafe. We dine at five" (*Letters* 7: 540). But like the sick boy in the Yiddische Mama joke, whose mother tells him to practice his violin in bed, Collins still managed some imaginary production of flâneurial boulevard images in the first part of his "Laid Up in Two Lodgings" (*HW* 7 June 1856): "At Paris as before in London I looked at the world about me."

Dickens and Collins's routine in Paris, then, up to a point at least, resembled that of contemporary Parisian *flâneurs*. In "Dr. Véron's Time" (*HW* 19 April 1856), George Augustus Sala describes the Palais Royal—their high temple—where Dickens would regularly dine at five at their high table, his favorite Parisian restaurant *Les Trois Frères Provençaux*: "in wet weather it supplies him [the *flâneur*] with an unequalled promenade, sheltered from the pattering rain, in the shape of four magnificent arcades, where he may lounge, loaf, or flâner at his leisure." And Douglas Jerrold describes the day as it is spent by a left-bank student practitioner of the art in "Near the Pantheon" (*HW* 12 August 1854) in terms that offer similarities to theirs. He too begins with "two dishes for breakfast, about ten," but after that the half bottle of *vin ordinaire* that accompanies them seems to prevent him from serious activity ("he should be off to his business—perhaps to the dissecting-room of a hospital, or to the studio of some great painter, his

master"). He finds that to "saunter into the Luxembourg gardens, to promenade while the band of one of the regiments is playing, is certainly a more pleasant proceeding." Yet as with Dickens and Collins there is artistic justification to hand: "if the stroller be an artist, may he not, in his walk, study character?"

Numerous writers about Paris in *Household Words* develop further defining features of what Sala calls "the legionary *flâneurs*" on "the much sauntered over Boulevards"("Arcadia," *HW* 18 June 1853), who provide the model for their own literary *personae*. In his article "Four Stories" (*HW* 26 June 1852), Sala uses a florid zoological and taxonomical metaphor to explain what he as a *flâneur* is doing: "I, the indigent philosopher, whose vocation it is to observe, and from the kennel of social peculiarities, fish, with the crook of reflection, queer fragments of life and manners." Flânerie is depicted as an art of divining social truths about France by reading the fleeting fragments of perception that are available on the boulevards. As such, it is a discipline of sorts, one that needs to be learned, if only through practice: in an article entitled "Monsieur Gogo's" for instance, the writer looks back on a time "when we were novices in the Trivia or art of walking the streets of Paris" (*HW* 31 January 1852), and thereby alludes to John Gay's poem *Trivia, or the Art of Walking the Streets of London,* of which Dickens was fond—he quotes it in a letter to Millais of 1855 for instance (*Letters* 7: 589). Blanchard's article "A Ball at the Barriers" (*HW* 17 May 1851), though, gives the game away when he characterizes the finished article, the mature and seasoned *flâneur,* as a kind of Bohemian, "an arrant philosophic, a true, observant, metaphysical vagabond." But elsewhere, going into greater detail, he presents the *flâneur* as a kind of sociologist, someone who walks in the crowd and reads in the gestures of those about him miniature epiphanies of the social upheavals taking place in the Paris of the 1850s: "who can walk about Paris for a couple of hours . . . without observing a thousand little revolutions, of a social and perhaps unimportant character, but which seem to concern him more than all the great political changes." ("More French Revolutions," *HW* 13 September 1851).

3. SPECTACLE

Where nowadays parents put their children in front of the TV set, Dickens chose in 1855 to take lodgings on the Champs Elysées because the view from the window would provide an admirable family spectacle to keep everyone busy and amused. He rejected first a lodging in the Rue Faubourg St. Honoré which looked out on a courtyard: "it would never have done for the children" (*Letters* 7: 720). Here, by contrast, they had "all Paris perpetually passing under the window" (*Letters* 7: 722). It offered, as he put it in a third letter, "a moving panorama outside which is Paris in itself" (*Letters* 7: 724).

Thus the family had front row seats for the spectacle of Parisian life. As tourists, they may have been responding unconsciously to the new accents of modern consumption that were gaining ground in Paris at that time, the drive towards the provision of that accessibility to the eye of everything in the field of vision at one single glance which Benjamin analyses in contemporary panoramas, or in contemporary Parisian department stores, where for the first time ticketed commodities (like Gustave in the Foundling Hospital) were presented simultaneously in broad and unencumbered space for the orgiastic delectation of the consumer's eye. "L'Europe s'est déplacé pour voir les marchandises" ("Europe came to see the merchandise"), wrote Hippolyte Taine in 1855 (Benjamin 50).

The variety and extent and uninterrupted continuity of the sights to be seen from 49 Champs Elysées provided a veritable "Parisian Nights Entertainments," to quote the title of an article by Sala that appeared in *The Train* on 1 January 1856 (see *Letters* 8: 20). It is Sala, too, again in "Dr. Véron's Time," who makes the connection in *Household Words* between such feasts for the eye and the exotic comestibles on display at the Palais Royal to the *flâneur,* who might gaze longingly but not partake, i.e. "train up his appetite in the way it should go by gazing at glowing panoramas of rare eatables and drinkables displayed in the larders of the great Restaurants, and in the window of the immortal Chevet." (*HW* 19 April 1856). As Kracauer suggests, the boulevards offered a kind of drug experience—literally so, perhaps, for invalid opium-consumers like Wilkie Collins who in "Laid up in Two Lodgings" comments on the "everlasting gaiety and bustle of the Champs Elysées' with its "confused phantasmagoria of gay colours and rushing forms" (*HW* 7 June 1856), and takes us into the world of impressionist painting.

Dickens's attitude towards the Parisian spectacle can be seen as ambivalent, or even contradictory. Of course he revelled in "the view without, astounding . . . the wonderful life perpetually flowing up and down" (*Letters* 7: 724). But in his psyche there were sensitivities about what it was like to be, not the voluntary observer, but the involuntarily observed. These might be said to center around the (for him) negative word "Exhibition," and a complex of emotions perhaps stemming from having felt himself as a boy to be an exhibit in a display case as he labelled blacking-bottles at a window—it was the reason his father removed him from that employment. He boycotted The Great Exhibition at the Crystal Palace in 1851, encased as it was in see-through glass, and didn't want to go to that in Paris in 1855, writing in May of the same year that "he had not the faintest idea of adding his personality to the French Exhibition, after flying one hundred miles from the English" (*Letters* 7: 606)—the point again, seemingly, that he did not want to make himself one of the exhibits.

For him it was a splendid thing to look out of windows, but his attitude to being looked at—whether the looks were invited or uninvited—was more complex.

But in the end Dickens did attend the art section of the Paris exhibition, where he was impressed by what he saw of contemporary French art, and about which he writes interestingly in his *Household Words* piece 'Insularities' (*HW* 19 January 1856). One may read in the discriminations he makes here and in the related letter to Forster (*Letters* 7: 742-4) between "the dramatic" and "the theatrical" a clue to his responses to Parisian street life. On the one hand he dismisses formal spectacle, as he finds it in English painting at the exhibition, even that of his friend Clarkson Stanfield—"too much like a set-scene" (*Letters* 7: 743). He is equally harsh, in Paris, on formal parades outdoors (such as those organized for political purposes during the Crimean War by Louis Napoleon) and classical theater indoors. What he admires at the exhibition are narrative genre scenes capturing spontaneous fleeting moments of contemporary life and manners, and it is worth remembering—to gauge the sensitivity to changing taste in his reactions—that, in Loyrette's words, "le succès de la scène de genre, établi depuis l'exposition universelle de 1855, a joué un role important dans l'adoption de plus en plus frequente des sujets tirés de la vie moderne" ("the success of the genre scene, which became established after the Universal Exhibition of 1855, played an important role in the increasingly frequent adoption of subjects drawn from modern life," Loyrette 270). In his article Dickens notes the insularity of English people who dismiss French painting as "theatrical," to which he retorts: "Conceiving the difference between a dramatic picture and a theatrical picture, to be, that in the former case a story is strikingly told, without apparent consciousness of a spectator, and that in the latter case the groups are obtrusively conscious of a spectator, and are obviously dressed up, and doing (or not doing) certain things with an eye to the spectator, and not for the sake of the story; we sought in vain for this defect" (*HW* 19 January 1856). French painting is dramatic, and therefore true, because French and other Continental European styles of self-expression are dramatic: as Forster puts it, summarizing Dickens's views, "the French themselves are a demonstrative and gesticulating people . . . and what thus is rendered by their artists is the truth through an immense part of the world" (*Letters* 7: 743). The *flâneur*/writer's delight in Parisian spectacle could certainly be justified if it focussed on its "dramatic" qualities' rather than its "theatrical" ones.

4. FROM *VANITY FAIR* TO *RAG FAIR*

One needs to retain these distinctions, together with a sense of the ambivalence of Parisian spectacle and of the Champs Elysées, as one examines the innumerable references to what W. H. Wills in the pages of *House-*

hold Words describes as "the love of ornament and the passion for display" in the French capital ("Paris Improved," *HW* 17 November 1855). Sidney Blanchard's piece "Painting the Lily" catches some of them, its title doing a part of the work—there is a lily in Paris, and/ but it is painted. His tone clearly shades into ironic criticism: "It was Easter, and a great gathering of the idleness of all nations was making an exhibition of itself in the *Champs Elysées,* assisting at the *fête* of Longchamps." (*HW* 31 May 1851). As W. M. Thomas puts it in "Sentimental Journalism," again with a hint of irony: "The French live, move, and have their being for 'effect'" (*HW* 28 February 1852), or, as Bernard Marchand puts it, describing the second half of the nineteenth century, "la bourgeoisie ne cacha plus sa fortune, mais l'exhiba de façon d'abord retenue, puis avec une exubérance croissante" ("the bourgeoisie no longer concealed its wealth; on the contrary, it began to display it, in a restrained way at first, then later with increasing exuberance," Marchand 93). In this context, too, Jerrold's "Paris Upon Wheels" introduces the big topic of sexual exhibition on the Paris boulevards by describing the carriages that ply along the Champs Elysées and elsewhere, "in which lorettes display the latest fashion." He gives clear hints that the purpose of their display is commercial: "so brisk is the business of love and show and vanity, that ample business is found within the fortifications for five thousand six hundred and seventy-one of these carriages" (*HW* 2 December 1854).

But the most resonant word in this passage is "vanity." The allegory that in *Household Words* integrates representations of the display on the boulevards into Dickensian city poetics stems, like most of Dickens's most powerful allegorical conceptions (the pilgrimage of Little Nell for instance), from Bunyan. It is Sala in his description in "Arcadia" of Burlington Arcade, of which the Arcades of Paris, where *flâneurs* saunter and observe the fashionable display, have reminded him, who makes the point explicit: "It was a little Vanity Fair. I have walked it many and many a time for years, thinking of John Bunyan" (*HW* 18 June 1853). E. S. Dixon's "The Hall of Wines" contains other direct allusion, when it describes the seclusion of the "Halle-aux-Vins," despite its proximity to the lively Quai St. Bernard on the banks of the Seine, "which allows it to gaze at the Vanity Fair, while it separates it from too familiar contact with the world" (*HW* 2 February 1856). But it is once more Costello, in the third of his major articles on Paris, "Rag Fair in Paris," who develops the metaphor in the most imaginative way, deflecting it away from "theatrical" commonplace in the direction of sharp probing into the "drama" of Parisian display (*HW* 25 November 1854).

He is not, to begin with, as taken in by the myth of intrinsic Parisian 'theatricality' as some of the contributors mentioned above seem to be—all he is prepared to

say is that "Parisians make more of themselves externally than we do," a modest assertion immediately qualified with the equivalent of the modern "and that's not hard": "a thing easily accomplished." His subject is clothes and fashion, but not only in its dandy connotation of newness and modernity: he satirizes a tailor in the Palais Royal who tries to sell him a suit "made of cashmere, of a bright, butter-cup yellow . . . profusely embroidered with scarlet braid, of a wormy pattern": "I invented that costume chiefly for in-doors wear; in the morning, at breakfast, for example, for study and for repose." His thoughts turn to the costume's 'progress' from cradle to grave, and on a flâneurial impulse he takes a cab to the second-hand clothes market on the Boulevard du Temple.

It is at this point that allegory becomes prominent. From now on he follows a Dantean downward spiral, first through the labyrinth of the streets: "cabmen have one common propensity in all great cities; they invariably choose their course through the narrowest and most obscure streets." Arriving at the market, he praises its brightness, practicality and utility, but his attention is especially fixed by allegorical emblems, the "painted signs ad libitum" attached to the stalls. "In the display of these they exhibit great brilliancy of imagination and richness of fancy"—sufficient, certainly, to interest a contemporary Lacanian:

> The next, "A la gueule dans (en) peine" is a painted rebus, explained by a bar of music (la), a mouth wide open (gueule), a set of teeth (dents), and a comb (peigne). All honour to the inventor of this hieroglyphic! Equally obscure in its application to her trade is the sign over the shop of Madame Meswinkal, who, for some unexplained reason, chooses to call herself a mouse (dite Souris). Her emblem, "A la petite souris," exhibits a lively representation of a ham, a loaf of bread, a knife, a tumbler, and a mouse and a mouse-trap. On looking at it, I asked myself these questions— not wishing to disturb Madame Meswinkal, who had fallen asleep while in the act of mending an old shoe— Why should the mouse be expected to go into the trap when the provisions are placed on the floor? And of what use to a mouse are an empty tumbler and a table-knife? Accessories, you will say, which convey to the mind a notion of the plenty which begets temptation; but again I ask, in what respect do they concern boots and shoes.

One is travelling, in this remarkably Dickensian comic writing, towards a Warren's Blacking cryptogram, the last sign mentioned being *Le coq et la botte* ("the cock and the boot"), "perhaps intended to impress one with the belief that a well-polished boot is many degrees superior to a looking-glass." And beyond that, to further social depths—past the Rotonde nearby, where second-hand clothes are recycled and sold for theatrical costumes, past the *chiffoniers* hunting for scraps of rag, towards someone whom Costello labels a *marchand de ficelle*: "he poked out a few discoloured rags, turned them over carefully, and then, as something caught his eye, stooped and picked it up. It was a piece of string, which he put into a basket, already half full of similar fragments . . . and very likely made a good thing of it." Whereupon the writer has reached, so to speak, the Rue de l'Enfer again: "As I did not expect to find a lower deep than this, I went back to my citadine and took leave of Rag Fair."

What writers like Costello or Henry Morley, the most serious and learned of all the contributors to *Household Words,* were able to perceive was that the France of the Second Empire had become a "theatrical" Vanity Fair, in which painted surface covered over scandal and social injustice at home and abroad. This was not something permanent and absolute, endemic in the nature of "the French," as that stereotype was constructed by the prejudices of the insular British public: it was a specific historical and social moment produced by a strikingly modern politics of entertainment and distraction. While there was gaiety in Paris, there was death in the Crimea: "Offiziere, die aus der Krim zurückkehrten, und einige oppositionelle Politiker beanstandeten zwar, daß sich Paris amüsierte, während man in den Gräben vor Sebastopol starb, aber der Kaiser wünschte es so" ("Officers back from the Crimea and a few opposition politicians protested that Paris was having fun while men were dying in the trenches at Sebastopol, but the Emperor wanted it like this," Kracauer 152). In Morley's article "The Theatres of Paris" (*HW* 2 October 1852), Louis Napoleon is described as "the temporary manager of France," a rather bad impresario who is losing customers to "the real drama" of contemporary Paris:

> Although the temporary manager of France deals largely himself in fireworks and pageants offered gratuitously to the public; yet his spectacles have, for the most part, failed through so much adversity of wind and weather, that the traditional doom of Vauxhall seems to be upon him; and, after all, the legitimate drama may not have suffered greatly through his competition.

This was the kind of society in which operetta could emerge, writes Kracauer, because the society in which it emerged had become operetta-like. ("Die Operette konnte entstehen, weil die Gesellschaft, in der sie entstand, operettenhaft war"—Kracauer 186). He calls it "Die Musik des Goldes"—the music of gold, or, of course, money. One of the jokes of the time referred to "les comptes fantastiques de Haussmann." The enormous cost of transforming Paris led to feverish Stock Market speculation, during which fortunes could be won and lost overnight.

This was part of the 'drama' of the Parisian Vanity Fair of the time that the *Household Words flâneurs* attempt to chronicle. "Every year the Bourse counts new lucky adventurers," writes Jerrold in "Paris Upon Wheels."

(*HW* 2 December 1854); he had given an example of one such in his "The French Waiter," which examines waiter-speculators in restaurants like *Les Trois Frères Provencaux*: "the most fortunate of them may be known to some of their visitors as jobbers on the Bourse" (*HW* 15 July 1854). Sala in "Four Stories," his portrait of the vertical allegory contained in the Parisian apartment house of the Second Empire, writes of "M. Ulysse de Saint-Flamm, forty-five years of age, decorated, wearing a white neckcloth": "he is not a stockbroker, though he is every day on the Bourse, frantic with financial combinations, bursting with bargains" (*HW* 26 June 1852). But the theme is already present in very early numbers of the journal—in Wills's "A New Joint-Stock Pandemonium Company" for instance, about a very Montague Tigglike Stock-Exchange prospectus in Paris seeking investors to make surefire profit by putting money into a scheme to construct, export and operate a casino in San Francisco (20 July 1850). Wills could see clearly the self-contradicting fantasies at work in the linking of gambling and stock exchange speculation: he calls it "gaming without risk, certainty in chance." No wonder, then, that Dickens found that *Martin Chuzzlewit* was a very popular book in Paris when he arrived at the moment of its serialisation in *Le Moniteur* in October 1855. He took note of what he saw, and moved on from Tigg to Merdle.

Notes

To be continued in December, at which time the list of Works Cited will appear.

Michael Hollington (essay date December 1997)

SOURCE: Hollington, Michael. "Dickens, *Household Words,* and the Paris Boulevards (Part Two)." *Dickens Quarterly* 14, no. 4 (December 1997): 199-212.

[*In the following second part of a two-part essay, Hollington outlines the writings of Charles Dickens and contributors to his periodical,* Household Words, *on the reconfiguration of Paris.*]

5. Carnival and Sexual Display

As Monte Carlo would again discover later in the century, where there were fortunes to be made through gambling and speculation, a flowering of prostitution of all kinds and at all levels would necessarily also follow. Zola remarks of Paris at this time in *La Curée* that "la ville n'était plus qu'une grande débauche de millions et de femmes" ("the city was no longer anything but a great debauch of millions and of women," Marchand 86); and Sala mentions more obliquely, in "Dr. Véron's Time" in *Household Words,* a certain gaming house in the Rue du Temple with the name "Maison Paphos."

The journal could and did write discreetly about prostitution and casual sex in Paris without having to make any direct reference to either simply by using French code words such as *lorette* and *grisette,* the one defined by Marchand as "simple prostituée ou grande cocotte" ("straightforward prostitutes or women of very easy virtue": the *lorettes* got their name because they first congregated in the vicinity of Notre-Dame-de-Lorette), the other as "petite ouvrière libre et galante qui aime pour le plaisir" ("humble free-and-easy working-class girls who made love for pleasure's sake," Marchand 12). Thus Blanchard's 'A Ball at The Barriers' urges "the student of character" (necessarily male of course) to "betake himself . . . to the haunts of the 'common people'" such as one of the *bals* at the Barrière du Montparnasse, of which Marchand comments: "les 'Vénus de barrière' y régnaient, mêlées aux familles d'ouvriers er d'artisan' ("the 'venuses of the barrières' ruled there, mingled amongst the families of workers and artisans,' Marchand 23).

Dickens's quite complex attitudes to prostitution in Paris again center around the question of public display. "In a great City, Prostitution *will be somewhere,*" he announces to Bulwer Lytton in August 1855 (*Letters* 7: 691). That somewhere should not be as public as the theater, he says—as had been the case in London in theaters like the Theatre Royal, Haymarket before 1843. Paris offers a better model—in February he had seen prostitutes at the theater, but "they were of the Audience, and conducted themselves like the rest of the Audience, and nobody was obliged to know the truth." Fortunately in London too a "Dancing Establishment" (the National Argyll Rooms) had come into existence after the banning of prostitutes from the Theatre Royal, and, according to Dickens, "the Police has shewn a sound discretion in not interfering with it."

Thus Dickens seems to have been in favor of the principle of the Parisian *bals* and *maisons closes* and the whole effort of Haussmann and Louis Napoleon to drive prostitution indoors: "les grandes percées d'Haussmann, en ouvrant Paris, avaient éclairé les voies publiques, assuré une meilleure sécurité et moralisé le trottoir" ("The great wedges driven by Haussmann opened up Paris, lit up the public ways, provided greater security and moralised the street pavements") writes Marchand (208). There were nearly 300 brothels during the Second Empire, many of them lavishly appointed, as prostitutes became luxury commodities like perfumes or expensive items of fashion. And despite his use of the allegorical capital letter 'P' in his letter to Bulwer Lytton, Dickens appears to have known a few of these establishments on the inside. He writes to Spencer Lyttleton in November about his disappointment that "the model (and moral) establishment *is* suppressed—the big number taken down—a dull honest trade driving under the gateway—a melancholy respectability has fallen on that fascinating mansion. I shed a tear, over the way, every Sunday" (*Letters* 7: 738). The Pilgrim House editors footnote a little timidly: "given Lyttelton's scapegrace reputation, perhaps a brothel"; I think we can be a little bit more definite than that, particularly if we take into account the letter to Collins dated 22 April 1856:

> On Saturday night, I paid three francs at the door of that place where we saw the wrestling, and went in, at 11 o-Clock, to a Ball. Much the same as our own National Argyll Rooms. Some pretty faces, but all of two classes—wicked and coldly calculating, or haggard, and wretched in their worn beauty. Among the latter, was a woman of thirty or so, in an Indian shawl, who never stirred from a seat in a corner at the time I was there. Handsome, regardless, brooding, and yet with some nobler qualities in her forehead. I mean to walk about tonight, and look for her. I didn't speak to her there, but I have a fancy I should like to know more about her. Never shall, I suppose.

> (*Letters* 8: 96)

This is fascinating material. It would not appear that Dickens is simply on a busman's holiday from his philanthropic activities on behalf of Miss Coutts for Urania Cottage; and even if he thought he was, there is Joachim Schlör's comment on the prostitute-reformers of the nineteenth century to take into account: "es kann durchaus sein, daß die Missionare . . . bei ihrer Tätigkeit ein—verdrängtes, verleugnetes, abgewehrtes—erotisches Vergnügen empfanden" ("it may very well be that the missionaries experienced erotic pleasure—repressed, denied, dismissed—during their activities," Schlör 250). Through his morgue-watching—we might compare Baudelaire's reply to a friend who asked him what he was up to as he scrutinised the girls on offer at the Casino: "mon cher ami, je regarde passer des têtes de mort!" ("my dear friend, I'm watching deaths-heads pass by!", Pichois and Avice 116)—he singles out a face he intends to stalk a second night, apparently this time outdoors.

The allegorizing of space here is rich and full of nuance. As Schlör remarks, the driving of prostitution indoors was part of the politics of the Second Empire, designed at establishing greater control over the 'dangerous' outdoors, parallel to the bulldozering of paved streets which might provide materials for the erection of barricades. Dickens approves of it, yet he seems to want to meet this exceptional person alone, outdoors, in the 'masculine' world of the street where after dark men might hunt, master and 'penetrate' the female night (Schlör pp. 166-68). On these visits to Paris, it might seem that all the ambiguities of Dickens's sympathy for victims on display in the streets—learned on the streets of London, and memorably expressed in a letter of November 1855, paraphrased by Forster, referring to a girl outside Whitechapel Workhouse to whom he gave a shilling: "Look at me", she said as she clutched the shilling and without thanks shuffled off (*Letters* 7: 742)—came to the fore.

As well as the spatial resonances of these excursions, we may also investigate their temporal peculiarities. As Ashford White remarks, "The winter visit, with evenings at the leading theatres, [became] almost a habit with the novelist." In Paris winter meant an increasing fear of crime (Chevalier notes that "elle atteint . . . en certains hivers de misère et de froid, sa plus grande intensité" ("it attains its greatest intensity in certain winters of misery and cold," Chevalier 35), and Dickens had to go home early after the winter of 1855-56 because his wife was upset by the number of crimes reported in the Champs Elysées area); but it also meant Carnival, a time outside time, transcending the everyday horrors of mud and snow.

Dickens was in Paris three times during the 1850s at the Carnival season, in 1851, 1855 and 1856. On the first two of these he was accompanied by rather *louche* companions: in 1851 Spencer Lyttelton, the Paris brothel connoisseur mentioned above, and in 1855 Wilkie Collins. Concerning the latter visit he announces his intentions with a reasonable degree of 'facetious' explicitness: "I want it to be pleasant and gay, and to throw myself en garçon on the festive diableries de Paris!" (*Letters* 7: 523)

But however 'diabolical' these bachelor activities may have been, the real point about them is that they took place once more under the constraints of the new régime. In the time of Louis-Philippe Carnival was an open-air occasion. Kracauer writes of the popularity of "Milord l'Arsouille," a masked figure who dispensed largesse generously amongst the crowds on the boulevards (Kracauer 35, 41). They (and Kracauer) thought he was Lord Seymour in disguise; but Martin-Fugier identifies him as Charles La Battut, the illegitimate son of a rich Englishman, a member of the dandy class who helped to make carnival at that time a kind of extension of dandyism (Martin-Fugier 341).

But as he had done with prostitution so he did with carnival—the showman Louis Napoleon took it indoors. Jerrold's "Paris with a mask on" is the appropriate *Household Words* reference; it is dated 19 April 1854, so Dickens must have known what to expect the following winter. Its *flâneur*-narrator is forced "to confess a decided disappointment"; he goes out to look for masks on the boulevards, and does not find any. But finally he tracks it down to its new lair:

> The fun of the old carnival, however, has now retired from the open streets. The police still annually issue stringent regulations, prohibiting all manner of indecorum, and restraining the old humourists who used to throw their yearly bag of flour from their windows upon the crowd below. Men will not mask in the streets with the police at their heels; but give them free way in a dancing hall, and it soon becomes obvious that the old spirit of masked revelry exists still in great vigour.

Thus carnival in 1855 was celebrated, not by men only, as it might seem from this account, in the *bals* where *lorettes* and *grisettes* and *vénus de barrières* were to be found in abundance. There Dickens, if not Collins, might find himself once again caught up in contradictions that the Paris of the 1850s fostered.

6. MUD

Dickens spent the next winter in Paris (1855-56) knee deep in allegorical mud. Its emotional significance for him can be gauged if we reflect that his childhood period of 'forced labour' in a boot blacking factory had been dedicated to producing a commodity to remove the traces of mud. In the intervening years, in part to erase the memory, perhaps, he had became a dandy, wearing polished boots instead of preparing polish for them. He had cultivated the friendship of Comte d'Orsay, the darling of the boulevards. In "French Domesticity" (*HW* 24 June 1854) Mrs. Eliza Lynn Linton gives a sharply focussed realization of this nexus of issues as she praises the French woman's capacity to negotiate her way through various kinds of physical and moral 'uncleanness': "she has a marvellous facility of walking clean through the dirty streets of Paris, and as marvellous a knack of holding up her skirts with one hand over her left hip . . . and a bewildering habit of mistaking her friend's husband for her own."[1]

That Paris should be specifically apt to evoke these associations was intrinsic in its name, or rather names. Hugo, like Costello a connoisseur of etymologies, had commented on this in ways that significantly illuminate the dualistic allegory seen above in *No Thoroughfare*: "L'Urbs des temps modernes . . . s'appelle *Lutetia*, ce qui vient de Lutus, *boue*, et elle s'appelle *Parisis*, ce qui vient d' *Isis*, la mystérieuse déesse de la Vérité" ("the 'urbis' of modern times . . . is called *Lutetia*, which comes from Lutus, *mud*, and is called *Parisis*, which comes from *Isis*, the mysterious goddess of truth," Hugo I, 1479; Labarthe 51). Its legendary muddiness centred upon the district around the Bastille, the Marais and the Faubourg St Antoine, which Dickens of course would vividly render in *A Tale of Two Cities*: "le plus fangeux de la ville: on le trouve encore boueux après des sécheresses de deux mois" ("the filthiest in the city; you still find mud there after a two month drought," Marchand 58). But a war of sorts was being waged upon the mud of Paris in the 1850s by the process of Haussmannisation. According to one's point of view, once could see it as a war to end wars, an annihilation of the medieval city and eradication through macadamization of the unpaved streets that had created the legendary 'Lutetia', or, in the short term at least, an orgiastic proliferation of mud, as Paris was turned for the time being into one nightmarish giant construction site. One thing is certain: Dickens was there at this precise moment in time, and experienced both the muddy horror and the hope of eventual salvation. He was witness to a kind of allegorical psychomachia waged between the forces of cleanliness, represented ostensibly by Haussmannisation, and the forces of city filth—Merdle, one is tempted to say.

And his response seems to have shifted with the passage of time, and prolonged firsthand exposure to the Haussmann process. At first, on his way to Italy in autumn 1853, it is thoroughly upbeat. He writes of the Haussmann projects:

> Paris is very full, extraordinarily gay, and wonderfully improving. Thousands of houses must have been pulled down for the construction of an immense street now making from the dirty old end of the Rue de Tivoli, past the Palais Royal, away beyond the Hotel de Ville. It will be the finest thing in Europe. The quays by the riverside are Macadamized and as clean as Regent Street. Indeed the general improvement in the essential articles of what is to be seen and what is to be smelt, is highly remarkable.
>
> (*Letters* 7: 163)

The mood lasts during and after the revisiting of Genoa, as Dickens reports in a letter to Leigh Hunt of January 1855, relating events of "some fifteen months ago when I went back to Genoa, and found it a stirring busy place, with miles of new Parisian-looking streets" (*Letters* 7: 519). At that time it would almost seem as if (in consonance with the perpetual negative comparisons of London and Paris throughout this period) it were London that were the muddier place, as a letter to Miss Burdett Coutts attests: "the condition of the streets to day, is inconceivable—mud and mire, in many places a foot deep" (*Letters* 7: 512).

But the winter of 1855-56 seems to have evoked another, more pessimistic response. That this was latent in Dickens anyway—the psychodrama of cleanliness versus filth carrying intense personal meaning—can be felt already in an incident in 1844 when he reached the hotel Bristol in Paris. "He was so beastly dirty," Ashford White recounts, that "he had quite lost all sense of his 'identity' and if he had been asked 'Are you Charles Dickens?' he would certainly have unblushingly answered. 'No, I never heard of him'" (Ashford White: 39). In 1855-56 he writes about getting covered in mud as if it meant losing one's face, features and identity (one's 'morgue,' to borrow one of Costello's suggestive etymologies.) Of one of his walks in January 1856 he writes to Mary Boyle how he ". . . came back with top-boots of mud on, and my very eyebrows smeared with mud. Georgina is usually invisible during the walking time of the day. A turned-up nose may be seen in the midst of a heap of splashes—nothing more." (*Letters* 8: 15).

We can trace the change of mood in these letters of that winter. One may start with the superficially breezy but oddly disconcerting announcement to Wills that the

apartment on the Champs Elysées has been licked into shape and is "exquisitely cheerful and vivacious—clean as anything human can be" (*Letters* 8: 725). The tone darkens in a letter to Mark Lemon, where the battle against defilement seems a losing one: "We are up to our knees in mud here. Literally in vehement despair. . . . Nothing will cleanse the streets. . . . Washing is awful." (*Letters* 8: 13). There is an apparent return of facetiousness to Wills on 19/20 January, with the announcement that "MUD" (underlined with short double strokes) "at Paris is 3 feet and 7/8 deep" (8: 32). But on the 20th, he appears to have lost faith in Haussmann: "It is difficult to picture the change made in this place by the removal of the paving stones (too ready for barricades) and macadamisation. It suits neither the climate nor the soil. We are again in a sea of mud" (8: 33).

Baudelaire shared these moods that same winter. In December 1855 he wrote to his mother: "je suis las des rhumes et des migraines et des fièvres, et surtout de la neige, et de la boue, et de la pluie" ("I am sick to death of colds and migraines and fevers, and above all of snow, mud, and rain"). Unlike Dickens he had no choice at this time but to walk in the mud as a pedestrian, and he hated what Haussmann was doing to Paris: "Encore s'est-il plaint de s'être souvent crotté: les travaux en cours . . . n'épargnent pas au piéton la boue et la fange" ("Once again he complained about frequently being covered in muck: work in progress doesn't spare the pedestrian from mud and filth"). Only he, when he could, chose not to look down at the street-level, where the mud was to be seen—in his one reasonably settled adult abode, from October 1843 to September 1845, he lived in a flat whose main room was "éclairée par une seule fenêtre dont les carreaux, jusqu'aux pénultièmes inclusivement, étaient dépolis 'afin de ne voir que le ciel,' disait-il" ("lit by a single window whose panes were obscured, right up the penultimate level, 'so that he'd only be able to see the sky,' he said" (Pichois and Avice 108, 91, 66).

7. BOTANIZING THE ASPHALT

Dickens was also in unconscious solidarity with Baudelaire in lamenting the passing of paving stones and their replacement by smooth macadamised tar and pitch. Baudelaire used the rhythm of his walk and the tap of his walking-stick against the uneven paving-stones as an aid to making subtle variations upon alexandrine metrics (Nadar describes him "choississant chaque pavé commes s'il eût à se garer d'y écraser un oeuf" ("choosing each paving-stone as if he had to be on his guard against smashing an egg," Benjamin 303). Sala, too, in his *Household Words* article "Music in Paving Stones," dedicated to what he describes as "the only boulevard of which London can boast," strives to gain inspiration from the contact between his boots and the pavement: "let me try, if, striking the paving stones with my iron heel, I cannot elicit some music. Let the stones of Regent Street, London, be my Rock Harmonicon, and let me essay to play upon them some few bars more of the musical tune" (*HW* 26 August 1854).

There seems little doubt that Dickens also formed and developed creative ideas for his novels in the process of his city walks. He refers to such a process on a number of occasions—in the very early stages of the evolution of *Little Dorrit,* for instance, when he writes to Miss Coutts from London of "having motes of new stories floating before my eyes in the dirty air" (*Letters* 7: 525). Then later from Paris he writes to Mark Lemon of his isolation, of missing his fellow playgoers on his nights out, "and when I go by myself, I come home stewing 'Little Dorrit' in my head" (*Letters* 8: 12).

The gestation of *Little Dorrit,* then, owes much to Dickens's Parisian *flânerie* in the years 1855 and 1856. After he had finished *Hard Times* in August 1854 he slowly began to germinate ideas for a new book. As the editors of the Pilgrim Letters suggest, Dickens at this time was beginning to find it easier to write in France than in England. He had finished both *Bleak House* and *Hard Times* in Boulogne-sur-mer: but now he needed to make a start, and for this, Paris was more appropriate. What it offered to him was "a new set of faces, a new set of streets," as an interesting article by Dixon in 1853, "The Phalansterian Menagerie," puts it in an analysis pertinent to the 'restlessness' Dickens regularly experienced with the onset of new creative writing, and of which he complains so frequently and vehemently in 1855:

> It is a luxury of ecstatic degree to make this kind of sudden escape, and to break loose out of the mill-round of duties which have daily to be done from morning to night. A new set of faces, a new set of streets, a new set of hedges and ditches and fields, are most effectual tonics. There are people in the world who would die, or go mad, if they could not freely and fairly take wing now and again. I am closely related to that family of migrants; and that, I suppose, was the reason why I happened so oddly to be strolling about Paris unconscious of the means which had conveyed me.
>
> (*HW* 17 September 1853)

So it is that not for the first time, one is tempted to use the word 'bohemian' in connection with Dickensian *flânerie,* especially in the context of this creative version thereof. Yet it would be difficult to apply the word 'bohemian' to Dickens himself in the 1850s: had he not mocked people like Baudelaire, constructing labyrinthine mazes through the streets of Paris to avoid meeting his creditors, in the figure of Dick Swiveller? Nonetheless, he seems during that period to have had quite a lot to do, one way and another, especially in Paris, with men—in particular writers—who might definitely be described as 'bohemian,' and to have allowed plenty of space in the columns of his journal for depiction of the 'bohemian' world.

The operative word for bohemianism in the Dickens circle is 'queer', used not in its modern sense, but certainly to describe unconventional and anti-bourgeois behavior. It is used for instance of Sala, who wasn't an intimate friend of Dickens, but who came to see him in Paris in January 1856 to ask for money: "I derived the idea that he was living very queerly here, and not doing himself much good. He knew nothing, I observed, about the pieces at the Theatres, and suggested a strong flavor of the wine shop and the billiard table" (*Letters* 8: 15). Collins, who certainly was, and who also liked eating on the left bank with students (see *Letters* 8: 78), is likewise described as "in a queer state" (*Letters* 7: 540). But Dickens also uses the word of himself, in particular to characterize his restless wanderings as he is in the process of composition: "I cannot relieve my mind or prepare myself for the morrow, unless I am perfectly free from promises and engagements, and can wander about in my own queer way" *Letters* 8: 55).

It is interesting, then, that although the Bohemian Sala is rather severe on his own kind living in the attic storey of his "Four Stories," Blanchard's "The True Bohemians of Paris" offers a reasonably sympathetic portrait of the same tribe. Based upon Murger, the article makes many criticisms of the Parisian *bohème*—he dismisses the idea of 'l'art pour l'art' for instance, and reproaches Bohemians with not being political enough—but insists upon its reality: it is not a fantasized gypsy land, such as that imagined by Hugo or Borrow, but the world of "unfortunate artists of all kinds—poets, painters, musicians, and dramatists—who haunt obscure *cafés* in all parts of Paris" (*HW* 15 November 1851).

It is Blanchard's belief, and Dickens's own, that France is a country where the arts are afforded much greater respect than they are in Britain, and that all genuine Bohemian artists must therefore eventually succeed. The crucial moment in Dickens's relationship with France occurred in 1847, when, as he told Féval, he started to feel fond of the country, "being moved by the funeral of the author Frédéric Soulié, at which a widespread popular respect for literature was manifest" (Collins 2, 292). That mindset was reinforced by a *Household Words* article Dickens admired, "Pierre Erard" by John Robertson (*HW* 6 October 1855; see also *Letters* 7: 705n), which describes the funeral cortège of a piano-maker crossing the Champs Elysées at a time when crowds were gathered to stare at Queen Victoria which "changed for a moment the thoughts of the sightseers." In the capital of modernity, despite the fixation upon fashion and novelty, the genuine artist could be assured of a moment of homage.

So Dickens wrote in November 1855 of his scepticism about the supposed discovery of a portrait claimed as the work of Porbus that had belonged to the actor Talma: "belonging once to Talma and being highly prized by him, I cannot believe (without much lucid explanation), that it would fade, in such a country as France, and fade for so long a time out of everybody's memory: being of any real worth" (*Letters* 7: 751). Blanchard likewise asserts, in his article on the Bohemians, that "most of them who have any real claims to distinction, attain it in the end. These are no days of 'mute inglorious Miltons,' especially in France, where talent must eventually make its way." Neither of them appears to have sufficiently taken the measure of Second Empire philistinism to have heard of Baudelaire; if they had, they might have acknowledged affinities between the French author who on his walks tapped out lines such as that addressing Paris in the second version of "Epilogue"—*Tu m'as donné ta boue et j'en ai fait de l'or* ("You have given me your mud and I have made gold from it")—and his English counterpart experiencing "stories floating before my eyes in the dirty air."

8. LEMAITRE AND ALLEGORY

This alchemically-produced gold, then, sometimes took the form of allegory. Dickens's imagination, as we have seen, often attempted to express and master the complexity of the modern city by seeing it in allegorical terms. Ashford White perceives this in his writings about the Paris Morgue when he observes that "in the grim winter of 1846-7 the aged white-haired victim of the river seemed to him an impersonation of the snowy season." (Ashford White 66) In 1851, in "A Monument of French Folly," comparing abattoirs in London with their counterparts in Paris, and mocking the kind of blind British jingoism in such matters that still has its echoes a century and a half later, allegory shades into ecological prophecy as it contemplates 'evil,' or inadequate slaughtering facilities, rising as a poisonous vapour to consume us all:

> Hard by Snow Hill and Warwick Lane, you shall see the little children, inured to sights of brutality from their birth, trotting along the alleys, mingled with troops of horribly busy pigs, up to their ankles in blood—but it makes the young rascals hardy. Into the imperfect sewers of this overgrown city, you shall have the immense mass of corruption, engendered by these practices, hastily thrown out of sight, to rise, in poisonous gases, into your house at night, when your sleeping children will most readily absorb them, and to find its languid way, at last into the river that you drink—but the French are a frog-eating people who wear wooden shoes, and it's O the roast beef of England, my boy, the jolly old English roast beef!'

> (*HW* 8 March 1851)

The 'trotting children' and the 'busy pigs' suggest the tangles of modern cities, where high and low, human and animal have got mixed up: in the same impressive piece Dickens address French cities as emblematic upward spirals with kennels at their center, surrounded by images of modernity: "I know your narrow, straggling winding streets, with a kennel in the midst, and lamps slung across. I know your picturesque street-corners, winding up-hill Heaven knows where!"

Perhaps this is why Dickens accepted so many Fourierist contributions to *Household Words* from Dixon, derived from Toussenel (despite commanding him to make it plain that he realized such thinking was pretty bizarre). Here all the animals are allegorical, and they express the vices of modernity. The series of five articles starts with the mole (whose identification with sex is continued in D. H. Lawrence's story *Second Best*); he is the "most complete allegorical expression of the absolute predominance of brutal over intellectual strength." ("The Mind of Brutes," *HW* 13 August 1853). In the same piece we have rats, "the emblem of those miserable and prolific populations which now cover the face of the globe, and which are driven by hunger;" the spider, "the emblem of the shopkeeper"; dormice, "the emblems of industrial parasites who spend three-quarters of their time in doing nothing up for their idleness by living upon the labours of others"; and many more. In "Equine Analogies" (*HW* 27 August 1853) the critical edge is honed a little in the contemplation of the mule as the "sad emblem of the feudalism of money," and especially in the recognition of how—in perverse continuation of heathen idolatry—both horses and young girls get commodified and consumed in Paris: "Paris consumes annually nearly fifteen thousand horses. About the same number of young girls are every year sacrificed there before the Minotaur of vice." This is the world of Costello's "Rag Fair" again, with its *imagerie populaire,* such as the "Au galant jardinier" sign representing "a spick-and-span new gardener, with a flower-pot in one hand and a spade in the other, selected as an emblem probably on account of a pair of highlows." The talented contributors to *Household Words,* such as Costello, savour the resonances of such words as "highlows."

But it is Ashford White's word "impersonation" that permits us to conclude. It was Dickens's regular Parisian winter evenings at the theater which, on occasions at least, enabled him to see the "drama of Parisian life" in terms not dissimilar from those Baudelaire employed to describe his ideal of the modern painter in the *Salon de 1845*: "Le peintre qui saura arracher à la vie actuelle son côté épique, et nous faire voir et comprendre avec de la couleur et du dessin, combien nous sommes grands et poétiques dans nos cruautés et nos bottes vernies" ("the painter who will be able to extract from contemporary life its epic side, and make us see and understand through colour and draughtsmanship how grand and poetic we are in our cruelties and polished boots," Pichois and Avice 69). Baudelaire meant Delacroix, and such drawings as that of "La Douleur," whereas for Dickens it was Lemaitre's acting, and his cry: "It wasn't I who murdered him—it was Misery!" (*Letters* 7: 537).

Notes

This article and its predecessor comprise the full text of a paper prepared for the International Dickens conference organized by Anny Sadrin in Dijon in June 1996, but read only in part on that occasion. An abbreviated version will appear in Anny Sadrin, ed, *Dickens, Europe and the New Worlds* (London: Macmillan, 1998).

1. It is interesting to note Mrs. Linton's characteristically robust reference to sexuality here. Dickens was squeamish about this aspect of her work on several occasions. "I don't know how it is but she gets so near the sexual side of things as to be a little dangerous for us at times," he writes to Wills in October 1854. The following month he writes again to tell him to reject one of her contributions: "The Actor is altogether out of the question. By Miss Lynn, I suppose. By whomsoever—unmitigated, bawdy Rot," and in January 1856: "Look to Langthwaite, to see there is no covert Bawdry in it" (*Letters* 7: 432, 753; 8: 16).

Works Cited

Benjamin, Walter. *Das Passagen-Werk.* Frankfurt: Suhrkamp Verlag, 1982.

Blanchard, Sydney. "A Ball at the Barriers." *Household Words* 3 (17 May 1851): 190-92.

———. "Painting the Lily." *Household Words* 3 (31 May 1851): 235-38.

———. "More French Revolutions." *Household Words* 3 (13 September 1851): 585-88.

———. "The True Bohemians of Paris." *Household Words* 4 (15 November 1852): 190-92.

Chevalier, Louis. *Classes laborieuses et Classes dangereuses.* Paris: Hachette, 1984 [Librairie Générale Française, 1978].

Collins, Philip. *Dickens: Interviews and Recollections.* 2 volumes. London: Macmillan, 1981.

Collins, Wilkie. "Laid Up in Two Lodgings." *Household Words* 13 (7 June 1856): 481-86.

Costello, Dudley. "Dead Reckoning in the Morgue." *Household Words* 8 (1 October 1853): 112-16.

———. "Blank Babies in Paris." *Household Words* 8 (17 December 1853), 379.

———. "Rag Fair in Paris." *Household Words* 10 (25 November 1854): 344-48.

Dickens, Charles. *The Letters of Charles Dickens. 1853-55.* The Pilgrim Edition. Vol. 7. Ed. Graham Storey, Kathleen Tillotson and Angus Easson. Oxford: Clarendon Press, 1993.

———. *The Letters of Charles Dickens. 1856-58.* The Pilgrim Edition. Vol. 8. Ed. Graham Storey and Kathleen Tillotson, 1995.

———. "Dullborough Town." The *Uncommercial Traveller & Reprinted Pieces.* Oxford: The New Oxford Illustrated Dickens, 1951.

———. "A Monument of French Folly." *Household Words* 2 (8 March 1851): 553-58.

———. "Insularities." *Household Words* 13 (19 January 1856): 1-4.

———. "Railway Dreaming." *Household Words* 13 (10 May 1856): 385-88.

———, and Collins, Wilkie. "No Thoroughfare." *Christmas Stories.* Oxford: The New Oxford Illustrated Dickens, 1952.

Dixon, E. S. "The Mind of Brutes." *Household Words* 7 (13 August 1853): 564-69.

———. "The Hall of Wines." *Household Words* 13 (2 February 1856): 66-70.

———. "The Phalansterian Menagerie." *Household Words* 8 (17 September 1853): 64-69.

———. "Equine Analogies." *Household Words* 7 (27 August 1853): 611-15.

Household Words, a weekly journal conducted by Charles Dickens. 19 volumes. London: Chapman & Hall, 1850-1859.

Hugo, Victor. *Œuvres poétiques.* Paris: Gallimard, Bibliothèque de la Pléiade, 1964.

Jerrold, Douglas. "Paris with a mask on." *Household Words* 9 (19 April 1854): 245-48

———. "The French Waiter." Household *Words* 9 (15 July 1854): 546-48.

———. "Near the Pantheon." *Household Words* 9 (12 August 1854): 612-14.

———. "Paris Upon Wheels." *Household Words* 10 (2 December 1854): 382-84. Kracauer, Siegfried. *Jacques Offenbach und das Paris seiner Zeit.* Frankfurt am Main: Suhrkamp Verlag 1994 [Amsterdam: Allert de Lange, 1937].

Labarthe, Patrick. "Paris comme décor allégorique." In *L'Année Baudelaire I:*

Baudelaire, Paris, l'Allégorie. Ed. Jean-Paul Avice and Claude Pichois. Paris: Editions Klincksieck, 1995.

Loyrette, Henri and Tinterow, Gary. *Impressionisme. Les origines 1859-1869.* Paris: Editions de la Réunion des musées nationaux, 1994.

Lynton, Eliza Lynn. "French Domesticity." *Household Words* 9 (17 June 1854): 434-48.

Marchand, Bernard. *Paris, histoire d'une ville: XIXe-XXe siècle.* Paris: Editions du Seuil, 1993.

Martin-Fugier, Anne. *La vie élégante ou la formation du Tout-Paris 1815-1848.* Paris: Editions du Seuil, 1993 [Fayard, 1990].

Morley, Henry. "The Theatres of Paris." *Household Words* 6 (2 October 1852): 63-69.

Pichois, Claude and Avice, Jean-Paul. *Baudelaire/Paris.* Paris: Editions Paris-Musées/Quai Voltaire, 1993.

Pontavice de Heussey, Robert. *L'Inimitable Boz: Etude historique et anécdotique.* Paris: Maison Quantin, 1889.

Robertson, John. "Pierre Erard." *Household Words* 12 (6 October 1855): 238-40.

Sala, George Augustus. "Monsieur Gogo's." *Household Words* 4 (21 January 1852): 444-48.

———. "Four Stories." *Household Words* 5 (26 June 1852): 336-42.

———. "Arcadia." *Household Words* 7 (18 June 1853): 376-80.

———. "Dr. Véron's Time." *Household Words* 13 (19 April 1856): 334-36.

———. "Parisian Nights Entertainment." *The Train* (1 January 1856).

Schlör, Joachim. *Nachts in der großen Stadt.* München: Artemis und Winkler, 1993.

Surveyer, Edouard F. "Dickens in France." *The Dickensian* 28 (1932): 46-56, 122-29, 197-201.

Thomas, W. M. "Sentimental Journalism." *Household Words* 4 (28 February 1852): 550-52.

White, F. Ashford. "In France with Charles Dickens." *The Dickensian* 9 (1913): 37-41, 64-68.

Wills, W. H. "A New Joint-Stock Pandemonium Company." *Household Words* 1 (20 July 1850): 403-04.

———. "Paris Improved." *Household Words* 12 (17 November 1855): 361-65.

ROME

George Bisztray (essay date June-December 1991)

SOURCE: Bisztray, George. "The Role of Rome in Hawthorne's *The Marble Faun* and Henry James's *Daisy Miller*." *Rivista di Studi Italiani* 9, nos. 1-2 (June-December 1991): 43-52.

[*In the following essay, Bisztray analyzes the historical significance of Nathaniel Hawthorne's depiction of* Rome in The Marble Faun *compared to Henry James's depiction of the city in* Daisy Miller.]

When Nathaniel Hawthorne arrived in Rome with his family on January 20, 1858, he found an anachronistic baroque city. It was the capital of the Papal State whose head had asked for French aid nine years before to put down a popular uprising. In the eighteen-fifties and sixties Rome was still ruled by an intolerant clergy that could preserve and exert its authority only by the continued presence of the occupying forces of Napoleon III, the pompous and unpopular French emperor. Political conditions were reflected in the cityscape. "Rome, as it now exists, has grown up under the Popes, and seems like nothing but a heap of rubbish," Hawthorne noted ungracefully in Chapter XII of his novel, which will be discussed in the ensuing pages.[1]

Twelve years later, when Henry James first visited Rome (between October 30 and December 28, 1869), more or less the same old-fashioned city awaited him. His impressions were entirely different, however, upon revisiting Rome on December 31, 1872, for a one-year stay. By then this city was the capital of an independent nation: an Italy unified for the first time after the fall of the Roman Empire. The secular spirit, the energy of a modernizing country could be sensed everywhere. Rome was no longer an anachronistic relic of past centuries but a thriving metropolis competing, like Berlin, with London and Paris for international prestige and influence. Rome "is an impossible modern city and will be a [. . .] modern capital, such as Victor Emmanuel is trying to make it," Henry wrote to his brother William two weeks after his arrival.[2]

Hawthorne wrote a novel, *The Marble Faun* (or, as it was titled in its first, British edition: *Transformation, or the Romance of Monte Beni*), in 1860. Its setting was Rome of the late 1850s. Henry James wrote several stories that took place in Rome. One of them was *Daisy Miller: A Study*—a short novel written in 1878, with contemporary Rome as background for most of the events.

Rome left deep and distinct impressions on both Hawthorne and James. Their works set in Italy, their travel diaries and their cultural differences have been compared by numerous American and some Italian scholars. Rome's image as a historically significant point of contrast between the two has, however, never been discussed before. The present article will concentrate on the artistic image of this city in two representative novels, utilizing the authors' direct admissions on Rome, uttered in their other works, only as secondary reference.

Knowing the historical events of the 1860s that separate Hawthorne's and James's generations and individual experience, one may expect to find information in the novels not only on Italian but also American intellectual history. While Italy stayed ready to complete the Risorgimento by incorporating the Papal State at an appropriate moment, the United States agonized through its four year long Civil War whose central issue was also unity, just as in Italy. These years brought forth profound changes in American life and ideas. Romanticism and late Puritanism had to yield to realism. It is interesting to notice that in *The Marble Faun* "Puritanism" often appears, both as a word and a principle. In *Daisy Miller* there is no trace of it.

What is common and what is distinct in these novels? Besides the setting the nationality of most of the main characters is another shared trait, inasmuch as the heroes in both novels are Americans. Besides Kenyon and Hilda, *The Marble Faun* contains two equally important European characters, while all those in *Daisy Miller* are Americans, with the only exception of Signore Giovanelli, Daisy's Italian date. The fate of the American heroes is closely connected to the Italian setting, which also has a significant role in shaping the personalities found in both novels.

At the same time, the effect of the milieu and the background of the American heroes in the two novels are different. As mentioned, the latter can be attributed mostly to historical and social changes in the United States. More interesting for our immediate purpose is the influence of the setting of Hawthorne's and James's characters.

Hawthorne was fascinated by Italy long before his first visit. In one of his earlier short stories titled "Rappaccini's Daughter," the setting could best be described as pseudo-Italian, imbuing the story with a spirit of Gothic horror. This particular setting, influenced as it was by such weird early Romantic English novelists as Horace Walpole and Mrs. Radcliffe, according to a Swedish critic, was one of Hawthorne's three images of Italy. The other two were the images of antiquity and that of the later Middle Ages, especially the period of Machiavelli. The same critic wrote on Hawthorne: "His approach to the country was one of mingled admiration and suspicion, and his actual experiences justified his expectations."[3]

Nothing reflects Hawthorne's ambivalent attitude more clearly than his two works, *Italian Note-Books* as well as *The Marble Faun*. Indeed, the latter also resembles at times a subjective travel log. By the time its passionate European protagonists, Donatello and Miriam, having committed "the crime," leave Rome, the scene has already changed frequently. The Capitol, the catacombs, the Villa Borghese, the Pincian Hill, the Corso, the Colisseum, the Forum, street life are just as vividly represented as the famous art treasures of the Roman museums, among which special attention is given to the

"Reposing Satyr," attributed to Praxiteles and housed in the Museo Capitolino. Two decades later, Henry James called Hawthorne's novel "part of the intellectual equipment of [every] Anglo-Saxon visitor to Rome."[4]

Besides the impact of Roman surroundings on Hawthorne, conscious artistic ideas motivated his choice for the main setting of the novel. He described his intentions in the preface as follows:

> Italy, as the site of [the author's] romance, was chiefly valuable to him as affording a sort of poetic or fairy precinct, where actualities would not be so terribly insisted upon as they are, and must needs be, in America. No author, without a trial, can conceive of the difficulty of writing a romance about a country where there is no shadow, no antiquity, no mystery, no picturesque and gloomy wrong, nor anything but a commonplace prosperity, in broad and simple daylight, as is happily the case with my dear native land. It will be very long, I trust, before romance writers may find congenial and easily handled themes, either in the annals of our stalwart republic, or in any characteristic and probable events of our individual lives. Romance and poetry, ivy, lichens, and wall-flowers, need ruin to make them grow.

No doubt, Rome, as the author experienced it in the late 1850s, was a convenient setting for a Hawthornian romance. It was a city of innumerable ruins, hiding places, mysterious old buildings and large public gardens full of shadows. All these furnished an atmosphere of suspense in the novel which the author enhanced with his biased outlook on the city that he chose to represent as a citadel of intrigue and corruption. After Donatello murdered the mysterious monk who had pursued his adored Miriam, the two have no difficulties with the authorities—no investigation is started after a man is found dead.[5] An atmosphere of gloom pervades this suppressed city haunted by the spirit of the past. Hawthorne repeatedly summed up his image of Rome in impressionistic description such as: "The ancient dust, the mouldiness of Rome, the dead atmosphere [. . .], the hard pavements, the smell of ruin and decaying generations, the chill palaces, the convent-bells, the heavy incense of altars, the life that he had led in those dark, narrow streets among priests, soldiers, nobles, artists, and women—" (Ch. VIII). In this milieu, even the present seems more unreal: "Side by side with the massiveness of the Roman Past, all matters that we handle or dream of nowadays look evanescent and visionary alike" (Ch. I).

How do Hawthorne's characters behave in this strange world? Hilda and Kenyon are young Puritans, citizens of a new country, glad to be unaffected by the sins of history, yet learning that they cannot gain understanding without experiencing sin. And just what place on earth would be more suitable to experience sin as it is defined in New England than Rome? In the beginning, they try to remain "innocent" in the middle of this crumbling city. They attempt to distance themselves from ordinary Italians, communicating only with other Anglo-American artists and tourists—their only European friends are the Italian Donatello and Miriam who has a mixed heritage. The symbol of this absurd self-isolation is Hilda who lives in her tower, with the Virgin's shrine, "above all the evil scent of Rome," feeding her doves. Paradoxically, even this seclusion indicates the influence that the city gradually exerts on her without her realizing it, since the Virgin's shrine and the doves are both recognizable Catholic symbols. Hilda and Kenyon cannot help but become fascinated with the city, this living museum thousands of years old in sharp contrast to the small, white, pure ("Puritan") and unbearably dull towns of their birthplace: New England, from which they fled in search of artistic inspiration and liberty. One leitmotif of the novel is the contrast between "the bleak but morally unencumbered prosperity of America and the aesthetically rich but morally heavy atmosphere of Rome haunted by the 'majestic and guilty shadows' of the past."[6]

As the reader can realize, Hawthorne utilized Rome in more than one way. The mysteries of the ancient city served as backdrop to his intended "romance." His personal memories from the time of his Roman sojourns (January 20-May 24, 1858, and October 17, 1858-May 26, 1859) provide a fascinating confirmation of his subjective reflections. The reader can only agree with Hawthorne's biographers and critics, however, who have univocally stated that his attitude toward Rome was "deeply ambivalent," in Wegelin's words.[7] The inner development of the novel went beyond the writer's intentions. Hawthorne clearly wanted to condemn the sinful capital of human past, but he did not manage to carry this through fully. His fate turned out to be almost the same as that of Hilda who, while rejecting Catholicism, eventually could barely "escape" her emotional subordination to it. Considering artistic intentions only, Wegelin is right in stating that Hawthorne failed to integrate moral and aesthetic values. The two remained a Platonic-Kierkegaardian dichotomy. Nearing the end of the novel, when we meet the two couples once again, Miriam and Donatello seem to have found consolation, if not redemption, in a simple country life as *contadino* and *contadina* (which must have been the only Italian words that Hawthorne used, repeatedly, in the novel.) In the meantime, Kenyon and Hilda contemplate sin, innocence and art—in all probability they will keep doing this together for the rest of their lives. Clearly, the European couple embody the "aesthetic attitude," the American the "ethical attitude." Is there an early expression of moralistic American chauvinism in the novel? Some critics would say yes. Extreme attitudes of North American visitors to Europe in more recent times—one awed, the other in various stages of moral shock—may provide the only "control data."

As it has been mentioned, both the literary and moral ideals of Hawthorne and James were markedly different. As for their literary views, Hawthorne was influenced by Romanticism and preferred writing in an allegoric-symbolic style, while Henry James mainly followed the principles of psychological realism. His heroes are character types (or "studies," according to the subtitle of *Daisy Miller*) rather than symbols. As for ethics, J. A. Ward points out some differences between the moral principles of Hawthorne and Henry James. Of these differences, two are relevant to the context at hand: 1) in James's fiction evil is not an active principle in the universe—there is no "evil according to nature"; and, 2) evil in James rarely exists beyond human relationships.[8] Both differences provide a useful focus for our discussion.

In the first place, *Daisy Miller* strikes the reader with a lack of any substantial description of Rome. City life and local customs are referred to only slightly more often. Could it be due to the brevity of the novel, which is also unique in James's *oeuvre*, being succinct, non-digressive and poignant? Or, is it possible to seek the explanation in the fact that the characters appear in Rome somewhat abruptly in Chapter III? These are perhaps less significant points. More important may be James's acute interest in the embedded psychocultural traits of his compatriots. The description of these traits reveals an ironically critical attitude toward his heroes. Daisy Miller, Mrs. Miller and Randolph are not artistic-minded people like the characters in *The Marble Faun*. Daisy is more interested in acquiring admirers, her mother in being accepted by local cosmopolitans, and her little brother in getting candy, than they are in the city itself. Maybe Henry James reflected in their figures the ironical stereotypes of the average American tourist and his image of Europe. Whereas in *The Marble Faun* there is not a single character recognizable to the modern reader, several heroes of *Daisy Miller* recall for us the overall impression Europeans have formed of American travellers in more recent times, even in the current era of mass tourism. The shallow treatment of local heritage and culture by the characters is a distinguishing attribute (true or false) of American tourists in the eyes of many contemporary Europeans.

All this does not mean the setting is of little or no importance in the novel. Its effect is latent and complex, but very real. Rome is present in the characters themselves: their behaviour and reaction to the events around them are reflections of their environment. This concerns more the human than the material setting, as in Hawthorne's case.

While the surroundings have an effect on the characters, in turn, they all have some effect on Daisy. In comparison with timid, chaste Hilda ("I am a poor, weak girl," Ch. L), Daisy appears as a strikingly different type of young American woman. She is living proof that decisive historical and cultural changes had also taken place in the United States since the writing of *The Marble Faun*. The twenty years which separate Hawthorne's and James's generations witnessed not only the rebirth of Italy but also the birth of a new American sensibility. Daisy herself is a child of the new generation. She is provokingly pretty, and as such, an image of American girls which prevailed in Europe long after James visited the continent. She is not only beautiful but also, by conservative standards, completely liberated, and, at the same time, innocent—a paradox that makes her absurd in the eyes of her acquaintances. In the words of S. B. Liljegren, Daisy is literally a lost child in Europe because of her "indefinable breath of independence."[9]

Daisy's fate is bound only indirectly to Europe. Those who cause her the most trouble are not the Italians but her own compatriots. James provides a wide range of typical American reactions to the Italian setting when describing the American characters. He tends to emphasize negative reactions: "their state of bewilderment, their helplessness in the face of European life, *their* lack of preparation for any but the most superficial relation with Europe as with an amusing and expensive toy, which performed for a change but to which, in consequence, one was in no need to feel any responsibility."[10]

James's American figures are terrible snobs. Their superficial awareness of the old traditions of Rome further reinforces this trait. As the author wrote in 1894, with indirect reference to *Daisy Miller,* he had intended to investigate "the eternal question of American snobbishness abroad."[11] The irony of this American attitude is that no Italian expects them to behave like Italians. Rome has the same lack of concern toward them as they have toward the real spirit of this city. The atmosphere is described by James as easygoing and slightly cynical, not overbearing and easily shocked. The Americans are acting out a naive play just for themselves, trying to be more Italian than the Italians while actually reinforcing their very American traits of prudishness and insecurity. James seems to pose an ironic question throughout the novel: before you attempt to copy a foreign way of life (for whatever reason), why don't you learn to know yourself and the real traditions of the country you visit?

While only of secondary importance, there are some references to particular Roman sites in the book. Once we are informed about the Villa Borghese and, at the end of the novel, about the Colosseum. It is interesting how some Italian critics ascribe great symbolic importance to certain details of the setting and how severely they judge the moral implications of these details. Umberto Mariani believes there is significance in the comparison of the first and last Roman scenes: the green Pincian Hill and the sinister swampy ground of the Col-

osseum surrounded by ruins that look like hills in the moonlight. Thus the two contrasted scenes are supposed to mark the beginning and the end of the process in the course of which the mysterious power of Rome destroys innocence.[12] Mario Praz states that Roman fever in *Daisy Miller* symbolizes a sort of moral malaise, just like cholera in Thomas Mann's *Death in Venice*.[13] The relevance of these interpretations is questionable. There is no reference in the novel to James's judging Daisy morally—as we have seen, his book is rather a critique of moral inhibitions. Neither can one find any evidence in the text of the author admonishing Romans for their immorality. As opposed to Hawthorne, James was neither a moralist nor a Romantic Platonist: aestheticism plays no role in *Daisy Miller,* and the aestheticethical dichotomy is gone entirely.

A summary comparison of the two novels has to take several aspects into consideration. One of these is the respective writer's artistic intention. Hawthorne utilized Rome as a picturesque abstraction—James as a vaguely characterized social milieu eliciting expectation of a certain behaviour among the Anglo-American heroes. Like most American romance writers, Hawthorne was more committed to certain principles than was James. In *The Marble Faun*, the author's social, moral, religious and artistic ideas are represented more recognizably than in James's ironic "study." Personality differences notwithstanding, Hawthorne's work can be read as a statement, while James's cannot.

In both novels, one can observe a polarity. In Hawthorne there is an ideal pattern serving as one pole: American (New England/Puritan) society and its moral/spiritual values. The other, sinful choice is symbolised by Rome. This city stands for more than one thing: Europe, Catholicism, past glory and present decay, and, eventually, for all of the above. It elicits a kind of naive fascination in Hawthorne's heroes: how could such a city, penetrated by the spirit of all possible "sins," produce such fantastic monuments of art? There are several variations of this question but it remains unanswered, which is a logical consequence of Hawthorne's speculative dichotomization of morals and the products of the human mind. Furthermore, it is also proof of Hawthorne's inability to understand cultures that are different from his. (At this point, one can better appreciate James's comment: Hawthorne was almost fifty years old when he first visited Europe and "exquisitely and consistently provincial."[14])

Also in Henry James's novels there are Americans on one side and Rome on the other, but neither represents an ideal. The city, especially its native dwellers and their social life, appear more through the eyes of the characters than directly. It confuses the American visitors who expect to be confronted with more complex moral expectations than they really are. At the same time, Rome is more sophisticated indeed than the so-journers from overseas, for whom only the moral criterion exists, could ever fathom. The target of the author's irony is the Americans rather than the Romans. At least James's Americans show a clumsy and exaggerated regard for ill-perceived local customs—something Hawthorne's characters consistently refused to do in their disdain of the locals. It was only the exotic folkloric element (such as the dance on the Pincian Hill) that Hawthorne deemed worthy to show contemporary Roman life. James's urbane and frivolous capital apparently no longer offered such archaic diversions from the countryside. Also, it is typical that while Hawthorne's Hilda and Kenyon do not associate with the Romans, Daisy Miller goes so far as to date one of them: Signore Giovanelli, the "polite little Roman," in the words of the snobbish and jealous Winterbourne.

These are some of the differences in the role played by the Italian capital in the two novels. More significant, however, is the unifying setting. In Rome, both Hawthorne and James found an appropriate expression of their respective views on America and Europe. This would have been impossible if James had not experienced the radical modernization of the archaic atmosphere that Hawthorne found twenty years before and himself on his first visit. But the new events in Italian history, the self-realization of its nationhood, was in accordance with the new chapter of American history which began after the Civil War. Both the Americans in *The Marble Faun* and those in *Daisy Miller* came from the morally most representative, almost archetypal regions of their country, for their respective time periods: New England, the citadel of Puritanism, and New York State, headquarters of the newly rich industrialists.[15] When presented in a European setting, these personalities had to be put into the most typical city. Hawthorne's Rome stood for almost the whole of terrorized post-revolutionary 1850s Europe, while that of James symbolized the new renaissance of continental nations in the 1870s.

Notes

1. Hawthorne's and James's novels exist in so many editions that a less precise but eventually more reliable reference to chapters, rather than pages, seems warranted to identify quotations.

2. H. James, *Letters,* edited by Leon Edel (Cambridge: Harvard University Press, 1974-), I, p. 324.

3. Jane Lundblad, *Nathaniel Hawthorne and European Literary Tradition* (Upsala: The American Institute in the University of Upsala, 1947), p. 62.

4. In chapter 6 of his book on *Hawthorne* ([London: Macmillan and Co.,] 1879).

5. In a "Postscript" to the novel, the author himself makes an appearance and chats with his heroes Hilda, Miriam and Kenyon. They tell him that there was an investigation after all, and Donatello is in prison. This addition to the novel is an obvious exercise in romantic irony, a favourite device of romance writers; however, it has nothing to do with the organic plausibility of the narrative.

6. Christof Wegelin, *The Image of Europe in Henry James* (Dallas: Southern Methodist University Press, 1958), p. 24. In critical retrospect, we may note that this dichotomy was symbolic and fully romanticized. American "innocence" was a long-lasting abstraction of the spiritual and cultural consciousness of that country, nurturing both pious self-satisfaction and an inferiority complex.

7. *Ibid.,* p. 24.

8. J. A. Ward, "Henry James and the Nature of Evil." Our source: reprint in *Critical Approaches to American Literature* (New York: Crowell, 1965), II, pp. 119-25.

9. S. B. Liljegren, "American and European in the Works of Henry James," *Lunds Universitets Årsskrift,* 15 (1919), 15.

10. Wegelin, *op cit.,* p. 58.

11. *The Notebooks of Henry James,* edited by F. O. Matthiessen and K. B. Murdock (New York: Oxford University Press, 1947), p. 167.

12. U. Mariani, "L'esperienza italiana di Henry James," *Studi Americani,* 6 (1960), 245.

13. M. Praz, "L'America e noi," in his *Cronache letterarie anglosassoni,* II: *Cronache americane* (Roma: Edizioni di Storia e Letteratura, 1951), pp. 272-5.

14. James, *Hawthorne,* Chapter 6.

15. In the words of Morton White, "After the Civil War, new social types entered American society" ("Coherence and Correspondence in American Thought," in *Paths of American Thought,* edited by A. M. Schlesinger and M. White. Boston: H. Mifflin Co., 1963, p. 4). The parvenu Millers are an example of these social types who would gradually swamp Rome as summer tourists, and are still arriving today.

Brigitte Bailey (essay date 2002)

SOURCE: Bailey, Brigitte. "Fuller, Hawthorne, and Imagining Urban Spaces in Rome." In *Roman Holidays: American Writers and Artists in Nineteenth-Century Italy,* edited by Robert K. Martin and Leland S. Person, pp. 175-90. Iowa City: University of Iowa Press, 2002.

[*In the following essay, Bailey maintains that in their "Roman texts" that combine tourist writing with jour-*

nalism and fiction, Margaret Fuller and Nathaniel Hawthorne provide commentary on "the mutually constituting elements of gender, city, and nation in the United States."]

Nineteenth-century urban space emerged as a category conceptualized through a web of contradictory discourses and visual practices. It was at once a cosmopolitan space and a national space, at once owned by an explicitly male gaze and traversed and looked at by women. And it was immediately both covered and shaped by an expansive print culture already in place, a culture whose most widely disseminated forms, the newspaper and the novel, embodied and at times analyzed the contradictory perspectives that composed the urban imaginary. Ever since Benedict Anderson's influential work on the cultural construction of nationhood, scholars have understood these two characteristic nineteenth-century genres as forms particularly appropriate for developing and disseminating a sense of national identity and for its successful internalization, that is, as helping to constitute a national imaginary;[1] similarly, a third popular bourgeois prose genre, travel writing, furthered the nationalist project by training what John Urry has called the "tourist gaze," a "socially organized" gaze "constructed through difference," on other nations.[2] Examining Margaret Fuller's and Nathaniel Hawthorne's Roman texts as overlapping genres, as conflations of tourist writing with journalism, on the one hand, and with fiction writing, on the other, reveals their engagement with what one might call a national city and their concerns, displaced onto the foreign scene of Italian urban space, about the mutually constituting elements of gender, city, and nation in the United States.

Fuller's dispatches to the *New-York Tribune* (1847-1849), during the period of the Roman Revolution, and Hawthorne's romance *The Marble Faun* (1860), derived from his Italian sojourn during a period of political repression in Rome, serve divergent purposes, but they are also linked through the nationalist function of their genres—journalism and fiction—in constructing what Anderson has called the "imagined community" of the modern nation-state. The novel carries out the tourist's agenda of the surveillance of foreign scenes in order to consolidate American national identity by contrast; as in most antebellum accounts, Italy in *The Marble Faun* is a posthistorical, aesthetic, feminized space whose transcendent status helps to solidify the identity of the United States as the province of language, masculine political agency, and contemporary history.[3] Fuller's newspaper account, on the other hand, focuses on present, political, and potentially nation-building action in Italy, on Italy's possible emergence as a nation-state in its own right. But both accounts are

also implicated in the related cultural effort of conceptualizing and representing the city, in developing an urban imaginary in antebellum American culture.

The significance of Fuller's and Hawthorne's representations of Roman spaces as specifically urban spaces emerges in such descriptive moments as their contrasting treatments of the view from one of the traditional vantage points overlooking the city: from the Pincian Hill onto the Piazza del Popolo immediately below.[4] Hawthorne gives us a panorama of Rome from the point of view of his American characters, Hilda and Kenyon:

> From the terrace where they now stood, there is an abrupt descent towards the Piazza del Popolo; and looking down into its broad space, they beheld the . . . palatial edifices . . . which grew . . . out of the thought of Michael Angelo. They saw, too, the red granite obelisk—eldest of things, even in Rome—which rises in the center of the piazza. . . . All Roman works . . . assume a transient . . . character, when we think that this indestructible monument supplied one of the recollections, which Moses, and the Israelites, bore from Egypt into the desert. . . .
>
> Lifting their eyes, Hilda and her companion gazed westward, and saw . . . the Castle of Sant'Angelo; that immense tomb of a pagan Emperor. . . . Still farther off, appeared a mighty pile of building, surmounted by the vast Dome [of St. Peter's]. . . . [A]t this distance, the entire outline of the world's Cathedral . . . is taken in at once.[5]

Their tourist gaze grasps the totality of the city and its major icons; their survey of the "varied prospect" (*MF*, 106) promises unlimited visual access to history (the Egyptian obelisk in the piazza prompts a cultural memory of Moses and the Israelites) and to architectural forms ("at this distance, the entire outline" of St. Peter's "is taken in at once"). As their gaze returns to the piazza below, they see the city's central avatar in the novel, the painter Miriam, kneeling ambiguously in the presence of her Model, and the difficulty of interpreting Rome returns; is she, as Hilda thinks, kneeling merely to get water from the fountain, or is she, as Kenyon argues and as the reader already knows, begging her persecutor for her freedom?

If Hawthorne emphasizes the promise and the limits of the tourist's gaze, especially as it is a function of the gazer's gender, Fuller, writing in December 1848 of revolutionary Rome, emphasizes the formation of contemporary history. She describes a gathering of troops, crowds, and government officials—all with republican sympathies—in the Piazza del Popolo and their movement to the Quirinal, the residence of the Pope, to demand political reforms:

> I passed along, toward the *Piazza del Popolo*. . . . I heard the drums beating, and, entering the Piazza, I found the troops of the line already assembled, and the

Civic Guard marching by in platoons; each *battaglione* saluted as it entered by trumpets and a fine strain from the hand of the Carbineers.

I climbed the Pincian to see better. There is no place so fine for anything of this kind as the Piazza del Popolo, it is so full of light, so fair and grand, the obelisk and fountain make so fine a center to all kinds of groups.

The object of the present meeting was for the Civic Guard and troops of the line to give pledges of sympathy preparatory to going to the Quirinal to demand a change of Ministry and of measures. The flag of the Union was placed in front of the obelisk; all present saluted it; some officials made addresses; the trumpets sounded, and all moved toward the Quirinal.[6]

The promise of access this passage makes is not to a totalizing panorama of history, arranged in fixed icons (the Egyptian obelisk, the classical tomb, and the baroque church), but to a theater of open-ended history in the making, a "fine," well-lit stage that serves as the backdrop to the ephemeral and fluid movements of flags, bodies, and trumpets.

Simon During offers a model for thinking about the urban imaginary in his account of an eighteenth-century English "civil Imaginary," a discursive formation that orders an emerging social world through the "production of narratives, moral cruxes, a linguistic decorum, and character types which cover the social field of the post-1688 world." The texts, especially novels and journalists' essays, produced by this eighteenth-century "civil Imaginary" "are a sympathetic attempt to circulate images of the forms of social existence available to the urban bourgeoisie of the time"; they also attempt to order this world by shaping the subjectivity of those who inhabit it and so, as During points out, are "ethical in the Foucauldian sense."[7] Antebellum American cities offered a similar "new cultural space." Historians have documented the explosive rate of urbanization in the northeastern United States during this period.[8] Accompanying this social change were discursive and visual strategies for seeing and ordering the city along middle- and upper-class lines. These strategies not only provided conceptual frameworks for seeing the city; they also normalized specific viewing positions, defined by gender and class, for the citizen of the city. And to the extent that they participated in the rhetoric of reform, they not only normalized but explicitly advocated ways of being in the city. Two approaches that define these positions and that I will draw on below are studies, derived from the work of Walter Benjamin, of the *flaneur,* the strolling male spectator of nineteenth-century city streets, and feminist histories of the place of women (physically and conceptually) in nineteenth-century cities.[9] The writings of this period participated in a broadly articulated urban imaginary, a bourgeois, gendered discourse whose function it was both to describe and to produce the city.

Fuller and Hawthorne participated in this discourse before they went abroad: Fuller through her writings covering New York social institutions during her two years there (1844-1846) and Hawthorne primarily through his Boston novel, *The Blithedale Romance* (1852). As a journalist, Fuller worked to render the city of New York visible to the reform-minded middle-class readers of the *Tribune;* as Joan Von Mehren says, Fuller "publicize[d] conditions in the city's charitable institutions": prisons, "almshouses, insane asylums, and homes for the blind and deaf."[10] Catherine C. Mitchell points out that Horace Greeley's *Tribune* advocated a reformist agenda that included temperance, the abolition of slavery, labor unions, and Fourier's vision of socialism. Fuller edited and was the main contributor to the first-page "literary department," a department that blended literary criticism, travel accounts, social analysis, and political correspondence.[11] Fuller's columns on New York produced for her readers over time an aggregate presence of cultural events (book publications, a concert at Castle Garden, an exhibition of an important painting), of the ongoing operations of disciplinary and benevolent institutions, and of architectural structures (such as Grace Church).[12] Her attention to forms of urban life and space that existed outside the domestic sphere and yet simultaneously with it complicated the reader's subjective experience of the city; her frequent contributions (three articles a week) covered and ordered the emerging "social field," to use During's phrase, of the American city and sought to mold the consciousness of her audience.[13]

The Blithedale Romance is, on the other hand, Hawthorne's sustained study, as Dana Brand puts it, of "an urban civilization on the point of becoming ubiquitous" and of "cosmopolitan modes of interacting with reality"; the novel is split between representations of Boston and representations of what Hawthorne emphasizes is an urban fantasy: the "return" to a communal, pastoral, unalienated mode of production and cultural expression at "Blithedale," modeled on the utopian agrarian community of Brook Farm, to which Hawthorne had briefly belonged.[14] Linking these two spaces is Hawthorne's narrator, Miles Coverdale, who appears as, according to Brand, the "representative subjectivity" of modernity—"that of the flaneur," the detached consumer of spectacle.[15] Unlike Fuller's persona of the reform writer, who seeks to intervene in the consciousness of her readers and to reorganize aspects of urban life, Hawthorne is interested in an urban subjectivity whose orientation to the city is primarily visual, a subjectivity that, as Griselda Pollock argues, is secured by gender and class hierarchies and located in middle- and upper-class male spectators: "The flaneur symbolizes the privilege or freedom to move about the public arenas of the city observing but never interacting, consuming the sights through a controlling but rarely acknowledged gaze."[16] The flaneur's impulse to type other urban characters—to know them through the eye—at once separates him from the crowd but also, in Benjamin's words, is an unsuccessful fantasy that viewing others can "break through" the actual isolation of urban inhabitants "by filling the hollow space created in him by such isolation, with the borrowed—and fictitious—isolations of strangers."[17] Hawthorne's exploration of Coverdale's modern position of visual privilege and social isolation is connected with his interest in the tourist's visual consumption of foreign parts.

During this period, Rome served both as posthistorical aesthetic spectacle and as an historical model for the idea of the U.S. national capital as either the political center of a republic or as imperial capital; it also served, more specifically, as a source of architectural models for the Capitol building in Washington.[18] Fuller's and Hawthorne's writings on Rome emphasize two possibilities for conceiving of American urban space: as political space or as consumable spectacle. Although Fuller imagines a political city, a polis, and Hawthorne is primarily engaged by the tourist's or flaneur's vision of the city, both aspects of these sometimes mutually contradictory components of the antebellum urban imaginary are present in both texts. Both writers seem at times aware of and yet enact the dominating, totalizing view of foreign sites that William W. Stowe finds characterizes the guidebooks of the period: "Tourists are sightseers: their subjugating gaze reduces individuals, institutions, art-works, and landscapes to bits of knowledge and elevates the tourists and their class, race, gender, and nation to the position of the authoritative knower."[19] As do philanthropic projects, tourism extends participation in a master gaze to women. Yet if Fuller wrestles with the contradictions between such a master gaze, this visual sampling of other regions, and her project of releasing Italy and Italians from static types to dynamic historical presences, Hawthorne writes, in effect, an analysis of what urban space looks like in which the political and historical have been repressed.

In his study of American urban literature, Sidney Bremer traces a variety of written responses to the nineteenth-century growth of the city from "polis" to "metropolis" to "megalopolis." He finds that the dominant conceptual model in the pre-Civil War period is still the older one of the polis, the "city-town." In this period, in which "fairly homogeneous, powerful mercantile elites dominated the economy and society of U.S. cities" and in which most published writers were members of this elite, the "city-town model in literature" is characterized by a voluntary sense of community, by a "strong sense of history," and by human agency; "the city-town's spaces form an environment that is shaped by human choices more than it shapes them."[20] Fuller draws on the city-town model to create an image of Rome as polis and as the emerging capital of the nation-state envisioned by the leaders of the Risorgimento. In doing so, she assumes the position of the elite republican writer, whose voice guides the formation of the community.[21]

Fuller traveled and lived in Europe in 1846-1850 as a foreign correspondent for the *Tribune*. During her travels in England, France, and Italy, Fuller met with a number of republican activists and exiles, including the Polish poet Adam Mickiewicz and Giuseppe Mazzini, the leader of the revolutionary republican movement, Young Italy. She arrived in Rome in 1847, in time to witness and report on the attempt by northern Italian states to throw off Austrian rule, on revolutionary activity throughout Italy, and on the brief exile of Pope Pius IX from Rome and the equally brief existence of a Roman Republic in 1849. Like Mazzini and others, Fuller understood the Roman Republic as a movement toward a unified Italy. And she understood herself as its historian; she was working on a manuscript of the history of the Roman Republic when she died in 1850.[22]

Fuller's letters to the *Tribune* repeatedly describe a city defined by citizens in motion, by political processions, funerals, troop movements, and religious festivals whose meaning is increasingly political. As William L. Vance says, "the People" become the hero of these letters.[23] Suppressing her private doubts about "the People," as Larry J. Reynolds points out,[24] Fuller publicly constructs a city increasingly "shaped by human choices" in the revolutionary days of self-determination. And she constructs a citizenry that, despite the lack of republican institutions and training, is already composed of self-regulating subjects. Her depictions of processions along the central thoroughfare of Rome, the Corso, deemphasize the architectural structure of the street (that is, external forms of order) and emphasize instead a naturalized image of voluntary community in motion. In May 1847, during a period when Pius IX briefly allied himself with the proponents of liberal reform, Fuller sent this description of voluntary political association and benevolent patriarchal support of such association to the *Tribune*:

> A week or two ago the Cardinal Secretary published a circular inviting the departments to measures which would give the people a sort of representative council. Nothing could seem more limited than this improvement but it was a great measure for Rome. At night the Corso . . . was illuminated, and many thousands passed through it in a torch-bearing procession . . . [A]s a river of fire, they streamed slowly through the Corso, on their way to the Quirinal to thank the Pope, upbearing a banner on which the edict was printed. . . . Ascending the Quirinal they made it a mount of light. . . . The Pope appeared on his balcony: the crowd shouted three vivas; he extended his arms; the crowd fell on their knees and received his benediction; he retired, and the torches were extinguished, and the multitude dispersed in an instant.

(*DFE*, 136-37)

Here, Fuller offers a way of conceptualizing the transition from paternal, Papal authority (signaled by the crowd's kneeling for the benediction) to the internalized law of the self-disciplining subject of the republican state;[25] the "multitude" shapes itself into a political community and then disperses by its own will, a motif Fuller constantly reiterates in her crowd descriptions. Such scenes draw on the concept of the polis, on the premetropolitan city-town shaped by the voluntary association of its inhabitants, to visualize the emergence of the agency of Rome's citizens.

Fuller is aware of the ethical thrust of the urban imaginary she is engaged in and helping to shape. She sees that the public sphere is discursively constructed; her reports repeatedly describe and often include translations of proclamations, accounts in the emerging liberal press of Italy, and the "news" orally transmitted from other regions of revolutionary Italy. The polis is invoked by language. The "circular" granting a limited representative body calls forth the procession, whose discursive origin is clear; the crowd carries the text of the edict printed on a banner. And citizens are also called into being through language; Fuller says that the first election in Rome (in early 1849 of the Constitutional Assembly for the Roman States) was a successful exercise of suffrage because of discussions held in the public sphere: "A few weeks' schooling at some popular meetings, the clubs, the conversations of the National Guards . . . was sufficient" (*DFE,* 255).

In *Paris As Revolution,* Priscilla Parkhurst Ferguson comments on Balzac's and Hugo's concept of the postrevolutionary writer's role in creating an urban imaginary. It is the task of the urban novelist to replace the gaze of the king, which had earlier given Paris unity, with that of the writer. The "urban imagination," she argues, is a "synecdochal imagination" that sees the apparent "fragments" of the city as parts of a whole: "Synecdoche thus bespeaks the aesthetic of integration. . . . Integration . . . create[s] [a] unity that . . . does not exist. . . . [T]his creation is the vocation of the writer."[26] In this respect like Balzac and Hugo, but also like the political leader of the Roman Republic, Mazzini, whose speeches and writings she includes in her dispatches, Fuller tries to call forth Rome as polis, as modern republican capital, through language. The processions she describes become synecdoches, parts standing in for the whole, an available image of the voluntary community she wants Rome to become and that she wants the American nation to reapproximate. Fuller attempts to revive American republicanism by means of an identification between her readers and Italian revolutionaries: "This cause is OURS" (*DFE,* 160). Both American aid to the Italians and the American national revival from the sins of slavery and the Mexican War will happen through the agency of "individuals" and small groups, who stand in for the whole of the

country and who represent the "Soul of our Nation" (*DFE,* 161); "voluntary association for improvement . . . will be the grand means for my country to grow" (*DFE,* 165). In such passages Fuller tries to call not only the modern Italian nation but also an American national subjectivity into being, a subjectivity characteristic of the polis. In doing so, she tries to connect, I would argue, the traditional, elite idea of the polis with the more revolutionary and egalitarian associationism of Fourier and his American exponents, a connection that elides the differences between older American republicanism and current European radicalism.[27]

Of course Fuller's Rome is also a spectacle, a theater of revolution that elicits aesthetic responses. Of the above torchlight procession, she describes the visual effect and notes, "I have never seen anything finer" (*DFE,* 137). And as she overlooks the gathering in the Piazza del Popolo, she describes this urban space as one especially fit for civic performances; to reiterate one sentence, "There is no place so fine for anything of this kind as the Piazza del Popolo, it is so full of light, so fair and grand, the obelisk and fountain make so fine a center to all kinds of groups" (*DFE,* 241). Such passages suggest that, like urban novels and urban journalism, public performances of republican solidarity can invent the modern national capital. The unified city and its citizens can be performed into being. But these passages also invoke the language of tourism and perhaps of more "modern," metropolitan forms of visual consumption. Indeed, Fuller's text vacillates between two modes of presenting revolution to her *Tribune* readers: the spectacular, romantic movements of the body of the citizenry in such passages as the one on the torchlight procession and deliberately sober, antispectacular accounts of the "tranquil[ity]" (*DFE,* 260) and ordinariness of life in revolutionary Rome. During the siege of Rome she comments on the "order of Rome": "I go from one end to the other . . . alone and on foot. My friends send out their little children alone with their nurses" (*DFE,* 284). Fuller's ambivalence about using a language of visual display to describe revolutionary activity may stem from her awareness that tourism operates in part by pictorializing characteristic events and people into types and therefore ultimately depriving them of agency—exactly the opposite of what she is trying to do. As she says of British tourists, the "vulgarity" that "snatches '*bits*' for a '*sketch*'" makes them "the most unseeing of all possible animals" (*DFE,* 132), a statement that associates the tourist gaze with reactionary politics.[28]

Hawthorne's Rome in *The Marble Faun,* as readers have pointed out, is primarily a series of tourist spaces: galleries, artists' studios, villa gardens, classical ruins, churches, catacombs.[29] As opposed to Fuller or Hugo, Hawthorne does not conceive of his writing as reinventing the city, and he visits Rome in 1859-1860 at a time of political repression, after the failure of the 1849 Roman Republic and before the final unification of Italy. The book itself represents for many readers divided impulses; Richard H. Brodhead finds that the novel, despite its considerable ambivalence about the process of creation, winds up supporting the stratification of art into high and low and, in giving Hilda the last word, effectively supports the authoritative repressions associated with "high" art and with "subordination-demanding institutions."[30] Robert Levine, who gives the novel perhaps its fullest recent reading as a text concerned with political issues and specifically with revolutionary activity, finds that despite Hawthorne's "partial sympathy" with Miriam's rebellion against "various reactionary forces depicted in the novel," he acquiesces with the recontainment of such rebellion at its end.[31] My argument is a similar one: that Hawthorne's urban imaginary is predicated on a gendered position, that *The Marble Faun* at once acknowledges and recontains the bid of women spectators for public participation in cities and in the informing gaze onto cities, and that Hawthorne reflects the effort by his contemporary male journalists and flaneurs to order the emerging metropolitan city through a gendered geography. Rome becomes a space where both revolution and women's gazes are evoked and repressed, indeed where urbanity comes to imply their simultaneous presence and nullification.

Mary P. Ryan identifies 1840 as "a rough benchmark in the gender geography of public urban space." At about this time, the separation of work from household space became increasingly standard for middle-class families and, as opposed to a greater "public mingling" that characterized earlier American urban life, public and private spheres became more fully separated and gendered. So just at the time that American cities grew into unzoned, apparently chaotic metropolises, gender became especially available as a category to decipher the city. As Ryan says, a mid-century "army of flaneurs cum journalists . . . impose[d] cognitive patterns on the heterogeneous spaces of the city" through a "cartography of gender":

> Relations with women, clearly the "other" in this largely male construction of urban geography, provided male writers with metaphors that neatly encapsulated the central problem of urban social space: how to create order and hierarchy in an environment where social differences existed in close physical proximity. Sexuality was perhaps the most powerful metaphor for the interplay of diversity and proximity in the big city.[32]

In this version of the urban imaginary, "dangerous" and "endangered" women became urban signs of class and ethnic difference.

As T. Walter Herbert persuasively argues, Hawthorne's visit to Rome coincided with a crisis in his faith in the coherence of the ideological and psychological structure of the middle-class family, and the romance is in part an attempt to recontain this crisis about authority and gender.[33] The novel features two women who move freely about the streets of Rome—Hilda and Miriam—one endangered and one dangerous. Hawthorne both lauds this freedom of movement and worries about it; by the end of the novel Hilda's ability to move freely has been undermined by her witnessing the crime of murder and her subsequent captivity experience.[34] The novel wants virtuous middle-class women to wander freely in urban spaces, but the city's capacity to taint this virtue seems too strong and Hilda is best relegated to safe spaces for such women: the home. Miriam also wanders but always less freely; as an expression of the city—with her mixed ethnic and national heritage, her antipatriarchal revolutionary impulses, as Levine points out, her masked identity, and her sexually ambiguous past—she is at once a victim of the city and linked to its subterranean power structures, even connected with someone in the Papal government, as the narrator states in the postscript (*MF,* 464).[35] The novel functions to separate these two women, to keep apart the possibilities for being in the city that they each represent. Leonardo Buonomo argues that Hawthorne meticulously keeps Hilda and Donatello separate as signs of two irreconcilable cultures;[36] it is also part of the cultural work of the novel to divide Hilda and Miriam, whom Hawthorne at first portrays as intimate. At the end Miriam is represented as being on the other side of an "abyss" (*MF,* 461) from Hilda, separated by categories of experience Hilda does not wish to acknowledge. Indeed, Hawthorne uses Hilda as an agent of repression for Miriam—Hilda's information leads to Miriam's loss of Donatello through his arrest and incarceration—and so cuts middle-class women off from their ethnic and experiential others. By doing so he represses the fact that middle-class women such as Fuller and Lydia Maria Child, who was briefly a journalist in New York in the 1840s, have already wandered through this emerging new metropolitan space and have assumed in their writings the gazing position generally held by men.[37]

Kenyon's and Hilda's contemplation of Miriam as part of their survey of Rome from the Pincian Hill anticipates the conclusion of the novel in its movement away from the mutual look of intimate relations that characterizes their relationship with Miriam in the beginning of the romance toward a reestablishment of the dominant and hierarchical tourist gaze. It is like Fuller's scene from the same spot in that both passages are turning points in their respective accounts; Miriam's despairing supplication to the Model, the mysterious agent of her oppression, immediately anticipates his murder (and her supplicating kneeling to Donatello, who kills the Model and liberates her), while the movement of the republican procession to the Quirinal precipitates Pope Pius IX's flight from Rome and the beginning of the Roman Republic, a liberty as short-lived as Miriam's and Donatello's. But here we have two interpretive gazers; whereas Hilda underinterprets the scene, Kenyon turns out to be a good reader of emblematic urban moments. His superior insight, even as it is presented as risky and in need of Hilda's domesticating discipline, permits him to continue to interact with Miriam, even to give her advice, that is, to shape the plot of her life. As Hilda breaks off her relationship with Miriam, Kenyon becomes the go-between, the mobile spectator and interpreter who can move between the two spheres they represent. In this scene Miriam—and other possibilities for women's cognitive grasp of the city—is returned to her status as a sign of the city; the possible woman gazer, as Fuller herself was for Hawthorne, moves from being a subject to being again an object of the gaze.

The city in *The Marble Faun* is the site of revolution repressed; Donatello, the pastoral, infantilized male Italian of much tourist writing, becomes in the city the violent revolutionary who destroys the Model, the figure of past modes of oppression, while Miriam's gaze, which triggers the murder, overthrows patriarchal authority. But these possible historical agents—the Italian man and the urban woman—become pictorialized, part of the gallery of masked figures and allegorical images Italy offers to tourists, by the end of the novel, as they disappear into the Roman carnival and, as Donatello does, into prison. In a reversal of Fuller's project, the early identification between the American characters and these figures is weakened and made abstract, even perhaps psychologized, as the paradigm of the tourist's vision returns. In an association Fuller might have understood, Hawthorne connects his most thorough tourist's survey of Rome in the novel, in which he calls Rome "the City of all time, and of all the world!" (*MF,* 111), with Kenyon's vision of Miriam kneeling in the Piazza del Popolo, metaphorically "shackled" like the "captive queen" Zenobia (*MF,* 108), that is, determined by her urban environment rather than shaping it through her gaze.

In the dreamwork of national building that tourist writings represent,[38] the tourist gaze is at once provisionally liberatory and disciplinary, releasing such figures as Miriam and Donatello and reincarcerating them. Similarly, the figure of Miriam/Zenobia speaks to the "dream-work" of imagining the national, even imperial city. Hawthorne draws here on his viewing of the American sculptor Harriet Hosmer's statue of Zenobia, which he admired while in Rome and mentions in his preface to *The Marble Faun* (*MF,* 4).[39] As Joy S. Kasson explains, Hosmer's statue, in its representation of a Syrian queen defeated by a Roman emperor and paraded through Rome in chains, evoked simultaneously the images of female power and captivity.[40] And it did so explicitly, I would add, in the context of Rome, cast here as imperial metropolis.

If the ambivalently rendered image of the shackled woman of power lies at the center of the spectacular metropolis for Hawthorne, just as similarly ambivalent images of women, according to Ryan, define the "gender geography" of the mid-century city for other male writers, Fuller, like Hosmer, at times participates in this trope and seeks to revise it. Larry J. Reynolds has argued that Fuller constructs a "public persona" in her dispatches, that she performs the "role of Liberty," the feminine embodiment of the spirit of revolution, an image available in European romantic culture.[41] If "Liberty" is defeated in the Roman Revolution, nevertheless, Fuller's adherence to this persona is an attempt to make a feminine sign speak, to merge image and discourse, representation and agency, and to do so in the context of political transformation played out in a national city.

As American cities moved toward a metropolitan identity at mid-century, the task of constructing an urban imaginary became urgent. Both texts show the tensions within such a cultural project. If Hawthorne's engagement with the gendered gaze of the urban spectator is more attuned to the emerging visual strategies of the metropolis, and so more "modern," Fuller's attempt to revive the concepts of city and citizenship defined by the republican polis is more "progressive." Their works may indicate less any clear historical shift from polis to the city of spectacle than a dialectical relation between these models of urbanity that continues to shape nineteenth-century American urban representations.

Notes

1. Benedict Anderson, *Imagined Communities: Reflections on the Origin and Spread of Nationalism,* rev. ed. (London: Verso, 1991). For a characteristic treatment of the relations between literary forms and the nation, see Timothy Brennan, who argues that novels were a "practical means of *creating* a people" in "The National Longing for Form," in *Nation and Narration,* ed. Homi K. Bhabha (London and New York: Routledge, 1990), 50. For an important distinction between an earlier role of print culture in elaborating a public sphere and the function of the novel, see Michael Warner, who argues that "although the nation-state was the product of the eighteenth century, the national imaginary was a product of the nineteenth" in *Letters of the Republic: Publication and the Public Sphere in Eighteenth-Century America* (Cambridge, Mass.: Harvard University Press, 1990), 120.

2. John Urry, *The Tourist Gaze: Leisure and Travel in Contemporary Societies* (London: Sage Publications, 1990), 1-4.

3. Brigitte Bailey, "The Protected Witness: Cole, Cooper, and the Tourist's View of the Italian Land-

scape," *American Iconology: New Approaches to Nineteenth-Century Art and Literature,* ed. David C. Miller. (New Haven, Conn.: Yale University Press, 1993), 92-94.

4. Eleanor L. Jones points out that the Pincian Hill was a "popular" site with "artists, photographers, and other travelers" in both the antebellum and post-Civil War periods ("Sanford Robinson Gifford," in *The Lure of Italy: American Artists and the Italian Experience 1760-1914,* ed. Theodore E. Stebbins, Jr. [Boston and New York: The Museum of Fine Arts, Boston, and Harry N. Abrams, Inc., 1992], 230).

5. Nathaniel Hawthorne, *The Marble Faun,* introduction by Richard H. Brodhead (New York: Penguin, 1990), 106-7. Subsequent citations will appear in the text abbreviated *MF.*

6. Margaret Fuller, *"These Sad But Glorious Days":* *Dispatches from Europe, 1846-1850,* ed. Larry J. Reynolds and Susan Belasco Smith (New Haven, Conn.: Yale University Press, 1991), 241. Subsequent citations will appear in the text abbreviated *DFE.*

7. Simon During, "Literature—Nationalism's Other? The Case for Revision," in *Nation and Narration,* ed. Homi Bhabha (London: Routledge, 1990), 142-43.

8. See, for example, James L. Machor, *Pastoral Cities: Urban Ideals and the Symbolic Landscape of America* (Madison: University of Wisconsin Press, 1987), 121-22.

9. Benjamin's articulation of Baudelaire's figure of the flaneur as the characteristic figure of modernity has informed both art historical accounts and literary criticism of the period (Walter Benjamin, *Charles Baudelaire: A Lyric Poet in the Era of High Capitalism,* trans. Harry Zohn [London: New Left Books, 1973]). In this essay I draw on Griselda Pollock's discussion of gender and the gaze in nineteenth-century French painting, *Vision and Difference: Femininity, Feminism and the Histories of Art* (London and New York: Routledge, 1988), and Dana Brand's reading of antebellum American male writers as flaneurs, *The Spectator and the City in Nineteenth-Century American Literature* (Cambridge: Cambridge University Press, 1991). The historical studies that have informed my thinking here are Mary P. Ryan's investigation of women and public space in three nineteenth-century American cities, *Women in Public: Between Banners and Ballots, 1825-1880* (Baltimore, Md.: Johns Hopkins University Press, 1990), and Christine Stansell's examination of women's lives and roles in antebellum New York, *City of Women:*

Sex and Class in New York, 1789-1860 (New York: Alfred A. Knopf, 1986).

10. Joan Von Mehren, *Minerva and the Muse: A Life of Margaret Fuller* (Amherst: University of Massachusetts Press, 1994), 218.

11. Catherine C. Mitchell, *Margaret Fuller's New York Journalism: A Biographical Essay and Key Writings* (Knoxville: University of Tennessee Press, 1995), 16-17.

12. I have taken these examples from Mitchell's edition of Fuller's New York journalism. See also Bell Gale Chevigny for more of Fuller's *Tribune* pieces: *The Woman and the Myth: Margaret Fuller's Life and Writings,* rev. ed. (Boston: Northeastern University Press, 1994). Just published, however, is the most authoritative and complete edition of Fuller's journalism while she lived in New York: *Margaret Fuller, Critic: Writings from the New-York Tribune, 1844-1846,* ed. Judith Mattson Bean and Joel Myerson (New York: Columbia University Press, 2000).

13. Mitchell points out that in the mid-1840s, the early days of its existence, the *Tribune* was still a relatively small newspaper that competed with two other papers for predominance in New York and not the nationally influential paper it would quickly become in the 1850s (*Margaret Fuller's New York Journalism,* 10, 13).

14. Brand, *The Spectator and the City,* 123. William E. Cain, in his recent edition of *The Blithedale Romance* (Boston: Bedford Books, 1996), has incorporated an illuminating set of documents from the period on social reform, utopian communal experiments, and related issues.

15. Brand, *The Spectator and the City,* 124-27. My thinking about *The Blithedale Romance* as an urban text has benefited not only from Brand's work but also from Nancy Von Rosk's thoughtful dissertation, "Domestic Visions and Shifting Identities: The Urban Novel and the Rise of a Consumer Culture in America, 1852-1925" (University of New Hampshire, 1999).

16. Pollock, *Vision and Difference,* 67.

17. Benjamin, *Charles Baudelaire,* 58.

18. Sidney H. Bremer, *Urban Intersections: Meetings of Life and Literature in United States Cities* (Urbana: University of Illinois Press, 1992), 30.

19. William W. Stowe, *Going Abroad: European Travel in Nineteenth-Century American Culture* (Princeton, N.J.: Princeton University Press, 1994), 48.

20. Bremer, *Urban Intersections,* 13.

21. In this way Fuller follows her father's example; as her biographers point out, Timothy Fuller was a self-made member of the New England elite, a Jeffersonian Republican twice elected to the U.S. Congress from Massachusetts who did not survive politically the transition to Jacksonian democracy. See Von Mehren, *Minerva and the Muse,* 13; and Charles Capper, *Margaret Fuller: An American Romantic Life* (New York and Oxford: Oxford University Press, 1992), 10-13.

22. A number of biographers and literary critics have discussed these final years in her life, as well as the (lost) manuscript. I cite here only the most recent biographer, Von Mehren, *Minerva and the Muse,* 230-339.

23. William L. Vance, *America's Rome,* vol. 2 (New Haven, Conn.: Yale University Press, 1989), 132-35.

24. Larry J. Reynolds, *European Revolutions and the American Literary Renaissance* (New Haven, Conn.: Yale University Press, 1988), 76.

25. One of the most recent treatments of the constitution of this subjectivity is Dana D. Nelson's study of early national manhood: *National Manhood: Capitalist Citizenship and the Imagined Fraternity of White Men* (Durham, N.C.: Duke University Press, 1998).

26. Priscilla Parkhurst Ferguson, *Paris As Revolution: Writing the Nineteenth-Century City* (Berkeley: University of California Press, 1994), 68-69.

27. See Von Mehren, *Minerva and the Muse,* 224, for a discussion of Fuller's Fourierist friends in New York, just before her trip to Europe. For a discussion of Fourier's influence on Fuller's feminism, see Christina Zwarg, *Feminist Conversations: Fuller, Emerson, and the Play of Reading* (Ithaca, N.Y.: Cornell University Press, 1995).

28. Fuller in general sees British interests as reactionary; of the *London Times* she says, "There exists not in Europe a paper more violently opposed to the cause of freedom" (*DFE,* 294).

29. See Richard H. Brodhead's introduction to *The Marble Faun,* xvii-xviii.

30. Richard H. Brodhead, *The School of Hawthorne* (New York: Oxford University Press, 1986), 73-75.

31. Robert S. Levine, "'Antebellum Rome' in *The Marble Faun,*" *American Literary History* 2 (Spring 1990): 31, 25.

32. Ryan, *Women in Public,* 61-68, 75.

33. T. Walter Herbert, *Dearest Beloved: The Hawthornes and the Making of the Middle-Class Family* (Berkeley: University of California Press, 1993), 215-72.

34. Jenny Franchot discusses Hilda's disappearance in terms of the conventions of the American Protestant "convent captivity narrative" in *Roads to Rome: The Antebellum Protestant Encounter with Catholicism* (Berkeley: University of California Press, 1994), 357.

35. Such characters are also staples of the "mysteries of the city" fiction by authors, such as George Lippard, who focused their novels on New York and Philadelphia in the 1840s and 1850s. See David S. Reynolds, *Beneath the American Renaissance: The Subversive Imagination in the Age of Emerson and Melville* (New York: Alfred A. Knopf, 1988), 82-84.

36. Leonardo Buonomo, *Backward Glances: Exploring Italy, Reinterpreting America (1831-1866)* (London: Associated University Presses, 1996), 52-53.

37. See Ryan, *Women in Public,* for a brief discussion of Child's urban explorations and her *Letters from New York* (82-83).

38. I draw here on W. J. T. Mitchell's discussion of landscape representations as the "'dreamwork' of imperialism," in "Imperial Landscape," in *Landscape and Power,* ed. W. J. T. Mitchell (Chicago: University of Chicago Press, 1994), 10.

39. Rita K. Gollin and John L. Idol, Jr., describe Hawthorne's response to Hosmer's statue in *Prophetic Pictures: Nathaniel Hawthorne's Uses of the Visual Arts* (Westport, Conn.: Greenwood Press, 1991), 96.

40. Joy S. Kasson, *Marble Queens and Captives: Women in Nineteenth-Century American Sculpture* (New Haven, Conn.: Yale University Press, 1990), 151.

41. Reynolds, *European Revolutions,* 74-76.

Elzbieta Foeller-Pituch (essay date fall 2003)

SOURCE: Foeller-Pituch, Elzbieta. "Henry James's Cosmopolitan Spaces: Rome as Global City." *The Henry James Review* 24, no. 3 (fall 2003): 291-97.

[*In the following essay, Foeller-Pituch closely examines Henry James's use of Rome and art in "The Last of the Valerii," Roderick Hudson, and* The Portrait of a Lady.]

"Rome's inexhaustible," states the consummate expatriate Gilbert Osmond (*PL* 401). And indeed Henry James's Rome is a global space where past and present,

Old World and New come together. The Eternal City—replete with monuments, art, and people, representing classical antiquity, the Renaissance, the Catholic Church, European social hierarchy, and European political upheavals—provides a quintessential cosmopolitan experience for his American travelers and expatriates. Although in the second half of the nineteenth century London emerged as the modern imperial metropolis where James finally felt most at home, Rome's aesthetic and historical eminence made it an ideal setting for his exploration of Americans' confrontations with the world and inspired the beginnings of his "anatomy of cosmopolitan culture [. . .] to trace the emerging outline of the global future" (Peyser 5). I would like to concentrate here on three earlier works—"The Last of the Valerii" (1874), *Roderick Hudson* (1878), and *The Portrait of a Lady* (1881)—and key scenes involving classical statues that echo and resonate against each other, in order to view James's engagement with the Eternal City as the crossroads of transatlantic alliances, cultural politics, and literary and artistic influences. For James Rome was a city in which "your sensation rarely begins and ends with itself; it reverberates—recalls, commemorates, resuscitates something else," which may have suggested to him the technique of introducing key repetitions and echoes in these works (*IH* 149).[1]

James's characters demonstrate a broad spectrum of feelings towards Rome. In *Roderick Hudson* the gamut ranges from old Mrs. Hudson's puritanical protest against "this wicked, infectious, heathenish place" (301) to the painter Sam Singleton's simple statement that "so long as one is not in Rome, pray what does it matter where one is?" (316). Words such as "bliss," "golden," and "brilliant" are used to describe life in Rome (52, 141, 159), while Hudson's newly arrived fiancée, Mary Garland, reverses the conventional order of Old World and New when she speaks of the city: "Before me lies a whole new world and it makes the old one, the poor little narrow familiar one I have always known, seem pitiful" (263).

James's own reactions to Rome are well known, from his first ecstatic 1869 message home ("At last—for the first time—I live!") to his 1907 letter addressed to Edith Wharton exclaiming against Rome as "perverted" and "vulgarized" (*HJL* 1: 160, 4: 457, 459). Mrs. Humphrey Ward admiringly commented that "Roman history and antiquities, Italian Art, Renaissance sculpture, the personalities and events of the Risorgimento, all these solid *connaissances* and many more were to be recognized perpetually as rich elements in the general wealth of Mr. James's mind," but contemporary critics compellingly argue that James did not have much first-hand knowledge of Italians and Italian society, was not really interested in the Risorgimento and the development of contemporary Italy, but rather constructed his Italy as a metaphor of art (qtd. in Tuttleton 43; Lombardo 230-

31). Rome, in this context, becomes the Eternal City, meeting place of paganism and Christianity, where classical ruins and sculptures mingle with the art and architecture of the Renaissance, and the majesty of the Catholic Church, embodied by the Vatican and St. Peter's Basilica, is superimposed on the splendors of the ancient Roman Empire. A classical locus of imperial conquest and aesthetic pleasure, it is a cosmopolis that provides a worthy space for James's American characters to work out their destinies.

James's expatriates are usually artists or young women. In "The Last of the Valerii" we have a combination of the two, as an older American artist observes his goddaughter's marriage to an Italian count, who succumbs to pagan worship of a superb classical statue of Juno that his rich American wife has unearthed in the family gardens. Martha Valerio's enthusiasm for all things Roman—her husband, the picturesque antiquity of his mansion and grounds, the might of his nominal Catholicism embodied by St. Peter's Basilica—all contribute to an energetic uprooting of herself from America and comfortable ensconcing in the role of elite Roman wife, suddenly to find herself helpless before the power of the ancient ways and branded a stranger still. Her archaeologist excludes foreigners from the dark influence of the past—"There's a pagan element in all of us,—I don't speak for you, *illustrissimi forestieri* [. . .]" (*LV* 115). The Count Valerio sums it up thus:

> There have been things seen and done here which leave strange influences behind! They don't touch you, doubtless, who come of another race. But they touch me, often, in the whisper of the leaves and the odor of the mouldy soil and the blank eyes of the old statues. I can't bear to look the statues in the face. I seem to see other strange eyes in the empty sockets, and I hardly know what they say to me.
>
> (98)

In his pagan stage the Count discovers the Pantheon, the Catholic church that used to be a temple to all the Olympian gods, and comments on it: "This is the best place in Rome [. . .]. But do you know I never came here till the other day? I left it to the *forestieri*. They go about with their red books, and read about this and that, and think they know it. Ah, you must *feel* it [. . .]" (110). This prompts the American narrator to meditate "on the strange ineffaceability of race-characteristics" (111). There is a careful differentiation here between the Anglo-Saxons and the Latins, the clear suggestion that the Americans are impervious to the influences native to the Old World and can only appreciate Rome as an intellectual exercise. The narrator's simultaneous exasperation and fascination with the Count reflect James's ambiguous feelings towards Americans' engagement with the Roman past and with contemporary Romans burdened by that past.

James is writing here under the influence of Prosper Mérimée's "La Vénus d'Ille" and a European folklore tradition of classical goddesses threatening mortal marriages, but the main emphasis is on the international theme. The story is also a partial reworking of Hawthorne's *Marble Faun,* with which it shares questions about the burden of history always present in Rome.[2] Martha Valerio is characterized by her godfather as "a more perfect experiment of nature, a riper fruit of time, than those primitive persons for whom Juno was a terror and Venus an example [. . .]" (*LV* 117). The hold she, as a modern, still has over her husband allows her to bury the statue and save their marriage, but a residue of Juno worship makes the Count keep the statue's hand as a relic in his curio cabinet, prompting the final anecdote of the story, when a visitor assumes the hand represents that of a former mistress. "'Ah,—a Roman?' said the gentleman, with a smirk. 'A Greek,' said the Count, with a frown" (122). This exchange reminds us that the classical statues are themselves "expatriates" in Rome, alien through distance of space and time. James plays with this notion in *Roderick Hudson* and *The Portrait of a Lady* as well, complicating any easy working out of "race" characteristics and allegiances.

In James's first notable full novel, the American sculptor Roderick Hudson, newly arrived in Rome from a small town in Massachusetts, comes under the spell of the Eternal City and starts to nurture vast artistic ambitions of a cosmopolitan nature. He expresses them in terms of classical statues and the emotional responses they may produce, echoing the effect of the Valerio Juno. "When Phidias and Praxiteles had their statues of goddesses unveiled in the temples of the Aegean, don't you suppose there was a passionate beating of hearts, a thrill of mysterious terror? I mean to bring it back; I mean to thrill the world again! I mean to produce a Juno that will make you tremble, a Venus that will make you grow faint" (*RH* 123-24). No hesitation here that his American origins make him too foreign to feel the power of the ancient deities. And again the two powerful goddesses are evoked—Juno and Venus, with clear echoes from "The Last of the Valerii," where the effect of the Juno is described as "almost terrible; beauty so eloquent could hardly be inanimate" (*LV* 114). Earlier in the novel Hudson sketches the head of the Ludovisi Juno, but imparts to it the features of the mysterious and beautiful Christina Light, whom he calls "a daughter of the elder world" and who is compared to a Greek goddess or nymph in several passages of the novel, despite her nominal Americanness (*RH* 110, 175, 181). She is said to be a worthy model for Phidias (151). A bust of Christina Light is one of Hudson's last great works before his decline and downfall. At the end we learn she is not just a truly cosmopolitan expatriate but a transnational, a product of both Old World and New. Like the Juno of "The Last of the Valerii," Christina Light, a contemporary goddess, embodies the power of

sexuality, and as such evokes passionate devotion and inspires true art.[3] The figure of Juno, classical patroness of marriage, appears in both works to subvert and question domestic arrangements—the transatlantic marriage of the Valerios and the New England engagement of Roderick Hudson and Mary Garland. Her threatening power is felt by all the principals, both Italian and American, though in varying degree. Rome as the resting place of the Greek statues, their haunting influences, and the temptations they embody, plays an important part in the education of Jamesian characters as they find themselves at the cultural and ethical crossroads offered by the Eternal City. As the Cavaliere Giacosa puts it: "Rome is Rome still: a place where strange things happen!," echoing Count Valerio's words (*RH* 167).

Christina may be a latter-day goddess or nymph, but she is put up for sale in the marriage market as if she were a statue or a slave; her mother regards her as a valuable commodity and at one point Mrs. Light is explicitly compared to a Turkish slave-dealer, which has interesting resonances to the recent American situation (163). When Christina fulfills her mother's and Roman society's expectations with a brilliant marriage to the fabulously wealthy and aristocratic Prince Casamassima, it is an exchange of title, power, and money for beauty and sophistication, brokered by Mrs. Light and undertaken by Christina under duress. The reification of people and the power of objects is a theme that recurs in James's fiction. Rome, with its marble statues, both ancient and contemporary, its palaces and gardens filled with art works, and its cosmopolitan parade of finery, is the locus of the commodified display and barter of objects and of people. As Thomas Peyser puts it in the context of *The Golden Bowl,* "for James and his American characters the habit of turning people into exhibits is inveterate" (137). In "The Last of the Valerii" the Count is described in terms of an ancient Roman bronze and the narrator teases his goddaughter about her idolatry—"I believed she had married the Count because he was like a statue of the Decadence"—in an interesting parallel to the power the Greek marble Juno has over him (*LV* 90, 93). In *Roderick Hudson* Christina Light is used by her mother as an object, fully aware of her own ornamental function and the voyeuristic pleasures her mother's guests derive from gazing at her, while Roderick's sculpture prolongs and increases that pleasure for American tourists and cosmopolitan Roman socialites. Isabel Archer of *The Portrait of a Lady* is unaware of herself as object, since she considers herself a free agent, abetted by several admirers who treat her as such; it is deeply ironic that she marries the one who does think of her as an ornament and financial aid rolled in one, prompting her later bitter reflections on "the dry staring fact that she had been an applied hung-up tool, as senseless and convenient as mere shaped wood and iron" (459). At this moment she sees herself not even as an ornamental object, but a purely utilitarian one.

Much earlier in the novel James sets his heroine in the Capitol gallery in the company of the ancient marbles,

> resting her eyes on their beautiful blank faces; listening, as it were, to their eternal silence. It is impossible, in Rome at least, to look long at a company of Greek sculptures without feeling the effect of their noble quietude; which, as with a high door closed for the ceremony, slowly drops on the spirit the large white mantle of peace. I say in Rome especially, because the Roman air is an exquisite medium for such impressions. The golden sunshine mingles with them, the deep stillness of the past, so vivid yet, though it is nothing but a void full of names, seems to throw a solemn spell over them. The blinds were partly closed in the windows of the capitol, and a clear, warm shadow rested on the figures and made them more mildly human. Isabel sat there a long time, under the charm of their motionless grace, wondering to what, of their experience, their absent eyes were open, and how, to our ears, their alien lips would sound. The dark red walls of the room threw them into relief: the polished marble floor reflected their beauty. She had seen them all before, but her enjoyment repeated itself, and it was all the greater because she was glad again, for the time, to be alone.
>
> (257-58)

This scene is obviously an important one in the novel, occurring as it does just after Isabel bids her rejected suitor Lord Warburton goodbye again and before she welcomes Gilbert Osmond to her side. I would even contend that it functions as a counterbalance to Isabel's famous musings on the failure of her marriage in chapter 42, both scenes outwardly static but important for the protagonist's internal development. Here the classical statues in the golden light of Rome offer the heroine a panorama of myth, history, and high art, the possibilities of esoteric knowledge and universal human truths. The contemplation of the statues is both soothing and a challenge. Isabel calls them the best company, and Osmond reveals his snobbery when he shows surprise that she should consider them "better company than an English peer," one of many instances when she ignores or gives a positive spin to a warning signal about Osmond's true character (258). Her puzzling over the statues' eyes echoes Count Valerio's words. Unlike the Roman, Isabel does not feel that the statues can speak directly to her about the past. As she is unable to fathom the experiences to which their "absent eyes were open" and how "their alien lips" would sound, so is she incapable of penetrating the character of the two Europeanized Americans who will use her—Osmond and Mme Merle, as impressive and as alien to her as the ancient Greek marbles.

The male statues she views—the Dying Gladiator, the Antinous, the Marble Faun (a clear gesture towards Hawthorne)—parallel the female goddesses that fasci-

nate James's male protagonists but are much less effective in stirring her emotions. These quiet marble sculptures may even be considered substitutes for and an escape from the all too active suitors she has been trying to avoid. The scene stresses her freedom before the definitive choice of marriage. She admires these famous sights of Rome as a tourist and visitor, but her feeling for them reveals her unique sensibilities, again contrasting the "sterile dilettante" Osmond's conventional fascination with "good things" and her own felt experience of the best company, foreshadowing her later expatriate married state with Osmond when they are settled in Rome (292). The ancient Greek "expatriate" statues for whom Rome is a mellow and golden site are also far from their homeland. Their grouping in the Capitoline museum, indicative of their "captive" state, parallels Isabel's later incarceration in the gloomy and glamorously decorated Palazzo Roccanera as one of the chief ornaments of her husband's house, to be gazed at by curious visitors. Isabel, as much as the other furnishings, makes Gilbert Osmond an envied leader of Roman cosmopolitan society, which flocks to the Palazzo Roccanera just as tourists come to Rome to see the historic marbles.

The Palazzo Roccanera is powerfully associated with the courtly intrigues and cruelties of the Renaissance. Daniel Mark Fogel has pointed out the parallels to Browning's dramatic monologue "My Last Duchess," while James explicitly describes Isabel's Roman home as a "kind of domestic fortress, a pile which bore a stern old Roman name, which smelt of historic deeds, of crime and craft and violence, which was mentioned in 'Murray' [a popular guidebook] and visited by tourists [. . .]" (Fogel 91-92; *PL* 307). This habitation, symbolic of Osmond's mental "house of darkness, [. . .] house of dumbness, [. . .] house of suffocation," unites different historic periods of Italian art and architecture to form for James a microcosm of the dark and stifling side of Rome—no golden sunlight here (360). Isabel finds respite by welcoming the burden of Rome's history and taking

> old Rome into her confidence, for in a world of ruins the ruin of her happiness seemed a less unnatural catastrophe. She rested her weariness upon things that had crumbled for centuries and yet still were upright; she dropped her secret sadness into the silence of lonely places, where its very modern quality detached itself and grew objective [. . .]. She had become deeply, tenderly acquainted with Rome; it interfused and moderated her passion. But she had grown to think of it chiefly as the place where people had suffered.
>
> (430)

Whereas contemplation of the Greek statues before her marriage marks for Isabel the potentialities and possibilities offered by Rome, here the burden of its history mitigates the effects of enclosure and claustrophobia.

Rome, home of inexhaustible possibility and stultifying convention, is both the scene of Isabel's triumph and of her entrapment.

In progressive works James's expatriates begin to engage more deeply with Rome in all its aspects, becoming more fully aware of it as a complex, historic entity and more willing to interact with it as a museum and as a seat of society. Isabel strikes us as more at home in Rome than Roderick Hudson and his friend and patron Rowland Mallet, or Martha Valerio and her godfather. In her later stages Isabel comes close to Christina Light in the effect she produces on observers, who see in her a great lady, but one more gracious and mature than the capricious Princess; she becomes as polished a cosmopolite as her husband or Mme Merle, but lives on a moral plane that these transplanted Americans can barely grasp, achieving a superb synthesis of American idealism and Old World refinement. Her return to Rome at the end of the novel marks her full engagement with the Eternal City and the burden of her own past that she has assumed. It is a victory for Rome that James's "heiress of all the ages" comes back—marking it as a locus that triumphantly condenses the world into its cosmopolitan spaces.

Notes

1. I am indebted to a number of works that I have not specifically quoted: Kaplan; Vance; Martin and Person; Bradbury; Winner; Tintner; and Edel.

2. Ziolkowski gives a succinct account of this motif, derived from a twelfth-century legend about a Roman nobleman, as manifested in folktales and literary works, including the stories of Mérimée and James, in his chapter "Image as Theme: Venus and the Ring" (in particular 61-65). See also Merivale. On the Hawthorne-James connection, see Bewley; Brodhead; and Rowe.

3. For an excellent discussion of the relationship between art and sexuality as represented by classical statuary in the Hawthornian context, see Baym.

Works Cited

WORKS BY HENRY JAMES

HJL—Henry James Letters. Ed. Leon Edel. 4 vols. Cambridge: Harvard UP, 1974.

LV—"The Last of the Valerii." The Complete Tales of Henry James. Vol. 3. Ed. Leon Edel. Philadelphia: Lippincott, 1962. 89-122.

PL—The Portrait of a Lady. Ed. Robert D. Bamberg. New York: Norton, 1975.

RH—Roderick Hudson. Ed. Geoffrey Moore. New York: Penguin, 1986.

IH—Italian Hours. Ed. John Auchard. University Park: Pennsylvania State UP, 1992. 139-51.

OTHER WORKS CITED

Baym, Nina. "The Marble Faun: Hawthorne's Elegy for Art." *Nathaniel Hawthorne.* Ed. Harold Bloom. New York: Chelsea, 1986. 99-114.

Bewley, Marius. *The Complex Fate.* London: Chatto and Windus, 1952.

Bradbury, Malcolm. *Dangerous Pilgrimages: Transatlantic Mythologies and the Novel.* New York: Viking, 1995.

Brodhead, Richard H. *The School of Hawthorne.* Oxford: Oxford UP, 1986.

Edel, Leon. *Henry James: A Life.* New York: Harper and Row, 1985.

Fogel, Daniel Mark. "Henry James's American Girls in Darkest Rome: The Abuse and Disabuse of Innocence." *The Sweetest Impressions of Life: The James Family and Italy.* Ed. James W. Tuttleton and Agostino Lombardo. New York: New York UP, 1990. 89-106.

Kaplan, Fred, ed. *Travelling in Italy with Henry James.* New York: Morrow, 1994.

Lombardo, Agostino. "Italy and the Artist in Henry James." *The Sweetest Impressions of Life: The James Family and Italy.* Ed. James W. Tuttleton and Agostino Lombardo. New York: New York UP, 1990. 228-39.

Martin, Robert K., and Leland S. Person, eds. *Roman Holidays: American Writers and Artists in Nineteenth-Century Italy.* Iowa City: U of Iowa P, 2002.

Merivale, Patricia. "The Raven and the Bust of Pallas: Classical Artefacts and the Gothic Tale." *PMLA* 89.5 (1974): 961-66.

Peyser, Thomas. *Utopia and Cosmopolis: Globalization in the Era of Literary Realism.* Durham: Duke UP, 1998.

Rowe, John Carlos. "Swept Away: Henry James, Margaret Fuller, and 'The Last of the Valerii.'" *Readers in History: Nineteenth-Century Literature and the Contexts of Response.* Ed. James L. Machor. Baltimore: Johns Hopkins UP, 1993.

Tintner, Adeline R. *The Museum World of Henry James.* Ann Arbor: UMI, 1986.

Tuttleton, James W. "'Dipped in the Sacred Stream': The James Family in Italy." *The Sweetest Impressions of Life: The James Family and Italy.* Ed. James W. Tuttleton and Agostino Lombardo. New York: New York UP, 1990. 22-47.

Vance, William L. *America's Rome.* 2 vols. New Haven: Yale UP, 1989.

Winner, Viola Hopkins. *Henry James and the Visual Arts.* Charlottesville: UP of Virginia, 1970.

Ziolkowski, Theodore. *Disenchanted Images: A Literary Iconology.* Princeton: Princeton UP, 1977.

Sanford E. Marovitz (essay date 2003)

SOURCE: Marovitz, Sanford E. "Hawthorne, Melville, and the Streets of Rome." *American Studies* 20 (2003): 25-36.

[*In the following essay, Marovitz studies the differences between the impressions of Rome expressed by Nathaniel Hawthorne and Herman Melville, and outlines the effect of Roman life and culture on each author.*]

Less than a year apart, two prominent American romancers traveled to Rome in the late 1850s. The first came as a tourist, visiting for less than a month, whereas the latter resided in the city for a total stay of nearly a year. The auctorial careers of both men had peaked by this time, at least in terms of popular appeal during their lifetimes. Herman Melville had continued to write and publish after the success of his early travel-adventure narratives, and *The Confidence-Man*—his last novel apart from the posthumous *Billy Budd*—was ready for publication, but he was no longer a major literary figure in the public eye when he sailed from New York late in 1856. In contrast, although Nathaniel Hawthorne's four years as U.S. consul in Liverpool had left him little time for new writing since 1853, his reputation as a distinguished author remained undimmed.

Both writers had long desired to visit Rome and actually to be in this center of western history and culture for well over two millennia, but the impetus behind their journeys differed for each. For Melville, it promised excitement in its way, but it was somewhat anticlimactic as part of his return trip from a disappointing pilgrimage to Egypt and the Holy Land, both of which enjoy a spiritual past that extends back into time far beyond that even of Rome. For Hawthorne, the Eternal City with its layers of tradition and history represented, through the art and architecture that remained from earlier ages, a long continuity of culture from which he had felt essentially detached and isolated in provincial Massachusetts, indeed in America itself. Yet his principal aim in establishing temporary residence in Rome was pragmatic. Fearful over the frail health of his wife, Sophia, he sought to spend the coming two winters with his family under more benign weather conditions than New England—or Old, for that matter—was likely to offer.

Melville, on his way to the eastern Mediterranean, stopped briefly in England, and while there paid Hawthorne what has become a well-known visit in Liverpool—well-known because of Hawthorne's trenchant account of their conversations during a long walk together. As has often been said, Hawthorne's insight into Melville's unsettled state of mind regarding faith and providence was very keen, as was his perception of Melville's integrity. But his delicately phrased complaint that Melville's "gentlemanly instincts" were limited only by his being "a little heterodox in the matter of clean linen"[1] possibly reveals his subject less meaningfully than himself. It betrays Hawthorne's almost obsessive preoccupation with cleanliness manifest in his letters from Rome as well as through much of the long daily notebook he kept there. This prissiness, this "inexorable demand for perfection in all things"—as noted by George Parsons Lathrop, Hawthorne's son-in-law, biographer, and editor of the 1883 Riverside Edition of the *Works*[2]—had a signal effect on the romancer's attitude throughout his year-and-a-half residence in Italy, especially his time spent in Rome.

Melville, on the other hand, was not hampered by an attitudinal problem during his relatively short Roman visit, but by physical ones. He had been under emotional and physical strain before leaving home, and by the time he reached Rome, having been on the move since early October, the traveling had taken an additional toll as well. Soon after his arrival in Rome, eye-strain began troubling him, at times seriously enough to be incapacitating, and in the final week of his stay in the city, he suffered from "a singular pain across [his] chest & in back" that kept him hotel-bound all day on March 15.[3] That concession to pain was unusual, however, for Melville rarely allowed physical distress to limit his program as a discerning traveler in the city; he intended to miss nothing worth noting, including the urban life around him.

Having traveled overnight by carriage from Naples, he arrived on the morning of February 25, 1857. He took a room at the Hotel Minerva, still situated a little southeast of the Pantheon, and remained there for the duration of his stay. Almost immediately, he set off on one of his walking tours, and typical of his behavior as a traveler, climbed to the top of the first tower he encountered, one centrally located on the Capitoline Hill, only about half a mile from the hotel. From there Melville could overlook the city, but either tired from the journey or in an unreceptive mood, he confessed that Rome "fell flat" on him and that his first view of St. Peter's had been "disappointing" (*J* 106).

Although such negativity implies an inauspicious beginning of his stay, Melville did not allow his colorless first impression to lessen his desire to explore the city, as his journal of the following weeks testifies. In accord with his usual practice, most of his journal entries are in the form of fragmentary notes rather than full statements, as if to serve more as reminders of what he had seen and occasionally heard than as reservoirs of detailed observations and thought.

Yet at times his few words suffice to convey a clear idea of what passed through his mind as he came upon specific sites, paintings, and sculptures. For example, after spending the day walking through the *loggie* of Raphael, the Sistine Chapel, and the Vatican Museum, he wrote that he was "Fagged out completely" and had to "set [a] long time . . . recovering from the stunning effect of a first visit" to the papal city (*J* 108). A few days earlier, the day after his arrival in Rome, while looking upon a statue of Tiberius in the Capitoline Hall of Emperors, he overheard a woman say, "That Tiberius? he don't look so bad at all". But Melville's own perception of the sculpture went beyond the surface to the character of its subject. Of the statue, he wrote simply: "It was he. A look of sickly evil,—intellect without manliness & sadness without goodness. Great brain overrefinements. Solitude" (*J* 106). Then in his lecture "Statues in Rome", first delivered in Lawrence, MA, the same year, he expanded the analysis:

> The arch dissembler Tiberius was handsome, refined, even pensive in expression . . . if he had *looked* bad, he could not have been Tiberius. His statue has such a sad and musing air . . . that . . . it might convey the impression of a man broken by great afflictions, of so pathetic a cast is it. Yet a close analysis brings out all his sinister features, and a close study of the statue will develop the monster portrayed by the historian. For Tiberius was melancholy without pity, and sensitive without affection. He was, perhaps, the most wicked of men.[4]
>
>   ("Statues" 402)

Here, as Howard C. Horsford has noted, is the portrait of a handsome, melancholic, dissembling monster of evil. Discussing Melville's general response to sculpture and painting, notably in this Greco-Roman context, Robert Milder observes that he regarded them "less with an eye to character than with tacit reference to history and the progress of civilization".[5] Milder rightly emphasizes that Melville was "thinking historically" (Milder 138) while wandering among the antiquities both in the museums and outside, yet he may be underestimating the impact on that meditative traveler of individualized busts and figures that enabled him to distinguish character traits and make moral assessments from them. This tendency is illustrated by his verbal portrait of Tiberius, although the marble sculpture he examined in the Capitoline Museum only reinforced his earlier view of the emperor. Melville returned more than thirty years later to that figure as he developed the character of Claggart in *Billy Budd*.

As for Billy himself, but a moment after demonizing Tiberius, Melville wrote a single word—"beautiful"—to describe a statue of Antinöus, which Gail Coffler persuasively argues was a principal source for his portrait of the heroic sailor.[6] In his lecture, Melville elaborated at length on the beauty of this sculpture. Between the citations on Tiberius and Antinöus appears a brief reference to the Dying Gladiator: "Shows that humanity existed amid the barbarians of the Roman time, as it [does] now among Christian barberousness" (*sic; J* 106). One need not stretch thematically to recognize how Captain Vere, himself a dying gladiator among Christian warriors, may be associated with the Roman statue. "None but a gentle heart could have conceived the idea of the Dying Gladiator", wrote Melville in his lecture ("Statues" 405), who had said in a letter six years earlier to Hawthorne: "I stand for the heart. To the dogs with the head!"[7]

Although he visited the studios of several English and American painters and sculptors in Rome, Melville had little companionship as he wandered about the city, and the journal reflects the way his solitude often affected his responses to things and places he saw. After a full day of site-visiting on February 28, for example, he returned at six o'clock to "dinner & to bed", as he succinctly described most of his evenings; his journal entry for that day concludes with "Silence and loneliness of long stretches of blank garden walls", which refers to the vast uninhabited areas within the original city limits (*J* 107). The following morning he walked immediately to Monte Cavallo, from where he observed "The private old palaces—The ruinous fountain of rocks, the vines & c trailing into pool. The mossy pillars and green ooze of loneliness.—The poor old statues in their niches" (*J* 108).

After seeing Melville briefly in Rome, his brother-in-law Samuel S. Shaw wrote to Lemuel Shaw—his father and Melville's father-in-law—that their kinsman "has been almost entirely alone" during his stay "but has found travelling companions, who are of service to him" (21 March 1857; *Correspondence* 310). Perhaps Shaw referred here to the artists and sculptors whom Melville met in Rome, but more likely he meant the Rousse family, whom Melville had befriended and who were also staying at the Minerva. On the afternoon or evening of March 8, Melville went to the Pincian, which he described as a "great Sunday resort", and after dining for seventeen cents, he sat and talked at length with Mr. Rousse, but there is no indication that they had spent part of the day together beforehand (*J* 110).

Melville had also been to the Pincian soon after his arrival in Rome, but his reaction to the activity there was not then as favorable, perhaps because his meditation over the statue of Tiberius had put him in a darker frame of mind. In his journal on that day, he had written: "Fashion & Rank—preposterous posturing [?] within stone's throw of Antinöus. How little influence has truth in the world!—Fashion everywhere ridiculous, but most so in Rome. No place where lonely man will feel more lonely than in Rome. (or Jerusalem)" (*J* 106).

A few days before leaving the city for Florence, Melville went out again amidst the crowds and gave more attention to people than to art and monuments. In the morning he wandered through the ghetto, which he described as filthy and crowded, as well it had to be.[8] Jews had been confined within the walls of the Roman ghetto from the mid-sixteenth century, and not for another thirteen years after Melville's visit—in 1870— would the walls come down. Located beside the Tiber, which Melville graphically depicted as "a ditch, yellow as saffron" (*J* 106), the lower streets of the ghetto were flooded whenever the river was high, so dirt and disease were difficult to control. Inevitably, it was overcrowded as well because Jews could not live elsewhere in the city. As he described the scene, the existence there does not seem much different from that of the Ashkenazic Jews living miserably then in their restricted *shtetlakh,* or villages, to the north in Eastern Europe.

In the evening of that day, Melville went to the Caffe Nuovo, where he noted, in complete contrast to his morning tour, the "Crowd of orderly, well-dressed people" and the "Magical guitarr [*sic*] man", to whom the audience responded with "Hush & applause" (*J* 213). He probably did not stay there listening until late, however, because at six the next morning he set off for a day's tour of Tivoli, almost twenty miles away, and on the following afternoon, March 21, Sam Shaw saw him off for Florence.

Eleven months less one day later, Nathaniel Hawthorne arrived in Rome from France. He entered the city with his wife and three children shortly before midnight, bitter over the cold, over having been cheated by his driver, and over having to bribe the customs officials to pass the family through without ado. They spent the first three nights at Spillman's Hotel, where Hawthorne was ill from cold and dampness. On February 23 the family moved to an apartment on Via Porta Pinciana, where they resided until the last week in May. The early entries in Hawthorne's Italian notebook leave no doubt that his introductory experience in Rome was even less auspicious than Melville's.

Nor did he ever free himself from his bitterness over those first few days. Unlike Melville, he recorded in his notebook an extended account of each day's activities, often describing in pages of graphic detail what and whom he had seen. (He also kept a pocket notebook in which he jotted a few specific data for each day as one does with a date book.) Time and again, from the beginning of his first stay in Rome to the end of his return trip in May of the following year, the entries included wrathful condemnations of Rome's pervasive cold, damp air; the filth he seemed to see wherever he went;

and the malignant atmosphere with the danger of Roman fever, a danger which materialized for the Hawthornes late in 1858 and nearly took the life of fourteen-year old Una, the eldest of the children.

Apart from this dreadful episode, Hawthorne himself ironically appears to have been more adversely affected by the air and weather than the rest of the family, including Sophia, whose relatively delicate health was of prime concern. "The climate is most detestable; it is full of poison", Hawthorne wrote in March 1858 to Francis Bennoch, a London merchant he had befriended in England.

> I feel no energy or enterprise. . . . Mrs. Hawthorne, on the contrary, is full of life and enterprise. . . . The children, too, are very well, and everybody flourishes except myself. . . . If my pen would but serve me as it has done of yore, I would send you such a description of this cold, rainy, filthy, stinking, rotten, rascally city as would avenge me for all the incommodities I have suffered here. I hate it worse than any other place in the whole world.[9]

Such childish vituperation also appears in the notebook, but it would be redundant to quote it further here.

To be sure, Hawthorne did not always feel such irrational depths of acerbity and hatred toward Rome. As he became more or less accustomed to the city—he never really became acclimatized to it—he sensed its almost magical draw on him, a kind of love inspired by the pervasive spirit of Rome, its aura of holiness emanating from the great churches, much of the artwork, indeed, from the papal city itself. On the day before the family set off to spend the summer in Florence, Hawthorne expressed alarm over Una's "fervor and love" for Rome, which she did not wish to leave, yet the next day—after first arguing violently with a servant and with porters who demanded more money, then departing amid a crowd of cursing beggars—he acknowledged "the sad embrace with which Rome takes possession of the soul." Indeed, he wrote, the whole family "felt the city pulling at our heart strings far more than London did".[10]

On returning in October, when they would settle in more satisfactory lodgings at Piazza Poli 68, Hawthorne again felt "a quiet, gentle comfortable pleasure", felt closer to Rome than to Concord and Salem, as if he were "drawing near home" (*N* 488). But a few days later he caught another cold and began to complain again. First the bread was too sour, then more seriously: "I do hate the Roman atmosphere; indeed, all my pleasure in getting back—all my home-feeling has already evaporated". He was depressed over "the languor of Rome,—its nastiness—its weary pavements—its little life pressed down by a weight of death" (*N,* 483, 485).

In none of his writings does Hawthorne expose his fundamental ambivalence as he does in those from and about Rome. Whereas Melville's response to the city was heavily influenced by moral predilections that colored whatever he saw and provoked meditation accordingly, Hawthorne persistently reacted angrily and defensively to what was unfamiliar and beyond his control. A telling contrast between the two travelers is evident in their strikingly different responses to the papal gardens at the Quirinale Palace. They held little appeal for Melville; he described them as "vast" and "cold", as a "paridise [*sic*] without the joy—freaks and caprices of endless wealth—rheumatics in gardener" (*J* 110). Hawthorne, on the other hand, found strangely attractive these extensive gardens

> laid out in straight avenues, bordered with walls of box, as impervious as if of stone,—not less than twenty feet high, . . . stiff and formal as its general arrangement is . . . it is a beautiful place—a delightful, sunny, and serene seclusion. . . . It would suit me well enough to have my daily walk along such straight paths; for I think them favorable to thought; which is apt to be disturbed by variety and unexpectedness.

(*N* 163)

Hawthorne's description and comments elicited by the scene could as well have been written by the "eminently *safe*" narrator of Melville's "Bartleby the Scrivener" as by the author of *The Marble Faun*.[11] His text connotes that boorish and predictable as Kenyon and Hilda may be in his final complete romance, Hawthorne invested more of his own tastes and personality in those two bland characters than most of his readers are inclined to accept.

If Hawthorne had always so strongly favored the invariable and expected, however, his fiction would not likely have gained literary acceptance in his own day or retained it in ours. In spite of his usual inclinations, even he could be surprised over a pleasure gained from the unanticipated. He experienced two Carnival seasons in Rome, for instance, and that he ordinarily found little pleasure in them is apparent from his comment following a dreary February day in 1858 when he rode with the family along the Corso to watch the festivities. One needs not only clear weather but a sunny disposition "to be joyous on such shallow provocation", he declared; particularly annoying to him was being hit by balls of confetti, one of which caught him directly in the eye and brought tears. Such antics are for children, he scoffed in his notebook and aptly concluded, "My cold criticism chills the life out of it" (*N* 71). But the following season brought a warmer response from him; he decided that merely watching the festivities is depressing, but participating even minimally reveals a source of satisfaction to be gained, and he better understood how young people could so delight in the Carnival (*N* 503-4). Such a concession, though, is less indicative of a real change in attitude than it is a throwback to an earlier Hawthorne, a reflection of the youthful author who amused some of the young women at Brook Farm in 1841 by joining them in a mild pillow fight.[12]

More typical of the romancer at this late stage of his career was the man of middle years set in his ways, still seeing himself as the disengaged observer, but he was too often overcome by a sharp emotional reaction to unfavorable circumstances that he could not control for his self-image to be a true one. Of course, in his long daily journal entries, the observer predominates; most of them convey detailed though relatively unsophisticated verbal pictures of artwork, gardens, churches, palaces, and so forth, but he also portrayed people he visited or simply watched on the street, speculating on their lives and motives, as he had done years before in "Footprints on the Sea-Shore", "Night Sketches: Beneath an Umbrella", "Sights from a Steeple", and, particularly, "The Old Apple-Dealer", among many other such familiar pieces.

Although Hawthorne was accompanied by his family, and he had many more acquaintances than Melville among the English and American artists in Rome, his emphasis on physical details in describing people, places, and things conveys an impression of detachment and therefore of psychological isolation amidst the multitude. This impression is intensified by his constant complaints about cold and darkness, which seem more often than not but a reflection of internalized disgust and dreariness.

Perhaps this attitude evolved from disappointment that Rome did not meet his idealized expectations, or perhaps from his inability to reconcile opposing qualities that regularly confronted him: past and present, ideal and real, sunshine and darkness, eternity and time, quiet and festivity, solitude and society, expectation and uncertainty, perfection and flaw, cleanliness and impurity, along with the many other such pairs that could be named.

Nothing that I have seen in Hawthorne's Italian notebook more effectively illustrates the dualities to which he was continuously subject, especially in Rome, than his account of visiting the site of a newly unearthed marble Venus in the area of Porta Portesi (now a giant flea-market) in Trastevere. On April 13, 1859, he was brought to the site by Mr. and Mrs. William Wetmore Story and Hamilton Gibbs Wilde, a less-noted American artist. Hawthorne's description of the incident is remarkably touching because the newly discovered figure is so lovely, comparable with the famed Venus de' Medici in Florence, despite its detached head and arms. When the head was found and placed atop the neck, Hawthorne, clearly moved by the admirable statue, wrote: "The earth still clung about her; her beautiful lips were full of it, till Mr. Story took a thin chip of wood and cleaned it away from between them" (*N* 517). Had he proceeded no farther with his description, the dual qualities would seem reconciled as complementary in his view of the figure: marble and dirt, heaven and earth, perfection and imperfection, ideality and reality. The marble goddess becomes an earthly beauty.

But the union is shattered when in the next few lines he describes the proprietor of the vineyard where the statue was found. Hawthorne portrays him as "a man with the most purple face and hugest and reddest nose that I ever beheld in my life. It must have taken innumerable hogsheads of his thin vintages to empurple his face in this manner. He chuckled much over the statue, and, I suppose, counts upon making his fortune by it". The romancer could not have improved upon this probably unintentional dual portrait of the immortal Aphrodite in marble under the control of the living Dionysus, huge phallic nose, obscene chuckle, and all. Even in his notebook, he could not represent the one without its gross and overpowering opposite, worse in this respect than Aminadab's fueling the fire for Aylmer as the modest Georgiana awaits her death in his story "The Birthmark". As Ishmael posits in *Moby-Dick,* every quality in this world is "what it is merely by contrast".[13] Whereas Ishmael could finally reconcile the opposites, however, Hawthorne, to his lasting discontent and discomfort, could not. In Marseilles about six weeks later, after he had left the city for the last time, his ambivalence was unresolved when he wrote, "although I have been very miserable there [in Rome], . . . and disgusted with a thousand things in daily life, still I cannot say I hate it. . . . But . . . I desire never to set eyes on it again" (*N* 506-07). As Terence Martin has put it, "All too often, [Hawthorne] could view the rich legacy of the Italian past only through the distracting lens of the Italian present" (Martin 25).

Yet his sustained irresolution in Rome did constitute a pendular balance of sorts that likely motivated Hawthorne toward writing another long romance. Initially, he had no thought of doing so, but over the course of time the idea germinated, and he commenced to sketch his romance out toward the end of July 1858 in Florence. As many scholars have shown, he eventually integrated extended passages of his Italian notebook into the growing manuscript of *The Marble Faun,* a worthy fiction in which different aspects of the author's conflicting values are explored. But his exploration there leads to no true synthesis of opposites.

For Melville, the Roman experience was not at first equally inspiring; it provided the substance of his first lecture, "Statues in Rome", now lost and meticulously reconstructed by Merton M. Sealts, Jr., from newspaper reports and letters. After attending the lecture, Melville's cousin Henry Gansevoort wrote to his father, Melville's Uncle Peter, that it "was well conceived and executed, but it lacked the force and beauty that characterize his early writings".[14] Reading the lecture now verifies this assessment, but it was not Melville's intention to romanticize what he had seen. Instead, he aimed to de-

scribe objectively many of the sculptures he had examined, then speculate on the aesthetic response likely to be generated by each work, and finally to discuss the statuary "as a whole". He concluded that the true nobility of the ancients endures, indeed, lives, through their sculptures as well as through the history of their actions. Although Hershel Parker criticizes the lecture as conventional in exposition, resembling that of a "superficial tour guide",[15] "Statues in Rome" accurately reflects Melville's meditative frame of mind as he scrutinized the sculptures on site with reference to their historical origins. Later on, other aspects of his Roman experience were incorporated in *Clarel,* several of his shorter poems, and, as already noted, *Billy Budd.*

But Hawthorne's romance and Melville's late writings present only a limited view of the two authors regarding their time passed in Rome as evident from their daily accounts of travel that both men kept with admirable regularity. Melville seems to have gained much in his understanding of the way that art relates to history and life beyond the level of signs and symbols. Incapacitated at times by ill health, he nevertheless visited one church, garden, gallery, and museum after another, absorbing all that he could during his three and a half weeks in the city until, as Laurie Robertson-Lorant phrases it, "he nearly drowned in the flood of history and art".[16] Always with him was a strong sense of past nobility in contrast to the superficiality he perceived in his own day. Despite weak vision and occasionally aching eyes, Melville examined art works in detail as if committing himself to losing nothing from them once he had left, and his prodigious memory was of infinite value to him in keeping his impressions of what he had seen alive in him for decades afterwards, as copious allusions to European paintings in his late poetry reveal.

Hawthorne's frame of mind was markedly different from Melville's, however, during his much longer stay in Rome. He seems to have felt more obligated to tour the galleries, churches, and palaces than driven by some internal force as Melville was. Parker believes that Hawthorne was too distressed in Italy over "the lack of perfection he saw: he was too sensitive for Italy" (733). He felt that he could not escape the cold and dampness in winter or the dirt, disorder, and beggary in all seasons. Henry James acknowledged that Hawthorne's Italian notebooks are "very pleasant reading" but of limited interest because "his contact with the life of the country, its people and its manners, was . . . extremely superficial".[17] He wrote that Hawthorne seems to have been "a good deal bored by the importunity of Italian art, for which his taste, naturally not keen, had never been cultivated" (James 160). That the "plastic sense was not strong in Hawthorne" (James 161) is confirmed by his distaste for nudity in statues; James said that generally Hawthorne found as much to admire in the smooth, white marble of a sculpture as he did in the sculpture itself and as much beauty in an antique frame as in the rare painting it holds (161). James's tone was much harsher seven years earlier in his anonymous review of *Passages from Hawthorne's French and Italian Notebooks,* where the entries represent the romancer as "superficial, uninformed, incurious, unappreciative" (quoted in Parker 772). The fact that James would write a book on Hawthorne, who was a major influence on the composition of his own fiction, testifies in itself to his admiration of the romancer's "genius," but James had little to say in favor of Hawthorne's taste in art, which he found altogether undeveloped.

Such criticism as this suggests that Hawthorne was considerably more sensitive and responsive to conditions than to art, especially art other than American, whereas Melville had developed a sophisticated sensitivity to European art amid its surroundings while responding but minimally to conditions. So distinctive a difference between these two American travelers in Rome notwithstanding, both authors benefited significantly from their experiences there. For Hawthorne, of course, the principal benefit was immediate as he incorporated much of it in his new romance, completed in England before his return to the U.S., but nothing in *The Marble Faun* or after its publication suggests that he was in any way deepened by the year he spent in the historic city. For Melville, on the other hand, the benefit was of a longer term because his receptiveness to and understanding of the visual arts and more broadly the Roman culture itself continued to fuse with his imagination to the extent that they became an integral component in the composition of his poetry for decades after his return to the U.S. until his death. Hawthorne's romance was in its second American edition and at least its third in England when he died. Melville earned virtually nothing from his poems, but by then dollars no longer damned him.

Notes

1. Quoted in James R. Mellow, *Nathaniel Hawthorne in His Times* (Boston: Houghton Mifflin, 1980) 472.

2. George Parsons Lathrop, ed., *Passages from the French and Italian Note-Books,* vol. 10 of *The Works of Nathaniel Hawthorne* (Boston: Houghton Mifflin, 1883) 119.

3. Herman Melville, *Journals,* ed. Howard C. Horsford with Lynn Horth, vol. 15 of *The Writings of Herman Melville* (Evanston and Chicago: Northwestern UP and the Newberry Library, 1989) 120; hereafter parenthetically cited in the text as *J.*

4. Herman Melville, "Statues in Rome", in *The Piazza Tales and Other Prose Pieces, 1839-1860,* ed. Harrison Hayford, Hershel Parker, and Thomas Tanselle; "Historical Note" and reconstructed

lectures by Merton M. Sealts, Jr., vol. 9 of *The Writings of Herman Melville* (Evanston and Chicago, Ill.: Northwestern UP and the Newberry Library, 1987) 402.

5. Robert Milder, "An Arch Between Two Lives: Melville and the Mediterranean, 1856-57", *Arizona Quarterly,* 55.4 (1999): 36. Milder uses the term *progress* here not to signify the *advance* of civilization but the way that culture transforms through ages of history; indeed, the remainder of his essay suggests that *retrogression* or *decline* may be more accurate in this context because he portrays Melville as increasingly disheartened during this period of his life over the lost grandeur and nobility that characterized the cultures of Greece and Rome.

6. Gail Coffler, "Classical Iconography in the Aesthetics of *Billy Budd, Sailor,*" in *Savage Eye: Melville and the Visual Arts,* ed. Christopher Sten (Kent, OH: Kent State Univ. Pr., 1991) 257, 261, 267.

7. Herman Melville, Letter to Nathaniel Hawthorne, 11 June 1851, *Correspondence,* ed. Lynn Horth, vol. 14 of *Writings* (1991) 192.

8. Hawthorne's repulsive description of the Roman Jews in chapter 42 of *The Marble Faun* has become notorious, so repeating it here should be unnecessary.

9. Nathaniel Hawthorne, Letter to Francis Bennoch, 16 March 1853, vol. 4 of *The Letters, 1857-1864,* ed. Thomas Woodson *et al.,* vol. 18 of the *Centenary Edition of the Works of Nathaniel Hawthorne* (Columbus: Ohio State UP, 1987) 138-39.

10. Nathaniel Hawthorne, *The French and Italian Notebooks,* ed. Thomas Woodson, vol. 14 of the *Centenary Edition of the Works* (1980) 230-33; hereafter abbreviated textually as *N.*

11. Herman Melville, "Bartleby the Scrivener," in *The Piazza Tales and Other Prose Pieces, 1839-1860,* ed. Hayford, Parker, Tanselle; vol. 9 of *The Writings* (1987) 14.

12. Anna Garrett Sedgwick, "A Girl of Sixteen at Brook Farm", *Autobiography of Brook Farm,* ed. Henry W. Sams (Englewood Cliffs, NJ: Prentice-Hall, 1958) 228.

13. Herman Melville, *Moby-Dick; or, The Whale,* ed. Hayford, Parker, Tanselle, vol. 6 of *The Writings* (1988) 53.

14. Eleanor Melville Metcalf, *Herman Melville: Cycle and Epicycle* (Cambridge, Mass.: Harvard UP, 1953) 167.

15. Hershel Parker, *Herman Melville: A Biography, Volume 2, 1851-1891* (Baltimore, MD: Johns Hopkins UP, 2002) 259, 362.

16. Laurie Robertson-Lorant, *Melville: A Biography* (New York: Clarkson-Potter, 1996) 393.

17. Henry James, Jr., *Hawthorne,* English Men of Letters Series (London: Macmillan, 1879) 159.

Sources

Coffler, Gail, "Classical Iconography in the Aesthetics of *Billy Budd, Sailor,*" in *Savage Eye: Melville and the Visual Arts,* ed. Christopher Sten. Kent, Ohio: Kent State Univ. Pr., 1991. Pp. 257-76.

Hawthorne, Nathaniel. *The French and Italian Notebooks,* ed. Thomas Woodson. Vol. 14 of *The Centenary Edition of the Works of Nathaniel Hawthorne.* Columbus: Ohio State UP, 1980.

ST. PETERSBURG

Alexandra Smith (essay date 2003)

SOURCE: Smith, Alexandra. "Pushkin's Imperial Image of St Petersburg Revisited." In *Two Hundred Years of Pushkin, Volume II: Alexander Pushkin: Myth and Monument,* edited by Robert Reid and Joe Andrew, pp. 117-38. Amsterdam and New York: Rodopi, 2003.

[*In the following essay, Smith offers a culturally-focused analysis of Pushkin's poetics as evidenced in his literary treatment of St. Petersburg.*]

Pushkin's portrayal of St Petersburg has attracted considerable attention among Pushkin scholars. It is possible to identify trends in their treatment of this topic. The trends include attempts to examine Pushkin's images of St Petersburg as part of the body of texts defined in Russian literary scholarship in these contexts: 'the Petersburg text' (Lotman and the Tartu school[1]); the descriptive approach (Tomashevskii[2]); the topographical approach (Mederskii[3]); the intertextual approach (Schwarzband, Kodjak[4]); and the mythological and mythopoetical approach (Jakobson[5], Bayley[6]).

These studies tend to focus on various aspects of Pushkin's Petersburg imagery. Yet they do not form a complete or coherent picture, and it remains unclear whether the topic 'Pushkin's Petersburg' has real credibility and whether Pushkin's texts with St Petersburg-bearing images actually have unity or display consistency.

To answer this it is necessary to have a closer look at Pushkin's poetics rather than ideological or socio-political issues which many scholars prefer to highlight.

There has been some re-assessment recently in Russian scholarship of Peter the Great, and it is becoming clearer why St Petersburg was depicted in nineteenth-century literature in an ambivalent and contradictory way, as will be discussed below. Nevertheless, Pushkin's portrayal of St Petersburg brings some coherence into the topic of literature's depiction of St Petersburg, if Pushkin's texts are discussed in their cultural rather than their socio-political context. Such a perspective allows us to re-discover some of the intertextual links between Pushkin's Petersburg texts and (on the one hand) the Petrine Baroque, and (on the other) the visual as well as literary representations of other European cities, chiefly London—with which comparisons of St Petersburg were sometimes made in the first half of the nineteenth century.

It is also argued that Pushkin's 'kinetic' poetic model of a young European city anticipates Bergson's metaphysical concept of 'duration' (*durée*). Such an interpretation could develop the cohesion of St Petersburg in Pushkin's imagery, imagery that exemplifies changing reality in a Bergsonian sense. Thus it may be possible to explain the irrational aspects of Pushkin's portrayal of St Petersburg as part of the inner consciousness, or 'intuition', to use Bergson's terminology. Such an approach helps bring together various aspects of Pushkin's imagery, which before were interpreted as conflicting and contradictory. As a result, Pushkin's art discloses more unity than disparity, and makes Pushkin's treatment of St Petersburg more consistent with his reputation for having a harmonizing influence, a reputation that has been firmly held among Russian poets of the twentieth century. In Aleksander Blok's famous speech 'The Poet's Role' he stresses Pushkin's preoccupation with inner concerns rather than with ideological or state affairs, one that underlines the child-like innocence embedded in Pushkin's writings. In the words of Blok, all Russians preserve in their memories from early childhood 'a happy name—Pushkin'.[7]

Blok's assessment of Pushkin's legacy in Russian culture defines Pushkin's work as part of national cultural memory. More importantly, Blok touches upon the universality of cultural memory, which he perceives as everlasting and dynamic. According to Blok, 'the poet is a child of harmony, and this gives him a role in the culture of the world. Three concerns are incumbent upon him: first, to liberate sounds from the native anarchic element in which they reside; second, to bring these sounds into harmony, or to give them form; and third, to transmit this harmony to the external world'.[8] This view of Pushkin as liberator of harmony enables Blok to highlight the dynamic mechanism of Pushkin's poetry, inviting a comparison of the poet with a composer who orchestrates the final transmission of harmony into the world. In other words the process, the dialogic nature of any poetic work results, in Blok's view, in participation in world culture.

Such a standpoint is very close to Bergson's view of memory and duration, and gives us an opportunity to assess Pushkin's work as part of the universal process of creativity. Bergson's concepts enable us to see the dynamic nature of Pushkin's work, leading us to the discovery of intertextual dialogism and reproduction of other cultural artefacts in his writings. Renata Lachmann has tested this approach in her analysis of Pushkin's poem *Monument,* linking intertextuality to cultural memory in general.[9] According to Lachmann, Acmeist poetics exemplifies Bergson's theory at its best, stressing the coexistence of all cultures (that is, producing a synchronic paradigm). In such a world-view, 'the past is grasped as becoming, as meaning that neither was nor is but that is, rather, always being projected into the future as deferred meaning. . . . Deferral prevents the death of culture, and mnemonic writing guarantees deferral'.[10] The concept of intertextuality as cultural memory can be easily extended to the discussion of Pushkin's St Petersburg including non-verbal images, as well as beliefs and imagery of contemporary popular urban culture. What appears to be paramount to the discussion of Pushkin's Petersburg is Bergson's idea of the inner unity of matter and spirit, achieved through the spatialization of time.

To a great extent, Pushkin was a creator of St Petersburg in the same manner as Peter the Great. The observation William Mills Todd III makes about Pushkin's *Evgenii Onegin* can be easily extended to all Pushkin's texts on St Petersburg, since they fit the paradigm usually defined as 'the text within the text'. Thus, Mills Todd concludes that life and novel form a unity in Pushkin's *Evgenii Onegin* because they both manifest the same creative process.[11] The semiotic terminology allows us to introduce here the term 'text' in a broader meaning, applying it to St Petersburg as a cultural space, a text in its own right. Inversely, it can be said that Pushkin's Petersburg creates its own cultural space. The relationship between Pushkin, the author of his Petersburg, and Peter the Great, the author of the city, can be best described as the anxiety of influence. To put it differently, Pushkin 'reads' St Petersburg as a book, as an evolving and open-ended text which can be used both for inscribing the poet's self and as a source of inspiration, as a context that helps Pushkin, the poet, to develop his own creative potential. This is especially true if we bear in mind that the St Petersburg of Pushkin's times was developing rapidly, changing its appearance in order to conform to the new Imperial image, with many features of the Petrine baroque being replaced with classical elements. Pushkin's vision of St Petersburg as expressed in *The Bronze Horseman* and in *The Queen of Spades* reflects the dynamic image of the

city's cultural space in which different memories and cultural imprints co-existed, and with the classical 'solemn' image still very much evolving.

This [essay] proposes to view Pushkin's writings on St Petersburg as mnemonic writing, preserving the city traditionally perceived as 'Westernized' cultural space with a strongly marked 'young' identity, in the face of the Old Believers' belief that the city was doomed to vanish. It can be argued that Blok's representation of Pushkin, as a poet of child-like qualities, owes a good deal to Pushkin's self-identification with the young and vibrant city, the child of Peter the Great. Pushkin's representation of St Petersburg is far from static and it also bears the stamp of Pushkin's self on the city landscape. Arguably, Pushkin's Petersburg text 'transgresses its own boundaries and opens up into the greater text of culture, macrotext' articulating the 'flowing movement that runs through texts and that constitutes them'.[12]

Two distinct periods in Pushkin's representation of St Petersburg in his texts are usually given special attention in Pushkin scholarship. One period comprises Pushkin's early years in Petersburg (1817-20) which may be characterized as the period of active intellectual and cultural life, when the young poet became increasingly involved in the social and cultural activities of the Russian capital. The second period runs from 1827 to 1837, marked by Pushkin's growing pessimism and somewhat split poetic persona. The latter arose from the failure of the Decembrist revolt and from Pushkin's social position as junior civil servant, humiliating in the eyes of the court and high society, as it did not match Pushkin's self-image of the first poet of Russia. It is important to bear in mind that most of Pushkin's poems on St Petersburg and Moscow before 1827 have not received much attention in Pushkin scholarship, and it is the second period which is known for the inscription of Petersburg urban life into Pushkin's texts. Such texts include *Evgenii Onegin, The Bronze Horseman* and *The Queen of Spades.*

In spite of the large body of work devoted to Pushkin's 'Petersburg texts', it remains unclear why the poet expressed such strong anxieties about the urban life in the capital when, after the end of the war with Napoleon (1812-15), St Petersburg was developing so rapidly. Pushkin captured the new appearance of the city in a number of poems, especially in the opening sections of *The Bronze Horseman,* in which he inscribes into the text the glorious appearance of the renovated Admiralty building. It was the most striking innovation of the St Petersburg urban landscape in the period 1806-1827. The image of the renovated and improved city must have had enormous appeal to Pushkin on his return to St Petersburg in 1827 after several years of exile, although some of the grand projects were still in progress. St Isaac's cathedral, for example, was completed only after Pushkin's death. Yet in the early 1830s the forty-eight supporting columns of the cathedral portico attracted many admirers. One newspaper wrote:

> This work is the highest example of human stamina, might and knowledge. The most courageous projects of the Middle Ages cannot be compared with it, and are much inferior. As a good comparison, one might refer to Ancient Egypt, which represents the youthful stage of our Universe.[13]

Curiously, there are no references in Pushkin's poetry to this or to several other city developments. Clearly, Pushkin's vision has its own mythopoetic aspects. It can be argued that after 1827 they are aspects developing into a coherent mythopoetic model.

A view prevalent in Pushkin studies (for example the Tartu school) states that Pushkin opposes Petersburg to Moscow, in the manner of the Biblical distinction between Jerusalem as the city of God and Babylon as scarlet woman and city of exile. In my view, this approach to Pushkin's Petersburg requires modification since some texts are exempt from this paradigm. In the words of one scholar, the binary opposition 'Jerusalem—Babylon' can be presented as follows:

> Jerusalem is the true home of the chosen, God's site for the Temple and the throne. Yet it is subject to corruption and wavering allegiance and thus condemned by the prophets, particularly Hosea and Jeremiah. Babylon in contrast is the fallen city of sensuality, greed, and disobedience to God's will; there men worship idols and false values.[14]

This attitude can be sensed in Pushkin's own reference to St Petersburg as a cursed city. It is known that upon receiving news of the flood in November 1824 Pushkin wrote to his brother: 'The very thing for cursed Petersburg'.[15] Indeed, Pushkin's image of the old Moscow and the new capital invites such an opposition, but their representation is ambivalent both in *The Bronze Horseman* and in *The Queen of Spades*. This might be explained by the Romantic fashion of the 1830s with its promotion of male genius as Romantic hero. Young Petersburg fitted their image. This view was reflected in Pushkin's differentiation of the two cities on the basis of gender principles. Thus in *Evgenii Onegin* Pushkin labels Moscow as grandmother. Furthermore, Pushkin does not see the two cities as equal any more, comparing the two capitals with two hearts that cannot co-exist in the same body.

In his essay 'The Journey from Moscow to St Petersburg' (1833-4) Pushkin summarizes his view thus: 'Peter the Great did not like Moscow . . . The decline of Moscow is the inevitable consequence of the rise of St Petersburg. Two capitals cannot flourish at the same time in the same state—just as two hearts cannot co-exist in one human body'.[16] Yet some of Pushkin's po-

ems do not distinguish strongly between the two cities. This is especially evident in the poem 'What a night! The hard frost . . .' ('К к о÷! Мо о еск ÷ий . . .') (1827) alluding to the execution of the rebellious *streltsy* by Peter the Great in Moscow's Red Square. The horse rider in this poem foreshadows the bronze horseman chasing Evgenii along the night streets of St Petersburg, yet the whole scene belongs to Moscow, the early capital of Russia, not St Petersburg. The Red Square that Pushkin depicts still bears all the marks of the bloody execution:

> . . . And the whole of Moscow sleeps quietly,
> Disturbing fear forgotten.
> And the square stands in the darkness of the night,
> Still full of the painful memories of execution.[17]

Yet the violent scene which Pushkin graphically depicts with dead bodies, blood, and the burning ashes of human bones is merged with the portrayal of a young executioner riding through the square to a meeting with his beloved. If anything it is the horse, not the rider, which conveys some disgust with the scene, as well as hesitation and anxiety. The rider persuades the horse to ride forward, forgetting the horror they both witnessed:

> '. . . What are you afraid of? What is it?
> Didn't we ride here yesterday,
> Stamping viciously on the traitors of the Tsar?
> . . . My swift horse, my fearless horse,
> Ride forward, fly! . . .' And the tired horse
> Ran through the pillars, underneath the hanging body
> . . .[18]

In this poem Pushkin's vision of Moscow is virtually indistinguishable from a similar scene of the chaos and violence in post-flood St Petersburg as presented in *The Bronze Horseman*. Therefore it is questionable whether *The Bronze Horseman* depends much on the imagery of Adam Mickiewicz who recorded his impressions of the flood in such poems as *The Monument of Peter the Great* (*Pomnik Piotra Wielkiego*) and *Oleszkiewiecz*. In the latter poem the Polish painter and freemason Oleszkiewiecz acts as a prophet, comparing St Petersburg with a new Babylon and predicting its demise. In the words of M. N. Virolainen, Pushkin's *The Bronze Horseman* contains polemical allusions to Mickiewicz's poems of which Pushkin was aware.[19] However, when juxtaposing these poems with Pushkin's poem about Moscow 'What a night! The hard frost . . .', it is difficult to agree with Schwarzband who insists on Pushkin's appropriation of these images from Mickiewicz's work. Schwarzband states that 'perhaps . . . Mickiewicz's poem *The Monument of Peter the Great* . . . inspired Pushkin to use the horse as an allegory of Russia, and the rider as an allegory of the autocracy'.[20] Clearly in 'What a night! The hard frost . . .' written about Moscow and preceding *The Bronze Horseman*, Pushkin had already created such an allegorical vision. This observation supports the view of John Bayley, who emphasizes that Pushkin knew Mickiewicz's poem *Forefathers' Eve (Dziady)* which describes St Petersburg; however everything about the poem must have outraged his æsthetic sense, but like the grit in the oyster it worked in him until the final casting of the pearl at Boldino in 1833. *The Bronze Horseman* is not a reply to Mickiewicz's poem, but it might not have been written without it.[21] Surprisingly, the possibility of self-reference in Pushkin's work has escaped scholars' attention. Yet 'What a night! The hard frost . . .' simply continues Pushkin's comparison of the Decembrist conspiracy in *Stanzas* (1826) with the mutiny of the Moscow *streltsy* at the beginning of Peter's reign. In this respect, Pushkin presents both cities as civilized urban places which had lost their innocence and appeal to the less privileged.

In many ways both Moscow and St Petersburg look equally appealing in Pushkin's verse novel *Evgenii Onegin,* boasting a huge range of social gatherings and cultural life, with a dynamic and diverse urban life. There are several scenes presented in a kinetic manner: as if the busy city life is seen through the eyes of a person taking a ride through the streets of Moscow and St Petersburg. The description in *Evgenii Onegin* of Moscow's busy Tverskaia Street as perceived by Tatiana (7: XXXVIII) strongly resembles, in its lively kaleidoscopic representation, St Petersburg's busy streets as seen by Onegin in the early hours of the morning (1: XXXV). Commenting on the liveliness and dynamism Pushkin employs in *Evgenii Onegin,* one of the most important Russian critics of the first half of the nineteenth century, N. I. Nadezhdin, compared Pushkin's portrayal of urban life with the paintings and engravings of the English artist William Hogarth (1697-1764). Hogarth's satirical realism and lively representation of life captured the imagination of Pushkin and his contemporaries. In his review of *Evgenii Onegin* Nadezhdin writes with great enthusiasm that Pushkin's 'portrayal of Moscow is truly Hogarthian! Pushkin's talent here is at its best'.[22] Hogarth's prints and engravings were well known in Russia in the first half of the nineteenth century. Petr Viazemskii mentions his name as being among the most influential artists in Russian cultural development of this period.[23] It is as if Nadezhdin was anxious to follow the example of the eighteenth-century English writers whose verbal portraits and interiors were imitative of Hogarth's art.

Nadezhdin's comments on the 'Englishness' and 'Hogarthian qualities' of Pushkin's artistic world extend to observations on a more general use of irony and parody in Pushkin's work. The critic defines Pushkin's poetics as 'simply a parody', claiming that

> Pushkin's muse is a mischievous young girl, who does not care tuppence for the world. Her element is to mock at everything, good and bad . . . not out of spite or

scorn, but simply out of desire to poke fun. It is this which shapes in a particular way Pushkin's poetic process and clearly distinguishes it from *Byronic* misanthropy or the humour of Jean-Paul Richter . . . There is nothing that can be done about it . . . what is true, is true . . . A master can mock and ridicule . . . provided, of course, he has a sense of honour and proportion. And if one can be great in small matters, then it is perfectly possible to call Pushkin a genius—*at caricature!*[24]

Nadezhdin's view of Pushkin has become increasingly credible in recent Russian studies on Pushkin,[25] despite being vigorously dismissed or marginalized in Soviet scholarship.[26] One scholar suggests the presence of carnivalesque qualities (in the Bakhtinian sense) in Pushkin's texts. It would not be overdoing it to take this point further and map out the co-presence of at least two pretexts, two stylistic influences in Pushkin's work that relate to the images of St Petersburg.

As Nadezhdin points out, Pushkin appropriates playfulness and dynamic impressionism in his poetry with great success. Both Pushkin and Hogarth share a great love for theatre and they both mock the theatrical in the everyday life of the middle class and the aristocracy. Hogarth's innovative techniques lie in reviving the baroque, introducing new themes and a vast new world of descriptive realism that occasionally blend irrational elements of fantasy which one critic said 'derived from popular art and from mannerism', and were 'in seeming contradiction with his inherent and increasing realism'.[27] To a great extent the same words can be applied to Pushkin. Pushkin's poem *Peter the Great's Feast* verbally reproduces some popular images of St Petersburg which appeared on many engravings of the two Russian eighteenth-century artists Ivan and Aleksei Zubov. Their engravings were imitative of the popular art of *lubok* and were promoting ideologically charged imperial images of the new Russian capital St Petersburg anxious to boost its trade with Europe.

The most famous engraving produced by Aleksei Zubov is the 1716 panorama of St Petersburg showing several important unfinished projects as being completed. In effect Zubov presented the future look of the city as its present one. In the same manner Pushkin wrote his utopian-like prophecy of St Petersburg's future diverse cultural space into *The Bronze Horseman*. The imagery of Zubov's engraving is politically charged and is a prototype image for Pushkin's *Peter the Great's Feast*. Lindsey Hughes describes the engraving:

> Like many views of the city, it focuses not on the buildings, which are confined to a narrow strip in the middle ground, but on the ships—warships, yachts, barges, and a sloop bearing Peter and Catherine—in the foreground. The sky takes up more than half the sheet, with hosts of heaven bearing a ribbon with the city's name. It shows St Petersburg from an 'impossible' angle, ignor-

ing the rules of aerial perspective, while at the same time showing buildings in their correct order as a strip of façades. Unfinished projects (for example, the spire of Peter-Paul Cathedral) are shown completed . . . Aleksei Zubov was able to capture the 'spirit of the age' as well as its concrete image.[28]

Peter the Great's Feast focuses primarily on the boats, yachts, Russian flags, military victories of Peter the Great and cargo ships, reproducing the festive atmosphere of the Petrine period:

> The multi-coloured flags of the ships
> Flutter joyfully above the Neva river,
> The loud harmonious songs of the rowers
> Reach the shores from the boats . . .
> What does the Russian tsar celebrate
> In the little city Petersburg?
> Why the shouts and loud shots,
> And the squadron is on the river? . . .
> Perhaps, our young fleet is greeting its father
> Brandt's old boat? . . .[29]

It is a commonplace to suggest that Pushkin's poem illustrates Peter the Great's ability to forgive his enemies, hinting that Nicholas I should pardon the Decembrist conspirators who were living in exile in Siberia. (The poem was written in 1835 and was intended to mark the anniversary of the Decembrist revolt.) While this is true, it is just as important to note that to achieve this Pushkin reproduces a very popular image of St Petersburg celebrating the young Russian Empire. Echoing Zubov's engraving, Pushkin refers to Catherine, Peter the Great's wife:

> Did Catherine give birth?
> Does she celebrate her Saint's day,
> This dark-browed wife
> Of the miracle-maker giant? . . .[30]

In this stanza Pushkin veils his allusion to the ever-increasing prosperity and fertility of the re-invented empire in overtones and imagery readily present in Russian popular culture (for example, 'dark-browed wife'; 'miracle-maker giant').

This is a twofold device. Pushkin's image of Empress Catherine I reflects the background of Peter the Great's wife that, together with his inclination towards democracy (including popular Yuletide festivities, fireworks, Russian court carnivals, the 'Drunken Assembly', parties, etc.), contributed to his image in popular literature as a tsar-craftsman, a people's tsar. Catherine progressed 'through the roles of camp-follower, mistress, official companion, wife, empress-consort, and, from 1725 to 1727, empress in her own right'.[31] Pushkin's image of Catherine as mother of the nation, a typical popular peasant goddess of fertility, so to speak, might be attributed to the fact that one of her pet names in Peter the Great's household was 'matka', meaning an old girl, mother and uterus—all at the same time. On the other hand, Pushkin as author of the poem inscribes his own voice into the festivities of Peter the Great, the Russian Bacchus. This point brings closer an understanding of the mechanism Pushkin employs, using the Petersburg setting, to promote his own hedonistic image (partially reflected in *Evgenii Onegin* and in some poems dedicated to various Petersburg friends, for example *To Galich*). This image produced a great effect on twentieth-century readers of Pushkin. As mentioned above, Blok associated Pushkin's name with the celebration of life and joyful carnival. In her essay 'My Pushkin' Tsvetaeva reflects on the excitement she felt as a child when reading Pushkin's *Peter the Great's Feast*. She found particularly striking and amusing the reference to the popular image of the Empress together with references to the noises produced by party-goers and cannons.[32] In spite of the fact that Pushkin declared England the 'fatherland of caricature and parody',[33] the Petrine culture was full of carnivalesque qualities that inspired parody and mockery. Furthermore, Pushkin draws attention to activities of Peter the Great that have highly questionable relevance to the state. It appears that Pushkin depicts with warmth and sympathy Peter the Great's whimsical and anarchistic qualities that would attract criticism from the more conservative representatives of Russian culture and from Western observers. Yet the image of the 'shaken' Neva at the end of the poem functions as a mark of the irony in this poem, alluding to the assault on the cultural memory of the nation and playing on the metaphor that, in popular cultural memory, associated Peter the Great with the pagan god of thunder who could strike again.

Here it may also be mentioned that Pushkin's *Peter the Great's Feast* conceals autobiographical overtones. Thus, Fedor Musin-Pushkin, one of Pushkin's ancestors, was executed by Peter the Great for participating in the 1697 conspiracy against the Tsar. Pushkin mentions Fedor in the poem *My Genealogy* (1830): 'My ancestor had a quarrel with Peter the Great'. Yet Ivan Musin-Pushkin, another Pushkin ancestor, took part in the greatest Peter the Great-organized spectacle—Zotov's 1715 wedding, a real landmark in the history of the orgies of the Drunken Assembly. Ivan Musin-Pushkin was dressed in Venetian costume.[34] Noting the carnivalesque overtones in Pushkin's texts that touch upon the theme of St Petersburg or of Peter the Great, it seems highly significant that Pushkin continues the Venetian motif in his representation of St Petersburg, introducing biographical allusions into his text.[35] As for the poem's setting, Pushkin refers to Peter the Great's celebrations of his 1714 victory at sea over Swedish war-ships, which led to the annexation of Finland. In his historical work *A History of Peter the Great* Pushkin details the victory celebrations of Peter the Great's 'naval' Poltava, with abundant gunfire across St Petersburg and Empress Catherine's giving birth to a daughter Margarita (wrongly mentioned by Pushkin as Natalia in his *History*).[36] A few months later, at the beginning of 1715, Peter the Great pardoned some officials involved in a financial scandal (members of Peter the Great's Treasury were sent to Siberia), celebrating it with gunfire and other festive activities. Just at this time Musin-Pushkin came to be dressed in Venetian costume for a carnival at the 'mock wedding' of a 'young groom', Zotov (who was over eighty years old), organized by Peter the Great in Moscow in January 1715. In the words of one of the witnesses, it was 'a world turned upside down', when the mock Tsar was carried in a sledge pulled by bears.[37]

Taking into account Pushkin's work in the archives as a historian, it is difficult to imagine that *Peter the Great's Feast* contains any of Pushkin's sincere admiration or sympathy. Pushkin's veiling of his didactic message to Nicholas I about the Decembrists sent to Siberia appears to be highly ambivalent. Could Pushkin really be celebrating such a carnival? Lindsey Hughes points out that there were many critical accounts of the forced and unspontaneous nature of the festivities: 'These and similar incidents confirm the suspicion that Peter's masquerades were not true carnival at all, in the sense that "people are liberated from authority, behaviour is unfettered and hierarchy is suspended". On the contrary, Peter's "courtly carnival" celebrated authority as sacred'.[38]

Contrary to the established view that Pushkin's *Peter the Great's Feast* contains a sympathetic account of the Russian Tsar, I argue that Pushkin's references to the popular image of Peter the Great suggest an imitation of the popular imagination to parodic effect. The great importance of the occasion for the Russian Empire is overshadowed in Pushkin's narration by actions of personal glorification. Thus, Pushkin's Peter, the autocratic leader, celebrates himself. Arguably Pushkin, the author in his own right, produces his own version of events to undermine the historical figure of Peter the Great, subverting Peter's pseudo-carnival. Pushkin ridicules as well as praises Peter the Great in a carnivalistic manner, developing Peter's masquerade into a true carnival.

This poem exemplifies, in my view, one of the most typical uses of irony, definable as *blame by praise*. It should be borne in mind, too, that Pushkin's *Peter the Great's Feast* mocks the naivety of popular belief in a benevolent autocrat. If anything, abundant references to cannons and guns produce a negative effect on readers. At the same time as playing on the popular motif of the benevolent Tsar, Pushkin conceals his doubts about the noble nature of Nicholas I, or for that matter any other Russian autocrat.

To support this observation, we can examine Pushkin's treatment of the theme of carnival and autocracy in an early Pushkin poem hitherto undiscussed in the context of the Petersburg theme. Pushkin conveys his doubts of

the true nature of Nicholas I's 'carnival' in the poem 'When the Tsar was frowning . . .' ('Бои х . . .') (1825). In this poem Pushkin's Nicholas I plays a practical joke on his audience, suggesting that Falconet's monument of Peter the Great has miraculously disappeared from its usual place:

> When the Tsar was frowning,
> He told his companion that, 'Yesterday
> The storm pushed down
> The monument to Peter'.
>
> The companion was frightened to death,
> Asking 'Is that so? I didn't know! . . .'
> The Tsar burst into laughter,
> Saying, 'It's an April Fool, my dear!'[39]

This poem implicitly links Nicholas I to Peter the Great in mentioning execution by hanging (a concealed homage to the hanged Decembrists), suggesting that the beginning of Nicholas' reign was marked with blood and victimization of some of his subjects, and repeating Pushkin's view of the tragedy of Peter the Great. The poem 'When the Tsar was frowning . . .' can be compared with observations Pushkin makes in his essay 'A Journey from Moscow to St Petersburg'. In this essay Pushkin states that 'Peter I did not like Moscow where everywhere he went he faced painful memories of revolts and executions, an extremely traditional way of life and the obstinate resistance of bigotry and prejudices'.[40] In 'When the Tsar was frowning . . .' Pushkin satirically conveys the Russian Tsar haunted by the legacy of his predecessor Peter, with whom he wanted to be compared. (The column marking the reign of Alexander I was built on the orders of Nicholas I, whose intention was to produce a grand monument that could overshadow Peter's fortress and its tall bell-tower.) Nicholas I was criticized by Pushkin and his contemporaries not only for his treatment of the Decembrists but also for his growing interference in censorship and failure to organize evacuation and help for victims of the famous St Petersburg flood of November 1824. Pushkin detects in Nicholas I signs of the anxiety of influence, as well as a tendency towards organizing ever more masquerades that act to confer sanctity on autocracy rather than to liberate the suppressed.

It is not coincidental that Pushkin employs irony in his depiction of Peter and Nicholas. In 'What a night! The hard frost . . .' Pushkin uses the first phrase as a mark of irony, suggesting that the poem contains a discourse on love (in the manner of many nineteenth-century love poems) but in the context of the poem its meaning unravels itself as pure mockery. Similarly in 'When the Tsar was frowning . . .' Pushkin makes a jester of the Tsar who pretends to be horrified rather than amused. This time St Petersburg with its famous monument to Peter the Great appears a perfect setting for such jokes.

The joke about the moving statue of Peter the Great appears in *The Bronze Horseman*. It has received extensive treatment in Pushkin scholarship. Virolainen, however, argues that there were many legends about the moving statue, including Count A. N. Golitsyn's dream, but all of them were likely to have been inspired by Pushkin's imagination as expressed in *The Bronze Horseman*.[41] The outline of this legend is important because Pushkin's 'When the Tsar was frowning . . .' supports an opposite view to Virolainen, that Pushkin was aware of the legend long before writing *The Bronze Horseman* (1833). According to the legend, in 1812 Alexander I intended to move the monument, but Count Golitsyn saw a 'good omen' in his dream and warned him not to do it. In Golitsyn's words, he saw himself walk towards Elagin Island to deliver a report to the Tsar. The Bronze Horseman chased Golitsyn on his way to the palace, and in front of the palace warned the Tsar and Golitsyn that it was not to be moved, because it served as the protector of the city. It is known Golitsyn recounted the dream to Alexander I who changed his mind about moving the monument.[42] Pushkin's version differs in that Alexander I spreads this legend himself, with the purpose of terrorizing his subordinates. Pushkin adds a humorous twist to the story, too.

There may have been many other legends of Peter the Great's statue circulating in St Petersburg, contributing to the growing body of urban tales that accompany the growth of any important trade centre or port city. Falconet himself was partly responsible for the impression his sculpture produced on its observers. First of all, the statue itself was to some extent a parody of Italian equestrian statues, bringing carnivalesque overtones to the city's landscape. According to the critic George Levitine, Falconet chose a simple concept, avoiding any overt symbolic detail:

> In this conception, Falconet departed from the main tradition of equestrian monuments, which took its source in the Roman statue of Marcus Aurelius, in the Capitoline square. This tradition was based on the image of a triumphant horseman mounted on a powerful steed, majestically advancing at a walking pace on the flat surface of a geometrically shaped pedestal. Exemplified during the Italian Renaissance by Donatello's 'Gattamelata' (Padua) and Verocchio's 'Colleoni' (Venice), this type of equestrian representation culminated in France in Girardon's famous statue of Louis XIV, which stood in the Place Vendôme, in Paris.[43]

There is an inner symbolic meaning in Falconet's equestrian statue, detectable to spectators, arising from Falconet's unusual placing of the monument on the edge of a rocky elevation. This added a certain twist to the old theme, producing an unprecedented dramatic context. However, Falconet explains in some of his letters that he portrayed 'Peter the Great not as a conqueror, but as a benevolent reformer and legislator; the monarch of

the "philosophers" and the benefactor of the new Russia'.[44] As Levitine points out:

> In his writings, Falconet repeatedly explained the meaning of various aspects of his statue. Instead of the traditional pseudo-Roman martial attire, the tsar is given a 'heroic' but nondescript garb which, according to the sculptor, belongs to 'men of all times'. The sculptor acknowledges the fact that this garb recalls the shirt worn by Volga boatmen, and one can note an additional, distinctly Russian, touch in the wolf skin used in the monarch's saddle . . . He has reached the summit of the rocky elevation that symbolizes the difficulties he has overcome.[45]

Surprisingly, the irony embedded in Falconet's monument has not been adequately discussed. Some distinctly 'barbaric' features of Falconet's horseman reflect the fact that Peter the Great was a jester, disguising himself as a 'people's Tsar'.

It should be noted that from the very beginning of the project there were several factors to inspire the creation of local legends. The monument itself was a living memory of the saga associated with the history of its creation. One of the most striking examples is the stone forming the statue's base. This was made from part of what was known in Russia as the 'Thunderstone' weighing over three million pounds. This gigantic monolith was brought from the Karelian swamp where according to Karelian legend Peter the Great had used it many times as an observation point. The monument itself became part of urban folklore. There were numerous accounts of people witnessing some movement of the statue. The vast space surrounding the monument chiefly contributed to this 'kinetic' effect, as did some important features of the monument itself. In Levitine's view:

> It is not a mere question of size. The arresting effect of this silhouette is also the result of the powerful ascending diagonal movement that abruptly releases its energy after having reached its apogee. Animated by a different rhythm, the theme of upward élan, culmination and break is repeated twice: in the bronze horseman, with the horse rearing over emptiness, and its mountain-like base, with the jutting shape of the cliff. Naturally this theme is the energizing force of the great triangle that gives the group its monumental character.[46]

The main achievement of the sculptor lies in the theatrically conceived staging. Some contemporaries, including Diderot, referred to Falconet's monument to Peter the Great as 'epic drama', or even 'Falconet's epic poem'.[47]

Theatricality formed an essential part of the Petrine period, and can be seen as part of the living legacy of Peter the Great in St Petersburg. It is not surprising that theatricality was on Pushkin's mind when he wrote such Petersburg tales as *The Queen of Spades, The Little House in Kolomna, The Bronze Horseman* and *The Lonely Little House on Vassilevskii Island.* It is interesting that the famous flood in St Petersburg significantly undermined popular belief in Peter the Great's God-like and miracle-making qualities. Falconet's monument became the embodiment of Peter the Great's qualities as a protector of the city (perhaps, in the same way as St George served as a protector of Moscow in popular culture).

As Levitine puts it, 'Benevolent or ominous, Peter the Great came to be popular as the jealous guardian of the destiny of the city, a kind of awesome palladium'.[48] As mentioned above, Pushkin's 'When the Tsar was frowning . . .' refers to an act of mockery concerning Falconet's statue. Alexander I's attitude was not unique. It is known that Countess Anna Tolstaia, a friend of Pushkin, visited Falconet's monument after the flood of St Petersburg on 7 November 1824, and expressed her disgust at the monument's failure to protect the city by sticking out her tongue at the statue.[49]

The flood produced mixed responses. Some reflected on this event with humour (see the satirical poem in the style of Béranger, written on the day after the event by Aleksandr Izmailov—'God decided to punish all the sinful here . . .'). Others described it in an apocalyptic vein. The number of the texts (especially prose tales) bearing the marks of the unravelling Apocalypse outweighs the number of more humorous or satirical texts. Such works include the historical tale *The Black Box* (1833) (е ый щик) by K. P. Massalskii, a novella *A Dead Man's Joke* (Жи ой е е) by V. F. Odoevskii (published in 1833 in the almanac *Dennitsa*), a Petersburg tale *The Feast of Death* (о Жес о с е и) by V. S. Pecherin (1833), to name just a few. It seems that Pushkin incorporated both tendencies in his Petersburg tales, embedding some parodies on existing texts, too. Among the sources Pushkin uses in *The Bronze Horseman,* Virolainen lists a great number of anecdotes and historical accounts of responses to the flood.[50]

In several ways Virolainen interprets *The Bronze Horseman* as an example of polyphony in the Bakhtinian sense. In Virolainen's view, the historical truth emerges as a collection of voices.[51] Virolainen's opinion appears far-fetched, stretching to some analogies with Dostoevskii's novels which Bakhtin examined in great detail. To support such a view one needs to rely on the evidence of the dialogical nature of the text. It is difficult, however, to find consistent evidence of dialogue in the narrative nature of *The Bronze Horseman.* The characteristics of Pushkin's narrative are still blurred. There is no agreement between scholars, for example, on which points of view are represented in *The Bronze Horseman.* In contrast to Pushkin's texts, Dostoevskii's novels contain various ideological trends and points of view with clear marks, that is, every voice is definable and distinctive. This is not the case with Pushkin. Evgenii's madness in *The Bronze Horseman* is not readily recognizable. Some scholars see this as the embodiment of realism, while others link it to Romantic tradition, to Shakespeare's drama, or to the representation of the holy fool in Russian popular culture.[52] Perhaps it is more appropriate to characterize *The Bronze Horseman* and other Petersburg tales by Pushkin as representation of cultural memory, expressing anxieties about the city's future destiny.

Under close examination Pushkin's Petersburg texts reveal many links with the popular mythology of the city not primarily centred on Falconet's statue. Thus, Ospovat and Timenchik relate people's fear of the monument to Alexander I, the new landmark of the city unveiled by Nicholas I to the public on 30 August 1834. Pushkin avoided the ceremony, finding it humiliating to appear there as a junior civil servant. Commenting on the enormous weight and height of the column, Countess Anna Tolstaia predicted that it would fall down, and avoided riding near it in her carriage. Alexander I's column became a target of many jokes.[53] Given both popular fears and jokes it is surprising that in the poem *The Monument* (1836) Pushkin chose Alexander's column in front of the Winter Palace for comparison with his own art, the non-verbal monument. Pushkin in referring to the column is suggesting that his own immortalized self be located in the space of St Petersburg. By placing himself in the cultural space of St Petersburg, Pushkin explored the opportunity of reaching a vast audience, making his image as popular and ambivalent as the image of the city itself. Thereby the poet secured his immortality: linking himself to the cultural memory of the city, advancing his ability to mimic different texts as the main virtue of his writing. Furthermore, Pushkin's characterization of himself in *The Monument* as a person who 'told the truth to the Tsars with a smile on his face' compares the poet with Evgenii, his protagonist in *The Bronze Horseman.* Both the prophetic and the humorous traits in Pushkin's art come together when his Petersburg tales are viewed as portraying the city as 'comic apocalypse' (to borrow the definition Mark Seiden applied to Dickens' London[54]).

Pushkin reflected the mood of his St Petersburg and European contemporaries when he expressed disillusion with the noise and growing commercialization of modern, European St Petersburg, the youngest of European capitals. Pushkin's contrasting view of Moscow and St Petersburg in *Evgenii Onegin,* manifesting the archetypal 'Jerusalem-Babylon' model, is comparable to the view of London found in late eighteenth-century British literary tradition. (The 'Babylonian' view of St Petersburg is strongly pronounced in Pushkin's tale *The Lonely Little House on Vassilevskii Island,* in which the protagonist is a victim of corrupting St Petersburg and withdraws from urban life as a result of his misfortunes.) As one critic concludes:

> Hence the ambivalence that marks the eighteenth-century's confrontation with the city and the deep nostalgia felt by many writers toward the past represented by the classical tradition. They would have liked to live in an idealized classical city, an Athens or Augustan Rome of their imagination—a city of culture in the truest sense. Yet the noise and perpetual whirl of commercial and criminal London kept closing in on them. They couldn't really reconcile the two images, although one has a sense of their having tried desperately to do so. It remained for the Romantics utterly to reject the city as a meaningless and trivial experience.[55]

These words are also applicable, with some modification, to Pushkin's world view. Anna Akhmatova noted the decaying atmosphere of Pushkin's St Petersburg and compared the image of the city in the first chapter of *Evgenii Onegin* with that presented in *The Bronze Horseman*:

> In the first example we see a charming native land through the eyes of Evgenii Onegin, the young exile; in the second example we see Petersburg as a pigsty as presented in Pushkin's letters; it is merciless and gloomy . . . The diversity and colourfulness of the scenes in *Eugene Onegin* had vanished in *The Bronze Horseman* . . . what is left is the impenetrable darkness and whores. It expresses Pushkin's cry over human life. What is felt is the displacement of the author of *The Bronze Horseman*.[56]

To Akhmatova's observations can be added Pushkin's thoughts about decaying St Petersburg in *Evgenii Onegin,* which she does not refer to. In the first chapter (stanza XXXV) Pushkin depicts the noisy scene of a St Petersburg morning in an ironic way. Pushkin refers to 'the pleasant noises of the morning' in the context of an unappealing St Petersburg setting: all images refer either to military training (allusions to the noises of drums—'St Petersburg, as busy as ever, had been woken up by drums') or to trade and business activities. We see these morning activities through the eyes of young Onegin returning home exhausted from the ball in the early hours of the morning, so it is difficult not to interpret Pushkin's remark about the pleasant noises of the morning as ironic. Pushkin's ironic viewpoint is also felt in the same chapter's allusion to the blue smoke of chimneys spiralling high into the sky. In this chapter the winter morning landscape is associated with pollution and a busy pace of life, not as enjoyable as the atmosphere Pushkin portrays in his other scenes that romantically idealize winter experiences in the country.

Scholars have overlooked one important aspect of Pushkin's Petersburg. As mentioned earlier, English writers developed the image of the classical city as a product of their imagination, ascribing to it the qualities of truly cultural space. In the context of this comparison, it is important to address the question of Pushkin's ideal city. Did he develop such a view of the classical city? In my view Pushkin expresses his longing for Venice, imagining it as a truly classical and peaceful cultural space. In the opening chapter of *Eugene Onegin* (1: XLIX) Pushkin vividly depicts Venice as a desirable location where he will be free and in love with a Venetian girl, enjoying a ride in a 'mysterious gondola'.[57] In the poem 'Near the places, where a golden Venice rules . . .'(1827) Pushkin reproduces the same dream of a peaceful and idyllic ride in a gondola through the canals of Venice. Pushkin compares himself to a young Venetian singing love songs and thinking of sacred poems. In the context of the European tradition of the representation of city life in the pre-Romantic and Romantic period, one may suggest that Pushkin's juxtaposition of Venice and St Petersburg is not coincidental and that it alludes to the image of the still evolving city. This view can be supported by reference to the concealed homage to Venice in *The Bronze Horseman.* Thus at the beginning of *The Bronze Horseman* Pushkin incorporates the words of Venetian citizen Francesco Algarotti, who in a letter in 1739 compared St Petersburg with 'the great window recently opened in the north through which Russia looks on Europe'.[58] In the Notes to *The Bronze Horseman* Pushkin identifies this quotation as a source of his metaphor attributed in the poem to Peter the Great: 'It is determined by Nature for us to cut a window here into Europe'. It is interesting that Pushkin depicts Peter as a mystic and a seer, as if the vision of the city came to him as an inspiration from Venice.

This point should not be overstated however, in the light of the fact that Peter the Great's acquaintance with Venice remains problematic. It is known, for example, that the mutiny of *streltsy* (reflected upon in 'What a night! The hard frost . . .') prevented Peter from visiting Venice (he was on his way to Venice but the news of mutiny made him cancel the trip). Pushkin's allusions to Venice are rare, but they do convey mystical overtones suggesting a Romantically idealized cultural space where poetry flourishes and enjoys freedom of expression, allowing spontaneity and exciting ground for mimicry. In this respect, Pushkin's ideal poet is Charskii, protagonist in the tale *Egyptian Nights* (1835). He is a somewhat mystical messenger, reminding Pushkin and his friends of Naples and other Italian locations, where free improvising is a commonplace. Perhaps, Pushkin uses the image of Venice as a political allusion too, fulfilling Mickiewicz's prophecy of the downfall of autocracy in Russia?[59] In the context of Pushkin's poetics, windows are associated with dreaming and seeing into the future. This is particularly evident in Pushkin's portrayal of Tatiana Larina in *Evgenii Onegin* and in the poem *To My Nanny,* where both women look through the window and into the future, anticipating events and visitors. By the same token,

Pushkin's appropriation of Algarotti's metaphor of St Petersburg as a window looking upon Europe in *The Bronze Horseman* can be treated in the same context, as if Pushkin adds to his list of visionaries not only Tatiana Larina, but Peter the Great, too, and even himself, since the city-window allows the poet to see horizons remote both in place and time (the ideal city of Venice, for example, with liberal atmosphere and free artistic expression).

The image of Venice in Pushkin's poetry can be best described in Bergsonian terms, as an intuitive vision of the future experienced by the poet as a mystical present (see for example, the usage discussed above of the word 'mystical' in Pushkin's references to Venice). It is also important to bear in mind that in Pushkin's dreaming of Venice in 'Near the places where a golden Venice rules . . .' the poet experiences a prophetic vision in the night, as if this state already foresees Bergson's concept of duration. In Bergson's words, it is a miraculous combination of 'a multiplicity of successive states of consciousness' and of 'a unity that binds them together': 'Duration will be the "synthesis" of this unity and this multiplicity, a mysterious operation which takes place in the darkness'.[60] Bergson brings together temporal and spatial concepts, talking of the flow of duration and comparing it with the flow of a river. In the light of this concept, Pushkin's presentation of himself in the poem 'Near the places where a golden Venice rules . . .' as a singer in a gondola/boat appears to be profound and far-reaching: he is a seer and a mystic who notices the unfolding images of future Time.

The juxtaposition of St Petersburg and Venice is fully developed in the Russian modernist and post-modernist poetic vision. Such a view contributes to a broader understanding of Pushkin's St Petersburg, the space where Pushkin located many themes and images which were to dominate Russian literature in the next hundred years. As Seiden comments:

> In *The Bronze Horseman* Pushkin shifted the focus of Russian literature from the planned, rational aspects of eighteenth-century Petersburg to the issue which was to dominate so much of nineteenth-century literature: the plight of the insulted and injured in the city.[61]

To modify the socio-political implications of Seiden's view, it should be added that Pushkin reflected on the ambivalent nature of the perception of the city in the nineteenth century, especially after 1825. Pushkin gave greater prominence than did his predecessors to the irrational fears and intuitive tendencies expressed in the urban popular culture of his time.

An extensive intertextual analysis of *The Bronze Horseman,* underlying many of the subtexts found in anecdotes and tales, has been undertaken by Timenchik and Ospovat.[62] Their study opens the possibility of examining further the role of metatextuality in Pushkin's works as regards the representation of St Petersburg. This [essay] has attempted to combine the intertextual approach with the psychoanalytical and philosophical, focusing on Pushkin's poetics. It suggests that Pushkin inscribes himself into the broader Petersburg text, making his text part of the cultural memory of the city, participating in both national and world cultures. Such an interpretation of Pushkin's Petersburg texts is possible if we compare Pushkin's inscription of visionary messages with, for example, that of William Blake, who predicted the downfall of London. John Bayley points to a significant difference between the two poets, stressing that in Blake's case:

> Like most poems of the great English romantics they are part of the complex and yet continuous life of the poet's consciousness, and must be understood in its total dimension. The reverse is true of Pushkin's poems. Inherently dramatic, each poem is complete in itself: to read it in the life of others will not extend or modify its meaning. In 'The Prophet' Pushkin incarnates himself as 'prophecy', not as the message a prophet brings.[63]

In the light of Bayley's observations, it would be appropriate to suggest that in his poem *The Monument* (1836) Pushkin reflects on precisely the fact that he incarnated himself as a prophecy in the cultural space of St Petersburg as conveyed in his Petersburg texts.

In *The Monument* the future image of the city unfolds: it is the city where the non-verbal, non-materialistic monument of the poet himself (represented, perhaps, as pure thought, or a part of the oral tradition and cultural memory) will produce a more overpowering effect upon the audience than the monuments of Pushkin's autocratic predecessors and other creators of the Petersburg text. It is as if Pushkin portrays himself in *The Monument* as witnessing how the false idols and inferior cultural landmarks are collapsing, thereby giving prominence to the immortal voice of the Pushkin, the Russian Orpheus, who so aptly compared himself with a Venetian singer-boatman.

Notes

1. See, for example, Iu. M. Lotman, 'Simvolika Peterburga i problemy semiotiki goroda', in Iu. M. Lotman, ed., Semiotika: Trudy po znakovym sistemam, *XVIII, Uchenye zapiski Tartuskogo gosudarstvennogo universiteta,* 664, Tartu, 1984, pp. 30-45; Z. G. Mintz et al., 'Peterburgskii tekst i russkii simvolism' in ibid., pp. 78-92.

2. B. Tomashevskii, 'Peterburg v tvorchestve Pushkina', in B. V. Tomashevskii, *Pushkinskii Peterburg,* Leningradskoe Gazetno-zhurnal'noe knizhnoe izdatel'stvo, Leningrad, 1949, pp. 3-40.

3. L. Mederskii, 'Arkhitekturnyi oblik pushkinskogo Peterburga', in ibid., pp. 285-352.

4. S. Schwarzband, *The Logic of Pushkin's Artistic Quest: From 'Yezersky' to 'The Queen of Spades'*, The Magnes Press, The Hebrew University, Jerusalem, 1988; Andrej Kodjak, '"The Queen of Spades" in the Context of the Faust Legend', in Andrej Kodjak et al., eds, *Alexander Pushkin: A Symposium on the 175th Anniversary of His Birth*, New York University Press, New York, 1976, pp. 87-118.

5. R. Jakobson, *Pushkin and His Sculptural Myth*, The Hague, Paris, 1975.

6. John Bayley, *Pushkin: A Comparative Commentary*, Cambridge University Press, Cambridge, 1971.

7. Aleksandr Blok, 'The Poet's Role', quoted from D. J. Richards and C. R. S. Cockrell, editors and translators, *Russian Views of Pushkin*, Willem A. Meeuws, Publisher, Oxford, 1976, pp. 127-134 (127).

8. Ibid., p. 129.

9. Renate Lachmann (translated by Roy Sellars and Antony Wall) 'Intertextuality as an Act of Memory: Pushkin's Transposition of Horace', in id., *Memory and Literature: Intertextuality in Russian Modernism*, University of Minnesota Press, 1997, pp. 194-221.

10. Ibid., p. 234.

11. William Mills Todd III, '"Evgenii Onegin": roman zhizni' in id., ed., *Sovremennoe amerikanskoe pushkinovedenie: sbornik statei*, 'Akademicheskii proekt', St Petersburg, 1999, p. 180.

12. Lachman, op. cit., p. 234.

13. Quoted from L. Mederskii, 'Arkhitekturnyi oblik pushkinskogo Peterburga', in B. V. Tomashevskii, ed., *Pushkinskii Peterburg*, Leningradskoe gazetno-zhurnal'noe knizhnoe izdatel'stvo, Leningrad, 1949, p. 304. (Translation is mine. Further quotations from Russian texts are given here in my translation, too.)

14. Arthur J. Witzman, 'Eighteenth-Century London: Urban Paradise or Fallen City?', *Journal of the History of Ideas*, XXXVI, 3, July-September 1975, p. 471.

15. Quoted from A. S. Pushkin, *The Bronze Horseman*, edited with introduction by T. E. Little, Bristol Classical Press, Bristol, 1991, p. xii.

16. A. S. Pushkin, 'Puteshestvie iz Moskvy v Peterburg' in *Sobranie sochinenii v desiati tomakh*, ed. D. D. Blagoi et al., VI, Gosudarstvennoe izdatel'stvo khudozhestvennoi literatury, Moscow, 1962, p. 383.

17. A. S. Pushkin, *Polnoe sobranie sochinenii v desiati tomakh*, second edition, ed. B. V. Tomashevskii, III (Stikhotvoreniia 1827-1836 gg.), Izdatel'stvo Akademii Nauk SSSR, Moscow, 1957, p. 484.

18. Loc. cit.

19. M. N. Virolainen, 'Mednyi vsadnik: peterburgskaia povest', *Zvezda*, 6, 1999, pp. 208-19 (208).

20. Schwarzband, op. cit., p. 76.

21. John Bayley, op. cit., p. 131.

22. N. Nadezhdin, *Vestnik Evropy*, CLXX, 7, 1830, pp. 195-223; quoted from S. Mashinskii, ed., *V mire Pushkina*, Sovetskii pisatel', Moscow, 1974, p. 350.

23. Thus, for example, Viazemskii comments on Smirnova-Rosset, as follows: 'Our beautiful lady could comprehend the art of Raphael, neither did she ignore the art of Turner and Hogarth'. Quoted from A. O. Smirnova-Rosset, *Dnevnik: Vospominaniia*, Nauka, Moscow, 1989, p. 589.

24. Quoted from Richards and Cockrell, op.cit., p. 246.

25. See, for example M. G. Sokolianskii, 'Ironiia v romane "Evgenii Onegin"', *Izvestiia Akademii nauk: seriia literatury i iazyka*, LVIII, 2, 1999, pp. 34-43; V. S. Baevskii, 'Dominanty khudozhestvennoi evoliutsii Pushkina', ibid., pp. 23-33.

26. See, for example, Blagoi's prescriptive recommendation to ignore such as view: 'To see in Pushkin's poetry merely the "elegance of a caricaturist", "amusing prattle", the masterly ability to "turn nature inside-out", and, as a result, to view him simply as a "genius of caricature", a "master of parody" is to misunderstand it completely. (Most of Nadezhdin's articles on Pushkin are an example of such a crude misinterpretation).' Quoted from Richards and Cockrell, op. cit., p. 246.

27. Frederick Antal, *Hogarth and His Place in European Art*, Routledge and Kegan Paul, London, 1962, p. 25.

28. Lindsey Hughes, *Russia In the Age of Peter the Great*, Yale University Press, New Haven and London, 1998, p. 233.

29. Pushkin, op. cit. (note 17), p. 350.

30. Ibid., p. 351.

31. Hughes, op. cit., p. 394.

32. Marina Tsvetaeva, *Moi Pushkin*, Sovetskii pisatel', Moscow, 1967, pp. 73-4.

33. A. S. Pushkin, *Sobranie sochinenie v desiati to-makh*, VII, 'Kritika i publitsistika', Nauka, Leningrad, 1978, p. 101.

34. Hughes, op. cit., p. 253.

35. Pushkin knew the history of the Petrine period very well, especially through his work on Peter the Great in the state archives. Pushkin contemplated writing a book on the history of Peter the Great's reign since 1827 but he started working officially in the archives in 1831. Ivan Musin-Pushkin was the last 'boyar' to be awarded this title by Peter the Great. Following heroic deeds during the battle in Poltava, Musin-Pushkin, a close ally of the Tsar, was promoted rapidly by Peter the Great, becoming one of the Senators of the newly created Senate. Pushkin refers to him extensively in his unfinished historical work *A History of Peter the Great* which was not approved for publication by Nicholas I because of its portrayal of crude and unflattering scenes from Peter the Great's life.

36. A. S. Pushkin, 'Istoriia Petra: podgotovitel'nye teksty', *Sobranie sochinenii v desiati tomakh*, IX, ed. B. V. Tomashevskii, Izdatel'stvo Akademii Nauk SSSR, Moscow, 1958, pp. 5-464 (337).

37. Hughes, op. cit., p. 253.

38. Ibid., p. 266.

39. Pushkin, op. cit. (note 17), II, p. 316.

40. Pushkin, 'Puteshestvie iz Peterburga v Moskvu', op. cit., p. 189.

41. Virolainen, op. cit., p. 213.

42. Loc. cit.

43. George Levitine, *The Sculpture of Falconet*, New York Graphic Society Ltd., Greenwich, Connecticut, 1972, p. 54. On Falconet more generally see chapter 6 of [*Two Hundred Years of Pushkin, Volume II*].

44. Ibid., p. 55.

45. Ibid., pp. 55-6.

46. Ibid., pp. 59-60.

47. Ibid., p. 60.

48. Ibid., p. 59.

49. See, for example, the discussion of this episode in A. L. Ospovat and R. D. Timenchik, *Pechal'nu povest' sokhranit'*, Kniga, Moscow, 1987, p. 24.

50. Virolainen, op. cit., p. 217.

51. Ibid., p. 219.

52. See the discussion of this point in Virolainen's article: ibid., p. 211.

53. Ospovat, op. cit., p. 47.

54. Mark Alexander Seiden, *Dickens' London: The City as Comic Apocalypsis*, unpublished PhD thesis, Cornell University, 1967.

55. Weitzman, op. cit., p. 479.

56. Quoted from Schwarzband, op. cit., p. 222.

57. Pushkin, op. cit. (Note 17), V, Moscow, 1957, p. 30.

58. Quoted from Hughes, op. cit., p. 210.

59. See the discussion of Mickiewicz's poem *Oleszkiewicz* in Little, ed., op. cit., p. 33.

60. Henri Bergson, *An Introduction to Metaphysics*, translated by T. E. Hulme, Macmillan and Co., Ltd, London, 1913, p. 49.

61. Seiden, op. cit., p. 2.

62. Ospovat, op. cit.

63. Bayley, op. cit. p. 145.

Nikolai Firtich (essay date 2004)

SOURCE: Firtich, Nikolai. "An Englishman in Wonderland: Lewis Carroll in St. Petersburg." *Zapiski Russkoi Akademicheskoi Gruppy v S.Sh.A./Transactions of the Association of Russian-American Scholars in the U.S.A.* 33 (2004): 157-65.

[*In the following essay, Firtich explores Lewis Carroll's journal of his trip to Russia in 1867 and assesses it as part of the body of literature known as the "Petersburg text" that captures and relates the unique mythology of St. Petersburg.*]

"It was much pleasanter at home," thought poor Alice "when one wasn't always growing larger and smaller, and being ordered around by mice and rabbits . . . and yet—and yet—it's rather curious, you know, this sort of life! I do wonder what can have happened to me . . . There ought to be a book written about me . . ."[1] This is how Alice reasons with herself after ending up in Wonderland. While this amazing book is familiar to most everybody, at present only few are aware of the fact that in 1867, two years after *Alice* appeared in print, the author of these lines, Lewis Carroll, embarked upon his one and only journey to the continent in order to visit Russia. And, with the punctuality typical of him, Carroll kept a fairly detailed journal, which was accordingly entitled *Journal of a Tour in Russia in 1867.*

Carroll did not intend these notes for publication, and the journal appeared in print only in the early 1930's, long after the writer's death in 1898.[2]

Although Carroll's journal has received passing mention in the works of several specialists, to date there exists neither a Russian translation nor an English-language scholarly edition.[3] Nor, to the best of my knowledge, have Lewis Carroll's notes appeared in any of the numerous collections of impressions of Russia left by foreign visitors.[4] It was suggested by one of Carroll's biographers that "the book is interesting only because Carroll's style never leaves him even in dealing with trivia, and because of the light it thinly sprays on his Anglophilia."[5]

Carroll's journal clearly deserves attention for more substantial reasons. The purpose of this article is to shed some light on the content of these notes and to look at them in the context of what has come to be called the "Petersburg text" and St. Petersburg mythology. But first a few words about Carroll himself, who is unquestionably one of the most mythologized personalities of the 19th century British literature, largely due to his supposed "dualism," a point which continues to stir debates about his biography.

Charles Ludwidge Dodgson was born in 1832 and died in 1898 having lived practically all of his life in Oxford. He received his degrees from Oxford University and eventually became a Lecturer of Mathematics at Christ Church College, simultaneously serving as Deacon in the college chapel. According to a number of sources, his math lectures as well as his sermons were distinguished by neither the spark of genius nor inspiration, and were in fact quite conservative.[6] The majority of his numerous works on mathematics are considered to be quite traditional, but a few writings on the problems of logic, although underestimated in his own time, are recognized as innovative by present-day specialists.[7] In general there is virtually nothing in the orderly and lonely lifestyle of Doctor Dodgson that betrayed the future author of the fantastic and deeply absurd adventures of Alice. Somewhat of an exception to this, perhaps, were his lifelong interests in theater and painting and his later occupation with photography in which he became an accomplished master.

Thus when Lewis Carroll, the eccentric author of *Alice in Wonderland* was "born," nobody apart from a few close friends could suspect any connection between that individual and the quite ordinary professor of mathematics Dodgson. This apparent discontinuity laid the foundation for the myth about the enigmatic duality of the author of *Alice,* a myth that was to a certain degree fueled by Dodgson himself who for a long time denied the authorship of *Alice,* calmly assuring the inquiring parties that all the questions should be addressed to

Lewis Carroll. This situation gave rise to a popular anecdote (although untrue) that Dodgson himself allowed to go unchallenged for many years. The story went that when news of *Alice* reached Queen Victoria, she approached the author with the request to send her his other books, and to her total astonishment she received a stack of Dodgson's works on mathematics.[8] As we know, this supposed duality, which in the opinion of some, including myself, was an absurdist game, eventually led to the entire series of Freudian psychoanalytical interpretations of Dodgson's life, as well as of the text of *Alice in Wonderland.*[9]

But let us turn now to the Dodgson-Carroll trip to Russia. Significantly, our hero traveled to Russia strictly as Doctor Dodgson,—professor and deacon of Oxford's Christ Church College and accompanying the dean of St. Paul's College, Canon Henry Parry Liddon. The official purpose of the trip was ecclesiastical in nature, since some circles in the Anglican and Orthodox Churches were then discussing the possibility of bringing the two churches closer together.[10] Dodgson and Liddon spent a month in Russia, visiting Petersburg, Moscow, Sergiev Posad, and Nizhnii Novgorod, meeting with Russian Orthodox clergy, viewing monasteries and cathedrals as well as museums. Dodgson also made several trips to the theater.

Dodgson knew no Russian, and seems to have had hardly any knowledge of Russian culture, but quite possibly because of that fact, and in contrast to many of his compatriots who visited Russia in the period after the Crimean War, Dodgson's reactions were marked by a lack of prejudice and a freshness of perception of the new and strange world that surrounded him. When referring to the characteristic lack of objective views of Russia on the part of the British travelers and their tendency to describe Russian life in the darkest possible tones, Francesca Wilson, the author of *Moscovy: Russia Through Foreign Eyes 1553-1900,* opted not to include them at all in her study because of their bias and unreliability.[11] It is a pity that Dodgson's Russian *Journal* which stands in total contrast to this tendency has escaped the author's attention.

However, the author of *Alice* also did not succumb to the kind of superficial fascination, which leads some travelers to write excitedly about every matreshka and balalaika. His journal is marked by the sense of quiet reflection and observation, as well as gentle humor in describing his surroundings, the local customs and the language.

On the train en route to St. Petersburg Dodgson tries to write down some Russian words, the first of which turns out to be the participle " щищ щихс ", the word that the author perceptively calls "alarming" (Carroll *Journal* 85).[12] Having arrived in St. Petersburg, Dodgson continues his linguistic experiments by energetically bargaining with the local cabbies with the help of a newly acquired vocabulary. As an example of his success he writes down the following dialogue that took place between a cab driver and himself:

DRIVER.

Tridsat' kopeek.

MYSELF.

Doatzat kopecki?

D.

(indignantly) Tritzat!

M.

(resolutely) Doatzat.

D.

(coaxingly) Doatzat pait?

M.

(with the air of one who has said his say, and wishes to be rid of the thing) Doatzat. (Here I take Liddon's arm, and we walk off together, entirely disregarding the shouts of the driver. When we have gone a few yards, we hear the droshky lumbering after us: he draws up alongside, and hails us)

M.

(gravely) Doatzat?

D.

(with a delighted grin). Da! Da! Doatzat! (and we get in).

(Carroll *Journal* 88)

Before turning to specific Petersburg-related entries of the author of *Alice,* however, I will try to summarize Dodgson's impressions of the country and its people. Perhaps the main human quality that struck him in the Russians with whom he became acquainted, was the generosity with which people offered their time and assistance to foreigners. In Moscow, searching for the Anglican chapel, Dodgson ran into a gentleman who could speak English and who to our hero's surprise not only explained how to get to the chapel but also personally escorted him there. During the visit to the Trinity monastery in Sergiev Posad, Dodgson and Liddon were shown around by a Russian gentleman who graciously explained everything to them in French and assisted them in the purchase of icons, an activity to which Dodgson dedicated a considerable portion of his time in Russia. "It was only after he had wished us a good day and left us," writes Dodgson, "that we discovered who it was that had shown us so much attention—more, I am afraid, than most Englishmen would show foreign-

ers—Prince Chirkoff" (Carroll *Journal* 100). Dodgson was deeply impressed by the icons in the monastery's icon studio and noted in his diary "that the difficulty was to decide, not so much what to buy, as what to leave unbought" (Carroll *Journal* 100). That same day the Moscow Bishop Leonid, who organized Dodgson's and Liddon's trip to the monastery, introduced the Englishmen to Metropolitan Philaret, who conversed with Liddon for over an hour and a half. Dodgson notes the patience of the Metropolitan, because "this discussion was conducted in a very original fashion—the Archbishop making a remark in Russian, which was put into English by the Bishop: Liddon then answered in French, and the Bishop repeated his answer in Russian to the Archbishop. So that a conversation carried on entirely between the two people required the use of three languages!" (Carroll *Journal* 101).

Among the impressions of Russia in Dodgson's journal his descriptions of Petersburg clearly have a central place. Amazement and excitement are apparent in the very first entry.

We only had time for a short stroll after dinner, but it was full of wonder and novelty. The enormous width of the streets (the secondary ones seem to be broader than anything in London), the little drozhkies, that went running about, seemingly quite indifferent as to running over anybody, (we soon found it was necessary to keep a very sharp lookout, as they never shouted, however close they were upon us)—the enormous illuminated signboards over the shops, and the gigantic churches, with their domes painted blue and covered with gold stars—. . . all contributed to the wonders of our first walk in St. Petersburg.

(Carroll *Journal* 86)

Two points are significant in this first entry. The first is that an Englishman, a citizen of the most technologically advanced modern empire of the period, is so struck by the modernity and the scale of Petersburg. The second point is painfully familiar to all Petersburgers. It turns out that the uncaring attitude towards pedestrians on the part of the drivers is not just a sign of the age of automobiles but is practically a topos of Petersburg's urbanism.

After the first impressions, the entries in Dodgson journal acquire a more reflexive and profound tone, showing how deeply he was moved by Petersburg. And at this point, in my opinion, the facade of Doctor Dodgson allows the emergence of Lewis Carroll, who had sensed the enigmatic spirit of the city and its metaphysical space. "In the afternoon we walked here and there about this marvelous city" writes Carroll. "It is so utterly unlike anything I have ever seen, that I feel as if I could and should be content to do nothing for many days but roam about it" (Carroll *Journal* 87). Nevsky Prospect in particular makes a strong impression on

Carroll, expressed in the following words: "We walked the whole length of the Nevsky, which is about 3 miles long, with many fine buildings along it, and must, I should think, be one of the finest streets in the world: it terminates in (probably) the largest square of in the world, the Admiralty platz" (Carroll *Journal* 88).

Here, without the slightest suspicion Carroll enters the Petersburg text by forging a link with Gogol's ironic, but nevertheless genuinely excited description of Nevsky Prospect. The typological connection between Gogol and Carroll, who of course were unaware of each other, clearly merits a separate investigation. Both were masters of the metaphysical absurd, striving to expose the mysterious side of things. Moreover, there are biographical correspondences. In their youth both wanted to become painters and throughout their lives were involved with the theater. Both were inclined towards certain theatricality and mystification. And, finally, both impressed their contemporaries by their seeming dualism—on the one hand, they were deeply religious people, tending towards social conservatism, and on the other hand they were the creators of the most enigmatic and absurd works of literature of their time. One can also find some intriguing textual correspondences. For example, the doubles Bobchinsky and Dobchinsky in Gogol's *Revizor* and Twidledee and Twidledum in Carroll's *Alice*.

But let us turn back to Carroll's Petersburg journal. Continuing his observations on Admiralty Square, he notes the following: "There is a fine equestrian statue of Peter the Great near the Admiralty. The lower part is not a pedestal but left shapeless and rough like a real rock. The horse is rearing, and has a serpent coiled about his hind feet, on which, I think it is treading." And here Carroll adds his own touch to the description of the Bronze Horseman. "If this had been put up in Berlin, Peter would no doubt have been actively engaged in killing the monster, but here he takes no notice of it: in fact the killing theory is not recognized" (Carroll *Journal* 88).

Carroll's comparison is based on personal impressions. While stopping in Berlin for a couple of days on his way to Russia, he entered the following reflections on the nature of local architecture in his journal:

> In fact the two principles of Berlin architecture appear to me to be these—"On the house tops, whenever there is a convenient place, put up the figure of a man; he is best placed standing on one leg. Whenever there is room on the ground, put either a circular group of busts on pedestals, in consultation, all looking inwards—or else the colossal figure of a man killing, about to kill, or having killed (the present tense is preferred) a beast; the more prickles the beast has, the better—in fact a dragon is the correct thing, but if it is beyond the artist, he may content himself with a lion or a pig." The beast-

killing principle has been carried out with a relentless monotony, which makes some parts of Berlin look like a fossil slaughterhouse.

(Carroll Journal 81)

So, the monument to Peter the Great attracts Carroll's attention, because of its difference from anything that our hero has seen in Europe on his way to Russia.

Being quite ignorant of Pushkin and not knowing anything about the mythological context of the Bronze Horseman, Carroll sees it with an historically untainted view and adds his own touch to the interpretation of the monument, in this way becoming a part of the "Petersburg text" of Russian culture. Free of the entire complex of Russian associations and interpretations connected with Peter the Great, Carroll suddenly points out the humane aspect of the Peter's image. In the same light he also sees the sculptures of lions (on one of which Pushkin's Evgenii had been sitting) on the Admiralty embankment: "We found two colossal figures of lions, which are so painfully mild, that each of them is rolling a ball about, like a kitten" (Carroll *Journal* 88).

Carroll continues his observations during his trip to Kronstadt and again strikes a mythological note.

> We then took a boat and rowed through the harbor, landing once to inspect a colossal dock yard in course of construction; the walls were being built of solid blocks of granite, with the outer face cut as smooth as if it were to decorate an interior of a building . . . On a general view the place looked something like an ant nest: hundreds of workmen swarming from end to end of the great hollow—and a constant tinkling of hammers sounding from all sides. It gave one an idea of what the scene must have been during the building of the Pyramids".

(Carroll Journal 111)

Thanks to his active imagination Carroll again senses an important element of the Petersburg's mythological make up—a link with the Egyptian Pyramids contained in the very history of this city's creation from rocks of granite in the middle of the deserted swamps.

And again Carroll is inclined towards positive interpretation, comparing Petersburg's constructions with one of the Wonders of the World. In general he sees Petersburg as miraculous and fantastic. A lover of long strolls, Carroll notes, after having walked more than 16 miles in this city that "the distances here are enormous: it is like walking about in the city of giants" (Carroll *Journal* 89). It is tempting to speculate that, perhaps, Carroll felt some connection between this fantastic city and the Wonderland in which his Alice travels, the land where all paradoxes are totally possible and moreover are quite acceptable.

There is one point at which Dodgson and Carroll would certainly be in total agreement—that is in their genuine affection for England. In the background of Dodgson's/

Carroll's travel notes one can always hear the notes of nostalgia for England that become especially audible towards the end of the journey. This unbending poetic attachment to England and the fact that Dodgson hardly ever mentioned his trip in his later diaries led all of the author's biographers to assert that this journey left no impression on Carroll's literary output. While this might be so, Carroll's own reflections on St. Petersburg clearly deserve a place in the St. Petersburg text of Russian culture.

Notes

1. Lewis Carroll, *The Annotated Alice: Alice's Adventures in Wonderland and through the Looking Glass.* Introduction and notes by Martin Gardner (New York: Wings Books, 1993) 58.

2. The first edition of this journal is the following: *The Russian Journal and Other Selections from Works of Lewis Carroll.* Edited and With the Introduction by John Francis, New York: McDermott. E. P. Dutton & Co. 1935.

3. While all of Carroll's biographers mention this journal since it documents Carroll's one and only trip abroad, the following works contain particularly relevant information about the context in which this journey took place: Derek Hudson, *An Illustrated Biography of Lewis Carroll.* (New York: Clarkson N. Potter, Inc./Publishers, 1977) 131-148; Richard Kelly, *Lewis Carroll* (Boston: Twayne Publishers, 1990) 18-20; Jean Gattegno, *Lewis Carroll. Fragments of a Looking Glass* (New York: Thomas Y. Crowell Company, 1976) 247-252.

4. In her detailed volume on foreign impressions of Russia, Francesca Wilson does not list Lewis Carroll. See Francesca Wilson, *Muscovy: Russia through Foreign Eyes 1553-1900.* (New York, 1970) 3-25.

5. Florence Becker Lennon, *Victoria through the Looking Glass: The Life of Lewis Carroll* (New York: Simon and Schuster, 1945) 140.

6. See N. M. Demurova, "Alisa v strane chudes i zazerkal'e" in Lewis Carroll, *Alisa v strane chudes. Alisa v zazerkal'e* (Moscow, 1978) 290-292; Warren Weaver, "Lewis Carroll Mathematician" *Scientific American,* April 1956; Gattegno, 141-150, 232-243.

7. Demurova, 284.

8. Cattegno, 287-290.

9. See Phylis Greenacre, *Swift and Carroll: A Psychoanalytic Study of Two Lives* (New York: International Universities Press, 1955); William Empson, *Some Versions of Pastoral* (New York: New Directions, 1960) 241-82.

10. For the outline of contacts between the Anglican and Orthodox Churches see Timothy Ware, *The Orthodox Church* (London: Penguin Books, 1997) 98-99, 317-21.

11. Francesca Wilson, 15.

12. The entire passage reads as follows: "The other gentleman we found to be an Englishman, who had lived in Petersburg for 15 years, and was returning from a visit to Paris and London. He was most kind in answering our questions and in giving us a great many hints as to seeing Petersburg, pronouncing the language, etc. but gave us rather dismal prospects of what is before us, as he says very few speak any language but Russian. As an instance of the extraordinary long words which the language contains, he spelt for me the following:

З И Ихс

which, written in English letters, is Zashtsheeshtshayoushtsheekhsya:—this alarming word is the genitive plural of a participle, and means 'of persons defending themselves.'

FURTHER READING

Criticism

Andrews, Howard F. "Nineteenth-Century St. Petersburg: Workpoints for an Exploration of Image and Place." In *Humanistic Geography and Literature: Essays on the Experience of Place,* edited by Douglas C. D. Pocock, pp. 173-89. London and Totowa, N.J.: Croom Helm and Barnes and Noble Books, 1981.

> Details the depiction of St. Petersburg in writings by Alexander Pushkin, Nikolai Gogol, Fyodor Dostoevsky, and Andrey Bely.

Buonomo, Leonardo. "Another Time, Another Place: Florence in the Writings of Margaret Fuller, Caroline Kirkland, and Constance Fenimore Woolson." In *The Poetics of Place: Florence Imagined,* edited by Irene Marchegiani Jones and Thomas Haeussler, pp. 99-123. Florence, Italy: Leo S. Olschki Editore, 2001.

> Surveys the contrasting views of Florence as either a unique Italian city or a typical Italian city in the works of Margaret Fuller, Caroline Kirkland, and Constance Fenimore Woolson.

Butler, Robert. "The City as Liberating Space in Life and Times of Frederick Douglass." In *The City in African-American Literature,* edited by Yoshinobu

Hakutani and Robert Butler, pp. 21-36. Madison, N.J. and London: Fairleigh Dickinson University Press and Associated University Presses, 1995.

    Illustrates how Frederick Douglass's favorable rendering of the city as offering opportunities to African Americans not available in rural areas differs from the view of the city presented in the works of other writers of the era.

Clarke, Graham, ed. *The American City: Literary and Cultural Perspectives.* New York and London: St. Martin's Press and Vision Press, 1988, 223 p.

    A collection of essays delineating the often paradoxical and widely varied treatment of American cities by American writers.

Gassenmeier, Michael, and Jens Martin Gurr. "The Experience of the City in British Romantic Poetry." In *Romantic Poetry,* edited by Angela Esterhammer, pp. 305-31. Amsterdam and Philadelphia, Pa.: John Benjamins, 2002.

    Surveys the treatment of London in Victorian Romantic poetry within "the context of seventeenth- and earlier eighteenth-century London poetry and the eminent political and ideological conflicts of the age of revolutions that the genre reflects and to which it owes its formation and development."

Kaganov, Grigorii. "Sight Riven and Restored: The Image of Petersburg Space, 1850-1900." *The Russian Review* 54, no. 2 (April 1995): 227-42.

    Describes the change in the literary presentation of St. Petersburg that began in the 1840s.

Kazin, Alfred. "New York from Melville to Mailer." In *Literature and the American Urban Experience: Essays on the City and Literature,* edited by Michael C. Jaye and Ann Chalmers Watts, pp. 81-92. New Brunswick, N.J., and Manchester, England: Rutgers University Press and Manchester University Press, 1981.

    Illustrates the treatment of New York City in works by Herman Melville, and in works by twentieth-century authors such as Ezra Pound, F. Scott Fitzgerald, Bernard Malamud, and Norman Mailer, emphasizing changes in literary style and culture.

Lloyd, William J. "A Social-Literary Geography of Late-Nineteenth-Century Boston." In *Humanistic Geography and Literature: Essays on the Experience of Place,* edited by Douglas C. D. Pocock, pp. 159-72. London and Totowa, N.J.: Croom Helm and Barnes and Noble Books, 1981.

    Outlines the sociological impact of the relationship between real life in various Boston districts and literary representations of Boston.

Thesing, William B. *The London Muse: Victorian Poetic Response to the City.* Athens: University of Georgia Press, 1982, 230 p.

    Provides a detailed analysis of Victorian poets' treatment of London in their works.

Motherhood in Nineteenth-Century Literature

The following entry provides commentary on the treatment of motherhood in nineteenth-century literature.

INTRODUCTION

The sentimental portrait of mothers as paragons of moral goodness was well-established during the nineteenth century; in addition, motherhood was often used as a symbol for nationhood, with the mother representing some form of the ideal or all-powerful state. Critics have noted that this ideal serves the dual purpose of keeping women focused on the domestic arena and of keeping men focused on the preservation of the family as well as of the nation. A rejection of sentimental motherhood characterizes much of nineteenth-century American literature; this rejection, critics argue, grew out of uncertainties regarding the future of democracy and democratic ideals. Because of the widespread belief in women's inability to govern or proceed without men's guidance, it seemed appropriate to Victorian writers to use mothers as symbols for uncertainty about developments, such as industrialization and democratization, that appear to be good and beneficial but which could go awry without proper direction and prudent leadership. During the nineteenth century, mothering was viewed as instinctual, based on the common belief that mothers were naturally guided in their efforts by their innate, unconditional love for their children. Mothers were expected to teach their children solely by example, rather than reasoned instruction. Critic Claire Chantell has pointed out that while many works of domestic fiction echo this belief in mothers endowed by nature to be perfect educators, writers such as Maria Cummins and Susan Warner challenged this notion in narratives such as *The Lamplighter* (1854) and *The Wide, Wide World* (1850) that depicted their young female heroines learning invaluable lessons outside of their homes and from individuals other than their biological mothers. Motherhood, or reproduction, in addition to serving as a symbol of the nation, was often used to represent artistic and scientific processes, and at times was set in opposition to these same processes.

Scholars have maintained that while Victorian society viewed the image of the saintly mother charged with a sacred mission to nurture and preserve her family and society at large as sacrosanct, the widely varying portraits of mothers and maternal archetypes in nineteenth-century literature reveal a complex and emotionally-charged system of beliefs underlying Victorian social, cultural, religious, and economic traditions. Critics such as Sally Shuttleworth have argued that demonic mother characters symbolize a widespread fear of the effect of women's empowerment on the patriarchal social order, and that angelic maternal characters are presented in an attempt to keep women informed of and focused upon their duties as wives and mothers, a proposed solution to the fear of the growing sphere of power and influence of the bourgeois class. Shuttleworth delineates the intense scrutiny and regulation to which Victorian bourgeois mothers were subjected in conduct books, domestic manuals, and popular fiction that offered meticulous attention to the minutest details of mothering and women's conduct in general. Similarly, as observed by critics, dead, dying, or otherwise physically absent maternal figures in Victorian literature serve as an expression of the anxiety inherent in the changing views of women by both themselves and men, as well as anxiety surrounding the changing nature of society in general. Often these absent mothers are present in spirit or in memory, and this view of motherhood mirrors the theories put forward by experts in the burgeoning field of psychology near the end of the nineteenth century. Numerous critics have analyzed Victorian fiction from a psychological perspective and have drawn parallels between the biographical facts of authors' childhood experiences and their representation of maternal figures in their works. Analyses of the treatment of motherhood by women authors, in particular, have shown that some offered alternatives to strict patriarchal order in their narratives by presenting nontraditional views of motherhood, including relations between mothers and sons; others dramatized the dilemma faced by Victorian women who were frequently forced to choose between being mothers and pursuing creative expression as writers, artists, or scholars. Both male and female authors often opted to use fictional mothers to offer commentary on weighty social issues such as slavery and the oppression of women; the great importance placed upon motherhood in Victorian society made employing mothers in the service of social justice uniquely effective.

REPRESENTATIVE WORKS

Mary Elizabeth Braddon
Lady Audley's Secret (novel) 1862

Anne Brontë

The Tenant of Wildfell Hall [as Acton Bell] (novel) 1848

Charlotte Brontë

Jane Eyre; an Autobiography [as Currer Bell] (novel) 1847

Shirley [as Currer Bell] (novel) 1849

Villette [as Currer Bell] (novel) 1853

Emily Brontë

*Wuthering Heights [as Ellis Bell] (novel) 1847

Fanny Burney

Evelina; or, A Young Lady's Entrance into the World (novel) 1778

Lydia Maria Child

The Mother's Book (handbook) 1829; revised and enlarged edition, 1844

A Romance of the Republic (novel) 1867; also published as *Rose and Flora*, 2 vols., 1867

Kate Chopin

The Awakening (novel) 1899

Wilkie Collins

No Name (novel) 1862

James Fenimore Cooper

The Last of the Mohicans. 2 vols. [published anonymously] (novel) 1826

The Deerslayer. 2 vols. [published anonymously] (novel) 1841

Maria Cummins

The Lamplighter [published anonymously] (novel) 1854

Charles Dickens

The Old Curiosity Shop (novel) 1841

Dealings with the Firm of Dombey and Son (novel) 1848

Bleak House (novel) 1853

Little Dorrit (novel) 1857

Great Expectations (novel) 1861

George Eliot

Adam Bede (novel) 1859

The Mill on the Floss (novel) 1860

Silas Marner, the Weaver of Raveloe (novel) 1861

Romola (novel) 1863

Felix Holt, the Radical (novel) 1866

Middlemarch: A Study of Provincial Life. 4 vols. (novel) 1871-72

Daniel Deronda. 4 vols. (novel) 1876

Elizabeth Cleghorn Gaskell

Ruth: A Novel. 3 vols. [published anonymously] 1853

North and South. 2 vols. [published anonymously] 1855

Juana Manuela Gorriti

La quena (novel) 1845

Nathaniel Hawthorne

The Scarlet Letter: A Romance (novel) 1850

A Wonder-Book for Girls and Boys (short stories) 1852

Harriet Jacobs

Incidents in the Life of a Slave Girl, Written by Herself [as Linda Brent] (autobiography) 1861

Herman Melville

Moby-Dick; or, The Whale (novel) 1851

Caroline Norton

The Separation of Mother and Child by the Laws of "Custody of Infants" Considered [published anonymously] (pamphlet) 1838

A Plain Letter to the Lord Chancellor on the Infant Custody Bill [as Pearce Stevenson, Esq.] (pamphlet) 1839

Margaret Oliphant

Innocent: A Tale of Modern Life (novel) 1873

Sir Tom (novel) 1883

Coventry Patmore

†*The Angel in the House: The Betrothal* (poetry) 1854; also published in *The Angel in the House: Book I, The Betrothal; Book II, The Espousals*, 1858

†*The Angel in the House: Book II, The Espousals* (poetry) 1856; also published in *The Angel in the House: Book I, The Betrothal; Book II, The Espousals*, 1858

†*Faithful for Ever* (poetry) 1860

†*The Victories of Love* (poetry) 1862

Edgar Allan Poe

"Ligeia" (short story) 1838; published in the journal *American Museum*

John Ruskin

‡*Sesame and Lilies: Two Lectures Delivered at Manchester in 1864* (lectures) 1865

George Sand

Valentine (novel) 1832

Mary Wollstonecraft Shelley

Frankenstein; or, The Modern Prometheus. 3 vols. (novel) 1818

Valperga: or, The Life and Adventures of Castruccio, Prince of Lucca. 3 vols. (novel) 1823

The Last Man. 2 vols. (novel) 1826

The Fortunes of Perkin Warbeck. 3 vols. (novel) 1830
Lodore. 3 vols. (novel) 1835
Falkner. 3 vols. (novel) 1837
#*Mathilda* [edited by Elizabeth Nitchie] (novella) 1959

Harriet Beecher Stowe
Uncle Tom's Cabin; or, Life among the Lowly. 2 vols.
   (novel) 1852

William Makepeace Thackeray
Vanity Fair: A Novel without a Hero (novel) 1848
The History of Pendennis: His Fortunes and Misfortunes, His Friends and His Greatest Enemy. 2 vols.
   (novel) 1849-50
The History of Henry Esmond, Esq., a Colonel in the Service of Her Majesty Q. Anne (novel) 1852

Anthony Trollope
Barchester Towers (novel) 1857

Susan Warner
The Wide, Wide World. 2 vols. (novel) 1850

Mrs. Henry Wood
East Lynne (novel) 1861
St. Martin's Eve (novel) 1866

Virginia Woolf
‖*Collected Essays.* 4 vols. (essays) 1966-67

*This edition of *Wuthering Heights* was published with Anne Brontë's novel *Agnes Grey.*

†These works were published together as *The Angel in the House* in 1863.

‡The lectures contained in this volume are "Of Kings' Treasuries" and "Of Queens' Gardens."

#Originally titled *The Fields of Fancy,* *Mathilda* is believed to have been written c. 1819.

‖This collection contains, among other essays, the essay "Professions for Women."

OVERVIEWS

Stephanie A. Smith (essay date 1994)

SOURCE: Smith, Stephanie A. Introduction to *Conceived by Liberty: Maternal Figures and Nineteenth-Century American Literature,* pp. 1-27. Ithaca, N.Y.: Cornell University Press, 1994.

[*In the following essay, an introduction to her book, Smith surveys the evolution of literary representations, critical assessments, and popular interpretations of maternal iconography during the nineteenth century.*]

Mid-nineteenth-century "American culture," wrote Ann Douglas, "seemed bent on establishing a perpetual Mother's Day."[1] As *The Public Ledger* declared in 1850, "a mother is, next to God, all powerful."[2] Yet despite how predominantly mothering figured as a trope for, among other things, morality—and despite the cultural currency of what G. J. Barker-Benfield dubbed the "maternal icon"[3]—quintessential American literature of the period has been defined, for the most part, as that which lacks or flees mother.[4] What impact would a sustained reconsideration of so pervasive a sign have on how to read American literature?

This was the foremost question that provoked *Conceived by Liberty.* To say that representations of a sanctified motherhood formed the primary cornerstone for commercially successful writing in the United States of the nineteenth century is a commonplace. But critical articulations of maternal iconography remain scarce. This lack is especially evident in considerations of work not designated commercial or sentimental. It is well, as Jane Tompkins writes in *Sensational Designs,* to talk about novelist Susan Warner's sentimental mothers, but Hester Prynne is quite another matter.[5] This point was brought home to me recently when a senior colleague said, "You know, I can't think of a single mother in American literature." "Hester Prynne?" I asked. "Oh, right," I was told, "but that's not what's really important about her, is it?"

Why is Hester Prynne's maternity so unimportant? Not all critics have thought so. In 1982 Daniel Cottom saw maternity as a central concern in *The Scarlet Letter.* Reading the novel as if it were a legal brief—Hawthorne v. Hester—on sexual/textual difference,[6] Cottom claimed that the text installed romance as an economy in which the maternal (reproductive) body signified the opposite of artistic production. However, if one should take Hawthorne's case as an incontrovertible proof, if maternal reproduction is the opposite of artistic production, then paying critical attention to how reproduction and the maternal body are themselves literary representations might damage the novel's artistic value. Best to skirt the issue (as it were), even though Hawthorne himself described Hester Prynne as "the image of Divine Maternity, which so many illustrious painters have vied with one another to represent."[7]

Reproducing my colleague's unintentionally punning question here—"Is there not a single mother in American literature?"—is meant less as an anecdotal indictment than as an index to the several aims of this book. The question, however simply, indicates that motherhood has consistently been regarded as less important than other features to an American literary heritage. After all, there is no maternity in Herman Melville's *Moby Dick.* But then again, how, without referring to representations of maternity, does one read Queequeg's "obstetrics" (in chapter 78)? Rescuing Tashtego from a decapitated whale's head, Queequeg "averred, that upon first thrusting in for him, a leg was presented; but well knowing that that was not as it ought to be, and might occasion great trouble;—he had thrust back the leg, and by a dexterous heave and toss, had wrought a somerset upon the Indian; so that with the next trial, he came forth in the good old way—head foremost."[8] Is maternity, or at the very least mid-wifery, not at issue in this description?

THE POLITICAL RELIGION OF THE NATION

Most critics of Anglo-American nineteenth-century culture and literature speak to the enormous, if paradoxical, pressure put on maternal iconography as emblematic for a stable, unfractured morality. It would be hard indeed for any sustained consideration of nineteenth-century cultural practices in the United States not to comment on the degree to which maternal iconography signaled utopian perfection, making "mother" a sacred, natural symbol of perfect, reciprocal relations. This symbol served as a self-regulating model for social and familial community and a source of creative generation. Woman performed what Leslie Fiedler characterized as the role of "sexless savior and . . . eternal Mama."[9] Thus by extension was the family, emphasizing maternity as the stabilizing icon of continuity in a (Christian) republic, woven into nineteenth-century discourses both public and private.

Logically, though, the use of the mother as both public and private figure undermined the supposed distance between political and domestic concerns.[10] Abraham Lincoln's 1837 speech to the Springfield Young Men's Lyceum, "The Perpetuation of our Political Institutions," indicates as much: "Let every man remember that to violate the law is to trample on the blood of his father, and to tear the charter of his own and his children's liberty. Let reverence for the laws be breathed by every American mother to the lisping babe that prattles on her lap, . . . in short, let it become the political religion of the nation."[11] Thus the (private) family, educated by a reverent, revered American motherhood, was construed as the moral linchpin in the structure of (public) liberty. And if Lincoln's speech is a public document, Henry David Thoreau's more private journal offers another example of the maternal icon would serve as pervasive cultural currency for ethical purity: "I lose my respect for the man who can make the mystery of sex the subject of a coarse jest, yet, when you speak earnestly and seriously on the subject, is silent. I feel this to be truly irreligious. Whatever may befall me, I trust that I may never lose my respect for purity in others. . . . I would preserve purity in act and thought, as I would cherish the memory of my mother."[12]

Elevated purity became discursively axiomatic for motherhood. Whether in speech or journal, behavior manual or instruction book, novel or autobiography, a cherished iconic memory of mother lifted the mind toward a better state and away from the sordid. This elevation would effect a clarity of purpose as well as social propriety. Keeping mother in mind meant keeping away from private unruliness that could lead, as Lincoln warned, to the destruction of public political liberty. Ignoring mother could be tantamount to both sociopolitical and personal suicide. Certainly Hester Prynne's demon child, Pearl, and Arthur Dimmesdale's and Roger Chillingsworth's tortured fates attest to the dangerous desires of a passionate, unruled, free body.

Yet if "mother" could intrude upon *Moby Dick* and *The Scarlet Letter* "she" raises the aesthetic spectre that perhaps sentimentality may not be confined to the pages of popular, domestic novels. Deemed aesthetically degrading because sentimental, mother has been left out of most critical assessments and lost or killed off in the narrative, and maternal iconography read, if at all, as banal. Pathetic and linked to, if not the very source of, an ever increasing consumer economy, maternal sentimentality supposedly came to demonstrate the "vitiation" of American culture, the shameful worst of nineteenth-century Victoriana—or so declared Ann Douglas. Since its publication in 1977 her *Feminization of American Culture* has provoked much disagreement, if not outright attack. And yet maternal sentimentality remains a by-word for banality. If, as Jane Tompkins labored to prove in *Sensational Designs,* domestic sentimentality was a politically expedient vehicle (primarily although not exclusively for white, middle-class women), invoking the sentimental functioned and can still function as a transparent sign of aesthetic paucity.

A few brief examples. In James Fenimore Cooper's sentimental novel *The Deerslayer* (1841), it is of profound and central importance that the mother of the Hutter girls is dead and deeply mourned. She is, in fact, doubly buried, both under the Hutter home and, because that home floats in the middle of Glimmerglass Lake, under the water. The sunken, lost Mrs. Hutter had also been sunk in her own estimation (and *her* mother's) because of her intimacy with a man "who came from Europe, and who could hardly be supposed to wish to form an honorable connection in America." The result of her "great error"? Two illegitimate daughters and a subsequent marriage to another man so far below this woman's social station and respectability in general that even her shameful grave had to be rendered invisible.[13] Still, despite that shame and invisibility, her memory animates the novel's action, and her fate determines that of Cooper's redoubtable Deerslayer.

The other mother in this novel is (chronologically) not yet a mother: Hist-oh!-Hist (Wah-ta-Wah), Chingachgook's beloved and the mother-to-be of Uncas, gives birth and dies in the narrative interstice between *The Deerslayer* and *The Last of the Mohicans.* But without her there would have been no "last" Mohican at all. In this second (chronologically) of the Leatherstocking Tales, published in 1826, both Munro girls have lost their mothers. Cora Munro's dead mother was "a lady whose misfortune it was . . . to be descended, remotely, from that unfortunate class who are so basely enslaved to administer to the wants of a luxurious people"; and consequently, even her doting father calls his daughter "degraded." Represented as inherently unable to have a proper (white) marriage—or, heaven forbid, children—Cora leaps off the famous cliff with the Mohican, Uncas, and so, according to Cooper's text, dies (out) with him and his tribe.[14]

By 1851 the situation of mothers and of those characters who, like Cora Munro, have become known as "tragic mulattas" had changed. They did not always have to die but were presented instead as living monuments of maternal virtue: Eliza Harris in *Uncle Tom's Cabin* and the later Rosabella Royal of Lydia Maria Child's *Romance of the Republic,* come to mind.[15] Yet even if Eliza and her lover, George Harris, do not die precipitously at each other's feet, they, with their children, do disappear from America to become the extratextual, utopic Adam and Eve of Liberia.

More significant for my argument, though, is the fact that none of these authors—Cooper, Stowe, and Child—have enjoyed reputations as "good" American writers. Both Nina Baym and Judith Fetterley have observed that "in the study of American literature there exists an equation between 'masculinity' and 'Americanness' parallel to the fusion . . . between 'male' and 'American writer.'"[16] Sentimentality has been part of that which is neither masculine nor artistic, and since maternity as a narrative focus is most apparent in the so-called women's sentimental texts, it is not surprising that it has been doubly ignored. Given how pervasively, since the 1940s, texts written by women have been excised from traditional notions of what constitutes America's literary heritage, the chance that maternal iconography might be viewed as a matrix of criticism has been slim.[17] Yet on what evaluative grounds are these sentimental texts being judged? Is sentimentality itself not also an issue for critical debate?

A partial answer as to how one can address the evaluative category "sentimental" is to question the relatively unproblematic vision of what might be said to constitute maternity. As both Judith Fetterley and Eve Kosofsky Sedgwick have noted, "sentimentality" has been an underdefined term, critical shorthand for the mundane of the everyday, the trivial.[18] Furthermore, the Emersonian metaphysical equation of perception with conception has, still, great definitive power; the maternal in the Western philosophical tradition has been overdetermined, to borrow from Julia Kristeva, as a space of material abjection,[19] while its supposed opposite, ab-stract conception, has been seen as the locus of unquestioned creativity. This represented disjunction between cerebral and corporeal conception affected the American writer particularly, insofar as an emerging nineteenth-century articulation of the uniquely "American" artist rested upon the core idea that to be able to conceptualize the future was to have a unique vision. This special perception would be to the advantage of America's national, cultural destiny. Transcendentalist in origin, clearly dependent on Cartesian metaphysics, this creative ideal was popularized through Ralph Waldo Emerson's works. As Oliver Wendell Holmes was to say, Emerson's essay *Nature* cut the cord that bound America culturally to Great Britain.[20]

Such idealist conceptualization is often claimed as the essence of a pragmatic American creativity, repeatedly identified with utopic "Americanness." As Emerson wrote, the American artist was "a conductor of the whole river of electricity. Nothing walks, or creeps, or grows or exists which must not in turn arise and walk before him as an exponent of meaning. . . . All the creatures, by pairs and by tribes, pour into his mind as into Noah's ark, to come forth again to people a new world."[21] Assimilating the world and peopling it properly with the spawn of a (Christian, American) mind, Emerson's artist gestates with electricity. He is a clean conductor, not bound to the temporal or to the mundane uncertainties of flesh. Those uncertainties are assigned rather to a discarded umbilical cord, or to the tribes and creatures that swarm and creep. At the heart of this national identity was the credo that to conceive an idea and give it shape in language was to birth a better world.

But the very term "conception" implies gender, and reproductive metaphors suggesting the maternal were invoked to represent it, even as the maternal itself was assigned to the monstrously multifarious, the uncertain, or the abject. "Conception" became a contested site of cultural value. When antebellum sentimental ideology focused on the maternal, it did so through rhetorical strategies of utopian beatification so that an iconographic economy celebrating the mother as an unconflicted image of utopian stability became dominant.

It was an unstable predominance, however. The sanctified icon of divine maternity kept invoking the scarlet adulteress, even as the icon served as a blind to underlying fears. Anxious questions arose. Who is the divine (demonic) mother's child—precious pearl or evil elf? Would the possibilities of democratic diversity merely precipitate fatal dismemberments—social, moral, and political? By examining ruptures in the dominant maternal iconographic economy, I will show how such fears of disunion shaped—and continue to shape—figurations of "the" maternal.

Moreover, the dominant rhetoric of nineteenth-century sentimental ideology which associated the maternal with "appropriate/d" excess[22]—whether that of beatific serenity or horrific rage—recurred in critical definitions of an American literary aesthetic. As a result, certain elements of the iconography—such as "nurturance"— were naturalized as instinctual rather than recognized as historically conditioned. Reified, sentimental maternal iconography has been situated in opposition to a more restrained "literary" practice and is still seen as such.[23] *Conceived by Liberty,* then, contends that maternal iconography is central both to how a nineteenth-century text such as *The Scarlet Letter* has been interpreted and to how such a text, as an artifact, works in relation to critical conflicts over aesthetic value and canonicity in the United States.

COULD IT BE POSSIBLE THAT SHE HAS NO MATERNAL INSTINCTS?

My choice of *The Scarlet Letter* as an opening emblem is unavoidable, not only because Hester Prynne is a mother but also because of the myriad critical meanings assigned to her playfully generative or promiscuously infamous signifier, the protean "A." Whether as Angel, Avenger, Adulteress, American, Animal, Anger, or Astonishment, this blazing "A" has been an avatar for the definition and study of an American literary aesthetic since 1879, when Henry James, in his Men of Letters biography *Hawthorne,* called *The Scarlet Letter* its author's "most substantial title to fame, . . . in the United States a literary event of the first importance. The book was the finest piece of imaginative writing yet put forth in the country, . . . America having produced a novel that belonged to literature, and to the forefront of it."[24]

But rather than writing yet another gloss on Mistress Prynne's ambiguous signifier, let me take a slightly circuitous route via two more recognizable icons of popular, national significance: the American bald eagle and the (younger) Statue of Liberty. In 1850, Salem's Custom House bore (as it still bears today) "an enormous specimen of the American eagle, with outspread wings, a shield before *her breast* and . . . a bunch of intermingled thunderbolts and barbed arrows in each claw" (*CH,* 6; emphasis added). Gendered as female in *The Scarlet Letter*'s prologue, this truculent spectacle is "vixenly." The narrator of "The Custom House" goes on to relate that the well-armed eagle's foolish progeny often mistake her viciousness for the protective instincts of a domestic hen. Our narrator knows better. Any who think "her bosom has all the softness and snugness of an eiderdown pillow" will find that this untender mother is "apt to fling off her nestlings with a scratch of her claw, a dab of her beak, or a rankling wound from her barbed arrows" (*CH,* 6).

Such an image of a maternalized demon is not surprising. Female monsters are as familiar a trope of nineteenth-century literature in the United States as the

Victorian Woman's calling to play Coventry Patmore's Angel-in-the-House.[25] Definitive polarities, these cultural twins the Demon/Angel and the Dark Lady/Light Lady, are densely impacted personifications of a variety of supposedly stable cultural borderlines dividing black from white, evil from good, upper from lower, normal from perverse. Thus the fate of the Dark Lady/Light Lady pair displays the catastrophes likely to result from a confusion or worse a fusion of such definitive oppositions. From Zenobia and Priscilla of *The Blithedale Romance* to Miriam and Hilda in *The Marble Faun,* Hawthorne's "women" enact this paradigm.[26]

Of course, Hawthorne was not alone in his use of a female Angel/Demon. Likewise, his casting of the eagle/ nation-state as both female and maternal was (and is) a broadly familiar device. Reconciliatory political narratives in the postcolonial, post-revolutionary nineteenth-century United States often figured Britain as Columbia's mother, or described Columbia herself as maternally protective of Liberty's children.[27] Indeed, a habit of personifying the nation-state as a mother, however transformed and reshaped by shifting historical contexts, has not vanished. Nor have this figure of speech and the associations it breeds lost their iconographic density or political efficacy. A recent resurgence of American patriotism has linked national pride to appropriate maternal and familial values, if the politically explosive image of American mother/soldiers in the Gulf War was any indication. Women like Captain Yolanda Huet-Vaughn, a family physician who left her son to serve in the Gulf, received both kudos for patriotism and censure for abandoning a child.[28]

Hawthorne's depiction of "The Custom House" eagle as a dangerous, wounding mother points to how its supposed opposite, a fantasy of homogeneous maternal love, was used as a prescriptive model. The ideal maternal icon would contain, and thus mask, any threat of disunion she might also represent. That is, to a republican democratic culture wherein the illusion of achieving univocal political consensus was deemed necessary, emblems of proliferation such as reproduction suggested the potential for squabbling diversity and so were scripted as dangerous—monstrous, perhaps, like Nathaniel Hawthorne's 1851 Medusa, from his collection *A Wonder-Book.*[29] Female, golden-winged, and brazen-clawed, Hawthorne's Gorgon inherited descriptive attributes from the republican "unhappy fowl" perched atop the Custom House. And both demons had "no great tenderness" for mortals (*WB* 41).

The American eagle a fatal Gorgon? Perhaps a more benign and embracing icon for democratic motherhood is the Statue of Liberty. Little more than a century old in the 1990s, Lady Liberty retains her fascination. For example, U.S. media coverage of the Chinese student uprising in Tiannanmen Square focused much of its attention on the students' replication of Lady Liberty; her subsequent dismemberment was presented as a horrific emblem of totalitarian oppression. In *The Anatomy of National Fantasy* Lauren Berlant persuasively argues that the Statue of Liberty inhabits a national fantasy of the timeless, indivisible iconic maternal body; however, says Berlant, when such a body is "employed symbolically to regulate or represent the field of national fantasy," her "positive 'agency' lies solely in her availability to be narrativized—controlled."[30] In August 1991 the logic of a campaign poster for the Children's Defense Fund seemed to exemplify this claim. The poster interrogated a photograph of the statue's head with the rhetorical question: "Could It Be Possible That She Has No Maternal Instincts?"[31] Addressed to Americans en masse, the poster's plea stands as a self-evident narrative. Lady Liberty cares.

But this image bears troubling antinomies. The bold rhetorical question may assume a prescripted (controlled) affirmative response—"Of course she has maternal instincts!"—but the poster's frame decapitates the statue, accentuating in close-up Lady-Mother Liberty's stony, frowning brow and her alarmingly spiked crown. Such a medusan image unsettles, threatening to arouse a response opposite the one the poster was presumably designed to evoke. Liberty with her toothy spikes seems to share in the *Wonder-Book* Gorgon's dream "of tearing some poor mortal all to pieces" (*WB,* 41).

Should my reading signal opposition, it also shares in the assumption that the word "maternal" is a synonym for (moral and instinctual) care, just as Hawthorne's sarcastic invocation of the motherly eiderdown pillow one could *not* find in the republican eagle's ample bosom presupposes that such an item ought to have been there in the first place. The Statue of Liberty, a hegemonic icon of sacred American motherhood, remains a seemingly unalloyed representation that helps instill, if not ensure, proper (hetero)social behaviors. In a national community that still identifies itself as Lady Liberty's ideal home but where traditional, rigidly enforced social and political boundaries are at least *theoretically* in flux, such maternal iconography can function as a conservative guarantee against a tide of unpredictable change. The mother, as a figure, can be used to reinforce conventional certitudes about racial, social, sexual, and political restrictions. Indeed, as Hazel Carby's *Reconstructing Womanhood: The Emergence of the Afro-American Woman Novelist* demonstrates, the nineteenth-century ideology of True Womanhood idealized Christian maternity and made the middle-class, legally married, heterosexual, domestic lady-mother supreme. This Woman, who passively reproduced without expressing sexual desire, and who exercised benevolent authority in the home, became a (white) icon against which any alternative patterns of mothering—or female behavior—were measured.[32]

And yet in the sheer replication of the icon's prescriptive function, the maternal angel points rather insistently toward her own demon and thus at her own fractured instability—or, as Berlant writes, "the unifying utopian figure, which in theory brings time and space into the realm of (discursive, systemic) perfection, shows, in relief, the impermanence and instability of the historical frames within which persons gain (self)knowledge and experience."[33] Maternal iconography was never as untroubled or as static as it was represented to be, rather, it was and is rife with moral, social, and politically charged tensions, subject to persistent conflict, and thus open to dynamic and strategic revisions.

Therefore, it is not surprising to find that "to mother," as Margaret Homans argues in *Bearing the Word: Language and Female Experience in Nineteenth Century Women's Writing,* was represented as both a prescriptive and an imperiled ideal. On one hand, "women's lives were increasingly defined in relation to a standard of motherhood, regardless of whether or not they were of childbearing age"; women who held jobs or who wrote "did so within a framework of dominant cultural myths in which writing contradicts mothering."[34] On the other hand, it is well documented that lower- and middle-class women (and mothers) during the mid-nineteenth century formed an increasingly large sector of the labor market in the United States, particularly in the textile and publishing industries.[35] The dominant maternal ideology did seek to confine women to (sacred) pregnancy and the physical duties of child rearing; popular wisdom held, as Lydia Maria Child's *The Mother's Book* did, that a girl who "feels interested in nothing but books . . . will in all probability be useless, or nearly so, in all the relations dearest to a good woman's heart"—these relations being maternal. Yet Child was herself a prolific author who insisted that "the power of finding enjoyment in reading is above all price, particularly to a woman."[36]

Reading, of course, is not the same activity as writing—or, indeed, as slave-laboring on a plantation. But Child's portrait of the useless girl does indicate that the iconic memory of mother, as Thoreau had imagined his nostalgic idealism, was especially pressing for those persons defined as women. As late as 1887 Mary Virginia Terhune—author of twenty-five novels and numerous short stories and essays, as well as the handbook *Common Sense in the Household*—could still claim that the "woman who rides her hobby of art, literature, social, religious or political reform rough-shod over the wreck of domestic comfort and happiness" was "diseased in perception and judgment."[37] As historian

Mary Ryan says, if "by the mid-nineteenth century maternity had assumed its honored position in the center of popular culture, right alongside a familiar variety of American pastry" so that "motherhood was invested with a new glory [and] . . . proclaimed the essence of femininity, 'woman's one duty and function . . . that alone for which she was created.'"[38] then "Mother," for all intents and purposes, meant "woman."

Furthermore, the figure of mother often reduced woman to another and even more restricted image: womb. Put simply, all women, regardless of circumstances, were expected to reproduce under the proper Christian aegis of marriage, and to mother their offspring carefully, in order to be defined as good, solid American women. Similarly, all men were expected to revere and uphold the purity of this maternal icon in order to be defined as true, patriotic, red-blooded American men. Otherwise? A potentially violent melange, potential dissolution—frequently figured in the "bad" woman/mother/womb such as Hawthorne's Custom House editor faces when he is positioned as a nestling seeking shelter at the mother eagle's breast.

But perhaps Hawthorne's brooding fowl-demon may best serve not as an allegorical reference in Western, neoclassical mythology but rather as an index to the sorts of maternal fantasies effective across a broad range of interconnected discourses in nineteenth-century American culture.[39] At the same time, the manner in which Hawthorne's eagle has been interpreted provides an example of how a variety of conflicting discourses not only were but still are readily accommodated by a trope of maternal reproduction as dire instrument of discord.

Liberty, That "Vixen of Contradictions"?

In *The Office of the Scarlet Letter* Sacvan Bercovitch welds the Custom House eagle to Hawthorne's later description—in his famously non-interventionist essay on the Civil War, "Chiefly about War Matters" (1862)—of the *Mayflower* as "the fated womb which in its first labor brought forth a brood of Pilgrims on Plymouth Rock, and, in a subsequent one, spawned slaves upon the Southern soil,—a monstrous birth, but one with which we have an instinctive sense of kindred, and so are stirred by an irresistible impulse to attend their rescue even at the cost of blood and ruin."[40] Bercovitch claims that this contains "all the major imaginative ingredients of the dominant culture," notably "the legend of the Puritan theocracy, womb of American democracy; the ambiguities of good and evil, agency of compromise; and the ironies of regeneration through violence, rationale for civil war." Hawthorne's tale of a fatal womb, he says, is "a parable of social conflict following upon cultural myth [which] reverberates with ambiguities at cross-purposes with each other—for ex-

ample, the recurrent American nightmare of miscegenation; the long literary procession of mutually destructive dark-white kin (from *Clotel* through *Clarel* and *Pudd'nhead Wilson* to *Absalom, Absalom!*); the biblical types of the elect and the damned through which the South defended its peculiar institution; and the racist use of the image of Christian sacrifice through which the North sanctified first the Union Cause and then the Martyrdom of Lincoln."[41]

Viewing Hawthorne's *Mayflower*-womb as rhetorical kin to the Custom House eagle, Bercovitch declares both to be versions of "a Frankenstein's monster of the culture: history returning in the guise of figures designed to control it—the most familiar of symbols . . . now streams forth disjunctions." Mother-eagle and womb-ship are (as are the Madonna/Whore Hester Prynne and her endlessly generative scarlet A) "uncannily" ambiguous signs, double-sided coins signifying above all a form of dynamic, if coercive, social continuity, or what Bercovitch calls "the American ideology" of "consensus founded upon the potential for dissent."[42]

Bercovitch's rendering of *The Scarlet Letter* as a definitive symbol of liberal ideology is remarkable for the breadth of concerns he identifies as embedded in the "Mayflower-eagle, mother of nationhood and vixen of contradictions."[43] Yet the interpretive telos of this argument, along with the metaphorics of Bercovitch's rhetoric, uncannily echoes the politics of consensual containment he explores. At certain key moments he presupposes an interpretive consensus without examining the terms of conflict. For example, the syntax of "mother of nationhood and vixen of contradictions" balances "mother" and "vixen" in a parallel construction that unquestioningly assumes the terms to be oppositional. But why has "vixen," a word that designates genus and sex, come to connote a vexatious or unruly quantity that can be opposed so easily to the term "mother"? And for whom, exactly, is miscegenation a "recurrent nightmare"? Is an American literary heritage indeed a "procession of mutually destructive dark-white kin," or might such kinships be described as mutually constitutive? Bercovitch's assertion that *Clotel, Clarel, Pudd'nhead Wilson,* and *Absalom, Absalom!* are tales of dark-white destruction is one way these texts have been read. But do these particular narratives measure the reach of "our" literary heritage? For instance, in her 1824 novel *Hobomok,* Lydia Maria Child offers a narrative in which interracial relations need not be read as altogether nightmarish.[44] Nor are the kinships of dark and light in Frances Watkins Harper's *Iola LeRoy* or Charles Chesnutt's *The Marrow of Tradition* well represented by the phrase "mutually destructive."

Indeed, the identification of miscegenation as a nightmare, though accurate with regard to many postbellum representations and indeed legalities, also neatly replicates Hawthorne's assertion that slaves were of monstrous, if kindred, birth to the Pilgrims, and that a "fated womb" was the fatal source of such twinned spawn of inevitable discord.[45] It leaves undisturbed the tenacious and intermeshed presuppositions that would read multiplicity, encoded in the words "brood" and "spawn," as associatively female and animalistic—a nightmare of improperly restrained, gendered reproduction.

In turn, those presuppositions serve to determine aesthetic categorization, affect how interpretive strategies operate, and ultimately form the basis upon which texts are chosen as representing "American" narratives. For instance, part of the elegance of Bercovitch's argumentive strategy is the rhetorical ease with which the *Mayflower*-eagle can both serve as the image of motherwomb, teeming with a brood of disjunctions, and be in and of itself a "monstrous birth, a Frankenstein's monster."[46] Using such a totemic Anglo-American cultural artifact as Frankenstein's monster proves a deft move for Bercovitch's argument, but it also enacts an interesting metaphoric collapse: it substitutes a later, widespread Anglo-American cultural fantasy for the particularity of Mary Shelley's text.[47] The appeal to Frankenstein's monster as metaphor begs a number of critical questions that must perforce redefine Bercovitch's interpretation. For is it not precisely a womb that is notoriously absent in Shelley's *Frankenstein*? Shelley made it clear that her monster was not born and did not consider itself monstrous until shown that it was *viewed* as horrific both by the parent who rejected it and by a hypocritical society that preached an ideal of disinterested Christian love. Shelley's novel figures maternity in various ways.[48] But what does the word "maternal" signify, how, and to whom? What sorts of maternities play through the novel? These are only a few of the suggestive questions that Bercovitch's facile cultural reference leaves out.

In fact, the unspoken source of logical connection that binds the *Mayflower* to the eagle is for Bercovitch the figuration of both as dangerously reproductive—fated wombs. If the ship and the bird are among the "most familiar of symbols"[49] in a national consciousness, and if mother is as "American as apple pie"[50] for the nineteenth century, all three slide together along a metonymic axis of maternal reproduction in Bercovitch's reading. Of course, my question as to why the notion of a fatal, Frankensteinian womb is available, without much critical mediation, as a metaphor for monstrosity is not meant to stand here as a definitive counterpoint to Sacvan Bercovitch's provocative reading of *The Scarlet Letter*. Still, it does serve as a telling reminder that reproduction can function as a metaphor of chaos. The womb remains a "feminized" image of an unquestioned, phantasmal horror about disunion.[51]

Moreover, such metaphors help to fuel contemporaneous arguments over whether cultural and interpretive diversity will mean pluralism or, worse, an "indeterminism"[52] that will dismember aesthetic judgment. The charge of indeterminism often implies that diversity means, ipso facto, a lack of intellectual integrity. Such a lack, it has been argued, will inevitably result in a sort of formless mess. "We" will lose sight of the value of "our" American culture in the pursuit of a spurious cultural relativity. "We" might lose the forest for the trees. The current tendency to cast either critical pluralism or, in more contemporary parlance, multicultural literacy as divisive Angel of Doom has appeared before in other guises. In fact, the treatment of *The Scarlet Letter* as an artifact bears the historical scars of a system of aesthetic evaluation activated by a presupposition that multiplicity must mean many-headed medusan monster.

When *The Scarlet Letter* was published in 1851, it contained "The Custom House," composed as the head note to a volume originally intended to include other works besides the novel. But as Henry James's 1879 discussion of it shows, this preface was first seen as integral to *The Scarlet Letter*.[53] Much subsequent critical debate, however, acting like Perseus, has quietly decapitated Hawthorne's novel by removing "The Custom House" as its head. Indeed "The Custom House" writes Nina Baym, has been silently ignored by most critics.[54] Yet even though Baym argues that the thematic continuities between the essay and the novel bind the pieces together, her article also treats them as separable entities insofar as she claims that "The Custom House" should be respected as a work "in its own right."[55]

But why the assumption that this sketch's ability to stand on its own serves to guarantee critical respect? In fact, a number of arguments designed to demonstrate the importance of "The Custom House" do so at the cost of the sketch's impact on and relation to *The Scarlet Letter* (and vice-versa) as if the political, autobiographical milieu as well as the unreliable tone of the jaunty (or jaundiced) narrator were either the buzzing of bothersome contingencies or just unnecessary detail. Indeed, one recent study declares that both novel and sketch are simply "twice their optimal length."[56] This supposed excess of "The Custom House," or what Baym called its "mundane materiality,"[57] has often been deemed incompatible with, or only obliquely related to, the balanced and artistically sound body of Hawthorne's most well-shaped tale.[58] For instance, in 1986 Jonathan Arac declared that "The Custom-House" occupies a space that "in its absence would not be recognized as vacant"; it adds "something gratuitous that was not required and thus destabilizes what it claims to support." So although it is a part of *The Scarlet Letter*, "The Custom House" also remains apart, is indeed declared a detriment to what Arac described as an unquestioned "self-sufficiency" of the tale that follows it.[59] Despite arguments demonstrating that the narrative perspective of *The Scarlet Letter* is shaped by the narrator of "The

Custom House"[60] and despite evidence that the sketch was composed in the midst of (as well as published with) *The Scarlet Letter,*[61] it still evidently poses aesthetic problems with regard to the question of appropriate form. Though considerable effort has been exerted to make the sketch an "organic part" of *The Scarlet Letter,*[62] it would appear that the organism still bears suspicious sutures.

It is undoubtedly true that issues other than form have long been at stake in critical assessments of *The Scarlet Letter,* and that "The Custom House" is usually taught as preface to, if not as a part of, the romance. What I am more concerned with is how a rhetoric of aesthetic cohesion can determine a structure of ideological, metaphorical logic which—under the rubric of reason, rationality, self-sufficiency, or, indeed, ordinary common sense—equates multiplicity with monstrosity. This equation, in turn, devalues discussion that seeks to explore the historical conflicts and contexts of diversity, specifically those concerning race, class, and gender. Such a logic continues to allow for the dismissal of particularity *as* particularity, on the grounds that multivalency eradicates standards of reliable value—without a murmur as to the basis of the supposedly reliable standards being upheld. This brand of common sense can render the everyday obsessions of Surveyor Hawthorne's "Custom House" wholly irrelevant to the scarlet romance of literatus M. de l'Aubépine, forcing a thematic separation between two interdependent texts.[63]

The amputation of mundane particularities from the stuff of sublime romance, I would argue, restricts what material can be viewed as valid or even useful for discussion. In addition, although more recent critical work on *The Scarlet Letter* has been aimed at precisely what earlier assessments would have struck off—that is, the "mundane materiality" of historical context (antebellum abolition, the politics of slavery, the women's rights movement, and the European revolutions of 1848)—such pleas for historical specificity themselves can slyly play Perseus.

Let me return, for a moment, to Jonathan Arac's "Politics of *The Scarlet Letter.*" Arac seeks a methodology that is historically and ideologically self-reflexive and that would also ground specific, incisive interpretation. In the course of his quest he takes issue with Frederick Crews and, through him, with larger critical debates about literary indeterminacy. In 1982 Crews had proclaimed that those debates which substituted the "empirically dubious sources of authority" of Marx, Nietzsche or Freud for authorial intent contributed to a wholesale "renunciation of rationally based choice between competing theories." Yet Crews, says Arac, "acted neither empirically nor rationally" in declaring authorial intent foundational. Arac calls Crews's declaration a "decapitation of literary studies by a debased pragma-

tism" intent upon keeping English departments, in a capitalist economy, up and running.[64]

Here I might stop and ask why Jonathan Arac uses decapitation—a politically charged image of formal execution—as an appropriately horrific image for the possible death of certain literary studies. I am more interested, however, in how Arac, despite his validation of the kinds of sociopolitical engagement represented by, say, the use of a Marxist conceptual framework, also performs a closure of debate not unlike the one with which he charges Crews. Although *The Scarlet Letter* addresses "the anonymous toil of women under the barbarism of patriarchy", he writes, "*we must go farther* to understand its immediate and continuing power long before feminism became an unavoidable presence. Slavery was the issue that agitated American politics more deeply in Hawthorne's time, and abolitionism made the young Henry Adams feel that Boston in 1850 was once again revolutionary (emphasis added).[65] Arac's identification of feminist debate about *The Scarlet Letter* as an obstacle to an understanding of slavery as *the* political issue curiously truncates his claim that refocusing on the "politics of *The Scarlet Letter*" will provide a more opened-out apprehension of Hawthorne's narrative. While distancing himself from a charge of indeterminacy, Arac's injunction to "go farther" places "feminism" in the position of a static ideology.

Indeed, Arac's vision of slavery and the abolitionist movement as somehow unmarked by gender politics tacitly severs antebellum abolition as a political movement from its relation to the women's rights movement and, in so doing, Arac disables a portion of the immediate and continuing power he wishes to locate in *The Scarlet Letter.*[66] Nineteenth-century abolition was hardly gender-neutral. The economics and ideology of slavery helped to shape—and were shaped by—the definitive cultural weight placed upon proper maternity. While domestic ideology strove to keep (free) women's labor restricted to the home just as a new, highly mobile marketplace economy demanded an influx of (unskilled, often female) laborers,[67] the slavocracy maintained that (female, slave) maternal reproduction was invisible (a slave supposedly could not be a true mother) even as it grounded economic security on that reproduction. Along similar lines, while medical theories concerning the radical instability of female anatomy were tying women ever more severely to a reproductive destiny—a biologically determined destiny that militated against the kind of social autonomy still named the American entrepreneurial spirit—many women were beginning to take political action with regard to abolition, suffrage and abortion.[68] Sojourner Truth's famous question "Ain't I a woman?" pinpoints the paradox of an antebellum (hetero)sexual orthodoxy insisting on the one hand, that to be truly feminine and maternal was to be anatomical weakness personified and on the other hand, enslaving some female bodies in enforced reproductive factories called plantations and working others to death in "Devil's Dungeon" papermills.[69]

Contrary to Arac's suggestion, feminism did not enter the picture merely as a result of twentieth-century critical practice. Not only was racial slavery marked by gender ideology, but abolition took shape through Arac's so-called "unavoidable presence." This would suggest that the relations between revolution, race, and reproduction need critical attention, an attention that Henry Adams was attuned to when he wrote *Democracy*'s story as that of a woman whose nurturance is dependent on the imperialist policies of late-nineteenth-century American politics.[70] At the very least, then, I would argue that Arac's American political history is a foreshortened one. It raises troubling questions as to which histories are lost, or remain untold, when "history" is used thus as a means of validating unquestionable truths. Slavery may have been *the* political issue agitating Hawthorne's time, as Arac insists, but it is shortsighted not to inquire how and to what end that issue was represented.[71]

REPRODUCTION, RACE, AND REVOLUTION

Conceived by Liberty addresses such foreshortenings in order to articulate the rhetoric of reproduction, race, and revolution that constructed and revised dominant, sentimental maternal iconography. The readings that follow seek first to demonstrate how a dominant antebellum maternal ideology put forward an illusion of a coherent, sanctified maternity, an ideology that marked both popular representations of motherhood and texts designated as literary. . . . Chapter 1 [of my book, *Conceived in Liberty,*] examines Lydia Maria Child's use of a maternal iconography to show how the creation of an obedient yet enterprising and bold citizenry fell most heavily on motherhood—both as pragmatic institution and as figurative symbol—and structured metaphorical and metaphysical debate. In the philosophical discussions that "occurred" between the writings of Sarah Margaret Fuller and Ralph Waldo Emerson, . . . the infrastructure of "an" American literature and culture was in the process of being constructed. Fuller's response to Emersonian metaphysics allowed for an aesthetics that demanded diversity as the basis for fecund creativity, an outlook that came to affect Emerson's later essays.

Antebellum maternal ideology was unstable, however. By examining specific representations that indicate rupture in texts that have been used critically, in one way or another, as central to argumentation about the shape of various contested American literatures, my readings propose that a supposedly seamless icon was not only conflicted but also a site of politicized, aesthetic con-

tention. Indeed, the beatified maternal as political and cultural icon, on which Emerson and Fuller relied to ground Transcendental metaphysics, also represented fears that the American democratic experiment might prove, as Henry James put it, a "many-headed monster of universal suffrage."[72] Should America lack appropriate controls, her unchecked reproductive capacity, deemed monstrous, would shatter the singularity of *e pluribus unum,* rendering a sublime ideal inchoate.

Such fears of maternalized duplicity can be seen most urgently in work directly addressing slavery and racial conflict as threats to the Union. Thus, . . . through a sustained discussion of sentimentality and slavery, I show how the underlying ideal of a homogeneous maternal love, because it both relied upon and masked fears of monstrosity, began to lose its symbolic force as a model of utopian unification during the Civil War. Sentimental maternity, often daring in its defiance of the expected, symbolized community for a dominant nineteenth-century American culture. Yet because it was unstable, its power to propose startling alternatives to convention was also uncertain.

Finally, I argue that in treating sentimental maternal iconography, critics have reinforced elements of the dominant ideology as natural. As a result, such criticism is often locked into the very ideology it seeks to expose. . . . I show how the Civil War's shattering of the maternal ideal as cultural icon allowed for the consolidation of a benevolent paternal ideology, which gained a definitive critical priority by providing a "new" principle of social and aesthetic unification. A univocal American cultural identity emerged as phantasmaly unscarred by conflict, fully coincident with Emerson's early credos of "Self-Reliance." In the project of renationalization, however, from Reconstruction to the turn of the century, the attributes of sentimental maternity were regendered: imaginative creativity, aesthetic purity, and moral idealism, all once associated with the maternal, became primarily paternal attributes.

Nevertheless, the reductive, rejecting denigration of the maternal upon which an emerging twentieth-century definition of quintessentially American identity would come to rest was a forced and painful process that left traces of agony. This agony and the system of paternalized aesthetics that it marks haunt the shape of late nineteenth-century narrative and, indeed, the ensuing shape of an American canon. Both the process of paternal reinstatement and the agony of maternal rejection are evidenced, albeit quite differently, in the work of Herman Melville and Henry James. Therefore, what became a prevailing twentieth-century definition of an American literary aesthetic was dependent upon but apparently unconnected to a previously central maternal icon, now lost. This book seeks to address both the conditions and the consequences of that loss.

Notes

1. Ann Douglas, *The Feminization of American Culture* (New York: Avon, 1977), 5.

2. Quoted in Gerda Lerner, *The Grimké Sisters from South Carolina* (New York: Schocken, 1971), 3.

3. G. J. Barker-Benfield, *The Horrors of the Half-Known Life: Attitudes toward Women and Sex in Nineteenth-Century America* (Boston: Harper and Row, 1976), 10-15.

4. Perhaps Leslie A. Fiedler's *Love and Death in the American Novel,* rev. ed. (New York: Dell, 1966) is the most widely known study proposing such a "flight." Other critics to whom I refer in this study have demonstrated how profoundly American literary history in the United States academy has been shaped by arguments structuring both American literature and the "American Renaissance" in opposition to sentimental motherhood as a trope.

5. Jane Tompkins, *Sensational Designs: The Cultural Work of American Fiction, 1790-1860* (New York: Oxford University Press, 1985).

6. Daniel Cottom, "Hawthorne versus Hester: The Ghostly Dialectic of Romance in *The Scarlet Letter,*" *Texas Studies in Literature and Language* 24 (Spring 1982): 62, with reference to Toril Moi, *Sexual/Textual Politics: Feminist Literary Theory* (New York: Methuen, 1985).

7. Nathaniel Hawthorne, *The Scarlet Letter* (New York: Norton, 1988), 41. "The Custom House" in this edition is cited hereafter as *CH* and *The Scarlet Letter* as *SL*.

8. Herman Melville, *Moby Dick* (London: Penguin, 1972), 451 (hereafter cited as *MD*). Earlier, Queequeg's famous matrimonial embrace has reminded Ishmael sharply and significantly of his stepmother and her disciplinary actions.

9. Fiedler, *Love and Death,* 90.

10. See also Mary Kelley, *Private Woman, Public Stage: Literary Domesticity in Nineteenth-Century America* (New York: Oxford University Press, 1984).

11. From *Abraham Lincoln's Speeches,* ed. L. E. Chittenden (New York: Dodd, Mead 1895), 21.

12. Henry David Thoreau, *Journal,* in *The Harper American Literature,* ed. Donald McQuade (New York: Harper & Row, 1987), 2:1500.

13. James Fenimore Cooper, *The Deerslayer* (New York: New American Library, 1963), 154, 165, 173.

14. James Fenimore Cooper, *The Last of the Mohicans* (New York: New American Library, 1963), 186-87. For discussions of Cooper's textual form of Native American genocide, see also Carolyn L. Karcher's introduction to Lydia Maria Child, *Hobomok and Other Writings on Indians,* ed. Carolyn L. Karcher (New Brunswick, N.J.: Rutgers University Press, 1986), esp. xxxvi-xxxvii; and Lora Romero's "Vanishing Americans: Gender, Empire, and New Historicism," *American Literature* 63, reprinted in *The Culture of Sentiment,* ed. Shirley Samuels (New York: Oxford University Press, 1992), 115-27.

15. It is interesting to note that in Lydia Maria Child's 1842 short story "The Quadroons" (*The Liberty Bell,* an annual giftbook that Maria Chapman edited for the Boston Female Anti-Slavery Society, 1842), which is widely credited with introducing the tragic mulatta as a literary archetype, both mother and daughter die as a result of their "condition"—whereas Child's later *A Romance of the Republic* insisted upon the survival of this figure. See also Karcher's critical introduction to Child, *Hobomok.* Karcher argues persuasively that Cooper's vision of racial antagonism became dominant not because it was any less sentimental than either Child's or Catharine Maria Sedgwick's in *Hope Leslie* but because its vision served the interests of a white, male ruling class. (For extended treatment of Child and Harriet Beecher Stowe, see Chapters 1 and 3 [of *Conceived in Liberty*].)

16. Judith Fetterley, *Provisions: A Reader from 19th-Century American Women* (Bloomington: Indiana University Press, 1985), 18. See also Nina Baym, "Melodramas of Beset Manhood: How Theories of American Fiction Exclude Women Authors," in *The New Feminist Criticism: Essays on Women, Literature, and Theory,* ed. Elaine Showalter (New York: Pantheon Books, 1985). Like Jane Tompkins, Baym delineates theories defining an American literary aesthetic which "in pursuit of the uniquely American . . . have arrived at a place where Americanness has vanished into the depths of what is alleged to be the universal male psyche" (79).

17. See Vincent B. Leitch, *American Literary Criticism* (New York: Columbia University Press, 1988).

18. See Fetterley, *Provisions,* 20; and Eve Kosofsky Sedgwick, *Epistemology of the Closet* (Berkeley: University of California Press, 1990), 144. I am indebted to Sedgwick, whose 1987 seminar at the University of California, Berkeley, prompted my examination of how the sentimental is still being constructed, and how those constructions might frame an understanding of nineteenth-century narratives. See also Susan K. Harris, "'But Is It Any Good?': Evaluating Nineteenth-Century American

Women's Fiction," *American Literature* 63 (March 1991): 43-61, which comments on Jane Tompkins's question as to whether sentimentality can ever be judged as aesthetically "good" writing.

19. See Julia Kristeva, *Powers of Horror: An Essay on Abjection* (New York: Columbia University Press, 1982).

20. Oliver Wendell Holmes, in *Critical Essays on Ralph Waldo Emerson,* ed. Robert E. Burkholder and Joel Myerson (Boston: G. K. Hall, 1983).

21. Ralph Waldo Emerson, "The Poet," in *The Harper American Literature,* ed. Donald McQuade (New York: Harper & Row, 1987), 1:1081.

22. I have borrowed Trinh T. Minh-ha's term "inappropriate/d" as a pertinent denotation for a site of appropriation that is resistant to the process. See Minh-ha, ed., "She, the Inappropriate/d Other" (special issue), *Discourse* 8 (Fall-Winter 1986-87). See also *Woman, Native, Other: Writing Postcoloniality and Feminism* (Bloomington: Indiana University Press, 1989).

23. See Leitch, *American Literary Criticism.* Although Tompkins's *Sensational Designs* restored to the previously belittled and often invisible maternal sentimentality the didactic power it possessed for nineteenth-century ideology, her revalorization has also served, ironically, to reinforce traditional and standard critical divisions between the sentimental and the serious, the popular and the literary. Calling for a critical reinvestment to validate didacticism within its historical context, rather than calling into question the categories of the "sentimental," "popular," and "didactic," *Sensational Designs* links political expediency to sentimental culture and demonstrates that the sentimental "is seen as a derogatory code name for female bodies and the female domestic and 'reproductive' preoccupations of birth, socialization, illness and death." But that linkage has not gotten very far beyond an aesthetic bind that Tompkins herself articulated. In asking in her final chapter "But is it any *good*?" Tompkins reasserts a traditional evaluative dichotomy prevalent in much American literary criticism, which insists on placing aesthetic literary value and political didactic intent in opposition. In addition, according to Susan K. Harris, "There appears to be an unspoken agreement not to submit nineteenth-century American women's novels to extended analytical evaluation . . . because the evaluative modes most of us were taught devalue this literature *a priori*" ("But Is It Any *Good*?" 44).

24. Henry James, *Hawthorne* (Ithaca: Cornell University Press, 1956), 86-87.

25. See Coventry Patmore, *The Angel in the House,* 2 vols. (London: Macmillan, 1863). See also Jean Fagan Yellin, "Nathaniel Hawthorne's *The Scarlet Letter,*" in *Women and Sisters: The Antislavery Feminists in American Culture* (New Haven: Yale University Press, 1989), esp. note 43.

26. Many critics have noted the prevalence of Dark Lady/Light Lady pairs in Hawthorne's works, particularly with regard to "Rappaccini's Daughter." See, e.g., Nina Baym, "Hawthorne's Women: The Tyranny of Social Myths," *Centennial Review* 15 (1971): 250-72; Judith Fryer, *The Faces of Eve: Women in the Nineteenth-Century American Novel* (New York: Oxford University Press, 1976); Gloria C. Erlich, *Family Themes and Hawthorne's Fiction: The Tenacious Web* (New Brunswick, N.J.: Rutgers University Press, 1984); Kristin Herzog, *Women, Ethnics, and Exotics: Images of Power in Mid-Nineteenth-Century American Fiction* (Knoxville: University of Tennessee Press, 1983); David Leverenz, "Devious Men: Hawthorne," in his *Manhood and the American Renaissance* (Ithaca: Cornell University Press, 1989), 227-58; and Yellin, "Hawthorne's *The Scarlet Letter,*" 125-52. Indeed, it is still common, particularly in films made in the United States, to find a "dark" woman of dubious sexuality—say, a "Black Widow"—cast as the dangerous opposite of her "light" and stereotypically innocent sister. Recent and self-conscious uses of Dark Lady/Light Lady pairs can be found in the film version of Bernard Malamud's novel *The Natural* (1984, Barry Levinson, dir., Tri-Star/Delphill), and in Michelle Pfeiffer's campy, schizophrenic Catwoman in *Batman Returns* (1992, Tim Burton, dir., Warner).

27. There are numerous and frequent references to Mother Britain, Columbia as a maternal figure, and of course the "motherhood" of the Statue of Liberty. See Martha Banta, *Imaging American Women: Idea and Ideals in Cultural History* (New York: Columbia University Press, 1987); and Annette Kolodny, *The Lay of the Land: Metaphor as Experience and History in American Life and Letters* (Chapel Hill: University of North Carolina Press, 1975). For an analysis of how such perceptions work in national iconography, see Lauren Berlant, *The Anatomy of National Fantasy: Hawthorne, Utopia, and Everyday Life* (Chicago: University of Chicago Press, 1991). For a highly suggestive feminist meditation on democratic theory, see Anne Phillips, *Engendering Democracy* (University Park: Pennsylvania State University Press, 1991).

28. The number of women in the American armed forces who served in this war was high; those who left small children behind were displayed in

photographs and discussed endlessly, it seemed. Huet-Vaughn caused even further debate when she deserted from Operation Desert Storm after deciding that the U.S. action was "immoral, inhumane, and unconstitutional." As a result, she was court-martialed, and although she was granted clemency, her medical license was revoked, despite the fact that her practice as a doctor had never been in question. See "Deserter Regrets War Protest Failed," *Gainesville Sun,* April 12, 1992. See also Valerie Hartouni, "Containing Women: Reproductive Discourse in the 1980s," in *Technoculture,* ed. Constance Penley and Andrew Ross (Minneapolis: University of Minnesota Press, 1991), 27-56.

29. Nathaniel Hawthorne, *A Wonder-Book,* p. 1 (New York: Houghton Mifflin, 1898), 21-48 (hereafter cited as as *WB*). Hawthorne describes the Gorgon as bearing "some distant resemblance to women . . . [with] wings, too, and exceedingly splendid ones, I can assure you; for every feather in them was pure, bright, glittering, burnished gold, and they looked very dazzlingly, no doubt, when the Gorgons were flying about in the sunshine" (*WB,* 24). The Custom House eagle, carved in 1826 by Jonathan True, is gilded.

30. Berlant, *The Anatomy of National Fantasy,* 26-27.

31. Children's Defense Fund Poster, August 1991. Then Vice-President J. Danforth Quayle's much publicized "attack" on the popular representation of single motherhood in the television series *Murphy Brown* is a brief but dense example of the efficacy, no matter whether one reads the consequences as trivial or no, of appealing to the mother-and-child icon in tensely political and conflictual socioeconomic times. Quayle's insistence that a loss of the moral qualities he finds transparently evident in the term "family values" (what sort of family? which values?) demonstrate that an appeal to utopian maternal iconography still masks social conflict.

32. Hazel Carby, *Reconstructing Womanhood: The Emergence of the Afro-American Woman Novelist* (New York: Oxford University Press, 1987), 60.

33. Berlant, *The Anatomy of National Fantasy,* 33.

34. Margaret Homans, *Bearing The Word: Language and Female Experience in Nineteenth-Century Women's Writing* (Chicago: University of Chicago Press, 1986), 22.

35. See Mary P. Ryan, *Womanhood in America* (New York: New Viewpoints, 1975); Carroll Smith-Rosenberg, *Disorderly Conduct: Visions of Gender in Victorian America* (New York: Oxford University Press, 1985).

36. Lydia Maria Child, *The Mother's Book* (Boston: Carter, Hendee & Babcock, 1831; rpt. New York: Arno Press, 1972), 20-21 (hereafter cited as *TMB*).

37. Quoted in Kelley, *Private Woman, Public Stage,* 333.

38. Ryan, *Womanhood,* 98-99. Ryan quotes Dr. William Dewees, *A Treatise on the Physical and Medical Treatment of Children* (Philadelphia, 1833), 64-65.

39. In fact the editor's fate—to become a version of Washington Irving's Headless Horseman—associatively draws mythological monster and republican icon closer together, at least insofar as Hawthorne's famous political execution (which rendered *The Scarlet Letter* a "Posthumous Paper of a Decapitated Surveyor:" *CH,* 33) was a beheading performed at the new administration's (medusan eagle's?) behest. For the political relation, within Enlightenment philosophy and pragmatics, between the Medusa and the threat of disorderly conduct, see also Neil Hertz, "Medusa's Head: Male Hysteria under Political Pressure," and related discussions by Joel Fineman, Catherine Gallagher, and Neil Hertz, "More about 'Medusa's Head,'" *Representations* 4 (Fall 1983): 27-55; and Larry J. Reynolds, "*The Scarlet Letter* and Revolutions Abroad," *American Literature* 77 (1985): 44-67; Yellin ("Hawthorne's *The Scarlet Letter*", in *Women & Sisters,* 133) also comments on Hawthorne's thorny relation to revolution and politics.

40. Nathaniel Hawthorne, "Chiefly about War Matters," *Atlantic Monthly* 10 (July 1862): 42.

41. Sacvan Bercovitch, *The Office of the Scarlet Letter* (Baltimore: Johns Hopkins Press, 1991), 158.

42. Ibid., 159.

43. Ibid.

44. Child's 1824 *Hobomok* features an interracial marriage that does not end violently. See also Yellin, *Women & Sisters*; and Carby, *Reconstructing Womanhood.*

45. Prior to 1864 amalgamation, not miscegenation, was the term used to designate interracial "commerce." I thank David Leverenz for calling this usage to my attention and John Mason for fleshing out the historical background to these terms.

46. Bercovitch, *Office,* 159.

47. For various considerations of both Shelley's text and the resulting cultural phenomenon of Frankenstein as a figure, see George Levine and U. C. Knoepflmacher, eds., *The Endurance of Frankenstein* (New York: Methuen, 1983).

48. Ellen Moers, "Female Gothic," in Levine and Knoepflmacher, *The Endurance of Frankenstein,* 11-35; makes the connections between the novel and Mary Shelley's own troubled maternity unmistakable. See also Anne K. Mellor, *Mary Shelley: Her Life, Her Fiction, Her Monsters* (New York: Routledge, 1987).

49. Bercovitch, *Office,* 159.

50. Ryan, *Womanhood,* 98-99.

51. For the cultural viability of the association between womb and phantasmal, dismembering horror, see Slavoj ˇZiˇzek, *The Sublime Object of Ideology* (London: Verso, 1989), 79.

52. As Jonathan Arac notes in "The Politics of *The Scarlet Letter,*" in *Ideology and Classic American Literature,* ed. Sacvan Bercovitch and Myra Jehlen (London: Cambridge University Press, 1987), 222-47, cries of horror concerning the problem of interpretive indeterminism have erupted all over the academy.

53. See James, *Hawthorne,* chap. 5. On the shape of later debates over how "The Custom House" should be treated, see *SL,* 249-78.

54. Nina Baym, "The Romantic *Malgré Lui*: Hawthorne in 'The Custom House,'" in *SL,* 265.

55. Ibid., 266.

56. Camille Paglia, *Sexual Personae* (New Haven: Yale University Press, 1990), 581. Paglia does not specify which parts should have been deleted or exactly why a perfect version would be a shorter one. Like Emperor Joseph of Austria speaking of Mozart (in the film *Amadeus*), Paglia has decided that Nathaniel Hawthorne used "too many notes."

57. Baym, "Romantic *Malgré Lui,*" 272.

58. For James, only *The Scarlet Letter* achieved the absolute "indefinable purity and lightness of conception, a quality which in a work of art affects one in the same way as the absence of grossness does in a human being" (*Hawthorne,* 88). Note his use of the term "conception" with reference to purity and lightness to denote both appropriate art and the appropriate human being, and his insistence that material grossness has no place in either.

59. Arac, "Politics," 252.

60. See Cottom, "Hawthorne versus Hester"; and David Leverenz, "Mrs. Hawthorne's Headache: Reading *The Scarlet Letter,*" *Nineteenth-Century Fiction* 37 (March 1983), 552-67.

61. See William Charvat, introduction to *The Scarlet Letter* (Columbus: Ohio State University Press, 1962), xxi-xxiii.

62. Robert L. Berner, "A Key to the 'Custom House'" in *SL,* 278.

63. Hawthorne lampoons his own literary aspirations with this parodic French rendition of his already anxiously revised last name: Hathorne to Hawthorne. The irony, of course, is that French can still connote cultural anxieties in an American critical context. I think particularly of how French "theory" (often monolithically imagined) is distrusted as ipso facto elitist, inappropriate to discussions of American texts.

64. Arac, "Politics" (citing Crews), 250.

65. Ibid., 248.

66. As Arac, Bercovitch, Yellin, Berlant, and T. Walter Herbert, Jr. (in *Dearest Beloved: The Hawthornes and the Making of the Middle-Class Family* [Berkeley: University of California Press, 1993]), among others, have claimed, Hawthorne was involved in the issues that agitated the politics of his time, although it is decidedly difficult to argue that he did anything but fence-sit with regard to abolition and the Civil War; indeed, in Yellin's estimation, Hawthorne's inactivity almost amounted to a pro-slavery position.

67. Ryan, *Womanhood,* 23-25.

68. In the antebellum courtroom, issues of a "free" mother's right to rear her offspring were being contested within a public discourse where issues of a slave's right to "own" himself (and later the hypocrisies of increasingly complex Jim Crow laws) had much to do with the legal status of any mother and her children. For example, in the slavocracy an African-American woman's child might be said, ironically, to belong to her alone under the euphemistic law that "a slave must follow the condition of its mother." But this provision allowed "mixed" children to be considered salable commodities, through organized (white male to black female) rape. Such "mass production" was predicated on several interlocking beliefs that structured the system of racial slavery: (1) that the woman bearing the salable child was not truly a mother, nor could she be or become (in the majority of cases) free; (2) that the woman bearing the salable child would, of course, never be white (suicide, infanticide, or a quick sale being preferable to an acknowledgment of such a birth); (3) that even if legally "free," the woman bearing the child would have no real or binding legal rights to her children, given the way property laws were written in both the North and the South. That is, since no woman had legal citizenship, a single woman's right to parent her children was no right at all. For instance, a white widow whose husband

left no clear will might have to file suit for custody of her children through a male member of
her family. Worse, a widow sometimes found her
deceased husband's male relations legally appointed heirs and guardians to her children; she
could even be turned out of her own home as a
burden on the household, and her children (given
the laxity of child-labor laws) sent out to work for
the new guardian. Such a patriarchal economy left
a black freedwoman legally powerless with regard
to her children, even if she had managed to "liberate" them from actual bondage. See Suzanne
Arms, *Immaculate Deception: A New Look at
Women and Childbirth in America* (Boston:
Houghton Mifflin, 1975); Michael Grossberg,
"Who Gets the Child? Custody, Guardianship, and
the Rise of a Judicial Patriarchy in Nineteenth-
Century America," *Feminist Studies* 9 (Summer
1983); Viviana A. Zelizer, *Pricing the Priceless
Child: The Changing Social Value of Children*
(New York: Basic Books, 1985); Sylvia D. Hof-
fert, *Private Matters: American Attitudes toward
Childbearing and Infant Nurture in the Urban
North, 1800-1860* (Chicago: University of Illinois
Press, 1989). Significantly, none of these works
address the particular situation of bi- or multira-
cial children in the nineteenth century.

69. Herman Melville, "The Paradise of Bachelors and
The Tartarus of Maids," in *Selected Tales and Poems* (New York: Holt, Rinehart & Winston, 1963),
206-30.

70. Henry Adams, *Democracy: An American Novel*
(London: Macmillan, 1882).

71. Joan Scott's persuasive and continuing argument
that history as a narrative needs attention with regard to gender is pertinent, particularly given that
Arac, for reasons he does not make clear, appears
to assume that "feminism" has no history or is a
univocal and ahistorical theoretical approach. See
Scott, "Gender as a Useful Category of Historical
Analysis," in *Gender and the Politics of History*
(New York: Columbia University Press, 1988),
28-52. Two useful works on the relation between
nineteenth-century feminism and the politics of
abolition are Yellin, *Women & Sisters,* and Smith-
Rosenberg, *Disorderly Conduct.*

72. James, *Hawthorne,* 111.

Claire Chantell (essay date autumn 2002)

SOURCE: Chantell, Claire. "The Limits of the Mother
at Home in *The Wide, Wide World* and *The Lamplighter.*" *Studies in American Fiction* 30, no. 2 (autumn
2002): 131-53.

[*In the following essay, Chantell discusses the Victorian
belief that mothers taught their children solely by example and illustrates how Susan Warner and Maria
Cummins "point out the limits of sentimental maternalism as an instrument for educating young women."*]

By the middle of the nineteenth century, domesticity
had gained a position of prominence, if not dominance,
in American culture; this discourse of home, family,
and private life influenced everything from home design to social reform movements.[1] A primary feature of
this ideology concerned the mother's role as child nurturer and educator, a role for which women were supposed to be divinely intended and biologically designed.
As historian Mary Ryan has observed, "the feminization
of child-rearing, in literature and in practice, dovetailed
neatly with the gender system enshrined in the cult of
domesticity. The true woman was the perfect candidate
for the role of child nurturer. She was loving, giving,
moral, pure, and consigned to the hearth."[2]

Much mid-nineteenth-century domestic literature, in the
form of advice manuals, articles in ladies' magazines,
and published sermons, reiterated and reinforced this
message through reverent portrayals of the mother as
"tutelary seraph," a home-bound figure who instills virtue and religion in her children through the medium of
her matchless love.[3] In his popular guide for parents,
Fireside Education (1838), Samuel Goodrich describes
the infant's early impressions of its mother, a "ministering spirit" who supplies all its inchoate needs: "If cold,
[she] brings it warmth; if hungry, she feeds it; if in
pain, she relieves it; if happy, she caresses it . . . The
mother is the DEITY OF INFANCY!"[4] As the child matures,
though, it begins to require more than food, warmth,
and affection. Now, according to Goodrich, the father
steps in:

> Hitherto, [the child] has been a creature of feeling; it
> now becomes a being of thought. The intellectual eye
> opens upon the world. . . . Curiosity is alive, and
> questions come thick and fast to the lisping lips . . .
> At this period, the child usually becomes fond of the
> society of his father. He can answer his questions. He
> can unfold the mysteries which excite the wonder of
> the childish intellect.
>
> (15)

This description typifies the view taken by many didactic writers who focus on the mother's role as child educator. In these texts, maternal instruction appears as an
instinctive, spontaneous reaction rather than a reasoned,
deliberate choice (a competency reserved for fathers).
Indeed, as a writer for *The Mother's Magazine* phrased
it in 1841, a mother was supposed not "to teach virtue
but to inspire it."[5] Taken together, these writings suggest that the ideal mother accomplished her work simply by loving her children; no more rigorous methods
were necessary. At its core, the antebellum cult of the
mother rested on the fundamentally emotional, irratio-

nal character of the mother's attitude towards her children. To underscore this point, I will use the term "sentimental maternalism" to refer to this cluster of beliefs.[6]

Most critics of nineteenth-century American literature conclude that the popular women's novels of mid-century bear the imprint of domesticity, including its emphasis on sentimental maternalism, although they debate the extent to which these texts advance or impede progressive political transformation.[7] Stephanie Smith, for example, deems it a "commonplace" to say that "representations of a sanctified motherhood formed the primary cornerstone for commercially successful writing in the United States of the nineteenth century."[8] But to suggest that domestic fictions uniformly or unequivocally promote sentimental maternalism misreads this genre. Detailed portraits of competent, capable motherhood (let alone the sanctified variety) rarely appear in most domestic fictions.[9] Far from promoting the mother's educative primacy, some of the nineteenth century's best-selling domestic novels demonstrate nothing so much as her superfluity.

This article shows how two popular domestic novels—Susan Warner's *The Wide, Wide World* (1850) and Maria Cummins' *The Lamplighter* (1854)—point out the limits of sentimental maternalism as an instrument for educating young women.[10] Though the heroines' training occupies these texts centrally, the novels minimize the mother's role in this work. These young women enjoy neither the tutelage of the seraphic mother nor the shelter of the sort of home into which she was usually projected. Instead, according to these novels the expertise required to cultivate exemplary women resides in many rather than one and in interaction with the world, not retreat from it. Ellen Montgomery and Gertrude Flint receive guidance from a series of surrogates, both male and female. Although like the archetypal sentimental mother in many ways, these surrogates evade the domestic isolation and extravagant emotion characteristic of the ideal. The reluctance of these fictions to embrace the fireside scenario—sanctified mother working within the intensely private setting of the middle-class home to inspire virtue in her children—registers their ambivalence about an ideology that, at first glance, they might seem to endorse.

Susan Warner's *The Wide, Wide World* has often been understood as a "prototype of the domestic bildungsroman."[11] Heroine Ellen Montgomery's spiritual, moral, and intellectual education occupies the text centrally. We first meet her as a ten-year-old girl; effectively orphaned soon thereafter, Ellen struggles on without the guidance of her idolized mother. Domesticity would suggest that Ellen's handicap is nearly insurmountable—the more so because Mrs. Montgomery perfectly embodies the characteristics of sentimental maternalism. Genteel, pious, submissive, and devoted to her child, the invalid Mrs. Montgomery clings to her parlor, where Ellen sews, reads aloud, and tends to the tea things. Indeed, Mrs. Montgomery ventures outside only once during her brief tenure in the novel.[12] Ellen's father, Captain Montgomery, inhabits an alien world outside the home; all Ellen and her mother seem to know of it is that in it there are lawsuits that force Captain and Mrs. Montgomery to leave for Europe. In the chapters preceding Ellen's separation from her mother, the two continually form and re-form a scene that can fairly be called the archetypal sentimental tableau: before the parlor fireplace of a genteel home, mother embraces child as the two pray, sing hymns, and discuss God's infinite goodness and wisdom.

Like the ideal fireside educator hailed by so many maternal advice books of the period, Mrs. Montgomery exploits the mother-child bond for the purpose of religious instruction—specifically, to teach Ellen to subdue her rebellious spirit and embrace the divine will lying behind every seeming injustice. And at first glance, it appears as though the novel vindicates the tutelary seraph; in the end, Ellen fulfills her mother's wishes, emerging as a model of Christian piety and submission to God's will. Both through her example and her instructions, Mrs. Montgomery lays the foundation for Ellen's future education; through her love, she embeds her authority within Ellen's conscience, continuing to regulate Ellen's behavior through the feelings aroused by the memory of that love. According to Richard Brodhead, Ellen's subsequent adventures and experiences testify to the power of the sentimental mother—so intolerable is her loss that Ellen spends the rest of the novel looking for new mothers.[13] Ellen's encounter with her first surrogate, Mr. George Marshman, seems to confirm this interpretation. Ellen meets Mr. Marshman on the boat that takes her away from her mother; as she sits wondering "Who is there to teach me now? Oh, what shall I do without you? Oh, mamma! How much I want you already," Mr. Marshman enters. He begins almost immediately to catechize Ellen in the same manner as her mother—giving her a book of hymns marked up just for her, like the specially inscribed Bible Ellen's mother leaves her (68).

But the surrogates who continue Ellen's education do more than merely bookmark the space left by her mother; they meet a far wider range of Ellen's needs, and they do so in ways that quietly highlight Mrs. Montgomery's weaknesses. Each of Ellen's guides—Mr. Marshman, siblings Alice and John Humphreys, Mr. Van Brunt—provides instruction that goes beyond religious indoctrination mediated through emotional manipulation. It is true that Mr. Marshman gives Ellen the hymns—but after he does so, he takes her all over the boat, explaining its different parts to her; "he was amused to find how far she pushed her inquiries into the how and why of things" (76). This scene introduces

Ellen's insatiable curiosity about things, particularly those of a scientific nature. Later, we see much more of Ellen's thirst for information about the world. Watching Alice make hot chocolate, Ellen "wanted to know what chocolate was made of—where it came from—where it was made best" (272). Observing while Mr. Van Brunt cures some freshly slaughtered hogs, Ellen quizzes him about why he salts the pork, if salt would preserve things besides pork, if the hams are salted too, how long the hams must smoke before they are done, and what's in the kettle over the fire. In short, nearly as often as Ellen gives in to the tears so derided by some twentieth-century critics, she asks her favorite question of all: "I wonder what is the reason of that?" (233).[14]

Although religion is always Ellen's most important subject, her primary mentors focus as much on satisfying Ellen's intellectual curiosity as overseeing her moral development. Walking in the woods with Alice, Ellen wonders aloud why the leaves fall in autumn, whether trees can live without leaves, and why evergreens don't drop their leaves. In response, Alice provides a botany lecture, explaining the role played by leaves in the tree's circulatory system (185-86). Similarly, Ellen queries John Humphreys at length on the meanings of unfamiliar words; "oracle" provides him an opportunity to hold forth on Greek mythological history. In that lecture, he uses the word "hieroglyphics," which provokes a curious look from Ellen; John asks if she wants to know what it means. "The pen was laid down while he explained, to a most eager little listener. Even the great business of the moment was forgotten. From hieroglyphics they went to the pyramids" (304). Well-read Alice capably teaches Ellen English and geography.[15] Schoolmasterly John sets Ellen at drawing lessons, teaches her to ride, and provides her with books like Weems' *Life of Washington* and Bunyan's *Pilgrim's Progress*. Encomiums like the following, voiced by Ellen's friend, abound—testimonials to the Humphreys' teaching skills: "She must be very clever; don't you think she is, mamma? Mamma, she beats me entirely in speaking French, and she knows all about English history; and arithmetic!—and did you ever hear her sing, mamma?" (417).

Ellen's surrogate mothers thus marry intellectual inquiry with religious exhortation in their approach to her education. By contrast, Mrs. Montgomery uses an exclusively emotional tutelary method, focusing on Ellen's heart, specifically its susceptibility to religious penetration. She exploits Ellen's adoration and her desire to please as a conduit for her moral lesson. This is not to say that emotion rages unchecked in the parlor. As frequently as Ellen or her mother give in to sorrow, equally often they struggle—eventually succeeding—to quell these signs of excessive feeling. By thus acknowledging the antebellum middle-class imperative to exercise self-restraint, an imperative heightened by Mrs. Montgom-

ery's physical fragility, this narrative clearly marks the unrestrained indulgence of intense feeling as undesirable and potentially dangerous. But though she well knows that her own health and the health of Ellen's character require emotional self-control, in the end Mrs. Montgomery betrays her own impulse towards indulgence. The night before Ellen leaves, Captain Montgomery breaks the solitude of his wife's parlor to tell her that Ellen will leave early the next morning. Though she conceals most of her agitation from her husband, Mrs. Montgomery frantically resolves to "waken Ellen immediately," despite the lateness of the hour (58). Mr. Montgomery quashes the plan as irrational and unwise. Having glimpsed Ellen's intensely passionate nature as well as the dangerous effect of emotion on Mrs. Montgomery's health, a reader might conclude that Mr. Montgomery's veto is rooted at least partially in reason, rather than wholly in indifference to human feeling. As he asks his wife, "Why in the world should you wake her up, just to spend the whole night in useless grieving?—unfitting her entirely for her journey, and doing yourself more harm than you can undo in a week" (59).

Separation only intensifies Mrs. Montgomery's power to provoke profound feeling from her daughter. Whenever Ellen receives a letter from her mother, her reaction is violently emotional, as in the following example: "Her transport was almost hysterical. She had opened the letter, but she was not able to read a word; and quitting Alice's arms, she threw herself upon the bed, sobbing in a mixture of joy and sorrow that seemed to take away her reason" (223). Mrs. Montgomery's presence, whether in person or mediated through writing, serves primarily to "take away" Ellen's reason and replace it with a highly emotional state that leaves her susceptible to penetration by her mother's religious precepts. The logic of sentimental maternalism as articulated in this novel defines the mother's greatest triumph as the implantation of her image in her child's mind, so that he or she may carry it throughout life as an emotional and spiritual touchstone. Given this logic, the sentimental mother can hardly afford to diffuse her focus; her child's emotional orientation requires all of her attention, to the exclusion of all other matters. It is only when Ellen leaves the shelter of her mother's parlor that her voracious intellectual curiosity emerges and can be satisfied.

Although she seems to live for nothing but these cloistered moments with her daughter, Mrs. Montgomery herself catches at the dilemma posed by their relationship. When Ellen worries about going to live with an aunt who she fears will "not be so likely to love me," her mother warns that she "must not expect . . . to find anybody as indulgent as I am, or as ready to overlook and excuse your faults" (21). The hallmark of sentimental motherhood—tender indulgence—stands simultaneously as Mrs. Montgomery's greatest strength and her principal flaw as a mother. It is telling that among the surrogates who take over Ellen's education she does not find a single one willing to "overlook and excuse" her faults, as her mother admits herself to be. Something more than maternal indulgence is required to bring Ellen to exemplary womanhood.

In arguing that this novel reveals the limitations of sentimental maternalism, I do not suggest that it rejects the ideal. Clearly, the novel indicates that affectionate bonding is the preferred mode of connection between all humans; Ellen's mentors all embed their instruction in a matrix of love and tenderness. For example, in Mr. Marshman, Ellen recognizes immediately a copy of that gentleness she misses; when he first addresses her, "there was no mistaking the look of kindness in the eyes that met hers. . . . All the floodgates of Ellen's heart were at once opened" (69). Ellen bursts into tears, and Mr. Marshman gently leads her away to a secluded part of the ship, where he holds her in his arms and speaks kind, soothing words to her. Though their encounter on the boat is brief, it simmers with an emotional intensity partly manifested in a tableau not unlike those of her mother's parlor: Mr. Marshman pets and hugs her, Ellen cries and falls asleep with her head on his chest.

Likewise, Ellen's most beloved surrogate mother, Alice Humphreys, treats her as tenderly as did Mrs. Montgomery. When Ellen first meets her, as with Mr. Marshman, she detects in Alice those characteristics her mother exhibited—characteristics Ellen absolutely requires from her mentors. Alice happens upon a sobbing Ellen; she asks the girl what is wrong:

> The tone found Ellen's heart and brought the water to her eyes again, though with a difference. She covered her face with her hands. But gentle hands were placed upon hers and drew them away; and the lady sitting down on Ellen's stone, took her in her arms; and Ellen hid her face in the bosom of a better friend than the cold earth had been like to prove her.
>
> (149)

The rest of Alice's and Ellen's encounters are characterized by a physical and emotional intimacy highly reminiscent of the sentimental tableau enacted in the Montgomery parlor.

But though sympathy and affection are necessary to the tutelary relationship, something more is required to bring a young girl to exemplary womanhood. I have already noted the intellectual and informational instruction Ellen receives from her mentors. We must also note that John Humphreys, who becomes Ellen's foremost earthly mentor, shows no difficulty at all reining in his tender feelings when it comes to Ellen. Indeed, Ellen remarks upon first meeting him that "she was quite sure from that one look into his eyes that he was a person to be feared" (275). Of course, it is only to be

expected that, as a male in a strongly patriarchal culture, John Humphreys would demonstrate control over his tender emotions; this fact alone is not remarkable. Rather, I point to the fact that Humphreys, among others, plays a significant role in bringing Ellen to maturity. In the end, *The Wide, Wide World* does not reject sentimental maternalism's emotionally intense model of instruction; it rejects this model as the *only* one to be used in educating a young woman. In order to produce the Ellen Montgomery that emerges at novel's end, Mrs. Montgomery must be replaced with this varied contingent of surrogates.

Published four years after Warner's novel, Maria Cummins' *The Lamplighter* also seems attuned to the tenets of sentimental maternalism, particularly in its depiction of the character Mrs. Sullivan. We never meet the biological mother of Gertrude Flint, the orphaned heroine; she dies when Gerty is three years old. At the age of eight, the child is informally adopted by the lamplighter Trueman Flint and jointly cared for by Flint and his neighbor, the widowed Mrs. Sullivan. Like Mrs. Montgomery, the figure of Mrs. Sullivan articulates cultural fears of dangerous female emotion even as she commands reverence as the iconic sentimental mother.

Though Mrs. Sullivan lives in more modest circumstances than Warner's Mrs. Montgomery, the hallmarks of the figure—domestic genius, boundless love—are present from the moment we first meet her. As Gerty lies sick in bed following her rescue from tenement life, she wakes to find a woman at her bedside. The novel at first offers little physical description of this caretaker, describing instead her actions: she fixes gruel for Gerty, sews on a child's frock, and soothes the child. Once Gerty regains her health, Mrs. Sullivan provides her first lesson in domesticity, directing her efforts to bring order and cleanliness to bachelor True's apartment. Mrs. Sullivan proves an excellent mentor in this regard, as the narrator takes pains to establish her domestic *bona fides*:

> Mrs. Sullivan was a little bit of a woman, but had more capability and energy than could have been found in any one among twenty others twice her size. She really pitied those whose home was such a mass of confusion; felt sure that they could not be happy; and inwardly determined, as soon as Gerty got well, to exert herself in the cause of cleanliness and order, which was in her eyes the cause of virtue and happiness, so completely did she identify outward neatness and purity with inward peace.
>
> (25)

Later in the novel, Gertrude proclaims Mrs. Sullivan "a living lesson of piety and patience . . . I know of no one who seems so fit for heaven" (169).

If Mrs. Sullivan seems to Gertrude a living angel, to her son, Willie, she assumes an even more exalted status. In an early scene, she prays aloud for Willie:

laying her hand on the head of her son, [she] offered up a simple, heart-felt prayer for the boy,—one of those mother's prayers, which the child listens to with reverence and love, and remembers in the far-off years; one of those prayers which *keep men from temptation, and deliver them from evil.*

(39, emphasis added)

In this scene, the sentimental mother becomes nearly indistinguishable from God; it is Mrs. Sullivan's prayer that promises to perform the work asked of God in the Lord's Prayer—to lead not into temptation but deliver from evil. Willie is thus bound to remember this prayer, mediated through his mother's selfless devotion, in those "far-off years" when she is no longer present.

The novel tests the efficacy of this mother's prayer before the story's end. Willie accepts an opportunity to develop a business career by travelling to India with a local merchant. While he is gone, Mrs. Sullivan becomes ill. Approaching death and aware that she will never see Willie again, Mrs. Sullivan shares with Gertrude a "beautiful dream" that she had. In the dream, she floats through the air until spotting Willie below in a crowded street. She trails him as he moves through scenes of decadence—"a dining-saloon, in the middle of which was a table covered with bottles, glasses, and the remains of a rich dessert"—among fine-looking but evil people (170). Recognizing that her son is tempted to accept a drink, Mrs. Sullivan's dream-self intervenes: "Just then I touched him on the shoulder. He turned, saw me, and instantly the glass fell from his hand and was broken into a thousand pieces." The mother's influence over her son is unassailable; Willie obediently follows her from that room despite the importuning of his new friends. Mrs. Sullivan has, literally, only to lift her finger to compel his obedience; as she recalls, "I placed myself in front of him, held up my finger menacingly, and shook my head. He hesitated no longer." The rest of the dream finds the two moving through the city together, with Mrs. Sullivan leading, Willie following. In this way, she guides him past snares, pitfalls, and dangers "into which, without me, he would surely have fallen" (171). She wakes from this dream finally at peace with her impending death, and expresses her relief to Gertrude: "I now believe that Willie's living mother might be powerless to turn him from temptation and evil; but the spirit of that mother will be mighty still" (172).

Mrs. Sullivan's dream celebrates the power of the sentimental mother to shape and control her child's character at the same time that it exposes her central flaw: she is more powerful absent than present. Just as Warner's novel hinted at Mrs. Montgomery's weakness as a tutor for her daughter Ellen, Cummins' novel illuminates the limitations of sentimental maternalism—namely, a tendency towards too-great tenderness. Like Mrs. Mont-

gomery, Mrs. Sullivan must be translated from corporeality into abstraction in order to achieve perfect influence over her child; living mothers, these novels imply, are limited mothers.

Take, for example, a scene that follows shortly after Uncle True's death. Hearing the news, Emily goes to the Sullivan home to see Gertrude. There she finds Mrs. Sullivan, who tells Emily the story "of Gertrude's agony of grief, the impossibility of comforting her, and the fears the kind little woman entertained lest the girl would die of sorrow" (96). She describes how Gerty huddled in the old man's chair for days on end, refusing to move or to eat. Mrs. Sullivan confesses to Emily, "I couldn't do anything with her myself . . . I couldn't bear to make her come away into my room, though I knew it would change the scene, and be better for her" (96). Though Mrs. Sullivan recognizes the danger of Gerty's brooding, she nonetheless can't steel herself to do the right thing. Only Willie's intervention breaks Gertrude's morbid trance; he does what Mrs. Sullivan cannot—removes Gertrude from the scene of sorrow—and so begins to cheer her up. Emily notes that "Willie shows good judgment . . . in trying to change the scene for her, and divert her thoughts" (97). It is a judgment that Mrs. Sullivan cannot exercise; though reason tells her it is best, her tenderness leads her to indulge Gerty's grief.

Mrs. Sullivan fails in similar ways when faced with her aged father's physical and mental decline. The adult Gertrude returns to assist Mrs. Sullivan at this time, believing that it is not "safe for such a timid, delicate woman as Mrs. Sullivan to be alone" with the increasingly senile man (130). Unwittingly, Gertrude indicts Mrs. Sullivan's distinctly maternal failing in this regard—her softness and indulgence: "He is *like a child* now, and full of whims. When he can possibly be indulged, Mrs. Sullivan will please him at any amount of convenience, and even danger, to herself" (130-31, emphasis added). It is true that Mrs. Sullivan's own health is failing at the same time; moreover, her father's behavior has become dangerously erratic. It is therefore not remarkable that Mrs. Sullivan needs help to manage her senile father. What stands out is rather that the novel portrays the sentimental mother as boundlessly powerful *in absentia*—memory of Mrs. Sullivan inspires Willie to heights of virtue—but compromised and even ineffectual in presence.

Gertrude herself provides the exemplary foil to Mrs. Sullivan's unchecked tenderness. Her great trial comes early in the novel, when Uncle True dies. Though still a child at this point, Gertrude commands her emotions as she faces the loss of one like a father to her. True asks Gerty to read him the prayer for the dying, and twelve-year-old Gerty trembles:

There *was* such a prayer, a beautiful one; and the thoughtful child, to whom the idea of death was familiar, knew it by heart,—but could she repeat the words? Could she command her voice? Her whole frame shook with agitation; but Uncle True wished to hear it, it would be comfort to him, and she would try. Concentrating all her energy and self-command, she began, and, gaining strength as she proceeded, went on to the end. Once or twice her voice faltered, but with new effort she succeeded . . . and her voice sounded so clear and calm that Uncle True's devotional spirit was not once disturbed by the thought of the girl's sufferings.

(93)

Gerty's performance here in subjugating her own sorrow for the sake of others demonstrates an emotional restraint that the novel clearly endorses. It stands in stark contrast to Mrs. Sullivan's inability to force Gerty from the scene of Uncle True's death and her breakdown in the face of her father's decline. In Gerty, we see the balance between emotion and self-control that the novel ascribes to the womanhood to which Gerty aspires. Although the novel honors Mrs. Sullivan's maternal love, we also see how sentiment circumscribes her in earthly matters. This set-piece demonstrating Gerty's self-command sets an example of steely sympathy incompatible, at this particular historical and cultural moment, with the ideal of sentimental motherhood. The cultural construction of sentimental motherhood emphasizes the emotionalism of the mother to a degree that hardly allows for easy self-command. Those features that make Mrs. Sullivan a formidable guardian after her death are exactly those features that circumscribe her power while alive.

Like Warner's novel, *The Lamplighter* provides its motherless heroine with extra-domestic, non-maternal surrogates who oversee her education and bring her to ideal womanhood. Indeed, it seems to take the proverbial village to transform Gerty from a hot-tempered waif into a paragon of emotional self-control. Lamplighter Trueman Flint is her first guide, taming Gerty's distrustful disposition with his love and kindness; she finds other teachers in Mrs. Sullivan and Willie. But it is the rich, blind Emily Graham who most centrally directs Gerty's transformation. Upon first meeting Gerty, Emily, we are told, "saw at once how totally neglected the little one had been, and the importance of her being educated and trained with care" (56). Thereafter, Emily lovingly guides and corrects Gerty's behavior; she oversees Gerty's intellectual education as well. Although *The Lamplighter* represents its heroine's reading matter and school subjects with far less specificity than *The Wide, Wide World,* nevertheless the novel firmly establishes not only that Gerty has formal schooling but also that Emily plays a major role in overseeing that aspect of her education. It is Emily who encourages Uncle True to send Gerty to school. Once Gerty learns to read (quickly, showing both an aptitude and an appetite for learning), Emily begins to supply her with books that she selects "carefully and judiciously [knowing] the

weight that such tales often carried with them to the hearts of children" (66).

Though Emily also attends to Gerty's spiritual education, we must note that before she leaves Gerty for the summer—their first separation—she gives Gerty a gift that speaks to the child's scholarly rather than spiritual education: "a book and a new slate" (68). And when Emily returns from the country, she establishes a routine whereby "Gerty should come every day and read to her for an hour" (70). This program of reading enriches and excites Gerty's intellect, all because Emily chooses the books carefully; "history, biography, and books of travels, were perused by Gerty at an age when most children's literary pursuits are confined to stories and pictures" (70). As with Alice Humphreys of *The Wide, Wide World,* the surrogate mother Emily Graham is inextricably associated with books and reading.

But even in intellectual development, Emily is not solely responsible for Gerty's growth—others contribute, in an ever-widening cluster of surrogates. Willie Sullivan helps Gerty to learn, and to love learning, in his role as childhood friend. When Emily and Gertrude are separated, Willie steps in and helps Gerty keep up her studies, so that "when Emily returned to the city in October, she could hardly understand how so much had been accomplished in what had seemed to her so short a time" (70). Indeed, Gerty and Willie mutually encourage one another's studies, with Willie routinely spending his evenings in the Flint home, studying side by side with Gerty. Willie takes up the study of French, so Emily provides French books for Gerty as well, with the result that Gerty "kept pace with him, oftentimes translating more during the week than he could find time to do" (72).

As these novels resist the idea of entrusting the sentimental mother fully with the work of educating daughters, they also reveal the shortcomings of the highly privatized middle-class home as a site for such an education. In *Cradle of the Middle Class,* Mary Ryan describes the development of a new ideal of privacy as part of the ideology of the emerging middle class. According to her account, while the "families of the agrarian era repeatedly interwove and overlapped with church and town" and "mingled together in the large network of face-to-face relations that formed the local community," by the middle of the nineteenth century "social space was often divided up between the 'home' and the 'streets,' warm, personal, and stable ties as opposed to cold, brittle, and threatening encounters" (233). One result of this division, Ryan contends, is the increasing idealization of the middle-class home as a private space, one possessing "a special sanctity, a privileged position remote from public contention and impenetrable to prying outsiders" (234).

Though this imagined evolution in the relationship of the family to the community may have been widely viewed as a welcome development, I suggest that these novels consider what might be lost as well as what might be gained. This is not to say that domestic fictions repudiate the idealization of privacy that accompanies the rise of middle-class culture. But by sending Ellen away from her fireside for the educational experiences that eventually render her exemplary, the novel draws the community, however ambivalently constructed, back into the picture. Strangers shepherd Ellen to her state of moral near-perfection, while her blood kin—Aunt Fortune, Uncle Lindsay, her father, even her mother—prove the greatest roadblocks to her development (or, considered more generously, they stand in as the trials and tribulations required to hone Ellen to perfection).

The thorny truth is that the same discourses that painted the home as a retreat from a selfish, striving world also magnified the sense of the home's isolation from the world. Whereas the "eager vigilance of the community" had checked selfish passions in an earlier era, the community was slowly ceding that role as an ideal of the home as retreat from the public gained ground.[16] The setting most closely associated with Mrs. Montgomery—the parlor—is notable for its insularity. Until the seventh chapter, when Ellen begins her journey to Aunt Fortune's, the narrative rarely strays far from this space, except for the shopping excursion that exhausts Mrs. Montgomery and Ellen's terrifying trip to the department store. Both of these trips, but particularly Ellen's solo flight, reinforce the sense in which the parlor functions as a haven from a chaotic, amoral world. In the parlor, mother and daughter cling to one another, focusing their attention inward. The narrator's first words directly addressed to the reader (following four lines of dialogue exchanged between Ellen and her mother) set the tone of both the parlor as well as the relationship between the two characters: "There was no one else in the room" (9). Outsiders rarely disturb their solitude; Mr. Montgomery himself never appears in the parlor with Ellen and her mother. In fact, we see Ellen going to great lengths to ensure that time spent with her mother remains untainted by her father's presence; twice she deliberately waits for him to leave the house before joining her mother in the parlor, despite her fierce longing for her mother's embrace. The two patiently endure the intrusions of Mrs. Montgomery's doctor, awaiting their reward; at last, "when evening came, they were again left to themselves . . . the mother and daughter were happily alone" (23). Even family functions simply defer the gratification to be had in the parlor: "When dinner was over and the table cleared away, the mother and daughter were left, as they always loved to be, alone" (36).

Although Ellen and her mother crave their parlor intimacy, the novel implies that in the physical and psychic seclusion of the parlor a dangerously unchallenged state of equilibrium exists between mother and daughter. Wholly enclosed in her mother's presence, Ellen hardly needs to assert herself at all. "I cannot thank you, mamma," Ellen begins, but her mother arrests her: "'It is not necessary, my dear child,' said Mrs. Montgomery . . . 'I know all that you would say'" (36). In the parlor, Ellen's primary occupations are to look out the window quietly, read aloud to her mother, and make tea in exactly the manner her mother prefers. When Mrs. Montgomery, for purposes of catechism, asks Ellen to describe the trust she reposes in her mother, Ellen replies, "I trust every word you say—entirely—I know nothing could be truer; if you were to tell me black is white, mamma, I should think my eyes had been mistaken" (18). Within the sentimental tableau represented by the parlor, Ellen has only to lean on her mother. As she confides, "I am glad to think I belong to you, and you have the management of me entirely, and I needn't manage myself, because I know I can't, and if I could, I'd rather you would, mamma" (18). As Ellen lies on the sofa next to her mother, we catch a glimpse of the central lesson she is learning in the parlor; "she thought it was greater happiness to lie there than any thing else in life could be—she thought she had rather even die so, on her mother's breast, than live long without her in the world" (38).

Though faithfully and perfectly articulating sentimental ideology, these scenes intimate that the sentimental mother will seduce her child away from engagement with any world beyond that of the cozy domestic enclosure.[17] Mrs. Montgomery herself explains that God is separating them because, as she puts it, "perhaps he sees, Ellen, that you never would seek him while you had me to cling to" (41). Mr. George Marshman, the gentleman on the boat, observes the same: "You love your mother better than you do the Saviour?" he asks. To Ellen's eagerly positive reply, he pointedly responds, "Then if he had left you your mother, Ellen, you would never have cared or thought about him?" (70). Though these two characters focus on the improved opportunities for religious growth that will result from separation, I suggest that the novel (perhaps inadvertently) makes a broader argument; for all the emotional power of the sentimental tableau, *The Wide, Wide World* reveals how it falls short as an educative milieu rich enough to produce a young woman prepared for a complex world.

It is important here to remember the important role played by "experience" in nineteenth-century educational ideals. Lockean notions of the impressionability of the mind sparked a turning away from rote learning, towards a conception instead of experience—physical and emotional—as the building block for character.

Mothers and teachers alike were to inculcate morality in their charges by constructing an environment in which all components conduced towards evoking the right feelings.[18] Education was widely defined *as* experience, and vice versa: as an editorial in *Godey's Lady's Book* from 1858 phrased it, "Everything is education— the trains of thought you are indulging in this hour; the society in which you will spend the evening, the conversations, walks, and incidents of tomorrow."[19]

Ellen Montgomery's experience follows this model. Once released from the cloistered captivity of her parlor world, Ellen sets out on a series of travels that demonstrate the existence of a widespread community of evangelical Christians—a ready-made family more crucial to her development than her biological family. On her journey to Thirlwall, Ellen meets the Reverend Mr. George Marshman on the boat; he takes up where her mother left off, giving Ellen a book of hymns and catechizing her on God's goodness. She first meets Alice Humphreys when she flees her aunt's house and literally climbs a mountain. And though Alice is without a doubt a paragon of domesticity, she is associated with the outdoors as well as with the intimate quarters of a parlor. Together, Alice and Ellen range about the countryside, climbing a mountain together to visit old Mrs. Vawse and descending in a snowstorm. Though critics may continue to speak, like Catharine O'Connell, for instance, of the novel's "absolute immersion in the female sphere of domesticity," any drawing of that sphere's boundaries must recognize that domesticity travels.[20]

Just as Ellen Montgomery could hardly have matured into the young woman we see at the novel's end had she remained embedded in the sentimental tableau, Gertrude Flint shows virtues that do not at all result from being sheltered in a home. From the beginning, she is quite literally associated with the streets. Though her salvation comes from Uncle True's taking her into a home, Gertrude remains linked to public and non-isolated spaces. She teaches school, takes a room in a boarding-house, and travels with the Jeremys. She demonstrates a level of comfort with being publicly observed that stems not from pride or a desire to be seen but from an acquaintance with public eyes. And though her work at the Graham home exhibits many of the hallmarks of domesticity—she helps with the housework, sews, nurses sick Emily, reads the newspaper aloud to Mr. Graham—the spaces with which she is associated do not seem isolated. Even Gertrude's own rooms are continually invaded by others, so that there are no closed-door tableaux like those of Mrs. Montgomery's parlor. Instead, Gertrude and Emily create a cheery space open to all who have the sense to value it.

If we wonder why domestic fictions might be reluctant to embrace the fireside ideal fully, we might look more closely at the product of this "more than maternal" labor—that is, the finished heroine herself. In many ways, the heroines who emerge at the end of these novels resemble the pious, pure, domestically gifted "true women" so frequently described in popular conduct literature of the antebellum period.[21] But though they possess these characteristics, Ellen and Gertrude depart from the model of womanhood offered by prescriptive literature. Erudition occupies a far more prominent place among their virtues, for example; I have already shown how these novels highlight Ellen's and Gerty's training in academic subjects, and how they quietly suggest that this work requires the superintendence of someone other than the sentimental mother. Moreover, these novels emphasize their heroine's gradual acquisition of an emotional self-control that contrasts sharply with the irrational tenderness characteristic of the sentimental ideal.

It is undeniable that a rhetoric of feeling—an imperative to act from the heart, a regard for the tender embrace—pervades these texts. The villains in *The Wide, Wide World* are those who do not immediately provoke or provide hugs and kisses—the hooligan Nancy Vawse, for one, but most notably Ellen's Aunt Fortune. Indeed, Fortune stands as the novel's Anti-Mother. From the very outset, we see that she fails Ellen's (and implicitly the narrator's) primary test when she declines to embrace Ellen physically and emotionally upon her arrival. Though Fortune is taken wholly by surprise at her niece's arrival, and though she provides Ellen with a good supper and a room, Ellen sees nothing but neglect in her aunt's behavior, crying in agony, "She did not kiss me! She didn't say she was glad to see me!" (101). Despite feeding Ellen, clothing her, and training her to perform a multitude of useful domestic tasks, in the end Fortune earns the novel's reproach because she does not convey this instruction through sympathy and affection.[22] And in *The Lamplighter,* Gertrude advises Fanny Bruce, a young admirer, that in order to learn to learn politeness, "you must cultivate your *heart,* Miss Bruce; you must cultivate your *heart*" (213). In this counsel Gertrude can fairly be said to speak for the implied narrators of both novels. But though these novels valorize an ethics of feeling, their heroines in fact model *rational* behavior.

Take, for example, Warner's Ellen Montgomery. As the novel nears its close and Ellen nears adulthood, we begin to see her hard-won control over her passions pay dividends beyond helping her submit to seeming injustices; it also enables her to conduct herself in a manner that an earlier century might well have characterized as rational. At the end of the novel, Ellen goes to Edinburgh to live with her mother's brother. This Scottish sojourn serves very much as a final test of Ellen's education to this point; how well has Ellen learned to trust God and submit outwardly to her uncle's authority while he assaults her attachment to her religion, her country, and her American friends, without inwardly forsaking any of her beliefs? The novel vindicates Ellen's education, of course. Significantly, however, Ellen meets her uncle's challenges with cool deliberation more often than she flees the room in tears. For example, in the following conversation with her uncle about the relative merits of America's Washington and Scotland's Bruce, Ellen maintains her argumentative equanimity.

> "Why do you prefer Washington?"
>
> "I should have to think to tell you that, sir."
>
> "Very well, then, think, and answer me."
>
> "One reason, I suppose, is because he was an American," said Ellen.
>
> "That is not reason enough for so reasonable a person as you are, Ellen; you must try again, or give up your preference."
>
> "I like Bruce, very much indeed," said Ellen musingly,—but he did what he did for *himself*;—Washington didn't."
>
> "Humph!—I am not quite sure as to either of your positions," said Mr. Lindsay.
>
> "And besides," said Ellen, "Bruce did one or two wrong things. Washington always did right."
>
> "He did, eh? What do you think of the murder of Andre?"
>
> "I think it was right," said Ellen firmly.
>
> (515)

My point here is not that Ellen in fact reasons like Descartes—indeed, her argument in regard to Washington is partisan rather than impartial. Nor do I suggest that Ellen no longer cries when she is upset. My point is that the narrator frames Ellen's confrontations with Mr. Lindsay as exchanges in which Ellen *reasons. The Wide, Wide World* idealizes an educational method that cultivates as much sense as sensibility. Ellen's argumentative confidence in this exchange and in others contrasts sharply with critical commentaries on the novel's—and the genre's—supposed hysteria.

Similarly, after an early struggle to master her youthful hot-headedness, *The Lamplighter*'s Gertrude Flint models a calm, deliberative approach to conflict. Consider the scene that occurs when Gertrude informs her present patron, Mr. Graham, that duty calls her to assist her earlier benefactor, Mrs. Sullivan. The exchange arouses intense feeling from both Gertrude and Mr. Graham, yet Gertrude manages to maintain the rational high ground. She earnestly minimizes the role played by emotion in her decision, stating that "it is not a matter of preference or choice, except as I feel it to be a duty." Mr. Graham, by contrast, angrily brushes off Emily's appeal to logic with his own assertion of wounded sensibility:

> "Father," said Emily, "I thought the object, in giving Gertrude a good education, was to make her independent of all the world, and not simply dependent upon us."

> "Emily," said Mr. Graham, "I tell you it is a matter of feeling,—you don't seem to look upon the thing in the light I do; but you are both against me, and I won't talk any more about it."
>
> (140)

Gertrude leaves "deeply wounded and grieved" and goes to her room where she "[gives] way to feelings that exhausted her spirit, and caused her a sleepless night" (141). During the night, the narrator informs us, "Gertrude had ample time to review and consider her own situation and circumstances" (143). She runs through a gamut of emotions, from grief and bitterness to—finally—a calm benevolence in which she gives Graham the benefit of the doubt but reaffirms her commitment to duty. Again, I do not argue here that this domestic heroine is not in fact motivated by her heart; clearly, Gertrude's affection for Mrs. Sullivan speaks as loudly as her sense of obligation to the Sullivan family. What draws my attention is the way the narrative characterizes Gertrude's response to an extremely upsetting situation—she reviews, she considers, she resolves. In an ironic contrast to Gertrude's composure, Mr. Graham is the one who gives in to violent expression of feeling.

In demonstrating the compatibility of rationality with more traditional "womanly" ideals, these texts silently emend the deficiencies of the sentimental model. Moreover, they demonstrate the incapacity of the fireside scenario, with its inward and exclusive focus on emotional nurture, to produce such exemplars.

According to the domestic rhetoric prevalent at mid-century, the individual mother held sole responsibility for childrearing; moreover, she was to perform this work at the fireside, that metaphor for the most private of all antebellum settings. The refusal of domestic fictions like *The Wide, Wide World* and *The Lamplighter* to fix responsibility for female education in "the mother at home" suggests serious ambivalence about the developing cult of motherhood. The surrogate system described in these texts, in which "strangers" take responsibility for tutoring the heroine in everything from Latin to Christian ethics, reintroduces an element lost in the valorization of family privacy. The path taken by Ellen and Gertrude on their way to maturity serves as a substitute for that "network of face-to-face relations" which Ryan claims is lost in the ideological division between public and private spaces. The "special sanctity" of the middle-class home could too easily slide into self-absorption or self-interest; these novels rescue young women from such private contexts and propel them out into the world, providing them a more useful and civic-minded education.

The fact that mothers in domestic fictions usually die young has not gone unnoticed by critics of antebellum literature. In her study of the role played by the discourse of affection in post-Revolutionary American literature, Elizabeth Barnes observes that "the mother often dies early in the domestic novel, and in her place is left a text—a Bible, a letter, a 'history'—that functions as a substitute for the mother and her wisdom . . . By the mid-nineteenth century, associations between mother and text render them practically interchangeable" (104). But interchangeable does not mean identical; though domestic fictions consistently replace the mother with a substitute, that substitute—whether text or surrogate—cannot perform exactly the same way that the mother would have. The slippage inevitable in this act of substitution opens up the way, in terms both of narrative and ideology, for someone or something else to perform the work supposedly exclusive to the mother. Ellen's and Gertrude's devoutly Christian surrogates are, like sentimental mothers, associated with the home and family and use primarily emotional means to shape the character of their young charges. But, I suggest, their freedom from literal maternalism—the surrogates rarely are themselves mothers—frees these figures from the negative associations with privacy, emotionalism, and self-absorption inextricable from antebellum treatments of motherhood.

Although Warner's and Cummins' novels seek something extra-maternal for the work of female education, they also embrace sentimental maternalism. They emphatically represent the middle-class home as the source of the greatest possible happiness and fulfillment, painting vivid portraits of such homes. This orientation is not incompatible with a simultaneous critique of domesticity. Lora Romero has reminded us to recognize "difference, contradiction, and dissent within the culture of domesticity," rather than reading the ideology as a unitary system uniformly applied and experienced (7). The fact that these novels choose figures other than mothers and sites other than the home for the work of shaping future generations of women suggests that the ideological enclosure of childrearing in highly privatized middle-class homes ruled by the mother sat uneasily with these writers. To the extent that the sentimental tableau enacts the developing middle-class ideal of privacy, *The Wide, Wide World* and *The Lamplighter* demonstrate the limitations of the work that can profitably be performed within the shelter provided by those four walls.

Notes

1. Mary P. Ryan's *Cradle of the Middle Class: The Family in Oneida County, New York, 1790-1865* (New York: Cambridge Univ. Press, 1981) argues cogently that the developing middle class depended for its identity on "domestic values and family practices" (15); hereafter cited parenthetically. For a study of both the character and the significance of the forming middle class, see Stuart M. Blumin, *The Emergence of the Middle Class: Social Experience in the American City, 1760-1900* (New York: Cambridge Univ. Press, 1989). And in *The Refinement of America: Persons, Houses, Cities* (New York: Vintage, 1992), Richard L. Bushman describes how the hallmarks of gentility—not synonymous with domesticity but overlapping in definition—served as a way for the expanding middle class to mark its distinction.

2. Mary P. Ryan, *The Empire of the Mother: American Writing about Domesticity, 1830-1860* (New York: Haworth, 1982), 56; hereafter cited parenthetically. Such was not universally the assumption before the mid-nineteenth century. In contrast to the rather utilitarian conception of motherhood prevalent before the American Revolution, as the nineteenth century opened motherly feeling was increasingly celebrated as exactly that which suited women to assume this burden. See Ruth H. Bloch, "American Feminine Ideals in Transition: The Rise of the Moral Mother, 1785-1815," *Feminist Studies* 4 (1978), 101-26.

3. The phrase comes from Lydia Sigourney's *Letters to Mothers* (New York: Harper and Brothers, 1839), 128. For a study of the breadth and impact of these kinds of domestic writings, see Ryan, *Empire,* particularly Chapter 4. Jan Lewis draws heavily from articles published in ladies' magazines between 1830 and 1865 in her "Mother's Love: The Construction of an Emotion in Nineteenth-Century America," *William and Mary Quarterly* 44 (1987), 689-721.

4. Samuel Goodrich, *Fireside Education* (London, 1841), 15; hereafter cited parenthetically.

5. Quoted in Lewis, 215.

6. As an ideology, sentimental maternalism overlaps with the transition to "intensive motherhood" described by Laurel Thatcher Ulrich, in which middle-class mothers of the nineteenth century began having fewer children to whom they devoted more attention. Intensive motherhood contrasts with "extensive motherhood," which Ulrich describes as a system in which women had more children to whom they dedicated relatively less attention. See her *Good Wives: Image and Reality in the Lives of Women in Northern New England, 1650-1750* (New York: Knopf, 1980).

7. Beginning with H. Ross Brown's *The Sentimental Novel in America, 1789-1860* (Durham: Duke Univ. Press, 1940), there has been a long line of literary critics who have dismissed the popular novels of nineteenth-century women writers as essentially conservative works, thoughtlessly complicit with an intellectually bankrupt dominant

culture. Ann Douglas renewed the vigor of this position with *The Feminization of American Culture* (New York: Knopf, 1977). Jane Tompkins directly addressed Douglas' view, arguing that these novels offered a radical alternative to the status quo, one shaped by domestic rather than marketplace values, in *Sensational Designs: The Cultural Work of American Fiction, 1790-1860* (New York: Oxford Univ. Press, 1985). More recently, Lora Romero has challenged the binary nature of the critical conversation about domesticity; see *Home Fronts: Domesticity and its Critics in the Antebellum United States* (Durham: Duke Univ. Press, 1997); hereafter cited parenthetically.

8. Stephanie Smith, *Conceived By Liberty: Maternal Figures and Nineteenth-Century American Literature* (Ithaca: Cornell Univ. Press, 1994), 1.

9. In *Woman's Fiction*, Nina Baym notes that many nineteenth-century novels written by women tell a single story—that of "a young girl who is deprived of the supports she had . . . depended on to sustain her throughout life and is faced with the necessity of winning her own way in the world." The "support" most often denied the young heroine is that of a competent, loving mother. See Baym, *Woman's Fiction: A Guide to Novels by and about Women in America, 1820-1870*, 2nd ed. (Urbana: Univ. of Illinois Press, 1993), 11.

10. Susan Warner, *The Wide, Wide World* (New York: The Feminist Press, 1987); hereafter cited parenthetically. Maria Susanna Cummins, *The Lamplighter,* ed. Nina Baym (New Brunswick: Rutgers Univ. Press, 1988); hereafter cited parenthetically.

11. See Elizabeth Barnes, *States of Sympathy: Seduction and Democracy in the American Novel,* (New York: Columbia Univ. Press, 1997), 105; hereafter cited parenthetically.

12. It must be noted at the outset that the Montgomerys rent their "home"; they live in a hotel. Nonetheless, the spaces in which Ellen and her mother act out their scenes, as well as the scenes themselves, are marked as middle-class, domestic, and intensely private. For the antebellum middle class, the parlor emblematized both the privacy and the aspirations to gentility characteristic of domesticity. See Karen Halttunen, *Confidence Men and Painted Women: A Study of Middle-Class Culture in America* (New Haven: Yale Univ. Press, 1982) and Bushman.

13. Richard Brodhead reads certain domestic fictions—among them Warner's—as participating in the "articulation of [a] correctional model that made warmly embracing parental love the preferred instrument for authority's exercise" (47).

He argues that a theory of "discipline through love" constituted the central normative model of character-formation of the antebellum middle-class, and he contends that mothers served as this disciplinary program's most powerful and effective instruments (18). See *Cultures of Letters: Scenes of Reading and Writing in Nineteenth-Century America* (Chicago: Univ. of Chicago Press, 1993), Chapter 3, "Sparing the Rod: Discipline and Fiction in Antebellum America." Hereafter cited parenthetically.

14. Nina Baym points out that Ellen's tears are "particularly associated with [her] early childhood—that is, with her condition as victimized and ineffectual orphan" (8) in arguing that Warner's novel portrays learning as a means of growing beyond sentimentalism. "Women's Novels, Women's Minds: An Unsentimental View of Nineteenth-Century American Women's Fiction," *Novel* 31 (Summer 1998), 335-50.

15. See pages 170-72 and 220, for example.

16. E. Anthony Rotundo, *American Manhood: Transformations in Masculinity from the Revolution to the Modern Era,* (New York: Basic Books, 1993), 22.

17. For Warner's novel, of course, the "world beyond" is the spiritual world consisting of Ellen's relationship with God.

18. See Bernard Wishy, *The Child and the Republic: The Dawn of Modern American Child Nurture* (Philadelphia: Univ. of Pennsylvania Press, 1968).

19. Quoted in Eleanor Wolf Thompson, *Education For Ladies, 1830-1860: Ideas on Education in Magazines for Women* (New York: King's Crown, 1947), 24.

20. Catherine O'Connell, "'We *Must* Sorrow': Silence, Suffering, and Sentimentality in Susan Warner's *The Wide, Wide World*," *Studies in American Fiction* 25 (1997), 23.

21. Barbara Welter's influential 1966 essay, "The Cult of True Womanhood: 1820-1860," identified in popular literature the existence of a particular stereotypical ideal, the virtues associated with which were domesticity, piety, purity, and submissiveness. The essay has been collected in her *Dimity Convictions: The American Woman in the Nineteenth Century* (Athens: Ohio Univ. Press, 1976). More recent works by feminist historians and literary critics have pointed out the extent to which Welter's analysis relied on prescriptive, rather than descriptive, texts.

22. Of course, Fortune's failing is also a class issue; she represents a world in which the constant pres-

ence of "rough work" renders middle-class gentility impossible. The reader searching for evidence of the distinction between Fortune and the genteel Alice Humphreys need look no further than the passage in which Alice shows Ellen her "large, well-appointed, and spotlessly neat kitchen." Alice explains the division that enables her to enjoy such a pleasant room: "Beyond this is a lower kitchen where Margery does all her rough work; nothing comes up the steps . . . to this but the very nicest and daintiest of kitchen matters" (167). Fortune, a single woman running a farm almost single-handedly, has neither time nor patience for daintiness. For a reading of Aunt Fortune as Warner's rebuttal to Emersonian notions of independence, see Lucinda L. Damon-Bach, "To Be a 'Parlor Soldier': Susan Warner's Answer to Emerson's 'Self-Reliance,'" in *Separate Spheres No More: Gender Convergence in American Literature, 1830-1930,* ed. Monika M. Elbert (Tuscaloosa: Univ. of Alabama Press, 2000), 29-49.

MATERNAL ARCHETYPES: GOOD, BAD, AND ABSENT

Sally Shuttleworth (essay date 1992)

SOURCE: Shuttleworth, Sally. "Demonic Mothers: Ideologies of Bourgeois Motherhood in the Mid-Victorian Era." In *Rewriting the Victorians: Theory, History, and the Politics of Gender,* edited by Linda M. Shires, pp. 31-51. New York and London: Routledge, 1992.

[*In the following essay, Shuttleworth examines the ways in which issues of class, sexuality, ideology, and bourgeois identity informed the beliefs and practices surrounding motherhood in Victorian society and literature.*]

Motherhood was set at the ideological centre of the Victorian bourgeois ideal. Virtually any reference to motherhood in the social texts of the era seemed to call forth, as if by necessity, yet one more recitation of the maternal creed. We hear endlessly of the mother's sacred mission to rear children, and of her spiritual grace which, filling the domestic sphere, uplifts her weary husband on his return from the corrupting world of Mammon. Few ideological constructs seem to arouse such uniform responses in the era; men and women, conservatives and reformers alike, seem to endorse this identical picture. Even with the beginnings of the wom-

en's movement in the 1860s, female reformers were reluctant to voice a challenge to the sacred ideals of motherhood. Yet the very ideological centrality of these ideals ensured that motherhood was not the still point around which other ideological contradictions might turn, but rather a field of potent conflict in itself. Far from guaranteeing, by its seemingly unchallengeable status, areas of overt ideological conflict, it acted as a focal point for many of the most problematic areas of Victorian ideology.

Ideals of motherhood had to perform important ideological labor: they helped constitute and maintain the gendered social hierarchy and its division of labor, they vindicated the middle class's claims to social leadership through moral superiority, and sanctioned, by their maintenance of a strict division between the realms of home and work, whatever questionable practices the bourgeois male might have to pursue in business. But motherhood was not solely a spiritual mission, as so many descriptions seemed to suggest. It was also an intensely physical process, and a mode of social productivity vital to the middle class's maintenance of power. From the beginnings of the foundation of the bourgeois ideal in the mid-eighteenth century, we start to hear dire warnings, which reach a crescendo in the Victorian era, that middle-class women are failing to fulfil their reproductive duties, producing sickly, puny children, while the threatening mass of the working classes are producing bouncing, healthy babes.

As Foucault (1984) has argued, the nineteenth century was an age dedicated to the regulation of the middle-class body, and perhaps even more than sexuality, the functions of maternity were the object of fierce scrutiny and control. Indeed maternity encompassed the domain of female sexuality, for all the workings of female sexual desire were traced directly to the operation of the reproductive system. Woman, the medical textbooks insisted, was ruled by her "uterine economy" from the first onset of puberty to the cessation of her reproductive life with the "climacteric," or menopause.[1] The maternal function dominated womanhood not only with the actual bearing of children, or the wild outbreaks of an "ovarian perversion of appetite" or puerperal insanity that childbirth might occasion, but in all the daily operations of the mind and body throughout a woman's reproductive life. Female emotion, whether hysterical and out of control, or spiritually elevated and refined, sprang from the seat of maternity; sexuality and tenderness were deemed equally the products of the uterine economy. The two seemingly opposed models of womanhood constructed in nineteenth-century bourgeois ideology—refined angel, or helpless prey to the workings of the body—come together in discourses on maternity, for woman's mission is both to ensure, physically, the healthy reproduction of the race, as well as the spiritual superiority of the middle class.

Contradictions within constructions of the maternal role were not confined to the split between materiality and spirituality, but were indeed legion. For example, conflicts between the projections of motherhood and wifehood abound. Emphasis on female domestic supremacy seemed to offer potentially dangerous images of female empowerment, while the intense ideological focus on woman's reproductive role threatened to marginalize male creativity. On a practical level, theorists were exercised by the problem of whether a woman's first concern should lie with the comfort of her husband or the upbringing of her children. Sarah Ellis solved the dilemma by producing two separate texts, *The Wives of England* (1843b) and *The Mothers of England* (1843a), both of which speak, to the virtual exclusion of the other sphere, of the all-encompassing centrality of their chosen theme. When conflict is unavoidable, Ellis pays lip service to the primary importance of the male, despite frequent projections of him as a spoilt and petulant child. The thinking underlying this priority is explicitly voiced in another contemporary text: Mrs Warren's semi-fictionalized account, *How I Managed My Children from Infancy to Marriage*:

> During all these years, though I became so devoted to my children, I never allowed them to interfere with my time when my husband came home. . . . I would suggest to every woman never to allow her children to usurp the time and loving attention due to the husband. If she does, home will be no home to him; he will become irritable and seek comfort elsewhere.
>
> (Warren 1865: 41-2)

Although a woman's central concern is with her children, self-interest dictates an outward subservience to the controller of the purse-strings.

The mother was not an unproblematic figure in Victorian discourse. The angel was shadowed by potent images of disruptive physicality, while wifehood and motherhood seemed to impose conflicting demands. This ideological confusion is perhaps best summarized in the details of a psychological case that seemed to haunt the male imagination of the era, being repeated frequently in medical texts of the time. It concerns a woman who, through an extreme "ovarian perversion of the appetite," developed "such a cannibalish longing for the flesh of her husband, that she killed him, ate as much of him as she could while fresh, and pickled the remainder" (Anon. 1851: 31).[2] In this monstrous concatenation of different ideological images, uncontrollable maternal urges unite with commendable attributes of housewifely zeal and economy literally to eat into and destroy male dominance. So absorbed is the woman with the needs of her reproducing body, and the fulfilment of her housewifely role, that her husband is efficiently and neatly subsumed, negated by the conjoined powers of maternity and domestic management. While

such demonic images are no doubt extreme, they are not unusual and highlight the ideological anxieties underlying the projections of female angelic subservience. Like the working classes, women represented to the bourgeois male imagination an ever-present threat to their dominance, a threat, moreover, that was enshrined within the sanctuary of their own home. In the following analysis I will look in more detail at some of the fears accruing around the middle-class female body, and attempts to regulate her maternal functions. The discourse of maternity was promulgated through a wide range of texts. This discussion will focus initially on the popular advice texts, and more specialized medical works which together laid the ideologically-riven ground of Victorian projections of motherhood, while the final section will consider the more complex textual terrain of fictional constructions.

HEALTHY REPRODUCTION

In his *Advice to Mothers* (1803), a text that laid the framework for later discussions in the Victorian era, William Buchan warned that "It is little short of intentional murder on the part of a weak, languid, nervous, or deformed woman to approach the marriage-bed" (Buchan 1809: 9). Not only would such a woman fail in her social duty of producing healthy offspring to perpetuate the nation's prosperity, she would also be burdened with ineradicable guilt for her heinous crime against the social good. This ideological construction of a languid, nervous woman who fails in her bounden duty to her country seems to shadow the bourgeois rise to social power. From the earliest stages, fears are voiced that "degeneracy" within these classes will impede industrial progress. Thus Thomas Trotter warns at the beginning of the nineteenth century that England's commercial ascendancy is under threat from "the increasing prevalence of nervous disorders; which, if not restrained soon, must inevitably sap our physical strength of constitution; make us an easy conquest to our invaders; and ultimately convert us into a nation of slaves and idiots" (Trotter 1812: x). As the century progressed, middle-class women, with their languid airs and nervous ailments, were increasingly singled out as the prime culprits of this feared decline (fears that were not in any way allayed by England's growing commercial success). The bourgeois woman was caught in an unyielding ideological double-bind: separated, increasingly, from the polluting domain of work, she was nevertheless then fiercely criticized for her debilitating idleness.

The era's advice books on womanhood and motherhood were virtually all directed to this social class of woman, and all carried the same message: idle, artificial habits, copied from a degenerate aristocracy, endangered the health and wealth of the nation. Sarah Ellis was uncompromisingly specific about the designated audience for

The Women of England. Other advice books, she observed, had been written for ladies, "while that estimable class of females who might be more specifically denominated *women,* and who yet enjoy the privilege of liberal education, with exemption from the pecuniary necessities of labour, are almost wholly overlooked" (Ellis 1838: preface). The category of true "womanhood" takes on an extraordinarily privileged status in her text: the true woman would be neither an aristocratic lady (a term that takes on increasingly pejorative connotations), nor subject to the degrading demands of pecuniary labour which helped to unsex the vulgar lower orders, but rather an educated member of the middle classes.

Like all her contemporaries, Ellis is not sparing of her strictures on "the sickly sensibilities, the feeble frames, and the useless habits of the rising generation" (1838: 11) which are threatening the "nation's moral wealth" (ibid.: 13). In a sweeping statement she asserts that:

> By far the greater portion of the young ladies (for they are no longer *women*) of the present day, are distinguished by a morbid listlessness of mind and body, except when under the influence of stimulus, a constant pining for excitement, and an eagerness to escape from every thing like practical and individual duty.

> (ibid.: 11-12)

Whereas an earlier generation were lambasted for not being true "ladies," the Victorian females were excoriated for not being true "women"—a category that encompassed both healthy reproduction and domestic usefulness. From a biological definition, "womanhood" has been transformed into a class-based moral assessment, but one that was nonetheless founded on the quality of biological performance with regard to reproduction.

The language of biological imperatives was pressed into service to underscore the middle-class concern with reproduction as a vehicle for the perpetuation of social dominance. According to J. M. Allan, "Woman craves to be a mother, knowing that she is an imperfect undeveloped being, until she has borne a child" (1869: 35). True selfhood, and indeed biological completion, only comes with successful maternity. But the latter was deemed to be threatened by the competing demands of wifehood. Thus Pye Henry Chavasse in his *Advice to a Wife on the Management of her own Health* endorsed the current ideological claim that a wife's highest duty was to bring healthy children into the world, but warned that if she pursued the customary round of marriage visits, she would irredeemably damage her own health and chances of reproductive success. A woman's conduct at this stage will determine "whether she shall be the mother of fine, healthy children—or—if, indeed, she be a mother at all—of sickly, undersized offspring" (Chavasse 1864: 1-2). As in all these works, "advice" seems to come in the guise of alarmist warnings. From the first hours of marriage, the young bride is faced with an impossible choice: if she fulfils her social duties as a wife, she will ensure her total failure as a mother.

Bourgeois motherhood was enshrined in sanctity but framed by prohibitions. The class basis of the criticism directed at the middle-class woman was quite specific: by aping the manners and vices of the upper classes she had weakened her constitution to such a degree that the debilitated middle classes were under threat from the rising vitality of the working classes. Women who miscarried, had puny infants, or failed to supply sufficient milk were directed to look at the working-class women who labored in the fields and yet still produced healthy offspring. While frequently vilified, in their roles as servants or wet-nurses, as vulgar corrupters of infant purity, working women were nonetheless held up to their middle-class counterparts as models of industry and reproductive success.

Behind all this concern with the middle-class mother's reproductive powers lay the beginnings of the eugenics debate. Long before Darwin's *Descent of Man* (1871), the idea of marital selection on the grounds of improving class and species health had been part of public discussion. Buchan, at the beginning of the nineteenth century, had observed that social degeneracy would be arrested if country squires could "be induced to pay half as much attention to the breed of men as to that of dogs, horses, and cattle" (1809: 107). By the mid-century, breeding anxiety was focused directly on the middle classes. T. J. Graham, in his treatise on the management of infancy, speaks confidently of the "laws of selection," and warns that the middle classes must be careful to avoid the mistakes which had precipitated the aristocracy into degeneracy: "It is only by attending to the law of selection, that the organization and qualities of offspring can be improved: and, on the other hand, that the disastrous consequences of improper intermarriages can be avoided" (Graham 1853: 28). Advice books abound with warnings about avoiding early marriages (which will entirely debilitate the women and produce puny children), marriages too close in blood, or ones where there is known to be a weak constitution, hereditary insanity, or morbid disposition in the family (Combe 1854: 18). John Reid, writing in 1821, had spoken of the "criminal indiscretion" of those who marry although "radically morbid in intellect," comparing the act unfavorably to that of shooting someone, which destroys only one life:

> But he who inflicts upon a single individual, the worse than deadly wound of insanity, knows not the numbers to which its venom may be communicated; he poisons a public stream out of which multitudes may drink; he is the enemy, not of one man, but of mankind.

> (Reid 1821: 285-6)

By the mid-century this secret poisoner and enemy of the public weal was more narrowly defined. Although some texts looked at the problems of weak mental or bodily constitutions in both sexes, the emphasis had shifted predominantly onto female weakness. Symbolic associations of women with disease were strengthened by the received wisdom that not only were women more prone to insanity than men, they were also more responsible for hereditary transmission: "insanity descends more often from the mother than the father, and from the mother to the daughters more often than to the sons" (Maudsley 1867: 216). Women, it seems, were the main pollutants, the primary poisoners of the public stream.

Sacred though the social role of motherhood might have been, the female body was seen as a fertile source of anarchic disruption. Bucknill and Tuke, in their influential *Manual of Psychological Medicine,* noted their surprise that even more women did not become insane under the pressures of pregnancy (Bucknill and Tuke 1874: 348). All stages of a woman's reproductive life were marked by potential violence: the cannibalish longings of pregnancy might be succeeded by the onset of puerperal insanity when murderous acts were frequently committed, usually against husbands and children. Bucknill and Tuke cite the case of a woman, thirteen days after her confinement, who "cut off the head of her child with a razor" (ibid.: 273). Even the operations of a woman's menstrual cycle could evoke equivalent violence—whether the blood flowed, or failed to appear. Maudsley cites the case of a woman who, afflicted with a desire to kill her children, was cured by the return of her menses, while another killed her three children when her menstrual blood started to flow (Maudsley 1867: 308-9). Motherhood, and all processes leading up to it, were firmly associated in Victorian eyes with murderous lust.

As physical body, vehicle of reproduction of the nation's wealth, the middle-class woman was subjected to extreme regulation. Failure to adhere to the strict regimes laid down by the medical establishment would lead to ideological reclassification: angel no longer, but a source of corruption and poison. In an era of appalling childbirth fatality, the medical establishment took no part of the blame, shifting the burden of guilt entirely onto the shoulders of the woman.[3] The mild Mrs Warren informs the reader how her ignorance and self-indulgence during her first pregnancy nearly killed both herself and her child. Should the expectant mother avoid exercise and resort to stimulants then "the child-spirit sent from the hand of God appears on the earth in human flesh, corrupt with the vices and taint of the mother" (Warren 1865: 8). A mother's guilt is such that it cannot be hidden. Both the temperament and physical constitution of a child, Andrew Combe declares, are "a legible transcript of the mother's condition and feelings during pregnancy" (Combe 1854: 26). Not only was it incumbent upon an expectant woman to control all physical aspects of her life, such as diet, social habits, and exercise, she also had to police her feelings, for these too would be inscribed upon the child, turning it into an informant, or public statement of her guilt.

All at costs, a pregnant woman was advised to avoid strong emotions and thoughts. Buchan, in his usual alarmist fashion, cited the case of a woman who, in a paroxysm of rage, "brought forth a child, with all its bowels hanging out of its little body" (1809: 12). Victorian texts warned of the dangers of anxiety, passion, and morbid thoughts during pregnancy, all of which could bring on miscarriage or mark the child for life. Pregnant women who were prey to anxiety, Combe observes, would give "birth to children who continued through life a prey to nervous, convulsive, or epileptic disease, or displayed a morbid timidity of character which no subsequent care could counteract" (1854: 24). Miscarriages could similarly be provoked by the slightest infringement of the rules for diet, social behavior, and exercise. As Thomas Bull warned in his *Hints to Mothers for the Management of Health,* an expectant mother should follow every rule and injunction laid down by her medical adviser, no matter how strict, for "by *one* act of disobedience she may blast every hope of success" (Bull 1837: 138). So perverted was the female body, one miscarriage was deemed to be sufficient to establish a "habit" which the woman could not break. Male discipline and female obedience was the name of the game, yet the woman was hedged around with so many restrictions that obedience itself seemed almost designed as a deliberate impossibility: a pregnant woman should take exercise but not too much, rest but not be idle, take cold baths but refrain from catching cold. All the rules seemed calculated to drive her into that very state of anxiety which she was warned was fatal, and a clear result of her own weakness and disobedience.

BREAST-FEEDING

The disciplining of the bourgeois mother's body did not cease with successful childbirth, but if anything increased in intensity. The image of the mother giving suck to her innocent babe was a potent one in Victorian ideology, but one that was riddled with class anxieties and demonic undertones. From the end of the eighteenth century, breast-feeding had been ideologically designated as a middle-class duty. Neither animals nor savages, Buchan had observed, were so monstrous as to withhold "the nutritive fluid" from their young (1809: 30). The Victorians similarly employed the discourse of the "natural" to enforce the bourgeois mother's obedience. Inability to breast-feed, like miscarriages, was again taken as a sign of her lack of discipline, her failure to forgo luxurious practices and the artificial round of social life (Combe 1854: 67). Mere feeding was insufficient, however; the *quality* of production also had to be strictly controlled. Cloaked beneath the rhetoric of the natural lie the assumptions and discourse of contemporary capitalist economics. Isabella Beeton advised the readers of her *Book of Household Management* that,

> As Nature has placed in the bosom of the mother the natural food of her offspring, it must be self-evident to every reflecting woman, that it becomes her duty to study, as far as lies in her power, to keep that reservoir of nourishment in as pure and invigorating condition as possible; for she must remember that the *quantity* is no proof of the *quality* of this aliment.
>
> (Beeton 1861: 1034)

This insidious distinction between quantity and quality performs a crucial role in class control: supplying milk of the correct class quality becomes a matter of conscious *study,* requiring the policing both of bodily habits and thought. Milk becomes a metonymic projection of womanhood; so seemingly pure and innocent, it can yet be a vehicle of class corruption. Unregulated emotion, mothers were warned, could turn their milk into a literal poison. Anger or a fretful temper would give the milk an "irritating quality" (Carpenter 1846 quoted in Graham 1853: 163). Nor does the emotion have to be extreme before such deleterious effects take place. Beeton's *Housewife's Treasury* paints a scenario of a mother confined upstairs with her new babe, listening to domestic turmoil below (the result, of course, of her previous faulty management): she "frets and fumes, and at last poor baby, the one least able to bear it, has to stand the consequences. Its food is upset and deranged, and turned into draughts of poison almost" (Beeton 1880?: 419). While extreme worry will most likely *kill* the child, readers are warned, even mild worry will have very harmful effects. Just as the physical state and temperament of the child when born is a "legible transcript" of a mother's self-regulation during pregnancy, the child's response to a mother's milk becomes one more moral indicator of a woman's self-control, or lack thereof. To this end, the milk is endowed with near magical powers of directly transcribing maternal emotional states into physical effects. Indeed it becomes the medium for the transmission of moral qualities, for the child was said to inherit the temperament of the mother or wet-nurse (Chavasse 1864: 169).

Although the texts extolled the delights of suckling one's own child, they also warned that it would be necessary to engage a wet-nurse if a mother came from a family with a "hereditary taint," whether a disposition to consumption or insanity, for "the milk of such mothers may be changed into a noxious agent,—even a deadly poison" (Conquest 1848 quoted in Graham 1853: 194). They should also instantly desist if their menses returned, for their milk would then be inevitably "de-

praved," a term which draws on the moral language of vice, taint, and corruption that pervades this discourse. On this occasion, the "depravity" seems to lie in the linking of the ideas of sexual activity and nursing, since menstruation was still regarded by some doctors as the time when women were sexually "on heat."[4] Discussion of the employment of wet-nurses is also sexually charged and produces an extreme ideological mystification of the milk, as all the fears of working-class pollution are condensed into this image of fluids circulating from the lower orders to the higher. Graham warns against the selection of a nurse with a less than perfect moral character:

> Her very blood, and therefore her milk, is commonly tainted by her bad disposition and evil tempers; and she never fails by her voice, manner, looks, etc., to stir up, more or less, the evil passions of the child, and thus to injure it physically, intellectually, and morally.
>
> (Graham 1853: 169)

Through the agency of the wet-nurse, the vulgarities and perversions of the working class are given physical imprint on the cherished minds and bodies of their masters.

The sexual undertones of this fear of working-class invasion are given overt articulation in the case Graham quotes from a Swedish physician: "in a respectable family in Stockholm the father, the mother, three children, the maid servant, and two clerks, were infected with the venereal disease by a nurse who was admitted into the family, without previous inquiry into her character" (1853: 191). As in the contemporary Aids scare, fear of pollution is enough to activate class, gender, and sexual prejudices to such a degree that all reasonable notions of cause and effect with regard to transmission are overturned: the very presence of a morally dubious working-class woman in a middle-class household, offering that highly sexualized organ, the breast, to one of its members, is enough to poison the blood of all who reside in it.

In making a connection between the transmission of "tainted milk" and that of venereal disease, Graham is drawing to the surface the class and sexual undertones which pervaded critiques of the bourgeois mother. In failing to fulfil her reproductive duty, in placing pleasure before the demands of motherhood and thus transmitting her own taints and vices to her children, she was in many ways falling out of her own class and thus joining the fallen sisterhood. The discourse which surrounded prostitution in the mid-Victorian era follows, significantly, exactly the bifurcation which characterized bourgeois ideologies of motherhood. In W. R. Greg's famous article in the 1850 *Westminster Review,* prostitutes are characterized initially as too womanly for their own good: perfect angels, they fall, not from evil desires, but from "pure unknowingness," and an exaggeration of woman's best qualities, a "strange and sublime unselfishness" (Greg 1850: 459). Their angelic nature is revealed even when fallen in the fact that they make excellent, affectionate mothers and nurses. With the mention of venereal disease, however, the whole tone of the article changes, and prostitutes become "the hundreds of female devils who prowl about day and night seeking for their prey" (ibid.: 478). The dramatic shift in representation, from tender angel to contaminating demon, follows exactly the same trajectory pursued by the ideological discourse on bourgeois motherhood. The same emotive images to be found in motherhood texts of poison being introduced into the very bosom of the family, and innocent babes being tainted from birth, are recycled in articles on venereal disease, which becomes one more version of the notion of women polluting the "public stream," only this time the source is the working-class female. This ready translatability of an existing discourse into different class terms, with the middle-class woman switching role from polluter to innocent victim, draws attention to the class and sexual concerns underpinning the discourses on bourgeois motherhood. Like the working class, the middle-class woman represented a disruptive and corrupting threat to class stability, a threat rendered all the more dangerous by her key position within that class formation. She stood accused, like the working class, of following her own desires, consulting her own pleasure rather than her duty to the nation.

SEXUALITY AND MATERNITY

The question of female pleasure, and of the relationship between sexuality and maternity, formed one more problematic area within Victorian ideologies of motherhood. Breast-feeding, although ideologically prescribed, was still an arena suffused with sexuality and worrying images of self-pleasuring. Medical texts and advice books spoke of the "positive pleasure derived from the act itself" (Graham 1853: 161) and suggested that "the pleasure of the young mother in her babe is said to be more exquisite than any other earthly bliss" (Chavasse 1864: 168, quoting *Good Words,* October 1861). Such exquisite pleasure was also dangerous, however, suggesting an unwelcome autonomy, an exclusion of the male from sexual gratification, and hence an activity crying out for external regulation.

As in all ages, breast-feeding highlighted the implicit conflict between a woman's marital and maternal roles, a conflict particularly pronounced in the Victorian era when the ideal of female beauty, with the exaggerated attention paid to the bust and hips, focused on woman's reproductive powers. According to one scientific commentator of the era, woman was most pleasing to man during "the period of activity of the reproductive organs," and her "greatest beauty of form" was to be found in "those parts peculiar to her organization": the bust and pelvis. The description of the bosom, "on which the organs for nutrition of the tender offspring are developed" spirals off into ecstatic, sexual contemplation:

> It is to her bosom that woman instinctively clasps all that she rightly loves—her bosom, remarkable for the unsurpassable beauty of its voluptuous contours and graceful inflexions, the white transparent surface of which is set off with an azure network, or tinged with the warm glow of the emotions and passions that make it heave in graceful undulations.
>
> (Anon. 1851: 19-20)

The woman's use of this bosom, so central to the Victorian male's sexual imagination, had to be severely regulated and controlled. Both the frequency and duration of breast-feeding were subject to rigid discipline. A mother should feed only at set, regulated times, and never on demand, like an animal. Some of the severest strictures are reserved for mothers who always have the child at their breast: overfeeding, all commentators agreed, could not only sow the seeds of later disease, but also kill outright (Graham 1853: 103). Breast-feeding should continue for nine months, but should quickly cease thereafter if the mother was not to become "nervous, emaciated, and hysterical" or the child to die of "water-on-the-brain, or, of consumption" (Chavasse 1864: 186).

One of the most significant prohibitions was against falling asleep while feeding, or allowing the infant to sleep in the maternal bed. Mrs Beeton speaks of

> that most injurious practice of letting the child *suck* after the mother has *fallen asleep,* a custom . . . which . . . is injurious to both mother and child. It is injurious to the infant by allowing it, without control, to imbibe to distension a fluid sluggishly secreted and deficient in those vital principles which the want of mental energy, and of the sympathetic appeals of the child on the mother, so powerfully produce on the secreted nutriment, while the mother wakes in a state of clammy exhaustion, with giddiness, dimness of sight, nausea, loss of appetite, and a dull aching pain through the back and between the shoulders. In fact, she wakes languid and unrefreshed from her sleep, with febrile symptoms and hectic flushes, caused by her baby vampire, who, while dragging from her her health and strength, has excited in itself a set of symptoms directly opposite, but fraught with the most injurious consequences— "functional derangement."
>
> (Beeton 1861: 1034)

In this extraordinary passage, the seemingly innocent picture of a mother asleep with her babe in her arms becomes a scene of uncontrolled debauchery. The baby becomes a sexualized demon, a vampire sucking at her breast, while her symptoms mirror those ascribed to women who indulged in "lesbian pleasures." Indeed, masturbation itself was similarly referred to in contemporary discourse as a vampire sucking away vital strength.[5] The milk itself is said to suffer, no longer expressing a mother's mental energy, or *conscious* sympathetic response to her child. The supreme sin actually lies in this state of unconsciousness: maternity is no longer being policed and externally controlled. From being a conscious, and hence socialized, mental response to the demands of her role, breast-feeding has become an instinctive, physical function, outside the sphere of social regulation. Hence the demonic sexual overtones. Breast-feeding remained unthreatening only to the degree that it functioned as a conscious social duty, prescribed and regulated from without, and not a pleasurably physical, solipsistic bonding of mother and child.

MATERNAL EXCESS

The final problematic area of maternal ideology I would like to consider is that of the mother who allows her feelings for her offspring to run to excess. Emotional immoderation in the mother, Buchan had warned, could produce an insidious "relaxing effeminacy" in her offspring which clearly threatened to undermine the moral fibre of the nation (Buchan 1809: 77-81). Sarah Ellis similarly speaks witheringly of mothers with "ungoverned springs of tenderness and love, which burst forth and exhaust themselves, without calculation or restraint" (Ellis 1843a: 106). Even maternal love should be subjected to an economic calculus. Ellis's imagery also suggests that maternal emotion partakes of the same volatile, disruptive nature, as female sexual passion, or insanity, which, women were warned, was liable to burst forth suddenly if not kept under constant watchful guard.

While fears of unregulated emotion, and especially female emotion, were rampant in the Victorian era, Ellis pins this particular form directly onto a conflict between the roles of mother and wife. "We must not forget," she warns with reference to maternal love, "that while wholly given up to this feeling, so sacred in itself, there is such a thing as neglecting, for the sake of the luxury it affords, the duty of a wife" (ibid.: 252). In a significant transposition, "luxury" ceases to denote an artificial social state, but designates instead a form of female emotional autonomy. The threat posed to a husband by a wife luxuriating in maternal feeling is overtly sexualized:

> wherever a mother thus doats upon her children, she is guilty of an act of unfaithfulness to her husband, at the same time that she places herself in a perilous position, from whence the first shock of disease, or the first symptom of ingratitude, may cast her down into utter wretchedness.
>
> (Ellis 1843a: 253)

Although the passage is enigmatic, it is perhaps not over-reading to suggest that this act of maternal "unfaithfulness" is rewarded by the husband "seeking comfort elsewhere," and the transmission of venereal disease. The undisciplined bourgeois mother is once more aligned with the fallen sisterhood. The affections, Ellis warns, must not "be concentrated into one focus, so as to burn with dangerous and destructive intensity" (ibid.). The image crystallizes many of the contradictions in Victorian projections of motherhood: the sacred passion can itself be demonized, turned into an avenging force which destroys both the angelic mother herself and the concord of the domestic hearth, revealing all too clearly the precarious balance of the patriarchal bourgeois order.

FICTIONAL REPRESENTATIONS

Mothers in Victorian fiction are distinguished by their absence. On the one hand this is a literal absence—heroes and heroines are notoriously motherless—and can be accounted for both in terms of hard historical fact, the high mortality rate associated with maternity, and in terms of generic fictional conventions: the romance structure dictated that the narrative end with marriage. Maternal absence also conferred, however, a form of shadowy power, allowing such figures to exert far more influence than that customarily given to the mothers permitted a more overt presence in the Victorian fictional text. Motherhood is simultaneously marginalized and given ideological centrality. This uneasy configuration is given literal embodiment in a series of novels which feature a mother who is yearned for in her absence, but who is actually present: Mrs Pryor in Charlotte Brontë's *Shirley* (1849) for example, or Lady Dedlock in Dickens's *Bleak House* (1853), or the Princess in Eliot's *Daniel Deronda* (1876). Perhaps the most extreme form of the absent/present mother is to be found in Mrs Henry Wood's *East Lynne* (1861), which features a mother who, presumed dead by her family, returns to look after her children in the guise of governess. *East Lynne* also differs from the other texts in this mode in that it focuses not on the offspring's emotional needs for a mother, but rather on the feelings of the mother herself.

The dramatic shift of narratorial focus revealed in *East Lynne* is typical of the genre of sensation fiction which emerged in the 1860s. While earlier fiction had not generally endorsed angelic notions of motherhood, neither had it foregrounded maternal emotion or explored the reverse, underside of bourgeois maternal ideology. Many of the sensation novels confronted these aspects of contemporary ideology head on, continuing into the vicissitudes of married life and producing representations of violent, undisciplined, or monstrous mothers which took to an extreme the negative formulations of the advice literature and medical texts. Perhaps the most famous example is Mary Braddon's *Lady Audley's Secret* (1862), where the heroine, whose only inheritance from her mother, she claims, is insanity, violates all the principles of motherhood in abandoning her child in order to pursue, under cover of her angelic appearance, a "demonic" career of self-interest. Wilkie Collins, in contrast, focuses in *Jezebel's Daughter* (1880) on an evil woman whose only redeeming quality is love for her daughter, while in the "thesis" novel, *The Legacy of Cain* (1888), he deliberately foregrounds the nature-nurture debate, directly paralleling the development of two girls, one the daughter of a convicted murderess, the other of a respectable, but selfish and unprincipled, woman.

In all these texts, contemporary medical debates on hereditary insanity, and the impact of maternity on the female mind and body, are explicitly highlighted. There is, however, a significant shift in the discourse. While the medical texts and advice books overtly promulgated contemporary ideology, sometimes seeking to reconcile contradictions, but more often letting conflicting constructions of womanhood stand side by side, the fictional texts actively explore and expose those contradictions. Structurally, they are also more complex than the other texts: overt agreement with dominant ideological projections, expressed directly by the narrator, or in the conformist endings adopted, is often undercut by the sympathies generated, or implicit critiques offered, in the course of the narrative. The two texts I would like to consider briefly, in conclusion, Mrs Henry Wood's *St Martin's Eve* (1866) and *East Lynne* (1861), both follow this pattern.

St Martin's Eve has all the ingredients of contemporary ideological debate: a "demonic" mother, in the figure of the primary heroine, Charlotte St John, and an insistent preoccupation with the "unwholesome" transmission of hereditary taints. In the opening section of the novel Charlotte's mother surprisingly opposes, for reasons she will not disclose, her daughter's marriage to the local lord, stating that, "I would almost rather see you die, than married to George St John" (Wood 1905: 27). The reason for such extraordinary vehemence soon becomes clear to the alert reader. Charlotte's father, we learn, died very suddenly in mysterious circumstances. Charlotte herself, however, appears oblivious of any causes for concern and, ignoring her mother's warnings, goes ahead with the marriage. Suspicions of hereditary insanity are confirmed when the birth of Charlotte's son calls forth a wild, jealous love. Charlotte is not the kind of demonic mother who rejects her child, but one who loves to excess. She will not leave her child to accompany her husband, a member of parliament, to London for,

> The frail little infant of a few days had become to her the greatest treasure earth ever gave; her love for him

was of that wild, impassioned, all-absorbing nature, known, it is hoped, but to few, for it never visits a well-regulated heart.

> (ibid.: 39-40)

Both the tone and substance of the comments echo contemporary advice books: Charlotte violates both her wifely duty and the requisite maternal self-regulation.

Charlotte's condition is exacerbated, and transformed into apparent madness by a crucial economic fact: her son is not the heir to the property, for there exists a previous heir, born to St John in his first marriage. Maternal passion leads to a jealous hatred of the heir, and to sudden outbursts of angry violence against him when Charlotte appears as one "mad," totally devoid of self-control. When the heir apparently burns himself to death we have our suspicions, shared by the surgeon and confirmed at the conclusion of the book, that Charlotte has been instrumental in his death. Her sins are not rewarded, for her own son dies shortly thereafter, not, interestingly, from the seeds of her own insanity, but from the hereditary taint of consumption which had destroyed his father. With such a fatal cocktail of inheritance, it is not surprising that the doctor remarks, in seemingly unfeeling vein, that it is best that the child die.

Throughout there is a reiterated suggestion that it is better to die than to transmit an unhealthy constitution, and thus poison the "public stream." In the secondary plot, which counterpoints that of Charlotte, the aristocratic and angelic Adeline dies of consumption (a disease associated with aristocratic overbreeding) and a broken heart. While Charlotte's unregulated energies find aggressive outward expression, Adeline's feelings implode. At her funeral, her lover Frederick, who was partly responsible for her death, thinks, in spite of his regrets, "that all things might still be for the best. Had she lived to bear him children—and to entail upon them her fragility of constitution—" (ibid.: 374). Contemporary ideological concerns with sexual selection, and the health of the ruling-class body, seem to ride rough-shod over dramatic sympathy. Frederick's subsequent opposition to the idea that Charlotte might marry his uncle (and thus disinherit him) is framed in similar terms. Any other woman, he tells himself, he would welcome, "But to marry *her*—with that possibility of taint in her blood . . ." (ibid.: 382). Both women, angel and demon alike, are to him potent sources of class pollution. Under his relentless pursuit and eagle eye, Charlotte's self-control cracks, signs of insanity emerge, and she is locked up in an asylum for good. The surgeon, Mr Pym, who has been a shadowy, all-knowing figure throughout, confirms the facts of her case. It was from her father, not her mother, that Charlotte inherited insanity, but his wild outburst four days before Charlotte was born clearly affected the mother and hence the baby in the womb.

On the surface, *St Martin's Eve* appears a textbook account of the dangers of maternal excess, and of transmitting hereditary "taints" to one's offspring. Wood follows with scrupulous care the precise details and language of contemporary medical accounts. Yet the sympathies generated in the novel run counter to this message: Charlotte's outbursts are all connected with the very obvious injustices of a patriarchal legal and economic system which insistently disinherits women, a fact which suggests justifiable rage rather than madness as the cause of her behavior. In addition, despite extensive narrational laudation, the hero Frederick, who gains all the wealth in the end, does not appear in a particularly appealing light. Although his uncontrolled outbreak of anger is partly responsible for Adeline's death, within a very short time he is pledging his love to a less aristocratic and hence healthier, more dynastically suitable bride. Prudence and common sense might dictate that we approve and applaud his actions, in line with Victorian concerns with the "law of selection," but the romantic sympathy generated by the novel lies firmly with the two heroines, for whose respective incarceration and death he is in part responsible. Female madness or consumption, outward demonic excess, or angelic repression are, the book suggests, but two sides of the same coin: the only responses permitted to women under patriarchal oppression. And both are equally fatal.

While contemporary ideologies of motherhood formed one of the central concerns of the sensation novel, they never receive straightforward endorsement. Mrs Henry Wood's *East Lynne,* which has driven successive generations of readers and theatre-goers to their handkerchiefs, brought such narrative ambiguity to a fine art. The novel highlights the class-based assumptions of contemporary advice texts: bourgeois prudence and self-control is set against aristocratic excess, but, as in *St Martin's Eve,* the overt message of the novel seems to run counter to its sympathies. Isabel, the delicate, aristocratic heroine, represents, on the surface, the worst excesses of a degenerate upper-class lineage, revealing a uterine economy entirely out of control. The forces of sexual desire (painted initially in very graphic terms, but subsequently masked under the morally more acceptable explanation of marital jealousy) cause her to violate the sacred code of motherhood and abandon her bourgeois home, husband, and children for the aristocratic rake, Francis Levison. Another form of excess, however, this time of maternal feeling, drives her back (having luckily suffered severe disfigurement in the mean time so as to render her virtually unrecognizable) to take up the post of governess to her own children, and to watch her ex-husband bestowing the same endearments as in her own marriage on his new, bourgeois bride. In behavioral terms, Isabel thus conforms to the most extreme aspects of aristocratic indiscipline held up to middle-class women as a terrifying model of

immoral, socially degenerate conduct. Although the narrator is careful to stress Isabel's mistakes, her suffering, as the Victorian critics were quick to point out, seems nonetheless to elevate her spiritually. The more she sins, the more angelic she becomes.

The descriptions of Isabel's insensate maternal longings parallel those of Charlotte St John, but the weakness is viewed in a more sympathetic light. Once installed as governess, Isabel's passion for her children, which she is never able to suppress or restrain, is contrasted sharply with the bourgeois, wifely restraint of Barbara. While the aristocratic Isabel is depicted primarily as a sexual being and a mother, the middle-class Barbara is primarily a wife. The conflict between maternal and wifely roles in Victorian ideology is here refracted across class lines, revealing, in the process, the direct connections between bourgeois economic and domestic ideology. The economic values of regulation, order, and restraint are associated with the middle class and with wifely subservience, while the messier, physical aspects of maternity and sexual desire are connected with upper-class indiscipline. Yet the novel is by no means clear cut in its ideological allegiances. Its troubled responses to the question of good motherhood are revealed most clearly in a long lecture that Barbara gives to Isabel on the correct way for a mother to bring up her children.

According to Barbara, mothers should not keep their children constantly about them, or as some mistaken mothers do, "wash them, dress them, feed them; rendering themselves slaves, and the nurse's office a sinecure" (Wood 1984: 341). Indeed the physical, troublesome daily care of children should be devolved onto the nurse so as not to weary the mother, who will then be more fitted for her daily duty of gathering the children round for "higher purposes," to instill in them a sense of Christian and moral duty. If the mother is too much with the children, her moral authority is weakened and indiscipline arises: "The children run wild; the husband is sick of it, and seeks peace and solace elsewhere" (ibid.). Barbara's highly regulated and hierarchical version of wifehood takes the separation of moral and physical upbringing to an extreme, while placing the comfort of the husband to the fore. Perhaps surprisingly, Isabel concurs, her agreement standing as a tacit acknowledgment of her own mistakes: "Lady Isabel silently assented. Mrs Carlyle's views were correct" (ibid.).

Such agreement, however, is conspicuously withheld when Barbara enters onto the subject of breast-feeding, which is linked, significantly, with the question of maternal versus wifely priorities. Breast-feeding, she insists, must give way before the claims of her husband: "If I and Mr Carlyle have to be out in the evening baby gives way. I should never give up my husband for my baby; never, dearly as I love him" (ibid.: 343). Isabel's ominous silence confirms the view that the text is not willing to endorse this assertion of wifely duty over the physical claims of maternity. Indeed, despite Isabel's own earlier agreement to Barbara's maternal system, when set against Isabel's passionate excess it appears cold and unfeeling, too calculating. As we view with Isabel's eyes, so we participate in all her exquisite maternal torture. Regulation itself comes to appear almost unseemly. Although Isabel comes from a line of consumptive, spendthrift aristocrats, she has all the sympathy of romance lacking in the healthy, self-controlled bourgeois class (whose qualities are aped by the lower-class Afy—a debased Aphrodite—who also lives with Francis Levison, but without shame, and out of sheer self-interested calculation). Like angelic mothers, restrained bourgeois wives do not generate much narrative excitement or interest.

Similarly, Archibald Carlyle, the hero of the tale, has, like his counterpart in *St Martin's Eve,* an unappealing side. Not only does he take advantage of the Earl of Mount Severn's debts and illness to buy himself an aristocratic estate on the cheap, he also puts the demands of his business before thoughts of Isabel. There is clearly a fine line to be drawn between self-interested calculation and responsible management. Despite narratorial insistence to the contrary, bourgeois prudence is not the stuff from which romantic heroes are made.

The romantic structure of the tale vindicates the values of passion, both sexual and maternal, over the controlled calculation which defines the bourgeois world: "Let people talk as they will, it is impossible to drive out human passions from the human heart. You may suppress them, deaden them, keep them in subjection, but you cannot root them out" (ibid.: 496). While Wood speaks of the need for constant self-watchfulness to keep the passions in check, the novel actually stresses the uncontrollability of passion. Against contemporary ideological projections, Wood insists that true passion *cannot* be controlled; Isabel preserves, and indeed increases, her angelic status precisely because she is powerless to control the workings of both sexual and maternal desire. Her powerlessness thus aligns her with the "angelic" fallen sisterhood who were too womanly for their own good. Barbara, although initially given to sexual excess, learns to regulate her feelings and is rewarded with wifedom and the subsequent extinction of all independence or narrative interest in her personality.

The writings of the sensation novels offer a fascinating insight into the workings of Victorian maternal ideology. We find here, writ large, all the demonic figures and anxious preoccupations with heredity which filled contemporary medical texts and advice literature. Notions of hereditary taints abound, and of woman as outwardly fair and controlled, but inwardly the hidden source of corruption of both her class and race. Yet the very excess with which some of these traits are painted draws attention to their unstable foundations. The sensation novel took the demonic underside of the Victorian bourgeois male's imagination and turned it back upon itself. The pages are full of unregulated motherhood: women who abandon their children or destroy them through love, who lash out in excesses of both sexual and maternal emotion, overturning all domestic peace around them. Yet the true villains of the piece, despite the "safe" moral commentary offered by the narrators, tend to be the calculating and colorless males who pursue these women to their doom, a pursuit frequently tied to their own economic or social advantage. The novels expose the degree to which the demonization of the maternal body is linked to the regulatory, economic ideologies of the era, and the maintenance of bourgeois male dominance.

Notes

1. For further details see, for example, Jalland and Hooper (1986), Showalter (1985), and Shuttleworth (1990).

2. The case is also cited, for example, sixteen years later by Henry Maudsley (1867: 303).

3. Andrew Combe opens his treatise with the alarming facts of infant mortality based on statistical data culled from the *Annual Reports of Births, Deaths and Marriages* in England in 1842-3: "of all the children born alive in England, 14 per cent die within the first year, and 20 per cent within the first two years" (Combe 1854: 2). In this work Combe does not express any interest in the rate of maternal deaths in childbirth.

4. For further details on this point, and a more general discussion of Victorian responses to menstruation, see Shuttleworth (1990).

5. Although Victorian fears of masturbation were focused primarily on the male, frequent concern was also expressed about female "self-pollution." For a popular treatment, and description of symptoms, see Goss (1829: 59-66). A description of onanism as "a vampire feeding on the life-blood of its victims" is to be found in another very popular "quack" text (Perry 1854: 54).

Works Cited

Allan, J. M. (1869) "On the Differences in the Minds of Men and Women," *Journal of the Anthropological Society of London* 7, cited in P. Jalland and J. Hooper, *Women from Birth to Death. The Female Life Cycle in Britain 1830-1914,* Brighton: Harvester, 1986.

Anon. (1851) "Woman in her Psychological Relations," *Journal of Psychological Medicine and Mental Pathology* 4: 18-50.

Beeton, I. (1861) *The Book of Household Management* London: S. O. Beeton.

———. (1880?) *Beeton's Housewife's Treasury of Domestic Information* London: Ward, Lock & Co.

Buchan, W. (1809) *Advice to Mothers, on the Subject of their own Health; and the Means of Promoting the Health, Strength, and Beauty of their Offspring,* Boston: J. Bumstead. First published 1803.

Bucknill, J. C. and Tuke, D. H. (1874) *A Manual of Psychological Medicine* 3rd edn, London: J. & A. Churchill.

Bull, T. (1837) *Hints to Mothers for the Management of Health,* cited in P. Jalland and J. Hooper, *Women from Birth to Death. The Female Life Cycle in Britain 1830-1914,* Brighton: Harvester, 1986.

Carpenter, W. B. (1846) *A Manual of Physiology,* London: J. & A. Churchill.

Chavasse, P. H. (1864) *Advice to a Wife on the Management of her own Health; and on the Treatment of some of the Complaints Incidental to Pregnancy, Labour and Suckling,* London: J. Churchill. First published 1839.

Combe, A. (1854) *A Treatise on the Physiological and Moral Management of Infancy, being a Practical Exposition of the Principles of Infant Training for the Uses of Parents,* Edinburgh: Machlachlan & Stewart. First published 1840.

Conquest, J. T. (1848) *Letters to a Mother,* London: Longman & Co.

Ellis, S. Stickney (1838) *The Women of England, their Social Duties, and Domestic Habits,* London: Fisher, Son, & Co.

———. (1843a) *The Mothers of England, their Influence and Responsibility,* London: Fisher, Son, & Co.

———. (1843b) *The Wives of England, their Relative Duties, Domestic Influence, and Social Obligations,* London: Fisher, Son & Co.

Foucault, M. (1984) *The History of Sexuality, Vol. 1,* trans. R. Hurley, Harmondsworth: Penguin.

Goss & Co. (1829) *Hygeniana: a Non-Medical Analysis of the Complaints Incidental to Females, in which are Offered Important Admonitions on the Peculiar Debilities Attending their Circumstances, Sympathies and Formation,* London: Sherwood & Co.

Graham, T. J. (1853) *On the Management and Disorders of Infancy and Childhood,* London: Simpkin, Marshall & Co.

Greg, W. R. (1850) "Prostitution" (Review Article), *Westminster Review* 53: 448-506.

Jalland, P. and Hooper, J. (1986) *Women from Birth to Death. The Female Life Cycle in Britain 1830-1914,* Brighton: Harvester.

Maudsley, H. (1867) *The Physiology and Pathology of the Mind,* London: Macmillan.

Perry, R. and L. & Co. (1854) *The Silent Friend: a Practical Work, Treating on the Anatomy and Physiology of the Organs of Generation, and their Diseases, with Observations on Onanism and its Baneful Results,* London.

Reid, J. (1821) *Essays on Hypochondriasis and other Nervous Afflictions,* 2nd edn, London: Longman, Brown, Green & Longman.

Showalter, E. (1985) *The Female Malady: Women, Madness, and English Culture, 1830-1980,* New York: Pantheon.

Shuttleworth, S. (1990) "Female Circulation: Medical Discourse and Popular Advertising in the Mid-Victorian Era." in M. Jacobus, E. Fox Keller, and S. Shuttleworth (eds) *Body/Politics: Women and the Discourses of Science,* London: Routledge.

Trotter, T. (1812) *A View of the Nervous Temperament; being a Practical Enquiry into the Increasing Prevalence, Prevention, and Treatment of those Diseases,* 3rd edn, London: Longman, Brown, Green & Longman.

Warren, Mrs. (1865) *How I Managed my Children from Infancy to Marriage,* London: Houlston & Wright.

Wood, Mrs H. [Ellen]. (1905) *St Martin's Eve,* London: Macmillan. First published 1866.

———. (1984) *East Lynne,* New Brunswick, Rutgers University Press. First published 1861.

Eva Cherniavsky (essay date 1995)

SOURCE: Cherniavsky, Eva. "Revivification and Utopian Time: Poe versus Stowe." In *That Pale Mother Rising: Sentimental Discourses and the Imitation of Motherhood in 19th-Century America,* pp. 41-60. Bloomington: Indiana University Press, 1995.

[*In the following essay, Cherniavsky discusses sentimental discourse on motherhood, maternal love, and the utopian ideal of the "Good Christian Mother."*]

It is only the utopian in some archetypes that enables their fruitful citation when looking forward, not backward. That has already occurred in the apparent interlocking of the phantasmagorias and in the dissolution of that appearance. All those rationalisms concerning mothers, *as those who are still giving birth,* show a light shining in from utopia, even during romanticism with the yearning graves and underworld lantern. The particular brooding in archetypes, and especially that, shows their incompleteness.

—Ernst Bloch

Bloch's remark about mothers, appended apparently by way of example to a discussion of the utopian components in certain archetypes, puts several terms into play: on the one hand, something he calls "rationalisms" of motherhood, associated here with a "utopian light"; on the other hand, the "phantasmagorias," or archetypal images, of the gothic romance.[1] Bloch fails to elucidate this odd configuration of terms. But in the very linking of "rationalisms" to gothicism (incidental as the locution "even during" makes their historical relation appear), a useful (re)construction of his elliptical allusion to motherhood emerges. The development of the gothic as a cultural genre in the late eighteenth and early nineteenth centuries intersects with a specifically modern rationalization of motherhood, one that participates in the Enlightenment project of rationalizing the social body. In this construction of motherhood, as I have argued, the mother becomes the mediator of democratic social and political forms, the producer of the rational citizen. The identification of the white middle-class mother with the social, to which her legal and political visibility is sacrificed, arguably engenders the antithetical and complementary excesses of the gothic, the imagery of subterranean maternal presence, of the "yearning grave." This kinship, or historical convergence, of the rationalized and the phantasmatic, of the socially reproductive mother and the not quite (not sufficiently) dead occupant of the "yearning grave," reveals itself decisively in the discourse of sentimentalism, and its figuration of the Good Christian Mother, as one whose moral influence extends beyond the grave, affecting her children's actions long after she herself is dead.

But where is the "utopian" in the bourgeois mother's (re)production of the rational social body? I insist on the question because it concerns more than the coherence of a particular, cryptic example: Bloch's apparently casual reference to the utopian resonance of the mother's (re)productive role conceals the *centrality* of this maternal function to his conception of a "utopian drive," as he elaborates it throughout *The Utopian Function of Art and Literature*. In Bloch's definition, the utopian drive inheres in particular signifiers that contain in embryo the possibility, or prospect, of difference. The utopian signifier incorporates that which is alien to it, in the form of the not-yet-known, of its "not-worked-through, non-mythical surplus." This "surplus" remains in excess of the signifier's historically delimited meaning, of the false, or merely partial, consciousness this signifier articulates.[2] To cite the "utopian in some archetypes" is to decipher in the archetype a latent, or immanent, alterity. The utopian function is thus organized, or informed, by a metaphorics of gestation: the utopian signifier brings to term within itself the potential form of the other. The "rationalisms concerning mothers, *as those who are still giving birth*," bearing new forms of being within, in fact furnish the conceptual model of

the utopian drive; as Bloch conceives it, the "utopian function" is a function of the rationalized maternal body.

Bloch's model for the cultural production of utopia is itself the product of the "rationalisms concerning mothers" which he acknowledges here, but only as an *example* of utopian signification. More precisely, Bloch's model is the product of such "rationalisms" at their point of juncture with the gothic archetype of "the yearning grave," a juncture which I am proposing to locate in the discourse of sentimentalism. By designating this more or less classically Marxist model of cultural production as sentimental,[3] I mean to suggest that Marxist critical discourse reproduces the logic of bourgeois rationalism to the extent that it, too, discovers in the essentialized maternal body the condition of its own transhistorical elaboration.[4] At the same time, I want to (re)read sentimentalism in the frame of Bloch's analysis, as a utopian/political discourse, insofar as its figuration of the Good Christian Mother is pregnant with a radically other possibility. Unlike Bloch, however, I align the good Christian mother's alterity, not with the rationalisms that shed light into the gothic crypt, but with something that at once inhabits and exceeds the rational and the gothic planes of the mother's sentimental portrait. Sentimental discourse can be seen to lead a varied life, as a "rationalism concerning mothers," operating in the service of a rationalized social and political order; as a (gothic) mythology of motherhood, which only reproduces the logic of a rationalized maternity; and finally, as the utopian, or "non-mythical surplus," of the sentimental portrait, where the "incompleteness" of the Good Christian Mother, and of the rational social order, is made legible.

To locate the "non-mythological surplus" of the white middle-class mother in the culture of nineteenth-century democracy is to see, not just beyond her domestication, but beyond her highly *mythologized* excess. The mythologized surplus of bourgeois motherhood arguably finds its privileged articulation in psychoanalysis, which takes up Bloch's rational/gothic binary, to insist both on the mother's absence (her lack) within the social (oedipal motherhood) and on her haunting anteriority (pre-oedipal motherhood). Inasmuch as the utopian component of sentimental motherhood is immanent within, but not reducible to, the imagery of the "yearning grave," however, it is also not reducible to the psychoanalytic decoding of the "yearning grave" as womb, as the edenic space of the mother-infant dyad. The point is that the preoedipal, or pretextual, mother embodies that which is constitutively absent in the speaking subject. To *represent* the preoedipal mother, one must be *outside* the dyadic enclosure, so that the representation of maternal origins signifies their loss. While Bloch's utopian prospect is there in what one says, un- or underheard, but always (potentially) enlightening, the maternal body, conceived as origin, is what is *not* there insofar as one is in a position to say anything at all.[5]

In fact, sentimental narrative frequently figures the mother as either dead or dying; she is the iconic absence in and of the sentimental narrative, the cameo, the memory, the deeply affecting, compulsively reproduced image of one who is, literally and symbolically, not of this world. And indelible memory, she haunts her progeny with the recollection of an infantile bliss, marked by her perfectly loving (angelic) presence. The "yearning" of this encrypted mother is socially (re)productive, in the sense that her memory imparts to (recuperates for) the individuated subject a feeling of integrity. In its alignment of rational and gothic motherhood, sentimental discourse offers this insight into democratic sociality: that the domestic angel best accomplishes her mission from the grave, insofar as she is always already a presence under erasure. This sentimental economy of motherhood comes nicely into focus in Margaret Fuller's construction of the mother as moral influence.

> Man is of Woman born, and her face bends over him in infancy with an expression he can never quite forget. Eminent men have delighted to pay tribute to this image. . . . The rudest tar brushes off a tear with his coat-sleeve at the hallowed name. . . . Some gleams of the same expression which shone down upon his infancy, angelically pure and benign, visit Man again with hopes of pure love, of a holy marriage. Or, if not before, in the eyes of the mother of his child they again are seen, and dim fancies pass before his mind, that Woman may not have been born for him alone, but have come from heaven, a commissioned soul, a messenger of truth and love; that she can only make for him a home in which he may lawfully repose, in so far as she is "True to the kindred points of Heaven and home."
>
> In gleams, in dim fancies, this thought visits the mind of common men. It is soon obscured by the mists of sensuality, the dust of routine, and he thinks it was only some meteor or ignis fatuus that shone. But as a Rosicrucian lamp, it burns unwearied, though condemned to the solitude of tombs.[6]

In a first moment, the mother here embodies the possibility of pre- or non-symbolic "expression"; her face, and metonymically her body, is itself a communication, so replete with meaning for the supine infant that its "message" never fully ceases. In Fuller's mythology, the originary maternal body is naturally or essentially significant—discloses its meanings without recourse to the order of signifiers. But remembering the mother's body, its mute and ineffable "expression," the sentimental "tar" only registers its loss—pays nostalgic tribute to a "hallowed *name*." More precisely, the remembered maternal body in this passage is divested of anything that might mark its "expression" as the mother's own:

maternal "expression" becomes the medium of the normative social imagination. Thus the mother's face is now "commissioned," made the bearer of another's message, the purveyor of the Father's truth, casting the sanction of divine authority on the domestic realm. From this perspective, the memory of his dead mother recalls her son to the "truth and love" of paternal law, the benignity of moral limits.

But if on one level, her son's evolving relation to the symbolic determines the mother's status (she is the subject's origin, and not herself a subject), on another level the mother Fuller envisions is something more, or something potentially other, than a recollected "expression" or a "hallowed name." Fuller's unforgettable mother is (also) a *visitation*, a spectral presence, a thing—a possibility—external to the son's psychic and corporeal boundaries. More exactly, this luminous mother is at once internal to the structures of the filial subject (a projection; a mere hallucination), and irreducibly other (an actual ghost). Positioned ambiguously within and without the son's psychic economy, Fuller's spectral mother erodes this limit, to expose the rational subject of democratic representation as a contingent entity, constituted within a complexly intersubjective field.

A "non-mythological surplus" arises from Fuller's portrait of the sentimental mother, something that inhabits but also (prospectively) derationalizes the maternal. A figure emerges in this portrait too present to be identified with the original/pretextual mother (symbolically constituted as absent), and too sensational, too invasive with respect to masculine corporeal boundaries to be identified with the iconic mother (whose remembered "expression" underwrites the integrity of the individuated subject). Rather this emergent figure occupies the fissure between these two mythologized positions, between the pre-rational mother and the domestic angel, and thereby "anticipates," to use Bloch's term, the potential difference of a maternal *subject*. It is not the mother's position in excess of the social and symbolic order—in the Eden of a lost expressiveness—that opens up a utopian perspective in Fuller's portrait of motherhood, but rather the mother's (spectral) existence in the present tense of historical time. This (re)animated mother, arisen from the grave, denaturalizes both prerational motherhood (that which is excluded from the social), and domesticated motherhood (that which embodies the social as affect).

If the formulas and set pieces of sentimental fiction are charged with a "non-mythological surplus," their "immanent alterity" arguably finds its expression in the weeping reader. The readers' dissolution in tears of sympathy not only maintains connection to what is lost, but also anticipates the dissolution of a rational subjectivity. Their weeping marks the readers' wordless recognition of the underheard alternative, of a purely prospective yet already affecting difference. Despite what sentimental authors liked to imagine, however, susceptibility to the portrait of ideal motherhood failed to transcend social divisions. In the figure of "the rudest tar," the wizened old sailor moved to tears at his mother's name, Fuller subtly argues for (by celebrating) the universally affecting qualities of sentimental motherhood. But the actual "rudest tar" was most likely no sentimentalist; sentimentalism is a race- and class-bound discourse, grounded in domestic ideology and middle-class family structures. As Christine Stansell has shown, for instance, the working-class women—whom the middle-class consumers of sentimental fiction periodically undertook to redeem—easily intuited that the discourse of sentimentalism couched as Christian charity what remained in fact a mission of "social domination."[7] While the tear of sympathy was *not* the glue that healed all social divisions, that bound together all races and classes, as sentimentalists sometimes sought to claim—while sentimentalism could indeed be made to serve egregiously racist and classist polemics (often in the very rhetoric with which it espoused such causes as abolition)—nevertheless sentimentalism does not reduce to a univocal affirmation of middle-class ideologies.[8]

Interestingly, the sentimental authors' claim for the socially leveling effect of sentimental writing reappears in the lament of modern mass culture critics, such as Ann Douglas, for whom the popularity of the sentimental novel marks a leveling of discursive forms, a "feminization" of United States culture.[9] But strangely, what turns out to have been "feminized," as this argument goes, is not the "high" cultural domain that is traditionally gendered masculine, but a popular discourse *conventionally* associated with effusion and excess. Sentimental fiction's mass circulation thus appears restricted, conveniently, to the "masses" and the masculine preserve of "high" culture, though marginalized, remains intact. If sentimentalism is a feminized discourse, it neither successfully colonizes the entire field of popular culture, nor does it entirely fail to colonize the imagination of a literary elite, composed of white middle- and upper-class male writers. Poe as well as Stowe writes the discourse of sentimentalism—even if, as I aim to show, the politics of "revivification" elide the utopian perspective onto which (re)animation opens.

POE'S "HIDEOUS DRAMA"

The tale of Ligeia's resurrection, her reincarnation in the body of another, represents, in the narrator's own words, "a hideous drama of revivification," hideous in the insistence of Ligeia's demand for life, a demand articulated in the corporeal idiom of the flush and the tremor, and in the resistance of Rowena's frame to these incursions of being.

> At length it became evident that a slight, a very feeble, and barely noticeable tinge of color had flushed up

within the cheeks, and along the sunken small veins of the eyelids. Through a species of unutterable horror and awe, for which the language of mortality has no sufficiently energetic expression, I felt my heart cease to beat, my limbs grow rigid where I sat. . . . In a short period it was certain, however, that a relapse had taken place; the color disappeared from both eyelid and cheek, leaving a wanness even more than that of marble; the lips became doubly shrivelled and pinched up in the ghastly expression of death; a repulsive clamminess and coldness rapidly overspread the surface of the body. . . . But why shall I minutely detail the unspeakable horrors of that night? Why shall I pause to relate how, time after time, until near the period of the gray dawn, this hideous drama of revivification was repeated; how each terrific relapse was only into a sterner and apparently more irredeemable death; how each agony wore the aspect of a struggle with some invisible foe; and how each struggle was succeeded by I know not what of wild changes in the personal appearance of the corpse?[10]

A twin horror shapes the narrator's sensations in this final section of "Ligeia," the horror of the corpse itself, of its cold and clammy flesh, a horror rehearsed, intensified with every reenactment of death, and the horror of its revivification, of a self-induced resurgence of being—a demand for life complicit with the narrator's longing, yet dangerously and appallingly alien. Even before Rowena's shroud comes undone to reveal Ligeia's distinctive features, the telltale "vehemence of desire for life," which the narrator earlier attributed to the dying Ligeia, informs the drama of revivification. Vehement desire thus betrays Ligeia's part in this drama prior to the body's actual unveiling. If from the first the narrator, like the reader, must intuit Ligeia's return, recognize in the transformations of Rowena's corpse Ligeia's indelible will to live, his intuition only accentuates the spectacle's horrific nature. In fact, it is exactly because the narrator discerns Ligeia's agency in the antics of Rowena's corpse that his own will is suspended, that the symptoms of life in the corpse produce in the teller of this tale the very symptoms of death. This relation of mutual exclusion, in which the masculine narrator cannot sustain his identity *vis-à-vis* an inflated feminine presence, is the hallmark of sentimentalism in its masculine (or elite cultural) inflection—as read and reproduced by a class of male writers who dissociate their own literary practice from that of contemporary women novelists. "Ligeia" is the narrative of sentimental motherhood told from the vantage of a rationalized masculinity, of a son whose desire for an impossible return *to* the original maternal body matches only his terror of that other possibility, that the maternal would *come (back) to him*. Inasmuch as the maternal origin figures as the site of a pre-symbolic complementarity, the fantasy of *the mother*'s return, of her eruption in the symbolic, is about the loss of origins in a radically different sense—about the denaturalization of the maternal body, released from pre-history into historical time, about the irreducible contingency of the masculine subject who seeks his wholeness in the m/other. The "lost" mother's return places us beyond the fetishizing double vision of mother-as-whole, mother-as-lack; the mother cannot return as what she was (as pre-symbolic unity), and having reappeared, will no longer reduce to what she is not, to (her) lack. The mother's (re)animation "gives birth" to the very thing that the phantasm of maternal origins functions to erase—namely, the mother as historical subject.

Kaja Silverman offers a particularly compelling account of how the maternal subject disappears in/from classic psychoanalytic discourse and thus by extension, I would argue, from the bourgeois cultural imaginary: "[T]he child's discursive exteriority—its emergence from the maternal enclosure—can be established only by placing the mother herself inside that enclosure, by relegating her to the interior of [Julia Kristeva's term for this enclosure] the *chora,* or—what is the same thing—by stripping her of all linguistic capabilities."[11] Thus, Silverman suggests, the positions of the mother and of her infant are conflated. Because in the psychoanalytic account of subject formation the child's *separation from* the mother inaugurates his *relation to* the symbolic, the mother's *own* relation to language is distorted. Rather than an individuated being, herself inserted in the symbolic order, whose body assumes specific affective dimensions *for her infant,* the mother is identified with the *space* of the maternal itself, with the space of infantile dependence and verbal incapacity. In this frame, the son's yearning to return to the origin, to the "maternal enclosure," may be read less as a desire for phantasmatic connection, a recuperation of the complementarity of self and (m)other, than as an extension of the desire for autonomy. Inasmuch as the mother assumes the infant's incompetence, the son's phantasmatic return to the maternal enclosure is less a fantasy of his own regression/unmaking, than an elaboration of his mastery: the son's "return" to the maternal origin can only terminate in a recapitulation of the mother's interiorization. In the fantasy of return, the son disavows, less his own position as a differentiated subject, than his mother's. Conversely, the "lost" mother's (re)animation (re)inscribes her in history, (re)instates her as a subject in and of discourse—neither in excess of, nor (therefore) at the limit of the social. If the originary mother embodies the beyond of the social (subject), the (re)animated mother displaces this beyond, and thus opens the utopian perspective where the contingency of existing social relations becomes visible.

The utopian perspective in Poe's "Ligeia" is as fragile and elusive as the status of Rowena's body is undecidable: as a masculinist discourse, sentimentalism at once opens and forecloses on the possibility of the mother's return. On the one hand, the masculine narrator represents himself in a more or less permanent state of psy-

chosis. The "chamber" he inhabits with Rowena and after her death is itself a Western phantasm of "oriental" luxury and decay, so that it remains finally uncertain whether the room actually exists as anything more than a projection of inner space. Likewise, Ligeia herself, as the figure whose loss this luxury both replaces and commemorates, is plausibly understood as a merely hallucinated presence in the room. On the other hand, when he reports his addiction to opium, his proneness to delusion, to the "waking visions of Ligeia" in which he indulges while sitting watch over Rowena's corpse, the narrator demonstrates a rationalist's skepticism concerning the reliability of his own senses. This conscientious acknowledgment of his impaired condition no less plausibly attests to the narrator's rationality, to his unimpeded capacity for self-evaluation, for distinguishing between "the waking vision" and the actual thing. By interrogating his own authority, the narrator underwrites the other possibility—that the sounds and motions from the bed, which have every appearance of *interrupting* his "revery," do in fact emanate from Ligeia herself.

Significantly, commentators on the tale, few in number and remarkably peremptory in their approach, bracket this carefully cultivated irresolution and subsume/subordinate Ligeia to the narrator in the most reductive and monological ways. Thus John Irwin, for instance, asserts that Ligeia is "a Psyche-figure for the narrator," a reading he derives, as far as textual evidence goes, solely from her description in the tale as a person of "gigantic volition."[12] On the contrary, Donald Pease identifies Ligeia with a primal loss, with an ineffable "something" the narrator no longer possesses: "[I]n such tales as 'Ligeia,' 'Morella,' and 'Berenice' . . . [Poe] created settings where fallen nobility could recover relation with someone or something lost."[13] The narrators of these tales "displace their present world by acting according to the demands of an archaic and infinitely more powerful past."[14] For Irwin, then, Ligeia's "gigantic volition" is identified with the masculine authorial voice, while for Pease, Ligeia's power is archaic, confined to the narrator's prelapsarian past, and hence no threat to his present discursive mastery.

Ironically, while neither Pease nor Irwin read the figure of Ligeia as a mother, they assign her a mother's destiny in democracy's rationalized symbolic order; she is either invisible (a manifestation of the narrator himself), or irretrievable (belongs to the narrator's pre-history).[15] But it is this destiny, precisely, and this order, that "Ligeia" ambiguously contests *and* (re)affirms. Certainly, the narrator's reminiscences of Ligeia, and of his relation to her, insist on her pre-textual status, and so on her necessary inscription as loss. Thus the narrator's enervated diction, his obsessively refined style of portraiture—the plainly feigned naïveté with which he aspires to a mimetic perfection that the very self-consciousness of this discursive posture undermines—functions to evacuate Ligeia from the site of her representation.

> In beauty of face no maiden ever equalled her. It was the radiance of an opium-dream—an airy and spirit-lifting vision more wildly divine than the phantasies which hovered about the slumbering souls of the daughters of Delos. Yet her features were not of that regular mould which we have been falsely taught to worship in the classical labors of the heathen. "There is no exquisite beauty," says Bacon, Lord Verulam, speaking truly of all the forms and *genera* of beauty, "without some strangeness in the proportion." [. . .] It might have been too that in these eyes of my beloved lay the secret to which Lord Verulam alludes. They were, I must believe, far larger than the ordinary eyes of our own race. . . . The "strangeness," however, which I found in the eyes was of a nature distinct from the formation, or the color, or the brilliancy of the features, and must, after all, be referred to the *expression*. Ah, word of no meaning! behind whose vast latitude of mere sound we intrench our ignorance of so much of the spiritual.
>
> ("LG" 176-78)

In the first moment of this portrait, Ligeia's physical beauty negates her materiality, as though perfection of form could only exist in the insubstantial medium of the vision, in the fluid dimensions of imaginary space. And while beauty in this initial moment still refers to form—Bacon's "strangeness" rests in proportions—the narrator ultimately deploys Bacon's aesthetic to locate Ligeia's beauty in what altogether exceeds her material "formation," in her "*expression*." Having transmuted Ligeia's beauty into a beauty of "*expression*," moreover, the narrator ambiguously registers the loss, abruptly empties her "*expression*" of its meaning, so that this signifier of excess, of *an excess* which still assumed at the outset a certain material specificity, becomes a cipher—the signifier of that which remains *in excess of* signification. Thus Poe, like Fuller, invests in the "expression" of a mother's face, with the fine if poignant distinction that what was in Fuller's portrait an "expression" replete with original presence becomes in Poe's a "vast latitude" of absence—an "expression" always already emptied of meaning.

But the essential significance Fuller associates with the mother attaches to Poe's Ligeia as well. As a body in excess of meaning, Ligeia becomes the repository of *all* meaning—the body of the signifiable itself:

> I have spoken of the learning of Ligeia: it was immense—such as I have never known in woman. In the classical tongues was she deeply proficient. . . . Indeed upon any theme of the most admired because simply the most abstruse of the boasted erudition of the Academy, have I *ever* found Ligeia at fault? [. . .] I said her knowledge was such as I have never known in woman—but where breathes the man who has tra-

versed, and successfully, *all* the wide areas of moral, physical, and mathematical science? I saw not then what I now clearly perceive, that the acquisitions of Ligeia were gigantic, were astounding; yet I was sufficiently aware of her infinite supremacy to resign myself, with a child-like confidence, to her guidance through the chaotic world of metaphysical investigation at which I was most busily occupied during the earlier years of our marriage. . . . Without Ligeia I was but as a child groping benighted.

> ("LG" 180-81)

Ligeia is thus coextensive with the space through which this "child-like" narrator moves "benighted"; she "traverse[s]," or spans, a universe that he merely inhabits. In the frame of her "gigantic acquisitions," moreover, the figure of Ligeia herself begins to elude us, as all possible articulations of her "gigantic volition" seem *a priori* exhausted. Ligeia vanishes in the face of her own "infinite supremacy," of an unboundedness that is the negation of her subjectivity, a plenitude that leaves no room for her partiality, for her voice. Instead, it is the figure of the narrator whom we distinguish, projecting himself down the "all untrodden path" of a strangely vacant "vista":

> With how vast a triumph—with how vivid a delight—with how much of all that is ethereal in hope—did I *feel*, as she bent over me in studies but little sought—but less known—that delicious vista by slow degrees expanding before me, down whose long, gorgeous, and all untrodden path, I might at length pass onward to the goal of a wisdom too divinely precious not to be forbidden.
>
> ("LG" 180)

In this pre-symbolic realm, where learning is encoded in sensory rather than discursive registers (knowledge is felt), the figure of the mother dissolves; less a guide, or interlocutor, than an environment, she is the matrix of a masculine proto-subject—of a not-yet-subject already invested here, however, with the social and discursive primacy of the normative (white middle-class) adult male.

Inasmuch as these maternal origins inform/are informed by a masculine subjectivity elaborated at the mother's expense, the imposition of paternal law remains a narrative inevitability. The crisis of Ligeia's loss assumes conventionally oedipal dimensions: thus death acquires a phallic shape in the verses of Poe's "Conqueror Worm"—which the narrator attributes to Ligeia in Poe's revision of the tale—while the dying Ligeia's frantic invocation of the Father on hearing her poem recited confirms the bearing of paternal authority on this narrative outcome. However, to the primal horror of the phallic worm's incursion ("But see, amid the mimic rout / A crawling shape intrude! / A blood-red thing that writhes from out / The scenic solitude!"), Ligeia responds with a rage ambiguously plaintive and admonitory in quality, at once providing and contesting the recognition of paternal ascendancy that this patriarchal God appears to exact:

> "Oh God!" half shrieked Ligeia, leaping to her feet and extending her arms aloft with a spasmodic movement, as I made an end to these lines—"Oh God! O Divine Father!—shall these things be undeviatingly so?—shall this conqueror be not once conquered?"
>
> ("LG" 183)

Ligeia's question is none the more answerable for being ostensibly rhetorical in nature; inasmuch as it solicits an unequivocal response, it asks for the resolution that this narrative drama of revivification defers. In its undecidability, Poe's "Ligeia" does not so much unravel as simply threaten to unravel the logic of democratic representation. To replace the socially unplaced figure of Ligeia—the narrator notes early in the tale that he never learned her "paternal name"—he purchases a bride whose title resonates with all the fine distinctions of social class, the "Lady Rowena Trevanion, of Tremaine." It is to Rowena's paternally inscribed body that Ligeia so dramatically, yet inconclusively, lays siege.

STOWE'S AUTHENTIC GHOST

In the chapters of *Uncle Tom's Cabin* set on Simon Legree's plantation, Poe's drama of revivification is rescripted to accommodate the possibility which "Ligeia" at once envisions and negates, the possibility, that is, of the lost mother's (re)animation—as an articulate, material presence. In assigning material existence to the spectral mother whose status Poe carefully refuses to determine, Stowe effectively divorces presence from identity: the possibility of the spectral mother's realization in the text hinges on the *non-identity* of her avatars, rather than on the congruence of her manifestations over time. In Stowe's initial account of Legree's "pale mother," whose silent image rises up to haunt his nights, the maternal spectre is the trace of a morality Legree suppresses, the indelible mark of maternal love on the reprobate soul. Like Poe's Ligeia, she is ambiguously the externalization of filial dread/desire, terrifying Legree with the *promise* of a coming retribution, and a figure irreducibly other to him, whose (re)appearance *effects* his psychic/corporeal dissolution. But what follows sets Stowe's narrative apart from Poe's, and foils the normative psychoanalytic understanding of the maternal body (as a lost origin(al)) that Poe's tale at least ambiguously supports. Perceiving the effect of his mother's influence on the otherwise implacable Legree, his black slave Cassy schemes to impersonate the spectre; draping herself in white, she (re)invests the dead white mother with life. Since Stowe designates as "an authentic ghost story" this travesty of white motherhood, in this episode of the novel at least, the Good Christian

Mother's authenticity comes to rest squarely on her difference from her prior incarnations. Legree's mother returns in a hybrid body, constituted in an articulation of affective motherhood and commodified reproduction. In claiming strategic possession of the white woman's spectral existence, Cassy engenders a non/white maternal subject, neither inside nor outside the order of democratic representation, but rather at the limit where this binary logic fails.

In contrast to Poe's narrator, whose terror of the mother's return is in direct proportion to his yearning for a return to the mother, Legree's distinction is his absolute lack of nostalgia for the maternal enclosure, an early and eager acquiescence in paternal law that results, paradoxically, in his repudiation of normative social forms—of the Father's (maternally mediated) message.

> Hard and reprobate as the godless man seemed now, there had been a time when he had been rocked on the bosom of a mother,—cradled with prayers and pious hymns,—his now seared brow bedewed with the waters of holy baptism. . . . Far in New England that mother had trained her only son, with long, unwearied love and patient prayers. Born of a hard-tempered sire, on whom that gentle woman had wasted a world of unvalued love, Legree had followed in the steps of his father . . . and at an early age, broke from her, to seek his fortunes at sea.[16]

What may appear by the standard of the realist novel as Stowe's flimsy characterization of Legree's innate evil points in another sense to the irrelevance of filial sentiment in the face of a structuring mythology of the masculine subject. As in Fuller's portrait, maternal love finds its expression in the pre-symbolic idiom of the essential maternal body, as it rocks and cradles the infant son. Here as well, the mother's presence reduces almost instantly to affect, operating in the service of a patriarchal authority. Legree is "cradled with prayers and pious hymns" to his heavenly Father. What distinguishes Legree from Fuller's sailor is not a respect for the paternal that leads him to follow in his earthly father's steps, but rather his failure to sentimentalize his mother's loss, to honor their affective tie. Legree is an unnatural son because he makes visible and violent the break which founds the rational subject.[17]

Legree's susceptibility to his dead mother's haunting appearance suggests the structural function of maternal love in the economy of rational subjectivity. Maternal love can be rejected as well as embraced, but never escaped. The point is that for the indifferent son, no less than for his feeling counterpart, the relation to the mother (as origin) is inescapably a relation to (the ground of) their own social subjectivity. From this perspective, the novel develops a utopian resonance at precisely the juncture where it seems most to lapse into banality:

[Having opened a letter in which his dying mother encloses as a keepsake a lock of her golden hair] Legree burned the hair, and burned the letter; and when he saw them hissing and crackling in the flame, inly shuddered as he thought of everlasting fires. He tried to drink, and revel, and swear away the memory; but often, in the deep night, whose solemn stillness arraigns the bad soul in forced communion with herself, he had seen that pale mother rising by his bedside, and felt the soft twining of that hair around his fingers, till the cold sweat would roll down his face, and he would spring from his bed in horror. Ye who have wondered to hear, in the same evangel, that God is love, and that God is consuming fire, see ye not how, to the soul resolved in evil, perfect love is the most fearful torture, the seal and sentence of the direst despair?

(*UTC* 529)

Legree cannot swear away the memory of maternal love because maternal affect mediates his relation to himself—or, in Stowe's religious teleology, to his soul. As the projection of an internal (social) limit, Legree's dead mother recalls him to himself (and to the impending consequences of his moral failing). At the same time, in the fact of the son's psychic and corporeal disarticulation, this passage registers the possibility of the mother's return: shocked past control of his body's functions, Legree breaks out in cold sweat and leaps up in inarticulate horror. His mother's appearance is ambiguously the occasion of Legree's reconstitution and decomposition as an accountable subject.

This is the scene into which Cassy inserts herself. Witness to his frenzy at the sight of little Eva's blond locks, which Legree's overseers have snatched from Tom and dutifully delivered to their master, Cassy infers the cause of Legree's terror and turns it to her own advantage. Concealing herself beneath a plain white sheet, she slips into his room by night; and when this visitation has reduced him to an impotent and inarticulate state, Cassy and her daughter substitute Emmeline, a young slave she has determined to protect from Legree's sexual advances, walk away from the plantation unmolested. Significantly, however, Cassy's affinity for the part of Legree's mother hinges for Stowe on the "influence" she already commands over Legree, an influence in turn attributed to Cassy's specifically verbal instability.

> The influence of Cassy over him was of a strange and singular kind. He was her owner, her tyrant and tormentor. . . . When he first bought her, she was, as she said, a woman delicately bred; and then he crushed her, without scruple, beneath the foot of his brutality. But, as time, and debasing influences, and despair, hardened womanhood within her, she had become in a measure his mistress, and he alternately tyrannized over and dreaded her. This influence had become more harassing and decided, since partial insanity had given *a strange, weird, unsettled cast to all her words and language.*

(*UTC* 567, emphasis added)

In this section of the novel, Stowe curiously falsifies the history of Cassy's "partial insanity" as Cassy herself tells it to Uncle Tom. In Cassy's rendition, Legree is only the last in a chain of abusive masters who have "crushed her, without scruple" in pursuit of their own interests. A lovely "quadroon," born of a white father and his black concubine and raised in luxury, Cassy's first episode of abandoned rage is directed at the master who sells off her children despite her careful negotiations to prevent it, and thus finally imparts to Cassy what her history of relative privilege had kept partially from view: her displacement from the social-symbolic order as commodity, which renders any legal, emotional or conventional claim to her children unintelligible. Cassy's "unsettled" language marks her liminal relation to an order in which to speak as a black mother is to *mean* nothing at all. As though reluctant to acknowledge the connection between the black mother's grief, her painfully acquired knowledge of her own social death, and her "unsettled" language, Stowe suddenly condenses a history that elsewhere she finds useful to develop.

To trace the genesis of Cassy's "unsettled" language in the frame of this elaborated history is to reverse Stowe's emphasis in the edited account she offers us here: in this frame, Cassy's lapse from the discourse of normative femininity and Good Christian Motherhood—a discourse unavailable as a mode of self-signification to the captive African-American mother—is less the point than Cassy's capacity to *enter into* this discourse, to address Legree in the essentially maternal idiom of "influence."

> It was a cloudy, misty moonlight, and there [Legree] saw it!—something white, gliding in! He heard the still rustle of its ghostly garments. It stood still by his bed;—a cold hand touched his; a voice said, three times, in a low fearful whisper "Come! come! come!" And, while he lay sweating with terror, he knew not when or how, the thing was gone. He sprang out of bed, and pulled at the door. It was shut and locked, and the man fell down in a swoon. After this, Legree became a harder drinker than ever before. . . . There were reports around the country, soon after, that he was sick and dying. Excess had brought on that frightful disease that *seems to throw the lurid shadows of a coming retribution back into the present life.*

(*UTC* 596, emphasis added)

Cassy not only performs (white) motherhood, she recodes it as a performative identity, a matter of style, of body surfaces. If in Stowe's abolitionist polemic black mothers are just like white mothers beneath the skin, essentially the same, Cassy's performance relocates white motherhood itself in the register of imitation. On the non/white body of the white-appearing slave, white motherhood is authenticated as a likeness, a repetition rather than an originary function. Sentimentalism expires here in the shoddy trappings and crude devices of a haunting that in the very banality of its artifice abdicates a mythologized essence and reveals the utopian remainder: a deadly command to which the vanquished master submits. No longer the mother's property, "excess" transfers to the son; remarkably, it is *Cassy* who marks the *white man*'s body with a condition "too frightful" to name.

Sheathed in white, Cassy's face marks the site where maternal "expression" goes blank. And while this non/ white figure has no destination in Stowe's narrative, she is equally impossible to efface. Notwithstanding Stowe's desire to redomesticate Cassy, to position her in the reconstituted familial sphere to which the freed black women in this novel accede, she remains beyond Stowe's power to recall. Seeking to reinscribe Cassy's face with the tender expression of white motherhood, Stowe arranges the unlikely reunion of Cassy with her daughter, who turns out to be none other than the heroic slave mother Eliza:

> Eliza's steady, consistent piety, regulated by the constant reading of the sacred word, made her a proper guide for the shattered and wearied mind of her mother. Cassy yielded at once, and with her whole soul, to every good influence, and became a devout and tender Christian.
>
> (*UTC* 607)

Despite if not *because* of this frantic recuperation, the figure of Cassy remains in Bloch's sense "incomplete," shattered. She sits askew in these scenes of domestic resolution that conclude the novel, a "strange, unsettled" presence, marking time on a utopian calendar.

Notes

1. Ernst Bloch, *The Utopian Function of Art and Literature*, 121.

2. Ernst Bloch, 120.

3. For a complementary discussion of Walter Benjamin and the gendering of history, see chapter 4 [in *That Pale Mother Rising*].

4. Thus I read the notable obscurity of Bloch's phrasing in this passage as the mark of his disavowal. Bloch blinds himself to the historical specificity of his critical practice at the very moment he is poised to acknowledge it.

5. It is helpful to compare Bloch's formulation of the utopian, as the "non-mythological surplus" of particular cultural signifiers, with Julia Kristeva's notion of the maternal, as a "heterogeneity that cannot be subsumed in the signifier" (Kristeva, "Stabat Mater," 259). For Bloch, unlike Kristeva, the utopian/maternal *inhabits* specific cultural codes, as a possibility historically *intrinsic* to them.

6. Fuller, *Women in the Nineteenth Century*, 49-51.

7. Stansell, *City of Women*, 66.

8. While I agree, then, with Hazel Carby's assertion that "the conventions of True Womanhood" serve to uphold a "racist, ideological system" (Carby, *Reconstructing Womanhood*, 50), I suggest that the discourse of sentimentalism is not finally *reducible* to the discourse of True Womanhood, though it does, certainly, *participate* in its fundamentally racist and classist assumptions. However, the extent to which nineteenth century African-American writers could appropriate and radically *reconfigure* sentimental narrative models argues for sentimentalism's dialogical structures.

9. Douglas, *The Feminization of American Culture*, passim.

10. Poe, "Ligeia," 190-92. Hereafter cited as "LG."

11. Silverman, *The Acoustic Mirror*, 105.

12. Irwin, *American Hieroglyphics*, 227.

13. Pease, *Visionary Compacts*, 189.

14. Ibid., 190.

15. With the notable exception of Daniel Hoffman, none of Poe's critics have remarked Ligeia's maternal characteristics. While Hoffman acknowledges Ligeia's function as "Mother-Figure" in the tale, he situates the narrator's relation to her within a strictly oedipal frame. The narrator's "problem," in Hoffman's analysis, turns out to be *Poe*'s impotence.

16. Stowe, *Uncle Tom's Cabin*, 528. Hereafter cited as *UTC*.

17. Interpreted in this way, Legree's violence should remind us of Margaret Homans's revisionist claim: "The symbolic order is founded, not merely on the regrettable loss of the mother, but on her active and overt murder" (Homans, *Bearing the Word*, 11).

Works Cited

Bloch, Ernst. *The Utopian Function of Art and Literature*. Trans. Jack Zipes and Frank Mecklenburg. Cambridge, Mass.: MIT Press, 1988.

Carby, Hazel V. *Reconstructing Womanhood: The Emergence of the Afro-American Novelist*. Oxford: Oxford University Press, 1987.

Douglas, Ann. *The Feminization of American Culture*. New York: Avon, 1978.

Fuller, Margaret. *Woman in the Nineteenth Century*. New York: Norton, 1971.

Hoffman, Daniel. *Poe Poe Poe Poe Poe Poe Poe*. Garden City, N.Y.: Doubleday, 1972.

Homans, Margaret. *Bearing the Word: Language and Female Experience in Nineteenth Century Women's Writing*. Chicago: University of Chicago Press, 1986.

Irwin, John. *American Hieroglyphics*. Baltimore: Johns Hopkins University Press, 1983.

Kristeva, Julia. "Stabat Mater." In *Tales of Love*. Trans Leon S. Roudiez. New York: Columbia University Press, 1987.

Pease, Donald. *Visionary Compacts: American Renaissance Writing in Cultural Context*. Madison: University of Wisconsin Press, 1987.

Poe, Edgar Allan. "Ligeia." In *Great Short Works of Edgar Allan Poe*. New York: Harper & Row, 1970.

Silverman, Kaja. *The Acoustic Mirror: The Female Voice in Psychoanalysis and Cinema*. Bloomington: Indiana University Press, 1988.

Stansell, Christine. *City of Women: Sex and Class in New York, 1789-1860*. Urbana: University of Illinois Press, 1987.

Stowe, Harriet Beecher. *Uncle Tom's Cabin*. New York: Penguin, 1981.

Lisa Hopkins (essay date 2002)

SOURCE: Hopkins, Lisa. "'A Medea, in More Senses than the More Obvious One': Motherhood in Mary Shelley's *Lodore* and *Falkner*." *The Eighteenth-Century Novel* 2 (2002): 383-405.

[*In the following essay, Hopkins examines Mary Shelley's novels* Lodore *and* Falkner, *and highlights Shelley's "profound ambivalence" toward motherhood, which Hopkins links to the works of Shelley's mother, Mary Wollstonecraft, and attributes to Wollstonecraft's absence in Shelley's life.*]

Many critics have pointed to the importance of ideas of motherhood both in Mary Shelley's first novel, *Frankenstein*, and in her own life, given the prominent public image of her dead mother, Mary Wollstonecraft, and her own disastrous experience with infant mortality.[1] Motherhood is of almost equally obvious importance in her second novel, *Valperga*,[2] and I have argued elsewhere that concerns associated with it are significant too in her third and fourth books, *The Last Man* and *The Fortunes of Perkin Warbeck*.[3] In her two last novels, *Lodore* and *Falkner*, she returns to the theme, and the pairing exhibits the full span of her contrasting attitudes. In *Lodore*, motherhood seems eventually to be redeemed, but is also covertly incriminated in the nov-

el's portrait of Lady Santerre; in *Falkner*, the dead mother is apparently idolized, but in fact what is fetishized is not the presence of a living mother, but her absence in her grave.

The pairing of these two novels reveals that the profound ambivalence of Mary Shelley's attitudes to mothering is rooted, as is so much of her writing, in the work of her mother. The girl who learned to read and write by tracing the letters on her mother's gravestone must surely have felt that the form of *The Wrongs of Woman*, in particular—letters of history and advice written by a mother to the daughter from whom she has been forcibly separated—spoke loudly to her own history and sense of identity, and her figuring of motherhood is always heavily inflected by memories of her own mother's life and writings.[4] Wollstonecraft herself was sharply double-edged in her literary depictions of motherhood. Though always happy to deploy it as a source of narrative pathos, she is equally happy to indict it, arguing that too many women had been educated only so as to be fit for a seraglio and thus could not be expected to "take care of the poor babes whom they bring into the world," and indeed at one time proposing a series of "Letters on the Management of Infants" in which she suggested that "while a third part of the human species . . . die during their infancy, . . . there is some error in the modes adopted by mothers and nurses."[5] The heroines of her fictions are cursed in their mothers. The opening paragraph of *Mary* is devoted almost entirely to a description of her ignorant and indolent mother, who loves only her son and not her daughter.[6] (Maria's mother also prefers her brother [*Wrongs of Woman*, 125], as does Henry Darnford's [*Mary*, 34].) *The Wrongs of Woman* is structured entirely around mothering and its legacy, with the heroine separated from her child, and Jemima the jailer suffering because "[a] deadly blight had met her at the very threshold of existence; and the wretchednes of her mother seemed a heavy weight fastened on her innocent neck, to drag her down to perdition" (79)—Jemima's mother having been seduced because of the faulty counsel of her own mother (102), leaving her daughter to be passed to a cruel stepmother before herself becoming pregnant and aborting the child, and finally completing the cycle by procuring the eviction and subsequent death of a pregnant woman (116). (We are also told that Maria's neighbor in the madhouse lost her senses while giving birth [p. 88].) Mary Shelley's dead, revered mother thus told her daughter not only that stepmothers are bad (a congenial message to the stepdaughter of the second Mrs. Godwin) but that mothers themselves are flawed; rarely can any texts have worked more strongly to reinforce Bettelheim's posited splitting into bad and alive or good and dead.

This model, albeit in a subtly complicated form, certainly comes close to what we find in *Lodore* and

Falkner. In her biography of Mary Shelley, Muriel Spark opines that *Lodore*

> is notable only for providing biographical confirmation, more or less literal: Professor Dowden and other commentators have already amply illustrated the points at which *Lodore* concurs with Mary Shelley's life-story. In all other respects, *Lodore* (successful in its time) represents a misdirected effort to reconcile things as they were in Mary's life with things as they might have been—an effort to fit the unorthodox facts into an orthodox moral system; and as a creative work it has no health.[7]

Without wishing to detract from Dowden's insights, one might well remark that the idea of relating *Lodore* to Mary Shelley's own life is in fact virtually redundant: she herself asked in a letter to Maria Gisborne, "did you recognize any of Shelley's & my early adventures—when we were in danger of being starved in Switzerland—& could get no dinner at an inn in London?"[8] But for Mary Shelley, these echoes of her own experiences do not by any means seem to have provided the main focus of the novel, for she also said of it:

> A Mother & Daughter are the heroines—The Mother who after safrifising [sic] *all* to the world at first—afterwards makes sacrifices not less entire, for her child—finding all to be Vanity, except the genuine affections of the heart. In the daughter I have tried to pourtray in its simplicity, & all the beauty I could muster, the *devotion* of a young wife for the husband of her choice—The disasters she goes through being described—& their result in awakening her Mother's affection, bringing about the conclusion of the tale.
>
>   (x)

It is not the relation between husband and wife but that between mother and child which lies at the heart of the novel, and this will be Mary Shelley's most sustained and complex treatment of it to date in her career.[9] If *Lodore* has no health, it is sick in very interesting ways.

Indeed, it claims for itself considerable resonances. Although it seems to be in so many ways the quietest of Mary Shelley's novels, with by far the fewest number of sensational events and an interest in the minutiae of bourgeois life in society which seems to bring it at times very close to the silver-fork novel, *Lodore* is steeped in the language and ethos of revolution. The very title of the book is derived from the name of Admiral Lord Lodore, who receives his barony for services rendered to the British government in the American War of Independence (6); but his son, the hero of the novel, seems little inclined to follow in his footsteps. Not only does he renounce the use of his title and go to live in America, under the name of Henry Fitzhenry, but at an earlier stage of the novel he intervenes to protect an Eton schoolfriend from their masters:

> This open rebellion astounded every one; a kind of consternation, which feared to show the gladness it felt, possessed the boyish subject of the tyro kingdom. Force conquered; Fitzhenry was led away, and the masters deliberated what sentence to pass on him. He saved them from coming to a conclusion by flight.
>
>   (31-32)

It is, however, ironic that it should be this "open rebellion" which should lead into some of the darkest and most closed areas of the novel's subtext, for although she is happy to use the language of rebellion which both her parents spoke so fluently, and to follow the practice of her mother's *Wrongs of Woman* in suggesting that individual narratives may be emblematic of larger social issues, Mary Shelley (still, in any case, financially dependent upon the goodwill of the arch-conservative Sir Timothy Shelley, her father-in-law) did not ultimately subscribe to the full panoply of Godwin's and Wollstonecraft's radical agenda; as she clearly shows in *The Fortunes of Perkin Warbeck,* where the pretender's legitimacy is affirmed but his steps to assert it condemned, she had no faith in the effectiveness of radical action even in a just cause, and she was skeptical of the motives of those who initiated it. Nor, however, did she wish openly to disavow the legacy of her parents. Indeed *Lodore* itself might be said to be "in a kind of consternation, which feared to show the gladness it felt," for these twin poles are typical of its complex attitudes towards revolution, in which apparent opposites are repeatedly blurred in ways which echo and are causally related to the novel's conflicted representations of mothers and their legacies.

This process begins early, when Lodore meets the widow of that contradictory being, an American royalist (78). Though the old régime may have passed, there are still those who feel its loss, as we also see much later when Lady Lodore wishes to retire from the world: "She often regretted that there were no convents, to which she might retire with safety and dignity. Conduct, such as she contemplated pursuing, would, under the old regime in France, have been recompensed by praise and gratitude" (264). Here Mary Wollstonecraft's condemnation of the irrationality of Catholicism and "the gross ritual of Romish ceremonies" (*Mary,* 30) gives way to a gentler sense of the respites and refuges that it was able to offer. Lady Lodore, moreover, bears the Christian name of Cornelia, which—as Mary Shelley, who was well versed in Roman history, would have known—associates her with Cornelia, mother of the Gracchi, a family of reformers.[10] This, too, works both to reinforce her status but also subtly to incriminate her, since their espousal of revolutionary tactics brought the sons of Cornelia to their deaths. Again Mary Shelley's difference from her own militantly reforming mother is clearly signalled here.

These are not the only revolutions which the language of *Lodore* remembers. The heroine's husband, Edward

Villiers, writes to her in a letter, "as Belvidera says, 'Remember twelve!'" (212); in Otway's *Venice Preserv'd,* the heroine Belvidera is married to one of the leaders of a conspiracy to overthrow the Venetian government (and her child is totally lost sight of by the narrative as the ramifications of the plot are pursued). Another passage recalls rather more recent events, also in ways inflected by Mary Shelley's personal history:

> There is no uninhabited desart so dreary as the peopled streets of London, to those who have no ties with its inhabitants, nor any pursuits in common with its busy crowds. A drop of water in the ocean is no symbol of the situation of an isolated individual thrown upon the stream of metropolitan life; that amalgamates with its kindred element; but the solitary being finds no pole of attraction to cause a union with its fellows, and bastilled by the laws of society, it is condemned to incommunicative solitude.
>
> (100)

The word "bastilled" can point in only one direction, France, but it is very notable here that the bastille in question is not a material, physical structure but the unwritten rules of social behavior. That is also in Wollstonecraft's *Wrongs of Woman,* where Maria laments that "[m]arriage had bastilled me for life" (154-55); here, however, it is being alone, not being married, which is thought of as a prison. Though *Lodore* thus directly reminds us of the French Revolution, and though the position of Lady Lodore in some respects recalls those of the women of Laclos's *Les Liaisons Dangereuses* (indeed she proposes to leave for Paris when it becomes particularly delicate), its real concerns lie elsewhere, as is indicated by a comment made by the narrator about Horatio Saville: "All abstracted and lofty as his speculations were, still his place had been in the hot-bed of patrician society, and he was familiar with the repetition of domestic revolutions, too frequent there" (119). It is with those domestic revolutions, and with gender politics rather than national government, that *Lodore* is most centrally concerned; but, as its use of the language of more public events suggests, this novel by the daughter of that most revolutionary of mothers never ceases to remember quite how revolutionary and momentous even the privately domestic may be, and quietly but insistently to suggest that it may, in the end, be wiser to seek to effect change from within society rather than from without.

The way in which it develops this idea is, above all, in its representations of mothering, all of which are both informed by the idea of the self-perpetuating cycle which Wollstonecraft limns in *The Wrongs of Woman* and also, covertly, reflect *on* Wollstonecraft even as they ostensibly reflect her. The keynote is soon heard, as we are introduced to Lodore and are informed that he has been orphaned in the same circumstances as Mary Shelley herself: his "recent birth had cost the life

of his hapless and lamented mother" (6). This is merely the first of many instances in the novel where birth is associated with privation, distress or death. When Lodore marries,

> Some few months after Mrs. Elizabeth [his sister] visited London on occasion of a christening, and then after a long interval, it was observed, that she never mentioned her brother, and that the name of his wife acted as a spell, to bring an expression of pain over her sedate features.
>
> (8)

A little later in the narrative, the reader begins to learn why this should be so:

> Within a year after her marriage, Lady Lodore gave birth to a daughter. This circumstance, which naturally tends to draw the parents nearer, unfortunately in this instance set them further apart . . . Her confinement was followed by a long illness; the child was nursed by a stranger, secluded in a distant part of the house, and during her slow recovery, the young mother seemed scarcely to remember that it existed.
>
> (47)

When the Lodores' daughter in turn grows up and marries, her husband's imprisonment for debt, and her determination to share all his hardships, mean that in the latter stages of her pregnancy, her husband Edward Villiers "fancied that he saw his young wife withering before his eyes, and looked forward to the birth of his child, under circumstances, that rendered even the necessary attendance difficult, if not impracticable" (257).

Even more dramatic is the fate of Clorinda, Neapolitan wife of Edward's cousin, Horatio Saville, who is obviously based at least in part on Emilia Viviani,[11] and whose death might therefore conceivably be seen as representing wish-fulfilment on the part of Mary Shelley. Jealous of her husband's affections, Clorinda flies into a furious rage and pulls a knife on him even though "she will at no distant period become a mother" (171); and though this crisis is weathered, when Clorinda finds herself "again in a situation to increase her family within a few months," she is precipitated into further turmoil because "while her safety depended on her being able to attain a state of calm, she feared a confinement in England, and believed that it was impossible that she should survive" (279). At the news that she must go to London "she raved through her house like a maniac; her servants even hid her child from her" (279), and almost as soon as she has embarked on the journey "she gave birth to a dead child. . . . By degrees her groans ceased, and she faded into death" (282). She is only twenty-one when she dies.

Ironically, this sad and premature death of one mother provides the narrative springboard which enables a happy ending to be contrived for another, Lady Lodore.

Despite the title's focus on her husband, Lady Lodore herself is arguably the most intriguing and fully realized character in the novel, and she and her daughter are certainly the central figures in its narrative. She is first introduced by her maiden name of Cornelia Santerre, and both names are rich in meaning: "sans-terre" figures her poverty and landless state, and Cornelia is a name associated not only with the mother of the Gracchi but with the mother of Vittoria, Flamineo, and Marcello in Webster's play *The White Devil* (since many of the epigraphs in the novel come from Renaissance drama, Mary Shelley seems likely to have been aware of the echo; it is also worth noting that, like the Gracchi, Marcello and Flamineo both die). It is, though, not as a mother but as a daughter that Lady Lodore seems first to be defined. She is devotedly attached to her mother, Lady Santerre, and puts this tie before any other, a fact which rapidly leads to the destruction of her marriage, since Lady Santerre, who "was a clever though uneducated woman: perfectly selfish, soured with the world, yet clinging to it" (44), is perpetually in the way of the young couple, displacing Lodore in her daughter's affections: "Once or twice at the beginning, he had attempted to withdraw his wife from this sinister influence, but Lady Lodore highly resented any effort of this kind, and saw in it an endeavour to make her neglect her first and dearest duties" (45). There is a slippery coupling of terms here, for though Lady Lodore's duties towards her mother were undoubtedly her "first," in the sense that they preceded the formation of any other attachment, they ought no longer to be her "dearest." Her persistence in continuing to define them as such, even after the birth of her child, leads directly to the break-up of her family, as is sharply revealed in the following exchange, after Cornelia has refused to leave her mother to accompany her husband and child:

> Even the cold Lady Santerre was moved—tears flowed from her eyes. 'My dear child!' she exclaimed.
>
> 'My dear child!'—the words found an echo in Lady Lodore's bosom;—'I am never to see my child more!'
>
>   (66)

Insisting on her "first" duties, Cornelia thus willingly sacrifices that which ought to be her "dearest."[12]

It is, I think, one of the novel's greatest distinctions—and also a mark of the delicate ambiguities of its agenda—that having thus relinquished her daughter, Lady Lodore is neither instantly prostrated with grief and remorse nor kept apart from her child by insuperable obstacles. *Lodore* is no *East Lynne*; indeed, it is not even a *Frankenstein,* and apart from the dramatic duel at the end of volume one and the death of Clorinda, the events are played out on a quieter, gentler scale than in Mary Shelley's previous novels, almost touching at times on the tone of a comedy of manners.

Cornelia does indeed find that "[t]he sight of a baby cradled in its mother's arms, or stretching out its little hands to her, had not unoften caused her to turn abruptly away, to hide her tears" (117); but she nevertheless completely fails to realize that Ethel will have grown, and, in a mark of her utter inability to engage imaginatively with the realities of her absent daughter, she has no idea that the young woman she sees at the theater can possibly be the little girl whom she sometimes thinks she might like to play with (130-31). Not only does she thus show herself deaf to any voice of instinct, she also instantly resolves that it would be socially inappropriate for them to get to know each other: "'One thing only I cannot endure,' said the lady hastily, 'to present a domestic tragedy or farce to the Opera House—we must not meet in public. I shall shut up my house and return to Paris'" (132). She speaks to her daughter only once at this stage of the novel, to tell her that her earring is loose, and in danger of falling out.

Eventually, however, nature triumphs. Lady Lodore is told that Ethel is living with Edward within the rules of the prison, and, although resenting the inconvenience, goes at once to visit her there. There she is so touched by Ethel's loyalty to her husband that she finds herself beginning to melt: "Yes, call me mother," said Lady Lo[do]re; "I may, at last, I hope, be allowed to prove myself one" (249), and soon she has decided virtually to beggar herself to provide for the young couple's future. Once she has made this resolve, she finds that she can at last, for the first time in many nights, sleep soundly, a detail which both evokes the spectre of Lady Macbeth and suggests that it has now been dispelled (252). Further, she begins to experience more general motherly impulses, reflecting that "if I earnestly desire to visit Lodore's grave, how gladly would I make a far longer pilgrimage to see Saville's child, and to devote myself to one who owes its existence to him" (269), and even when she is finally united with Saville "her love for her daughter was the master passion" (309). It seems merely appropriate that when she does indeed visit Lodore's grave, she should find there "on high a niche containing the holy mother and divine child" (306). True, unselfish motherhood, it may well seem, is divinely sanctioned, and will bring a woman her real happiness.

What, though, will it do to her child? When Edward hears that Lady Lodore has roused his agent to work, he exclaims, "She has inspired Gayland with energy and activity!—O, then, she must be a Medea, in more senses than the more obvious one" (255). It is suggestive that it is at the moment of her self-sacrifice that Cornelia should be imaged as a Medea, for if she is about to guarantee the material prosperity of the young couple, she may also be seen as beginning to pose a more subtle threat to their welfare, that of reproducing the uneasy triangle which has once before obtained among husband, wife, and wife's mother. Lady Lodore has always been opposed to Ethel's marriage with Edward, on the grounds that it was financially imprudent, an attitude of which Mary Shelley herself seems to be critical, since she has Ethel fail utterly to suspect anything of her mother's interference because Ethel "had not the remotest suspicion that it would be considered as conducive to her welfare to banish the only friend that she had in the world" (148). Even on her way to visit Ethel within the prison rules, Lady Lodore is busy reflecting that "[i]f Ethel had been entrusted to her guardianship, she certainly had never become the wife of Edward Villiers" (248), and she cannot imagine that Ethel will seriously propose to remain with her husband when she is offered asylum by her mother (247). It is ominous, too, that while Ethel thinks tenderly of her mother, Edward resists her, as Lodore had done Lady Santerre: "[s]he could not inspire him with the tenderness that warmed her heart towards her mother" (256).

It is in keeping with this ambiguity that while the act of mothering provides personal satisfaction and narrative *telos,* the novel's images of being mothered are not positive. When Horatio Saville first meets Clorinda, she has been "shut up in [a] convent through the heartless vanity of her mother, who dreaded her as a rival" (164), and although a "young travelled gentleman" says of Clorinda that "to see her with her child, is positively a finer tableau than any Raphael or Correggio in the world" (245), we soon see the falsity of the image: although "the birth of her child operated a beneficial change for a time" (277), Clorinda, in a cyclical repetition of bad mothering of the kind shown in Wollstonecraft's *Wrongs of Woman,* "soon grew jealous even of her own child" (278), and when she dies the little girl is largely indifferent—"she had always loved her father, and now she clung to his bosom and pressed her infant lips to his cheek" (283). Francis Derham refuses to escape from the cruelty he experiences at Eton because "'My mother,' he said, 'I have promised my mother to bear all;' and tears gushed from his large light blue eyes; 'but for her, the green grass of this spring were growing on my grave. I dare not pain her'" (32). In contrast, Lodore can get away because "I am leaving this wretched place, where men rule because they are strong, for my father's house. I never yet asked for a thing that I ought to have, that it was not granted me. I am a boy here, there I am a man" (32). Mothers, it seems, condemn one to suffering; fathers liberate. Later, there is more unsympathetic mothering in Derham's family, this time towards his daughter Fanny (212-13).

Other, more subtle indictments of being mothered are also to be found. Mary Shelley takes a chapter epigraph from *A Woman Killed with Kindness* (69), a play in which an adulterous mother is deprived of her children, and maternal tradition is disregarded when the narrative voice dismisses "the tapestry of our grandmothers" (23). When Lodore is jealous of Casimir—who is in fact his illegitimate son—he receives no support from the boy's mother: "[t]he Countess appeared to observe him indeed, and sometimes it seemed as if she regarded the angry workings of his heart with malicious pleasure" (52). Indeed, it is indirectly because of the manipulative nature of the Countess that Lodore falls prey to Lady Santerre: "Lodore had been accustomed to feminine controul, and he yielded with docility to her silken fetters" (43). The inadequacy of Lady Santerre's own conception of motherhood is tellingly revealed by her language when she assures Cornelia that "[e]ven if he remain away, he will quickly become weary of being accompanied by an infant and its nurse, and too glad to find that you will still be willing to act the mother towards his child" (67). To "act the mother" is, indeed, what she has been concerned to do, and a similar failure of agency is evidenced in the terms of Cornelia's letter to her husband, "[i]t is cruelty beyond compare, to separate one so young from maternal tenderness and fosterage" (67). Lodore himself has originally believed that "to deprive a mother of her child were barbarity beyond that of savages" (61), but the word "fosterage" undoes the naturalness of the bond completely. The extent of the alienation thus induced is revealed in the dislocation inherent in two images applied to Ethel: first, we are told that "[s]he earnestly desired to leave England, which had treated her with but a step-mother's welcome" (156), and then that when Edward returns to court her, Ethel "felt it like a return to a natural state of things, after unnatural deprivation. As if, a young nestling, she had been driven from her mother's side, and was now restored to the dear fosterage of her care" (159). The inability even to accept that this is what has happened without the cushion of an "as if" tellingly suggests the devastation of its impact.

The exception to this pattern of bad mothering is Ethel herself. Initially, Ethel reprises with variations the history of her mother; although superficially unlike her, "she had gestures, smiles, and tones, which were all Lady Lodore" (167), and although devoted to Edward, she is also ready to love her mother. After Lady Lodore does something even as mundane as warning her that her earring is in danger of falling out, Ethel is rhapsodic: "Her mother was no longer a semi-gorgon, hid behind a deceptive mask—a Medea, without a touch of human pity. She was a lovely, soft-voiced, angelic-looking woman, whom she would have given worlds to be permitted to love and wait upon" (179). Her potential likeness to her mother is sharply underlined when one of the images in this passage is shortly afterwards applied to herself: after she joins Edward in London and sees how happy this makes him, Ethel feels that "Medea, with all her potent herbs, was less of a magician than she, in the power of infusing the sparkling spirit of life into one human frame" (197), which, in its

Medea reference and its suggestion of birth, serves doubly to pair her with her mother.

Ultimately, however, Ethel breaks the novel's destructive patterns of bad or fatal mothering. Firstly, unlike Clorinda, she looks forward to the birth of her child: "the prospect of becoming a mother within a few months, opened another source of tenderness" (237). She has no qualms about her ability to care for it, being sure that "[h]er babe, if destined to open its eyes first on such a scene, would be still less acted upon by its apparent cheerlessness. Cradled in her arms, and nourished at her bosom, what more benign fate could await the little stranger?" (256-57). Her confidence is amply rewarded: "In less than a month after their liberation, she gave birth to a son. The mingled danger and rejoicing attendant on this event, imparted fresh strength to the attachment that united Edward to her; and the little stranger himself was a new object of tenderness and interest" (275). Unlike the other babies of the novel, Ethel's is indeed "new" and a "stranger": he is a boy, the first to be born in the narrative since Lodore himself. Perhaps a male child is Ethel's reward; certainly it reverses the pattern begun with Lady Santerre, who "was the mother of a daughter only; and her hopes and prospects died with her husband" (40), and seen also in *The Wrongs of Woman*, where Maria is "led . . . to lament that she had given birth to a daughter" (*Wrongs*, 120). Moreover, this switch from the relentless bearing of daughters to this crowning son can serve to draw our attention to a pattern in the novel almost as persistent as its depictions of mothering, a repeated imaging of gender reversal.

At an early stage in the book, Cornelia thinks of Lodore as exhibiting "the resolves, changeable as the moon, of a man governed by no sane purpose" (67). It is more usually women's behavior which is said to be governed by the moon; the passage, with *her* condemning *his* irrationality, thus effects an interesting switch. A similar reversal may be suggested in the description of how "Fanny nursed her father, watched over his health and humours, with the tenderness and indulgence of a mother" (79), which also inverts the natural order of the generations. Later, Cornelia refuses to leave her mother because "I should hold myself a parricide" (120), where the noun silently masculinizes Lady Santerre, while genders are unsettled again when we are told that "[i]t was often the custom of Aunt Bessy, like the father of Hamlet, to sleep after dinner" (150). *Hamlet* is also at the root of two more such instances: we are told that in Ethel "[t]here was an affectionateness of disposition kneaded up in the very texture of her soul, which gave it its 'very form and pressure'" (15), and that "[t]he fair girl had been brought up . . . to view society as the glass by which she was to set her feelings" (44). Both passages incorporate phrases directly or indirectly echoing Ophelia's soliloquy on Hamlet, but here they are

applied not to a man but to a woman. Though Cornelia may opine that "[t]he worst thing that can happen to a girl, is to have her prejudices and principles unhinged" (132), the language of the novel does not hesitate to do some unhinging of its own, just as Wollstonecraft had had her Mary quote Macbeth rather than Lady Macbeth—"to-morrow, and to-morrow" (*Mary*, 44) and her Maria threaten, like Hamlet's father, to divulge "the secrets of her prison-house" to her child (*Wrongs*, 185).

This is also the case with the heavily Miltonic and Shakespearean imagery of the first part of the narrative, which consistently depends for its effect upon various types of inversion.[13] Ethel, like Miranda, is just three when they come to Illinois, and the epigraph to the chapter consists of an exchange between Miranda and Prospero; but Ethel, unlike Miranda, and contrary to her father's expectation, has a memory of her mother (28-29), just as the allusions to *Paradise Lost* work not only to reinforce the authority of the patriarch but also to recall the mother, since Wollstonecraft's Mary had also educated herself by reading Milton, and Maria beguiles herself with *Paradise Lost* in the madhouse (*Mary*, 10; *The Wrongs of Woman*, 85). Indeed Milton is specifically associated with maternal inheritance when we are told how when her painter master hopes to capture her affections, "Ethel listened—Eve listened to the serpent, and since then, her daughters have been accused of an aptitude to give ear to forbidden discourses" (25); but despite this potent precedent—in a way, the avatar of all bad mothering—Ethel does not succumb to this temptation, and fittingly she also reverses Eve's destiny, since when they are to leave America "[s]he felt as if about to enter Paradise" (87). Finally, the very presence of Miltonic imagery problematizes the depiction of the relationship between Lodore and Ethel, since it automatically aligns it with one of husband and wife, especially when we read that "[t]he world was before him" (26) and that "[a] few natural tears Ethel shed—they were not many" (27), in which they exactly reproduce the roles of Adam and Eve.

Such a resonance may well seem to bring *Lodore* very close to the incestuous world of *Mathilda*, and it is certainly true that if the novel largely indicts mothering, it is by no means that much kinder to fathering. The narrator does concede that "[t]here is a peculiarity in the education of a daughter, brought up by a father only, which tends to develop early a thousand of those portions of mind, which are folded up, and often destroyed, under mere feminine tuition" (15). However, when we are told that "Fitzhenry drew his chief ideas from Milton's Eve" (18), we are surely meant to remember, as Fiona Stafford points out, that "[i]n the second chapter of *A Vindication of the Rights of Woman* (1792), Mary Wollstonecraft takes the contradictions inherent in Milton's portrayal of Eve as the starting point for her attack on male tyranny" (18, note b); here the voice of the mother implicitly castigates the actions of the father. Indeed there are several outright denunciations of Lodore's parenting:

> He would have knelt to kiss her footsteps as she bounded across the grass, and tears glistened in his eyes as she embraced his knees on his return from any excursion; but her prattle often wearied him, and her very presence was sometimes the source of intense pain.
>
> (15)

> It cannot be doubted, but that it were for the happiness of the other sex that she were taught more to rely on and act for herself. But in the cultivation of this feeling, the education of Fitzhenry was lamentably deficient.
>
> (19)

> [T]he paternal protection is never entirely efficient. A father avenges an insult; but he has seldom watchfulness enough to prevent it.
>
> (24-25)

Notably, Edward has a very difficult relationship with his father: the two of them know only "the portion of filial and paternal affection which their relative position but too usually inspires" (139), and it is his father's extravagance, selfishness, and untrustworthiness which leads to Edward's imprisonment. As the narrator of *Lodore* remarks, though without the resonances which the words carry for modern ears, "There is something so awful in a father. His words are laws" (83).

The distant echoing of the plot of *Mathilda,* the implicit allusion to Mary Wollstonecraft, and the numerous details in the novel which Mary Shelley freely volunteered to be based on her own life, all bring the discussion of parenting back full circle to the issue on which criticism of *Lodore* has so often focused, the relationship of the novel to Mary Shelley's biography. What interest me, however, are not so much one-to-one correspondences of the kind which Dowden thought he had found,[14] but more blurred and conflicted identifications. As Fiona Stafford points out, Lady Lodore at the end of the novel is 34, Mary Shelley's own age when she wrote it (xi); but so is Lodore at the outset (42). Ultimately, I think, the gender ambiguity which is at the heart of so many of Mary Shelley's novels has resurfaced here once more, and precludes any simple identification or endorsement of either the mother or the father figure; indeed Katherine Hill-Miller argues that "Shelley is careful to portray Lodore and Cornelia as mirror images of each other" (150). However much at war with each other Lodore and Lady Lodore may be, their daughter can make no choice between them, and while she finds that when "she entered her father's library . . . his image appeared to rise before her, to regulate and purify her thoughts" (26), she also discovers that "[t]urning

her thoughts from Villiers, she would have been glad to discover any link that might enchain her to the mass. She reverted to her mother" (156). Mary Shelley certainly reverts to her own mother when she comments on Lodore's reliance on Milton's Eve, but she does so only to indict her fictional father. Moreover, in sending Lodore to America—and there introducing him to a girl named Fanny—she also surely remembers her mother's first love, Gilbert Imlay, father of Wollstonecraft's daughter Fanny, and in some sense a possible alternative father for Mary Shelley herself; and Godwin's adherence to Lockean tabula rasa theory is critiqued here—as elsewhere in Mary Shelley's novels—in its appropriation for Lodore's attitude to his wife: "[h]e found the lovely girl somewhat ignorant; but white paper to be written upon at will, is a favourite metaphor among those men who have described the ideal of a wife" (41). It is the impossibility of forgetting either parent, the difficulty of reconciling their memory with finding one's own identity as mother, wife, and woman, and a deep-seated scepticism about the wisdom and practicality of their revolutionary agenda, that animates and energizes *Lodore,* together with a fear that all daughters are doomed simultaneously to disappoint and to reduplicate their mothers, and the fact that this text is less openly concerned with monstrosity than Mary Shelley's earlier novels means only that the ever-latent fear of monstrosity may have found more subtle but also more insidious manifestations.

Mary Shelley conceived of her last novel, *Falkner,* as "in the style of *Lodore,*" and expected it to be her best.[15] It is indeed a fitting culmination to her oeuvre, because it brings together a number of the themes and concerns of her previous fiction: it shares with *Frankenstein* the heroine's name, Elizabeth, the images of a bride dead in a storm, of a devilish male, and of pale faces lit by lightning (187), and a concern with the mother's grave and the fate of her dead body; with *Lodore* an ostensibly redemptive portrait of motherhood; and with *The Last Man* a significant forgetfulness.

Falkner is above all centered on the graves of mothers, climaxing, indeed, in the actual exhumation of one.[16] Those of the hero and heroine dominate, but Lady Cecil's mother too is dead, and Falkner's whole life has been colored by the early loss of his (157). Though Mary Shelley herself thought that *Falkner* was indelibly marked by the fact that her father had died during its composition (ix), it is her mother whom the novel much more obviously remembers, particularly the young Mary's habit of frequenting her grave.[17] Indeed, the very cemetery where Elizabeth Raby's parents are buried can be seen as replicating this configuration: there are

> two graves, of which one only was distinguished by a simple headstone, to commemorate the name of him who mouldered beneath. This tomb was inscribed to

the memory of Edwin Raby, but the neighbouring and less honoured grave claimed more of the child's attention—for her mother lay beneath the unrecorded turf.

(6)

It is, indeed, consistently her mother whom Elizabeth mourns more: though "these two graves were all of relationship she knew upon the earth," it is from only one of them that she derives comfort—"'Mamma' was there beneath, and still she could love and feel herself beloved" (15). This marked preference inaugurates the novel's overwhelming emphasis on passionate adoration and almost apotheosis of the lost and lamented figure of the mother. At the same time, however, a slightly different note is sounded. Elizabeth is the only person in the village who ever visits the graveyard, "except on Sunday, after evening service, when a mother might linger for a few moments near the fresh grave of a lately lost child" (6). Children may have long memories for their mothers, but mothers themselves, it seems, have rather short ones for their children.

Elizabeth first meets Rupert Falkner as he is about to shoot himself on her mother's grave. She stops him, and he befriends and adopts her. Having already destroyed one mother, Falkner thus becomes in loco parentis to Elizabeth, and she consistently terms him her father. This is, it seems, enough for her: indeed she explicitly declares, "I can't have a new mamma—I won't have any but my own mamma" (26). It is, though, perhaps unclear whether Falkner is to be seen more as the manifestation of the marginalized, replaceable father, or of the mother from whose grave he metaphorically springs, especially given that he is motivated partly by the desire to fulfil the duties which would otherwise have devolved on the dead Alithea (28). As in *Lodore,* there is thus much interest in the extent to which a man can be a mother. We are told that Elizabeth's own mother had struggled against her disease "with a fortitude a mother only could practise" (22); but Falkner seems to identify himself rather with mothers than with fathers, as when we are told that he "had always loved children. In the Indian wilds, which for many years he had inhabited, the sight of a young native mother, with her babe, had moved him to envious tears" (26)—a memory to which the narrative will later return. When he meets Elizabeth, he "pitied the mother who had been forced to desert so sweet a flower" (27), but says nothing of her father, and when she falls ill, "[n]o mother could have attended on her more assiduously than Falkner" (35). The question of men's femininity is, too, further stressed by having it raised in connection with Gerard, who has "grown kind as a woman" (86).

If Falkner seems able to take the place of Elizabeth's own mother, however, it will be far more difficult for him to "replace" Alithea (28). Indeed even Miss Jervis,

Elizabeth's governess, can rival him in some respects: she teaches her charge needlework, "and thus Elizabeth escaped for ever the danger she had hitherto run of wanting those feminine qualities without which every woman must be unhappy—and, to a certain degree, unsexed" (40). Alithea represents a far more serious challenge. Ostensibly, she is the ideal mother; as Katherine Hill-Miller points out, "[a]ll the characters, and especially the males closest to her, refer to Alithea in divine terms."[18] In our first introduction to her, Mrs. Raby calls her "incomparable as a mother" (11) and recommends her own daughter to her care, since then "I should die in the belief that I left my child another mother in you" (12). After the death of both women, the tables are in a sense turned: instead of Alithea being able to succor Mrs. Raby's child, it is Elizabeth who says to Falkner of the neglected and unhappy Gerard Neville, Alithea's son, "Oh! how I wish you would save him as you saved me" (44). But no-one can stand *in loco parentis* to Alithea's son, for "she had loved [him] with passion inexpressible": "[t]he tenderness of her disposition, joined to her great talents and sweetness, rendered her unparalleled in the attention she paid to his happiness and education. No mother ever equalled her—for no woman ever possessed at once equal virtues and equal capacities" (46). Unlucky in her marriage, Alithea turns instead to her son: "Gerard was all in all to her—her hope, her joy, her idol, and he returned her love with more than a child's affection" (95). When Falkner proposes elopement, she silences him with, "[n]ever, dear Rupert, speak thus to me again, or we must part—I have a son," and she seems to him at that moment to express "the maternal nature, such as Catholics imagine it, without a tincture of the wife, a girlish, yet enthusiastic rapture at the very thought of her child" (181). Alithea herself confirms that this is how she feels: "[a] mother is, in my eyes, a more sacred name than wife. My life is wrapped in my boy, in him I find blameless joy" (182). Indeed it was her overwhelming devotion to her son that directly caused her death, and her despair at being parted from him also highlights another difference between men and mothers: while Alithea has lived a life of self-sacrifice for Gerard's sake, Falkner abducts her because "I never could force myself to do the thing I hated; I never could persuade myself to relinquish the thing I desired" (186).

Alithea's unparalleled attachment to her son, however, is notably not present in her attitude to her daughter. As in *The Last Man,* where the gender of Juliet's baby is forgotten by the narrator within the course of a few pages, this child seems predominantly presented as the victim of forgetfulness, and a hasty reading of the novel might hardly reveal her existence. She is first mentioned by Gerard, but in terms which suggest she might be as much an embodiment of the Romantic fantasy of the sibling/lover, almost another aspect of Elizabeth herself, as a real person: he says he remembers Elizabeth at Baden as "a beautiful girl—and I thought such would have been my sister, and I had not been alone—if fate, if cruel, inexorable, horrible destiny had not deprived me of her as well as all—all that made my childish existence Paradise" (75). The question of her existence is further confused by the fact that he calls Lady Cecil his sister, although they are in fact unrelated, while Lady Cecil herself blurs the boundaries still further by being so markedly maternal—she calls her children "dear little angels" (80). The next mention of Gerard's nameless sister, however, leaves no doubt of her reality: he tells Elizabeth that he cannot believe that his mother could "have deserted me, her child, whom she so fondly loved—and who even in that unconscious age adored her—and her poor little girl, who died neglected" (87). We later learn that "the carelessness of a nurse during a childish illness caused her death" (110), but one might well say that the neglect had begun well before the departure of the mother, and is continued by the novel itself; certainly as Alithea is borne away her cry is for "My child! my son!" (99) rather than for her *children,* and though Falkner proposed taking Gerard away with them, he spared no thought for the daughter (185). Moreover, Alithea's conduct, however high-minded, is, arguably, blameworthy in one other respect: in unlocking the garden gate "with her own key" (99) and going out to where a gentleman awaited her, she recalls Eve, Austen's Maria Bertram, and, most closely, Richardson's Clarissa, who was also abducted and died as a result of leaving the garden: not for nothing does Elizabeth imagine her ultimate drowning as the result of "a false step" (195). Even within Alithea, "mourned for, as never mother was mourned before" (135), lurks monstrosity; and when we recall that Wollstonecraft's Maria too, escaping from the asylum intending to live openly with a man not her husband, feared "that she should never get out at the garden gate" (*Wrongs,* 190), we again catch glimpses of some of the conflicts which make this so.

Perhaps part of this difference in Alithea's parenting of her son and her daughter may be ascribed to the extent to which she is a composite representation of the different phases of Mary Shelley's own life. Mary Wollstonecraft, however guiltlessly, left behind a daughter; Mary Shelley too lost daughters—one of them, like Alithea's, never named—but she could, by this stage in her life, reasonably claim that she had successfully brought up a son. It is notable that when Elizabeth imagines Alithea's last moments and then, with her own voice blurring into that of the narrator, silently rhapsodizes on motherhood, it is only the male child that is imagined as the object of the mother's affections:

> There is something so beautiful in a young mother's feelings. Usually a creature to be fostered and protected—taught to look to another for aid and safety; yet a woman is the undaunted guardian of her little child. She will expose herself to a thousand dangers to shield his fragile being from harm. If sickness or injury approach him, her heart is transfixed by terror: readily, joyfully, she would give her own blood to sustain him. The world is a hideous desert when she is threatened to be deprived of him; and when he is near, and she takes him to the shelter of her bosom, and wraps him in her soft, warm embrace, she cares for nothing beyond that circle; and his smiles and infantine caresses are the light of their life.
>
> (195)

What, though, if the child is a girl? *Falkner* answers the question silently and powerfully: as in *Lodore,* sons flourish, but daughters wither and die.

Nor is this the extent of the novel's quiet case against Alithea. If Falkner cannot rival her, someone else can. As the narrative progresses, Elizabeth moves increasingly from her early worship of her mother to assuming a maternal role herself: indeed Katherine Hill-Miller suggests that both here and in *Lodore,* "the daughter paradoxically eludes the father's control by apparently becoming precisely what he asks: a conventional, supportive, maternal figure" (14), behavior which ultimately "punishes him" (192). When Falkner is wounded in Greece, "she drew nearer the litter, as a lonely mother might to the cradle of her child, when in the stillness of night some ravenous beast intruded on a savage solitude" (62)—a striking image of devotion and courage. Falkner certainly associates her with Alithea: both women are carried by him and sheltered from storms (34 and 164); both are seen as mother figures—recalling and amplifying on his earlier reference, he later records that "I never saw a young Indian mother with her infant but my soul dissolved in tender fancies of domestic union and bliss with Alithea" (173),[19] while after his confession Elizabeth "watched him as a mother may a child" (223); and he takes each away with him in the name of their mothers (28 and 179). After reading Falkner's narrative of Alithea's death and of the events leading up to it, Elizabeth, in a powerful passage, virtually relives Alithea's experiences (194-95), and towards the end of the book she has almost become Alithea: Gerard, echoing *Frankenstein*'s blurring of another Elizabeth with the corpse of his mother, tells her that "[y]ou haunted my dreams, accompanied by every image of horror—sometimes you were bleeding, ghastly, dying—sometimes you took my poor mother's form, as Falkner describes it, snatched cold and pale from the waves" (258), while Falkner, imagining a shape, wonders "[w]as it Alithea or Elizabeth?" (280).

Perhaps because Elizabeth is now available to replace her, the novel in its closing stages seems almost indecently glad to be firmly rid of Alithea, and to be assured that, unlike the mother in *Frankenstein,* she really is permanently in her grave: what Katherine Hill-Miller argues of *Lodore*—that "Ethel calls Cornelia to the salvation of sacrifice; she also calls Cornelia to her grave"

(162) seems doubly true here. Though Falkner's narrative, confirmed by what Hoskins has already told Gerard, surely makes the matter abundantly clear, further confirmation is nevertheless sought, and the grave itself opened:

> With one consent, though in silence, everyone gathered nearer, and looked in—they saw a human skeleton. The action of the elements, which the sands had not been able to impede, had destroyed every vestige of a human frame, except those discoloured bones, and long tresses of dark hair, which were wound around the skull. A universal yet suppressed groan burst from all. Gerard felt inclined to leap into the grave, but the thought of the many eyes all gazing, acted as a check.
>
> (215)

With Mary Shelley refusing to soften any details, Alithea's mortality is made abundantly, even shockingly, clear—and surprisingly, perhaps, Gerard does not shrink from it, is indeed "desirous to stay to look again on what had been his mother" (216). Later, the grave is opened once again and the body explored yet further: though the sight may be "abhorrent to the eye" (220), we cannot, it seems, get enough of it. It does not even put Gerard or his father off their dinner (220). Ultimately, the unity which Falkner, Elizabeth and Gerard achieve at the end of the novel is informed and enabled by the loss of Alithea; Gerard can even "take my mother's destroyer by the hand, and live with him on terms of intimacy and friendship" (295). Though the cry of "Come back, mamma" echoes at various times from both Gerard and Elizabeth (13 and 98), this novel, unlike *Frankenstein,* willingly accepts, and indeed ensures, that the mother stays dead; and although ostensibly seeming to celebrate her memory and her virtues, it also powerfully critiques them.

Notes

1. See for instance Mary Poovey, "My Hideous Progeny: Mary Shelley and the Feminisation of Romance," *Publications of the Modern Language Association of America,* 95 (1980), reprinted in *The Gothick,* ed. Sage, 163; Judy Simons, *Diaries and Journals of Literary Women from Fanny Burney to Virginia Woolf* (Basingstoke: Macmillan, 1990), 69; and U. C. Knoepflmacher, "Thoughts on the Aggression of Daughters," in *The Endurance of Frankenstein,* ed. George Levine and U. C. Knoepflmacher (Berkeley: U of California P, 1979): 94. It was also taken as a significant factor in Kenneth Branagh's recent film of the book, in which Victor's mother dies in childbirth and amniotic fluid from a birthing-stool is used in the creation of the monster.

2. See for instance Joseph W. Lew, "God's Sister: History and Ideology in *Valperga,*" in *The Other Mary Shelley: Beyond Frankenstein,* ed. Audrey

A. Fisch, Anne K. Mellor, and Esther H. Schor (Oxford: Oxford UP, 1993), 159-81, and Daniel E. White, "'The God Undeified': Mary Shelley's *Valperga,* Italy, and the Aesthetic of Desire," *Romanticism on the Net* 6 (May, 1997).

3. In "The Self and the Monstrous: *The Fortunes of Perkin Warbeck,*" in *Iconoclastic Departures: Mary Shelley after 'Frankenstein',* ed. Syndy Conger, Frederick Frank and Gregory O'Dea (Associated University Presses, 1997), 260-74, and "Memory at the End of History: Mary Shelley's *The Last Man,*" *Romanticism on the Net* 6 (May, 1997).

4. See for instance Clarissa Campbell Orr, "Mary Shelley's *Rambles in Germany and Italy,* the Celebrity Author, and the Undiscovered Country of the Human Heart," *Romanticism on the Net* 11 (August 1998) [May 18, 2001], http://users.ox.ac.uk/~scat0385/rambles.html, on the way in which in Mary's *Rambles in Germany and Italy,* which pays conscious homage to her mother's travel writing, "the personal is presented to a great degree as part of the experience of motherhood in general; this also makes it a philosophical kind of projection of motherhood" (9).

5. Mary Wollstonecraft, "Letters on the Management of Infants," in *A Wollstonecraft Anthology,* ed. Janet Todd (Oxford: Polity, 1989), 86 and 60.

6. Mary Wollstonecraft, *Mary* and *The Wrongs of Woman,* ed. Gary Kelly (Oxford: Oxford UP, 1976), 1, 4. All further quotations from both *Mary* and *The Wrongs of Woman* will be taken from this edition and reference will be given in the text.

7. Muriel Spark, *Mary Shelley* (London: Cardinal, 1989), 150-51.

8. Mary Shelley, *Lodore,* ed. Fiona Stafford (London: William Pickering, 1996), introductory note, x. All quotations from the novel will be taken from this edition and reference will be given in the text.

9. Kate Ferguson Ellis also points out the thematic continuity between *Frankenstein* and *Lodore,* suggesting that *Lodore* "could be called *Frankenstein* without the science" ("Subversive Surfaces: The Limits of Domestic Affection in Mary Shelley's Later Fiction," in *The Other Mary Shelley*: 230).

10. See H. H. Scullard, *From the Gracchi to Nero* (London: Routledge, 1988), 23-24.

11. The representation of Clorinda also has features in common with Wollstonecraft's airy dismissal of the Portuguese as Catholic and therefore "uncivilized" (30).

12. Katherine Hill-Miller argues that another mother is also being invoked here: she calls Lady San-

terre "a living embodiment of Mary Woll-stonecraft's warning in *A Vindication of the Rights of Woman*" (*"My Hideous Progeny": Mary Shelley, William Godwin, and the Father-Daughter Relationship* [Newark: U of Delaware P, 1995], 156). For Hill-Miller, "Lady Santerre symbolizes . . . an inversion of natural maternal feelings for a child" (155).

13. For comment on these, see Introduction, xi.

14. See Introduction, x-xi, for a list of these: Clorinda is seen as Emilia Viviani, Cornelia and Lady Santerre as Percy Shelley's first wife and her sister, Lodore as Byron, and Derham, Horatio Saville, and Edward Villiers as all having elements of Percy Shelley himself.

15. Mary Shelley, *Falkner*, ed. Pamela Clemit (London: William Pickering, 1996), ix. All further quotations from the novel will be taken from this edition and reference will be given in the text.

16. Though Elisabeth Bronfen does not discuss *Falkner*, her comments on the importance of dead women's bodies in *Frankenstein* are pertinent here too (*Over Her Dead Body: Death, Femininity and the Aesthetic* [Manchester: Manchester UP, 1992], 132-33).

17. For an argument that it is also informed by Mary's memories of her dealings with her father-in-law, Sir Timothy Shelley, see Bonnie Rayford Neumann, *The Lonely Muse: A Critical Biography of Mary Wollstonecraft Shelley* (Salzburg: Salzburg Studie, 1979), 147.

18. Hill-Miller, *"My Hideous Progeny,"* 175.

19. For comment on this passage, see Hill-Miller, 195.

MOTHERHOOD, PATRIARCHY, AND THE SOCIAL ORDER

Elizabeth Langland (essay date fall 1987)

SOURCE: Langland, Elizabeth. "Patriarchal Ideology and Marginal Motherhood in Victorian Novels by Women." *Studies in the Novel* 19, no. 3 (fall 1987): 381-94.

[*In the following essay, Langland argues that an analysis of the representation of mother-son relations in Victorian women's writing reveals an alternative to strict patriarchal traditions.*]

Although feminist criticism has analyzed the relationship between mothers and daughters and between fathers and daughters, it has ignored the relationship between mothers and sons as depicted by women writers. Two assumptions are implicit in this omission: first, that women writers inevitably identify with the role of daughter, either in recuperating possibilities through their literal and literary mothers or in struggling with the patriarchal imprimatur represented by their literal and literary fathers; and second, that the Oedipal model which has dominated our study of mothers and sons, emphasizing the son's sexual attraction toward and ultimate rejection of the mother in favor of the father, does justice to this intricate relationship. Neither of these dual assumptions reveals the rich insights available to us when we study representations of the mother/son relationship from the mother's point of view, my focus in this essay. Taking this view, we discover a persistent dialogic between patriarchy's dutiful daughter and its marginal mother, a dialogic that demythologizes Victorian ideology and interrogates the conventions of narrative form.

I

I shall begin by outlining some of the most prevalent ideologies of womanhood in the Victorian era, then summarize briefly the ways in which contemporary feminist criticism has interpreted those ideologies, and finally, before turning to the analysis of individual novels, reexamine the influence of the ideologies upon the self-fashionings of the Victorians.

After approximately 1840, Victorians were engaged in a significant debate over the roles, rights, and responsibilities of women. Informing and fueling these debates were assumptions about a woman's particular "nature" and its differences from a man's. This "Woman Question" was not merely a matter for idle discussion but a genuine *question,* which, by the 1860s, "had become one of the most important topics of the day,"[1] its importance generated by historical circumstances, particularly religious doubts and the "viciously competitive atmosphere of business."[2] The Victorians' thoughts on the subject led to articulations of differences between masculine and feminine nature, most memorably, perhaps, in Sarah Lewis' *Woman's Mission* (1839), Coventry Patmore's *The Angel in the House* (1854-62), and John Ruskin's "Of Queen's Gardens" (1865), works extolling woman's special role as the moral regenerator of mankind.

Basically, four distinct but related myths about women fed the Victorian imagination.[3] Significantly, all of these myths postulate woman's moral efficacy in the world at the same time as they limit her sphere for action in that world. "The Angel in the House" of Coventry Patmore's poem has become the most famous stereotype, one that

Virginia Woolf, in "Professions for Women," both ridiculed and respected as a potent force to be killed. Even if Victorians did not subscribe to the idea of the Angel in the House, they were attracted to the implicit ideal of woman's redemptive or salvatory potential. Victorian fiction is peopled by a variety of idealistic, high-minded, and compassionate heroines who embody values that are seen as distinctively feminine in contrast to masculine aggressiveness and competitiveness.

The variety and persistence of myths on a similar theme quickly reveal the Victorian preoccupation with and investment in woman's special nature, a nature characterized by nurture, compassion, and a humanized community. This preoccupation developed into an ideology that legitimized unequal power relations in the economic and political sphere even as it glorified women's role in the domestic and "moral" sphere. It is easy to see, therefore, how the myth of women's salvatory and redemptive potential victimized women. It is equally easy to see, as Nina Auerbach notes in *Woman and the Demon,* why feminist criticism began its life in the early 1970s by "pinioning just such myths . . . Gleefully, in the classroom and in print, we identified pernicious 'myths' and 'images' of women, certain that we knew what the reality was: it was us, solid, sullen, and victimized."[4] Auerbach's response was to reexamine the myth of woman's redemptive potential "in order to retrieve a less tangible, but also less restricting, facet of woman's history than the social sciences can encompass" and ultimately to define a "myth crowning a disobedient woman in her many guises as heir of the ages and demonic savior of the race."[5] She exposes the Victorians' own self-division, their tendency to locate the transformative power of woman within the repressive image of the Angel in the House.

I wish to probe still further the workings of the ideology of woman's salvatory and transformative potential to observe that what Auerbach defines as the "rich foundation of mythic perception" may ultimately, in fact, have actually served the patriarchy as the spoonful of sugar that helps the medicine of patriarchal repression go down. That is, women would accept the conditions of their suppression if the repressive myth also articulated extraordinary and fearful powers of women. The myth of transformative powers ultimately made palatable the real, social victimization.

But after recognizing the subtle and not-so-subtle means by which this ideology repressed women, we must also acknowledge the historical ways in which it was a necessary precondition to any liberation women may ultimately have experienced and articulated. A significant part of Victorian self-fashioning is its conscious emphasis on morality. In her recent book, *Marriage and Morals Among the Victorians,* Gertrude Himmelfarb explores the gap between public pronouncement and private behavior—not to expose the "hypocrisy" latent in Victorian self-representations, but to argue for the Victorians' serious investment in certain moral ideologies as a response to the "profound crisis produced by Darwinism": "If the Victorians had no dogmatic social ideology, no binding religious faith, they did have a compelling, almost obsessive faith in morality . . . Those eminent Victorians who no longer believed in God believed all the more in man. They deified man, not, like Feuerbach, to 'de-alienate' him, or, like Marx, to 'socialize' him, but, like Comte, to moralize him."[6] The Victorians' moral self-representations were not, then, evidence of hypocrisy, but rather were serious attempts to reinterpret the moral irregularities of their personal lives following the breakdown of traditional systems of morality. Obviously, women had an equal historical investment in images of female ideality; the problem, of course, was that the image carried a very different impact for women than for men. The woman writer was ideally poised to articulate such contradictions, contradictions evident even in her stance toward writing itself, which also had to be reinterpreted within the female salvatory ideology. Not surprisingly, we discover women novelists like Gaskell and George Eliot speaking of writing as a logical extension of woman's moral role within the family, a fulfillment of her salvatory mission in the world. So, George Eliot noted in a letter after the publication of her first novel, *Adam Bede,* "I have written a novel which people say has stirred them very deeply—and *not a few people,* but almost all reading England."[7]

Literary representations of women writers testify to their seduction by Victorian self-fashionings and, perhaps more important, to their own investment in them. Ultimately, however, women must have perceived the limitations of self-fashionings that defined self-realization as reproduction of the patriarchy. Of course, one source of man's fear of woman derives from her part in the reproductive process—a woman must produce the sons who will become the patriarchs of the next generation. A mother is a point of potential vulnerability in the system. Her repression must, therefore, be the more complete. In women's portraits of the mother/son relationship, we discover the demystification of the myth of the morally efficacious heroine. In their representations of mothers, female writers reveal the ways in which patriarchy ensures that a woman bearing a son, rather than inscribing her potential in the world, initiates her own marginalization through the culture's appropriation of her body's fruits.

II

Although through their representations of mothers and sons Victorian women novelists dramatize the demystification of the myth of motherhood and its pernicious, seductive ramifications, the power of the ideology is such that the myth continues in the texts as a potent presence, deconstructing its own critique and reinscribing itself in the novels' conclusions in the myths of the dutiful daughters. The result, in Bakhtin's terms, is a dialogic discourse—a doubleness in women's fiction, a tendency toward double-seeing and double-speaking that reflects a continual, unresolvable tension between images that at once liberate and enslave.[8] In women's novels, there is a prominent dialogue between externally persuasive and internally persuasive voices, or between the culture's imperatives of the dutiful daughter who is to marry and produce sons and the actual experiences of the marginal mother who, in acting out the dutiful daughter myth, is displaced and ignored.

Not only does the story of the marginal mother challenge the ideology of the dutiful daughter but that challenge provides the foundation for a questioning of the ideological character of genre. The movement toward narrative closure in the daughter's story is contradicted by the opposing impulse toward radical instability and openness in the mother's tale. The result is a novel that questions the very nature of the conventions it uses and thus forces us to consider the ways in which ideologies undergird those narrative conventions. The new narrative space generated by the disruption of the conventions constitutes an important innovation and is a significant achievement of women's fiction.[9] My purpose in the ensuing analyses is to articulate the dutiful daughter/marginal mother dialogic and to explore the narrative gaps and tensions it exposes.

A discussion of Anne Brontë's *The Tenant of Wildfell Hall* and Elizabeth Gaskell's *North and South* will set the stage for an analysis of George Eliot's later novels: *Felix Holt* and *Daniel Deronda*. In these novels of George Eliot's artistic maturity, written after she had earned wide social respect and recognition and had been adopted as a "mother" by young men and women alike, we ironically discover a preoccupation with the marginality of mothers, the utter ineffectuality of their plans and dreams. A brief examination of Charlotte Brontë's *Villette* will follow because I see it as sharing *Daniel Deronda*'s impulse to expose the ideological character of genre.

Anne Brontë's *The Tenant of Wildfell Hall* is today relatively unread, but it deserves a greater audience both for the maturity of its artistry and for its trenchant grasp of cultural ideology. Although we might want to argue that Victorian novels maintain so profound a disjunction between the daughter heroine and the marginal mother that the Victorian heroine rarely grows up to be a mother, Anne Brontë deliberately collapses the two categories into one character to dispel the illusion of difference and to show them as a continuum.

In *The Tenant*, Helen, an idealistic girl called an "angel" by her prospective husband, wakes to the reality that she is married to a dissolute rake whose power over her is absolute. She takes control of her own life by fleeing into seclusion, and she returns only to seize ultimate control as the demon at his deathbed, reminding him by her presence of his guilt and imminent damnation. Here we find a portrayal of woman's transformative power as she achieves an innocent revenge in returning to her husband out of a duty that becomes his punishment. Indeed, she seems here a tormenting demon to be feared.

However, the ultimate conflict between wife and husband is enacted over the body of their son. In fighting her husband for her son, Helen is fighting the entire Victorian patriarchal system that produced him. Brontë's grasp of her culture's ideology allows her to mount a trenchant attack on the status quo, both the indulgence of men and the consequent subjugation of women. Brontë understands perfectly the dialectical relationship between these twin evils, which she relentlessly exposes. From the beginning of the novel, we find portrait after portrait of indulged men who have become, as a consequence, sensualists, coxcombs, or self-righteous prigs. But the very women who produced them and who suffer by their selfishness continue to defend them, perpetuating the system in invidious ways. One wife praises her now-deceased husband in these terms: "He always said I was a good wife, and did my duty; and he always did his—bless him!—he was steady and punctual, seldom found fault without reason, always did justice to my good dinners, and hardly ever spoiled my cookery by delay—and that's as much as any woman can expect of any man."[10]

Anne Brontë also understands that, when a man bonds with his son, he does so over the body of the mother. Once the adored object, she must be made foolish and contemptible. Huntingdon's indoctrination of his little son into manhood means that he "learnt to tipple wine like papa, to swear like Mr. Hattersley, and to have his own way like a man, and sent mamma to the devil when she tried to prevent him" (*TWH*, p. 356). When Helen tries to eradicate the pernicious influence of her husband, she finds only criticism, strongest from the women whom she would liberate from male tyranny. She is urged against "the fatal error . . . of taking that boy's education upon [herself]," and she responds with spirit: "I am to send him to school, I suppose, to learn to despise his mother's authority and affection!" (*TWH*, p. 55). It is a telling response; to make a man of a boy means to teach him to despise his mother, to despise all women. Anne Brontë thus anticipates by almost two decades John Stuart Mill's remark in "The Subjection of Women": "Such people are little aware . . . how early the notion of [a boy's] inherent superiority to a girl arises in his mind; how it grows with his growth and strengthens with his strength; how it is inoculated by one schoolboy upon another; how early the youth thinks himself superior to his mother, owing her perhaps forbearance, but no real respect."[11]

Despite the radical nature of Brontë's thesis—her understanding of the way in which the indulgence of men leads them to become tyrants over women and ensures female subjugation—Brontë must legitimize her heroine by enclosing her narrative within that of the man destined to become her second husband. Although Helen struggles to forestall her son's traditional assimilation within the patriarchy, Brontë needs to legitimize Helen's rebellion against her first husband by giving it a patriarchal imprimatur in the form of Gilbert Markham. Thus, Helen Graham's narrative is enclosed within Gilbert's. His reinscription of her story and his accompanying interpretations of events legitimize her as the violated Angel in the House. To compensate for his appropriation of Helen's story, Brontë attempts in Markham to present a feminist reformation of the indulged son of patriarchy by having him educated through Helen's journals and her life. But the possibility of Helen's marginalization remains in the ideological imperative of the dutiful daughter of patriarchy and forces us to feel that the traditional narrative resolution of marriage raises as many questions as it answers.

Gaskell's *North and South* is like *The Tenant of Wildfell Hall* in proposing male education as a possible means of interrupting the destructive dialectic of patriarchy's dutiful daughter and marginal mother. Mrs. Thornton, the mother, clearly fears displacement by Margaret Hale, and Gaskell provides a moving account of her anguished love: "A terrible pain—a pang of vain jealousy—shot through her: she hardly knew whether it was more physical or mental; but it forced her to sit down."[12] When her son returns, his proposal rejected by Margaret, he murmurs, "No one loves me,—no one cares for me, but you, mother," and she responds, "Mother's love is given by God, John. It holds fast for ever and ever" (*NS*, p. 271). Although the usurpation of Mrs. Thornton's place ultimately seems inevitable, it is only so within patriarchy's hierarchical imperative: a man replaces his mother with his wife. As Mr. Thornton is forced through Margaret's agency to recognize the destructive nature of the master/worker hierarchy with its explosive potential for violence, he is simultaneously questioning other such hierarchies. He recognizes that, "no mere institutions . . . can attach class to class as they should be attached, unless the working out of such institutions brings the individuals of the different classes into actual personal contact. Such intercourse is the very breath of life" (*NS*, p. 525). And this recognition enables him to turn to his mother in the crisis of his business failure and to find solace and support in their communion: "It was a great comfort to have had this conversation with his mother" (*NS*, p. 518). Further, it prepares for his immediate and entire acceptance of Margaret's offer of financial aid, an acceptance which is distinctive in that Thornton does not make the demurrers common to male protagonists when accepting a wife of vastly superior financial means. Cooperation and social intercourse replace competition and self-assertion.

One subtle feature of Gaskell's text anticipates this dismantling of patriarchal categories. In descriptions of her heroine, Margaret Hale, Gaskell often has recourse to oxymorons. When Thornton meets her he is impressed with her movements, "full of a soft feminine defiance," and her eyes, "meeting his with quiet maiden freedom" (*NS*, p. 100). "Soft feminine" and "defiance" jar, as we expect to read something like "soft feminine delicacy"; "quiet maiden" and "freedom" arrest us because we anticipate a phrase like "quiet maiden modesty." The stereotype of the dutiful daughter is introduced only to be suddenly exposed by its radical revision. Not surprisingly, the concluding paragraphs of Gaskell's novel display this same tendency toward oxymoronic description of Margaret and her actions. She is "glowing with beautiful shame" and she tries to wrest flowers out of Thornton's hands "with gentle violence" (*NS*, p. 530). The traditional ideology of patriarchal narrative closure is undermined in the descriptive oxymorons. We expect the heroine to be enfolded in the hero's arms as she will be enclosed in his life, her meaning and purpose circumscribed by his. But in Margaret's acceptance lies the possibility of defiance, in her submission is latent violence. The tension between terms generates an open space for the action of Margaret and the continued presence of Mrs. Thornton.

Gaskell's resolution is more positive than any George Eliot can construct with the possible exception of that in *Middlemarch*. But, even there, the novel's resolution fulfills the ideology of patriarchal narrative closure because Dorothea is enclosed within Will's life: "Many who knew her, thought it a pity that so substantive and rare a creature should have been absorbed into the life of another."[13] The resolution to *Adam Bede*, which also initially appears positive, requires both the death of Lizbeth Bede and the cessation of Dinah's preaching, much approved by Adam, who thinks it right for her "to set th' example o' submitting."[14]

In Eliot, I note a significant division between the early and later novels in the representation of the mother/son relationship. In "Janet's Repentance" (Mamsey and Dempster), *Silas Marner* (Dolly and Adam Winthrop), *Adam Bede* (Lizbeth and Adam Bede), and *The Mill on the Floss* (Bessie and Tom Tulliver), the mother looks to her son as a replacement for the father, accepting his authority (even his brutality, in the case of Dempster) uncritically. The mothers are usually querulous, weak, and foolish women, acknowledging their dependent and marginal status. In *Romola*, a transitional novel, Eliot does not represent any mother/son relationships, but

Romola herself emerges as a madonna, mother to a community, and we find her in the novel's conclusion instructing Tito's son by Tessa. Romola has become, ironically, the *pater familias* and prepares the way for Eliot's strong, authoritative mothers to follow. I would suggest that, with increasing fame, George Eliot discovered a confidence that enabled her to move from the position of dutiful daughter seeking to placate the father to a position of moral authority that was signaled historically by her assumption of the role of "wise woman" in the salon. But the "wise woman" was a maternal role that perhaps made more evident woman's marginality. The novels of George Eliot's artistic maturity—*Felix Holt, Middlemarch,* and *Daniel Deronda*—all present mothers who have asserted themselves in the world. In *Middlemarch,* many of the significant mothers of sons—Lydgate's, Casaubon's, Ladislaw's—are absent, but of Ladislaw's we know a crucial detail. Both she and her own mother were rebels and their rebellions have become a value for Ladislaw, who wishes to preserve their inheritance and is therefore willing to reject patriarchal identification and appropriation. Ladislaw, described as an "Italian with white mice" (*M,* p. 359), a "Daphnis in coat and waistcoat" (*M,* p. 264), and the "slim young fellow with his girl's complexion" (*M,* p. 446), is both feminized and marginalized. He and his mother provide a poignant contrast to the more fully dramatized mother/son relationships in *Felix Holt* and *Daniel Deronda,* where the sons seem incapable of learning or valuing the mothers' lessons.

In *Felix Holt,* Mrs. Holt's quarrels with her son parody Mrs. Transome's more serious sense of loss and violation in a world made threatening by the maturity and ascension to the head of the estate by her son. In *Daniel Deronda,* the Princess Halm-Eberstein's cruel fate is to watch her son reclaim the patriarchal heritage of Judaism from which she has sought to release both herself and him. The novels suggest that the patriarchal bias is so deeply ingrained in our culture and world view that for women to challenge it is a futile and tragic exercise. A mother's yearning love for her son within a patriarchal structure dictates a self-suppression that the son, socialized by the same ideology, will happily escape, and we witness the pain and poignancy of the ways mothers have been implicated in enforcing their own marginalization.

The son's relation to his mother in Eliot's *Felix Holt* and *Daniel Deronda* paints a dark picture of woman's transformative potential in the world, a picture in stark contrast to the Victorian myths of women's moral powers of suasion. Ironically, too, both Esther Lyon and Gwendolen Harleth, through their choices of male mentors, find themselves endorsing the very values that have culminated in such misery for their mothers. The result is a conflicting pattern of values where the story of the marginal mother demystifies and exposes that of the dutiful daughter.

The opening chapters of *Felix Holt* impress us with a mother's painful sense of her utter inconsequence to her son. Mrs. Transome eagerly anticipates the return of Harold after a fifteen-year absence, only to be stunned by the discovery that she who "had been used to rule in virtue of acknowledged superiority" is "completely . . . excluded from her son's inward world."[15] "I am a hag!" she says to herself, "an ugly old woman who happens to be his mother. That is what he sees in me . . . I shall count for nothing" (*FH,* p. 22). And later the narrator says, "The shadow which had fallen over Mrs. Transome in this first interview with her son was the presentiment of her powerlessness" (*FH,* p. 26). She ultimately must submit to her son's lecture: "Women, very properly, don't change their views, but keep to the notions in which they have been brought up. It doesn't signify what they think—they are not called upon to judge or to act. You must really leave me to take my own course in these matters, which properly belong to men" (*FH,* p. 40). Her response is eloquent: "I don't know who would be a mother if she could foresee what a slight thing she will be to her son when she is old" (*FH,* p. 40). When Mrs. Transome confides to her personal maid, "A woman never has seen the worst till she is old," she is answered with the consolation, "It mayn't be good luck to be a woman . . . But one begins with it from a baby: one gets used to it" (*FH,* pp. 379, 380). It is tempting to multiply examples from this novel. Mrs. Transome is the fallen woman—fallen by virtue of her adultery; she is supposedly mythic in her transformative power, heir to the ages, and yet she is utterly inconsequential, heir to nothing. The demonic woman might be able to transform society, but not if she is a mother.

The supposedly kinder son, the eponymous hero of *Felix Holt,* is really only more indulgent with a mother who is also depicted as irrelevant to his life. When she complains of her son's pride and obstinacy, she is counselled that "many eminent servants of God have been led by ways as strange" (*FH,* p. 59). Her querulous rejoinder—"Then I'm sorry for their mothers"—anticipates Mrs. Transome's bitter remark: "God was cruel when he made women" (*FH,* p. 380). Jacob's patriarchal ladder may extend to heaven, but women are denied the first rung.

Esther Lyon, the ultimately idealized heroine of this novel, relinquishes her vanity under Felix's tutelage. Her vivacity is curbed as she is stung by Felix's criticism, first into a new sense of duty toward her father and then into a resolution not to become, in Felix's words, one of those "foolish women who spoil men's lives" because "Men can't help loving them" (*FH,* p.

129). The total absolution of men and the notion that this innocent girl might ruin a man's life are made bitterly ironic by the spectacle of the discarded mothers who gave life to these patriarchal giants. The narrator urges us, on the one hand, to accept that "The best part of a woman's love is worship" (*FH*, pp. 362-63); but, on the other hand, she regrets that, "After all, she was a woman and could not make her own lot" (*FH*, p. 419). Sometimes the narrator of *Felix Holt* speaks eloquently of Esther's love for Felix, extolling her angelic nature: "When a woman feels purely and nobly, that ardour of hers which breaks through formulas too rigorously urged on men by daily practical needs, makes one of her most precious influences: she is the added impulse that shatters the stiffening crust of cautious experience" (*FH*, p. 456). At the same time the narrator depicts a shattered Mrs. Transome facing a cruel son who has now learned of her adultery: "She seemed as if age were striking her with a sudden wand—as if her trembling face were getting haggard before him. She was mute. But her eyes had not fallen; they looked up in helpless misery at her son. Her son turned away his eyes from her, and left her" (*FH*, p. 468).

The dialogue between the dutiful daughter and marginal mother, where the fate of each challenges that of the other, remains an informing tension in the novel. The obedience of Esther becomes all the more peremptory in the face of Mrs. Transome's disobedience and unhappiness. Thus, the novel, in its presentation of Esther's life, insists on the ideology inherent in narrative closure that the haunted, lonely spectacle of Mrs. Transome's life rejects, a dialogic representation that reflects George Eliot's simultaneous investment in and rebellion against Victorian self-fashionings that made women powerless icons.

Whereas Eliot wants to preserve the notion of marriage as resolution to the conflicts *Felix Holt* has presented, she does not persist in that fiction in her last novel, *Daniel Deronda*. Critics have commented on the irresolution of this work, which leaves Gwendolen Harleth's fate uncertain, raising the question of what a woman's fate can be within the patriarchy. In a novel that treats of inheritances—financial and spiritual—women inherit nothing. They are the "makeshift feminine offspring" of Sir Hugo, the "daughters, little better than no children,"[16] whose "sex was announced as a melancholy alternative, the offspring desired being a son" (*DD*, p. 214). The one heiress in the novel, Catherine Arrowpoint, insists on the freedom to choose her own husband, and, once married, disappears from the novel as her husband appropriates the authority of her position.

Of course, the issue of inheritance is focused most sharply on the Princess Halm-Eberstein and her frustrated desire to release her son, Daniel Deronda, from the grasp of his Jewish heritage. Judaism for her has meant an inheritance of even greater patriarchal restriction. She speaks of "slavery," of her father's "fettering [her] into obedience" (*DD*, p. 692). But though she has sought to defy her father, as she approaches death she finds his will inexorable and feels a coercion to tell Daniel of his heritage. This beaten, suffering woman is characterized by Joseph Kalonymos as the author of "that wicked contrivance" that would have robbed Daniel of his kindred and heritage. Kalonymos gloats, "I have restored to [Daniel Charisi] the offspring they had robbed him of" (*DD*, p. 789). Daniel is not his mother's son; he is his grandfather's and Mordecai's. The Princess's words to Daniel echo poignantly: "Poor boy! . . . I wonder how it would have been if I had kept you with me . . . whether you would have turned your heart to the old things . . . against mine . . . and we should have quarrelled . . . your grandfather would have been in you . . . and you would have hampered my life with your young growth from the old root" (*DD*, pp. 729-30). She has the prescience to see that Mirah, the woman Daniel loves, is "not ambitious . . . not one who must have a path of her own"; and she concludes, "Why, she is made for you, then . . . I can see that you would never have let yourself be merged in a wife, as your father was" (*DD*, pp. 728, 729).

Whereas the submission of Daniel's wife must be all the more absolute in the face of his mother's rebellion—like Esther's obedience in the face of Mrs. Transome's disobedience—Eliot's female protagonist, Gwendolen Harleth, ultimately stands outside the ideological closure of marriage. Neither dutiful daughter nor marginal mother, she inhabits the open space this dialogic has created. Her final letter to Daniel bespeaks the indeterminacy of her life:

> I have remembered your words—that I may live to be one of the best of women, who make others glad that they were born. I do not yet see how that can be, but you know better than I. If it ever comes true, it will be because you helped me. I only thought of myself, and I made you grieve. It hurts me now to think of your grief. You must not grieve any more for me. It is better—it shall be better with me because I have known you.
>
> (*DD*, p. 882)

Gwendolen's irresolution—"I do not yet see how that can be"—pinpoints the ideological character of marriage as narrative closure; her failure of traditional vocation within patriarchy exposes the abyss beyond.

Charlotte Brontë's *Villette*, a last novel like Eliot's *Daniel Deronda*, reaches a similar narrative and ideological impasse. In this work, Brontë depicts her only sympathetic mother/son relationship, that between Louisa and Graham Bretton. Yet I would argue that, through a significant process of displacement, Lucy Snowe replaces Louisa Bretton, precisely because Lucy conceives of herself as ineligible and negligible, just as a mother must. Lucy seeks to dress herself in the sober browns of the older woman and is acutely uncomfortable in youthful pink. A would-be lover to Graham, she is easily eclipsed by Polly Home. We experience Lucy's jealousy, not Louisa's. Graham himself links Lucy with his mother, commenting, "My mother is good; *she* is divine; and *you* are as true as steel."[17] Although he refers to her as a "god-sister," her emotions are those of the displaced mother. Mrs. Bretton largely disappears from the story as Lucy witnesses the accord among Polly, Graham, and Mr. Home. The jealous father relinquishes his prize and bonds with the son-to-be, preserving Polly as his dutiful daughter even as she becomes Graham's wife. Their trinity is symbolized by Polly's weaving the "grey lock" and "the blonde wave" with "a tress of her own hair," and then securing the whole in her locket.

The dutiful daughter Polly moves toward absolute closure in her submission to patriarchal ideology: "She kept her husband's love, she aided his progress—of his happiness, she was the cornerstone." Lucy tells us further, "These two lives of Graham and Polly were blessed . . . It was so, for God saw that it was good" (*V*, p. 533). Irony peeks through this traditional resolution blessed by a traditional patriarchal God. That denouement gives way to a second—Lucy's—where indeterminacy prevails, dominated by what Charlotte Brontë called the "little puzzle" of M. Paul's fate. God is summoned as his guardian, too: "God watch that sail! Oh! guard it!" (*V*, p. 595). But here we pause, "pause at once . . . leave sunny imaginations hope" (*V*, 596). In displacing the marginal mother with Lucy Snowe and in stressing the indeterminacy of Lucy's fate, Charlotte Brontë, like her sister authors, exposes yet more fully the ways in which the patriarchal ideology of women's lives undergirds conventions of narrative closure.

III

Victorian women writers persistently reveal a dialogic imagination in their representations of dutiful daughters and marginal mothers, testifying to the centrality of this conflict in their lives. Their dialogic narratives both challenge patriarchal ideologies and make traditional narrative closure problematic. In spite of pervasive myths regarding the morally suasive power of women, Victorian women writers saw that the myth of motherhood continuously demanded the mother's displacement by patriarchy's dutiful daughter and effectively blocked a woman's influence in the world. Their narratives detail that process and, in so doing, expose the patriarchal bias of narrative closures that require a heroine's submission to male definition and her conscription within a man's life. The richly dialogic narratives that result from the depiction of marginal mothers with dutiful daughters opened up a space in which Victorian women writers could investigate and rewrite narrative closure.

Perhaps, then, those literary mothers would have rejoiced to find a new affirmation available to their literary daughter, Virginia Woolf. In *To the Lighthouse*, Lily Briscoe wrestles with the presence and the spirit of Mrs. Ramsay and the mother's dictum that "They [Lily and William Bankes] must marry."[18] In a moment of illumination, daughter Lily reconceptualizes her duty: "She need not marry, thank heaven: she need not undergo that degradation. She was saved from that dilution. She would move the tree more to the middle" (*TL*, p. 154). Woolf affirms art as a wholly satisfying alternative to marriage yet she preserves the value of the mother who enables the final resolution—Cam's, James's, and Mr. Ramsay's landing at the lighthouse and Lily's definitive brush stroke. In so doing, Woolf takes possession of the narrative space that her precursors had opened up, a space where sons need not reject the mothers' visions, where daughters are released from traditional patterns of duty, and where narratives can experiment with new modes of resolution.

Notes

1. See Elizabeth Helsinger et al., eds., *The Woman Question: Defining Voices, 1837-1883* (New York and London: Garland Publishing, Inc., 1983), p. xi; and Martha Vicinus, ed., *A Widening Sphere: Changing Roles of Victorian Women* (Bloomington and London: Indiana Univ. Press, 1980), p. ix.

2. Carol Christ, "Victorian Masculinity and the Angel in the House," in *A Widening Sphere*, p. 146.

3. I have used the definitions set out by Helsinger et al. They postulate first the Angel in the House; loving and self-sacrificing, she "provides continuity and moral strength in a rapidly changing society." The second myth, in antithesis, postulated men and women as completely equal but because it was "so much at odds with the widespread interest in women's special nature . . . it seems to have played a smaller role in the public debate." The other two myths might be called the "Angel out of the House" and the "Female Savior," both related to the Angel in the House so that "distinctions . . . are often particularly difficult to draw." In brief, the Angel out of the House extended her duties beyond the home, not entering "man's" sphere but "ministering to the needs of the world at large through philanthropy or social service." The Female Saviour is a radical version of the angelic ideal: "a female saviour leading the way to a fuller humanity and ushering in a new era of community and love" (pp. xiv-xv).

4. Nina Auerbach, *Woman and the Demon: The Life of a Victorian Myth* (Cambridge: Harvard Univ. Press, 1982), pp. 2-3.

5. Auerbach, pp. 2, 3.

6. Gertrude Himmelfarb, *Marriage and Morals Among the Victorians* (New York: Alfred A. Knopf, 1986), pp. 78-79.

7. *Selections from George Eliot's Letters,* ed. Gordon Haight (New Haven and London: Yale Univ. Press, 1985), p. 230. Margaret Homans, *Bearing the Word: Language and Female Experience in Nineteenth-Century Women's Writing* (Chicago and London: Univ. of Chicago Press, 1986), has persuasively argued for the pressure that Victorian "exhortations placed on women to embrace motherhood as a vocation—or, at the very least, to define any other vocation in terms of motherhood." She adds, "Both Eliot and Gaskell attempt to accommodate at once their own desires to write and the expectation that they perform the roles that accumulate around the idea of mother in Victorian England" (p. 153).

8. The work of Mikhail Bakhtin provides a vocabulary and a theoretical framework for interpreting women's novels. See, particularly, *The Dialogic Imagination: Four Essays,* trans. Caryl Emerson and Michael Holquist, ed. Michael Holquist (Austin: Univ. of Texas Press, 1981), and *Problems of Dostoevsky's Poetics,* ed. Caryl Emerson (Minneapolis: Univ. of Minnesota Press, 1984).

9. I am indebted in my formulation to the suggestiveness of Nancy Miller's article, "Emphasis Added: Plots and Plausibilities in Women's Fiction," *PMLA* 96 (1981), 36-48, which speaks of the ideological character of narrative conventions.

10. Anne Brontë, *The Tenant of Wildfell Hall* (Harmondsworth: Penguin, 1979), p. 79. Subsequent citations to the novel will be from this edition and page numbers will be preceded by *TWH.*

11. John Stuart Mill, "The Subjection of Women," in *Essays on Sex Equality,* ed. Alice S. Rossi (Chicago and London: Univ. of Chicago Press, 1970), pp. 218-19.

12. Elizabeth Gaskell, *North and South* (Harmondsworth: Penguin, 1970), p. 269. Subsequent citations to the novel will be from this edition and page numbers will be preceded by *NS.*

13. George Eliot, *Middlemarch* (Boston: Houghton Mifflin, 1956), p. 611. Subsequent citations to the novel will be from this edition and page numbers will be preceded by *M.*

14. George Eliot, *Adam Bede* (Boston: Houghton Mifflin, 1968), p. 449.

15. George Eliot, *Felix Holt The Radical* (New York: Norton, 1970), pp. 17, 20. Subsequent citations to the novel will be from this edition and page numbers will be preceded by *FH.*

16. George Eliot, *Daniel Deronda* (Harmondsworth: Penguin, 1967), p. 498. Subsequent citations to the novel will be from this edition and page numbers will be preceded by *DD.*

17. Charlotte Brontë, *Villette* (Harmondsworth: Penguin, 1979), p. 529. Subsequent citations to the novel will be from this edition and page numbers will be preceded by *V.*

18. Virginia Woolf, *To the Lighthouse* (New York: Harcourt, Brace and World, 1955), p. 109. Subsequent citations to the novel will be from this edition and page numbers will be preceded by *TL.*

Marianne Hirsch (essay date 1994)

SOURCE: Hirsch, Marianne. "Jane's Family Romances." In *Borderwork: Feminist Engagements with Comparative Literature,* edited by Margaret R. Higonnet, pp. 162-85. Ithaca, N.Y. and London: Cornell University Press, 1994.

[*In the following essay, Hirsch views* Jane Eyre *as a family romance and analyzes Brontë's representation of maternity in the novel, arguing that such an approach reveals a deeper understanding of feminist and comparative readings of the text.*]

Narrative is, in sum, the most elaborate kind of attempt, on the part of the speaking subject, after syntactic competence, to situate his or her self among his or her desires and their taboos, that is, at the interior of the oedipal triangle.

—Julia Kristeva

The urge to intellectual and artistic creation and the productivity of motherhood spring from common sources, and it seems very natural that one should be capable of replacing the other.

—Helene Deutsch

Although most mothers have been and are women, mothering is potentially work for men and women. . . . There is no reason to believe that one sex rather than the other is more capable of doing maternal work.

—Sara Ruddick

"When his first-born was put into his arms, he could see that the boy had inherited his own eyes, as they once were—large, brilliant and black."[1] Paradoxically, the novel's only hint of Jane Eyre's maternity actually serves to affirm the paternity of Edward Rochester: his gaze at his son, and the male line of transmission by which the son inherits his father's eyes and therefore this same gaze. This affirmation of paternity is all the more incongruous in a paragraph that seems to challenge masculine dominance. In revealing Rochester's regained eyesight, the novel still reserves access and control of the symbolic for Jane and grants her husband the discernment of nature, not of books: "He cannot read or write much; but he can find his way without being led by the hand: the sky is no longer a blank to him—the earth no longer a void" (397).

Exploring this incongruity and looking, in particular, at how maternal and paternal functions are deployed in Brontë's novel provides an opportunity for a new look at a novel that has become a classic, if not a cult text, in the women's studies canon. It is possible to trace, through readings of *Jane Eyre,* the evolution of feminist literary interpretation: all the major trends are clearly represented. For feminist comparatists, however, *Jane Eyre* is more than such a touchstone. In reading the novel through the perspective of the family romance, I hope to bring together the formalist, generic, and cultural interests of the comparatist with the psychoanalytic focus of the feminist literary critic, and to bring them to bear on a text which, set at the moment of European imperial expansion, in itself raises questions about any comparatist, cross-cultural venture. As I teach this novel—and I have taught it in both comparative literature and women's studies courses—and as I write about it, I still feel as though I were shuttling back and forth between my two identities, my comparatist and my feminist selves. I hope that this reading will show some of that discursive disjointedness even as it helps to bridge it. I also hope that it will allow me to write into it my personal as well as my theoretical commitments.

Jane Eyre offers an especially radical elaboration of a *female* family romance model present in a number of Victorian novels by women writers: Brontë gives Jane the possibility not only of becoming a mother, but also of combining maternity with a different, and in the ideology of the period a contradictory, labor—the imaginative and self-engendering act of writing her own story. What makes it possible for Jane to become a mother, a condition that most nineteenth-century women writers will do anything to avoid for their heroines, is connected to the ways in which maternity is defined and deployed in the text. One key factor in this deployment is the distribution of a parental role to Edward Rochester, which enables us to read the father-son dyad described in the quoted passage as a sign not of Rochester's *paternity* but of what we might think of as his *male maternity.* Other factors include the particular class structure that underlies the novel and the specific definitions of what constitutes the labor of mothering in the first place. These definitions, however, raise certain literary questions as well; for example, one might ask whether Jane's maternity allows her to adopt a maternal voice in the text and to develop a maternal textuality, or whether, in spite of her motherhood, she continues to write her childhood fantasies and experiences.

In bringing *Jane Eyre* into the comparatist canon, and in reading it through the generic lens of the family romance, I hope also to bring it *back* to women's studies, transformed. Why the family romance? One genre where comparatist and feminist concerns have intersected frequently and fruitfully for me and for others is the bildungsroman, and one might wonder what a shift from the bildungsroman to the family romance might open up for comparatist readers of this text and of other realist novels. This shift is meant to venture a response to recent revisions in feminist readings of *Jane Eyre,* for in the late 1980s and 1990s earlier celebrations of the novel's feminist rebelliousness have been seriously challenged and reformulated. Jane Lazarre's reading of Jane as the "rebel girl," Sandra Gilbert and Susan Gubar's use of Brontë's representation of the woman writer as the "madwoman in the attic," Sandra Gilbert's reading of Jane as a female "pilgrim's progress," Adrienne Rich's demonstration of how successfully Jane overcomes the "temptations of a motherless daughter" all represent a specific moment in the practice of feminist reading, a moment that highlights individual achievement and psychological growth and development as unquestioned values for women.[2] More recently the novel has been cast instead as a portrait of a feminist individualist heroine whose marginality allows her to develop an oppositional discourse which *seem* to challenge but which actually *participates* in hegemonic ideology—Western, imperialist, racist, middle class, heterosexist, familial, psychological. Readings by Gayatri Spivak, Nancy Armstrong, and Mary Childers, among others, brilliantly explore the novel's blindnesses to its own collusions and "otherings."[3] Spivak's essay is especially pertinent in a comparatist framework, not only because it reads *Jane Eyre* against the background of European imperial expansion, but also because it confronts the nineteenth-century feminist individualism of the "marginal" Jane with the persona of the other, native, female subject. Spivak demands a comparatist reading that is fully cognizant of imperialism as the background for academic comparatism, and a feminist reading that reveals the problematic relationship between the feminist heroine and the "other" woman, her double or her victim.

Although I have found these essays illuminating, I am also concerned about how quickly they dismiss the novel's radical aspects, and with them the feminism of the 1970s for which *Jane Eyre* has come to stand. Here I agree with Cora Kaplan's suggestion that "Jane Eyre is in danger of displacing Bertha Mason as a new 'monstrous feminine'—the anti-text of what eighties and nineties feminism should be."[4] Kaplan's strategy—reading the novel as a thematization of contemporary British politics, firmly rooted in its 1840s context, which reveals it to be anti-imperialist, though still racist and nationalist—is very different from Spivak's, and the two together can illustrate the distance between English department new historicism and a comparatist approach informed by the cultural critique of the 1980s. In what follows I confront the more recent revisionist critical readings of *Jane Eyre* with earlier approaches highlighting the novel's subversive strategies. I do this neither in order to reinscribe *Jane Eyre* into an unquestioned feminist or comparatist canon, nor so as to claim that *Jane Eyre* is unquestionably "radical," a term that, in itself, needs reflection and contextualization. My aim is to see how some "new" comparatist questions in feminist theory concerning race, class, and empire can relocate and redefine without totally displacing "older" concerns with family, identity, and authority. It is precisely a comparatist perspective that may be able to bring out points of connection between what has come to appear as two separate moves and two separate moments in feminist criticism and theory. *Family,* in my reading, functions as a nexus organizing a variety of issues in this family romance. In responding to both older and more recent feminist concerns (maternity/paternity and class issues in relation to work and authorship), such a reading tries to envision a mother-inclusive and class-conscious feminism as well as a gender, class, and race-conscious comparatist genre theory.

FAMILY ROMANCES

The "female family romance" model I have identified in nineteenth-century novels by women writers is based on Freud's notion of the *Familienroman* and the strange ways in which it echoes, by both repeating and distorting, the texts of nineteenth-century realism. In making this connection I assert my belief that Freud's analysis responds to the same cultural plots as nineteenth-century fiction, and that in a number of his essays he clarifies and elucidates not only those underlying cultural plots but also the very structures of the realist novel's presentation of individual development and familial fantasies. Predictably, however, Freud is clearer on spelling out a male model, one that fits Balzac's Rastignac, Dickens's Pip, or Keller's Heinrich much more readily than Brontë's Jane; a female model has to be extrapolated from his essays and read back into and against the work of women writers. My analysis does not aim to privilege Freud's insights into female psychology. I read him as a reader of fictional plots which he brings out, elaborates, and reformulates into theory, or into theoretical fiction.

In spite of its Freudian source, the notion of the family romance, more than the notion of the bildungsroman, facilitates a consciousness of the intersections of textuality with gender, class, and race. The bildungsroman is concerned with the growth and development of the individual; its source is the bourgeois culture of eighteenth-century Germany, with its idealist belief in the perfectibility of the human spirit. Its focus, as critics have charged, is indeed individualist. Even though it

places individual development in the context of familial and social structures, its goal is the formation of an integrated psychological and social subject. The critic who approaches a novel through the generic rubric of bildungsroman does risk psychologizing social, political, and economic issues. Not only have feminist redefinitions of the bildungsroman raised questions about the individualist goals of *Bildung* as the traditional genre defines them, but they have looked critically at the very notion of "individual." Feminist revisionist criticism, much of it comparatist in nature, has indeed redefined *Bildung* in ways that make it more attuned to women's lives and more congruent with female-authored texts. *Bildung,* in the eyes of feminist critics, is less child-centered, less aimed toward autonomy, more affiliative and relational. It needs to be contextualized and historicized; it needs to be confronted with the insights of feminist psychology. Even a redefined individuality, however, even an individuality that is inflected by the differences that gender makes in the social, cannot easily respond to the critiques of class, race, and imperial bias; it remains privileged and informed by first world middle-class values. In continuing to be a narrative of emancipation, it fosters certain relationships and certain aspects of individuality over others. We can see these values in the readings of *Jane Eyre* that were published in the 1970s and early 1980s, although not all of those readings were informed by generic criticism and the bildungsroman. They stressed friendship and sisterhood, nurturance and affiliation, care for others and care for self. But they also stressed individuality, self-reliance, self-preservation, choice, and self-expression.[5]

It may seem paradoxical that the notion of family romance, adapted from Freud and from feminist revisions of Freud, should offer a more satisfactory alternative to the bildungsroman as a generic lens through which to read women's fiction, yet I believe that for the nineteenth-century European novel it does. In Freud's terms, the *Familienroman* is still an individual interrogation of origins, one that embeds the engenderment of narrative within the structure of family. The family romance thus combines and reveals as indistinguishable the experience of family and the process of narrative. Precisely because the family romance is the *fantasied story* of the individual place within the family unit, it is alterable and manipulable, adaptable to varied circumstances. In fact, the individual ability to shift familial circumstance, to dream of alternatives, is the essence of the family romance. The narrating subject is but a member of the unit of family, and all of the relations within that unit impinge on his or her activity of fabulation. And, as those relations shift, so can the family romance: each life story is shaped by more than one familial fantasy. Fantasies might begin in childhood and be characteristic of childhood, but they can mature to adulthood; they can even concern aging and adult development. Objecting to the family romance construct from a feminist or Marxist perspective, one might argue that family is a unit that is inherently bourgeois and conservative; that it is the agent of the transmission of property and the safeguarding of values. One might argue as well that family, at least in the psychoanalytic narrative, is still first and foremost a psychological unit. Yet, even in the Freudian schema, family is what the individual wants to manipulate, to transform, and to escape. The constraints of family are precisely what motivates the desire for liberation, social transformation, even revolution. Thus, the generic rubric of family romance shows both the power that family holds as a hegemonic mythos in the period of nineteenth-century realism and the pain, even the violence, that any transformation of its traditional oedipal and patriarchal shapes can cause.

The fantasy of family is a fantasy of relationship; it can be a collective rather than a uniquely individual fantasy. Family, moreover, is a larger unit than the nuclear one; it includes extended kin relations, and even for Freud it included servants and governesses. The narrative of family is embedded in a narrative of class aspiration and economic fantasies of enrichment. And the character of patriarchal family relations is, in the family romance, applicable to other relations, whether they be intergroup, international, or intercultural. Family structures can therefore be used as metaphors of colonial relations. I realize, however, as I adopt and adapt this model, that it remains problematic in a number of ways: it forces us to begin with Freud; it does continue to promote familial values even as it transforms and critiques them; it does weight the analysis toward the psychological even as it allows an expansion to the social and political. What is more, it reinforces the family as model and metaphor, whether positive or negative, for other forms of relation. Yet in doing so it merely reveals something that is indeed central to European realism. In spite of its problems, I believe that the generic rubric of family romance opens up certain aspects of nineteenth-century novels by women writers to scrutiny and to critique. It permits us to ask, for example, how Jane can combine the act of writing with the labor of maternity, and it permits us to see what desires shape Brontë's representation of her heroine's developmental course. It also permits us to see in a new light the transformations that Rochester undergoes in the novel. Tangentially, it permits us to evaluate anew the role of Bertha Mason and the novel's position on St. John's imperialist project. Yet I would propose this model not as transhistorically or cross-culturally valid but as applicable specifically to nineteenth-century European and American realism.

The nineteenth-century heroine's female family romance, as extrapolated from Freud, comprises three principal elements: (1) the condition of motherlessness and therefore the freedom to develop beyond the limitations of the maternal story and maternal transmission; (2) the replacement of maternal nurturance with a paternal/fraternal bond, which turns into a quasi-incestuous heterosexual romance/marriage, affording the heroine access to plot and to the symbolic; and (3) the avoidance of maternity, most often made possible by this conflation of husband with brother/father, and thereby the possibility of remaining in the plot.

For most nineteenth-century heroines maternal absence actually engenders feminine fictions. Plot demands the separation of heroines from the messages of powerlessness and disinheritance which mothers tend to transmit. Maternal stories are stories not to be repeated: from the perspective of fictional plot, mothers can only be examples not to be emulated. The somewhat unconventional though severely truncated story of Jane's mother provides an apt example. Adored by her brother, disowned by her family for making a "low" marriage to a penniless clergyman, she dies of the typhus fever he caught from the poor he visited in a large manufacturing town, leaving her daughter Jane to the care of her more conventional brother, Mr. Reed. In Mrs. Eyre's case the break with her home and family embeds her in the economically based institution of marriage and motherhood, which proves to be fatal. She is the victim of the social constraints that delimit women's lives; but, from a different perspective, she has to die so that her daughter might have a story. The benefits of Jane's motherlessness are only confirmed by the other disastrous portraits of mothers the novel presents. Mrs. Reed, Céline Varens, Antoinetta Mason, even Mrs. Ingram turn out to be debilitating obstacles to their daughters' successful development. The earlier they are eliminated, the better chance their daughters have; the deeper the mother-daughter bond, the more devastating it proves to be. From contact with their mothers, daughters inherit madness, intemperance, and savagery at worst, incompetence and flightiness at best.

Freud's analysis in "Family Romances," however, implies that mothers need to be eliminated from feminine fictions for deeper reasons.[6] The family romance, as Freud describes it, provides for the developing individual a necessary escape from the "authority of his parents," and it is this conflict over authority and legitimacy which becomes the basis for fantasy and mythmaking. Read in conjunction with Marthe Robert's gloss, *Origins of the Novel,* Freud's essay becomes the paradigm for a more extensive theory of fiction making.[7] "Indeed, the whole process of society rests upon the opposition between successive generations," Freud asserts. Two stages define this process of liberation. First, the child, feeling slighted and in competition with siblings, and seeing that his parents are not unique and incomparable as he had at first supposed, imagines that he might be a stepchild or adopted. He frees himself from his parents by imaginatively replacing them with richer, more noble, aristocratic ones. Robert calls this the "foundling plot" and discusses it as the basis for the fantastic narratives and romances of Chrétien de Troyes, Cervantes, Hoffmann, Novalis, Melville, and Kafka. At this stage in his explanation of the "foundling fantasy," Freud introduces a gender distinction, arguing that "a boy is far more inclined to feel hostile impulses toward his father than toward his mother and has a far more intense desire to get free from *him* than from *her.* In this respect the imagination of girls is apt to show itself much weaker."[8] For Freud, the fantasies surrounding the child's relation to his or her origin, and the rebellious refusal of parental authority, processes intimately connected to the creation of fiction, are more available to the boy because they are embedded in the conflicts over authority between father and son. Because the girl fails to participate in the struggle over authority, or in the anxiety over legitimacy, she evinces, in Freud's terms, a weaker imagination.

At the second stage of the family romance a beginning awareness of "the difference in the parts played by fathers and mothers in their sexual relations" begins to inform fantasy. When the child realizes that *"pater semper incertus est,* while the mother is *certissima,* the family romance undergoes a curious curtailment: it contents itself with exalting the child's father, but no longer casts any doubts on his maternal origin, which is regarded as something unalterable." The child's fantasies, Freud insists, become sexual at this stage and take the mother as sexual object. Freud suggests that they have "two principal aims, an erotic and an ambitious one."[9] Robert classifies this plot as the "bastard" plot—the origins of the realist fiction of Balzac, Dostoyevski, Tolstoy, Proust, Faulkner, Dickens. But because of the different roles mothers and fathers play in the process of reproduction, the father alone enters into the realm of fantasy while the mother remains firmly and certainly planted in reality, excluded from the process of "fictionalization." While imagination can alter her *status* and explore her *sexuality,* it cannot replace her *identity.* This "real" mother does become the object of the child's manipulative fantasy, which turns her into an adulteress, the agent of his own social elevation. Typically the mother falls in status while the father is elevated to royalty. Ultimately, the mother is no more than an instrument in the central drama between father and son. Men thus participate more directly in the plot of class aspiration, which is an inherent aspect of the family romance, while women have only a mediated access to class mobility.

Freud and Robert do not explore the gender asymmetry of this second model. If these daydreams and fantasies are the bases for creativity, what are the implications of this shift in the family romance for the girl, especially for the girl who also wants to develop her imagination and wants to write? If the mother's identity is certain, then the girl lacks the important opportunity to replace imaginatively the same-sex parent, a process on which, Freud's model insists, imagination and creativity depend. The father's presence, since his identity is uncertain, does not preclude fantasies of illegitimacy which can constitute a new self, free from familial and class constraints. The mother's presence, however, makes such fantasies impossible; therefore, we might extrapolate, in order to make possible the "opposition between successive generations" and to free the girl's imaginative play, the mother must be eliminated from the fiction. Yet even eliminating the mother from her plots cannot offer the girl a story that is parallel to the boy's: the drama of father and son, so fundamentally a conflict about authority and economic success in the public world, could never translate into a drama between mother and daughter. The girl's plot, if it is to have any import, must, like the boy's, revolve around the males in the family, who hold the keys to the power and ambition where plot resides.

Whereas the boy uses the mother as an instrument in the conflict with his father, however, and ultimately replaces his erotic fantasies with ambitious ones, the girl's fantasies revolve around the father in at once a more direct and a more conflicted manner. Since the father is *semper incertus,* the girl's heterosexual erotic relationships, unlike the boy's, are always potentially incestuous. *All* men are possible brothers, uncles, or fathers. Thus Freud's model implies that the danger of incest is more pronounced for the girl; the conditions for it lie at the basis of Freud's familial construction, making any marriage potentially incestuous, and, conversely, any father or brother a potentially safe erotic and sexual partner. In the female plot the father and his power *are* the object; what is more, fathers, brothers, uncles, and husbands are, in this particular psychic economy, interchangeable. Their precise *identity* is *semper incertus,* even as their *position* is forever desirable. Unlike the boy, who dreams of gaining authority by taking the father's place, the girl hopes to gain access to it by marrying him.

Thus, the "female family romance" implied in Freud's essay is founded on the elimination of the mother and the attachment to a husband/father. The feminine fiction then revolves not around the drama of same-sex parent-child relations but around marriage, which alone can place women's stories in a position of participating in the dynamics of power, authority, success, and legitimacy which constitute the plots of realist fiction. And in the marriage plot fathers, brothers, uncles, and husbands are conflated in complicated ways, and masculine representations often combine and modulate these roles.

Predictably, however, women writers do not simply hand over their heroines from mother to father/husband; they attempt to compensate for the loss of maternal nurturance by replacing the father with another man who offers an alternative to patriarchal power and dominance. Here is where women writers, to varying degrees, challenge the model implied in Freud's essay. I have understood the female fantasy that emerges from this will to difference in Adrienne Rich's terms as the fantasy of "the-man-who-would-understand,"[10] the man who, unlike a distant and authoritarian father, would combine maternal nurturance with paternal power. The male object, in this transformation of the marriage plot, takes the form of a "brother" or "uncle" who can be nurturing even as he provides access to the issues of legitimacy and authority central to plotting. Most important, perhaps, his fraternal, incestuous status can protect the heroine from becoming a mother and thereby can help her, in spite of the closure of marriage, to remain a subject, not to disappear from plot as the object of her child's fantasy. It is thus that women writers, in a gesture of resistance, attempt to revise a cultural plot leading, with certainty and inevitability, not only to marriage but most especially to maternity, a developmental plot Freud traces in his later essays, "Female Sexuality" and "Femininity." Here Freud asserts, of course, that mature femininity means not only the replacement of the mother with the father as libidinal object, but the replacement of the wish for a penis with a wish for a child. In resisting this developmental course, women writers offer their heroines an alternative direction—and the possibility of remaining in the plot.

Yet, whereas the male foundling and bastard fantasies revolve around the self and guarantee the hero's agency, the revisionary fantasy of the-man-who-would-understand revolves around the attachment to another person, and can at best promise only a mediated access to plotting. Moreover, the fraternal lover or husband ultimately offers the heroine a limited alternative to the father's patriarchal power. The fraternal marriage, even when it comes about, is at best a qualified solution to the heroine's desire for a continuing plot. In fact, although the fraternal man-who-would-understand cannot literally become the husband of the heroine's children, he most often eventually assumes a patriarchal power that may have been veiled but that certainly was not absent during the courtship plot.[11] He frequently has to be eliminated from the heroine's life so that she will be forced to determine her own course.[12] And although the heroine's childlessness does not necessarily offer a solution that ensures her survival and imaginative creativity, her course, we assume, would be insurmountably impeded by maternity.[13]

"MY SEARED VISION! MY CRIPPLED STRENGTH!"

Jane Eyre appears to be the epitome of the family romance: the orphan child, raised in a hostile counterfamily, freed imaginatively to dream of alternative familial contexts, to transform those dreams into fictions and those fictions into autobiography. As she sits in her window seat, Jane dreams her way into the family, only to realize that she is "less than a servant," brutally and unfairly cast out of their midst. Yet her healthy sense of injustice, coupled with her firm knowledge of her legitimacy, with her class affiliation, and with her education—a security that appears to be unshakable, resistant even to abuse and confinement—enhances Jane's freedom to imagine as well as her ability to analyze her situation and to speak out assertively against it. With father and mother dead, then, and with this combination of class security, clear-cut mistreatment, and, later, her education, Jane can fantasize various family romances. Her fantastic analysis of her situation appears most vividly in the dream-paintings Rochester later so admires, paintings that give us an insight into her "inward eye" and the familial landscapes it can dream up (109-11). The first, a drowned female corpse whose arm sticks out of the water below a powerful cormorant who holds her gold bracelet is perhaps her dead mother, marked by the sign of economic security representing female victimization and masculine dominance. The second, a soft pastel female bust with stars in her hair and dark, wild eyes, is clearly an alternative maternal figure of her imagination, an angry mother-goddess perhaps. The third, a colossal diademed head with hollow, despairing eyes, draped in a dark turban, could represents a patriarchal specter whose power she challenges and whose vitality she removes: his ring is of white flame, and his sparkles have a lurid tinge.

Jane is motherless, and indeed Brontë replaces the mother with other parental figures. Jane is not unnurtured: Bessie, Miss Temple, Helen Burns, the memory of Mr. Reed all contribute to her relative psychic security, although none assumes an importance she cannot fantasize herself away from. She even enjoys the spiritual nurture of the moon, which appears to her on a number of occasions as an alternative presence to the Christian spirituality represented in the novel by St. John. Until we get to Rochester, the novel conforms perfectly to the female family romance pattern: Jane is an orphan; her father's family's economic status is uncertain, but her mother's identity and position is *certissima*. Even though she is told that she is less than a servant, she knows to assert her right to be treated as an individual, and her individuality is firmly upheld by the class allegiance she can claim through maternal certainty. In the Reed household, as well as later at school, at Thornfield, and at Marsh's End, Jane has the opportunity to fantasize various familial configurations that would improve her condition. Through those fantasies Jane develops the imagination that so characterizes her.

But in Brontë's novel Edward Rochester is not the fraternal man-who-would-understand. Although at their first encounter Rochester falls off his horse and relies on Jane's assistance, although he appeals for her help on other occasions, although he cross-dresses as the Gypsy, although he "understands" Jane down to her deepest spirit and she can assert that they are "equals" as her spirit addresses his spirit, although, in other words, the novel works hard to establish their mutual understanding and in some sense their equality, Rochester never for a moment relinquishes his masculine patriarchal power, never surrenders his sexual otherness. And even though his economic, experiential, sexual, and generational power is unambiguously established early in the novel, even though it is accepted by Jane, who calls herself his dependent and calls him "master," he uses every opportunity to bolster it even further. The Gypsy scene and his charade about the impending marriage to Miss Ingram are good examples of Rochester's shameless abuse of power and status and his distance from the persona of the fraternal lover. Rochester's secrecy, his insistence about dressing Jane, about transforming her as quickly as possible into Mrs. Rochester, the "iron grip" with which he hurries her to church all leave no doubt as to his distant and powerful masculinity and to Jane's "mistake" in her choice of partner, a mistake which his violent "marital" struggle with Bertha and his hubristic attempts to defy religious and state law only serve to underscore.

Whereas in other novels the fraternal lover eventually turns into the patriarchal husband, however, veiling his phallic power only then to display it with surprising force, Rochester actually travels an opposite course: with the loss of his eyesight and his limb, he also definitively loses the dominance which made him unworthy of marrying Jane. The physical disabilities caused by the fire at Thornfield are metaphors for the harsh and painful psychological and spiritual transformations he undergoes. At Ferndean he again and again reminds Jane of his dependence, his weakness, his "seared vision and crippled strength" (391). Jane rewards him by insisting: "I love you better now, when I can really be useful to you, than I did in your state of proud independence when you disdained every part but that of the giver and protector" (392). As she becomes the intermediary by which Rochester sees, feels, and interprets the world in and around him, Jane gains the power Rochester has lost: "He saw nature—he saw books through me; and never did I weary of gazing on his behalf, and of putting into words the effect of field, tree, town, river, cloud, sunbeam: never did I weary of reading to him" (397). They reverse roles, as she now teases him and makes him jealous of St. John. And she maintains full control of her story, to the point of keeping to herself, and to her reader, a crucial moment in her tale: her own participation in the supernatural between them reported by Rochester: "I listened to Mr. Rochester's narrative; but made no disclosure in return. The coincidence struck me as too awful and inexplicable to be communicated or discussed. If I told anything, my tale would be such as must necessarily make a profound im-

pression on the mind of my hearer: and that mind . . . needed not the deeper shade of the supernatural. I kept these things then and pondered them in my heart" (394). Through these reversals, through Jane's increased control and authority, Rochester becomes the twin man-who-would-understand. "No woman was ever nearer to her mate than I am; ever more absolutely bone of his bone and flesh of his flesh" (396, 397).[14]

But unlike other fraternal husbands or lovers who become quasi-incestuous and thereby protect the heroine from maternity,[15] Rochester maintains enough distance and enough masculine potency literally to become the father of Jane's child. "His form was of the same strong and stalwart contour as ever: his port was still erect, his hair was still raven-black, nor were his features altered or sunk: not in one year's space, by any sorrow, could his athletic strength be quelled, or his vigorous prime blighted" (387). Rochester is a "caged eagle," a "royal eagle chained to a perch." And when he expresses openly his anxieties about his potency, Jane explicitly reassures him: "You are green and vigorous. Plants will grow about your roots, whether you ask them or not, because they take delight in your bountiful shadow; and as they grow they will lean towards you, and wind around you, because your strength offers them so safe a prop" (391). This, we might say, is the ultimate fantasy of the man-who-would-understand. Characterizing the penis and not the phallus, Rochester's is a potency without oppressive patriarchal privilege. Whereas at Thornfield Rochester had to drag Jane to be married with an "iron grip," here at Ferndean he can humbly wait for "plants" to "wind around him" gladly and voluntarily, seeking his "safe prop" on their own.

Such potency is clearly dangerous, however. For Jane that danger lies in the fact that it arouses her sexuality, a condition which, as the representation of the sensual and sexual Bertha demonstrates, is frought with pitfalls. Its only possible redemption, maternity, is also a condition that cannot, in the context of this novel, or of Victorian fiction more generally, be either a welcome or a safe one. In order to confront this double danger and to find a course allowing its heroine's survival, *Jane Eyre* needs to reshape further the female family romance fantasy.

Dreaming of Children

"To dream of children was a sure sign of trouble, either to oneself or one's kin," Jane assures us as her obsessive dreams begin (193). She has learned this, like many other things, from Bessie and Miss Abbott, the servants at Gateshead, and, as much as the novel works hard at establishing Jane's difference from servant women, she does share with them this fear of birth and maternity. Jane dreams of children on two separate occasions: first, there is a week-long series of dreams preceding the call for a return to the Reed household. Next there are two dreams preceding her planned marriage, dreamt on the same night during which Rochester is away on a trip. These dreams are usually read as delayed expressions of Jane's unprocessed childhood anger and rage. Directed at her mistreatment and her dependency, the rage of the red room stays with her as an internal barrier separating her from the possibility of marriage and adulthood. It can be argued, however, that in these dreams of children Jane plays both the role of the child and the role of the caretaker, that she sees herself not only as the helpless child but also as its mother. And in the role of mother Jane is also helpless and alone. She associates her dreams with scenes of violence and death, all familial scenes such as Richard Mason's injury at the hands of his sister, and John Reed's suicide and his mother's illness. These scenes clarify the violence that resides within familial structures, exposing the mother, in particular, to danger. The second two dreams, preceding Jane's "marriage," associate adult femininity and especially maternity with solitude, weariness, and peril. Jane feels the child to be a barrier between herself and Rochester. In both dreams she chases Rochester, but is impeded from catching up to him by the burden of the child. In both dreams he is free to leave for distant countries, or just to walk down the road, while she remains in charge of the wailing infant. And in the second dream she fails to protect the child; the wall on which she perches crumbles, and the child rolls off her knee. Her solitary maternity becomes lethal, for both mother and child.

It is at this point, as she awakens from this dream, or while still dreaming, that Jane encounters the mysterious monster Bertha, though the association of Bertha with the child dream was already established earlier. In previous readings Bertha was seen to represent a warning to Jane that she must overcome and repress her childhood rage lest she should wish to turn into the monstrous and uncontained bundle of passions which Bertha embodies, and which is reinforced by Bertha's Jamaican and Creole origins. If we read the dream as representing Jane's maternity and not her childhood anger, however, then what does the connection to Bertha mean? In this reading Bertha becomes for Jane an image of the reproduction of mothering. First, Bertha is, of course, the "infamous daughter of an infamous mother." She is also, by oedipal association, Rochester's wife, and therefore a maternal figure to Jane, a figure Jane must displace. Thus for Jane, as she imagines herself married to Rochester, and either a sexual adult woman or a mother, the rage of the red room comes back in the figure of Bertha, the married woman abandoned by her husband for her uncontrolled appetite, the woman who is doomed to repeat the mad life of her own mother. Jane's rage, then, is not the rage of the abandoned child but the rage of the abandoned adult woman who could never imagine combining sexuality

and maternity, and for whom either course appears potentially ruinous. If we look at Grace Poole, Bertha's alternate persona, this association is borne out: Grace, the lone caretaker of her wailing, heavy, unpredictable charge, is the figure Jane invokes in her dream as she falls off the roof. Jane is both, of course, the neglectful caretaker and the neglected infant, both Grace and Bertha. Her unconscious anxiety and fear are aimed at the position of lone caretaker, at her sole responsibility for her own life and for the life of another who is dependent on her as she has been dependent on others.

These dreams of children are the underside of Jane's other familial fantasies, both the orphan fantasy and the fantasy of the man-who-would-understand. Whereas these are fantasies of freedom and result in creativity, the other is a fantasy of confinement and destructiveness, a fantasy of both destroying and being destroyed. And yet, at the end of the novel Jane describes her firstborn. How does she circumvent the threats and dangers of motherhood? How does she combine maternity, sexuality, and creativity? I would suggest that the novel offsets the dreams of children and the disastrous maternal portraits they paint with more reassuring visions of what maternal work might entail. If she thinks back on her history, Jane will note that if she were to have children as Mrs. Rochester, she would not in fact be the one to care for them. She herself and her cousins are raised not by Mrs. Reed but by Bessie and Miss Abbott, who feed them, dress them, tell them stories, sing to them, and even administer moral lessons to them. Mrs. Reed might bear the responsibility for overseeing their work and training them, but, like many Victorian fictional mothers, she acts overwhelmed and helpless, and she does not do the actual caretaking work. As in the Reed household, maternal functions are scattered throughout the novel, and, except in the case of the young Bessie charged with the infant Jane, and that of Grace Poole, women with whom Jane only very partially identifies, they never rest too firmly or burdensomely on a single woman.

Jane herself is cleverly protected from the worst parts of her own "maternal" work as a teacher or governess. When she teaches at Lowood, she has the leisure to paint her watercolors and do a lot of dreaming. When she is engaged as Adele's governess, she can always send her off to her nurse, or ask Mrs. Fairfax to take her. When Adele models her new dresses, for example, Jane, even while pretending to be present, does not pay attention. Rochester describes the scene thus: "I observed you . . . for half an hour, while you played with Adele in the gallery. . . . Adele claimed your outward attention for a while; yet I fancied your thoughts were elsewhere: but you were patient with her, my little Jane; you talked to her and amused her a long time. When at last she left you you lapsed at once into deep reverie . . . you paced gently on and dreamed" (275). Teaching

Adele and playing with her need not interfere with Jane's dreaming, with her imaginative and creative activities. The same is true of her work as a schoolteacher at Marsh's End: Jane teaches but has the time and leisure to study with St. John. The duties of the governess or the teacher are not represented in the novel as a form of work that invades or threatens one's identity or interferes with one's creativity. Brontë uses Jane's roles as governess and teacher effectively to establish her dependence and marginality, but she also protects Jane from any deeper contamination by the world of work: her functions and investments remain as vague, diffused, and scattered throughout the novel as possible. And, surprisingly, this remains true as Jane moves up the class and economic ladder from pupil to governess, to teacher, and eventually to mother.

Brontë exploits the liminal position of the governess within the family, so brilliantly analyzed by Mary Poovey, and also what that liminality implies—the actual caretaking functions of servants.[16] Poovey distinguishes between the mother (the idealized unemployed) and the governess (who does for wages what the mother should be doing for free and who thereby destabilizes and threatens familial boundaries). We need to see, however, that the mother is after all employed: she supervises the household, including often very young servants and governesses. Although that work is different from the actual caretaking function of servants, it is work nevertheless.[17] We also need to distinguish the governess (who in this novel can move into the role of the "underemployed" mother, whose boundary from her is tenuous and can be crossed) from the servant (who cannot because she is separated by class). In this novel, then, as in other novels of the period, maternity is a threat not because of the work middle-class mothers do, for in fact the work of middle-class mothering is only tangentially related to the physical and emotional care of children. Maternity is a threat for other, deeper reasons of identity, and those reasons interestingly and subversively connect women of different classes and backgrounds. In fact, we best see the danger of maternity in the person of Grace Poole, the caretaker contaminated by her charge. Through most of the novel Grace *is* the insane woman on the third floor, who laughs, haunts, and stabs people. We see the danger of maternity in the Creole woman, Antoinetta Mason, who transmits her insanity to her daughter, and in the French woman, Céline Varens, who abandons her child to poverty rather than raise her. We see to what lengths Mrs. Reed goes to protect herself from these dangers of maternal contamination, by hiring servants and by adopting rigid principles of patriarchal Christian education, and ultimately how devastating and lethal her maternity proves to be nonetheless.

The dangers of maternity for Jane are most clearly manifested in her relation to St. John and in her re-

sponse to his demands. Although he appears in the novel primarily as the fraternal patriarch, St. John's demands on Jane resemble a child's demands. Jane nearly loses herself in a relation which is dictated by convention, which involves the bodily threat of contamination in the East, and which attracts her with a nearly irresistible compulsion. In all three respects this relationship resembles maternity. Opposed to her caretaking relation to Rochester, which is adult, mutual, and self-enriching rather than self-diminishing, her connection to St. John is profoundly endangering. The investment in maternity as identity is akin to Jane's investment in St. John, threatening the loss of the self Jane so firmly knows she has to take care of herself. But in this novel Brontë begins to redefine the shapes of maternal work and identity in such a way as to propose it as a viable possibility for Jane.

THE REPRODUCTION OF FATHERING

"He would send for the baby; though I entreated him rather to put it out to nurse and pay for its maintenance. I hated it the first time I set my eyes on it—a sickly, whining, pining thing! It would wail in its cradle all night long—not screaming heartily like any other child, but whimpering and moaning. Reed pitied it; and he used to nurse it and notice it as if it had been his own: more, indeed, than he ever noticed his own at that age. . . . In his last illness, he had it brought continually to his bedside" (203, 204). This account of Jane's infancy by the dying Mrs. Reed clarifies aspects of the family romance plot and Brontë's transformations of it. As Mr. Reed adopts Jane, and attempts to get his wife to promise to take care of her, the illegitimate family is made legitimate, thereby restoring his incestuous bond with his sister, broken by her marriage. The account is especially striking, however, because, except for Jane's dream, it is the novel's only account of actual nurturing behavior. Consoling a wailing child, in waking life, is left to a man, an uncle. This differs from but is related to other paternal and avuncular acts in the novel: Rochester's adoption of Adele, whom he does not like but pities enough to provide for her and raise her in his house; Mr. Eyre's intervention on behalf of Jane, also financial and moral, though not directly physical; to a much lesser degree the nurturing presence and moral intervention of Mr. Lloyd on behalf of Jane; and St. John's intervention to rescue Jane from the threshold of death on the moors.

These acts of paternal nurturance are powerful enough in the novel to threaten Mrs. Reed utterly. She fails to keep her promise to Mr. Reed, a promise that would extend his protection of his niece beyond his death. She cannot bear to help Mr. Eyre establish a connection with Jane and reports her dead. What does she have to gain from this lie, which follows her to her grave? Nothing but to circumvent a form of relation she perceives as more powerful than any other: the connection between uncle and niece, a connection that can "lift [Jane] to prosperity" (210) and legitimacy within the family, and can move her firmly into the space of plot.

In sending Jane to Lowood, Mrs. Reed substitutes a different, a dominant, authoritarian and patriarchal form of paternity, Mr. Brocklehurst's domineering and oppressive child rearing practices, for Mr. Reed's nurturing care. Lowood is designed to control and contain all aspects of feminine desire, all female appetite, whether it be for food, material possessions, pleasure, imaginative play, or even knowledge exceeding the conventional canon of acceptability. Body, intellect, soul, and will have to be regimented and regulated to become smooth instruments of the reproduction of traditional values and norms. All passion needs painfully to be eliminated through humiliation and correction. Brocklehurst's authoritarian power is echoed later in the novel by St. John and his mission, associated in the novel with institutionalized Christianity. St. John functions both as Jane's demanding child and as an exacting father, much more than as the brother, as she and he want to define their relation:

> By degrees, he acquired a certain influence over me that took away my liberty of mind: his praise and notice were more restraining than his indifference. I could no longer talk or laugh freely when he was by, because a tiresomely importunate instinct reminded me that vivacity . . . was distasteful to him. I was so fully aware that only serious moods and occupations were acceptable, that in his presence every effort to sustain or follow any other became vain: I fell under a freezing spell. When he said "go," I went; "come," I came; "do this," I did it. But I did not love my servitude.
>
> (354)

Marriage to such a man is lethal: "If I were to marry you, you would kill me. You are killing me now" (363), Jane insists, realizing that St. John represents the opposite of sensual desire or sexual passion and that marital relation should not be based on such thorough repression of desire and the body.

St. John's protective and repressive paternal functions extend not only over Jane and the rest of his family but also over "his race." The manner in which St. John works for humanity is distinctly paternal and patriarchal: "Firm, faithful, and devoted; full of energy, and zeal, and truth, he labors for his race: he clears their painful way to improvement: he hews down like a giant the prejudices of creed and caste that encumber it. He may be stern; he may be exacting: he may be ambitious yet; . . . but his is the ambition of the high master-spirit, which aims to fill a place in the first rank of those who are redeemed from the earth" (398). As "master" and father, St. John inserts himself in an apostolic line of sons and fathers, beginning with Jesus and God.

This is St. John's authoritarian paternity, a paternity the novel sharply and definitively contrasts to another form of refigured paternity—that of Mr. Reed, Mr. Lloyd, Mr. Eyre, and Edward Rochester. As it reshapes paternity, the novel also distances itself from the patriarchal and imperialist civilizing mission St. John undertakes on behalf of "his race." With the critique of Brocklehurst's and St. John's paternity, the novel wants to imagine a different form of spiritual content and relation, one that is perhaps best approximated by the communication Jane achieves with the moon, or the supernatural "conversation" she has with Rochester. These are both based on a deep empathy rather than on the need to improve or correct.

Rochester is the agent of the novel's refigured paternity. From the protector of Adele who does not like children, Rochester turns into the father who hold his child in his arms and stares into his eyes. With his vulnerability Rochester gains in nurturance, and as we have seen, his nurturance is enriched by his potency. This male nurturance, built up in the novel through the figures of Reed, Lloyd, and Eyre, makes it possible for Jane to become a mother and not to claim her child but to hand it over, instead, directly to its father. In developing, ever so suggestively, Rochester's redeemed paternity, Brontë adds another dimension to the female family romance. For Rochester is a different paternal figure from the other fathers in the novel. He has money like Mr. Eyre and Mr. Reed, but he lacks the moral authority of Mr. Lloyd, and, most important, he lacks the relation to the symbolic that all three share. That contact the novel reserves for Jane: "He cannot read or write much; but he can find his way without being led by the hand: the sky is no longer a blank to him—the earth no longer a void." Whereas the other three nurturing paternal figures remain distant, disembodied, benevolent, Rochester is definitively embodied in his disability. He describes himself as a "sightless block," insisting: "'On this arm I have neither hand nor nails,' he said drawing the mutilated limb from his breast, and showing it to me. 'It is a mere stump and ghastly sight'" (384). Thus embodied, thus responsible for earth and sky and not for books, holding his child in his arms, Rochester differs both from the authoritarian/authoritative and from the nurturing fathers. He is, and the novel suggests this ever so subtly, the "male mother," whose nurturance, obviously relieved by the caretaking work of servants and governesses, could free Jane to continue her imaginative labor and to write her story. This male mother is the figure Jane chased after in her dreams; this is the parent, the partner fantasized in an adult female family romance. He is both dependent and to be depended upon; he is weak and also strong. He is the embodied father, the vulnerable father, the humble father.

Why, however, is Jane's "firstborn," the only child she mentions in the novel, a boy? Why, like most other nineteenth-century heroines, is Jane unable to reproduce herself? Why does the novel displace a reproduction of daughters?[18] Does the novel still fear the daughter-father bond, a bond always profoundly threatening to both mothers and daughters, and especially so if the father is nurturing as well as powerful? Does Jane fear it because of its seductions, its threats of incest and daughterly exchange? Or does she, like Mrs. Reed, fear it because it would exclude her as a mother from a bond she can never equal for her daughters? Or is it, conversely, that in highlighting the son's mirroring moment with a male rather than a female "mother" ("he could see that the boy had inherited his own eyes, as they once were—large, brilliant and black"), Brontë envisions a "reproduction of fathering" which becomes a "male mothering" and a different masculinity? If this last is true, then the novel even more radically distances itself from St. John's patriarchal Christian imperialist vision, outlined contiguously to it in the text. Linking these two visions of fathering, St. John's paternity and Rochester's male maternity, is Rochester's acknowledgment of a God who had "tempered judgment with mercy" (397) and Jane's happy picture of an extended egalitarian family connected through the sisterhood of Jane, Diana, and Mary, a sisterhood that thrives in the absence of the brother, St. John. This family successfully functions within the law because, as far as the novel reveals, it is not tested: Rochester's son is his "firstborn," but we are not privy to whatever conflict over inheritance and exchange might threaten to reproduce the disastrous familial situations of Jane and Rochester's own families of origin.

It seems, moreover, that although this family romance fantasizes a way of reproducing and changing the father, to the point of casting him as a male mother, it still cannot reproduce female mothering or a female line of transmission. Here it reaches one limit of its radical potential. No legitimate daughter is mentioned in the novel; Adele is rather cleverly removed from the family; and Jane never herself adopts a maternal voice. The story she writes, like the pictures she draws, keeps her firmly intricated in her infantile identity and in her own uniqueness and unreproducibility. And although her family romance fantasies do mature to adulthood, they stop short of detailing a vision of herself as a mother who is also a sexual woman and a writer.

If Jane is able to write, if she is able to appropriate from Rochester the access to the symbolic, she may be able do so in spite of being a mother, but she cannot do so *as a mother*. Jane's family romances have transcended the individualist bildungsroman by refiguring masculinity as well as femininity, and by situating individual development in the midst of pressing social, economic, and historical issues of class and empire which shape and reshape the story of *Bildung*. Yet Jane as narrator does remain the separating daughter, the abused

and neglected rebel child. It is as daughter and as rebel child, in fact, that she continues to appeal to contemporary feminist readings, whether those readings are celebratory or critical. Although she can envision a male mother who can transmit to his son the contact with the earth and the sky, Brontë is unable to envision a female mother who can write her story in a maternal voice, who can write about the mother and the daughter in the different family romance she fantasizes.[19] Jane's limited ability to adopt the perspective of maternity and adulthood also limits the range of the family romances she can fantasize and enact.

Nor does *Jane Eyre* enable us to step out of the bounds of the familial, and here is where the family romance paradigm reveals both its strengths and its limitations of view. At the end of her plot Jane is firmly based in the new and admittedly renewed family she has forged. The setting of her familial life is inauspicious: Ferndean is Rochester's least attractive property, deemed too damp and unhealthy even to house the mad Bertha. Other than Diana, Mary, and their husbands and children, the Rochesters seem to associate with no one; whatever familial transformation Brontë was able to envision had to remain utopian and limited in scale. Yet the bases of the envisioned transformations also had to remain unexamined. As a new family consolidates itself, it practices its own blindness and exclusions. Adele comes dangerously close to repeating the status of Jane in the Reed household; her removal from the family seems to be rather cruel. Jane's status in her new family is ensured by the financial security she achieves by means of her uncle's colonial possessions, though this source is never questioned in the space of the text. Rochester's transformation is made possible, however painfully, by Bertha's convenient death and her destruction of their tainted past life. St. John himself, moreover, is excluded from the fold of his metropolitan family and left to absorb the colonial guilt and the civilizing labor which actually facilitate the family's consolidation on both economic and moral grounds. As much as they allow for revision and manipulation, familial fantasies and the family romance paradigm which enables us to analyze them continue to perpetuate structures separating inside from outside which may well be basic to the realist novel. And even as a feminist revision of the family romance allows us to perceive these structures, it does not allow us to step outside them.

Notes

Part of this essay is based on my discussion of the family romance in the introduction and chap. 2 of *The Mother-Daughter Plot: Narrative, Psychoanalysis, Feminism* (Bloomington: Indiana University Press, 1989). The essay was written in 1991.

1. Charlotte Brontë, *Jane Eyre* (New York: Norton, 1971), p. 397; subsequent references are cited in the text.

2. Jane Lazarre, "Charlotte's Web: Reading *Jane Eyre* over Time," in *Between Women,* ed. Carol Ascher, Louise de Salvo, and Sara Ruddick (Boston: Beacon, 1984); Sandra Gilbert and Susan Gubar, *The Madwoman in the Attic: The Woman Writer and the Nineteenth-Century Literary Imagination* (New Haven: Yale University Press, 1979); Adrienne Rich, "The Temptations of a Motherless Daughter," in *On Lies, Secrets, and Silence: Selected Prose, 1966-1978* (New York: Norton, 1979).

3. Gayatri Spivak, "Three Women's Texts and a Critique of Imperialism," *Critical Inquiry* 12.1 (Autumn 1985): 243-61; Nancy Armstrong and Leonard Tennenhouse, "Introduction: Representing Violence, or 'How the West Was Won,'" in *The Violence of Representation: Literature and the History of Violence* (New York: Routledge, 1989); Mary Childers, "Lady Monsters and Woman Servants," unpublished manuscript.

4. Cora Kaplan, "Fostering 'Chartism and Rebellion': Race, Class, and Feminism in *Jane Eyre*," unpublished manuscript.

5. For feminist studies of the bildungsroman, see Elizabeth Abel, Marianne Hirsch, and Elizabeth Langland, eds., *The Voyage In: Fictions of Female Development* (Hanover, N.H.: University Press of New England, 1983); Rita Felski, *Beyond Feminist Aesthetics: Feminist Literature and Social Change* (Cambridge: Harvard University Press, 1989), chap. 4; and Susan Fraiman, *Unbecoming Women: British Women Writers and the Novel of Development* (New York: Columbia University Press, 1993).

6. Sigmund Freud, "Family Romances" ("Der Familienroman der Neurotiker" [1908]), in *The Standard Edition of the Complete Works of Sigmund Freud,* ed. James Strachey, 24 vols. (London: Hogarth, 1953), 9:237-41.

7. Marthe Robert, *Origins of the Novel,* trans. Sacha Rabinowitch (Bloomington: Indiana University Press, 1980). For another extensive discussion of the family romance as fictional genre, see Christine van Boheemen, *The Novel as Family Romance: Language, Gender, and Authority from Fielding to Joyce* (Ithaca: Cornell University Press, 1987). Robert does not consider gender as a category; van Boheemen includes a brief discussion on gender in her introduction.

8. Freud, "Family Romances," 238.

9. Ibid., 239, 238.

10. See Adrienne Rich, "Natural Resources," in *The Dream of a Common Language: Poems, 1974-1977* (New York: Norton, 1978).

11. Jane Austen's *Emma* provides a good example; see my discussion of Mr. Knightley in *Mother-Daughter Plot,* 60-61.

12. See, for example, Charlotte Brontë's *Villette.*

13. Kate Chopin's *Awakening,* ed. Margo Culley (New York: Norton, 1976), movingly illustrates this point.

14. For a different reading of Rochester's masculinity, see Jean Wyatt, *Reconstructing Desire: The Role of the Unconscious in Women's Reading and Writing* (Chapel Hill: University of North Carolina Press, 1990). Wyatt sees Rochester as providing for Jane a chance actually to marry the father and to experience a paternal nurturance that most women desire but cannot get.

15. For example, Mr. Knightley, Heathcliff in Emily Brontë's *Wuthering Heights,* and Benedict in George Sand's *Valentine.*

16. Mary Poovey, *Uneven Developments: The Ideological Work of Gender in Mid-Victorian England* (Chicago: University of Chicago Press, 1990), esp. 126-63.

17. I am indebted to Mary Childers for allowing me to read her unpublished analysis of the structure of work in Brontë's novel, which constitutes a fundamental disagreement with Poovey's reading.

18. Some novels allow the heroine an indirect form of reproduction, through a niece or the child of a friend, but never a direct one. See the little niece Valentine at the end of Sand's *Valentine,* and the little Emma, daughter of Miss Taylor, at the end of Austen's *Emma.*

19. In *Mother-Daughter Plot* I reflect in more detail on the absence of maternal perspectives in women's fiction, especially in nineteenth-century realism. See esp. chaps. 1-3.

Barbara Z. Thaden (essay date 1997)

SOURCE: Thaden, Barbara Z. Introduction to *The Maternal Voice in Victorian Fiction: Rewriting the Patriarchal Family,* pp. 3-15. New York and London: Garland Publishing, Inc., 1997.

[*In the following essay, an introduction to her book, Thaden highlights the unique commentary and perspective on motherhood offered in works by nineteenth-century authors—such as Margaret Oliphant, Elizabeth Gaskell, and Frances Trollope—who were mothers themselves.*]

Is there such a thing as the writing mother's fantasy? And if so, what transformations does the fantasy undergo in the process of its fictionalization?

(Susan Suleiman 372)

Whether or not, as Edward Shorter claims, good mothering is an invention of modern culture,[1] surely the urge to dictate new and better methods of taking care of children is a recent obsession. The disintegration of traditional familial and communal lifestyles wrought by industrialization had led to great instability and insecurity about child-raising practices in the industrialized world. Every generation of twentieth-century mothers has been handed professional advice, child-rearing manuals, and new, scientifically-authorized child development theories. According to Jessie Bernard, modern middle-class motherhood, which assigns "sole responsibility for child care to the mother" and attributes the social, moral, physical, and spiritual development, positive or negative, of the child almost exclusively to the quality of the mother-child relationship, is "new and unique" to our century. This image of the ideal, ever-present, ever-loving, all-responsible mother was, according to Bernard, "a nineteenth-century Victorian creation" (cited Helterline 590-591). An examination of the ways in which British Victorian novelists who were mothers themselves contributed to this new idealization of motherhood can help us to understand not only how a functional model of motherhood was created and came to be accepted in our century but also how our mid- and late-twentieth-century ideology of motherhood has affected how we interpret Victorian representations of motherhood.

The British under Queen Victoria's reign are often thought of as exalting motherhood. The queen herself was saluted as "Mother, Wife, and Queen" after fifty years of rule by crowds who seemed to agree that the queen's position as supreme mother and wife elevated her even more than her position as political head of her country (Honig 11). Every mother was a queen. Elaine Showalter writes that a proper mother was "a Perfect Lady, an Angel in the House, contentedly submissive to men, but strong in her inner purity and religiosity, queen in her own realm of the Home" (*Literature of Their Own* 14). Nina Auerbach writes that childless women in the nineteenth century were "struggling against the universal approval of large families and paeans to the holiness of motherhood," for "motherhood was not merely a biological fact, but a spiritual essence inseparable from pure womanhood" (174).

But despite this apparent emphasis on pure and self-sacrificing mothers within the dominant cultural ideology, good mothers are not a staple of canonized Victorian literature, even among the female authors. Too often, mothers are either dead, unimportant, ineffective, or destructive. For example, Charlotte Brontë's Jane Eyre and Lucy Snowe are both motherless, and the former suffers from persecution by an evil mother-substitute. In Emily Brontë's *Wuthering Heights,* the mothers of Catherine Earnshaw and Edgar Linton die without affecting the action in any way, and Heathcliff

is a foundling. Eliot presents ineffective or pernicious mothers for many of her main characters, including Maggie Tulliver, Daniel Deronda, Gwendolen Harleth, and Felix Holt. Many of her other main characters have dead mothers, including Dorothea Brooke and Dinah Morris. Among the male writers most read today, Dickens presents few portraits of good mothers, and Thackeray, in *Vanity Fair,* actually mocks the stereotype of the good mother in his portrait of Amelia Osborne. Trollope comes closest to portraying the stereotypical good mother with his portrait of Mrs. Bold in *Barchester Towers,* but this is a briefly sketched characterization.

Many reasons for the absence of the ideal mother as a character in fiction have been proffered. It may be, as psychoanalytical theory claims, that a good mother simply has little place in the stories we tell ourselves because psychological maturing involves separating ourselves from our mothers. It may be simply that an ideal mother does not make an interesting fictional character. A dead, absent, or distant mother may also be necessary to allow the main character, especially if she is a young woman, greater scope for action, as mothers are often conservative forces in life and literature, and novels depend on plot. The adventures of the orphan thrown upon the world can often provide more colorful plot twists than can the adventures of the drawing room, and the parentless hero or heroine is a literary convention older than the novel itself.

Perhaps, however, we find few mothers as main characters in Victorian fiction, and few representations of good mothers, because the Victorian novelists most studied today were not mothers themselves and were not usually interested in exploring this ideological territory. Of the major novelists, only Thackeray, in *Vanity Fair,* compares two mothers and makes pointed comments about the stereotypes dominating the public mind concerning motherhood. As Merryn Williams points out, "it is significant that the four really great women novelists of the nineteenth century—Jane Austen, the two Brontës, and George Eliot—were all childless and married late or not at all" (*Women in the English Novel* 15). Perhaps, however, the significance of this statement lies in our own twentieth-century tastes, prejudices, and aversions, since many popular nineteenth-century British novelists, including Frances Trollope, Elizabeth Gaskell, Margaret Oliphant, Ellen Price Wood, Caroline Norton, Anne Marsh, and Mary Elizabeth Braddon, were the mothers of legitimate or illegitimate children.

Whether or not these mother/authors offer a different perspective on Victorian motherhood precisely because they were biological mothers is a politically charged question. While Marjorie McCormick claims that "there is no question mothers experience the world somewhat differently from any other group" precisely because of their reproductive function (xiii), most feminists struggle to discount sex-based differences as *significant*.[2] However, while not claiming that the mother/authors experience life differently for biological reasons, I do claim that the social and legal position of mothers, married and unmarried, can best be understood and appreciated by an author who is in the position of being defined, by her society, as a mother. Ideological constructions of reality obviously change, and the way these changes occur is in part the subject of [*The Maternal Voice in Victorian Fiction*]. Mother/authors, whether consciously or unconsciously, were aware of problems in their society's construction of the ideal mother. Their fiction does in fact offer more varied representations of motherhood than the fiction of the more canonized authors. Their non-stereotypical, highly subversive, and controversial representations may have remained unacknowledged for so long because they did not easily fit into the world view of male academics or that of the first waves of feminist academics who began to recover and revive Victorian women's fiction. The fiction of Gaskell, Oliphant, Norton, and Wood sheds new light on the personal, social, and legal conflicts Victorian mothers faced, but it is only now, in the late twentieth century, that we are prepared to interpret their idealized representations of motherhood as subversive and not complicit to the dominant ideology.

How much did the Victorian idealization of motherhood influence the representation of mothers in fiction? Some feminist literary critics start with the assumption that the ideology which surrounded women and mothers had a greater influence on the representation of female characters in fiction than had the actual experiences of the authors, not only because of the pervasive effect of the cultural ideal but also because Victorian authors were anxious to ensure the acceptance of publishers and lending libraries, both of which exercised a conservative influence. Françoise Basch, for example, found that representations of women in Victorian fiction are almost without exception more stereotyped, more conventional, and less shockingly sordid than reports from commissions and other nonfiction writing, including the biographies and letters of eminent and less than eminent ladies. Basch feels that novelists celebrated the role of wife-mother, while the real wife-mother, "far from celebrating her role . . . often seemed to suffer in it" (269). Mother/authors often do depict good, self-sacrificing, devoted mothers, even though more recent critics such as Marianne Hirsch, Susan Peck McDonald, and Marjorie McCormick have noted the lack of good living mother/characters, not their idealization, in the best-known novels written before the twentieth century.

Whether through her presence or her absence, the ideal mother had a place of her own in Victorian fiction which, if not filled, implied a great void. Nancy Armstrong believes that the family unit as we know it today,

in which children are socialized by their mothers, "existed mainly as a fiction" before it existed as a fact: "through fiction . . . this kind of household first acquired its power to reproduce a particular form of social relations rooted in gender" (217). Many historians who employ what Anderson calls the "sentiments" approach to history argue that the concept of mother as we know it today was in fact created during the eighteenth and nineteenth centuries. Laurence Stone, for example, speculates that maternal breast-feeding, which had long been out of style and only became popular again in the eighteenth century, led mothers to love their children in a more "exclusive, monopolistic" way (*Family,* 112), which in turn led to a more child-centered society (431). He believes that "natural maternal instincts were allowed to develop" only if mothers breast-fed and had daily physical contact with their infants and children (*Family,* 114), implying that the quality of maternal attachment must have been different if not altogether lacking in those pre-eighteenth-century mothers who sent their children out to wet nurse for a year or two and then left them to be brought up by members of their household staff, sent them to boarding schools, or sent them to live with relatives. Like Stone, Monique Plaza claims that our present day functional definition of a mother as the one who provides "material and affective attendance on the children in the heart of the family" (78), a definition which implies the mother's almost constant "material proximity with the child," was created during the eighteenth and nineteenth centuries (79). However, Marilyn Helterline and others remind us that middle-class Victorian mothers were not expected to physically care for their children: while this "functional" definition of motherhood was being created during the nineteenth century, it was not accepted as natural—that is, did not become the dominant ideology—until the mid-twentieth century.

Philosophers, doctors, political pamphleteers, and authors of moral, religious, and general advice manuals had been barraging women with propaganda urging them to stay home and take care of their children since the beginning of the eighteenth century. A long aristocratic tradition (more prevalent on the continent than in England, but still well represented even in nineteenth-century British novels) which held that children were "an inconvenience that should be kept from interfering with the pleasures and intrigues of their mothers" (Robertson 11) was under attack on all fronts. Nineteenth-century wives were often advised to devote themselves exclusively to their husband, home, and children, perhaps as a reaction to the growing feminist movement. Since being a wife and mother, as shown by Barbara Leavy's analysis of *The British Mother's Magazine,* was beginning to be considered not only a full-time job in itself but a sacred profession, Victorian men and women often believed that writing novels interfered with that duty: "women who wrote did so within a framework of dominant cultural myths in which writing contradicts mothering" (Homans 22). Showalter and Homans believe that women authors were often led to assume male pseudonyms during this period because writing as a vocation was "in direct conflict with their status as women" (*Literature of Their Own* 22).

While it may be true that some women writers such as the Brontës and George Eliot chose to write under a male pseudonym because "their feeling that to write is necessarily to be, or to impersonate, a man" (Homans 22), this is not true of most of the mother/authors of the period, the very authors whose two full-time professions could most obviously be seen to interfere with each other. These authors often chose to publish under their own name or anonymously (without a male pseudonym) and thus, I believe, were writing with another audience and another tradition in mind than those female authors who felt the need to disguise their sex. A male *nom de plume* did not generate a wider reading audience—only, perhaps, greater critical attention. When Gaskell was trying to think of a pseudonym under which to publish her first novel, William Howitt, who was negotiating her contract with Chapman and Hall, suggested a lady's name in order to make the book more popular, which suggests that those female authors who chose a male pseudonym did not do so to increase the *sale* of their novels.

Even though most of the mother/authors did not disguise their identity or their sex, they did not usually represent the conflict generated by their dual and culturally incompatible roles; for example, no novels by Gaskell or Oliphant have a mother/author as a main character, although both have working mothers as main characters. The primary conflicts these authors chose to represent were not those between working and motherhood, but those which would plague any nineteenth-century middle-class mother, conflicts created by the family structure, by the duties and responsibilities of a bourgeois wife, and by the legal status of married women, all of which made it impossible for a bourgeois woman to realize anything approaching the idealized role she was expected to play within her household. She had no legal say over the education of her children or over any other matter pertaining to their upbringing; her social and legal status made her role as moral arbiter questionable if not ludicrous to anyone over the age of six, while the educational system from cradle to college ensured the ever-widening gulf between male and female spheres of employment, interests, and empathies, ensuring that a mother's sons would become strangers and her daughters victims. Both Gaskell and Oliphant oppose these tendencies by writing novels which stress the importance of good mothering because only a revolution in the way mothering was regarded could contribute to the social and legal emancipation of mothers.

Even though Gaskell remained married throughout her adulthood, apparently happily, to a Unitarian minister, several of her novels subvert the ideals of patriarchal marriage through heroines who insist on raising their children outside of the marriage bond. Although Gaskell's life centered on her own role as wife and mother, her fiction as well as her letters and a diary written during the early years of her daughter Marianne's life reveal the perhaps unconscious desires and frustrations of married motherhood. Like Gaskell, Oliphant, the author of more than 90 novels, often portrays female protagonists who undermine what we consider to be her age's assumptions about marriage and motherhood. Some of her novels offer the most penetrating and startling representations of maternal desire and its fulfillment available in Victorian fiction.

Victorian mother/authors remind us that while nineteenth-century mothers were expected to make a great emotional investment in every child, social and legal conventions made it very unlikely that they themselves would gain any *return* on their investment. One of the painful contradictions facing married mothers was the way a patriarchal society which propagandized the importance of breast-feeding and maternal care at the same time forced women to privilege the wifely role over the maternal role and forced them to break their primary libidinal bonds with their infants. Stone reminds us that even parents of the classes most likely to exhibit child-centered behavior "did not personally attend to the day-to-day needs of their children, who were looked after by nurses, maids, governesses and tutors" (*Family* 449). The diaries and letters left by both Gaskell and Oliphant testify that these two authors were indeed extremely child centered, believing that their maternal duties were far more important than their professional work. Yet both authors had several servants as part of their middle-class households, and both had nurses for their children. Something as seemingly innocuous as a nurse can interfere with the primary libidinal bond between even a breast-feeding mother and her child, and Gaskell's diary of the first years of her daughter Marianne testifies to the types of emotional conflicts which often resulted from live-in childcare arrangements.

These conflicts were not the same mother-child conflicts which we so often read about today, which are generated in the nuclear family and represented as being the result of too much, too close, and too "fusional" mothering. We must constantly remember that the bourgeois Victorian household was very different from most modern-day British or American middle-class homes, and that although many historians and literary critics claim that the mid-Victorian period was the time when mothers were most idealized, the type of idealization to which they were subject was very different from that inflicted upon twentieth-century mothers. Although

nineteenth-century married women became more confined to the home because not actively involved in their
husband's businesses, they were not confined to the
home *in the same way* that mothers were confined to
the home after World War II in Britain or after both
world wars in America, when they were *literally* unable
to leave their homes during the day, confined by small
children, no household help, and the uniquely twentieth-
century concept that a mother should be always in close
physical proximity to her child.

Ann Dally shows how the idealization of the mother
which followed World War II in Britain, when
government-established day nurseries were closed and
women were no longer needed in the workplace, was
supported by the seminal studies of John Bowlby on
maternal deprivation, conducted for the World Health
Organization following World War II. Bowlby's studies
of war orphans and other institutionalized children
seemed to show that maternal deprivation had devastating effects on intellectual and social development. He
claimed that children could develop healthy egos only
if they had love and "constant attention day and night,
seven days a week and 365 in the year" from their
mother or permanent mother-substitute (Bowlby 67)
and recommended, among other things, that day care be
replaced by subsidies for single mothers of young children who could not support themselves. His findings,
which have resulted in a half century of follow-up studies, contributed to a whole generation of British mothers staying home and taking care of their young children. The significant factor here is that this was the first
generation of middle-class mothers in Britain who had
ever had primary and sole responsibility for their own
children. Before World War II in England, labor-saving
devices had been few and labor cheap. A household
would not be considered middle class unless it had at
least one servant, and if small children were at home, a
nurse or nanny was always employed, no matter what
the family's other economic constraints. Of course the
upper classes had an entire array of servants. In post-
World War II Britain, however, servants became almost
impossible to hire because full employment and the
new perception that private service was demeaning allowed the former servant class to obtain different types
of work.

This new total confinement to the home, unique to the
twentieth century, which required mothers to have full
responsibility for all household tasks and all childcare,
may have been so radically oppressing that we are still
today in the process of attempting to challenge or overturn the assumptions which led to this state of affairs
(Rich's *Of Woman Born*, Badinter, Chodorow, and Dinnerstein seem especially relevant here). It is easy to see
how Bowlby's views, which became the culture's accepted standards, affected authors such as Shorter and
Badinter in their interpretation of French mothering—

especially in Shorter, we can almost feel the dismay
and horror at practices which he equates literally with
murder. It is also apparent, in my opinion, that the back-
lash against such idealization of the mother has influenced many histories of Victorian literature written since
1950. The idea that women of the mid-nineteenth century were prisoners in their husbands' or fathers' homes
permeates so many historical and critical studies of the
nineteenth century that we must become suspicious that
this historical interpretation may be biased by the experiences of twentieth-century women. Biographies of
nineteenth-century middle-class mothers show that they
may in fact have been more free to travel for extended
periods without husband and/or children and to work at
home, because of the availability of inexpensive household help and because they were not expected to stay
with their children twenty-four hours a day.

Karl Mannheim's sociology of knowledge helps explain
the cultural relativism involved in any act of historical
criticism. He writes that when the analyst seeks to examine historical epochs which have "fundamentally divergent thought-systems and . . . widely differing
modes of experience and interpretation," he needs to
have "the courage to subject not just the adversary's
point of view but all points of view, including his own,
to the ideological analysis" (Mannheim 51, 69). We
need to examine how the Victorian experience of motherhood differed from the post-World War II British and
American middle-class experience of motherhood and
how those differences affected the types of desires and
frustrations mothers experienced. We must remember
that the ideology of motherhood generated by the research of John Bowlby and the string of psychoana-
lysts, psychologists, and scientists, from Winnicott to
Harlow, who attempted to validate his basic premise
that a mother and her infant should never be separated
for the first years of the latter's life, had yet to be *created* during the nineteenth century. I would like to argue that mother/authors such as Oliphant and Gaskell
were instrumental in the creation of this very ideology,
one which has profoundly affected the life of almost every woman in this century (whether positively or negatively is, of course, a matter of opinion), because they
depicted in their fiction the mother's so often repressed
desire for ownership of the child during a historical period in which children born in wedlock were the in-
alienable property of their fathers, to do with and dispose of as they saw fit. A wife's bondage to home and
hearth in nineteenth-century Britain was in most cases
not so much physical as psychological, the result of the
legal status of married women which gave almost total
control of their bodies, their assets, and their children to
their husbands.

While Stone claims that by the 1750's the sentimental
child-centered family with breast-feeding mother sensu-
ally attached to her infant was well established in En-

gland, he also claims that the Victorian period "was marked by a strong revival of moral reform, paternal authority and sexual repression" (*Family* 666). Nowhere was this trend more evident than in child custody decisions. Towards the end of the eighteenth century, the Court of King's Bench began to refuse to place children into the custody of abusive fathers, and this "discretion" of the court became the basis of child custody decisions in many countries, including America, during the nineteenth century—except, ironically, in England, which in 1802 reverted completely to upholding the inalienability of a father's right to his children, to such an extent that "it had the effect of creating new paternal rights, the existence of which had only been vaguely hinted at" in the eighteenth century (Zainaldin 1063 n. 97).

Children born in wedlock had always, under common law, been the legal property of their fathers in England, and child custody remained a problematic issue and a key target of feminist reform efforts throughout the nineteenth century. While a private separation agreement might give the wife custody, especially of girls and babies, these separation agreements did not hold up in court. An 1820 court decision denied "the legal validity of conceding custody to a wife" and "declared that the inherent power of a father over his children could not be abrogated by any private agreement he might enter into" (Stone, *Road* 172), a decision which was upheld until the passage of the Infant Custody Act of 1873 (Shanley 139). "The common law courts always gave full patriarchal power to any father, however unworthy, until his children had reached maturity" (Stone, *Road* 171) even after the passage of the first Infant Custody Act, initiated by the pleadings of Caroline Norton and passed in 1839, which only gave mothers who were rich enough to initiate a suit the right to *petition* the Court of Chancery for custody of their children ages seven and younger (custody was still *automatically* granted to the father) in cases of separation or divorce. Only after 1857 did courts sometimes allow mothers to retain custody of their children under age 14 in cases of separation or divorce and only if the mothers were not guilty of adultery. A man living with his wife, however, could still do as he liked with his minor children, including sending them to live elsewhere and completely denying his wife access to them. The father could appoint a guardian other than the mother (before or after his own death); if he died intestate, the mother could not appoint a guardian of her choice; after her death, the children became wards of the Court.

Caroline Norton was appalled to discover, when her husband denied her access to her children and sent them to live with his relatives, that she had no legal recourse. In her pamphlets urging the passage of the first Infant Custody Bill, she used the contemporary concept of a natural biological motherhood to argue for changes in child custody laws. Norton reiterates a single, striking image, that of a husband who "may stand on his own hearth and tear from the very breast of the nursing mother, the little unconscious infant whose lips were drawing from her bosom the nourishment of life" (Norton, *Pamphlets* 24). The case to which she refers, in which a husband snatched away his infant to force his wife into a property settlement more to his advantage, and others in which children were abducted from their mothers and placed into the hands of mistresses and unknown governesses are reminiscent of the image which had opened Mary Wollstonecraft's novel *The Wrongs of Women,* published in 1798. Throughout the nineteenth century a wife and mother in a less-than-ideal marriage could live in constant fear of losing all access to her children, which common law seemed to consider hostages held by the husband to ensure his wife's good behavior. Legal opinion against granting separated wives the right to their property or children usually cited the inevitable collapse of the family and the nation which would ensue if wives were granted these rights. While custody law in cases of separation or divorce was gradually modified during the course of the nineteenth century to allow mothers a chance to gain or retain custody of their children, Parliament continued to refuse to grant married wives living with their husbands any legal right to control of their children.

Despite these legal constraints, Harriet Blodgett found that nineteenth-century Englishwomen's private diaries did not reveal dissatisfaction with marriage and motherhood. "Most of the diarists paint a flattering picture of female fate as marriage and motherhood . . . Most declare the happiness they have experienced in marriage, or propose nothing to imply that they are discontent. Nor do they complain about the burden of motherhood. The women affirm the roles in which their culture has taught them they matter most and from which usually, even if not invariably, they do derive satisfaction" (148-149). While this is usually also true in the diaries and letters left by Gaskell and Oliphant, a close reading of some of their novels in combination with a close examination of their autobiographical writings reveals cracks in the seemingly smooth facade of the Victorian ideology of motherhood, cracks which I believe could best be perceived by those who were in a position to compare the actual role a mother was called upon to play with that prescribed for her by conduct books, religious, philosophical, and medical texts, and household management and advice books. The novels I am considering by these two women were all written after they had been married and had raised their children for some time. Gaskell and Oliphant are therefore not looking forward to some paradise promised by the popular press, but, as they write their fictions about mothers, looking backward upon the actual experience of marriage and motherhood in their day. In addition, these novels are all written after several highly publicized cases (beginning in the nineteenth century with *Rex vs. de Manneville,* 1804) in which judges were powerless to grant custody of infants and young children to mothers forced to leave their husbands for cruelty or whose husbands denied them access to their infants and children for even the most selfish and abominable reasons (Pinchbeck 370-373). These cases included that of Caroline Norton, which resulted in her writing "Separation of Mother and Child by the Law of Custody of Infants Considered" (1837) and *A Plain Letter to the Lord Chancellor* (1839). The publicity surrounding these cases contributed to placing the issue of a married mother's status under common law into such a negative light that even many anti-feminists agreed reform was necessary.

Despite their very different circumstances as mothers, in their fiction Gaskell and Oliphant idealize the mother's role in similar ways. This idealization—this insistence upon the indispensability of mother love—helped to ameliorate the married mother's legal status in Britain and to give separated and divorced mothers a better chance to gain or retain custody of their children. Although the fiction of Norton and Wood also addresses the conflicts faced by wives and mothers, we learn more from their novels by what they do not allow to happen than by what they represent. Gaskell and Oliphant take more risks in writing new roles for mothers in their fiction. Even though they may have been jeopardizing the popularity of their novels, they seem to have been compelled to explore the conflicts created within the "pre-nuclear" family, and to develop, even more than the popular press, a functional definition of motherhood.

In the case of the domestic novel's representation of women's role in society, representation often preceded practice, and most historians agree that Rousseau, for example, represented a certain type of mother in order to bring her into existence. The creation of a new type of mother seems to have been the goal of many of the conduct manuals and medical treatises of the eighteenth and nineteenth centuries as well. Gaskell and Oliphant do not seem to have been engaging in this type of social engineering; instead, they point out the pain and suffering created by an ideology of motherhood which conflicted with social practice. They seem to have been yearning, through their fiction, for a closer, undisturbed mother/infant bond and more maternal influence in a child's emotional and intellectual life. Their fiction shows how mothers themselves began to change the ideology of motherhood during the nineteenth century so that it better met the needs of mothers and children.

[The first chapter of my *The Maternal Voice in Victorian Fiction*] shows how mother/authors rewrite the classic story of the orphaned heroine from the mother's perspective. A comparison of Burney's *Evelina* with Gaskell's *Ruth* or Oliphant's *Innocent* shows a remarkable difference in treatment. Burney can write a social comedy about a heroine whose mother's death while giving birth to the heroine was caused by that mother's ill treatment by the heroine's grandmother and father. Such a beginning as Evelina's would be considered more properly the opening of a tragedy in novels by Gaskell and Oliphant, as it would in most novels written since the end of the nineteenth century, because having had a (good and alive) mother is now considered essential for an *adult*'s emotional and psychological well-being, a concept Gaskell and Oliphant (unlike other well-known Victorian authors) reinforce in their fiction. Having no mother has come to be seen as a tragedy in itself, and never having had a good mother or mother-substitute is now perceived as not only an insurmountable obstacle to happiness but even to normal cognitive and emotional development. An examination of the canonized Victorian fiction will show that this idea was far from accepted by most Victorians, however. Gaskell and Oliphant concentrate on the significance of the lost mother, on what her loss has meant to the heroine, and how it has left her unprotected or even undeveloped as a human being. The memory of a good mother can serve as a source of strength, and a heroine who has no good mother to remember is not capable of overcoming this liability. We can compare this type of idealization of the mother with the depiction, by non-mother/authors, of motherless heroines such as Jane Eyre, who have no memory of their mothers but who nonetheless prevail over adversity.

[The second chapter of my *The Maternal Voice in Victorian Fiction*] shows how mothers in Gaskell and Oliphant are also often a source of spiritual solace or represent an alternative God of loving kindness and forgiveness when their children are judged harshly by the world. These fictional representations of the importance of good mothering are perhaps the only nineteenth-century fictional representations which support the rhetoric of the advice manuals, philosophical tracts, and physician's prescriptions which stressed the importance of good mothering and attempted to convince mothers to stay home with their children. Because so many other nineteenth-century novels depict mothers as unimportant or harmful and because mothers continued to be denied an equal chance at custody and an equal say in the management of their children throughout the century, we must question how deeply the culture believed in the importance of good mothering, despite all the rhetoric it created and digested. Perhaps authors such as Gaskell and Oliphant, through imaginatively representing the consequences of good and bad mothering, contributed more to a heartfelt belief in the importance of good mothering than all the philosophical tracts and education manuals combined. I would argue that these representations helped lead to some of the profound transformations in the definition of "mothering" which we have experienced and continue to experience in this century. They emphasize the importance of a mother's role in bringing up happy, hopeful, and faithful children. They also show, as I discuss in [the third chapter of my *The Maternal Voice in Victorian Fiction*], mothers seizing responsibility for their children from husbands, lovers, and nursemaids, and setting up alternative living arrangements, which I call "maternal circles," in which children can be raised without the pernicious influence of less-than-ideal fathers.

In dramatizing the conflict between wifely and maternal duties, Norton and Wood tend to concentrate on the more conservative, more typical Victorian view that a wife's primary responsibility was to her husband, not to her child or children, despite the fact that neither author lived the life of a typical Victorian wife and mother. [The fourth chapter of my *The Maternal Voice in Victorian Fiction*] shows how Wood's immensely popular *East Lynne* and Oliphant's *Sir Tom* poignantly dramatize the contradictions a married mother faced between her duties as a wife and as a mother. They both show how impelling, and how dangerous, it was for married mothers to devote themselves to their children rather than to their husbands.

These mother/authors helped to validate and reinforce a new way of thinking about the mother/infant bond, and the role of the mother in rearing her children. This belief in the indispensability of a mother's love and care was implied in the writings of Rousseau and in the conduct literature which made raising her children a wife's most important duty, but the legal status of women during the nineteenth century shows that at a certain level, British society was unwilling to concede this indispensability, unwilling to allow mothers any right to their children or even to their own lives which would enable them to fulfill their duty effectively. Mother/authors saw a need for an idealization of motherhood which would leave no question in the public mind that mothers needed their children and children needed their mothers. They helped to create a new ideology of motherhood which was necessary to free married mothers from the legal bondage they suffered under the common law doctrine of "coverture," to allow separated and divorced mothers an equal chance at child custody, to make the best interests of the child the primary concern in child custody disputes, and to convince an all-male legal system that in most cases the best interests of children were served by allowing them access to their mothers. These mother/authors performed a valuable service for their time, even if the ideology they helped to create came to be epitomized, in the twentieth century, by the work of John Bowlby and identified with a completely different type of feminine bondage to the home and hearth.

Notes

1. Shorter defines modern culture as culture created by the Industrial Revolution, which modified the traditional, communal, authoritarian family structure of agrarian village life. While these changes in family and culture took place (and are still taking place) at different rates, in different time periods, in different parts of the world, Southern England was one of the first European societies to "scrape against the modern world," by the early eighteenth century (21).

2. Claire Kahane offers a typical example of the anti-essentialist argument in "Questioning the Maternal Voice," *Genders* 3 (Fall 1988): 82-91. See also the introduction to Martha McMahon's *Engendering Motherhood,* New York: Guilford, 1995, for a discussion of the argument between essentialism and anti-essentialism.

Works Cited

Armstrong, Nancy. *Desire and Domestic Fiction.* New York: Oxford UP, 1987.

Auerbach, Nina. "Artists and Mothers: A False Alliance." *Romantic Imprisonment: Women and Other Glorified Outcasts.* New York: Columbia UP, 1985. 171-183.

———. *Communities of Women: An Idea in Fiction.* Cambridge: Harvard UP, 1978.

Badinter, Elizabeth. *The Myth of Motherhood.* Trans. Roger De Garis. London: Souvenir Press, 1981.

Basch, Françoise. *Relative Creatures: Victorian Women in Society and the Novel.* New York: Schocken Books, 1974.

Blodgett, Harriet. *Centuries of Female Days: Englishwomen's Private Diaries.* New Brunswick: Rutgers UP, 1988.

Bowlby, John. *Maternal Care and Mental Health.* 1951. New York: Schocken Books, 1966. Published in the same volume with D. Ainsworth, et al., *Deprivation of Maternal Care.*

Brontë, Anne. *The Tenant of Wildfell Hall.* 1848. Ed. G. D. Hargreaves. New York: Penguin, 1985.

Brontë, Charlotte. *Jane Eyre.* 1847. Ed. Richard J. Dunn. New York: W. W. Norton, 1987.

———. *Shirley.* 1849. Ed. Andrew and Judith Hook. New York: Penguin, 1974.

———. *Villette.* 1853. Ed. Mark Lilly. London: Penguin, 1985.

Brontë, Emily. *Wuthering Heights.* 1847. Ed. David Daiches. Harmondsworth, Middlesex, England: Penguin, 1965.

Burney, Frances. *Evelina.* 1778. Ed. Edward A. Bloom. New York: Oxford UP, 1970.

Chodorow, Nancy. *The Reproduction of Mothering. Psychoanalysis and the Sociology of Gender.* Berkeley: U of California P, 1978.

————, and Susan Contratto. "The Fantasy of the Perfect Mother." *Rethinking the Family.* Eds. Barrie Thorne and Marilyn Tolum. New York: Longman, 1982.

Dally, Ann. *Inventing Motherhood: The Consequences of an Ideal.* New York: Schocken Books, 1983.

Dinnerstein, Dorothy. *The Mermaid and the Minotaur.* New York: Harper and Row, 1976.

Eliot, George. *Adam Bede.* 1859. Ed. Stephen Gill. Harmondsworth, Middlesex: Penguin, 1980.

————. *Daniel Deronda.* 1874-6. Ed. Barbara Hardy. Harmondsworth, Middlesex: Penguin, 1967.

————. *Felix Holt.* 1866. Ed. Peter Coveney. Harmondsworth, Middlesex: Penguin, 1972.

————. *Middlemarch.* 1871-2. Ed. Gordon S. Haight. Boston: Houghton Mifflin, 1956.

————. *The Mill on the Floss.* 1860. New York: Oxford UP, 1980.

Gaskell, Elizabeth. *The Letters of Mrs. Gaskell.* Eds. J. A. V. Chapple and Arthur Pollard. Cambridge: Harvard UP, 1967.

————. "Lizzie Leigh." 1850. *Four Short Stories.* Ed. Anna Walters. Boston: Pandora Press (Routledge and Kegan Paul), 1983.

————. *Mary Barton.* 1848. Ed. Edgar Wright. Oxford: Oxford UP, 1987.

————. *My Diary: The Early Years of My Daughter Marianne.* London: privately printed by Clement Shorter, 1923.

————. *North and South.* 1855. Knutsford Edition. New York: G. P. Putnam's Sons, 1906.

————. *Ruth.* 1852. Ed. Alan Shelston. New York: Oxford UP, 1985.

————. *Sylvia's Lovers.* 1863. Ed. Andrew Sanders. New York: Oxford UP, 1982.

————. *Wives and Daughters.* 1866. Ed. Frank Glover Smith. Middlesex, England: Penguin, 1969.

Helterline, Marilyn. "The Emergence of Modern Motherhood: Motherhood in England 1899-1959." *International Journal of Women's Studies* 3:6 (1980): 590-614.

Hirsch, Marianne. *The Mother/Daughter Plot: Narrative, Psychoanalysis, Feminism.* Bloomington: Indiana UP, 1989.

Homans, Margaret. *Bearing the Word: Language and Female Experience in Nineteenth Century Woman's Writing.* Chicago: U of Chicago Press, 1986.

Honig, Edith Lazaros. *Breaking the Angelic Image: Woman Power in Victorian Children's Fantasy.* New York: Greenwood Press, 1988.

Kahane, Claire. "Questioning the Maternal Voice." *Genders* 3 (Fall 1988): 82-91.

Leavy, Barbara Fass. "Fathering and The British Mother's Magazine, 1845-1864." *Victorian Periodicals Review* 1980 13 (1-2): 10-17.

Mannheim, Karl. *Ideology and Utopia: An Introduction to the Sociology of Knowledge.* Trans. Louis Wirth and Edward Shils. London: Routledge and Kegan Paul, 1936.

McCormick, Marjorie. *Mothers in the English Novel: From Stereotype to Archetype.* New York: Garland, 1991.

McDonald, Susan Peck. "Jane Austen and the Tradition of the Absent Mother." Davidson and Broner. 58-69.

McMahon, Martha. *Engendering Motherhood: Identity and Self Transformation in Women's Lives.* New York: Guilford Press, 1995.

Norton, Caroline. *A Letter to the Queen on Lord Chancellor Cranworth's Marriage and Divorce Bill.* London: Longman, Brown, Green and Longmans, 1855. Reproduced in *Selected Writings of Caroline Norton: Facsimile Reproductions with an Introduction and Notes by James O. Hoge and Jane Marcus.* Delmar, New York: Scholars' Facsimiles and Reprints, 1978,

————. *Lost and Saved.* 1863. Delmar, NY: Scholars' Facsimiles and Reprints, 1988.

————. *Stuart of Dunleath.* New York: Harper and Brothers, 1851.

Oliphant, Margaret. *The Autobiography of Margaret Oliphant: The Complete Text.* Ed. Elisabeth Jay. New York: Oxford UP, 1990.

————. *A Country Gentleman and His Family.* 1886. London: Macmillan, 1887.

————. *Innocent: A Tale of Modern Life.* London: Sampson Low, Marson, Low and Learle, 1873.

————. *Kirsteen.* 1890. 2nd ed. London: Macmillan, 1900.

————. *The Ladies Lindores.* 1883. Chicago and New York: Belford, Clarke & Co., 188?

————. *Lady Car.* London: Longmans, Green, 1889.

————. *The Marriage of Elinor.* London: Macmillan & Co., and New York, 1892.

————. *The Rector and The Doctor's Family.* Edinburgh: W. Blackwood, 1863. New York: Garland, 1975.

————. *Sir Tom.* 1884. London: Macmillan, 1893.

Pinchbeck, Ivy, and Margaret Hewitt. *Children in English Society.* Vol. 2. London: Routledge and Kegan Paul, 1973.

Plaza, Monique. "The Mother/The Same: Hatred of the Mother in Psychoanalysis." *Feminist Issues* 2:1 (Spring 1992): 75-99.

Rich, Adrienne. *Of Woman Born. Motherhood as Experience and Institution.* New York: W. W. Norton, 1976.

Shanley, Mary Lyndon. *Feminism, Marriage, and the Law in Victorian England, 1850-1895.* Princeton: Princeton UP, 1989.

Shorter, Edward. *The Making of the Modern Family.* New York: Basic Books, 1975.

Showalter, Elaine. *A Literature of Their Own: British Women Novelists from Brontë to Lessing.* Princeton: Princeton UP, 1977.

Stone, Laurence. *The Family, Sex and Marriage in England 1500-1800.* NY: Harper and Row, 1977.

———. *Road to Divorce.* New York: Oxford UP, 1990.

Suleiman, Susan. "Writing and Motherhood." *The (M)other Tongue: Essays in Feminist Psychoanalytic Interpretation.* Ed. Shirley Nelson Garner, Claire Kahane, and Madelon Sprengnether. Ithaca: Cornell UP, 1986.

Williams, Merryn. *Women in the English Novel, 1800-1900.* New York: St. Martin's Press, 1984.

Winnicott, D. W., "The Theory of the Parent-Infant Relationship." *International Journal of Psycho-Analysis* 41 (1960): 585-595.

Wood, Ellen Price (Mrs. Henry). *East Lynne.* 1861. New Brunswick: Rutgers UP, 1984.

Zainaldin, Jamil. "The Emergence of a Modern American Family Law: Child Custody, Adoption, and the Courts, 1796-1851." *Northwestern University Law Review* 73 (1979).

MOTHERHOOD AND OPPRESSION

Magda T. Vergara (essay date spring 1996)

SOURCE: Vergara, Magda T. "In Defense of Motherhood: Juana Manuela Gorriti's Ambivalent Portrayal of a Slave Woman in *La quena.*" *Romance Notes* 36, no. 3 (spring 1996): 277-82.

[*In the following essay, Vergara traces Juana Manuela Gorriti's portrayal of an enslaved woman who betrays her mistress to save her children and gain freedom for her family in* La quena *as a commentary on the ways in which slavery destroys families and threatens the social order.*]

Nineteenth-century Latin American literature, best known for the works of Esteban Echeverría, Domingo Faustino Sarmiento, and José Hernández, produced other notable authors who have since fallen into obscurity. This is particularly true of the female writers of that century. Although there is a growing body of criticism that focuses on women authors, in general, few are studied and acknowledged for their work and contribution to nineteenth-century Latin American literature. Juana Manuela Gorriti (Argentina, 1818-1892) is one of these.[1] In her time, she was a highly acclaimed author of short stories, articles, and journals. She also hosted a reputable and respected literary salon in Lima, Peru. Today, however, knowledge of her work is limited to a few small circles.

The need to reevaluate the literature and history of past centuries, along with feminist criticism, has led to the rediscovery of female writers such as Gorriti. A renewed interest in Gorriti has led critics such as Francine Masiello, Mary Berg, and Thomas Meehan, to note the inclusion of women and Indians and the use of the fantastic as distinguishable characteristics in her narrative. Nevertheless, Gorriti's works merit greater attention and recognition. Her feminine discourse and recurrent themes clearly set her work apart from the canonical narratives. As a whole, her narrative offers a female perspective to the predominantly male view of nineteenth-century Latin America as it is studied today.

Gorriti earned a reputation as a writer with her first narrative, *La quena* (1845).[2] Based on an Indian legend and set during the colonial period in Peru, it is the tragic love story of a mestizo man, Hernán, and a criolla woman, Rosa.[3] The plot development is reminiscent of *Romeo and Juliet*; the main characters are star-crossed lovers whose parents oppose their relationship. Hernán is the bastard son of a Spaniard and an Inca princess, while Rosa is from a powerful criolla family.[4] Her father is an "oidor" for the Spanish court. The plot also includes the villains and the intrigue found in *Othello*. Rosa's slave Francisca is a conniving figure, similar to Iago, who contributes to the tragic outcome of the narrative. Her main role is to intercept the lovers' letters and exchange them for ones that tell of infidelity and death. This sets the tragedy in motion.

Francisca's character, however, serves additional purposes that go beyond that of intermediary. The character allows Gorriti to include a slave's tale in the narrative, a common characteristic of Latin American Romanticism. Many of these tales, such as the story of Nay and Sinar in Jorge Issac's *María*, were incorporated into the narrative as an element of exoticism. These slave tales typically depicted a harmonious society where the slaves were happy and treated well in captivity regardless of the hardships they had endured during their enslavement. Their lives in Africa were

considered fond memories to be shared with their own-
ers. Francisca, therefore, is initially presented as the dutiful slave who does not harbor any ill feelings towards
Rosa. Rather, she serves and loves her mistress and acts
in her defense. In chapter five, for example, Francisca
stands guard all night to warn Rosa of her father's
awakening while Rosa clandestinely meets with Hernán.
Upon hearing Francisca's warning signal, a whistle,
Rosa comments to Hernán: "—es Francisca, mi esclava
favorita, la depositaria de nuestro secreto que me anun-
cia que mi padre se ha levantado ya" (35). ("It's Francisca, my favorite slave, the depository of our secret
who announces that my father has woken".) Rosa's
words imply that there is a relationship of trust between
the two women, thereby minimizing the political implications and the actual relationship of slave owner and
slave. Ironically, it is this same "favorite and trustworthy" slave who, six months later, betrays the couple.

Francisca's tale is fully developed in chapter 6, entitled
"La esclava" (The Slave). As the narrative progresses,
the perspective of the slave is introduced and a more
realistic picture of society emerges. Francisca is fully
aware of her social condition and has not forgotten the
suffering that she and her children have endured during
her five years of captivity. She yearns for her freedom
and is willing to go to any lengths to acquire it. In the
notable absence of a positive male figure to offer protection and aid, a feature characteristic of Gorriti's narratives, Francisca accepts a proposition from a negative
male character. Specifically, she accepts two hundred
ounces of gold from Ramírez, Rosa's evil and corrupt
suitor, for her betrayal. Thus, Francisca is quickly transformed from an obedient slave to that of Judas Iscariot
and is no longer aligned with Rosa but rather appears in
contrast to her. Francisca then represents a threat to heterosexual love. Furthermore, she is symbolic of a barbaric element in the society, slavery, that must be addressed and resolved in order for love to flourish and
for the nation to progress. Ultimately, slavery is the
stumbling block that interferes with the unification and
civilization of the country.

At first reading, Francisca's description appears to reflect Gorriti's racial prejudice. The focus on the slavewoman's eyes and teeth, combined with her subsequent
actions, present a negative portrayal of the character,
especially when considered from a twentieth-century
perspective. The narrator comments: ". . . en vez del
blanco, suave y adorable rostro de Rosa, la amante y
bellísima novia . . . se vieron brillar, rodeados de tinie-
blas, los ojos ardientes y los dientes blancos de una
negra" (37). (". . . rather than Rosa's soft, white, adorable face, the loving and beautiful lover . . . shining,
surrounded by darkness, were the burning eyes and
white teeth of a black woman".) The description builds
to resemble that of a dark and sinister being, a demon
who brings about tragedy. Her physical description cap-

tures the character's lust for vengeance and her determination to escape slavery:

> . . . sus albos dientes se entrechocaron; hincháronse
> los músculos de su cuello; y con la mano estendida, se-
> mejante á un genio maléfico cirniéndose sobre aquel
> palacio y amenazándolo: ¡Blancos! exclamó ¡vosotros
> no tuvisteis piedad de mí; yo no la tengo de vosotros!
> vosotros me arrebatasteis mi felicidad, yo la he res-
> catado vendiendo la vuestra.
>
> (41)

> . . . her white teeth collided, the muscles of her neck
> grew tense, and with an extended hand, similar to that
> of an evil genie hovering threateningly over the palace:
> Whites!, she exclaimed, you didn't have any pity on
> me; I don't have any for you! You stole my happiness,
> I have rescued it selling yours.

Francisca consciously dishonors an entire family in order to achieve her goals. She is fully aware that Rosa
will suffer upon hearing of Hernán's death and will
subsequently enter a loveless marriage. However, she
demonstrates only slight remorse for the heartache her
actions will cause. Furthermore, she anticipates
Hernán's suicide and is actually surprised to hear that
he has joined the priesthood instead. Nevertheless, Francisca justifies her actions in the name of motherhood.
She comments: "Por una madre restituida á sus hijos,
dos amantes han sido hundidos en una inmensa deses-
peración, un padre, una esposa y un marido serán des-
honrados . . ." (41) ("For a mother restored to her children, two lovers have been plunged into an immense
despair, a father, a wife and a husband have been
dishonored").

Francisca's attitude and actions might seem appropriate
to modern readers given the conditions of slavery. However, it probably was not the case during the nineteenth-
century. If anything, her attitude and behavior might
seem offensive and appalling to the readers, an educated class, many of whom owned slaves.[5] How dare
this slave betray her owner who trusted her and treated
her fairly? Yet, Gorriti makes the reader sympathize
with the slave woman's plight by emphasizing her redeeming qualities and familial values: her role as a
mother and the strength of her maternal love. Francisca's goal is to be reunited with her children and end
their suffering caused by her enslavement. The full nature of her rebellion and internal anguish reaches a crescendo in a gripping monologue. She exclaims:

> . . . ¡Aibar! ¡Leila! ¡hijos adorados! mis hermosos pe-
> queñitos gemelos! ¿quién me hubiese dicho, cuando
> para ir á la fuente fatal de donde me arrebataron, os
> acosté dormidos en vuestra cuna de mimbres á la som-
> bra de los palmeros de nuestra cabaña, que tantas veces
> he visto en sueños: ¿quién me hubiese dicho que
> pasarían cinco años sin veros? Pero nuestra buena Fet-
> iche se ha compadecido al fin de mi desesperacion; va

á restituiros vuestra madre, y dentro de poco tiempo, ll-
evando como antes uno de vosotros en cada uno de mis
brazos, iré á cantar nuestra felicidad á los ecos del
desierto . . .

(40)

(. . . Aibar! Leila! my adored children! my beautiful
twins! Who would have told me when I layed you down
in your wicker crib under the shade of the palm trees
by our hut, which I have seen many times in my
dreams, that five years would pass without seeing you?
But our good Fetish has finally had pity on my despair,
is going to return your mother, and soon, as before,
with each of you in my arms, I will sing our happiness
to the echoes of the desert . . .)

Upon justifying Francisca's actions in the name of
motherhood, Gorriti adds greater ambiguity and contradiction to her negative portrayal of Francisca. On one
hand, Francisca's betrayal of heterosexual love is repre-
hensible; on the other, it is a worthy sacrifice in the
name of maternal love. For Gorriti, maternal love was
ineffable. It surpassed all others and justified all actions,
even betrayal.

Francisca's act of vengeance is further legitimized by
her desire to return to her homeland. As the narrative
unfolds, it is clear that she seeks freedom in order to reclaim her previous life. The money that she receives for
her betrayal is not merely a bounty, but rather provides
her with the necessary financial resources for passage to
Africa. Prior to her enslavement, she lived with her
children in what is described as a terrestrial paradise.
They lived peacefully in a cabin shaded by palm trees.
Francisca only becomes a "vengeful demon" as a direct
result of her enslavement. The Europeans began the
slave trade which carried over to the New World. They
and their ancestors humiliated, gagged, and chained her,
forcing her to act in self defense. As such, Francisca's
story demonstrates the tragic consequences of slavery
for society as a whole. It is interesting to note that in
La quena Gorriti does not promote the equality of the
slaves. Slavery is unacceptable due to its societal implications rather than its political implications per se.[6] Her
criticism lies in its destructive powers within families
and consequently, the entire society. As a direct result
of slavery, families are dishonored (Rosa's family),
mothers are torn away from their children (Francisca
and her children), and lovers are tragically separated
(Rosa and Hernán).

Although in many ways *La quena* is a representative
romantic work, its fundamental feminine discourse distinguishes it from its contemporaries. Francisca's negative portrayal, associated with her race, undoubtedly
represents a biased description characteristic of the era.
However, the ambivalent element associated with Francisca's role as a mother serves to overshadow Gorriti's
apparent racial prejudice. The unconditional defense of

motherhood makes the initial negative portrayal of Francisca tenuous at best. Gorriti endorsed destructive actions against her own society at a time when this was
uncommon. She legitimized a slavewoman's betrayal of
her mistress and accepted the dishonor of a prominent
criolla family. Essentially, Gorriti sided with barbarism
in order to defend familial and familiar values that were
being threatened by the political and patriarchal discourse that dominated the country. In *La quena*, a slavewoman's vengeance and betrayal provided a mother's
freedom and her actions were justified in the name of
motherhood.

Notes

1. Gertrudis Gómez de Avellaneda (Cuba, 1814-
   1873) and Clorinda Matto de Turner (Peru, 1854-
   1909) are two of the more widely recognized female authors of the period.

2. *La quena* was later published in serial form in
   1865. The quotes used here maintain the spelling
   of the 1865 text included in *Sueños y Realidades*.

3. According to Mariano Pelliza, cited by W. G.
   Weyland in his introduction of *Narraciones,* the
   narrative is based on an Inca Indian legend which
   appears in Marmontel's work *Les Incas ou la destruction de l'empire,* Paris (1777).

4. In *Foundational Fictions*, Doris Sommer considers these types of romances a symbolic attempt to
   unify the different nations since the love relationships were representative of different sectors of
   society.

5. After independence, many Latin American countries took steps to eliminate slavery. In most cases,
   this was accomplished by mid-century. For further
   information see David Bushnell and Neill
   Macaulay, *The Emergence of Latin America in the
   Nineteenth-Century* (New York: Oxford UP, 1988)
   243-45.

6. The most familiar antislavery novels of the period
   are *Sab* (1841) by Gertrudis Gómez de Avellanda
   (Cuba, 1814-1873) and *Cecilia Valdés* (first part
   1839, completed in 1879, final version 1882) by
   Cirilio Villaverde (Cuba, 1812-1894).

Works Cited

Berg, Mary G. "Juana Manuela Gorriti." *Spanish American Women Writers: A Bio-Bibliographical Source Book.*
Ed. Diane Marting. New York: Greenwood Press, 1990.
226-240.

Gorriti, Juana Manuela. *La quena.* Included in *Sueños y
Realidades.* Ed. Vicente G. Quesada. Intro. Jose María
Torres Caicedo. 2 vols. Buenos Aires: Casavalle, 1865.
3-67.

Masiello, Francine. "Between Civilization and Barbarism: Women, Family and Literary Culture in Mid-Nineteenth Century Argentina." *Historical Grounding for Hispanic and Luso-Brazilian Feminist Literary Criticism*. Ed. Hernán Vidal. Lit. and Human Rights. 4th ser. Minneapolis: Inst. for the Study of Ideol. and Lit., 1989. 517-66.

Meehan, Thomas C. "Una olvidada precursora de la literatura fantástica argentina: Juana Manuela Gorriti." *Chasqui: Revista de Literatura Latinoamericana* 10.2-3 (Feb-May 1981) 3-19.

Sommer, Doris. *Foundational Fictions: The National Romances of Latin America*. Berkeley: U of California P, 1991.

Andrea O'Reilly Herrera (essay date 1997)

SOURCE: Herrera, Andrea O'Reilly. "'Herself Beheld': Marriage, Motherhood, and Oppression in Brontë's *Villette* and Jacobs's *Incidents in the Life of a Slave Girl*." In *Family Matters in the British and American Novel*, edited by Andrea O'Reilly Herrera, Elizabeth Mahn Nollen, and Sheila Reitzel Foor, pp. 55-77. Bowling Green, Ohio: Bowling Green State University Popular Press, 1997.

[*In the following essay, Herrera illustrates how marriage and motherhood are explored within the context of the oppression of women in Charlotte Brontë's* Villette *and Harriet Jacobs's* Incidents in the Life of a Slave Girl.]

> Some will object, that a comparison cannot fairly be made between the government of the male sex and the forms of unjust power . . . But was there ever any domination which did not appear natural to those who possessed it? . . . Did not the slaveowners of the Southern United States maintain the same doctrine, with all the fanaticism with which men cling to the theories that justify their passions and legitimate their personal interests?
>
> —John Stuart Mill, *The Subjection of Women* (1869)

In 1853 Charlotte Brontë published her last and perhaps her most controversial novel, *Villette,* a semiautobiographical work written in the form of an autobiography. Less than four years after the publication of *Villette,* Harriet Jacobs, a woman born into slavery, completed her now famous autobiography, *Incidents in the Life of a Slave Girl, Written by Herself* (though it was not actually published until 1861). Although both of their "autobiographies" are written out of clearly different circumstances and are, therefore, ostensibly distinct from one another, when approached in a refracted light it soon becomes apparent that Brontë's and Jacobs's works actually mirror one another in surprising and ex-

traordinary ways, for both put into relief the issues of marriage, motherhood, and oppression against the larger social attitude toward women. In short, both Brontë's and Jacobs's works stand as powerful commentaries on women's positions during the mid-nineteenth century.

In order to pursue such a reading, one must first establish the prevailing attitude toward middle-class white women's positions and female deportment both in Britain and in the United States during the period in which Brontë and Jacobs were writing, for this ideology provides the undergirding for both of their works. As scores of historians and critics have pointed out, the middle-class ideal of domesticity and womanhood during the nineteenth century, often referred to as "home idealism" and the "cult of true womanhood" (respectively), enjoined females to be sexually and socially passive, modest, self-effacing, self-sacrificing, pious, and pure in body and mind.[1]

In addition, women were denied entrance into most universities and were barred from most professions, excluding teaching, acting as a governess, and nursing, all of which essentially were extensions of their domestic duties. Because they were not expected (or allowed in many cases) to earn wages outside of the home and frequently did not have any direct claim to property, the large majority of middle- to upper-class women were entirely dependent upon men both for economic support and for intellectual stimulus, a social reality that has prompted many students of the period to claim that white middle-class women were little more than chattel.

Perhaps Martha Vicinus best sums up middle-class women's positions during the period when she says, "In her most perfect form," the ideal woman was expected to "[combine] total sexual innocence, conspicuous consumption and the worship of the family hearth."[2] The female ideal that Vicinus refers to was advocated both in works of fiction and nonfiction. A good example is John Ruskin's essay "Of Queens Gardens" (1865).[3] In it Ruskin—dubbed by many as the Victorian "interpreter" of art and culture—sketches an idyllic portrait of the domestic sphere which figures home as an enclosed garden, a kind of prelapsarian asylum where women rear children and reform, or even redeem, irascible and bellicose men. Home, according to Ruskin, is the locus of peace, security, and morality, and woman is rooted at the center of that order.

Visions of home and womanhood such as Ruskin's helped typify nineteenth-century attitudes toward women's role within the domestic sphere and her position in British and American society. A great portion of the writing produced during the period carved out male and female spheres of activity and advocated in very specific terms modes of female deportment. Not only was female propriety and chastity emphasized, but both novels and conduct books alike were preoccupied with preparing women for the wedded state, for only in marriage could they fully assume their Ruskinian roles as ministering angels. However, despite the fact that wifehood and motherhood had come to be regarded—in the popular imagination at least—as quasi-religious vocations and marriage was viewed as the fulfillment of a woman's destiny, in reality economic and social circumstances precluded many females, such as Brontë and Jacobs, from realizing these ideals.

* * *

In some sense Brontë's *Villette* can be read as a rebuke against the narrowness and the limitations of the female domestic ideal Ruskin, among others, had laid out for women to emulate. During the time at which Brontë was writing, middle-class women such as herself were faced with the undeniable fact that British society was teeming with increasing numbers of "superfluous" or "redundant" women.[4] By mid-century nearly one out of every four English women was dependent upon her own resources; by 1850 there were over half a million more women than men in England. As a result, unmarried women who had passed their prime or lacked the economic, social, or physical attributes that would enable them to compete in the marriage market were forced to seek other ways to support themselves.

Though marriage was the preferred vocation for women, there were actually several alternative occupations to the wedded state. Often, "displaced" women either became governesses or companions to elderly widows. By the early 1840s single women were encouraged to pursue careers such as nursing or ministering to the poor. Aside from marriage, teaching, and social or charitable work, there was one other legitimate, though much disputed, alternative for middle-class Victorian spinsters during the period: entering the nunnery. However, the revival of the Roman Catholic religious orders and the establishment of Anglican nunneries during the 1840s stirred a furious debate that persisted nearly throughout the Victorian period, for female religious life represented, for many, a rejection of women's "natural" roles and functions as wives and mothers. In effect, the woman who willingly professed a vow of chastity and consciously abjured the "noisy" secular world of men not only failed to fulfill her (procreative) duty but, moreover, leveled a threat at the very underpinnings of British society: home and family.

Charlotte Brontë was well aware of the career options open to English women. Perhaps as a direct result of her own painful circumstances, she was extremely concerned with validating the solitary woman's experiences and activities and endowing her with a status comparable to that of the married woman. In an 1846 letter addressed to Miss Wooler, the headmistress of the boarding school where Brontë herself matriculated and later taught, she wrote:

> . . . it seems that even a lone woman can be happy, as well as cherished wives and proud mothers. . . . I speculate much on the existence of unmarried and never-to-be married women nowadays; and I have already got to the point of considering that there is no more respectable character on this earth than an unmarried woman, who makes her own way through life quietly, perseveringly, without support of husband or brother; and who, having attained the age of forty-five or upwards, retains in her possession a well-regulated mind, a disposition to enjoy simple pleasures, and fortitude to support inevitable pains, sympathy with the suffering of others, and willingness to relieve want as far as means extend.[5]

In her final novel, *Villette,* Charlotte Brontë dramatizes the plight of the genteel Victorian spinster and orphan Lucy Snowe, a woman who seeks to define an independent identity for herself in a society that devalues unmarried or "displaced" women and virtually denies them visibility outside of a domestic context.[6] That *Villette* is centrally concerned with the subject of personal, as opposed to public, identity is suggested by its autobiographical form—a narrative form that implicitly and consciously entails the exploration and exposure of the self for public display. *Villette* is, more specifically, profoundly concerned with the idea of women's social identity, as opposed to private identity, and the novel "plays" with the idea of artifice or self-fashioning—allowing people to see what they want to see or what we want them to see—and its narrator, Lucy, is the queen of masking.[7] Lucy's narrative is not only filled with mysteries, conspiracies, and confusing relativities, but it is shot through with strategic omissions, silences, and concealments. Lucy repeatedly withholds important information from the reader, such as the identity of Dr. John, thus establishing and maintaining her authorial control both over her own narrative and over her audience. In effect, she presents for the reader's scrutiny only selective incidents in her life. Even those who appear to be closest to her do not really seem to know Lucy at all. Graham Bretton, for example, fails to perceive her painfully obvious romantic attraction to him. In addition to puzzling those around her, Lucy evades our gaze as well. Though she provides us with a relatively detailed, though highly subjective, portrait of her surroundings and the people whom she encounters in her travels, we are never given a clear description of her physical appearance, and we must continuously adjust and readjust our impression of her mental state. Lucy's shifting, fragmented identity is further underscored by her unreliable narrative and by the multiple nicknames the people whom she encounters in her travels give her, such as Ginevra Fanshawe, M. Paul, and Graham Bretton, among others. Her lack of identity is also emphasized by the fact that the first part of her autobiography chronicles the activities in the Bretton household and provides little to no insight into the inner life of Lucy herself. In the first part of her narrative, Lucy accounts for her own thoughts and actions only as they relate to others.

As many critics have observed, Lucy's social invisibility and displacement—her lack of identity—are highlighted at the very outset of Brontë's novel. Unlike her foster family, the Brettons (a name that obviously suggests that they represent all of Britain), whose social identity is so firmly established that the house and the town that they live in is named after them, Lucy has no fixed identity. She not only lacks a physical home or family of her own, but she is neither at home in her native England, nor, as her agitated first person narrative suggests, at "home" with herself. She is, in other words, both physically and psychically homeless. In the first quarter of the novel she, like Jane Eyre, moves peripatetically from manor house to manor house, ever conscious of her marginalization and her comparative insignificance to those who take her in. In Lucy's own words, she is a "placeless person," who is as inconsequential and "unobtrusive" as a piece of "furniture" simply because she lacks all of the attributes that would establish her social identity, such as money, title, pedigree, and physical beauty (135).[8]

In each "foster" home that Lucy temporarily inhabits, she assumes many of the roles or careers available to single women such as herself. At the outset she is the Bretton's ward; after leaving their home she takes a post as a companion-nursemaid to the wealthy elderly spinster Miss Marchmont, who Sandra Gilbert and Susan Gubar describe as a "nun" who "lives in confinement, a perpetual virgin dedicated to the memory of the lover she lost."[9] When the latter dies, leaving her unexpectedly destitute, Lucy's physical and psychic alienation, coupled with her absolute penury, prompt her to abandon England and sail to Villette, the "great" capital of the imaginary kingdom of Labassecour, "the land of convents and confessionals."

In Villette the social displacement and alienation that Lucy experienced in England is temporarily magnified, for she is literally an alien on foreign turf. Not only is she friendless and without references, but she lacks even the most basic and essential tool to establish her identity: language. In desperation, Lucy seeks shelter in a girls' school located on the grounds of a former convent: Madame Beck's Pensionnat de Demoiselles on the Rue de Fossette. There she dons a dark *grissete*, like a kind of secular nun immured behind the high convent walls that surround the Pensionnat, and assumes the only other roles available to her, aside from marriage: governess and teacher.

At the outset the Pensionnat, like the newly established monasteries in England, functions for Lucy as a secular protective haven—a home away from home—for desti-

tute females who share her plight. Madame Beck acts as her surrogate mother, and the demi-convent functions as her surrogate home, complete with an extended secular family. However, Madame Beck, who is often characterized as a kind of abbess, runs her boarding school like a monastery.[10] Much like a Mother Superior, she maintains constant surveillance over her community, wielding the arbitrary authority that the Protestant Brontë associated with the Catholic Church.[11] Her presence is ubiquitous. Calling for unquestioning obedience, she administers her school with absolute control; Lucy tells us, she kept all but her own children "in distrustful restraint, in blind ignorance, and under a surveillance that left no moment and no corner for retirement" (99). Despite its shortcomings, the demi-convent protects Lucy from "the perils of darkness" and the "new Gothic" world she depicts as being peopled with "dreaded [male] hunters" who pursue her through the streets (89, 86).[12] In effect, the demi-convent attracts and shelters those who, like Lucy, are unsuccessfully socialized and unable to regulate their own lives or cope in the outside world.

Cloistered within the convent walls, Lucy struggles to overcome her sense of alienation. There, she aspires toward an ideal of passionlessness that female religious life purportedly demanded, an ideal that was also enjoined upon women by the Victorian establishment.[13] It is at this point that Brontë yokes together her feminist concerns with the overarching theme of institutional restraint, for as one critic has noted, "the female monastery represented patriarchal institutional restraint on a large scale in the British imagination."[14] Mistakenly, Lucy perceives that the only way to establish an independent identity, without compromising or losing respectability or social integrity, is to remain completely detached from life, "cool" and "calm" and "stoical," she tells us, "about [her] future" (151). Clearly, Lucy is well-schooled in the Victorian notions that in order for a woman to preserve her intellectual and social integrity, she must suppress her natural sentiments and passions; unrestrained desire portends female ruin; and female sexuality is simply "an aspect of women's social function." In effect, Lucy struggles with an ideology which suggests that emotional capacity and desire in a woman are signs of weakness or inferiority, an ideology which functioned as a means of maintaining control over female sexuality and ambition, for it "kept" women in their "places."

In her struggle to exercise self-restraint and suppress her natural inclinations, Lucy measures herself against the potential female and male role models whom she encounters on her "journey." Although she represents an extreme, Modeste (modest?) Beck embodies the rational, reserved ideal toward which Lucy aspires, rather than the frivolous and self-indulgent Ginevra Fanshawe, who consents to play the role of the coquette, or the subservient and self-effacing Polly *Home* (my emphasis), who dedicates herself to domesticity and to pleasing men. In Lucy's view, not only is she morally and intellectually superior to women like Ginevra, but she regards the latter, along with Polly Home, as puppets or playthings for men who maintain absolute authority over them, though they claim to endow them with a morally superior or "angelic" status.

Just as Lucy systematically rejects the standards and ideals against which women were expected to measure themselves, so is her identity "tested" against two types of men: Dr. John, the embodiment of the Victorian ideal of manhood, and M. Paul, a foreigner and a Roman Catholic, who functions as the physical and emotional antithesis of the fair physician.[15] The passion and personal desire that she feels first for Graham Bretton, and then for M. Paul proves to be completely incompatible with her Victorian education and poses a very real threat to her beliefs regarding female behavior. Though Lucy has willingly cloistered herself within the old demi-convent and adopted the garb and the lifestyle of a nun, to her great dismay she discovers that more often than not her passionate and sometimes irrational inward sensibility is at odds with the dispassionate, rational social or external personage she believes she must be in order to establish an identity that is independent of the expectations placed upon her by her society.[16] The ability to conceal and suppress her emotions and disavow her natural inclinations toward both Graham Bretton and M. Paul become, simultaneously, the source of her power and her demise. The oppressive environment of the demi-convent, coupled with the emotional and physical isolation of the life Lucy has chosen to lead, cause her to undergo an identity crisis which pits her authentic or natural emotional self against her passionless social self, a crisis which leads her to the very brink of madness.[17]

Brontë carefully traces the steps Lucy takes to overcome both her psychic and emotional fragmentation and to get beyond the damaging, artificial notion of cultural and religious propriety; the images of the convent and the nun figure largely in this process. Lucy's various encounters in the demi-convent with the spectral nuns mark her progress toward independence and self-realization; both Graham Bretton and M. Paul are linked, either through direct experience or association, to a separate nun.

There are two deceased nuns in *Villette*: the phantom nun who haunts the Pensionnat on the Rue de Fossette and M. Paul's former lover, the "sainted nun" Justine Marie, who represents in the novel a kind of latter-day version of Miss Marchmont.[18] Both women have been victims of their passion; their marginalization is emphasized by the fact that they are ghosts, literally relegated to a state of virtual invisibility, which is akin to Lucy's

insignificant status in Victorian society. The former, according to legend, was buried alive for committing some nameless "sin," presumably of passion, against her vow; and the latter opted to take a vow of poverty and chastity—as a sign of her fidelity—because she was forbidden to marry the then impecunious M. Paul. In effect, the nun of legend and Justine Marie embody the two combating aspects of Lucy Snowe: the first represents indulgence and unrestraint, and the second the renunciation and sublimation of worldly passion.

Lucy encounters the nuns, individually, on five separate occasions: the nun at the demi-convent haunts her three times as she struggles to suppress her feelings for Dr. John (Graham Bretton), and the spirit of Justine Marie torments her during her "courtship" with M. Paul. The first and second visitations take place in the *grenier* of the Rue de Fossette. There, the nameless phantom interrupts her while she is reading Dr. John's letter and frightens her as she searches for a dress to wear on an unchaperoned outing to the theater. Significantly, the second visitation takes place during the same evening that she witnesses Vashti's overtly passionate and (literally) inflammatory performance. Lucy is then confronted with the spectral nun a third time just after she has grown disillusioned with Dr. John and buries (an obvious metaphor for repression) his letters beneath the "dryad skelton" of the old pear tree (which she refers to in her narrative as Methuselah) where the young nun was purportedly interred (422). (The pear, with its curved, hour glass shape, suggests the female form.) Gathering her courage at this third meeting, Lucy attempts to determine the nun's identity. "Who are you? and why do you come to me?" she asks, but the shrouded figure remains silent (426). As the nun rushes past her, Lucy vainly stretches out her hand to determine whether the figure is real or illusory, since Dr. John had repeatedly assured her that the nun was merely a product of her overwrought imagination. She calls after it into the darkness, "If you have any real errand to me, come back and deliver it." Once again, Lucy receives no response.

Although Lucy has yet to decipher it, the spectral nun has a clearly defined errand in the novel; however, Brontë denies her heroine knowledge of the true identity of the specter at this juncture, for Lucy has yet to have fully undergone her "education." In other words, Lucy's disappointment with the physician—a man who clearly prefers a woman with domestic "talents," rather than one with intellectual aspirations, such as Polly Home(body?)—represents only the first stage of her development; she must also confront M. Paul and, by association, the second nun—Justine Marie—whom she encounters on two separate occasions.

The fourth visitation occurs shortly after Lucy's disillusionment with, and consequent rejection of, the English Dr. John and the onset of her emotional/intellectual attachment to M. Paul. The nun intrudes upon M. Paul and Lucy while they are sharing a relatively intimate moment in the *allée défendue* in the garden of the demi-convent. It is he who suggests that the phantom is not the nun of legend but, rather, his deceased lover, Justine Marie. He tells Lucy, "her business is as much with you as with me" (531). As they continue to discuss the "nature" of the apparition, the nun sweeps past them in the alley; Lucy proclaims, "never had [she] seen her so clearly" (534). Although Lucy is still deceived, for she has yet to "see" the nun for what she really is, it is at this point in her narrative that she first entertains the possibility that the ghost is something more than a "nervous malady," something that lies outside of herself.

Lucy's final encounter with a nun follows the incident in the park where she sees M. Paul with his young and beautiful ward, a woman whom Lucy mistakes for his lover. Upon discovering the couple, Lucy undergoes a severe nervous breakdown. It is this second disillusionment which prepares her for her last confrontation with the specter of the nun. Even though Lucy misreads the scene—thinking at the time that M. Paul was engaged to the girl—in retrospect she reflects upon the absurdity of her romantic "infatuation" with the professor, an infatuation that parallels her idealized vision of Graham Bretton. The revelation is liberating for her, and she suggests:

> In my infatuation, I said, Truth, you are a good mistress to your faithful servants! While a lie pressed me, how I suffered! Even when the falsehood was still sweet, still flattering to the fancy, and warm to the feelings, it wasted me with hourly torment. The persuasion that affection was won could not be divorced from the dread that, by another turn of wheel, it might be lost. Truth stripped away Falsehood, and Flattery, and Expectancy, and here I stand—free!'
>
> Nothing remained now but to take my freedom to my chamber, to carry it with me to my bed and see what I could make of it. The play was not yet indeed quite played out. . . .
>
> (677)

Indeed, Brontë's play was not yet played out. Having undergone this second disillusionment, despite the fact that it was prompted by her own misapprehension, Lucy is prepared to free herself of the romantic notion that the only way for a woman to find happiness is through love for a man—any man. Her final awakening takes place in two stages. Upon returning to the dormitory, the dark "nun's cell," to meditate upon her new-found freedom, Lucy encounters the specter of Justine Marie lying across her bed—the emotionally barren woman, who had sacrificed her self for love, that Lucy had almost allowed herself to become. Provoked by jealousy, rage, perhaps self-hatred and a sense of inexplicable guilt, she engages in a symbolic struggle with the nun.[19] In this final encounter, Brontë uses the ghost nun to sig-

nify the ambiguous, contradictory images of womanhood that have haunted Lucy. In one respect the supine nun represents the Victorian ideal of female passionlessness that Lucy has attempted to internalize, simply by virtue of the fact that Justine Marie is a nun. On the other hand, however, she is an amorous young woman who consciously buried her passion for her lover by entering the convent. In effect, she simultaneously functions as the very embodiment of the contradictory impulses with which Lucy is battling: passion vs. reason and restraint. However, because Brontë fails to identify which nun lies stretched across Lucy's bed in this episode, there resides the possibility that she may also be the phantom who haunts the demi-convent—the passionate woman who submitted to her desire and was punished. In the conflated figure of the nun, therefore, Brontë brings together and encapsulates a triad of conflicting cultural ideologies that have contributed to, or perhaps caused, Lucy's fragmented identity.

When she first finds the nun lying on her bed, Lucy perceives that she is a figment of her own imagination; then she quickly discovers that it is a "spectra" which has material form, something other than, or apart from, herself:

> I defied the spectra. In a moment, without exclamation, I had rushed on the haunted couch; nothing leaped out or sprang, or stirred; all the movement was mine, so was all the life, the reality, the substance, the force; as my instinct felt. I tore her up—the incubus! I held her on high—the goblin! I shook her loose—the mystery! And down she fell—down all around me—down in shreds and fragments—and I trode upon her.
>
> (681)

In that moment Lucy discovers that the nun is neither illusory, nor is she a specter; rather, "the long nun proved a long bolster dressed in a long black stole, and artfully invested with a white veil." Moreover, she herself endows the black stole and the white veil with life, or so she thinks.

By allowing Lucy to struggle with the pillow-nun, which she believes is another woman, before discovering that it is a bolster covered with a stole and a veil, Brontë subtly suggests that the notion of the impropriety of female passion or desire to which Lucy adheres (and the nuns represent) is a sham, a myth. Her unconscious complicity in animating and perpetuating the ideology that the nuns represent, coupled with her realization that she has been deceived yet again, causes Lucy to ask two central questions: "*Whence* came these vestments? *Who* contrived this artifice?" (my emphasis). In framing these questions, Lucy reveals her sudden awareness of the fact that the specter is—beyond the "shadow" of a doubt—not the product of her own imagination but, rather, an illusion created by another. Only then can she, like a neo-Radcliffian heroine, lift the "veil" that conceals the ultimate "mystery" in Villette and penetrate the "homely web of truth": the fact that the nun, in all of her manifestations, is nothing more than a male creation, contrived—in a spectacular act of spectral transvestism—by Ginevra Fanshawe's foppish lover, Alfred de Hamal, so that he might gain access to and possess the object of his affections. With this revelation Brontë brilliantly suggests that the stultifying notion of female propriety that Lucy perceives she has violated is a myth or illusion. And so, just as the struggle with the pillow-nun marks the moment at which Lucy acknowledges that her physical and emotional confinement is self-administered, the final demystification of the phantom represents the point at which she recognizes that she has been victimized or haunted by a perversely sentimental image of womanhood. In effect, the phantom nuns, with their multiple and conflated associations, are scarecrows set up by men in the "Queen's Garden."

The final sequence in *Villette* projects Lucy beyond the domestic sphere and the demi-convent into the wider world where she establishes herself as an independent agent. Despite her linguistic and cultural displacement in Villette, the foreign setting functions as a positive distancing factor which allows Lucy to acknowledge and overcome the seemingly insurmountable obstacles and limitations placed upon her by British patriarchal culture. In other words, her journey away from her native homeland ultimately serves as a catalyst for self-discovery. On foreign turf, her social invisibility becomes a source of power, rather than a debilitating attribute as it was in Britain. In some sense, however, Brontë subtly avoids a direct challenge to patriarchal ideology by allowing Lucy to remain abroad, at a safe distance from British shores; moreover, we learn that she has taken up a "respectable" career that does not disrupt traditional notions of woman's ministering role within the public domain: teaching. What remains notable, however, is the fact that Lucy struck out on her own, albeit with the assistance of M. Paul, and established herself outside the context of marriage and the convent. In so doing, she neither denied herself the experience of love, nor did she renounce her femininity.[20] That Lucy attained her economic and personal independence partly as a result of M. Paul's interventions seems to signify Brontë's recognition of the social reality that even under the most propitious circumstances most women remained reliant upon male esteem and, more often than not, male financial support for their success. However, M. Paul was for her only a temporary "savior." Not only does Lucy literally outlive him, but his death does not leave her helpless like Miss Marchmont, who confined herself to the domestic sphere after the loss of her lover, or without future ambitions like Justine Marie, who renounced the possibility of happiness and chose convent life because of her thwarted love. In the same vein, M. Paul was not solely responsible for

Lucy's ultimate success. Though he established her in a "cot" with a small classroom, it was actually Miss Marchmont's legacy that enabled her to expand her *externat* (day school) into a *pensionnat* (boarding school) (594). At the conclusion of her narrative—which marks the passage of many years since the death of M. Paul—it becomes apparent that although Lucy had been enriched by their brief relationship, she had also managed to go on quite happily and successfully without him.

* * *

Like Charlotte Brontë, Harriet Jacobs also wrote in response to her own painful circumstances. Acutely conscious of her tenuous position in society, she employed a pseudonym (Linda Brent), like Charlotte Brontë (Currer Bell), to write about the unspeakables of her plight as a woman during the period; however, her story is complicated by the fact that she was a black woman born into slavery in the South during the pre-Civil War period.

Incidents in the Life of a Slave Girl, Written by Herself dramatizes the plight of a black female slave who is both genteel and educated. Unlike Lucy Snowe, Linda Brent (aka Harriet Jacobs) is a woman who seeks to define an identity for herself independent of her race but not necessarily independent of her gender, for as many critics have noted Jacobs portrays herself in her narrative as a "maternal icon" and a "heroic," "suffering," and "outraged" slave mother.[21] Unlike *Villette*, which aims to validate the life of the single woman, *Incidents* sets out to justify the life of the single slave mother. Though its final vision is different from *Villette*'s, *Incidents* also functions as a critique against the ideals of womanhood and domesticity that white patriarchal society institutionalized during the period—impossible ideals to which Linda Brent, like Lucy Snowe, could not conform.[22] In short, it too exposes the limitations and the narrowness of these ideals. As Jean Fagan Yellin states,

> Like all slave narratives, *Incidents* was shaped by the empowering impulse that created the American Renaissance. Jacobs' book expressed democratic ideals and embodied a dual critique of nineteenth-century America: it challenged the institution of chattel slavery with its supporting ideology of white racism, as well as traditional patriarchal institutions and ideologies.[23]

Although the distinctions between their "plights" are self-evident, and the intention of this essay is not to suggest that the obstacles white middle-class spinsters faced were equivalent to or greater than those with which female slaves were confronted, Brontë's and Jacobs's accounts bear striking resemblances to one another. On the most obvious level both employ an autobiographical narrative form. In addition, *Villette* and

Incidents are written in a "confessional mode" which, ironically, frees the narrators of their "social" guilt and sins, which neither one is responsible for having committed. Although she is openly emotional, Linda, like Lucy, maintains a controlled, rational tone as she recounts the horrors of slavery; her self-control is put into relief against the semi-hysterical ranting of Mrs. Flint. In the same vein, both narratives contain, to borrow Franny Nudelman's words, "strategic concealments" that insure the heroines' "authorial liberty" and control.[24] For Jacobs, the adoption of this form, coupled with the fact that she portrays herself as a fictional character, is especially significant, for she positions herself at the center of a narrative from which black women had traditionally been marginalized; like Lucy Snowe, Brent simultaneously assumes the role of an insider and an outsider in her own story and, as many critics have noted, she transforms herself from object to subject.[25] More important, as Nudelman has pointed out, by privileging both the voice and the experience of a female slave, Jacobs "radically alters the structure of a discourse that typically constructs the slave as a mute [and tragic] subject whose experience must be translated by an empathetic white observer" (924). Perhaps what is most noteworthy, however, is Jacobs's mastery of language itself, the most basic tool, as noted above, for shaping and controlling identity.

Although one should never lose sight of the very human story behind Jacobs's account, her autobiography is generally treated as a carefully crafted and edited abolitionist statement. As Fagan Yellin observes, Jacobs's narrator "utilizes standard abolitionist rhetoric to lament the inadequacy of her descriptions of slavery and to urge her audience to involve themselves in anti-slavery efforts" (xiv). Not only is *Incidents* filled with abolitionist "sentimentality" and rhetoric, but Jacobs draws upon and transforms a literary paradigm previously established in other slave narratives, such as Frederick Douglass's.[26] Like *Villette*, *Incidents* also manipulates the conventions of sentimental domestic fiction as well as overturns the traditional power relations in the seduction novel.

Linda Brent's narrative also follows a trajectory that is quite similar to Lucy Snowe's. At the outset of her narrative, Linda establishes her "communal identity."[27] Contrary to the plight of most slaves, she has a clear sense of her connections and her origins. Unlike the young Lucy Snowe, who is only a temporary ward in the Bretton's home, Linda grows up in the house that she was born in and gives birth to her own children in that same house. In some sense her grandmother's (Aunt Martha Horniblow) home can be likened to Mrs. Bretton's in that it functions, at least in Linda's memory, as a kind of safe haven which temporarily shelters her from the realities of the outside world. As Linda herself notes, she was "fondly shielded" in that house from the

fact that she was a slave until six years of age, when she learned that in the eyes of white society she was little more than "a piece of merchandise" (5).[28]

In some sense the Brent/Horniblow household mirrors the white bourgeois ideal of domesticity, for it consists of an extended family which includes Linda's maternal grandmother and great aunt, her parents, and her brother. Though she is taken from her family prematurely, Linda's mother is characterized as being warm and loving; Martha Horniblow replaces her daughter after her death, thus functioning as a kind of wise surrogate mother. Unlike the typical slave father, who was robbed of his paternal authority and his role as protector and bread winner, Linda's father is an accomplished carpenter who maintains absolute authority over his household even after his wife's death. Although Linda's family embodies the vision of domesticity her bourgeois audience prized, it is soon undercut and robbed of its "status" by the harsh realities of slavery. As Linda repeatedly points out, slavery not only robs black Americans of the "right to family ties," but it prevents even the strongest men from "protecting their wives and children" and women from fulfilling their maternal duties, and denies her own children "lawful claim to their own name" (43, 38, 78). In her own words, families were sent to the auction block where "Husbands were torn from wives, parents from children, never to look upon each other again this side of the grave" (106). Paralleling the scene in which Lucy Snowe discovers that her recently deceased employer, Miss Marchmont, failed to leave her a (monetary) legacy—something which would have insured her independence in English society—Linda's happiness and future prospects are "blighted" when she discovers that her slave-mistress had broken her death-bed promise to free her and her brother, William (53). At the reading of the will she learns, moreover, that she is "bequeathed" to her mistress's five-year-old niece, Emily Flint. Like Lucy Snowe, Linda thus begins an odyssey in search of freedom and her own "hearthstone."

Linda's second "home"—the household of the physician Dr. Flint—is, theoretically, the "genuine" embodiment of the white Southern bourgeois ideal of domesticity. However, Linda reveals that in reality it is a "cage of obscene birds" (52). Though Dr. Flint maintains the outward appearance of a healer and a pious Christian, he embodies the very worst characteristics of a Southern slave holder. She states,

> Reader, I draw no imaginary picture of Southern homes. I am telling you the plain truth. . . . The young wife soon learns that the husband in whose hands she has placed her happiness pays no regard to his marriage vows. Children of every shade of complexion play with

her own fair babes, and too well she knows that they are born unto him of his own household. Jealousy and hatred enter the flowery home, and it is ravaged of its loveliness.

(36)

At a later juncture in her narrative she observes,

I can testify from my own experience and observation, that slavery is a curse to whites as well as blacks. It makes the white fathers cruel and sensual; the sons violent and licentious; it contaminates the daughters and makes the wives wretched.

(52)

In Hazel Carby's words, *Incidents* is a "sophisticated sustained narrative dissection of the conventions of true womanhood."[29] In Dr. Flint's home, Linda is confronted with the irreconcilable incongruities between the prevailing conception of female identity and "true womanhood" and her own condition as a female slave. From the very outset it is made clear that despite her lowly status she possesses many of the attributes which would make her "marketable" in genteel society, such as piety and beauty. But Linda quickly discovers that these very attributes make her vulnerable to exploitation. In vain, she attempts to uphold the values advocated by bourgeois society and model herself after the very same ideals or virtues against which Lucy measured herself: modesty, chastity, passionlessness, and domesticity. However, she soon discovers that slavery "deemed" it a "crime" for a black woman to "wish to be virtuous" (31). Moreover beauty, a coveted attribute for a white woman, becomes her "greatest curse," for it makes her the object of Dr. Flint's desire and Mrs. Flint's jealousy and scorn. Rejecting her grandmother's form of piety, which advocates passive acceptance and compliance with "God's will," or one's "lot in life," Linda sidesteps the female ideals of silence and submissiveness in order to combat her master-pursuer. Not only does she repeatedly rebuke Dr. Flint's advances, but she attempts to exert her own will by pursuing a relationship with a "young colored carpenter" in her neighborhood who was born a free man. Linda soon discovers that the "dream of her youth" is thwarted by the realities of her own plight, for the civil laws to which she is subject as a slave give no sanction to marriage or love. In her description of her first disappointment with love, Jacobs cleverly parodies the plot of the sentimental romance novel, which often centers around the combatting tropes of marriage based on love and mutual respect as opposed to the idea of arranged marriages, which are tantamount to political or economic exchanges. Linda describes her relationship with her "lover" as one founded on "mutual attachment" and love; however, she undercuts this vision by pointing out that in order for them to realize their dream of happiness, her lover must offer to buy her (37). Denying her the right to choose her own

partner, Dr. Flint, like an autocratic father, punctures Linda's "love dream" by denying the young carpenter's offer and suggesting instead that he arrange for her a union—though not sanctioned by law—with one of his own slaves, whom he would choose for her. In this episode Linda must come to terms with the fact that she is an object, a possession, much like a "piece of [parlor] furniture" which can be moved from place to place—a description which echoes the very language employed in Brontë's *Villette* (141).

As Beth Maclay Doriani points out in "Black Womanhood in Nineteenth Century America," Linda, being a black female slave, is faced with "a more complex standard of morality" than a white woman (210). For her, the ideals of silence, pious submissiveness and sexual passivity—all of which her free grandmother embodies—are tantamount to consenting to sexual exploitation and rape. Moreover, as Maclay Doriani has observed "bearing children does not define the slave as a true woman, since children are mere commodities" to the slave master (211). In self-defense, Linda thus breaks her vow of silence and rebukes her master.[30] After refusing his "proposal" with a verbal barrage which leaves the doctor almost speechless with anger, Flint offers her an opportunity to "redeem her character" by giving in to his advances (40). Defying the notion that a black woman's destiny lies not in legitimate marriage and motherhood but in rape and in her potential as a breeder of a new generation of slaves, Linda thus chooses her own sexual partner—Mr. Sands—and bears him a son and a daughter. In her own words,

I wanted to keep myself pure; and under the most adverse circumstances, I tried hard to preserve my self-respect . . . but to be an object of interest to a man who is not married, and is not her master, is agreeable to the pride and feelings of a slave, if her miserable situation has left her any pride or sentiment. It seems less degrading to give one's self, than to submit to compulsion. There is something akin to freedom in having a lover who has no control over you, except that which he gains by kindness and attachment.

(54-55)

Despite her defiance and her extraordinary assertion of will, Dr. Flint continues to persecute Linda. He repeatedly offers to "make her into a lady" by setting her up with her children in a cottage on his property, where he promises to leave her in "peace," though he would have constant access to her. In effect, he offers her a kind of perverse inversion of the Ruskinian, or perhaps it would be more correct to say Cowperian, ideal of domesticity (35).[31] Conscious that she cannot hold out much longer against this "fiend who bears the shape of [a man]," nor can she protect her own children, Linda conceals herself in the attic of her grandmother's garret—a claustrophobic space that recalls the nun's cell in the demiconvent which protected Lucy—and awaits an opportunity to flee to the North (27). As Nudelman observes, for Linda "visibility is a form of vulnerability and invisibility a means of freedom," much in the same way that cultural anonymity functioned for Lucy Snowe (959).

Upon discovering that Mr. Sands had failed to make good on his promise to free their children, Linda determines that she cannot remain in her hiding place any longer. Despite the fact that her grandmother's attic provides her with sanctuary and "freedom" from Dr. Flint's persecution and surveillance, she imagines that her only chance at true freedom both for herself and her children lies in the North, a territory as "foreign" to Linda as Villette was to Lucy. Just as Lucy Snowe abandons her native England, Linda flees her birthplace at the first opportunity; but upon her arrival in the North she too becomes disillusioned. Not only is she a stranger without references—a prerequisite for employment in polite society—but Linda quickly discovers that she is still pursued by, and subject to, the feared slave "hunters," a reality which was intensified by the passage of the Fugitive Slave Law, and that the "spectres" of slavery are everywhere evident (158, 186). Recalling Lucy's experience in Villette, Linda realizes, with great disappointment, that even though she is north of the Mason-Dixon line she must continue to be on her guard, for in her own words, "slaves, being surrounded by mysteries, deceptions, and dangers, early learn to be suspicious and watchful, and prematurely cautious and cunning" (155). However, Linda also encounters friends among strangers who are willing to protect and assist her.

Like *Villette,* Linda's narrative fails to resolve in the "usual way" with marriage. Rather, it concludes with Linda's having attained her primary goal—freedom—with the assistance of her benefactress, the second Mrs. Bruce. Like Lucy Snowe, Linda Brent "refuses to be destroyed by guilt" and forgives herself; by relying on her audience's empathetic identification and reaction, she both asks their forgiveness and calls them to political action.[32] In the closing paragraphs Linda expresses her desire to become financially independent in order to attain "the dream of [her] life": a home of her own, where she can educate her own children. Although her narrative steps beyond the "confines of genre," and Jacobs's narrator redefines not only true womanhood but motherhood as well, Jacobs, despite her independence, will always be "excluded" from white "domestic culture," as Nudelman points out.[33] Nevertheless critics continue to claim that Jacobs has created an "original" definition of motherhood and has "define[d] a womanhood different from the definitions advanced by the white world." Jacobs's narrative clearly demonstrates that black women could not be "judged by the same standards" as white women; however, scholars categorically fail to acknowledge that although she critiques patriarchal institutions and ideologies which support slavery and "articulate[s] the limitations of those standards," as Nudelman suggests, at no time does Jacobs reject the ideals of womanhood advocated by white bourgeois society (56). What she does do is point out the fact that her race, and consequently her position in society, precludes her from fulfilling these ideals. Again and again Jacobs's narrator "indulge[s] the hope" of attaining her "love dream"—to marry the man of her choice—and fulfilling her destiny as a "useful woman and a good mother"—traditional female destinies which Charlotte Brontë seems to reject (37-38, 133). By embracing and advocating the ideals of wifeliness and motherhood, Jacobs avoided a complete denunciation of patriarchal ideology just as Brontë did by establishing Lucy in a teaching career. In other words, in attempting to gain her audience's empathy by establishing not only her womanhood but her humanity as well, Jacobs posits a kind of counter-myth which, ironically, embraced the very ideals which white female writers such as Charlotte Brontë dismissed. In some sense, therefore, Jacobs simply reconstituted the terms and the conditions of her own slavery, for the sexist patriarchal system to which she—as a woman—was subject, regardless of her race, predetermined both her role, her behavior, and her prospects. Eventually, black female authors, such as Zora Neale Hurston, revised the traditional view of female destiny and women's social position and function that Jacobs seemed to advocate and disavowed the prescribed codes and mores that ultimately defined and limited women's role. However, one cannot lose sight of the fact that writers like Harriet Jacobs paved the way for later generations of female authors to protest the manner in which females in general were "enslaved" by patriarchy. Through her autobiography she advocated the black slave's fundamental human rights by establishing the fact that black women were capable of all of the functions and emotions that white society not only associated with being a woman, but with being a human being as well, rights and assumptions which Charlotte Brontë never dreamed of having to defend.

Notes

1. For more on the cult of the home and women's deportment during the Victorian period see Eric Trudgill, *Madonnas and Magdalens* (New York: Homes & Meier, 1976); Barbara Welter, "The Cult of True Womanhood," *Dimity Convictions: The American Woman in the Nineteenth Century.* Ed. Barbara Welter (Athens: Ohio UP, 1977) 21-41; Nancy Cott, "Passionlessness: An Interpretation of Victorian Sexual Ideology, 1790-1850," *Signs* 4.2 (1979): 219-36.

2. *Suffer and Be Still: Women in the Victorian Age* (Bloomington: Indiana UP, 1972) xi.

3. New York: Wiley, 1889.

4. See Martha Vicinus for more on this subject, *Independent Women: Work and Community for Single Women, 1850-1920* (Chicago: U of Chicago P, 1985).

5. See Vol. 1, chapter 14 of Elizabeth Gaskell's *The Life of Charlotte Brontë* (New York: Penguin, 1975) 289-90.

6. There are several stretches of time that go unaccounted for in Lucy Snowe's narrative, gaps that she often directly acknowledges and suggests that the reader imaginatively fill in.

7. That Charlotte Brontë was conscious of the artificial and contrived nature of gender roles seems to be indicated by the fact that Lucy literally takes on the role of a man in a play staged at the demi-convent. Although she appears on stage dressed as a man, Lucy insists upon wearing her own clothes beneath her costume, indicating, as some critics have suggested, the type of charading women like the Brontë sisters had to engage in (by assuming male pseudonyms) in order to compete in a public arena largely dominated by men. Brontë also seems to imply that the social roles allotted to women are pure artifice through the paintings that are mentioned, each of which depicts women in various stereotypical roles: the Cleopatra, the series *La vie d'une femme,* and the portrait of the "sainted" Justine Marie. Finally, note the reference to "play" on page 677 when Lucy struggles with the pillow-nun.

8. All quotations are taken from the Oxford edition of *Villette* (London: Clarendon, 1984).

9. *The Madwoman in the Attic: The Woman Writer and the Nineteenth-Century Literary Imagination* (New Haven: Yale UP, 1979) 209.

10. With the exception of M. Paul, the girls are not allowed to receive male visitors, and their daily schedules are divided up into three distinct periods—work or study, prayer, and a short interlude for rest or relaxation—which recall the Augustinian rules Edward Pusey adapted and then sought to impose upon his female religious communities. Though Madame Beck tends to be quite nasty, Lucy frequently praises her for her charitable benevolence and her maternal qualities. Like the Superior of a convent, she functions as a kind of surrogate mother; and like a demanding spiritual mother, she makes certain that her charges adhere to a strict disciplinary code. In the same vein, Brontë designates Paul Emanuel—whose surname translates as "God is with us" and Christian name recalls the biblical Saul, who was struck blind on the road to Damascus—as a kind of resident secular priest, whom Lucy refers to as a "lay Jesuit."

11. Reinforcing this notion, Lucy repeatedly links Madame Beck with the spectral nun who haunts the demi-convent. Upon their first meeting she comments, "No ghost stood beside me, nor anything of spectral aspect; merely a motherly, dumpy little woman, in a large shawl, a wrapping-gown, and a clean, trim night-cap" (88). Nevertheless, Madame Beck "glides ghost-like through the house," and she appears and disappears, "noisless as a shadow" in her "shoes of silence" (100, 95, 88).

12. Robert B. Heilman was the first to identify Brontë's works as "new Gothic." See Heilman's "Charlotte Brontë's 'New' Gothic," *From Jane Austen to Joseph Conrad.* Ed. Charles Rathburn (Minneapolis: U of Minneapolis P, 1958) 118-32.

13. See Nancy Cott's "Passionlessness: An Interpretation of Victorian Sexual Ideology," 219-36.

14. Lucy's façade of self-possession and internalized restraint may also be viewed as a product of her Protestant upbringing. See especially Rosemary Clark-Beattie's essay "Fables of Rebellion: Anti-Catholicism and the Structure of *Villette,*" *English Literary History* 53 (1986); and Ruth Bernard Yeazell's *Fictions of Modesty* (Chicago: U of Chicago P, 1984) 169-93. As Nina Auerbach observes in *Communities of Women* (Cambridge: Harvard UP, 1978), Charlotte Brontë depicts the Catholic Church in a pejorative way in *Jane Eyre* as well. She states, "Eliza Reed, whom Jane defines as an anti-human personification of 'judgment without feeling' . . . embrace[s] the tenets of Rome and takes the veil" (102).

15. In his essay "The Brontës: The Self Defined, Redefined, and Refined," which appears in *The Victorian Experience: The Novelists,* ed. Richard A. Levine (Athens: Ohio UP, 1976), Frederick R. Karl comments, "All Brontë heroines must be tested by their confrontation with a male. They must, in a sense, pass through male experience" (129).

16. For more on this subject see especially Christina Crosby's "Charlotte Brontë's Haunted Text," *Studies in English Literature, 1500-1900* 24 (1984): 705-15; Linda Hunt's "*Villette*: The Inward and Outward Life," *Victorians Institute Journal* 11 (1982-83): 23-31; John Kucich's "Passionate Reserve and Reserved Passion in the Works of Charlotte Brontë," *English Literary History* 52 (1985): 913-37; and Ruth Bernard Yeazell's *Fictions of Modesty* 169-93.

17. As many critics have observed, Lucy Snowe's name (*luz* and snow) suggests this conflict. For more on the significance of names in *Villette* see

George S. Dunbar's "Proper Names in *Villette*," *Nineteenth-Century Fiction* 15 (June 1960): 77-80.

18. The nun in *Villette* has traditionally been treated as a single figure. (In general, commentators who have acknowledged that there are, indeed, two nuns, have placed little to no importance on this fact.) In the past, critics such as W. A. Craik, have dismissed "her" as a silly "neo Gothic" device "too trite for serious consideration," *The Brontë Novels* (London: Methuen, 1968) 187. Others have stressed the idea that the phantom nun appears to Lucy at key moments in her emotional development, an argument with which I concur. However, according to most accounts, she is merely a projection of Lucy's psychic state. See especially E. D. H. Johnson's "'Daring the Dread Glance': Charlotte Brontë's Treatment of the Supernatural in *Villette*," *Nineteenth-Century Fiction* 20 (1965-66): 325-36.

19. Lucy's almost masochistic sense of her own guilt and sinfulness or imperfection is encapsulated in the "mad" scene in which she goes into the Catholic church; when she reaches the confessional she discovers that she has nothing to say. As Robert Keefe observes in *Charlotte Brontë's World of Death* (Austin: U of Texas P, 1979), "Lucy buries herself before she can sin"; the only sin she has committed is against her own natural instincts (165).

20. In "The Brontës: The Self Defined, Redefined, and Refined," Frederick R. Karl points out that Lucy's desire to attain (male) independence without forfeiting her "feminine role" is epitomized in the scene, previously mentioned, in which she acts out a male role in a "vest, a collar, and a cravat, and a paletot" while "retaining" her "woman's garb," which she wears beneath her costume (209).

21. For more on this subject see for example Jean Fagan Yellin's introduction to the 1987 edition of *Incidents in the Life of a Slave Girl, Written by Herself* (Cambridge: Harvard UP) xiii-xxxiv; Deborah M. Garfield's "Speech, Listening, and Female Sexuality in *Incidents in the Life of a Slave Girl*," *Arizona Quarterly* 50.2 (1994):19-49; Joanne M. Braxton's *Black Women Writing Autobiography: A Tradition within a Tradition* (Philadelphia: Temple UP, 1989) 18-38.

22. Although many critics have written on this subject, see especially Hazel Carby's *Reconstructing Womanhood: The Emergence of the Afro-American Woman Novelist* (New York: Oxford UP, 1987).

23. See Fagan Yellin's introduction to the 1987 edition of Jacobs's *Incidents in the Life of a Slave Girl, Written by Herself* (Cambridge: Harvard UP) xiii.

24. "Harriet Jacobs and the Sentimental Politics of Female Suffering," *English Literary History* 59.4 (1992): 959.

25. See note 39 of Jean Fagan Yellin's introduction to the 1987 edition of *Incidents* 257.

26. For more on this subject see especially Joanne Braxton's *Black Women Writing Autobiography* and Beth Maclay Doriani's "Black Womanhood in Nineteenth-Century America: Subversion and Self-Construction in Two Women's Autobiographies," *American Quarterly* 43.2 (1991): 199-222.

27. For more on this subject see Beth Maclay Doriani's "Black Womanhood in Nineteenth-Century America," *American Quarterly* 43.2 (1991): 218-19.

28. All quotations are taken from the 1987 edition of *Incidents in the Life of a Slave Girl, Written by Herself* (Cambridge: Harvard UP).

29. *Reconstructing Womanhood: The Emergence of the Black Woman Novelist* (New York: Oxford UP, 1987) 47.

30. Granted, as critic Valerie Smith, among others, has observed, Harriet Jacobs had to observe these injunctions to some measure, as manifest in the gaps or silences in her work, in order to make her text palatable to her genteel white audience. As Smith notes in her 1988 introduction to *Incidents in the Life of a Slave Girl,* Jacobs's account is curbed by "cultural injunctions against woman's assertiveness and directness and speech" (New York: Oxford UP) xxxiii.

31. As Franny Nudelman points out, Linda dubs her hiding space "The Loophole Retreat," an ironic reference to William Cowper's "The Task," a poem that paints an idealized image of domesticity akin to Ruskin's, p. 958. In it, the domestic sphere is depicted as a safe haven from the chaotic outside world for women and children. According to Jean Fagan Yellin, Jacobs was not the first American to employ Cowper's phrase. See note 1, chapter 21, p. 277 in her edition of Jacobs's autobiography.

32. See Elizabeth C. Becker's "Harriet Jacobs's Search for Home," *College Language Association Journal* 35.5 (1992) 416 for more on Jacobs's guilt regarding her relationship with Mr. Sands. On the subject of the ability of "maternal sorrow" to override social and racial barriers, see especially Franny Nudelman's "Harriet Jacobs and the Sentimental Politics of Female Suffering."

33. See Becker's "Harriet Jacobs's Search for Home," 413; and Nudelman's "Harriet Jacobs and the Sentimental Politics of Female Suffering," 960.

Works Cited

Brontë, Charlotte. *Villette*. London: Oxford UP, 1984.

Carby, Hazel. *Reconstructing Womanhood: The Emergence of the Afro-American Woman Novelist*. New York: Oxford UP, 1987.

Doriani, Beth Maclay. "Black Womanhood in Nineteenth-Century America: Subversion and Self-Construction in Two Women's Autobiographies." *American Quarterly* 43.2 (1991): 199-222.

Gaskell, Elizabeth. *The Life of Charlotte Brontë*. New York: Penguin, 1975.

Gilbert, Sandra, and Susan Gubar. *The Madwoman in the Attic: The Woman Writer and the Nineteenth-Century Literary Imagination*. New Haven: Yale UP, 1979.

Jacobs, Harriet. *Incidents in the Life of a Slave Girl, Written by Herself*. Cambridge: Harvard UP, 1987.

Nudelman, Franny. "Harriet Jacobs and the Sentimental Politics of Female Suffering." *English Literary History* 59.4 (1992): 939-64.

Vicinus, Martha. *Suffer and Be Still: Women in the Victorian Age*. Bloomington: Indiana UP, 1972.

Yellin, Jean Fagan. Introduction. *Incidents in the Life of a Slave Girl, Written by Herself*. Cambridge: Harvard UP, 1987.

Debra Morris (essay date 1998)

SOURCE: Morris, Debra. "Maternal Roles and the Production of Name in Wilkie Collins's *No Name*." *Dickens Studies Annual* 27 (1998): 271-86.

[*In the following essay, Morris explores Wilkie Collins's treatment of maternal characters in* No Name *as a means of illuminating the author's attitudes toward man-woman relations and his sympathetic view of women's experience.*]

Critical treatment of Collins's use of family to signify larger cultural issues, particularly the claustrophobic nature of domesticity, offers a strong departure point for my argument about maternal figures in *No Name*. Helena Michie examines sisterhood in *No Name* as one of Victorian society's "mechanisms for coping with the specter of female difference," and Jenny Bourne Taylor indicates that Magdalen enacts roles that are "exaggerated re-enactments of the world that she has lost" and suggests that "Magdalen's transgression is transformed into adaptation by pushing the codes of moral management through their own limits" when she plays various roles such as "'a [y]oung lady at home,'" a governess,

and an "innocent middle-class girl" (Michie 401, Taylor 137, 138). Both Michie and Taylor explore the family's construction of female identity without showing how fully mothers, and the role culturally assigned them, haunt Collins's novel. Tamar Heller examines the Gothic, a genre which places mothers and daughters at its center, and explores Collins's use of a traditionally female genre. She shows how female sexuality, rebellion, and revolution are linked and suppressed in Collins's major novels, and thus marginalized, mirroring the status of Collins's works in the literary marketplace (introduction). Like Heller, I think Collins's maternal figures are important. They provide a way to assess his sympathy toward women and their effacement in a society that places so much meaning on inheritance and name, the cultural domain assigned to the father. I will argue that a culturally determined narrative which draws strength from a traditional, Western vision of motherhood underlies the actions Collins's strong heroines exhibit as they try to carve out less traditional existences for themselves. I think more emphasis needs to be placed on how maternal power is threatening not only to men but to the women who find themselves trapped in maternal discourse simply by virtue of being daughters themselves.

Offering a more concrete basis for the maternal influence unconsciously realized in *No Name*, Catherine Peters's recent biography of Wilkie Collins' *The King of Inventors* uses his mother's "substantial autobiographical manuscript," a document "until now never identified or discussed by her son's biographers" (4). This document locates Collins's debt to his mother as it "gives a very different picture of [Collins's mother's] background and early life from the publicly accepted one, rapidly sketched in Wilkie Collins's life of his father, and repeated by his own biographers" (4). Importantly for my argument, Peters identifies traces of Collins's own mother in *No Name*, suggesting that "the description of the eighteen-year-old Magdalen, before the family disasters, is very similar to Harriet's (Collins's mother) self-portrait of a giddy girl, witty, lively and attractive, her father's favourite" (250). Peters indicates further that Harriet's passion for acting reveals the ways in which Collins's characterization of Magdalen bears a maternal resemblance (250). Harriet, when "[f]aced with family catastrophe and the need to earn her own living . . . proposed to become an actress. She was persuaded, with great reluctance, to become a governess instead" (250). As Peters suggests, Harriet never tests the Magdalen in her and instead becomes like the "docile Norah" (250). In "renounc[ing]" all personal ambition during marriage," Harriet supported her husband in his career as a painter and "taught the children their early lessons" (31). Harriet's devotion to her role as mother, and the similarities Peters traces between Collins's mother and especially Magdalen suggest that Collins's maternal characters, those silent, enigmatic figures, are worth exploring as keys to his view of the relationship between the sexes, as well as what has been recognized as his sympathy toward women.[1]

I.

No Name (1862) is particularly important to this argument because it shows one strong daughter figure trying to escape the implicit loss of voice embedded in her culture's narrative of motherhood. Before analyzing the trap Magdalen's society imposes on her, let me summarize the novel's plot. In *No Name,* Norah and Magdalen's parents, while legally unmarried, share a household as husband and wife and raise their daughters in the semblance of a legally bound family. Although Mr. Vanstone eventually takes Mrs. Vanstone as his wife when his legally recognized wife dies, he is killed before he has a chance to change the terms of his will and provide for those he can now identify as family. Thus Norah and Magdalen lose their name when their parents die and when they fall victim to a legal system that undermines their moral right to their father's inheritance. I will argue that the substance of *No Name,* detailing Magdalen's quest for revenge, allows her to engage in roles in which she uses her sexuality, making herself a projection of male desire, to ensnare others, and for a purpose other than what society would view as the conventional production of her father's name, the role a woman is traditionally expected to assume. The roles Magdalen takes on indicate her desire to keep herself from becoming one of patriarchy's victims and follow her changing attitude towards the name of the father and all that a relationship to the symbolic embodies. Throughout her adventures Magdalen plays out various maternal narratives before embracing the traditional one, and these narratives fail specifically *because* they allow her to express herself as a sexual subject.

To understand the limitations Magdalen faces as one expected to become a mother, I will be drawing from Kristeva's vision of the myth of motherhood as outlined in her essay "Stabat Mater" since it articulates the loss of voice and sexual self Collins's text explores. Kristeva identifies the Virgin Mary as the "traditional representation of motherhood" (160). In this vision, the mother, "impregnat[ed] without sexuality; . . . , preserved from masculine intervention, conceives alone with a 'third party', an non-person, the Spirit," thus denying the mother "the flesh" and insuring that "the symbolic link alone is to last" (164). Sexuality is undermined in that the Virgin "assumes her feminine denial of the other sex (of man) but overcomes him by setting up a third person: I do not conceive with you but with Him" (180). The Virgin Mary then provides no model for intimacy between the sexes and minimizes the integral role a woman's sexuality plays in furthering lineage. Further questioning the components inherent to the myth of

motherhood, Nancy Chodorow and Margaret Homans add to my discussion as well by emphasizing a division between a young girl's development and a young boy's, a distinction mirrored by Collins's division between the world of sons and the world of daughters.

II.

In this argument I look at *No Name*'s exploration of the trap embodied in motherhood, like the one Kristeva, Chodorow, and Homans uphold. This view of motherhood suggests that the power mothers hold over themselves and others is strikingly limited because that power is contingent on absence. *No Name* emphasizes the distinct effects the maternal and paternal legacies have on Magdalen's search for justice in a society that erases the maternal and limits the forms of its expression to insure a reliance on the paternal, as it is both psychologically and legally defined.

Collins's preface foreshadows the terms of Magdalen's problematic return to the familial when he tells us that the world of this novel holds no long hidden mystery. Its characters do not keep secrets from the audience for a prolonged period of time as happens in *The Woman in White.* The linear quality of Collins's plot in which "all the main events of the story are purposely foreshadowed, before they take place" suggests that Collins's text is constructed like a well-linked chain, a neat uncluttered movement from one event to the next like that which characterizes the paradigmatic relationship between fathers and sons (preface). This departure then is interesting in a novel so preoccupied with inheritance, wills, and the family name. It could be argued then that in presenting *No Name* in this manner, Collins's text reveals a world that sees patriarchy as necessarily defining every aspect of life. The text then impresses upon us that while Magdalen might perceive herself as adventuring outside this paradigm, her maneuverings ultimately only lead her closer to its embrace. This text, constructed like Magdalen's world, manipulates Magdalen and by extension mothers in general, into what is culturally conceived of as their "appropriate" place in Victorian society.

Collins begins his story about the Vanstone daughters with an example of a father and son relationship. Mr. Clare, the Vanstones' neighbor, raises three sons alone after his own wife dies. Here Collins's text provides an extreme example of a family governed by patriarchy. While this family is obviously not to be measured as a model, it would seem to serve as an indicator of how society at large treats women and how it conceives of the "appropriate" place for mothers in general. The mother of this family, figuratively and literally negated, inhabits that space beyond the borders of this predominately male world defined by fathers and sons. This, Kristeva scholar Kelly Oliver would suggest, is an extreme reenactment of the primary separation, the distance that a child creates between himself and that threatening maternal body, a body, that "threatens identity," as it makes the borders between self and other increasingly fragile (57). Preserving this distance, Mr. Clare thinks about his loss in the abstract and remains "philosophically resign[ed]" to it (26). His memory of his wife is secondary to his preoccupation with his library as Mr. Clare "abandoned the entire direction of his household to the slatternly old woman who was his only servant, on the condition that she was never to venture near his books, with a duster in her hand, from one year's end to the other" (26). His wife is kept from language because of her death, but the "slatternly old woman" through Mr. Clare's orders remains distant from the symbolic, the world that seemingly provides access to power in this society.

Mr. Clare's household, with an absent maternal figure, is less than ideal, as is his attitude towards parenting: "As a father, he regarded his family of three sons in the light of a necessary domestic evil, which perpetually threatened the sanctity of his study and the safety of his books" (26). He sees his sons as an immediate threat to the private time he uses to explore the world of language in general. His library "not only filled all the rooms in his modest little dwelling, but lined the staircases and passages as well" (26). Chodorow would argue that Clare is typically masculine in his self-definition as a "boy has engaged, and been required to engage, in a more emphatic individuation and a more defensive firming of experienced ego boundaries" (166-67). Unlike a girl's, a boy's sense of self is based neither on his capacity to build relationships nor on his capacity to provide empathy. The world of language insulates Clare from sources of connection, the means he has to build relationships within his home. Collins's text then suggests that the very structure that keeps fathers and sons tied together also ironically keeps them from substantially assuming the role of caretaker. This sense of self further lets Clare create both himself and others in very much a "male" model: "His views of human nature were the views of Diogenes, tempered by Rochefoucault" (26). His views of humanity are derived not by experiencing others, but through sources which keep him fully removed from them. While Clare hides behind the symbolic values his culture creates, Collins suggests his internal emptiness. Books isolate him and keep him from connecting to those he is meant to love. Through Mr. Clare's character Collins shows how shallow the ties between these family members are and by extension he criticizes those connections based on lineage. While the name of the father holds this family together, the abstract label it depends upon also allows him to place his dead wife far into the distance and it allows him to "'dismiss the unimportant accident of [his sons'] birth from all consideration'" (27).

The child he raises, Francis Clare, the man Magdalen falls in love with, is both passive and lazy. Appropriately, Magdalen and Frank fall in love under the spell of the theater and their roles as lovers in the play *The Rivals*. Frank lets Magdalen lead him, and her power over him makes it clear that she acts in a way Victorian society would find unnatural, as she manages his opinions and directs the course of their intimacy. Magdalen's acting allows her to display her body to others and to fashion herself, expressing what Michie describes as "the promiscuous multiplication of . . . identity."[2] She gives life to her sexuality and recreates herself on the stage rather than in a culturally accepted way, in the capacity of a mother like the paradigm Kristeva describes. Although Magdelen on some level preserves her alliance with the traditional vision of motherhood the Virgin Mary represents by denying the other sex in her act of reproduction, she too "inappropriately" delights in herself as a sexual subject.

When Magdalen manipulates the other actors into allowing her to play both Julia and Lucy, Frank makes clear his passivity in the activities: "I said nothing—I only agreed with the ladies'" (46). Frank compliantly allows Magdalen to reproduce herself, to use her creative powers for something other than the furthering of culture as society would define it. In this way Collins's text suggests that marrying Francis Clare is not an appropriate choice for Magdalen: Collins's text reveals that when Magdalen manages his opinions, and later when she controls his presentation of self in helping him rehearse for the play, she fails to assume her "appropriate" place in relation to him. However, I would argue that ironically while no one would want Magdalen trapped in marriage to Frances Claire, it would seem that Magdalen expresses herself more freely in this relationship than she does in the one that results in her more "appropriate" marriage, a marriage that ultimately destroys the strong presence that makes her such an interesting heroine.

When Frank passively succumbs to Magdalen's charms and her desire for his participation in the play, it is clear that Magdalen is not yet resigned to her appropriate role in relation to the symbolic:

> When Frank presented himself in the evening, ignorant of the first elements of his part, she took him in hand as a middle-aged school-mistress might have taken in hand a backward little boy. The few attempts he made to vary the sternly practical nature of the evening's occupation by slipping in compliments sidelong, she put away from her with the contemptuous self-possession of a woman of twice her age.
>
> (40-41)

In this scene, as she mediates between the masculine and the feminine, it could be argued that Magdalen actively tries to control Frank's language rather than conceiving herself as the passive bearer of his name or his language, a Madonna figure in its truest sense. The text too, because it describes her as a "middle-aged-school-mistress" characterizes her as spinster-like and thus aligns her to one who has not borne children to further the name of the father in society. By detaching herself from a culturally acceptable maternal discourse, Magdalen attempts to exert the kind of control over another's word she pursues later, a power viewed as inhibiting rather than promoting family.

At this point in the novel it would seem as though the bond between Mr. Vanstone, and his daughter, Magdalen, is the strongest one Collins's text presents. When Magdalen tries to manipulate her father into giving her permission to act, she coyly suggests to him that, "'there is never any difference of opinion between us'" (33). Even more noteworthy is the final tactic she employs with her father, a tactic that echoes Shakespeare's *Much Ado About Nothing.* Significantly, Magdalen mimics the words Benedick speaks to Beatrice at the play's conclusion: "'fourthly, because I give him a kiss, which naturally stops his mouth and settles the whole question'" (33). She takes on a man's role, seeing herself in control of stopping rather than bearing her father's words and his impact on society, taking on an active rather than passive role in her relationship to him. More important, her early action reverses the culturally "proper" role she later assumes with Captain Kirke, who stops her mouth with a kiss at the novel's conclusion and controls her flow of words before taking her as his wife.

Magdalen first turns to her father when she discovers her youthful love for Frank and realizes that he is being sent to China. She actively proposes a marriage to Frank, telling her father that "'There is nobody to speak for us, . . . except me'" (68). Again she speaks of her union with another in an active rather than passive manner, suppressing Frank's voice, his language, with her own as though their voices are one. Mr. Vanstone, in hearing his daughter's words, realizes she is growing. When she expresses her interest in another, Mr. Vanstone begins to dwell on the natural world and in particular on its death. Collins's narrator tells his readers:

> If the summer scene which then spread before Mr. Vanstone's eyes had suddenly changed to a dreary winter view—if the trees had lost all their leaves, and the green fields had turned white with snow in an instant—his face could not have expressed greater amazement . . .
>
> (68)

Collins uses an appropriate metaphor to express Mr. Vanstone's surprise at his daughter's growth. Collins's text, in aligning her budding sexuality with the transformation of summer into winter, represents the way mas-

culine desire constructs its objects, and thus the way in which a mother's sexuality is unconsciously erased. Homans suggests in her discussion of the acquisition of representation language that for a male child "learning representational language (and discovering some of its implications)" can be connected with "a loss that is equivalent to the mother's death," the mother who is often associated with nature (4). Representational language allows a male child to pursue substitutes for his mother's forbidden body, to fulfill with another the desire he feels for her. Collins's text suggests that Mr. Vanstone perceives Magdalen's sexuality in terms of a narrative that distanced him from his mother and her sexuality, foreshadowing the way Magdalen will allow her sexuality to be negated to insure her own survival in this particular culture.

While Magdalen seems to be closely allied with her father, it appears that Norah holds a closer relationship to her mother, and a closer allegiance to the culturally assigned role her mother embodies. Adding to this distinction between sisters, Norah's first love, George Bartram, unlike Magdalen's, is a man whose appearance "presented the likeness [of her father] in his younger days" and thus keeps Norah's narrative confined to the structure of lineage (529). In keeping with this distinction between sisters, Collins's narrator describes the relationship between mother and daughter: "Her eldest child, now descending the stairs by her side, was the mirror in which she could look back, and see again the reflection of her own youth" (6). The mother and daughter are tied by a mirror through which the mother can envision her past. Collins's text also implies that Norah's mother is the mirror in which Norah can envision her own future. This portrait upholds a unity between mother and daughter, so it makes sense that Norah changes little after her mother's death, for she, within herself, possesses marks of her mother's "identity." She never wholly loses that sense of herself as a fragmented extension of others, a mediator for the symbolic realm without a clarified voice of her own.

While the text upholds the distinctions between sisters, it also indicates how clearly their choices are similarly limited simply because they are daughters. When Magdalen begins the process of revenge, she takes on a disguise. Initially she disguises herself as Miss Garth, her governess. While referred to as "'our second mother,'" Miss Garth is a governess whose children under her care are importantly not her own (135). This first disguise that Magdalen adopts is suggestive, as she stays in touch, at least on an artificial level, with those who are most representative of maternal qualities and yet distant from the actual process of birth.

While Magdalen takes on the disguise of a governess and fails to achieve what she desires, Norah literally becomes a governess herself and fails to show control over the children in her charge (230). She too in her failure becomes an object of vision and of judgment:

> The people in the street stopped and laughed; some of them jestingly advised a little wholesome correction; one woman asked Norah if she was the child's mother, another pitied her audibly for being the child's governess.
>
> (221)

Norah as a governess has little impact on the household she is a part of or the children who are under her charge. Her ineffectiveness, her inability to shape the children, is made even clearer when Norah defines happiness for Magdalen:

> "The way to happiness is often very hard to find; harder, I almost think, for women than for men. But if we try patiently, and try long enough, we reach it at last-in Heaven, if not on earth."
>
> (253)

Although actively seeking happiness, Norah suggests that happiness for a woman can only be experienced in an invisible, spiritual, and indeed, empty world like the one her mother now inhabits. Collins's text shows how closely society has aligned the two sisters, not because their personality would lead them to follow the same path, but because society has denied them the chance to explore their individual voices outside the boundaries of the law.

Because Norah accepts the law, she is not defined by the boundaries the novel uses to define the realm Magdalen attempts to control. Norah's story, unlike Magdalen's, remains a part of the background in the form of letters. She is once removed from Magdalen's story, placed in the distance like her mother, and denied direct access to the main action of the novel. As Oliver suggests, a daughter, always bound to her mother, "makes her mother abject in order to reject her," and in the process "also makes herself abject, rejects herself" (61). In keeping with this erasure of boundaries defining the self, Norah's tale is relegated to sections of the novel called "Between the Scenes, Progress of the Story through the Post." Collins's text separates Norah's life taking place "Between the Scenes," moving it away from the boundaries and the bodily that is a part of the world Magdalen inhabits, suggesting their differences in terms of the presentation of self. Norah is passive to the extent that even though George Bartram reads her emotions correctly, she ultimately needs another to explain her love and to undo the words she has spoken, indicting their inherent lack of value and thus her allegiance to a narrative that undermines her control over voice and language. In getting George Bartram and Norah back together, Miss Garth does so at the expense of Norah's capacity to act and her capacity to speak in a way reflective of her desires when she tells George to

pursue his marriage proposal further: "'Don't take No for an answer . . . [Women] act on impulse; and, in nine cases out of ten, they are heartily sorry for it afterward'" (563). In the economy of the narrative, Norah earns love and money through her passivity and by ultimately embracing Victorian society's traditional vision of motherhood.

Magdalen, unlike Norah, refuses to be passive and tries to maintain control over her presentation of self. When she becomes an actress, creating herself as an object of vision, she plays two different parts. For one of these roles, Magdalen creates a caricature of her sister, one which Michie suggests emphasizes their sexual differences, "the difference between the fallen and the unfallen, the sexual and the pure woman" (404). Magdalen goes on to discuss why she performed this particular role "'to an audience of strangers'" (52). Magdalen herself suggests the unity between sisters when she tells Norah: "'In your place, I should have felt flattered by the selection'" (52). Magdalen fictionalizes herself in the image of another, namely Norah, one who is aligned to and comfortable with the maternal as her culture defines it. Magdalen then, it could be argued, superficially assumes the traditional narrative of the maternal without making herself subject to its laws. By empowering herself as a sexual subject, she lingers between the world of the feminine and the world of the masculine as they are culturally delineated, each of which promises her nothing but a living death.

As the secrets of the family are revealed, Collins's text further elaborates on the role of the maternal and the role Magdalen eventually unconsciously assumes. When Magdalen's father dies, her mother becomes tragically ill. Collins's text emphasizes Mrs. Vanstone's dependence on her husband:

> Before another hour had passed, the disclosure of the husband's sudden death was followed by the suspense of the wife's mortal peril. She lay helpless on her widowed bed; her own life, and the life of her unborn child, trembling in the balance.
>
> (83)

Yet, as Oliver in her analysis of Kristeva would suggest, the important union here is not the one that connects husband and wife. Rather, the union between mother and child even in death establishes a mother's one area of control, that she is "master" of a life that once born demands her loss of self (Oliver 66). The novel's unsettling account of this union reveals the power mothers have over their children as they bear them and, tragically, the futility of that capacity to control, accompanied as it is by her own death. This "mastery" then affords women a power to be revered because it furthers lineage, but one that has to be concealed because it involves the sexuality that is seen as threatening. Mrs. Vanstone does produce a "frail little life—faint and feeble from the first" which "survived her till the evening was on the wane, and the sunset was dim in the quiet western heaven" (90). This image, I would argue, indicates the trap Magdalen faces. By assuming roles that do not further her role as a mother in the traditional paradigm Kristeva outlines, she actually loses control over those she believes are under her power. Yet in producing life the mother must give up her sense of self and disappear to have any form of power.

After Magdalen's father dies and her mother's death appears imminent, Collins describes each daughter's reaction to her personal tragedy. Miss Garth senses a distinction between Norah's and Magdalen's responses to their loss: "Her least anxiety was for the elder sister. The agony of Norah's grief had forced its way outward to the natural relief of tears. It was not so with Magdalen" (83). Norah, at this point in the novel, produces tears, indicating her natural alignment to cultural perceptions of the feminine and her emotional tie to another. She makes herself vulnerable to others, expressing the emotions she feels. Even at the death of her father, the man to whom she seemed so close, Magdalen remains "tearless" (83). Incredibly, "[n]othing roused, nothing melted her" (83). As she keeps her capacity for empathy hidden from public view, and tries to be a less traditional woman, Magdalen instead takes a culturally traditional masculine pose.

Magdalen's attempt to control the vision she produces for others and her belief in her own separateness surface after the loss of her parents. After running away she seeks to reclaim her inheritance. She meets Captain Wragge, a man for whom "not even the widest stretch of courtesy could have included him at any time in the list of Mrs. Vanstone's relatives" even though he claims to be a distant relation (21). Magdalen decides to place herself under a contract to Captain Wragge when he asks her to "'Place your departure from York, your dramatic career, and your private inquiries under my care'" and she answers "'I do'" (181). The relationship between them figuratively relies on the prostitution of her body and provides a bleak measure of the relationship between the sexes. It suggests that even Magdalen's attempt to escape the symbolic places her under contract, binding her to the words of others. I would argue that even more importantly, this marriage does not further her escape as much as she would imagine and indeed foreshadows her marriage to a more socially acceptable Captain, who while clearly more honest, will control her presentation of self even more completely.

When trying on a role for Captain Wragge to show him her capacity for disguise, Magdalen imagines

> Frank came back to her from the sea, and the face of her dead father looked at her with the smile of happy

old times. The voices of her mother and her sister talked gently in the fragrant country stillness, and the garden-walks at Combe-Raven opened once more on her view.

> (183)

When she hears the disembodied voices of the female members of her family as they are associated with the natural world she makes them less and less corporeal, while she sees her father in terms of his face, the part of the body most fully associated with spoken language. Ironically, however, she gives her mother and her sister a voice and a relational language embodied in a conversation, while her imagination does not associate language with either her lover Frank or her father, whom she places in the far removed distance as "dead" (a designation she does not give her mother even though she is no longer alive). She rescues them from the "milk and tears," the "metaphor of non-speech, of a 'semiotics' that linguistic communication does not account for" that Kristeva sees as associated with the Virgin Mary (174). Magdalen also gives them a voice rather than defining them in her imagination as only the "holder of sound" (Kristeva 173). For as Kristeva suggests, "We are entitled only to the ear of the virginal body, the tears and the breast. With the female sexual organ changed into an innocent shell, holder of sound, there arises a possible tendency to eroticize hearing, voice or even understanding" (172-73). She gives her mother value in death, trying to change the problematic path her society has determined for her, significantly a sexuality embodied in a voice Magdalen herself will be denied in life when she later marries.

When Magdalen meets Captain Wragge's wife, she continues to enact maternal qualities that do not require her to actually become a mother. The gigantic infantilized Mrs. Wragge, as Deidre David states, "feels herself deprived of identity by the incessant discipline of male directions; she becomes, in a sense, somewhat like Magdalen, a woman deprived of her identity as inheriting daughter and disciplined by laws that legislate legitimacy and correct irregularity" (193). Captain Wragge describes his wife as "'the crookedest woman I ever met with'" (163). She disturbs the kind of linearity one would associate with legacy and with the paradigm that allows for society's continuation although even she in the end becomes contained in a portrait announcing her husband's words. While around her husband, Mrs. Wragge complains of a buzzing in her head, a buzzing which begins when she loses herself in her motherly concerns for others. This is especially apparent when she describes her previous employment to Magdalen: "'The gentlemen all came together; the gentlemen were all hungry together; the gentlemen all gave their orders together—'" (164). She becomes confused as she makes herself available to the demands of anonymous men and conceives herself as merely a "holder of sound" (Kristeva 173).

While Magdalen also comes to lose herself in the words of others, she initially uses her sexuality to maintain control over her place in society. Her adventures outside the traditional paradigm of motherhood lead her to her cousin Noel Vanstone, the son of the man who has kept her from her rightful inheritance, and Mrs. Lecount, his housekeeper. Noel upholds the worst values of patriarchy and enacts them to the extreme. He thinks of his father in terms of the bargains he has brought into the house and thus merely in terms of the legacy he leaves behind as it is shallowly conceived:

> "All these things are my father's bargains. There is not another house in England which has such curiosities as these. . . . Mrs. Lecount is like the curiosities, . . . she is one of my father's bargains."
>
> (230)

Despite his preoccupation with money, his name is associated with birth—ironic in a man so frightened of life itself. In a sense Collins's name for this character is representative of the ways in which birth has been co-opted by the male world of legacy that denies the important presence of the mother. Noel's potential legacy has little to do with heart as Mrs. Lecount describes his physical weaknesses to Magdalen: "'There is no positive disease; there is only a chronic feebleness . . . a want of vital power in the organ [heart] itself'" (227). Lacking the empathy a heart gives life to, Noel cannot see himself in relation to others and thus only views Magdalen as an object of desire.

Noel is infatuated with Magdalen and seeks her hand in marriage. He is "enchanted" when Magdalen coquettishly imitates Mrs. Lecount's "smooth voice, and Mrs. Lecount's insinuating graces of manner" (364). Magdalen's choice of Mrs. Lecount as an object to feed Noel Vanstone's desire is suggestive. Mrs. Lecount has taken care of him and "has lived in [Michael Vanstone's] service ever since his wife's death," and as Collins's text tells us "has acquired a strong influence over both father and son" (197). She even goes so far as to compose Noel's will, dictating it to him, indicating that her power, unlike that of the Virgin Mary, is not subsumed by her acknowledgment of the power the world of the symbolic holds over her (465). Like Magdalen, she has tried to remove herself from the demand that she actually become a mother. Because Mrs. Lecount's legacy has little to do with furthering the name of the father, it is defined by death: "'I had no other legacy. There is the Tank. All the Subjects died but this quiet little fellow—this nice little toad'" (227). By imitating Mrs. Lecount, Magdalen actively controls language and produces it in the guise of one who has become a guardian figure and has replaced Noel Vanstone's mother without producing heirs to bear the father's name, thus allowing her to perpetuate her ambiguous relationship to the maternal discourse her society values.

When Magdalen realizes that she is becoming increasingly compromised, that indeed she has "'lost something,'" she cries to "'Mother Earth: The only mother [she has] left'" (273). Her overt despair coincides with the time when Captain Kirke is initially bewitched by her beauty, a man who distinctly makes the point, "'I'm old enough to be her father'" (284). In making this allusion to their age difference Kirke points to his capacity to renew her association with traditional family. When she laments "'Mother Earth'" as the only mother she has left, he points to himself as her potential father. Although Captain Kirke indicates the power Magdalen has over him, he also uses words that describe her in an otherworldly manner, creating her as an abstraction. While he is attracted to Magdalen, he at first runs away from any involvement with her. He prefers the sea, telling his sister: "'The only sweetheart I have any business with at my age is my ship'" and remains in pursuit of the abstract representation of female sexuality which he can control (285).

Captain Kirke does save Magdalen, and as her savior he appropriately links the daughter's narrative to the father's, showing how fully the father's story determines the daughter's. The name Kirke first enters the Vanstone narrative when after making a less than ideal marriage, Mr. Vanstone becomes involved with another woman, Magdalen's mother, a woman who acts the role of wife even though legally she is not his wife. The woman who is legally Mr. Vanstone's wife marries him only for money and is tarnished by her "'misconduct prior to the ceremony'" (99). A Major Kirke, father of Magdalen's future husband, saves Magdalen's father from suicide. While Magdalen is busy setting out her plans for revenge, Captain Kirke recognizes Vanstone as "'a name my father used often to speak of in his time'" when going over the visitor's list in trying to identify Magdalen and seeing Noel Vanstone's name on it (281). Collins's text emphasizes the name she inherits from her father in defining her and eventually saving her. Thus Magdalen relies on the Kirkes, their lineage, and the narrative this particular father shares with his son for her renewal in society, a renewal that involves marriage and the death of her control over language. The text then upholds patriarchy's power to act as nurturing caretaker, while at the same time subversively suggesting that it is this very power that disenfranchises women and thus limits the choices they actually have.

Magdalen begins yielding to the traditional maternal paradigm when Mrs. Lecount discovers the plot against Noel Vanstone and Magdalen is forces to make a quick marriage. At this time Magdalen's passivity is emphasized: "Magdalen passively put on her hat; passively accompanied her companion along the public walk, until they reached its northward extremity" (393). Her passivity finally leads to a suicide attempt. The words she envisions as her last are to Captain Wragge and are those of a caretaker: "'be kind to your wife for my sake'" (406). She enacts those nurturing manners so important to a mother toward a woman old enough to be her mother, finally becoming a passive woman without control over the vision or language of another.

Further indicating her surrender to the values of her society, Magdalen assumes the role of a maid, at which time her employer changes her name to "'Lucy'" (513). She has come full circle, as the name is reminiscent, as Taylor observes, of her role in the play *The Rivals,* although this time she has so little social or psychic power that she does not name herself (137). She takes on the identity of Louisa, her maid, a woman who is not married and has her lover's child out of wedlock. Magdalen not only takes on the role of a mother, but one whose circumstances resemble that of her own parents (497). When "[h]er whole nervous system [gives] way," she finally reclaims her role within family (580).

Captain Kirke, symbolic of this traditional family, saves her and nurses her back to health. When she is sick, she connects Captain Kirke to her father:

> He stooped, and lifted Magdalen in his arms. Her head rested gently on the sailor's breast; her eyes looked up wonderingly into the sailor's face. . . . Her mind had wandered back to old days at home; and her few broken words showed that she fancied herself a child again in her father's arms.
>
> (576)

During her recovery, she learns to listen as Captain Kirke saves her and becomes her constant caretaker: "Her questions were endless. Every thing that he could tell her of himself and his life she drew form him delicately and insensibly" (593). She no longer is valued for her words, but rather she becomes the passive source that brings his words to life. He becomes an "egoist" in her hands, implying her final loss of identity even before she marries him (593). Having restored a father figure in her life, Magdalen becomes completely passive. She is silenced in the last words of the text, this time with a kiss and thus finally succumbs to her place in society.

In conclusion, Collins's text gives an account of a mother's power in *No Name,* and connects it to the effacement women experience. In her biography, Peters cites Collins's thoughts as they appeared in *The Guilty River, Arrowsmith's Christmas Annual* (1886, 3) about the relationship of parents and children:

> Our mothers have the most sacred of all claims on our gratitude and our love. They have nourished us with their blood; they have risked their lives in bringing us into the world; they have preserved and guided our helpless infancy with divine patience and love. What claim equally strong and equally tender does the other parent establish on his offspring? What motive does the instinct of his young children find for preferring their father before any other person who may be a familiar object in their daily lives? They love him—naturally and rightly love him—because he lives in their remembrance (if he is a good man) as the first, the best, the dearest of their friends.
>
> (as cited in Peters 75)

Collins's language describing the distinction between a mother's and a father's hold over a child is suggestive. The mother's is "sacred" and otherworldly while the father remains grounded in the world as an unthreatening "friend" (as cited in Peters 75). The mother "nourishes [a child] with blood" as though in raising a child she moves increasingly closer to death. This language too reveals the immense gap between the worlds of mothers and that of fathers, and shows then why Magdalen fails as she attempts to define herself. For although throughout her journeys Magdalen uses the language more typical of the male realm to escape the effects of the law, to escape the narrative of traditional motherhood, it fails to empower her. Rather, Collins's text reveals that Magdalen has no choice but to embrace her assigned role as her steps outside the law only draw her closer to its terms.

Notes

1. See, for example, Robert Ashley's *Wilkie Collins* (New York: Roy, 1952), pages 70-80 for a discussion of a Collins's relationships with women.

2. Helena Michie, "'There is No Friend like a Sister': Sisterhood as Sexual Difference," *ELH,* 56 (Summer 1989), 412. Michie indicates the history behind Collins's use of the theater: "Amateur theatricals are used, of course, from *Mansfield Park* onward, . . . for the expression of inappropriate erotic feelings." Also consider Céline Varens of Jane Eyre and Charlotte Brontë's use of acting in *Villette.*

Works Cited

Ashley, Robert. *Wilkie Collins.* New York: Roy, 1952.

Chodorow, Nancy. *The Reproduction of Mothering: Psychoanalysis and the Sociology of Gender.* Berkeley: U. of California P, 1978.

Collins, Wilkie. *No Name.* Ed. Mark Ford. London: Penguin, 1994.

David, Deidre. "Rewriting Male Plot in Wilkie Collins's *No Name*: Captain Wragge Orders an Omelette and Mrs. Wragge Goes into Custody," *Out of Bounds: Male Writers and Gender[ed] Criticism.* Eds. Laura Claridge and Elizabeth Langland. Amherst: U of Massachusetts P, 1990.

Heller, Tamar. *Dead Secrets: Wilkie Collins and The Female Gothic.* New Haven: Yale UP, 1992.

Homans, Margaret. *Bearing the Word: Language and Female Experience in Nineteenth-Century Women's Writing.* Chicago: U of Chicago P, 1986.

Kristeva, Julia. *The Kristeva Reader.* Ed. Toril Moi. Tr. León S. Roudiez. New York: Columbia UP, 1986.

Michie, Helena. "'There is no Friend like a Sister': Sisterhood as Sexual Difference." *ELH* 56 (Summer 1989): 401-21.

Oliver, Kelly. *Reading Kristeva: Unraveling the Doublebind.* Bloomington: Indiana UP, 1993.

Peters, Catherine. *The King of Inventors: A Life of Wilkie Collins.* New Jersey: Princeton UP, 1991.

Taylor, Jenny Bourne. *In the Secret Theatre of Home: Wilkie Collins, Sensation Narrative and Nineteenth Century Psychology.* New York: Routledge, 1988.

FURTHER READING

Criticism

Gelder, Ann. "Reforming the Body: 'Experience' and the Architecture of Imagination in Harriet Jacobs's *Incidents in the Life of a Slave Girl.*" In *Inventing Maternity: Politics, Science, and Literature, 1650-1865,* edited by Susan C. Greenfield and Carol Barash, pp. 252-66. Lexington: University Press of Kentucky, 1999.

> Examines Jacobs's attitude toward slavery, motherhood, and the female body in *Incidents in the Life of a Slave Girl.*

Hadlock, Philip G. "The Semiotics of Maternity in Maupassant's *Une vie.*" In *The Mother in/and French Literature,* edited by Buford Norman, pp. 93-113. Amsterdam and Atlanta, Ga.: Rodopi, 2000.

> Argues that the case of Jeanne in Maupassant's *Une vie* "seems to call for a reconsideration of what motherhood means for Maupassant."

Homans, Margaret. "Bearing Demons: *Frankenstein's* Circumvention of the Maternal." In *Frankenstein: Mary Shelley,* edited by Fred Botting, pp. 140-65. New York: St. Martin's Press, 1995.

> Illustrates that Shelley's treatment of motherhood in *Frankenstein* reveals the author's views of the contradictory roles of mothering and being a daughter, and the effect of this conflict on her own and other women's writing.

Jones, Shirley. "Motherhood and Melodrama: *Salem Chapel* and Sensation Fiction." *Women's Writing* 6, no. 2 (1999): 239-50.

> Places Margaret Oliphant's *Salem Chapel* within the context of Victorian sensation fiction and delineates Oliphant's uniquely varied characters, arguing that "*Salem Chapel* is a distinctive contribution to Oliphant's extensive and complex scrutiny of the personal and cultural meaning of motherhood."

Matus, Jill L. *Unstable Bodies: Victorian Representations of Sexuality and Maternity.* Manchester, England and New York: Manchester University Press, 1995, 280 p.

> Book-length study that compares various Victorian authors' approaches to the subject of women's sexuality and maternity.

McKnight, Natalie J. "Mothering Theory and Miserable or Missing Mothers in Victorian Novels." In *Suffering Mothers in Mid-Victorian Novels,* pp. 23-35. New York: St. Martin's Press, 1997.

> Employs various psychological theories of mothering to provide a detailed analysis of the portrayals of mothers and of maternal ideals in some nineteenth-century novels.

Roulin, Jean-Marie. "Mothers in Revolution: Political Representations of Maternity in Nineteenth-Century France." *Yale French Studies,* no. 101 (2001): 182-200.

> Discusses the use of women and mothers in nineteenth-century French literature as symbols of the republic, and the social and political implications of this symbolism.

How to Use This Index

The main references

list all author entries in the following Thomson Gale Literary Criticism series:

AAL = *Asian American Literature*
BG = *The Beat Generation: A Gale Critical Companion*
BLC = *Black Literature Criticism*
BLCS = *Black Literature Criticism Supplement*
CLC = *Contemporary Literary Criticism*
CLR = *Children's Literature Review*
CMLC = *Classical and Medieval Literature Criticism*
DC = *Drama Criticism*
FL = *Feminism in Literature: A Gale Critical Companion*
GL = *Gothic Literature: A Gale Critical Companion*
HLC = *Hispanic Literature Criticism*
HLCS = *Hispanic Literature Criticism Supplement*
HR = *Harlem Renaissance: A Gale Critical Companion*
LC = *Literature Criticism from 1400 to 1800*
NCLC = *Nineteenth-Century Literature Criticism*
NNAL = *Native North American Literature*
PC = *Poetry Criticism*
SSC = *Short Story Criticism*
TCLC = *Twentieth-Century Literary Criticism*
WLC = *World Literature Criticism, 1500 to the Present*
WLCS = *World Literature Criticism Supplement*

The cross-references

list all author entries in the following Thomson Gale biographical and literary sources:

AAYA = *Authors & Artists for Young Adults*
AFAW = *African American Writers*
AFW = *African Writers*
AITN = *Authors in the News*
AMW = *American Writers*
AMWR = *American Writers Retrospective Supplement*
AMWS = *American Writers Supplement*
ANW = *American Nature Writers*
AW = *Ancient Writers*
BEST = *Bestsellers*
BPFB = *Beacham's Encyclopedia of Popular Fiction: Biography and Resources*
BRW = *British Writers*
BRWS = *British Writers Supplement*
BW = *Black Writers*
BYA = *Beacham's Guide to Literature for Young Adults*
CA = *Contemporary Authors*
CAAS = *Contemporary Authors Autobiography Series*
CABS = *Contemporary Authors Bibliographical Series*
CAD = *Contemporary American Dramatists*
CANR = *Contemporary Authors New Revision Series*
CAP = *Contemporary Authors Permanent Series*
CBD = *Contemporary British Dramatists*
CCA = *Contemporary Canadian Authors*
CD = *Contemporary Dramatists*
CDALB = *Concise Dictionary of American Literary Biography*

CDALBS = *Concise Dictionary of American Literary Biography Supplement*
CDBLB = *Concise Dictionary of British Literary Biography*
CMW = *St. James Guide to Crime & Mystery Writers*
CN = *Contemporary Novelists*
CP = *Contemporary Poets*
CPW = *Contemporary Popular Writers*
CSW = *Contemporary Southern Writers*
CWD = *Contemporary Women Dramatists*
CWP = *Contemporary Women Poets*
CWRI = *St. James Guide to Children's Writers*
CWW = *Contemporary World Writers*
DA = *DISCovering Authors*
DA3 = *DISCovering Authors 3.0*
DAB = *DISCovering Authors: British Edition*
DAC = *DISCovering Authors: Canadian Edition*
DAM = *DISCovering Authors: Modules*
   DRAM: *Dramatists Module;* **MST:** *Most-studied Authors Module;*
   MULT: *Multicultural Authors Module;* **NOV:** *Novelists Module;*
   POET: *Poets Module;* **POP:** *Popular Fiction and Genre Authors Module*
DFS = *Drama for Students*
DLB = *Dictionary of Literary Biography*
DLBD = *Dictionary of Literary Biography Documentary Series*
DLBY = *Dictionary of Literary Biography Yearbook*
DNFS = *Literature of Developing Nations for Students*
EFS = *Epics for Students*
EXPN = *Exploring Novels*
EXPP = *Exploring Poetry*
EXPS = *Exploring Short Stories*
EW = *European Writers*
FANT = *St. James Guide to Fantasy Writers*
FW = *Feminist Writers*
GFL = *Guide to French Literature,* Beginnings to 1789, 1798 to the Present
GLL = *Gay and Lesbian Literature*
HGG = *St. James Guide to Horror, Ghost & Gothic Writers*
HW = *Hispanic Writers*
IDFW = *International Dictionary of Films and Filmmakers: Writers and Production Artists*
IDTP = *International Dictionary of Theatre: Playwrights*
LAIT = *Literature and Its Times*
LAW = *Latin American Writers*
JRDA = *Junior DISCovering Authors*
MAICYA = *Major Authors and Illustrators for Children and Young Adults*
MAICYAS = *Major Authors and Illustrators for Children and Young Adults Supplement*
MAWW = *Modern American Women Writers*
MJW = *Modern Japanese Writers*
MTCW = *Major 20th-Century Writers*
NCFS = *Nonfiction Classics for Students*
NFS = *Novels for Students*
PAB = *Poets: American and British*
PFS = *Poetry for Students*
RGAL = *Reference Guide to American Literature*
RGEL = *Reference Guide to English Literature*
RGSF = *Reference Guide to Short Fiction*
RGWL = *Reference Guide to World Literature*
RHW = *Twentieth-Century Romance and Historical Writers*
SAAS = *Something about the Author Autobiography Series*
SATA = *Something about the Author*
SFW = *St. James Guide to Science Fiction Writers*
SSFS = *Short Stories for Students*
TCWW = *Twentieth-Century Western Writers*
WLIT = *World Literature and Its Times*
WP = *World Poets*
YABC = *Yesterday's Authors of Books for Children*
YAW = *St. James Guide to Young Adult Writers*

Literary Criticism Series
Cumulative Author Index

Affable Hawk
 See MacCarthy, Sir (Charles Otto) Desmond
Africa, Ben
 See Bosman, Herman Charles
Afton, Effie
 See Harper, Frances Ellen Watkins
Agapida, Fray Antonio
 See Irving, Washington
Agee, James (Rufus) 1909-1955 ...... **TCLC 1, 19, 180**
 See also AAYA 44; AITN 1; AMW; CA 108; 148; CANR 131; CDALB 1941-1968; DAM NOV; DLB 2, 26, 152; DLBY 1989; EWL 3; LAIT 3; LATS 1:2; MAL 5; MTCW 2; MTFW 2005; NFS 22; RGAL 4; TUS
Aghill, Gordon
 See Silverberg, Robert
Agnon, S(hmuel) Y(osef Halevi) 1888-1970 .... **CLC 4, 8, 14; SSC 30; TCLC 151**
 See also CA 17-18; 25-28R; CANR 60, 102; CAP 2; DLB 329; EWL 3; MTCW 1, 2; RGHL; RGSF 2; RGWL 2, 3; WLIT 6
Agrippa von Nettesheim, Henry Cornelius 1486-1535 .... **LC 27**
Aguilera Malta, Demetrio 1909-1981 .... **HLCS 1**
 See also CA 111; 124; CANR 87; DAM MULT, NOV; DLB 145; EWL 3; HW 1; RGWL 3
Agustini, Delmira 1886-1914 .... **HLCS 1**
 See also CA 166; DLB 290; HW 1, 2; LAW
Aherne, Owen
 See Cassill, R(onald) V(erlin)
Ai 1947- .... **CLC 4, 14, 69; PC 72**
 See also CA 85-88; CAAS 13; CANR 70; CP 6, 7; DLB 120; PFS 16
Aickman, Robert (Fordyce) 1914-1981 .... **CLC 57**
 See also CA 5-8R; CANR 3, 72, 100; DLB 261; HGG; SUFW 1, 2
Aidoo, (Christina) Ama Ata 1942- .... **BLCS; CLC 177**
 See also AFW; BW 1; CA 101; CANR 62, 144; CD 5, 6; CDWLB 3; CN 6, 7; CWD; CWP; DLB 117; DNFS 1, 2; EWL 3; FW; WLIT 2
Aiken, Conrad (Potter) 1889-1973 .... **CLC 1, 3, 5, 10, 52; PC 26; SSC 9**
 See also AMW; CA 5-8R; 45-48; CANR 4, 60; CDALB 1929-1941; CN 1; CP 1; DAM NOV, POET; DLB 9, 45, 102; EWL 3; EXPS; HGG; MAL 5; MTCW 1, 2; MTFW 2005; PFS 24; RGAL 4; RGSF 2; SATA 3, 30; SSFS 8; TUS
Aiken, Joan (Delano) 1924-2004 ...... **CLC 35**
 See also AAYA 1, 25; CA 9-12R, 182; 223; CAAE 182; CANR 4, 23, 34, 64, 121; CLR 1, 19, 90; DLB 161; FANT; HGG; JRDA; MAICYA 1, 2; MTCW 1; RHW; SAAS 1; SATA 2, 30, 73; SATA-Essay 109; SATA-Obit 152; SUFW 2; WYA; YAW
Ainsworth, William Harrison 1805-1882 .... **NCLC 13**
 See also DLB 21; HGG; RGEL 2; SATA 24; SUFW 1
Aitmatov, Chingiz (Torekulovich) 1928- .... **CLC 71**
 See Aytmatov, Chingiz
 See also CA 103; CANR 38; CWW 2; DLB 302; MTCW 1; RGSF 2; SATA 56
Akers, Floyd
 See Baum, L(yman) Frank
Akhmadulina, Bella Akhatovna 1937- .... **CLC 53; PC 43**
 See also CA 65-68; CWP; CWW 2; DAM POET; EWL 3

Akhmatova, Anna 1888-1966 ..... **CLC 11, 25, 64, 126; PC 2, 55**
 See also CA 19-20; 25-28R; CANR 35; CAP 1; DA3; DAM POET; DLB 295; EW 10; EWL 3; FL 1:5; MTCW 1, 2; PFS 18; RGWL 2, 3
Aksakov, Sergei Timofeyvich 1791-1859 .... **NCLC 2**
 See also DLB 198
Aksenov, Vasilii (Pavlovich)
 See Aksyonov, Vassily (Pavlovich)
 See also CWW 2
Aksenov, Vassily
 See Aksyonov, Vassily (Pavlovich)
Akst, Daniel 1956- .... **CLC 109**
 See also CA 161; CANR 110
Aksyonov, Vassily (Pavlovich) 1932- .... **CLC 22, 37, 101**
 See Aksenov, Vasilii (Pavlovich)
 See also CA 53-56; CANR 12, 48, 77; DLB 302; EWL 3
Akutagawa Ryunosuke 1892-1927 ... **SSC 44; TCLC 16**
 See also CA 117; 154; DLB 180; EWL 3; MJW; RGSF 2; RGWL 2, 3
Alabaster, William 1568-1640 .... **LC 90**
 See also DLB 132; RGEL 2
Alain 1868-1951 .... **TCLC 41**
 See also CA 163; EWL 3; GFL 1789 to the Present
Alain de Lille c. 1116-c. 1203 .... **CMLC 53**
 See also DLB 208
Alain-Fournier .... **TCLC 6**
 See Fournier, Henri-Alban
 See also DLB 65; EWL 3; GFL 1789 to the Present; RGWL 2, 3
Al-Amin, Jamil Abdullah 1943- .... **BLC 1**
 See also BW 1, 3; CA 112; 125; CANR 82; DAM MULT
Alanus de Insluis
 See Alain de Lille
Alarcon, Pedro Antonio de 1833-1891 .... **NCLC 1; SSC 64**
Alas (y Urena), Leopoldo (Enrique Garcia) 1852-1901 .... **TCLC 29**
 See also CA 113; 131; HW 1; RGSF 2
Albee, Edward (III) 1928- ..... **CLC 1, 2, 3, 5, 9, 11, 13, 25, 53, 86, 113; DC 11; WLC 1**
 See also AAYA 51; AITN 1; AMW; CA 5-8R; CABS 3; CAD; CANR 8, 54, 74, 124; CD 5, 6; CDALB 1941-1968; DA; DA3; DAB; DAC; DAM DRAM, MST; DFS 2, 3, 8, 10, 13, 14; DLB 7, 266; EWL 3; INT CANR-8; LAIT 4; LMFS 2; MAL 5; MTCW 1, 2; MTFW 2005; RGAL 4; TUS
Alberti (Merello), Rafael
 See Alberti, Rafael
 See also CWW 2
Alberti, Rafael 1902-1999 .... **CLC 7**
 See Alberti (Merello), Rafael
 See also CA 85-88; 185; CANR 81; DLB 108; EWL 3; HW 2; RGWL 2, 3
Albert the Great 1193(?)-1280 ...... **CMLC 16**
 See also DLB 115
Alcaeus c. 620B.C.- .... **CMLC 65**
 See also DLB 176
Alcala-Galiano, Juan Valera y
 See Valera y Alcala-Galiano, Juan
Alcayaga, Lucila Godoy
 See Godoy Alcayaga, Lucila
Alciato, Andrea 1492-1550 .... **LC 116**
Alcott, Amos Bronson 1799-1888 ... **NCLC 1, 167**
 See also DLB 1, 223

Alcott, Louisa May 1832-1888 . **NCLC 6, 58, 83; SSC 27; WLC 1**
 See also AAYA 20; AMWS 1; BPFB 1; BYA 2; CDALB 1865-1917; CLR 1, 38, 109; DA; DA3; DAB; DAC; DAM MST, NOV; DLB 1, 42, 79, 223, 239, 242; DLBD 14; FL 1:2; FW; JRDA; LAIT 2; MAICYA 1, 2; NFS 12; RGAL 4; SATA 100; TUS; WCH; WYA; YABC 1; YAW
Alcuin c. 730-804 .... **CMLC 69**
 See also DLB 148
Aldanov, M. A.
 See Aldanov, Mark (Alexandrovich)
Aldanov, Mark (Alexandrovich) 1886-1957 .... **TCLC 23**
 See also CA 118; 181; DLB 317
Aldington, Richard 1892-1962 .... **CLC 49**
 See also CA 85-88; CANR 45; DLB 20, 36, 100, 149; LMFS 2; RGEL 2
Aldiss, Brian W. 1925- .. **CLC 5, 14, 40; SSC 36**
 See also AAYA 42; CA 5-8R, 190; CAAE 190; CAAS 2; CANR 5, 28, 64, 121; CN 1, 2, 3, 4, 5, 6, 7; DAM NOV; DLB 14, 261, 271; MTCW 1, 2; MTFW 2005; SATA 34; SCFW 1, 2; SFW 4
Aldrich, Bess Streeter 1881-1954 .... **TCLC 125**
 See also CLR 70; TCWW 2
Alegria, Claribel
 See Alegria, Claribel
 See also CWW 2; DLB 145, 283
Alegria, Claribel 1924- .... **CLC 75; HLCS 1; PC 26**
 See Alegria, Claribel
 See also CA 131; CAAS 15; CANR 66, 94, 134; DAM MULT; EWL 3; HW 1; MTCW 2; MTFW 2005; PFS 21
Alegria, Fernando 1918-2005 .... **CLC 57**
 See also CA 9-12R; CANR 5, 32, 72; EWL 3; HW 1, 2
Aleichem, Sholom .... **SSC 33; TCLC 1, 35**
 See Rabinovitch, Sholem
 See also TWA
Aleixandre, Vicente 1898-1984 .... **HLCS 1; TCLC 113**
 See also CANR 81; DLB 108, 329; EWL 3; HW 2; MTCW 1, 2; RGWL 2, 3
Alekseev, Konstantin Sergeivich
 See Stanislavsky, Constantin
Alekseyer, Konstantin Sergeyevich
 See Stanislavsky, Constantin
Aleman, Mateo 1547-1615(?) .... **LC 81**
Alencar, Jose de 1829-1877 .... **NCLC 157**
 See also DLB 307; LAW; WLIT 1
Alencon, Marguerite d'
 See de Navarre, Marguerite
Alepoudelis, Odysseus
 See Elytis, Odysseus
 See also CWW 2
Aleshkovsky, Joseph 1929-
 See Aleshkovsky, Yuz
 See also CA 121; 128
Aleshkovsky, Yuz .... **CLC 44**
 See Aleshkovsky, Joseph
 See also DLB 317
Alexander, Lloyd (Chudley) 1924- ... **CLC 35**
 See also AAYA 1, 27; BPFB 1; BYA 5, 6, 7, 9, 10, 11; CA 1-4R; CANR 1, 24, 38, 55, 113; CLR 1, 5, 48; CWRI 5; DLB 52; FANT; JRDA; MAICYAS 1; MTCW 1; SAAS 19; SATA 3, 49, 81, 129, 135; SUFW; TUS; WYA; YAW
Alexander, Meena 1951- .... **CLC 121**
 See also CA 115; CANR 38, 70, 146; CP 5, 6, 7; CWP; DLB 323; FW
Alexander, Samuel 1859-1938 .... **TCLC 77**
Alexeiev, Konstantin
 See Stanislavsky, Constantin

Alexeyev, Constantin Sergeivich
See Stanislavsky, Constantin
Alexeyev, Konstantin Sergeyevich
See Stanislavsky, Constantin
Alexie, Sherman 1966- .... **CLC 96, 154; NNAL; PC 53**
See also AAYA 28; BYA 15; CA 138; CANR 65, 95, 133; CN 7; DA3; DAM MULT; DLB 175, 206, 278; LATS 1:2; MTCW 2; MTFW 2005; NFS 17; SSFS 18
al-Farabi 870(?)-950 .... **CMLC 58**
See also DLB 115
Alfau, Felipe 1902-1999 .... **CLC 66**
See also CA 137
Alfieri, Vittorio 1749-1803 .... **NCLC 101**
See also EW 4; RGWL 2, 3; WLIT 7
Alfonso X 1221-1284 .... **CMLC 78**
Alfred, Jean Gaston
See Ponge, Francis
Alger, Horatio, Jr. 1832-1899 .... **NCLC 8, 83**
See also CLR 87; DLB 42; LAIT 2; RGAL 4; SATA 16; TUS
Al-Ghazali, Muhammad ibn Muhammad
1058-1111 .... **CMLC 50**
See also DLB 115
Algren, Nelson 1909-1981 ..... **CLC 4, 10, 33; SSC 33**
See also AMWS 9; BPFB 1; CA 13-16R; 103; CANR 20, 61; CDALB 1941-1968; CN 1, 2; DLB 9; DLBY 1981, 1982, 2000; EWL 3; MAL 5; MTCW 1, 2; MTFW 2005; RGAL 4; RGSF 2
al-Hariri, al-Qasim ibn 'Ali Abu Muhammad al-Basri
1054-1122 .... **CMLC 63**
See also RGWL 3
Ali, Ahmed 1908-1998 .... **CLC 69**
See also CA 25-28R; CANR 15, 34; CN 1, 2, 3, 4, 5; DLB 323; EWL 3
Ali, Tariq 1943- .... **CLC 173**
See also CA 25-28R; CANR 10, 99
Alighieri, Dante
See Dante
See also WLIT 7
al-Kindi, Abu Yusuf Ya'qub ibn Ishaq c. 801-c. 873 .... **CMLC 80**
Allan, John B.
See Westlake, Donald E.
Allan, Sidney
See Hartmann, Sadakichi
Allan, Sydney
See Hartmann, Sadakichi
Allard, Janet .... **CLC 59**
Allen, Edward 1948- .... **CLC 59**
Allen, Fred 1894-1956 .... **TCLC 87**
Allen, Paula Gunn 1939- .... **CLC 84, 202; NNAL**
See also AMWS 4; CA 112; 143; CANR 63, 130; CWP; DA3; DAM MULT; DLB 175; FW; MTCW 2; MTFW 2005; RGAL 4; TCWW 2
Allen, Roland
See Ayckbourn, Alan
Allen, Sarah A.
See Hopkins, Pauline Elizabeth
Allen, Sidney H.
See Hartmann, Sadakichi
Allen, Woody 1935- .... **CLC 16, 52, 195**
See also AAYA 10, 51; AMWS 15; CA 33-36R; CANR 27, 38, 63, 128; DAM POP; DLB 44; MTCW 1; SSFS 21
Allende, Isabel 1942- ... **CLC 39, 57, 97, 170; HLC 1; SSC 65; WLCS**
See also AAYA 18, 70; CA 125; 130; CANR 51, 74, 129; CDWLB 3; CLR 99; CWW 2; DA3; DAM MULT, NOV; DLB 145; DNFS 1; EWL 3; FL 1:5; FW; HW 1, 2; INT CA-130; LAIT 5; LAWS 1; LMFS 2;

MTCW 1, 2; MTFW 2005; NCFS 1; NFS 6, 18; RGSF 2; RGWL 3; SATA 163; SSFS 11, 16; WLIT 1
Alleyn, Ellen
See Rossetti, Christina
Alleyne, Carla D. .... **CLC 65**
Allingham, Margery (Louise)
1904-1966 .... **CLC 19**
See also CA 5-8R; 25-28R; CANR 4, 58; CMW 4; DLB 77; MSW; MTCW 1, 2
Allingham, William 1824-1889 ..... **NCLC 25**
See also DLB 35; RGEL 2
Allison, Dorothy E. 1949- .... **CLC 78, 153**
See also AAYA 53; CA 140; CANR 66, 107; CN 7; CSW; DA3; FW; MTCW 2; MTFW 2005; NFS 11; RGAL 4
Alloula, Malek .... **CLC 65**
Allston, Washington 1779-1843 .... **NCLC 2**
See also DLB 1, 235
Almedingen, E. M. .... **CLC 12**
See Almedingen, Martha Edith von
See also SATA 3
Almedingen, Martha Edith von 1898-1971
See Almedingen, E. M.
See also CA 1-4R; CANR 1
Almodovar, Pedro 1949(?)- .... **CLC 114, 229; HLCS 1**
See also CA 133; CANR 72, 151; HW 2
Almqvist, Carl Jonas Love
1793-1866 .... **NCLC 42**
al-Mutanabbi, Ahmad ibn al-Husayn Abu al-Tayyib al-Jufi al-Kindi
915-965 .... **CMLC 66**
See Mutanabbi, Al-
See also RGWL 3
Alonso, Damaso 1898-1990 .... **CLC 14**
See also CA 110; 131; 130; CANR 72; DLB 108; EWL 3; HW 1, 2
Alov
See Gogol, Nikolai (Vasilyevich)
al'Sadaawi, Nawal
See El Saadawi, Nawal
See also FW
al-Shaykh, Hanan 1945- .... **CLC 218**
See Shaykh, al- Hanan
See also CA 135; CANR 111; WLIT 6
Al Siddik
See Rolfe, Frederick (William Serafino Austin Lewis Mary)
See also GLL 1; RGEL 2
Alta 1942- .... **CLC 19**
See also CA 57-60
Alter, Robert B(ernard) 1935- .... **CLC 34**
See also CA 49-52; CANR 1, 47, 100
Alther, Lisa 1944- .... **CLC 7, 41**
See also BPFB 1; CA 65-68; CAAS 30; CANR 12, 30, 51; CN 4, 5, 6, 7; CSW; GLL 2; MTCW 1
Althusser, L.
See Althusser, Louis
Althusser, Louis 1918-1990 .... **CLC 106**
See also CA 131; 132; CANR 102; DLB 242
Altman, Robert 1925-2006 .... **CLC 16, 116**
See also CA 73-76; CANR 43
Alurista .... **HLCS 1; PC 34**
See Urista (Heredia), Alberto (Baltazar)
See also CA 45-48R; DLB 82; LLW
Alvarez, A. 1929- .... **CLC 5, 13**
See also CA 1-4R; CANR 3, 33, 63, 101, 134; CN 3, 4, 5, 6; CP 1, 2, 3, 4, 5, 6, 7; DLB 14, 40; MTFW 2005
Alvarez, Alejandro Rodriguez 1903-1965
See Casona, Alejandro
See also CA 131; 93-96; HW 1

Alvarez, Julia 1950- .... **CLC 93; HLCS 1**
See also AAYA 25; AMWS 7; CA 147; CANR 69, 101, 133; DA3; DLB 282; LATS 1:2; LLW; MTCW 2; MTFW 2005; NFS 5, 9; SATA 129; WLIT 1
Alvaro, Corrado 1896-1956 .... **TCLC 60**
See also CA 163; DLB 264; EWL 3
Amado, Jorge 1912-2001 ... **CLC 13, 40, 106; HLC 1**
See also CA 77-80; 201; CANR 35, 74, 135; CWW 2; DAM MULT, NOV; DLB 113, 307; EWL 3; HW 2; LAW; LAWS 1; MTCW 1, 2; MTFW 2005; RGWL 2, 3; TWA; WLIT 1
Ambler, Eric 1909-1998 .... **CLC 4, 6, 9**
See also BRWS 4; CA 9-12R; 171; CANR 7, 38, 74; CMW 4; CN 1, 2, 3, 4, 5, 6; DLB 77; MSW; MTCW 1, 2; TEA
Ambrose, Stephen E. 1936-2002 .... **CLC 145**
See also AAYA 44; CA 1-4R; 209; CANR 3, 43, 57, 83, 105; MTFW 2005; NCFS 2; SATA 40, 138
Amichai, Yehuda 1924-2000 .. **CLC 9, 22, 57, 116; PC 38**
See also CA 85-88; 189; CANR 46, 60, 99, 132; CWW 2; EWL 3; MTCW 1, 2; MTFW 2005; PFS 24; RGHL; WLIT 6
Amichai, Yehudah
See Amichai, Yehuda
Amiel, Henri Frederic 1821-1881 .... **NCLC 4**
See also DLB 217
Amis, Kingsley 1922-1995 . **CLC 1, 2, 3, 5, 8, 13, 40, 44, 129**
See also AITN 2; BPFB 1; BRWS 2; CA 9-12R; 150; CANR 8, 28, 54; CDBLB 1945-1960; CN 1, 2, 3, 4, 5, 6; CP 1, 2, 3, 4; DA; DA3; DAB; DAC; DAM MST, NOV; DLB 15, 27, 100, 139, 326; DLBY 1996; EWL 3; HGG; INT CANR-8; MTCW 1, 2; MTFW 2005; RGEL 2; RGSF 2; SFW 4
Amis, Martin 1949- ... **CLC 4, 9, 38, 62, 101, 213**
See also BEST 90:3; BRWS 4; CA 65-68; CANR 8, 27, 54, 73, 95, 132; CN 5, 6, 7; DA3; DLB 14, 194; EWL 3; INT CANR-27; MTCW 2; MTFW 2005
Ammianus Marcellinus c. 330-c. 395 .... **CMLC 60**
See also AW 2; DLB 211
Ammons, A.R. 1926-2001 .. **CLC 2, 3, 5, 8, 9, 25, 57, 108; PC 16**
See also AITN 1; AMWS 7; CA 9-12R; 193; CANR 6, 36, 51, 73, 107, 156; CP 1, 2, 3, 4, 5, 6, 7; CSW; DAM POET; DLB 5, 165; EWL 3; MAL 5; MTCW 1, 2; PFS 19; RGAL 4; TCLE 1:1
Ammons, Archie Randolph
See Ammons, A.R.
Amo, Tauraatua i
See Adams, Henry (Brooks)
Amory, Thomas 1691(?)-1788 .... **LC 48**
See also DLB 39
Anand, Mulk Raj 1905-2004 ...... **CLC 23, 93**
See also CA 65-68; 231; CANR 32, 64; CN 1, 2, 3, 4, 5, 6, 7; DAM NOV; DLB 323; EWL 3; MTCW 1, 2; MTFW 2005; RGSF 2
Anatol
See Schnitzler, Arthur
Anaximander c. 611B.C.-c. 546B.C. .... **CMLC 22**
Anaya, Rudolfo A. 1937- .... **CLC 23, 148; HLC 1**
See also AAYA 20; BYA 13; CA 45-48; CAAS 4; CANR 1, 32, 51, 124; CN 4, 5, 6, 7; DAM MULT, NOV; DLB 82, 206, 278; HW 1; LAIT 4; LLW; MAL 5; MTCW 1, 2; MTFW 2005; NFS 12; RGAL 4; RGSF 2; TCWW 2; WLIT 1

Andersen, Hans Christian
1805-1875 .... **NCLC 7, 79; SSC 6, 56; WLC 1**
See also AAYA 57; CLR 6, 113; DA; DA3; DAB; DAC; DAM MST, POP; EW 6; MAICYA 1, 2; RGSF 2; RGWL 2, 3; SATA 100; TWA; WCH; YABC 1

Anderson, C. Farley
See Mencken, H(enry) L(ouis); Nathan, George Jean

Anderson, Jessica (Margaret) Queale
1916- .... **CLC 37**
See also CA 9-12R; CANR 4, 62; CN 4, 5, 6, 7; DLB 325

Anderson, Jon (Victor) 1940- .... **CLC 9**
See also CA 25-28R; CANR 20; CP 1, 3, 4, 5; DAM POET

Anderson, Lindsay (Gordon)
1923-1994 .... **CLC 20**
See also CA 125; 128; 146; CANR 77

Anderson, Maxwell 1888-1959 .... **TCLC 2, 144**
See also CA 105; 152; DAM DRAM; DFS 16, 20; DLB 7, 228; MAL 5; MTCW 2; MTFW 2005; RGAL 4

Anderson, Poul 1926-2001 .... **CLC 15**
See also AAYA 5, 34; BPFB 1; BYA 6, 8, 9; CA 1-4R, 181; 199; CAAE 181; CAAS 2; CANR 2, 15, 34, 64, 110; CLR 58; DLB 8; FANT; INT CANR-15; MTCW 1, 2; MTFW 2005; SATA 90; SATA-Brief 39; SATA-Essay 106; SCFW 1, 2; SFW 4; SUFW 1, 2

Anderson, Robert (Woodruff)
1917- .... **CLC 23**
See also AITN 1; CA 21-24R; CANR 32; CD 6; DAM DRAM; DLB 7; LAIT 5

Anderson, Roberta Joan
See Mitchell, Joni

Anderson, Sherwood 1876-1941 ... **SSC 1, 46, 91; TCLC 1, 10, 24, 123; WLC 1**
See also AAYA 30; AMW; AMWC 2; BPFB 1; CA 104; 121; CANR 61; CDALB 1917-1929; DA; DA3; DAB; DAC; DAM MST, NOV; DLB 4, 9, 86; DLBD 1; EWL 3; EXPS; GLL 2; MAL 5; MTCW 1, 2; MTFW 2005; NFS 4; RGAL 4; RGSF 2; SSFS 4, 10, 11; TUS

Anderson, Wes 1969- .... **CLC 227**
See also CA 214

Andier, Pierre
See Desnos, Robert

Andouard
See Giraudoux, Jean(-Hippolyte)

Andrade, Carlos Drummond de ..... **CLC 18**
See Drummond de Andrade, Carlos
See also EWL 3; RGWL 2, 3

Andrade, Mario de .... **TCLC 43**
See de Andrade, Mario
See also DLB 307; EWL 3; LAW; RGWL 2, 3; WLIT 1

Andreae, Johann V(alentin)
1586-1654 .... **LC 32**
See also DLB 164

Andreas Capellanus fl. c. 1185- .... **CMLC 45**
See also DLB 208

Andreas-Salome, Lou 1861-1937 ... **TCLC 56**
See also CA 178; DLB 66

Andreev, Leonid
See Andreyev, Leonid (Nikolaevich)
See also DLB 295; EWL 3

Andress, Lesley
See Sanders, Lawrence

Andrewes, Lancelot 1555-1626 .... **LC 5**
See also DLB 151, 172

Andrews, Cicily Fairfield
See West, Rebecca

Andrews, Elton V.
See Pohl, Frederik

Andrews, Peter
See Soderbergh, Steven

Andreyev, Leonid (Nikolaevich)
1871-1919 .... **TCLC 3**
See Andreev, Leonid
See also CA 104; 185

Andric, Ivo 1892-1975 .... **CLC 8; SSC 36; TCLC 135**
See also CA 81-84; 57-60; CANR 43, 60; CDWLB 4; DLB 147, 329; EW 11; EWL 3; MTCW 1; RGSF 2; RGWL 2, 3

Androvar
See Prado (Calvo), Pedro

Angela of Foligno 1248(?)-1309 .... **CMLC 76**

Angelique, Pierre
See Bataille, Georges

Angell, Roger 1920- .... **CLC 26**
See also CA 57-60; CANR 13, 44, 70, 144; DLB 171, 185

Angelou, Maya 1928- ... **BLC 1; CLC 12, 35, 64, 77, 155; PC 32; WLCS**
See also AAYA 7, 20; AMWS 4; BPFB 1; BW 2, 3; BYA 2; CA 65-68; CANR 19, 42, 65, 111, 133; CDALBS; CLR 53; CP 4, 5, 6, 7; CPW; CSW; CWP; DA; DA3; DAB; DAC; DAM MST, MULT, POET, POP; DLB 38; EWL 3; EXPN; EXPP; FL 1:5; LAIT 4; MAICYA 2; MAICYAS 1; MAL 5; MBL; MTCW 1, 2; MTFW 2005; NCFS 2; NFS 2; PFS 2, 3; RGAL 4; SATA 49, 136; TCLE 1:1; WYA; YAW

Angouleme, Marguerite d'
See de Navarre, Marguerite

Anna Comnena 1083-1153 .... **CMLC 25**

Annensky, Innokentii Fedorovich
See Annensky, Innokenty (Fyodorovich)
See also DLB 295

Annensky, Innokenty (Fyodorovich)
1856-1909 .... **TCLC 14**
See also CA 110; 155; EWL 3

Annunzio, Gabriele d'
See D'Annunzio, Gabriele

Anodos
See Coleridge, Mary E(lizabeth)

Anon, Charles Robert
See Pessoa, Fernando (Antonio Nogueira)

Anouilh, Jean 1910-1987 ..... **CLC 1, 3, 8, 13, 40, 50; DC 8, 21**
See also AAYA 67; CA 17-20R; 123; CANR 32; DAM DRAM; DFS 9, 10, 19; DLB 321; EW 13; EWL 3; GFL 1789 to the Present; MTCW 1, 2; MTFW 2005; RGWL 2, 3; TWA

Anselm of Canterbury
1033(?)-1109 .... **CMLC 67**
See also DLB 115

Anthony, Florence
See Ai

Anthony, John
See Ciardi, John (Anthony)

Anthony, Peter
See Shaffer, Anthony; Shaffer, Peter

Anthony, Piers 1934- .... **CLC 35**
See also AAYA 11, 48; BYA 7; CA 200; CAAE 200; CANR 28, 56, 73, 102, 133; CLR 118; CPW; DAM POP; DLB 8; FANT; MAICYA 2; MAICYAS 1; MTCW 1, 2; MTFW 2005; SAAS 22; SATA 84, 129; SATA-Essay 129; SFW 4; SUFW 1, 2; YAW

Anthony, Susan B(rownell)
1820-1906 .... **TCLC 84**
See also CA 211; FW

Antiphon c. 480B.C.-c. 411B.C. .... **CMLC 55**

Antoine, Marc
See Proust, (Valentin-Louis-George-Eugene) Marcel

Antoninus, Brother
See Everson, William (Oliver)
See also CP 1

Antonioni, Michelangelo 1912- .... **CLC 20, 144**
See also CA 73-76; CANR 45, 77

Antschel, Paul 1920-1970
See Celan, Paul
See also CA 85-88; CANR 33, 61; MTCW 1; PFS 21

Anwar, Chairil 1922-1949 .... **TCLC 22**
See Chairil Anwar
See also CA 121; 219; RGWL 3

Anzaldua, Gloria (Evanjelina)
1942-2004 .... **CLC 200; HLCS 1**
See also CA 175; 227; CSW; CWP; DLB 122; FW; LLW; RGAL 4; SATA-Obit 154

Apess, William 1798-1839(?) .... **NCLC 73; NNAL**
See also DAM MULT; DLB 175, 243

Apollinaire, Guillaume 1880-1918 .... **PC 7; TCLC 3, 8, 51**
See Kostrowitzki, Wilhelm Apollinaris de
See also CA 152; DAM POET; DLB 258, 321; EW 9; EWL 3; GFL 1789 to the Present; MTCW 2; PFS 24; RGWL 2, 3; TWA; WP

Apollonius of Rhodes
See Apollonius Rhodius
See also AW 1; RGWL 2, 3

Apollonius Rhodius c. 300B.C.-c. 220B.C. .... **CMLC 28**
See Apollonius of Rhodes
See also DLB 176

Appelfeld, Aharon 1932- ... **CLC 23, 47; SSC 42**
See also CA 112; 133; CANR 86; CWW 2; DLB 299; EWL 3; RGHL; RGSF 2; WLIT 6

Apple, Max (Isaac) 1941- .... **CLC 9, 33; SSC 50**
See also CA 81-84; CANR 19, 54; DLB 130

Appleman, Philip (Dean) 1926- .... **CLC 51**
See also CA 13-16R; CAAS 18; CANR 6, 29, 56

Appleton, Lawrence
See Lovecraft, H. P.

Apteryx
See Eliot, T(homas) S(tearns)

Apuleius, (Lucius Madaurensis) c. 125-c. 164 .... **CMLC 1, 84**
See also AW 2; CDWLB 1; DLB 211; RGWL 2, 3; SUFW; WLIT 8

Aquin, Hubert 1929-1977 .... **CLC 15**
See also CA 105; DLB 53; EWL 3

Aquinas, Thomas 1224(?)-1274 ..... **CMLC 33**
See also DLB 115; EW 1; TWA

Aragon, Louis 1897-1982 .... **CLC 3, 22; TCLC 123**
See also CA 69-72; 108; CANR 28, 71; DAM NOV, POET; DLB 72, 258; EW 11; EWL 3; GFL 1789 to the Present; GLL 2; LMFS 2; MTCW 1, 2; RGWL 2, 3

Arany, Janos 1817-1882 .... **NCLC 34**

Aranyos, Kakay 1847-1910
See Mikszath, Kalman

Aratus of Soli c. 315B.C.-c. 240B.C. .... **CMLC 64**
See also DLB 176

Arbuthnot, John 1667-1735 .... **LC 1**
See also DLB 101

Archer, Herbert Winslow
See Mencken, H(enry) L(ouis)

Archer, Jeffrey 1940- .... **CLC 28**
See also AAYA 16; BEST 89:3; BPFB 1; CA 77-80; CANR 22, 52, 95, 136; CPW; DA3; DAM POP; INT CANR-22; MTFW 2005

Bakhtin, M. M.
See Bakhtin, Mikhail Mikhailovich
Bakhtin, Mikhail
See Bakhtin, Mikhail Mikhailovich
Bakhtin, Mikhail Mikhailovich
1895-1975 .... **CLC 83; TCLC 160**
See also CA 128; 113; DLB 242; EWL 3
Bakshi, Ralph 1938(?)- .... **CLC 26**
See also CA 112; 138; IDFW 3
Bakunin, Mikhail (Alexandrovich)
1814-1876 .... **NCLC 25, 58**
See also DLB 277
Baldwin, James 1924-1987 ... **BLC 1; CLC 1,**
2, 3, 4, 5, 8, 13, 15, 17, 42, 50, 67, 90,
127; DC 1; SSC 10, 33; WLC 1
See also AAYA 4, 34; AFAW 1, 2; AMWR
2; AMWS 1; BPFB 1; BW 1; CA 1-4R;
124; CABS 1; CAD; CANR 3, 24;
CDALB 1941-1968; CN 1, 2, 3, 4; CPW;
DA; DA3; DAB; DAC; DAM MST,
MULT, NOV, POP; DFS 11, 15; DLB 2,
7, 33, 249, 278; DLBY 1987; EWL 3;
EXPS; LAIT 5; MAL 5; MTCW 1, 2;
MTFW 2005; NCFS 4; NFS 4; RGAL 4;
RGSF 2; SATA 9; SATA-Obit 54; SSFS
2, 18; TUS
Baldwin, William c. 1515-1563 .... **LC 113**
See also DLB 132
Bale, John 1495-1563 .... **LC 62**
See also DLB 132; RGEL 2; TEA
Ball, Hugo 1886-1927 .... **TCLC 104**
Ballard, J.G. 1930- .... **CLC 3, 6, 14, 36, 137;**
SSC 1, 53
See also AAYA 3, 52; BRWS 5; CA 5-8R;
CANR 15, 39, 65, 107, 133; CN 1, 2, 3,
4, 5, 6, 7; DA3; DAM NOV, POP; DLB
14, 207, 261, 319; EWL 3; HGG; MTCW
1, 2; MTFW 2005; NFS 8; RGEL 2;
RGSF 2; SATA 93; SCFW 1, 2; SFW 4
Balmont, Konstantin (Dmitriyevich)
1867-1943 .... **TCLC 11**
See also CA 109; 155; DLB 295; EWL 3
Baltausis, Vincas 1847-1910
See Mikszath, Kalman
Balzac, Honore de 1799-1850 ... **NCLC 5, 35,**
53, 153; SSC 5, 59; WLC 1
See also DA; DA3; DAB; DAC; DAM
MST, NOV; DLB 119; EW 5; GFL 1789
to the Present; LMFS 1; RGSF 2; RGWL
2, 3; SSFS 10; SUFW; TWA
Bambara, Toni Cade 1939-1995 .... **BLC 1;**
CLC 19, 88; SSC 35; TCLC 116;
WLCS
See also AAYA 5, 49; AFAW 2; AMWS 11;
BW 2, 3; BYA 12, 14; CA 29-32R; 150;
CANR 24, 49, 81; CDALBS; DA; DA3;
DAC; DAM MST, MULT; DLB 38, 218;
EXPS; MAL 5; MTCW 1, 2; MTFW
2005; RGAL 4; RGSF 2; SATA 112; SSFS
4, 7, 12, 21
Bamdad, A.
See Shamlu, Ahmad
Bamdad, Alef
See Shamlu, Ahmad
Banat, D. R.
See Bradbury, Ray
Bancroft, Laura
See Baum, L(yman) Frank
Banim, John 1798-1842 .... **NCLC 13**
See also DLB 116, 158, 159; RGEL 2
Banim, Michael 1796-1874 .... **NCLC 13**
See also DLB 158, 159
Banjo, The
See Paterson, A(ndrew) B(arton)
Banks, Iain
See Banks, Iain M.
See also BRWS 11

Banks, Iain M. 1954- .... **CLC 34**
See Banks, Iain
See also CA 123; 128; CANR 61, 106; DLB
194, 261; EWL 3; HGG; INT CA-128;
MTFW 2005; SFW 4
Banks, Lynne Reid .... **CLC 23**
See Reid Banks, Lynne
See also AAYA 6; BYA 7; CLR 86; CN 4,
5, 6
Banks, Russell 1940- . **CLC 37, 72, 187; SSC**
42
See also AAYA 45; AMWS 5; CA 65-68;
CAAS 15; CANR 19, 52, 73, 118; CN 4,
5, 6, 7; DLB 130, 278; EWL 3; MAL 5;
MTCW 2; MTFW 2005; NFS 13
Banville, John 1945- .... **CLC 46, 118, 224**
See also CA 117; 128; CANR 104, 150; CN
4, 5, 6, 7; DLB 14, 271, 326; INT CA-
128
Banville, Theodore (Faullain) de
1832-1891 .... **NCLC 9**
See also DLB 217; GFL 1789 to the Present
Baraka, Amiri 1934- .... **BLC 1; CLC 1, 2, 3,**
5, 10, 14, 33, 115, 213; DC 6; PC 4;
WLCS
See Jones, LeRoi
See also AAYA 63; AFAW 1, 2; AMWS 2;
BW 2, 3; CA 21-24R; CABS 3; CAD;
CANR 27, 38, 61, 133; CD 3, 5, 6;
CDALB 1941-1968; CP 4, 5, 6, 7; CPW;
DA; DA3; DAC; DAM MST, MULT,
POET, POP; DFS 3, 11, 16; DLB 5, 7,
16, 38; DLBD 8; EWL 3; MAL 5; MTCW
1, 2; MTFW 2005; PFS 9; RGAL 4;
TCLE 1:1; TUS; WP
Baratynsky, Evgenii Abramovich
1800-1844 .... **NCLC 103**
See also DLB 205
Barbauld, Anna Laetitia
1743-1825 .... **NCLC 50**
See also DLB 107, 109, 142, 158; RGEL 2
Barbellion, W. N. P. .... **TCLC 24**
See Cummings, Bruce F(rederick)
Barber, Benjamin R. 1939- .... **CLC 141**
See also CA 29-32R; CANR 12, 32, 64, 119
Barbera, Jack (Vincent) 1945- .... **CLC 44**
See also CA 110; CANR 45
Barbey d'Aurevilly, Jules-Amedee
1808-1889 .... **NCLC 1; SSC 17**
See also DLB 119; GFL 1789 to the Present
Barbour, John c. 1316-1395 .... **CMLC 33**
See also DLB 146
Barbusse, Henri 1873-1935 .... **TCLC 5**
See also CA 105; 154; DLB 65; EWL 3;
RGWL 2, 3
Barclay, Alexander c. 1475-1552 .... **LC 109**
See also DLB 132
Barclay, Bill
See Moorcock, Michael
Barclay, William Ewert
See Moorcock, Michael
Barea, Arturo 1897-1957 .... **TCLC 14**
See also CA 111; 201
Barfoot, Joan 1946- .... **CLC 18**
See also CA 105; CANR 141
Barham, Richard Harris
1788-1845 .... **NCLC 77**
See also DLB 159
Baring, Maurice 1874-1945 .... **TCLC 8**
See also CA 105; 168; DLB 34; HGG
Baring-Gould, Sabine 1834-1924 ... **TCLC 88**
See also DLB 156, 190
Barker, Clive 1952- .... **CLC 52, 205; SSC 53**
See also AAYA 10, 54; BEST 90:3; BPFB
1; CA 121; 129; CANR 71, 111, 133;
CPW; DA3; DAM POP; DLB 261; HGG;
INT CA-129; MTCW 1, 2; MTFW 2005;
SUFW 2

Barker, George Granville
1913-1991 .... **CLC 8, 48**
See also CA 9-12R; 135; CANR 7, 38; CP
1, 2, 3, 4, 5; DAM POET; DLB 20; EWL
3; MTCW 1
Barker, Harley Granville
See Granville-Barker, Harley
See also DLB 10
Barker, Howard 1946- .... **CLC 37**
See also CA 102; CBD; CD 5, 6; DLB 13,
233
Barker, Jane 1652-1732 .... **LC 42, 82**
See also DLB 39, 131
Barker, Pat 1943- .... **CLC 32, 94, 146**
See also BRWS 4; CA 117; 122; CANR 50,
101, 148; CN 6, 7; DLB 271, 326; INT
CA-122
Barker, Patricia
See Barker, Pat
Barlach, Ernst (Heinrich)
1870-1938 .... **TCLC 84**
See also CA 178; DLB 56, 118; EWL 3
Barlow, Joel 1754-1812 .... **NCLC 23**
See also AMWS 2; DLB 37; RGAL 4
Barnard, Mary (Ethel) 1909- .... **CLC 48**
See also CA 21-22; CAP 2; CP 1
Barnes, Djuna 1892-1982 .... **CLC 3, 4, 8, 11,**
29, 127; SSC 3
See Steptoe, Lydia
See also AMWS 3; CA 9-12R; 107; CAD;
CANR 16, 55; CN 1, 2, 3; CWD; DLB 4,
9, 45; EWL 3; GLL 1; MAL 5; MTCW 1,
2; MTFW 2005; RGAL 4; TCLE 1:1;
TUS
Barnes, Jim 1933- .... **NNAL**
See also CA 108; 175; CAAE 175; CAAS
28; DLB 175
Barnes, Julian 1946- .... **CLC 42, 141**
See also BRWS 4; CA 102; CANR 19, 54,
115, 137; CN 4, 5, 6, 7; DAB; DLB 194;
DLBY 1993; EWL 3; MTCW 2; MTFW
2005; SSFS 24
Barnes, Julian Patrick
See Barnes, Julian
Barnes, Peter 1931-2004 .... **CLC 5, 56**
See also CA 65-68; 230; CAAS 12; CANR
33, 34, 64, 113; CBD; CD 5, 6; DFS 6;
DLB 13, 233; MTCW 1
Barnes, William 1801-1886 .... **NCLC 75**
See also DLB 32
Baroja, Pio 1872-1956 .... **HLC 1; TCLC 8**
See also CA 104; 247; EW 9
Baroja y Nessi, Pio
See Baroja, Pio
Baron, David
See Pinter, Harold
Baron Corvo
See Rolfe, Frederick (William Serafino Aus-
tin Lewis Mary)
Barondess, Sue K(aufman)
1926-1977 .... **CLC 8**
See Kaufman, Sue
See also CA 1-4R; 69-72; CANR 1
Baron de Teive
See Pessoa, Fernando (Antonio Nogueira)
Baroness Von S.
See Zangwill, Israel
Barres, (Auguste-)Maurice
1862-1923 .... **TCLC 47**
See also CA 164; DLB 123; GFL 1789 to
the Present
Barreto, Afonso Henrique de Lima
See Lima Barreto, Afonso Henrique de
Barrett, Andrea 1954- .... **CLC 150**
See also CA 156; CANR 92; CN 7; SSFS
24
Barrett, Michele .... **CLC 65**
Barrett, (Roger) Syd 1946-2006 .... **CLC 35**

Barrett, William (Christopher) 1913-1992 .... **CLC 27**
See also CA 13-16R; 139; CANR 11, 67; INT CANR-11

Barrett Browning, Elizabeth 1806-1861 ...... **NCLC 1, 16, 61, 66, 170; PC 6, 62; WLC 1**
See also AAYA 63; BRW 4; CDBLB 1832-1890; DA; DA3; DAB; DAC; DAM MST, POET; DLB 32, 199; EXPP; FL 1:2; PAB; PFS 2, 16, 23; TEA; WLIT 4; WP

Barrie, J(ames) M(atthew) 1860-1937 .... **TCLC 2, 164**
See also BRWS 3; BYA 4, 5; CA 104; 136; CANR 77; CDBLB 1890-1914; CLR 16; CWRI 5; DA3; DAB; DAM DRAM; DFS 7; DLB 10, 141, 156; EWL 3; FANT; MAICYA 1, 2; MTCW 2; MTFW 2005; SATA 100; SUFW; WCH; WLIT 4; YABC 1

Barrington, Michael
See Moorcock, Michael

Barrol, Grady
See Bograd, Larry

Barry, Mike
See Malzberg, Barry N(athaniel)

Barry, Philip 1896-1949 .... **TCLC 11**
See also CA 109; 199; DFS 9; DLB 7, 228; MAL 5; RGAL 4

Bart, Andre Schwarz
See Schwarz-Bart, Andre

Barth, John (Simmons) 1930- ... **CLC 1, 2, 3, 5, 7, 9, 10, 14, 27, 51, 89, 214; SSC 10, 89**
See also AITN 1, 2; AMW; BPFB 1; CA 1-4R; CABS 1; CANR 5, 23, 49, 64, 113; CN 1, 2, 3, 4, 5, 6, 7; DAM NOV; DLB 2, 227; EWL 3; FANT; MAL 5; MTCW 1; RGAL 4; RGSF 2; RHW; SSFS 6; TUS

Barthelme, Donald 1931-1989 ... **CLC 1, 2, 3, 5, 6, 8, 13, 23, 46, 59, 115; SSC 2, 55**
See also AMWS 4; BPFB 1; CA 21-24R; 129; CANR 20, 58; CN 1, 2, 3, 4; DA3; DAM NOV; DLB 2, 234; DLBY 1980, 1989; EWL 3; FANT; LMFS 2; MAL 5; MTCW 1, 2; MTFW 2005; RGAL 4; RGSF 2; SATA 7; SATA-Obit 62; SSFS 17

Barthelme, Frederick 1943- ...... **CLC 36, 117**
See also AMWS 11; CA 114; 122; CANR 77; CN 4, 5, 6, 7; CSW; DLB 244; DLBY 1985; EWL 3; INT CA-122

Barthes, Roland (Gerard) 1915-1980 .... **CLC 24, 83; TCLC 135**
See also CA 130; 97-100; CANR 66; DLB 296; EW 13; EWL 3; GFL 1789 to the Present; MTCW 1, 2; TWA

Bartram, William 1739-1823 .... **NCLC 145**
See also ANW; DLB 37

Barzun, Jacques (Martin) 1907- ..... **CLC 51, 145**
See also CA 61-64; CANR 22, 95

Bashevis, Isaac
See Singer, Isaac Bashevis

Bashkirtseff, Marie 1859-1884 .... **NCLC 27**

Basho, Matsuo
See Matsuo Basho
See also RGWL 2, 3; WP

Basil of Caesaria c. 330-379 .... **CMLC 35**

Basket, Raney
See Edgerton, Clyde (Carlyle)

Bass, Kingsley B., Jr.
See Bullins, Ed

Bass, Rick 1958- .... **CLC 79, 143; SSC 60**
See also AMWS 16; ANW; CA 126; CANR 53, 93, 145; CSW; DLB 212, 275

Bassani, Giorgio 1916-2000 .... **CLC 9**
See also CA 65-68; 190; CANR 33; CWW 2; DLB 128, 177, 299; EWL 3; MTCW 1; RGHL; RGWL 2, 3

Bastian, Ann .... **CLC 70**

Bastos, Augusto Roa
See Roa Bastos, Augusto

Bataille, Georges 1897-1962 .... **CLC 29; TCLC 155**
See also CA 101; 89-92; EWL 3

Bates, H(erbert) E(rnest) 1905-1974 .... **CLC 46; SSC 10**
See also CA 93-96; 45-48; CANR 34; CN 1; DA3; DAB; DAM POP; DLB 162, 191; EWL 3; EXPS; MTCW 1, 2; RGSF 2; SSFS 7

Bauchart
See Camus, Albert

Baudelaire, Charles 1821-1867 . **NCLC 6, 29, 55, 155; PC 1; SSC 18; WLC 1**
See also DA; DA3; DAB; DAC; DAM MST, POET; DLB 217; EW 7; GFL 1789 to the Present; LMFS 2; PFS 21; RGWL 2, 3; TWA

Baudouin, Marcel
See Peguy, Charles (Pierre)

Baudouin, Pierre
See Peguy, Charles (Pierre)

Baudrillard, Jean 1929- .... **CLC 60**
See also DLB 296

Baum, L(yman) Frank 1856-1919 .. **TCLC 7, 132**
See also AAYA 46; BYA 16; CA 108; 133; CLR 15, 107; CWRI 5; DLB 22; FANT; JRDA; MAICYA 1, 2; MTCW 1, 2; NFS 13; RGAL 4; SATA 18, 100; WCH

Baum, Louis F.
See Baum, L(yman) Frank

Baumbach, Jonathan 1933- .... **CLC 6, 23**
See also CA 13-16R; CAAS 5; CANR 12, 66, 140; CN 3, 4, 5, 6, 7; DLBY 1980; INT CANR-12; MTCW 1

Bausch, Richard (Carl) 1945- .... **CLC 51**
See also AMWS 7; CA 101; CAAS 14; CANR 43, 61, 87; CN 7; CSW; DLB 130; MAL 5

Baxter, Charles 1947- .... **CLC 45, 78**
See also CA 57-60; CANR 40, 64, 104, 133; CPW; DAM POP; DLB 130; MAL 5; MTCW 2; MTFW 2005; TCLE 1:1

Baxter, George Owen
See Faust, Frederick (Schiller)

Baxter, James K(eir) 1926-1972 .... **CLC 14**
See also CA 77-80; CP 1; EWL 3

Baxter, John
See Hunt, E(verette) Howard, (Jr.)

Bayer, Sylvia
See Glassco, John

Bayle, Pierre 1647-1706 .... **LC 126**
See also DLB 268, 313; GFL Beginnings to 1789

Baynton, Barbara 1857-1929 .... **TCLC 57**
See also DLB 230; RGSF 2

Beagle, Peter S. 1939- .... **CLC 7, 104**
See also AAYA 47; BPFB 1; BYA 9, 10, 16; CA 9-12R; CANR 4, 51, 73, 110; DA3; DLBY 1980; FANT; INT CANR-4; MTCW 2; MTFW 2005; SATA 60, 130; SUFW 1, 2; YAW

Beagle, Peter Soyer
See Beagle, Peter S.

Bean, Normal
See Burroughs, Edgar Rice

Beard, Charles A(ustin) 1874-1948 .... **TCLC 15**
See also CA 115; 189; DLB 17; SATA 18

Beardsley, Aubrey 1872-1898 .... **NCLC 6**

Beattie, Ann 1947- ..... **CLC 8, 13, 18, 40, 63, 146; SSC 11**
See also AMWS 5; BEST 90:2; BPFB 1; CA 81-84; CANR 53, 73, 128; CN 4, 5, 6, 7; CPW; DA3; DAM NOV, POP; DLB 218, 278; DLBY 1982; EWL 3; MAL 5; MTCW 1, 2; MTFW 2005; RGAL 4; RGSF 2; SSFS 9; TUS

Beattie, James 1735-1803 .... **NCLC 25**
See also DLB 109

Beauchamp, Kathleen Mansfield 1888-1923
See Mansfield, Katherine
See also CA 104; 134; DA; DA3; DAC; DAM MST; MTCW 2; TEA

Beaumarchais, Pierre-Augustin Caron de 1732-1799 .... **DC 4; LC 61**
See also DAM DRAM; DFS 14, 16; DLB 313; EW 4; GFL Beginnings to 1789; RGWL 2, 3

Beaumont, Francis 1584(?)-1616 .. **DC 6; LC 33**
See also BRW 2; CDBLB Before 1660; DLB 58; TEA

Beauvoir, Simone de 1908-1986 .... **CLC 1, 2, 4, 8, 14, 31, 44, 50, 71, 124; SSC 35; WLC 1**
See also BPFB 1; CA 9-12R; 118; CANR 28, 61; DA; DA3; DAB; DAC; DAM MST, NOV; DLB 72; DLBY 1986; EW 12; EWL 3; FL 1:5; FW; GFL 1789 to the Present; LMFS 2; MTCW 1, 2; MTFW 2005; RGSF 2; RGWL 2, 3; TWA

Beauvoir, Simone Lucie Ernestine Marie Bertrand de
See Beauvoir, Simone de

Becker, Carl (Lotus) 1873-1945 ..... **TCLC 63**
See also CA 157; DLB 17

Becker, Jurek 1937-1997 .... **CLC 7, 19**
See also CA 85-88; 157; CANR 60, 117; CWW 2; DLB 75, 299; EWL 3; RGHL

Becker, Walter 1950- .... **CLC 26**

Becket, Thomas a 1118(?)-1170 ..... **CMLC 83**

Beckett, Samuel 1906-1989 ... **CLC 1, 2, 3, 4, 6, 9, 10, 11, 14, 18, 29, 57, 59, 83; DC 22; SSC 16, 74; TCLC 145; WLC 1**
See also BRWC 2; BRWR 1; BRWS 1; CA 5-8R; 130; CANR 33, 61; CBD; CDBLB 1945-1960; CN 1, 2, 3, 4; CP 1, 2, 3, 4; DA; DA3; DAB; DAC; DAM DRAM, MST, NOV; DFS 2, 7, 18; DLB 13, 15, 233, 319, 321, 329; DLBY 1990; EWL 3; GFL 1789 to the Present; LATS 1:2; LMFS 2; MTCW 1, 2; MTFW 2005; RGSF 2; RGWL 2, 3; SSFS 15; TEA; WLIT 4

Beckford, William 1760-1844 .... **NCLC 16**
See also BRW 3; DLB 39, 213; GL 2; HGG; LMFS 1; SUFW

Beckham, Barry (Earl) 1944- .... **BLC 1**
See also BW 1; CA 29-32R; CANR 26, 62; CN 1, 2, 3, 4, 5, 6; DAM MULT; DLB 33

Beckman, Gunnel 1910- .... **CLC 26**
See also CA 33-36R; CANR 15, 114; CLR 25; MAICYA 1, 2; SAAS 9; SATA 6

Becque, Henri 1837-1899 .... **DC 21; NCLC 3**
See also DLB 192; GFL 1789 to the Present

Becquer, Gustavo Adolfo 1836-1870 .... **HLCS 1; NCLC 106**
See also DAM MULT

Beddoes, Thomas Lovell 1803-1849 .. **DC 15; NCLC 3, 154**
See also BRWS 11; DLB 96

Bede c. 673-735 .... **CMLC 20**
See also DLB 146; TEA

Bedford, Denton R. 1907-(?) .... **NNAL**

Bedford, Donald F.
See Fearing, Kenneth (Flexner)

Beecher, Catharine Esther
1800-1878 .... **NCLC 30**
See also DLB 1, 243

Beecher, John 1904-1980 .... **CLC 6**
See also AITN 1; CA 5-8R; 105; CANR 8;
CP 1, 2, 3

Beer, Johann 1655-1700 .... **LC 5**
See also DLB 168

Beer, Patricia 1924- .... **CLC 58**
See also CA 61-64; 183; CANR 13, 46; CP
1, 2, 3, 4, 5, 6; CWP; DLB 40; FW

Beerbohm, Max
See Beerbohm, (Henry) Max(imilian)

Beerbohm, (Henry) Max(imilian)
1872-1956 .... **TCLC 1, 24**
See also BRWS 2; CA 104; 154; CANR 79;
DLB 34, 100; FANT; MTCW 2

Beer-Hofmann, Richard
1866-1945 .... **TCLC 60**
See also CA 160; DLB 81

Beg, Shemus
See Stephens, James

Begiebing, Robert J(ohn) 1946- .... **CLC 70**
See also CA 122; CANR 40, 88

Begley, Louis 1933- .... **CLC 197**
See also CA 140; CANR 98; DLB 299;
RGHL; TCLE 1:1

Behan, Brendan (Francis)
1923-1964 .... **CLC 1, 8, 11, 15, 79**
See also BRWS 2; CA 73-76; CANR 33,
121; CBD; CDBLB 1945-1960; DAM
DRAM; DFS 7; DLB 13, 233; EWL 3;
MTCW 1, 2

Behn, Aphra 1640(?)-1689 .. **DC 4; LC 1, 30,
42; PC 13; WLC 1**
See also BRWS 3; DA; DA3; DAB; DAC;
DAM DRAM, MST, NOV, POET; DFS
16; DLB 39, 80, 131; FW; TEA; WLIT 3

Behrman, S(amuel) N(athaniel)
1893-1973 .... **CLC 40**
See also CA 13-16; 45-48; CAD; CAP 1;
DLB 7, 44; IDFW 3; MAL 5; RGAL 4

Bekederemo, J. P. Clark
See Clark Bekederemo, J.P.
See also CD 6

Belasco, David 1853-1931 .... **TCLC 3**
See also CA 104; 168; DLB 7; MAL 5;
RGAL 4

Belcheva, Elisaveta Lyubomirova
1893-1991 .... **CLC 10**
See Bagryana, Elisaveta

Beldone, Phil "Cheech"
See Ellison, Harlan

Beleno
See Azuela, Mariano

Belinski, Vissarion Grigoryevich
1811-1848 .... **NCLC 5**
See also DLB 198

Belitt, Ben 1911- .... **CLC 22**
See also CA 13-16R; CAAS 4; CANR 7,
77; CP 1, 2, 3, 4, 5, 6; DLB 5

Belknap, Jeremy 1744-1798 .... **LC 115**
See also DLB 30, 37

Bell, Gertrude (Margaret Lowthian)
1868-1926 .... **TCLC 67**
See also CA 167; CANR 110; DLB 174

Bell, J. Freeman
See Zangwill, Israel

Bell, James Madison 1826-1902 .... **BLC 1;
TCLC 43**
See also BW 1; CA 122; 124; DAM MULT;
DLB 50

Bell, Madison Smartt 1957- ..... **CLC 41, 102,
223**
See also AMWS 10; BPFB 1; CA 111, 183;
CAAE 183; CANR 28, 54, 73, 134; CN
5, 6, 7; CSW; DLB 218, 278; MTCW 2;
MTFW 2005

Bell, Marvin (Hartley) 1937- .... **CLC 8, 31**
See also CA 21-24R; CAAS 14; CANR 59,
102; CP 1, 2, 3, 4, 5, 6, 7; DAM POET;
DLB 5; MAL 5; MTCW 1

Bell, W. L. D.
See Mencken, H(enry) L(ouis)

Bellamy, Atwood C.
See Mencken, H(enry) L(ouis)

Bellamy, Edward 1850-1898 ..... **NCLC 4, 86,
147**
See also DLB 12; NFS 15; RGAL 4; SFW
4

Belli, Gioconda 1948- .... **HLCS 1**
See also CA 152; CANR 143; CWW 2;
DLB 290; EWL 3; RGWL 3

Bellin, Edward J.
See Kuttner, Henry

Bello, Andres 1781-1865 .... **NCLC 131**
See also LAW

**Belloc, (Joseph) Hilaire (Pierre Sebastien
Rene Swanton)** 1870-1953 .... **PC 24;
TCLC 7, 18**
See also CA 106; 152; CLR 102; CWRI 5;
DAM POET; DLB 19, 100, 141, 174;
EWL 3; MTCW 2; MTFW 2005; SATA
112; WCH; YABC 1

Belloc, Joseph Peter Rene Hilaire
See Belloc, (Joseph) Hilaire (Pierre Sebastien Rene Swanton)

Belloc, Joseph Pierre Hilaire
See Belloc, (Joseph) Hilaire (Pierre Sebastien Rene Swanton)

Belloc, M. A.
See Lowndes, Marie Adelaide (Belloc)

Belloc-Lowndes, Mrs.
See Lowndes, Marie Adelaide (Belloc)

Bellow, Saul 1915-2005 ...... **CLC 1, 2, 3, 6, 8,
10, 13, 15, 25, 33, 34, 63, 79, 190, 200;
SSC 14; WLC 1**
See also AITN 2; AMW; AMWC 2; AMWR
2; BEST 89:3; BPFB 1; CA 5-8R; 238;
CABS 1; CANR 29, 53, 95, 132; CDALB
1941-1968; CN 1, 2, 3, 4, 5, 6, 7; DA;
DA3; DAB; DAC; DAM MST, NOV,
POP; DLB 2, 28, 299, 329; DLBD 3;
DLBY 1982; EWL 3; MAL 5; MTCW 1,
2; MTFW 2005; NFS 4, 14; RGAL 4;
RGHL; RGSF 2; SSFS 12, 22; TUS

Belser, Reimond Karel Maria de 1929-
See Ruyslinck, Ward
See also CA 152

Bely, Andrey .... **PC 11; TCLC 7**
See Bugayev, Boris Nikolayevich
See also DLB 295; EW 9; EWL 3

Belyi, Andrei
See Bugayev, Boris Nikolayevich
See also RGWL 2, 3

Bembo, Pietro 1470-1547 .... **LC 79**
See also RGWL 2, 3

Benary, Margot
See Benary-Isbert, Margot

Benary-Isbert, Margot 1889-1979 .... **CLC 12**
See also CA 5-8R; 89-92; CANR 4, 72;
CLR 12; MAICYA 1, 2; SATA 2; SATA-
Obit 21

Benavente (y Martinez), Jacinto
1866-1954 .... **DC 26; HLCS 1; TCLC 3**
See also CA 106; 131; CANR 81; DAM
DRAM, MULT; DLB 329; EWL 3; GLL
2; HW 1, 2; MTCW 1, 2

Benchley, Peter 1940-2006 .... **CLC 4, 8**
See also AAYA 14; AITN 2; BPFB 1; CA
17-20R; 248; CANR 12, 35, 66, 115;
CPW; DAM NOV, POP; HGG; MTCW 1,
2; MTFW 2005; SATA 3, 89, 164

Benchley, Peter Bradford
See Benchley, Peter

Benchley, Robert (Charles)
1889-1945 .... **TCLC 1, 55**
See also CA 105; 153; DLB 11; MAL 5;
RGAL 4

Benda, Julien 1867-1956 .... **TCLC 60**
See also CA 120; 154; GFL 1789 to the
Present

Benedict, Ruth 1887-1948 .... **TCLC 60**
See also CA 158; CANR 146; DLB 246

Benedict, Ruth Fulton
See Benedict, Ruth

Benedikt, Michael 1935- .... **CLC 4, 14**
See also CA 13-16R; CANR 7; CP 1, 2, 3,
4, 5, 6, 7; DLB 5

Benet, Juan 1927-1993 .... **CLC 28**
See also CA 143; EWL 3

Benet, Stephen Vincent 1898-1943 ..... **PC 64;
SSC 10, 86; TCLC 7**
See also AMWS 11; CA 104; 152; DA3;
DAM POET; DLB 4, 48, 102, 249, 284;
DLBY 1997; EWL 3; HGG; MAL 5;
MTCW 2; MTFW 2005; RGAL 4; RGSF
2; SSFS 22; SUFW; WP; YABC 1

Benet, William Rose 1886-1950 ..... **TCLC 28**
See also CA 118; 152; DAM POET; DLB
45; RGAL 4

Benford, Gregory (Albert) 1941- ..... **CLC 52**
See also BPFB 1; CA 69-72; 175; CAAE
175; CAAS 27; CANR 12, 24, 49, 95,
134; CN 7; CSW; DLBY 1982; MTFW
2005; SCFW 2; SFW 4

Bengtsson, Frans (Gunnar)
1894-1954 .... **TCLC 48**
See also CA 170; EWL 3

Benjamin, David
See Slavitt, David R(ytman)

Benjamin, Lois
See Gould, Lois

Benjamin, Walter 1892-1940 .... **TCLC 39**
See also CA 164; DLB 242; EW 11; EWL
3

Ben Jelloun, Tahar 1944-
See Jelloun, Tahar ben
See also CA 135; CWW 2; EWL 3; RGWL
3; WLIT 2

Benn, Gottfried 1886-1956 .. **PC 35; TCLC 3**
See also CA 106; 153; DLB 56; EWL 3;
RGWL 2, 3

Bennett, Alan 1934- .... **CLC 45, 77**
See also BRWS 8; CA 103; CANR 35, 55,
106, 157; CBD; CD 5, 6; DAB; DAM
MST; DLB 310; MTCW 1, 2; MTFW
2005

Bennett, (Enoch) Arnold
1867-1931 .... **TCLC 5, 20**
See also BRW 6; CA 106; 155; CDBLB
1890-1914; DLB 10, 34, 98, 135; EWL 3;
MTCW 2

Bennett, Elizabeth
See Mitchell, Margaret (Munnerlyn)

Bennett, George Harold 1930-
See Bennett, Hal
See also BW 1; CA 97-100; CANR 87

Bennett, Gwendolyn B. 1902-1981 .... **HR 1:2**
See also BW 1; CA 125; DLB 51; WP

Bennett, Hal .... **CLC 5**
See Bennett, George Harold
See also CAAS 13; DLB 33

Bennett, Jay 1912- .... **CLC 35**
See also AAYA 10; CA 69-72; CANR 11,
42, 79; JRDA; SAAS 4; SATA 41, 87;
SATA-Brief 27; WYA; YAW

Bennett, Louise 1919-2006 .. **BLC 1; CLC 28**
See also BW 2, 3; CA 151; CDWLB 3; CP
1, 2, 3, 4, 5, 6, 7; DAM MULT; DLB 117;
EWL 3

Bennett-Coverley, Louise
See Bennett, Louise

Binchy, Maeve 1940- .... **CLC 153**
See also BEST 90:1; BPFB 1; CA 127; 134; CANR 50, 96, 134; CN 5, 6, 7; CPW; DA3; DAM POP; DLB 319; INT CA-134; MTCW 2; MTFW 2005; RHW

Binyon, T(imothy) J(ohn)
1936-2004 .... **CLC 34**
See also CA 111; 232; CANR 28, 140

Bion 335B.C.-245B.C. .... **CMLC 39**

Bioy Casares, Adolfo 1914-1999 ... **CLC 4, 8, 13, 88; HLC 1; SSC 17**
See Casares, Adolfo Bioy; Miranda, Javier; Sacastru, Martin
See also CA 29-32R; 177; CANR 19, 43, 66; CWW 2; DAM MULT; DLB 113; EWL 3; HW 1, 2; LAW; MTCW 1, 2; MTFW 2005

Birch, Allison .... **CLC 65**

Bird, Cordwainer
See Ellison, Harlan

Bird, Robert Montgomery
1806-1854 .... **NCLC 1**
See also DLB 202; RGAL 4

Birkerts, Sven 1951- .... **CLC 116**
See also CA 128; 133, 176; CAAE 176; CAAS 29; CANR 151; INT CA-133

Birney, (Alfred) Earle 1904-1995 .. **CLC 1, 4, 6, 11; PC 52**
See also CA 1-4R; CANR 5, 20; CN 1, 2, 3, 4; CP 1, 2, 3, 4, 5, 6; DAC; DAM MST, POET; DLB 88; MTCW 1; PFS 8; RGEL 2

Biruni, al 973-1048(?) .... **CMLC 28**

Bishop, Elizabeth 1911-1979 ..... **CLC 1, 4, 9, 13, 15, 32; PC 3, 34; TCLC 121**
See also AMWR 2; AMWS 1; CA 5-8R; 89-92; CABS 2; CANR 26, 61, 108; CDALB 1968-1988; CP 1, 2, 3; DA; DA3; DAC; DAM MST, POET; DLB 5, 169; EWL 3; GLL 2; MAL 5; MBL; MTCW 1, 2; PAB; PFS 6, 12; RGAL 4; SATA-Obit 24; TUS; WP

Bishop, John 1935- .... **CLC 10**
See also CA 105

Bishop, John Peale 1892-1944 ..... **TCLC 103**
See also CA 107; 155; DLB 4, 9, 45; MAL 5; RGAL 4

Bissett, Bill 1939- .... **CLC 18; PC 14**
See also CA 69-72; CAAS 19; CANR 15; CCA 1; CP 1, 2, 3, 4, 5, 6, 7; DLB 53; MTCW 1

Bissoondath, Neil (Devindra)
1955- .... **CLC 120**
See also CA 136; CANR 123; CN 6, 7; DAC

Bitov, Andrei (Georgievich) 1937- ... **CLC 57**
See also CA 142; DLB 302

Biyidi, Alexandre 1932-
See Beti, Mongo
See also BW 1, 3; CA 114; 124; CANR 81; DA3; MTCW 1, 2

Bjarme, Brynjolf
See Ibsen, Henrik (Johan)

Bjoernson, Bjoernstjerne (Martinius)
1832-1910 .... **TCLC 7, 37**
See also CA 104

Black, Benjamin
See Banville, John

Black, Robert
See Holdstock, Robert P.

Blackburn, Paul 1926-1971 .... **CLC 9, 43**
See also BG 1:2; CA 81-84; 33-36R; CANR 34; CP 1; DLB 16; DLBY 1981

Black Elk 1863-1950 .... **NNAL; TCLC 33**
See also CA 144; DAM MULT; MTCW 2; MTFW 2005; WP

Black Hawk 1767-1838 .... **NNAL**

Black Hobart
See Sanders, (James) Ed(ward)

Blacklin, Malcolm
See Chambers, Aidan

Blackmore, R(ichard) D(oddridge)
1825-1900 .... **TCLC 27**
See also CA 120; DLB 18; RGEL 2

Blackmur, R(ichard) P(almer)
1904-1965 .... **CLC 2, 24**
See also AMWS 2; CA 11-12; 25-28R; CANR 71; CAP 1; DLB 63; EWL 3; MAL 5

Black Tarantula
See Acker, Kathy

Blackwood, Algernon (Henry)
1869-1951 .... **TCLC 5**
See also CA 105; 150; DLB 153, 156, 178; HGG; SUFW 1

Blackwood, Caroline (Maureen)
1931-1996 .... **CLC 6, 9, 100**
See also BRWS 9; CA 85-88; 151; CANR 32, 61, 65; CN 3, 4, 5, 6; DLB 14, 207; HGG; MTCW 1

Blade, Alexander
See Hamilton, Edmond; Silverberg, Robert

Blaga, Lucian 1895-1961 .... **CLC 75**
See also CA 157; DLB 220; EWL 3

Blair, Eric (Arthur) 1903-1950 .... **TCLC 123**
See Orwell, George
See also CA 104; 132; DA; DA3; DAB; DAC; DAM MST, NOV; MTCW 1, 2; MTFW 2005; SATA 29

Blair, Hugh 1718-1800 .... **NCLC 75**

Blais, Marie-Claire 1939- .... **CLC 2, 4, 6, 13, 22**
See also CA 21-24R; CAAS 4; CANR 38, 75, 93; CWW 2; DAC; DAM MST; DLB 53; EWL 3; FW; MTCW 1, 2; MTFW 2005; TWA

Blaise, Clark 1940- .... **CLC 29**
See also AITN 2; CA 53-56, 231; CAAE 231; CAAS 3; CANR 5, 66, 106; CN 4, 5, 6, 7; DLB 53; RGSF 2

Blake, Fairley
See De Voto, Bernard (Augustine)

Blake, Nicholas
See Day Lewis, C(ecil)
See also DLB 77; MSW

Blake, Sterling
See Benford, Gregory (Albert)

Blake, William 1757-1827 . **NCLC 13, 37, 57, 127, 173; PC 12, 63; WLC 1**
See also AAYA 47; BRW 3; BRWR 1; CD-BLB 1789-1832; CLR 52; DA; DA3; DAB; DAC; DAM MST, POET; DLB 93, 163; EXPP; LATS 1:1; LMFS 1; MAICYA 1, 2; PAB; PFS 2, 12, 24; SATA 30; TEA; WCH; WLIT 3; WP

Blanchot, Maurice 1907-2003 .... **CLC 135**
See also CA 117; 144; 213; CANR 138; DLB 72, 296; EWL 3

Blasco Ibanez, Vicente 1867-1928 . **TCLC 12**
See Ibanez, Vicente Blasco
See also BPFB 1; CA 110; 131; CANR 81; DA3; DAM NOV; EW 8; EWL 3; HW 1, 2; MTCW 1

Blatty, William Peter 1928- .... **CLC 2**
See also CA 5-8R; CANR 9, 124; DAM POP; HGG

Bleeck, Oliver
See Thomas, Ross (Elmore)

Blessing, Lee (Knowlton) 1949- .... **CLC 54**
See also CA 236; CAD; CD 5, 6; DFS 23

Blight, Rose
See Greer, Germaine

Blish, James (Benjamin) 1921-1975 . **CLC 14**
See also BPFB 1; CA 1-4R; 57-60; CANR 3; CN 2; DLB 8; MTCW 1; SATA 66; SCFW 1, 2; SFW 4

Bliss, Frederick
See Card, Orson Scott

Bliss, Reginald
See Wells, H(erbert) G(eorge)

Blixen, Karen (Christentze Dinesen)
1885-1962
See Dinesen, Isak
See also CA 25-28; CANR 22, 50; CAP 2; DA3; DLB 214; LMFS 1; MTCW 1, 2; SATA 44; SSFS 20

Bloch, Robert (Albert) 1917-1994 .... **CLC 33**
See also AAYA 29; CA 5-8R, 179; 146; CAAE 179; CAAS 20; CANR 5, 78; DA3; DLB 44; HGG; INT CANR-5; MTCW 2; SATA 12; SATA-Obit 82; SFW 4; SUFW 1, 2

Blok, Alexander (Alexandrovich)
1880-1921 .... **PC 21; TCLC 5**
See also CA 104; 183; DLB 295; EW 9; EWL 3; LMFS 2; RGWL 2, 3

Blom, Jan
See Breytenbach, Breyten

Bloom, Harold 1930- .... **CLC 24, 103, 221**
See also CA 13-16R; CANR 39, 75, 92, 133; DLB 67; EWL 3; MTCW 2; MTFW 2005; RGAL 4

Bloomfield, Aurelius
See Bourne, Randolph S(illiman)

Bloomfield, Robert 1766-1823 ..... **NCLC 145**
See also DLB 93

Blount, Roy (Alton), Jr. 1941- .... **CLC 38**
See also CA 53-56; CANR 10, 28, 61, 125; CSW; INT CANR-28; MTCW 1, 2; MTFW 2005

Blowsnake, Sam 1875-(?) .... **NNAL**

Bloy, Leon 1846-1917 .... **TCLC 22**
See also CA 121; 183; DLB 123; GFL 1789 to the Present

Blue Cloud, Peter (Aroniawenrate)
1933- .... **NNAL**
See also CA 117; CANR 40; DAM MULT

Bluggage, Oranthy
See Alcott, Louisa May

Blume, Judy (Sussman) 1938- .... **CLC 12, 30**
See also AAYA 3, 26; BYA 1, 8, 12; CA 29-32R; CANR 13, 37, 66, 124; CLR 2, 15, 69; CPW; DA3; DAM NOV, POP; DLB 52; JRDA; MAICYA 1, 2; MAICYAS 1; MTCW 1, 2; MTFW 2005; NFS 24; SATA 2, 31, 79, 142; WYA; YAW

Blunden, Edmund (Charles)
1896-1974 .... **CLC 2, 56; PC 66**
See also BRW 6; BRWS 11; CA 17-18; 45-48; CANR 54; CAP 2; CP 1, 2; DLB 20, 100, 155; MTCW 1; PAB

Bly, Robert (Elwood) 1926- .... **CLC 1, 2, 5, 10, 15, 38, 128; PC 39**
See also AMWS 4; CA 5-8R; CANR 41, 73, 125; CP 1, 2, 3, 4, 5, 6, 7; DA3; DAM POET; DLB 5; EWL 3; MAL 5; MTCW 1, 2; MTFW 2005; PFS 6, 17; RGAL 4

Boas, Franz 1858-1942 .... **TCLC 56**
See also CA 115; 181

Bobette
See Simenon, Georges (Jacques Christian)

Boccaccio, Giovanni 1313-1375 ... **CMLC 13, 57; SSC 10, 87**
See also EW 2; RGSF 2; RGWL 2, 3; TWA; WLIT 7

Bochco, Steven 1943- .... **CLC 35**
See also AAYA 11, 71; CA 124; 138

Bode, Sigmund
See O'Doherty, Brian

Bodel, Jean 1167(?)-1210 .... **CMLC 28**

Bodenheim, Maxwell 1892-1954 .... **TCLC 44**
See also CA 110; 187; DLB 9, 45; MAL 5; RGAL 4

Bodenheimer, Maxwell
See Bodenheim, Maxwell

Bodker, Cecil 1927-
See Bodker, Cecil

Boyd, William (Andrew Murray)
1952- .... **CLC 28, 53, 70**
See also CA 114; 120; CANR 51, 71, 131;
CN 4, 5, 6, 7; DLB 231

Boyesen, Hjalmar Hjorth
1848-1895 .... **NCLC 135**
See also DLB 12, 71; DLBD 13; RGAL 4

Boyle, Kay 1902-1992 .... **CLC 1, 5, 19, 58,
121; SSC 5**
See also CA 13-16R; 140; CAAS 1; CANR
29, 61, 110; CN 1, 2, 3, 4, 5; CP 1, 2, 3,
4, 5; DLB 4, 9, 48, 86; DLBY 1993; EWL
3; MAL 5; MTCW 1, 2; MTFW 2005;
RGAL 4; RGSF 2; SSFS 10, 13, 14

Boyle, Mark
See Kienzle, William X.

Boyle, Patrick 1905-1982 .... **CLC 19**
See also CA 127

Boyle, T. C.
See Boyle, T. Coraghessan
See also AMWS 8

Boyle, T. Coraghessan 1948- ..... **CLC 36, 55,
90; SSC 16**
See Boyle, T. C.
See also AAYA 47; BEST 90:4; BPFB 1;
CA 120; CANR 44, 76, 89, 132; CN 6, 7;
CPW; DA3; DAM POP; DLB 218, 278;
DLBY 1986; EWL 3; MAL 5; MTCW 2;
MTFW 2005; SSFS 13, 19

Boz
See Dickens, Charles (John Huffam)

Brackenridge, Hugh Henry
1748-1816 .... **NCLC 7**
See also DLB 11, 37; RGAL 4

Bradbury, Edward P.
See Moorcock, Michael
See also MTCW 2

Bradbury, Malcolm (Stanley)
1932-2000 .... **CLC 32, 61**
See also CA 1-4R; CANR 1, 33, 91, 98,
137; CN 1, 2, 3, 4, 5, 6, 7; CP 1; DA3;
DAM NOV; DLB 14, 207; EWL 3;
MTCW 1, 2; MTFW 2005

Bradbury, Ray 1920- ... **CLC 1, 3, 10, 15, 42,
98; SSC 29, 53; WLC 1**
See also AAYA 15; AITN 1, 2; AMWS 4;
BPFB 1; BYA 4, 5, 11; CA 1-4R; CANR
2, 30, 75, 125; CDALB 1968-1988; CN
1, 2, 3, 4, 5, 6, 7; CPW; DA; DA3; DAB;
DAC; DAM MST, NOV, POP; DLB 2, 8;
EXPN; EXPS; HGG; LAIT 3, 5; LATS
1:2; LMFS 2; MAL 5; MTCW 1, 2;
MTFW 2005; NFS 1, 22; RGAL 4; RGSF
2; SATA 11, 64, 123; SCFW 1, 2; SFW 4;
SSFS 1, 20; SUFW 1, 2; TUS; YAW

Braddon, Mary Elizabeth
1837-1915 .... **TCLC 111**
See also BRWS 8; CA 108; 179; CMW 4;
DLB 18, 70, 156; HGG

Bradfield, Scott 1955- .... **SSC 65**
See also CA 147; CANR 90; HGG; SUFW
2

Bradfield, Scott Michael
See Bradfield, Scott

Bradford, Gamaliel 1863-1932 .... **TCLC 36**
See also CA 160; DLB 17

Bradford, William 1590-1657 .... **LC 64**
See also DLB 24, 30; RGAL 4

Bradley, David (Henry), Jr. 1950- .... **BLC 1;
CLC 23, 118**
See also BW 1, 3; CA 104; CANR 26, 81;
CN 4, 5, 6, 7; DAM MULT; DLB 33

Bradley, John Ed 1958- .... **CLC 55**
See also CA 139; CANR 99; CN 6, 7; CSW

Bradley, John Edmund, Jr.
See Bradley, John Ed

Bradley, Marion Zimmer
1930-1999 .... **CLC 30**
See Chapman, Lee; Dexter, John; Gardner,
Miriam; Ives, Morgan; Rivers, Elfrida
See also AAYA 40; BPFB 1; CA 57-60; 185;
CAAS 10; CANR 7, 31, 51, 75, 107;
CPW; DA3; DAM POP; DLB 8; FANT;
FW; MTCW 1, 2; MTFW 2005; SATA 90,
139; SATA-Obit 116; SFW 4; SUFW 2;
YAW

Bradshaw, John 1933- .... **CLC 70**
See also CA 138; CANR 61

Bradstreet, Anne 1612(?)-1672 .... **LC 4, 30,
130; PC 10**
See also AMWS 1; CDALB 1640-1865;
DA; DA3; DAC; DAM MST, POET; DLB
24; EXPP; FW; PFS 6; RGAL 4; TUS;
WP

Brady, Joan 1939- .... **CLC 86**
See also CA 141

Bragg, Melvyn 1939- .... **CLC 10**
See also BEST 89:3; CA 57-60; CANR 10,
48, 89; CN 1, 2, 3, 4, 5, 6, 7; DLB 14,
271; RHW

Brahe, Tycho 1546-1601 .... **LC 45**
See also DLB 300

Braine, John (Gerard) 1922-1986 . **CLC 1, 3,
41**
See also CA 1-4R; 120; CANR 1, 33; CD-
BLB 1945-1960; CN 1, 2, 3, 4; DLB 15;
DLBY 1986; EWL 3; MTCW 1

Braithwaite, William Stanley (Beaumont)
1878-1962 .... **BLC 1; HR 1:2; PC 52**
See also BW 1; CA 125; DAM MULT; DLB
50, 54; MAL 5

Bramah, Ernest 1868-1942 .... **TCLC 72**
See also CA 156; CMW 4; DLB 70; FANT

Brammer, Billy Lee
See Brammer, William

Brammer, William 1929-1978 .... **CLC 31**
See also CA 235; 77-80

Brancati, Vitaliano 1907-1954 .... **TCLC 12**
See also CA 109; DLB 264; EWL 3

Brancato, Robin F(idler) 1936- .... **CLC 35**
See also AAYA 9, 68; BYA 6; CA 69-72;
CANR 11, 45; CLR 32; JRDA; MAICYA
2; MAICYAS 1; SAAS 9; SATA 97;
WYA; YAW

Brand, Dionne 1953- .... **CLC 192**
See also BW 2; CA 143; CANR 143; CWP

Brand, Max
See Faust, Frederick (Schiller)
See also BPFB 1; TCWW 1, 2

Brand, Millen 1906-1980 .... **CLC 7**
See also CA 21-24R; 97-100; CANR 72

Branden, Barbara .... **CLC 44**
See also CA 148

Brandes, Georg (Morris Cohen)
1842-1927 .... **TCLC 10**
See also CA 105; 189; DLB 300

Brandys, Kazimierz 1916-2000 .... **CLC 62**
See also CA 239; EWL 3

Branley, Franklyn M(ansfield)
1915-2002 .... **CLC 21**
See also CA 33-36R; 207; CANR 14, 39;
CLR 13; MAICYA 1, 2; SAAS 16; SATA
4, 68, 136

Brant, Beth (E.) 1941- .... **NNAL**
See also CA 144; FW

Brant, Sebastian 1457-1521 .... **LC 112**
See also DLB 179; RGWL 2, 3

Brathwaite, Edward Kamau
1930- .... **BLCS; CLC 11; PC 56**
See also BRWS 12; BW 2, 3; CA 25-28R;
CANR 11, 26, 47, 107; CDWLB 3; CP 1,
2, 3, 4, 5, 6, 7; DAM POET; DLB 125;
EWL 3

Brathwaite, Kamau
See Brathwaite, Edward Kamau

Brautigan, Richard (Gary)
1935-1984 .... **CLC 1, 3, 5, 9, 12, 34, 42;
TCLC 133**
See also BPFB 1; CA 53-56; 113; CANR
34; CN 1, 2, 3; CP 1, 2, 3, 4; DA3; DAM
NOV; DLB 2, 5, 206; DLBY 1980, 1984;
FANT; MAL 5; MTCW 1; RGAL 4;
SATA 56

Brave Bird, Mary .... **NNAL**
See Crow Dog, Mary

Braverman, Kate 1950- .... **CLC 67**
See also CA 89-92; CANR 141

Brecht, (Eugen) Bertolt (Friedrich)
1898-1956 ..... **DC 3; TCLC 1, 6, 13, 35,
169; WLC 1**
See also CA 104; 133; CANR 62; CDWLB
2; DA; DA3; DAB; DAC; DAM DRAM,
MST; DFS 4, 5, 9; DLB 56, 124; EW 11;
EWL 3; IDTP; MTCW 1, 2; MTFW 2005;
RGHL; RGWL 2, 3; TWA

Brecht, Eugen Berthold Friedrich
See Brecht, (Eugen) Bertolt (Friedrich)

Bremer, Fredrika 1801-1865 .... **NCLC 11**
See also DLB 254

Brennan, Christopher John
1870-1932 .... **TCLC 17**
See also CA 117; 188; DLB 230; EWL 3

Brennan, Maeve 1917-1993 ... **CLC 5; TCLC
124**
See also CA 81-84; CANR 72, 100

Brenner, Jozef 1887-1919
See Csath, Geza
See also CA 240

Brent, Linda
See Jacobs, Harriet A(nn)

Brentano, Clemens (Maria)
1778-1842 .... **NCLC 1**
See also DLB 90; RGWL 2, 3

Brent of Bin Bin
See Franklin, (Stella Maria Sarah) Miles
(Lampe)

Brenton, Howard 1942- .... **CLC 31**
See also CA 69-72; CANR 33, 67; CBD;
CD 5, 6; DLB 13; MTCW 1

Breslin, James 1930-
See Breslin, Jimmy
See also CA 73-76; CANR 31, 75, 139;
DAM NOV; MTCW 1, 2; MTFW 2005

Breslin, Jimmy .... **CLC 4, 43**
See Breslin, James
See also AITN 1; DLB 185; MTCW 2

Bresson, Robert 1901(?)-1999 .... **CLC 16**
See also CA 110; 187; CANR 49

Breton, Andre 1896-1966 .. **CLC 2, 9, 15, 54;
PC 15**
See also CA 19-20; 25-28R; CANR 40, 60;
CAP 2; DLB 65, 258; EW 11; EWL 3;
GFL 1789 to the Present; LMFS 2;
MTCW 1, 2; MTFW 2005; RGWL 2, 3;
TWA; WP

Breton, Nicholas c. 1554-c. 1626 .... **LC 133**
See also DLB 136

Breytenbach, Breyten 1939(?)- .. **CLC 23, 37,
126**
See also CA 113; 129; CANR 61, 122;
CWW 2; DAM POET; DLB 225; EWL 3

Bridgers, Sue Ellen 1942- .... **CLC 26**
See also AAYA 8, 49; BYA 7, 8; CA 65-68;
CANR 11, 36; CLR 18; DLB 52; JRDA;
MAICYA 1, 2; SAAS 1; SATA 22, 90;
SATA-Essay 109; WYA; YAW

Bridges, Robert (Seymour)
1844-1930 .... **PC 28; TCLC 1**
See also BRW 6; CA 104; 152; CDBLB
1890-1914; DAM POET; DLB 19, 98

Bridie, James .... **TCLC 3**
See Mavor, Osborne Henry
See also DLB 10; EWL 3

Brown, William Hill 1765-1793 .... **LC 93**
    See also DLB 37
Brown, William Wells 1815-1884 ...... **BLC 1;**
    DC 1; NCLC 2, 89
    See also DAM MULT; DLB 3, 50, 183,
    248; RGAL 4
Browne, (Clyde) Jackson 1948(?)- ... **CLC 21**
    See also CA 120
Browne, Sir Thomas 1605-1682 .... **LC 111**
    See also BRW 2; DLB 151
Browning, Robert 1812-1889 . **NCLC 19, 79;**
    PC 2, 61; WLCS
    See also BRW 4; BRWC 2; BRWR 2; CD-
    BLB 1832-1890; CLR 97; DA; DA3;
    DAB; DAC; DAM MST, POET; DLB 32,
    163; EXPP; LATS 1:1; PAB; PFS 1, 15;
    RGEL 2; TEA; WLIT 4; WP; YABC 1
Browning, Tod 1882-1962 .... **CLC 16**
    See also CA 141; 117
Brownmiller, Susan 1935- .... **CLC 159**
    See also CA 103; CANR 35, 75, 137; DAM
    NOV; FW; MTCW 1, 2; MTFW 2005
Brownson, Orestes Augustus
    1803-1876 .... **NCLC 50**
    See also DLB 1, 59, 73, 243
Bruccoli, Matthew J(oseph) 1931- ... **CLC 34**
    See also CA 9-12R; CANR 7, 87; DLB 103
Bruce, Lenny .... **CLC 21**
    See Schneider, Leonard Alfred
Bruchac, Joseph 1942- .... **NNAL**
    See also AAYA 19; CA 33-36R; CANR 13,
    47, 75, 94, 137; CLR 46; CWRI 5; DAM
    MULT; JRDA; MAICYA 2; MAICYAS 1;
    MTCW 2; MTFW 2005; SATA 42, 89,
    131, 172
Bruin, John
    See Brutus, Dennis
Brulard, Henri
    See Stendhal
Brulls, Christian
    See Simenon, Georges (Jacques Christian)
Brunetto Latini c. 1220-1294 .... **CMLC 73**
Brunner, John (Kilian Houston)
    1934-1995 .... **CLC 8, 10**
    See also CA 1-4R; 149; CAAS 8; CANR 2,
    37; CPW; DAM POP; DLB 261; MTCW
    1, 2; SCFW 1, 2; SFW 4
Bruno, Giordano 1548-1600 .... **LC 27**
    See also RGWL 2, 3
Brutus, Dennis 1924- ... **BLC 1; CLC 43; PC**
    24
    See also AFW; BW 2, 3; CA 49-52; CAAS
    14; CANR 2, 27, 42, 81; CDWLB 3; CP
    1, 2, 3, 4, 5, 6, 7; DAM MULT, POET;
    DLB 117, 225; EWL 3
Bryan, C(ourtlandt) D(ixon) B(arnes)
    1936- .... **CLC 29**
    See also CA 73-76; CANR 13, 68; DLB
    185; INT CANR-13
Bryan, Michael
    See Moore, Brian
    See also CCA 1
Bryan, William Jennings
    1860-1925 .... **TCLC 99**
    See also DLB 303
Bryant, William Cullen 1794-1878 . **NCLC 6,**
    46; PC 20
    See also AMWS 1; CDALB 1640-1865;
    DA; DAB; DAC; DAM MST, POET;
    DLB 3, 43, 59, 189, 250; EXPP; PAB;
    RGAL 4; TUS
Bryusov, Valery Yakovlevich
    1873-1924 .... **TCLC 10**
    See also CA 107; 155; EWL 3; SFW 4
Buchan, John 1875-1940 .... **TCLC 41**
    See also CA 108; 145; CMW 4; DAB;
    DAM POP; DLB 34, 70, 156; HGG;
    MSW; MTCW 2; RGEL 2; RHW;
    YABC 2

Buchanan, George 1506-1582 .... **LC 4**
    See also DLB 132
Buchanan, Robert 1841-1901 .... **TCLC 107**
    See also CA 179; DLB 18, 35
Buchheim, Lothar-Guenther 1918- .... **CLC 6**
    See also CA 85-88
Buchner, (Karl) Georg
    1813-1837 .... **NCLC 26, 146**
    See also CDWLB 2; DLB 133; EW 6;
    RGSF 2; RGWL 2, 3; TWA
Buchwald, Art 1925- .... **CLC 33**
    See also AITN 1; CA 5-8R; CANR 21, 67,
    107; MTCW 1, 2; SATA 10
Buchwald, Arthur
    See Buchwald, Art
Buck, Pearl S(ydenstricker)
    1892-1973 .... **CLC 7, 11, 18, 127**
    See also AAYA 42; AITN 1; AMWS 2;
    BPFB 1; CA 1-4R; 41-44R; CANR 1, 34;
    CDALBS; CN 1; DA; DA3; DAB; DAC;
    DAM MST, NOV; DLB 9, 102, 329; EWL
    3; LAIT 3; MAL 5; MTCW 1, 2; MTFW
    2005; RGAL 4; RHW; SATA 1, 25; TUS
Buckler, Ernest 1908-1984 .... **CLC 13**
    See also CA 11-12; 114; CAP 1; CCA 1;
    CN 1, 2, 3; DAC; DAM MST; DLB 68;
    SATA 47
Buckley, Christopher 1952- .... **CLC 165**
    See also CA 139; CANR 119
Buckley, Christopher Taylor
    See Buckley, Christopher
Buckley, Vincent (Thomas)
    1925-1988 .... **CLC 57**
    See also CA 101; CP 1, 2, 3, 4; DLB 289
Buckley, William F., Jr. 1925- ..... **CLC 7, 18,**
    37
    See also AITN 1; BPFB 1; CA 1-4R; CANR
    1, 24, 53, 93, 133; CMW 4; CPW; DA3;
    DAM POP; DLB 137; DLBY 1980; INT
    CANR-24; MTCW 1, 2; MTFW 2005;
    TUS
Buechner, Frederick 1926- ..... **CLC 2, 4, 6, 9**
    See also AMWS 12; BPFB 1; CA 13-16R;
    CANR 11, 39, 64, 114, 138; CN 1, 2, 3,
    4, 5, 6, 7; DAM NOV; DLBY 1980; INT
    CANR-11; MAL 5; MTCW 1, 2; MTFW
    2005; TCLE 1:1
Buell, John (Edward) 1927- .... **CLC 10**
    See also CA 1-4R; CANR 71; DLB 53
Buero Vallejo, Antonio 1916-2000 ... **CLC 15,**
    46, 139, 226; DC 18
    See also CA 106; 189; CANR 24, 49, 75;
    CWW 2; DFS 11; EWL 3; HW 1; MTCW
    1, 2
Bufalino, Gesualdo 1920-1996 .... **CLC 74**
    See also CA 209; CWW 2; DLB 196
Bugayev, Boris Nikolayevich
    1880-1934 .... **PC 11; TCLC 7**
    See Bely, Andrey; Belyi, Andrei
    See also CA 104; 165; MTCW 2; MTFW
    2005
Bukowski, Charles 1920-1994 ... **CLC 2, 5, 9,**
    41, 82, 108; PC 18; SSC 45
    See also CA 17-20R; 144; CANR 40, 62,
    105; CN 4, 5; CP 1, 2, 3, 4; CPW; DA3;
    DAM NOV, POET; DLB 5, 130, 169;
    EWL 3; MAL 5; MTCW 1, 2; MTFW
    2005
Bulgakov, Mikhail 1891-1940 .... **SSC 18;**
    TCLC 2, 16, 159
    See also BPFB 1; CA 105; 152; DAM
    DRAM, NOV; DLB 272; EWL 3; MTCW
    2; MTFW 2005; NFS 8; RGSF 2; RGWL
    2, 3; SFW 4; TWA
Bulgakov, Mikhail Afanasevich
    See Bulgakov, Mikhail

Bulgya, Alexander Alexandrovich
    1901-1956 .... **TCLC 53**
    See Fadeev, Aleksandr Aleksandrovich;
    Fadeev, Alexandr Alexandrovich; Fadeyev,
    Alexander
    See also CA 117; 181
Bullins, Ed 1935- ... **BLC 1; CLC 1, 5, 7; DC**
    6
    See also BW 2, 3; CA 49-52; CAAS 16;
    CAD; CANR 24, 46, 73, 134; CD 5, 6;
    DAM DRAM, MULT; DLB 7, 38, 249;
    EWL 3; MAL 5; MTCW 1, 2; MTFW
    2005; RGAL 4
Bulosan, Carlos 1911-1956 .... **AAL**
    See also CA 216; DLB 312; RGAL 4
Bulwer-Lytton, Edward (George Earle
    Lytton) 1803-1873 .... **NCLC 1, 45**
    See also DLB 21; RGEL 2; SFW 4; SUFW
    1; TEA
Bunin, Ivan
    See Bunin, Ivan Alexeyevich
Bunin, Ivan Alekseevich
    See Bunin, Ivan Alexeyevich
Bunin, Ivan Alexeyevich 1870-1953 ... **SSC 5;**
    TCLC 6
    See also CA 104; DLB 317, 329; EWL 3;
    RGSF 2; RGWL 2, 3; TWA
Bunting, Basil 1900-1985 ...... **CLC 10, 39, 47**
    See also BRWS 7; CA 53-56; 115; CANR
    7; CP 1, 2, 3, 4; DAM POET; DLB 20;
    EWL 3; RGEL 2
Bunuel, Luis 1900-1983 ... **CLC 16, 80; HLC**
    1
    See also CA 101; 110; CANR 32, 77; DAM
    MULT; HW 1
Bunyan, John 1628-1688 .. **LC 4, 69; WLC 1**
    See also BRW 2; BYA 5; CDBLB 1660-
    1789; DA; DAB; DAC; DAM MST; DLB
    39; RGEL 2; TEA; WCH; WLIT 3
Buravsky, Alexandr .... **CLC 59**
Burckhardt, Jacob (Christoph)
    1818-1897 .... **NCLC 49**
    See also EW 6
Burford, Eleanor
    See Hibbert, Eleanor Alice Burford
Burgess, Anthony . **CLC 1, 2, 4, 5, 8, 10, 13,**
    15, 22, 40, 62, 81, 94
    See Wilson, John (Anthony) Burgess
    See also AAYA 25; AITN 1; BRWS 1; CD-
    BLB 1960 to Present; CN 1, 2, 3, 4, 5;
    DAB; DLB 14, 194, 261; DLBY 1998;
    EWL 3; RGEL 2; RHW; SFW 4; YAW
Burke, Edmund 1729(?)-1797 .... **LC 7, 36;**
    WLC 1
    See also BRW 3; DA; DA3; DAB; DAC;
    DAM MST; DLB 104, 252; RGEL 2;
    TEA
Burke, Kenneth (Duva) 1897-1993 ... **CLC 2,**
    24
    See also AMW; CA 5-8R; 143; CANR 39,
    74, 136; CN 1, 2; CP 1, 2, 3, 4, 5; DLB
    45, 63; EWL 3; MAL 5; MTCW 1, 2;
    MTFW 2005; RGAL 4
Burke, Leda
    See Garnett, David
Burke, Ralph
    See Silverberg, Robert
Burke, Thomas 1886-1945 .... **TCLC 63**
    See also CA 113; 155; CMW 4; DLB 197
Burney, Fanny 1752-1840 .... **NCLC 12, 54,**
    107
    See also BRWS 3; DLB 39; FL 1:2; NFS
    16; RGEL 2; TEA
Burney, Frances
    See Burney, Fanny

Callimachus c. 305B.C.-c.
240B.C. .... **CMLC 18**
See also AW 1; DLB 176; RGWL 2, 3
Calvin, Jean
See Calvin, John
See also DLB 327; GFL Beginnings to 1789
Calvin, John 1509-1564 .... **LC 37**
See Calvin, Jean
Calvino, Italo 1923-1985 .... **CLC 5, 8, 11, 22,**
33, 39, 73; SSC 3, 48; TCLC 183
See also AAYA 58; CA 85-88; 116; CANR
23, 61, 132; DAM NOV; DLB 196; EW
13; EWL 3; MTCW 1, 2; MTFW 2005;
RGHL; RGSF 2; RGWL 2, 3; SFW 4;
SSFS 12; WLIT 7
Camara Laye
See Laye, Camara
See also EWL 3
Camden, William 1551-1623 .... **LC 77**
See also DLB 172
Cameron, Carey 1952- .... **CLC 59**
See also CA 135
Cameron, Peter 1959- .... **CLC 44**
See also AMWS 12; CA 125; CANR 50,
117; DLB 234; GLL 2
Camoens, Luis Vaz de 1524(?)-1580
See Camoes, Luis de
See also EW 2
Camoes, Luis de 1524(?)-1580 . **HLCS 1; LC**
62; PC 31
See Camoens, Luis Vaz de
See also DLB 287; RGWL 2, 3
Campana, Dino 1885-1932 .... **TCLC 20**
See also CA 117; 246; DLB 114; EWL 3
Campanella, Tommaso 1568-1639 .... **LC 32**
See also RGWL 2, 3
Campbell, John W(ood, Jr.)
1910-1971 .... **CLC 32**
See also CA 21-22; 29-32R; CANR 34;
CAP 2; DLB 8; MTCW 1; SCFW 1, 2;
SFW 4
Campbell, Joseph 1904-1987 .... **CLC 69;**
TCLC 140
See also AAYA 3, 66; BEST 89:2; CA 1-4R;
124; CANR 3, 28, 61, 107; DA3; MTCW
1, 2
Campbell, Maria 1940- .... **CLC 85; NNAL**
See also CA 102; CANR 54; CCA 1; DAC
Campbell, (John) Ramsey 1946- ..... **CLC 42;**
SSC 19
See also AAYA 51; CA 57-60, 228; CAAE
228; CANR 7, 102; DLB 261; HGG; INT
CANR-7; SUFW 1, 2
Campbell, (Ignatius) Roy (Dunnachie)
1901-1957 .... **TCLC 5**
See also AFW; CA 104; 155; DLB 20, 225;
EWL 3; MTCW 2; RGEL 2
Campbell, Thomas 1777-1844 .... **NCLC 19**
See also DLB 93, 144; RGEL 2
Campbell, Wilfred .... **TCLC 9**
See Campbell, William
Campbell, William 1858(?)-1918
See Campbell, Wilfred
See also CA 106; DLB 92
Campbell, William Edward March
1893-1954
See March, William
See also CA 108
Campion, Jane 1954- .... **CLC 95, 229**
See also AAYA 33; CA 138; CANR 87
Campion, Thomas 1567-1620 .... **LC 78**
See also CDBLB Before 1660; DAM POET;
DLB 58, 172; RGEL 2
Camus, Albert 1913-1960 ...... **CLC 1, 2, 4, 9,**
11, 14, 32, 63, 69, 124; DC 2; SSC 9,
76; WLC 1
See also AAYA 36; AFW; BPFB 1; CA 89-
92; CANR 131; DA; DA3; DAB; DAC;
DAM DRAM, MST, NOV; DLB 72, 321,

329; EW 13; EWL 3; EXPN; EXPS; GFL
1789 to the Present; LATS 1:2; LMFS 2;
MTCW 1, 2; MTFW 2005; NFS 6, 16;
RGHL; RGSF 2; RGWL 2, 3; SSFS 4;
TWA
Canby, Vincent 1924-2000 .... **CLC 13**
See also CA 81-84; 191
Cancale
See Desnos, Robert
Canetti, Elias 1905-1994 .. **CLC 3, 14, 25, 75,**
86; TCLC 157
See also CA 21-24R; 146; CANR 23, 61,
79; CDWLB 2; CWW 2; DA3; DLB 85,
124, 329; EW 12; EWL 3; MTCW 1, 2;
MTFW 2005; RGWL 2, 3; TWA
Canfield, Dorothea F.
See Fisher, Dorothy (Frances) Canfield
Canfield, Dorothea Frances
See Fisher, Dorothy (Frances) Canfield
Canfield, Dorothy
See Fisher, Dorothy (Frances) Canfield
Canin, Ethan 1960- .... **CLC 55; SSC 70**
See also CA 131; 135; MAL 5
Cankar, Ivan 1876-1918 .... **TCLC 105**
See also CDWLB 4; DLB 147; EWL 3
Cannon, Curt
See Hunter, Evan
Cao, Lan 1961- .... **CLC 109**
See also CA 165
Cape, Judith
See Page, P(atricia) K(athleen)
See also CCA 1
Capek, Karel 1890-1938 .... **DC 1; SSC 36;**
TCLC 6, 37; WLC 1
See also CA 104; 140; CDWLB 4; DA;
DA3; DAB; DAC; DAM DRAM, MST,
NOV; DFS 7, 11; DLB 215; EW 10; EWL
3; MTCW 2; MTFW 2005; RGSF 2;
RGWL 2, 3; SCFW 1, 2; SFW 4
Capella, Martianus fl. 4th cent. - .. **CMLC 84**
Capote, Truman 1924-1984 . **CLC 1, 3, 8, 13,**
19, 34, 38, 58; SSC 2, 47, 93; TCLC
164; WLC 1
See also AAYA 61; AMWS 3; BPFB 1; CA
5-8R; 113; CANR 18, 62; CDALB 1941-
1968; CN 1, 2, 3; CPW; DA; DA3; DAB;
DAC; DAM MST, NOV, POP; DLB 2,
185, 227; DLBY 1980, 1984; EWL 3;
EXPS; GLL 1; LAIT 3; MAL 5; MTCW
1, 2; MTFW 2005; NCFS 2; RGAL 4;
RGSF 2; SATA 91; SSFS 2; TUS
Capra, Frank 1897-1991 .... **CLC 16**
See also AAYA 52; CA 61-64; 135
Caputo, Philip 1941- .... **CLC 32**
See also AAYA 60; CA 73-76; CANR 40,
135; YAW
Caragiale, Ion Luca 1852-1912 ...... **TCLC 76**
See also CA 157
Card, Orson Scott 1951- .... **CLC 44, 47, 50**
See also AAYA 11, 42; BPFB 1; BYA 5, 8;
CA 102; CANR 27, 47, 73, 102, 106, 133;
CLR 116; CPW; DA3; DAM POP; FANT;
INT CANR-27; MTCW 1, 2; MTFW
2005; NFS 5; SATA 83, 127; SCFW 2;
SFW 4; SUFW 2; YAW
Cardenal, Ernesto 1925- .... **CLC 31, 161;**
HLC 1; PC 22
See also CA 49-52; CANR 2, 32, 66, 138;
CWW 2; DAM MULT, POET; DLB 290;
EWL 3; HW 1, 2; LAWS 1; MTCW 1, 2;
MTFW 2005; RGWL 2, 3
Cardinal, Marie 1929-2001 .... **CLC 189**
See also CA 177; CWW 2; DLB 83; FW
Cardozo, Benjamin N(athan)
1870-1938 .... **TCLC 65**
See also CA 117; 164

Carducci, Giosue (Alessandro Giuseppe)
1835-1907 .... **PC 46; TCLC 32**
See also CA 163; DLB 329; EW 7; RGWL
2, 3
Carew, Thomas 1595(?)-1640 . **LC 13; PC 29**
See also BRW 2; DLB 126; PAB; RGEL 2
Carey, Ernestine Gilbreth
1908-2006 .... **CLC 17**
See also CA 5-8R; CANR 71; SATA 2
Carey, Peter 1943- .... **CLC 40, 55, 96, 183**
See also BRWS 12; CA 123; 127; CANR
53, 76, 117, 157; CN 4, 5, 6, 7; DLB 289,
326; EWL 3; INT CA-127; MTCW 1, 2;
MTFW 2005; RGSF 2; SATA 94
Carleton, William 1794-1869 .... **NCLC 3**
See also DLB 159; RGEL 2; RGSF 2
Carlisle, Henry (Coffin) 1926- .... **CLC 33**
See also CA 13-16R; CANR 15, 85
Carlsen, Chris
See Holdstock, Robert P.
Carlson, Ron 1947- .... **CLC 54**
See also CA 105, 189; CAAE 189; CANR
27, 155; DLB 244
Carlson, Ronald F.
See Carlson, Ron
Carlyle, Thomas 1795-1881 ..... **NCLC 22, 70**
See also BRW 4; CDBLB 1789-1832; DA;
DAB; DAC; DAM MST; DLB 55, 144,
254; RGEL 2; TEA
Carman, (William) Bliss 1861-1929 ... **PC 34;**
TCLC 7
See also CA 104; 152; DAC; DLB 92;
RGEL 2
Carnegie, Dale 1888-1955 .... **TCLC 53**
See also CA 218
Carossa, Hans 1878-1956 .... **TCLC 48**
See also CA 170; DLB 66; EWL 3
Carpenter, Don(ald Richard)
1931-1995 .... **CLC 41**
See also CA 45-48; 149; CANR 1, 71
Carpenter, Edward 1844-1929 .... **TCLC 88**
See also CA 163; GLL 1
Carpenter, John (Howard) 1948- ... **CLC 161**
See also AAYA 2; CA 134; SATA 58
Carpenter, Johnny
See Carpenter, John (Howard)
Carpentier (y Valmont), Alejo
1904-1980 . **CLC 8, 11, 38, 110; HLC 1;**
SSC 35
See also CA 65-68; 97-100; CANR 11, 70;
CDWLB 3; DAM MULT; DLB 113; EWL
3; HW 1, 2; LAW; LMFS 2; RGSF 2;
RGWL 2, 3; WLIT 1
Carr, Caleb 1955- .... **CLC 86**
See also CA 147; CANR 73, 134; DA3
Carr, Emily 1871-1945 .... **TCLC 32**
See also CA 159; DLB 68; FW; GLL 2
Carr, John Dickson 1906-1977 .... **CLC 3**
See Fairbairn, Roger
See also CA 49-52; 69-72; CANR 3, 33,
60; CMW 4; DLB 306; MSW; MTCW 1,
2
Carr, Philippa
See Hibbert, Eleanor Alice Burford
Carr, Virginia Spencer 1929- .... **CLC 34**
See also CA 61-64; DLB 111
Carrere, Emmanuel 1957- .... **CLC 89**
See also CA 200
Carrier, Roch 1937- .... **CLC 13, 78**
See also CA 130; CANR 61, 152; CCA 1;
DAC; DAM MST; DLB 53; SATA 105,
166
Carroll, James Dennis
See Carroll, Jim
Carroll, James P. 1943(?)- .... **CLC 38**
See also CA 81-84; CANR 73, 139; MTCW
2; MTFW 2005

Damas, Leon-Gontran 1912-1978 .... **CLC 84**
  See also BW 1; CA 125; 73-76; EWL 3
Dana, Richard Henry Sr.
  1787-1879 .... **NCLC 53**
Daniel, Samuel 1562(?)-1619 .... **LC 24**
  See also DLB 62; RGEL 2
Daniels, Brett
  See Adler, Renata
Dannay, Frederic 1905-1982 .... **CLC 11**
  See Queen, Ellery
  See also CA 1-4R; 107; CANR 1, 39; CMW
  4; DAM POP; DLB 137; MTCW 1
D'Annunzio, Gabriele 1863-1938 ... **TCLC 6,**
  40
  See also CA 104; 155; EW 8; EWL 3;
  RGWL 2, 3; TWA; WLIT 7
Danois, N. le
  See Gourmont, Remy(-Marie-Charles) de
Dante 1265-1321 .... **CMLC 3, 18, 39, 70; PC**
  21; WLCS
  See Alighieri, Dante
  See also DA; DA3; DAB; DAC; DAM
  MST, POET; EFS 1; EW 1; LAIT 1;
  RGWL 2, 3; TWA; WP
d'Antibes, Germain
  See Simenon, Georges (Jacques Christian)
Danticat, Edwidge 1969- ... **CLC 94, 139, 228**
  See also AAYA 29; CA 152; 192; CAAE
  192; CANR 73, 129; CN 7; DNFS 1;
  EXPS; LATS 1:2; MTCW 2; MTFW
  2005; SSFS 1; YAW
Danvers, Dennis 1947- .... **CLC 70**
Danziger, Paula 1944-2004 .... **CLC 21**
  See also AAYA 4, 36; BYA 6, 7, 14; CA
  112; 115; 229; CANR 37, 132; CLR 20;
  JRDA; MAICYA 1, 2; MTFW 2005;
  SATA 36, 63, 102, 149; SATA-Brief 30;
  SATA-Obit 155; WYA; YAW
Da Ponte, Lorenzo 1749-1838 .... **NCLC 50**
d'Aragona, Tullia 1510(?)-1556 .... **LC 121**
Dario, Ruben 1867-1916 .... **HLC 1; PC 15;**
  TCLC 4
  See also CA 131; CANR 81; DAM MULT;
  DLB 290; EWL 3; HW 1, 2; LAW;
  MTCW 1, 2; MTFW 2005; RGWL 2, 3
Darley, George 1795-1846 .... **NCLC 2**
  See also DLB 96; RGEL 2
Darrow, Clarence (Seward)
  1857-1938 .... **TCLC 81**
  See also CA 164; DLB 303
Darwin, Charles 1809-1882 .... **NCLC 57**
  See also BRWS 7; DLB 57, 166; LATS 1:1;
  RGEL 2; TEA; WLIT 4
Darwin, Erasmus 1731-1802 .... **NCLC 106**
  See also DLB 93; RGEL 2
Daryush, Elizabeth 1887-1977 ...... **CLC 6, 19**
  See also CA 49-52; CANR 3, 81; DLB 20
Das, Kamala 1934- .... **CLC 191; PC 43**
  See also CA 101; CANR 27, 59; CP 1, 2, 3,
  4, 5, 6, 7; CWP; DLB 323; FW
Dasgupta, Surendranath
  1887-1952 .... **TCLC 81**
  See also CA 157
Dashwood, Edmee Elizabeth Monica de la
  Pasture 1890-1943
  See Delafield, E. M.
  See also CA 119; 154
da Silva, Antonio Jose
  1705-1739 .... **NCLC 114**
Daudet, (Louis Marie) Alphonse
  1840-1897 .... **NCLC 1**
  See also DLB 123; GFL 1789 to the Present;
  RGSF 2
Daudet, Alphonse Marie Leon
  1867-1942 .... **SSC 94**
  See also CA 217
d'Aulnoy, Marie-Catherine c.
  1650-1705 .... **LC 100**

Daumal, Rene 1908-1944 .... **TCLC 14**
  See also CA 114; 247; EWL 3
Davenant, William 1606-1668 .... **LC 13**
  See also DLB 58, 126; RGEL 2
Davenport, Guy (Mattison, Jr.)
  1927-2005 .... **CLC 6, 14, 38; SSC 16**
  See also CA 33-36R; 235; CANR 23, 73;
  CN 3, 4, 5, 6; CSW; DLB 130
David, Robert
  See Nezval, Vitezslav
Davidson, Avram (James) 1923-1993
  See Queen, Ellery
  See also CA 101; 171; CANR 26; DLB 8;
  FANT; SFW 4; SUFW 1, 2
Davidson, Donald (Grady)
  1893-1968 .... **CLC 2, 13, 19**
  See also CA 5-8R; 25-28R; CANR 4, 84;
  DLB 45
Davidson, Hugh
  See Hamilton, Edmond
Davidson, John 1857-1909 .... **TCLC 24**
  See also CA 118; 217; DLB 19; RGEL 2
Davidson, Sara 1943- .... **CLC 9**
  See also CA 81-84; CANR 44, 68; DLB
  185
Davie, Donald (Alfred) 1922-1995 .... **CLC 5,**
  8, 10, 31; PC 29
  See also BRWS 6; CA 1-4R; 149; CAAS 3;
  CANR 1, 44; CP 1, 2, 3, 4, 5, 6; DLB 27;
  MTCW 1; RGEL 2
Davie, Elspeth 1918-1995 .... **SSC 52**
  See also CA 120; 126; 150; CANR 141;
  DLB 139
Davies, Ray(mond Douglas) 1944- ... **CLC 21**
  See also CA 116; 146; CANR 92
Davies, Rhys 1901-1978 .... **CLC 23**
  See also CA 9-12R; 81-84; CANR 4; CN 1,
  2; DLB 139, 191
Davies, Robertson 1913-1995 .. **CLC 2, 7, 13,**
  25, 42, 75, 91; WLC 2
  See Marchbanks, Samuel
  See also BEST 89:2; BPFB 1; CA 33-36R;
  150; CANR 17, 42, 103; CN 1, 2, 3, 4, 5,
  6; CPW; DA; DA3; DAB; DAC; DAM
  MST, NOV, POP; DLB 68; EWL 3; HGG;
  INT CANR-17; MTCW 1, 2; MTFW
  2005; RGEL 2; TWA
Davies, Sir John 1569-1626 .... **LC 85**
  See also DLB 172
Davies, Walter C.
  See Kornbluth, C(yril) M.
Davies, William Henry 1871-1940 ... **TCLC 5**
  See also BRWS 11; CA 104; 179; DLB 19,
  174; EWL 3; RGEL 2
Da Vinci, Leonardo 1452-1519 ..... **LC 12, 57,**
  60
  See also AAYA 40
Davis, Angela (Yvonne) 1944- .... **CLC 77**
  See also BW 2, 3; CA 57-60; CANR 10,
  81; CSW; DA3; DAM MULT; FW
Davis, B. Lynch
  See Bioy Casares, Adolfo; Borges, Jorge
  Luis
Davis, Frank Marshall 1905-1987 ...... **BLC 1**
  See also BW 2, 3; CA 125; 123; CANR 42,
  80; DAM MULT; DLB 51
Davis, Gordon
  See Hunt, E(verette) Howard, (Jr.)
Davis, H(arold) L(enoir) 1896-1960 . **CLC 49**
  See also ANW; CA 178; 89-92; DLB 9,
  206; SATA 114; TCWW 1, 2
Davis, Hart
  See Poniatowska, Elena
Davis, Natalie Zemon 1928- .... **CLC 204**
  See also CA 53-56; CANR 58, 100

Davis, Rebecca (Blaine) Harding
  1831-1910 .... **SSC 38; TCLC 6**
  See also AMWS 16; CA 104; 179; DLB 74,
  239; FW; NFS 14; RGAL 4; TUS
Davis, Richard Harding
  1864-1916 .... **TCLC 24**
  See also CA 114; 179; DLB 12, 23, 78, 79,
  189; DLBD 13; RGAL 4
Davison, Frank Dalby 1893-1970 ..... **CLC 15**
  See also CA 217; 116; DLB 260
Davison, Lawrence H.
  See Lawrence, D(avid) H(erbert Richards)
Davison, Peter (Hubert) 1928-2004 . **CLC 28**
  See also CA 9-12R; 234; CAAS 4; CANR
  3, 43, 84; CP 1, 2, 3, 4, 5, 6, 7; DLB 5
Davys, Mary 1674-1732 .... **LC 1, 46**
  See also DLB 39
Dawson, (Guy) Fielding (Lewis)
  1930-2002 .... **CLC 6**
  See also CA 85-88; 202; CANR 108; DLB
  130; DLBY 2002
Dawson, Peter
  See Faust, Frederick (Schiller)
  See also TCWW 1, 2
Day, Clarence (Shepard, Jr.)
  1874-1935 .... **TCLC 25**
  See also CA 108; 199; DLB 11
Day, John 1574(?)-1640(?) .... **LC 70**
  See also DLB 62, 170; RGEL 2
Day, Thomas 1748-1789 .... **LC 1**
  See also DLB 39; YABC 1
Day Lewis, C(ecil) 1904-1972 . **CLC 1, 6, 10;**
  PC 11
  See Blake, Nicholas; Lewis, C. Day
  See also BRWS 3; CA 13-16; 33-36R;
  CANR 34; CAP 1; CP 1; CWRI 5; DAM
  POET; DLB 15, 20; EWL 3; MTCW 1, 2;
  RGEL 2
Dazai Osamu .... **SSC 41; TCLC 11**
  See Tsushima, Shuji
  See also CA 164; DLB 182; EWL 3; MJW;
  RGSF 2; RGWL 2, 3; TWA
de Andrade, Carlos Drummond
  See Drummond de Andrade, Carlos
de Andrade, Mario 1892(?)-1945
  See Andrade, Mario de
  See also CA 178; HW 2
Deane, Norman
  See Creasey, John
Deane, Seamus (Francis) 1940- ...... **CLC 122**
  See also CA 118; CANR 42
de Beauvoir, Simone
  See Beauvoir, Simone de
de Beer, P.
  See Bosman, Herman Charles
De Botton, Alain 1969- .... **CLC 203**
  See also CA 159; CANR 96
de Brissac, Malcolm
  See Dickinson, Peter (Malcolm de Brissac)
de Campos, Alvaro
  See Pessoa, Fernando (Antonio Nogueira)
de Chardin, Pierre Teilhard
  See Teilhard de Chardin, (Marie Joseph)
  Pierre
de Crenne, Helisenne c. 1510-c.
  1560 .... **LC 113**
Dee, John 1527-1608 .... **LC 20**
  See also DLB 136, 213
Deer, Sandra 1940- .... **CLC 45**
  See also CA 186
De Ferrari, Gabriella 1941- .... **CLC 65**
  See also CA 146
de Filippo, Eduardo 1900-1984 ... **TCLC 127**
  See also CA 132; 114; EWL 3; MTCW 1;
  RGWL 2, 3

Defoe, Daniel 1660(?)-1731 .... LC 1, 42, 108;
WLC 2
See also AAYA 27; BRW 3; BRWR 1; BYA
4; CDBLB 1660-1789; CLR 61; DA;
DA3; DAB; DAC; DAM MST, NOV;
DLB 39, 95, 101; JRDA; LAIT 1; LMFS
1; MAICYA 1, 2; NFS 9, 13; RGEL 2;
SATA 22; TEA; WCH; WLIT 3

de Gouges, Olympe
See de Gouges, Olympe

de Gouges, Olympe 1748-1793 .... LC 127
See also DLB 313

de Gourmont, Remy(-Marie-Charles)
See Gourmont, Remy(-Marie-Charles) de

de Gournay, Marie le Jars
1566-1645 .... LC 98
See also DLB 327; FW

de Hartog, Jan 1914-2002 .... CLC 19
See also CA 1-4R; 210; CANR 1; DFS 12

de Hostos, E. M.
See Hostos (y Bonilla), Eugenio Maria de

de Hostos, Eugenio M.
See Hostos (y Bonilla), Eugenio Maria de

Deighton, Len .... CLC 4, 7, 22, 46
See Deighton, Leonard Cyril
See also AAYA 6; BEST 89:2; BPFB 1; CD-
BLB 1960 to Present; CMW 4; CN 1, 2,
3, 4, 5, 6, 7; CPW; DLB 87

Deighton, Leonard Cyril 1929-
See Deighton, Len
See also AAYA 57; CA 9-12R; CANR 19,
33, 68; DA3; DAM NOV, POP; MTCW
1, 2; MTFW 2005

Dekker, Thomas 1572(?)-1632 ..... DC 12; LC
22
See also CDBLB Before 1660; DAM
DRAM; DLB 62, 172; LMFS 1; RGEL 2

de Laclos, Pierre Ambroise Franois
See Laclos, Pierre-Ambroise Francois

Delacroix, (Ferdinand-Victor-)Eugene
1798-1863 .... NCLC 133
See also EW 5

Delafield, E. M. .... TCLC 61
See Dashwood, Edmee Elizabeth Monica
de la Pasture
See also DLB 34; RHW

de la Mare, Walter (John)
1873-1956 . SSC 14; TCLC 4, 53; WLC
2
See also CA 163; CDBLB 1914-1945; CLR
23; CWRI 5; DA3; DAB; DAC; DAM
MST, POET; DLB 19, 153, 162, 255, 284;
EWL 3; EXPP; HGG; MAICYA 1, 2;
MTCW 2; MTFW 2005; RGEL 2; RGSF
2; SATA 16; SUFW 1; TEA; WCH

de Lamartine, Alphonse (Marie Louis Prat)
See Lamartine, Alphonse (Marie Louis Prat)
de

Delaney, Franey
See O'Hara, John (Henry)

Delaney, Shelagh 1939- .... CLC 29
See also CA 17-20R; CANR 30, 67; CBD;
CD 5, 6; CDBLB 1960 to Present; CWD;
DAM DRAM; DFS 7; DLB 13; MTCW 1

Delany, Martin Robison
1812-1885 .... NCLC 93
See also DLB 50; RGAL 4

Delany, Mary (Granville Pendarves)
1700-1788 .... LC 12

Delany, Samuel R., Jr. 1942- ... BLC 1; CLC
8, 14, 38, 141
See also AAYA 24; AFAW 2; BPFB 1; BW
2, 3; CA 81-84; CANR 27, 43, 116; CN
2, 3, 4, 5, 6, 7; DAM MULT; DLB 8, 33;
FANT; MAL 5; MTCW 1, 2; RGAL 4;
SATA 92; SCFW 1, 2; SFW 4; SUFW 2

De la Ramee, Marie Louise (Ouida)
1839-1908
See Ouida
See also CA 204; SATA 20

de la Roche, Mazo 1879-1961 .... CLC 14
See also CA 85-88; CANR 30; DLB 68;
RGEL 2; RHW; SATA 64

De La Salle, Innocent
See Hartmann, Sadakichi

de Laureamont, Comte
See Lautreamont

Delbanco, Nicholas 1942- ..... CLC 6, 13, 167
See also CA 17-20R, 189; CAAE 189;
CAAS 2; CANR 29, 55, 116, 150; CN 7;
DLB 6, 234

Delbanco, Nicholas Franklin
See Delbanco, Nicholas

del Castillo, Michel 1933- .... CLC 38
See also CA 109; CANR 77

Deledda, Grazia (Cosima)
1875(?)-1936 .... TCLC 23
See also CA 123; 205; DLB 264, 329; EWL
3; RGWL 2, 3; WLIT 7

Deleuze, Gilles 1925-1995 .... TCLC 116
See also DLB 296

Delgado, Abelardo (Lalo) B(arrientos)
1930-2004 .... HLC 1
See also CA 131; 230; CAAS 15; CANR
90; DAM MST, MULT; DLB 82; HW 1,
2

Delibes, Miguel .... CLC 8, 18
See Delibes Setien, Miguel
See also DLB 322; EWL 3

Delibes Setien, Miguel 1920-
See Delibes, Miguel
See also CA 45-48; CANR 1, 32; CWW 2;
HW 1; MTCW 1

DeLillo, Don 1936- ..... CLC 8, 10, 13, 27, 39,
54, 76, 143, 210, 213
See also AMWC 2; AMWS 6; BEST 89:1;
BPFB 1; CA 81-84; CANR 21, 76, 92,
133; CN 3, 4, 5, 6, 7; CPW; DA3; DAM
NOV, POP; DLB 6, 173; EWL 3; MAL 5;
MTCW 1, 2; MTFW 2005; RGAL 4; TUS

de Lisser, H. G.
See De Lisser, H(erbert) G(eorge)
See also DLB 117

De Lisser, H(erbert) G(eorge)
1878-1944 .... TCLC 12
See de Lisser, H. G.
See also BW 2; CA 109; 152

Deloire, Pierre
See Peguy, Charles (Pierre)

Deloney, Thomas 1543(?)-1600 .... LC 41
See also DLB 167; RGEL 2

Deloria, Ella (Cara) 1889-1971(?) ..... NNAL
See also CA 152; DAM MULT; DLB 175

Deloria, Vine, Jr. 1933-2005 .... CLC 21, 122;
NNAL
See also CA 53-56; 245; CANR 5, 20, 48,
98; DAM MULT; DLB 175; MTCW 1;
SATA 21; SATA-Obit 171

Deloria, Vine Victor, Jr.
See Deloria, Vine, Jr.

del Valle-Inclan, Ramon (Maria)
See Valle-Inclan, Ramon (Maria) del
See also DLB 322

Del Vecchio, John M(ichael) 1947- .. CLC 29
See also CA 110; DLBD 9

de Man, Paul (Adolph Michel)
1919-1983 .... CLC 55
See also CA 128; 111; CANR 61; DLB 67;
MTCW 1, 2

DeMarinis, Rick 1934- .... CLC 54
See also CA 57-60, 184; CAAE 184; CAAS
24; CANR 9, 25, 50; DLB 218; TCWW 2

de Maupassant, (Henri Rene Albert) Guy
See Maupassant, (Henri Rene Albert)
Guy de

Dembry, R. Emmet
See Murfree, Mary Noailles

Demby, William 1922- .... BLC 1; CLC 53
See also BW 1, 3; CA 81-84; CANR 81;
DAM MULT; DLB 33

de Menton, Francisco
See Chin, Frank (Chew, Jr.)

Demetrius of Phalerum c.
307B.C.- .... CMLC 34

Demijohn, Thom
See Disch, Thomas M.

De Mille, James 1833-1880 .... NCLC 123
See also DLB 99, 251

Deming, Richard 1915-1983
See Queen, Ellery
See also CA 9-12R; CANR 3, 94; SATA 24

Democritus c. 460B.C.-c. 370B.C. . CMLC 47

de Montaigne, Michel (Eyquem)
See Montaigne, Michel (Eyquem) de

de Montherlant, Henry (Milon)
See Montherlant, Henry (Milon) de

Demosthenes 384B.C.-322B.C. ...... CMLC 13
See also AW 1; DLB 176; RGWL 2, 3;
WLIT 8

de Musset, (Louis Charles) Alfred
See Musset, Alfred de

de Natale, Francine
See Malzberg, Barry N(athaniel)

de Navarre, Marguerite 1492-1549 ... LC 61;
SSC 85
See Marguerite d'Angouleme; Marguerite
de Navarre
See also DLB 327

Denby, Edwin (Orr) 1903-1983 .... CLC 48
See also CA 138; 110; CP 1

de Nerval, Gerard
See Nerval, Gerard de

Denham, John 1615-1669 .... LC 73
See also DLB 58, 126; RGEL 2

Denis, Julio
See Cortazar, Julio

Denmark, Harrison
See Zelazny, Roger

Dennis, John 1658-1734 .... LC 11
See also DLB 101; RGEL 2

Dennis, Nigel (Forbes) 1912-1989 ...... CLC 8
See also CA 25-28R; 129; CN 1, 2, 3, 4;
DLB 13, 15, 233; EWL 3; MTCW 1

Dent, Lester 1904-1959 .... TCLC 72
See also CA 112; 161; CMW 4; DLB 306;
SFW 4

De Palma, Brian 1940- .... CLC 20
See also CA 109

De Palma, Brian Russell
See De Palma, Brian

de Pizan, Christine
See Christine de Pizan
See also FL 1:1

De Quincey, Thomas 1785-1859 ..... NCLC 4,
87
See also BRW 4; CDBLB 1789-1832; DLB
110, 144; RGEL 2

Deren, Eleanora 1908(?)-1961
See Deren, Maya
See also CA 192; 111

Deren, Maya .... CLC 16, 102
See Deren, Eleanora

Derleth, August (William)
1909-1971 .... CLC 31
See also BPFB 1; BYA 9, 10; CA 1-4R; 29-
32R; CANR 4; CMW 4; CN 1; DLB 9;
DLBD 17; HGG; SATA 5; SUFW 1

Der Nister 1884-1950 .... TCLC 56
See Nister, Der

de Routisie, Albert
See Aragon, Louis

Derrida, Jacques 1930-2004 ...... **CLC 24, 87, 225**
See also CA 124; 127; 232; CANR 76, 98, 133; DLB 242; EWL 3; LMFS 2; MTCW 2; TWA

Derry Down Derry
See Lear, Edward

Dersonnes, Jacques
See Simenon, Georges (Jacques Christian)

Der Stricker c. 1190-c. 1250 .... **CMLC 75**
See also DLB 138

Desai, Anita 1937- .... **CLC 19, 37, 97, 175**
See also BRWS 5; CA 81-84; CANR 33, 53, 95, 133; CN 1, 2, 3, 4, 5, 6, 7; CWRI 5; DA3; DAB; DAM NOV; DLB 271, 323; DNFS 2; EWL 3; FW; MTCW 1, 2; MTFW 2005; SATA 63, 126

Desai, Kiran 1971- .... **CLC 119**
See also BYA 16; CA 171; CANR 127

de Saint-Luc, Jean
See Glassco, John

de Saint Roman, Arnaud
See Aragon, Louis

Desbordes-Valmore, Marceline
1786-1859 .... **NCLC 97**
See also DLB 217

Descartes, Rene 1596-1650 .... **LC 20, 35**
See also DLB 268; EW 3; GFL Beginnings to 1789

Deschamps, Eustache 1340(?)-1404 .. **LC 103**
See also DLB 208

De Sica, Vittorio 1901(?)-1974 .... **CLC 20**
See also CA 117

Desnos, Robert 1900-1945 .... **TCLC 22**
See also CA 121; 151; CANR 107; DLB 258; EWL 3; LMFS 2

Destouches, Louis-Ferdinand
1894-1961 .... **CLC 9, 15**
See Celine, Louis-Ferdinand
See also CA 85-88; CANR 28; MTCW 1

de Tolignac, Gaston
See Griffith, D(avid Lewelyn) W(ark)

Deutsch, Babette 1895-1982 .... **CLC 18**
See also BYA 3; CA 1-4R; 108; CANR 4, 79; CP 1, 2, 3; DLB 45; SATA 1; SATA-Obit 33

Devenant, William 1606-1649 .... **LC 13**

Devkota, Laxmiprasad 1909-1959 . **TCLC 23**
See also CA 123

De Voto, Bernard (Augustine)
1897-1955 .... **TCLC 29**
See also CA 113; 160; DLB 9, 256; MAL 5; TCWW 1, 2

De Vries, Peter 1910-1993 ..... **CLC 1, 2, 3, 7, 10, 28, 46**
See also CA 17-20R; 142; CANR 41; CN 1, 2, 3, 4, 5; DAM NOV; DLB 6; DLBY 1982; MAL 5; MTCW 1, 2; MTFW 2005

Dewey, John 1859-1952 .... **TCLC 95**
See also CA 114; 170; CANR 144; DLB 246, 270; RGAL 4

Dexter, John
See Bradley, Marion Zimmer
See also GLL 1

Dexter, Martin
See Faust, Frederick (Schiller)

Dexter, Pete 1943- .... **CLC 34, 55**
See also BEST 89:2; CA 127; 131; CANR 129; CPW; DAM POP; INT CA-131; MAL 5; MTCW 1; MTFW 2005

Diamano, Silmang
See Senghor, Leopold Sedar

Diamond, Neil 1941- .... **CLC 30**
See also CA 108

Diaz del Castillo, Bernal c. 1496-1584 .... **HLCS 1; LC 31**
See also DLB 318; LAW

di Bassetto, Corno
See Shaw, George Bernard

Dick, Philip K. 1928-1982 ... **CLC 10, 30, 72; SSC 57**
See also AAYA 24; BPFB 1; BYA 11; CA 49-52; 106; CANR 2, 16, 132; CN 2, 3; CPW; DA3; DAM NOV, POP; DLB 8; MTCW 1, 2; MTFW 2005; NFS 5; SCFW 1, 2; SFW 4

Dick, Philip Kindred
See Dick, Philip K.

Dickens, Charles (John Huffam)
1812-1870 .... **NCLC 3, 8, 18, 26, 37, 50, 86, 105, 113, 161; SSC 17, 49, 88; WLC 2**
See also AAYA 23; BRW 5; BRWC 1, 2; BYA 1, 2, 3, 13, 14; CDBLB 1832-1890; CLR 95; CMW 4; DA; DA3; DAB; DAC; DAM MST, NOV; DLB 21, 55, 70, 159, 166; EXPN; GL 2; HGG; JRDA; LAIT 1, 2; LATS 1:1; LMFS 1; MAICYA 1, 2; NFS 4, 5, 10, 14, 20; RGEL 2; RGSF 2; SATA 15; SUFW 1; TEA; WCH; WLIT 4; WYA

Dickey, James (Lafayette)
1923-1997 .... **CLC 1, 2, 4, 7, 10, 15, 47, 109; PC 40; TCLC 151**
See also AAYA 50; AITN 1, 2; AMWS 4; BPFB 1; CA 9-12R; 156; CABS 2; CANR 10, 48, 61, 105; CDALB 1968-1988; CP 1, 2, 3, 4, 5, 6; CPW; CSW; DA3; DAM NOV, POET, POP; DLB 5, 193; DLBD 7; DLBY 1982, 1993, 1996, 1997, 1998; EWL 3; INT CANR-10; MAL 5; MTCW 1, 2; NFS 9; PFS 6, 11; RGAL 4; TUS

Dickey, William 1928-1994 .... **CLC 3, 28**
See also CA 9-12R; 145; CANR 24, 79; CP 1, 2, 3, 4; DLB 5

Dickinson, Charles 1951- .... **CLC 49**
See also CA 128; CANR 141

Dickinson, Emily (Elizabeth)
1830-1886 ..... **NCLC 21, 77, 171; PC 1; WLC 2**
See also AAYA 22; AMW; AMWR 1; CDALB 1865-1917; DA; DA3; DAB; DAC; DAM MST, POET; DLB 1, 243; EXPP; FL 1:3; MBL; PAB; PFS 1, 2, 3, 4, 5, 6, 8, 10, 11, 13, 16; RGAL 4; SATA 29; TUS; WP; WYA

Dickinson, Mrs. Herbert Ward
See Phelps, Elizabeth Stuart

Dickinson, Peter (Malcolm de Brissac)
1927- .... **CLC 12, 35**
See also AAYA 9, 49; BYA 5; CA 41-44R; CANR 31, 58, 88, 134; CLR 29; CMW 4; DLB 87, 161, 276; JRDA; MAICYA 1, 2; SATA 5, 62, 95, 150; SFW 4; WYA; YAW

Dickson, Carr
See Carr, John Dickson

Dickson, Carter
See Carr, John Dickson

Diderot, Denis 1713-1784 .... **LC 26, 126**
See also DLB 313; EW 4; GFL Beginnings to 1789; LMFS 1; RGWL 2, 3

Didion, Joan 1934- . **CLC 1, 3, 8, 14, 32, 129**
See also AITN 1; AMWS 4; CA 5-8R; CANR 14, 52, 76, 125; CDALB 1968-1988; CN 2, 3, 4, 5, 6, 7; DA3; DAM NOV; DLB 2, 173, 185; DLBY 1981, 1986; EWL 3; MAL 5; MBL; MTCW 1, 2; MTFW 2005; NFS 3; RGAL 4; TCLE 1:1; TCWW 2; TUS

di Donato, Pietro 1911-1992 .... **TCLC 159**
See also CA 101; 136; DLB 9

Dietrich, Robert
See Hunt, E(verette) Howard, (Jr.)

Difusa, Pati
See Almodovar, Pedro

Dillard, Annie 1945- ...... **CLC 9, 60, 115, 216**
See also AAYA 6, 43; AMWS 6; ANW; CA 49-52; CANR 3, 43, 62, 90, 125; DA3; DAM NOV; DLB 275, 278; DLBY 1980; LAIT 4, 5; MAL 5; MTCW 1, 2; MTFW 2005; NCFS 1; RGAL 4; SATA 10, 140; TCLE 1:1; TUS

Dillard, R(ichard) H(enry) W(ilde)
1937- .... **CLC 5**
See also CA 21-24R; CAAS 7; CANR 10; CP 2, 3, 4, 5, 6, 7; CSW; DLB 5, 244

Dillon, Eilis 1920-1994 .... **CLC 17**
See also CA 9-12R; 182; 147; CAAE 182; CAAS 3; CANR 4, 38, 78; CLR 26; MAI-CYA 1, 2; MAICYAS 1; SATA 2, 74; SATA-Essay 105; SATA-Obit 83; YAW

Dimont, Penelope
See Mortimer, Penelope (Ruth)

Dinesen, Isak ..... **CLC 10, 29, 95; SSC 7, 75**
See Blixen, Karen (Christentze Dinesen)
See also EW 10; EWL 3; EXPS; FW; GL 2; HGG; LAIT 3; MTCW 1; NCFS 2; NFS 9; RGSF 2; RGWL 2, 3; SSFS 3, 6, 13; WLIT 2

Ding Ling .... **CLC 68**
See Chiang, Pin-chin
See also DLB 328; RGWL 3

Diphusa, Patty
See Almodovar, Pedro

Disch, Thomas M. 1940- .... **CLC 7, 36**
See Disch, Tom
See also AAYA 17; BPFB 1; CA 21-24R; CAAS 4; CANR 17, 36, 54, 89; CLR 18; CP 5, 6, 7; DA3; DLB 8; HGG; MAICYA 1, 2; MTCW 1, 2; MTFW 2005; SAAS 15; SATA 92; SCFW 1, 2; SFW 4; SUFW 2

Disch, Tom
See Disch, Thomas M.
See also DLB 282

d'Isly, Georges
See Simenon, Georges (Jacques Christian)

Disraeli, Benjamin 1804-1881 ... **NCLC 2, 39, 79**
See also BRW 4; DLB 21, 55; RGEL 2

Ditcum, Steve
See Crumb, R.

Dixon, Paige
See Corcoran, Barbara (Asenath)

Dixon, Stephen 1936- .... **CLC 52; SSC 16**
See also AMWS 12; CA 89-92; CANR 17, 40, 54, 91; CN 4, 5, 6, 7; DLB 130; MAL 5

Dixon, Thomas, Jr. 1864-1946 ..... **TCLC 163**
See also RHW

Djebar, Assia 1936- .... **CLC 182**
See also CA 188; EWL 3; RGWL 3; WLIT 2

Doak, Annie
See Dillard, Annie

Dobell, Sydney Thompson
1824-1874 .... **NCLC 43**
See also DLB 32; RGEL 2

Doblin, Alfred .... **TCLC 13**
See Doeblin, Alfred
See also CDWLB 2; EWL 3; RGWL 2, 3

Dobroliubov, Nikolai Aleksandrovich
See Dobrolyubov, Nikolai Alexandrovich
See also DLB 277

Dobrolyubov, Nikolai Alexandrovich
1836-1861 .... **NCLC 5**
See Dobroliubov, Nikolai Aleksandrovich

Dobson, Austin 1840-1921 .... **TCLC 79**
See also DLB 35, 144

Dobyns, Stephen 1941- .... **CLC 37**
See also AMWS 13; CA 45-48; CANR 2, 18, 99; CMW 4; CP 4, 5, 6, 7; PFS 23

Doctorow, Edgar Laurence
See Doctorow, E.L.

Doctorow, E.L. 1931- . CLC **6, 11, 15, 18, 37, 44, 65, 113, 214**
 See also AAYA 22; AITN 2; AMWS 4; BEST 89:3; BPFB 1; CA 45-48; CANR 2, 33, 51, 76, 97, 133; CDALB 1968-1988; CN 3, 4, 5, 6, 7; CPW; DA3; DAM NOV, POP; DLB 2, 28, 173; DLBY 1980; EWL 3; LAIT 3; MAL 5; MTCW 1, 2; MTFW 2005; NFS 6; RGAL 4; RGHL; RHW; TCLE 1:1; TCWW 1, 2; TUS
Dodgson, Charles L(utwidge) 1832-1898
 See Carroll, Lewis
 See also CLR 2; DA; DA3; DAB; DAC; DAM MST, NOV, POET; MAICYA 1, 2; SATA 100; YABC 2
Dodsley, Robert 1703-1764 .... LC **97**
 See also DLB 95; RGEL 2
Dodson, Owen (Vincent) 1914-1983 .. BLC **1;** CLC **79**
 See also BW 1; CA 65-68; 110; CANR 24; DAM MULT; DLB 76
Doeblin, Alfred 1878-1957 .... TCLC **13**
 See Doblin, Alfred
 See also CA 110; 141; DLB 66
Doerr, Harriet 1910-2002 .... CLC **34**
 See also CA 117; 122; 213; CANR 47; INT CA-122; LATS 1:2
Domecq, H(onorio Bustos)
 See Bioy Casares, Adolfo
Domecq, H(onorio) Bustos
 See Bioy Casares, Adolfo; Borges, Jorge Luis
Domini, Rey
 See Lorde, Audre
 See also GLL 1
Dominique
 See Proust, (Valentin-Louis-George-Eugene) Marcel
Don, A
 See Stephen, Sir Leslie
Donaldson, Stephen R(eeder)
 1947- .... CLC **46, 138**
 See also AAYA 36; BPFB 1; CA 89-92; CANR 13, 55, 99; CPW; DAM POP; FANT; INT CANR-13; SATA 121; SFW 4; SUFW 1, 2
Donleavy, J(ames) P(atrick) 1926- .... CLC **1, 4, 6, 10, 45**
 See also AITN 2; BPFB 1; CA 9-12R; CANR 24, 49, 62, 80, 124; CBD; CD 5, 6; CN 1, 2, 3, 4, 5, 6, 7; DLB 6, 173; INT CANR-24; MAL 5; MTCW 1, 2; MTFW 2005; RGAL 4
Donnadieu, Marguerite
 See Duras, Marguerite
Donne, John 1572-1631 ... LC **10, 24, 91;** PC **1, 43;** WLC **2**
 See also AAYA 67; BRW 1; BRWC 1; BRWR 2; CDBLB Before 1660; DA; DAB; DAC; DAM MST, POET; DLB 121, 151; EXPP; PAB; PFS 2, 11; RGEL 3; TEA; WLIT 3; WP
Donnell, David 1939(?)- .... CLC **34**
 See also CA 197
Donoghue, Denis 1928- .... CLC **209**
 See also CA 17-20R; CANR 16, 102
Donoghue, P. S.
 See Hunt, E(verette) Howard, (Jr.)
Donoso (Yanez), Jose 1924-1996 ... CLC **4, 8, 11, 32, 99;** HLC **1;** SSC **34;** TCLC **133**
 See also CA 81-84; 155; CANR 32, 73; CD-WLB 3; CWW 2; DAM MULT; DLB 113; EWL 3; HW 1, 2; LAW; LAWS 1; MTCW 1, 2; MTFW 2005; RGSF 2; WLIT 1
Donovan, John 1928-1992 .... CLC **35**
 See also AAYA 20; CA 97-100; 137; CLR 3; MAICYA 1, 2; SATA 72; SATA-Brief 29; YAW

Don Roberto
 See Cunninghame Graham, Robert (Gallnigad) Bontine
Doolittle, Hilda 1886-1961 . CLC **3, 8, 14, 31, 34, 73;** PC **5;** WLC **3**
 See H. D.
 See also AAYA 66; AMWS 1; CA 97-100; CANR 35, 131; DA; DAC; DAM MST, POET; DLB 4, 45; EWL 3; FW; GLL 1; LMFS 2; MAL 5; MBL; MTCW 1, 2; MTFW 2005; PFS 6; RGAL 4
Doppo, Kunikida .... TCLC **99**
 See Kunikida Doppo
Dorfman, Ariel 1942- .... CLC **48, 77, 189;** HLC **1**
 See also CA 124; 130; CANR 67, 70, 135; CWW 2; DAM MULT; DFS 4; EWL 3; HW 1, 2; INT CA-130; WLIT 1
Dorn, Edward (Merton)
 1929-1999 .... CLC **10, 18**
 See also CA 93-96; 187; CANR 42, 79; CP 1, 2, 3, 4, 5, 6, 7; DLB 5; INT CA-93-96; WP
Dor-Ner, Zvi .... CLC **70**
Dorris, Michael 1945-1997 .... CLC **109;** NNAL
 See also AAYA 20; BEST 90:1; BYA 12; CA 102; 157; CANR 19, 46, 75; CLR 58; DA3; DAM MULT, NOV; DLB 175; LAIT 5; MTCW 2; MTFW 2005; NFS 3; RGAL 4; SATA 75; SATA-Obit 94; TCWW 2; YAW
Dorris, Michael A.
 See Dorris, Michael
Dorsan, Luc
 See Simenon, Georges (Jacques Christian)
Dorsange, Jean
 See Simenon, Georges (Jacques Christian)
Dorset
 See Sackville, Thomas
Dos Passos, John (Roderigo)
 1896-1970 ... CLC **1, 4, 8, 11, 15, 25, 34, 82;** WLC **2**
 See also AMW; BPFB 1; CA 1-4R; 29-32R; CANR 3; CDALB 1929-1941; DA; DA3; DAB; DAC; DAM MST, NOV; DLB 4, 9, 274, 316; DLBD 1, 15; DLBY 1996; EWL 3; MAL 5; MTCW 1, 2; MTFW 2005; NFS 14; RGAL 4; TUS
Dossage, Jean
 See Simenon, Georges (Jacques Christian)
Dostoevsky, Fedor Mikhailovich
 1821-1881 .. NCLC **2, 7, 21, 33, 43, 119, 167;** SSC **2, 33, 44;** WLC **2**
 See Dostoevsky, Fyodor
 See also AAYA 40; DA; DA3; DAB; DAC; DAM MST, NOV; EW 7; EXPN; NFS 3, 8; RGSF 2; RGWL 2, 3; SSFS 8; TWA
Dostoevsky, Fyodor
 See Dostoevsky, Fedor Mikhailovich
 See also DLB 238; LATS 1:1; LMFS 1, 2
Doty, M. R.
 See Doty, Mark (Alan)
Doty, Mark
 See Doty, Mark (Alan)
Doty, Mark (Alan) 1953(?)- .... CLC **176;** PC **53**
 See also AMWS 11; CA 161, 183; CAAE 183; CANR 110; CP 7
Doty, Mark A.
 See Doty, Mark (Alan)
Doughty, Charles M(ontagu)
 1843-1926 .... TCLC **27**
 See also CA 115; 178; DLB 19, 57, 174
Douglas, Ellen .... CLC **73**
 See Haxton, Josephine Ayres; Williamson, Ellen Douglas
 See also CN 5, 6, 7; CSW; DLB 292

Douglas, Gavin 1475(?)-1522 .... LC **20**
 See also DLB 132; RGEL 2
Douglas, George
 See Brown, George Douglas
 See also RGEL 2
Douglas, Keith (Castellain)
 1920-1944 .... TCLC **40**
 See also BRW 7; CA 160; DLB 27; EWL 3; PAB; RGEL 2
Douglas, Leonard
 See Bradbury, Ray
Douglas, Michael
 See Crichton, Michael
Douglas, (George) Norman
 1868-1952 .... TCLC **68**
 See also BRW 6; CA 119; 157; DLB 34, 195; RGEL 2
Douglas, William
 See Brown, George Douglas
Douglass, Frederick 1817(?)-1895 ..... BLC **1;** NCLC **7, 55, 141;** WLC **2**
 See also AAYA 48; AFAW 1, 2; AMWC 1; AMWS 3; CDALB 1640-1865; DA; DA3; DAC; DAM MST, MULT; DLB 1, 43, 50, 79, 243; FW; LAIT 2; NCFS 2; RGAL 4; SATA 29
Dourado, (Waldomiro Freitas) Autran
 1926- .... CLC **23, 60**
 See also CA 25-28R; 179; CANR 34, 81; DLB 145, 307; HW 2
Dourado, Waldomiro Freitas Autran
 See Dourado, (Waldomiro Freitas) Autran
Dove, Rita 1952- .. BLCS; CLC **50, 81;** PC **6**
 See Dove, Rita Frances
 See also AAYA 46; AMWS 4; BW 2; CA 109; CAAS 19; CANR 27, 42, 68, 76, 97, 132; CDALBS; CP 5, 6, 7; CSW; CWP; DA3; DAM MULT, POET; DLB 120; EWL 3; EXPP; MAL 5; MTCW 2; MTFW 2005; PFS 1, 15; RGAL 4
Doveglion
 See Villa, Jose Garcia
Dowell, Coleman 1925-1985 .... CLC **60**
 See also CA 25-28R; 117; CANR 10; DLB 130; GLL 1
Dowson, Ernest (Christopher)
 1867-1900 .... TCLC **4**
 See also CA 105; 150; DLB 19, 135; RGEL 2
Doyle, A. Conan
 See Doyle, Sir Arthur Conan
Doyle, Sir Arthur Conan
 1859-1930 ..... SSC **12, 83, 95;** TCLC **7;** WLC **2**
 See Conan Doyle, Arthur
 See also AAYA 14; BRWS 2; CA 104; 122; CANR 131; CDBLB 1890-1914; CLR 106; CMW 4; DA; DA3; DAB; DAC; DAM MST, NOV; DLB 18, 70, 156, 178; EXPS; HGG; LAIT 2; MSW; MTCW 1, 2; MTFW 2005; RGEL 2; RGSF 2; RHW; SATA 24; SCFW 1, 2; SFW 4; SSFS 2; TEA; WCH; WLIT 4; WYA; YAW
Doyle, Conan
 See Doyle, Sir Arthur Conan
Doyle, John
 See Graves, Robert
Doyle, Roddy 1958- .... CLC **81, 178**
 See also AAYA 14; BRWS 5; CA 143; CANR 73, 128; CN 6, 7; DA3; DLB 194, 326; MTCW 2; MTFW 2005
Doyle, Sir A. Conan
 See Doyle, Sir Arthur Conan
Dr. A
 See Asimov, Isaac; Silverstein, Alvin; Silverstein, Virginia B(arbara Opshelor)

Epicurus 341B.C.-270B.C. .... **CMLC 21**
See also DLB 176
Epsilon
See Betjeman, John
Epstein, Daniel Mark 1948- .... **CLC 7**
See also CA 49-52; CANR 2, 53, 90
Epstein, Jacob 1956- .... **CLC 19**
See also CA 114
Epstein, Jean 1897-1953 .... **TCLC 92**
Epstein, Joseph 1937- .... **CLC 39, 204**
See also AMWS 14; CA 112; 119; CANR
50, 65, 117
Epstein, Leslie 1938- .... **CLC 27**
See also AMWS 12; CA 73-76, 215; CAAE
215; CAAS 12; CANR 23, 69; DLB 299;
RGHL
Equiano, Olaudah 1745(?)-1797 . **BLC 2; LC
16**
See also AFAW 1, 2; CDWLB 3; DAM
MULT; DLB 37, 50; WLIT 2
Erasmus, Desiderius 1469(?)-1536 ..... **LC 16,
93**
See also DLB 136; EW 2; LMFS 1; RGWL
2, 3; TWA
Erdman, Paul E(mil) 1932- .... **CLC 25**
See also AITN 1; CA 61-64; CANR 13, 43,
84
Erdrich, Karen Louise
See Erdrich, Louise
Erdrich, Louise 1954- .... **CLC 39, 54, 120,
176; NNAL; PC 52**
See also AAYA 10, 47; AMWS 4; BEST
89:1; BPFB 1; CA 114; CANR 41, 62,
118, 138; CDALBS; CN 5, 6, 7; CP 6, 7;
CPW; CWP; DA3; DAM MULT, NOV,
POP; DLB 152, 175, 206; EWL 3; EXPP;
FL 1:5; LAIT 5; LATS 1:2; MAL 5;
MTCW 1, 2; MTFW 2005; NFS 5; PFS
14; RGAL 4; SATA 94, 141; SSFS 14,
22; TCWW 2
Erenburg, Ilya (Grigoryevich)
See Ehrenburg, Ilya (Grigoryevich)
Erickson, Stephen Michael 1950-
See Erickson, Steve
See also CA 129; SFW 4
Erickson, Steve .... **CLC 64**
See Erickson, Stephen Michael
See also CANR 60, 68, 136; MTFW 2005;
SUFW 2
Erickson, Walter
See Fast, Howard
Ericson, Walter
See Fast, Howard
Eriksson, Buntel
See Bergman, (Ernst) Ingmar
Eriugena, John Scottus c.
810-877 .... **CMLC 65**
See also DLB 115
Ernaux, Annie 1940- .... **CLC 88, 184**
See also CA 147; CANR 93; MTFW 2005;
NCFS 3, 5
Erskine, John 1879-1951 .... **TCLC 84**
See also CA 112; 159; DLB 9, 102; FANT
Eschenbach, Wolfram von
See von Eschenbach, Wolfram
See also RGWL 3
Eseki, Bruno
See Mphahlele, Ezekiel
Esenin, S.A.
See Esenin, Sergei
See also EWL 3
Esenin, Sergei 1895-1925 .... **TCLC 4**
See Esenin, S.A.
See also CA 104; RGWL 2, 3
Esenin, Sergei Aleksandrovich
See Esenin, Sergei

Eshleman, Clayton 1935- .... **CLC 7**
See also CA 33-36R, 212; CAAE 212;
CAAS 6; CANR 93; CP 1, 2, 3, 4, 5, 6,
7; DLB 5
Espada, Martin 1957- .... **PC 74**
See also CA 159; CANR 80; CP 7; EXPP;
LLW; MAL 5; PFS 13, 16
Espriella, Don Manuel Alvarez
See Southey, Robert
Espriu, Salvador 1913-1985 .... **CLC 9**
See also CA 154; 115; DLB 134; EWL 3
Espronceda, Jose de 1808-1842 ..... **NCLC 39**
Esquivel, Laura 1951(?)- ... **CLC 141; HLCS
1**
See also AAYA 29; CA 143; CANR 68, 113;
DA3; DNFS 2; LAIT 3; LMFS 2; MTCW
2; MTFW 2005; NFS 5; WLIT 1
Esse, James
See Stephens, James
Esterbrook, Tom
See Hubbard, L. Ron
Estleman, Loren D. 1952- .... **CLC 48**
See also AAYA 27; CA 85-88; CANR 27,
74, 139; CMW 4; CPW; DA3; DAM
NOV, POP; DLB 226; INT CANR-27;
MTCW 1, 2; MTFW 2005; TCWW 1, 2
Etherege, Sir George 1636-1692 . **DC 23; LC
78**
See also BRW 2; DAM DRAM; DLB 80;
PAB; RGEL 2
Euclid 306B.C.-283B.C. .... **CMLC 25**
Eugenides, Jeffrey 1960(?)- .... **CLC 81, 212**
See also AAYA 51; CA 144; CANR 120;
MTFW 2005; NFS 24
Euripides c. 484B.C.-406B.C. .... **CMLC 23,
51; DC 4; WLCS**
See also AW 1; CDWLB 1; DA; DA3;
DAB; DAC; DAM DRAM, MST; DFS 1,
4, 6; DLB 176; LAIT 1; LMFS 1; RGWL
2, 3; WLIT 8
Evan, Evin
See Faust, Frederick (Schiller)
Evans, Caradoc 1878-1945 ... **SSC 43; TCLC
85**
See also DLB 162
Evans, Evan
See Faust, Frederick (Schiller)
Evans, Marian
See Eliot, George
Evans, Mary Ann
See Eliot, George
See also NFS 20
Evarts, Esther
See Benson, Sally
Everett, Percival
See Everett, Percival L.
See also CSW
Everett, Percival L. 1956- .... **CLC 57**
See Everett, Percival
See also BW 2; CA 129; CANR 94, 134;
CN 7; MTFW 2005
Everson, R(onald) G(ilmour)
1903-1992 .... **CLC 27**
See also CA 17-20R; CP 1, 2, 3, 4; DLB 88
Everson, William (Oliver)
1912-1994 .... **CLC 1, 5, 14**
See Antoninus, Brother
See also BG 1:2; CA 9-12R; 145; CANR
20; CP 2, 3, 4, 5; DLB 5, 16, 212; MTCW
1
Evtushenko, Evgenii Aleksandrovich
See Yevtushenko, Yevgeny (Alexandrovich)
See also CWW 2; RGWL 2, 3
Ewart, Gavin (Buchanan)
1916-1995 .... **CLC 13, 46**
See also BRWS 7; CA 89-92; 150; CANR
17, 46; CP 1, 2, 3, 4, 5, 6; DLB 40;
MTCW 1

Ewers, Hanns Heinz 1871-1943 ..... **TCLC 12**
See also CA 109; 149
Ewing, Frederick R.
See Sturgeon, Theodore (Hamilton)
Exley, Frederick (Earl) 1929-1992 .... **CLC 6,
11**
See also AITN 2; BPFB 1; CA 81-84; 138;
CANR 117; DLB 143; DLBY 1981
Eynhardt, Guillermo
See Quiroga, Horacio (Sylvestre)
Ezekiel, Nissim (Moses) 1924-2004 .. **CLC 61**
See also CA 61-64; 223; CP 1, 2, 3, 4, 5, 6,
7; DLB 323; EWL 3
Ezekiel, Tish O'Dowd 1943- .... **CLC 34**
See also CA 129
Fadeev, Aleksandr Aleksandrovich
See Bulgya, Alexander Alexandrovich
See also DLB 272
Fadeev, Alexandr Alexandrovich
See Bulgya, Alexander Alexandrovich
See also EWL 3
Fadeyev, A.
See Bulgya, Alexander Alexandrovich
Fadeyev, Alexander .... **TCLC 53**
See Bulgya, Alexander Alexandrovich
Fagen, Donald 1948- .... **CLC 26**
Fainzilberg, Ilya Arnoldovich 1897-1937
See Ilf, Ilya
See also CA 120; 165
Fair, Ronald L. 1932- .... **CLC 18**
See also BW 1; CA 69-72; CANR 25; DLB
33
Fairbairn, Roger
See Carr, John Dickson
Fairbairns, Zoe (Ann) 1948- .... **CLC 32**
See also CA 103; CANR 21, 85; CN 4, 5,
6, 7
Fairfield, Flora
See Alcott, Louisa May
Fairman, Paul W. 1916-1977
See Queen, Ellery
See also CA 114; SFW 4
Falco, Gian
See Papini, Giovanni
Falconer, James
See Kirkup, James
Falconer, Kenneth
See Kornbluth, C(yril) M.
Falkland, Samuel
See Heijermans, Herman
Fallaci, Oriana 1930-2006 .... **CLC 11, 110**
See also CA 77-80; CANR 15, 58, 134; FW;
MTCW 1
Faludi, Susan 1959- .... **CLC 140**
See also CA 138; CANR 126; FW; MTCW
2; MTFW 2005; NCFS 3
Faludy, George 1913- .... **CLC 42**
See also CA 21-24R
Faludy, Gyoergy
See Faludy, George
Fanon, Frantz 1925-1961 .... **BLC 2; CLC 74**
See also BW 1; CA 116; 89-92; DAM
MULT; DLB 296; LMFS 2; WLIT 2
Fanshawe, Ann 1625-1680 .... **LC 11**
Fante, John (Thomas) 1911-1983 .... **CLC 60;
SSC 65**
See also AMWS 11; CA 69-72; 109; CANR
23, 104; DLB 130; DLBY 1983
Far, Sui Sin .... **SSC 62**
See Eaton, Edith Maude
See also SSFS 4
Farah, Nuruddin 1945- ...... **BLC 2; CLC 53,
137**
See also AFW; BW 2, 3; CA 106; CANR
81, 148; CDWLB 3; CN 4, 5, 6, 7; DAM
MULT; DLB 125; EWL 3; WLIT 2

Forez
See Mauriac, Francois (Charles)

Forman, James
See Forman, James D(ouglas)

Forman, James D(ouglas) 1932- .... **CLC 21**
See also AAYA 17; CA 9-12R; CANR 4,
19, 42; JRDA; MAICYA 1, 2; SATA 8,
70; YAW

Forman, Milos 1932- .... **CLC 164**
See also AAYA 63; CA 109

Fornes, Maria Irene 1930- .... **CLC 39, 61,
187; DC 10; HLCS 1**
See also CA 25-28R; CAD; CANR 28, 81;
CD 5, 6; CWD; DLB 7; HW 1, 2; INT
CANR-28; LLW; MAL 5; MTCW 1;
RGAL 4

Forrest, Leon (Richard)
1937-1997 .... **BLCS; CLC 4**
See also AFAW 2; BW 2; CA 89-92; 162;
CAAS 7; CANR 25, 52, 87; CN 4, 5, 6;
DLB 33

Forster, E(dward) M(organ)
1879-1970 ...... **CLC 1, 2, 3, 4, 9, 10, 13,
15, 22, 45, 77; SSC 27; TCLC 125;
WLC 2**
See also AAYA 2, 37; BRW 6; BRWR 2;
BYA 12; CA 13-14; 25-28R; CANR 45;
CAP 1; CDBLB 1914-1945; DA; DA3;
DAB; DAC; DAM MST, NOV; DLB 34,
98, 162, 178, 195; DLBD 10; EWL 3;
EXPN; LAIT 3; LMFS 1; MTCW 1, 2;
MTFW 2005; NCFS 1; NFS 3, 10, 11;
RGEL 2; RGSF 2; SATA 57; SUFW 1;
TEA; WLIT 4

Forster, John 1812-1876 .... **NCLC 11**
See also DLB 144, 184

Forster, Margaret 1938- .... **CLC 149**
See also CA 133; CANR 62, 115; CN 4, 5,
6, 7; DLB 155, 271

Forsyth, Frederick 1938- .... **CLC 2, 5, 36**
See also BEST 89:4; CA 85-88; CANR 38,
62, 115, 137; CMW 4; CN 3, 4, 5, 6, 7;
CPW; DAM NOV, POP; DLB 87; MTCW
1, 2; MTFW 2005

Forten, Charlotte L. 1837-1914 .... **BLC 2;
TCLC 16**
See Grimke, Charlotte L(ottie) Forten
See also DLB 50, 239

Fortinbras
See Grieg, (Johan) Nordahl (Brun)

Foscolo, Ugo 1778-1827 .... **NCLC 8, 97**
See also EW 5; WLIT 7

Fosse, Bob 1927-1987
See Fosse, Robert L.
See also CA 110; 123

Fosse, Robert L. .... **CLC 20**
See Fosse, Bob

Foster, Hannah Webster
1758-1840 .... **NCLC 99**
See also DLB 37, 200; RGAL 4

Foster, Stephen Collins
1826-1864 .... **NCLC 26**
See also RGAL 4

Foucault, Michel 1926-1984 . **CLC 31, 34, 69**
See also CA 105; 113; CANR 34; DLB 242;
EW 13; EWL 3; GFL 1789 to the Present;
GLL 1; LMFS 2; MTCW 1, 2; TWA

**Fouque, Friedrich (Heinrich Karl) de la
Motte** 1777-1843 .... **NCLC 2**
See also DLB 90; RGWL 2, 3; SUFW 1

Fourier, Charles 1772-1837 .... **NCLC 51**

Fournier, Henri-Alban 1886-1914
See Alain-Fournier
See also CA 104; 179

Fournier, Pierre 1916-1997 .... **CLC 11**
See Gascar, Pierre
See also CA 89-92; CANR 16, 40

Fowles, John 1926-2005 .... **CLC 1, 2, 3, 4, 6,
9, 10, 15, 33, 87; SSC 33**
See also BPFB 1; BRWS 1; CA 5-8R; 245;
CANR 25, 71, 103; CDBLB 1960 to
Present; CN 1, 2, 3, 4, 5, 6, 7; DA3; DAB;
DAC; DAM MST; DLB 14, 139, 207;
EWL 3; HGG; MTCW 1, 2; MTFW 2005;
NFS 21; RGEL 2; RHW; SATA 22; SATA-
Obit 171; TEA; WLIT 4

Fowles, John Robert
See Fowles, John

Fox, Paula 1923- .... **CLC 2, 8, 121**
See also AAYA 3, 37; BYA 3, 8; CA 73-76;
CANR 20, 36, 62, 105; CLR 1, 44, 96;
DLB 52; JRDA; MAICYA 1, 2; MTCW
1; NFS 12; SATA 17, 60, 120, 167; WYA;
YAW

Fox, William Price (Jr.) 1926- .... **CLC 22**
See also CA 17-20R; CAAS 19; CANR 11,
142; CSW; DLB 2; DLBY 1981

Foxe, John 1517(?)-1587 .... **LC 14**
See also DLB 132

Frame, Janet .. **CLC 2, 3, 6, 22, 66, 96; SSC
29**
See Clutha, Janet Paterson Frame
See also CN 1, 2, 3, 4, 5, 6, 7; CP 2, 3, 4;
CWP; EWL 3; RGEL 2; RGSF 2; TWA

France, Anatole .... **TCLC 9**
See Thibault, Jacques Anatole Francois
See also DLB 123, 330; EWL 3; GFL 1789
to the Present; RGWL 2, 3; SUFW 1

Francis, Claude .... **CLC 50**
See also CA 192

Francis, Dick
See Francis, Richard Stanley
See also CN 2, 3, 4, 5, 6

Francis, Richard Stanley 1920- ... **CLC 2, 22,
42, 102**
See Francis, Dick
See also AAYA 5, 21; BEST 89:3; BPFB 1;
CA 5-8R; CANR 9, 42, 68, 100, 141; CD-
BLB 1960 to Present; CMW 4; CN 7;
DA3; DAM POP; DLB 87; INT CANR-9;
MSW; MTCW 1, 2; MTFW 2005

Francis, Robert (Churchill)
1901-1987 .... **CLC 15; PC 34**
See also AMWS 9; CA 1-4R; 123; CANR
1; CP 1, 2, 3, 4; EXPP; PFS 12; TCLE
1:1

Francis, Lord Jeffrey
See Jeffrey, Francis
See also DLB 107

Frank, Anne(lies Marie)
1929-1945 .... **TCLC 17; WLC 2**
See also AAYA 12; BYA 1; CA 113; 133;
CANR 68; CLR 101; DA; DA3; DAB;
DAC; DAM MST; LAIT 4; MAICYA 2;
MAICYAS 1; MTCW 1, 2; MTFW 2005;
NCFS 2; RGHL; SATA 87; SATA-Brief
42; WYA; YAW

Frank, Bruno 1887-1945 .... **TCLC 81**
See also CA 189; DLB 118; EWL 3

Frank, Elizabeth 1945- .... **CLC 39**
See also CA 121; 126; CANR 78, 150; INT
CA-126

Frankl, Viktor E(mil) 1905-1997 ...... **CLC 93**
See also CA 65-68; 161; RGHL

Franklin, Benjamin
See Hasek, Jaroslav (Matej Frantisek)

Franklin, Benjamin 1706-1790 .... **LC 25;
WLCS**
See also AMW; CDALB 1640-1865; DA;
DA3; DAB; DAC; DAM MST; DLB 24,
43, 73, 183; LAIT 1; RGAL 4; TUS

**Franklin, (Stella Maria Sarah) Miles
(Lampe)** 1879-1954 .... **TCLC 7**
See also CA 104; 164; DLB 230; FW;
MTCW 2; RGEL 2; TWA

Franzen, Jonathan 1959- .... **CLC 202**
See also AAYA 65; CA 129; CANR 105

Fraser, Antonia 1932- .... **CLC 32, 107**
See also AAYA 57; CA 85-88; CANR 44,
65, 119; CMW; DLB 276; MTCW 1, 2;
MTFW 2005; SATA-Brief 32

Fraser, George MacDonald 1925- ...... **CLC 7**
See also AAYA 48; CA 45-48, 180; CAAE
180; CANR 2, 48, 74; MTCW 2; RHW

Fraser, Sylvia 1935- .... **CLC 64**
See also CA 45-48; CANR 1, 16, 60; CCA
1

Frayn, Michael 1933- .... **CLC 3, 7, 31, 47,
176; DC 27**
See also AAYA 69; BRWC 2; BRWS 7; CA
5-8R; CANR 30, 69, 114, 133; CBD; CD
5, 6; CN 1, 2, 3, 4, 5, 6, 7; DAM DRAM,
NOV; DFS 22; DLB 13, 14, 194, 245;
FANT; MTCW 1, 2; MTFW 2005; SFW
4

Fraze, Candida (Merrill) 1945- .... **CLC 50**
See also CA 126

Frazer, Andrew
See Marlowe, Stephen

Frazer, J(ames) G(eorge)
1854-1941 .... **TCLC 32**
See also BRWS 3; CA 118; NCFS 5

Frazer, Robert Caine
See Creasey, John

Frazer, Sir James George
See Frazer, J(ames) G(eorge)

Frazier, Charles 1950- .... **CLC 109, 224**
See also AAYA 34; CA 161; CANR 126;
CSW; DLB 292; MTFW 2005

Frazier, Ian 1951- .... **CLC 46**
See also CA 130; CANR 54, 93

Frederic, Harold 1856-1898 ... **NCLC 10, 175**
See also AMW; DLB 12, 23; DLBD 13;
MAL 5; NFS 22; RGAL 4

Frederick, John
See Faust, Frederick (Schiller)
See also TCWW 2

Frederick the Great 1712-1786 .... **LC 14**

Fredro, Aleksander 1793-1876 .... **NCLC 8**

Freeling, Nicolas 1927-2003 .... **CLC 38**
See also CA 49-52; 218; CAAS 12; CANR
1, 17, 50, 84; CMW 4; CN 1, 2, 3, 4, 5,
6; DLB 87

Freeman, Douglas Southall
1886-1953 .... **TCLC 11**
See also CA 109; 195; DLB 17; DLBD 17

Freeman, Judith 1946- .... **CLC 55**
See also CA 148; CANR 120; DLB 256

Freeman, Mary E(leanor) Wilkins
1852-1930 .... **SSC 1, 47; TCLC 9**
See also CA 106; 177; DLB 12, 78, 221;
EXPS; FW; HGG; MBL; RGAL 4; RGSF
2; SSFS 4, 8; SUFW 1; TUS

Freeman, R(ichard) Austin
1862-1943 .... **TCLC 21**
See also CA 113; CANR 84; CMW 4; DLB
70

French, Albert 1943- .... **CLC 86**
See also BW 3; CA 167

French, Antonia
See Kureishi, Hanif

French, Marilyn 1929- .. **CLC 10, 18, 60, 177**
See also BPFB 1; CA 69-72; CANR 3, 31,
134; CN 5, 6, 7; CPW; DAM DRAM,
NOV, POP; FL 1:5; FW; INT CANR-31;
MTCW 1, 2; MTFW 2005

French, Paul
See Asimov, Isaac

Freneau, Philip Morin 1752-1832 .. **NCLC 1,
111**
See also AMWS 2; DLB 37, 43; RGAL 4

Freud, Sigmund 1856-1939 .... **TCLC 52**
See also CA 115; 133; CANR 69; DLB 296;
EW 8; EWL 3; LATS 1:1; MTCW 1, 2;
MTFW 2005; NCFS 3; TWA

Freytag, Gustav 1816-1895 .... **NCLC 109**
See also DLB 129

Friedan, Betty 1921-2006 .... **CLC 74**
See also CA 65-68; 248; CANR 18, 45, 74;
DLB 246; FW; MTCW 1, 2; MTFW
2005; NCFS 5

Friedan, Betty Naomi
See Friedan, Betty

Friedlander, Saul 1932- .... **CLC 90**
See also CA 117; 130; CANR 72; RGHL

Friedman, B(ernard) H(arper)
1926- .... **CLC 7**
See also CA 1-4R; CANR 3, 48

Friedman, Bruce Jay 1930- ...... **CLC 3, 5, 56**
See also CA 9-12R; CAD; CANR 25, 52,
101; CD 5, 6; CN 1, 2, 3, 4, 5, 6, 7; DLB
2, 28, 244; INT CANR-25; MAL 5; SSFS
18

Friel, Brian 1929- .... **CLC 5, 42, 59, 115; DC
8; SSC 76**
See also BRWS 5; CA 21-24R; CANR 33,
69, 131; CBD; CD 5, 6; DFS 11; DLB
13, 319; EWL 3; MTCW 1; RGEL 2; TEA

Friis-Baastad, Babbis Ellinor
1921-1970 .... **CLC 12**
See also CA 17-20R; 134; SATA 7

Frisch, Max 1911-1991 ...... **CLC 3, 9, 14, 18,
32, 44; TCLC 121**
See also CA 85-88; 134; CANR 32, 74; CD-
WLB 2; DAM DRAM, NOV; DLB 69,
124; EW 13; EWL 3; MTCW 1, 2; MTFW
2005; RGHL; RGWL 2, 3

Fromentin, Eugene (Samuel Auguste)
1820-1876 .... **NCLC 10, 125**
See also DLB 123; GFL 1789 to the Present

Frost, Frederick
See Faust, Frederick (Schiller)

Frost, Robert 1874-1963 . **CLC 1, 3, 4, 9, 10,
13, 15, 26, 34, 44; PC 1, 39, 71; WLC 2**
See also AAYA 21; AMW; AMWR 1; CA
89-92; CANR 33; CDALB 1917-1929;
CLR 67; DA; DA3; DAB; DAC; DAM
MST, POET; DLB 54, 284; DLBD 7;
EWL 3; EXPP; MAL 5; MTCW 1, 2;
MTFW 2005; PAB; PFS 1, 2, 3, 4, 5, 6,
7, 10, 13; RGAL 4; SATA 14; TUS; WP;
WYA

Frost, Robert Lee
See Frost, Robert

Froude, James Anthony
1818-1894 .... **NCLC 43**
See also DLB 18, 57, 144

Froy, Herald
See Waterhouse, Keith (Spencer)

Fry, Christopher 1907-2005 ... **CLC 2, 10, 14**
See also BRWS 3; CA 17-20R; 240; CAAS
23; CANR 9, 30, 74, 132; CBD; CD 5, 6;
CP 1, 2, 3, 4, 5, 6, 7; DAM DRAM; DLB
13; EWL 3; MTCW 1, 2; MTFW 2005;
RGEL 2; SATA 66; TEA

Frye, (Herman) Northrop
1912-1991 .... **CLC 24, 70; TCLC 165**
See also CA 5-8R; 133; CANR 8, 37; DLB
67, 68, 246; EWL 3; MTCW 1, 2; MTFW
2005; RGAL 4; TWA

Fuchs, Daniel 1909-1993 .... **CLC 8, 22**
See also CA 81-84; 142; CAAS 5; CANR
40; CN 1, 2, 3, 4, 5; DLB 9, 26, 28;
DLBY 1993; MAL 5

Fuchs, Daniel 1934- .... **CLC 34**
See also CA 37-40R; CANR 14, 48

Fuentes, Carlos 1928- .. **CLC 3, 8, 10, 13, 22,
41, 60, 113; HLC 1; SSC 24; WLC 2**
See also AAYA 4, 45; AITN 2; BPFB 1;
CA 69-72; CANR 10, 32, 68, 104, 138;
CDWLB 3; CWW 2; DA; DA3; DAB;
DAC; DAM MST, MULT, NOV; DLB
113; DNFS 2; EWL 3; HW 1, 2; LAIT 3;

LATS 1:2; LAW; LAWS 1; LMFS 2;
MTCW 1, 2; MTFW 2005; NFS 8; RGSF
2; RGWL 2, 3; TWA; WLIT 1

Fuentes, Gregorio Lopez y
See Lopez y Fuentes, Gregorio

Fuertes, Gloria 1918-1998 .... **PC 27**
See also CA 178, 180; DLB 108; HW 2;
SATA 115

Fugard, (Harold) Athol 1932- . **CLC 5, 9, 14,
25, 40, 80, 211; DC 3**
See also AAYA 17; AFW; CA 85-88; CANR
32, 54, 118; CD 5, 6; DAM DRAM; DFS
3, 6, 10; DLB 225; DNFS 1, 2; EWL 3;
LATS 1:2; MTCW 1; MTFW 2005; RGEL
2; WLIT 2

Fugard, Sheila 1932- .... **CLC 48**
See also CA 125

Fujiwara no Teika 1162-1241 .... **CMLC 73**
See also DLB 203

Fukuyama, Francis 1952- .... **CLC 131**
See also CA 140; CANR 72, 125

Fuller, Charles (H.), (Jr.) 1939- .... **BLC 2;
CLC 25; DC 1**
See also BW 2; CA 108; 112; CAD; CANR
87; CD 5, 6; DAM DRAM, MULT; DFS
8; DLB 38, 266; EWL 3; INT CA-112;
MAL 5; MTCW 1

Fuller, Henry Blake 1857-1929 .... **TCLC 103**
See also CA 108; 177; DLB 12; RGAL 4

Fuller, John (Leopold) 1937- .... **CLC 62**
See also CA 21-24R; CANR 9, 44; CP 1, 2,
3, 4, 5, 6, 7; DLB 40

Fuller, Margaret
See Ossoli, Sarah Margaret (Fuller)
See also AMWS 2; DLB 183, 223, 239; FL
1:3

Fuller, Roy (Broadbent) 1912-1991 ... **CLC 4,
28**
See also BRWS 7; CA 5-8R; 135; CAAS
10; CANR 53, 83; CN 1, 2, 3, 4, 5; CP 1,
2, 3, 4, 5; CWRI 5; DLB 15, 20; EWL 3;
RGEL 2; SATA 87

Fuller, Sarah Margaret
See Ossoli, Sarah Margaret (Fuller)

Fuller, Sarah Margaret
See Ossoli, Sarah Margaret (Fuller)
See also DLB 1, 59, 73

Fuller, Thomas 1608-1661 .... **LC 111**
See also DLB 151

Fulton, Alice 1952- .... **CLC 52**
See also CA 116; CANR 57, 88; CP 5, 6, 7;
CWP; DLB 193

Furphy, Joseph 1843-1912 .... **TCLC 25**
See Collins, Tom
See also CA 163; DLB 230; EWL 3; RGEL
2

Fuson, Robert H(enderson) 1927- .... **CLC 70**
See also CA 89-92; CANR 103

Fussell, Paul 1924- .... **CLC 74**
See also BEST 90:1; CA 17-20R; CANR 8,
21, 35, 69, 135; INT CANR-21; MTCW
1, 2; MTFW 2005

Futabatei, Shimei 1864-1909 .... **TCLC 44**
See Futabatei Shimei
See also CA 162; MJW

Futabatei Shimei
See Futabatei, Shimei
See also DLB 180; EWL 3

Futrelle, Jacques 1875-1912 .... **TCLC 19**
See also CA 113; 155; CMW 4

Gaboriau, Emile 1835-1873 .... **NCLC 14**
See also CMW 4; MSW

Gadda, Carlo Emilio 1893-1973 ...... **CLC 11;
TCLC 144**
See also CA 89-92; DLB 177; EWL 3;
WLIT 7

Gaddis, William 1922-1998 ... **CLC 1, 3, 6, 8,
10, 19, 43, 86**
See also AMWS 4; BPFB 1; CA 17-20R;
172; CANR 21, 48, 148; CN 1, 2, 3, 4, 5,
6; DLB 2, 278; EWL 3; MAL 5; MTCW
1, 2; MTFW 2005; RGAL 4

Gaelique, Moruen le
See Jacob, (Cyprien-)Max

Gage, Walter
See Inge, William (Motter)

Gaiman, Neil 1960- .... **CLC 195**
See also AAYA 19, 42; CA 133; CANR 81,
129; CLR 109; DLB 261; HGG; MTFW
2005; SATA 85, 146; SFW 4; SUFW 2

Gaiman, Neil Richard
See Gaiman, Neil

Gaines, Ernest J. 1933- .. **BLC 2; CLC 3, 11,
18, 86, 181; SSC 68**
See also AAYA 18; AFAW 1, 2; AITN 1;
BPFB 2; BW 2, 3; BYA 6; CA 9-12R;
CANR 6, 24, 42, 75, 126; CDALB 1968-
1988; CLR 62; CN 1, 2, 3, 4, 5, 6, 7;
CSW; DA3; DAM MULT; DLB 2, 33,
152; DLBY 1980; EWL 3; EXPN; LAIT
5; LATS 1:2; MAL 5; MTCW 1, 2;
MTFW 2005; NFS 5, 7, 16; RGAL 4;
RGSF 2; RHW; SATA 86; SSFS 5; YAW

Gaitskill, Mary 1954- .... **CLC 69**
See also CA 128; CANR 61, 152; DLB 244;
TCLE 1:1

Gaitskill, Mary Lawrence
See Gaitskill, Mary

Gaius Suetonius Tranquillus
See Suetonius

Galdos, Benito Perez
See Perez Galdos, Benito
See also EW 7

Gale, Zona 1874-1938 .... **TCLC 7**
See also CA 105; 153; CANR 84; DAM
DRAM; DFS 17; DLB 9, 78, 228; RGAL
4

Galeano, Eduardo (Hughes) 1940- . **CLC 72;
HLCS 1**
See also CA 29-32R; CANR 13, 32, 100;
HW 1

Galiano, Juan Valera y Alcala
See Valera y Alcala-Galiano, Juan

Galilei, Galileo 1564-1642 .... **LC 45**

Gallagher, Tess 1943- .... **CLC 18, 63; PC 9**
See also CA 106; CP 3, 4, 5, 6, 7; CWP;
DAM POET; DLB 120, 212, 244; PFS 16

Gallant, Mavis 1922- ..... **CLC 7, 18, 38, 172;
SSC 5, 78**
See also CA 69-72; CANR 29, 69, 117;
CCA 1; CN 1, 2, 3, 4, 5, 6, 7; DAC; DAM
MST; DLB 53; EWL 3; MTCW 1, 2;
MTFW 2005; RGEL 2; RGSF 2

Gallant, Roy A(rthur) 1924- .... **CLC 17**
See also CA 5-8R; CANR 4, 29, 54, 117;
CLR 30; MAICYA 1, 2; SATA 4, 68, 110

Gallico, Paul (William) 1897-1976 ..... **CLC 2**
See also AITN 1; CA 5-8R; 69-72; CANR
23; CN 1, 2; DLB 9, 171; FANT; MAI-
CYA 1, 2; SATA 13

Gallo, Max Louis 1932- .... **CLC 95**
See also CA 85-88

Gallois, Lucien
See Desnos, Robert

Gallup, Ralph
See Whitemore, Hugh (John)

Galsworthy, John 1867-1933 .... **SSC 22;
TCLC 1, 45; WLC 2**
See also BRW 6; CA 104; 141; CANR 75;
CDBLB 1890-1914; DA; DA3; DAB;
DAC; DAM DRAM, MST, NOV; DLB
10, 34, 98, 162, 330; DLBD 16; EWL 3;
MTCW 2; RGEL 2; SSFS 3; TEA

Galt, John 1779-1839 .... **NCLC 1, 110**
See also DLB 99, 116, 159; RGEL 2; RGSF
2

Galvin, James 1951- .... **CLC 38**
See also CA 108; CANR 26

Gamboa, Federico 1864-1939 .... **TCLC 36**
See also CA 167; HW 2; LAW

Gandhi, M. K.
See Gandhi, Mohandas Karamchand

Gandhi, Mahatma
See Gandhi, Mohandas Karamchand

Gandhi, Mohandas Karamchand
1869-1948 .... **TCLC 59**
See also CA 121; 132; DA3; DAM MULT;
DLB 323; MTCW 1, 2

Gann, Ernest Kellogg 1910-1991 ..... **CLC 23**
See also AITN 1; BPFB 2; CA 1-4R; 136;
CANR 1, 83; RHW

Gao Xingjian 1940- .... **CLC 167**
See Xingjian, Gao
See also MTFW 2005

Garber, Eric 1943(?)-
See Holleran, Andrew
See also CANR 89

Garcia, Cristina 1958- .... **CLC 76**
See also AMWS 11; CA 141; CANR 73,
130; CN 7; DLB 292; DNFS 1; EWL 3;
HW 2; LLW; MTFW 2005

Garcia Lorca, Federico 1898-1936 ...... **DC 2;**
HLC 2; PC 3; TCLC 1, 7, 49, 181;
WLC 2
See Lorca, Federico Garcia
See also AAYA 46; CA 104; 131; CANR
81; DA; DA3; DAB; DAC; DAM DRAM,
MST, MULT, POET; DFS 4, 10; DLB
108; EWL 3; HW 1, 2; LATS 1:2; MTCW
1, 2; MTFW 2005; TWA

Garcia Marquez, Gabriel 1928- .... **CLC 2, 3,**
8, 10, 15, 27, 47, 55, 68, 170; HLC 1;
SSC 8, 83; WLC 3
See also AAYA 3, 33; BEST 89:1, 90:4;
BPFB 2; BYA 12, 16; CA 33-36R; CANR
10, 28, 50, 75, 82, 128; CDWLB 3; CPW;
CWW 2; DA; DA3; DAB; DAC; DAM
MST, MULT, NOV, POP; DLB 113, 330;
DNFS 1, 2; EWL 3; EXPN; EXPS; HW
1, 2; LAIT 2; LATS 1:2; LAW; LAWS 1;
LMFS 2; MTCW 1, 2; MTFW 2005;
NCFS 3; NFS 1, 5, 10; RGSF 2; RGWL
2, 3; SSFS 1, 6, 16, 21; TWA; WLIT 1

Garcia Marquez, Gabriel Jose
See Garcia Marquez, Gabriel

Garcilaso de la Vega, El Inca
1539-1616 .... **HLCS 1; LC 127**
See also DLB 318; LAW

Gard, Janice
See Latham, Jean Lee

Gard, Roger Martin du
See Martin du Gard, Roger

Gardam, Jane (Mary) 1928- .... **CLC 43**
See also CA 49-52; CANR 2, 18, 33, 54,
106; CLR 12; DLB 14, 161, 231; MAI-
CYA 1, 2; MTCW 1; SAAS 9; SATA 39,
76, 130; SATA-Brief 28; YAW

Gardner, Herb(ert George)
1934-2003 .... **CLC 44**
See also CA 149; 220; CAD; CANR 119;
CD 5, 6; DFS 18, 20

Gardner, John, Jr. 1933-1982 ... **CLC 2, 3, 5,**
7, 8, 10, 18, 28, 34; SSC 7
See also AAYA 45; AITN 1; AMWS 6;
BPFB 2; CA 65-68; 107; CANR 33, 73;
CDALBS; CN 2, 3; CPW; DA3; DAM
NOV, POP; DLB 2; DLBY 1982; EWL 3;
FANT; LATS 1:2; MAL 5; MTCW 1, 2;
MTFW 2005; NFS 3; RGAL 4; RGSF 2;
SATA 40; SATA-Obit 31; SSFS 8

Gardner, John (Edmund) 1926- .... **CLC 30**
See also CA 103; CANR 15, 69, 127; CMW
4; CPW; DAM POP; MTCW 1

Gardner, Miriam
See Bradley, Marion Zimmer
See also GLL 1

Gardner, Noel
See Kuttner, Henry

Gardons, S. S.
See Snodgrass, W.D.

Garfield, Leon 1921-1996 .... **CLC 12**
See also AAYA 8, 69; BYA 1, 3; CA 17-
20R; 152; CANR 38, 41, 78; CLR 21;
DLB 161; JRDA; MAICYA 1, 2; MAIC-
YAS 1; SATA 1, 32, 76; SATA-Obit 90;
TEA; WYA; YAW

Garland, (Hannibal) Hamlin
1860-1940 .... **SSC 18; TCLC 3**
See also CA 104; DLB 12, 71, 78, 186;
MAL 5; RGAL 4; RGSF 2; TCWW 1, 2

Garneau, (Hector de) Saint-Denys
1912-1943 .... **TCLC 13**
See also CA 111; DLB 88

Garner, Alan 1934- .... **CLC 17**
See also AAYA 18; BYA 3, 5; CA 73-76,
178; CAAE 178; CANR 15, 64, 134; CLR
20; CPW; DAB; DAM POP; DLB 161,
261; FANT; MAICYA 1, 2; MTCW 1, 2;
MTFW 2005; SATA 18, 69; SATA-Essay
108; SUFW 1, 2; YAW

Garner, Hugh 1913-1979 .... **CLC 13**
See Warwick, Jarvis
See also CA 69-72; CANR 31; CCA 1; CN
1, 2; DLB 68

Garnett, David 1892-1981 .... **CLC 3**
See also CA 5-8R; 103; CANR 17, 79; CN
1, 2; DLB 34; FANT; MTCW 2; RGEL 2;
SFW 4; SUFW 1

Garnier, Robert c. 1545-1590 .... **LC 119**
See also DLB 327; GFL Beginnings to 1789

Garrett, George (Palmer, Jr.) 1929- . **CLC 3,**
11, 51; SSC 30
See also AMWS 7; BPFB 2; CA 1-4R, 202;
CAAE 202; CAAS 5; CANR 1, 42, 67,
109; CN 1, 2, 3, 4, 5, 6, 7; CP 1, 2, 3, 4,
5, 6, 7; CSW; DLB 2, 5, 130, 152; DLBY
1983

Garrick, David 1717-1779 .... **LC 15**
See also DAM DRAM; DLB 84, 213;
RGEL 2

Garrigue, Jean 1914-1972 .... **CLC 2, 8**
See also CA 5-8R; 37-40R; CANR 20; CP
1; MAL 5

Garrison, Frederick
See Sinclair, Upton

Garrison, William Lloyd
1805-1879 .... **NCLC 149**
See also CDALB 1640-1865; DLB 1, 43,
235

Garro, Elena 1920(?)-1998 .. **HLCS 1; TCLC**
153
See also CA 131; 169; CWW 2; DLB 145;
EWL 3; HW 1; LAWS 1; WLIT 1

Garth, Will
See Hamilton, Edmond; Kuttner, Henry

Garvey, Marcus (Moziah, Jr.)
1887-1940 ... **BLC 2; HR 1:2; TCLC 41**
See also BW 1; CA 120; 124; CANR 79;
DAM MULT

Gary, Romain .... **CLC 25**
See Kacew, Romain
See also DLB 83, 299; RGHL

Gascar, Pierre .... **CLC 11**
See Fournier, Pierre
See also EWL 3; RGHL

Gascoigne, George 1539-1577 .... **LC 108**
See also DLB 136; RGEL 2

Gascoyne, David (Emery)
1916-2001 .... **CLC 45**
See also CA 65-68; 200; CANR 10, 28, 54;
CP 1, 2, 3, 4, 5, 6, 7; DLB 20; MTCW 1;
RGEL 2

Gaskell, Elizabeth Cleghorn
1810-1865 .... **NCLC 5, 70, 97, 137; SSC**
25
See also BRW 5; CDBLB 1832-1890; DAB;
DAM MST; DLB 21, 144, 159; RGEL 2;
RGSF 2; TEA

Gass, William H. 1924- . **CLC 1, 2, 8, 11, 15,**
39, 132; SSC 12
See also AMWS 6; CA 17-20R; CANR 30,
71, 100; CN 1, 2, 3, 4, 5, 6, 7; DLB 2,
227; EWL 3; MAL 5; MTCW 1, 2; MTFW
2005; RGAL 4

Gassendi, Pierre 1592-1655 .... **LC 54**
See also GFL Beginnings to 1789

Gasset, Jose Ortega y
See Ortega y Gasset, Jose

Gates, Henry Louis, Jr. 1950- ... **BLCS; CLC**
65
See also BW 2, 3; CA 109; CANR 25, 53,
75, 125; CSW; DA3; DAM MULT; DLB
67; EWL 3; MAL 5; MTCW 2; MTFW
2005; RGAL 4

Gatos, Stephanie
See Katz, Steve

Gautier, Theophile 1811-1872 .. **NCLC 1, 59;**
PC 18; SSC 20
See also DAM POET; DLB 119; EW 6;
GFL 1789 to the Present; RGWL 2, 3;
SUFW; TWA

Gay, John 1685-1732 .... **LC 49**
See also BRW 3; DAM DRAM; DLB 84,
95; RGEL 2; WLIT 3

Gay, Oliver
See Gogarty, Oliver St. John

Gay, Peter 1923- .... **CLC 158**
See also CA 13-16R; CANR 18, 41, 77,
147; INT CANR-18; RGHL

Gay, Peter Jack
See Gay, Peter

Gaye, Marvin (Pentz, Jr.)
1939-1984 .... **CLC 26**
See also CA 195; 112

Gebler, Carlo 1954- .... **CLC 39**
See also CA 119; 133; CANR 96; DLB 271

Gee, Maggie 1948- .... **CLC 57**
See also CA 130; CANR 125; CN 4, 5, 6,
7; DLB 207; MTFW 2005

Gee, Maurice 1931- .... **CLC 29**
See also AAYA 42; CA 97-100; CANR 67,
123; CLR 56; CN 2, 3, 4, 5, 6, 7; CWRI
5; EWL 3; MAICYA 2; RGSF 2; SATA
46, 101

Gee, Maurice Gough
See Gee, Maurice

Geiogamah, Hanay 1945- .... **NNAL**
See also CA 153; DAM MULT; DLB 175

Gelbart, Larry
See Gelbart, Larry (Simon)
See also CAD; CD 5, 6

Gelbart, Larry (Simon) 1928- .... **CLC 21, 61**
See Gelbart, Larry
See also CA 73-76; CANR 45, 94

Gelber, Jack 1932-2003 ...... **CLC 1, 6, 14, 79**
See also CA 1-4R; 216; CAD; CANR 2;
DLB 7, 228; MAL 5

Gellhorn, Martha (Ellis)
1908-1998 .... **CLC 14, 60**
See also CA 77-80; 164; CANR 44; CN 1,
2, 3, 4, 5, 6 7; DLBY 1982, 1998

Genet, Jean 1910-1986 .. **CLC 1, 2, 5, 10, 14,**
44, 46; DC 25; TCLC 128
See also CA 13-16R; CANR 18; DA3;
DAM DRAM; DFS 10; DLB 72, 321;
DLBY 1986; EW 13; EWL 3; GFL 1789
to the Present; GLL 1; LMFS 2; MTCW
1, 2; MTFW 2005; RGWL 2, 3; TWA

Genlis, Stephanie-Felicite Ducrest
1746-1830 .... **NCLC 166**
See also DLB 313

Gladkov, Fyodor (Vasilyevich)
1883-1958 .... **TCLC 27**
See Gladkov, Fedor Vasil'evich
See also CA 170; EWL 3

Glancy, Diane 1941- .... **CLC 210; NNAL**
See also CA 136, 225; CAAE 225; CAAS
24; CANR 87; DLB 175

Glanville, Brian (Lester) 1931- .... **CLC 6**
See also CA 5-8R; CAAS 9; CANR 3, 70;
CN 1, 2, 3, 4, 5, 6, 7; DLB 15, 139; SATA
42

Glasgow, Ellen (Anderson Gholson)
1873-1945 .... **SSC 34; TCLC 2, 7**
See also AMW; CA 104; 164; DLB 9, 12;
MAL 5; MBL; MTCW 2; MTFW 2005;
RGAL 4; RHW; SSFS 9; TUS

Glaspell, Susan 1882(?)-1948 ..... **DC 10; SSC
41; TCLC 55, 175**
See also AMWS 3; CA 110; 154; DFS 8,
18; DLB 7, 9, 78, 228; MBL; RGAL 4;
SSFS 3; TCWW 2; TUS; YABC 2

Glassco, John 1909-1981 .... **CLC 9**
See also CA 13-16R; 102; CANR 15; CN
1, 2; CP 1, 2, 3; DLB 68

Glasscock, Amnesia
See Steinbeck, John (Ernst)

Glasser, Ronald J. 1940(?)- .... **CLC 37**
See also CA 209

Glassman, Joyce
See Johnson, Joyce

Gleick, James (W.) 1954- .... **CLC 147**
See also CA 131; 137; CANR 97; INT CA-
137

Glendinning, Victoria 1937- .... **CLC 50**
See also CA 120; 127; CANR 59, 89; DLB
155

Glissant, Edouard (Mathieu)
1928- .... **CLC 10, 68**
See also CA 153; CANR 111; CWW 2;
DAM MULT; EWL 3; RGWL 3

Gloag, Julian 1930- .... **CLC 40**
See also AITN 1; CA 65-68; CANR 10, 70;
CN 1, 2, 3, 4, 5, 6

Glowacki, Aleksander
See Prus, Boleslaw

Gluck, Louise 1943- .... **CLC 7, 22, 44, 81,
160; PC 16**
See also AMWS 5; CA 33-36R; CANR 40,
69, 108, 133; CP 1, 2, 3, 4, 5, 6, 7; CWP;
DA3; DAM POET; DLB 5; MAL 5;
MTCW 2; MTFW 2005; PFS 5, 15;
RGAL 4; TCLE 1:1

Glyn, Elinor 1864-1943 .... **TCLC 72**
See also DLB 153; RHW

Gobineau, Joseph-Arthur
1816-1882 .... **NCLC 17**
See also DLB 123; GFL 1789 to the Present

Godard, Jean-Luc 1930- .... **CLC 20**
See also CA 93-96

Godden, (Margaret) Rumer
1907-1998 .... **CLC 53**
See also AAYA 6; BPFB 2; BYA 2, 5; CA
5-8R; 172; CANR 4, 27, 36, 55, 80; CLR
20; CN 1, 2, 3, 4, 5, 6; CWRI 5; DLB
161; MAICYA 1, 2; RHW; SAAS 12;
SATA 3, 36; SATA-Obit 109; TEA

Godoy Alcayaga, Lucila 1899-1957 .. **HLC 2;
PC 32; TCLC 2**
See Mistral, Gabriela
See also BW 2; CA 104; 131; CANR 81;
DAM MULT; DNFS; HW 1, 2; MTCW 1,
2; MTFW 2005

Godwin, Gail 1937- ...... **CLC 5, 8, 22, 31, 69,
125**
See also BPFB 2; CA 29-32R; CANR 15,
43, 69, 132; CN 3, 4, 5, 6, 7; CPW; CSW;
DA3; DAM POP; DLB 6, 234; INT
CANR-15; MAL 5; MTCW 1, 2; MTFW
2005

Godwin, Gail Kathleen
See Godwin, Gail

Godwin, William 1756-1836 .. **NCLC 14, 130**
See also CDBLB 1789-1832; CMW 4; DLB
39, 104, 142, 158, 163, 262; GL 2; HGG;
RGEL 2

Goebbels, Josef
See Goebbels, (Paul) Joseph

Goebbels, (Paul) Joseph
1897-1945 .... **TCLC 68**
See also CA 115; 148

Goebbels, Joseph Paul
See Goebbels, (Paul) Joseph

Goethe, Johann Wolfgang von
1749-1832 . **DC 20; NCLC 4, 22, 34, 90,
154; PC 5; SSC 38; WLC 3**
See also CDWLB 2; DA; DA3; DAB;
DAC; DAM DRAM, MST, POET; DLB
94; EW 5; GL 2; LATS 1; LMFS 1:1;
RGWL 2, 3; TWA

Gogarty, Oliver St. John
1878-1957 .... **TCLC 15**
See also CA 109; 150; DLB 15, 19; RGEL
2

Gogol, Nikolai (Vasilyevich)
1809-1852 .... **DC 1; NCLC 5, 15, 31,
162; SSC 4, 29, 52; WLC 3**
See also DA; DAB; DAC; DAM DRAM,
MST; DFS 12; DLB 198; EW 6; EXPS;
RGSF 2; RGWL 2, 3; SSFS 7; TWA

Goines, Donald 1937(?)-1974 ... **BLC 2; CLC
80**
See also AITN 1; BW 1, 3; CA 124; 114;
CANR 82; CMW 4; DA3; DAM MULT,
POP; DLB 33

Gold, Herbert 1924- ... **CLC 4, 7, 14, 42, 152**
See also CA 9-12R; CANR 17, 45, 125; CN
1, 2, 3, 4, 5, 6, 7; DLB 2; DLBY 1981;
MAL 5

Goldbarth, Albert 1948- .... **CLC 5, 38**
See also AMWS 12; CA 53-56; CANR 6,
40; CP 3, 4, 5, 6, 7; DLB 120

Goldberg, Anatol 1910-1982 .... **CLC 34**
See also CA 131; 117

Goldemberg, Isaac 1945- .... **CLC 52**
See also CA 69-72; CAAS 12; CANR 11,
32; EWL 3; HW 1; WLIT 1

Golding, Arthur 1536-1606 .... **LC 101**
See also DLB 136

Golding, William 1911-1993 . **CLC 1, 2, 3, 8,
10, 17, 27, 58, 81; WLC 3**
See also AAYA 5, 44; BPFB 2; BRWR 1;
BRWS 1; BYA 2; CA 5-8R; 141; CANR
13, 33, 54; CD 5; CDBLB 1945-1960;
CLR 94; CN 1, 2, 3, 4; DA; DA3; DAB;
DAC; DAM MST, NOV; DLB 15, 100,
255, 326, 330; EWL 3; EXPN; HGG;
LAIT 4; MTCW 1, 2; MTFW 2005; NFS
2; RGEL 2; RHW; SFW 4; TEA; WLIT
4; YAW

Goldman, Emma 1869-1940 .... **TCLC 13**
See also CA 110; 150; DLB 221; FW;
RGAL 4; TUS

Goldman, Francisco 1954- .... **CLC 76**
See also CA 162

Goldman, William 1931- .... **CLC 1, 48**
See also BPFB 2; CA 9-12R; CANR 29,
69, 106; CN 1, 2, 3, 4, 5, 6, 7; DLB 44;
FANT; IDFW 3, 4

Goldman, William W.
See Goldman, William

Goldmann, Lucien 1913-1970 .... **CLC 24**
See also CA 25-28; CAP 2

Goldoni, Carlo 1707-1793 .... **LC 4**
See also DAM DRAM; EW 4; RGWL 2, 3;
WLIT 7

Goldsberry, Steven 1949- .... **CLC 34**
See also CA 131

Goldsmith, Oliver 1730-1774 .... **DC 8; LC 2,
48, 122; WLC 3**
See also BRW 3; CDBLB 1660-1789; DA;
DAB; DAC; DAM DRAM, MST, NOV,
POET; DFS 1; DLB 39, 89, 104, 109, 142;
IDTP; RGEL 2; SATA 26; TEA; WLIT 3

Goldsmith, Peter
See Priestley, J(ohn) B(oynton)

Gombrowicz, Witold 1904-1969 .... **CLC 4, 7,
11, 49**
See also CA 19-20; 25-28R; CANR 105;
CAP 2; CDWLB 4; DAM DRAM; DLB
215; EW 12; EWL 3; RGWL 2, 3; TWA

Gomez de Avellaneda, Gertrudis
1814-1873 .... **NCLC 111**
See also LAW

Gomez de la Serna, Ramon
1888-1963 .... **CLC 9**
See also CA 153; 116; CANR 79; EWL 3;
HW 1, 2

Goncharov, Ivan Alexandrovich
1812-1891 .... **NCLC 1, 63**
See also DLB 238; EW 6; RGWL 2, 3

Goncourt, Edmond (Louis Antoine Huot) de
1822-1896 .... **NCLC 7**
See also DLB 123; EW 7; GFL 1789 to the
Present; RGWL 2, 3

Goncourt, Jules (Alfred Huot) de
1830-1870 .... **NCLC 7**
See also DLB 123; EW 7; GFL 1789 to the
Present; RGWL 2, 3

Gongora (y Argote), Luis de
1561-1627 .... **LC 72**
See also RGWL 2, 3

Gontier, Fernande 19(?)- .... **CLC 50**

Gonzalez Martinez, Enrique
See Gonzalez Martinez, Enrique
See also DLB 290

Gonzalez Martinez, Enrique
1871-1952 .... **TCLC 72**
See Gonzalez Martinez, Enrique
See also CA 166; CANR 81; EWL 3; HW
1, 2

Goodison, Lorna 1947- .... **PC 36**
See also CA 142; CANR 88; CP 5, 6, 7;
CWP; DLB 157; EWL 3

Goodman, Paul 1911-1972 ..... **CLC 1, 2, 4, 7**
See also CA 19-20; 37-40R; CAD; CANR
34; CAP 2; CN 1; DLB 130, 246; MAL
5; MTCW 1; RGAL 4

GoodWeather, Harley
See King, Thomas

Googe, Barnabe 1540-1594 .... **LC 94**
See also DLB 132; RGEL 2

Gordimer, Nadine 1923- ...... **CLC 3, 5, 7, 10,
18, 33, 51, 70, 123, 160, 161; SSC 17,
80; WLCS**
See also AAYA 39; AFW; BRWS 2; CA
5-8R; CANR 3, 28, 56, 88, 131; CN 1, 2,
3, 4, 5, 6, 7; DA; DA3; DAB; DAC; DAM
MST, NOV; DLB 225, 326, 330; EWL 3;
EXPS; INT CANR-28; LATS 1:2; MTCW
1, 2; MTFW 2005; NFS 4; RGEL 2;
RGSF 2; SSFS 2, 14, 19; TWA; WLIT 2;
YAW

Gordon, Adam Lindsay
1833-1870 .... **NCLC 21**
See also DLB 230

Gordon, Caroline 1895-1981 . **CLC 6, 13, 29,
83; SSC 15**
See also AMW; CA 11-12; 103; CANR 36;
CAP 1; CN 1, 2; DLB 4, 9, 102; DLBD
17; DLBY 1981; EWL 3; MAL 5; MTCW
1, 2; MTFW 2005; RGAL 4; RGSF 2

Gordon, Charles William 1860-1937
See Connor, Ralph
See also CA 109

Hobson, Laura Z(ametkin)
1900-1986 .... **CLC 7, 25**
See also BPFB 2; CA 17-20R; 118; CANR
55; CN 1, 2, 3, 4; DLB 28; SATA 52

Hoccleve, Thomas c. 1368-c. 1437 ...... **LC 75**
See also DLB 146; RGEL 2

Hoch, Edward D(entinger) 1930-
See Queen, Ellery
See also CA 29-32R; CANR 11, 27, 51, 97;
CMW 4; DLB 306; SFW 4

Hochhuth, Rolf 1931- .... **CLC 4, 11, 18**
See also CA 5-8R; CANR 33, 75, 136;
CWW 2; DAM DRAM; DLB 124; EWL
3; MTCW 1, 2; MTFW 2005; RGHL

Hochman, Sandra 1936- .... **CLC 3, 8**
See also CA 5-8R; CP 1, 2, 3, 4, 5; DLB 5

Hochwaelder, Fritz 1911-1986 .... **CLC 36**
See Hochwalder, Fritz
See also CA 29-32R; 120; CANR 42; DAM
DRAM; MTCW 1; RGWL 3

Hochwalder, Fritz
See Hochwaelder, Fritz
See also EWL 3; RGWL 2

Hocking, Mary (Eunice) 1921- .... **CLC 13**
See also CA 101; CANR 18, 40

Hodgins, Jack 1938- .... **CLC 23**
See also CA 93-96; CN 4, 5, 6, 7; DLB 60

Hodgson, William Hope
1877(?)-1918 .... **TCLC 13**
See also CA 111; 164; CMW 4; DLB 70,
153, 156, 178; HGG; MTCW 2; SFW 4;
SUFW 1

Hoeg, Peter 1957- .... **CLC 95, 156**
See also CA 151; CANR 75; CMW 4; DA3;
DLB 214; EWL 3; MTCW 2; MTFW
2005; NFS 17; RGWL 3; SSFS 18

Hoffman, Alice 1952- .... **CLC 51**
See also AAYA 37; AMWS 10; CA 77-80;
CANR 34, 66, 100, 138; CN 4, 5, 6, 7;
CPW; DAM NOV; DLB 292; MAL 5;
MTCW 1, 2; MTFW 2005; TCLE 1:1

Hoffman, Daniel (Gerard) 1923- . **CLC 6, 13,
23**
See also CA 1-4R; CANR 4, 142; CP 1, 2,
3, 4, 5, 6, 7; DLB 5; TCLE 1:1

Hoffman, Eva 1945- .... **CLC 182**
See also AMWS 16; CA 132; CANR 146

Hoffman, Stanley 1944- .... **CLC 5**
See also CA 77-80

Hoffman, William 1925- .... **CLC 141**
See also CA 21-24R; CANR 9, 103; CSW;
DLB 234; TCLE 1:1

Hoffman, William M.
See Hoffman, William M(oses)
See also CAD; CD 5, 6

Hoffman, William M(oses) 1939- ..... **CLC 40**
See Hoffman, William M.
See also CA 57-60; CANR 11, 71

Hoffmann, E(rnst) T(heodor) A(madeus)
1776-1822 .... **NCLC 2; SSC 13, 92**
See also CDWLB 2; DLB 90; EW 5; GL 2;
RGSF 2; RGWL 2, 3; SATA 27; SUFW
1; WCH

Hofmann, Gert 1931-1993 .... **CLC 54**
See also CA 128; CANR 145; EWL 3;
RGHL

Hofmannsthal, Hugo von 1874-1929 ... **DC 4;
TCLC 11**
See also CA 106; 153; CDWLB 2; DAM
DRAM; DFS 17; DLB 81, 118; EW 9;
EWL 3; RGWL 2, 3

Hogan, Linda 1947- ..... **CLC 73; NNAL; PC
35**
See also AMWS 4; ANW; BYA 12; CA 120,
226; CAAE 226; CANR 45, 73, 129;
CWP; DAM MULT; DLB 175; SATA
132; TCWW 2

Hogarth, Charles
See Creasey, John

Hogarth, Emmett
See Polonsky, Abraham (Lincoln)

Hogarth, William 1697-1764 .... **LC 112**
See also AAYA 56

Hogg, James 1770-1835 .... **NCLC 4, 109**
See also BRWS 10; DLB 93, 116, 159; GL
2; HGG; RGEL 2; SUFW 1

Holbach, Paul-Henri Thiry
1723-1789 .... **LC 14**
See also DLB 313

Holberg, Ludvig 1684-1754 .... **LC 6**
See also DLB 300; RGWL 2, 3

Holcroft, Thomas 1745-1809 .... **NCLC 85**
See also DLB 39, 89, 158; RGEL 2

Holden, Ursula 1921- .... **CLC 18**
See also CA 101; CAAS 8; CANR 22

Holderlin, (Johann Christian) Friedrich
1770-1843 .... **NCLC 16; PC 4**
See also CDWLB 2; DLB 90; EW 5; RGWL
2, 3

Holdstock, Robert
See Holdstock, Robert P.

Holdstock, Robert P. 1948- .... **CLC 39**
See also CA 131; CANR 81; DLB 261;
FANT; HGG; SFW 4; SUFW 1

Holinshed, Raphael fl. 1580- .... **LC 69**
See also DLB 167; RGEL 2

Holland, Isabelle (Christian)
1920-2002 .... **CLC 21**
See also AAYA 11, 64; CA 21-24R; 205;
CAAE 181; CANR 10, 25, 47; CLR 57;
CWRI 5; JRDA; LAIT 4; MAICYA 1, 2;
SATA 8, 70; SATA-Essay 103; SATA-Obit
132; WYA

Holland, Marcus
See Caldwell, (Janet Miriam) Taylor
(Holland)

Hollander, John 1929- .... **CLC 2, 5, 8, 14**
See also CA 1-4R; CANR 1, 52, 136; CP 1,
2, 3, 4, 5, 6, 7; DLB 5; MAL 5; SATA 13

Hollander, Paul
See Silverberg, Robert

Holleran, Andrew .... **CLC 38**
See Garber, Eric
See also CA 144; GLL 1

Holley, Marietta 1836(?)-1926 .... **TCLC 99**
See also CA 118; DLB 11; FL 1:3

Hollinghurst, Alan 1954- .... **CLC 55, 91**
See also BRWS 10; CA 114; CN 5, 6, 7;
DLB 207, 326; GLL 1

Hollis, Jim
See Summers, Hollis (Spurgeon, Jr.)

Holly, Buddy 1936-1959 .... **TCLC 65**
See also CA 213

Holmes, Gordon
See Shiel, M(atthew) P(hipps)

Holmes, John
See Souster, (Holmes) Raymond

Holmes, John Clellon 1926-1988 ...... **CLC 56**
See also BG 1:2; CA 9-12R; 125; CANR 4;
CN 1, 2, 3, 4; DLB 16, 237

Holmes, Oliver Wendell, Jr.
1841-1935 .... **TCLC 77**
See also CA 114; 186

Holmes, Oliver Wendell
1809-1894 .... **NCLC 14, 81; PC 71**
See also AMWS 1; CDALB 1640-1865;
DLB 1, 189, 235; EXPP; PFS 24; RGAL
4; SATA 34

Holmes, Raymond
See Souster, (Holmes) Raymond

Holt, Victoria
See Hibbert, Eleanor Alice Burford
See also BPFB 2

Holub, Miroslav 1923-1998 .... **CLC 4**
See also CA 21-24R; 169; CANR 10; CD-
WLB 4; CWW 2; DLB 232; EWL 3;
RGWL 3

Holz, Detlev
See Benjamin, Walter

Homer c. 8th cent. B.C.- .... **CMLC 1, 16, 61;
PC 23; WLCS**
See also AW 1; CDWLB 1; DA; DA3;
DAB; DAC; DAM MST, POET; DLB
176; EFS 1; LAIT 1; LMFS 1; RGWL 2,
3; TWA; WLIT 8; WP

Hongo, Garrett Kaoru 1951- .... **PC 23**
See also CA 133; CAAS 22; CP 5, 6, 7;
DLB 120, 312; EWL 3; EXPP; RGAL 4

Honig, Edwin 1919- .... **CLC 33**
See also CA 5-8R; CAAS 8; CANR 4, 45,
144; CP 1, 2, 3, 4, 5, 6, 7; DLB 5

Hood, Hugh (John Blagdon) 1928- . **CLC 15,
28; SSC 42**
See also CA 49-52; CAAS 17; CANR 1,
33, 87; CN 1, 2, 3, 4, 5, 6, 7; DLB 53;
RGSF 2

Hood, Thomas 1799-1845 .... **NCLC 16**
See also BRW 4; DLB 96; RGEL 2

Hooker, (Peter) Jeremy 1941- .... **CLC 43**
See also CA 77-80; CANR 22; CP 2, 3, 4,
5, 6, 7; DLB 40

Hooker, Richard 1554-1600 .... **LC 95**
See also BRW 1; DLB 132; RGEL 2

hooks, bell 1952(?)- .... **CLC 94**
See also BW 2; CA 143; CANR 87, 126;
DLB 246; MTCW 2; MTFW 2005; SATA
115, 170

Hope, A(lec) D(erwent) 1907-2000 .... **CLC 3,
51; PC 56**
See also BRWS 7; CA 21-24R; 188; CANR
33, 74; CP 1, 2, 3, 4, 5; DLB 289; EWL
3; MTCW 1, 2; MTFW 2005; PFS 8;
RGEL 2

Hope, Anthony 1863-1933 .... **TCLC 83**
See also CA 157; DLB 153, 156; RGEL 2;
RHW

Hope, Brian
See Creasey, John

Hope, Christopher (David Tully)
1944- .... **CLC 52**
See also AFW; CA 106; CANR 47, 101;
CN 4, 5, 6, 7; DLB 225; SATA 62

Hopkins, Gerard Manley
1844-1889 .... **NCLC 17; PC 15; WLC 3**
See also BRW 5; BRWR 2; CDBLB 1890-
1914; DA; DA3; DAB; DAC; DAM MST,
POET; DLB 35, 57; EXPP; PAB; RGEL
2; TEA; WP

Hopkins, John (Richard) 1931-1998 .. **CLC 4**
See also CA 85-88; 169; CBD; CD 5, 6

Hopkins, Pauline Elizabeth
1859-1930 .... **BLC 2; TCLC 28**
See also AFAW 2; BW 2, 3; CA 141; CANR
82; DAM MULT; DLB 50

Hopkinson, Francis 1737-1791 .... **LC 25**
See also DLB 31; RGAL 4

Hopley-Woolrich, Cornell George 1903-1968
See Woolrich, Cornell
See also CA 13-14; CANR 58, 156; CAP 1;
CMW 4; DLB 226; MTCW 2

Horace 65B.C.-8B.C. .... **CMLC 39; PC 46**
See also AW 2; CDWLB 1; DLB 211;
RGWL 2, 3; WLIT 8

Horatio
See Proust, (Valentin-Louis-George-Eugene)
Marcel

Horgan, Paul (George Vincent
O'Shaughnessy) 1903-1995 .. **CLC 9, 53**
See also BPFB 2; CA 13-16R; 147; CANR
9, 35; CN 1, 2, 3, 4, 5; DAM NOV; DLB
102, 212; DLBY 1985; INT CANR-9;
MTCW 1, 2; MTFW 2005; SATA 13;
SATA-Obit 84; TCWW 1, 2

Horkheimer, Max 1895-1973 .... **TCLC 132**
See also CA 216; 41-44R; DLB 296

Horn, Peter
See Kuttner, Henry

Horne, Frank (Smith) 1899-1974 ...... **HR 1:2**
See also BW 1; CA 125; 53-56; DLB 51;
WP

Horne, Richard Henry Hengist
1802(?)-1884 .... **NCLC 127**
See also DLB 32; SATA 29

Hornem, Horace Esq.
See Byron, George Gordon (Noel)

Horney, Karen (Clementine Theodore
Danielsen) 1885-1952 .... **TCLC 71**
See also CA 114; 165; DLB 246; FW

Hornung, E(rnest) W(illiam)
1866-1921 .... **TCLC 59**
See also CA 108; 160; CMW 4; DLB 70

Horovitz, Israel (Arthur) 1939- .... **CLC 56**
See also CA 33-36R; CAD; CANR 46, 59;
CD 5, 6; DAM DRAM; DLB 7; MAL 5

Horton, George Moses
1797(?)-1883(?) .... **NCLC 87**
See also DLB 50

Horvath, odon von 1901-1938
See von Horvath, Odon
See also EWL 3

Horvath, Oedoen von -1938
See von Horvath, Odon

Horwitz, Julius 1920-1986 .... **CLC 14**
See also CA 9-12R; 119; CANR 12

Horwitz, Ronald
See Harwood, Ronald

Hospital, Janette Turner 1942- .... **CLC 42,
145**
See also CA 108; CANR 48; CN 5, 6, 7;
DLB 325; DLBY 2002; RGSF 2

Hostos, E. M. de
See Hostos (y Bonilla), Eugenio Maria de

Hostos, Eugenio M. de
See Hostos (y Bonilla), Eugenio Maria de

Hostos, Eugenio Maria
See Hostos (y Bonilla), Eugenio Maria de

Hostos (y Bonilla), Eugenio Maria de
1839-1903 .... **TCLC 24**
See also CA 123; 131; HW 1

Houdini
See Lovecraft, H. P.

Houellebecq, Michel 1958- .... **CLC 179**
See also CA 185; CANR 140; MTFW 2005

Hougan, Carolyn 1943- .... **CLC 34**
See also CA 139

Household, Geoffrey (Edward West)
1900-1988 .... **CLC 11**
See also CA 77-80; 126; CANR 58; CMW
4; CN 1, 2, 3, 4; DLB 87; SATA 14;
SATA-Obit 59

Housman, A(lfred) E(dward)
1859-1936 .... **PC 2, 43; TCLC 1, 10;
WLCS**
See also AAYA 66; BRW 6; CA 104; 125;
DA; DA3; DAB; DAC; DAM MST,
POET; DLB 19, 284; EWL 3; EXPP;
MTCW 1, 2; MTFW 2005; PAB; PFS 4,
7; RGEL 2; TEA; WP

Housman, Laurence 1865-1959 .... **TCLC 7**
See also CA 106; 155; DLB 10; FANT;
RGEL 2; SATA 25

Houston, Jeanne Wakatsuki 1934- .... **AAL**
See also AAYA 49; CA 103, 232; CAAE
232; CAAS 16; CANR 29, 123; LAIT 4;
SATA 78, 168; SATA-Essay 168

Howard, Elizabeth Jane 1923- ..... **CLC 7, 29**
See also BRWS 11; CA 5-8R; CANR 8, 62,
146; CN 1, 2, 3, 4, 5, 6, 7

Howard, Maureen 1930- .... **CLC 5, 14, 46,
151**
See also CA 53-56; CANR 31, 75, 140; CN
4, 5, 6, 7; DLBY 1983; INT CANR-31;
MTCW 1, 2; MTFW 2005

Howard, Richard 1929- .... **CLC 7, 10, 47**
See also AITN 1; CA 85-88; CANR 25, 80,
154; CP 1, 2, 3, 4, 5, 6, 7; DLB 5; INT
CANR-25; MAL 5

Howard, Robert E 1906-1936 .... **TCLC 8**
See also BPFB 2; BYA 5; CA 105; 157;
CANR 155; FANT; SUFW 1; TCWW 1,
2

Howard, Robert Ervin
See Howard, Robert E

Howard, Warren F.
See Pohl, Frederik

Howe, Fanny (Quincy) 1940- .... **CLC 47**
See also CA 117, 187; CAAE 187; CAAS
27; CANR 70, 116; CP 6, 7; CWP; SATA-
Brief 52

Howe, Irving 1920-1993 .... **CLC 85**
See also AMWS 6; CA 9-12R; 141; CANR
21, 50; DLB 67; EWL 3; MAL 5; MTCW
1, 2; MTFW 2005

Howe, Julia Ward 1819-1910 .... **TCLC 21**
See also CA 117; 191; DLB 1, 189, 235;
FW

Howe, Susan 1937- .... **CLC 72, 152; PC 54**
See also AMWS 4; CA 160; CP 5, 6, 7;
CWP; DLB 120; FW; RGAL 4

Howe, Tina 1937- .... **CLC 48**
See also CA 109; CAD; CANR 125; CD 5,
6; CWD

Howell, James 1594(?)-1666 .... **LC 13**
See also DLB 151

Howells, W. D.
See Howells, William Dean

Howells, William D.
See Howells, William Dean

Howells, William Dean 1837-1920 ... **SSC 36;
TCLC 7, 17, 41**
See also AMW; CA 104; 134; CDALB
1865-1917; DLB 12, 64, 74, 79, 189;
LMFS 1; MAL 5; MTCW 2; RGAL 4;
TUS

Howes, Barbara 1914-1996 .... **CLC 15**
See also CA 9-12R; 151; CAAS 3; CANR
53; CP 1, 2, 3, 4, 5, 6; SATA 5; TCLE 1:1

Hrabal, Bohumil 1914-1997 ...... **CLC 13, 67;
TCLC 155**
See also CA 106; 156; CAAS 12; CANR
57; CWW 2; DLB 232; EWL 3; RGSF 2

Hrabanus Maurus 776(?)-856 .... **CMLC 78**
See also DLB 148

Hrotsvit of Gandersheim c. 935-c.
1000 .... **CMLC 29**
See also DLB 148

Hsi, Chu 1130-1200 .... **CMLC 42**

Hsun, Lu
See Lu Hsun

Hubbard, L. Ron 1911-1986 .... **CLC 43**
See also AAYA 64; CA 77-80; 118; CANR
52; CPW; DA3; DAM POP; FANT;
MTCW 2; MTFW 2005; SFW 4

Hubbard, Lafayette Ronald
See Hubbard, L. Ron

Huch, Ricarda (Octavia)
1864-1947 .... **TCLC 13**
See also CA 111; 189; DLB 66; EWL 3

Huddle, David 1942- .... **CLC 49**
See also CA 57-60; CAAS 20; CANR 89;
DLB 130

Hudson, Jeffrey
See Crichton, Michael

Hudson, W(illiam) H(enry)
1841-1922 .... **TCLC 29**
See also CA 115; 190; DLB 98, 153, 174;
RGEL 2; SATA 35

Hueffer, Ford Madox
See Ford, Ford Madox

Hughart, Barry 1934- .... **CLC 39**
See also CA 137; FANT; SFW 4; SUFW 2

Hughes, Colin
See Creasey, John

Hughes, David (John) 1930-2005 ..... **CLC 48**
See also CA 116; 129; 238; CN 4, 5, 6, 7;
DLB 14

Hughes, Edward James
See Hughes, Ted
See also DA3; DAM MST, POET

Hughes, (James Mercer) Langston
1902-1967 ..... **BLC 2; CLC 1, 5, 10, 15,
35, 44, 108; DC 3; HR 1:2; PC 1, 53;
SSC 6, 90; WLC 3**
See also AAYA 12; AFAW 1, 2; AMWR 1;
AMWS 1; BW 1, 3; CA 1-4R; 25-28R;
CANR 1, 34, 82; CDALB 1929-1941;
CLR 17; DA; DA3; DAB; DAC; DAM
DRAM, MST, MULT, POET; DFS 6, 18;
DLB 4, 7, 48, 51, 86, 228, 315; EWL 3;
EXPP; EXPS; JRDA; LAIT 3; LMFS 2;
MAICYA 1, 2; MAL 5; MTCW 1, 2;
MTFW 2005; NFS 21; PAB; PFS 1, 3, 6,
10, 15; RGAL 4; RGSF 2; SATA 4, 33;
SSFS 4, 7; TUS; WCH; WP; YAW

Hughes, Richard (Arthur Warren)
1900-1976 .... **CLC 1, 11**
See also CA 5-8R; 65-68; CANR 4; CN 1,
2; DAM NOV; DLB 15, 161; EWL 3;
MTCW 1; RGEL 2; SATA 8; SATA-Obit
25

Hughes, Ted 1930-1998 . **CLC 2, 4, 9, 14, 37,
119; PC 7**
See Hughes, Edward James
See also BRWC 2; BRWR 2; BRWS 1; CA
1-4R; 171; CANR 1, 33, 66, 108; CLR 3;
CP 1, 2, 3, 4, 5, 6; DAB; DAC; DLB 40,
161; EWL 3; EXPP; MAICYA 1, 2;
MTCW 1, 2; MTFW 2005; PAB; PFS 4,
19; RGEL 2; SATA 49; SATA-Brief 27;
SATA-Obit 107; TEA; YAW

Hugo, Richard
See Huch, Ricarda (Octavia)

Hugo, Richard F(ranklin)
1923-1982 .... **CLC 6, 18, 32; PC 68**
See also AMWS 6; CA 49-52; 108; CANR
3; CP 1, 2, 3; DAM POET; DLB 5, 206;
EWL 3; MAL 5; PFS 17; RGAL 4

Hugo, Victor (Marie) 1802-1885 .... **NCLC 3,
10, 21, 161; PC 17; WLC 3**
See also AAYA 28; DA; DA3; DAB; DAC;
DAM DRAM, MST, NOV, POET; DLB
119, 192, 217; EFS 2; EW 6; EXPN; GFL
1789 to the Present; LAIT 1, 2; NFS 5,
20; RGWL 2, 3; SATA 47; TWA

Huidobro, Vicente
See Huidobro Fernandez, Vicente Garcia
See also DLB 283; EWL 3; LAW

Huidobro Fernandez, Vicente Garcia
1893-1948 .... **TCLC 31**
See Huidobro, Vicente
See also CA 131; HW 1

Hulme, Keri 1947- .... **CLC 39, 130**
See also CA 125; CANR 69; CN 4, 5, 6, 7;
CP 6, 7; CWP; DLB 326; EWL 3; FW;
INT CA-125; NFS 24

Hulme, T(homas) E(rnest)
1883-1917 .... **TCLC 21**
See also BRWS 6; CA 117; 203; DLB 19

Humboldt, Alexander von
1769-1859 .... **NCLC 170**
See also DLB 90

Humboldt, Wilhelm von
1767-1835 .... **NCLC 134**
See also DLB 90

Hume, David 1711-1776 .... **LC 7, 56**
See also BRWS 3; DLB 104, 252; LMFS 1;
TEA

Humphrey, William 1924-1997 .... **CLC 45**
See also AMWS 9; CA 77-80; 160; CANR
68; CN 1, 2, 3, 4, 5, 6; CSW; DLB 6, 212,
234, 278; TCWW 1, 2

Humphreys, Emyr Owen 1919- .... **CLC 47**
    See also CA 5-8R; CANR 3, 24; CN 1, 2,
    3, 4, 5, 6, 7; DLB 15
Humphreys, Josephine 1945- ..... **CLC 34, 57**
    See also CA 121; 127; CANR 97; CSW;
    DLB 292; INT CA-127
Huneker, James Gibbons
    1860-1921 .... **TCLC 65**
    See also CA 193; DLB 71; RGAL 4
Hungerford, Hesba Fay
    See Brinsmead, H(esba) F(ay)
Hungerford, Pixie
    See Brinsmead, H(esba) F(ay)
Hunt, E(verette) Howard, (Jr.)
    1918- .... **CLC 3**
    See also AITN 1; CA 45-48; CANR 2, 47,
    103; CMW 4
Hunt, Francesca
    See Holland, Isabelle (Christian)
Hunt, Howard
    See Hunt, E(verette) Howard, (Jr.)
Hunt, Kyle
    See Creasey, John
Hunt, (James Henry) Leigh
    1784-1859 .... **NCLC 1, 70; PC 73**
    See also DAM POET; DLB 96, 110, 144;
    RGEL 2; TEA
Hunt, Marsha 1946- .... **CLC 70**
    See also BW 2, 3; CA 143; CANR 79
Hunt, Violet 1866(?)-1942 .... **TCLC 53**
    See also CA 184; DLB 162, 197
Hunter, E. Waldo
    See Sturgeon, Theodore (Hamilton)
Hunter, Evan 1926-2005 .... **CLC 11, 31**
    See McBain, Ed
    See also AAYA 39; BPFB 2; CA 5-8R; 241;
    CANR 5, 38, 62, 97, 149; CMW 4; CN 1,
    2, 3, 4, 5, 6, 7; CPW; DAM POP; DLB
    306; DLBY 1982; INT CANR-5; MSW;
    MTCW 1; SATA 25; SATA-Obit 167;
    SFW 4
Hunter, Kristin
    See Lattany, Kristin (Elaine Eggleston)
    Hunter
    See also CN 1, 2, 3, 4, 5, 6
Hunter, Mary
    See Austin, Mary (Hunter)
Hunter, Mollie 1922- .... **CLC 21**
    See McIlwraith, Maureen Mollie Hunter
    See also AAYA 13, 71; BYA 6; CANR 37,
    78; CLR 25; DLB 161; JRDA; MAICYA
    1, 2; SAAS 7; SATA 54, 106, 139; SATA-
    Essay 139; WYA; YAW
Hunter, Robert (?)-1734 .... **LC 7**
Hurston, Zora Neale 1891-1960 .... **BLC 2;**
    CLC 7, 30, 61; DC 12; HR 1:2; SSC 4,
    80; TCLC 121, 131; WLCS
    See also AAYA 15, 71; AFAW 1, 2; AMWS
    6; BW 1, 3; BYA 12; CA 85-88; CANR
    61; CDALBS; DA; DA3; DAC; DAM
    MST, MULT, NOV; DFS 6; DLB 51, 86;
    EWL 3; EXPN; EXPS; FL 1:6; FW; LAIT
    3; LATS 1:1; LMFS 2; MAL 5; MBL;
    MTCW 1, 2; MTFW 2005; NFS 3; RGAL
    4; RGSF 2; SSFS 1, 6, 11, 19, 21; TUS;
    YAW
Husserl, E. G.
    See Husserl, Edmund (Gustav Albrecht)
Husserl, Edmund (Gustav Albrecht)
    1859-1938 .... **TCLC 100**
    See also CA 116; 133; DLB 296
Huston, John (Marcellus)
    1906-1987 .... **CLC 20**
    See also CA 73-76; 123; CANR 34; DLB
    26
Hustvedt, Siri 1955- .... **CLC 76**
    See also CA 137; CANR 149
Hutten, Ulrich von 1488-1523 .... **LC 16**
    See also DLB 179

Huxley, Aldous (Leonard)
    1894-1963 .... **CLC 1, 3, 4, 5, 8, 11, 18,**
    35, 79; SSC 39; WLC 3
    See also AAYA 11; BPFB 2; BRW 7; CA
    85-88; CANR 44, 99; CDBLB 1914-1945;
    DA; DA3; DAB; DAC; DAM MST, NOV;
    DLB 36, 100, 162, 195, 255; EWL 3;
    EXPN; LAIT 5; LMFS 2; MTCW 1, 2;
    MTFW 2005; NFS 6; RGEL 2; SATA 63;
    SCFW 1, 2; SFW 4; TEA; YAW
Huxley, T(homas) H(enry)
    1825-1895 .... **NCLC 67**
    See also DLB 57; TEA
Huygens, Constantijn 1596-1687 .... **LC 114**
    See also RGWL 2, 3
Huysmans, Joris-Karl 1848-1907 ... **TCLC 7,**
    69
    See also CA 104; 165; DLB 123; EW 7;
    GFL 1789 to the Present; LMFS 2; RGWL
    2, 3
Hwang, David Henry 1957- .... **CLC 55, 196;**
    DC 4, 23
    See also CA 127; 132; CAD; CANR 76,
    124; CD 5, 6; DA3; DAM DRAM; DFS
    11, 18; DLB 212, 228, 312; INT CA-132;
    MAL 5; MTCW 2; MTFW 2005; RGAL
    4
Hyde, Anthony 1946- .... **CLC 42**
    See Chase, Nicholas
    See also CA 136; CCA 1
Hyde, Margaret O(ldroyd) 1917- ..... **CLC 21**
    See also CA 1-4R; CANR 1, 36, 137; CLR
    23; JRDA; MAICYA 1, 2; SAAS 8; SATA
    1, 42, 76, 139
Hynes, James 1956(?)- .... **CLC 65**
    See also CA 164; CANR 105
Hypatia c. 370-415 .... **CMLC 35**
Ian, Janis 1951- .... **CLC 21**
    See also CA 105; 187
Ibanez, Vicente Blasco
    See Blasco Ibanez, Vicente
    See also DLB 322
Ibarbourou, Juana de
    1895(?)-1979 .... **HLCS 2**
    See also DLB 290; HW 1; LAW
Ibarguengoitia, Jorge 1928-1983 ..... **CLC 37;**
    TCLC 148
    See also CA 124; 113; EWL 3; HW 1
Ibn Battuta, Abu Abdalla
    1304-1368(?) .... **CMLC 57**
    See also WLIT 2
Ibn Hazm 994-1064 .... **CMLC 64**
Ibsen, Henrik (Johan) 1828-1906 .... **DC 2;**
    TCLC 2, 8, 16, 37, 52; WLC 3
    See also AAYA 46; CA 104; 141; DA; DA3;
    DAB; DAC; DAM DRAM, MST; DFS 1,
    6, 8, 10, 11, 15, 16; EW 7; LAIT 2; LATS
    1:1; MTFW 2005; RGWL 2, 3
Ibuse, Masuji 1898-1993 .... **CLC 22**
    See Ibuse Masuji
    See also CA 127; 141; MJW; RGWL 3
Ibuse Masuji
    See Ibuse, Masuji
    See also CWW 2; DLB 180; EWL 3
Ichikawa, Kon 1915- .... **CLC 20**
    See also CA 121
Ichiyo, Higuchi 1872-1896 .... **NCLC 49**
    See also MJW
Idle, Eric 1943- .... **CLC 21**
    See Monty Python
    See also CA 116; CANR 35, 91, 148
Idris, Yusuf 1927-1991 .... **SSC 74**
    See also AFW; EWL 3; RGSF 2, 3; RGWL
    3; WLIT 2
Ignatow, David 1914-1997 .... **CLC 4, 7, 14,**
    40; PC 34
    See also CA 9-12R; 162; CAAS 3; CANR
    31, 57, 96; CP 1, 2, 3, 4, 5, 6; DLB 5;
    EWL 3; MAL 5

Ignotus
    See Strachey, (Giles) Lytton
Ihimaera, Witi (Tame) 1944- .... **CLC 46**
    See also CA 77-80; CANR 130; CN 2, 3, 4,
    5, 6, 7; RGSF 2; SATA 148
Ilf, Ilya .... **TCLC 21**
    See Fainzilberg, Ilya Arnoldovich
    See also EWL 3
Illyes, Gyula 1902-1983 .... **PC 16**
    See also CA 114; 109; CDWLB 4; DLB
    215; EWL 3; RGWL 2, 3
Imalayen, Fatima-Zohra
    See Djebar, Assia
Immermann, Karl (Lebrecht)
    1796-1840 .... **NCLC 4, 49**
    See also DLB 133
Ince, Thomas H. 1882-1924 .... **TCLC 89**
    See also IDFW 3, 4
Inchbald, Elizabeth 1753-1821 ...... **NCLC 62**
    See also DLB 39, 89; RGEL 2
Inclan, Ramon (Maria) del Valle
    See Valle-Inclan, Ramon (Maria) del
Infante, G(uillermo) Cabrera
    See Cabrera Infante, G.
Ingalls, Rachel 1940- .... **CLC 42**
    See also CA 123; 127; CANR 154
Ingalls, Rachel Holmes
    See Ingalls, Rachel
Ingamells, Reginald Charles
    See Ingamells, Rex
Ingamells, Rex 1913-1955 .... **TCLC 35**
    See also CA 167; DLB 260
Inge, William (Motter) 1913-1973 ..... **CLC 1,**
    8, 19
    See also CA 9-12R; CAD; CDALB 1941-
    1968; DA3; DAM DRAM; DFS 1, 3, 5,
    8; DLB 7, 249; EWL 3; MAL 5; MTCW
    1, 2; MTFW 2005; RGAL 4; TUS
Ingelow, Jean 1820-1897 .... **NCLC 39, 107**
    See also DLB 35, 163; FANT; SATA 33
Ingram, Willis J.
    See Harris, Mark
Innaurato, Albert (F.) 1948(?)- ... **CLC 21, 60**
    See also CA 115; 122; CAD; CANR 78;
    CD 5, 6; INT CA-122
Innes, Michael
    See Stewart, J(ohn) I(nnes) M(ackintosh)
    See also DLB 276; MSW
Innis, Harold Adams 1894-1952 .... **TCLC 77**
    See also CA 181; DLB 88
Insluis, Alanus de
    See Alain de Lille
Iola
    See Wells-Barnett, Ida B(ell)
Ionesco, Eugene 1912-1994 ... **CLC 1, 4, 6, 9,**
    11, 15, 41, 86; DC 12; WLC 3
    See also CA 9-12R; 144; CANR 55, 132;
    CWW 2; DA; DA3; DAB; DAC; DAM
    DRAM, MST; DFS 4, 9; DLB 321; EW
    13; EWL 3; GFL 1789 to the Present;
    LMFS 2; MTCW 1, 2; MTFW 2005;
    RGWL 2, 3; SATA 7; SATA-Obit 79;
    TWA
Iqbal, Muhammad 1877-1938 .... **TCLC 28**
    See also CA 215; EWL 3
Ireland, Patrick
    See O'Doherty, Brian
Irenaeus St. 130- .... **CMLC 42**
Irigaray, Luce 1930- .... **CLC 164**
    See also CA 154; CANR 121; FW
Iron, Ralph
    See Schreiner, Olive (Emilie Albertina)
Irving, John 1942- . **CLC 13, 23, 38, 112, 175**
    See also AAYA 8, 62; AMWS 6; BEST
    89:3; BPFB 2; CA 25-28R; CANR 28, 73,
    112, 133; CN 3, 4, 5, 6, 7; CPW; DA3;
    DAM NOV, POP; DLB 6, 278; DLBY
    1982; EWL 3; MAL 5; MTCW 1, 2;
    MTFW 2005; NFS 12, 14; RGAL 4; TUS

Jefferson, Janet
See Mencken, H(enry) L(ouis)

Jefferson, Thomas 1743-1826 . **NCLC 11, 103**
See also AAYA 54; ANW; CDALB 1640-1865; DA3; DLB 31, 183; LAIT 1; RGAL 4

Jeffrey, Francis 1773-1850 .... **NCLC 33**
See Francis, Lord Jeffrey

Jelakowitch, Ivan
See Heijermans, Herman

Jelinek, Elfriede 1946- .... **CLC 169**
See also AAYA 68; CA 154; DLB 85, 330; FW

Jellicoe, (Patricia) Ann 1927- .... **CLC 27**
See also CA 85-88; CBD; CD 5, 6; CWD; CWRI 5; DLB 13, 233; FW

Jelloun, Tahar ben 1944- .... **CLC 180**
See Ben Jelloun, Tahar
See also CA 162; CANR 100

Jemyma
See Holley, Marietta

Jen, Gish .... **AAL; CLC 70, 198**
See Jen, Lillian
See also AMWC 2; CN 7; DLB 312

Jen, Lillian 1955-
See Jen, Gish
See also CA 135; CANR 89, 130

Jenkins, (John) Robin 1912- .... **CLC 52**
See also CA 1-4R; CANR 1, 135; CN 1, 2, 3, 4, 5, 6, 7; DLB 14, 271

Jennings, Elizabeth (Joan)
1926-2001 .... **CLC 5, 14, 131**
See also BRWS 5; CA 61-64; 200; CAAS 5; CANR 8, 39, 66, 127; CP 1, 2, 3, 4, 5, 6, 7; CWP; DLB 27; EWL 3; MTCW 1; SATA 66

Jennings, Waylon 1937-2002 .... **CLC 21**

Jensen, Johannes V(ilhelm)
1873-1950 .... **TCLC 41**
See also CA 170; DLB 214, 330; EWL 3; RGWL 3

Jensen, Laura (Linnea) 1948- .... **CLC 37**
See also CA 103

Jerome, Saint 345-420 .... **CMLC 30**
See also RGWL 3

Jerome, Jerome K(lapka)
1859-1927 .... **TCLC 23**
See also CA 119; 177; DLB 10, 34, 135; RGEL 2

Jerrold, Douglas William
1803-1857 .... **NCLC 2**
See also DLB 158, 159; RGEL 2

Jewett, (Theodora) Sarah Orne
1849-1909 .... **SSC 6, 44; TCLC 1, 22**
See also AMW; AMWC 2; AMWR 2; CA 108; 127; CANR 71; DLB 12, 74, 221; EXPS; FL 1:3; FW; MAL 5; MBL; NFS 15; RGAL 4; RGSF 2; SATA 15; SSFS 4

Jewsbury, Geraldine (Endsor)
1812-1880 .... **NCLC 22**
See also DLB 21

Jhabvala, Ruth Prawer 1927- . **CLC 4, 8, 29, 94, 138; SSC 91**
See also BRWS 5; CA 1-4R; CANR 2, 29, 51, 74, 91, 128; CN 1, 2, 3, 4, 5, 6, 7; DAB; DAM NOV; DLB 139, 194, 323, 326; EWL 3; IDFW 3, 4; INT CANR-29; MTCW 1, 2; MTFW 2005; RGSF 2; RGWL 2; RHW; TEA

Jibran, Kahlil
See Gibran, Kahlil

Jibran, Khalil
See Gibran, Kahlil

Jiles, Paulette 1943- .... **CLC 13, 58**
See also CA 101; CANR 70, 124; CP 5; CWP

Jimenez (Mantecon), Juan Ramon
1881-1958 .... **HLC 1; PC 7; TCLC 4, 183**
See also CA 104; 131; CANR 74; DAM MULT, POET; DLB 134, 330; EW 9; EWL 3; HW 1; MTCW 1, 2; MTFW 2005; RGWL 2, 3

Jimenez, Ramon
See Jimenez (Mantecon), Juan Ramon

Jimenez Mantecon, Juan
See Jimenez (Mantecon), Juan Ramon

Jin, Ba 1904-2005
See Pa Chin
See also CA 244; CWW 2; DLB 328

Jin, Xuefei
See Ha Jin

Jodelle, Etienne 1532-1573 .... **LC 119**
See also DLB 327; GFL Beginnings to 1789

Joel, Billy .... **CLC 26**
See Joel, William Martin

Joel, William Martin 1949-
See Joel, Billy
See also CA 108

John, Saint 10(?)-100 .... **CMLC 27, 63**

John of Salisbury c. 1115-1180 ..... **CMLC 63**

John of the Cross, St. 1542-1591 .... **LC 18**
See also RGWL 2, 3

John Paul II, Pope 1920-2005 .... **CLC 128**
See also CA 106; 133; 238

Johnson, B(ryan) S(tanley William)
1933-1973 .... **CLC 6, 9**
See also CA 9-12R; 53-56; CANR 9; CN 1; CP 1, 2; DLB 14, 40; EWL 3; RGEL 2

Johnson, Benjamin F., of Boone
See Riley, James Whitcomb

Johnson, Charles (Richard) 1948- .... **BLC 2; CLC 7, 51, 65, 163**
See also AFAW 2; AMWS 6; BW 2, 3; CA 116; CAAS 18; CANR 42, 66, 82, 129; CN 5, 6, 7; DAM MULT; DLB 33, 278; MAL 5; MTCW 2; MTFW 2005; RGAL 4; SSFS 16

Johnson, Charles S(purgeon)
1893-1956 .... **HR 1:3**
See also BW 1, 3; CA 125; CANR 82; DLB 51, 91

Johnson, Denis 1949- . **CLC 52, 160; SSC 56**
See also CA 117; 121; CANR 71, 99; CN 4, 5, 6, 7; DLB 120

Johnson, Diane 1934- .... **CLC 5, 13, 48**
See also BPFB 2; CA 41-44R; CANR 17, 40, 62, 95, 155; CN 4, 5, 6, 7; DLBY 1980; INT CANR-17; MTCW 1

Johnson, E(mily) Pauline 1861-1913 . **NNAL**
See also CA 150; CCA 1; DAC; DAM MULT; DLB 92, 175; TCWW 2

Johnson, Eyvind (Olof Verner)
1900-1976 .... **CLC 14**
See also CA 73-76; 69-72; CANR 34, 101; DLB 259, 330; EW 12; EWL 3

Johnson, Fenton 1888-1958 .... **BLC 2**
See also BW 1; CA 118; 124; DAM MULT; DLB 45, 50

Johnson, Georgia Douglas (Camp)
1880-1966 .... **HR 1:3**
See also BW 1; CA 125; DLB 51, 249; WP

Johnson, Helene 1907-1995 .... **HR 1:3**
See also CA 181; DLB 51; WP

Johnson, J. R.
See James, C(yril) L(ionel) R(obert)

Johnson, James Weldon 1871-1938 .. **BLC 2; HR 1:3; PC 24; TCLC 3, 19, 175**
See also AFAW 1, 2; BW 1, 3; CA 104; 125; CANR 82; CDALB 1917-1929; CLR 32; DA3; DAM MULT, POET; DLB 51; EWL 3; EXPP; LMFS 2; MAL 5; MTCW 1, 2; MTFW 2005; NFS 22; PFS 1; RGAL 4; SATA 31; TUS

Johnson, Joyce 1935- .... **CLC 58**
See also BG 1:3; CA 125; 129; CANR 102

Johnson, Judith (Emlyn) 1936- .... **CLC 7, 15**
See Sherwin, Judith Johnson
See also CA 25-28R; 153; CANR 34; CP 6, 7

Johnson, Lionel (Pigot)
1867-1902 .... **TCLC 19**
See also CA 117; 209; DLB 19; RGEL 2

Johnson, Marguerite Annie
See Angelou, Maya

Johnson, Mel
See Malzberg, Barry N(athaniel)

Johnson, Pamela Hansford
1912-1981 .... **CLC 1, 7, 27**
See also CA 1-4R; 104; CANR 2, 28; CN 1, 2, 3; DLB 15; MTCW 1, 2; MTFW 2005; RGEL 2

Johnson, Paul 1928- .... **CLC 147**
See also BEST 89:4; CA 17-20R; CANR 34, 62, 100, 155

Johnson, Paul Bede
See Johnson, Paul

Johnson, Robert .... **CLC 70**

Johnson, Robert 1911(?)-1938 .... **TCLC 69**
See also BW 3; CA 174

Johnson, Samuel 1709-1784 . **LC 15, 52, 128; WLC 3**
See also BRW 3; BRWR 1; CDBLB 1660-1789; DA; DAB; DAC; DAM MST; DLB 39, 95, 104, 142, 213; LMFS 1; RGEL 2; TEA

Johnson, Uwe 1934-1984 .. **CLC 5, 10, 15, 40**
See also CA 1-4R; 112; CANR 1, 39; CD-WLB 2; DLB 75; EWL 3; MTCW 1; RGWL 2, 3

Johnston, Basil H. 1929- .... **NNAL**
See also CA 69-72; CANR 11, 28, 66; DAC; DAM MULT; DLB 60

Johnston, George (Benson) 1913- .... **CLC 51**
See also CA 1-4R; CANR 5, 20; CP 1, 2, 3, 4, 5, 6, 7; DLB 88

Johnston, Jennifer (Prudence)
1930- .... **CLC 7, 150, 228**
See also CA 85-88; CANR 92; CN 4, 5, 6, 7; DLB 14

Joinville, Jean de 1224(?)-1317 ..... **CMLC 38**

Jolley, (Monica) Elizabeth 1923- ..... **CLC 46; SSC 19**
See also CA 127; CAAS 13; CANR 59; CN 4, 5, 6, 7; DLB 325; EWL 3; RGSF 2

Jones, Arthur Llewellyn 1863-1947
See Machen, Arthur
See also CA 104; 179; HGG

Jones, D(ouglas) G(ordon) 1929- ..... **CLC 10**
See also CA 29-32R; CANR 13, 90; CP 1, 2, 3, 4, 5, 6, 7; DLB 53

Jones, David (Michael) 1895-1974 .... **CLC 2, 4, 7, 13, 42**
See also BRW 6; BRWS 7; CA 9-12R; 53-56; CANR 28; CDBLB 1945-1960; CP 1, 2; DLB 20, 100; EWL 3; MTCW 1; PAB; RGEL 2

Jones, David Robert 1947-
See Bowie, David
See also CA 103; CANR 104

Jones, Diana Wynne 1934- .... **CLC 26**
See also AAYA 12; BYA 6, 7, 9, 11, 13, 16; CA 49-52; CANR 4, 26, 56, 120; CLR 23, 120; DLB 161; FANT; JRDA; MAICYA 1, 2; MTFW 2005; SAAS 7; SATA 9, 70, 108, 160; SFW 4; SUFW 2; YAW

Jones, Edward P. 1950- .... **CLC 76, 223**
See also AAYA 71; BW 2, 3; CA 142; CANR 79, 134; CSW; MTFW 2005

Jones, Gayl 1949- ...... **BLC 2; CLC 6, 9, 131**
See also AFAW 1, 2; BW 2, 3; CA 77-80; CANR 27, 66, 122; CN 4, 5, 6, 7; CSW; DA3; DAM MULT; DLB 33, 278; MAL 5; MTCW 1, 2; MTFW 2005; RGAL 4

Jones, James 1921-1977 ...... **CLC 1, 3, 10, 39**
See also AITN 1, 2; AMWS 11; BPFB 2; CA 1-4R; 69-72; CANR 6; CN 1, 2; DLB 2, 143; DLBD 17; DLBY 1998; EWL 3; MAL 5; MTCW 1; RGAL 4

Jones, John J.
See Lovecraft, H. P.

Jones, LeRoi .... **CLC 1, 2, 3, 5, 10, 14**
See Baraka, Amiri
See also CN 1, 2; CP 1, 2, 3; MTCW 2

Jones, Louis B. 1953- .... **CLC 65**
See also CA 141; CANR 73

Jones, Madison (Percy, Jr.) 1925- ...... **CLC 4**
See also CA 13-16R; CAAS 11; CANR 7, 54, 83; CN 1, 2, 3, 4, 5, 6, 7; CSW; DLB 152

Jones, Mervyn 1922- .... **CLC 10, 52**
See also CA 45-48; CAAS 5; CANR 1, 91; CN 1, 2, 3, 4, 5, 6, 7; MTCW 1

Jones, Mick 1956(?)- .... **CLC 30**

Jones, Nettie (Pearl) 1941- .... **CLC 34**
See also BW 2; CA 137; CAAS 20; CANR 88

Jones, Peter 1802-1856 .... **NNAL**

Jones, Preston 1936-1979 .... **CLC 10**
See also CA 73-76; 89-92; DLB 7

Jones, Robert F(rancis) 1934-2003 .... **CLC 7**
See also CA 49-52; CANR 2, 61, 118

Jones, Rod 1953- .... **CLC 50**
See also CA 128

Jones, Terence Graham Parry
1942- .... **CLC 21**
See Jones, Terry; Monty Python
See also CA 112; 116; CANR 35, 93; INT CA-116; SATA 127

Jones, Terry
See Jones, Terence Graham Parry
See also SATA 67; SATA-Brief 51

Jones, Thom (Douglas) 1945(?)- ..... **CLC 81; SSC 56**
See also CA 157; CANR 88; DLB 244; SSFS 23

Jong, Erica 1942- .... **CLC 4, 6, 8, 18, 83**
See also AITN 1; AMWS 5; BEST 90:2; BPFB 2; CA 73-76; CANR 26, 52, 75, 132; CN 3, 4, 5, 6, 7; CP 2, 3, 4, 5, 6, 7; CPW; DA3; DAM NOV, POP; DLB 2, 5, 28, 152; FW; INT CANR-26; MAL 5; MTCW 1, 2; MTFW 2005

Jonson, Ben(jamin) 1572(?)-1637 . **DC 4; LC 6, 33, 110; PC 17; WLC 3**
See also BRW 1; BRWC 1; BRWR 1; CD-BLB Before 1660; DA; DAB; DAC; DAM DRAM, MST, POET; DFS 4, 10; DLB 62, 121; LMFS 1; PFS 23; RGEL 2; TEA; WLIT 3

Jordan, June 1936-2002 .. **BLCS; CLC 5, 11, 23, 114, 230; PC 38**
See also AAYA 2, 66; AFAW 1, 2; BW 2, 3; CA 33-36R; 206; CANR 25, 70, 114, 154; CLR 10; CP 3, 4, 5, 6, 7; CWP; DAM MULT, POET; DLB 38; GLL 2; LAIT 5; MAICYA 1, 2; MTCW 1; SATA 4, 136; YAW

Jordan, June Meyer
See Jordan, June

Jordan, Neil 1950- .... **CLC 110**
See also CA 124; 130; CANR 54, 154; CN 4, 5, 6, 7; GLL 2; INT CA-130

Jordan, Neil Patrick
See Jordan, Neil

Jordan, Pat(rick M.) 1941- .... **CLC 37**
See also CA 33-36R; CANR 121

Jorgensen, Ivar
See Ellison, Harlan

Jorgenson, Ivar
See Silverberg, Robert

Joseph, George Ghevarughese .... **CLC 70**

Josephson, Mary
See O'Doherty, Brian

Josephus, Flavius c. 37-100 .... **CMLC 13**
See also AW 2; DLB 176; WLIT 8

Josiah Allen's Wife
See Holley, Marietta

Josipovici, Gabriel (David) 1940- ...... **CLC 6, 43, 153**
See also CA 37-40R, 224; CAAE 224; CAAS 8; CANR 47, 84; CN 3, 4, 5, 6, 7; DLB 14, 319

Joubert, Joseph 1754-1824 .... **NCLC 9**

Jouve, Pierre Jean 1887-1976 .... **CLC 47**
See also CA 65-68; DLB 258; EWL 3

Jovine, Francesco 1902-1950 .... **TCLC 79**
See also DLB 264; EWL 3

Joyce, James (Augustine Aloysius)
1882-1941 .... **DC 16; PC 22; SSC 3, 26, 44, 64; TCLC 3, 8, 16, 35, 52, 159; WLC 3**
See also AAYA 42; BRW 7; BRWC 1; BRWR 1; BYA 11, 13; CA 104; 126; CD-BLB 1914-1945; DA; DA3; DAB; DAC; DAM MST, NOV, POET; DLB 10, 19, 36, 162, 247; EWL 3; EXPN; EXPS; LAIT 3; LMFS 1, 2; MTCW 1, 2; MTFW 2005; NFS 7; RGSF 2; SSFS 1, 19; TEA; WLIT 4

Jozsef, Attila 1905-1937 .... **TCLC 22**
See also CA 116; 230; CDWLB 4; DLB 215; EWL 3

Juana Ines de la Cruz, Sor
1651(?)-1695 ...... **HLCS 1; LC 5; PC 24**
See also DLB 305; FW; LAW; RGWL 2, 3; WLIT 1

Juana Inez de La Cruz, Sor
See Juana Ines de la Cruz, Sor

Judd, Cyril
See Kornbluth, C(yril) M.; Pohl, Frederik

Juenger, Ernst 1895-1998 .... **CLC 125**
See Junger, Ernst
See also CA 101; 167; CANR 21, 47, 106; DLB 56

Julian of Norwich 1342(?)-1416(?) . **LC 6, 52**
See also BRWS 12; DLB 146; LMFS 1

Julius Caesar 100B.C.-44B.C.
See Caesar, Julius
See also CDWLB 1; DLB 211

Junger, Ernst
See Juenger, Ernst
See also CDWLB 2; EWL 3; RGWL 2, 3

Junger, Sebastian 1962- .... **CLC 109**
See also AAYA 28; CA 165; CANR 130; MTFW 2005

Juniper, Alex
See Hospital, Janette Turner

Junius
See Luxemburg, Rosa

Junzaburo, Nishiwaki
See Nishiwaki, Junzaburo
See also EWL 3

Just, Ward 1935- .... **CLC 4, 27**
See also CA 25-28R; CANR 32, 87; CN 6, 7; INT CANR-32

Just, Ward Swift
See Just, Ward

Justice, Donald (Rodney)
1925-2004 .... **CLC 6, 19, 102; PC 64**
See also AMWS 7; CA 5-8R; 230; CANR 26, 54, 74, 121, 122; CP 1, 2, 3, 4, 5, 6, 7; CSW; DAM POET; DLBY 1983; EWL 3; INT CANR-26; MAL 5; MTCW 2; PFS 14; TCLE 1:1

Juvenal c. 60-c. 130 .... **CMLC 8**
See also AW 2; CDWLB 1; DLB 211; RGWL 2, 3; WLIT 8

Juvenis
See Bourne, Randolph S(illiman)

K., Alice
See Knapp, Caroline

Kabakov, Sasha .... **CLC 59**

Kabir 1398(?)-1448(?) .... **LC 109; PC 56**
See also RGWL 2, 3

Kacew, Romain 1914-1980
See Gary, Romain
See also CA 108; 102

Kadare, Ismail 1936- .... **CLC 52, 190**
See also CA 161; EWL 3; RGWL 3

Kadohata, Cynthia (Lynn)
1956(?)- .... **CLC 59, 122**
See also AAYA 71; CA 140; CANR 124; SATA 155

Kafka, Franz 1883-1924 ... **SSC 5, 29, 35, 60; TCLC 2, 6, 13, 29, 47, 53, 112, 179; WLC 3**
See also AAYA 31; BPFB 2; CA 105; 126; CDWLB 2; DA; DA3; DAB; DAC; DAM MST, NOV; DLB 81; EW 9; EWL 3; EXPS; LATS 1:1; LMFS 2; MTCW 1, 2; MTFW 2005; NFS 7; RGSF 2; RGWL 2, 3; SFW 4; SSFS 3, 7, 12; TWA

Kahanovitsch, Pinkhes
See Der Nister

Kahn, Roger 1927- .... **CLC 30**
See also CA 25-28R; CANR 44, 69, 152; DLB 171; SATA 37

Kain, Saul
See Sassoon, Siegfried (Lorraine)

Kaiser, Georg 1878-1945 .... **TCLC 9**
See also CA 106; 190; CDWLB 2; DLB 124; EWL 3; LMFS 2; RGWL 2, 3

Kaledin, Sergei .... **CLC 59**

Kaletski, Alexander 1946- .... **CLC 39**
See also CA 118; 143

Kalidasa fl. c. 400-455 .... **CMLC 9; PC 22**
See also RGWL 2, 3

Kallman, Chester (Simon)
1921-1975 .... **CLC 2**
See also CA 45-48; 53-56; CANR 3; CP 1, 2

Kaminsky, Melvin .... **CLC 12, 217**
See Brooks, Mel
See also AAYA 13, 48; DLB 26

Kaminsky, Stuart M. 1934- .... **CLC 59**
See also CA 73-76; CANR 29, 53, 89; CMW 4

Kaminsky, Stuart Melvin
See Kaminsky, Stuart M.

Kamo no Chomei 1153(?)-1216 .... **CMLC 66**
See also DLB 203

Kamo no Nagaakira
See Kamo no Chomei

Kandinsky, Wassily 1866-1944 .... **TCLC 92**
See also AAYA 64; CA 118; 155

Kane, Francis
See Robbins, Harold

Kane, Henry 1918-
See Queen, Ellery
See also CA 156; CMW 4

Kane, Paul
See Simon, Paul

Kanin, Garson 1912-1999 .... **CLC 22**
See also AITN 1; CA 5-8R; 177; CAD; CANR 7, 78; DLB 7; IDFW 3, 4

Kaniuk, Yoram 1930- .... **CLC 19**
See also CA 134; DLB 299; RGHL

Kant, Immanuel 1724-1804 ..... **NCLC 27, 67**
See also DLB 94

Kantor, MacKinlay 1904-1977 .... **CLC 7**
See also CA 61-64; 73-76; CANR 60, 63;
CN 1, 2; DLB 9, 102; MAL 5; MTCW 2;
RHW; TCWW 1, 2

Kanze Motokiyo
See Zeami

Kaplan, David Michael 1946- .... **CLC 50**
See also CA 187

Kaplan, James 1951- .... **CLC 59**
See also CA 135; CANR 121

Karadzic, Vuk Stefanovic
1787-1864 .... **NCLC 115**
See also CDWLB 4; DLB 147

Karageorge, Michael
See Anderson, Poul

Karamzin, Nikolai Mikhailovich
1766-1826 .... **NCLC 3, 173**
See also DLB 150; RGSF 2

Karapanou, Margarita 1946- .... **CLC 13**
See also CA 101

Karinthy, Frigyes 1887-1938 .... **TCLC 47**
See also CA 170; DLB 215; EWL 3

Karl, Frederick R(obert)
1927-2004 .... **CLC 34**
See also CA 5-8R; 226; CANR 3, 44, 143

Karr, Mary 1955- .... **CLC 188**
See also AMWS 11; CA 151; CANR 100;
MTFW 2005; NCFS 5

Kastel, Warren
See Silverberg, Robert

Kataev, Evgeny Petrovich 1903-1942
See Petrov, Evgeny
See also CA 120

Kataphusin
See Ruskin, John

Katz, Steve 1935- .... **CLC 47**
See also CA 25-28R; CAAS 14, 64; CANR
12; CN 4, 5, 6, 7; DLBY 1983

Kauffman, Janet 1945- .... **CLC 42**
See also CA 117; CANR 43, 84; DLB 218;
DLBY 1986

Kaufman, Bob (Garnell)
1925-1986 .... **CLC 49; PC 74**
See also BG 1:3; BW 1; CA 41-44R; 118;
CANR 22; CP 1; DLB 16, 41

Kaufman, George S. 1889-1961 ...... **CLC 38;
DC 17**
See also CA 108; 93-96; DAM DRAM;
DFS 1, 10; DLB 7; INT CA-108; MTCW
2; MTFW 2005; RGAL 4; TUS

Kaufman, Moises 1964- .... **DC 26**
See also CA 211; DFS 22; MTFW 2005

Kaufman, Sue .... **CLC 3, 8**
See Barondess, Sue K(aufman)

Kavafis, Konstantinos Petrou 1863-1933
See Cavafy, C(onstantine) P(eter)
See also CA 104

Kavan, Anna 1901-1968 .... **CLC 5, 13, 82**
See also BRWS 7; CA 5-8R; CANR 6, 57;
DLB 255; MTCW 1; RGEL 2; SFW 4

Kavanagh, Dan
See Barnes, Julian

Kavanagh, Julie 1952- .... **CLC 119**
See also CA 163

Kavanagh, Patrick (Joseph)
1904-1967 .... **CLC 22; PC 33**
See also BRWS 7; CA 123; 25-28R; DLB
15, 20; EWL 3; MTCW 1; RGEL 2

Kawabata, Yasunari 1899-1972 ..... **CLC 2, 5,
9, 18, 107; SSC 17**
See Kawabata Yasunari
See also CA 93-96; 33-36R; CANR 88;
DAM MULT; DLB 330; MJW; MTCW 2;
MTFW 2005; RGSF 2; RGWL 2, 3

Kawabata Yasunari
See Kawabata, Yasunari
See also DLB 180; EWL 3

Kaye, M.M. 1908-2004 .... **CLC 28**
See also CA 89-92; 223; CANR 24, 60, 102,
142; MTCW 1, 2; MTFW 2005; RHW;
SATA 62; SATA-Obit 152

Kaye, Mollie
See Kaye, M.M.

Kaye-Smith, Sheila 1887-1956 .... **TCLC 20**
See also CA 118; 203; DLB 36

Kaymor, Patrice Maguilene
See Senghor, Leopold Sedar

Kazakov, Iurii Pavlovich
See Kazakov, Yuri Pavlovich
See also DLB 302

Kazakov, Yuri Pavlovich 1927-1982 . **SSC 43**
See Kazakov, Iurii Pavlovich; Kazakov,
Yury
See also CA 5-8R; CANR 36; MTCW 1;
RGSF 2

Kazakov, Yury
See Kazakov, Yuri Pavlovich
See also EWL 3

Kazan, Elia 1909-2003 .... **CLC 6, 16, 63**
See also CA 21-24R; 220; CANR 32, 78

Kazantzakis, Nikos 1883(?)-1957 .... **TCLC 2,
5, 33, 181**
See also BPFB 2; CA 105; 132; DA3; EW
9; EWL 3; MTCW 1, 2; MTFW 2005;
RGWL 2, 3

Kazin, Alfred 1915-1998 ..... **CLC 34, 38, 119**
See also AMWS 8; CA 1-4R; CAAS 7;
CANR 1, 45, 79; DLB 67; EWL 3

Keane, Mary Nesta (Skrine) 1904-1996
See Keane, Molly
See also CA 108; 114; 151; RHW

Keane, Molly .... **CLC 31**
See Keane, Mary Nesta (Skrine)
See also CN 5, 6; INT CA-114; TCLE 1:1

Keates, Jonathan 1946(?)- .... **CLC 34**
See also CA 163; CANR 126

Keaton, Buster 1895-1966 .... **CLC 20**
See also CA 194

Keats, John 1795-1821 ...... **NCLC 8, 73, 121;
PC 1; WLC 3**
See also AAYA 58; BRW 4; BRWR 1; CD-
BLB 1789-1832; DA; DA3; DAB; DAC;
DAM MST, POET; DLB 96, 110; EXPP;
LMFS 1; PAB; PFS 1, 2, 3, 9, 17; RGEL
2; TEA; WLIT 3; WP

Keble, John 1792-1866 .... **NCLC 87**
See also DLB 32, 55; RGEL 2

Keene, Donald 1922- .... **CLC 34**
See also CA 1-4R; CANR 5, 119

Keillor, Garrison 1942- ..... **CLC 40, 115, 222**
See also AAYA 2, 62; AMWS 16; BEST
89:3; BPFB 2; CA 111; 117; CANR 36,
59, 124; CPW; DA3; DAM POP; DLBY
1987; EWL 3; MTCW 1, 2; MTFW 2005;
SATA 58; TUS

Keith, Carlos
See Lewton, Val

Keith, Michael
See Hubbard, L. Ron

Keller, Gottfried 1819-1890 .... **NCLC 2; SSC
26**
See also CDWLB 2; DLB 129; EW; RGSF
2; RGWL 2, 3

Keller, Nora Okja 1965- .... **CLC 109**
See also CA 187

Kellerman, Jonathan 1949- .... **CLC 44**
See also AAYA 35; BEST 90:1; CA 106;
CANR 29, 51, 150; CMW 4; CPW; DA3;
DAM POP; INT CANR-29

Kelley, William Melvin 1937- .... **CLC 22**
See also BW 1; CA 77-80; CANR 27, 83;
CN 1, 2, 3, 4, 5, 6, 7; DLB 33; EWL 3

Kellogg, Marjorie 1922-2005 .... **CLC 2**
See also CA 81-84; 246

Kellow, Kathleen
See Hibbert, Eleanor Alice Burford

Kelly, Lauren
See Oates, Joyce Carol

Kelly, M(ilton) T(errence) 1947- ...... **CLC 55**
See also CA 97-100; CAAS 22; CANR 19,
43, 84; CN 6

Kelly, Robert 1935- .... **SSC 50**
See also CA 17-20R; CAAS 19; CANR 47;
CP 1, 2, 3, 4, 5, 6, 7; DLB 5, 130, 165

Kelman, James 1946- .... **CLC 58, 86**
See also BRWS 5; CA 148; CANR 85, 130;
CN 5, 6, 7; DLB 194, 319, 326; RGSF 2;
WLIT 4

Kemal, Yasar
See Kemal, Yashar
See also CWW 2; EWL 3; WLIT 6

Kemal, Yashar 1923(?)- .... **CLC 14, 29**
See also CA 89-92; CANR 44

Kemble, Fanny 1809-1893 .... **NCLC 18**
See also DLB 32

Kemelman, Harry 1908-1996 .... **CLC 2**
See also AITN 1; BPFB 2; CA 9-12R; 155;
CANR 6, 71; CMW 4; DLB 28

Kempe, Margery 1373(?)-1440(?) ... **LC 6, 56**
See also BRWS 12; DLB 146; FL 1:1;
RGEL 2

Kempis, Thomas a 1380-1471 .... **LC 11**

Kendall, Henry 1839-1882 .... **NCLC 12**
See also DLB 230

Keneally, Thomas 1935- .... **CLC 5, 8, 10, 14,
19, 27, 43, 117**
See also BRWS 4; CA 85-88; CANR 10,
50, 74, 130; CN 1, 2, 3, 4, 5, 6, 7; CPW;
DA3; DAM NOV; DLB 289, 299, 326;
EWL 3; MTCW 1, 2; MTFW 2005; NFS
17; RGEL 2; RGHL; RHW

Kennedy, A(lison) L(ouise) 1965- ... **CLC 188**
See also CA 168, 213; CAAE 213; CANR
108; CD 5, 6; CN 6, 7; DLB 271; RGSF
2

Kennedy, Adrienne (Lita) 1931- .... **BLC 2;
CLC 66; DC 5**
See also AFAW 2; BW 2, 3; CA 103; CAAS
20; CABS 3; CAD; CANR 26, 53, 82;
CD 5, 6; DAM MULT; DFS 9; DLB 38;
FW; MAL 5

Kennedy, John Pendleton
1795-1870 .... **NCLC 2**
See also DLB 3, 248, 254; RGAL 4

Kennedy, Joseph Charles 1929-
See Kennedy, X. J.
See also CA 1-4R, 201; CAAE 201; CANR
4, 30, 40; CWRI 5; MAICYA 2; MAIC-
YAS 1; SATA 14, 86, 130; SATA-Essay
130

Kennedy, William 1928- ... **CLC 6, 28, 34, 53**
See also AAYA 1; AMWS 7; BPFB 2; CA
85-88; CANR 14, 31, 76, 134; CN 4, 5, 6,
7; DA3; DAM NOV; DLB 143; DLBY
1985; EWL 3; INT CANR-31; MAL 5;
MTCW 1, 2; MTFW 2005; SATA 57

Kennedy, X. J. .... **CLC 8, 42**
See Kennedy, Joseph Charles
See also AMWS 15; CAAS 9; CLR 27; CP
1, 2, 3, 4, 5, 6, 7; DLB 5; SAAS 22

Kenny, Maurice (Francis) 1929- ..... **CLC 87;
NNAL**
See also CA 144; CAAS 22; CANR 143;
DAM MULT; DLB 175

Kent, Kelvin
See Kuttner, Henry

Kenton, Maxwell
See Southern, Terry

Kenyon, Jane 1947-1995 .... **PC 57**
See also AAYA 63; AMWS 7; CA 118; 148;
CANR 44, 69; CP 6, 7; CWP; DLB 120;
PFS 9, 17; RGAL 4

Kenyon, Robert O.
See Kuttner, Henry

Kepler, Johannes 1571-1630 .... **LC 45**

Ker, Jill
See Conway, Jill K(er)

Kerkow, H. C.
See Lewton, Val

Kerouac, Jack 1922-1969 ...... **CLC 1, 2, 3, 5, 14, 29, 61; TCLC 117; WLC**
See Kerouac, Jean-Louis Lebris de
See also AAYA 25; AMWC 1; AMWS 3; BG 3; BPFB 2; CDALB 1941-1968; CP 1; CPW; DLB 2, 16, 237; DLBD 3; DLBY 1995; EWL 3; GLL 1; LATS 1:2; LMFS 2; MAL 5; NFS 8; RGAL 4; TUS; WP

Kerouac, Jean-Louis Lebris de 1922-1969
See Kerouac, Jack
See also AITN 1; CA 5-8R; 25-28R; CANR 26, 54, 95; DA; DA3; DAB; DAC; DAM MST, NOV, POET, POP; MTCW 1, 2; MTFW 2005

Kerr, (Bridget) Jean (Collins)
1923(?)-2003 .... **CLC 22**
See also CA 5-8R; 212; CANR 7; INT CANR-7

Kerr, M. E. .... **CLC 12, 35**
See Meaker, Marijane
See also AAYA 2, 23; BYA 1, 7, 8; CLR 29; SAAS 1; WYA

Kerr, Robert .... **CLC 55**

Kerrigan, (Thomas) Anthony 1918- .. **CLC 4, 6**
See also CA 49-52; CAAS 11; CANR 4

Kerry, Lois
See Duncan, Lois

Kesey, Ken 1935-2001 .... **CLC 1, 3, 6, 11, 46, 64, 184; WLC 3**
See also AAYA 25; BG 1:3; BPFB 2; CA 1-4R; 204; CANR 22, 38, 66, 124; CDALB 1968-1988; CN 1, 2, 3, 4, 5, 6, 7; CPW; DA; DA3; DAB; DAC; DAM MST, NOV, POP; DLB 2, 16, 206; EWL 3; EXPN; LAIT 4; MAL 5; MTCW 1, 2; MTFW 2005; NFS 2; RGAL 4; SATA 66; SATA-Obit 131; TUS; YAW

Kesselring, Joseph (Otto)
1902-1967 .... **CLC 45**
See also CA 150; DAM DRAM, MST; DFS 20

Kessler, Jascha (Frederick) 1929- ...... **CLC 4**
See also CA 17-20R; CANR 8, 48, 111; CP 1

Kettelkamp, Larry (Dale) 1933- .... **CLC 12**
See also CA 29-32R; CANR 16; SAAS 3; SATA 2

Key, Ellen (Karolina Sofia)
1849-1926 .... **TCLC 65**
See also DLB 259

Keyber, Conny
See Fielding, Henry

Keyes, Daniel 1927- .... **CLC 80**
See also AAYA 23; BYA 11; CA 17-20R; 181; CAAE 181; CANR 10, 26, 54, 74; DA; DA3; DAC; DAM MST, NOV; EXPN; LAIT 4; MTCW 1; MTFW 2005; NFS 2; SATA 37; SFW 4

Keynes, John Maynard
1883-1946 .... **TCLC 64**
See also CA 114; 162, 163; DLBD 10; MTCW 2; MTFW 2005

Khanshendel, Chiron
See Rose, Wendy

Khayyam, Omar 1048-1131 ... **CMLC 11; PC 8**
See Omar Khayyam
See also DA3; DAM POET; WLIT 6

Kherdian, David 1931- .... **CLC 6, 9**
See also AAYA 42; CA 21-24R; 192; CAAE 192; CAAS 2; CANR 39, 78; CLR 24; JRDA; LAIT 3; MAICYA 1, 2; SATA 16, 74; SATA-Essay 125

Khlebnikov, Velimir .... **TCLC 20**
See Khlebnikov, Viktor Vladimirovich
See also DLB 295; EW 10; EWL 3; RGWL 2, 3

Khlebnikov, Viktor Vladimirovich 1885-1922
See Khlebnikov, Velimir
See also CA 117; 217

Khodasevich, V.F.
See Khodasevich, Vladislav

Khodasevich, Vladislav
1886-1939 .... **TCLC 15**
See also CA 115; DLB 317; EWL 3

Khodasevich, Vladislav Felitsianovich
See Khodasevich, Vladislav

Kielland, Alexander Lange
1849-1906 .... **TCLC 5**
See also CA 104

Kiely, Benedict 1919- ... **CLC 23, 43; SSC 58**
See also CA 1-4R; CANR 2, 84; CN 1, 2, 3, 4, 5, 6, 7; DLB 15, 319; TCLE 1:1

Kienzle, William X. 1928-2001 .... **CLC 25**
See also CA 93-96; 203; CAAS 1; CANR 9, 31, 59, 111; CMW 4; DA3; DAM POP; INT CANR-31; MSW; MTCW 1, 2; MTFW 2005

Kierkegaard, Soren 1813-1855 ..... **NCLC 34, 78, 125**
See also DLB 300; EW 6; LMFS 2; RGWL 3; TWA

Kieslowski, Krzysztof 1941-1996 .... **CLC 120**
See also CA 147; 151

Killens, John Oliver 1916-1987 .... **CLC 10**
See also BW 2; CA 77-80; 123; CAAS 2; CANR 26; CN 1, 2, 3, 4; DLB 33; EWL 3

Killigrew, Anne 1660-1685 .... **LC 4, 73**
See also DLB 131

Killigrew, Thomas 1612-1683 .... **LC 57**
See also DLB 58; RGEL 2

Kim
See Simenon, Georges (Jacques Christian)

Kincaid, Jamaica 1949- ...... **BLC 2; CLC 43, 68, 137; SSC 72**
See also AAYA 13, 56; AFAW 2; AMWS 7; BRWS 7; BW 2, 3; CA 125; CANR 47, 59, 95, 133; CDALBS; CDWLB 3; CLR 63; CN 4, 5, 6, 7; DA3; DAM MULT, NOV; DLB 157, 227; DNFS 1; EWL 3; EXPS; FW; LATS 1:2; LMFS 2; MAL 5; MTCW 2; MTFW 2005; NCFS 1; NFS 3; SSFS 5, 7; TUS; WWE 1; YAW

King, Francis (Henry) 1923- .... **CLC 8, 53, 145**
See also CA 1-4R; CANR 1, 33, 86; CN 1, 2, 3, 4, 5, 6, 7; DAM NOV; DLB 15, 139; MTCW 1

King, Kennedy
See Brown, George Douglas

King, Martin Luther, Jr. 1929-1968 . **BLC 2; CLC 83; WLCS**
See also BW 2, 3; CA 25-28; CANR 27, 44; CAP 2; DA; DA3; DAB; DAC; DAM MST, MULT; LAIT 5; LATS 1:2; MTCW 1, 2; MTFW 2005; SATA 14

King, Stephen 1947- .... **CLC 12, 26, 37, 61, 113, 228; SSC 17, 55**
See also AAYA 1, 17; AMWS 5; BEST 90:1; BPFB 2; CA 61-64; CANR 1, 30, 52, 76, 119, 134; CN 7; CPW; DA3; DAM NOV, POP; DLB 143; DLBY 1980; HGG; JRDA; LAIT 5; MTCW 1, 2; MTFW 2005; RGAL 4; SATA 9, 55, 161; SUFW 1, 2; WYAS 1; YAW

King, Stephen Edwin
See King, Stephen

King, Steve
See King, Stephen

King, Thomas 1943- .... **CLC 89, 171; NNAL**
See also CA 144; CANR 95; CCA 1; CN 6, 7; DAC; DAM MULT; DLB 175; SATA 96

Kingman, Lee .... **CLC 17**
See Natti, (Mary) Lee
See also CWRI 5; SAAS 3; SATA 1, 67

Kingsley, Charles 1819-1875 .... **NCLC 35**
See also CLR 77; DLB 21, 32, 163, 178, 190; FANT; MAICYA 2; MAICYAS 1; RGEL 2; WCH; YABC 2

Kingsley, Henry 1830-1876 .... **NCLC 107**
See also DLB 21, 230; RGEL 2

Kingsley, Sidney 1906-1995 .... **CLC 44**
See also CA 85-88; 147; CAD; DFS 14, 19; DLB 7; MAL 5; RGAL 4

Kingsolver, Barbara 1955- .... **CLC 55, 81, 130, 216**
See also AAYA 15; AMWS 7; CA 129; 134; CANR 60, 96, 133; CDALBS; CN 7; CPW; CSW; DA3; DAM POP; DLB 206; INT CA-134; LAIT 5; MTCW 2; MTFW 2005; NFS 5, 10, 12, 24; RGAL 4; TCLE 1:1

Kingston, Maxine Hong 1940- .... **AAL; CLC 12, 19, 58, 121; WLCS**
See also AAYA 8, 55; AMWS 5; BPFB 2; CA 69-72; CANR 13, 38, 74, 87, 128; CDALBS; CN 6, 7; DA3; DAM MULT, NOV; DLB 173, 212, 312; DLBY 1980; EWL 3; FL 1:6; FW; INT CANR-13; LAIT 5; MAL 5; MBL; MTCW 1, 2; MTFW 2005; NFS 6; RGAL 4; SATA 53; SSFS 3; TCWW 2

Kinnell, Galway 1927- ..... **CLC 1, 2, 3, 5, 13, 29, 129; PC 26**
See also AMWS 3; CA 9-12R; CANR 10, 34, 66, 116, 138; CP 1, 2, 3, 4, 5, 6, 7; DLB 5; DLBY 1987; EWL 3; INT CANR-34; MAL 5; MTCW 1, 2; MTFW 2005; PAB; PFS 9; RGAL 4; TCLE 1:1; WP

Kinsella, Thomas 1928- .... **CLC 4, 19, 138; PC 69**
See also BRWS 5; CA 17-20R; CANR 15, 122; CP 1, 2, 3, 4, 5, 6, 7; DLB 27; EWL 3; MTCW 1, 2; MTFW 2005; RGEL 2; TEA

Kinsella, W.P. 1935- .... **CLC 27, 43, 166**
See also AAYA 7, 60; BPFB 2; CA 97-100, 222; CAAE 222; CAAS 7; CANR 21, 35, 66, 75, 129; CN 4, 5, 6, 7; CPW; DAC; DAM NOV, POP; FANT; INT CANR-21; LAIT 5; MTCW 1, 2; MTFW 2005; NFS 15; RGSF 2

Kinsey, Alfred C(harles)
1894-1956 .... **TCLC 91**
See also CA 115; 170; MTCW 2

Kipling, (Joseph) Rudyard 1865-1936 . **PC 3; SSC 5, 54; TCLC 8, 17, 167; WLC 3**
See also AAYA 32; BRW 6; BRWC 1, 2; BYA 4; CA 105; 120; CANR 33; CDBLB 1890-1914; CLR 39, 65; CWRI 5; DA; DA3; DAB; DAC; DAM MST, POET; DLB 19, 34, 141, 156, 330; EWL 3; EXPS; FANT; LAIT 3; LMFS 1; MAICYA 1, 2; MTCW 1, 2; MTFW 2005; NFS 21; PFS 22; RGEL 2; RGSF 2; SATA 100; SFW 4; SSFS 8, 21, 22; SUFW 1; TEA; WCH; WLIT 4; YABC 2

Kircher, Athanasius 1602-1680 .... **LC 121**
See also DLB 164

Kirk, Russell (Amos) 1918-1994 .. **TCLC 119**
See also AITN 1; CA 1-4R; 145; CAAS 9; CANR 1, 20, 60; HGG; INT CANR-20; MTCW 1, 2

Kirkham, Dinah
See Card, Orson Scott

Kirkland, Caroline M. 1801-1864 . **NCLC 85**
See also DLB 3, 73, 74, 250, 254; DLBD 13

Kirkup, James 1918- .... **CLC 1**
    See also CA 1-4R; CAAS 4; CANR 2; CP
    1, 2, 3, 4, 5, 6, 7; DLB 27; SATA 12

Kirkwood, James 1930(?)-1989 .... **CLC 9**
    See also AITN 2; CA 1-4R; 128; CANR 6,
    40; GLL 2

Kirsch, Sarah 1935- .... **CLC 176**
    See also CA 178; CWW 2; DLB 75; EWL
    3

Kirshner, Sidney
    See Kingsley, Sidney

Kis, Danilo 1935-1989 .... **CLC 57**
    See also CA 109; 118; 129; CANR 61; CD-
    WLB 4; DLB 181; EWL 3; MTCW 1;
    RGSF 2; RGWL 2, 3

Kissinger, Henry A(lfred) 1923- ..... **CLC 137**
    See also CA 1-4R; CANR 2, 33, 66, 109;
    MTCW 1

Kittel, Frederick August
    See Wilson, August

Kivi, Aleksis 1834-1872 .... **NCLC 30**

Kizer, Carolyn 1925- ..... **CLC 15, 39, 80; PC
    66**
    See also CA 65-68; CAAS 5; CANR 24,
    70, 134; CP 1, 2, 3, 4, 5, 6, 7; CWP; DAM
    POET; DLB 5, 169; EWL 3; MAL 5;
    MTCW 2; MTFW 2005; PFS 18; TCLE
    1:1

Klabund 1890-1928 .... **TCLC 44**
    See also CA 162; DLB 66

Klappert, Peter 1942- .... **CLC 57**
    See also CA 33-36R; CSW; DLB 5

Klein, A(braham) M(oses)
    1909-1972 .... **CLC 19**
    See also CA 101; 37-40R; CP 1; DAB;
    DAC; DAM MST; DLB 68; EWL 3;
    RGEL 2; RGHL

Klein, Joe
    See Klein, Joseph

Klein, Joseph 1946- .... **CLC 154**
    See also CA 85-88; CANR 55

Klein, Norma 1938-1989 .... **CLC 30**
    See also AAYA 2, 35; BPFB 2; BYA 6, 7,
    8; CA 41-44R; 128; CANR 15, 37; CLR
    2, 19; INT CANR-15; JRDA; MAICYA
    1, 2; SAAS 1; SATA 7, 57; WYA; YAW

Klein, T(heodore) E(ibon) D(onald)
    1947- .... **CLC 34**
    See also CA 119; CANR 44, 75; HGG

Kleist, Heinrich von 1777-1811 ...... **NCLC 2,
    37; SSC 22**
    See also CDWLB 2; DAM DRAM; DLB
    90; EW 5; RGSF 2; RGWL 2, 3

Klima, Ivan 1931- .... **CLC 56, 172**
    See also CA 25-28R; CANR 17, 50, 91;
    CDWLB 4; CWW 2; DAM NOV; DLB
    232; EWL 3; RGWL 3

Klimentev, Andrei Platonovich
    See Klimentov, Andrei Platonovich

Klimentov, Andrei Platonovich
    1899-1951 .... **SSC 42; TCLC 14**
    See Platonov, Andrei Platonovich; Platonov,
    Andrey Platonovich
    See also CA 108; 232

Klinger, Friedrich Maximilian von
    1752-1831 .... **NCLC 1**
    See also DLB 94

Klingsor the Magician
    See Hartmann, Sadakichi

Klopstock, Friedrich Gottlieb
    1724-1803 .... **NCLC 11**
    See also DLB 97; EW 4; RGWL 2, 3

Kluge, Alexander 1932- .... **SSC 61**
    See also CA 81-84; DLB 75

Knapp, Caroline 1959-2002 .... **CLC 99**
    See also CA 154; 207

Knebel, Fletcher 1911-1993 .... **CLC 14**
    See also AITN 1; CA 1-4R; 140; CAAS 3;
    CANR 1, 36; CN 1, 2, 3, 4, 5; SATA 36;
    SATA-Obit 75

Knickerbocker, Diedrich
    See Irving, Washington

Knight, Etheridge 1931-1991 ... **BLC 2; CLC
    40; PC 14**
    See also BW 1, 3; CA 21-24R; 133; CANR
    23, 82; CP 1, 2, 3, 4, 5; DAM POET; DLB
    41; MTCW 2; MTFW 2005; RGAL 4;
    TCLE 1:1

Knight, Sarah Kemble 1666-1727 .... **LC 7**
    See also DLB 24, 200

Knister, Raymond 1899-1932 .... **TCLC 56**
    See also CA 186; DLB 68; RGEL 2

Knowles, John 1926-2001 ... **CLC 1, 4, 10, 26**
    See also AAYA 10; AMWS 12; BPFB 2;
    BYA 3; CA 17-20R; 203; CANR 40, 74,
    76, 132; CDALB 1968-1988; CLR 98; CN
    1, 2, 3, 4, 5, 6, 7; DA; DAC; DAM MST,
    NOV; DLB 6; EXPN; MTCW 1, 2;
    MTFW 2005; NFS 2; RGAL 4; SATA 8,
    89; SATA-Obit 134; YAW

Knox, Calvin M.
    See Silverberg, Robert

Knox, John c. 1505-1572 .... **LC 37**
    See also DLB 132

Knye, Cassandra
    See Disch, Thomas M.

Koch, C(hristopher) J(ohn) 1932- .... **CLC 42**
    See also CA 127; CANR 84; CN 3, 4, 5, 6,
    7; DLB 289

Koch, Christopher
    See Koch, C(hristopher) J(ohn)

Koch, Kenneth 1925-2002 .... **CLC 5, 8, 44**
    See also AMWS 15; CA 1-4R; 207; CAD;
    CANR 6, 36, 57, 97, 131; CD 5, 6; CP 1,
    2, 3, 4, 5, 6, 7; DAM POET; DLB 5; INT
    CANR-36; MAL 5; MTCW 2; MTFW
    2005; PFS 20; SATA 65; WP

Kochanowski, Jan 1530-1584 .... **LC 10**
    See also RGWL 2, 3

Kock, Charles Paul de 1794-1871 . **NCLC 16**

Koda Rohan
    See Koda Shigeyuki

Koda Rohan
    See Koda Shigeyuki
    See also DLB 180

Koda Shigeyuki 1867-1947 .... **TCLC 22**
    See Koda Rohan
    See also CA 121; 183

Koestler, Arthur 1905-1983 ... **CLC 1, 3, 6, 8,
    15, 33**
    See also BRWS 1; CA 1-4R; 109; CANR 1,
    33; CDBLB 1945-1960; CN 1, 2, 3;
    DLBY 1983; EWL 3; MTCW 1, 2; MTFW
    2005; NFS 19; RGEL 2

Kogawa, Joy Nozomi 1935- ...... **CLC 78, 129**
    See also AAYA 47; CA 101; CANR 19, 62,
    126; CN 6, 7; CP 1; CWP; DAC; DAM
    MST, MULT; FW; MTCW 2; MTFW
    2005; NFS 3; SATA 99

Kohout, Pavel 1928- .... **CLC 13**
    See also CA 45-48; CANR 3

Koizumi, Yakumo
    See Hearn, (Patricio) Lafcadio (Tessima
    Carlos)

Kolmar, Gertrud 1894-1943 .... **TCLC 40**
    See also CA 167; EWL 3; RGHL

Komunyakaa, Yusef 1947- .. **BLCS; CLC 86,
    94, 207; PC 51**
    See also AFAW 2; AMWS 13; CA 147;
    CANR 83; CP 6, 7; CSW; DLB 120; EWL
    3; PFS 5, 20; RGAL 4

Konrad, George
    See Konrad, Gyorgy

Konrad, Gyorgy 1933- .... **CLC 4, 10, 73**
    See also CA 85-88; CANR 97; CDWLB 4;
    CWW 2; DLB 232; EWL 3

Konwicki, Tadeusz 1926- .... **CLC 8, 28, 54,
    117**
    See also CA 101; CAAS 9; CANR 39, 59;
    CWW 2; DLB 232; EWL 3; IDFW 3;
    MTCW 1

Koontz, Dean R. 1945- .... **CLC 78, 206**
    See also AAYA 9, 31; BEST 89:3, 90:2; CA
    108; CANR 19, 36, 52, 95, 138; CMW 4;
    CPW; DA3; DAM NOV, POP; DLB 292;
    HGG; MTCW 1; MTFW 2005; SATA 92,
    165; SFW 4; SUFW 2; YAW

Koontz, Dean Ray
    See Koontz, Dean R.

Kopernik, Mikolaj
    See Copernicus, Nicolaus

Kopit, Arthur (Lee) 1937- ...... **CLC 1, 18, 33**
    See also AITN 1; CA 81-84; CABS 3;
    CAD; CD 5, 6; DAM DRAM; DFS 7, 14;
    DLB 7; MAL 5; MTCW 1; RGAL 4

Kopitar, Jernej (Bartholomaus)
    1780-1844 .... **NCLC 117**

Kops, Bernard 1926- .... **CLC 4**
    See also CA 5-8R; CANR 84; CBD; CN 1,
    2, 3, 4, 5, 6, 7; CP 1, 2, 3, 4, 5, 6, 7; DLB
    13; RGHL

Kornbluth, C(yril) M. 1923-1958 .... **TCLC 8**
    See also CA 105; 160; DLB 8; SCFW 1, 2;
    SFW 4

Korolenko, V.G.
    See Korolenko, Vladimir G.

Korolenko, Vladimir
    See Korolenko, Vladimir G.

Korolenko, Vladimir G.
    1853-1921 .... **TCLC 22**
    See also CA 121; DLB 277

Korolenko, Vladimir Galaktionovich
    See Korolenko, Vladimir G.

Korzybski, Alfred (Habdank Skarbek)
    1879-1950 .... **TCLC 61**
    See also CA 123; 160

Kosinski, Jerzy 1933-1991 ..... **CLC 1, 2, 3, 6,
    10, 15, 53, 70**
    See also AMWS 7; BPFB 2; CA 17-20R;
    134; CANR 9, 46; CN 1, 2, 3, 4; DA3;
    DAM NOV; DLB 2, 299; DLBY 1982;
    EWL 3; HGG; MAL 5; MTCW 1, 2;
    MTFW 2005; NFS 12; RGAL 4; RGHL;
    TUS

Kostelanetz, Richard (Cory) 1940- .. **CLC 28**
    See also CA 13-16R; CAAS 8; CANR 38,
    77; CN 4, 5, 6; CP 2, 3, 4, 5, 6, 7

Kostrowitzki, Wilhelm Apollinaris de
    1880-1918
    See Apollinaire, Guillaume
    See also CA 104

Kotlowitz, Robert 1924- .... **CLC 4**
    See also CA 33-36R; CANR 36

Kotzebue, August (Friedrich Ferdinand) von
    1761-1819 .... **NCLC 25**
    See also DLB 94

Kotzwinkle, William 1938- ..... **CLC 5, 14, 35**
    See also BPFB 2; CA 45-48; CANR 3, 44,
    84, 129; CLR 6; CN 7; DLB 173; FANT;
    MAICYA 1, 2; SATA 24, 70, 146; SFW
    4; SUFW 2; YAW

Kowna, Stancy
    See Szymborska, Wislawa

Kozol, Jonathan 1936- .... **CLC 17**
    See also AAYA 46; CA 61-64; CANR 16,
    45, 96; MTFW 2005

Kozoll, Michael 1940(?)- .... **CLC 35**

Kramer, Kathryn 19(?)- .... **CLC 34**

Kramer, Larry 1935- .... **CLC 42; DC 8**
    See also CA 124; 126; CANR 60, 132;
    DAM POP; DLB 249; GLL 1

Krasicki, Ignacy 1735-1801 .... **NCLC 8**

Laishley, Alex
See Booth, Martin

Lamartine, Alphonse (Marie Louis Prat) de
1790-1869 .... **NCLC 11; PC 16**
See also DAM POET; DLB 217; GFL 1789
to the Present; RGWL 2, 3

Lamb, Charles 1775-1834 ..... **NCLC 10, 113;
WLC 3**
See also BRW 4; CDBLB 1789-1832; DA;
DAB; DAC; DAM MST; DLB 93, 107,
163; RGEL 2; SATA 17; TEA

Lamb, Lady Caroline 1785-1828 ... **NCLC 38**
See also DLB 116

Lamb, Mary Ann 1764-1847 .... **NCLC 125**
See also DLB 163; SATA 17

Lame Deer 1903(?)-1976 .... **NNAL**
See also CA 69-72

Lamming, George (William) 1927- ... **BLC 2;
CLC 2, 4, 66, 144**
See also BW 2, 3; CA 85-88; CANR 26,
76; CDWLB 3; CN 1, 2, 3, 4, 5, 6, 7; CP
1; DAM MULT; DLB 125; EWL 3;
MTCW 1, 2; MTFW 2005; NFS 15;
RGEL 2

L'Amour, Louis 1908-1988 .... **CLC 25, 55**
See also AAYA 16; AITN 2; BEST 89:2;
BPFB 2; CA 1-4R; 125; CANR 3, 25, 40;
CPW; DA3; DAM NOV, POP; DLB 206;
DLBY 1980; MTCW 1, 2; MTFW 2005;
RGAL 4; TCWW 1, 2

Lampedusa, Giuseppe (Tomasi) di
.... **TCLC 13**
See Tomasi di Lampedusa, Giuseppe
See also CA 164; EW 11; MTCW 2; MTFW
2005; RGWL 2, 3

Lampman, Archibald 1861-1899 ... **NCLC 25**
See also DLB 92; RGEL 2; TWA

Lancaster, Bruce 1896-1963 .... **CLC 36**
See also CA 9-10; CANR 70; CAP 1; SATA
9

Lanchester, John 1962- .... **CLC 99**
See also CA 194; DLB 267

Landau, Mark Alexandrovich
See Aldanov, Mark (Alexandrovich)

Landau-Aldanov, Mark Alexandrovich
See Aldanov, Mark (Alexandrovich)

Landis, Jerry
See Simon, Paul

Landis, John 1950- .... **CLC 26**
See also CA 112; 122; CANR 128

Landolfi, Tommaso 1908-1979 .... **CLC 11, 49**
See also CA 127; 117; DLB 177; EWL 3

Landon, Letitia Elizabeth
1802-1838 .... **NCLC 15**
See also DLB 96

Landor, Walter Savage
1775-1864 .... **NCLC 14**
See also BRW 4; DLB 93, 107; RGEL 2

Landwirth, Heinz 1927-
See Lind, Jakov
See also CA 9-12R; CANR 7

Lane, Patrick 1939- .... **CLC 25**
See also CA 97-100; CANR 54; CP 3, 4, 5,
6, 7; DAM POET; DLB 53; INT CA-97-
100

Lane, Rose Wilder 1887-1968 ...... **TCLC 177**
See also CA 102; CANR 63; SATA 29;
SATA-Brief 28; TCWW 2

Lang, Andrew 1844-1912 .... **TCLC 16**
See also CA 114; 137; CANR 85; CLR 101;
DLB 98, 141, 184; FANT; MAICYA 1, 2;
RGEL 2; SATA 16; WCH

Lang, Fritz 1890-1976 .... **CLC 20, 103**
See also AAYA 65; CA 77-80; 69-72;
CANR 30

Lange, John
See Crichton, Michael

Langer, Elinor 1939- .... **CLC 34**
See also CA 121

Langland, William 1332(?)-1400(?) .... **LC 19,
120**
See also BRW 1; DA; DAB; DAC; DAM
MST, POET; DLB 146; RGEL 2; TEA;
WLIT 3

Langstaff, Launcelot
See Irving, Washington

Lanier, Sidney 1842-1881 . **NCLC 6, 118; PC
50**
See also AMWS 1; DAM POET; DLB 64;
DLBD 13; EXPP; MAICYA 1; PFS 14;
RGAL 4; SATA 18

Lanyer, Aemilia 1569-1645 .... **LC 10, 30, 83;
PC 60**
See also DLB 121

Lao Tzu c. 6th cent. B.C.-3rd cent.
B.C. .... **CMLC 7**

Lao-Tzu
See Lao Tzu

Lapine, James (Elliot) 1949- .... **CLC 39**
See also CA 123; 130; CANR 54, 128; INT
CA-130

Larbaud, Valery (Nicolas)
1881-1957 .... **TCLC 9**
See also CA 106; 152; EWL 3; GFL 1789
to the Present

Lardner, Ring
See Lardner, Ring(gold) W(ilmer)
See also BPFB 2; CDALB 1917-1929; DLB
11, 25, 86, 171; DLBD 16; MAL 5;
RGAL 4; RGSF 2

Lardner, Ring W., Jr.
See Lardner, Ring(gold) W(ilmer)

Lardner, Ring(gold) W(ilmer)
1885-1933 .... **SSC 32; TCLC 2, 14**
See Lardner, Ring
See also AMW; CA 104; 131; MTCW 1, 2;
MTFW 2005; TUS

Laredo, Betty
See Codrescu, Andrei

Larkin, Maia
See Wojciechowska, Maia (Teresa)

Larkin, Philip (Arthur) 1922-1985 ... **CLC 3,
5, 8, 9, 13, 18, 33, 39, 64; PC 21**
See also BRWS 1; CA 5-8R; 117; CANR
24, 62; CDBLB 1960 to Present; CP 1, 2,
3, 4; DA3; DAB; DAM MST, POET;
DLB 27; EWL 3; MTCW 1, 2; MTFW
2005; PFS 3, 4, 12; RGEL 2

La Roche, Sophie von
1730-1807 .... **NCLC 121**
See also DLB 94

La Rochefoucauld, Francois
1613-1680 .... **LC 108**

Larra (y Sanchez de Castro), Mariano Jose
de 1809-1837 .... **NCLC 17, 130**

Larsen, Eric 1941- .... **CLC 55**
See also CA 132

Larsen, Nella 1893(?)-1963 .... **BLC 2; CLC
37; HR 1:3**
See also AFAW 1, 2; BW 1; CA 125; CANR
83; DAM MULT; DLB 51; FW; LATS
1:1; LMFS 2

Larson, Charles R(aymond) 1938- ... **CLC 31**
See also CA 53-56; CANR 4, 121

Larson, Jonathan 1960-1996 .... **CLC 99**
See also AAYA 28; CA 156; DFS 23;
MTFW 2005

La Sale, Antoine de c. 1386-1460(?) . **LC 104**
See also DLB 208

Las Casas, Bartolome de
1474-1566 .... **HLCS; LC 31**
See Casas, Bartolome de las
See also DLB 318; LAW

Lasch, Christopher 1932-1994 .... **CLC 102**
See also CA 73-76; 144; CANR 25, 118;
DLB 246; MTCW 1, 2; MTFW 2005

Lasker-Schueler, Else 1869-1945 ... **TCLC 57**
See Lasker-Schuler, Else
See also CA 183; DLB 66, 124

Lasker-Schuler, Else
See Lasker-Schueler, Else
See also EWL 3

Laski, Harold J(oseph) 1893-1950 . **TCLC 79**
See also CA 188

Latham, Jean Lee 1902-1995 .... **CLC 12**
See also AITN 1; BYA 1; CA 5-8R; CANR
7, 84; CLR 50; MAICYA 1, 2; SATA 2,
68; YAW

Latham, Mavis
See Clark, Mavis Thorpe

Lathen, Emma .... **CLC 2**
See Hennissart, Martha; Latsis, Mary J(ane)
See also BPFB 2; CMW 4; DLB 306

Lathrop, Francis
See Leiber, Fritz (Reuter, Jr.)

Latsis, Mary J(ane) 1927-1997
See Lathen, Emma
See also CA 85-88; 162; CMW 4

Lattany, Kristin
See Lattany, Kristin (Elaine Eggleston)
Hunter

Lattany, Kristin (Elaine Eggleston) Hunter
1931- .... **CLC 35**
See Hunter, Kristin
See also AITN 1; BW 1; BYA 3; CA 13-
16R; CANR 13, 108; CLR 3; CN 7; DLB
33; INT CANR-13; MAICYA 1, 2; SAAS
10; SATA 12, 132; YAW

Lattimore, Richmond (Alexander)
1906-1984 .... **CLC 3**
See also CA 1-4R; 112; CANR 1; CP 1, 2,
3; MAL 5

Laughlin, James 1914-1997 .... **CLC 49**
See also CA 21-24R; 162; CAAS 22; CANR
9, 47; CP 1, 2, 3, 4, 5, 6; DLB 48; DLBY
1996, 1997

Laurence, Margaret 1926-1987 ..... **CLC 3, 6,
13, 50, 62; SSC 7**
See also BYA 13; CA 5-8R; 121; CANR
33; CN 1, 2, 3, 4; DAC; DAM MST; DLB
53; EWL 3; FW; MTCW 1, 2; MTFW
2005; NFS 11; RGEL 2; RGSF 2; SATA-
Obit 50; TCWW 2

Laurent, Antoine 1952- .... **CLC 50**

Lauscher, Hermann
See Hesse, Hermann

Lautreamont 1846-1870 .. **NCLC 12; SSC 14**
See Lautreamont, Isidore Lucien Ducasse
See also GFL 1789 to the Present; RGWL
2, 3

Lautreamont, Isidore Lucien Ducasse
See Lautreamont
See also DLB 217

Lavater, Johann Kaspar
1741-1801 .... **NCLC 142**
See also DLB 97

Laverty, Donald
See Blish, James (Benjamin)

Lavin, Mary 1912-1996 . **CLC 4, 18, 99; SSC
4, 67**
See also CA 9-12R; 151; CANR 33; CN 1,
2, 3, 4, 5, 6; DLB 15, 319; FW; MTCW
1; RGEL 2; RGSF 2; SSFS 23

Lavond, Paul Dennis
See Kornbluth, C(yril) M.; Pohl, Frederik

Lawes, Henry 1596-1662 .... **LC 113**
See also DLB 126

Lawler, Ray
See Lawler, Raymond Evenor
See also DLB 289

Lawler, Raymond Evenor 1922- .... **CLC 58**
See Lawler, Ray
See also CA 103; CD 5, 6; RGEL 2

Leimbach, Martha 1963-
See Leimbach, Marti
See also CA 130

Leimbach, Marti .... **CLC 65**
See Leimbach, Martha

Leino, Eino .... **TCLC 24**
See Lonnbohm, Armas Eino Leopold
See also EWL 3

Leiris, Michel (Julien) 1901-1990 ..... **CLC 61**
See also CA 119; 128; 132; EWL 3; GFL 1789 to the Present

Leithauser, Brad 1953- .... **CLC 27**
See also CA 107; CANR 27, 81; CP 5, 6, 7; DLB 120, 282

le Jars de Gournay, Marie
See de Gournay, Marie le Jars

Lelchuk, Alan 1938- .... **CLC 5**
See also CA 45-48; CAAS 20; CANR 1, 70, 152; CN 3, 4, 5, 6, 7

Lem, Stanislaw 1921-2006 ..... **CLC 8, 15, 40, 149**
See also CA 105; 249; CAAS 1; CANR 32; CWW 2; MTCW 1; SCFW 1, 2; SFW 4

Lemann, Nancy (Elise) 1956- .... **CLC 39**
See also CA 118; 136; CANR 121

Lemonnier, (Antoine Louis) Camille 1844-1913 .... **TCLC 22**
See also CA 121

Lenau, Nikolaus 1802-1850 .... **NCLC 16**

L'Engle, Madeleine 1918- .... **CLC 12**
See also AAYA 28; AITN 2; BPFB 2; BYA 2, 4, 5, 7; CA 1-4R; CANR 3, 21, 39, 66, 107; CLR 1, 14, 57; CPW; CWRI 5; DA3; DAM POP; DLB 52; JRDA; MAICYA 1, 2; MTCW 1, 2; MTFW 2005; SAAS 15; SATA 1, 27, 75, 128; SFW 4; WYA; YAW

Lengyel, Jozsef 1896-1975 .... **CLC 7**
See also CA 85-88; 57-60; CANR 71; RGSF 2

Lenin 1870-1924
See Lenin, V. I.
See also CA 121; 168

Lenin, V. I. .... **TCLC 67**
See Lenin

Lennon, John (Ono) 1940-1980 .. **CLC 12, 35**
See also CA 102; SATA 114

Lennox, Charlotte Ramsay 1729(?)-1804 .... **NCLC 23, 134**
See also DLB 39; RGEL 2

Lentricchia, Frank, Jr.
See Lentricchia, Frank

Lentricchia, Frank 1940- .... **CLC 34**
See also CA 25-28R; CANR 19, 106, 148; DLB 246

Lenz, Gunter .... **CLC 65**

Lenz, Jakob Michael Reinhold 1751-1792 .... **LC 100**
See also DLB 94; RGWL 2, 3

Lenz, Siegfried 1926- .... **CLC 27; SSC 33**
See also CA 89-92; CANR 80, 149; CWW 2; DLB 75; EWL 3; RGSF 2; RGWL 2, 3

Leon, David
See Jacob, (Cyprien-)Max

Leonard, Elmore 1925- .... **CLC 28, 34, 71, 120, 222**
See also AAYA 22, 59; AITN 1; BEST 89:1, 90:4; BPFB 2; CA 81-84; CANR 12, 28, 53, 76, 96, 133; CMW 4; CN 5, 6, 7; CPW; DA3; DAM POP; DLB 173, 226; INT CANR-28; MSW; MTCW 1, 2; MTFW 2005; RGAL 4; SATA 163; TCWW 1, 2

Leonard, Hugh .... **CLC 19**
See Byrne, John Keyes
See also CBD; CD 5, 6; DFS 13; DLB 13

Leonov, Leonid (Maximovich) 1899-1994 .... **CLC 92**
See Leonov, Leonid Maksimovich
See also CA 129; CANR 76; DAM NOV; EWL 3; MTCW 1, 2; MTFW 2005

Leonov, Leonid Maksimovich
See Leonov, Leonid (Maximovich)
See also DLB 272

Leopardi, (Conte) Giacomo 1798-1837 .... **NCLC 22, 129; PC 37**
See also EW 5; RGWL 2, 3; WLIT 7; WP

Le Reveler
See Artaud, Antonin (Marie Joseph)

Lerman, Eleanor 1952- .... **CLC 9**
See also CA 85-88; CANR 69, 124

Lerman, Rhoda 1936- .... **CLC 56**
See also CA 49-52; CANR 70

Lermontov, Mikhail Iur'evich
See Lermontov, Mikhail Yuryevich
See also DLB 205

Lermontov, Mikhail Yuryevich 1814-1841 .... **NCLC 5, 47, 126; PC 18**
See Lermontov, Mikhail Iur'evich
See also EW 6; RGWL 2, 3; TWA

Leroux, Gaston 1868-1927 .... **TCLC 25**
See also CA 108; 136; CANR 69; CMW 4; MTFW 2005; NFS 20; SATA 65

Lesage, Alain-Rene 1668-1747 ...... **LC 2, 28**
See also DLB 313; EW 3; GFL Beginnings to 1789; RGWL 2, 3

Leskov, N(ikolai) S(emenovich) 1831-1895
See Leskov, Nikolai (Semyonovich)

Leskov, Nikolai (Semyonovich) 1831-1895 .... **NCLC 25, 174; SSC 34**
See Leskov, Nikolai Semenovich

Leskov, Nikolai Semenovich
See Leskov, Nikolai (Semyonovich)
See also DLB 238

Lesser, Milton
See Marlowe, Stephen

Lessing, Doris 1919- .. **CLC 1, 2, 3, 6, 10, 15, 22, 40, 94, 170; SSC 6, 61; WLCS**
See also AAYA 57; AFW; BRWS 1; CA 9-12R; CAAS 14; CANR 33, 54, 76, 122; CBD; CD 5, 6; CDBLB 1960 to Present; CN 1, 2, 3, 4, 5, 6, 7; CWD; DA; DA3; DAB; DAC; DAM MST, NOV; DFS 20; DLB 15, 139; DLBY 1985; EWL 3; EXPS; FL 1:6; FW; LAIT 4; MTCW 1, 2; MTFW 2005; RGEL 2; RGSF 2; SFW 4; SSFS 1, 12, 20; TEA; WLIT 2, 4

Lessing, Gotthold Ephraim 1729-1781 .... **DC 26; LC 8, 124**
See also CDWLB 2; DLB 97; EW 4; RGWL 2, 3

Lester, Richard 1932- .... **CLC 20**

Levenson, Jay .... **CLC 70**

Lever, Charles (James) 1806-1872 .... **NCLC 23**
See also DLB 21; RGEL 2

Leverson, Ada Esther 1862(?)-1933(?) .... **TCLC 18**
See Elaine
See also CA 117; 202; DLB 153; RGEL 2

Levertov, Denise 1923-1997 .. **CLC 1, 2, 3, 5, 8, 15, 28, 66; PC 11**
See also AMWS 3; CA 1-4R, 178; 163; CAAE 178; CAAS 19; CANR 3, 29, 50, 108; CDALBS; CP 1, 2, 3, 4, 5, 6; CWP; DAM POET; DLB 5, 165; EWL 3; EXPP; FW; INT CANR-29; MAL 5; MTCW 1, 2; PAB; PFS 7, 17; RGAL 4; RGHL; TUS; WP

Levi, Carlo 1902-1975 .... **TCLC 125**
See also CA 65-68; 53-56; CANR 10; EWL 3; RGWL 2, 3

Levi, Jonathan .... **CLC 76**
See also CA 197

Levi, Peter (Chad Tigar) 1931-2000 .... **CLC 41**
See also CA 5-8R; 187; CANR 34, 80; CP 1, 2, 3, 4, 5, 6, 7; DLB 40

Levi, Primo 1919-1987 ...... **CLC 37, 50; SSC 12; TCLC 109**
See also CA 13-16R; 122; CANR 12, 33, 61, 70, 132; DLB 177, 299; EWL 3; MTCW 1, 2; MTFW 2005; RGHL; RGWL 2, 3; WLIT 7

Levin, Ira 1929- .... **CLC 3, 6**
See also CA 21-24R; CANR 17, 44, 74, 139; CMW 4; CN 1, 2, 3, 4, 5, 6, 7; CPW; DA3; DAM POP; HGG; MTCW 1, 2; MTFW 2005; SATA 66; SFW 4

Levin, Meyer 1905-1981 .... **CLC 7**
See also AITN 1; CA 9-12R; 104; CANR 15; CN 1, 2, 3; DAM POP; DLB 9, 28; DLBY 1981; MAL 5; RGHL; SATA 21; SATA-Obit 27

Levine, Albert Norman 1923-2005
See Levine, Norman
See also CN 7

Levine, Norman 1923-2005 .... **CLC 54**
See also CA 73-76; 240; CAAS 23; CANR 14, 70; CN 1, 2, 3, 4, 5, 6; CP 1; DLB 88

Levine, Norman Albert
See Levine, Norman

Levine, Philip 1928- .. **CLC 2, 4, 5, 9, 14, 33, 118; PC 22**
See also AMWS 5; CA 9-12R; CANR 9, 37, 52, 116, 156; CP 1, 2, 3, 4, 5, 6, 7; DAM POET; DLB 5; EWL 3; MAL 5; PFS 8

Levinson, Deirdre 1931- .... **CLC 49**
See also CA 73-76; CANR 70

Levi-Strauss, Claude 1908- .... **CLC 38**
See also CA 1-4R; CANR 6, 32, 57; DLB 242; EWL 3; GFL 1789 to the Present; MTCW 1, 2; TWA

Levitin, Sonia (Wolff) 1934- .... **CLC 17**
See also AAYA 13, 48; CA 29-32R; CANR 14, 32, 79; CLR 53; JRDA; MAICYA 1, 2; SAAS 2; SATA 4, 68, 119, 131; SATA-Essay 131; YAW

Levon, O. U.
See Kesey, Ken

Levy, Amy 1861-1889 .... **NCLC 59**
See also DLB 156, 240

Lewes, George Henry 1817-1878 ... **NCLC 25**
See also DLB 55, 144

Lewis, Alun 1915-1944 .... **SSC 40; TCLC 3**
See also BRW 7; CA 104; 188; DLB 20, 162; PAB; RGEL 2

Lewis, C. Day
See Day Lewis, C(ecil)
See also CN 1

Lewis, Cecil Day
See Day Lewis, C(ecil)

Lewis, Clive Staples
See Lewis, C.S.

Lewis, C.S. 1898-1963 ... **CLC 1, 3, 6, 14, 27, 124; WLC 4**
See also AAYA 3, 39; BPFB 2; BRWS 3; BYA 15, 16; CA 81-84; CANR 33, 71, 132; CDBLB 1945-1960; CLR 3, 27, 109; CWRI 5; DA; DA3; DAB; DAC; DAM MST, NOV, POP; DLB 15, 100, 160, 255; EWL 3; FANT; JRDA; LMFS 2; MAICYA 1, 2; MTCW 1, 2; MTFW 2005; NFS 24; RGEL 2; SATA 13, 100; SCFW 1, 2; SFW 4; SUFW 1; TEA; WCH; WYA; YAW

Lewis, Janet 1899-1998 .... **CLC 41**
See Winters, Janet Lewis
See also CA 9-12R; 172; CANR 29, 63; CAP 1; CN 1, 2, 3, 4, 5, 6; DLBY 1987; RHW; TCWW 2

Loewinsohn, Ron(ald William)
1937- .... **CLC 52**
See also CA 25-28R; CANR 71; CP 1, 2, 3, 4

Logan, Jake
See Smith, Martin Cruz

Logan, John (Burton) 1923-1987 .... **CLC 5**
See also CA 77-80; 124; CANR 45; CP 1, 2, 3, 4; DLB 5

Lo Kuan-chung 1330(?)-1400(?) .... **LC 12**

Lombard, Nap
See Johnson, Pamela Hansford

Lombard, Peter 1100(?)-1160(?) ... **CMLC 72**

Lombino, Salvatore
See Hunter, Evan

London, Jack 1876-1916 .. **SSC 4, 49; TCLC 9, 15, 39; WLC 4**
See London, John Griffith
See also AAYA 13; AITN 2; AMW; BPFB 2; BYA 4, 13; CDALB 1865-1917; CLR 108; DLB 8, 12, 78, 212; EWL 3; EXPS; LAIT 8; MAL 5; NFS 8; RGAL 4; RGSF 2; SATA 18; SFW 4; SSFS 7; TCWW 1, 2; TUS; WYA; YAW

London, John Griffith 1876-1916
See London, Jack
See also CA 110; 119; CANR 73; DA; DA3; DAB; DAC; DAM MST, NOV; JRDA; MAICYA 1, 2; MTCW 1, 2; MTFW 2005; NFS 19

Long, Emmett
See Leonard, Elmore

Longbaugh, Harry
See Goldman, William

Longfellow, Henry Wadsworth
1807-1882 .... **NCLC 2, 45, 101, 103; PC 30; WLCS**
See also AMW; AMWR 2; CDALB 1640-1865; CLR 99; DA; DA3; DAB; DAC; DAM MST, POET; DLB 1, 59, 235; EXPP; PAB; PFS 2, 7, 17; RGAL 4; SATA 19; TUS; WP

Longinus c. 1st cent. - .... **CMLC 27**
See also AW 2; DLB 176

Longley, Michael 1939- .... **CLC 29**
See also BRWS 8; CA 102; CP 1, 2, 3, 4, 5, 6, 7; DLB 40

Longstreet, Augustus Baldwin
1790-1870 .... **NCLC 159**
See also DLB 3, 11, 74, 248; RGAL 4

Longus fl. c. 2nd cent. - .... **CMLC 7**

Longway, A. Hugh
See Lang, Andrew

Lonnbohm, Armas Eino Leopold 1878-1926
See Leino, Eino
See also CA 123

Lonnrot, Elias 1802-1884 .... **NCLC 53**
See also EFS 1

Lonsdale, Roger ed. .... **CLC 65**

Lopate, Phillip 1943- .... **CLC 29**
See also CA 97-100; CANR 88, 157; DLBY 1980; INT CA-97-100

Lopez, Barry (Holstun) 1945- .... **CLC 70**
See also AAYA 9, 63; ANW; CA 65-68; CANR 7, 23, 47, 68, 92; DLB 256, 275; INT CANR-7, -23; MTCW 1; RGAL 4; SATA 67

Lopez de Mendoza, Inigo
See Santillana, Inigo Lopez de Mendoza, Marques de

Lopez Portillo (y Pacheco), Jose
1920-2004 .... **CLC 46**
See also CA 129; 224; HW 1

Lopez y Fuentes, Gregorio
1897(?)-1966 .... **CLC 32**
See also CA 131; EWL 3; HW 1

Lorca, Federico Garcia
See Garcia Lorca, Federico
See also DFS 4; EW 11; PFS 20; RGWL 2, 3; WP

Lord, Audre
See Lorde, Audre
See also EWL 3

Lord, Bette Bao 1938- .... **AAL; CLC 23**
See also BEST 90:3; BPFB 2; CA 107; CANR 41, 79; INT CA-107; SATA 58

Lord Auch
See Bataille, Georges

Lord Brooke
See Greville, Fulke

Lord Byron
See Byron, George Gordon (Noel)

Lorde, Audre 1934-1992 .... **BLC 2; CLC 18, 71; PC 12; TCLC 173**
See Domini, Rey; Lord, Audre
See also AFAW 1, 2; BW 1, 3; CA 25-28R; 142; CANR 16, 26, 46, 82; CP 2, 3, 4, 5; DA3; DAM MULT, POET; DLB 41; FW; MAL 5; MTCW 1, 2; MTFW 2005; PFS 16; RGAL 4

Lord Houghton
See Milnes, Richard Monckton

Lord Jeffrey
See Jeffrey, Francis

Loreaux, Nichol .... **CLC 65**

Lorenzini, Carlo 1826-1890
See Collodi, Carlo
See also MAICYA 1, 2; SATA 29, 100

Lorenzo, Heberto Padilla
See Padilla (Lorenzo), Heberto

Loris
See Hofmannsthal, Hugo von

Loti, Pierre .... **TCLC 11**
See Viaud, (Louis Marie) Julien
See also DLB 123; GFL 1789 to the Present

Lou, Henri
See Andreas-Salome, Lou

Louie, David Wong 1954- .... **CLC 70**
See also CA 139; CANR 120

Louis, Adrian C. .... **NNAL**
See also CA 223

Louis, Father M.
See Merton, Thomas (James)

Louise, Heidi
See Erdrich, Louise

Lovecraft, H. P. 1890-1937 .... **SSC 3, 52; TCLC 4, 22**
See also AAYA 14; BPFB 2; CA 104; 133; CANR 106; DA3; DAM POP; HGG; MTCW 1, 2; MTFW 2005; RGAL 4; SCFW 1, 2; SFW 4; SUFW

Lovecraft, Howard Phillips
See Lovecraft, H. P.

Lovelace, Earl 1935- .... **CLC 51**
See also BW 2; CA 77-80; CANR 41, 72, 114; CD 5, 6; CDWLB 3; CN 1, 2, 3, 4, 5, 6, 7; DLB 125; EWL 3; MTCW 1

Lovelace, Richard 1618-1657 . **LC 24; PC 69**
See also BRW 2; DLB 131; EXPP; PAB; RGEL 2

Lowe, Pardee 1904- .... **AAL**

Lowell, Amy 1874-1925 ... **PC 13; TCLC 1, 8**
See also AAYA 57; AMW; CA 104; 151; DAM POET; DLB 54, 140; EWL 3; EXPP; LMFS 2; MAL 5; MBL; MTCW 2; MTFW 2005; RGAL 4; TUS

Lowell, James Russell 1819-1891 ... **NCLC 2, 90**
See also AMWS 1; CDALB 1640-1865; DLB 1, 11, 64, 79, 189, 235; RGAL 4

Lowell, Robert (Traill Spence, Jr.)
1917-1977 .... **CLC 1, 2, 3, 4, 5, 8, 9, 11, 15, 37, 124; PC 3; WLC 4**
See also AMW; AMWC 2; AMWR 2; CA 9-12R; 73-76; CABS 2; CAD; CANR 26, 60; CDALBS; CP 1, 2; DA; DA3; DAB; DAC; DAM MST, NOV; DLB 5, 169; EWL 3; MAL 5; MTCW 1, 2; MTFW 2005; PAB; PFS 6, 7; RGAL 4; WP

Lowenthal, Michael (Francis)
1969- .... **CLC 119**
See also CA 150; CANR 115

Lowndes, Marie Adelaide (Belloc)
1868-1947 .... **TCLC 12**
See also CA 107; CMW 4; DLB 70; RHW

Lowry, (Clarence) Malcolm
1909-1957 .... **SSC 31; TCLC 6, 40**
See also BPFB 2; BRWS 3; CA 105; 131; CANR 62, 105; CDBLB 1945-1960; DLB 15; EWL 3; MTCW 1, 2; MTFW 2005; RGEL 2

Lowry, Mina Gertrude 1882-1966
See Loy, Mina
See also CA 113

Lowry, Sam
See Soderbergh, Steven

Loxsmith, John
See Brunner, John (Kilian Houston)

Loy, Mina .... **CLC 28; PC 16**
See Lowry, Mina Gertrude
See also DAM POET; DLB 4, 54; PFS 20

Loyson-Bridet
See Schwob, Marcel (Mayer Andre)

Lucan 39-65 .... **CMLC 33**
See also AW 2; DLB 211; EFS 2; RGWL 2, 3

Lucas, Craig 1951- .... **CLC 64**
See also CA 137; CAD; CANR 71, 109, 142; CD 5, 6; GLL 2; MTFW 2005

Lucas, E(dward) V(errall)
1868-1938 .... **TCLC 73**
See also CA 176; DLB 98, 149, 153; SATA 20

Lucas, George 1944- .... **CLC 16**
See also AAYA 1, 23; CA 77-80; CANR 30; SATA 56

Lucas, Hans
See Godard, Jean-Luc

Lucas, Victoria
See Plath, Sylvia

Lucian c. 125-c. 180 .... **CMLC 32**
See also AW 2; DLB 176; RGWL 2, 3

Lucilius c. 180B.C.-102B.C. .... **CMLC 82**
See also DLB 211

Lucretius c. 94B.C.-c. 49B.C. .... **CMLC 48**
See also AW 2; CDWLB 1; DLB 211; EFS 2; RGWL 2, 3; WLIT 8

Ludlam, Charles 1943-1987 .... **CLC 46, 50**
See also CA 85-88; 122; CAD; CANR 72, 86; DLB 266

Ludlum, Robert 1927-2001 .... **CLC 22, 43**
See also AAYA 10, 59; BEST 89:1, 90:3; BPFB 2; CA 33-36R; 195; CANR 25, 41, 68, 105, 131; CMW 4; CPW; DA3; DAM NOV, POP; DLBY 1982; MSW; MTCW 1, 2; MTFW 2005

Ludwig, Ken 1950- .... **CLC 60**
See also CA 195; CAD; CD 6

Ludwig, Otto 1813-1865 .... **NCLC 4**
See also DLB 129

Lugones, Leopoldo 1874-1938 .... **HLCS 2; TCLC 15**
See also CA 116; 131; CANR 104; DLB 283; EWL 3; HW 1; LAW

Lu Hsun .... **SSC 20; TCLC 3**
See Shu-Jen, Chou
See also EWL 3

Lukacs, George .... **CLC 24**
See Lukacs, Gyorgy (Szegeny von)

Macleod, Fiona
See Sharp, William
See also RGEL 2; SUFW

MacNeice, (Frederick) Louis
1907-1963 .... **CLC 1, 4, 10, 53; PC 61**
See also BRW 7; CA 85-88; CANR 61;
DAB; DAM POET; DLB 10, 20; EWL 3;
MTCW 1, 2; MTFW 2005; RGEL 2

MacNeill, Dand
See Fraser, George MacDonald

Macpherson, James 1736-1796 .... **LC 29**
See Ossian
See also BRWS 8; DLB 109; RGEL 2

Macpherson, (Jean) Jay 1931- .... **CLC 14**
See also CA 5-8R; CANR 90; CP 1, 2, 3, 4,
6, 7; CWP; DLB 53

Macrobius fl. 430- .... **CMLC 48**

MacShane, Frank 1927-1999 .... **CLC 39**
See also CA 9-12R; 186; CANR 3, 33; DLB
111

Macumber, Mari
See Sandoz, Mari(e Susette)

Madach, Imre 1823-1864 .... **NCLC 19**

Madden, (Jerry) David 1933- .... **CLC 5, 15**
See also CA 1-4R; CAAS 3; CANR 4, 45;
CN 3, 4, 5, 6, 7; CSW; DLB 6; MTCW 1

Maddern, Al(an)
See Ellison, Harlan

Madhubuti, Haki R. 1942- ... **BLC 2; CLC 6,
73; PC 5**
See Lee, Don L.
See also BW 2, 3; CA 73-76; CANR 24,
51, 73, 139; CP 6, 7; CSW; DAM MULT,
POET; DLB 5, 41; DLBD 8; EWL 3;
MAL 5; MTCW 2; MTFW 2005; RGAL
4

Madison, James 1751-1836 .... **NCLC 126**
See also DLB 37

Maepenn, Hugh
See Kuttner, Henry

Maepenn, K. H.
See Kuttner, Henry

Maeterlinck, Maurice 1862-1949 ..... **TCLC 3**
See also CA 104; 136; CANR 80; DAM
DRAM; DLB 192; EW 8; EWL 3; GFL
1789 to the Present; LMFS 2; RGWL 2,
3; SATA 66; TWA

Maginn, William 1794-1842 .... **NCLC 8**
See also DLB 110, 159

Mahapatra, Jayanta 1928- .... **CLC 33**
See also CA 73-76; CAAS 9; CANR 15,
33, 66, 87; CP 4, 5, 6, 7; DAM MULT;
DLB 323

Mahfouz, Naguib 1911(?)-2006 ..... **CLC 153;
SSC 66**
See Mahfuz, Najib
See also AAYA 49; BEST 89:2; CA 128;
CANR 55, 101; DA3; DAM NOV;
MTCW 1, 2; MTFW 2005; RGWL 2, 3;
SSFS 9

Mahfouz, Naguib Abdel Aziz Al-Sabilgi
See Mahfouz, Naguib

Mahfuz, Najib .... **CLC 52, 55**
See Mahfouz, Naguib
See also AFW; CWW 2; DLBY 1988; EWL
3; RGSF 2; WLIT 6

Mahon, Derek 1941- .... **CLC 27; PC 60**
See also BRWS 6; CA 113; 128; CANR 88;
CP 1, 2, 3, 4, 5, 6, 7; DLB 40; EWL 3

Maiakovskii, Vladimir
See Mayakovski, Vladimir (Vladimirovich)
See also IDTP; RGWL 2, 3

Mailer, Norman 1923- ... **CLC 1, 2, 3, 4, 5, 8,
11, 14, 28, 39, 74, 111**
See also AAYA 31; AITN 2; AMW; AMWC
2; AMWR 2; BPFB 2; CA 9-12R; CABS
1; CANR 28, 74, 77, 130; CDALB 1968-
1988; CN 1, 2, 3, 4, 5, 6, 7; CPW; DA;
DA3; DAB; DAC; DAM MST, NOV,

POP; DLB 2, 16, 28, 185, 278; DLBD 3;
DLBY 1980, 1983; EWL 3; MAL 5;
MTCW 1, 2; MTFW 2005; NFS 10;
RGAL 4; TUS

Mailer, Norman Kingsley
See Mailer, Norman

Maillet, Antonine 1929- .... **CLC 54, 118**
See also CA 115; 120; CANR 46, 74, 77,
134; CCA 1; CWW 2; DAC; DLB 60;
INT CA-120; MTCW 2; MTFW 2005

Maimonides, Moses 1135-1204 ..... **CMLC 76**
See also DLB 115

Mais, Roger 1905-1955 .... **TCLC 8**
See also BW 1, 3; CA 105; 124; CANR 82;
CDWLB 3; DLB 125; EWL 3; MTCW 1;
RGEL 2

Maistre, Joseph 1753-1821 .... **NCLC 37**
See also GFL 1789 to the Present

Maitland, Frederic William
1850-1906 .... **TCLC 65**

Maitland, Sara (Louise) 1950- .... **CLC 49**
See also BRWS 11; CA 69-72; CANR 13,
59; DLB 271; FW

Major, Clarence 1936- ... **BLC 2; CLC 3, 19,
48**
See also AFAW 2; BW 2, 3; CA 21-24R;
CAAS 6; CANR 13, 25, 53, 82; CN 3, 4,
5, 6, 7; CP 2, 3, 4, 5, 6, 7; CSW; DAM
MULT; DLB 33; EWL 3; MAL 5; MSW

Major, Kevin (Gerald) 1949- .... **CLC 26**
See also AAYA 16; CA 97-100; CANR 21,
38, 112; CLR 11; DAC; DLB 60; INT
CANR-21; JRDA; MAICYA 1, 2; MAIC-
YAS 1; SATA 32, 82, 134; WYA; YAW

Maki, James
See Ozu, Yasujiro

Makine, Andrei 1957- .... **CLC 198**
See also CA 176; CANR 103; MTFW 2005

Malabaila, Damiano
See Levi, Primo

Malamud, Bernard 1914-1986 .. **CLC 1, 2, 3,
5, 8, 9, 11, 18, 27, 44, 78, 85; SSC 15;
TCLC 129; WLC 4**
See also AAYA 16; AMWS 1; BPFB 2;
BYA 15; CA 5-8R; 118; CABS 1; CANR
28, 62, 114; CDALB 1941-1968; CN 1, 2,
3, 4; CPW; DA; DA3; DAB; DAC; DAM
MST, NOV, POP; DLB 2, 28, 152; DLBY
1980, 1986; EWL 3; EXPS; LAIT 4;
LATS 1:1; MAL 5; MTCW 1, 2; MTFW
2005; NFS 4, 9; RGAL 4; RGHL; RGSF
2; SSFS 8, 13, 16; TUS

Malan, Herman
See Bosman, Herman Charles; Bosman,
Herman Charles

Malaparte, Curzio 1898-1957 .... **TCLC 52**
See also DLB 264

Malcolm, Dan
See Silverberg, Robert

Malcolm, Janet 1934- .... **CLC 201**
See also CA 123; CANR 89; NCFS 1

Malcolm X .... **BLC 2; CLC 82, 117; WLCS**
See Little, Malcolm
See also LAIT 5; NCFS 3

Malebranche, Nicolas 1638-1715 .... **LC 133**
See also GFL Beginnings to 1789

Malherbe, Francois de 1555-1628 .... **LC 5**
See also DLB 327; GFL Beginnings to 1789

Mallarme, Stephane 1842-1898 ...... **NCLC 4,
41; PC 4**
See also DAM POET; DLB 217; EW 7;
GFL 1789 to the Present; LMFS 2; RGWL
2, 3; TWA

Mallet-Joris, Francoise 1930- .... **CLC 11**
See also CA 65-68; CANR 17; CWW 2;
DLB 83; EWL 3; GFL 1789 to the Present

Malley, Ern
See McAuley, James Phillip

Mallon, Thomas 1951- .... **CLC 172**
See also CA 110; CANR 29, 57, 92

Mallowan, Agatha Christie
See Christie, Agatha (Mary Clarissa)

Maloff, Saul 1922- .... **CLC 5**
See also CA 33-36R

Malone, Louis
See MacNeice, (Frederick) Louis

Malone, Michael (Christopher)
1942- .... **CLC 43**
See also CA 77-80; CANR 14, 32, 57, 114

Malory, Sir Thomas 1410(?)-1471(?) . **LC 11,
88; WLCS**
See also BRW 1; BRWR 2; CDBLB Before
1660; DA; DAB; DAC; DAM MST; DLB
146; EFS 2; RGEL 2; SATA 59; SATA-
Brief 33; TEA; WLIT 3

Malouf, David 1934- .... **CLC 28, 86**
See also BRWS 12; CA 124; CANR 50, 76;
CN 3, 4, 5, 6, 7; CP 1, 3, 4, 5, 6, 7; DLB
289; EWL 3; MTCW 2; MTFW 2005;
SSFS 24

Malraux, (Georges-)Andre
1901-1976 .... **CLC 1, 4, 9, 13, 15, 57**
See also BPFB 2; CA 21-22; 69-72; CANR
34, 58; CAP 2; DA3; DAM NOV; DLB
72; EW 12; EWL 3; GFL 1789 to the
Present; MTCW 1, 2; MTFW 2005;
RGWL 2, 3; TWA

Malthus, Thomas Robert
1766-1834 .... **NCLC 145**
See also DLB 107, 158; RGEL 2

Malzberg, Barry N(athaniel) 1939- ... **CLC 7**
See also CA 61-64; CAAS 4; CANR 16;
CMW 4; DLB 8; SFW 4

Mamet, David 1947- .. **CLC 9, 15, 34, 46, 91,
166; DC 4, 24**
See also AAYA 3, 60; AMWS 14; CA 81-
84; CABS 3; CAD; CANR 15, 41, 67, 72,
129; CD 5, 6; DA3; DAM DRAM; DFS
2, 3, 6, 12, 15; DLB 7; EWL 3; IDFW 4;
MAL 5; MTCW 1, 2; MTFW 2005;
RGAL 4

Mamet, David Alan
See Mamet, David

Mamoulian, Rouben (Zachary)
1897-1987 .... **CLC 16**
See also CA 25-28R; 124; CANR 85

Mandelshtam, Osip
See Mandelstam, Osip (Emilievich)
See also EW 10; EWL 3; RGWL 2, 3

Mandelstam, Osip (Emilievich)
1891(?)-1943(?) .... **PC 14; TCLC 2, 6**
See Mandelshtam, Osip
See also CA 104; 150; MTCW 2; TWA

Mander, (Mary) Jane 1877-1949 ... **TCLC 31**
See also CA 162; RGEL 2

Mandeville, Bernard 1670-1733 .... **LC 82**
See also DLB 101

Mandeville, Sir John fl. 1350- ...... **CMLC 19**
See also DLB 146

Mandiargues, Andre Pieyre de .... **CLC 41**
See Pieyre de Mandiargues, Andre
See also DLB 83

Mandrake, Ethel Belle
See Thurman, Wallace (Henry)

Mangan, James Clarence
1803-1849 .... **NCLC 27**
See also RGEL 2

Maniere, J.-E.
See Giraudoux, Jean(-Hippolyte)

Mankiewicz, Herman (Jacob)
1897-1953 .... **TCLC 85**
See also CA 120; 169; DLB 26; IDFW 3, 4

Manley, (Mary) Delariviere
1672(?)-1724 .... **LC 1, 42**
See also DLB 39, 80; RGEL 2

Mann, Abel
See Creasey, John

Martineau, Harriet 1802-1876 ...... **NCLC 26, 137**
  See also DLB 21, 55, 159, 163, 166, 190; FW; RGEL 2; YABC 2

Martines, Julia
  See O'Faolain, Julia

Martinez, Enrique Gonzalez
  See Gonzalez Martinez, Enrique

Martinez, Jacinto Benavente y
  See Benavente (y Martinez), Jacinto

Martinez de la Rosa, Francisco de Paula
  1787-1862 .... **NCLC 102**
  See also TWA

Martinez Ruiz, Jose 1873-1967
  See Azorin; Ruiz, Jose Martinez
  See also CA 93-96; HW 1

Martinez Sierra, Gregorio
  See Martinez Sierra, Maria

Martinez Sierra, Gregorio
  1881-1947 .... **TCLC 6**
  See also CA 115; EWL 3

Martinez Sierra, Maria 1874-1974 .. **TCLC 6**
  See also CA 250; 115; EWL 3

Martinsen, Martin
  See Follett, Ken

Martinson, Harry (Edmund)
  1904-1978 .... **CLC 14**
  See also CA 77-80; CANR 34, 130; DLB 259; EWL 3

Martyn, Edward 1859-1923 .... **TCLC 131**
  See also CA 179; DLB 10; RGEL 2

Marut, Ret
  See Traven, B.

Marut, Robert
  See Traven, B.

Marvell, Andrew 1621-1678 .... **LC 4, 43; PC 10; WLC 4**
  See also BRW 2; BRWR 2; CDBLB 1660-1789; DA; DAB; DAC; DAM MST, POET; DLB 131; EXPP; PFS 5; RGEL 2; TEA; WP

Marx, Karl (Heinrich)
  1818-1883 .... **NCLC 17, 114**
  See also DLB 129; LATS 1:1; TWA

Masaoka, Shiki -1902 .... **TCLC 18**
  See Masaoka, Tsunenori
  See also RGWL 3

Masaoka, Tsunenori 1867-1902
  See Masaoka, Shiki
  See also CA 117; 191; TWA

Masefield, John (Edward)
  1878-1967 .... **CLC 11, 47**
  See also CA 19-20; 25-28R; CANR 33; CAP 2; CDBLB 1890-1914; DAM POET; DLB 10, 19, 153, 160; EWL 3; EXPP; FANT; MTCW 1, 2; PFS 5; RGEL 2; SATA 19

Maso, Carole 1955(?)- .... **CLC 44**
  See also CA 170; CANR 148; CN 7; GLL 2; RGAL 4

Mason, Bobbie Ann 1940- ... **CLC 28, 43, 82, 154; SSC 4**
  See also AAYA 5, 42; AMWS 8; BPFB 2; CA 53-56; CANR 11, 31, 58, 83, 125; CDALBS; CN 5, 6, 7; CSW; DA3; DLB 173; DLBY 1987; EWL 3; EXPS; INT CANR-31; MAL 5; MTCW 1, 2; MTFW 2005; NFS 4; RGAL 4; RGSF 2; SSFS 3, 8, 20; TCLE 1:2; YAW

Mason, Ernst
  See Pohl, Frederik

Mason, Hunni B.
  See Sternheim, (William Adolf) Carl

Mason, Lee W.
  See Malzberg, Barry N(athaniel)

Mason, Nick 1945- .... **CLC 35**

Mason, Tally
  See Derleth, August (William)

Mass, Anna .... **CLC 59**

Mass, William
  See Gibson, William

Massinger, Philip 1583-1640 .... **LC 70**
  See also BRWS 11; DLB 58; RGEL 2

Master Lao
  See Lao Tzu

Masters, Edgar Lee 1868-1950 ...... **PC 1, 36; TCLC 2, 25; WLCS**
  See also AMWS 1; CA 104; 133; CDALB 1865-1917; DA; DAC; DAM MST, POET; DLB 54; EWL 3; EXPP; MAL 5; MTCW 1, 2; MTFW 2005; RGAL 4; TUS; WP

Masters, Hilary 1928- .... **CLC 48**
  See also CA 25-28R, 217; CAAE 217; CANR 13, 47, 97; CN 6, 7; DLB 244

Mastrosimone, William 1947- .... **CLC 36**
  See also CA 186; CAD; CD 5, 6

Mathe, Albert
  See Camus, Albert

Mather, Cotton 1663-1728 .... **LC 38**
  See also AMWS 2; CDALB 1640-1865; DLB 24, 30, 140; RGAL 4; TUS

Mather, Increase 1639-1723 .... **LC 38**
  See also DLB 24

Mathers, Marshall
  See Eminem

Mathers, Marshall Bruce
  See Eminem

Matheson, Richard (Burton) 1926- .. **CLC 37**
  See also AAYA 31; CA 97-100; CANR 88, 99; DLB 8, 44; HGG; INT CA-97-100; SCFW 1, 2; SFW 4; SUFW 2

Mathews, Harry (Burchell) 1930- ..... **CLC 6, 52**
  See also CA 21-24R; CAAS 6; CANR 18, 40, 98; CN 5, 6, 7

Mathews, John Joseph 1894-1979 .. **CLC 84; NNAL**
  See also CA 19-20; 142; CANR 45; CAP 2; DAM MULT; DLB 175; TCWW 1, 2

Mathias, Roland (Glyn) 1915- .... **CLC 45**
  See also CA 97-100; CANR 19, 41; CP 1, 2, 3, 4, 5, 6, 7; DLB 27

Matsuo Basho 1644(?)-1694 ...... **LC 62; PC 3**
  See Basho, Matsuo
  See also DAM POET; PFS 2, 7, 18

Mattheson, Rodney
  See Creasey, John

Matthews, (James) Brander
  1852-1929 .... **TCLC 95**
  See also CA 181; DLB 71, 78; DLBD 13

Matthews, Greg 1949- .... **CLC 45**
  See also CA 135

Matthews, William (Procter III)
  1942-1997 .... **CLC 40**
  See also AMWS 9; CA 29-32R; 162; CAAS 18; CANR 12, 57; CP 2, 3, 4, 5, 6; DLB 5

Matthias, John (Edward) 1941- .... **CLC 9**
  See also CA 33-36R; CANR 56; CP 4, 5, 6, 7

Matthiessen, F(rancis) O(tto)
  1902-1950 .... **TCLC 100**
  See also CA 185; DLB 63; MAL 5

Matthiessen, Peter 1927- ... **CLC 5, 7, 11, 32, 64**
  See also AAYA 6, 40; AMWS 5; ANW; BEST 90:4; BPFB 2; CA 9-12R; CANR 21, 50, 73, 100, 138; CN 1, 2, 3, 4, 5, 6, 7; DA3; DAM NOV; DLB 6, 173, 275; MAL 5; MTCW 1, 2; MTFW 2005; SATA 27

Maturin, Charles Robert
  1780(?)-1824 .... **NCLC 6, 169**
  See also BRWS 8; DLB 178; GL 3; HGG; LMFS 1; RGEL 2; SUFW

Matute (Ausejo), Ana Maria 1925- .. **CLC 11**
  See also CA 89-92; CANR 129; CWW 2; DLB 322; EWL 3; MTCW 1; RGSF 2

Maugham, W. S.
  See Maugham, W(illiam) Somerset

Maugham, W(illiam) Somerset
  1874-1965 .. **CLC 1, 11, 15, 67, 93; SSC 8, 94; WLC 4**
  See also AAYA 55; BPFB 2; BRW 6; CA 5-8R; 25-28R; CANR 40, 127; CDBLB 1914-1945; CMW 4; DA; DA3; DAB; DAC; DAM DRAM, MST, NOV; DFS 22; DLB 10, 36, 77, 100, 162, 195; EWL 3; LAIT 3; MTCW 1, 2; MTFW 2005; NFS 23; RGEL 2; RGSF 2; SATA 54; SSFS 17

Maugham, William Somerset
  See Maugham, W(illiam) Somerset

Maupassant, (Henri Rene Albert) Guy de
  1850-1893 . **NCLC 1, 42, 83; SSC 1, 64; WLC 4**
  See also BYA 14; DA; DA3; DAB; DAC; DAM MST; DLB 123; EW 7; EXPS; GFL 1789 to the Present; LAIT 2; LMFS 1; RGSF 2; RGWL 2, 3; SSFS 4, 21; SUFW; TWA

Maupin, Armistead 1944- .... **CLC 95**
  See also CA 125; 130; CANR 58, 101; CPW; DA3; DAM POP; DLB 278; GLL 1; INT CA-130; MTCW 2; MTFW 2005

Maupin, Armistead Jones, Jr.
  See Maupin, Armistead

Maurhut, Richard
  See Traven, B.

Mauriac, Claude 1914-1996 .... **CLC 9**
  See also CA 89-92; 152; CWW 2; DLB 83; EWL 3; GFL 1789 to the Present

Mauriac, Francois (Charles)
  1885-1970 .... **CLC 4, 9, 56; SSC 24**
  See also CA 25-28; CAP 2; DLB 65; EW 10; EWL 3; GFL 1789 to the Present; MTCW 1, 2; MTFW 2005; RGWL 2, 3; TWA

Mavor, Osborne Henry 1888-1951
  See Bridie, James
  See also CA 104

Maxwell, William (Keepers, Jr.)
  1908-2000 .... **CLC 19**
  See also AMWS 8; CA 93-96; 189; CANR 54, 95; CN 1, 2, 3, 4, 5, 6, 7; DLB 218, 278; DLBY 1980; INT CA-93-96; MAL 5; SATA-Obit 128

May, Elaine 1932- .... **CLC 16**
  See also CA 124; 142; CAD; CWD; DLB 44

Mayakovski, Vladimir (Vladimirovich)
  1893-1930 .... **TCLC 4, 18**
  See Maiakovskii, Vladimir; Mayakovsky, Vladimir
  See also CA 104; 158; EWL 3; MTCW 2; MTFW 2005; SFW 4; TWA

Mayakovsky, Vladimir
  See Mayakovski, Vladimir (Vladimirovich)
  See also EW 11; WP

Mayhew, Henry 1812-1887 .... **NCLC 31**
  See also DLB 18, 55, 190

Mayle, Peter 1939(?)- .... **CLC 89**
  See also CA 139; CANR 64, 109

Maynard, Joyce 1953- .... **CLC 23**
  See also CA 111; 129; CANR 64

Mayne, William (James Carter)
  1928- .... **CLC 12**
  See also AAYA 20; CA 9-12R; CANR 37, 80, 100; CLR 25; FANT; JRDA; MAI-CYA 1, 2; MAICYAS 1; SAAS 11; SATA 6, 68, 122; SUFW 2; YAW

Mayo, Jim
  See L'Amour, Louis

Maysles, Albert 1926- .... **CLC 16**
  See also CA 29-32R

Maysles, David 1932-1987 .... CLC 16
    See also CA 191
Mazer, Norma Fox 1931- .... CLC 26
    See also AAYA 5, 36; BYA 1, 8; CA 69-72;
    CANR 12, 32, 66, 129; CLR 23; JRDA;
    MAICYA 1, 2; SAAS 1; SATA 24, 67,
    105, 168; WYA; YAW
Mazzini, Guiseppe 1805-1872 .... NCLC 34
McAlmon, Robert (Menzies)
    1895-1956 .... TCLC 97
    See also CA 107; 168; DLB 4, 45; DLBD
    15; GLL 1
McAuley, James Phillip 1917-1976 .. CLC 45
    See also CA 97-100; CP 1, 2; DLB 260;
    RGEL 2
McBain, Ed
    See Hunter, Evan
    See also MSW
McBrien, William (Augustine)
    1930- .... CLC 44
    See also CA 107; CANR 90
McCabe, Patrick 1955- .... CLC 133
    See also BRWS 9; CA 130; CANR 50, 90;
    CN 6, 7; DLB 194
McCaffrey, Anne 1926- .... CLC 17
    See also AAYA 6, 34; AITN 2; BEST 89:2;
    BPFB 2; BYA 5; CA 25-28R, 227; CAAE
    227; CANR 15, 35, 55, 96; CLR 49;
    CPW; DA3; DAM NOV, POP; DLB 8;
    JRDA; MAICYA 1, 2; MTCW 1, 2;
    MTFW 2005; SAAS 11; SATA 8, 70, 116,
    152; SATA-Essay 152; SFW 4; SUFW 2;
    WYA; YAW
McCaffrey, Anne Inez
    See McCaffrey, Anne
McCall, Nathan 1955(?)- .... CLC 86
    See also AAYA 59; BW 3; CA 146; CANR
    88
McCann, Arthur
    See Campbell, John W(ood, Jr.)
McCann, Edson
    See Pohl, Frederik
McCarthy, Charles, Jr.
    See McCarthy, Cormac
McCarthy, Cormac 1933- .... CLC 4, 57, 101,
    204
    See also AAYA 41; AMWS 8; BPFB 2; CA
    13-16R; CANR 10, 42, 69, 101; CN 6, 7;
    CPW; CSW; DA3; DAM POP; DLB 6,
    143, 256; EWL 3; LATS 1:2; MAL 5;
    MTCW 2; MTFW 2005; TCLE 1:2;
    TCWW 2
McCarthy, Mary (Therese)
    1912-1989 .. CLC 1, 3, 5, 14, 24, 39, 59;
    SSC 24
    See also AMW; BPFB 2; CA 5-8R; 129;
    CANR 16, 50, 64; CN 1, 2, 3, 4; DA3;
    DLB 2; DLBY 1981; EWL 3; FW; INT
    CANR-16; MAL 5; MBL; MTCW 1, 2;
    MTFW 2005; RGAL 4; TUS
McCartney, James Paul
    See McCartney, Paul
McCartney, Paul 1942- .... CLC 12, 35
    See also CA 146; CANR 111
McCauley, Stephen (D.) 1955- .... CLC 50
    See also CA 141
McClaren, Peter .... CLC 70
McClure, Michael (Thomas) 1932- ... CLC 6,
    10
    See also BG 1:3; CA 21-24R; CAD; CANR
    17, 46, 77, 131; CD 5, 6; CP 1, 2, 3, 4, 5,
    6, 7; DLB 16; WP
McCorkle, Jill (Collins) 1958- .... CLC 51
    See also CA 121; CANR 113; CSW; DLB
    234; DLBY 1987; SSFS 24
McCourt, Frank 1930- .... CLC 109
    See also AAYA 61; AMWS 12; CA 157;
    CANR 97, 138; MTFW 2005; NCFS 1

McCourt, James 1941- .... CLC 5
    See also CA 57-60; CANR 98, 152
McCourt, Malachy 1931- .... CLC 119
    See also SATA 126
McCoy, Horace (Stanley)
    1897-1955 .... TCLC 28
    See also AMWS 13; CA 108; 155; CMW 4;
    DLB 9
McCrae, John 1872-1918 .... TCLC 12
    See also CA 109; DLB 92; PFS 5
McCreigh, James
    See Pohl, Frederik
McCullers, (Lula) Carson (Smith)
    1917-1967 .... CLC 1, 4, 10, 12, 48, 100;
    SSC 9, 24; TCLC 155; WLC 4
    See also AAYA 21; AMW; AMWC 2; BPFB
    2; CA 5-8R; 25-28R; CABS 1, 3; CANR
    18, 132; CDALB 1941-1968; DA; DA3;
    DAB; DAC; DAM MST, NOV; DFS 5,
    18; DLB 2, 7, 173, 228; EWL 3; EXPS;
    FW; GLL 1; LAIT 3, 4; MAL 5; MBL;
    MTCW 1, 2; MTFW 2005; NFS 6, 13;
    RGAL 4; RGSF 2; SATA 27; SSFS 5;
    TUS; YAW
McCulloch, John Tyler
    See Burroughs, Edgar Rice
McCullough, Colleen 1937- ...... CLC 27, 107
    See also AAYA 36; BPFB 2; CA 81-84;
    CANR 17, 46, 67, 98, 139; CPW; DA3;
    DAM NOV, POP; MTCW 1, 2; MTFW
    2005; RHW
McCunn, Ruthanne Lum 1946- .... AAL
    See also CA 119; CANR 43, 96; DLB 312;
    LAIT 2; SATA 63
McDermott, Alice 1953- .... CLC 90
    See also CA 109; CANR 40, 90, 126; CN
    7; DLB 292; MTFW 2005; NFS 23
McElroy, Joseph 1930- .... CLC 5, 47
    See also CA 17-20R; CANR 149; CN 3, 4,
    5, 6, 7
McElroy, Joseph Prince
    See McElroy, Joseph
McEwan, Ian 1948- .... CLC 13, 66, 169
    See also BEST 90:4; BRWS 4; CA 61-64;
    CANR 14, 41, 69, 87, 132; CN 3, 4, 5, 6,
    7; DAM NOV; DLB 14, 194, 319, 326;
    HGG; MTCW 1, 2; MTFW 2005; RGSF
    2; SUFW 2; TEA
McFadden, David 1940- .... CLC 48
    See also CA 104; CP 1, 2, 3, 4, 5, 6, 7; DLB
    60; INT CA-104
McFarland, Dennis 1950- .... CLC 65
    See also CA 165; CANR 110
McGahern, John 1934-2006 .... CLC 5, 9, 48,
    156; SSC 17
    See also CA 17-20R; 249; CANR 29, 68,
    113; CN 1, 2, 3, 4, 5, 6, 7; DLB 14, 231,
    319; MTCW 1
McGinley, Patrick (Anthony) 1937- . CLC 41
    See also CA 120; 127; CANR 56; INT CA-
    127
McGinley, Phyllis 1905-1978 .... CLC 14
    See also CA 9-12R; 77-80; CANR 19; CP
    1, 2; CWRI 5; DLB 11, 48; MAL 5; PFS
    9, 13; SATA 2, 44; SATA-Obit 24
McGinniss, Joe 1942- .... CLC 32
    See also AITN 2; BEST 89:2; CA 25-28R;
    CANR 26, 70, 152; CPW; DLB 185; INT
    CANR-26
McGivern, Maureen Daly
    See Daly, Maureen
McGrath, Patrick 1950- .... CLC 55
    See also CA 136; CANR 65, 148; CN 5, 6,
    7; DLB 231; HGG; SUFW 2
McGrath, Thomas (Matthew)
    1916-1990 .... CLC 28, 59
    See also AMWS 10; CA 9-12R; 132; CANR
    6, 33, 95; CP 1, 2, 3, 4, 5; DAM POET;
    MAL 5; MTCW 1; SATA 41;
    SATA-Obit 66

McGuane, Thomas 1939- .. CLC 3, 7, 18, 45,
    127
    See also AITN 2; BPFB 2; CA 49-52;
    CANR 5, 24, 49, 94; CN 2, 3, 4, 5, 6, 7;
    DLB 2, 212; DLBY 1980; EWL 3; INT
    CANR-24; MAL 5; MTCW 1; MTFW
    2005; TCWW 1, 2
McGuckian, Medbh 1950- .... CLC 48, 174;
    PC 27
    See also BRWS 5; CA 143; CP 4, 5, 6, 7;
    CWP; DAM POET; DLB 40
McHale, Tom 1942(?)-1982 .... CLC 3, 5
    See also AITN 1; CA 77-80; 106; CN 1, 2,
    3
McHugh, Heather 1948- .... PC 61
    See also CA 69-72; CANR 11, 28, 55, 92;
    CP 4, 5, 6, 7; CWP; PFS 24
McIlvanney, William 1936- .... CLC 42
    See also CA 25-28R; CANR 61; CMW 4;
    DLB 14, 207
McIlwraith, Maureen Mollie Hunter
    See Hunter, Mollie
    See also SATA 2
McInerney, Jay 1955- .... CLC 34, 112
    See also AAYA 18; BPFB 2; CA 116; 123;
    CANR 45, 68, 116; CN 5, 6, 7; CPW;
    DA3; DAM POP; DLB 292; INT CA-123;
    MAL 5; MTCW 2; MTFW 2005
McIntyre, Vonda N. 1948- .... CLC 18
    See also CA 81-84; CANR 17, 34, 69;
    MTCW 1; SFW 4; YAW
McIntyre, Vonda Neel
    See McIntyre, Vonda N.
McKay, Claude .... BLC 3; HR 1:3; PC 2;
    TCLC 7, 41; WLC 4
    See McKay, Festus Claudius
    See also AFAW 1, 2; AMWS 10; DAB;
    DLB 4, 45, 51, 117; EWL 3; EXPP; GLL
    2; LAIT 3; LMFS 2; MAL 5; PAB; PFS
    4; RGAL 4; WP
McKay, Festus Claudius 1889-1948
    See McKay, Claude
    See also BW 1, 3; CA 104; 124; CANR 73;
    DA; DAC; DAM MST, MULT, NOV,
    POET; MTCW 1, 2; MTFW 2005; TUS
McKuen, Rod 1933- .... CLC 1, 3
    See also AITN 1; CA 41-44R; CANR 40;
    CP 1
McLoughlin, R. B.
    See Mencken, H(enry) L(ouis)
McLuhan, (Herbert) Marshall
    1911-1980 .... CLC 37, 83
    See also CA 9-12R; 102; CANR 12, 34, 61;
    DLB 88; INT CANR-12; MTCW 1, 2;
    MTFW 2005
McManus, Declan Patrick Aloysius
    See Costello, Elvis
McMillan, Terry 1951- .. BLCS; CLC 50, 61,
    112
    See also AAYA 21; AMWS 13; BPFB 2;
    BW 2, 3; CA 140; CANR 60, 104, 131;
    CN 7; CPW; DA3; DAM MULT, NOV,
    POP; MAL 5; MTCW 2; MTFW 2005;
    RGAL 4; YAW
McMurtry, Larry 1936- .... CLC 2, 3, 7, 11,
    27, 44, 127
    See also AAYA 15; AITN 2; AMWS 5;
    BEST 89:2; BPFB 2; CA 5-8R; CANR
    19, 43, 64, 103; CDALB 1968-1988; CN
    2, 3, 4, 5, 6, 7; CPW; CSW; DA3; DAM
    NOV, POP; DLB 2, 143, 256; DLBY
    1980, 1987; EWL 3; MAL 5; MTCW 1,
    2; MTFW 2005; RGAL 4; TCWW 1, 2
McMurtry, Larry Jeff
    See McMurtry, Larry
McNally, Terrence 1939- ... CLC 4, 7, 41, 91;
    DC 27
    See also AAYA 62; AMWS 13; CA 45-48;
    CAD; CANR 2, 56, 116; CD 5, 6; DA3;
    DAM DRAM; DFS 16, 19; DLB 7, 249;
    EWL 3; GLL 1; MTCW 2; MTFW 2005

McNally, Thomas Michael
See McNally, T.M.
McNally, T.M. 1961- .... **CLC 82**
See also CA 246
McNamer, Deirdre 1950- .... **CLC 70**
McNeal, Tom .... **CLC 119**
McNeile, Herman Cyril 1888-1937
See Sapper
See also CA 184; CMW 4; DLB 77
McNickle, (William) D'Arcy
1904-1977 .... **CLC 89; NNAL**
See also CA 9-12R; 85-88; CANR 5, 45;
DAM MULT; DLB 175, 212; RGAL 4;
SATA-Obit 22; TCWW 1, 2
McPhee, John 1931- .... **CLC 36**
See also AAYA 61; AMWS 3; ANW; BEST
90:1; CA 65-68; CANR 20, 46, 64, 69,
121; CPW; DLB 185, 275; MTCW 1, 2;
MTFW 2005; TUS
McPherson, James Alan 1943- . **BLCS; CLC
19, 77; SSC 95**
See also BW 1, 3; CA 25-28R; CAAS 17;
CANR 24, 74, 140; CN 3, 4, 5; CSW;
DLB 38, 244; EWL 3; MTCW 1, 2;
MTFW 2005; RGAL 4; RGSF 2; SSFS
23
McPherson, William (Alexander)
1933- .... **CLC 34**
See also CA 69-72; CANR 28; INT
CANR-28
McTaggart, J. McT. Ellis
See McTaggart, John McTaggart Ellis
McTaggart, John McTaggart Ellis
1866-1925 .... **TCLC 105**
See also CA 120; DLB 262
Mead, George Herbert 1863-1931 . **TCLC 89**
See also CA 212; DLB 270
Mead, Margaret 1901-1978 .... **CLC 37**
See also AITN 1; CA 1-4R; 81-84; CANR
4; DA3; FW; MTCW 1, 2; SATA-Obit 20
Meaker, Marijane 1927-
See Kerr, M. E.
See also CA 107; CANR 37, 63, 145; INT
CA-107; JRDA; MAICYA 1, 2; MAIC-
YAS 1; MTCW 1; SATA 20, 61, 99, 160;
SATA-Essay 111; YAW
Medoff, Mark (Howard) 1940- .... **CLC 6, 23**
See also AITN 1; CA 53-56; CAD; CANR
5; CD 5, 6; DAM DRAM; DFS 4; DLB
7; INT CANR-5
Medvedev, P. N.
See Bakhtin, Mikhail Mikhailovich
Meged, Aharon
See Megged, Aharon
Meged, Aron
See Megged, Aharon
Megged, Aharon 1920- .... **CLC 9**
See also CA 49-52; CAAS 13; CANR 1,
140; EWL 3; RGHL
Mehta, Deepa 1950- .... **CLC 208**
Mehta, Gita 1943- .... **CLC 179**
See also CA 225; CN 7; DNFS 2
Mehta, Ved 1934- .... **CLC 37**
See also CA 1-4R, 212; CAAE 212; CANR
2, 23, 69; DLB 323; MTCW 1; MTFW
2005
Melanchthon, Philipp 1497-1560 .... **LC 90**
See also DLB 179
Melanter
See Blackmore, R(ichard) D(oddridge)
Meleager c. 140B.C.-c. 70B.C. ...... **CMLC 53**
Melies, Georges 1861-1938 .... **TCLC 81**
Melikow, Loris
See Hofmannsthal, Hugo von
Melmoth, Sebastian
See Wilde, Oscar (Fingal O'Flahertie Wills)
Melo Neto, Joao Cabral de
See Cabral de Melo Neto, Joao
See also CWW 2; EWL 3

Meltzer, Milton 1915- .... **CLC 26**
See also AAYA 8, 45; BYA 2, 6; CA 13-
16R; CANR 38, 92, 107; CLR 13; DLB
61; JRDA; MAICYA 1, 2; SAAS 1; SATA
1, 50, 80, 128; SATA-Essay 124; WYA;
YAW
Melville, Herman 1819-1891 ..... **NCLC 3, 12,
29, 45, 49, 91, 93, 123, 157; SSC 1, 17,
46, 95; WLC 4**
See also AAYA 25; AMW; AMWR 1;
CDALB 1640-1865; DA; DA3; DAB;
DAC; DAM MST, NOV; DLB 3, 74, 250,
254; EXPN; EXPS; GL 3; LAIT 1, 2; NFS
7, 9; RGAL 4; RGSF 2; SATA 59; SSFS
3; TUS
Members, Mark
See Powell, Anthony
Membreno, Alejandro .... **CLC 59**
Menand, Louis 1952- .... **CLC 208**
See also CA 200
Menander c. 342B.C.-c. 293B.C. .... **CMLC 9,
51; DC 3**
See also AW 1; CDWLB 1; DAM DRAM;
DLB 176; LMFS 1; RGWL 2, 3
Menchu, Rigoberta 1959- .. **CLC 160; HLCS
2**
See also CA 175; CANR 135; DNFS 1;
WLIT 1
Mencken, H(enry) L(ouis)
1880-1956 .... **TCLC 13**
See also AMW; CA 105; 125; CDALB
1917-1929; DLB 11, 29, 63, 137, 222;
EWL 3; MAL 5; MTCW 1, 2; MTFW
2005; NCFS 4; RGAL 4; TUS
Mendelsohn, Jane 1965- .... **CLC 99**
See also CA 154; CANR 94
Mendoza, Inigo Lopez de
See Santillana, Inigo Lopez de Mendoza,
Marques de
Menton, Francisco de
See Chin, Frank (Chew, Jr.)
Mercer, David 1928-1980 .... **CLC 5**
See also CA 9-12R; 102; CANR 23; CBD;
DAM DRAM; DLB 13, 310; MTCW 1;
RGEL 2
Merchant, Paul
See Ellison, Harlan
Meredith, George 1828-1909 .. **PC 60; TCLC
17, 43**
See also CA 117; 153; CANR 80; CDBLB
1832-1890; DAM POET; DLB 18, 35, 57,
159; RGEL 2; TEA
Meredith, William (Morris) 1919- .... **CLC 4,
13, 22, 55; PC 28**
See also CA 9-12R; CAAS 14; CANR 6,
40, 129; CP 1, 2, 3, 4, 5, 6, 7; DAM
POET; DLB 5; MAL 5
Merezhkovsky, Dmitrii Sergeevich
See Merezhkovsky, Dmitry Sergeyevich
See also DLB 295
Merezhkovsky, Dmitry Sergeyevich
See Merezhkovsky, Dmitry Sergeyevich
See also EWL 3
Merezhkovsky, Dmitry Sergeyevich
1865-1941 .... **TCLC 29**
See Merezhkovsky, Dmitrii Sergeevich;
Merezhkovsky, Dmitry Sergeyevich
See also CA 169
Merimee, Prosper 1803-1870 ... **NCLC 6, 65;
SSC 7, 77**
See also DLB 119, 192; EW 6; EXPS; GFL
1789 to the Present; RGSF 2; RGWL 2,
3; SSFS 8; SUFW
Merkin, Daphne 1954- .... **CLC 44**
See also CA 123
Merleau-Ponty, Maurice
1908-1961 .... **TCLC 156**
See also CA 114; 89-92; DLB 296; GFL
1789 to the Present

Merlin, Arthur
See Blish, James (Benjamin)
Mernissi, Fatima 1940- .... **CLC 171**
See also CA 152; FW
Merrill, James 1926-1995 ...... **CLC 2, 3, 6, 8,
13, 18, 34, 91; PC 28; TCLC 173**
See also AMWS 3; CA 13-16R; 147; CANR
10, 49, 63, 108; CP 1, 2, 3, 4; DA3; DAM
POET; DLB 5, 165; DLBY 1985; EWL 3;
INT CANR-10; MAL 5; MTCW 1, 2;
MTFW 2005; PAB; PFS 23; RGAL 4
Merriman, Alex
See Silverberg, Robert
Merriman, Brian 1747-1805 .... **NCLC 70**
Merritt, E. B.
See Waddington, Miriam
Merton, Thomas (James)
1915-1968 . **CLC 1, 3, 11, 34, 83; PC 10**
See also AAYA 61; AMWS 8; CA 5-8R;
25-28R; CANR 22, 53, 111, 131; DA3;
DLB 48; DLBY 1981; MAL 5; MTCW 1,
2; MTFW 2005
Merwin, W.S. 1927- ..... **CLC 1, 2, 3, 5, 8, 13,
18, 45, 88; PC 45**
See also AMWS 3; CA 13-16R; CANR 15,
51, 112, 140; CP 1, 2, 3, 4, 5, 6, 7; DA3;
DAM POET; DLB 5, 169; EWL 3; INT
CANR-15; MAL 5; MTCW 1, 2; MTFW
2005; PAB; PFS 5, 15; RGAL 4
Metastasio, Pietro 1698-1782 .... **LC 115**
See also RGWL 2, 3
Metcalf, John 1938- .... **CLC 37; SSC 43**
See also CA 113; CN 4, 5, 6, 7; DLB 60;
RGSF 2; TWA
Metcalf, Suzanne
See Baum, L(yman) Frank
Mew, Charlotte (Mary) 1870-1928 .. **TCLC 8**
See also CA 105; 189; DLB 19, 135; RGEL
2
Mewshaw, Michael 1943- .... **CLC 9**
See also CA 53-56; CANR 7, 47, 147;
DLBY 1980
Meyer, Conrad Ferdinand
1825-1898 .... **NCLC 81; SSC 30**
See also DLB 129; EW; RGWL 2, 3
Meyer, Gustav 1868-1932
See Meyrink, Gustav
See also CA 117; 190
Meyer, June
See Jordan, June
Meyer, Lynn
See Slavitt, David R(ytman)
Meyers, Jeffrey 1939- .... **CLC 39**
See also CA 73-76, 186; CAAE 186; CANR
54, 102; DLB 111
**Meynell, Alice (Christina Gertrude
Thompson)** 1847-1922 .... **TCLC 6**
See also CA 104; 177; DLB 19, 98; RGEL
2
Meyrink, Gustav .... **TCLC 21**
See Meyer, Gustav
See also DLB 81; EWL 3
Michaels, Leonard 1933-2003 ..... **CLC 6, 25;
SSC 16**
See also AMWS 16; CA 61-64; 216; CANR
21, 62, 119; CN 3, 4, 5, 6, 7; DLB 130;
MTCW 1; TCLE 1:2
Michaux, Henri 1899-1984 .... **CLC 8, 19**
See also CA 85-88; 114; DLB 258; EWL 3;
GFL 1789 to the Present; RGWL 2, 3
Micheaux, Oscar (Devereaux)
1884-1951 .... **TCLC 76**
See also BW 3; CA 174; DLB 50; TCWW
2
Michelangelo 1475-1564 .... **LC 12**
See also AAYA 43
Michelet, Jules 1798-1874 .... **NCLC 31**
See also EW 5; GFL 1789 to the Present

Michels, Robert 1876-1936 .... **TCLC 88**
See also CA 212

Michener, James A. 1907(?)-1997 . **CLC 1, 5, 11, 29, 60, 109**
See also AAYA 27; AITN 1; BEST 90:1; BPFB 2; CA 5-8R; 161; CANR 21, 45, 68; CN 1, 2, 3, 4, 5, 6; CPW; DA3; DAM NOV, POP; DLB 6; MAL 5; MTCW 1, 2; MTFW 2005; RHW; TCWW 1, 2

Mickiewicz, Adam 1798-1855 . **NCLC 3, 101; PC 38**
See also EW 5; RGWL 2, 3

Middleton, (John) Christopher 1926- .... **CLC 13**
See also CA 13-16R; CANR 29, 54, 117; CP 1, 2, 3, 4, 5, 6, 7; DLB 40

Middleton, Richard (Barham) 1882-1911 .... **TCLC 56**
See also CA 187; DLB 156; HGG

Middleton, Stanley 1919- .... **CLC 7, 38**
See also CA 25-28R; CAAS 23; CANR 21, 46, 81, 157; CN 1, 2, 3, 4, 5, 6, 7; DLB 14, 326

Middleton, Thomas 1580-1627 ...... **DC 5; LC 33, 123**
See also BRW 2; DAM DRAM, MST; DFS 18, 22; DLB 58; RGEL 2

Migueis, Jose Rodrigues 1901-1980 . **CLC 10**
See also DLB 287

Mikszath, Kalman 1847-1910 .... **TCLC 31**
See also CA 170

Miles, Jack .... **CLC 100**
See also CA 200

Miles, John Russiano
See Miles, Jack

Miles, Josephine (Louise) 1911-1985 .... **CLC 1, 2, 14, 34, 39**
See also CA 1-4R; 116; CANR 2, 55; CP 1, 2, 3, 4; DAM POET; DLB 48; MAL 5; TCLE 1:2

Militant
See Sandburg, Carl (August)

Mill, Harriet (Hardy) Taylor 1807-1858 .... **NCLC 102**
See also FW

Mill, John Stuart 1806-1873 .... **NCLC 11, 58**
See also CDBLB 1832-1890; DLB 55, 190, 262; FW 1; RGEL 2; TEA

Millar, Kenneth 1915-1983 .... **CLC 14**
See Macdonald, Ross
See also CA 9-12R; 110; CANR 16, 63, 107; CMW 4; CPW; DA3; DAM POP; DLB 2, 226; DLBD 6; DLBY 1983; MTCW 1, 2; MTFW 2005

Millay, E. Vincent
See Millay, Edna St. Vincent

Millay, Edna St. Vincent 1892-1950 ..... **PC 6, 61; TCLC 4, 49, 169; WLCS**
See Boyd, Nancy
See also AMW; CA 104; 130; CDALB 1917-1929; DA; DA3; DAB; DAC; DAM MST, POET; DLB 45, 249; EWL 3; EXPP; FL 1:6; MAL 5; MBL; MTCW 1, 2; MTFW 2005; PAB; PFS 3, 17; RGAL 4; TUS; WP

Miller, Arthur 1915-2005 ..... **CLC 1, 2, 6, 10, 15, 26, 47, 78, 179; DC 1; WLC 4**
See also AAYA 15; AITN 1; AMW; AMWC 1; CA 1-4R; 236; CABS 3; CAD; CANR 2, 30, 54, 76, 132; CD 5, 6; CDALB 1941-1968; DA; DA3; DAB; DAC; DAM DRAM, MST; DFS 1, 3, 8; DLB 7, 266; EWL 3; LAIT 1, 4; LATS 1:2; MAL 5; MTCW 1, 2; MTFW 2005; RGAL 4; RGHL; TUS; WYAS 1

Miller, Henry (Valentine) 1891-1980 .... **CLC 1, 2, 4, 9, 14, 43, 84; WLC 4**
See also AMW; BPFB 2; CA 9-12R; 97-100; CANR 33, 64; CDALB 1929-1941; CN 1, 2; DA; DA3; DAB; DAC; DAM MST, NOV; DLB 4, 9; DLBY 1980; EWL 3; MAL 5; MTCW 1, 2; MTFW 2005; RGAL 4; TUS

Miller, Hugh 1802-1856 .... **NCLC 143**
See also DLB 190

Miller, Jason 1939(?)-2001 .... **CLC 2**
See also AITN 1; CA 73-76; 197; CAD; CANR 130; DFS 12; DLB 7

Miller, Sue 1943- .... **CLC 44**
See also AMWS 12; BEST 90:3; CA 139; CANR 59, 91, 128; DA3; DAM POP; DLB 143

Miller, Walter M(ichael, Jr.) 1923-1996 .... **CLC 4, 30**
See also BPFB 2; CA 85-88; CANR 108; DLB 8; SCFW 1, 2; SFW 4

Millett, Kate 1934- .... **CLC 67**
See also AITN 1; CA 73-76; CANR 32, 53, 76, 110; DA3; DLB 246; FW; GLL 1; MTCW 1, 2; MTFW 2005

Millhauser, Steven 1943- ... **CLC 21, 54, 109; SSC 57**
See also CA 110; 111; CANR 63, 114, 133; CN 6, 7; DA3; DLB 2; FANT; INT CA-111; MAL 5; MTCW 2; MTFW 2005

Millhauser, Steven Lewis
See Millhauser, Steven

Millin, Sarah Gertrude 1889-1968 ... **CLC 49**
See also CA 102; 93-96; DLB 225; EWL 3

Milne, A. A. 1882-1956 .... **TCLC 6, 88**
See also BRWS 5; CA 104; 133; CLR 1, 26, 108; CMW 4; CWRI 5; DA3; DAB; DAC; DAM MST; DLB 10, 77, 100, 160; FANT; MAICYA 1, 2; MTCW 1, 2; MTFW 2005; RGEL 2; SATA 100; WCH; YABC 1

Milne, Alan Alexander
See Milne, A. A.

Milner, Ron(ald) 1938-2004 ..... **BLC 3; CLC 56**
See also AITN 1; BW 1; CA 73-76; 230; CAD; CANR 24, 81; CD 5, 6; DAM MULT; DLB 38; MAL 5; MTCW 1

Milnes, Richard Monckton 1809-1885 .... **NCLC 61**
See also DLB 32, 184

Milosz, Czeslaw 1911-2004 .... **CLC 5, 11, 22, 31, 56, 82; PC 8; WLCS**
See also AAYA 62; CA 81-84; 230; CANR 23, 51, 91, 126; CDWLB 4; CWW 2; DA3; DAM MST, POET; DLB 215; EW 13; EWL 3; MTCW 1, 2; MTFW 2005; PFS 16; RGHL; RGWL 2, 3

Milton, John 1608-1674 ..... **LC 9, 43, 92; PC 19, 29; WLC 4**
See also AAYA 65; BRW 2; BRWR 2; CD-BLB 1660-1789; DA; DA3; DAB; DAC; DAM MST, POET; DLB 131, 281; EFS 1; EXPP; LAIT 1; PAB; PFS 3, 17; RGEL 2; TEA; WLIT 3; WP

Min, Anchee 1957- .... **CLC 86**
See also CA 146; CANR 94, 137; MTFW 2005

Minehaha, Cornelius
See Wedekind, Frank

Miner, Valerie 1947- .... **CLC 40**
See also CA 97-100; CANR 59; FW; GLL 2

Minimo, Duca
See D'Annunzio, Gabriele

Minot, Susan (Anderson) 1956- ...... **CLC 44, 159**
See also AMWS 6; CA 134; CANR 118; CN 6, 7

Minus, Ed 1938- .... **CLC 39**
See also CA 185

Mirabai 1498(?)-1550(?) .... **PC 48**
See also PFS 24

Miranda, Javier
See Bioy Casares, Adolfo
See also CWW 2

Mirbeau, Octave 1848-1917 .... **TCLC 55**
See also CA 216; DLB 123, 192; GFL 1789 to the Present

Mirikitani, Janice 1942- .... **AAL**
See also CA 211; DLB 312; RGAL 4

Mirk, John (?)-c. 1414 .... **LC 105**
See also DLB 146

Miro (Ferrer), Gabriel (Francisco Victor) 1879-1930 .... **TCLC 5**
See also CA 104; 185; DLB 322; EWL 3

Misharin, Alexandr .... **CLC 59**

Mishima, Yukio ... **CLC 2, 4, 6, 9, 27; DC 1; SSC 4; TCLC 161; WLC 4**
See Hiraoka, Kimitake
See also AAYA 50; BPFB 2; GLL 1; MJW; RGSF 2; RGWL 2, 3; SSFS 5, 12

Mistral, Frederic 1830-1914 .... **TCLC 51**
See also CA 122; 213; GFL 1789 to the Present

Mistral, Gabriela
See Godoy Alcayaga, Lucila
See also DLB 283; DNFS 1; EWL 3; LAW; RGWL 2, 3; WP

Mistry, Rohinton 1952- ... **CLC 71, 196; SSC 73**
See also BRWS 10; CA 141; CANR 86, 114; CCA 1; CN 6, 7; DAC; SSFS 6

Mitchell, Clyde
See Ellison, Harlan

Mitchell, Emerson Blackhorse Barney 1945- .... **NNAL**
See also CA 45-48

Mitchell, James Leslie 1901-1935
See Gibbon, Lewis Grassic
See also CA 104; 188; DLB 15

Mitchell, Joni 1943- .... **CLC 12**
See also CA 112; CCA 1

Mitchell, Joseph (Quincy) 1908-1996 .... **CLC 98**
See also CA 77-80; 152; CANR 69; CN 1, 2, 3, 4, 5, 6; CSW; DLB 185; DLBY 1996

Mitchell, Margaret (Munnerlyn) 1900-1949 .... **TCLC 11, 170**
See also AAYA 23; BPFB 2; BYA 1; CA 109; 125; CANR 55, 94; CDALBS; DA3; DAM NOV, POP; DLB 9; LAIT 2; MAL 5; MTCW 1, 2; MTFW 2005; NFS 9; RGAL 4; RHW; TUS; WYAS 1; YAW

Mitchell, Peggy
See Mitchell, Margaret (Munnerlyn)

Mitchell, S(ilas) Weir 1829-1914 .... **TCLC 36**
See also CA 165; DLB 202; RGAL 4

Mitchell, W(illiam) O(rmond) 1914-1998 .... **CLC 25**
See also CA 77-80; 165; CANR 15, 43; CN 1, 2, 3, 4, 5, 6; DAC; DAM MST; DLB 88; TCLE 1:2

Mitchell, William (Lendrum) 1879-1936 .... **TCLC 81**
See also CA 213

Mitford, Mary Russell 1787-1855 ... **NCLC 4**
See also DLB 110, 116; RGEL 2

Mitford, Nancy 1904-1973 .... **CLC 44**
See also BRWS 10; CA 9-12R; CN 1; DLB 191; RGEL 2

Miyamoto, (Chujo) Yuriko 1899-1951 .... **TCLC 37**
See Miyamoto Yuriko
See also CA 170, 174

Miyamoto Yuriko
See Miyamoto, (Chujo) Yuriko
See also DLB 180

Miyazawa, Kenji 1896-1933 .... **TCLC 76**
See Miyazawa Kenji
See also CA 157; RGWL 3

Miyazawa Kenji
　　See Miyazawa, Kenji
　　See also EWL 3
Mizoguchi, Kenji 1898-1956 .... **TCLC 72**
　　See also CA 167
Mo, Timothy (Peter) 1950- .... **CLC 46, 134**
　　See also CA 117; CANR 128; CN 5, 6, 7;
　　DLB 194; MTCW 1; WLIT 4; WWE 1
Modarressi, Taghi (M.) 1931-1997 ... **CLC 44**
　　See also CA 121; 134; INT CA-134
Modiano, Patrick (Jean) 1945- .... **CLC 18,
　　218**
　　See also CA 85-88; CANR 17, 40, 115;
　　CWW 2; DLB 83, 299; EWL 3; RGHL
Mofolo, Thomas (Mokopu)
　　1875(?)-1948 .... **BLC 3; TCLC 22**
　　See also AFW; CA 121; 153; CANR 83;
　　DAM MULT; DLB 225; EWL 3; MTCW
　　2; MTFW 2005; WLIT 2
Mohr, Nicholasa 1938- .... **CLC 12; HLC 2**
　　See also AAYA 8, 46; CA 49-52; CANR 1,
　　32, 64; CLR 22; DAM MULT; DLB 145;
　　HW 1, 2; JRDA; LAIT 5; LLW; MAICYA
　　2; MAICYAS 1; RGAL 4; SAAS 8; SATA
　　8, 97; SATA-Essay 113; WYA; YAW
Moi, Toril 1953- .... **CLC 172**
　　See also CA 154; CANR 102; FW
Mojtabai, A(nn) G(race) 1938- ..... **CLC 5, 9,
　　15, 29**
　　See also CA 85-88; CANR 88
Moliere 1622-1673 ..... **DC 13; LC 10, 28, 64,
　　125, 127; WLC 4**
　　See also DA; DA3; DAB; DAC; DAM
　　DRAM, MST; DFS 13, 18, 20; DLB 268;
　　EW 3; GFL Beginnings to 1789; LATS
　　1:1; RGWL 2, 3; TWA
Molin, Charles
　　See Mayne, William (James Carter)
Molnar, Ferenc 1878-1952 .... **TCLC 20**
　　See also CA 109; 153; CANR 83; CDWLB
　　4; DAM DRAM; DLB 215; EWL 3;
　　RGWL 2, 3
Momaday, N. Scott 1934- ...... **CLC 2, 19, 85,
　　95, 160; NNAL; PC 25; WLCS**
　　See also AAYA 11, 64; AMWS 4; ANW;
　　BPFB 2; BYA 12; CA 25-28R; CANR 14,
　　34, 68, 134; CDALBS; CN 2, 3, 4, 5, 6,
　　7; CPW; DA; DA3; DAB; DAC; DAM
　　MST, MULT, NOV, POP; DLB 143, 175,
　　256; EWL 3; EXPP; INT CANR-14;
　　LAIT 4; LATS 1:2; MAL 5; MTCW 1, 2;
　　MTFW 2005; NFS 10; PFS 2, 11; RGAL
　　4; SATA 48; SATA-Brief 30; TCWW 1,
　　2; WP; YAW
Monette, Paul 1945-1995 .... **CLC 82**
　　See also AMWS 10; CA 139; 147; CN 6;
　　GLL 1
Monroe, Harriet 1860-1936 .... **TCLC 12**
　　See also CA 109; 204; DLB 54, 91
Monroe, Lyle
　　See Heinlein, Robert A.
Montagu, Elizabeth 1720-1800 .... **NCLC 7,
　　117**
　　See also FW
Montagu, Mary (Pierrepont) Wortley
　　1689-1762 .... **LC 9, 57; PC 16**
　　See also DLB 95, 101; FL 1:1; RGEL 2
Montagu, W. H.
　　See Coleridge, Samuel Taylor
Montague, John (Patrick) 1929- ..... **CLC 13,
　　46**
　　See also CA 9-12R; CANR 9, 69, 121; CP
　　1, 2, 3, 4, 5, 6, 7; DLB 40; EWL 3;
　　MTCW 1; PFS 12; RGEL 2; TCLE 1:2
Montaigne, Michel (Eyquem) de
　　1533-1592 .... **LC 8, 105; WLC 4**
　　See also DA; DAB; DAC; DAM MST;
　　DLB 327; EW 2; GFL Beginnings to
　　1789; LMFS 1; RGWL 2, 3; TWA

Montale, Eugenio 1896-1981 ... **CLC 7, 9, 18;
　　PC 13**
　　See also CA 17-20R; 104; CANR 30; DLB
　　114; EW 11; EWL 3; MTCW 1; PFS 22;
　　RGWL 2, 3; TWA; WLIT 7
Montesquieu, Charles-Louis de Secondat
　　1689-1755 .... **LC 7, 69**
　　See also DLB 314; EW 3; GFL Beginnings
　　to 1789; TWA
Montessori, Maria 1870-1952 ...... **TCLC 103**
　　See also CA 115; 147
Montgomery, (Robert) Bruce 1921(?)-1978
　　See Crispin, Edmund
　　See also CA 179; 104; CMW 4
Montgomery, L(ucy) M(aud)
　　1874-1942 .... **TCLC 51, 140**
　　See also AAYA 12; BYA 1; CA 108; 137;
　　CLR 8, 91; DA3; DAC; DAM MST; DLB
　　92; DLBD 14; JRDA; MAICYA 1, 2;
　　MTCW 2; MTFW 2005; RGEL 2; SATA
　　100; TWA; WCH; WYA; YABC 1
Montgomery, Marion H., Jr. 1925- .... **CLC 7**
　　See also AITN 1; CA 1-4R; CANR 3, 48;
　　CSW; DLB 6
Montgomery, Max
　　See Davenport, Guy (Mattison, Jr.)
Montherlant, Henry (Milon) de
　　1896-1972 .... **CLC 8, 19**
　　See also CA 85-88; 37-40R; DAM DRAM;
　　DLB 72, 321; EW 11; EWL 3; GFL 1789
　　to the Present; MTCW 1
Monty Python
　　See Chapman, Graham; Cleese, John
　　(Marwood); Gilliam, Terry; Idle, Eric;
　　Jones, Terence Graham Parry; Palin,
　　Michael (Edward)
　　See also AAYA 7
Moodie, Susanna (Strickland)
　　1803-1885 .... **NCLC 14, 113**
　　See also DLB 99
Moody, Hiram 1961-
　　See Moody, Rick
　　See also CA 138; CANR 64, 112; MTFW
　　2005
Moody, Minerva
　　See Alcott, Louisa May
Moody, Rick .... **CLC 147**
　　See Moody, Hiram
Moody, William Vaughan
　　1869-1910 .... **TCLC 105**
　　See also CA 110; 178; DLB 7, 54; MAL 5;
　　RGAL 4
Mooney, Edward 1951-
　　See Mooney, Ted
　　See also CA 130
Mooney, Ted .... **CLC 25**
　　See Mooney, Edward
Moorcock, Michael 1939- .... **CLC 5, 27, 58**
　　See Bradbury, Edward P.
　　See also AAYA 26; CA 45-48; CAAS 5;
　　CANR 2, 17, 38, 64, 122; CN 5, 6, 7;
　　DLB 14, 231, 261, 319; FANT; MTCW 1,
　　2; MTFW 2005; SATA 93, 166; SCFW 1,
　　2; SFW 4; SUFW 1, 2
Moorcock, Michael John
　　See Moorcock, Michael
Moore, Alan 1953- .... **CLC 230**
　　See also AAYA 51; CA 204; CANR 138;
　　DLB 261; MTFW 2005; SFW 4
Moore, Brian 1921-1999 ... **CLC 1, 3, 5, 7, 8,
　　19, 32, 90**
　　See Bryan, Michael
　　See also BRWS 9; CA 1-4R; 174; CANR 1,
　　25, 42, 63; CCA 1; CN 1, 2, 3, 4, 5, 6;
　　DAB; DAC; DAM MST; DLB 251; EWL
　　3; FANT; MTCW 1, 2; MTFW 2005;
　　RGEL 2
Moore, Edward
　　See Muir, Edwin
　　See also RGEL 2

Moore, G. E. 1873-1958 .... **TCLC 89**
　　See also DLB 262
Moore, George Augustus
　　1852-1933 .... **SSC 19; TCLC 7**
　　See also BRW 6; CA 104; 177; DLB 10,
　　18, 57, 135; EWL 3; RGEL 2; RGSF 2
Moore, Lorrie .... **CLC 39, 45, 68**
　　See Moore, Marie Lorena
　　See also AMWS 10; CN 5, 6, 7; DLB 234;
　　SSFS 19
Moore, Marianne (Craig)
　　1887-1972 .... **CLC 1, 2, 4, 8, 10, 13, 19,
　　47; PC 4, 49; WLCS**
　　See also AMW; CA 1-4R; 33-36R; CANR
　　3, 61; CDALB 1929-1941; CP 1; DA;
　　DA3; DAB; DAC; DAM MST, POET;
　　DLB 45; DLBD 7; EWL 3; EXPP; FL 1:6;
　　MAL 5; MBL; MTCW 1, 2; MTFW 2005;
　　PAB; PFS 14, 17; RGAL 4; SATA 20;
　　TUS; WP
Moore, Marie Lorena 1957- .... **CLC 165**
　　See Moore, Lorrie
　　See also CA 116; CANR 39, 83, 139; DLB
　　234; MTFW 2005
Moore, Michael 1954- .... **CLC 218**
　　See also AAYA 53; CA 166; CANR 150
Moore, Thomas 1779-1852 ... **NCLC 6, 110**
　　See also DLB 96, 144; RGEL 2
Moorhouse, Frank 1938- .... **SSC 40**
　　See also CA 118; CANR 92; CN 3, 4, 5, 6,
　　7; DLB 289; RGSF 2
Mora, Pat 1942- .... **HLC 2**
　　See also AMWS 13; CA 129; CANR 57,
　　81, 112; CLR 58; DAM MULT; DLB 209;
　　HW 1, 2; LLW; MAICYA 2; MTFW
　　2005; SATA 92, 134
Moraga, Cherrie 1952- .... **CLC 126; DC 22**
　　See also CA 131; CANR 66, 154; DAM
　　MULT; DLB 82, 249; FW; GLL 1; HW 1,
　　2; LLW
Morand, Paul 1888-1976 .... **CLC 41; SSC 22**
　　See also CA 184; 69-72; DLB 65; EWL 3
Morante, Elsa 1918-1985 .... **CLC 8, 47**
　　See also CA 85-88; 117; CANR 35; DLB
　　177; EWL 3; MTCW 1, 2; MTFW 2005;
　　RGHL; RGWL 2, 3; WLIT 7
Moravia, Alberto .... **CLC 2, 7, 11, 27, 46;
　　SSC 26**
　　See Pincherle, Alberto
　　See also DLB 177; EW 12; EWL 3; MTCW
　　2; RGSF 2; RGWL 2, 3; WLIT 7
More, Hannah 1745-1833 ...... **NCLC 27, 141**
　　See also DLB 107, 109, 116, 158; RGEL 2
More, Henry 1614-1687 .... **LC 9**
　　See also DLB 126, 252
More, Sir Thomas 1478(?)-1535 .... **LC 10, 32**
　　See also BRWC 1; BRWS 7; DLB 136, 281;
　　LMFS 1; RGEL 2; TEA
Moreas, Jean .... **TCLC 18**
　　See Papadiamantopoulos, Johannes
　　See also GFL 1789 to the Present
Moreton, Andrew Esq.
　　See Defoe, Daniel
Morgan, Berry 1919-2002 .... **CLC 6**
　　See also CA 49-52; 208; DLB 6
Morgan, Claire
　　See Highsmith, Patricia
　　See also GLL 1
Morgan, Edwin (George) 1920- .... **CLC 31**
　　See also BRWS 9; CA 5-8R; CANR 3, 43,
　　90; CP 1, 2, 3, 4, 5, 6, 7; DLB 27
Morgan, (George) Frederick
　　1922-2004 .... **CLC 23**
　　See also CA 17-20R; 224; CANR 21, 144;
　　CP 2, 3, 4, 5, 6, 7
Morgan, Harriet
　　See Mencken, H(enry) L(ouis)
Morgan, Jane
　　See Cooper, James Fenimore

NOV; DLB 53; EWL 3; MTCW 1, 2;
MTFW 2005; RGEL 2; RGSF 2; SATA
29; SSFS 5, 13, 19; TCLE 1:2; WWE 1

Munro, H(ector) H(ugh) 1870-1916
See Saki
See also AAYA 56; CA 104; 130; CANR
104; CDBLB 1890-1914; DA; DA3;
DAB; DAC; DAM MST, NOV; DLB 34,
162; EXPS; MTCW 1, 2; MTFW 2005;
RGEL 2; SSFS 15

Murakami, Haruki 1949- .... **CLC 150**
See Murakami Haruki
See also CA 165; CANR 102, 146; MJW;
RGWL 3; SFW 4; SSFS 23

Murakami Haruki
See Murakami, Haruki
See also CWW 2; DLB 182; EWL 3

Murasaki, Lady
See Murasaki Shikibu

Murasaki Shikibu 978(?)-1026(?) .. **CMLC 1, 79**
See also EFS 2; LATS 1:1; RGWL 2, 3

Murdoch, Iris 1919-1999 .. **CLC 1, 2, 3, 4, 6, 8, 11, 15, 22, 31, 51; TCLC 171**
See also BRWS 1; CA 13-16R; 179; CANR
8, 43, 68, 103, 142; CBD; CDBLB 1960
to Present; CN 1, 2, 3, 4, 5, 6; CWD;
DA3; DAB; DAC; DAM MST, NOV;
DLB 14, 194, 233, 326; EWL 3; INT
CANR-8; MTCW 1, 2; MTFW 2005; NFS
18; RGEL 2; TCLE 1:2; TEA; WLIT 4

Murfree, Mary Noailles 1850-1922 .. **SSC 22; TCLC 135**
See also CA 122; 176; DLB 12, 74; RGAL
4

Murglie
See Murnau, F.W.

Murnau, Friedrich Wilhelm
See Murnau, F.W.

Murnau, F.W. 1888-1931 .... **TCLC 53**
See also CA 112

Murphy, Richard 1927- .... **CLC 41**
See also BRWS 5; CA 29-32R; CP 1, 2, 3,
4, 5, 6, 7; DLB 40; EWL 3

Murphy, Sylvia 1937- .... **CLC 34**
See also CA 121

Murphy, Thomas (Bernard) 1935- ... **CLC 51**
See Murphy, Tom
See also CA 101

Murphy, Tom
See Murphy, Thomas (Bernard)
See also DLB 310

Murray, Albert L. 1916- .... **CLC 73**
See also BW 2; CA 49-52; CANR 26, 52,
78; CN 7; CSW; DLB 38; MTFW 2005

Murray, James Augustus Henry
1837-1915 .... **TCLC 117**

Murray, Judith Sargent
1751-1820 .... **NCLC 63**
See also DLB 37, 200

Murray, Les(lie Allan) 1938- .... **CLC 40**
See also BRWS 7; CA 21-24R; CANR 11,
27, 56, 103; CP 1, 2, 3, 4, 5, 6, 7; DAM
POET; DLB 289; DLBY 2001; EWL 3;
RGEL 2

Murry, J. Middleton
See Murry, John Middleton

Murry, John Middleton
1889-1957 .... **TCLC 16**
See also CA 118; 217; DLB 149

Musgrave, Susan 1951- .... **CLC 13, 54**
See also CA 69-72; CANR 45, 84; CCA 1;
CP 2, 3, 4, 5, 6, 7; CWP

Musil, Robert (Edler von)
1880-1942 .... **SSC 18; TCLC 12, 68**
See also CA 109; CANR 55, 84; CDWLB
2; DLB 81, 124; EW 9; EWL 3; MTCW
2; RGSF 2; RGWL 2, 3

Muske, Carol .... **CLC 90**
See Muske-Dukes, Carol (Anne)

Muske-Dukes, Carol (Anne) 1945-
See Muske, Carol
See also CA 65-68, 203; CAAE 203; CANR
32, 70; CWP; PFS 24

Musset, Alfred de 1810-1857 . **DC 27; NCLC 7, 150**
See also DLB 192, 217; EW 6; GFL 1789
to the Present; RGWL 2, 3; TWA

Musset, Louis Charles Alfred de
See Musset, Alfred de

Mussolini, Benito (Amilcare Andrea)
1883-1945 .... **TCLC 96**
See also CA 116

Mutanabbi, Al-
See al-Mutanabbi, Ahmad ibn al-Husayn
Abu al-Tayyib al-Jufi al-Kindi
See also WLIT 6

My Brother's Brother
See Chekhov, Anton (Pavlovich)

Myers, L(eopold) H(amilton)
1881-1944 .... **TCLC 59**
See also CA 157; DLB 15; EWL 3; RGEL
2

Myers, Walter Dean 1937- .. **BLC 3; CLC 35**
See Myers, Walter M.
See also AAYA 4, 23; BW 2; BYA 6, 8, 11;
CA 33-36R; CANR 20, 42, 67, 108; CLR
4, 16, 35, 110; DAM MULT, NOV; DLB
33; INT CANR-20; JRDA; LAIT 5; MAI-
CYA 1, 2; MAICYAS 1; MTCW 2;
MTFW 2005; SAAS 2; SATA 41, 71, 109,
157; SATA-Brief 27; WYA; YAW

Myers, Walter M.
See Myers, Walter Dean

Myles, Symon
See Follett, Ken

Nabokov, Vladimir (Vladimirovich)
1899-1977 .... **CLC 1, 2, 3, 6, 8, 11, 15, 23, 44, 46, 64; SSC 11, 86; TCLC 108; WLC 4**
See also AAYA 45; AMW; AMWC 1;
AMWR 1; BPFB 2; CA 5-8R; 69-72;
CANR 20, 102; CDALB 1941-1968; CN
1, 2; CP 2; DA; DA3; DAB; DAC; DAM
MST, NOV; DLB 2, 244, 278, 317; DLBD
3; DLBY 1980, 1991; EWL 3; EXPS;
LATS 1:2; MAL 5; MTCW 1, 2; MTFW
2005; NCFS 4; NFS 9; RGAL 4; RGSF
2; SSFS 6, 15; TUS

Naevius c. 265B.C.-201B.C. .... **CMLC 37**
See also DLB 211

Nagai, Kafu .... **TCLC 51**
See Nagai, Sokichi
See also DLB 180

Nagai, Sokichi 1879-1959
See Nagai, Kafu
See also CA 117

Nagy, Laszlo 1925-1978 .... **CLC 7**
See also CA 129; 112

Naidu, Sarojini 1879-1949 .... **TCLC 80**
See also EWL 3; RGEL 2

Naipaul, Shiva 1945-1985 .... **CLC 32, 39; TCLC 153**
See also CA 110; 112; 116; CANR 33; CN
2, 3; DA3; DAM NOV; DLB 157; DLBY
1985; EWL 3; MTCW 1, 2; MTFW 2005

Naipaul, V.S. 1932- .. **CLC 4, 7, 9, 13, 18, 37, 105, 199; SSC 38**
See also BPFB 2; BRWS 1; CA 1-4R;
CANR 1, 33, 51, 91, 126; CDBLB 1960
to Present; CDWLB 3; CN 1, 2, 3, 4, 5,
6, 7; DA3; DAB; DAC; DAM MST,
NOV; DLB 125, 204, 207, 326; DLBY
1985, 2001; EWL 3; LATS 1:2; MTCW
1, 2; MTFW 2005; RGEL 2; RGSF 2;
TWA; WLIT 4; WWE 1

Nakos, Lilika 1903(?)-1989 .... **CLC 29**

Napoleon
See Yamamoto, Hisaye

Narayan, R.K. 1906-2001 ...... **CLC 7, 28, 47, 121, 211; SSC 25**
See also BPFB 2; CA 81-84; 196; CANR
33, 61, 112; CN 1, 2, 3, 4, 5, 6, 7; DA3;
DAM NOV; DLB 323; DNFS 1; EWL 3;
MTCW 1, 2; MTFW 2005; RGEL 2;
RGSF 2; SATA 62; SSFS 5; WWE 1

Nash, (Frediric) Ogden 1902-1971 . **CLC 23; PC 21; TCLC 109**
See also CA 13-14; 29-32R; CANR 34, 61;
CAP 1; CP 1; DAM POET; DLB 11;
MAICYA 1, 2; MAL 5; MTCW 1, 2;
RGAL 4; SATA 2, 46; WP

Nashe, Thomas 1567-1601(?) .... **LC 41, 89**
See also DLB 167; RGEL 2

Nathan, Daniel
See Dannay, Frederic

Nathan, George Jean 1882-1958 .... **TCLC 18**
See Hatteras, Owen
See also CA 114; 169; DLB 137; MAL 5

Natsume, Kinnosuke
See Natsume, Soseki

Natsume, Soseki 1867-1916 .... **TCLC 2, 10**
See Natsume Soseki; Soseki
See also CA 104; 195; RGWL 2, 3; TWA

Natsume Soseki
See Natsume, Soseki
See also DLB 180; EWL 3

Natti, (Mary) Lee 1919-
See Kingman, Lee
See also CA 5-8R; CANR 2

Navarre, Marguerite de
See de Navarre, Marguerite

Naylor, Gloria 1950- ..... **BLC 3; CLC 28, 52, 156; WLCS**
See also AAYA 6, 39; AFAW 1, 2; AMWS
8; BW 2, 3; CA 107; CANR 27, 51, 74,
130; CN 4, 5, 6, 7; CPW; DA; DA3;
DAC; DAM MST, MULT, NOV, POP;
DLB 173; EWL 3; FW; MAL 5; MTCW
1, 2; MTFW 2005; NFS 4, 7; RGAL 4;
TCLE 1:2; TUS

Neal, John 1793-1876 .... **NCLC 161**
See also DLB 1, 59, 243; FW; RGAL 4

Neff, Debra .... **CLC 59**

Neihardt, John Gneisenau
1881-1973 .... **CLC 32**
See also CA 13-14; CANR 65; CAP 1; DLB
9, 54, 256; LAIT 2; TCWW 1, 2

Nekrasov, Nikolai Alekseevich
1821-1878 .... **NCLC 11**
See also DLB 277

Nelligan, Emile 1879-1941 .... **TCLC 14**
See also CA 114; 204; DLB 92; EWL 3

Nelson, Willie 1933- .... **CLC 17**
See also CA 107; CANR 114

Nemerov, Howard 1920-1991 .... **CLC 2, 6, 9, 36; PC 24; TCLC 124**
See also AMW; CA 1-4R; 134; CABS 2;
CANR 1, 27, 53; CN 1, 2, 3; CP 1, 2, 3,
4, 5; DAM POET; DLB 5, 6; DLBY 1983;
EWL 3; INT CANR-27; MAL 5; MTCW
1, 2; MTFW 2005; PFS 10, 14; RGAL 4

Neruda, Pablo 1904-1973 .. **CLC 1, 2, 5, 7, 9, 28, 62; HLC 2; PC 4, 64; WLC 4**
See also CA 19-20; 45-48; CANR 131; CAP
2; DA; DA3; DAB; DAC; DAM MST,
MULT, POET; DLB 283; DNFS 1; EWL
3; HW 1; LAW; MTCW 1, 2; MTFW
2005; PFS 11; RGWL 2, 3; TWA; WLIT
1; WP

Nerval, Gerard de 1808-1855 ... **NCLC 1, 67; PC 13; SSC 18**
See also DLB 217; EW 6; GFL 1789 to the
Present; RGSF 2; RGWL 2, 3

Norway, Nevil Shute 1899-1960
See Shute, Nevil
See also CA 102; 93-96; CANR 85; MTCW
2

Norwid, Cyprian Kamil
1821-1883 .... **NCLC 17**
See also RGWL 3

Nosille, Nabrah
See Ellison, Harlan

Nossack, Hans Erich 1901-1977 .... **CLC 6**
See also CA 93-96; 85-88; CANR 156;
DLB 69; EWL 3

Nostradamus 1503-1566 .... **LC 27**

Nosu, Chuji
See Ozu, Yasujiro

Notenburg, Eleanora (Genrikhovna) von
See Guro, Elena (Genrikhovna)

Nova, Craig 1945- .... **CLC 7, 31**
See also CA 45-48; CANR 2, 53, 127

Novak, Joseph
See Kosinski, Jerzy

Novalis 1772-1801 .... **NCLC 13**
See also CDWLB 2; DLB 90; EW 5; RGWL
2, 3

Novick, Peter 1934- .... **CLC 164**
See also CA 188

Novis, Emile
See Weil, Simone (Adolphine)

Nowlan, Alden (Albert) 1933-1983 ... **CLC 15**
See also CA 9-12R; CANR 5; CP 1, 2, 3;
DAC; DAM MST; DLB 53; PFS 12

Noyes, Alfred 1880-1958 ...... **PC 27; TCLC 7**
See also CA 104; 188; DLB 20; EXPP;
FANT; PFS 4; RGEL 2

Nugent, Richard Bruce
1906(?)-1987 .... **HR 1:3**
See also BW 1; CA 125; DLB 51; GLL 2

Nunn, Kem .... **CLC 34**
See also CA 159

Nussbaum, Martha Craven 1947- .. **CLC 203**
See also CA 134; CANR 102

Nwapa, Flora (Nwanzuruaha)
1931-1993 .... **BLCS; CLC 133**
See also BW 2; CA 143; CANR 83; CD-
WLB 3; CWRI 5; DLB 125; EWL 3;
WLIT 2

Nye, Robert 1939- .... **CLC 13, 42**
See also BRWS 10; CA 33-36R; CANR 29,
67, 107; CN 1, 2, 3, 4, 5, 6, 7; CP 1, 2, 3,
4, 5, 6, 7; CWRI 5; DAM NOV; DLB 14,
271; FANT; HGG; MTCW 1; RHW;
SATA 6

Nyro, Laura 1947-1997 .... **CLC 17**
See also CA 194

Oates, Joyce Carol 1938- .. **CLC 1, 2, 3, 6, 9,
11, 15, 19, 33, 52, 108, 134; SSC 6, 70;
WLC 4**
See also AAYA 15, 52; AITN 1; AMWS 2;
BEST 89:2; BPFB 3; BYA 11; CA 5-8R;
CANR 25, 45, 74, 113, 129, 228; CDALB
1968-1988; CN 1, 2, 3, 4, 5, 6, 7; CP 5,
6, 7; CPW; CWP; DA; DA3; DAB; DAC;
DAM MST, NOV, POP; DLB 2, 5, 130;
DLBY 1981; EWL 3; EXPS; FL 1:6; FW;
GL 3; HGG; INT CANR-25; LAIT 4;
MAL 5; MBL; MTCW 1, 2; MTFW 2005;
NFS 8, 24; RGAL 4; RGSF 2; SATA 159;
SSFS 1, 8, 17; SUFW 2; TUS

O'Brian, E. G.
See Clarke, Arthur C.

O'Brian, Patrick 1914-2000 .... **CLC 152**
See also AAYA 55; BRWS 12; CA 144; 187;
CANR 74; CPW; MTCW 2; MTFW 2005;
RHW

O'Brien, Darcy 1939-1998 .... **CLC 11**
See also CA 21-24R; 167; CANR 8, 59

O'Brien, Edna 1932- ..... **CLC 3, 5, 8, 13, 36,
65, 116; SSC 10, 77**
See also BRWS 5; CA 1-4R; CANR 6, 41,
65, 102; CDBLB 1960 to Present; CN 1,
2, 3, 4, 5, 6, 7; DA3; DAM NOV; DLB
14, 231, 319; EWL 3; FW; MTCW 1, 2;
MTFW 2005; RGSF 2; WLIT 4

O'Brien, Fitz-James 1828-1862 ..... **NCLC 21**
See also DLB 74; RGAL 4; SUFW

O'Brien, Flann .... **CLC 1, 4, 5, 7, 10, 47**
See O Nuallain, Brian
See also BRWS 2; DLB 231; EWL 3;
RGEL 2

O'Brien, Richard 1942- .... **CLC 17**
See also CA 124

O'Brien, Tim 1946- .... **CLC 7, 19, 40, 103,
211; SSC 74**
See also AAYA 16; AMWS 5; CA 85-88;
CANR 40, 58, 133; CDALBS; CN 5, 6,
7; CPW; DA3; DAM POP; DLB 152;
DLBD 9; DLBY 1980; LATS 1:2; MAL
5; MTCW 2; MTFW 2005; RGAL 4;
SSFS 5, 15; TCLE 1:2

Obstfelder, Sigbjoern 1866-1900 .... **TCLC 23**
See also CA 123

O'Casey, Sean 1880-1964 .... **CLC 1, 5, 9, 11,
15, 88; DC 12; WLCS**
See also BRW 7; CA 89-92; CANR 62;
CBD; CDBLB 1914-1945; DA3; DAB;
DAC; DAM DRAM, MST; DFS 19; DLB
10; EWL 3; MTCW 1, 2; MTFW 2005;
RGEL 2; TEA; WLIT 4

O'Cathasaigh, Sean
See O'Casey, Sean

Occom, Samson 1723-1792 .... **LC 60; NNAL**
See also DLB 175

Occomy, Marita (Odette) Bonner
1899(?)-1971
See Bonner, Marita
See also BW 2; CA 142; DFS 13; DLB 51,
228

Ochs, Phil(ip David) 1940-1976 .... **CLC 17**
See also CA 185; 65-68

O'Connor, Edwin (Greene)
1918-1968 .... **CLC 14**
See also CA 93-96; 25-28R; MAL 5

O'Connor, (Mary) Flannery
1925-1964 .... **CLC 1, 2, 3, 6, 10, 13, 15,
21, 66, 104; SSC 1, 23, 61, 82; TCLC
132; WLC 4**
See also AAYA 7; AMW; AMWR 2; BPFB
3; BYA 16; CA 1-4R; CANR 3, 41;
CDALB 1941-1968; DA; DA3; DAB;
DAC; DAM MST, NOV; DLB 2, 152;
DLBD 12; DLBY 1980; EWL 3; EXPS;
LAIT 5; MAL 5; MBL; MTCW 1, 2;
MTFW 2005; NFS 3, 21; RGAL 4; RGSF
2; SSFS 2, 7, 10, 19; TUS

O'Connor, Frank .... **CLC 23; SSC 5**
See O'Donovan, Michael Francis
See also DLB 162; EWL 3; RGSF 2; SSFS
5

O'Dell, Scott 1898-1989 .... **CLC 30**
See also AAYA 3, 44; BPFB 3; BYA 1, 2,
3, 5; CA 61-64; 129; CANR 12, 30, 112;
CLR 1, 16; DLB 52; JRDA; MAICYA 1,
2; SATA 12, 60, 134; WYA; YAW

Odets, Clifford 1906-1963 ..... **CLC 2, 28, 98;
DC 6**
See also AMWS 2; CA 85-88; CAD; CANR
62; DAM DRAM; DFS 3, 17, 20; DLB 7,
26; EWL 3; MAL 5; MTCW 1, 2; MTFW
2005; RGAL 4; TUS

O'Doherty, Brian 1928- .... **CLC 76**
See also CA 105; CANR 108

O'Donnell, K. M.
See Malzberg, Barry N(athaniel)

O'Donnell, Lawrence
See Kuttner, Henry

O'Donovan, Michael Francis
1903-1966 .... **CLC 14**
See O'Connor, Frank
See also CA 93-96; CANR 84

Oe, Kenzaburo 1935- .. **CLC 10, 36, 86, 187;
SSC 20**
See Oe Kenzaburo
See also CA 97-100; CANR 36, 50, 74, 126;
DA3; DAM NOV; DLB 182; DLBY 1994;
LATS 1:2; MJW; MTCW 1, 2; MTFW
2005; RGSF 2; RGWL 2, 3

Oe Kenzaburo
See Oe, Kenzaburo
See also CWW 2; EWL 3

O'Faolain, Julia 1932- .... **CLC 6, 19, 47, 108**
See also CA 81-84; CAAS 2; CANR 12,
61; CN 2, 3, 4, 5, 6, 7; DLB 14, 231, 319;
FW; MTCW 1; RHW

O'Faolain, Sean 1900-1991 ...... **CLC 1, 7, 14,
32, 70; SSC 13; TCLC 143**
See also CA 61-64; 134; CANR 12, 66; CN
1, 2, 3, 4; DLB 15, 162; MTCW 1, 2;
MTFW 2005; RGEL 2; RGSF 2

O'Flaherty, Liam 1896-1984 .... **CLC 5, 34;
SSC 6**
See also CA 101; 113; CANR 35; CN 1, 2,
3; DLB 36, 162; DLBY 1984; MTCW 1,
2; MTFW 2005; RGEL 2; RGSF 2; SSFS
5, 20

Ogai
See Mori Ogai
See also MJW

Ogilvy, Gavin
See Barrie, J(ames) M(atthew)

O'Grady, Standish (James)
1846-1928 .... **TCLC 5**
See also CA 104; 157

O'Grady, Timothy 1951- .... **CLC 59**
See also CA 138

O'Hara, Frank 1926-1966 .... **CLC 2, 5, 13,
78; PC 45**
See also CA 9-12R; 25-28R; CANR 33;
DA3; DAM POET; DLB 5, 16, 193; EWL
3; MAL 5; MTCW 1, 2; MTFW 2005;
PFS 8, 12; RGAL 4; WP

O'Hara, John (Henry) 1905-1970 . **CLC 1, 2,
3, 6, 11, 42; SSC 15**
See also AMW; BPFB 3; CA 5-8R; 25-28R;
CANR 31, 60; CDALB 1929-1941; DAM
NOV; DLB 9, 86, 324; DLBD 2; EWL 3;
MAL 5; MTCW 1, 2; MTFW 2005; NFS
11; RGAL 4; RGSF 2

O'Hehir, Diana 1929- .... **CLC 41**
See also CA 245

Ohiyesa
See Eastman, Charles A(lexander)

Okada, John 1923-1971 .... **AAL**
See also BYA 14; CA 212; DLB 312

Okigbo, Christopher 1930-1967 .... **BLC 3;
CLC 25, 84; PC 7; TCLC 171**
See also AFW; BW 1, 3; CA 77-80; CANR
74; CDWLB 3; DAM MULT, POET; DLB
125; EWL 3; MTCW 1, 2; MTFW 2005;
RGEL 2

Okigbo, Christopher Ifenayichukwu
See Okigbo, Christopher

Okri, Ben 1959- .... **CLC 87, 223**
See also AFW; BRWS 5; BW 2, 3; CA 130;
138; CANR 65, 128; CN 5, 6, 7; DLB
157, 231, 319, 326; EWL 3; INT CA-138;
MTCW 2; MTFW 2005; RGSF 2; SSFS
20; WLIT 2; WWE 1

Olds, Sharon 1942- .. **CLC 32, 39, 85; PC 22**
See also AMWS 10; CA 101; CANR 18,
41, 66, 98, 135; CP 5, 6, 7; CPW; CWP;
DAM POET; DLB 120; MAL 5; MTCW
2; MTFW 2005; PFS 17

Oldstyle, Jonathan
See Irving, Washington

Oz, Amos 1939- ...... **CLC 5, 8, 11, 27, 33, 54; SSC 66**
See also CA 53-56; CANR 27, 47, 65, 113, 138; CWW 2; DAM NOV; EWL 3; MTCW 1, 2; MTFW 2005; RGHL; RGSF 2; RGWL 3; WLIT 6

Ozick, Cynthia 1928- .... **CLC 3, 7, 28, 62, 155; SSC 15, 60**
See also AMWS 5; BEST 90:1; CA 17-20R; CANR 23, 58, 116; CN 3, 4, 5, 6, 7; CPW; DA3; DAM NOV, POP; DLB 28, 152, 299; DLBY 1982; EWL 3; EXPS; INT CANR-23; MAL 5; MTCW 1, 2; MTFW 2005; RGAL 4; RGHL; RGSF 2; SSFS 3, 12, 22

Ozu, Yasujiro 1903-1963 .... **CLC 16**
See also CA 112

Pabst, G. W. 1885-1967 .... **TCLC 127**

Pacheco, C.
See Pessoa, Fernando (Antonio Nogueira)

Pacheco, Jose Emilio 1939- .... **HLC 2**
See also CA 111; 131; CANR 65; CWW 2; DAM MULT; DLB 290; EWL 3; HW 1, 2; RGSF 2

Pa Chin .... **CLC 18**
See Jin, Ba
See also EWL 3

Pack, Robert 1929- .... **CLC 13**
See also CA 1-4R; CANR 3, 44, 82; CP 1, 2, 3, 4, 5, 6, 7; DLB 5; SATA 118

Padgett, Lewis
See Kuttner, Henry

Padilla (Lorenzo), Heberto
1932-2000 .... **CLC 38**
See also AITN 1; CA 123; 131; 189; CWW 2; EWL 3; HW 1

Page, James Patrick 1944-
See Page, Jimmy
See also CA 204

Page, Jimmy 1944- .... **CLC 12**
See Page, James Patrick

Page, Louise 1955- .... **CLC 40**
See also CA 140; CANR 76; CBD; CD 5, 6; CWD; DLB 233

Page, P(atricia) K(athleen) 1916- ...... **CLC 7, 18; PC 12**
See Cape, Judith
See also CA 53-56; CANR 4, 22, 65; CP 1, 2, 3, 4, 5, 6, 7; DAC; DAM MST; DLB 68; MTCW 1; RGEL 2

Page, Stanton
See Fuller, Henry Blake

Page, Stanton
See Fuller, Henry Blake

Page, Thomas Nelson 1853-1922 .... **SSC 23**
See also CA 118; 177; DLB 12, 78; DLBD 13; RGAL 4

Pagels, Elaine
See Pagels, Elaine Hiesey

Pagels, Elaine Hiesey 1943- .... **CLC 104**
See also CA 45-48; CANR 2, 24, 51, 151; FW; NCFS 4

Paget, Violet 1856-1935
See Lee, Vernon
See also CA 104; 166; GLL 1; HGG

Paget-Lowe, Henry
See Lovecraft, H. P.

Paglia, Camille 1947- .... **CLC 68**
See also CA 140; CANR 72, 139; CPW; FW; GLL 2; MTCW 2; MTFW 2005

Paige, Richard
See Koontz, Dean R.

Paine, Thomas 1737-1809 .... **NCLC 62**
See also AMWS 1; CDALB 1640-1865; DLB 31, 43, 73, 158; LAIT 1; RGAL 4; RGEL 2; TUS

Pakenham, Antonia
See Fraser, Antonia

Palamas, Costis
See Palamas, Kostes

Palamas, Kostes 1859-1943 .... **TCLC 5**
See Palamas, Kostis
See also CA 105; 190; RGWL 2, 3

Palamas, Kostis
See Palamas, Kostes
See also EWL 3

Palazzeschi, Aldo 1885-1974 .... **CLC 11**
See also CA 89-92; 53-56; DLB 114, 264; EWL 3

Pales Matos, Luis 1898-1959 .... **HLCS 2**
See Pales Matos, Luis
See also DLB 290; HW 1; LAW

Paley, Grace 1922- .. **CLC 4, 6, 37, 140; SSC 8**
See also AMWS 6; CA 25-28R; CANR 13, 46, 74, 118; CN 2, 3, 4, 5, 6, 7; CPW; DA3; DAM POP; DLB 28, 218; EWL 3; EXPS; FW; INT CANR-13; MAL 5; MBL; MTCW 1, 2; MTFW 2005; RGAL 4; RGSF 2; SSFS 3, 20

Palin, Michael (Edward) 1943- .... **CLC 21**
See Monty Python
See also CA 107; CANR 35, 109; SATA 67

Palliser, Charles 1947- .... **CLC 65**
See also CA 136; CANR 76; CN 5, 6, 7

Palma, Ricardo 1833-1919 .... **TCLC 29**
See also CA 168; LAW

Pamuk, Orhan 1952- .... **CLC 185**
See also CA 142; CANR 75, 127; CWW 2; WLIT 6

Pancake, Breece Dexter 1952-1979
See Pancake, Breece D'J
See also CA 123; 109

Pancake, Breece D'J .... **CLC 29; SSC 61**
See Pancake, Breece Dexter
See also DLB 130

Panchenko, Nikolai .... **CLC 59**

Pankhurst, Emmeline (Goulden)
1858-1928 .... **TCLC 100**
See also CA 116; FW

Panko, Rudy
See Gogol, Nikolai (Vasilyevich)

Papadiamantis, Alexandros
1851-1911 .... **TCLC 29**
See also CA 168; EWL 3

Papadiamantopoulos, Johannes 1856-1910
See Moreas, Jean
See also CA 117; 242

Papini, Giovanni 1881-1956 .... **TCLC 22**
See also CA 121; 180; DLB 264

Paracelsus 1493-1541 .... **LC 14**
See also DLB 179

Parasol, Peter
See Stevens, Wallace

Pardo Bazan, Emilia 1851-1921 .... **SSC 30**
See also EWL 3; FW; RGSF 2; RGWL 2, 3

Pareto, Vilfredo 1848-1923 .... **TCLC 69**
See also CA 175

Paretsky, Sara 1947- .... **CLC 135**
See also AAYA 30; BEST 90:3; CA 125; 129; CANR 59, 95; CMW 4; CPW; DA3; DAM POP; DLB 306; INT CA-129; MSW; RGAL 4

Parfenie, Maria
See Codrescu, Andrei

Parini, Jay (Lee) 1948- .... **CLC 54, 133**
See also CA 97-100, 229; CAAE 229; CAAS 16; CANR 32, 87

Park, Jordan
See Kornbluth, C(yril) M.; Pohl, Frederik

Park, Robert E(zra) 1864-1944 ..... **TCLC 73**
See also CA 122; 165

Parker, Bert
See Ellison, Harlan

Parker, Dorothy (Rothschild)
1893-1967 . **CLC 15, 68; PC 28; SSC 2; TCLC 143**
See also AMWS 9; CA 19-20; 25-28R; CAP 2; DA3; DAM POET; DLB 11, 45, 86; EXPP; FW; MAL 5; MBL; MTCW 1, 2; MTFW 2005; PFS 18; RGAL 4; RGSF 2; TUS

Parker, Robert B. 1932- .... **CLC 27**
See also AAYA 28; BEST 89:4; BPFB 3; CA 49-52; CANR 1, 26, 52, 89, 128; CMW 4; CPW; DAM NOV, POP; DLB 306; INT CANR-26; MSW; MTCW 1; MTFW 2005

Parker, Robert Brown
See Parker, Robert B.

Parkin, Frank 1940- .... **CLC 43**
See also CA 147

Parkman, Francis, Jr. 1823-1893 .. **NCLC 12**
See also AMWS 2; DLB 1, 30, 183, 186, 235; RGAL 4

Parks, Gordon 1912-2006 .... **BLC 3; CLC 1, 16**
See also AAYA 36; AITN 2; BW 2, 3; CA 41-44R; 249; CANR 26, 66, 145; DA3; DAM MULT; DLB 33; MTCW 2; MTFW 2005; SATA 8, 108

Parks, Gordon Alexander Buchanan
See Parks, Gordon

Parks, Suzan-Lori 1964(?)- .... **DC 23**
See also AAYA 55; CA 201; CAD; CD 5, 6; CWD; DFS 22; RGAL 4

Parks, Tim(othy Harold) 1954- ...... **CLC 147**
See also CA 126; 131; CANR 77, 144; CN 7; DLB 231; INT CA-131

Parmenides c. 515B.C.-c.
450B.C. .... **CMLC 22**
See also DLB 176

Parnell, Thomas 1679-1718 .... **LC 3**
See also DLB 95; RGEL 2

Parr, Catherine c. 1513(?)-1548 .... **LC 86**
See also DLB 136

Parra, Nicanor 1914- ... **CLC 2, 102; HLC 2; PC 39**
See also CA 85-88; CANR 32; CWW 2; DAM MULT; DLB 283; EWL 3; HW 1; LAW; MTCW 1

Parra Sanojo, Ana Teresa de la
1890-1936 .... **HLCS 2**
See de la Parra, (Ana) Teresa (Sonojo)
See also LAW

Parrish, Mary Frances
See Fisher, M(ary) F(rances) K(ennedy)

Parshchikov, Aleksei 1954- .... **CLC 59**
See Parshchikov, Aleksei Maksimovich

Parshchikov, Aleksei Maksimovich
See Parshchikov, Aleksei
See also DLB 285

Parson, Professor
See Coleridge, Samuel Taylor

Parson Lot
See Kingsley, Charles

Parton, Sara Payson Willis
1811-1872 .... **NCLC 86**
See also DLB 43, 74, 239

Partridge, Anthony
See Oppenheim, E(dward) Phillips

Pascal, Blaise 1623-1662 .... **LC 35**
See also DLB 268; EW 3; GFL Beginnings to 1789; RGWL 2, 3; TWA

Pascoli, Giovanni 1855-1912 .... **TCLC 45**
See also CA 170; EW 7; EWL 3

Pasolini, Pier Paolo 1922-1975 .. **CLC 20, 37, 106; PC 17**
See also CA 93-96; 61-64; CANR 63; DLB 128, 177; EWL 3; MTCW 1; RGWL 2, 3

Pasquini
See Silone, Ignazio

Peretz, Yitzkhok Leibush
See Peretz, Isaac Loeb
Perez Galdos, Benito 1843-1920 ..... **HLCS 2;**
TCLC 27
See Galdos, Benito Perez
See also CA 125; 153; EWL 3; HW 1;
RGWL 2, 3
Peri Rossi, Cristina 1941- .. **CLC 156; HLCS**
2
See also CA 131; CANR 59, 81; CWW 2;
DLB 145, 290; EWL 3; HW 1, 2
Perlata
See Peret, Benjamin
Perloff, Marjorie G(abrielle)
1931- .... **CLC 137**
See also CA 57-60; CANR 7, 22, 49, 104
Perrault, Charles 1628-1703 .... **LC 2, 56**
See also BYA 4; CLR 79; DLB 268; GFL
Beginnings to 1789; MAICYA 1, 2;
RGWL 2, 3; SATA 25; WCH
Perry, Anne 1938- .... **CLC 126**
See also CA 101; CANR 22, 50, 84, 150;
CMW 4; CN 6, 7; CPW; DLB 276
Perry, Brighton
See Sherwood, Robert E(mmet)
Perse, St.-John
See Leger, (Marie-Rene Auguste) Alexis
Saint-Leger
Perse, Saint-John
See Leger, (Marie-Rene Auguste) Alexis
Saint-Leger
See also DLB 258; RGWL 3
Persius 34-62 .... **CMLC 74**
See also AW 2; DLB 211; RGWL 2, 3
Perutz, Leo(pold) 1882-1957 .... **TCLC 60**
See also CA 147; DLB 81
Peseenz, Tulio F.
See Lopez y Fuentes, Gregorio
Pesetsky, Bette 1932- .... **CLC 28**
See also CA 133; DLB 130
Peshkov, Alexei Maximovich 1868-1936
See Gorky, Maxim
See also CA 105; 141; CANR 83; DA;
DAC; DAM DRAM, MST, NOV; MTCW
2; MTFW 2005
Pessoa, Fernando (Antonio Nogueira)
1888-1935 ..... **HLC 2; PC 20; TCLC 27**
See also CA 125; 183; DAM MULT; DLB
287; EW 10; EWL 3; RGWL 2, 3; WP
Peterkin, Julia Mood 1880-1961 ...... **CLC 31**
See also CA 102; DLB 9
Peters, Joan K(aren) 1945- .... **CLC 39**
See also CA 158; CANR 109
Peters, Robert L(ouis) 1924- .... **CLC 7**
See also CA 13-16R; CAAS 8; CP 1, 5, 6,
7; DLB 105
Petofi, Sandor 1823-1849 .... **NCLC 21**
See also RGWL 2, 3
Petrakis, Harry Mark 1923- .... **CLC 3**
See also CA 9-12R; CANR 4, 30, 85, 155;
CN 1, 2, 3, 4, 5, 6, 7
Petrarch 1304-1374 .... **CMLC 20; PC 8**
See also DA3; DAM POET; EW 2; LMFS
1; RGWL 2, 3; WLIT 7
Petronius c. 20-66 .... **CMLC 34**
See also AW 2; CDWLB 1; DLB 211;
RGWL 2, 3; WLIT 8
Petrov, Evgeny .... **TCLC 21**
See Kataev, Evgeny Petrovich
Petry, Ann (Lane) 1908-1997 .. **CLC 1, 7, 18;**
TCLC 112
See also AFAW 1, 2; BPFB 3; BW 1, 3;
BYA 2; CA 5-8R; 157; CAAS 6; CANR
4, 46; CLR 12; CN 1, 2, 3, 4, 5, 6; DLB
76; EWL 3; JRDA; LAIT 1; MAICYA 1,
2; MAICYAS 1; MTCW 1; RGAL 4;
SATA 5; SATA-Obit 94; TUS
Petursson, Halligrimur 1614-1674 .... **LC 8**

Peychinovich
See Vazov, Ivan (Minchov)
Phaedrus c. 15B.C.-c. 50 .... **CMLC 25**
See also DLB 211
Phelps (Ward), Elizabeth Stuart
See Phelps, Elizabeth Stuart
See also FW
Phelps, Elizabeth Stuart
1844-1911 .... **TCLC 113**
See Phelps (Ward), Elizabeth Stuart
See also CA 242; DLB 74
Philips, Katherine 1632-1664 . **LC 30; PC 40**
See also DLB 131; RGEL 2
Philipson, Morris H. 1926- .... **CLC 53**
See also CA 1-4R; CANR 4
Phillips, Caryl 1958- ..... **BLCS; CLC 96, 224**
See also BRWS 5; BW 2; CA 141; CANR
63, 104, 140; CBD; CD 5, 6; CN 5, 6, 7;
DA3; DAM MULT; DLB 157; EWL 3;
MTCW 2; MTFW 2005; WLIT 4; WWE
1
Phillips, David Graham
1867-1911 .... **TCLC 44**
See also CA 108; 176; DLB 9, 12, 303;
RGAL 4
Phillips, Jack
See Sandburg, Carl (August)
Phillips, Jayne Anne 1952- .... **CLC 15, 33,**
139; SSC 16
See also AAYA 57; BPFB 3; CA 101;
CANR 24, 50, 96; CN 4, 5, 6, 7; CSW;
DLBY 1980; INT CANR-24; MTCW 1,
2; MTFW 2005; RGAL 4; RGSF 2; SSFS
4
Phillips, Richard
See Dick, Philip K.
Phillips, Robert (Schaeffer) 1938- .... **CLC 28**
See also CA 17-20R; CAAS 13; CANR 8;
DLB 105
Phillips, Ward
See Lovecraft, H. P.
Philostratus, Flavius c. 179-c.
244 .... **CMLC 62**
Piccolo, Lucio 1901-1969 .... **CLC 13**
See also CA 97-100; DLB 114; EWL 3
Pickthall, Marjorie L(owry) C(hristie)
1883-1922 .... **TCLC 21**
See also CA 107; DLB 92
Pico della Mirandola, Giovanni
1463-1494 .... **LC 15**
See also LMFS 1
Piercy, Marge 1936- .... **CLC 3, 6, 14, 18, 27,**
62, 128; PC 29
See also BPFB 3; CA 21-24R, 187; CAAE
187; CAAS 1; CANR 13, 43, 66, 111; CN
3, 4, 5, 6, 7; CP 1, 2, 3, 4, 5, 6, 7; CWP;
DLB 120, 227; EXPP; FW; MAL 5;
MTCW 1, 2; MTFW 2005; PFS 9, 22;
SFW 4
Piers, Robert
See Anthony, Piers
Pieyre de Mandiargues, Andre 1909-1991
See Mandiargues, Andre Pieyre de
See also CA 103; 136; CANR 22, 82; EWL
3; GFL 1789 to the Present
Pilnyak, Boris 1894-1938 . **SSC 48; TCLC 23**
See Vogau, Boris Andreyevich
See also EWL 3
Pinchback, Eugene
See Toomer, Jean
Pincherle, Alberto 1907-1990 ...... **CLC 11, 18**
See Moravia, Alberto
See also CA 25-28R; 132; CANR 33, 63,
142; DAM NOV; MTCW 1; MTFW 2005
Pinckney, Darryl 1953- .... **CLC 76**
See also BW 2, 3; CA 143; CANR 79

Pindar 518(?)B.C.-438(?)B.C. .... **CMLC 12;**
PC 19
See also AW 1; CDWLB 1; DLB 176;
RGWL 2
Pineda, Cecile 1942- .... **CLC 39**
See also CA 118; DLB 209
Pinero, Arthur Wing 1855-1934 .... **TCLC 32**
See also CA 110; 153; DAM DRAM; DLB
10; RGEL 2
Pinero, Miguel (Antonio Gomez)
1946-1988 .... **CLC 4, 55**
See also CA 61-64; 125; CAD; CANR 29,
90; DLB 266; HW 1; LLW
Pinget, Robert 1919-1997 .... **CLC 7, 13, 37**
See also CA 85-88; 160; CWW 2; DLB 83;
EWL 3; GFL 1789 to the Present
Pink Floyd
See Barrett, (Roger) Syd; Gilmour, David;
Mason, Nick; Waters, Roger; Wright, Rick
Pinkney, Edward 1802-1828 .... **NCLC 31**
See also DLB 248
Pinkwater, D. Manus
See Pinkwater, Daniel Manus
Pinkwater, Daniel
See Pinkwater, Daniel Manus
Pinkwater, Daniel M.
See Pinkwater, Daniel Manus
Pinkwater, Daniel Manus 1941- .... **CLC 35**
See also AAYA 1, 46; BYA 9; CA 29-32R;
CANR 12, 38, 89, 143; CLR 4; CSW;
FANT; JRDA; MAICYA 1, 2; SAAS 3;
SATA 8, 46, 76, 114, 158; SFW 4; YAW
Pinkwater, Manus
See Pinkwater, Daniel Manus
Pinsky, Robert 1940- .... **CLC 9, 19, 38, 94,**
121, 216; PC 27
See also AMWS 6; CA 29-32R; CAAS 4;
CANR 58, 97, 138; CP 3, 4, 5, 6, 7; DA3;
DAM POET; DLBY 1982, 1998; MAL 5;
MTCW 2; MTFW 2005; PFS 18; RGAL
4; TCLE 1:2
Pinta, Harold
See Pinter, Harold
Pinter, Harold 1930- .. **CLC 1, 3, 6, 9, 11, 15,**
27, 58, 73, 199; DC 15; WLC 4
See also BRWR 1; BRWS 1; CA 5-8R;
CANR 33, 65, 112, 145; CBD; CD 5, 6;
CDBLB 1960 to Present; CP 1; DA; DA3;
DAB; DAC; DAM DRAM, MST; DFS 3,
5, 7, 14; DLB 13, 310; EWL 3; IDFW 3,
4; LMFS 2; MTCW 1, 2; MTFW 2005;
RGEL 2; RGHL; TEA
Piozzi, Hester Lynch (Thrale)
1741-1821 .... **NCLC 57**
See also DLB 104, 142
Pirandello, Luigi 1867-1936 .. **DC 5; SSC 22;**
TCLC 4, 29, 172; WLC 4
See also CA 104; 153; CANR 103; DA;
DA3; DAB; DAC; DAM DRAM, MST;
DFS 4, 9; DLB 264; EW 8; EWL 3;
MTCW 2; MTFW 2005; RGSF 2; RGWL
2, 3; WLIT 7
Pirsig, Robert M(aynard) 1928- ... **CLC 4, 6,**
73
See also CA 53-56; CANR 42, 74; CPW 1;
DA3; DAM POP; MTCW 1, 2; MTFW
2005; SATA 39
Pisan, Christine de
See Christine de Pizan
Pisarev, Dmitrii Ivanovich
See Pisarev, Dmitry Ivanovich
See also DLB 277
Pisarev, Dmitry Ivanovich
1840-1868 .... **NCLC 25**
See Pisarev, Dmitrii Ivanovich
Pix, Mary (Griffith) 1666-1709 .... **LC 8**
See also DLB 80

Potok, Herman Harold
　　See Potok, Chaim
Potter, Dennis (Christopher George)
　　1935-1994 .... **CLC 58, 86, 123**
　　See also BRWS 10; CA 107; 145; CANR
　　33, 61; CBD; DLB 233; MTCW 1
Pound, Ezra (Weston Loomis)
　　1885-1972 .. **CLC 1, 2, 3, 4, 5, 7, 10, 13,**
　　18, 34, 48, 50, 112; PC 4; WLC 5
　　See also AAYA 47; AMW; AMWR 1; CA
　　5-8R; 37-40R; CANR 40; CDALB 1917-
　　1929; CP 1; DA; DA3; DAB; DAC; DAM
　　MST, POET; DLB 4, 45, 63; DLBD 15;
　　EFS 2; EWL 3; EXPP; LMFS 2; MAL 5;
　　MTCW 1, 2; MTFW 2005; PAB; PFS 2,
　　8, 16; RGAL 4; TUS; WP
Povod, Reinaldo 1959-1994 .... **CLC 44**
　　See also CA 136; 146; CANR 83
Powell, Adam Clayton, Jr.
　　1908-1972 .... **BLC 3; CLC 89**
　　See also BW 1, 3; CA 102; 33-36R; CANR
　　86; DAM MULT
Powell, Anthony 1905-2000 ... **CLC 1, 3, 7, 9,**
　　10, 31
　　See also BRW 7; CA 1-4R; 189; CANR 1,
　　32, 62, 107; CDBLB 1945-1960; CN 1, 2,
　　3, 4, 5, 6; DLB 15; EWL 3; MTCW 1, 2;
　　MTFW 2005; RGEL 2; TEA
Powell, Dawn 1896(?)-1965 .... **CLC 66**
　　See also CA 5-8R; CANR 121; DLBY 1997
Powell, Padgett 1952- .... **CLC 34**
　　See also CA 126; CANR 63, 101; CSW;
　　DLB 234; DLBY 01
Powell, (Oval) Talmage 1920-2000
　　See Queen, Ellery
　　See also CA 5-8R; CANR 2, 80
Power, Susan 1961- .... **CLC 91**
　　See also BYA 14; CA 160; CANR 135; NFS
　　11
Powers, J(ames) F(arl) 1917-1999 ..... **CLC 1,**
　　4, 8, 57; SSC 4
　　See also CA 1-4R; 181; CANR 2, 61; CN
　　1, 2, 3, 4, 5, 6; DLB 130; MTCW 1;
　　RGAL 4; RGSF 2
Powers, John J(ames) 1945-
　　See Powers, John R.
　　See also CA 69-72
Powers, John R. .... **CLC 66**
　　See Powers, John J(ames)
Powers, Richard 1957- .... **CLC 93**
　　See also AMWS 9; BPFB 3; CA 148;
　　CANR 80; CN 6, 7; MTFW 2005; TCLE
　　1:2
Pownall, David 1938- .... **CLC 10**
　　See also CA 89-92, 180; CAAS 18; CANR
　　49, 101; CBD; CD 5, 6; CN 4, 5, 6, 7;
　　DLB 14
Powys, John Cowper 1872-1963 ... **CLC 7, 9,**
　　15, 46, 125
　　See also CA 85-88; CANR 106; DLB 15,
　　255; EWL 3; FANT; MTCW 1, 2; MTFW
　　2005; RGEL 2; SUFW
Powys, T(heodore) F(rancis)
　　1875-1953 .... **TCLC 9**
　　See also BRWS 8; CA 106; 189; DLB 36,
　　162; EWL 3; FANT; RGEL 2; SUFW
Pozzo, Modesta
　　See Fonte, Moderata
Prado (Calvo), Pedro 1886-1952 ... **TCLC 75**
　　See also CA 131; DLB 283; HW 1; LAW
Prager, Emily 1952- .... **CLC 56**
　　See also CA 204
Pratchett, Terry 1948- .... **CLC 197**
　　See also AAYA 19, 54; BPFB 3; CA 143;
　　CANR 87, 126; CLR 64; CN 6, 7; CPW;
　　CWRI 5; FANT; MTFW 2005; SATA 82,
　　139; SFW 4; SUFW 2

Pratolini, Vasco 1913-1991 .... **TCLC 124**
　　See also CA 211; DLB 177; EWL 3; RGWL
　　2, 3
Pratt, E(dwin) J(ohn) 1883(?)-1964 . **CLC 19**
　　See also CA 141; 93-96; CANR 77; DAC;
　　DAM POET; DLB 92; EWL 3; RGEL 2;
　　TWA
Premchand .... **TCLC 21**
　　See Srivastava, Dhanpat Rai
　　See also EWL 3
Prescott, William Hickling
　　1796-1859 .... **NCLC 163**
　　See also DLB 1, 30, 59, 235
Preseren, France 1800-1849 .... **NCLC 127**
　　See also CDWLB 4; DLB 147
Preussler, Otfried 1923- .... **CLC 17**
　　See also CA 77-80; SATA 24
Prevert, Jacques (Henri Marie)
　　1900-1977 .... **CLC 15**
　　See also CA 77-80; 69-72; CANR 29, 61;
　　DLB 258; EWL 3; GFL 1789 to the
　　Present; IDFW 3, 4; MTCW 1; RGWL 2,
　　3; SATA-Obit 30
Prevost, (Antoine Francois)
　　1697-1763 .... **LC 1**
　　See also DLB 314; EW 4; GFL Beginnings
　　to 1789; RGWL 2, 3
Price, Reynolds 1933- .. **CLC 3, 6, 13, 43, 50,**
　　63, 212; SSC 22
　　See also AMWS 6; CA 1-4R; CANR 1, 37,
　　57, 87, 128; CN 1, 2, 3, 4, 5, 6, 7; CSW;
　　DAM NOV; DLB 2, 218, 278; EWL 3;
　　INT CANR-37; MAL 5; MTFW 2005;
　　NFS 18
Price, Richard 1949- .... **CLC 6, 12**
　　See also CA 49-52; CANR 3, 147; CN 7;
　　DLBY 1981
Prichard, Katharine Susannah
　　1883-1969 .... **CLC 46**
　　See also CA 11-12; CANR 33; CAP 1; DLB
　　260; MTCW 1; RGEL 2; RGSF 2; SATA
　　66
Priestley, J(ohn) B(oynton)
　　1894-1984 .... **CLC 2, 5, 9, 34**
　　See also BRW 7; CA 9-12R; 113; CANR
　　33; CDBLB 1914-1945; CN 1, 2, 3; DA3;
　　DAM DRAM, NOV; DLB 10, 34, 77,
　　100, 139; DLBY 1984; EWL 3; MTCW
　　1, 2; MTFW 2005; RGEL 2; SFW 4
Prince 1958- .... **CLC 35**
　　See also CA 213
Prince, F(rank) T(empleton)
　　1912-2003 .... **CLC 22**
　　See also CA 101; 219; CANR 43, 79; CP 1,
　　2, 3, 4, 5, 6, 7; DLB 20
Prince Kropotkin
　　See Kropotkin, Peter (Aleksieevich)
Prior, Matthew 1664-1721 .... **LC 4**
　　See also DLB 95; RGEL 2
Prishvin, Mikhail 1873-1954 .... **TCLC 75**
　　See Prishvin, Mikhail Mikhailovich
Prishvin, Mikhail Mikhailovich
　　See Prishvin, Mikhail
　　See also DLB 272; EWL 3
Pritchard, William H(arrison)
　　1932- .... **CLC 34**
　　See also CA 65-68; CANR 23, 95; DLB
　　111
Pritchett, V(ictor) S(awdon)
　　1900-1997 ... **CLC 5, 13, 15, 41; SSC 14**
　　See also BPFB 3; BRWS 3; CA 61-64; 157;
　　CANR 31, 63; CN 1, 2, 3, 4, 5, 6; DA3;
　　DAM NOV; DLB 15, 139; EWL 3;
　　MTCW 1, 2; MTFW 2005; RGEL 2;
　　RGSF 2; TEA
Private 19022
　　See Manning, Frederic
Probst, Mark 1925- .... **CLC 59**
　　See also CA 130

Procaccino, Michael
　　See Cristofer, Michael
Proclus c. 412-c. 485 .... **CMLC 81**
Prokosch, Frederic 1908-1989 ...... **CLC 4, 48**
　　See also CA 73-76; 128; CANR 82; CN 1,
　　2, 3, 4; CP 1, 2, 3, 4; DLB 48; MTCW 2
Propertius, Sextus c. 50B.C.-c.
　　16B.C. .... **CMLC 32**
　　See also AW 2; CDWLB 1; DLB 211;
　　RGWL 2, 3; WLIT 8
Prophet, The
　　See Dreiser, Theodore
Prose, Francine 1947- .... **CLC 45**
　　See also AMWS 16; CA 109; 112; CANR
　　46, 95, 132; DLB 234; MTFW 2005;
　　SATA 101, 149
Protagoras c. 490B.C.-420B.C. ...... **CMLC 85**
　　See also DLB 176
Proudhon
　　See Cunha, Euclides (Rodrigues Pimenta)
　　da
Proulx, Annie
　　See Proulx, E. Annie
Proulx, E. Annie 1935- .... **CLC 81, 158**
　　See also AMWS 7; BPFB 3; CA 145;
　　CANR 65, 110; CN 6, 7; CPW 1; DA3;
　　DAM POP; MAL 5; MTCW 2; MTFW
　　2005; SSFS 18, 23
Proulx, Edna Annie
　　See Proulx, E. Annie
Proust, (Valentin-Louis-George-Eugene)
　　Marcel 1871-1922 ..... **SSC 75; TCLC 7,**
　　13, 33; WLC 5
　　See also AAYA 58; BPFB 3; CA 104; 120;
　　CANR 110; DA; DA3; DAB; DAC; DAM
　　MST, NOV; DLB 65; EW 9; EWL 3; GFL
　　1789 to the Present; MTCW 1, 2; MTFW
　　2005; RGWL 2, 3; TWA
Prowler, Harley
　　See Masters, Edgar Lee
Prudentius, Aurelius Clemens 348-c.
　　405 .... **CMLC 78**
　　See also EW 1; RGWL 2, 3
Prus, Boleslaw 1845-1912 .... **TCLC 48**
　　See also RGWL 2, 3
Pryor, Aaron Richard
　　See Pryor, Richard
Pryor, Richard 1940-2005 .... **CLC 26**
　　See also CA 122; 152; 246
Pryor, Richard Franklin Lenox Thomas
　　See Pryor, Richard
Przybyszewski, Stanislaw
　　1868-1927 .... **TCLC 36**
　　See also CA 160; DLB 66; EWL 3
Pteleon
　　See Grieve, C(hristopher) M(urray)
　　See also DAM POET
Puckett, Lute
　　See Masters, Edgar Lee
Puig, Manuel 1932-1990 .... **CLC 3, 5, 10, 28,**
　　65, 133; HLC 2
　　See also BPFB 3; CA 45-48; CANR 2, 32,
　　63; CDWLB 3; DA3; DAM MULT; DLB
　　113; DNFS 1; EWL 3; GLL 1; HW 1, 2;
　　LAW; MTCW 1, 2; MTFW 2005; RGWL
　　2, 3; TWA; WLIT 1
Pulitzer, Joseph 1847-1911 .... **TCLC 76**
　　See also CA 114; DLB 23
Purchas, Samuel 1577(?)-1626 .... **LC 70**
　　See also DLB 151
Purdy, A(lfred) W(ellington)
　　1918-2000 .... **CLC 3, 6, 14, 50**
　　See also CA 81-84; 189; CAAS 17; CANR
　　42, 66; CP 1, 2, 3, 4, 5, 6, 7; DAC; DAM
　　MST, POET; DLB 88; PFS 5; RGEL 2

Rampling, Anne
See Rice, Anne
See also GLL 2

Ramsay, Allan 1686(?)-1758 .... **LC 29**
See also DLB 95; RGEL 2

Ramsay, Jay
See Campbell, (John) Ramsey

Ramuz, Charles-Ferdinand
1878-1947 .... **TCLC 33**
See also CA 165; EWL 3

Rand, Ayn 1905-1982 ...... **CLC 3, 30, 44, 79; WLC 5**
See also AAYA 10; AMWS 4; BPFB 3; BYA 12; CA 13-16R; 105; CANR 27, 73; CDALBS; CN 1, 2, 3; CPW; DA; DA3; DAC; DAM MST, NOV, POP; DLB 227, 279; MTCW 1, 2; MTFW 2005; NFS 10, 16; RGAL 4; SFW 4; TUS; YAW

Randall, Dudley (Felker) 1914-2000 . **BLC 3; CLC 1, 135**
See also BW 1, 3; CA 25-28R; 189; CANR 23, 82; CP 1, 2, 3, 4, 5; DAM MULT; DLB 41; PFS 5

Randall, Robert
See Silverberg, Robert

Ranger, Ken
See Creasey, John

Rank, Otto 1884-1939 .... **TCLC 115**

Ransom, John Crowe 1888-1974 .. **CLC 2, 4, 5, 11, 24; PC 61**
See also AMW; CA 5-8R; 49-52; CANR 6, 34; CDALBS; CP 1, 2; DA3; DAM POET; DLB 45, 63; EWL 3; EXPP; MAL 5; MTCW 1, 2; MTFW 2005; RGAL 4; TUS

Rao, Raja 1908-2006 .... **CLC 25, 56**
See also CA 73-76; CANR 51; CN 1, 2, 3, 4, 5, 6; DAM NOV; DLB 323; EWL 3; MTCW 1, 2; MTFW 2005; RGEL 2; RGSF 2

Raphael, Frederic (Michael) 1931- ... **CLC 2, 14**
See also CA 1-4R; CANR 1, 86; CN 1, 2, 3, 4, 5, 6, 7; DLB 14, 319; TCLE 1:2

Ratcliffe, James P.
See Mencken, H(enry) L(ouis)

Rathbone, Julian 1935- .... **CLC 41**
See also CA 101; CANR 34, 73, 152

Rattigan, Terence (Mervyn)
1911-1977 .... **CLC 7; DC 18**
See also BRWS 7; CA 85-88; 73-76; CBD; CDBLB 1945-1960; DAM DRAM; DFS 8; DLB 13; IDFW 3, 4; MTCW 1, 2; MTFW 2005; RGEL 2

Ratushinskaya, Irina 1954- .... **CLC 54**
See also CA 129; CANR 68; CWW 2

Raven, Simon (Arthur Noel)
1927-2001 .... **CLC 14**
See also CA 81-84; 197; CANR 86; CN 1, 2, 3, 4, 5, 6; DLB 271

Ravenna, Michael
See Welty, Eudora

Rawley, Callman 1903-2004
See Rakosi, Carl
See also CA 21-24R; 228; CANR 12, 32, 91

Rawlings, Marjorie Kinnan
1896-1953 .... **TCLC 4**
See also AAYA 20; AMWS 10; ANW; BPFB 3; BYA 3; CA 104; 137; CANR 74; CLR 63; DLB 9, 22, 102; DLBD 17; JRDA; MAICYA 1, 2; MAL 5; MTCW 2; MTFW 2005; RGAL 4; SATA 100; WCH; YABC 1; YAW

Ray, Satyajit 1921-1992 .... **CLC 16, 76**
See also CA 114; 137; DAM MULT

Read, Herbert Edward 1893-1968 ..... **CLC 4**
See also BRW 6; CA 85-88; 25-28R; DLB 20, 149; EWL 3; PAB; RGEL 2

Read, Piers Paul 1941- .... **CLC 4, 10, 25**
See also CA 21-24R; CANR 38, 86, 150; CN 2, 3, 4, 5, 6, 7; DLB 14; SATA 21

Reade, Charles 1814-1884 .... **NCLC 2, 74**
See also DLB 21; RGEL 2

Reade, Hamish
See Gray, Simon (James Holliday)

Reading, Peter 1946- .... **CLC 47**
See also BRWS 8; CA 103; CANR 46, 96; CP 5, 6, 7; DLB 40

Reaney, James 1926- .... **CLC 13**
See also CA 41-44R; CAAS 15; CANR 42; CD 5, 6; CP 1, 2, 3, 4, 5, 6, 7; DAC; DAM MST; DLB 68; RGEL 2; SATA 43

Rebreanu, Liviu 1885-1944 .... **TCLC 28**
See also CA 165; DLB 220; EWL 3

Rechy, John 1934- ..... **CLC 1, 7, 14, 18, 107; HLC 2**
See also CA 5-8R, 195; CAAE 195; CAAS 4; CANR 6, 32, 64, 152; CN 1, 2, 3, 4, 5, 6, 7; DAM MULT; DLB 122, 278; DLBY 1982; HW 1, 2; INT CANR-6; LLW; MAL 5; RGAL 4

Rechy, John Francisco
See Rechy, John

Redcam, Tom 1870-1933 .... **TCLC 25**

Reddin, Keith 1956- .... **CLC 67**
See also CAD; CD 6

Redgrove, Peter (William)
1932-2003 .... **CLC 6, 41**
See also BRWS 6; CA 1-4R; 217; CANR 3, 39, 77; CP 1, 2, 3, 4, 5, 6, 7; DLB 40; TCLE 1:2

Redmon, Anne .... **CLC 22**
See Nightingale, Anne Redmon
See also DLBY 1986

Reed, Eliot
See Ambler, Eric

Reed, Ishmael 1938- ..... **BLC 3; CLC 2, 3, 5, 6, 13, 32, 60, 174; PC 68**
See also AFAW 1, 2; AMWS 10; BPFB 3; BW 2, 3; CA 21-24R; CANR 25, 48, 74, 128; CN 1, 2, 3, 4, 5, 6, 7; CP 1, 2, 3, 4, 5, 6, 7; CSW; DA3; DAM MULT; DLB 2, 5, 33, 169, 227; DLBD 8; EWL 3; LMFS 2; MAL 5; MSW; MTCW 1, 2; MTFW 2005; PFS 6; RGAL 4; TCWW 2

Reed, John (Silas) 1887-1920 .... **TCLC 9**
See also CA 106; 195; MAL 5; TUS

Reed, Lou .... **CLC 21**
See Firbank, Louis

Reese, Lizette Woodworth
1856-1935 .... **PC 29; TCLC 181**
See also CA 180; DLB 54

Reeve, Clara 1729-1807 .... **NCLC 19**
See also DLB 39; RGEL 2

Reich, Wilhelm 1897-1957 .... **TCLC 57**
See also CA 199

Reid, Christopher (John) 1949- .... **CLC 33**
See also CA 140; CANR 89; CP 4, 5, 6, 7; DLB 40; EWL 3

Reid, Desmond
See Moorcock, Michael

Reid Banks, Lynne 1929-
See Banks, Lynne Reid
See also AAYA 49; CA 1-4R; CANR 6, 22, 38, 87; CLR 24; CN 1, 2, 3, 7; JRDA; MAICYA 1, 2; SATA 22, 75, 111, 165; YAW

Reilly, William K.
See Creasey, John

Reiner, Max
See Caldwell, (Janet Miriam) Taylor (Holland)

Reis, Ricardo
See Pessoa, Fernando (Antonio Nogueira)

Reizenstein, Elmer Leopold
See Rice, Elmer (Leopold)
See also EWL 3

Remarque, Erich Maria 1898-1970 . **CLC 21**
See also AAYA 27; BPFB 3; CA 77-80; 29-32R; CDWLB 2; DA; DA3; DAB; DAC; DAM MST, NOV; DLB 56; EWL 3; EXPN; LAIT 3; MTCW 1, 2; MTFW 2005; NFS 4; RGHL; RGWL 2, 3

Remington, Frederic S(ackrider)
1861-1909 .... **TCLC 89**
See also CA 108; 169; DLB 12, 186, 188; SATA 41; TCWW 2

Remizov, A.
See Remizov, Aleksei (Mikhailovich)

Remizov, A. M.
See Remizov, Aleksei (Mikhailovich)

Remizov, Aleksei (Mikhailovich)
1877-1957 .... **TCLC 27**
See Remizov, Alexey Mikhaylovich
See also CA 125; 133; DLB 295

Remizov, Alexey Mikhaylovich
See Remizov, Aleksei (Mikhailovich)
See also EWL 3

Renan, Joseph Ernest 1823-1892 . **NCLC 26, 145**
See also GFL 1789 to the Present

Renard, Jules(-Pierre) 1864-1910 .. **TCLC 17**
See also CA 117; 202; GFL 1789 to the Present

Renart, Jean fl. 13th cent. - .... **CMLC 83**

Renault, Mary .... **CLC 3, 11, 17**
See Challans, Mary
See also BPFB 3; BYA 2; CN 1, 2, 3; DLBY 1983; EWL 3; GLL 1; LAIT 1; RGEL 2; RHW

Rendell, Ruth 1930- .... **CLC 28, 48**
See Vine, Barbara
See also BPFB 3; BRWS 9; CA 109; CANR 32, 52, 74, 127; CN 5, 6, 7; CPW; DAM POP; DLB 87, 276; INT CANR-32; MSW; MTCW 1, 2; MTFW 2005

Rendell, Ruth Barbara
See Rendell, Ruth

Renoir, Jean 1894-1979 .... **CLC 20**
See also CA 129; 85-88

Resnais, Alain 1922- .... **CLC 16**

Revard, Carter 1931- .... **NNAL**
See also CA 144; CANR 81, 153; PFS 5

Reverdy, Pierre 1889-1960 .... **CLC 53**
See also CA 97-100; 89-92; DLB 258; EWL 3; GFL 1789 to the Present

Rexroth, Kenneth 1905-1982 .... **CLC 1, 2, 6, 11, 22, 49, 112; PC 20**
See also BG 1:3; CA 5-8R; 107; CANR 14, 34, 63; CDALB 1941-1968; CP 1, 2, 3; DAM POET; DLB 16, 48, 165, 212; DLBY 1982; EWL 3; INT CANR-14; MAL 5; MTCW 1, 2; MTFW 2005; RGAL 4

Reyes, Alfonso 1889-1959 .... **HLCS 2; TCLC 33**
See also CA 131; EWL 3; HW 1; LAW

Reyes y Basoalto, Ricardo Eliecer Neftali
See Neruda, Pablo

Reymont, Wladyslaw (Stanislaw)
1868(?)-1925 .... **TCLC 5**
See also CA 104; EWL 3

Reynolds, John Hamilton
1794-1852 .... **NCLC 146**
See also DLB 96

Reynolds, Jonathan 1942- .... **CLC 6, 38**
See also CA 65-68; CANR 28

Reynolds, Joshua 1723-1792 .... **LC 15**
See also DLB 104

Reynolds, Michael S(hane)
1937-2000 .... **CLC 44**
See also CA 65-68; 189; CANR 9, 89, 97

Reznikoff, Charles 1894-1976 .... **CLC 9**
See also AMWS 14; CA 33-36; 61-64; CAP 2; CP 1, 2; DLB 28, 45; RGHL; WP

Roberts, Elizabeth Madox
1886-1941 .... **TCLC 68**
See also CA 111; 166; CLR 100; CWRI 5;
DLB 9, 54, 102; RGAL 4; RHW; SATA
33; SATA-Brief 27; TCWW 2; WCH

Roberts, Kate 1891-1985 .... **CLC 15**
See also CA 107; 116; DLB 319

Roberts, Keith (John Kingston)
1935-2000 .... **CLC 14**
See also BRWS 10; CA 25-28R; CANR 46;
DLB 261; SFW 4

Roberts, Kenneth (Lewis)
1885-1957 .... **TCLC 23**
See also CA 109; 199; DLB 9; MAL 5;
RGAL 4; RHW

Roberts, Michele (Brigitte) 1949- .... **CLC 48,
178**
See also CA 115; CANR 58, 120; CN 6, 7;
DLB 231; FW

Robertson, Ellis
See Ellison, Harlan; Silverberg, Robert

Robertson, Thomas William
1829-1871 .... **NCLC 35**
See Robertson, Tom
See also DAM DRAM

Robertson, Tom
See Robertson, Thomas William
See also RGEL 2

Robeson, Kenneth
See Dent, Lester

Robinson, Edwin Arlington
1869-1935 .... **PC 1, 35; TCLC 5, 101**
See also AMW; CA 104; 133; CDALB
1865-1917; DA; DAC; DAM MST,
POET; DLB 54; EWL 3; EXPP; MAL 5;
MTCW 1, 2; MTFW 2005; PAB; PFS 4;
RGAL 4; WP

Robinson, Henry Crabb
1775-1867 .... **NCLC 15**
See also DLB 107

Robinson, Jill 1936- .... **CLC 10**
See also CA 102; CANR 120; INT CA-102

Robinson, Kim Stanley 1952- .... **CLC 34**
See also AAYA 26; CA 126; CANR 113,
139; CN 6, 7; MTFW 2005; SATA 109;
SCFW 2; SFW 4

Robinson, Lloyd
See Silverberg, Robert

Robinson, Marilynne 1944- ...... **CLC 25, 180**
See also AAYA 69; CA 116; CANR 80, 140;
CN 4, 5, 6, 7; DLB 206; MTFW 2005;
NFS 24

Robinson, Mary 1758-1800 .... **NCLC 142**
See also DLB 158; FW

Robinson, Smokey .... **CLC 21**
See Robinson, William, Jr.

Robinson, William, Jr. 1940-
See Robinson, Smokey
See also CA 116

Robison, Mary 1949- .... **CLC 42, 98**
See also CA 113; 116; CANR 87; CN 4, 5,
6, 7; DLB 130; INT CA-116; RGSF 2

Roches, Catherine des 1542-1587 ...... **LC 117**
See also DLB 327

Rochester
See Wilmot, John
See also RGEL 2

Rod, Edouard 1857-1910 .... **TCLC 52**

Roddenberry, Eugene Wesley 1921-1991
See Roddenberry, Gene
See also CA 110; 135; CANR 37; SATA 45;
SATA-Obit 69

Roddenberry, Gene .... **CLC 17**
See Roddenberry, Eugene Wesley
See also AAYA 5; SATA-Obit 69

Rodgers, Mary 1931- .... **CLC 12**
See also BYA 5; CA 49-52; CANR 8, 55,
90; CLR 20; CWRI 5; INT CANR-8;
JRDA; MAICYA 1, 2; SATA 8, 130

Rodgers, W(illiam) R(obert)
1909-1969 .... **CLC 7**
See also CA 85-88; DLB 20; RGEL 2

Rodman, Eric
See Silverberg, Robert

Rodman, Howard 1920(?)-1985 .... **CLC 65**
See also CA 118

Rodman, Maia
See Wojciechowska, Maia (Teresa)

Rodo, Jose Enrique 1871(?)-1917 .... **HLCS 2**
See also CA 178; EWL 3; HW 2; LAW

Rodolph, Utto
See Ouologuem, Yambo

Rodriguez, Claudio 1934-1999 .... **CLC 10**
See also CA 188; DLB 134

Rodriguez, Richard 1944- .... **CLC 155; HLC
2**
See also AMWS 14; CA 110; CANR 66,
116; DAM MULT; DLB 82, 256; HW 1,
2; LAIT 5; LLW; MTFW 2005; NCFS 3;
WLIT 1

Roelvaag, O(le) E(dvart) 1876-1931
See Rolvaag, O(le) E(dvart)
See also CA 117; 171

Roethke, Theodore (Huebner)
1908-1963 .... **CLC 1, 3, 8, 11, 19, 46,
101; PC 15**
See also AMW; CA 81-84; CABS 2;
CDALB 1941-1968; DA3; DAM POET;
DLB 5, 206; EWL 3; EXPP; MAL 5;
MTCW 1, 2; PAB; PFS 3; RGAL 4; WP

Rogers, Carl R(ansom)
1902-1987 .... **TCLC 125**
See also CA 1-4R; 121; CANR 1, 18;
MTCW 1

Rogers, Samuel 1763-1855 .... **NCLC 69**
See also DLB 93; RGEL 2

Rogers, Thomas Hunton 1927- .... **CLC 57**
See also CA 89-92; INT CA-89-92

Rogers, Will(iam Penn Adair)
1879-1935 .... **NNAL; TCLC 8, 71**
See also CA 105; 144; DA3; DAM MULT;
DLB 11; MTCW 2

Rogin, Gilbert 1929- .... **CLC 18**
See also CA 65-68; CANR 15

Rohan, Koda
See Koda Shigeyuki

Rohlfs, Anna Katharine Green
See Green, Anna Katharine

Rohmer, Eric .... **CLC 16**
See Scherer, Jean-Marie Maurice

Rohmer, Sax .... **TCLC 28**
See Ward, Arthur Henry Sarsfield
See also DLB 70; MSW; SUFW

Roiphe, Anne 1935- .... **CLC 3, 9**
See also CA 89-92; CANR 45, 73, 138;
DLBY 1980; INT CA-89-92

Roiphe, Anne Richardson
See Roiphe, Anne

Rojas, Fernando de 1475-1541 ... **HLCS 1, 2;
LC 23**
See also DLB 286; RGWL 2, 3

Rojas, Gonzalo 1917- .... **HLCS 2**
See also CA 178; HW 2; LAWS 1

Roland (de la Platiere), Marie-Jeanne
1754-1793 .... **LC 98**
See also DLB 314

**Rolfe, Frederick (William Serafino Austin
Lewis Mary)** 1860-1913 .... **TCLC 12**
See Al Siddik
See also CA 107; 210; DLB 34, 156; RGEL
2

Rolland, Romain 1866-1944 .... **TCLC 23**
See also CA 118; 197; DLB 65, 284; EWL
3; GFL 1789 to the Present; RGWL 2, 3

Rolle, Richard c. 1300-c. 1349 ...... **CMLC 21**
See also DLB 146; LMFS 1; RGEL 2

Rolvaag, O(le) E(dvart) .... **TCLC 17**
See Roelvaag, O(le) E(dvart)
See also DLB 9, 212; MAL 5; NFS 5;
RGAL 4

Romain Arnaud, Saint
See Aragon, Louis

Romains, Jules 1885-1972 .... **CLC 7**
See also CA 85-88; CANR 34; DLB 65,
321; EWL 3; GFL 1789 to the Present;
MTCW 1

Romero, Jose Ruben 1890-1952 .... **TCLC 14**
See also CA 114; 131; EWL 3; HW 1; LAW

Ronsard, Pierre de 1524-1585 . **LC 6, 54; PC
11**
See also DLB 327; EW 2; GFL Beginnings
to 1789; RGWL 2, 3; TWA

Rooke, Leon 1934- .... **CLC 25, 34**
See also CA 25-28R; CANR 23, 53; CCA
1; CPW; DAM POP

Roosevelt, Franklin Delano
1882-1945 .... **TCLC 93**
See also CA 116; 173; LAIT 3

Roosevelt, Theodore 1858-1919 .... **TCLC 69**
See also CA 115; 170; DLB 47, 186, 275

Roper, William 1498-1578 .... **LC 10**

Roquelaure, A. N.
See Rice, Anne

Rosa, Joao Guimaraes 1908-1967 ... **CLC 23;
HLCS 1**
See Guimaraes Rosa, Joao
See also CA 89-92; DLB 113, 307; EWL 3;
WLIT 1

Rose, Wendy 1948- . **CLC 85; NNAL; PC 13**
See also CA 53-56; CANR 5, 51; CWP;
DAM MULT; DLB 175; PFS 13; RGAL
4; SATA 12

Rosen, R. D.
See Rosen, Richard (Dean)

Rosen, Richard (Dean) 1949- .... **CLC 39**
See also CA 77-80; CANR 62, 120; CMW
4; INT CANR-30

Rosenberg, Isaac 1890-1918 .... **TCLC 12**
See also BRW 6; CA 107; 188; DLB 20,
216; EWL 3; PAB; RGEL 2

Rosenblatt, Joe .... **CLC 15**
See Rosenblatt, Joseph
See also CP 3, 4, 5, 6, 7

Rosenblatt, Joseph 1933-
See Rosenblatt, Joe
See also CA 89-92; CP 1, 2; INT CA-89-92

Rosenfeld, Samuel
See Tzara, Tristan

Rosenstock, Sami
See Tzara, Tristan

Rosenstock, Samuel
See Tzara, Tristan

Rosenthal, M(acha) L(ouis)
1917-1996 .... **CLC 28**
See also CA 1-4R; 152; CAAS 6; CANR 4,
51; CP 1, 2, 3, 4, 5, 6; DLB 5; SATA 59

Ross, Barnaby
See Dannay, Frederic; Lee, Manfred B.

Ross, Bernard L.
See Follett, Ken

Ross, J. H.
See Lawrence, T(homas) E(dward)

Ross, John Hume
See Lawrence, T(homas) E(dward)

Ross, Martin 1862-1915
See Martin, Violet Florence
See also DLB 135; GLL 2; RGEL 2; RGSF
2

Ross, (James) Sinclair 1908-1996 ... **CLC 13;
SSC 24**
See also CA 73-76; CANR 81; CN 1, 2, 3,
4, 5, 6; DAC; DAM MST; DLB 88;
RGEL 2; RGSF 2; TCWW 1, 2

Ryga, George 1932-1987 .... **CLC 14**
See also CA 101; 124; CANR 43, 90; CCA
1; DAC; DAM MST; DLB 60
Rymer, Thomas 1643(?)-1713 .... **LC 132**
See also DLB 101
S. H.
See Hartmann, Sadakichi
S. S.
See Sassoon, Siegfried (Lorraine)
Sa'adawi, al- Nawal
See El Saadawi, Nawal
See also AFW; EWL 3
Saadawi, Nawal El
See El Saadawi, Nawal
See also WLIT 2
Saba, Umberto 1883-1957 .... **TCLC 33**
See also CA 144; CANR 79; DLB 114;
EWL 3; RGWL 2, 3
Sabatini, Rafael 1875-1950 .... **TCLC 47**
See also BPFB 3; CA 162; RHW
Sabato, Ernesto 1911- ... **CLC 10, 23; HLC 2**
See also CA 97-100; CANR 32, 65; CD-
WLB 3; CWW 2; DAM MULT; DLB 145;
EWL 3; HW 1, 2; LAW; MTCW 1, 2;
MTFW 2005
Sa-Carneiro, Mario de 1890-1916 . **TCLC 83**
See also DLB 287; EWL 3
Sacastru, Martin
See Bioy Casares, Adolfo
See also CWW 2
Sacher-Masoch, Leopold von
1836(?)-1895 .... **NCLC 31**
Sachs, Hans 1494-1576 .... **LC 95**
See also CDWLB 2; DLB 179; RGWL 2, 3
Sachs, Marilyn 1927- .... **CLC 35**
See also AAYA 2; BYA 6; CA 17-20R;
CANR 13, 47, 150; CLR 2; JRDA; MAI-
CYA 1, 2; SAAS 2; SATA 3, 68, 164;
SATA-Essay 110; WYA; YAW
Sachs, Marilyn Stickle
See Sachs, Marilyn
Sachs, Nelly 1891-1970 .... **CLC 14, 98**
See also CA 17-18; 25-28R; CANR 87;
CAP 2; EWL 3; MTCW 2; MTFW 2005;
PFS 20; RGHL; RGWL 2, 3
Sackler, Howard (Oliver)
1929-1982 .... **CLC 14**
See also CA 61-64; 108; CAD; CANR 30;
DFS 15; DLB 7
Sacks, Oliver 1933- .... **CLC 67, 202**
See also CA 53-56; CANR 28, 50, 76, 146;
CPW; DA3; INT CANR-28; MTCW 1, 2;
MTFW 2005
Sacks, Oliver Wolf
See Sacks, Oliver
Sackville, Thomas 1536-1608 .... **LC 98**
See also DAM DRAM; DLB 62, 132;
RGEL 2
Sadakichi
See Hartmann, Sadakichi
Sa'dawi, Nawal al-
See El Saadawi, Nawal
See also CWW 2
Sade, Donatien Alphonse Francois
1740-1814 .... **NCLC 3, 47**
See also DLB 314; EW 4; GFL Beginnings
to 1789; RGWL 2, 3
Sade, Marquis de
See Sade, Donatien Alphonse Francois
Sadoff, Ira 1945- .... **CLC 9**
See also CA 53-56; CANR 5, 21, 109; DLB
120
Saetone
See Camus, Albert
Safire, William 1929- .... **CLC 10**
See also CA 17-20R; CANR 31, 54, 91, 148

Sagan, Carl 1934-1996 .... **CLC 30, 112**
See also AAYA 2, 62; CA 25-28R; 155;
CANR 11, 36, 74; CPW; DA3; MTCW 1,
2; MTFW 2005; SATA 58; SATA-Obit 94
Sagan, Francoise .... **CLC 3, 6, 9, 17, 36**
See Quoirez, Francoise
See also CWW 2; DLB 83; EWL 3; GFL
1789 to the Present; MTCW 2
Sahgal, Nayantara (Pandit) 1927- .... **CLC 41**
See also CA 9-12R; CANR 11, 88; CN 1,
2, 3, 4, 5, 6, 7; DLB 323
Said, Edward W. 1935-2003 .... **CLC 123**
See also CA 21-24R; 220; CANR 45, 74,
107, 131; DLB 67; MTCW 2; MTFW
2005
Saint, H(arry) F. 1941- .... **CLC 50**
See also CA 127
St. Aubin de Teran, Lisa 1953-
See Teran, Lisa St. Aubin de
See also CA 118; 126; CN 6, 7; INT CA-
126
Saint Birgitta of Sweden c.
1303-1373 .... **CMLC 24**
Sainte-Beuve, Charles Augustin
1804-1869 .... **NCLC 5**
See also DLB 217; EW 6; GFL 1789 to the
Present
Saint-Exupery, Antoine de
1900-1944 .... **TCLC 2, 56, 169; WLC**
See also AAYA 63; BPFB 3; BYA 3; CA
108; 132; CLR 10; DA3; DAM NOV;
DLB 72; EW 12; EWL 3; GFL 1789 to
the Present; LAIT 3; MAICYA 1, 2;
MTCW 1, 2; MTFW 2005; RGWL 2, 3;
SATA 20; TWA
**Saint-Exupery, Antoine Jean Baptiste Marie
Roger de**
See Saint-Exupery, Antoine de
St. John, David
See Hunt, E(verette) Howard, (Jr.)
St. John, J. Hector
See Crevecoeur, Michel Guillaume Jean de
Saint-John Perse
See Leger, (Marie-Rene Auguste) Alexis
Saint-Leger
See also EW 10; EWL 3; GFL 1789 to the
Present; RGWL 2
Saintsbury, George (Edward Bateman)
1845-1933 .... **TCLC 31**
See also CA 160; DLB 57, 149
Sait Faik .... **TCLC 23**
See Abasiyanik, Sait Faik
Saki .... **SSC 12; TCLC 3; WLC 5**
See Munro, H(ector) H(ugh)
See also BRWS 6; BYA 11; LAIT 2; RGEL
2; SSFS 1; SUFW
Sala, George Augustus 1828-1895 . **NCLC 46**
Saladin 1138-1193 .... **CMLC 38**
Salama, Hannu 1936- .... **CLC 18**
See also CA 244; EWL 3
Salamanca, J(ack) R(ichard) 1922- .. **CLC 4,
15**
See also CA 25-28R, 193; CAAE 193
Salas, Floyd Francis 1931- .... **HLC 2**
See also CA 119; CAAS 27; CANR 44, 75,
93; DAM MULT; DLB 82; HW 1, 2;
MTCW 2; MTFW 2005
Sale, J. Kirkpatrick
See Sale, Kirkpatrick
Sale, John Kirkpatrick
See Sale, Kirkpatrick
Sale, Kirkpatrick 1937- .... **CLC 68**
See also CA 13-16R; CANR 10, 147
Salinas, Luis Omar 1937- ... **CLC 90; HLC 2**
See also AMWS 13; CA 131; CANR 81,
153; DAM MULT; DLB 82; HW 1, 2
Salinas (y Serrano), Pedro
1891(?)-1951 .... **TCLC 17**
See also CA 117; DLB 134; EWL 3

Salinger, J.D. 1919- . **CLC 1, 3, 8, 12, 55, 56,
138; SSC 2, 28, 65; WLC 5**
See also AAYA 2, 36; AMW; AMWC 1;
BPFB 3; CA 5-8R; CANR 39, 129;
CDALB 1941-1968; CLR 18; CN 1, 2, 3,
4, 5, 6, 7; CPW 1; DA; DA3; DAB; DAC;
DAM MST, NOV, POP; DLB 2, 102, 173;
EWL 3; EXPN; LAIT 4; MAICYA 1, 2;
MAL 5; MTCW 1, 2; MTFW 2005; NFS
1; RGAL 4; RGSF 2; SATA 67; SSFS 17;
TUS; WYA; YAW
Salisbury, John
See Caute, (John) David
Sallust c. 86B.C.-35B.C. .... **CMLC 68**
See also AW 2; CDWLB 1; DLB 211;
RGWL 2, 3
Salter, James 1925- .. **CLC 7, 52, 59; SSC 58**
See also AMWS 9; CA 73-76; CANR 107;
DLB 130
Saltus, Edgar (Everton) 1855-1921 . **TCLC 8**
See also CA 105; DLB 202; RGAL 4
Saltykov, Mikhail Evgrafovich
1826-1889 .... **NCLC 16**
See also DLB 238:
Saltykov-Shchedrin, N.
See Saltykov, Mikhail Evgrafovich
Samarakis, Andonis
See Samarakis, Antonis
See also EWL 3
Samarakis, Antonis 1919-2003 .... **CLC 5**
See Samarakis, Andonis
See also CA 25-28R; 224; CAAS 16; CANR
36
Sanchez, Florencio 1875-1910 .... **TCLC 37**
See also CA 153; DLB 305; EWL 3; HW 1;
LAW
Sanchez, Luis Rafael 1936- .... **CLC 23**
See also CA 128; DLB 305; EWL 3; HW 1;
WLIT 1
Sanchez, Sonia 1934- .... **BLC 3; CLC 5, 116,
215; PC 9**
See also BW 2, 3; CA 33-36R; CANR 24,
49, 74, 115; CLR 18; CP 2, 3, 4, 5, 6, 7;
CSW; CWP; DA3; DAM MULT; DLB 41;
DLBD 8; EWL 3; MAICYA 1, 2; MAL 5;
MTCW 1, 2; MTFW 2005; SATA 22, 136;
WP
Sancho, Ignatius 1729-1780 .... **LC 84**
Sand, George 1804-1876 ..... **NCLC 2, 42, 57,
174; WLC 5**
See also DA; DA3; DAB; DAC; DAM
MST, NOV; DLB 119, 192; EW 6; FL 1:3;
FW; GFL 1789 to the Present; RGWL 2,
3; TWA
Sandburg, Carl (August) 1878-1967 . **CLC 1,
4, 10, 15, 35; PC 2, 41; WLC 5**
See also AAYA 24; AMW; BYA 1, 3; CA
5-8R; 25-28R; CANR 35; CDALB 1865-
1917; CLR 67; DA; DA3; DAB; DAC;
DAM MST, POET; DLB 17, 54, 284;
EWL 3; EXPP; LAIT 2; MAICYA 1, 2;
MAL 5; MTCW 1, 2; MTFW 2005; PAB;
PFS 3, 6, 12; RGAL 4; SATA 8; TUS;
WCH; WP; WYA
Sandburg, Charles
See Sandburg, Carl (August)
Sandburg, Charles A.
See Sandburg, Carl (August)
Sanders, (James) Ed(ward) 1939- .... **CLC 53**
See Sanders, Edward
See also BG 1:3; CA 13-16R; CAAS 21;
CANR 13, 44, 78; CP 1, 2, 3, 4, 5, 6, 7;
DAM POET; DLB 16, 244
Sanders, Edward
See Sanders, (James) Ed(ward)
See also DLB 244
Sanders, Lawrence 1920-1998 .... **CLC 41**
See also BEST 89:4; BPFB 3; CA 81-84;
165; CANR 33, 62; CMW 4; CPW; DA3;
DAM POP; MTCW 1

Schneider, Leonard Alfred 1925-1966
  See Bruce, Lenny
  See also CA 89-92

Schnitzler, Arthur 1862-1931 ..... **DC 17; SSC 15, 61; TCLC 4**
  See also CA 104; CDWLB 2; DLB 81, 118; EW 8; EWL 3; RGSF 2; RGWL 2, 3

Schoenberg, Arnold Franz Walter 1874-1951 .... **TCLC 75**
  See also CA 109; 188

Schonberg, Arnold
  See Schoenberg, Arnold Franz Walter

Schopenhauer, Arthur 1788-1860 . **NCLC 51, 157**
  See also DLB 90; EW 5

Schor, Sandra (M.) 1932(?)-1990 ..... **CLC 65**
  See also CA 132

Schorer, Mark 1908-1977 .... **CLC 9**
  See also CA 5-8R; 73-76; CANR 7; CN 1, 2; DLB 103

Schrader, Paul (Joseph) 1946- . **CLC 26, 212**
  See also CA 37-40R; CANR 41; DLB 44

Schreber, Daniel 1842-1911 .... **TCLC 123**

Schreiner, Olive (Emilie Albertina) 1855-1920 .... **TCLC 9**
  See also AFW; BRWS 2; CA 105; 154; DLB 18, 156, 190, 225; EWL 3; FW; RGEL 2; TWA; WLIT 2; WWE 1

Schulberg, Budd (Wilson) 1914- .. **CLC 7, 48**
  See also BPFB 3; CA 25-28R; CANR 19, 87; CN 1, 2, 3, 4, 5, 6, 7; DLB 6, 26, 28; DLBY 1981, 2001; MAL 5

Schulman, Arnold
  See Trumbo, Dalton

Schulz, Bruno 1892-1942 .. **SSC 13; TCLC 5, 51**
  See also CA 115; 123; CANR 86; CDWLB 4; DLB 215; EWL 3; MTCW 2; MTFW 2005; RGSF 2; RGWL 2, 3

Schulz, Charles M. 1922-2000 .... **CLC 12**
  See also AAYA 39; CA 9-12R; 187; CANR 6, 132; INT CANR-6; MTFW 2005; SATA 10; SATA-Obit 118

Schulz, Charles Monroe
  See Schulz, Charles M.

Schumacher, E(rnst) F(riedrich) 1911-1977 .... **CLC 80**
  See also CA 81-84; 73-76; CANR

Schumann, Robert 1810-1856 ...... **NCLC 143**

Schuyler, George Samuel 1895-1977 . **HR 1:3**
  See also BW 2; CA 81-84; 73-76; CANR 42; DLB 29, 51

Schuyler, James Marcus 1923-1991 .. **CLC 5, 23**
  See also CA 101; 134; CP 1, 2, 3, 4, 5; DAM POET; DLB 5, 169; EWL 3; INT CA-101; MAL 5; WP

Schwartz, Delmore (David) 1913-1966 ... **CLC 2, 4, 10, 45, 87; PC 8**
  See also AMWS 2; CA 17-18; 25-28R; CANR 35; CAP 2; DLB 28, 48; EWL 3; MAL 5; MTCW 1, 2; MTFW 2005; PAB; RGAL 4; TUS

Schwartz, Ernst
  See Ozu, Yasujiro

Schwartz, John Burnham 1965- .... **CLC 59**
  See also CA 132; CANR 116

Schwartz, Lynne Sharon 1939- .... **CLC 31**
  See also CA 103; CANR 44, 89; DLB 218; MTCW 2; MTFW 2005

Schwartz, Muriel A.
  See Eliot, T(homas) S(tearns)

Schwarz-Bart, Andre 1928-2006 .... **CLC 2, 4**
  See also CA 89-92; CANR 109; DLB 299; RGHL

Schwarz-Bart, Simone 1938- . **BLCS; CLC 7**
  See also BW 2; CA 97-100; CANR 117; EWL 3

Schwerner, Armand 1927-1999 .... **PC 42**
  See also CA 9-12R; 179; CANR 50, 85; CP 2, 3, 4, 5, 6; DLB 165

Schwitters, Kurt (Hermann Edward Karl Julius) 1887-1948 .... **TCLC 95**
  See also CA 158

Schwob, Marcel (Mayer Andre) 1867-1905 .... **TCLC 20**
  See also CA 117; 168; DLB 123; GFL 1789 to the Present

Sciascia, Leonardo 1921-1989 .. **CLC 8, 9, 41**
  See also CA 85-88; 130; CANR 35; DLB 177; EWL 3; MTCW 1; RGWL 2, 3

Scoppettone, Sandra 1936- .... **CLC 26**
  See Early, Jack
  See also AAYA 11, 65; BYA 8; CA 5-8R; CANR 41, 73, 157; GLL 1; MAICYA 1; MAICYAS 1; SATA 9, 92; WYA; YAW

Scorsese, Martin 1942- .... **CLC 20, 89, 207**
  See also AAYA 38; CA 110; 114; CANR 46, 85

Scotland, Jay
  See Jakes, John

Scott, Duncan Campbell 1862-1947 .... **TCLC 6**
  See also CA 104; 153; DAC; DLB 92; RGEL 2

Scott, Evelyn 1893-1963 .... **CLC 43**
  See also CA 104; 112; CANR 64; DLB 9, 48; RHW

Scott, F(rancis) R(eginald) 1899-1985 .... **CLC 22**
  See also CA 101; 114; CANR 87; CP 1, 2, 3, 4; DLB 88; INT CA-101; RGEL 2

Scott, Frank
  See Scott, F(rancis) R(eginald)

Scott, Joan .... **CLC 65**

Scott, Joanna 1960- .... **CLC 50**
  See also CA 126; CANR 53, 92

Scott, Paul (Mark) 1920-1978 ...... **CLC 9, 60**
  See also BRWS 1; CA 81-84; 77-80; CANR 33; CN 1, 2; DLB 14, 207, 326; EWL 3; MTCW 1; RGEL 2; RHW; WWE 1

Scott, Ridley 1937- .... **CLC 183**
  See also AAYA 13, 43

Scott, Sarah 1723-1795 .... **LC 44**
  See also DLB 39

Scott, Sir Walter 1771-1832 .... **NCLC 15, 69, 110; PC 13; SSC 32; WLC 5**
  See also AAYA 22; BRW 4; BYA 2; CD-BLB 1789-1832; DA; DAB; DAC; DAM MST, NOV, POET; DLB 93, 107, 116, 144, 159; GL 3; HGG; LAIT 1; RGEL 2; RGSF 2; SSFS 10; SUFW 1; TEA; WLIT 3; YABC 2

Scribe, (Augustin) Eugene 1791-1861 . **DC 5; NCLC 16**
  See also DAM DRAM; DLB 192; GFL 1789 to the Present; RGWL 2, 3

Scrum, R.
  See Crumb, R.

Scudery, Georges de 1601-1667 .... **LC 75**
  See also GFL Beginnings to 1789

Scudery, Madeleine de 1607-1701 .. **LC 2, 58**
  See also DLB 268; GFL Beginnings to 1789

Scum
  See Crumb, R.

Scumbag, Little Bobby
  See Crumb, R.

Seabrook, John
  See Hubbard, L. Ron

Seacole, Mary Jane Grant 1805-1881 .... **NCLC 147**
  See also DLB 166

Sealy, I(rwin) Allan 1951- .... **CLC 55**
  See also CA 136; CN 6, 7

Search, Alexander
  See Pessoa, Fernando (Antonio Nogueira)

Sebald, W(infried) G(eorg) 1944-2001 .... **CLC 194**
  See also BRWS 8; CA 159; 202; CANR 98; MTFW 2005; RGHL

Sebastian, Lee
  See Silverberg, Robert

Sebastian Owl
  See Thompson, Hunter S.

Sebestyen, Igen
  See Sebestyen, Ouida

Sebestyen, Ouida 1924- .... **CLC 30**
  See also AAYA 8; BYA 7; CA 107; CANR 40, 114; CLR 17; JRDA; MAICYA 1, 2; SAAS 10; SATA 39, 140; WYA; YAW

Sebold, Alice 1963(?)- .... **CLC 193**
  See also AAYA 56; CA 203; MTFW 2005

Second Duke of Buckingham
  See Villiers, George

Secundus, H. Scriblerus
  See Fielding, Henry

Sedges, John
  See Buck, Pearl S(ydenstricker)

Sedgwick, Catharine Maria 1789-1867 .... **NCLC 19, 98**
  See also DLB 1, 74, 183, 239, 243, 254; FL 1:3; RGAL 4

Sedulius Scottus 9th cent. -c. 874 .. **CMLC 86**

Seelye, John (Douglas) 1931- .... **CLC 7**
  See also CA 97-100; CANR 70; INT CA-97-100; TCWW 1, 2

Seferiades, Giorgos Stylianou 1900-1971
  See Seferis, George
  See also CA 5-8R; 33-36R; CANR 5, 36; MTCW 1

Seferis, George .... **CLC 5, 11; PC 66**
  See Seferiades, Giorgos Stylianou
  See also EW 12; EWL 3; RGWL 2, 3

Segal, Erich (Wolf) 1937- .... **CLC 3, 10**
  See also BEST 89:1; BPFB 3; CA 25-28R; CANR 20, 36, 65, 113; CPW; DAM POP; DLBY 1986; INT CANR-20; MTCW 1

Seger, Bob 1945- .... **CLC 35**

Seghers, Anna .... **CLC 7**
  See Radvanyi, Netty
  See also CDWLB 2; DLB 69; EWL 3

Seidel, Frederick (Lewis) 1936- .... **CLC 18**
  See also CA 13-16R; CANR 8, 99; CP 1, 2, 3, 4, 5, 6, 7; DLBY 1984

Seifert, Jaroslav 1901-1986 . **CLC 34, 44, 93; PC 47**
  See also CA 127; CDWLB 4; DLB 215; EWL 3; MTCW 1, 2

Sei Shonagon c. 966-1017(?) .... **CMLC 6**

Sejour, Victor 1817-1874 .... **DC 10**
  See also DLB 50

Sejour Marcou et Ferrand, Juan Victor
  See Sejour, Victor

Selby, Hubert, Jr. 1928-2004 ..... **CLC 1, 2, 4, 8; SSC 20**
  See also CA 13-16R; 226; CANR 33, 85; CN 1, 2, 3, 4, 5, 6, 7; DLB 2, 227; MAL 5

Selzer, Richard 1928- .... **CLC 74**
  See also CA 65-68; CANR 14, 106

Sembene, Ousmane
  See Ousmane, Sembene
  See also AFW; EWL 3; WLIT 2

Senancour, Etienne Pivert de 1770-1846 .... **NCLC 16**
  See also DLB 119; GFL 1789 to the Present

Sender, Ramon (Jose) 1902-1982 ...... **CLC 8; HLC 2; TCLC 136**
  See also CA 5-8R; 105; CANR 8; DAM MULT; DLB 322; EWL 3; HW 1; MTCW 1; RGWL 2, 3

Seneca, Lucius Annaeus c. 4B.C.-c. 65 .... **CMLC 6; DC 5**
  See also AW 2; CDWLB 1; DAM DRAM; DLB 211; RGWL 2, 3; TWA; WLIT 8

Simenon, Georges (Jacques Christian)
1903-1989 .... CLC 1, 2, 3, 8, 18, 47
See also BPFB 3; CA 85-88; 129; CANR
35; CMW 4; DA3; DAM POP; DLB 72;
DLBY 1989; EW 12; EWL 3; GFL 1789
to the Present; MSW; MTCW 1, 2; MTFW
2005; RGWL 2, 3

Simic, Charles 1938- .... CLC 6, 9, 22, 49, 68,
130; PC 69
See also AMWS 8; CA 29-32R; CAAS 4;
CANR 12, 33, 52, 61, 96, 140; CP 2, 3, 4,
5, 6, 7; DA3; DAM POET; DLB 105;
MAL 5; MTCW 2; MTFW 2005; PFS 7;
RGAL 4; WP

Simmel, Georg 1858-1918 .... TCLC 64
See also CA 157; DLB 296

Simmons, Charles (Paul) 1924- .... CLC 57
See also CA 89-92; INT CA-89-92

Simmons, Dan 1948- .... CLC 44
See also AAYA 16, 54; CA 138; CANR 53,
81, 126; CPW; DAM POP; HGG; SUFW
2

Simmons, James (Stewart Alexander)
1933- .... CLC 43
See also CA 105; CAAS 21; CP 1, 2, 3, 4,
5, 6, 7; DLB 40

Simms, William Gilmore
1806-1870 .... NCLC 3
See also DLB 3, 30, 59, 73, 248, 254;
RGAL 4

Simon, Carly 1945- .... CLC 26
See also CA 105

Simon, Claude 1913-2005 ... CLC 4, 9, 15, 39
See also CA 89-92; 241; CANR 33, 117;
CWW 2; DAM NOV; DLB 83; EW 13;
EWL 3; GFL 1789 to the Present; MTCW
1

Simon, Claude Eugene Henri
See Simon, Claude

Simon, Claude Henri Eugene
See Simon, Claude

Simon, Marvin Neil
See Simon, Neil

Simon, Myles
See Follett, Ken

Simon, Neil 1927- .... CLC 6, 11, 31, 39, 70;
DC 14
See also AAYA 32; AITN 1; AMWS 4; CA
21-24R; CAD; CANR 26, 54, 87, 126;
CD 5, 6; DA3; DAM DRAM; DFS 2, 6,
12, 18; DLB 7, 266; LAIT 4; MAL 5;
MTCW 1, 2; MTFW 2005; RGAL 4; TUS

Simon, Paul 1941(?)- .... CLC 17
See also CA 116; 153; CANR 152

Simon, Paul Frederick
See Simon, Paul

Simonon, Paul 1956(?)- .... CLC 30

Simonson, Rick ed. .... CLC 70

Simpson, Harriette
See Arnow, Harriette (Louisa) Simpson

Simpson, Louis 1923- ... CLC 4, 7, 9, 32, 149
See also AMWS 9; CA 1-4R; CAAS 4;
CANR 1, 61, 140; CP 1, 2, 3, 4, 5, 6, 7;
DAM POET; DLB 5; MAL 5; MTCW 1,
2; MTFW 2005; PFS 7, 11, 14; RGAL 4

Simpson, Mona 1957- .... CLC 44, 146
See also CA 122; 135; CANR 68, 103; CN
6, 7; EWL 3

Simpson, Mona Elizabeth
See Simpson, Mona

Simpson, N(orman) F(rederick)
1919- .... CLC 29
See also CA 13-16R; CBD; DLB 13; RGEL
2

Sinclair, Andrew (Annandale) 1935- . CLC 2,
14
See also CA 9-12R; CAAS 5; CANR 14,
38, 91; CN 1, 2, 3, 4, 5, 6, 7; DLB 14;
FANT; MTCW 1

Sinclair, Emil
See Hesse, Hermann

Sinclair, Iain 1943- .... CLC 76
See also CA 132; CANR 81, 157; CP 5, 6,
7; HGG

Sinclair, Iain MacGregor
See Sinclair, Iain

Sinclair, Irene
See Griffith, D(avid Lewelyn) W(ark)

Sinclair, Julian
See Sinclair, May

Sinclair, Mary Amelia St. Clair (?)-
See Sinclair, May

Sinclair, May 1865-1946 .... TCLC 3, 11
See also CA 104; 166; DLB 36, 135; EWL
3; HGG; RGEL 2; RHW; SUFW

Sinclair, Roy
See Griffith, D(avid Lewelyn) W(ark)

Sinclair, Upton 1878-1968 ...... CLC 1, 11, 15,
63; TCLC 160; WLC 5
See also AAYA 63; AMWS 5; BPFB 3;
BYA 2; CA 5-8R; 25-28R; CANR 7;
CDALB 1929-1941; DA; DA3; DAB;
DAC; DAM MST, NOV; DLB 9; EWL 3;
INT CANR-7; LAIT 3; MAL 5; MTCW
1, 2; MTFW 2005; NFS 6; RGAL 4;
SATA 9; TUS; YAW

Sinclair, Upton Beall
See Sinclair, Upton

Singe, (Edmund) J(ohn) M(illington)
1871-1909 .... WLC

Singer, Isaac
See Singer, Isaac Bashevis

Singer, Isaac Bashevis 1904-1991 .. CLC 1, 3,
6, 9, 11, 15, 23, 38, 69, 111; SSC 3, 53,
80; WLC 5
See also AAYA 32; AITN 1, 2; AMW;
AMWR 2; BPFB 3; BYA 1, 4; CA 1-4R;
134; CANR 1, 39, 106; CDALB 1941-
1968; CLR 1; CN 1, 2, 3, 4; CWRI 5;
DA; DA3; DAB; DAC; DAM MST, NOV;
DLB 6, 28, 52, 278; DLBY 1991; EWL
3; EXPS; HGG; JRDA; LAIT 3; MAI-
CYA 1, 2; MAL 5; MTCW 1, 2; MTFW
2005; RGAL 4; RGHL; RGSF 2; SATA 3,
27; SATA-Obit 68; SSFS 2, 12, 16; TUS;
TWA

Singer, Israel Joshua 1893-1944 .... TCLC 33
See also CA 169; EWL 3

Singh, Khushwant 1915- .... CLC 11
See also CA 9-12R; CAAS 9; CANR 6, 84;
CN 1, 2, 3, 4, 5, 6, 7; DLB 323; EWL 3;
RGEL 2

Singleton, Ann
See Benedict, Ruth

Singleton, John 1968(?)- .... CLC 156
See also AAYA 50; BW 2, 3; CA 138;
CANR 67, 82; DAM MULT

Siniavskii, Andrei
See Sinyavsky, Andrei (Donatevich)
See also CWW 2

Sinjohn, John
See Galsworthy, John

Sinyavsky, Andrei (Donatevich)
1925-1997 .... CLC 8
See Siniavskii, Andrei; Sinyavsky, Andrey
Donatovich; Tertz, Abram
See also CA 85-88; 159

Sinyavsky, Andrey Donatovich
See Sinyavsky, Andrei (Donatevich)
See also EWL 3

Sirin, V.
See Nabokov, Vladimir (Vladimirovich)

Sissman, L(ouis) E(dward)
1928-1976 .... CLC 9, 18
See also CA 21-24R; 65-68; CANR 13; CP
2; DLB 5

Sisson, C(harles) H(ubert)
1914-2003 .... CLC 8
See also BRWS 11; CA 1-4R; 220; CAAS
3; CANR 3, 48, 84; CP 1, 2, 3, 4, 5, 6, 7;
DLB 27

Sitting Bull 1831(?)-1890 .... NNAL
See also DA3; DAM MULT

Sitwell, Dame Edith 1887-1964 ..... CLC 2, 9,
67; PC 3
See also BRW 7; CA 9-12R; CANR 35;
CDBLB 1945-1960; DAM POET; DLB
20; EWL 3; MTCW 1, 2; MTFW 2005;
RGEL 2; TEA

Siwaarmill, H. P.
See Sharp, William

Sjoewall, Maj 1935- .... CLC 7
See Sjowall, Maj
See also CA 65-68; CANR 73

Sjowall, Maj
See Sjoewall, Maj
See also BPFB 3; CMW 4; MSW

Skelton, John 1460(?)-1529 ..... LC 71; PC 25
See also BRW 1; DLB 136; RGEL 2

Skelton, Robin 1925-1997 .... CLC 13
See Zuk, Georges
See also AITN 2; CA 5-8R; 160; CAAS 5;
CANR 28, 89; CCA 1; CP 1, 2, 3, 4, 5, 6;
DLB 27, 53

Skolimowski, Jerzy 1938- .... CLC 20
See also CA 128

Skram, Amalie (Bertha)
1847-1905 .... TCLC 25
See also CA 165

Skvorecky, Josef 1924- . CLC 15, 39, 69, 152
See also CA 61-64; CAAS 1; CANR 10,
34, 63, 108; CDWLB 4; CWW 2; DA3;
DAC; DAM NOV; DLB 232; EWL 3;
MTCW 1, 2; MTFW 2005

Slade, Bernard 1930- .... CLC 11, 46
See Newbound, Bernard Slade
See also CAAS 9; CCA 1; CD 6; DLB 53

Slaughter, Carolyn 1946- .... CLC 56
See also CA 85-88; CANR 85; CN 5, 6, 7

Slaughter, Frank G(ill) 1908-2001 ... CLC 29
See also AITN 2; CA 5-8R; 197; CANR 5,
85; INT CANR-5; RHW

Slavitt, David R(ytman) 1935- ...... CLC 5, 14
See also CA 21-24R; CAAS 3; CANR 41,
83; CN 1, 2; CP 1, 2, 3, 4, 5, 6, 7; DLB
5, 6

Slesinger, Tess 1905-1945 .... TCLC 10
See also CA 107; 199; DLB 102

Slessor, Kenneth 1901-1971 .... CLC 14
See also CA 102; 89-92; DLB 260; RGEL
2

Slowacki, Juliusz 1809-1849 .... NCLC 15
See also RGWL 3

Smart, Christopher 1722-1771 . LC 3; PC 13
See also DAM POET; DLB 109; RGEL 2

Smart, Elizabeth 1913-1986 .... CLC 54
See also CA 81-84; 118; CN 4; DLB 88

Smiley, Jane (Graves) 1949- ...... CLC 53, 76,
144
See also AAYA 66; AMWS 6; BPFB 3; CA
104; CANR 30, 50, 74, 96; CN 6, 7; CPW
1; DA3; DAM POP; DLB 227, 234; EWL
3; INT CANR-30; MAL 5; MTFW 2005;
SSFS 19

Smith, A(rthur) J(ames) M(arshall)
1902-1980 .... CLC 15
See also CA 1-4R; 102; CANR 4; CP 1, 2,
3; DAC; DLB 88; RGEL 2

Smith, Adam 1723(?)-1790 .... LC 36
See also DLB 104, 252; RGEL 2

Smith, Alexander 1829-1867 .... NCLC 59
See also DLB 32, 55

Smith, Anna Deavere 1950- .... CLC 86
See also CA 133; CANR 103; CD 5, 6; DFS
2, 22

Smith, Betty (Wehner) 1904-1972 .... **CLC 19**
See also BPFB 3; BYA 3; CA 5-8R; 33-36R; DLBY 1982; LAIT 3; RGAL 4; SATA 6

Smith, Charlotte (Turner)
1749-1806 .... **NCLC 23, 115**
See also DLB 39, 109; RGEL 2; TEA

Smith, Clark Ashton 1893-1961 .... **CLC 43**
See also CA 143; CANR 81; FANT; HGG; MTCW 2; SCFW 1, 2; SFW 4; SUFW

Smith, Dave .... **CLC 22, 42**
See Smith, David (Jeddie)
See also CAAS 7; CP 3, 4, 5, 6, 7; DLB 5

Smith, David (Jeddie) 1942-
See Smith, Dave
See also CA 49-52; CANR 1, 59, 120; CSW; DAM POET

Smith, Iain Crichton 1928-1998 .... **CLC 64**
See also BRWS 9; CA 21-24R; 171; CN 1, 2, 3, 4, 5, 6; CP 1, 2, 3, 4, 5, 6; DLB 40, 139, 319; RGSF 2

Smith, John 1580(?)-1631 .... **LC 9**
See also DLB 24, 30; TUS

Smith, Johnston
See Crane, Stephen (Townley)

Smith, Joseph, Jr. 1805-1844 .... **NCLC 53**

Smith, Kevin 1970- .... **CLC 223**
See also AAYA 37; CA 166; CANR 131

Smith, Lee 1944- .... **CLC 25, 73**
See also CA 114; 119; CANR 46, 118; CN 7; CSW; DLB 143; DLBY 1983; EWL 3; INT CA-119; RGAL 4

Smith, Martin
See Smith, Martin Cruz

Smith, Martin Cruz 1942- .. **CLC 25; NNAL**
See also BEST 89:4; BPFB 3; CA 85-88; CANR 6, 23, 43, 65, 119; CMW 4; CPW; DAM MULT, POP; HGG; INT CANR-23; MTCW 2; MTFW 2005; RGAL 4

Smith, Patti 1946- .... **CLC 12**
See also CA 93-96; CANR 63

Smith, Pauline (Urmson)
1882-1959 .... **TCLC 25**
See also DLB 225; EWL 3

Smith, Rosamond
See Oates, Joyce Carol

Smith, Sheila Kaye
See Kaye-Smith, Sheila

Smith, Stevie 1902-1971 .... **CLC 3, 8, 25, 44; PC 12**
See also BRWS 2; CA 17-18; 29-32R; CANR 35; CAP 2; CP 1; DAM POET; DLB 20; EWL 3; MTCW 1, 2; PAB; PFS 3; RGEL 2; TEA

Smith, Wilbur 1933- .... **CLC 33**
See also CA 13-16R; CANR 7, 46, 66, 134; CPW; MTCW 1, 2; MTFW 2005

Smith, William Jay 1918- .... **CLC 6**
See also AMWS 13; CA 5-8R; CANR 44, 106; CP 1, 2, 3, 4, 5, 6, 7; CSW; CWRI 5; DLB 5; MAICYA 1, 2; SAAS 22; SATA 2, 68, 154; SATA-Essay 154; TCLE 1:2

Smith, Woodrow Wilson
See Kuttner, Henry

Smith, Zadie 1975- .... **CLC 158**
See also AAYA 50; CA 193; MTFW 2005

Smolenskin, Peretz 1842-1885 .... **NCLC 30**

Smollett, Tobias (George) 1721-1771 ... **LC 2, 46**
See also BRW 3; CDBLB 1660-1789; DLB 39, 104; RGEL 2; TEA

Snodgrass, W.D. 1926- .... **CLC 2, 6, 10, 18, 68; PC 74**
See also AMWS 6; CA 1-4R; CANR 6, 36, 65, 85; CP 1, 2, 3, 4, 5, 6, 7; DAM POET; DLB 5; MAL 5; MTCW 1, 2; MTFW 2005; RGAL 4; TCLE 1:2

Snorri Sturluson 1179-1241 .... **CMLC 56**
See also RGWL 2, 3

Snow, C(harles) P(ercy) 1905-1980 ... **CLC 1, 4, 6, 9, 13, 19**
See also BRW 7; CA 5-8R; 101; CANR 28; CDBLB 1945-1960; CN 1, 2; DAM NOV; DLB 15, 77; DLBD 17; EWL 3; MTCW 1, 2; MTFW 2005; RGEL 2; TEA

Snow, Frances Compton
See Adams, Henry (Brooks)

Snyder, Gary 1930- . **CLC 1, 2, 5, 9, 32, 120; PC 21**
See also AMWS 8; ANW; BG 1:3; CA 17-20R; CANR 30, 60, 125; CP 1, 2, 3, 4, 5, 6, 7; DA3; DAM POET; DLB 5, 16, 165, 212, 237, 275; EWL 3; MAL 5; MTCW 2; MTFW 2005; PFS 9, 19; RGAL 4; WP

Snyder, Zilpha Keatley 1927- .... **CLC 17**
See also AAYA 15; BYA 1; CA 9-12R; CANR 38; CLR 31; JRDA; MAICYA 1, 2; SAAS 2; SATA 1, 28, 75, 110, 163; SATA-Essay 112, 163; YAW

Soares, Bernardo
See Pessoa, Fernando (Antonio Nogueira)

Sobh, A.
See Shamlu, Ahmad

Sobh, Alef
See Shamlu, Ahmad

Sobol, Joshua 1939- .... **CLC 60**
See Sobol, Yehoshua
See also CA 200; RGHL

Sobol, Yehoshua 1939-
See Sobol, Joshua
See also CWW 2

Socrates 470B.C.-399B.C. .... **CMLC 27**

Soderberg, Hjalmar 1869-1941 ...... **TCLC 39**
See also DLB 259; EWL 3; RGSF 2

Soderbergh, Steven 1963- .... **CLC 154**
See also AAYA 43; CA 243

Soderbergh, Steven Andrew
See Soderbergh, Steven

Sodergran, Edith (Irene) 1892-1923
See Soedergran, Edith (Irene)
See also CA 202; DLB 259; EW 11; EWL 3; RGWL 2, 3

Soedergran, Edith (Irene)
1892-1923 .... **TCLC 31**
See Sodergran, Edith (Irene)

Softly, Edgar
See Lovecraft, H. P.

Softly, Edward
See Lovecraft, H. P.

Sokolov, Alexander V(sevolodovich) 1943-
See Sokolov, Sasha
See also CA 73-76

Sokolov, Raymond 1941- .... **CLC 7**
See also CA 85-88

Sokolov, Sasha .... **CLC 59**
See Sokolov, Alexander V(sevolodovich)
See also CWW 2; DLB 285; EWL 3; RGWL 2, 3

Solo, Jay
See Ellison, Harlan

Sologub, Fyodor .... **TCLC 9**
See Teternikov, Fyodor Kuzmich
See also EWL 3

Solomons, Ikey Esquir
See Thackeray, William Makepeace

Solomos, Dionysios 1798-1857 .... **NCLC 15**

Solwoska, Mara
See French, Marilyn

Solzhenitsyn, Aleksandr I. 1918- .. **CLC 1, 2, 4, 7, 9, 10, 18, 26, 34, 78, 134; SSC 32; WLC 5**
See Solzhenitsyn, Aleksandr Isayevich
See also AAYA 49; AITN 1; BPFB 3; CA 69-72; CANR 40, 65, 116; DA; DA3; DAB; DAC; DAM MST, NOV; DLB 302; EW 13; EXPS; LAIT 4; MTCW 1, 2; MTFW 2005; NFS 6; RGSF 2; RGWL 2, 3; SSFS 9; TWA

Solzhenitsyn, Aleksandr Isayevich
See Solzhenitsyn, Aleksandr I.
See also CWW 2; EWL 3

Somers, Jane
See Lessing, Doris

Somerville, Edith Oenone
1858-1949 .... **SSC 56; TCLC 51**
See also CA 196; DLB 135; RGEL 2; RGSF 2

Somerville & Ross
See Martin, Violet Florence; Somerville, Edith Oenone

Sommer, Scott 1951- .... **CLC 25**
See also CA 106

Sommers, Christina Hoff 1950- ...... **CLC 197**
See also CA 153; CANR 95

Sondheim, Stephen (Joshua) 1930- . **CLC 30, 39, 147; DC 22**
See also AAYA 11, 66; CA 103; CANR 47, 67, 125; DAM DRAM; LAIT 4

Sone, Monica 1919- .... **AAL**
See also DLB 312

Song, Cathy 1955- .... **AAL; PC 21**
See also CA 154; CANR 118; CWP; DLB 169, 312; EXPP; FW; PFS 5

Sontag, Susan 1933-2004 ... **CLC 1, 2, 10, 13, 31, 105, 195**
See also AMWS 3; CA 17-20R; 234; CANR 25, 51, 74, 97; CN 1, 2, 3, 4, 5, 6, 7; CPW; DA3; DAM POP; DLB 2, 67; EWL 3; MAL 5; MBL; MTCW 1, 2; MTFW 2005; RGAL 4; RHW; SSFS 10

Sophocles 496(?)B.C.-406(?)B.C. .... **CMLC 2, 47, 51, 86; DC 1; WLCS**
See also AW 1; CDWLB 1; DA; DA3; DAB; DAC; DAM DRAM, MST; DFS 1, 4, 8; DLB 176; LAIT 1; LATS 1:1; LMFS 1; RGWL 2, 3; TWA; WLIT 8

Sordello 1189-1269 .... **CMLC 15**

Sorel, Georges 1847-1922 .... **TCLC 91**
See also CA 118; 188

Sorel, Julia
See Drexler, Rosalyn

Sorokin, Vladimir .... **CLC 59**
See Sorokin, Vladimir Georgievich

Sorokin, Vladimir Georgievich
See Sorokin, Vladimir
See also DLB 285

Sorrentino, Gilbert 1929-2006 .... **CLC 3, 7, 14, 22, 40**
See also CA 77-80; 250; CANR 14, 33, 115, 157; CN 3, 4, 5, 6, 7; CP 1, 2, 3, 4, 5, 6, 7; DLB 5, 173; DLBY 1980; INT CANR-14

Soseki
See Natsume, Soseki
See also MJW

Soto, Gary 1952- ... **CLC 32, 80; HLC 2; PC 28**
See also AAYA 10, 37; BYA 11; CA 119; 125; CANR 50, 74, 107, 157; CLR 38; CP 4, 5, 6, 7; DAM MULT; DLB 82; EWL 3; EXPP; HW 1, 2; INT CA-125; JRDA; LLW; MAICYA 1; MAICYAS 1; MAL 5; MTCW 2; MTFW 2005; PFS 7; RGAL 4; SATA 80, 120; WYA; YAW

Soupault, Philippe 1897-1990 .... **CLC 68**
See also CA 116; 147; 131; EWL 3; GFL 1789 to the Present; LMFS 2

Souster, (Holmes) Raymond 1921- .... **CLC 5, 14**
See also CA 13-16R; CAAS 14; CANR 13, 29, 53; CP 1, 2, 3, 4, 5, 6, 7; DA3; DAC; DAM POET; DLB 88; RGEL 2; SATA 63

Southern, Terry 1924(?)-1995 .... **CLC 7**
See also AMWS 11; BPFB 3; CA 1-4R; 150; CANR 1, 55, 107; CN 1, 2, 3, 4, 5, 6; DLB 2; IDFW 3, 4

Stegner, Wallace (Earle) 1909-1993 .. **CLC 9, 49, 81; SSC 27**
See also AITN 1; AMWS 4; ANW; BEST 90:3; BPFB 3; CA 1-4R; CAAS 9; CANR 1, 21, 46; CN 1, 2, 3, 4, 5; DAM NOV; DLB 9, 206, 275; DLBY 1993; EWL 3; MAL 5; MTCW 1, 2; MTFW 2005; RGAL 4; TCWW 1, 2; TUS

Stein, Gertrude 1874-1946 .... **DC 19; PC 18; SSC 42; TCLC 1, 6, 28, 48; WLC 5**
See also AAYA 64; AMW; AMWC 2; CA 104; 132; CANR 108; CDALB 1917-1929; DA; DA3; DAB; DAC; DAM MST, NOV, POET; DLB 4, 54, 86, 228; DLBD 15; EWL 3; EXPS; FL 1:6; GLL 1; MAL 5; MBL; MTCW 1, 2; MTFW 2005; NCFS 4; RGAL 4; RGSF 2; SSFS 5; TUS; WP

Steinbeck, John (Ernst) 1902-1968 ... **CLC 1, 5, 9, 13, 21, 34, 45, 75, 124; SSC 11, 37, 77; TCLC 135; WLC 5**
See also AAYA 12; AMW; BPFB 3; BYA 2, 3, 13; CA 1-4R; 25-28R; CANR 1, 35; CDALB 1929-1941; DA; DA3; DAB; DAC; DAM DRAM, MST, NOV; DLB 7, 9, 212, 275, 309; DLBD 2; EWL 3; EXPS; LAIT 3; MAL 5; MTCW 1, 2; MTFW 2005; NFS 1, 5, 7, 17, 19; RGAL 4; RGSF 2; RHW; SATA 9; SSFS 3, 6, 22; TCWW 1, 2; TUS; WYA; YAW

Steinem, Gloria 1934- .... **CLC 63**
See also CA 53-56; CANR 28, 51, 139; DLB 246; FL 1:1; FW; MTCW 1, 2; MTFW 2005

Steiner, George 1929- .... **CLC 24, 221**
See also CA 73-76; CANR 31, 67, 108; DAM NOV; DLB 67, 299; EWL 3; MTCW 1, 2; MTFW 2005; RGHL; SATA 62

Steiner, K. Leslie
See Delany, Samuel R., Jr.

Steiner, Rudolf 1861-1925 .... **TCLC 13**
See also CA 107

Stendhal 1783-1842 .. **NCLC 23, 46; SSC 27; WLC 5**
See also DA; DA3; DAB; DAC; DAM MST, NOV; DLB 119; EW 5; GFL 1789 to the Present; RGWL 2, 3; TWA

Stephen, Adeline Virginia
See Woolf, (Adeline) Virginia

Stephen, Sir Leslie 1832-1904 .... **TCLC 23**
See also BRW 5; CA 123; DLB 57, 144, 190

Stephen, Sir Leslie
See Stephen, Sir Leslie

Stephen, Virginia
See Woolf, (Adeline) Virginia

Stephens, James 1882(?)-1950 .... **SSC 50; TCLC 4**
See also CA 104; 192; DLB 19, 153, 162; EWL 3; FANT; RGEL 2; SUFW

Stephens, Reed
See Donaldson, Stephen R(eeder)

Steptoe, Lydia
See Barnes, Djuna
See also GLL 1

Sterchi, Beat 1949- .... **CLC 65**
See also CA 203

Sterling, Brett
See Bradbury, Ray; Hamilton, Edmond

Sterling, Bruce 1954- .... **CLC 72**
See also CA 119; CANR 44, 135; CN 7; MTFW 2005; SCFW 2; SFW 4

Sterling, George 1869-1926 .... **TCLC 20**
See also CA 117; 165; DLB 54

Stern, Gerald 1925- .... **CLC 40, 100**
See also AMWS 9; CA 81-84; CANR 28, 94; CP 3, 4, 5, 6, 7; DLB 105; RGAL 4

Stern, Richard (Gustave) 1928- ... **CLC 4, 39**
See also CA 1-4R; CANR 1, 25, 52, 120; CN 1, 2, 3, 4, 5, 6, 7; DLB 218; DLBY 1987; INT CANR-25

Sternberg, Josef von 1894-1969 .... **CLC 20**
See also CA 81-84

Sterne, Laurence 1713-1768 .... **LC 2, 48; WLC 5**
See also BRW 3; BRWC 1; CDBLB 1660-1789; DA; DAB; DAC; DAM MST, NOV; DLB 39; RGEL 2; TEA

Sternheim, (William Adolf) Carl 1878-1942 .... **TCLC 8**
See also CA 105; 193; DLB 56, 118; EWL 3; IDTP; RGWL 2, 3

Stevens, Margaret Dean
See Aldrich, Bess Streeter

Stevens, Mark 1951- .... **CLC 34**
See also CA 122

Stevens, Wallace 1879-1955 . **PC 6; TCLC 3, 12, 45; WLC 5**
See also AMW; AMWR 1; CA 104; 124; CDALB 1929-1941; DA; DA3; DAB; DAC; DAM MST, POET; DLB 54; EWL 3; EXPP; MAL 5; MTCW 1, 2; PAB; PFS 13, 16; RGAL 4; TUS; WP

Stevenson, Anne (Katharine) 1933- .. **CLC 7, 33**
See also BRWS 6; CA 17-20R; CAAS 9; CANR 9, 33, 123; CP 3, 4, 5, 6, 7; CWP; DLB 40; MTCW 1; RHW

Stevenson, Robert Louis (Balfour) 1850-1894 ...... **NCLC 5, 14, 63; SSC 11, 51; WLC 5**
See also AAYA 24; BPFB 3; BRW 5; BRWC 1; BRWR 1; BYA 1, 2, 4, 13; CD-BLB 1890-1914; CLR 10, 11, 107; DA; DA3; DAB; DAC; DAM MST, NOV; DLB 18, 57, 141, 156, 174; DLBD 13; GL 3; HGG; JRDA; LAIT 1, 3; MAICYA 1, 2; NFS 11, 20; RGEL 2; RGSF 2; SATA 100; SUFW; TEA; WCH; WLIT 4; WYA; YABC 2; YAW

Stewart, J(ohn) I(nnes) M(ackintosh) 1906-1994 .... **CLC 7, 14, 32**
See Innes, Michael
See also CA 85-88; 147; CAAS 3; CANR 47; CMW 4; CN 1, 2, 3, 4, 5; MTCW 1, 2

Stewart, Mary (Florence Elinor) 1916- .... **CLC 7, 35, 117**
See also AAYA 29; BPFB 3; CA 1-4R; CANR 1, 59, 130; CMW 4; CPW; DAB; FANT; RHW; SATA 12; YAW

Stewart, Mary Rainbow
See Stewart, Mary (Florence Elinor)

Stifle, June
See Campbell, Maria

Stifter, Adalbert 1805-1868 .. **NCLC 41; SSC 28**
See also CDWLB 2; DLB 133; RGSF 2; RGWL 2, 3

Still, James 1906-2001 .... **CLC 49**
See also CA 65-68; 195; CAAS 17; CANR 10, 26; CSW; DLB 9; DLBY 01; SATA 29; SATA-Obit 127

Sting 1951-
See Sumner, Gordon Matthew
See also CA 167

Stirling, Arthur
See Sinclair, Upton

Stitt, Milan 1941- .... **CLC 29**
See also CA 69-72

Stockton, Francis Richard 1834-1902
See Stockton, Frank R.
See also AAYA 68; CA 108; 137; MAICYA 1, 2; SATA 44; SFW 4

Stockton, Frank R. .... **TCLC 47**
See Stockton, Francis Richard
See also BYA 4, 13; DLB 42, 74; DLBD 13; EXPS; SATA-Brief 32; SSFS 3; SUFW; WCH

Stoddard, Charles
See Kuttner, Henry

Stoker, Abraham 1847-1912
See Stoker, Bram
See also CA 105; 150; DA; DA3; DAC; DAM MST, NOV; HGG; MTFW 2005; SATA 29

Stoker, Bram . **SSC 62; TCLC 8, 144; WLC 6**
See Stoker, Abraham
See also AAYA 23; BPFB 3; BRWS 3; BYA 5; CDBLB 1890-1914; DAB; DLB 304; GL 3; LATS 1:1; NFS 18; RGEL 2; SUFW; TEA; WLIT 4

Stolz, Mary (Slattery) 1920- .... **CLC 12**
See also AAYA 8; AITN 1; CA 5-8R; CANR 13, 41, 112; JRDA; MAICYA 1, 2; SAAS 3; SATA 10, 71, 133; YAW

Stone, Irving 1903-1989 .... **CLC 7**
See also AITN 1; BPFB 3; CA 1-4R; 129; CAAS 3; CANR 1, 23; CN 1, 2, 3, 4; CPW; DA3; DAM POP; INT CANR-23; MTCW 1, 2; MTFW 2005; RHW; SATA 3; SATA-Obit 64

Stone, Oliver 1946- .... **CLC 73**
See also AAYA 15, 64; CA 110; CANR 55, 125

Stone, Oliver William
See Stone, Oliver

Stone, Robert 1937- .... **CLC 5, 23, 42, 175**
See also AMWS 5; BPFB 3; CA 85-88; CANR 23, 66, 95; CN 4, 5, 6, 7; DLB 152; EWL 3; INT CANR-23; MAL 5; MTCW 1; MTFW 2005

Stone, Ruth 1915- .... **PC 53**
See also CA 45-48; CANR 2, 91; CP 5, 6, 7; CSW; DLB 105; PFS 19

Stone, Zachary
See Follett, Ken

Stoppard, Tom 1937- ... **CLC 1, 3, 4, 5, 8, 15, 29, 34, 63, 91; DC 6; WLC 6**
See also AAYA 63; BRWC 1; BRWR 2; BRWS 1; CA 81-84; CANR 39, 67, 125; CBD; CD 5, 6; CDBLB 1960 to Present; DA; DA3; DAB; DAC; DAM DRAM, MST; DFS 2, 5, 8, 11, 13, 16; DLB 13, 233; DLBY 1985; EWL 3; LATS 1:2; MTCW 1, 2; MTFW 2005; RGEL 2; TEA; WLIT 4

Storey, David (Malcolm) 1933- . **CLC 2, 4, 5, 8**
See also BRWS 1; CA 81-84; CANR 36; CBD; CD 5, 6; CN 1, 2, 3, 4, 5, 6; DAM DRAM; DLB 13, 14, 207, 245, 326; EWL 3; MTCW 1; RGEL 2

Storm, Hyemeyohsts 1935- ... **CLC 3; NNAL**
See also CA 81-84; CANR 45; DAM MULT

Storm, (Hans) Theodor (Woldsen) 1817-1888 .... **NCLC 1; SSC 27**
See also CDWLB 2; DLB 129; EW; RGSF 2; RGWL 2, 3

Storni, Alfonsina 1892-1938 . **HLC 2; PC 33; TCLC 5**
See also CA 104; 131; DAM MULT; DLB 283; HW 1; LAW

Stoughton, William 1631-1701 .... **LC 38**
See also DLB 24

Stout, Rex (Todhunter) 1886-1975 ..... **CLC 3**
See also AITN 2; BPFB 3; CA 61-64; CANR 71; CMW 4; CN 2; DLB 306; MSW; RGAL 4

Stow, (Julian) Randolph 1935- ... **CLC 23, 48**
See also CA 13-16R; CANR 33; CN 1, 2, 3, 4, 5, 6, 7; CP 1, 2, 3, 4; DLB 260; MTCW 1; RGEL 2

Swift, Graham 1949- .... **CLC 41, 88**
See also BRWC 2; BRWS 5; CA 117; 122; CANR 46, 71, 128; CN 4, 5, 6, 7; DLB 194, 326; MTCW 2; MTFW 2005; NFS 18; RGSF 2

Swift, Jonathan 1667-1745 ..... **LC 1, 42, 101; PC 9; WLC 6**
See also AAYA 41; BRW 3; BRWC 1; BRWR 1; BYA 5, 14; CDBLB 1660-1789; CLR 53; DA; DA3; DAB; DAC; DAM MST, NOV, POET; DLB 39, 95, 101; EXPN; LAIT 1; NFS 6; RGEL 2; SATA 19; TEA; WCH; WLIT 3

Swinburne, Algernon Charles 1837-1909 ... **PC 24; TCLC 8, 36; WLC 6**
See also BRW 5; CA 105; 140; CDBLB 1832-1890; DA; DA3; DAB; DAC; DAM MST, POET; DLB 35, 57; PAB; RGEL 2; TEA

Swinfen, Ann .... **CLC 34**
See also CA 202

Swinnerton, Frank (Arthur) 1884-1982 .... **CLC 31**
See also CA 202; 108; CN 1, 2, 3; DLB 34

Swinnerton, Frank Arthur 1884-1982 .... **CLC 31**
See also CA 108; DLB 34

Swithen, John
See King, Stephen

Sylvia
See Ashton-Warner, Sylvia (Constance)

Symmes, Robert Edward
See Duncan, Robert

Symonds, John Addington 1840-1893 .... **NCLC 34**
See also DLB 57, 144

Symons, Arthur 1865-1945 .... **TCLC 11**
See also CA 107; 189; DLB 19, 57, 149; RGEL 2

Symons, Julian (Gustave) 1912-1994 .... **CLC 2, 14, 32**
See also CA 49-52; 147; CAAS 3; CANR 3, 33, 59; CMW 4; CN 1, 2, 3, 4, 5; CP 1, 3, 4; DLB 87, 155; DLBY 1992; MSW; MTCW 1

Synge, (Edmund) J(ohn) M(illington) 1871-1909 .... **DC 2; TCLC 6, 37**
See also BRW 6; BRWR 1; CA 104; 141; CDBLB 1890-1914; DAM DRAM; DFS 18; DLB 10, 19; EWL 3; RGEL 2; TEA; WLIT 4

Syruc, J.
See Milosz, Czeslaw

Szirtes, George 1948- .... **CLC 46; PC 51**
See also CA 109; CANR 27, 61, 117; CP 4, 5, 6, 7

Szymborska, Wislawa 1923- ... **CLC 99, 190; PC 44**
See also CA 154; CANR 91, 133; CDWLB 4; CWP; CWW 2; DA3; DLB 232; DLBY 1996; EWL 3; MTCW 2; MTFW 2005; PFS 15; RGHL; RGWL 3

T. O., Nik
See Annensky, Innokenty (Fyodorovich)

Tabori, George 1914- .... **CLC 19**
See also CA 49-52; CANR 4, 69; CBD; CD 5, 6; DLB 245; RGHL

Tacitus c. 55-c. 117 .... **CMLC 56**
See also AW 2; CDWLB 1; DLB 211; RGWL 2, 3; WLIT 8

Tagore, Rabindranath 1861-1941 .... **PC 8; SSC 48; TCLC 3, 53**
See also CA 104; 120; DA3; DAM DRAM, POET; DLB 323; EWL 3; MTCW 1, 2; MTFW 2005; PFS 18; RGEL 2; RGSF 2; RGWL 2, 3; TWA

Taine, Hippolyte Adolphe 1828-1893 .... **NCLC 15**
See also EW 7; GFL 1789 to the Present

Talayesva, Don C. 1890-(?) .... **NNAL**

Talese, Gay 1932- .... **CLC 37**
See also AITN 1; CA 1-4R; CANR 9, 58, 137; DLB 185; INT CANR-9; MTCW 1, 2; MTFW 2005

Tallent, Elizabeth 1954- .... **CLC 45**
See also CA 117; CANR 72; DLB 130

Tallmountain, Mary 1918-1997 .... **NNAL**
See also CA 146; 161; DLB 193

Tally, Ted 1952- .... **CLC 42**
See also CA 120; 124; CAD; CANR 125; CD 5, 6; INT CA-124

Talvik, Heiti 1904-1947 .... **TCLC 87**
See also EWL 3

Tamayo y Baus, Manuel 1829-1898 .... **NCLC 1**

Tammsaare, A(nton) H(ansen) 1878-1940 .... **TCLC 27**
See also CA 164; CDWLB 4; DLB 220; EWL 3

Tam'si, Tchicaya U
See Tchicaya, Gerald Felix

Tan, Amy 1952- ...... **AAL; CLC 59, 120, 151**
See also AAYA 9, 48; AMWS 10; BEST 89:3; BPFB 3; CA 136; CANR 54, 105, 132; CDALBS; CN 6, 7; CPW 1; DA3; DAM MULT, NOV, POP; DLB 173, 312; EXPN; FL 1:6; FW; LAIT 3, 5; MAL 5; MTCW 2; MTFW 2005; NFS 1, 13, 16; RGAL 4; SATA 75; SSFS 9; YAW

Tandem, Carl Felix
See Spitteler, Carl

Tandem, Felix
See Spitteler, Carl

Tanizaki, Jun'ichiro 1886-1965 ... **CLC 8, 14, 28; SSC 21**
See Tanizaki Jun'ichiro
See also CA 93-96; 25-28R; MJW; MTCW 2; MTFW 2005; RGSF 2; RGWL 2

Tanizaki Jun'ichiro
See Tanizaki, Jun'ichiro
See also DLB 180; EWL 3

Tannen, Deborah 1945- .... **CLC 206**
See also CA 118; CANR 95

Tannen, Deborah Frances
See Tannen, Deborah

Tanner, William
See Amis, Kingsley

Tante, Dilly
See Kunitz, Stanley

Tao Lao
See Storni, Alfonsina

Tapahonso, Luci 1953- .... **NNAL; PC 65**
See also CA 145; CANR 72, 127; DLB 175

Tarantino, Quentin (Jerome) 1963- .... **CLC 125, 230**
See also AAYA 58; CA 171; CANR 125

Tarassoff, Lev
See Troyat, Henri

Tarbell, Ida M(inerva) 1857-1944 . **TCLC 40**
See also CA 122; 181; DLB 47

Tarkington, (Newton) Booth 1869-1946 .... **TCLC 9**
See also BPFB 3; BYA 3; CA 110; 143; CWRI 5; DLB 9, 102; MAL 5; MTCW 2; RGAL 4; SATA 17

Tarkovskii, Andrei Arsen'evich
See Tarkovsky, Andrei (Arsenyevich)

Tarkovsky, Andrei (Arsenyevich) 1932-1986 .... **CLC 75**
See also CA 127

Tartt, Donna 1964(?)- .... **CLC 76**
See also AAYA 56; CA 142; CANR 135; MTFW 2005

Tasso, Torquato 1544-1595 .... **LC 5, 94**
See also EFS 2; EW 2; RGWL 2, 3; WLIT 7

Tate, (John Orley) Allen 1899-1979 .. **CLC 2, 4, 6, 9, 11, 14, 24; PC 50**
See also AMW; CA 5-8R; 85-88; CANR 32, 108; CN 1, 2; CP 1; DLB 4, 45, 63; DLBD 17; EWL 3; MAL 5; MTCW 1, 2; MTFW 2005; RGAL 4; RHW

Tate, Ellalice
See Hibbert, Eleanor Alice Burford

Tate, James (Vincent) 1943- ..... **CLC 2, 6, 25**
See also CA 21-24R; CANR 29, 57, 114; CP 1, 2, 3, 4, 5, 6, 7; DLB 5, 169; EWL 3; PFS 10, 15; RGAL 4; WP

Tate, Nahum 1652(?)-1715 .... **LC 109**
See also DLB 80; RGEL 2

Tauler, Johannes c. 1300-1361 ...... **CMLC 37**
See also DLB 179; LMFS 1

Tavel, Ronald 1940- .... **CLC 6**
See also CA 21-24R; CAD; CANR 33; CD 5, 6

Taviani, Paolo 1931- .... **CLC 70**
See also CA 153

Taylor, Bayard 1825-1878 .... **NCLC 89**
See also DLB 3, 189, 250, 254; RGAL 4

Taylor, C(ecil) P(hilip) 1929-1981 ...... **CLC 27**
See also CA 25-28R; 105; CANR 47; CBD

Taylor, Edward 1642(?)-1729 . **LC 11; PC 63**
See also AMW; DA; DAB; DAC; DAM MST, POET; DLB 24; EXPP; RGAL 4; TUS

Taylor, Eleanor Ross 1920- .... **CLC 5**
See also CA 81-84; CANR 70

Taylor, Elizabeth 1912-1975 ..... **CLC 2, 4, 29**
See also CA 13-16R; CANR 9, 70; CN 1, 2; DLB 139; MTCW 1; RGEL 2; SATA 13

Taylor, Frederick Winslow 1856-1915 .... **TCLC 76**
See also CA 188

Taylor, Henry (Splawn) 1942- .... **CLC 44**
See also CA 33-36R; CAAS 7; CANR 31; CP 6, 7; DLB 5; PFS 10

Taylor, Kamala 1924-2004
See Markandaya, Kamala
See also CA 77-80; 227; MTFW 2005; NFS 13

Taylor, Mildred D. 1943- .... **CLC 21**
See also AAYA 10, 47; BW 1; BYA 3, 8; CA 85-88; CANR 25, 115, 136; CLR 9, 59, 90; CSW; DLB 52; JRDA; LAIT 3; MAICYA 1, 2; MTFW 2005; SAAS 5; SATA 135; WYA; YAW

Taylor, Peter (Hillsman) 1917-1994 .. **CLC 1, 4, 18, 37, 44, 50, 71; SSC 10, 84**
See also AMWS 5; BPFB 3; CA 13-16R; 147; CANR 9, 50; CN 1, 2, 3, 4, 5; CSW; DLB 218, 278; DLBY 1981, 1994; EWL 3; EXPS; INT CANR-9; MAL 5; MTCW 1, 2; MTFW 2005; RGSF 2; SSFS 9; TUS

Taylor, Robert Lewis 1912-1998 .... **CLC 14**
See also CA 1-4R; 170; CANR 3, 64; CN 1, 2; SATA 10; TCWW 1, 2

Tchekhov, Anton
See Chekhov, Anton (Pavlovich)

Tchicaya, Gerald Felix 1931-1988 .. **CLC 101**
See Tchicaya U Tam'si
See also CA 129; 125; CANR 81

Tchicaya U Tam'si
See Tchicaya, Gerald Felix
See also EWL 3

Teasdale, Sara 1884-1933 .... **PC 31; TCLC 4**
See also CA 104; 163; DLB 45; GLL 1; PFS 14; RGAL 4; SATA 32; TUS

Tecumseh 1768-1813 .... **NNAL**
See also DAM MULT

Tegner, Esaias 1782-1846 .... **NCLC 2**

Teilhard de Chardin, (Marie Joseph) Pierre 1881-1955 .... **TCLC 9**
See also CA 105; 210; GFL 1789 to the Present

Temple, Ann
See Mortimer, Penelope (Ruth)
Tennant, Emma (Christina) 1937- .. **CLC 13, 52**
See also BRWS 9; CA 65-68; CAAS 9; CANR 10, 38, 59, 88; CN 3, 4, 5, 6, 7; DLB 14; EWL 3; SFW 4
Tenneshaw, S. M.
See Silverberg, Robert
Tenney, Tabitha Gilman
1762-1837 .... **NCLC 122**
See also DLB 37, 200
Tennyson, Alfred 1809-1892 ... **NCLC 30, 65, 115; PC 6; WLC 6**
See also AAYA 50; BRW 4; CDBLB 1832-1890; DA; DA3; DAB; DAC; DAM MST, POET; DLB 32; EXPP; PAB; PFS 1, 2, 4, 11, 15, 19; RGEL 2; TEA; WLIT 4; WP
Teran, Lisa St. Aubin de .... **CLC 36**
See St. Aubin de Teran, Lisa
Terence c. 184B.C.-c. 159B.C. ...... **CMLC 14; DC 7**
See also AW 1; CDWLB 1; DLB 211; RGWL 2, 3; TWA; WLIT 8
Teresa de Jesus, St. 1515-1582 .... **LC 18**
Teresa of Avila, St.
See Teresa de Jesus, St.
Terkel, Louis .... **CLC 38**
See Terkel, Studs
See also AAYA 32; AITN 1; MTCW 2; TUS
Terkel, Studs 1912-
See Terkel, Louis
See also CA 57-60; CANR 18, 45, 67, 132; DA3; MTCW 1, 2; MTFW 2005
Terry, C. V.
See Slaughter, Frank G(ill)
Terry, Megan 1932- .... **CLC 19; DC 13**
See also CA 77-80; CABS 3; CAD; CANR 43; CD 5, 6; CWD; DFS 18; DLB 7, 249; GLL 2
Tertullian c. 155-c. 245 .... **CMLC 29**
Tertz, Abram
See Sinyavsky, Andrei (Donatevich)
See also RGSF 2
Tesich, Steve 1943(?)-1996 .... **CLC 40, 69**
See also CA 105; 152; CAD; DLBY 1983
Tesla, Nikola 1856-1943 .... **TCLC 88**
Teternikov, Fyodor Kuzmich 1863-1927
See Sologub, Fyodor
See also CA 104
Tevis, Walter 1928-1984 .... **CLC 42**
See also CA 113; SFW 4
Tey, Josephine .... **TCLC 14**
See Mackintosh, Elizabeth
See also DLB 77; MSW
Thackeray, William Makepeace
1811-1863 ...... **NCLC 5, 14, 22, 43, 169; WLC 6**
See also BRW 5; BRWC 2; CDBLB 1832-1890; DA; DA3; DAB; DAC; DAM MST, NOV; DLB 21, 55, 159, 163; NFS 13; RGEL 2; SATA 23; TEA; WLIT 3
Thakura, Ravindranatha
See Tagore, Rabindranath
Thames, C. H.
See Marlowe, Stephen
Tharoor, Shashi 1956- .... **CLC 70**
See also CA 141; CANR 91; CN 6, 7
Thelwall, John 1764-1834 .... **NCLC 162**
See also DLB 93, 158
Thelwell, Michael Miles 1939- .... **CLC 22**
See also BW 2; CA 101
Theobald, Lewis, Jr.
See Lovecraft, H. P.
Theocritus c. 310B.C.- .... **CMLC 45**
See also AW 1; DLB 176; RGWL 2, 3
Theodorescu, Ion N. 1880-1967
See Arghezi, Tudor
See also CA 116

Theriault, Yves 1915-1983 .... **CLC 79**
See also CA 102; CANR 150; CCA 1; DAC; DAM MST; DLB 88; EWL 3
Theroux, Alexander (Louis) 1939- .... **CLC 2, 25**
See also CA 85-88; CANR 20, 63; CN 4, 5, 6, 7
Theroux, Paul 1941- .... **CLC 5, 8, 11, 15, 28, 46, 159**
See also AAYA 28; AMWS 8; BEST 89:4; BPFB 3; CA 33-36R; CANR 20, 45, 74, 133; CDALBS; CN 1, 2, 3, 4, 5, 6, 7; CP 1; CPW 1; DA3; DAM POP; DLB 2, 218; EWL 3; HGG; MAL 5; MTCW 1, 2; MTFW 2005; RGAL 4; SATA 44, 109; TUS
Thesen, Sharon 1946- .... **CLC 56**
See also CA 163; CANR 125; CP 5, 6, 7; CWP
Thespis fl. 6th cent. B.C.- .... **CMLC 51**
See also LMFS 1
Thevenin, Denis
See Duhamel, Georges
Thibault, Jacques Anatole Francois
1844-1924
See France, Anatole
See also CA 106; 127; DA3; DAM NOV; MTCW 1, 2; TWA
Thiele, Colin 1920-2006 .... **CLC 17**
See also CA 29-32R; CANR 12, 28, 53, 105; CLR 27; CP 1, 2; DLB 289; MAICYA 1, 2; SAAS 2; SATA 14, 72, 125; YAW
Thistlethwaite, Bel
See Wetherald, Agnes Ethelwyn
Thomas, Audrey (Callahan) 1935- .... **CLC 7, 13, 37, 107; SSC 20**
See also AITN 2; CA 21-24R, 237; CAAE 237; CAAS 19; CANR 36, 58; CN 2, 3, 4, 5, 6, 7; DLB 60; MTCW 1; RGSF 2
Thomas, Augustus 1857-1934 .... **TCLC 97**
See also MAL 5
Thomas, D.M. 1935- ..... **CLC 13, 22, 31, 132**
See also BPFB 3; BRWS 4; CA 61-64; CAAS 11; CANR 17, 45, 75; CDBLB 1960 to Present; CN 4, 5, 6, 7; CP 1, 2, 3, 4, 5, 6, 7; DA3; DLB 40, 207, 299; HGG; INT CANR-17; MTCW 1, 2; MTFW 2005; RGHL; SFW 4
Thomas, Dylan (Marlais) 1914-1953 .... **PC 2, 52; SSC 3, 44; TCLC 1, 8, 45, 105; WLC 6**
See also AAYA 45; BRWS 1; CA 104; 120; CANR 65; CDBLB 1945-1960; DA; DA3; DAB; DAC; DAM DRAM, MST, POET; DLB 13, 20, 139; EWL 3; EXPP; LAIT 3; MTCW 1, 2; MTFW 2005; PAB; PFS 1, 3, 8; RGEL 2; RGSF 2; SATA 60; TEA; WLIT 4; WP
Thomas, (Philip) Edward 1878-1917 . **PC 53; TCLC 10**
See also BRW 6; BRWS 3; CA 106; 153; DAM POET; DLB 19, 98, 156, 216; EWL 3; PAB; RGEL 2
Thomas, Joyce Carol 1938- .... **CLC 35**
See also AAYA 12, 54; BW 2, 3; CA 113; 116; CANR 48, 114, 135; CLR 19; DLB 33; INT CA-116; JRDA; MAICYA 1, 2; MTCW 1, 2; MTFW 2005; SAAS 7; SATA 40, 78, 123, 137; SATA-Essay 137; WYA; YAW
Thomas, Lewis 1913-1993 .... **CLC 35**
See also ANW; CA 85-88; 143; CANR 38, 60; DLB 275; MTCW 1, 2
Thomas, M. Carey 1857-1935 .... **TCLC 89**
See also FW
Thomas, Paul
See Mann, (Paul) Thomas
Thomas, Piri 1928- .... **CLC 17; HLCS 2**
See also CA 73-76; HW 1; LLW

Thomas, R(onald) S(tuart)
1913-2000 .... **CLC 6, 13, 48**
See also CA 89-92; 189; CAAS 4; CANR 30; CDBLB 1960 to Present; CP 1, 2, 3, 4, 5, 6, 7; DAB; DAM POET; DLB 27; EWL 3; MTCW 1; RGEL 2
Thomas, Ross (Elmore) 1926-1995 .. **CLC 39**
See also CA 33-36R; 150; CANR 22, 63; CMW 4
Thompson, Francis (Joseph)
1859-1907 .... **TCLC 4**
See also BRW 5; CA 104; 189; CDBLB 1890-1914; DLB 19; RGEL 2; TEA
Thompson, Francis Clegg
See Mencken, H(enry) L(ouis)
Thompson, Hunter S. 1937(?)-2005 .. **CLC 9, 17, 40, 104, 229**
See also AAYA 45; BEST 89:1; BPFB 3; CA 17-20R; 236; CANR 23, 46, 74, 77, 111, 133; CPW; CSW; DA3; DAM POP; DLB 185; MTCW 1, 2; MTFW 2005; TUS
Thompson, James Myers
See Thompson, Jim (Myers)
Thompson, Jim (Myers)
1906-1977(?) .... **CLC 69**
See also BPFB 3; CA 140; CMW 4; CPW; DLB 226; MSW
Thompson, Judith (Clare Francesca)
1954- .... **CLC 39**
See also CA 143; CD 5, 6; CWD; DFS 22
Thomson, James 1700-1748 .... **LC 16, 29, 40**
See also BRWS 3; DAM POET; DLB 95; RGEL 2
Thomson, James 1834-1882 .... **NCLC 18**
See also DAM POET; DLB 35; RGEL 2
Thoreau, Henry David 1817-1862 .. **NCLC 7, 21, 61, 138; PC 30; WLC 6**
See also AAYA 42; AMW; ANW; BYA 3; CDALB 1640-1865; DA; DA3; DAB; DAC; DAM MST; DLB 1, 183, 223, 270, 298; LAIT 2; LMFS 1; NCFS 3; RGAL 4; TUS
Thorndike, E. L.
See Thorndike, Edward L(ee)
Thorndike, Edward L(ee)
1874-1949 .... **TCLC 107**
See also CA 121
Thornton, Hall
See Silverberg, Robert
Thorpe, Adam 1956- .... **CLC 176**
See also CA 129; CANR 92; DLB 231
Thubron, Colin (Gerald Dryden)
1939- .... **CLC 163**
See also CA 25-28R; CANR 12, 29, 59, 95; CN 5, 6, 7; DLB 204, 231
Thucydides c. 455B.C.-c. 395B.C. . **CMLC 17**
See also AW 1; DLB 176; RGWL 2, 3; WLIT 8
Thumboo, Edwin Nadason 1933- .... **PC 30**
See also CA 194; CP 1
Thurber, James (Grover)
1894-1961 .. **CLC 5, 11, 25, 125; SSC 1, 47**
See also AAYA 56; AMWS 1; BPFB 3; BYA 5; CA 73-76; CANR 17, 39; CDALB 1929-1941; CWRI 5; DA; DA3; DAB; DAC; DAM DRAM, MST, NOV; DLB 4, 11, 22, 102; EWL 3; EXPS; FANT; LAIT 3; MAICYA 1, 2; MAL 5; MTCW 1, 2; MTFW 2005; RGAL 4; RGSF 2; SATA 13; SSFS 1, 10, 19; SUFW; TUS
Thurman, Wallace (Henry)
1902-1934 ..... **BLC 3; HR 1:3; TCLC 6**
See also BW 1, 3; CA 104; 124; CANR 81; DAM MULT; DLB 51
Tibullus c. 54B.C.-c. 18B.C. .... **CMLC 36**
See also AW 2; DLB 211; RGWL 2, 3; WLIT 8

Ticheburn, Cheviot
See Ainsworth, William Harrison
Tieck, (Johann) Ludwig
1773-1853 .... **NCLC 5, 46; SSC 31**
See also CDWLB 2; DLB 90; EW 5; IDTP;
RGSF 2; RGWL 2, 3; SUFW
Tiger, Derry
See Ellison, Harlan
Tilghman, Christopher 1946- .... **CLC 65**
See also CA 159; CANR 135, 151; CSW;
DLB 244
Tillich, Paul (Johannes)
1886-1965 .... **CLC 131**
See also CA 5-8R; 25-28R; CANR 33;
MTCW 1, 2
Tillinghast, Richard (Williford)
1940- .... **CLC 29**
See also CA 29-32R; CAAS 23; CANR 26,
51, 96; CP 2, 3, 4, 5, 6, 7; CSW
Timrod, Henry 1828-1867 .... **NCLC 25**
See also DLB 3, 248; RGAL 4
Tindall, Gillian (Elizabeth) 1938- ...... **CLC 7**
See also CA 21-24R; CANR 11, 65, 107;
CN 1, 2, 3, 4, 5, 6, 7
Tiptree, James, Jr. .... **CLC 48, 50**
See Sheldon, Alice Hastings Bradley
See also DLB 8; SCFW 1, 2; SFW 4
Tirone Smith, Mary-Ann 1944- .... **CLC 39**
See also CA 118; 136; CANR 113; SATA
143
Tirso de Molina 1580(?)-1648 .... **DC 13;**
HLCS 2; LC 73
See also RGWL 2, 3
Titmarsh, Michael Angelo
See Thackeray, William Makepeace
Tocqueville, Alexis (Charles Henri Maurice
Clerel Comte) de 1805-1859 .. **NCLC 7,**
63
See also EW 6; GFL 1789 to the Present;
TWA
Toer, Pramoedya Ananta
1925-2006 .... **CLC 186**
See also CA 197; 251; RGWL 3
Toffler, Alvin 1928- .... **CLC 168**
See also CA 13-16R; CANR 15, 46, 67;
CPW; DAM POP; MTCW 1, 2
Toibin, Colm 1955- .... **CLC 162**
See also CA 142; CANR 81, 149; CN 7;
DLB 271
Tolkien, J(ohn) R(onald) R(euel)
1892-1973 .... **CLC 1, 2, 3, 8, 12, 38;**
TCLC 137; WLC 6
See also AAYA 10; AITN 1; BPFB 3;
BRWC 2; BRWS 2; CA 17-18; 45-48;
CANR 36, 134; CAP 2; CDBLB 1914-
1945; CLR 56; CN 1; CPW 1; CWRI 5;
DA; DA3; DAB; DAC; DAM MST, NOV,
POP; DLB 15, 160, 255; EFS 2; EWL 3;
FANT; JRDA; LAIT 1; LATS 1:2; LMFS
2; MAICYA 1, 2; MTCW 1, 2; MTFW
2005; NFS 8; RGEL 2; SATA 2, 32, 100;
SATA-Obit 24; SFW 4; SUFW; TEA;
WCH; WYA; YAW
Toller, Ernst 1893-1939 .... **TCLC 10**
See also CA 107; 186; DLB 124; EWL 3;
RGWL 2, 3
Tolson, M. B.
See Tolson, Melvin B(eaunorus)
Tolson, Melvin B(eaunorus)
1898(?)-1966 .... **BLC 3; CLC 36, 105**
See also AFAW 1, 2; BW 1, 3; CA 124; 89-
92; CANR 80; DAM MULT, POET; DLB
48, 76; MAL 5; RGAL 4
Tolstoi, Aleksei Nikolaevich
See Tolstoy, Alexey Nikolaevich
Tolstoi, Lev
See Tolstoy, Leo (Nikolaevich)
See also RGSF 2; RGWL 2, 3

Tolstoy, Aleksei Nikolaevich
See Tolstoy, Alexey Nikolaevich
See also DLB 272
Tolstoy, Alexey Nikolaevich
1882-1945 .... **TCLC 18**
See Tolstoy, Aleksei Nikolaevich
See also CA 107; 158; EWL 3; SFW 4
Tolstoy, Leo (Nikolaevich)
1828-1910 . **SSC 9, 30, 45, 54; TCLC 4,**
11, 17, 28, 44, 79, 173; WLC 6
See Tolstoi, Lev
See also AAYA 56; CA 104; 123; DA; DA3;
DAB; DAC; DAM MST, NOV; DLB 238;
EFS 2; EW 7; EXPS; IDTP; LAIT 2;
LATS 1:1; LMFS 1; NFS 10; SATA 26;
SSFS 5; TWA
Tolstoy, Count Leo
See Tolstoy, Leo (Nikolaevich)
Tomalin, Claire 1933- .... **CLC 166**
See also CA 89-92; CANR 52, 88; DLB
155
Tomasi di Lampedusa, Giuseppe 1896-1957
See Lampedusa, Giuseppe (Tomasi) di
See also CA 111; DLB 177; EWL 3; WLIT
7
Tomlin, Lily 1939(?)-
See Tomlin, Mary Jean
See also CA 117
Tomlin, Mary Jean .... **CLC 17**
See Tomlin, Lily
Tomline, F. Latour
See Gilbert, W(illiam) S(chwenck)
Tomlinson, (Alfred) Charles 1927- .... **CLC 2,**
4, 6, 13, 45; PC 17
See also CA 5-8R; CANR 33; CP 1, 2, 3, 4,
5, 6, 7; DAM POET; DLB 40; TCLE 1:2
Tomlinson, H(enry) M(ajor)
1873-1958 .... **TCLC 71**
See also CA 118; 161; DLB 36, 100, 195
Tonna, Charlotte Elizabeth
1790-1846 .... **NCLC 135**
See also DLB 163
Tonson, Jacob fl. 1655(?)-1736 .... **LC 86**
See also DLB 170
Toole, John Kennedy 1937-1969 ..... **CLC 19,**
64
See also BPFB 3; CA 104; DLBY 1981;
MTCW 2; MTFW 2005
Toomer, Eugene
See Toomer, Jean
Toomer, Eugene Pinchback
See Toomer, Jean
Toomer, Jean 1894-1967 .. **BLC 3; CLC 1, 4,**
13, 22; HR 1:3; PC 7; SSC 1, 45;
TCLC 172; WLCS
See also AFAW 1, 2; AMWS 3, 9; BW 1;
CA 85-88; CDALB 1917-1929; DA3;
DAM MULT; DLB 45, 51; EWL 3; EXPP;
EXPS; LMFS 2; MAL 5; MTCW 1, 2;
MTFW 2005; NFS 11; RGAL 4; RGSF 2;
SSFS 5
Toomer, Nathan Jean
See Toomer, Jean
Toomer, Nathan Pinchback
See Toomer, Jean
Torley, Luke
See Blish, James (Benjamin)
Tornimparte, Alessandra
See Ginzburg, Natalia
Torre, Raoul della
See Mencken, H(enry) L(ouis)
Torrence, Ridgely 1874-1950 .... **TCLC 97**
See also DLB 54, 249; MAL 5
Torrey, E(dwin) Fuller 1937- .... **CLC 34**
See also CA 119; CANR 71
Torsvan, Ben Traven
See Traven, B.
Torsvan, Benno Traven
See Traven, B.

Torsvan, Berick Traven
See Traven, B.
Torsvan, Berwick Traven
See Traven, B.
Torsvan, Bruno Traven
See Traven, B.
Torsvan, Traven
See Traven, B.
Tourneur, Cyril 1575(?)-1626 .... **LC 66**
See also BRW 2; DAM DRAM; DLB 58;
RGEL 2
Tournier, Michel 1924- .... **CLC 6, 23, 36, 95;**
SSC 88
See also CA 49-52; CANR 3, 36, 74, 149;
CWW 2; DLB 83; EWL 3; GFL 1789 to
the Present; MTCW 1, 2; SATA 23
Tournier, Michel Edouard
See Tournier, Michel
Tournimparte, Alessandra
See Ginzburg, Natalia
Towers, Ivar
See Kornbluth, C(yril) M.
Towne, Robert (Burton) 1936(?)- ..... **CLC 87**
See also CA 108; DLB 44; IDFW 3, 4
Townsend, Sue .... **CLC 61**
See Townsend, Susan Lilian
See also AAYA 28; CA 119; 127; CANR
65, 107; CBD; CD 5, 6; CPW; CWD;
DAB; DAC; DAM MST; DLB 271; INT
CA-127; SATA 55, 93; SATA-Brief 48;
YAW
Townsend, Susan Lilian 1946-
See Townsend, Sue
Townshend, Pete
See Townshend, Peter (Dennis Blandford)
Townshend, Peter (Dennis Blandford)
1945- .... **CLC 17, 42**
See also CA 107
Tozzi, Federigo 1883-1920 .... **TCLC 31**
See also CA 160; CANR 110; DLB 264;
EWL 3; WLIT 7
Tracy, Don(ald Fiske) 1905-1970(?)
See Queen, Ellery
See also CA 1-4R; 176; CANR 2
Trafford, F. G.
See Riddell, Charlotte
Traherne, Thomas 1637(?)-1674 .. **LC 99; PC**
70
See also BRW 2; BRWS 11; DLB 131;
PAB; RGEL 2
Traill, Catharine Parr 1802-1899 .. **NCLC 31**
See also DLB 99
Trakl, Georg 1887-1914 .... **PC 20; TCLC 5**
See also CA 104; 165; EW 10; EWL 3;
LMFS 2; MTCW 2; RGWL 2, 3
Trambley, Estela Portillo .... **TCLC 163**
See Portillo Trambley, Estela
See also CA 77-80; RGAL 4
Tranquilli, Secondino
See Silone, Ignazio
Transtroemer, Tomas Gosta
See Transtromer, Tomas (Goesta)
Transtromer, Tomas (Gosta)
See Transtromer, Tomas (Goesta)
See also CWW 2
Transtromer, Tomas (Goesta)
1931- .... **CLC 52, 65**
See Transtromer, Tomas (Gosta)
See also CA 117; 129; CAAS 17; CANR
115; DAM POET; DLB 257; EWL 3; PFS
21
Transtromer, Tomas Gosta
See Transtromer, Tomas (Goesta)
Traven, B. 1882(?)-1969 .... **CLC 8, 11**
See also CA 19-20; 25-28R; CAP 2; DLB
9, 56; EWL 3; MTCW 1; RGAL 4
Trediakovsky, Vasilii Kirillovich
1703-1769 .... **LC 68**
See also DLB 150

von Horvath, Oedoen
See von Horvath, Odon
See also CA 184

von Kleist, Heinrich
See Kleist, Heinrich von

Vonnegut, Kurt, Jr.
See Vonnegut, Kurt

Vonnegut, Kurt 1922- ... **CLC 1, 2, 3, 4, 5, 8, 12, 22, 40, 60, 111, 212; SSC 8; WLC 6**
See also AAYA 6, 44; AITN 1; AMWS 2; BEST 90:4; BPFB 3; BYA 3, 14; CA 1-4R; CANR 1, 25, 49, 75, 92; CDALB 1968-1988; CN 1, 2, 3, 4, 5, 6, 7; CPW 1; DA; DA3; DAB; DAC; DAM MST, NOV, POP; DLB 2, 8, 152; DLBD 3; DLBY 1980; EWL 3; EXPN; EXPS; LAIT 4; LMFS 2; MAL 5; MTCW 1, 2; MTFW 2005; NFS 3; RGAL 4; SCFW; SFW 4; SSFS 5; TUS; YAW

Von Rachen, Kurt
See Hubbard, L. Ron

von Sternberg, Josef
See Sternberg, Josef von

Vorster, Gordon 1924- .... **CLC 34**
See also CA 133

Vosce, Trudie
See Ozick, Cynthia

Voznesensky, Andrei (Andreievich)
1933- .... **CLC 1, 15, 57**
See Voznesensky, Andrey
See also CA 89-92; CANR 37; CWW 2; DAM POET; MTCW 1

Voznesensky, Andrey
See Voznesensky, Andrei (Andreievich)
See also EWL 3

Wace, Robert c. 1100-c. 1175 .... **CMLC 55**
See also DLB 146

Waddington, Miriam 1917-2004 .... **CLC 28**
See also CA 21-24R; 225; CANR 12, 30; CCA 1; CP 1, 2, 3, 4, 5, 6, 7; DLB 68

Wagman, Fredrica 1937- .... **CLC 7**
See also CA 97-100; INT CA-97-100

Wagner, Linda W.
See Wagner-Martin, Linda (C.)

Wagner, Linda Welshimer
See Wagner-Martin, Linda (C.)

Wagner, Richard 1813-1883 ..... **NCLC 9, 119**
See also DLB 129; EW 6

Wagner-Martin, Linda (C.) 1936- .... **CLC 50**
See also CA 159; CANR 135

Wagoner, David (Russell) 1926- .... **CLC 3, 5, 15; PC 33**
See also AMWS 9; CA 1-4R; CAAS 3; CANR 2, 71; CN 1, 2, 3, 4, 5, 6, 7; CP 1, 2, 3, 4, 5, 6, 7; DLB 5, 256; SATA 14; TCWW 1, 2

Wah, Fred(erick James) 1939- .... **CLC 44**
See also CA 107; 141; CP 1, 6, 7; DLB 60

Wahloo, Per 1926-1975 .... **CLC 7**
See also BPFB 3; CA 61-64; CANR 73; CMW 4; MSW

Wahloo, Peter
See Wahloo, Per

Wain, John (Barrington) 1925-1994 . **CLC 2, 11, 15, 46**
See also CA 5-8R; 145; CAAS 4; CANR 23, 54; CDBLB 1960 to Present; CN 1, 2, 3, 4, 5; CP 1, 2, 3, 4, 5; DLB 15, 27, 139, 155; EWL 3; MTCW 1, 2; MTFW 2005

Wajda, Andrzej 1926- .... **CLC 16, 219**
See also CA 102

Wakefield, Dan 1932- .... **CLC 7**
See also CA 21-24R; 211; CAAE 211; CAAS 7; CN 4, 5, 6, 7

Wakefield, Herbert Russell
1888-1965 .... **TCLC 120**
See also CA 5-8R; CANR 77; HGG; SUFW

Wakoski, Diane 1937- ...... **CLC 2, 4, 7, 9, 11, 40; PC 15**
See also CA 13-16R, 216; CAAE 216; CAAS 1; CANR 9, 60, 106; CP 1, 2, 3, 4, 5, 6, 7; CWP; DAM POET; DLB 5; INT CANR-9; MAL 5; MTCW 2; MTFW 2005

Wakoski-Sherbell, Diane
See Wakoski, Diane

Walcott, Derek 1930- ... **BLC 3; CLC 2, 4, 9, 14, 25, 42, 67, 76, 160; DC 7; PC 46**
See also BW 2; CA 89-92; CANR 26, 47, 75, 80, 130; CBD; CD 5, 6; CDWLB 3; CP 1, 2, 3, 4, 5, 6, 7; DA3; DAB; DAC; DAM MST, MULT, POET; DLB 117; DLBY 1981; DNFS 1; EFS 1; EWL 3; LMFS 2; MTCW 1, 2; MTFW 2005; PFS 6; RGEL 2; TWA; WWE 1

Waldman, Anne (Lesley) 1945- .... **CLC 7**
See also BG 1:3; CA 37-40R; CAAS 17; CANR 34, 69, 116; CP 1, 2, 3, 4, 5, 6, 7; CWP; DLB 16

Waldo, E. Hunter
See Sturgeon, Theodore (Hamilton)

Waldo, Edward Hamilton
See Sturgeon, Theodore (Hamilton)

Walker, Alice 1944- ...... **BLC 3; CLC 5, 6, 9, 19, 27, 46, 58, 103, 167; PC 30; SSC 5; WLCS**
See also AAYA 3, 33; AFAW 1, 2; AMWS 3; BEST 89:4; BPFB 3; BW 2, 3; CA 37-40R; CANR 9, 27, 49, 66, 82, 131; CDALB 1968-1988; CN 4, 5, 6, 7; CPW; CSW; DA; DA3; DAB; DAC; DAM MST, MULT, NOV, POET, POP; DLB 6, 33, 143; EWL 3; EXPN; EXPS; FL 1:6; FW; INT CANR-27; LAIT 3; MAL 5; MBL; MTCW 1, 2; MTFW 2005; NFS 5; RGAL 4; RGSF 2; SATA 31; SSFS 2, 11; TUS; YAW

Walker, Alice Malsenior
See Walker, Alice

Walker, David Harry 1911-1992 ...... **CLC 14**
See also CA 1-4R; 137; CANR 1; CN 1, 2; CWRI 5; SATA 8; SATA-Obit 71

Walker, Edward Joseph 1934-2004
See Walker, Ted
See also CA 21-24R; 226; CANR 12, 28, 53

Walker, George F(rederick) 1947- .. **CLC 44, 61**
See also CA 103; CANR 21, 43, 59; CD 5, 6; DAB; DAC; DAM MST; DLB 60

Walker, Joseph A. 1935-2003 .... **CLC 19**
See also BW 1, 3; CA 89-92; CAD; CANR 26, 143; CD 5, 6; DAM DRAM, MST; DFS 12; DLB 38

Walker, Margaret 1915-1998 .. **BLC; CLC 1, 6; PC 20; TCLC 129**
See also AFAW 1, 2; BW 2, 3; CA 73-76; 172; CANR 26, 54, 76, 136; CN 1, 2, 3, 4, 5, 6; CP 1, 2, 3, 4, 5, 6; CSW; DAM MULT; DLB 76, 152; EXPP; FW; MAL 5; MTCW 1, 2; MTFW 2005; RGAL 4; RHW

Walker, Ted .... **CLC 13**
See Walker, Edward Joseph
See also CP 1, 2, 3, 4, 5, 6, 7; DLB 40

Wallace, David Foster 1962- ... **CLC 50, 114; SSC 68**
See also AAYA 50; AMWS 10; CA 132; CANR 59, 133; CN 7; DA3; MTCW 2; MTFW 2005

Wallace, Dexter
See Masters, Edgar Lee

Wallace, (Richard Horatio) Edgar
1875-1932 .... **TCLC 57**
See also CA 115; 218; CMW 4; DLB 70; MSW; RGEL 2

Wallace, Irving 1916-1990 .... **CLC 7, 13**
See also AITN 1; BPFB 3; CA 1-4R; 132; CAAS 1; CANR 1, 27; CPW; DAM NOV, POP; INT CANR-27; MTCW 1, 2

Wallant, Edward Lewis 1926-1962 ... **CLC 5, 10**
See also CA 1-4R; CANR 22; DLB 2, 28, 143, 299; EWL 3; MAL 5; MTCW 1, 2; RGAL 4; RGHL

Wallas, Graham 1858-1932 .... **TCLC 91**

Waller, Edmund 1606-1687 .... **LC 86; PC 72**
See also BRW 2; DAM POET; DLB 126; PAB; RGEL 2

Walley, Byron
See Card, Orson Scott

Walpole, Horace 1717-1797 .... **LC 2, 49**
See also BRW 3; DLB 39, 104, 213; GL 3; HGG; LMFS 1; RGEL 2; SUFW 1; TEA

Walpole, Hugh (Seymour)
1884-1941 .... **TCLC 5**
See also CA 104; 165; DLB 34; HGG; MTCW 2; RGEL 2; RHW

Walrond, Eric (Derwent) 1898-1966 . **HR 1:3**
See also BW 1; CA 125; DLB 51

Walser, Martin 1927- .... **CLC 27, 183**
See also CA 57-60; CANR 8, 46, 145; CWW 2; DLB 75, 124; EWL 3

Walser, Robert 1878-1956 ..... **SSC 20; TCLC 18**
See also CA 118; 165; CANR 100; DLB 66; EWL 3

Walsh, Gillian Paton
See Paton Walsh, Gillian

Walsh, Jill Paton .... **CLC 35**
See Paton Walsh, Gillian
See also CLR 2, 65; WYA

Walter, William Christian
See Andersen, Hans Christian

Walters, Anna L(ee) 1946- .... **NNAL**
See also CA 73-76

Walther von der Vogelweide c.
1170-1228 .... **CMLC 56**

Walton, Izaak 1593-1683 .... **LC 72**
See also BRW 2; CDBLB Before 1660; DLB 151, 213; RGEL 2

Wambaugh, Joseph (Aloysius), Jr.
1937- .... **CLC 3, 18**
See also AITN 1; BEST 89:3; BPFB 3; CA 33-36R; CANR 42, 65, 115; CMW 4; CPW 1; DA3; DAM NOV, POP; DLB 6; DLBY 1983; MSW; MTCW 1, 2

Wang Wei 699(?)-761(?) .... **PC 18**
See also TWA

Warburton, William 1698-1779 .... **LC 97**
See also DLB 104

Ward, Arthur Henry Sarsfield 1883-1959
See Rohmer, Sax
See also CA 108; 173; CMW 4; HGG

Ward, Douglas Turner 1930- .... **CLC 19**
See also BW 1; CA 81-84; CAD; CANR 27; CD 5, 6; DLB 7, 38

Ward, E. D.
See Lucas, E(dward) V(errall)

Ward, Mrs. Humphry 1851-1920
See Ward, Mary Augusta
See also RGEL 2

Ward, Mary Augusta 1851-1920 ... **TCLC 55**
See Ward, Mrs. Humphry
See also DLB 18

Ward, Nathaniel 1578(?)-1652 .... **LC 114**
See also DLB 24

Ward, Peter
See Faust, Frederick (Schiller)

Warhol, Andy 1928(?)-1987 .... **CLC 20**
See also AAYA 12; BEST 89:4; CA 89-92; 121; CANR 34

Warner, Francis (Robert le Plastrier)
1937- .... **CLC 14**
See also CA 53-56; CANR 11; CP 1, 2, 3, 4

Warner, Marina 1946- .... **CLC 59**
See also CA 65-68; CANR 21, 55, 118; CN
5, 6, 7; DLB 194; MTFW 2005

Warner, Rex (Ernest) 1905-1986 ...... **CLC 45**
See also CA 89-92; 119; CN 1, 2, 3, 4; CP
1, 2, 3, 4; DLB 15; RGEL 2; RHW

Warner, Susan (Bogert)
1819-1885 .... **NCLC 31, 146**
See also DLB 3, 42, 239, 250, 254

Warner, Sylvia (Constance) Ashton
See Ashton-Warner, Sylvia (Constance)

Warner, Sylvia Townsend
1893-1978 .. **CLC 7, 19; SSC 23; TCLC
131**
See also BRWS 7; CA 61-64; 77-80; CANR
16, 60, 104; CN 1, 2; DLB 34, 139; EWL
3; FANT; FW; MTCW 1, 2; RGEL 2;
RGSF 2; RHW

Warren, Mercy Otis 1728-1814 ..... **NCLC 13**
See also DLB 31, 200; RGAL 4; TUS

Warren, Robert Penn 1905-1989 .. **CLC 1, 4,
6, 8, 10, 13, 18, 39, 53, 59; PC 37; SSC
4, 58; WLC 6**
See also AITN 1; AMW; AMWC 2; BPFB
3; BYA 1; CA 13-16R; 129; CANR 10,
47; CDALB 1968-1988; CN 1, 2, 3, 4;
CP 1, 2, 3, 4; DA; DA3; DAB; DAC;
DAM MST, NOV, POET; DLB 2, 48, 152,
320; DLBY 1980, 1989; EWL 3; INT
CANR-10; MAL 5; MTCW 1, 2; MTFW
2005; NFS 13; RGAL 4; RGSF 2; RHW;
SATA 46; SATA-Obit 63; SSFS 8; TUS

Warrigal, Jack
See Furphy, Joseph

Warshofsky, Isaac
See Singer, Isaac Bashevis

Warton, Joseph 1722-1800 ... **LC 128; NCLC
118**
See also DLB 104, 109; RGEL 2

Warton, Thomas 1728-1790 .... **LC 15, 82**
See also DAM POET; DLB 104, 109;
RGEL 2

Waruk, Kona
See Harris, (Theodore) Wilson

Warung, Price .... **TCLC 45**
See Astley, William
See also DLB 230; RGEL 2

Warwick, Jarvis
See Garner, Hugh
See also CCA 1

Washington, Alex
See Harris, Mark

Washington, Booker T(aliaferro)
1856-1915 .... **BLC 3; TCLC 10**
See also BW 1; CA 114; 125; DA3; DAM
MULT; LAIT 2; RGAL 4; SATA 28

Washington, George 1732-1799 .... **LC 25**
See also DLB 31

Wassermann, (Karl) Jakob
1873-1934 .... **TCLC 6**
See also CA 104; 163; DLB 66; EWL 3

Wasserstein, Wendy 1950-2006 . **CLC 32, 59,
90, 183; DC 4**
See also AMWS 15; CA 121; 129; 247;
CABS 3; CAD; CANR 53, 75, 128; CD
5, 6; CWD; DA3; DAM DRAM; DFS 3,
17; DLB 228; EWL 3; FW; INT CA-129;
MAL 5; MTCW 2; MTFW 2005; SATA
94; SATA-Obit 174

Waterhouse, Keith (Spencer) 1929- . **CLC 47**
See also CA 5-8R; CANR 38, 67, 109;
CBD; CD 6; CN 1, 2, 3, 4, 5, 6, 7; DLB
13, 15; MTCW 1, 2; MTFW 2005

Waters, Frank (Joseph) 1902-1995 .. **CLC 88**
See also CA 5-8R; 149; CAAS 13; CANR
3, 18, 63, 121; DLB 212; DLBY 1986;
RGAL 4; TCWW 1, 2

Waters, Mary C. .... **CLC 70**

Waters, Roger 1944- .... **CLC 35**

Watkins, Frances Ellen
See Harper, Frances Ellen Watkins

Watkins, Gerrold
See Malzberg, Barry N(athaniel)

Watkins, Gloria Jean
See hooks, bell

Watkins, Paul 1964- .... **CLC 55**
See also CA 132; CANR 62, 98

Watkins, Vernon Phillips
1906-1967 .... **CLC 43**
See also CA 9-10; 25-28R; CAP 1; DLB
20; EWL 3; RGEL 2

Watson, Irving S.
See Mencken, H(enry) L(ouis)

Watson, John H.
See Farmer, Philip Jose

Watson, Richard F.
See Silverberg, Robert

Watts, Ephraim
See Horne, Richard Henry Hengist

Watts, Isaac 1674-1748 .... **LC 98**
See also DLB 95; RGEL 2; SATA 52

Waugh, Auberon (Alexander)
1939-2001 .... **CLC 7**
See also CA 45-48; 192; CANR 6, 22, 92;
CN 1, 2, 3; DLB 14, 194

Waugh, Evelyn (Arthur St. John)
1903-1966 .. **CLC 1, 3, 8, 13, 19, 27, 44,
107; SSC 41; WLC 6**
See also BPFB 3; BRW 7; CA 85-88; 25-
28R; CANR 22; CDBLB 1914-1945; DA;
DA3; DAB; DAC; DAM MST, NOV,
POP; DLB 15, 162, 195; EWL 3; MTCW
1, 2; MTFW 2005; NFS 13, 17; RGEL 2;
RGSF 2; TEA; WLIT 4

Waugh, Harriet 1944- .... **CLC 6**
See also CA 85-88; CANR 22

Ways, C. R.
See Blount, Roy (Alton), Jr.

Waystaff, Simon
See Swift, Jonathan

Webb, Beatrice (Martha Potter)
1858-1943 .... **TCLC 22**
See also CA 117; 162; DLB 190; FW

Webb, Charles (Richard) 1939- .... **CLC 7**
See also CA 25-28R; CANR 114

Webb, Frank J. .... **NCLC 143**
See also DLB 50

Webb, James, Jr.
See Webb, James

Webb, James 1946- .... **CLC 22**
See also CA 81-84; CANR 156

Webb, James H.
See Webb, James

Webb, James Henry
See Webb, James

Webb, Mary Gladys (Meredith)
1881-1927 .... **TCLC 24**
See also CA 182; 123; DLB 34; FW; RGEL
2

Webb, Mrs. Sidney
See Webb, Beatrice (Martha Potter)

Webb, Phyllis 1927- .... **CLC 18**
See also CA 104; CANR 23; CCA 1; CP 1,
2, 3, 4, 5, 6, 7; CWP; DLB 53

Webb, Sidney (James) 1859-1947 .. **TCLC 22**
See also CA 117; 163; DLB 190

Webber, Andrew Lloyd .... **CLC 21**
See Lloyd Webber, Andrew
See also DFS 7

Weber, Lenora Mattingly
1895-1971 .... **CLC 12**
See also CA 19-20; 29-32R; CAP 1; SATA
2; SATA-Obit 26

Weber, Max 1864-1920 .... **TCLC 69**
See also CA 109; 189; DLB 296

Webster, John 1580(?)-1634(?) ...... **DC 2; LC
33, 84, 124; WLC 6**
See also BRW 2; CDBLB Before 1660; DA;
DAB; DAC; DAM DRAM, MST; DFS
17, 19; DLB 58; IDTP; RGEL 2; WLIT 3

Webster, Noah 1758-1843 .... **NCLC 30**
See also DLB 1, 37, 42, 43, 73, 243

Wedekind, Benjamin Franklin
See Wedekind, Frank

Wedekind, Frank 1864-1918 .... **TCLC 7**
See also CA 104; 153; CANR 121, 122;
CDWLB 2; DAM DRAM; DLB 118; EW
8; EWL 3; LMFS 2; RGWL 2, 3

Wehr, Demaris .... **CLC 65**

Weidman, Jerome 1913-1998 .... **CLC 7**
See also AITN 2; CA 1-4R; 171; CAD;
CANR 1; CD 1, 2, 3, 4, 5; DLB 28

Weil, Simone (Adolphine)
1909-1943 .... **TCLC 23**
See also CA 117; 159; EW 12; EWL 3; FW;
GFL 1789 to the Present; MTCW 2

Weininger, Otto 1880-1903 .... **TCLC 84**

Weinstein, Nathan
See West, Nathanael

Weinstein, Nathan von Wallenstein
See West, Nathanael

Weir, Peter (Lindsay) 1944- .... **CLC 20**
See also CA 113; 123

Weiss, Peter (Ulrich) 1916-1982 .. **CLC 3, 15,
51; TCLC 152**
See also CA 45-48; 106; CANR 3; DAM
DRAM; DFS 3; DLB 69, 124; EWL 3;
RGHL; RGWL 2, 3

Weiss, Theodore (Russell)
1916-2003 .... **CLC 3, 8, 14**
See also CA 9-12R; 189; 216; CAAE 189;
CAAS 2; CANR 46, 94; CP 1, 2, 3, 4, 5,
6, 7; DLB 5; TCLE 1:2

Welch, (Maurice) Denton
1915-1948 .... **TCLC 22**
See also BRWS 8, 9; CA 121; 148; RGEL
2

Welch, James (Phillip) 1940-2003 ..... **CLC 6,
14, 52; NNAL; PC 62**
See also CA 85-88; 219; CANR 42, 66, 107;
CN 5, 6, 7; CP 2, 3, 4, 5, 6, 7; CPW;
DAM MULT, POP; DLB 175, 256; LATS
1:1; NFS 23; RGAL 4; TCWW 1, 2

Weldon, Fay 1931- . **CLC 6, 9, 11, 19, 36, 59,
122**
See also BRWS 4; CA 21-24R; CANR 16,
46, 63, 97, 137; CDBLB 1960 to Present;
CN 3, 4, 5, 6, 7; CPW; DAM POP; DLB
14, 194, 319; EWL 3; FW; HGG; INT
CANR-16; MTCW 1, 2; MTFW 2005;
RGEL 2; RGSF 2

Wellek, Rene 1903-1995 .... **CLC 28**
See also CA 5-8R; 150; CAAS 7; CANR 8;
DLB 63; EWL 3; INT CANR-8

Weller, Michael 1942- .... **CLC 10, 53**
See also CA 85-88; CAD; CD 5, 6

Weller, Paul 1958- .... **CLC 26**

Wellershoff, Dieter 1925- .... **CLC 46**
See also CA 89-92; CANR 16, 37

Welles, (George) Orson 1915-1985 .. **CLC 20,
80**
See also AAYA 40; CA 93-96; 117

Wellman, John McDowell 1945-
See Wellman, Mac
See also CA 166; CD 5

Wellman, Mac .... **CLC 65**
See Wellman, John McDowell; Wellman,
John McDowell
See also CAD; CD 6; RGAL 4

Wellman, Manly Wade 1903-1986 ... **CLC 49**
See also CA 1-4R; 118; CANR 6, 16, 44;
FANT; SATA 6; SATA-Obit 47; SFW 4;
SUFW

Wells, Carolyn 1869(?)-1942 .... **TCLC 35**
See also CA 113; 185; CMW 4; DLB 11

Wells, H(erbert) G(eorge) 1866-1946 . **SSC 6, 70; TCLC 6, 12, 19, 133; WLC 6**
See also AAYA 18; BPFB 3; BRW 6; CA 110; 121; CDBLB 1914-1945; CLR 64; DA; DA3; DAB; DAC; DAM MST, NOV; DLB 34, 70, 156, 178; EWL 3; EXPS; HGG; LAIT 3; LMFS 2; MTCW 1, 2; MTFW 2005; NFS 17, 20; RGEL 2; RGSF 2; SATA 20; SCFW 1, 2; SFW 4; SSFS 3; SUFW; TEA; WCH; WLIT 4; YAW

Wells, Rosemary 1943- .... **CLC 12**
See also AAYA 13; BYA 7, 8; CA 85-88; CANR 48, 120; CLR 16, 69; CWRI 5; MAICYA 1, 2; SAAS 1; SATA 18, 69, 114, 156; YAW

Wells-Barnett, Ida B(ell)
1862-1931 .... **TCLC 125**
See also CA 182; DLB 23, 221

Welsh, Irvine 1958- .... **CLC 144**
See also CA 173; CANR 146; CN 7; DLB 271

Welty, Eudora 1909-2001 .... **CLC 1, 2, 5, 14, 22, 33, 105, 220; SSC 1, 27, 51; WLC 6**
See also AAYA 48; AMW; AMWR 1; BPFB 3; CA 9-12R; 199; CABS 1; CANR 32, 65, 128; CDALB 1941-1968; CN 1, 2, 3, 4, 5, 6, 7; CSW; DA; DA3; DAB; DAC; DAM MST, NOV; DLB 2, 102, 143; DLBD 12; DLBY 1987, 2001; EWL 3; EXPS; HGG; LAIT 3; MAL 5; MBL; MTCW 1, 2; MTFW 2005; NFS 13, 15; RGAL 4; RGSF 2; RHW; SSFS 2, 10; TUS

Welty, Eudora Alice
See Welty, Eudora

Wen I-to 1899-1946 .... **TCLC 28**
See also EWL 3

Wentworth, Robert
See Hamilton, Edmond

Werfel, Franz (Viktor) 1890-1945 ... **TCLC 8**
See also CA 104; 161; DLB 81, 124; EWL 3; RGWL 2, 3

Wergeland, Henrik Arnold
1808-1845 .... **NCLC 5**

Wersba, Barbara 1932- .... **CLC 30**
See also AAYA 2, 30; BYA 6, 12, 13; CA 29-32R, 182; CAAE 182; CANR 16, 38; CLR 3, 78; DLB 52; JRDA; MAICYA 1, 2; SAAS 2; SATA 1, 58; SATA-Essay 103; WYA; YAW

Wertmueller, Lina 1928- .... **CLC 16**
See also CA 97-100; CANR 39, 78

Wescott, Glenway 1901-1987 .. **CLC 13; SSC 35**
See also CA 13-16R; 121; CANR 23, 70; CN 1, 2, 3, 4; DLB 4, 9, 102; MAL 5; RGAL 4

Wesker, Arnold 1932- .... **CLC 3, 5, 42**
See also CA 1-4R; CAAS 7; CANR 1, 33; CBD; CD 5, 6; CDBLB 1960 to Present; DAB; DAM DRAM; DLB 13, 310, 319; EWL 3; MTCW 1; RGEL 2; TEA

Wesley, Charles 1707-1788 .... **LC 128**
See also DLB 95; RGEL 2

Wesley, John 1703-1791 .... **LC 88**
See also DLB 104

Wesley, Richard (Errol) 1945- .... **CLC 7**
See also BW 1; CA 57-60; CAD; CANR 27; CD 5, 6; DLB 38

Wessel, Johan Herman 1742-1785 .... **LC 7**
See also DLB 300

West, Anthony (Panther)
1914-1987 .... **CLC 50**
See also CA 45-48; 124; CANR 3, 19; CN 1, 2, 3, 4; DLB 15

West, C. P.
See Wodehouse, P(elham) G(renville)

West, Cornel (Ronald) 1953- .... **BLCS; CLC 134**
See also CA 144; CANR 91; DLB 246

West, Delno C(loyde), Jr. 1936- .... **CLC 70**
See also CA 57-60

West, Dorothy 1907-1998 ...... **HR 1:3; TCLC 108**
See also BW 2; CA 143; 169; DLB 76

West, (Mary) Jessamyn 1902-1984 ... **CLC 7, 17**
See also CA 9-12R; 112; CANR 27; CN 1, 2, 3; DLB 6; DLBY 1984; MTCW 1, 2; RGAL 4; RHW; SATA-Obit 37; TCWW 2; TUS; YAW

West, Morris L(anglo) 1916-1999 ..... **CLC 6, 33**
See also BPFB 3; CA 5-8R; 187; CANR 24, 49, 64; CN 1, 2, 3, 4, 5, 6; CPW; DLB 289; MTCW 1, 2; MTFW 2005

West, Nathanael 1903-1940 .. **SSC 16; TCLC 1, 14, 44**
See also AMW; AMWR 2; BPFB 3; CA 104; 125; CDALB 1929-1941; DA3; DLB 4, 9, 28; EWL 3; MAL 5; MTCW 1, 2; MTFW 2005; NFS 16; RGAL 4; TUS

West, Owen
See Koontz, Dean R.

West, Paul 1930- .... **CLC 7, 14, 96, 226**
See also CA 13-16R; CAAS 7; CANR 22, 53, 76, 89, 136; CN 1, 2, 3, 4, 5, 6, 7; DLB 14; INT CANR-22; MTCW 2; MTFW 2005

West, Rebecca 1892-1983 ... **CLC 7, 9, 31, 50**
See also BPFB 3; BRWS 3; CA 5-8R; 109; CANR 19; CN 1, 2, 3; DLB 36; DLBY 1983; EWL 3; FW; MTCW 1, 2; MTFW 2005; NCFS 4; RGEL 2; TEA

Westall, Robert (Atkinson)
1929-1993 .... **CLC 17**
See also AAYA 12; BYA 2, 6, 7, 8, 9, 15; CA 69-72; 141; CANR 18, 68; CLR 13; FANT; JRDA; MAICYA 1, 2; MAICYAS 1; SAAS 2; SATA 23, 69; SATA-Obit 75; WYA; YAW

Westermarck, Edward 1862-1939 . **TCLC 87**

Westlake, Donald E. 1933- .... **CLC 7, 33**
See also BPFB 3; CA 17-20R; CAAS 13; CANR 16, 44, 65, 94, 137; CMW 4; CPW; DAM POP; INT CANR-16; MSW; MTCW 2; MTFW 2005

Westmacott, Mary
See Christie, Agatha (Mary Clarissa)

Weston, Allen
See Norton, Andre

Wetcheek, J. L.
See Feuchtwanger, Lion

Wetering, Janwillem van de
See van de Wetering, Janwillem

Wetherald, Agnes Ethelwyn
1857-1940 .... **TCLC 81**
See also CA 202; DLB 99

Wetherell, Elizabeth
See Warner, Susan (Bogert)

Whale, James 1889-1957 .... **TCLC 63**

Whalen, Philip (Glenn) 1923-2002 .... **CLC 6, 29**
See also BG 1:3; CA 9-12R; 209; CANR 5, 39; CP 1, 2, 3, 4, 5, 6, 7; DLB 16; WP

Wharton, Edith (Newbold Jones)
1862-1937 ... **SSC 6, 84; TCLC 3, 9, 27, 53, 129, 149; WLC 6**
See also AAYA 25; AMW; AMWC 2; AMWR 1; BPFB 3; CA 104; 132; CDALB 1865-1917; DA; DA3; DAB; DAC; DAM MST, NOV; DLB 4, 9, 12, 78, 189; DLBD 13; EWL 3; EXPS; FL 1:6; GL 3; HGG; LAIT 2, 3; LATS 1:1; MAL 5; MBL; MTCW 1, 2; MTFW 2005; NFS 5, 11, 15, 20; RGAL 4; RGSF 2; RHW; SSFS 6, 7; SUFW; TUS

Wharton, James
See Mencken, H(enry) L(ouis)

Wharton, William (a pseudonym)
1925- .... **CLC 18, 37**
See also CA 93-96; CN 4, 5, 6, 7; DLBY 1980; INT CA-93-96

Wheatley (Peters), Phillis
1753(?)-1784 ... **BLC 3; LC 3, 50; PC 3; WLC 6**
See also AFAW 1, 2; CDALB 1640-1865; DA; DA3; DAC; DAM MST, MULT, POET; DLB 31, 50; EXPP; FL 1:1; PFS 13; RGAL 4

Wheelock, John Hall 1886-1978 .... **CLC 14**
See also CA 13-16R; 77-80; CANR 14; CP 1, 2; DLB 45; MAL 5

Whim-Wham
See Curnow, (Thomas) Allen (Monro)

Whitaker, Rod 1931-2005
See Trevanian
See also CA 29-32R; 246; CANR 45, 153; CMW 4

White, Babington
See Braddon, Mary Elizabeth

White, E. B. 1899-1985 .... **CLC 10, 34, 39**
See also AAYA 62; AITN 2; AMWS 1; CA 13-16R; 116; CANR 16, 37; CDALBS; CLR 1, 21, 107; CPW; DA3; DAM POP; DLB 11, 22; EWL 3; FANT; MAICYA 1, 2; MAL 5; MTCW 1, 2; MTFW 2005; NCFS 5; RGAL 4; SATA 2, 29, 100; SATA-Obit 44; TUS

White, Edmund 1940- .... **CLC 27, 110**
See also AAYA 7; CA 45-48; CANR 3, 19, 36, 62, 107, 133; CN 5, 6, 7; DA3; DAM POP; DLB 227; MTCW 1, 2; MTFW 2005

White, Elwyn Brooks
See White, E. B.

White, Hayden V. 1928- .... **CLC 148**
See also CA 128; CANR 135; DLB 246

White, Patrick (Victor Martindale)
1912-1990 ...... **CLC 3, 4, 5, 7, 9, 18, 65, 69; SSC 39; TCLC 176**
See also BRWS 1; CA 81-84; 132; CANR 43; CN 1, 2, 3, 4; DLB 260; EWL 3; MTCW 1; RGEL 2; RGSF 2; RHW; TWA; WWE 1

White, Phyllis Dorothy James 1920-
See James, P. D.
See also CA 21-24R; CANR 17, 43, 65, 112; CMW 4; CN 7; CPW; DA3; DAM POP; MTCW 1, 2; MTFW 2005; TEA

White, T(erence) H(anbury)
1906-1964 .... **CLC 30**
See also AAYA 22; BPFB 3; BYA 4, 5; CA 73-76; CANR 37; DLB 160; FANT; JRDA; LAIT 1; MAICYA 1, 2; RGEL 2; SATA 12; SUFW 1; YAW

White, Terence de Vere 1912-1994 ... **CLC 49**
See also CA 49-52; 145; CANR 3

White, Walter
See White, Walter F(rancis)

White, Walter F(rancis) 1893-1955 ... **BLC 3; HR 1:3; TCLC 15**
See also BW 1; CA 115; 124; DAM MULT; DLB 51

White, William Hale 1831-1913
See Rutherford, Mark
See also CA 121; 189

Whitehead, Alfred North
1861-1947 .... **TCLC 97**
See also CA 117; 165; DLB 100, 262

Whitehead, E(dward) A(nthony)
1933- .... **CLC 5**
See Whitehead, Ted
See also CA 65-68; CANR 58, 118; CBD; CD 5; DLB 310

Whitehead, Ted
See Whitehead, E(dward) A(nthony)
See also CD 6

Whiteman, Roberta J. Hill 1947- ...... **NNAL**
See also CA 146

Whitemore, Hugh (John) 1936- .... **CLC 37**
See also CA 132; CANR 77; CBD; CD 5,
6; INT CA-132

Whitman, Sarah Helen (Power)
1803-1878 .... **NCLC 19**
See also DLB 1, 243

Whitman, Walt(er) 1819-1892 .. **NCLC 4, 31,
81; PC 3; WLC 6**
See also AAYA 42; AMW; AMWR 1;
CDALB 1640-1865; DA; DA3; DAB;
DAC; DAM MST, POET; DLB 3, 64,
224, 250; EXPP; LAIT 2; LMFS 1; PAB;
PFS 2, 3, 13, 22; RGAL 4; SATA 20;
TUS; WP; WYAS 1

Whitney, Isabella fl. 1565-fl. 1575 ..... **LC 130**
See also DLB 136

Whitney, Phyllis A(yame) 1903- .... **CLC 42**
See also AAYA 36; AITN 2; BEST 90:3;
CA 1-4R; CANR 3, 25, 38, 60; CLR 59;
CMW 4; CPW; DA3; DAM POP; JRDA;
MAICYA 1, 2; MTCW 2; RHW; SATA 1,
30; YAW

Whittemore, (Edward) Reed, Jr.
1919- .... **CLC 4**
See also CA 9-12R, 219; CAAE 219; CAAS
8; CANR 4, 119; CP 1, 2, 3, 4, 5, 6, 7;
DLB 5; MAL 5

Whittier, John Greenleaf
1807-1892 .... **NCLC 8, 59**
See also AMWS 1; DLB 1, 243; RGAL 4

Whittlebot, Hernia
See Coward, Noel (Peirce)

Wicker, Thomas Grey 1926-
See Wicker, Tom
See also CA 65-68; CANR 21, 46, 141

Wicker, Tom .... **CLC 7**
See Wicker, Thomas Grey

Wideman, John Edgar 1941- ... **BLC 3; CLC
5, 34, 36, 67, 122; SSC 62**
See also AFAW 1, 2; AMWS 10; BPFB 4;
BW 2, 3; CA 85-88; CANR 14, 42, 67,
109, 140; CN 4, 5, 6, 7; DAM MULT;
DLB 33, 143; MAL 5; MTCW 2; MTFW
2005; RGAL 4; RGSF 2; SSFS 6, 12, 24;
TCLE 1:2

Wiebe, Rudy (Henry) 1934- .. **CLC 6, 11, 14,
138**
See also CA 37-40R; CANR 42, 67, 123;
CN 1, 2, 3, 4, 5, 6, 7; DAC; DAM MST;
DLB 60; RHW; SATA 156

Wieland, Christoph Martin
1733-1813 .... **NCLC 17**
See also DLB 97; EW 4; LMFS 1; RGWL
2, 3

Wiene, Robert 1881-1938 .... **TCLC 56**

Wieners, John 1934- .... **CLC 7**
See also BG 1:3; CA 13-16R; CP 1, 2, 3, 4,
5, 6, 7; DLB 16; WP

Wiesel, Elie 1928- ...... **CLC 3, 5, 11, 37, 165;
WLCS**
See also AAYA 7, 54; AITN 1; CA 5-8R;
CAAS 4; CANR 8, 40, 65, 125; CDALBS;
CWW 2; DA; DA3; DAB; DAC; DAM
MST, NOV; DLB 83, 299; DLBY 1987;
EWL 3; INT CANR-8; LAIT 4; MTCW
1, 2; MTFW 2005; NCFS 4; NFS 4;
RGHL; RGWL 3; SATA 56; YAW

Wiesel, Eliezer
See Wiesel, Elie

Wiggins, Marianne 1947- .... **CLC 57**
See also AAYA 70; BEST 89:3; CA 130;
CANR 60, 139; CN 7

Wigglesworth, Michael 1631-1705 .... **LC 106**
See also DLB 24; RGAL 4

Wiggs, Susan .... **CLC 70**
See also CA 201

Wight, James Alfred 1916-1995
See Herriot, James
See also CA 77-80; SATA 55; SATA-Brief
44

Wilbur, Richard 1921- .. **CLC 3, 6, 9, 14, 53,
110; PC 51**
See also AMWS 3; CA 1-4R; CABS 2;
CANR 2, 29, 76, 93, 139; CDALBS; CP
1, 2, 3, 4, 5, 6, 7; DA; DAB; DAC; DAM
MST, POET; DLB 5, 169; EWL 3; EXPP;
INT CANR-29; MAL 5; MTCW 1, 2;
MTFW 2005; PAB; PFS 11, 12, 16;
RGAL 4; SATA 9, 108; WP

Wild, Peter 1940- .... **CLC 14**
See also CA 37-40R; CP 1, 2, 3, 4, 5, 6, 7;
DLB 5

Wilde, Oscar (Fingal O'Flahertie Wills)
1854(?)-1900 .... **DC 17; SSC 11, 77;
TCLC 1, 8, 23, 41, 175; WLC 6**
See also AAYA 49; BRW 5; BRWC 1, 2;
BRWR 2; BYA 15; CA 104; 119; CANR
112; CDBLB 1890-1914; CLR 114; DA;
DA3; DAB; DAC; DAM DRAM, MST,
NOV; DFS 4, 8, 9, 21; DLB 10, 19, 34,
57, 141, 156, 190; EXPS; FANT; GL 3;
LATS 1:1; NFS 20; RGEL 2; RGSF 2;
SATA 24; SSFS 7; SUFW; TEA; WCH;
WLIT 4

Wilder, Billy .... **CLC 20**
See Wilder, Samuel
See also AAYA 66; DLB 26

Wilder, Samuel 1906-2002
See Wilder, Billy
See also CA 89-92; 205

Wilder, Stephen
See Marlowe, Stephen

Wilder, Thornton (Niven)
1897-1975 .. **CLC 1, 5, 6, 10, 15, 35, 82;
DC 1, 24; WLC 6**
See also AAYA 29; AITN 2; AMW; CA 13-
16R; 61-64; CAD; CANR 40, 132;
CDALBS; CN 1, 2; DA; DA3; DAB;
DAC; DAM DRAM, MST, NOV; DFS 1,
4, 16; DLB 4, 7, 9, 228; DLBY 1997;
EWL 3; LAIT 3; MAL 5; MTCW 1, 2;
MTFW 2005; NFS 24; RGAL 4; RHW;
WYAS 1

Wilding, Michael 1942- ...... **CLC 73; SSC 50**
See also CA 104; CANR 24, 49, 106; CN
4, 5, 6, 7; DLB 325; RGSF 2

Wiley, Richard 1944- .... **CLC 44**
See also CA 121; 129; CANR 71

Wilhelm, Kate .... **CLC 7**
See Wilhelm, Katie
See also AAYA 20; BYA 16; CAAS 5; DLB
8; INT CANR-17; SCFW 2

Wilhelm, Katie 1928-
See Wilhelm, Kate
See also CA 37-40R; CANR 17, 36, 60, 94;
MTCW 1; SFW 4

Wilkins, Mary
See Freeman, Mary E(leanor) Wilkins

Willard, Nancy 1936- .... **CLC 7, 37**
See also BYA 5; CA 89-92; CANR 10, 39,
68, 107, 152; CLR 5; CP 2, 3, 4, 5; CWP;
CWRI 5; DLB 5, 52; FANT; MAICYA 1,
2; MTCW 1; SATA 37, 71, 127; SATA-
Brief 30; SUFW 2; TCLE 1:2

William of Malmesbury c. 1090B.C.-c.
1140B.C. .... **CMLC 57**

William of Ockham 1290-1349 ..... **CMLC 32**

Williams, Ben Ames 1889-1953 ..... **TCLC 89**
See also CA 183; DLB 102

Williams, Charles
See Collier, James Lincoln

Williams, Charles (Walter Stansby)
1886-1945 .... **TCLC 1, 11**
See also BRWS 9; CA 104; 163; DLB 100,
153, 255; FANT; RGEL 2; SUFW 1

Williams, C.K. 1936- .... **CLC 33, 56, 148**
See also CA 37-40R; CAAS 26; CANR 57,
106; CP 1, 2, 3, 4, 5, 6, 7; DAM POET;
DLB 5; MAL 5

Williams, Ella Gwendolen Rees
See Rhys, Jean

Williams, (George) Emlyn
1905-1987 .... **CLC 15**
See also CA 104; 123; CANR 36; DAM
DRAM; DLB 10, 77; IDTP; MTCW 1

Williams, Hank 1923-1953 .... **TCLC 81**
See Williams, Hiram King

Williams, Helen Maria
1761-1827 .... **NCLC 135**
See also DLB 158

Williams, Hiram Hank
See Williams, Hank

Williams, Hiram King
See Williams, Hank
See also CA 188

Williams, Hugo (Mordaunt) 1942- ... **CLC 42**
See also CA 17-20R; CANR 45, 119; CP 1,
2, 3, 4, 5, 6, 7; DLB 40

Williams, J. Walker
See Wodehouse, P(elham) G(renville)

Williams, John A(lfred) 1925- . **BLC 3; CLC
5, 13**
See also AFAW 2; BW 2, 3; CA 53-56, 195;
CAAE 195; CAAS 3; CANR 6, 26, 51,
118; CN 1, 2, 3, 4, 5, 6, 7; CSW; DAM
MULT; DLB 2, 33; EWL 3; INT CANR-6;
MAL 5; RGAL 4; SFW 4

Williams, Jonathan (Chamberlain)
1929- .... **CLC 13**
See also CA 9-12R; CAAS 12; CANR 8,
108; CP 1, 2, 3, 4, 5, 6, 7; DLB 5

Williams, Joy 1944- .... **CLC 31**
See also CA 41-44R; CANR 22, 48, 97

Williams, Norman 1952- .... **CLC 39**
See also CA 118

Williams, Roger 1603(?)-1683 .... **LC 129**
See also DLB 24

Williams, Sherley Anne 1944-1999 ... **BLC 3;
CLC 89**
See also AFAW 2; BW 2, 3; CA 73-76; 185;
CANR 25, 82; DAM MULT, POET; DLB
41; INT CANR-25; SATA 78; SATA-Obit
116

Williams, Shirley
See Williams, Sherley Anne

Williams, Tennessee 1911-1983 . **CLC 1, 2, 5,
7, 8, 11, 15, 19, 30, 39, 45, 71, 111; DC
4; SSC 81; WLC 6**
See also AAYA 31; AITN 1, 2; AMW;
AMWC 1; CA 5-8R; 108; CABS 3; CAD;
CANR 31, 132; CDALB 1941-1968; CN
1, 2, 3; DA; DA3; DAB; DAC; DAM
DRAM, MST; DFS 17; DLB 7; DLBD 4;
DLBY 1983; EWL 3; GLL 1; LAIT 4;
LATS 1:2; MAL 5; MTCW 1, 2; MTFW
2005; RGAL 4; TUS

Williams, Thomas (Alonzo)
1926-1990 .... **CLC 14**
See also CA 1-4R; 132; CANR 2

Williams, William C.
See Williams, William Carlos

Williams, William Carlos
1883-1963 .... **CLC 1, 2, 5, 9, 13, 22, 42,
67; PC 7; SSC 31; WLC 6**
See also AAYA 46; AMW; AMWR 1; CA
89-92; CANR 34; CDALB 1917-1929;
DA; DA3; DAB; DAC; DAM MST,
POET; DLB 4, 16, 54, 86; EWL 3; EXPP;
MAL 5; MTCW 1, 2; MTFW 2005; NCFS
4; PAB; PFS 1, 6, 11; RGAL 4; RGSF 2;
TUS; WP

Yonge, Charlotte (Mary)
1823-1901 .... **TCLC 48**
See also CA 109; 163; DLB 18, 163; RGEL
2; SATA 17; WCH
York, Jeremy
See Creasey, John
York, Simon
See Heinlein, Robert A.
Yorke, Henry Vincent 1905-1974 ..... **CLC 13**
See Green, Henry
See also CA 85-88; 49-52
Yosano, Akiko 1878-1942 ... **PC 11; TCLC 59**
See also CA 161; EWL 3; RGWL 3
Yoshimoto, Banana .... **CLC 84**
See Yoshimoto, Mahoko
See also AAYA 50; NFS 7
Yoshimoto, Mahoko 1964-
See Yoshimoto, Banana
See also CA 144; CANR 98; SSFS 16
Young, Al(bert James) 1939- ... **BLC 3; CLC 19**
See also BW 2, 3; CA 29-32R; CANR 26,
65, 109; CN 2, 3, 4, 5, 6, 7; CP 1, 2, 3, 4,
5, 6, 7; DAM MULT; DLB 33
Young, Andrew (John) 1885-1971 ...... **CLC 5**
See also CA 5-8R; CANR 7, 29; CP 1;
RGEL 2
Young, Collier
See Bloch, Robert (Albert)
Young, Edward 1683-1765 .... **LC 3, 40**
See also DLB 95; RGEL 2
Young, Marguerite (Vivian)
1909-1995 .... **CLC 82**
See also CA 13-16; 150; CAP 1; CN 1, 2,
3, 4, 5, 6
Young, Neil 1945- .... **CLC 17**
See also CA 110; CCA 1
Young Bear, Ray A. 1950- ... **CLC 94; NNAL**
See also CA 146; DAM MULT; DLB 175;
MAL 5
Yourcenar, Marguerite 1903-1987 ... **CLC 19, 38, 50, 87**
See also BPFB 3; CA 69-72; CANR 23, 60,
93; DAM NOV; DLB 72; DLBY 1988;
EW 12; EWL 3; GFL 1789 to the Present;
GLL 1; MTCW 1, 2; MTFW 2005;
RGWL 2, 3
Yuan, Chu 340(?)B.C.-278(?)B.C. . **CMLC 36**
Yurick, Sol 1925- .... **CLC 6**
See also CA 13-16R; CANR 25; CN 1, 2,
3, 4, 5, 6, 7; MAL 5
Zabolotsky, Nikolai Alekseevich
1903-1958 .... **TCLC 52**
See Zabolotsky, Nikolay Alekseevich
See also CA 116; 164
Zabolotsky, Nikolay Alekseevich
See Zabolotsky, Nikolai Alekseevich
See also EWL 3
Zagajewski, Adam 1945- .... **PC 27**
See also CA 186; DLB 232; EWL 3
Zalygin, Sergei -2000 .... **CLC 59**

Zalygin, Sergei (Pavlovich)
1913-2000 .... **CLC 59**
See also DLB 302
Zamiatin, Evgenii
See Zamyatin, Evgeny Ivanovich
See also RGSF 2; RGWL 2, 3
Zamiatin, Evgenii Ivanovich
See Zamyatin, Evgeny Ivanovich
See also DLB 272
Zamiatin, Yevgenii
See Zamyatin, Evgeny Ivanovich
Zamora, Bernice (B. Ortiz) 1938- .. **CLC 89; HLC 2**
See also CA 151; CANR 80; DAM MULT;
DLB 82; HW 1, 2
Zamyatin, Evgeny Ivanovich
1884-1937 .... **SSC 89; TCLC 8, 37**
See Zamiatin, Evgenii; Zamiatin, Evgenii
Ivanovich; Zamyatin, Yevgeny Ivanovich
See also CA 105; 166; SFW 4
Zamyatin, Yevgeny Ivanovich
See Zamyatin, Evgeny Ivanovich
See also EW 10; EWL 3
Zangwill, Israel 1864-1926 ... **SSC 44; TCLC 16**
See also CA 109; 167; CMW 4; DLB 10,
135, 197; RGEL 2
Zanzotto, Andrea 1921- .... **PC 65**
See also CA 208; CWW 2; DLB 128; EWL
3
Zappa, Francis Vincent, Jr. 1940-1993
See Zappa, Frank
See also CA 108; 143; CANR 57
Zappa, Frank .... **CLC 17**
See Zappa, Francis Vincent, Jr.
Zaturenska, Marya 1902-1982 ..... **CLC 6, 11**
See also CA 13-16R; 105; CANR 22; CP 1,
2, 3
Zayas y Sotomayor, Maria de 1590-c.
1661 .... **LC 102; SSC 94**
See also RGSF 2
Zeami 1363-1443 .... **DC 7; LC 86**
See also DLB 203; RGWL 2, 3
Zelazny, Roger 1937-1995 .... **CLC 21**
See also AAYA 7, 68; BPFB 3; CA 21-24R;
148; CANR 26, 60; CN 6; DLB 8; FANT;
MTCW 1, 2; MTFW 2005; SATA 57;
SATA-Brief 39; SCFW 1, 2; SFW 4;
SUFW 1, 2
Zhang Ailing
See Chang, Eileen
See also CWW 2; DLB 328; RGSF 2
Zhdanov, Andrei Alexandrovich
1896-1948 .... **TCLC 18**
See also CA 117; 167
Zhukovsky, Vasilii Andreevich
See Zhukovsky, Vasily (Andreevich)
See also DLB 205
Zhukovsky, Vasily (Andreevich)
1783-1852 .... **NCLC 35**
See Zhukovsky, Vasilii Andreevich

Ziegenhagen, Eric .... **CLC 55**
Zimmer, Jill Schary
See Robinson, Jill
Zimmerman, Robert
See Dylan, Bob
Zindel, Paul 1936-2003 ...... **CLC 6, 26; DC 5**
See also AAYA 2, 37; BYA 2, 3, 8, 11, 14;
CA 73-76; 213; CAD; CANR 31, 65, 108;
CD 5, 6; CDALBS; CLR 3, 45, 85; DA;
DA3; DAB; DAC; DAM DRAM, MST,
NOV; DFS 12; DLB 7, 52; JRDA; LAIT
5; MAICYA 1, 2; MTCW 1, 2; MTFW
2005; NFS 14; SATA 16, 58, 102; SATA-
Obit 142; WYA; YAW
Zinn, Howard 1922- .... **CLC 199**
See also CA 1-4R; CANR 2, 33, 90
Zinov'Ev, A.A.
See Zinoviev, Alexander
Zinov'ev, Aleksandr
See Zinoviev, Alexander
See also DLB 302
Zinoviev, Alexander 1922-2006 .... **CLC 19**
See Zinov'ev, Aleksandr
See also CA 116; 133; 250; CAAS 10
Zinoviev, Alexander Aleksandrovich
See Zinoviev, Alexander
Zizek, Slavoj 1949- .... **CLC 188**
See also CA 201; MTFW 2005
Zoilus
See Lovecraft, H. P.
Zola, Emile (Edouard Charles Antoine)
1840-1902 .. **TCLC 1, 6, 21, 41; WLC 6**
See also CA 104; 138; DA; DA3; DAB;
DAC; DAM MST, NOV; DLB 123; EW
7; GFL 1789 to the Present; IDTP; LMFS
1, 2; RGWL 2; TWA
Zoline, Pamela 1941- .... **CLC 62**
See also CA 161; SFW 4
Zoroaster 628(?)B.C.-551(?)B.C. ... **CMLC 40**
Zorrilla y Moral, Jose 1817-1893 .... **NCLC 6**
Zoshchenko, Mikhail (Mikhailovich)
1895-1958 .... **SSC 15; TCLC 15**
See also CA 115; 160; EWL 3; RGSF 2;
RGWL 3
Zuckmayer, Carl 1896-1977 .... **CLC 18**
See also CA 69-72; DLB 56, 124; EWL 3;
RGWL 2, 3
Zuk, Georges
See Skelton, Robin
See also CCA 1
Zukofsky, Louis 1904-1978 ... **CLC 1, 2, 4, 7, 11, 18; PC 11**
See also AMWS 3; CA 9-12R; 77-80;
CANR 39; CP 1, 2; DAM POET; DLB 5,
165; EWL 3; MAL 5; MTCW 1; RGAL 4
Zweig, Paul 1935-1984 .... **CLC 34, 42**
See also CA 85-88; 113
Zweig, Stefan 1881-1942 .... **TCLC 17**
See also CA 112; 170; DLB 81, 118; EWL
3; RGHL
Zwingli, Huldreich 1484-1531 .... **LC 37**
See also DLB 179

Literary Criticism Series
Cumulative Topic Index

This index lists all topic entries in Thompson Gale's *Children's Literature Review* (CLR), *Classical and Medieval Literature Criticism* (CMLC), *Contemporary Literary Criticism* (CLC), *Drama Criticism* (DC), *Literature Criticism from 1400 to 1800* (LC), *Nineteenth-Century Literature Criticism* (NCLC), *Short Story Criticism* (SSC), and *Twentieth-Century Literary Criticism* (TCLC). The index also lists topic entries in the Gale Critical Companion Collection, which includes the following publications: *The Beat Generation* (BG), *Feminism in Literature* (FL), *Gothic Literature* (GL), and *Harlem Renaissance* (HR).

Topic Index

Topic Index

NCLC Cumulative Nationality Index

AMERICAN

Adams, John **106**
Adams, John Quincy **175**
Alcott, Amos Bronson **1, 167**
Alcott, Louisa May **6, 58, 83**
Alger, Horatio Jr. **8, 83**
Allston, Washington **2**
Apess, William **73**
Audubon, John James **47**
Barlow, Joel **23**
Bartram, William **145**
Beecher, Catharine Esther **30**
Bellamy, Edward **4, 86, 147**
Bird, Robert Montgomery **1**
Boker, George Henry **125**
Boyesen, Hjalmar Hjorth **135**
Brackenridge, Hugh Henry **7**
Brentano, Clemens (Maria) **1**
Brown, Charles Brockden **22, 74, 122**
Brown, William Wells **2, 89**
Brownson, Orestes Augustus **50**
Bryant, William Cullen **6, 46**
Calhoun, John Caldwell **15**
Channing, William Ellery **17**
Child, Francis James **173**
Child, Lydia Maria **6, 73**
Chivers, Thomas Holley **49**
Cooke, John Esten **5**
Cooke, Rose Terry **110**
Cooper, James Fenimore **1, 27, 54**
Cooper, Susan Fenimore **129**
Cranch, Christopher Pearse **115**
Crèvecoeur, Michel Guillaume Jean de **105**
Crockett, David **8**
Cummins, Maria Susanna **139**
Dana, Richard Henry Sr. **53**
Delany, Martin Robinson **93**
Dickinson, Emily (Elizabeth) **21, 77, 171**
Douglass, Frederick **7, 55, 141**
Dunlap, William **2**
Dwight, Timothy **13**
Emerson, Mary Moody **66**
Emerson, Ralph Waldo **1, 38, 98**
Field, Eugene **3**
Foster, Hannah Webster **99**
Foster, Stephen Collins **26**
Frederic, Harold **10, 175**
Freneau, Philip Morin **1, 111**
Garrison, William Lloyd **149**
Hale, Sarah Josepha (Buell) **75**
Halleck, Fitz-Greene **47**
Hamilton, Alexander **49**
Hammon, Jupiter **5**
Harris, George Washington **23, 165**
Hawthorne, Nathaniel **2, 10, 17, 23, 39, 79, 95, 158, 171**
Hawthorne, Sophia Peabody **150**
Hayne, Paul Hamilton **94**
Holmes, Oliver Wendell **14, 81**
Horton, George Moses **87**
Irving, Washington **2, 19, 95**
Jackson, Helen Hunt **90**

Jacobs, Harriet A(nn) **67, 162**
James, Henry Sr. **53**
Jefferson, Thomas **11, 103**
Kennedy, John Pendleton **2**
Kirkland, Caroline M. **85**
Lanier, Sidney **6, 118**
Lazarus, Emma **8, 109**
Lincoln, Abraham **18**
Longfellow, Henry Wadsworth **2, 45, 101, 103**
Longstreet, Augustus Baldwin **159**
Lowell, James Russell **2, 90**
Madison, James **126**
Melville, Herman **3, 12, 29, 45, 49, 91, 93, 123, 157**
Mowatt, Anna Cora **74**
Murray, Judith Sargent **63**
Neal, John **161**
Osgood, Frances Sargent **141**
Parkman, Francis Jr. **12**
Parton, Sara Payson Willis **86**
Paulding, James Kirke **2**
Peabody, Elizabeth Palmer **169**
Pinkney, Edward **31**
Poe, Edgar Allan **1, 16, 55, 78, 94, 97, 117**
Prescott, William Hickling **163**
Rowson, Susanna Haswell **5, 69**
Sedgwick, Catharine Maria **19, 98**
Shaw, Henry Wheeler **15**
Sigourney, Lydia Howard (Huntley) **21, 87**
Simms, William Gilmore **3**
Smith, Joseph Jr. **53**
Solomon, Northup **105**
Southworth, Emma Dorothy Eliza Nevitte **26**
Stowe, Harriet (Elizabeth) Beecher **3, 50, 133**
Taylor, Bayard **89**
Tenney, Tabitha Gilman **122**
Thoreau, Henry David **7, 21, 61, 138**
Timrod, Henry **25**
Trumbull, John **30**
Truth, Sojourner **94**
Tyler, Royall **3**
Very, Jones **9**
Warner, Susan (Bogert) **31, 146**
Warren, Mercy Otis **13**
Webster, Noah **30**
Webb, Frank J. **143**
Whitman, Sarah Helen (Power) **19**
Whitman, Walt(er) **4, 31, 81**
Whittier, John Greenleaf **8, 59**
Wilson, Harriet E. Adams **78**
Winnemucca, Sarah **79**

ARGENTINIAN

Echeverria, (Jose) Esteban (Antonino) **18**
Hernández, José **17**
Sarmiento, Domingo Faustino **123**

AUSTRALIAN

Adams, Francis **33**
Clarke, Marcus (Andrew Hislop) **19**

Gordon, Adam Lindsay **21**
Harpur, Charles **114**
Kendall, Henry **12**

AUSTRIAN

Grillparzer, Franz **1, 102**
Lenau, Nikolaus **16**
Nestroy, Johann **42**
Raimund, Ferdinand Jakob **69**
Sacher-Masoch, Leopold von **31**
Stifter, Adalbert **41**

BRAZILIAN

Alencar, Jose de **157**

CANADIAN

Crawford, Isabella Valancy **12, 127**
De Mille, James **123**
Haliburton, Thomas Chandler **15, 149**
Lampman, Archibald **25**
Moodie, Susanna (Strickland) **14, 113**
Richardson, John **55**
Traill, Catharine Parr **31**

CHINESE

Li Ju-chen **137**

COLOMBIAN

Isaacs, Jorge Ricardo **70**
Silva, José Asunción **114**

CUBAN

Avellaneda, Gertrudis Gómez de **111**
Casal, Julián del **131**
Manzano, Juan Francisco **155**
Martí (y Pérez), José (Julian) **63**
Villaverde, Cirilo **121**

CZECH

Macha, Karel Hynek **46**

DANISH

Andersen, Hans Christian **7, 79**
Grundtvig, Nicolai Frederik Severin **1, 158**
Jacobsen, Jens Peter **34**
Kierkegaard, Søren **34, 78, 125**

DUTCH

Multatuli (Eduard Douwes Dekker) **165**

ENGLISH

Ainsworth, William Harrison **13**
Arnold, Matthew **6, 29, 89, 126**
Arnold, Thomas **18**
Austen, Jane **1, 13, 19, 33, 51, 81, 95, 119, 150**
Bagehot, Walter **10**
Barbauld, Anna Laetitia **50**
Barham, Richard Harris **77**

ISBN-13: 978-0-7876-9847-8
ISBN-10: 0-7876-9847-4